Lateinische Schulgrammatik

von **Dr. Carl Stegmann,**

Oberlehrer am Königl. Ulrichs-Gymnasium zu Norden.

Sechste Doppel-Auflage.

[XII u. 250 S.] gr. 8. 1893. In Leinwand geb. *M.* 2.40.

☞ Selten hat wohl ein neues Schulbuch einen so bedeutenden und schnellen Erfolg gehabt wie Stegmanns lateinische Grammatik; dieselbe erfüllt die Forderungen der neuen Lehrpläne vollkommen.

Lateinische Lese- und Übungsbücher

für Sexta bis Tertia

von

Ph. Kautzmann,

Professor am Gymnasium zu Mannheim,

Dr. K. Pfaff und T. Schmidt,

Professoren am Gymnasium zu Heidelberg.

I. Teil, für Sexta. 2. Auflage. 1894. *M.* 1.60.
II. Teil, für Quinta. 2. Auflage. 1895. *M.* 1.60.
III. Teil, für Quarta 1894. *M.* 1.40.
IV. Teil, für Tertia. [Unter der Presse.]

☞ Diese, wie allgemein anerkannt, nach gesunden Grundsätzen gearbeiteten Übungsbücher haben nicht nur in Baden, sondern auch in norddeutschen Anstalten vielfach Eingang gefunden.

Freiexemplare zur Prüfung behufs event. Einführung stehen auf Wunsch bereitwilligst zur Verfügung.

BIBLIOTHECA

* SCHULTEXTE *

TEUBNERIANA

DEMOSTHENES'
NEUN PHILIPPISCHE REDEN.

TEXTAUSGABE

FÜR DEN SCHULGEBRAUCH

VON

TH. THALHEIM,

DIREKTOR DES KGL. GYMNASIUMS ZU HIRSCHBERG/SCHL.

LEIPZIG,

DRUCK UND VERLAG VON B. G. TEUBNER.

1896.

Einleitung.

Entwickelung der griechischen Beredsamkeit.

Anfänge. Wenngleich das öffentliche Leben der griechischen Staaten naturgemäſs bedeutende Redner ausbildete (Perikles), so hat die eigentliche Redekunst ihren Ursprung in Sikilien, wo kurz vorher auch eine besondere Gattung des Lustspiels, die megarische Posse (Epicharmos von Kos) entstanden war. In den vielen Eigentumsstreitigkeiten, welche dem Sturz der Tyrannen (Hieron und Thrasybulos) 466 folgten, entwickelte sich in der aufgeweckten Bevölkerung die kunstmäſsige Rede. Ihre ersten Lehrer waren Korax und Teisias, aber erst Gorgias von Leontinoi wies einen besonderen Stil auf, indem er die Rede mit dichterischen Worten schmückte und zur Klarstellung des Gedankens den Gegensatz aufsuchte Dieser Mann kam 427 als Gesandter seiner Vaterstadt nach Athen, um Hilfe gegen die Syrakusier zu erbitten; seine Kunst machte einen gewaltigen Eindruck und erweckte sofort Nacheiferung. Gorgias lebte fortan als Lehrer seiner Kunst im eigentlichen Griechenland umherziehend und gebrauchte in seinen Schriften den attischen Dialekt.

Einteilung. Die Alten unterschieden drei Gattungen der Rede, das $\gamma\acute{\epsilon}\nu o\varsigma$ $\delta\iota\varkappa\alpha\nu\iota\varkappa\grave{o}\nu$ die Prozeſsrede, das $\gamma\acute{\epsilon}\nu o\varsigma$ $\sigma\upsilon\mu\beta o\upsilon\lambda\epsilon\upsilon\tau\iota\varkappa\grave{o}\nu$ die politische Rede, das $\gamma\acute{\epsilon}\nu o\varsigma$ $\grave{\epsilon}\pi\iota\delta\epsilon\iota\varkappa\tau\iota\varkappa\grave{o}\nu$ die Prunk- oder Festrede.

a*

Die Dekas der attischen Redner. Die Weiter-
entwickelung der Kunst erfolgte in Athen und wird von
den Alten selbst an folgende zehn Namen geknüpft: Antiphon, Andokides — Lysias, Isokrates, Isaios — Lykurgos,
Hypereides, Aischines, Demosthenes, Deinarchos, von
denen die beiden ersten zur Zeit des peloponnesischen
Krieges lebten, die übrigen wesentlich dem vierten Jahr-
hundert angehörten. Andokides und Aischines verdanken
ihren Platz mehr natürlicher Anlage als kunstmäfsiger
Ausbildung, Lysias, Isaios, Deinarchos waren Nichtbürger
und als solche von aller staatsmännischen Wirksamkeit
ausgeschlossen. Sie schrieben als λογογράφοι Prozefs-
reden für andere, da in Athen vor Gericht ein jeder
seine Sache selbst führen mufste.

Antiphon, ein Staatsmann, das Haupt der Vier-
hundert im Jahre 411, wurde nach ihrem Sturze trotz
einer ausgezeichneten Verteidigungsrede wegen Hoch-
verrats hingerichtet. Erhalten sind 15 Reden, sämtlich
in Blutprozessen, zwölf davon sind Übungsreden, je vier
auf einen Fall bezüglich, daher Tetralogien genannt, je
zwei vom Ankläger und Angeklagten. Gerade diese
sind durch Scharfsinn ausgezeichnet, wenn auch das
Streben nach Gegensätzen dem Gedanken mitunter Gewalt anthut.

Andokides, aus angesehener Familie, war 415 in
den Mysterienfrevel verwickelt, rettete sich und mehrere
Verwandte vor Hinrichtung durch Geständnis und Anzeige, mufste dann aber Athen verlassen und kehrte erst
nach dem Sturze der Dreifsig zurück. Im korinthischen
Kriege gehörte er 391 zu einer Gesandtschaft nach Sparta
und suchte den Frieden zu vermitteln. Erhalten sind
drei Reden, darunter περὶ τῶν μυστηρίων.

Lysias gehört einer vermögenden Kaufmannsfamilie
an, die durch Perikles aus Syrakus nach Athen gezogen

worden war. Sein Vater Kephalos stand in freundschaft-
lichem Verkehr mit Sophokles und Sokrates. Lysias
wanderte jung mit seinen Brüdern nach Thurioi aus,
kehrte jedoch bald nach dem unglücklichen Ausgange
des sikilischen Unternehmens zurück und lebte in behag-
lichem Wohlstande, den eine bedeutende Schildfabrik mit
120 Sklaven mehrte. Dieser Reichtum jedoch erregte
den Neid der Dreifsig, sein Bruder Polemarchos fiel
ihnen zum Opfer, Lysias selbst entzog sich durch Flucht
und unterstützte die heimkehrende Volkspartei in ihrem
Kampfe gegen die Machthaber durch Waffen, Söldner
und Geld. Schriftstellerische Neigungen hatte Lysias stets
gehabt, jetzt führte ihn das Schicksal zu dem Gegen-
stande, der seiner Natur gemäfs war. Er klagte den
Eratosthenes, ein Mitglied der Dreifsig, des Mordes an
seinem Bruder an und lieh von da ab seine Feder denen,
die in Prozessen seines Beistandes bedurften. In schlichter
einfacher Sprache stellt er vor allem den Thatbestand
meisterhaft dar, dann versteht er vortrefflich seine Per-
sonen zu kennzeichnen, dafs man sie vor sich zu sehen
glaubt, den jungen, selbstbewufsten Politiker (16), dem
man den Eintritt in den Rat streitig macht, den vermögenden Grundbesitzer (7), der sich an den heiligen
Ölbäumen vergriffen haben soll, den Krüppel (24), dem
man seine Staatsunterstützung rauben will. Jede Rede
wirkt wie ein Bild, aus dem vollen Leben heraus-
geschnitten. Überliefert sind 31 Reden, darunter 7 wahrscheinlich unecht.

Isokrates, aus mittlerem Stande, sah sich durch
Schüchternheit und eine schwache Stimme von dem Be-
rufe eines Staatsmannes ausgeschlossen; er wandte sich,
als seine Familie durch den dekeleischen Krieg verarmt
war, dem Unterricht des Gorgias und demnächst der
Thätigkeit eines Logographen zu, die ihm jedoch wenig

behagte. Er gründete deshalb eine Schule der Bered-
samkeit, welche ihm Ansehn und Vermögen eintrug,
und verfaßte Kunstreden, welche stilistisch auf das sorg-
fältigste durchgebildet und geglättet Muster griechischer
Prosa geworden sind. Obwohl sie staatsmännische Ziele
verfolgen, haben sie thatsächliche Erfolge nicht gehabt.
Er starb nahezu 100 Jahre alt, bald nach der Schlacht
bei Chaironeia, bis zuletzt frischen Geistes und schrift-
stellerisch thätig. Wir haben 21 Reden, darunter den
Panegyrikos, der die Berechtigung Athens zur Seeherrschaft
nachweist und zu einem gemeinsamen Kriege gegen die
Perser auffordert, und den Panathenaikos, eine Lobrede
auf Athen, im höchsten Alter verfaßt.

Von des Isaios Lebensumständen ist fast nichts
sicher überliefert, er war als schlauer Beistand in Erb-
und Besitzstreitigkeiten berühmt, daher suchte auch der
junge Demosthenes seine Unterweisung. Die erhaltenen
11 Reden betreffen alle Erbschaftsprozesse, sie zeigen
den Redner in schlichter Sprache dem Lysias ähnlich,
aber zugleich versteht er die knappen und oft dunklen
Gesetzesbestimmungen sehr zu gunsten seiner Partei zu
drehen und zu wenden.

Lykurgos, aus dem priesterlichen Geschlechte der
Eteobutaden, war streng gegen sich und andre, von spar-
tanischer Einfachheit, unermüdlich in seinem öffentlichen
Wirken. Besonders trat er nach der Schlacht bei Chaironeia hervor, als andere verzagten; er hat von da ab
zwölf Jahre mit glänzendem Erfolge die Finanzen Athens
geleitet, dabei große Bauten ausgeführt, wie die Schiffshäuser, ein Zeughaus und das dionysische Theater vollendet. Vermöge seines unbestechlichen Charakters besaß
er großes Ansehn beim Volke. Er war ein Verehrer
der Dichter, zumal der drei großen Tragiker, denen er
Bildsäulen setzte und deren Werke er in einem Exemplar

im Staatsarchiv bewahren liefs, um sie vor willkürlichen
Veränderungen zu schützen. Als Ankläger war er ge-
fürchtet, weil er auf strenge Strafen antrug. Erhalten
hat sich nur eine Rede gegen Leokrates, den er auf den
Tod anklagte, weil er gleich nach der Schlacht bei
Chaironeia Athen verlassen hatte.

Gleich unbestechlich war Hypereides, aber ein
Lebemann, den Genüssen der Tafel, dem Spiel und den
Frauen zugethan. Freimütig und opferwillig hat er
lange an des Demosthenes Seite gekämpft, er war es,
der 343 die Verurteilung des bestochenen Philokrates
erwirkte. Als aber Demosthenes die Gelegenheit ver-
säumte mit des Harpalos Geld gegen die Makedonier
aufzustehen (324), trennte sich der hitzige Hypereides
von ihm und bewirkte seinen Sturz. Dann betrieb er
den lamischen Krieg, flüchtete nach dessen unglücklichem
Ausgang, wurde aber ergriffen und von Antipatros hingerichtet. Als Redner war er schlicht und nüchtern,
ähnlich dem Lysias, aber voll Witz und Geist. Von
seinen Reden ist in Handschriften keine überliefert, da-
gegen sind auf Papyrusrollen aus ägyptischen Gräbern
nach und nach sechs derselben zum Vorschein gekommen,
darunter die gegen Demosthenes und jüngst die gegen
Athenogenes, die einen jungen Athener in den Händen
eines ägyptischen Wucherers zeigt.

Wie diese beiden etwa fünf Jahr älter als Demosthenes
war auch Aischines, aus verarmter Familie, ohne tiefere
Bildung. Er begann seine Laufbahn als Schreiber bei
den Behörden, versuchte sich als tragischer Schauspieler,
schlofs sich dann an Eubulos an und wurde 346 Mitglied der Friedensgesandtschaften. Hier wurde Aischines
von Philipp gewonnen und war fortan das Haupt der
makedonischen Partei in Athen und als solches der er-
bitterte Gegner des Demosthenes. Auf diesen Streit be-

ziehen sich auch seine drei Reden. Als er bei der Anklage gegen Ktesiphon, der für Demosthenes einen
goldenen Kranz beantragt hatte, einen völligen Mifs-
erfolg erlebte, ging er 330 freiwillig in die Verbannung
nach Ephesos und Rhodos und soll in Samos gestorben sein.

Demosthenes, des Demosthenes Sohn, aus dem
Gau Paiania, um 384 geboren, verlor seinen Vater früh
und wurde durch gewissenlose Vormünder um den gröfsten
Teil des väterlichen Erbes betrogen. Das Verlangen, sie
zur Rechenschaft zu ziehen, führte ihn zur Beschäftigung
mit der Redekunst und zum Unterrichte des Isaios. Die
Klage des 20 jährigen Jünglings erwirkte die Verurteilung
des Aphobos zu zehn Talenten Schadenersatz, und wenn
er auch von dem verlorenen Vermögen nur einen Teil
wiedererhielt, so war dieser Erfolg für seine Zukunft
entscheidend. Mit der unbeugsamsten Thatkraft über-
wand er die Mängel seiner Naturanlage und bildete sich
zum gröfsten Redner des Altertums. Die erworbene
Übung und Rechtskenntnis verwertete er zunächst als
Sachwalter. Mit dreifsig Jahren trat er selbst mit Ge-
richts- und Staatsreden auf, aber erst 351 mit der ersten
Philippika fand er den Gegner, dessen Bekämpfung, wenngleich nicht von Erfolg gekrönt, ihm Unsterblichkeit ver-
leihen sollte. Einen ärgerlichen Handel hatte er mit
Meidias, der ihn, den Choregen seiner Phyle, während
der Feier der grofsen Dionysien thätlich beleidigte. Nachdem das Volk durch eine Abstimmung das Verfahren des
Gegners gemifsbilligt hatte, liefs sich Demosthenes zu
einem Vergleich herbei.

Bei Chaironeia nahm er als Hoplit am Kampfe teil
und hielt bei der Leichenfeier den Gefallenen die Grab-
rede. Zwei Jahre darauf stellte Ktesiphon den Antrag,
des Demosthenes Verdienste mit einem goldenen Kranze
zu ehren, und wenn es auch der Anklage des Aischines

gelang, die Ausführung sechs Jahre hinzuhalten, so erlitt er doch bei der Verhandlung (Rede $\pi\varepsilon\varrho\grave{\iota}$ $\sigma\tau\varepsilon\varphi\acute{\alpha}\nu o\upsilon$) eine entscheidende Niederlage.

Im Jahre 324 kam Harpalos, der ungetreue Schatzmeister des Königs Alexandros, nach Athen mit vielem Gelde, und als von makedonischer Seite seine Auslieferung verlangt wurde, verhaftete man ihn und liefs sein Geld auf die Burg bringen. Da aber fehlte fast die Hälfte des Geldes, und der Areopag, dem die Untersuchung übertragen war, nannte unter den Empfängern auch Demosthenes mit 20 Talenten. Dieser erkannte den Empfang an, behauptete aber das Geld zu einem Vorschufs an die Theorikenkasse verwandt zu haben. Er wurde zu 50 Talenten verurteilt und, da er nicht zahlen konnte, ins Gefängnis geworfen, entkam jedoch nach dem Peloponnes. Während des lamischen Krieges wurde er nach Athen zurückgerufen, floh nach dem Siege des Antipatros, wurde im Poseidontempel auf der Insel Kalauria bei Troizen aufgefunden und entzog sich der Abführung durch Gift (322).

Deinarchos stammte aus Korinth und gelangte in Athen als Sachwalter zu Wohlstand und Einflufs. Er wurde 307 nach dem Sturze der makedonischen Oligarchie angeklagt, entzog sich dem Gericht und lebte 15 Jahre in Chalkis auf Euboia in der Verbannung. Die drei erhaltenen Reden, darunter eine gegen Demosthenes, beziehen sich auf den harpalischen Prozefs.

Geschichtliches.

König Philippos von Makedonien hatte nach seiner Thronbesteigung 359 die Athener, die einen anderen Thronbewerber unterstützten, durch Versprechungen beschwichtigt, ihre Gefangenen ohne Lösegeld zurückgeschickt und unter Verzicht auf Amphipolis Frieden

geschlossen. Als er Herr im eignen Hause war und die
Athener durch den Bundesgenossenkrieg 357—55 ander-
weit beschäftigt wuſste, eroberte Philippos Amphipolis,
Pydna, bald auch Poteidaia. Die attischen Kleruchen
des letzteren Gebietes schickte er zwar ungefährdet nach
Hause, überlieſs aber die zerstörte Stadt ebenso wie
Anthemus den Olynthiern, um sie von Athen zu trennen.
Dann bemächtigte er sich der Goldbergwerke des Pan-
gaion, die ihm reichen Ertrag, an 1000 Talente jährlich,
für seine Kriege und Bestechungen lieferten, und gründete
die Stadt Philippoi. Endlich 353 eroberte und zerstörte
er das mit Athen verbündete Methone, athenische Hilfe
kam überall zu spät.

Darauf wurde Philippos von den Aleuaden von Larisa
nach Thessalien gerufen gegen die Tyrannen von Pherai,
welche von den Phokern unterstützt wurden. Anfangs
gegen diese unglücklich, schlug er sie 352 entscheidend
und besetzte den Hafen Pagasai und die Landschaft
Magnesia. Ein Vorstoſs gegen die Thermopylen wurde
durch eine rechtzeitig eingetroffene Flotte der Athener
vereitelt, worauf sich Philippos nach Thrakien wandte.
Die Nachricht von seinen dortigen Fortschritten, ins-
besondere von der Belagerung Heraions, die im November 352 nach Athen gelangte, verursachte groſse
Aufregung und viele stürmische Volksversammlungen
(III 4). Bei dieser Gelegenheit, wahrscheinlich Anfang 351, trat Demosthenes mit seiner ersten Philippika hervor, welche im Gegensatze zu einzelnen Hilfssendungen einen dauernden Krieg mit Philippos und ein
Heer, zu einem Vierteil aus Bürgern bestehend, fordert.
Es erfolgte auch ein kräftiger Beschluſs, vierzig Trieren,
die Bürger bis zu 45 Jahren auszusenden, 60 Talente
zu steuern. Aber die Nachricht von des Königs Er-
krankung lähmte die Ausführung, im Herbst fuhr Chari-

demos mit zehn unbewehrten Schiffen und fünf Talenten
aus (III 5).

Auch die Stadt Olynthos, anfangs von Philippos
mit Wohlthaten überhäuft, sah sich durch seine Fort-
schritte in Thessalien und Thrakien bedroht und schloſs
352 einen Vertrag mit Athen. Darauf erfolgte wirklich
ein Angriff von seiten des Königs, doch wandte er sich
bald ab nach Illyrien und Epeiros. Erst 349 begann
er den Kampf gegen Olynthos, zunächst noch unter
Friedensversicherungen. Die Stadt suchte Hilfe bei
Athen. Aus diesem Anlaſs hielt Demosthenes seine drei
olynthischen Reden: a) eine doppelte Kriegsrüstung
nach Olynthos und gegen Philippos' Land ist erforder-
lich, b) Philippos' Macht beruht auf Lug und Trug,
weder seine Bundesgenossen, noch seine eigenen Unter-
thanen sind zuverlässig, c) vor allem thut Euch eine
anderweite Regelung der Finanzverwaltung not. Die
Athener schickten auch nach Olynthos drei Hilfssendungen,
welche jedoch teils unzureichend waren, teils zu spät
kamen. Sie hatten sich zudem in eine Unternehmung
auf Euboia (348) eingelassen, welche trotz Phokions Sieg
bei Tamynai übel genug ablief. Olynthos fiel durch
Verrat und wurde zerstört, ebenso erorberte Philippos
die übrigen Städte der Chalkidike.

Nach diesem groſsen Erfolge wandte sich der König
wieder nach Thrakien, wohin auch die Athener ihren Feld-
herrn Chares sandten. Bald jedoch machte er Friedens-
anträge. Zehn Gesandte gingen Anfang 346 nach Pella
und wurden gröſstenteils von Philippos gewonnen. Auf
Philokrates' Antrag wurde sodann in Athen ein Friede
auf der Grundlage des gegenwärtigen Besitzstandes ab-
geschlossen und von den Athenern sofort beschworen,
während die Gesandten nochmals zum Könige gingen,
um ihm den Eid abzunehmen. Diese wurden in Pella

zurückgehalten, während Philippos in Thrakien neue Eroberungen machte, die dann durch den Frieden ihm gesichert wurden. Demosthenes widersetzte sich vergebens,
ebensowenig hörte man in Athen seinen nüchternen und
mifstrauischen Bericht (V 10), sondern glaubte denen,
die, von Philippos gewonnen, den Athenern für die Zukunft vom Könige die gröfsten Vorteile in Aussicht
stellten. Die Athener gaben die Phoker preis, diese
streckten die Waffen, Philippos rückte durch die Thermopylen, und in einer Versammlung der Amphiktyonen
wurden die Phoker geächtet, ihre Stimmen und die
Leitung der pythischen Spiele auf Philippos übertragen. Da sahen sich die Athener bitter getäuscht
und nahmen eine drohende Haltung an, und als eine
Gesandtschaft mit der Aufforderung erschien, man
solle Philippos' Eintritt in den Amphiktyonenbund an-
erkennen, da warnte Demosthenes, als die Volksstimmung
schwankte, in der Rede vom Frieden dringend davor,
dafs man durch eine Ablehnung nicht die versammelten
Amphiktyonen zu einem gemeinsamen Kriege gegen
Athen reize.

Nach dem Frieden befestigte Philippos seine
Stellung in Thessalien und griff in den Peloponnes
über, indem er dort die Messenier und Argeier zu
gewinnen suchte, welche sich trotz der Warnungen der
Athener (VI 19) ihm anschlossen. Den Athenern gegenüber beteuerte er seine Friedensliebe und bei Gelegenheit einer solchen Gesandtschaft scheint im Jahre 344
die zweite philippische Rede gehalten, welche die
gesamte Politik des Königs als gegen Athen gerichtet
darstellt.

In der That stieg in der nächsten Zeit der Einflufs
des Redners und seiner Partei; Philokrates entzog sich
der Strafe durch freiwillige Verbannung; 343 hielt es

Philippos für angezeigt durch Python von Byzanz, einen gewandten Redner, in Athen die Vorwürfe seiner Gegner zu widerlegen und zu einer Abänderung des Friedensvertrages seine Hand zu bieten (VII 19). Die Beschwerden rechtfertigte demgegenüber Demosthenes in glänzender Rede; mit anderweiten Vertragsvorschlägen wurde Hegesippos, ein entschiedener Gegner der makedonischen Partei, zu Philippos entsandt, aber sehr unfreundlich empfangen. Die Antwort gab erst im folgenden Jahre ein Brief des Königs, gegen welchen die Rede über Halonnesos von Hegesippos gehalten ist. Sie geht das Antwortschreiben Punkt für Punkt durch, um es zu widerlegen.

Kurz vorher hatten die Athener unter Diopeithes Kleruchen nach dem Chersonnes entsandt, welche mit den Bewohnern von Kardia in Streit gerieten. Diopeithes warb Söldner, verschaffte sich durch Anhalten der Handelsschiffe die Mittel zu ihrem Unterhalt und plünderte die thrakische Umgegend. Darauf erfolgten Beschwerden des Philippos in Athen, die von seinen dortigen Anhängern unterstützt wurden. Deshalb wies Demosthenes in der Rede über die Angelegenheiten im Chersonnes (Frühjahr 341) nach, dafs der König in Wahrheit der Friedensstörer sei und dafs Diopeithes als Vertreter der Sache Athens Unterstützung verdiene. Darauf wurde in der That Diopeithes mit Geld und Kriegsbedarf versehen.

Nur kurze Zeit später ist die dritte Philippika gehalten, welche nachweist, dafs trotz des anscheinenden Friedens Philippos sich in vollem Kriege mit Athen befinde, dafs er seine Macht der straflosen Bestechlichkeit, der Schlaffheit und Sorglosigkeit seiner Gegner verdanke, dafs man vor allem selbst rüsten, dann aber auch die anderen Staaten, selbst Chios, Rhodos, sogar den Perser-

könig gegen Philippos aufrufen müsse. Das Volk stimmte
den Anträgen des Redners zu und setzte sie im folgenden
Jahre durch zahlreiche Gesandtschaften ins Werk, mit
dem besten Erfolge, bis Philippos durch den amphik-
tyonischen Krieg gegen die amphissäischen Lokrer der
Weg nach Böotien geöffnet wurde.

ΟΛΥΝΘΙΑΚΟΣ Α.

Ἀντὶ πολλῶν ἂν, ὦ ἄνδρες Ἀθηναῖοι, χρημάτων **1**
ὑμᾶς ἑλέσθαι νομίζω, εἰ φανερὸν γένοιτο τὸ μέλλον
συνοίσειν τῇ πόλει περὶ ὧν νυνὶ σκοπεῖτε. ὅτε
τοίνυν τοῦθ᾽ οὕτως ἔχει, προσήκει προθύμως **5**
ἐθέλειν ἀκούειν τῶν βουλομένων συμβουλεύειν·
οὐ γὰρ μόνον εἴ τι χρήσιμον ἐσκεμμένος ἥκει τις,
τοῦτ᾽ ἂν ἀκούσαντες λάβοιτε, ἀλλὰ καὶ τῆς ὑμετέρας τύχης ὑπολαμβάνω, πολλὰ τῶν δεόντων ἐκ
τοῦ παραχρῆμ᾽ ἐνίοις ἂν ἐπελθεῖν εἰπεῖν, ὥστ᾽ ἐξ **10**
ἁπάντων ῥᾳδίαν τὴν τοῦ συμφέροντος ὑμῖν αἵρεσιν
γενέσθαι.

Ὁ μὲν οὖν παρὼν καιρός, ὦ ἄνδρες Ἀθηναῖοι, **2**
μόνον οὐχὶ λέγει φωνὴν ἀφιείς, ὅτι τῶν πραγμάτων ὑμῖν ἐκείνων αὐτοῖς ἀντιληπτέον **15**
ἐστίν, εἴπερ ὑπὲρ σωτηρίας αὐτῶν φροντίζετε·
ἡμεῖς δ᾽ οὐκ οἶδ᾽ ὅντινά μοι δοκοῦμεν ἔχειν τρόπον
πρὸς αὐτά. ἔστι δὴ τά γ᾽ ἐμοὶ δοκοῦντα, ψηφίσασθαι μὲν ἤδη τὴν βοήθειαν, καὶ παρασκευάσα-
σθαι τὴν ταχίστην, ὅπως ἐνθένδε βοηθήσητε καὶ **20**
μὴ πάθητε ταὐτὸν ὅπερ καὶ πρότερον, πρεσβείαν **III, 4.**

δὲ πέμπειν, ἥτις ταῦτ᾽ ἐρεῖ καὶ παρέσται τοῖς
3 πράγμασιν· ὡς ἔστι μάλιστα τοῦτο δέος, μὴ πα-
νοῦργος ὢν καὶ δεινὸς ἄνθρωπος πράγμασι χρῆσθαι,
τὰ μὲν εἴκων, ἡνίκ᾽ ἂν τύχῃ, τὰ δ᾽ ἀπειλῶν (ἀξιό-
5 πιστος δ᾽ ἂν εἰκότως φαίνοιτο), τὰ δ᾽ ἡμᾶς δια-
βάλλων καὶ τὴν ἀπουσίαν τὴν ἡμετέραν, τρέψηται
4 καὶ παρασπάσηταί τι τῶν ὅλων πραγμάτων. οὐ μὴν
ἀλλ᾽ ἐπιεικῶς, ὦ ἄνδρες Ἀθηναῖοι, τοῦθ᾽ ὃ δυσ-
μαχώτατόν ἐστι τῶν Φιλίππου πραγμάτων,
10 καὶ βέλτιστον ὑμῖν. τὸ γὰρ εἶναι πάντων
ἐκεῖνον ἕν᾽ ὄντα κύριον καὶ ῥητῶν καὶ ἀπορρήτων
καὶ ἅμα στρατηγὸν καὶ δεσπότην καὶ ταμίαν, καὶ
πανταχοῦ αὐτὸν παρεῖναι τῷ στρατεύματι, πρὸς
μὲν τὸ τὰ τοῦ πολέμου ταχὺ καὶ κατὰ καιρὸν
15 πράττεσθαι πολλῷ προέχει, πρὸς δὲ τὰς καταλλαγάς,
ἃς ἂν ἐκεῖνος ποιήσαιτ᾽ ἄσμενος πρὸς Ὀλυνθίους,
5 ἐναντίως ἔχει. δῆλον γάρ ἐστι τοῖς Ὀλυνθίοις,
ὅτι νῦν οὐ περὶ δόξης οὐδ᾽ ὑπὲρ μέρους χώρας
πολεμοῦσιν, ἀλλ᾽ ἀναστάσεως καὶ ἀνδραποδισμοῦ
20 τῆς πατρίδος, καὶ ἴσασιν ἅ τ᾽ Ἀμφιπολιτῶν ἐποίησε
357 τοὺς παραδόντας αὐτῷ τὴν πόλιν καὶ Πυδναίων
τοὺς ὑποδεξαμένους· καὶ ὅλως ἄπιστον, οἶμαι, ταῖς
πολιτείαις ἡ τυραννίς, ἄλλως τε κἂν ὅμορον χώραν
6 ἔχωσιν. ταῦτ᾽ οὖν ἐγνωκότας ὑμᾶς, ὦ ἄνδρες
25 Ἀθηναῖοι, καὶ τἄλλ᾽ ἃ προσήκει πάντ᾽ ἐνθυμουμένους φημὶ δεῖν ἐθελῆσαι καὶ παροξυνθῆναι καὶ
τῷ πολέμῳ προσέχειν, εἴπερ ποτέ, καὶ νῦν, χρήματ᾽
εἰσφέροντας προθύμως καὶ αὐτοὺς ἐξιόντας καὶ
μηδὲν ἐλλείποντας. οὐδὲ γὰρ λόγος οὐδὲ σκῆψις

ἔϑ᾽ ὑμῖν τοῦ μὴ τὰ δέοντα ποιεῖν ἐθέλειν ὑπολείπεται.

Νυνὶ γάρ, ὃ πάντες ἐθρυλεῖτε, ὡς Ὀλυνθίους 7 ἐκπολεμῆσαι δεῖ Φιλίππῳ, γέγονεν αὐτό- ματον, καὶ ταῦϑ᾽ ὡς ἂν ὑμῖν μάλιστα συμφέροι. 5 εἰ μὲν γὰρ ὑφ᾽ ὑμῶν πεισθέντες ἀνείλοντο τὸν πόλεμον, σφαλεροὶ σύμμαχοι καὶ μέχρι του ταῦτ᾽ ἂν ἐγνωκότες ἦσαν ἴσως· ἐπειδὴ δ᾽ ἐκ τῶν πρὸς αὐτοὺς ἐγκλημάτων μισοῦσι, βεβαίαν εἰκὸς τὴν ἔχθραν αὐτοὺς ὑπὲρ ὧν φοβοῦνται καὶ πεπόνθασιν 10 ἔχειν. οὐ δεῖ δὴ τοιοῦτον, ὦ ἄνδρες Ἀθηναῖοι, 8 παραπεπτωκότα καιρὸν ἀφεῖναι, οὐδὲ παθεῖν ταὐτόν, ὅπερ ἤδη πολλάκις πρότερον πεπόνθατε. εἰ γάρ, ὅϑ᾽ ἥκομεν Εὐβοεῦσι βεβοηθηκότες καὶ παρῆσαν Ἀμφιπολιτῶν Ἱέραξ καὶ Στρατοκλῆς ἐπὶ τουτὶ τὸ 357 βῆμα, κελεύοντες ἡμᾶς πλεῖν καὶ παραλαμβάνειν 16 τὴν πόλιν, τὴν αὐτὴν παρειχόμεϑ᾽ ἡμεῖς ὑπὲρ ἡμῶν αὐτῶν προθυμίαν, ἥνπερ ὑπὲρ τῆς Εὐβοέων σωτηρίας, εἴχετ᾽ ἂν Ἀμφίπολιν τότε καὶ πάντων τῶν μετὰ ταῦτ᾽ ἂν ἦτ᾽ ἀπηλλαγμένοι πραγμάτων. 20 καὶ πάλιν, ἡνίκα Πύδνα, Ποτείδαια, Μεθώνη, 9 Παγασαί, τἆλλα, ἵνα μὴ καϑ᾽ ἕκαστα λέγων διατρίβω, 357/53 πολιορκούμεν᾽ ἀπηγγέλλετο, εἰ τότε τούτων ἑνὶ τῷ πρώτῳ προθύμως καὶ ὡς προσῆκεν ἐβοηθήσαμεν αὐτοί, ῥᾷονι καὶ πολὺ ταπεινοτέρῳ νῦν ἂν ἐχρώ- 25 μεθα τῷ Φιλίππῳ. νῦν δὲ τὸ μὲν παρὸν ἀεὶ προϊέμενοι, τὰ δὲ μέλλοντ᾽ αὐτόματ᾽ οἰόμενοι σχήσειν καλῶς, ηὐξήσαμεν, ὦ ἄνδρες Ἀθηναῖοι, Φίλιππον ἡμεῖς καὶ κατεστήσαμεν τηλικοῦτον,

1*

ἡλίκος οὐδείς πω βασιλεὺς γέγονε Μακεδονίας.
νυνὶ δὴ καιρὸς ἥκει τις, οὗτος ὁ τῶν Ὀλυνθίων,
αὐτόματος τῇ πόλει, ὃς οὐδενός ἐστιν ἐλάττων τῶν
πρότερον ἐκείνων.

10 Καὶ ἔμοιγε δοκεῖ τις ἂν, ὦ ἄνδρες Ἀθηναῖοι,
6 δίκαιος λογιστὴς τῶν παρὰ τῶν θεῶν ἡμῖν ὑπηργ-
μένων καταστάς, καίπερ οὐκ ἐχόντων ὡς δεῖ
πολλῶν, ὅμως μεγάλην ἂν ἔχειν αὐτοῖς χάριν,
εἰκότως· τὸ μὲν γὰρ πόλλ' ἀπολωλεκέναι κατὰ
10 τὸν πόλεμον τῆς ἡμετέρας ἀμελείας ἄν τις θείη
δικαίως, τὸ δὲ μήτε πάλαι τοῦτο πεπονθέναι, πε-
φηνέναι τέ τιν' ἡμῖν συμμαχίαν τούτων ἀντίρροπον,
ἂν βουλώμεθα χρῆσθαι, τῆς παρ' ἐκείνων εὐνοίας
11 εὐεργέτημ' ἂν ἔγωγε θείην. ἀλλ' οἶμαι, παρόμοιόν
15 ἐστιν, ὅπερ καὶ περὶ τῆς τῶν χρημάτων κτήσεως·
ἂν μὲν γάρ, ὅσ' ἄν τις λάβῃ, καὶ σώσῃ, μεγάλην
ἔχει τῇ τύχῃ τὴν χάριν, ἂν δ' ἀναλώσας λάθῃ,
συνανήλωσε καὶ τὸ μεμνῆσθαι τὴν χάριν. καὶ
περὶ τῶν πραγμάτων οὕτως οἱ μὴ χρησάμενοι
20 τοῖς καιροῖς ὀρθῶς οὐδ', εἰ συνέβη τι παρὰ τῶν
θεῶν χρηστόν, μνημονεύουσιν· πρὸς γὰρ τὸ
τελευταῖον ἐκβὰν ἕκαστον τῶν πρὶν ὑπαρξάντων
κρίνεται. διὸ καὶ σφόδρα δεῖ τῶν λοιπῶν ἡμᾶς,
ὦ ἄνδρες Ἀθηναῖοι, φροντίσαι, ἵνα ταῦτ' ἐπανορ-
25 θωσάμενοι τὴν ἐπὶ τοῖς πεπραγμένοις ἀδοξίαν
ἀποτριψώμεθα.

12 Εἰ δὲ προησόμεθα, ὦ ἄνδρες Ἀθηναῖοι, καὶ
τούτους τοὺς ἀνθρώπους, εἶτ' Ὄλυνθον ἐκεῖνος
καταστρέψεται, φρασάτω τις ἐμοί, τί τὸ κωλῦον

ἔτ᾽ αὐτὸν ἔσται βαδίζειν ὅποι βούλεται.
ἆρά γε λογίζεταί τις ὑμῶν, ὦ ἄνδρες Ἀθηναῖοι,
καὶ θεωρεῖ τὸν τρόπον, δι᾽ ὃν μέγας γέγονεν
ἀσθενὴς ὢν τὸ κατ᾽ ἀρχὰς Φίλιππος; τὸ πρῶτον 357/53
Ἀμφίπολιν λαβών, μετὰ ταῦτα Πύδναν, πάλιν 5
Ποτείδαιαν, Μεθώνην αὖθις, εἶτα Θετταλίας ἐπέβη·
μετὰ ταῦτα Φεράς, Παγασάς, Μαγνησίαν, πάνθ᾽ 13
352
ὃν ἐβούλετ᾽ εὐτρεπίσας τρόπον, ᾤχετ᾽ εἰς Θρᾴκην.
εἶτ᾽ ἐκεῖ τοὺς μὲν ἐκβαλών, τοὺς δὲ καταστήσας
τῶν βασιλέων ἠσθένησεν· πάλιν ῥᾴσας οὐκ ἐπὶ 352/51
τὸ ῥᾳθυμεῖν ἀπέκλινεν, ἀλλ᾽ εὐθὺς Ὀλυνθίοις 11
ἐπεχείρησεν. τὰς δ᾽ ἐπ᾽ Ἰλλυριοὺς καὶ Παίονας
358/51
αὐτοῦ καὶ πρὸς Ἀρύββαν καὶ ὅποι τις ἂν εἴποι
παραλείπω στρατείας. Τί οὖν, ἄν τις εἴποι, ταῦτα 14
λέγεις ἡμῖν νῦν; ἵνα γνῶτε, ὦ ἄνδρες Ἀθηναῖοι, 15
καὶ αἴσθησθ᾽ ἀμφότερα, καὶ τὸ προΐεσθαι καθ᾽
ἕκαστον ἀεί τι τῶν πραγμάτων ὡς ἀλυσιτελές,
καὶ τὴν φιλοπραγμοσύνην, ᾗ χρῆται καὶ συζῇ
Φίλιππος, ὑφ᾽ ἧς οὐκ ἔστιν ὅπως ἀγαπήσας τοῖς
πεπραγμένοις ἡσυχίαν σχήσει. εἰ δ᾽ ὁ μὲν ὡς ἀεί 20
τι μεῖζον τῶν ὑπαρχόντων δεῖ πράττειν ἐγνωκὼς
ἔσται, ἡμεῖς δ᾽ ὡς οὐδενὸς ἀντιληπτέον ἐρρωμένως
τῶν πραγμάτων, σκοπεῖσθ᾽ εἰς τί ποτ᾽ ἐλπὶς ταῦτα
τελευτῆσαι. πρὸς θεῶν, τίς οὕτως εὐήθης ἐστὶν 15
ὑμῶν, ὅστις ἀγνοεῖ τὸν ἐκεῖθεν πόλεμον δεῦρ᾽ 25
ἥξοντα, ἂν ἀμελήσωμεν; ἀλλὰ μὴν εἰ τοῦτο γενήσεται, δέδοικα, ὦ ἄνδρες Ἀθηναῖοι, μὴ τὸν
αὐτὸν τρόπον, ὥσπερ οἱ δανειζόμενοι ῥᾳδίως ἐπὶ
τοῖς μεγάλοις τόκοις, μικρὸν εὐπορήσαντες χρόνον,

ὕστερον καὶ τῶν ἀρχαίων ἀπέστησαν, οὕτω καὶ
ἡμεῖς, ἂν ἐπὶ πολλῷ φανῶμεν ἐρραθυμηκότες καὶ
ἅπαντα πρὸς ἡδονὴν ζητοῦντες, πολλὰ καὶ χαλεπὰ
ὧν οὐκ ἠβουλόμεθ᾿ ὕστερον εἰς ἀνάγκην ἔλθωμεν
5 ποιεῖν, καὶ κινδυνεύσωμεν περὶ τῶν ἐν αὐτῇ τῇ χώρᾳ.

16   Τὸ μὲν οὖν ἐπιτιμᾶν ἴσως φῆσαι τις ἂν
ῥᾴδιον καὶ παντὸς εἶναι, τὸ δ᾿ ὑπὲρ τῶν παρόντων
ὅ τι δεῖ πράττειν ἀποφαίνεσθαι, τοῦτ᾿ εἶναι
συμβούλου. ἐγὼ δ᾿ οὐκ ἀγνοῶ μέν, ὦ ἄνδρες
10 Ἀθηναῖοι, τοῦθ᾿, ὅτι πολλάκις ὑμεῖς οὐ τοὺς
αἰτίους, ἀλλὰ τοὺς ὑστάτους περὶ τῶν πραγμάτων
εἰπόντας ἐν ὀργῇ ποιεῖσθε, ἄν τι μὴ κατὰ γνώμην
ἐκβῇ· οὐ μὴν οἶμαι δεῖν τὴν ἰδίαν ἀσφάλειαν
σκοποῦνθ᾿ ὑποστείλασθαι περὶ ὧν ὑμῖν συμφέρειν
17 ἡγοῦμαι.   φημὶ δὴ διχῇ βοηθητέον εἶναι τοῖς
16 πράγμασιν ὑμῖν, τῷ τε τὰς πόλεις τοῖς Ὀλυνθίοις
σῴζειν καὶ τοὺς τοῦτο ποιήσοντας στρατιώτας
ἐκπέμπειν, καὶ τῷ τὴν ἐκείνου χώραν κακῶς ποιεῖν
καὶ τριήρεσι καὶ στρατιώταις ἑτέροις· εἰ δὲ θατέρου
20 τούτων ὀλιγωρήσετε, ὀκνῶ μὴ μάταιος ἡμῖν ἡ
18 στρατεία γένηται.   εἴτε γὰρ ὑμῶν τὴν ἐκείνου
κακῶς ποιούντων ὑπομείνας τοῦτ᾿ Ὄλυνθον παρα-
στήσεται, ῥᾳδίως ἐπὶ τὴν οἰκείαν ἐλθὼν ἀμυνεῖται.
εἴτε βοηθησάντων μόνον ὑμῶν εἰς Ὄλυνθον ἀκιν-
25 δύνως ὁρῶν ἔχοντα τὰ οἴκοι προσκαθεδεῖται καὶ
προσεδρεύσει τοῖς πράγμασι, περιέσται τῷ χρόνῳ
τῶν πολιορκουμένων. δεῖ δὴ πολλὴν καὶ διχῇ
τὴν βοήθειαν εἶναι.

Καὶ περὶ μὲν τῆς βοηθείας ταῦτα γιγνώσκω· 19
περὶ δὲ χρημάτων πόρου, ἔστιν, ὦ ἄνδρες
Ἀθηναῖοι, χρήμαθ᾽ ὑμῖν, ἔστιν ὅσ᾽ οὐδενὶ τῶν
ἄλλων ἀνθρώπων στρατιωτικά· ταῦτα δ᾽ ὑμεῖς
οὕτως ὡς βούλεσθε λαμβάνετε. εἰ μὲν οὖν ταῦτα 5
τοῖς στρατευομένοις ἀποδώσετε, οὐδενὸς ὑμῖν
προσδεῖ πόρου, εἰ δὲ μή, προσδεῖ, μᾶλλον δ᾽
ἅπαντος ἐνδεῖ τοῦ πόρου. τί οὖν, ἄν τις εἴποι,
σὺ γράφεις ταῦτ᾽ εἶναι στρατιωτικά; μὰ Δί᾽ οὐκ 20
ἔγωγε· ἐγὼ μὲν γὰρ ἡγοῦμαι στρατιώτας δεῖν 10
κατασκευασθῆναι καὶ εἶναι στρατιωτικὰ καὶ μίαν
σύνταξιν εἶναι τὴν αὐτὴν τοῦ τε λαμβάνειν καὶ
τοῦ ποιεῖν τὰ δέοντα· ὑμεῖς δ᾽ οὕτω πως ἄνευ
πραγμάτων λαμβάνειν εἰς τὰς ἑορτάς. ἔστι δὴ
λοιπόν, οἶμαι, πάντας εἰσφέρειν, ἂν πολλῶν δέῃ, 15
πολλά, ἂν ὀλίγων, ὀλίγα. δεῖ δὲ χρημάτων, καὶ
ἄνευ τούτων οὐδὲν ἔστι γενέσθαι τῶν δεόντων.
λέγουσι δὲ καὶ ἄλλους τινὰς ἄλλοι πόρους, ὧν
ἕλεσθ᾽ ὅστις ὑμῖν συμφέρειν δοκεῖ· καὶ ἕως ἐστὶ
καιρός, ἀντιλάβεσθε τῶν πραγμάτων. 20

Ἄξιον δ᾽ ἐνθυμηθῆναι καὶ λογίσασθαι τὰ 21
πράγματ᾽ ἐν ᾧ καθέστηκε νυνὶ τὰ Φιλίππου.
οὔτε γάρ, ὡς δοκεῖ καὶ φήσειέ τις ἂν μὴ σκοπῶν
ἀκριβῶς, εὐτρεπῶς οὐδ᾽ ὡς ἂν κάλλιστ᾽ αὐτῷ τὰ
παρόντ᾽ ἔχει, οὔτ᾽ ἂν ἐξήνεγκε τὸν πόλεμόν ποτε 25
τοῦτον ἐκεῖνος, εἰ πολεμεῖν ᾠήθη δεήσειν αὐτόν,
ἀλλ᾽ ὡς ἐπιὼν ἅπαντα τότ᾽ ἤλπιζε τὰ πράγματ᾽
ἀναιρήσεσθαι, κᾆτα διέψευσται. τοῦτο δὴ πρῶτον

αὐτὸν ταράττει παρὰ γνώμην γεγονὸς καὶ πολλὴν
ἀθυμίαν αὐτῷ παρέχει, εἶτα τὰ τῶν Θετταλῶν.
22 ταῦτα γὰρ ἄπιστα μὲν ἦν δήπου φύσει καὶ ἀεὶ
πᾶσιν ἀνθρώποις, κομιδῇ δ᾿, ὥσπερ ἦν, καὶ ἔστι
5 νῦν τούτῳ. καὶ γὰρ Παγασὰς ἀπαιτεῖν αὐτόν
εἰσιν ἐψηφισμένοι καὶ Μαγνησίαν κεκωλύκασι
τειχίζειν. ἤκουον δ᾿ ἔγωγέ τινων, ὡς οὐδὲ τοὺς
λιμένας καὶ τὰς ἀγορὰς ἔτι δώσοιεν αὐτῷ καρ-
ποῦσθαι· τὰ γὰρ κοινὰ τὰ Θετταλῶν ἀπὸ τούτων
10 δέοι διοικεῖν, οὐ Φίλιππον λαμβάνειν. εἰ δὲ
τούτων ἀποστερηθήσεται τῶν χρημάτων, εἰς στενὸν
κομιδῇ τὰ τῆς τροφῆς τοῖς ξένοις αὐτῷ καταστήσεται.
23 ἀλλὰ μὴν τόν γε Παίονα καὶ τὸν Ἰλλυριὸν καὶ
ἁπλῶς τούτους ἅπαντας ἡγεῖσθαι χρὴ αὐτονόμους
15 ἥδιον᾿ ἂν καὶ ἐλευθέρους ἢ δούλους εἶναι· καὶ
γὰρ ἀήθεις τοῦ κατακούειν τινός εἰσι, καὶ ἄνθρωπος ὑβριστής, ὥς φασιν. καὶ μὰ Δί᾿ οὐδὲν ἄπιστον
ἴσως· τὸ γὰρ εὖ πράττειν παρὰ τὴν ἀξίαν ἀφορμὴ
τοῦ κακῶς φρονεῖν τοῖς ἀνοήτοις γίγνεται, διόπερ
20 πολλάκις δοκεῖ τὸ φυλάξαι τἀγαθὰ τοῦ κτήσασθαι
24 χαλεπώτερον εἶναι. δεῖ τοίνυν ὑμᾶς, ὦ ἄνδρες
Ἀθηναῖοι, τὴν ἀκαιρίαν τὴν ἐκείνου καιρὸν ὑμέτερον
νομίσαντας ἑτοίμως συνάρασθαι τὰ πράγματα, καὶ
πρεσβευομένους ἐφ᾿ ἃ δεῖ καὶ στρατευομένους
25 αὐτοὺς καὶ παροξύνοντας τοὺς ἄλλους ἅπαντας,
λογιζομένους, εἰ Φίλιππος λάβοι καθ᾿ ὑμῶν τοιοῦτον
καιρὸν καὶ πόλεμος γένοιτο πρὸς τῇ χώρᾳ — πῶς
ἂν αὐτὸν οἴεσθ᾿ ἑτοίμως ἐφ᾿ ὑμᾶς ἐλθεῖν; εἶτ᾿ οὐκ
αἰσχύνεσθε, εἰ μηδ᾿ ἃ πάθοιτ᾿ ἄν, εἰ δύναιτ᾿

ἐκεῖνος — ταῦτα ποιῆσαι καιρὸν ἔχοντες ⟨οὐ⟩ τολμήσετε;

Ἔτι τοίνυν, ὦ ἄνδρες Ἀθηναῖοι, μηδὲ τοῦθ' 25
ὑμᾶς λανθανέτω, ὅτι νῦν αἵρεσίς ἐστιν ὑμῖν,
πότερ' ὑμᾶς ἐκεῖ χρὴ πολεμεῖν ἢ παρ' ὑμῖν 5
ἐκεῖνον. ἐὰν μὲν γὰρ ἀντέχῃ τὰ τῶν Ὀλυνθίων,
ὑμεῖς ἐκεῖ πολεμήσετε καὶ τὴν ἐκείνου κακῶς
ποιήσετε, τὴν ὑπάρχουσαν καὶ τὴν οἰκείαν ταύτην
ἀδεῶς καρπούμενοι· ἂν δ' ἐκεῖνα Φίλιππος λάβῃ,
τίς αὐτὸν κωλύσει δεῦρο βαδίζειν; Θηβαῖοι; (μὴ 26
λίαν πικρὸν εἰπεῖν ᾖ) καὶ συνεισβαλοῦσιν ἑτοίμως. 11
ἀλλὰ Φωκεῖς; οἱ τὴν οἰκείαν οὐχ οἷοί τ' ὄντες
φυλάττειν, ἐὰν μὴ βοηθήσηθ' ὑμεῖς. ἢ ἄλλος τις;
— ἀλλ', ὦ τᾶν, οὐχὶ βουλήσεται. τῶν ἀτοπω-
τάτων μεντἂν εἴη, εἰ, ἃ νῦν ἄνοιαν ὀφλι- 15
σκάνων ὅμως ἐκλαλεῖ, ταῦτα δυνηθεὶς μὴ πράξει.
ἀλλὰ μὴν ἡλίκα γ' ἐστὶ τὰ διάφορα ἐνθάδ' ἢ 'κεῖ 27
πολεμεῖν, οὐδὲ λόγου προσδεῖν ἡγοῦμαι. εἰ γὰρ
ὑμᾶς δεήσειεν αὐτοὺς τριάκονθ' ἡμέρας μόνας ἔξω
γενέσθαι καί, ὅσ' ἀνάγκη στρατοπέδῳ χρωμένους, 20
τῶν ἐκ τῆς χώρας λαμβάνειν, μηδενὸς ὄντος ἐν
αὐτῇ πολεμίου λέγω, πλέον ἂν οἶμαι ζημιωθῆναι
τοὺς γεωργοῦντας ὑμῶν, ἢ ὅσ' εἰς ἅπαντα τὸν
πρὸ τοῦ πόλεμον δεδαπάνησθε. εἰ δὲ δὴ πόλεμός
τις ἥξει, πόσα χρὴ νομίσαι ζημιώσεσθαι; καὶ πρόσ- 25
εσθ' ἡ ὕβρις καὶ ἔθ' ἡ τῶν πραγμάτων αἰσχύνη,
οὐδεμιᾶς ἐλάττων ζημία τοῖς γε σώφροσιν.

28   *Πάντα δὴ ταῦτα δεῖ συνιδόντας ἅπαντας*
βοηθεῖν καὶ ἀπωθεῖν ἐκεῖσε τὸν πόλεμον, τοὺς
μὲν εὐπόρους, ἵν᾽ ὑπὲρ τῶν πολλῶν ὧν καλῶς
ποιοῦντες ἔχουσι, μίκρ᾽ ἀναλίσκοντες τὰ λοιπὰ
5 *καρπῶνται ἀδεῶς, τοὺς δ᾽ ἐν ἡλικίᾳ, ἵνα τὴν τοῦ*
πολεμεῖν ἐμπειρίαν ἐν τῇ Φιλίππου χώρᾳ κτη-
σάμενοι φοβεροὶ φύλακες τῆς οἰκείας ἀκεραίου
γένωνται, τοὺς δὲ λέγοντας, ἵν᾽ αἱ τῶν πεπολιτευ-
μένων αὐτοῖς εὔθυναι ῥᾴδιαι γένωνται, ὡς ὁποῖ᾽
10 *ἅττ᾽ ἂν ὑμᾶς περιστῇ τὰ πράγματα, τοιοῦτοι*
κριταὶ καὶ τῶν πεπραγμένων αὐτοῖς ἔσεσθε. χρηστὰ
δ᾽ εἴη παντὸς ἕνεκα.

ΟΛΥΝΘΙΑΚΟΣ Β.

Ἐπὶ πολλῶν μὲν ἄν τις ἰδεῖν, ὦ ἄνδρες 1
Ἀθηναῖοι, δοκεῖ μοι τὴν παρὰ τῶν θεῶν εὔνοιαν
φανερὰν γιγνομένην τῇ πόλει, οὐχ ἥκιστα δ᾽ ἐν
τοῖς παροῦσι πράγμασιν· τὸ γὰρ τοὺς πολεμή- 5
σοντας Φιλίππῳ γεγενῆσθαι καὶ χώραν ὅμορον
καὶ δύναμίν τινα κεκτημένους, καὶ τὸ μέγιστον
ἁπάντων, τὴν ὑπὲρ τοῦ πολέμου γνώμην τοιαύτην
ἔχοντας, ὥστε τὰς πρὸς ἐκεῖνον διαλλαγὰς πρῶτον
μὲν ἀπίστους, εἶτα τῆς ἑαυτῶν πατρίδος νομίζειν 10
ἀνάστασιν, δαιμονίᾳ τινὶ καὶ θείᾳ παντάπασιν
ἔοικεν εὐεργεσίᾳ. δεῖ τοίνυν, ὦ ἄνδρες Ἀθηναῖοι, 2
τοῦτ᾽ ἤδη σκοπεῖν αὐτούς, ὅπως μὴ χείρους περὶ
ἡμᾶς αὐτοὺς εἶναι δόξομεν τῶν ὑπαρχόντων, ὡς
ἔστι τῶν αἰσχρῶν, μᾶλλον δὲ τῶν αἰσχίστων, μὴ 15
μόνον πόλεων καὶ τόπων, ὧν ἦμέν ποτε κύριοι,
φαίνεσθαι προϊεμένους, ἀλλὰ καὶ τῶν ὑπὸ τῆς
τύχης παρασκευασθέντων συμμάχων καὶ καιρῶν.

Τὸ μὲν οὖν, ὦ ἄνδρες Ἀθηναῖοι, τὴν 3
Φιλίππου ῥώμην διεξιέναι, καὶ διὰ τούτων 20
τῶν λόγων προτρέπειν τὰ δέοντα ποιεῖν ὑμᾶς,
οὐχὶ καλῶς ἔχειν ἡγοῦμαι. διὰ τί; ὅτι μοι δοκεῖ

πάνθ᾽, ὅσ᾽ ἂν εἴποι τις ὑπὲρ τούτων, ἐκείνῳ μὲν
ἔχειν φιλοτιμίαν, ἡμῖν δ᾽ οὐχὶ καλῶς πεπρᾶχθαι.
ὁ μὲν γάρ, ὅσῳ πλείον᾽ ὑπὲρ τὴν ἀξίαν πεποίηκε
τὴν αὑτοῦ, τοσούτῳ θαυμαστότερος παρὰ πᾶσι
5 νομίζεται. ὑμεῖς δ᾽, ὅσῳ χεῖρον ἢ προσῆκε κέχρησθε
τοῖς πράγμασι, τοσούτῳ πλείον᾽ αἰσχύνην ὠφλή-
4 κατε. ταῦτα μὲν οὖν παραλείψω. καὶ γὰρ εἰ μετ᾽
ἀληθείας τις, ὦ ἄνδρες Ἀθηναῖοι, σκοποῖτο, ἐνθένδ᾽
ἂν αὐτὸν ἴδοι μέγαν γεγενημένον, οὐχὶ παρ᾽
10 αὐτοῦ. ὧν οὖν ἐκεῖνος μὲν ὀφείλει τοῖς ὑπὲρ
αὑτοῦ πεπολιτευμένοις χάριν, ὑμῖν δὲ δίκην προσήκει λαβεῖν, τούτων οὐχὶ νῦν ὁρῶ τὸν καιρὸν
τοῦ λέγειν· ἃ δὲ καὶ χωρὶς τούτων ἔνι, καὶ
βέλτιόν ἐστιν ἀκηκοέναι πάντας ὑμᾶς, καὶ μεγάλα,
15 ὦ ἄνδρες Ἀθηναῖοι, κατ᾽ ἐκείνου φαίνοιτ᾽ ἂν
ὀνείδη βουλομένοις ὀρθῶς δοκιμάζειν, ταῦτ᾽ εἰπεῖν
πειράσομαι.

5   Τὸ μὲν οὖν ἐπίορκον καὶ ἄπιστον καλεῖν, ἄνευ
τοῦ τὰ πεπραγμένα δεικνύναι, λοιδορίαν εἶναί τις
20 ἂν φήσειε κενὴν δικαίως, τὸ δὲ πάνθ᾽, ὅσα πώποτ᾽
ἔπραξε, διεξιόντ᾽ ἐφ᾽ ἅπασι τοιοῦτον ἐλέγχειν, καὶ
βραχέος λόγου συμβαίνει δεῖσθαι, καὶ δυοῖν ἕνεχ᾽
ἡγοῦμαι συμφέρειν εἰρῆσθαι, τοῦ τ᾽ ἐκεῖνον, ὅπερ
καὶ ἀληθὲς ὑπάρχει, φαῦλον φαίνεσθαι καὶ τοὺς
25 ὑπερεκπεπληγμένους ὡς ἄμαχόν τινα τὸν Φίλιππον ἰδεῖν, ὅτι πάντα διεξελήλυθεν, οἷς πρότερον
παρακρουόμενος μέγας ηὐξήθη, καὶ πρὸς αὐτὴν
6 ἥκει τὴν τελευτὴν τὰ πράγματ᾽ αὐτῷ. ἐγὼ

γάρ, ὦ ἄνδρες Ἀθηναῖοι, σφόδρ᾽ ἂν ἡγούμην καὶ
αὐτὸς φοβερὸν τὸν Φίλιππον καὶ θαυμαστόν, εἰ
τὰ δίκαια πράττονθ᾽ ἑώρων ηὐξημένον· νῦν δὲ
θεωρῶν καὶ σκοπῶν εὑρίσκω τὴν μὲν ἡμετέραν
εὐήθειαν τὸ κατ᾽ ἀρχάς, ὅτ᾽ Ὀλυνθίους ἀπήλαυνόν 5
τινες ἐνθένδε βουλομένους ὑμῖν διαλεχθῆναι, τῷ τὴν
Ἀμφίπολιν φάσκειν παραδώσειν καὶ τὸ θρυλούμενόν 358
ποτ᾽ ἀπόρρητον ἐκεῖνο κατασκευάσαι, τούτῳ προσαγα-
γόμενον, τὴν δ᾽ Ὀλυνθίων φιλίαν μετὰ ταῦτα τῷ 7
Ποτείδαιαν οὖσαν ὑμετέραν ἐξελεῖν καὶ τοὺς μὲν 356
πρότερον συμμάχους ὑμᾶς ἀδικῆσαι, παραδοῦναι δ᾽ 11
ἐκείνοις, Θετταλοὺς δὲ νῦν τὰ τελευταῖα τῷ Μαγνησίαν παραδώσειν ὑποσχέσθαι καὶ τὸν Φωκικὸν 353
πόλεμον πολεμήσειν ὑπὲρ αὐτῶν ἀναδέξασθαι.
ὅλως δ᾽ οὐδεὶς ἔστιν ὅντιν᾽ οὐ πεφενάκικεν ἐκεῖνος 15
τῶν αὐτῷ χρησαμένων. τὴν γὰρ ἑκάστων ἄνοιαν
ἀεὶ τῶν ἀγνοούντων αὐτὸν ἐξαπατῶν καὶ προσ-
λαμβάνων οὕτως ηὐξήθη. ὥσπερ οὖν διὰ τούτων 8
ἤρθη μέγας, ἡνίχ᾽ ἕκαστοι συμφέρον αὐτὸν ἑαυτοῖς
ᾤοντό τι πράξειν, οὕτως ὀφείλει διὰ τῶν αὐτῶν 20
τούτων καὶ καθαιρεθῆναι πάλιν, ἐπειδὴ πάνθ᾽
ἕνεχ᾽ ἑαυτοῦ ποιῶν ἐξελήλεγκται. καιροῦ μὲν δή,
ὦ ἄνδρες Ἀθηναῖοι, πρὸς τοῦτο πάρεστι Φιλίππῳ
τὰ πράγματα· ἢ παρελθών τις ἐμοί, μᾶλλον δ᾽
ὑμῖν δειξάτω, ὡς οὐκ ἀληθῆ ταῦτ᾽ ἐγὼ λέγω, ἢ 25
ὡς οἱ τὰ πρῶτ᾽ ἐξηπατημένοι τὰ λοιπὰ πιστεύσουσιν,
ἢ ὡς οἱ παρὰ τὴν αὐτῶν ἀξίαν δεδουλωμένοι
Θετταλοὶ νῦν οὐκ ἂν ἐλεύθεροι γένοιντ᾽ ἄσμενοι.

Καὶ μὴν εἴ τις ὑμῶν ταῦτα μὲν οὕτως ἔχειν 9

ἡγεῖται, οἴεται δὲ βίᾳ καθέξειν αὐτὸν τὰ πράγματα τῷ τὰ χωρία καὶ λιμένας καὶ τὰ τοιαῦτα
προειληφέναι, οὐκ ὀρθῶς οἴεται. ὅταν μὲν γὰρ ὑπ᾽
εὐνοίας τὰ πράγματα συστῇ καὶ πᾶσι ταὐτὰ συμφέρῃ
5 τοῖς μετέχουσι τοῦ πολέμου, καὶ συμπονεῖν καὶ φέρειν τὰς συμφορὰς καὶ μένειν ἐθέλουσιν ἄνθρωποι·
ὅταν δ᾽ ἐκ πλεονεξίας καὶ πονηρίας τις ὥσπερ οὗτος
ἰσχύσῃ, ἡ πρώτη πρόφασις καὶ μικρὸν πταῖσμ᾽
10 ἅπαντ᾽ ἀνεχαίτισεν καὶ διέλυσεν. οὐ γὰρ ἔστιν,
10 οὐκ ἔστιν, ὦ ἄνδρες Ἀθηναῖοι, ἀδικοῦντα καὶ ἐπιορ-
κοῦντα καὶ ψευδόμενον δύναμιν βεβαίαν κτήσασθαι,
ἀλλὰ τὰ τοιαῦτ᾽ εἰς μὲν ἅπαξ καὶ βραχὺν χρόνον
ἀντέχει, καὶ σφόδρα γ᾽ ἤνθησεν ἐπὶ ταῖς ἐλπίσιν,
ἂν τύχῃ, τῷ χρόνῳ δὲ φωρᾶται καὶ περὶ αὐτὰ καταρ-
15 ρεῖ. ὥσπερ γὰρ οἰκίας, οἶμαι, καὶ πλοίου καὶ τῶν
ἄλλων τῶν τοιούτων τὰ κάτωθεν ἰσχυρότατ᾽ εἶναι
δεῖ, οὕτω καὶ τῶν πράξεων τὰς ἀρχὰς καὶ τὰς ὑπο-
θέσεις ἀληθεῖς καὶ δικαίας εἶναι προσήκει. τοῦτο
δ᾽ οὐκ ἔνι νῦν ἐν τοῖς πεπραγμένοις Φιλίππῳ.

11   Φημὶ δὴ δεῖν ἡμᾶς τοῖς μὲν Ὀλυνθίους βοη-
21 θεῖν (καὶ ὅπως τις λέγει κάλλιστα καὶ τάχιστα,
οὕτως ἀρέσκει μοι), πρὸς δὲ Θετταλοὺς πρεσβείαν
πέμπειν, ἣ τοὺς μὲν διδάξει ταῦτα, τοὺς δὲ παρ-
οξυνεῖ· καὶ γὰρ νῦν εἰσιν ἐψηφισμένοι Παγασὰς
25 ἀπαιτεῖν καὶ περὶ Μαγνησίας λόγους ποιεῖσθαι.
12 σκοπεῖσθε μέντοι τοῦτο, ὦ ἄνδρες Ἀθηναῖοι, ὅπως
μὴ λόγους ἐροῦσι μόνον οἱ παρ᾽ ἡμῶν πρέσβεις,
ἀλλὰ καὶ ἔργον τι δεικνύειν ἕξουσιν, ἐξεληλυθότων
ὑμῶν ἀξίως τῆς πόλεως καὶ ὄντων ἐπὶ τοῖς πρά-

γμασιν· ὡς ἅπας μὲν λόγος, ἂν ἀπῇ τὰ πράγματα,
μάταιόν τι φαίνεται καὶ κενόν, μάλιστα δ᾽ ὁ παρὰ
τῆς ἡμετέρας πόλεως· ὅσῳ γὰρ ἑτοιμότατ᾽ αὐτῷ
δοκοῦμεν χρῆσθαι, τοσούτῳ μᾶλλον ἀπιστοῦσι
πάντες αὐτῷ. πολλὴν δὴ τὴν μετάστασιν καὶ **13**
μεγάλην δεικτέον τὴν μεταβολήν, εἰσφέροντας, ἐξι- 6
όντας, ἅπαντα ποιοῦντας ἑτοίμως, εἴπερ τις ὑμῖν
προσέξει τὸν νοῦν. κἂν ταῦτ᾽ ἐθελήσηθ᾽, ὡς
προσήκει, καὶ δὴ περαίνειν, οὐ μόνον, ὦ ἄνδρες
Ἀθηναῖοι, τὰ συμμαχικὰ ἀσθενῶς καὶ ἀπίστως 10
ἔχοντα φανήσεται Φιλίππῳ, ἀλλὰ καὶ τὰ τῆς
οἰκείας ἀρχῆς καὶ δυνάμεως κακῶς ἔχοντ᾽
ἐξελεγχθήσεται.

Ὅλως μὲν γὰρ ἡ Μακεδονικὴ δύναμις καὶ **14**
ἀρχὴ ἐν μὲν προσθήκῃ μερίς ἐστί τις οὐ μικρά, 15
οἷον ὑπῆρξέ ποθ᾽ ὑμῖν ἐπὶ Τιμοθέου πρὸς Ὀλυν- 364
θίους· πάλιν αὖ πρὸς Ποτείδαιαν Ὀλυνθίοις· ἐφάνη 356
τι τοῦτο συναμφότερον· νυνὶ δὲ Θετταλοῖς στασιά- 353
ζουσι καὶ τεταραγμένοις ἐπὶ τὴν τυραννικὴν οἰκίαν
ἐβοήθησε· καὶ ὅποι τις ἂν, οἶμαι, προσθῇ κἂν 20
μικρὰν δύναμιν, πάντ᾽ ὠφελεῖ· αὐτὴ δὲ καθ᾽
αὑτὴν ἀσθενὴς καὶ πολλῶν κακῶν ἐστι μεστή.
καὶ γὰρ οὗτος ἅπασι τούτοις, οἷς ἄν τις μέγαν **15**
αὐτὸν ἡγήσαιτο, τοῖς πολέμοις καὶ ταῖς στρατείαις,
ἔτ᾽ ἐπισφαλεστέραν, ἢ ὑπῆρχε φύσει, κατεσκεύακεν 25
αὐτῷ. μὴ γὰρ οἴεσθε, ὦ ἄνδρες Ἀθηναῖοι, τοῖς
αὐτοῖς Φίλιππόν τε χαίρειν καὶ τοὺς ἀρχο-
μένους, ἀλλ᾽ ὁ μὲν δόξης ἐπιθυμεῖ, καὶ τοῦτ᾽

ἐζήλωκε καὶ προῄρηται πράττων καὶ κινδυνεύων,
16 ἂν συμβῇ τι, παθεῖν, τὴν τοῦ διαπράξασθαι ταῦθ᾽,
ἃ μηδεὶς πώποτ᾽ ἄλλος Μακεδόνων βασιλεύς, δόξαν
ἀντὶ τοῦ ζῆν ἀσφαλῶς ᾑρημένος· τοῖς δὲ τῆς μὲν
5 φιλοτιμίας τῆς ἀπὸ τούτων οὐ μέτεστι, κοπτόμενοι
δ᾽ ἀεὶ ταῖς στρατείαις ταύταις ταῖς ἄνω κάτω
λυποῦνται καὶ συνεχῶς ταλαιπωροῦσιν, οὔτ᾽ ἐπὶ
τοῖς ἔργοις οὔτ᾽ ἐπὶ τοῖς αὐτῶν ἰδίοις ἐώμενοι δια-
τρίβειν, οὔθ᾽ ὅσ᾽ ἂν ποιήσωσιν οὕτως, ὅπως ἂν
10 δύνωνται, ταῦτ᾽ ἔχοντες διαθέσθαι κεκλειμένων
τῶν ἐμπορίων τῶν ἐν τῇ χώρᾳ διὰ τὸν πόλεμον.

17   Οἱ μὲν οὖν πολλοὶ Μακεδόνων πῶς ἔχουσι
Φιλίππῳ, ἐκ τούτων ἄν τις σκέψαιτ᾽ οὐ χαλεπῶς·
οἱ δὲ δὴ περὶ αὐτὸν ὄντες ξένοι καὶ πεζέται-
15 ροι δόξαν μὲν ἔχουσιν, ὡς εἰσὶ θαυμαστοὶ καὶ
συγκεκροτημένοι τὰ τοῦ πολέμου, ὡς δ᾽ ἐγὼ τῶν
ἐν αὐτῇ τῇ χώρᾳ γεγενημένων τινὸς ἤκουον, ἀνδρὸς
οὐδαμῶς οἵου τε ψεύδεσθαι, οὐδένων εἰσὶ βελτίους.
18 εἰ μὲν γάρ τις ἀνήρ ἐστιν ἐν αὐτοῖς οἷος ἔμπειρος
20 πολέμου καὶ ἀγώνων, τούτους μὲν φιλοτιμίᾳ πάντας
ἀπωθεῖν αὐτὸν ἔφη, βουλόμενον πάνθ᾽ αὑτοῦ
δοκεῖν εἶναι τὰ ἔργα (πρὸς γὰρ αὖ τοῖς ἄλλοις καὶ
τὴν φιλοτιμίαν ἀνυπέρβλητον εἶναι)· εἰ δέ τις
σώφρων ἢ δίκαιος ἄλλως, τὴν καθ᾽ ἡμέραν ἀκρα-
25 σίαν τοῦ βίου καὶ μέθην καὶ κορδακισμοὺς οὐ
δυνάμενος φέρειν, παρεῶσθαι καὶ ἐν οὐδενὸς εἶναι
19 μέρει τὸν τοιοῦτον. λοιποὺς δὴ περὶ αὐτὸν εἶναι
λῃστὰς καὶ κόλακας καὶ τοιούτους ἀνθρώπους, οἵους
μεθυσθέντας ὀρχεῖσθαι τοιαῦτα, οἷ᾽ ἐγὼ νῦν ὀκνῶ

πρὸς ὑμᾶς ὀνομάσαι. δῆλον δ᾽ ὅτι ταῦτ᾽ ἐστὶν
ἀληθῆ· καὶ γὰρ οὓς ἐνθένδε πάντες ἀπήλαυνον
ὡς πολὺ τῶν θαυματοποιῶν ἀσελγεστέρους ὄντας,
Καλλίαν ἐκεῖνον τὸν δημόσιον καὶ τοιούτους ἀνθρώπους, μίμους γελοίων καὶ ποιητὰς αἰσχρῶν ᾀσμάτων, 5
ὧν εἰς τοὺς συνόντας ποιοῦσιν ἕνεκα τοῦ γελα-
σθῆναι, τούτους ἀγαπᾷ καὶ περὶ αὐτὸν ἔχει.

Καίτοι ταῦτα, εἰ καὶ μικρά τις ἡγεῖται, μεγάλα, **20**
ὦ ἄνδρες Ἀθηναῖοι, δείγματα τῆς ἐκείνου γνώμης
καὶ κακοδαιμονίας ἐστὶ τοῖς εὖ φρονοῦσιν. ἀλλ᾽, 10
οἶμαι, νῦν μὲν ἐπισκοτεῖ τούτοις τὸ κατορθοῦν·
αἱ γὰρ εὐπραξίαι δειναὶ συγκρύψαι τὰ τοιαῦτ᾽
ὀνείδη· εἰ δέ τι πταίσει, τότ᾽ ἀκριβῶς αὐτοῦ ταῦτ᾽
ἐξετασθήσεται. δοκεῖ δ᾽ ἔμοιγε, ὦ ἄνδρες Ἀθηναῖοι, δείξειν οὐκ εἰς μακράν, ἂν οἵ τε θεοὶ θέλωσι 15
καὶ ὑμεῖς βούλησθε. ὥσπερ γὰρ ἐν τοῖς σώμασιν, **21**
τέως μὲν ἂν ἐρρωμένος ᾖ τις, οὐδὲν ἐπαισθάνεται,
ἐπὰν δ᾽ ἀρρώστημά τι συμβῇ, πάντα κινεῖται, κἂν
ῥῆγμα κἂν στρέμμα κἂν ἄλλο τι τῶν ὑπαρχόντων
σαθρῶν ᾖ, οὕτω καὶ τῶν πόλεων καὶ τῶν τυράννων, 20
ἕως μὲν ἂν ἔξω πολεμῶσιν, ἀφανῆ τὰ κακὰ τοῖς
πολλοῖς ἐστιν, ἐπειδὰν δ᾽ ὅμορος πόλεμος συμπλακῇ,
πάντ᾽ ἐποίησεν ἔκδηλα.

Εἰ δέ τις ὑμῶν, ὦ ἄνδρες Ἀθηναῖοι, τὸν **22**
Φίλιππον εὐτυχοῦνθ᾽ ὁρῶν, ταύτῃ φοβερὸν προσ- 25
πολεμῆσαι νομίζει, σώφρονος μὲν ἀνθρώπου λογισμῷ
χρῆται· μεγάλη γὰρ ῥοπή, μᾶλλον δ᾽ ὅλον ἡ τύχη
παρὰ πάντ᾽ ἐστὶ τὰ τῶν ἀνθρώπων πράγματα· οὐ

μὴν ἀλλ᾽ ἔγωγε, εἴ τις αἵρεσίν μοι δοίη, τὴν τῆς
ἡμετέρας πόλεως τύχην ἂν ἑλοίμην, ἐθελόντων ἃ
προσήκει ποιεῖν ὑμῶν αὐτῶν καὶ κατὰ μικρόν, ἢ
τὴν ἐκείνου· πολὺ γὰρ πλείους ἀφορμὰς εἰς τὸ
5 τὴν παρὰ τῶν θεῶν εὔνοιαν ἔχειν ὁρῶ ὑμῖν
23 ἐνούσας ἢ ᾽κείνῳ. ἀλλ᾽, οἶμαι, καθήμεθ᾽ οὐδὲν
ποιοῦντες· οὐκ ἔνι δ᾽ αὐτὸν ἀργοῦντ᾽ οὐδὲ τοῖς
φίλοις ἐπιτάττειν ὑπὲρ αὐτοῦ τι ποιεῖν, μή τί γε
δὴ τοῖς θεοῖς. οὐ δὴ θαυμαστόν ἐστιν, εἰ στρα-
10 τευόμενος καὶ πονῶν ἐκεῖνος αὐτὸς καὶ παρὼν ἐφ᾽
ἅπασι καὶ μηδένα καιρὸν μηδ᾽ ὥραν παραλείπων
ἡμῶν μελλόντων καὶ ψηφιζομένων καὶ πυνθανομέ-
νων περιγίγνεται. οὐδὲ θαυμάζω τοῦτ᾽ ἐγώ· τοὐναντίον γὰρ ἂν ἦν θαυμαστόν, εἰ μηδὲν ποιοῦντες ἡμεῖς,
15 ὧν τοῖς πολεμοῦσι προσήκει, τοῦ πάντα ποιοῦντος
24 περιῆμεν. ἀλλ᾽ ἐκεῖνο θαυμάζω, εἰ Λακεδαιμονίοις
μέν ποτε, ὦ ἄνδρες Ἀθηναῖοι, ὑπὲρ τῶν Ἑλληνικῶν δικαίων ἀντήρατε, καὶ πόλλ᾽ ἰδίᾳ πλεονεκτῆσαι πολλάκις ὑμῖν ἐξὸν οὐκ ἠθελήσατε, ἀλλ᾽ ἵν᾽ οἱ
20 ἄλλοι τύχωσι τῶν δικαίων, τὰ ὑμέτερ᾽ αὐτῶν ἀνη-
λίσκετ᾽ εἰσφέροντες καὶ προεκινδυνεύετε στρατευόμενοι, νυνὶ δ᾽ ὀκνεῖτ᾽ ἐξιέναι καὶ μέλλετ᾽ εἰσφέρειν
ὑπὲρ τῶν ὑμετέρων αὐτῶν κτημάτων, καὶ τοὺς μὲν
ἄλλους σεσώκατε πολλάκις πάντας καὶ καθ᾽ ἕν᾽ αὐτῶν
25 ἐν μέρει, τὰ δ᾽ ὑμέτερ᾽ αὐτῶν ἀπολωλεκότες κά-
25 θησθε. ταῦτα θαυμάζω, καὶ ἔτι πρὸς τούτοις, εἰ μηδεὶς ὑμῶν, ὦ ἄνδρες Ἀθηναῖοι, δύναται λογίσασθαι,
πόσον πολεμεῖτε χρόνον Φιλίππῳ καὶ τί ποιούντων
ὑμῶν ὁ χρόνος διελήλυθεν οὗτος. ἴστε γὰρ δήπου

τοῦϑ᾽, ὅτι μελλόντων αὐτῶν, ἑτέρους τινὰς ἐλπιζόντων πράξειν, αἰτιωμένων ἀλλήλους, κρινόντων,
πάλιν ἐλπιζόντων, σχεδὸν ταὐτὰ ἅπερ νυνὶ ποιούντων
ἅπας ὁ χρόνος διελήλυθεν. εἶϑ᾽ οὕτως ἀγνωμόνως 26
ἔχετε, ὦ ἄνδρες Ἀθηναῖοι, ὥστε δι᾽ ὧν ἐκ χρηστῶν 5
φαῦλα τὰ πράγματα τῆς πόλεως γέγονεν, διὰ
τούτων ἐλπίζετε τῶν αὐτῶν ἐκ φαύλων αὐτὰ
χρηστὰ γενήσεσθαι; ἀλλ᾽ οὔτ᾽ εὔλογον οὔτ᾽ ἔχον
ἐστὶ φύσιν τοῦτό γε· πολὺ γὰρ ῥᾷον ἔχοντας φυλάττειν ἢ κτήσασθαι πάντα πέφυκεν. νῦν δ᾽ ὅ 10
τι μὲν φυλάξομεν, οὐδέν ἐστιν ὑπὸ τοῦ πολέμου
λοιπὸν τῶν πρότερον, κτήσασθαι δὲ δεῖ. αὐτῶν
οὖν ἡμῶν ἔργον τοῦτ᾽ ἤδη.

   Φημὶ δὴ δεῖν εἰσφέρειν χρήματα, αὐτοὺς ἐξ- 27
ιέναι προθύμως, μηδέν᾽ αἰτιᾶσθαι, πρὶν ἂν τῶν 15
πραγμάτων κρατήσητε, τηνικαῦτα δ᾽ ἀπ᾽ αὐτῶν
τῶν ἔργων κρίναντας, τοὺς μὲν ἀξίους ἐπαίνου
τιμᾶν, τοὺς δ᾽ ἀδικοῦντας κολάζειν, τὰς προφάσεις δ᾽ ἀφελεῖν καὶ τὰ καθ᾽ ὑμᾶς ἐλλείμ-
ματα· οὐ γὰρ ἔστι πικρῶς ἐξετάσαι, τί πέπρακται 20
τοῖς ἄλλοις, ἂν μὴ παρ᾽ ὑμῶν αὐτῶν πρῶτον
ὑπάρξῃ τὰ δέοντα. τίνος γὰρ ἕνεκα, ὦ ἄνδρες 28
Ἀθηναῖοι, νομίζετε τοῦτον μὲν φεύγειν τὸν πόλεμον πάντας ὅσους ἂν ἐκπέμψητε στρατηγούς,
ἰδίους δ᾽ εὑρίσκειν πολέμους, εἰ δεῖ τι τῶν 25
ὄντων καὶ περὶ τῶν στρατηγῶν εἰπεῖν; ὅτι ἐνταῦθα μέν ἐστι τἆθλα, ὑπὲρ ὧν ἐστιν ὁ πόλεμος,
ὑμέτερα, καὶ ἃ ἂν ληφθῇ, παραχρῆμ᾽ ὑμεῖς κομι-
εῖσθε· οἱ δὲ κίνδυνοι τῶν ἐφεστηκότων ἴδιοι,

2*

μισθὸς δ᾽ οὐκ ἔστιν· ἐκεῖ δὲ κίνδυνοι μὲν
ἐλάττους, τὰ δὲ λήμματα τῶν ἐφεστηκότων καὶ
τῶν στρατιωτῶν, Λάμψακος, Σίγειον, τὰ πλοῖα
ἃ συλῶσιν. ἐπ᾽ οὖν τὸ λυσιτελοῦν αὐτοῖς
29 ἕκαστοι χωροῦσιν. ὑμεῖς δ᾽, ὅταν μὲν εἰς τὰ
6 πράγματ᾽ ἀποβλέψητε φαύλως ἔχοντα, τοὺς
ἐφεστηκότας κρίνετε, ὅταν δὲ δόντες λόγον τὰς
ἀνάγκας ἀκούσητε ταύτας, ἀφίετε. περίεστι τοίνυν
ὑμῖν ἀλλήλοις ἐρίζειν καὶ διεστάναι, τοῖς μὲν
10 ταῦτα πεπεισμένοις, τοῖς δὲ ταῦτα, τὰ κοινὰ
δ᾽ ἔχειν φαύλως. πρότερον μὲν γὰρ, ὦ ἄνδρες
Ἀθηναῖοι, εἰσεφέρετε κατὰ συμμορίας, νυνὶ δὲ
πολιτεύεσθε κατὰ συμμορίας. ῥήτωρ ἡγεμὼν
ἑκατέρων, καὶ στρατηγὸς ὑπὸ τούτῳ καὶ οἱ βοησό-
15 μενοι τριακόσιοι· οἱ δ᾽ ἄλλοι προσνενέμησθ᾽ οἱ
30 μὲν ὡς τούτους, οἱ δ᾽ ὡς ἐκείνους. δεῖ δὴ ταῦτ᾽
ἐπανέντας καὶ ὑμῶν αὐτῶν ἔτι καὶ νῦν γενο-
μένους κοινὸν καὶ τὸ λέγειν καὶ τὸ βουλεύεσθαι
καὶ τὸ πράττειν ποιῆσαι. εἰ δὲ τοῖς μὲν ὥσπερ
20 ἐκ τυραννίδος ὑμῶν ἐπιτάττειν ἀποδώσετε, τοῖς δ᾽
ἀναγκάζεσθαι τριηραρχεῖν, εἰσφέρειν, στρατεύεσθαι,
τοῖς δὲ ψηφίζεσθαι κατὰ τούτων μόνον, ἄλλο δὲ
μηδ᾽ ὁτιοῦν συμπονεῖν, οὐχὶ γενήσεται τῶν δεόντων ὑμῖν οὐδὲν ἐν καιρῷ· τὸ γὰρ ἠδικημένον ἀεὶ
25 μέρος ἐλλείψει, εἶθ᾽ ὑμῖν τούτους κολάζειν ἀντὶ
τῶν ἐχθρῶν ἐξέσται.

31 Λέγω δὴ κεφάλαιον, πάντας εἰσφέρειν ἀφ᾽
ὅσων ἕκαστος ἔχει τὸ ἴσον· πάντας ἐξιέναι κατὰ
μέρος, ἕως ἂν ἅπαντες στρατεύσησθε· πᾶσι τοῖς

παριοῦσι λόγον διδόναι, καὶ τὰ βέλτισθ᾽ ὧν ἂν
ἀκούσηθ᾽ αἱρεῖσθαι, μὴ ἃ ἂν ὁ δεῖν᾽ ἢ ὁ δεῖν᾽ εἴπῃ.
κἂν ταῦτα ποιῆτε, οὐ τὸν εἰπόντα μόνον παραχρῆμ᾽
ἐπαινέσεσθε, ἀλλὰ καὶ ὑμᾶς αὐτοὺς ὕστερον, βέλτιον τῶν ὅλων πραγμάτων ὑμῖν ἐχόντων.   5

ΟΛΥΝΘΙΑΚΟΣ Γ.

1   Οὐχὶ ταὐτὰ παρίσταταί μοι γιγνώσκειν, ὦ
ἄνδρες Ἀθηναῖοι, ὅταν τ᾽ εἰς τὰ πράγματ᾽ ἀπο-
βλέψω καὶ ὅταν πρὸς τοὺς λόγους, οὓς ἀκούω·
5 τοὺς μὲν γὰρ λόγους περὶ τοῦ τιμωρήσασθαι
Φίλιππον ὁρῶ γιγνομένους, τὰ δὲ πράγματ᾽ εἰς
τοῦτο προήκοντα, ὥσθ᾽ ὅπως μὴ πεισόμεθ᾽ αὐτοὶ
πρότερον κακῶς σκέψασθαι δέον. οὐδὲν οὖν ἄλλο
μοι δοκοῦσιν οἱ τὰ τοιαῦτα λέγοντες ἢ τὴν ὑπό-
10 θεσιν, περὶ ἧς βουλεύεσθε, οὐχὶ τὴν οὖσαν
2 παριστάντες ὑμῖν ἁμαρτάνειν. ἐγὼ δ᾽ ὅτι
μὲν ποτ᾽ ἐξῆν τῇ πόλει καὶ τὰ αὑτῆς ἔχειν ἀσφαλῶς καὶ Φίλιππον τιμωρήσασθαι, καὶ μάλ᾽ ἀκριβῶς
οἶδα· ἐπ᾽ ἐμοῦ γάρ, οὐ πάλαι γέγονε ταῦτ᾽ ἀμφό-
15 τερα· νῦν μέντοι πέπεισμαι τοῦθ᾽ ἱκανὸν προλαβεῖν ἡμῖν εἶναι τὴν πρώτην, ὅπως τοὺς
συμμάχους σώσομεν. ἐὰν γὰρ τοῦτο βεβαίως
ὑπάρξῃ, τότε καὶ περὶ τοῦ τίνα τιμωρήσεταί τις
ἐκεῖνον τρόπον ἐξέσται σκοπεῖν· πρὶν δὲ τὴν ἀρχὴν
20 ὀρθῶς ὑποθέσθαι, μάταιον ἡγοῦμαι περὶ τῆς τελευ-
τῆς ὁντινοῦν ποιεῖσθαι λόγον.

3   Ὁ μὲν οὖν παρὼν καιρός, ὦ ἄνδρες Ἀθηναῖοι,

εἴπερ ποτέ, πολλῆς φροντίδος καὶ βουλῆς δεῖται·
ἐγὼ δ᾽ οὐχ ὅ τι χρὴ περὶ τῶν παρόντων συμβουλεῦσαι χαλεπώτατον ἡγοῦμαι, ἀλλ᾽ ἐκεῖν᾽ ἀπορῶ,
τίνα χρὴ τρόπον, ὦ ἄνδρες Ἀθηναῖοι, πρὸς ὑμᾶς
περὶ αὐτῶν εἰπεῖν. πέπεισμαι γὰρ ἐξ ὧν παρὼν 5
καὶ ἀκούων σύνοιδα, τὰ πλείω τῶν πραγμάτων
ἡμᾶς ἐκπεφευγέναι τῷ μὴ βούλεσθαι τὰ δέοντα
ποιεῖν ἢ τῷ μὴ συνιέναι. ἀξιῶ δ᾽ ὑμᾶς, ἂν μετὰ
παρρησίας ποιῶμαι τοὺς λόγους, ὑπομένειν,
τοῦτο θεωροῦντας, εἰ τἀληθῆ λέγω καὶ διὰ τοῦτο, 10
ἵνα τὰ λοιπὰ βελτίω γένηται. ὁρᾶτε γὰρ ὡς ἐκ
τοῦ πρὸς χάριν δημηγορεῖν ἐνίους εἰς πᾶν προελή-
λυθε μοχθηρίας τὰ παρόντα.

Ἀναγκαῖον δ᾽ ὑπολαμβάνω μικρὰ τῶν γεγενη- 4
μένων πρῶτον ὑμᾶς ὑπομνῆσαι. μέμνησθε, ὦ 15
ἄνδρες Ἀθηναῖοι, ὅτ᾽ ἀπηγγέλθη Φίλιππος ὑμῖν
ἐν Θρᾴκῃ, τρίτον ἢ τέταρτον ἔτος τουτί, Ἡραῖον 352
τεῖχος πολιορκῶν. τότε τοίνυν μὴν μὲν ἦν μαι-
μακτηριών· πολλῶν δὲ λόγων καὶ θορύβου γιγνο-
μένου παρ᾽ ὑμῖν ἐψηφίσασθε τετταράκοντα τριήρεις 20
καθέλκειν καὶ τοὺς μέχρι πέντε καὶ τετταράκοντ᾽
ἐτῶν αὐτοὺς ἐμβαίνειν καὶ τάλανθ᾽ ἑξήκοντ᾽
εἰσφέρειν. καὶ μετὰ ταῦτα διελθόντος τοῦ ἐνι- 5
αυτοῦ τούτου ἑκατομβαιών, μεταγειτνιών, βοηδρο-
μιών· τούτου τοῦ μηνὸς μόγις μετὰ τὰ μυστήρια 25
δέκα ναῦς ἀπεστείλατ᾽ ἔχοντα κενὰς Χαρίδημον 351
καὶ πέντε τάλαντ᾽ ἀργυρίου. ὡς γὰρ ἠγγέλθη
Φίλιππος ἀσθενῶν ἢ τεθνεώς (ἦλθε γὰρ ἀμφό-

τερα), οὐκέτι καιρὸν οὐδένα τοῦ βοηθεῖν νομί-
σαντες ἀφίετε, ὦ ἄνδρες Ἀθηναῖοι, τὸν ἀπόστολον.
ἦν δ᾽ οὗτος ὁ καιρὸς αὐτός· εἰ γὰρ τότ᾽ ἐκεῖσ᾽
ἐβοηθήσαμεν, ὥσπερ ἐψηφισάμεθα, προθύμως,
5 οὐκ ἂν ἠνώχλει νῦν ἡμῖν ὁ Φίλιππος σωθείς.

6   Τὰ μὲν δὴ τότε πραχθέντ᾽ οὐκ ἂν ἄλλως
ἔχοι· νῦν δ᾽ ἑτέρου πολέμου καιρὸς ἥκει τις,
δι᾽ ὃν καὶ περὶ τούτων ἐμνήσθην, ἵνα μὴ ταὐτὰ
πάθητε. τί δὴ χρησόμεθα, ὦ ἄνδρες Ἀθηναῖοι,
10 τούτῳ; εἰ γὰρ μὴ βοηθήσετε παντὶ σθένει κατὰ
τὸ δυνατόν, θεάσασθ᾽ ὃν τρόπον ὑμεῖς ἐστρατη-
7 γηκότες πάντ᾽ ἔσεσθ᾽ ὑπὲρ Φιλίππου. ὑπῆρχον
Ὀλύνθιοι δύναμίν τινα κεκτημένοι, καὶ διέκειθ᾽
οὕτω τὰ πράγματα· οὔτε Φίλιππος ἐθάρρει τούτους,
15 οὔθ᾽ οὗτοι Φίλιππον. ἐπράξαμεν ἡμεῖς κἀκεῖνοι
πρὸς ἡμᾶς εἰρήνην· ἦν τοῦθ᾽ ὥσπερ ἐμπόδισμά τι
τῷ Φιλίππῳ καὶ δυσχερές, πόλιν μεγάλην ἐφορ-
μεῖν τοῖς ἑαυτοῦ καιροῖς διηλλαγμένην πρὸς ἡμᾶς.
ἐκπολεμῆσαι δεῖν ᾠόμεθα τοὺς ἀνθρώπους ἐκ παν-
20 τὸς τρόπου, καὶ ἅπαντες ἐθρύλουν τοῦτο· πέπρακται
νυνὶ τοῦθ᾽ ὁπωσδήποτε.

8   Τί οὖν ὑπόλοιπον, ὦ ἄνδρες Ἀθηναῖοι, πλὴν
βοηθεῖν ἐρρωμένως καὶ προθύμως; ἐγὼ μὲν οὐχ
ὁρῶ· χωρὶς γὰρ τῆς περιστάσης ἂν ἡμᾶς αἰσχύνης,
25 εἰ καθυφείμεθά τι τῶν πραγμάτων, οὐδὲ τὸν
φόβον, ὦ ἄνδρες Ἀθηναῖοι, μικρὸν ὁρῶ τὸν
τῶν μετὰ ταῦτα, ἐχόντων μὲν ὡς ἔχουσι
Θηβαίων ἡμῖν, ἀπειρηκότων δὲ χρήμασι Φωκέων,
μηδενὸς δ᾽ ἐμποδὼν ὄντος Φιλίππῳ τὰ παρόντα

καταστρεψαμένῳ πρὸς ταῦτ᾽ ἐπικλῖναι τὰ πράγματα. ἀλλὰ μὴν εἴ τις ὑμῶν εἰς τοῦτ᾽ ἀναβάλλεται 9
ποιήσειν τὰ δέοντα, ἰδεῖν ἐγγύθεν βούλεται τὰ
δεινά, ἐξὸν ἀκούειν ἄλλοθι γιγνόμενα, καὶ βοηθοὺς
ἑαυτῷ ζητεῖν, ἐξὸν νῦν ἑτέροις αὐτὸν βοηθεῖν· 5
ὅτι γὰρ εἰς τοῦτο περιστήσεται τὰ πράγματα, ἐὰν
τὰ παρόντα προώμεθα, σχεδὸν ἴσμεν ἅπαντες
δήπου.

Ἀλλ᾽ ὅτι μὲν δὴ δεῖ βοηθεῖν, εἴποι τις ἄν, 10
πάντες ἐγνώκαμεν καὶ βοηθήσομεν· τὸ δ᾽ ὅπως, 10
τοῦτο λέγε. μὴ τοίνυν, ὦ ἄνδρες Ἀθηναῖοι,
θαυμάσητε, ἂν παράδοξον εἴπω τι τοῖς πολλοῖς.
νομοθέτας καθίσατε. ἐν δὲ τούτοις τοῖς νομο-
θέταις μὴ θῆσθε νόμον μηδένα (εἰσὶ γὰρ ὑμῖν
ἱκανοί), ἀλλὰ τοὺς εἰς τὸ παρὸν βλάπτοντας 15
ὑμᾶς λύσατε. λέγω τοὺς περὶ τῶν θεωρικῶν, 11
σαφῶς οὑτωσί, καὶ τοὺς περὶ τῶν στρατευομένων
ἐνίους, ὧν οἱ μὲν τὰ στρατιωτικὰ τοῖς οἴκοι μένουσι
διανέμουσι θεωρικά, οἱ δὲ τοὺς ἀτακτοῦντας
ἀθῴους καθιστᾶσιν, εἶτα καὶ τοὺς τὰ δέοντα 20
ποιεῖν βουλομένους ἀθυμοτέρους ποιοῦσιν. ἐπειδὰν δὲ ταῦτα λύσητε καὶ τὴν τοῦ τὰ βέλτιστα
λέγειν ὁδὸν παράσχητ᾽ ἀσφαλῆ, τηνικαῦτα τὸν
γράψονθ᾽, ἃ πάντες ἴσθ᾽ ὅτι συμφέρει, ζητεῖτε.
πρὶν δὲ ταῦτα πρᾶξαι, μὴ σκοπεῖτε, τίς εἰπὼν τὰ 12
βέλτισθ᾽ ὑπὲρ ὑμῶν ὑφ᾽ ὑμῶν ἀπολέσθαι βουλή- 26
σεται· οὐ γὰρ εὑρήσετε, ἄλλως τε καὶ τούτου μόνου
περιγίγνεσθαι μέλλοντος, παθεῖν ἀδίκως τι κακὸν

τὸν ταῦτ᾽ εἰπόντα καὶ γράψαντα, μηδὲν δ᾽ ὠφε-
λῆσαι τὰ πράγματα, ἀλλὰ καὶ εἰς τὸ λοιπὸν μᾶλλον
ἔτι ἢ νῦν τὸ τὰ βέλτιστα λέγειν φοβερώτερον
ποιῆσαι. καὶ λύειν γ᾽, ὦ ἄνδρες Ἀθηναῖοι, τοὺς
5 νόμους δεῖ τούτους τοὺς αὐτοὺς ἀξιοῦν, οἵπερ καὶ
13 τεθήκασιν· οὐ γάρ ἐστι δίκαιον τὴν μὲν χάριν, ἣ
πᾶσαν ἔβλαπτε τὴν πόλιν, τοῖς τότε θεῖσιν ὑπάρχειν, τὴν δ᾽ ἀπέχθειαν, δι᾽ ἧς ἂν ἅπαντες
ἄμεινον πράξαιμεν, τῷ νῦν τὰ βέλτιστ᾽ εἰπόντι
10 ζημίαν γενέσθαι. πρὶν δὲ ταῦτ᾽ εὐτρεπίσαι, μηδα-
μῶς, ὦ ἄνδρες Ἀθηναῖοι, μηδέν᾽ ἀξιοῦτε τηλικοῦτον
εἶναι παρ᾽ ὑμῖν, ὥστε τοὺς νόμους τούτους παρα-
βάντα μὴ δοῦναι δίκην, μηδ᾽ οὕτως ἀνόητον, ὥστ᾽
εἰς προῦπτον κακὸν αὑτὸν ἐμβαλεῖν.

14   Οὐ μὴν οὐδ᾽ ἐκεῖνό γ᾽ ὑμᾶς ἀγνοεῖν δεῖ, ὦ
16 ἄνδρες Ἀθηναῖοι, ὅτι ψήφισμ᾽ οὐδενὸς ἄξιόν ἐστιν,
ἂν μὴ προσγένηται τὸ ποιεῖν ἐθέλειν τά γε
δόξαντα προθύμως ὑμᾶς. εἰ γὰρ αὐτάρκη τὰ
ψηφίσματ᾽ ἦν ἢ ὑμᾶς ἀναγκάζειν, ἃ προσήκει,
20 πράττειν ἤ, περὶ ὧν γραφείη, διαπράξασθαι, οὔτ᾽
ἂν ὑμεῖς πολλὰ ψηφιζόμενοι μικρά, μᾶλλον δ᾽
οὐδὲν ἐπράττετε τούτων, οὔτε Φίλιππος τοσοῦτον
ὑβρίκει χρόνον· πάλαι γὰρ ἂν ἕνεκά γε ψηφι-
15 σμάτων ἐδεδώκει δίκην. ἀλλ᾽ οὐχ οὕτω ταῦτ᾽ ἔχει·
25 τὸ γὰρ πράττειν, τοῦ λέγειν καὶ χειροτονεῖν
ὕστερον ὂν τῇ τάξει, πρότερον τῇ δυνάμει καὶ
κρεῖττόν ἐστιν. τοῦτ᾽ οὖν δεῖ προσεῖναι, τὰ δ᾽ ἄλλ᾽
ὑπάρχει· καὶ γὰρ εἰπεῖν τὰ δέοντα παρ᾽ ὑμῖν εἰσιν,
ὦ ἄνδρες Ἀθηναῖοι, δυνάμενοι, καὶ γνῶναι πάν-

των ὑμεῖς ὀξύτατοι τὰ ῥηθέντα· καὶ πρᾶξαι δὲ
δυνήσεσθε νῦν, ἐὰν ὀρθῶς ποιῆτε. τίνα γὰρ 16
χρόνον ἢ τίνα καιρόν, ὦ ἄνδρες Ἀθηναῖοι, τοῦ
παρόντος βελτίω ζητεῖτε; ἢ πόθ᾽ ἃ δεῖ πράξετε,
εἰ μὴ νῦν; οὐχ ἅπαντα μὲν ἡμῶν προείληφε τὰ 5
χωρί᾽ ἄνθρωπος, εἰ δὲ καὶ ταύτης κύριος τῆς
χώρας γενήσεται, πάντων αἴσχιστα πεισόμεθα; οὐχ
οὓς, εἰ πολεμήσαιεν, ἑτοίμως σώσειν ὑπισχνούμεθα,
οὗτοι νῦν πολεμοῦσιν; οὐκ ἐχθρός; οὐκ ἔχων τὰ
ἡμέτερα; οὐ βάρβαρος; οὐχ ὅ τι ἂν εἴποι τις; ἀλλὰ 17
πρὸς θεῶν πάντ᾽ ἐάσαντες καὶ μόνον οὐχὶ 11
συγκατασκευάσαντες αὐτῷ, τότε τοὺς αἰτίους οἵτινες
τούτων ζητήσομεν; οὐ γὰρ αὐτοί γ᾽ αἴτιοι φήσομεν
εἶναι· σαφῶς οἶδα τοῦτ᾽ ἐγώ. οὐδὲ γὰρ ἐν τοῖς
τοῦ πολέμου κινδύνοις τῶν φυγόντων οὐδεὶς 15
ἑαυτοῦ κατηγορεῖ, ἀλλὰ τοῦ στρατηγοῦ καὶ τῶν
πλησίον καὶ πάντων μᾶλλον, ἥττηνται δ᾽ ὅμως
διὰ πάντας τοὺς φυγόντας δήπου· μένειν γὰρ
ἐξῆν τῷ κατηγοροῦντι τῶν ἄλλων· εἰ δὲ τοῦτ᾽
ἐποίει ἕκαστος, ἐνίκων ἄν. 20

Καὶ νῦν, οὐ λέγει τις τὰ βέλτιστα· ἀναστὰς 18
ἄλλος εἰπάτω, μὴ τοῦτον αἰτιάσθω. ἕτερος λέγει
τις βελτίω· ταῦτα ποιεῖτ᾽ ἀγαθῇ τύχῃ. ἀλλ᾽ οὐχ
ἡδέα ταῦτα· οὐκέτι τοῦθ᾽ ὁ λέγων ἀδικεῖ, πλὴν
εἰ δέον εὔξασθαι παραλείπει· εὔξασθαι μὲν γάρ, 25
ὦ ἄνδρες Ἀθηναῖοι, ῥᾴδιον, εἰς ταὐτὸ πάνθ᾽, ὅσα
βούλεταί τις, ἀθροίσαντ᾽ ἐν ὀλίγῳ· ἑλέσθαι δέ,
ὅταν περὶ πραγμάτων προτεθῇ σκοπεῖν, οὐκέθ᾽
ὁμοίως εὔπορον, ἀλλὰ δεῖ τὰ βέλτιστ᾽ ἀντὶ τῶν

ἡδέων, ἂν μὴ συναμφότερ᾽ ἐξῇ, λαμβάνειν.
19 εἰ δέ τις ἡμῖν ἔχει καὶ τὰ θεωρικὰ ἐᾶν καὶ πόρους
ἑτέρους λέγειν στρατιωτικούς, οὐχ οὗτος κρείττων;
εἴποι τις ἄν. φήμ᾽ ἔγωγε, εἴπερ ἔστιν, ὦ ἄνδρες
5 Ἀθηναῖοι· ἀλλὰ θαυμάζω, εἴ τῳ ποτ᾽ ἀνθρώπων
ἢ γέγονεν ἢ γενήσεται, ἂν τὰ παρόντ᾽ ἀναλώσῃ,
πρὸς ἃ μὴ δεῖ, τῶν ἀπόντων εὐπορῆσαι, πρὸς ἃ
δεῖ. ἀλλ᾽ οἶμαι, μέγα τοῖς τοιούτοις ὑπάρχει λόγοις
ἡ παρ᾽ ἑκάστου βούλησις, διόπερ ῥᾷστον ἁπάντων
10 ἐστὶν αὐτὸν ἐξαπατῆσαι· ὃ γὰρ βούλεται, τοῦθ᾽
ἕκαστος καὶ οἴεται, τὰ δὲ πράγματα πολλάκις οὐχ
20 οὕτω πέφυκεν. ὁρᾶτ᾽ οὖν, ὦ ἄνδρες Ἀθηναῖοι,
ταῦθ᾽ οὕτως, ὅπως καὶ τὰ πράγματ᾽ ἐνδέχεται καὶ
δυνήσεσθ᾽ ἐξιέναι καὶ μισθὸν ἕξετε. οὔ τοι σωφρό-
15 νων οὐδὲ γενναίων ἐστὶν ἀνθρώπων, ἐλλείποντάς
τι δι᾽ ἔνδειαν χρημάτων τῶν τοῦ πολέμου, εὐχερῶς
τὰ τοιαῦτ᾽ ὀνείδη φέρειν, οὐδ᾽ ἐπὶ μὲν Κορινθίους
καὶ Μεγαρέας ἁρπάσαντας τὰ ὅπλα πορεύεσθαι,
Φίλιππον δ᾽ ἐᾶν πόλεις Ἑλληνίδας ἀνδραποδίζεσθαι
20 δι᾽ ἀπορίαν ἐφοδίων τοῖς στρατευομένοις.

21   Καὶ ταῦτ᾽ οὐχ ἵν᾽ ἀπέχθωμαί τισιν ὑμῶν,
τὴν ἄλλως προῄρημαι λέγειν· οὐ γὰρ οὕτως
ἄφρων οὐδ᾽ ἀτυχής εἰμ᾽ ἐγώ, ὥστ᾽ ἀπεχθάνεσθαι
βούλεσθαι μηδὲν ὠφελεῖν νομίζων· ἀλλὰ δικαίου
25 πολίτου κρίνω τὴν τῶν πραγμάτων σωτηρίαν ἀντὶ
τῆς ἐν τῷ λέγειν χάριτος αἱρεῖσθαι· καὶ γὰρ τοὺς
ἐπὶ τῶν προγόνων ἡμῶν λέγοντας ἀκούω, ὥσπερ
ἴσως καὶ ὑμεῖς, οὓς ἐπαινοῦσι μὲν οἱ παριόντες

ἅπαντες, μιμοῦνται δ᾽ οὐ πάνυ, τούτῳ τῷ ἔθει
καὶ τῷ τρόπῳ τῆς πολιτείας χρῆσθαι, τὸν Ἀρι-
στείδην ἐκεῖνον, τὸν Νικίαν, τὸν ὁμώνυμον ἐμαυτῷ,
τὸν Περικλέα. ἐξ οὗ δ᾽ οἱ διερωτῶντες ὑμᾶς 22
οὗτοι πεφήνασι ῥήτορες „τί βούλεσθε; τί γράψω; 5
τί ὑμῖν χαρίσωμαι"; προπέποται τῆς παραυτίκα
χάριτος τὰ τῆς πόλεως πράγματα καὶ τοιαυτὶ συμβαίνει, καὶ τὰ μὲν τούτων πάντα καλῶς ἔχει, τὰ
δ᾽ ὑμέτερ᾽ αἰσχρῶς. καίτοι σκέψασθ᾽, ὦ ἄνδρες 23
Ἀθηναῖοι, ἅ τις ἂν κεφάλαι᾽ εἰπεῖν ἔχοι τῶν τ᾽ 10
ἐπὶ τῶν προγόνων ἔργων καὶ τῶν ἐφ᾽ ὑμῶν.
ἔσται δὲ βραχὺς καὶ γνώριμος ὑμῖν ὁ λόγος. οὐ γὰρ
ἀλλοτρίοις ὑμῖν χρωμένοις παραδείγμασιν, ἀλλ᾽
οἰκείοις, ὦ ἄνδρες Ἀθηναῖοι, εὐδαίμοσιν ἔξεστι
γενέσθαι. ἐκεῖνοι τοίνυν, οἷς οὐκ ἐχαρίζονθ᾽ οἱ 24
λέγοντες οὐδ᾽ ἐφίλουν αὐτούς, ὥσπερ ὑμᾶς οὗτοι 16
νῦν, πέντε μὲν καὶ τετταράκοντ᾽ ἔτη τῶν Ἑλλήνων
ἦρξαν ἑκόντων, πλείω δ᾽ ἢ μύρια τάλαντ᾽ εἰς τὴν
ἀκρόπολιν ἀνήγαγον, ὑπήκουε δ᾽ ὁ ταύτην τὴν
χώραν ἔχων αὐτοῖς βασιλεύς, ὥσπερ ἐστὶ προσῆκον 20
βάρβαρον Ἕλλησι, πολλὰ δὲ καὶ καλὰ καὶ πεζῇ καὶ
ναυμαχοῦντες ἔστησαν τρόπαι᾽ αὐτοὶ στρατευόμενοι,
μόνοι δ᾽ ἀνθρώπων κρείττω τὴν ἐπὶ τοῖς ἔργοις
δόξαν τῶν φθονούντων κατέλιπον. ἐπὶ μὲν δὴ 25
τῶν Ἑλληνικῶν ἦσαν τοιοῦτοι, ἐν δὲ τοῖς κατὰ 25
τὴν πόλιν αὐτὴν θεάσασθ᾽ ὁποῖοι ἔν τε τοῖς
κοινοῖς κἂν τοῖς ἰδίοις. δημοσίᾳ μὲν τοίνυν
οἰκοδομήματα καὶ κάλλη τοιαῦτα καὶ τοσαῦτα κατ-
εσκεύασαν ἡμῖν ἱερῶν καὶ τῶν ἐν τούτοις ἀνα-

θημάτων, ὥστε μηδενὶ τῶν ἐπιγιγνομένων ὑπερ-
26 βολὴν λελεῖφθαι· ἰδίᾳ δ᾽ οὕτω σώφρονες ἦσαν
καὶ σφόδρ᾽ ἐν τῷ τῆς πολιτείας ἤθει μένοντες,
ὥστε τὴν Ἀριστείδου καὶ τὴν Μιλτιάδου καὶ τῶν
5 τότε λαμπρῶν οἰκίαν, εἴ τις ἄρ᾽ οἶδεν ὑμῶν ὁποία
ποτ᾽ ἐστίν, ὁρᾷ τῆς τοῦ γείτονος οὐδὲν σεμνοτέραν
οὖσαν· οὐ γὰρ εἰς περιουσίαν ἐπράττετ᾽ αὐτοῖς
τὰ τῆς πόλεως, ἀλλὰ τὸ κοινὸν αὔξειν ἕκαστος
ᾤετο δεῖν. ἐκ δὲ τοῦ τὰ μὲν Ἑλληνικὰ πιστῶς,
10 τὰ δὲ πρὸς τοὺς θεοὺς εὐσεβῶς, τὰ δ᾽ ἐν αὑτοῖς
ἴσως διοικεῖν μεγάλην εἰκότως ἐκτήσαντ᾽ εὐδαι-
27 μονίαν. τότε μὲν δὴ τοῦτον τὸν τρόπον εἶχε τὰ
πράγματ᾽ ἐκείνοις, χρωμένοις οἷς εἶπον προστάταις·
νυνὶ δὲ πῶς ἡμῖν ὑπὸ τῶν χρηστῶν τῶν νῦν τὰ
15 πράγματ᾽ ἔχει; ἆρά γ᾽ ὁμοίως καὶ παραπλησίως;
οἷς — τὰ μὲν ἄλλα σιωπῶ, πόλλ᾽ ἂν ἔχων εἰπεῖν,
ἀλλ᾽ ὅσης ἅπαντες ὁρᾶτ᾽ ἐρημίας ἐπειλημμένοι, καὶ
Λακεδαιμονίων μὲν ἀπολωλότων, Θηβαίων δ᾽
ἀσχόλων ὄντων, τῶν δ᾽ ἄλλων οὐδενὸς ὄντος
20 ἀξιόχρεω περὶ τῶν πρωτείων ἡμῖν ἀντιτάξασθαι,
ἐξὸν ἡμῖν καὶ τὰ ἡμέτερ᾽ αὐτῶν ἀσφαλῶς ἔχειν
καὶ τὰ τῶν ἄλλων δίκαια βραβεύειν, ἀπεστερήμεθα
28 μὲν χώρας οἰκείας, πλείω δ᾽ ἢ χίλια καὶ πεντα-
κόσια τάλαντ᾽ ἀνηλώκαμεν εἰς οὐδὲν δέον, οὓς δ᾽
25 ἐν τῷ πολέμῳ συμμάχους ἐκτησάμεθα, εἰρήνης
οὔσης ἀπολωλέκασιν οὗτοι, ἐχθρὸν δ᾽ ἐφ᾽ ἡμᾶς
αὐτοὺς τηλικοῦτον ἠσκήκαμεν. ἢ φρασάτω τις
ἐμοὶ παρελθών, πόθεν ἄλλοθεν ἰσχυρὸς γέγονεν
29 ἢ παρ᾽ ἡμῶν αὐτῶν Φίλιππος. ἀλλ᾽, ὦ τᾶν, εἰ

ταῦτα φαύλως, τὰ γ᾽ ἐν αὐτῇ τῇ πόλει νῦν
ἄμεινον ἔχει. καὶ τί ἂν εἰπεῖν τις ἔχοι; τὰς
ἐπάλξεις ἃς κονιῶμεν, καὶ τὰς ὁδοὺς ἃς ἐπισκευ-
άζομεν, καὶ κρήνας καὶ λήρους; ἀποβλέψατε δὴ
πρὸς τοὺς ταῦτα πολιτευομένους, ὧν οἱ μὲν ἐκ 5
πτωχῶν πλούσιοι γεγόνασιν, οἱ δ᾽ ἐξ ἀδόξων
ἔντιμοι, ἔνιοι δὲ τὰς ἰδίας οἰκίας τῶν δημοσίων
οἰκοδομημάτων σεμνοτέρας εἰσὶ κατεσκευασμένοι·
ὅσῳ δὲ τὰ τῆς πόλεως ἐλάττω γέγονεν, τοσούτῳ
τὰ τούτων ηὔξηται.   10

Τί δὴ τὸ πάντων αἴτιον τούτων, καὶ τί 30
δή ποθ᾽ ἅπαντ᾽ εἶχε καλῶς τότε καὶ νῦν οὐκ
ὀρθῶς; ὅτι τότε μὲν πράττειν καὶ στρατεύεσθαι
τολμῶν αὐτὸς ὁ δῆμος δεσπότης τῶν πολιτευομένων ἦν καὶ κύριος αὐτὸς ἁπάντων τῶν ἀγαθῶν, καὶ 15
ἀγαπητὸν ἦν παρὰ τοῦ δήμου τῶν ἄλλων ἑκάστῳ
καὶ τιμῆς καὶ ἀρχῆς καὶ ἀγαθοῦ τινος μεταλαβεῖν·
νῦν δὲ τοὐναντίον κύριοι μὲν οἱ πολιτευόμενοι τῶν 31
ἀγαθῶν καὶ διὰ τούτων ἅπαντα πράττεται, ὑμεῖς
δ᾽ ὁ δῆμος ἐκνενευρισμένοι καὶ περιηρημένοι χρή- 20
ματα, συμμάχους ἐν ὑπηρέτου καὶ προσθήκης
μέρει γεγένησθε, ἀγαπῶντες, ἐὰν μεταδιδῶσι
θεωρικῶν ὑμῖν ἢ Βοηδρόμια πέμψωσιν οὗτοι, καὶ
τὸ πάντων ἀνδρειότατον, τῶν ὑμετέρων αὐτῶν
χάριν προσοφείλετε. οἱ δ᾽ ἐν αὐτῇ τῇ πόλει 25
καθείρξαντες ὑμᾶς ἐπάγουσιν ἐπὶ ταῦτα καὶ τιθα-
σεύουσι χειροήθεις αὐτοῖς ποιοῦντες. ἔστι δ᾽ 32
οὐδέποτ᾽, οἶμαι, μέγα καὶ νεανικὸν φρόνημα λαβεῖν
μικρὰ καὶ φαῦλα πράττοντας· ὁποῖ᾽ ἄττα γὰρ ἂν

τἀπιτηδεύματα τῶν ἀνθρώπων ᾖ, τοιοῦτον ἀνάγκη
καὶ τὸ φρόνημ᾽ ἔχειν. ταῦτα μὰ τὴν Δήμητρ᾽
οὐκ ἂν θαυμάσαιμι εἰ μείζων εἰπόντι ἐμοὶ γένοιτο
παρ᾽ ὑμῶν βλάβη τῶν πεποιηκότων αὐτὰ γενέσθαι·
5 οὐδὲ γὰρ παρρησία περὶ πάντων ἀεὶ παρ᾽ ὑμῖν
ἐστιν, ἀλλ᾽ ἔγωγ᾽, ὅτι καὶ νῦν γέγονε, θαυμάζω.

33   Ἐὰν οὖν ἀλλὰ νῦν γ᾽ ἔτ᾽ ἀπαλλαγέντες τούτων
τῶν ἐθῶν ἐθελήσητε στρατεύεσθαί τε καὶ
πράττειν ἀξίως ὑμῶν αὐτῶν καὶ ταῖς περιου-
10 σίαις ταῖς οἴκοι ταύταις ἀφορμαῖς ἐπὶ τὰ ἔξω τῶν
ἀγαθῶν χρήσησθε, ἴσως ἂν, ἴσως, ὦ ἄνδρες
Ἀθηναῖοι, τέλειόν τι καὶ μέγα κτήσαισθ᾽ ἀγαθὸν
καὶ τῶν τοιούτων λημμάτων ἀπαλλαγείητε, ἃ τοῖς
ἀσθενοῦσι παρὰ τῶν ἰατρῶν σιτίοις διδομένοις
15 ἔοικεν. καὶ γὰρ ἐκεῖν᾽ οὔτ᾽ ἰσχὺν ἐντίθησιν οὔτ᾽
ἀποθνήσκειν ἐᾷ. καὶ ταῦθ᾽, ἃ νέμεσθε νῦν ὑμεῖς,
οὔτε τοσαῦτ᾽ ἐστίν, ὥστ᾽ ὠφέλειαν ἔχειν τινὰ
διαρκῆ, οὔτ᾽ ἀπογνόντας ἄλλο τι πράττειν ἐᾷ, ἀλλ᾽
ἔστι ταῦτα τὴν ἑκάστου ῥᾳθυμίαν ὑμῶν ἐπαυ-
34 ξάνοντα. οὐκοῦν σὺ μισθοφορὰν λέγεις; φήσει
21 τις. καὶ παραχρῆμά γε τὴν αὐτὴν σύνταξιν
ἁπάντων, ὦ ἄνδρες Ἀθηναῖοι, ἵνα τῶν κοινῶν
ἕκαστος τὸ μέρος λαμβάνων, ὅτου δέοιθ᾽ ἡ πόλις,
τοῦθ᾽ ὑπάρχοι· ἔξεστιν ἄγειν ἡσυχίαν· οἴκοι
25 μένων βελτίων, τοῦ δι᾽ ἔνδειαν ἀνάγκη τι ποιεῖν
αἰσχρὸν ἀπηλλαγμένος· συμβαίνει τι τοιοῦτον
οἷον καὶ τὰ νῦν· στρατιώτης αὐτὸς ὑπάρχων ἀπὸ
τῶν αὐτῶν τούτων λημμάτων, ὥσπερ ἐστὶ δίκαιον

ὑπὲρ τῆς πατρίδος· ἔστι τις ἔξω τῆς ἡλικίας ὑμῶν·
ὅσ᾽ οὗτος ἀτάκτως νῦν λαμβάνων οὐκ ὠφελεῖ,
ταῦτ᾽ ἐν ἴσῃ τάξει λαμβάνων, πάντ᾽ ἐφορῶν καὶ
διοικῶν ἃ χρὴ πράττεσθαι. ὅλως δ᾽ οὔτ᾽ ἀφελὼν **35**
οὔτε προσθείς, πλὴν μικρὸν τὴν ἀταξίαν ἀνελών, 5
εἰς τάξιν ἤγαγον τὴν πόλιν τὴν αὐτὴν τοῦ λαβεῖν,
τοῦ στρατεύεσθαι, τοῦ δικάζειν, τοῦ ποιεῖν τοῦθ᾽,
ὅ τι καθ᾽ ἡλικίαν ἕκαστος ἔχοι καὶ ὅτου καιρὸς
εἴη, τάξιν ποιήσας. οὐκ ἔστιν ὅπου μηδὲν ἐγὼ
ποιοῦσιν τὰ τῶν ποιούντων εἶπον ὡς δεῖ νέμειν, 10
οὐδ᾽ αὐτοὺς μὲν ἀργεῖν καὶ σχολάζειν καὶ ἀπορεῖν,
ὅτι δ᾽ οἱ τοῦ δεῖνος νικῶσι ξένοι, ταῦτα πυνθάνε-
σθαι· ταῦτα γὰρ νυνὶ γίγνεται. καὶ οὐχὶ μέμφομαι **36**
τὸν ποιοῦντά τι τῶν δεόντων ὑπὲρ ὑμῶν, ἀλλὰ
καὶ ὑμᾶς ὑπὲρ ὑμῶν αὐτῶν ἀξιῶ πράττειν ταῦθ᾽, 15
ἐφ᾽ οἷς ἑτέρους τιμᾶτε, καὶ μὴ παραχωρεῖν, ὦ
ἄνδρες Ἀθηναῖοι, τῆς τάξεως, ἣν ὑμῖν οἱ πρόγονοι
τῆς ἀρετῆς μετὰ πολλῶν καὶ καλῶν κινδύνων
κτησάμενοι κατέλιπον.

Σχεδὸν εἴρηκα, ἃ νομίζω συμφέρειν, ὑμεῖς δ᾽ 20
ἕλοισθ᾽, ὅ τι καὶ τῇ πόλει καὶ ἅπασι συνοίσειν
ὑμῖν μέλλει.

ΚΑΤΑ ΦΙΛΙΠΠΟΥ Α.

1   Εἰ μὲν περὶ καινοῦ τινος πράγματος προὐτί-
θετο, ὦ ἄνδρες Ἀθηναῖοι, λέγειν, ἐπισχὼν ἄν,
ἕως οἱ πλεῖστοι τῶν εἰωθότων γνώμην ἀπεφήναντο,
5 εἰ μὲν ἤρεσκέ τί μοι τῶν ὑπὸ τούτων ῥηθέντων,
ἡσυχίαν ἂν ἦγον, εἰ δὲ μή, τότ᾽ ἂν αὐτὸς ἐπει-
ρώμην ἃ γιγνώσκω λέγειν. ἐπειδὴ δ᾽, ὑπὲρ ὧν
πολλάκις εἰρήκασιν οὗτοι πρότερον, συμβαίνει καὶ
νυνὶ σκοπεῖν, ἡγοῦμαι καὶ πρῶτος ἀναστὰς
10 εἰκότως ἂν συγγνώμης τυγχάνειν. εἰ γὰρ ἐκ
τοῦ παρεληλυθότος χρόνου τὰ δέονθ᾽ οὗτοι συνε-
βούλευσαν, οὐδὲν ἂν ὑμᾶς νῦν ἔδει βουλεύεσθαι.

2   Πρῶτον μὲν οὖν οὐκ ἀθυμητέον, ὦ ἄνδρες
Ἀθηναῖοι, τοῖς παροῦσι πράγμασιν, οὐδ᾽ εἰ πάνυ
15 φαύλως ἔχειν δοκεῖ. ὃ γάρ ἐστι χείριστον αὐτῶν ἐκ
τοῦ παρεληλυθότος χρόνου, τοῦτο πρὸς τὰ μέλλοντα
βέλτιστον ὑπάρχει. τί οὖν ἐστι τοῦτο; ὅτι οὐδέν,
ὦ ἄνδρες Ἀθηναῖοι, τῶν δεόντων ποιούντων ὑμῶν
κακῶς τὰ πράγματ᾽ ἔχει· ἐπεί τοι, εἰ πάνθ᾽ ἃ
20 προσῆκε πραττόντων οὕτως εἶχεν, οὐδ᾽ ἂν ἐλπὶς
3 ἦν αὐτὰ βελτίω γενέσθαι. ἔπειτ᾽ ἐνθυμητέον καὶ

παρ' ἄλλων ἀκούουσι καὶ τοῖς εἰδόσιν αὐτοῖς ἀνα-
μιμνησκομένοις, ἡλίκην ποτ' ἐχόντων δύναμιν
Λακεδαιμονίων — ἐξ οὗ χρόνος οὐ πολύς — ὡς
καλῶς καὶ προσηκόντως οὐδὲν ἀνάξιον ὑμεῖς ἐπρά-
ξατε τῆς πόλεως, ἀλλ' ὑπεμείναθ' ὑπὲρ τῶν δικαίων ₅
τὸν πρὸς ἐκείνους πόλεμον. τίνος οὖν ἕνεκα ταῦτα ₃₇₈
λέγω; ἵν' εἰδῆτ', ὦ ἄνδρες Ἀθηναῖοι, καὶ θεάσησθε,
ὅτι οὐδὲν οὔτε φυλαττομένοις ὑμῖν ἐστι φοβερὸν οὔτ', ἂν ὀλιγωρῆτε, τοιοῦτον, οἷον ἂν ὑμεῖς
βούλοισθε, παραδείγμασι χρώμενοι τῇ τότε ῥώμῃ ₁₀
τῶν Λακεδαιμονίων, ἧς ἐκρατεῖτ' ἐκ τοῦ προσέχειν
τοῖς πράγμασι τὸν νοῦν, καὶ τῇ νῦν ὕβρει τούτου,
δι' ἣν ταραττόμεθ' ἐκ τοῦ μηδὲν φροντίζειν ὧν
ἐχρῆν.

Εἰ δέ τις ὑμῶν, ὦ ἄνδρες Ἀθηναῖοι, δυσπολέ- ₄
μητον οἴεται τὸν Φίλιππον εἶναι, σκοπῶν τό τε ₁₆
πλῆθος τῆς ὑπαρχούσης αὐτῷ δυνάμεως καὶ τὸ τὰ
χωρία πάντ' ἀπολωλέναι τῇ πόλει, ὀρθῶς μὲν
οἴεται, λογισάσθω μέντοι τοῦθ', ὅτι εἴχομέν ποθ'
ἡμεῖς, ὦ ἄνδρες Ἀθηναῖοι, Πύδναν καὶ Ποτείδαιαν ₂₀
καὶ Μεθώνην καὶ πάντα τὸν τόπον τοῦτον οἰκεῖον
κύκλῳ, καὶ πολλὰ τῶν μετ' ἐκείνου νῦν ὄντων
ἐθνῶν αὐτονομούμενα καὶ ἐλεύθερ' ὑπῆρχε καὶ
μᾶλλον ἡμῖν ἐβούλετ' ἔχειν οἰκείως ἢ 'κείνῳ. εἰ ₅
τοίνυν ὁ Φίλιππος τότε ταύτην ἔσχε τὴν γνώμην, ₂₅
ὡς χαλεπὸν πολεμεῖν ἐστιν Ἀθηναίοις ἔχουσι τοσαῦτ'
ἐπιτειχίσματα τῆς αὐτοῦ χώρας ἔρημον ὄντα συμμάχων, οὐδὲν ἂν ὧν νυνὶ πεποίηκεν ἔπραξεν οὐδὲ
τοσαύτην ἐκτήσατο δύναμιν. ἀλλ' εἶδεν, ὦ ἄνδρες

3*

Ἀθηναῖοι, τοῦτο καλῶς ἐκεῖνος, ὅτι ταῦτα μὲν
ἐστιν ἅπαντα τὰ χωρὶ ἆθλα τοῦ πολέμου κείμεν᾽
ἐν μέσῳ, φύσει δ᾽ ὑπάρχει τοῖς παροῦσι τὰ τῶν
ἀπόντων καὶ τοῖς ἐθέλουσι πονεῖν καὶ κινδυνεύειν
6 τὰ τῶν ἀμελούντων. καὶ γάρ τοι ταύτῃ χρησά-
6 μενος τῇ γνώμῃ πάντα κατέστραπται καὶ ἔχει, τὰ
μὲν ὡς ἂν ἑλών τις ἔχοι πολέμῳ, τὰ δὲ σύμμαχα
καὶ φίλα ποιησάμενος. ⟨⟩ καὶ γὰρ συμμαχεῖν καὶ
προσέχειν τὸν νοῦν τούτοις ἐθέλουσιν ἅπαντες, οὓς
10 ἂν ὁρῶσι παρεσκευασμένους καὶ πράττειν ἐθέλοντας
7 ἃ χρή. ἂν τοίνυν, ὦ ἄνδρες Ἀθηναῖοι, καὶ ὑμεῖς
ἐπὶ τῆς τοιαύτης ἐθελήσητε γενέσθαι γνώμης νῦν,
ἐπειδήπερ οὐ πρότερον, καὶ ἕκαστος ὑμῶν, οὗ δεῖ
καὶ δύναιτ᾽ ἂν παρασχεῖν αὐτὸν χρήσιμον τῇ πόλει,
15 πᾶσαν ἀφεὶς τὴν εἰρωνείαν ἕτοιμος πράττειν ὑπάρξῃ,
ὁ μὲν χρήματ᾽ ἔχων εἰσφέρειν, ὁ δ᾽ ἐν ἡλικίᾳ
στρατεύεσθαι, — συνελόντι δ᾽ ἁπλῶς, ἂν ὑμῶν
αὐτῶν ἐθελήσητε γενέσθαι καὶ παύσησθ᾽ αὐτὸς
μὲν οὐδὲν ἕκαστος ποιήσειν ἐλπίζων, τὸν δὲ πλησίον
20 πάνθ᾽ ὑπὲρ αὐτοῦ πράξειν, καὶ τὰ ὑμέτερ᾽ αὐτῶν
κομιεῖσθε, ἂν θεὸς θέλῃ, καὶ τὰ κατερραθυμημένα
8 πάλιν ἀναλήψεσθε, κἀκεῖνον τιμωρήσεσθε. μὴ γὰρ
ὡς θεῷ νομίζετ᾽ ἐκείνῳ τὰ παρόντα πεπηγέ-
ναι πράγματ᾽ ἀθάνατα, ἀλλὰ καὶ μισεῖ τις ἐκεῖ-
25 νον καὶ δέδιεν, ὦ ἄνδρες Ἀθηναῖοι, καὶ φθονεῖ καὶ
τῶν πάνυ νῦν δοκούντων οἰκείως ἔχειν, καὶ ἅπανθ᾽,
ὅσα περ καὶ ἐν ἄλλοις τισὶν ἀνθρώποις ἔνι, ταῦτα
κἂν τοῖς μετ᾽ ἐκείνου χρὴ νομίζειν ἐνεῖναι. κατέ-
πτηχε μέντοι πάντα ταῦτα νῦν, οὐκ ἔχοντ᾽ ἀπο-

στροφὴν διὰ τὴν ὑμετέραν βραδυτῆτα καὶ ῥαθυμίαν,
ἣν ἀποθέσθαι φημὶ δεῖν ἤδη. ὁρᾶτε γάρ, ὦ ἄνδρες 9
Ἀθηναῖοι, τὸ πρᾶγμα, οἷ προελήλυθεν ἀσελγείας
ἄνθρωπος, ὃς οὐδ᾽ αἵρεσιν ὑμῖν δίδωσι τοῦ πράττειν
ἢ ἄγειν ἡσυχίαν, ἀλλ᾽ ἀπειλεῖ καὶ λόγους ὑπερη- 5
φάνους, ὥς φασι, λέγει, καὶ οὐχ οἷός ἐστιν ἔχων
ἃ κατέστραπται μένειν ἐπὶ τούτων, ἀλλ᾽ ἀεί τι
προσπεριβάλλεται καὶ κύκλῳ πανταχῇ μέλλοντας
ἡμᾶς καὶ καθημένους περιστοιχίζεται.

Πότ᾽ οὖν, ὦ ἄνδρες Ἀθηναῖοι, πόθ᾽ ἃ χρὴ 10
πράξετε; ἐπειδὰν τί γένηται; ἐπειδὰν νὴ Δι᾽ ἀνάγκη 11
τις ᾖ. νῦν δὲ τί χρὴ τὰ γιγνόμεν᾽ ἡγεῖσθαι; ἐγὼ
μὲν γὰρ οἶμαι τοῖς ἐλευθέροις μεγίστην ἀνάγκην τὴν ὑπὲρ τῶν πραγμάτων αἰσχύνην
εἶναι. ἢ βούλεσθε, εἰπέ μοι, περιόντες αὐτῶν 15
πυνθάνεσθαι· „λέγεταί τι καινόν;" γένοιτο γὰρ ἂν
τι καινότερον ἢ Μακεδὼν ἀνὴρ Ἀθηναίους κατα-
πολεμῶν καὶ τὰ τῶν Ἑλλήνων διοικῶν; „τέθνηκε
Φίλιππος;" „οὐ μὰ Δι᾽, ἀλλ᾽ ἀσθενεῖ." τί δ᾽ ὑμῖν 11
351
διαφέρει; καὶ γὰρ ἂν οὗτός τι πάθῃ, ταχέως ὑμεῖς 20
ἕτερον Φίλιππον ποιήσετε, ἄνπερ οὕτω προσέχητε
τοῖς πράγμασι τὸν νοῦν· οὐδὲ γὰρ οὗτος παρὰ τὴν
αὑτοῦ ῥώμην τοσοῦτον ἐπηύξηται, ὅσον παρὰ τὴν
ἡμετέραν ἀμέλειαν. καίτοι καὶ τοῦτο· εἴ τι πάθοι 12
καὶ τὰ τῆς τύχης ἡμῖν, ἥπερ ἀεὶ βέλτιον ἢ ἡμεῖς 25
ἡμῶν αὐτῶν ἐπιμελούμεθα, καὶ τοῦτ᾽ ἐξεργάσαιτο,
ἴσθ᾽ ὅτι πλησίον μὲν ὄντες, ἅπασιν ἂν τοῖς πράγμασι τεταραγμένοις ἐπιστάντες ὅπως βούλεσθε
διοικήσαισθε, ὡς δὲ νῦν ἔχετε, οὐδὲ διδόντων τῶν

καιρῶν Ἀμφίπολιν δέξασθαι δύναισθ᾽ ἄν, ἀπηρτη-
μένοι καὶ ταῖς παρασκευαῖς καὶ ταῖς γνώμαις.

13   Ὡς μὲν οὖν δεῖ τὰ προσήκοντα ποιεῖν
ἐθέλοντας ὑπάρχειν ἅπαντας ἑτοίμως, ὡς
5 ἐγνωκότων ὑμῶν καὶ πεπεισμένων, παύομαι λέγων·
τὸν δὲ τρόπον τῆς παρασκευῆς, ἣν ἀπαλλάξαι
ἂν τῶν τοιούτων πραγμάτων ἡμᾶς οἴομαι, καὶ τὸ
πλῆθος ὅσον, καὶ πόρους οὕστινας χρημάτων, καὶ
τἆλλ᾽ ὡς ἂν μοι βέλτιστα καὶ τάχιστα δοκεῖ παρα-
10 σκευασθῆναι, καὶ δὴ πειράσομαι λέγειν, δεηθεὶς
14 ὑμῶν, ὦ ἄνδρες Ἀθηναῖοι, τοσοῦτον. ἐπειδὰν
ἅπαντ᾽ ἀκούσητε, κρίνατε, μὴ πρότερον προ-
λαμβάνετε· μηδ᾽ ἂν ἐξ ἀρχῆς δοκῶ τινι καινὴν
παρασκευὴν λέγειν, ἀναβάλλειν με τὰ πράγμαθ᾽
15 ἡγείσθω. οὐ γὰρ οἱ „ταχύ“ καὶ „τήμερον“ εἰπόντες
μάλιστ᾽ εἰς δέον λέγουσιν (οὐ γὰρ ἂν τά γ᾽ ἤδη
γεγενημένα τῇ νυνὶ βοηθείᾳ κωλῦσαι δυνηθείημεν),
15 ἀλλ᾽ ὃς ἂν δείξῃ, τίς πορισθεῖσα παρασκευὴ καὶ
πόση καὶ πόθεν διαμεῖναι δυνήσεται, ἕως ἂν ἢ
20 διαλυσώμεθα πεισθέντες τὸν πόλεμον ἢ περι-
γενώμεθα τῶν ἐχθρῶν· οὕτω γὰρ οὐκέτι τοῦ
λοιποῦ πάσχοιμεν ἂν κακῶς. οἶμαι τοίνυν ἐγὼ
ταῦτα λέγειν ἔχειν, μὴ κωλύων εἴ τις ἄλλος ἐπαγ-
γέλλεταί τι. ἡ μὲν οὖν ὑπόσχεσις οὕτω μεγάλη,
25 τὸ δὲ πρᾶγμ᾽ ἤδη τὸν ἔλεγχον δώσει, κριταὶ δ᾽
ὑμεῖς ἔσεσθε.

16   Πρῶτον μὲν τοίνυν, ὦ ἄνδρες Ἀθηναῖοι,
τριήρεις πεντήκοντα παρασκευάσασθαί φημι δεῖν,

εἶτ᾽ αὐτοὺς οὕτω τὰς γνώμας ἔχειν ὡς, ἐάν τι δέῃ,
πλευστέον εἰς ταύτας αὐτοῖς ἐμβᾶσιν. πρὸς δὲ
τούτοις τοῖς ἡμίσεσι τῶν ἱππέων ἱππαγωγοὺς τριήρεις καὶ πλοῖ᾽ ἱκανὰ εὐτρεπίσαι κελεύω· ταῦτα 17
μὲν οἶμαι δεῖν ὑπάρχειν ἐπὶ τὰς ἐξαίφνης 5
ταύτας ἀπὸ τῆς οἰκείας χώρας αὐτοῦ στρατείας
εἰς Πύλας καὶ Χερρόνησον καὶ Ὄλυνθον καὶ ὅποι
βούλεται· δεῖ γὰρ ἐκείνῳ τοῦτ᾽ ἐν τῇ γνώμῃ παρα-
στῆσαι, ὡς ὑμεῖς ἐκ τῆς ἀμελείας ταύτης τῆς ἄγαν, 9
ὥσπερ εἰς Εὔβοιαν καὶ πρότερόν ποτέ φασιν εἰς 357
Ἁλίαρτον καὶ τὰ τελευταῖα πρώην εἰς Πύλας, ἴσως 395. 352
ἂν ὁρμήσαιτε· (οὗτοι παντελῶς οὐδ᾽ εἰ μὴ ποιήσαιτ᾽ 18
ἂν τοῦτο, ὡς ἔγωγέ φημι δεῖν, εὐκαταφρόνητόν
ἐστιν) ἵν᾽ ἢ διὰ τὸν φόβον εἰδὼς εὐτρεπεῖς ὑμᾶς
(εἴσεται γὰρ ἀκριβῶς· εἰσὶ γάρ, εἰσὶν οἱ πάντ᾽ 15
ἐξαγγέλλοντες ἐκείνῳ παρ᾽ ἡμῶν αὐτῶν πλείους τοῦ
δέοντος) ἡσυχίαν ἔχῃ, ἢ παριδὼν ταῦτ᾽ ἀφύλακτος
ληφθῇ, μηδενὸς ὄντος ἐμποδὼν πλεῖν ἐπὶ τὴν
ἐκείνου χώραν ὑμῖν, ἂν ἐνδῷ καιρόν. ταῦτα μέν 19
ἐστιν ἃ πᾶσι δεδόχθαι φημὶ δεῖν καὶ παρεσκευάσθαι 20
προσήκειν οἴομαι· πρὸ δὲ τούτων δύναμίν τινα,
ὦ ἄνδρες Ἀθηναῖοι, φημὶ προχειρίσασθαι δεῖν
ὑμᾶς, ἣ συνεχῶς πολεμήσει καὶ κακῶς ἐκεῖνον
ποιήσει. μή μοι μυρίους μηδὲ δισμυρίους ξένους,
μηδὲ τὰς ἐπιστολιμαίους ταύτας δυνάμεις, ἀλλ᾽ ἣ 25
τῆς πόλεως ἔσται, κἂν ὑμεῖς ἕνα κἂν πλείους κἂν
τὸν δεῖνα κἂν ὁντινοῦν χειροτονήσητε στρατηγόν,
τούτῳ πείσεται καὶ ἀκολουθήσει. καὶ τροφὴν ταύτῃ
πορίσαι κελεύω. ἔσται δ᾽ αὕτη τίς ἡ δύναμις καὶ 20

πόση; καὶ πόθεν τὴν τροφὴν ἕξει; καὶ πῶς ταῦτ᾽
ἐθελήσει ποιεῖν; ἐγὼ φράσω, καθ᾽ ἕκαστον τούτων
διεξιὼν χωρίς· ξένους μὲν λέγω — καὶ ὅπως μὴ
ποιήσεθ᾽ ὃ πολλάκις ὑμᾶς ἔβλαψεν· πάντ᾽ ἐλάττω
5 νομίζοντες εἶναι τοῦ δέοντος, καὶ τὰ μέγιστ᾽ ἐν
τοῖς ψηφίσμασιν αἱρούμενοι, ἐπὶ τῷ πράττειν οὐδὲ
τὰ μικρὰ ποιεῖτε· ἀλλὰ τὰ μικρὰ ποιήσαντες καὶ
πορίσαντες, τούτοις προστίθετε, ἂν ἐλάττω φαίνηται.
21 λέγω δὴ τοὺς πάντας στρατιώτας δισχιλίους, τούτων
10 δ᾽ Ἀθηναίους φημὶ δεῖν εἶναι πεντακοσίους, ἐξ ἧς
ἂν τινος ὑμῖν ἡλικίας καλῶς ἔχειν δοκῇ, χρόνον
τακτὸν στρατευομένους, μὴ μακρὸν τοῦτον, ἀλλ᾽
ὅσον ἂν δοκῇ καλῶς ἔχειν, ἐκ διαδοχῆς ἀλλήλοις·
τοὺς δ᾽ ἄλλους ξένους εἶναι κελεύω. καὶ μετὰ τού-
15 των ἱππέας διακοσίους, καὶ τούτων πεντήκοντ᾽
Ἀθηναίους τοὐλάχιστον, ὥσπερ τοὺς πεζούς, τὸν
αὐτὸν τρόπον στρατευομένους, καὶ ἱππαγωγοὺς τού-
22 τοις.   εἶεν· τί πρὸς τούτοις ἔτι; ταχείας τριήρεις
δέκα· δεῖ γάρ, ἔχοντος ἐκείνου ναυτικόν, καὶ τα-
20 χειῶν τριήρων ἡμῖν, ὅπως ἀσφαλῶς ἡ δύναμις πλέῃ.
πόθεν δὴ τούτοις ἡ τροφὴ γενήσεται; ἐγὼ καὶ τοῦτο
φράσω καὶ δείξω, ἐπειδάν, διότι τηλικαύτην ἀποχρῆν οἶμαι τὴν δύναμιν καὶ πολίτας τοὺς
στρατευομένους εἶναι κελεύω, διδάξω.

23   Τοσαύτην μέν, ὦ ἄνδρες Ἀθηναῖοι, διὰ ταῦτα,
26 ὅτι οὐκ ἔνι νῦν ἡμῖν πορίσασθαι δύναμιν τὴν
ἐκείνῳ παραταξομένην, ἀλλὰ λῃστεύειν ἀνάγκη καὶ
τούτῳ τῷ τρόπῳ τοῦ πολέμου χρῆσθαι τὴν πρώτην.
οὐ τοίνυν ὑπέρογκον αὐτήν (οὐ γὰρ ἔστι μισθὸς

οὐδὲ τροφή), οὐδὲ παντελῶς ταπεινὴν εἶναι δεῖ. πολίτας δὲ παρεῖναι καὶ συμπλεῖν διὰ ταῦτα κελεύω, ὅτι καὶ πρότερόν ποτ᾽ ἀκούω ξενικὸν τρέφειν ἐν Κορίνθῳ τὴν πόλιν, οὗ Πολύστρατος 393/90 ἡγεῖτο καὶ Ἰφικράτης καὶ Χαβρίας καὶ ἄλλοι τινές, 5 καὶ αὐτοὺς ὑμᾶς συστρατεύεσθαι· καὶ οἶδ᾽ ἀκούων, 24 ὅτι Λακεδαιμονίους παρατασσόμενοι μεθ᾽ ὑμῶν ἐνίκων οὗτοι οἱ ξένοι καὶ ὑμεῖς μετ᾽ ἐκείνων. ἐξ οὗ δ᾽ αὐτὰ καθ᾽ αὑτὰ τὰ ξενικὰ ὑμῖν στρατεύεται, τοὺς φίλους νικᾷ καὶ τοὺς συμμάχους, οἱ δ᾽ 10 ἐχθροὶ μείζους τοῦ δέοντος γεγόνασιν. καὶ παρακύψαντ᾽ ἐπὶ τὸν τῆς πόλεως πόλεμον, πρὸς Ἀρτάβαζον καὶ πανταχοῖ μᾶλλον οἴχεται πλέοντα, ὁ δὲ στρατηγὸς ἀκολουθεῖ, εἰκότως· οὐ γὰρ ἔστ᾽ ἄρχειν μὴ διδόντα μισθόν. τί οὖν κελεύω; τὰς προφάσεις 25 ἀφελεῖν καὶ τοῦ στρατηγοῦ καὶ τῶν στρατιωτῶν, 16 μισθὸν πορίσαντας καὶ στρατιώτας οἰκείους ὥσπερ ἐπόπτας τῶν στρατηγουμένων παρακαταστήσαντας, ἐπεὶ νῦν γε γέλως ἔσθ᾽ ὡς χρώμεθα τοῖς πράγμασιν. εἰ γὰρ ἔροιτό τις ὑμᾶς, „εἰρήνην ἄγετε, 20 ὦ ἄνδρες Ἀθηναῖοι;“ „μὰ Δί᾽ οὐχ ἡμεῖς γε,“ εἴποιτ᾽ ἄν, „ἀλλὰ Φιλίππῳ πολεμοῦμεν.“ οὐκ 26 ἐχειροτονεῖτε δ᾽ ἐξ ὑμῶν αὐτῶν δέκα ταξιάρχους καὶ στρατηγοὺς καὶ φυλάρχους καὶ ἱππάρχους δύο; τί οὖν οὗτοι ποιοῦσιν; πλὴν ἑνὸς ἀνδρός, ὃν ἂν 25 ἐκπέμψητ᾽ ἐπὶ τὸν πόλεμον, οἱ λοιποὶ τὰς πομπὰς πέμπουσιν ὑμῖν μετὰ τῶν ἱεροποιῶν· ὥσπερ γὰρ οἱ πλάττοντες τοὺς πηλίνους, εἰς τὴν ἀγορὰν χειροτονεῖτε τοὺς ταξιάρχους καὶ τοὺς φυλάρχους, οὐκ

27 ἐπὶ τὸν πόλεμον. οὐ γὰρ ἐχρῆν, ὦ ἄνδρες Ἀθηναῖοι,
ταξιάρχους παρ᾽ ὑμῶν, ἵππαρχον παρ᾽ ὑμῶν, ἄρχον-
τας οἰκείους εἶναι, ἵν᾽ ἦν ὡς ἀληθῶς τῆς πόλεως
ἡ δύναμις; ἀλλ᾽ εἰς μὲν Λῆμνον τὸν παρ᾽ ὑμῶν
5 ἵππαρχον δεῖ πλεῖν, τῶν δ᾽ ὑπὲρ τῶν τῆς πόλεως
κτημάτων ἀγωνιζομένων Μενέλαον ἱππαρχεῖν. καὶ
οὐ τὸν ἄνδρα μεμφόμενος ταῦτα λέγω, ἀλλ᾽ ὑφ᾽
ὑμῶν ἔδει κεχειροτονημένον εἶναι τοῦτον, ὅστις ἂν ᾖ.

28   Ἴσως δὲ ταῦτα μὲν ὀρθῶς ἡγεῖσθε λέγεσθαι,
10 τὸ δὲ τῶν χρημάτων, πόσα καὶ πόθεν ἔσται,
μάλιστα ποθεῖτ᾽ ἀκοῦσαι. τοῦτο δὴ καὶ περαίνω.
χρήματα τοίνυν — ἔστι μὲν ἡ τροφή, σιτηρέσιον
μόνον, τῇ δυνάμει ταύτῃ τάλαντ᾽ ἐνενήκοντα καὶ
μικρόν τι πρός· δέκα μὲν ναυσὶ ταχείαις τετταρά-
15 κοντα τάλαντα, εἴκοσιν εἰς τὴν ναῦν μναῖ τοῦ
μηνὸς ἑκάστου, στρατιώταις δὲ δισχιλίοις τοσαῦθ᾽
ἕτερα, ἵνα δέκα τοῦ μηνὸς ὁ στρατιώτης δραχμὰς
σιτηρέσιον λαμβάνῃ, τοῖς δ᾽ ἱππεῦσι διακοσίοις
οὖσιν, ἐὰν τριάκοντα δραχμὰς ἕκαστος λαμβάνῃ
29 τοῦ μηνός, δώδεκα τάλαντα. εἰ δέ τις οἴεται
21 μικρὰν ἀφορμὴν εἶναι, σιτηρέσιον τοῖς στρατευομένοις ὑπάρχειν, οὐκ ὀρθῶς ἔγνωκεν· ἐγὼ γὰρ
οἶδα σαφῶς ὅτι, τοῦτ᾽ ἂν γένηται, προσποριεῖ τὰ
λοίπ᾽ αὐτὸ τὸ στράτευμ᾽ ἀπὸ τοῦ πολέμου, οὐδένα
25 τῶν Ἑλλήνων ἀδικοῦν οὐδὲ τῶν συμμάχων, ὥστ᾽
ἔχειν μισθὸν ἐντελῆ. ἐγὼ συμπλέων ἐθελοντὴς
πάσχειν ὁτιοῦν ἕτοιμος, ἐὰν μὴ ταῦθ᾽ οὕτως ἔχῃ.
πόθεν οὖν ὁ πόρος τῶν χρημάτων ἃ παρ᾽ ὑμῶν
κελεύω γενέσθαι, τοῦτ᾽ ἤδη λέξω.

ΠΟΡΟΥ ΑΠΟΔΕΙΞΙΣ.

Ἃ μὲν ἡμεῖς, ὦ ἄνδρες Ἀθηναῖοι, δεδυνήμεθ᾽ 30
εὑρεῖν, ταῦτ᾽ ἐστίν. ἐπειδὰν δ᾽ ἐπιχειροτονῆτε
τὰς γνώμας, ἂν ὑμῖν ἀρέσκῃ, χειροτονήσετε, ἵνα
μὴ μόνον ἐν τοῖς ψηφίσμασι καὶ ταῖς ἐπιστολαῖς 5
πολεμῆτε Φιλίππῳ, ἀλλὰ καὶ τοῖς ἔργοις. Δοκεῖτε 31
δὲ μοι πολὺ βέλτιον ἂν περὶ τοῦ πολέμου καὶ
ὅλης τῆς παρασκευῆς βουλεύσασθαι, εἰ τὸν τόπον,
ὦ ἄνδρες Ἀθηναῖοι, τῆς χώρας, πρὸς ἣν πολεμεῖτε,
ἐνθυμηθείητε καὶ λογίσαισθε, ὅτι τοῖς πνεύμασι 10
καὶ ταῖς ὥραις τοῦ ἔτους τὰ πολλὰ προλαμβάνων
διαπράττεται Φίλιππος, καὶ φυλάξας τοὺς ἐτησίας
ἢ τὸν χειμῶν᾽ ἐπιχειρεῖ, ἡνίκ᾽ ἂν ἡμεῖς μὴ δυναί-
μεθ᾽ ἐκεῖσ᾽ ἀφικέσθαι. δεῖ τοίνυν ταῦτ᾽ ἐνθυμου- 32
μένους μὴ βοηθείαις πολεμεῖν (ὑστεριοῦμεν γὰρ 15
ἁπάντων), ἀλλὰ παρασκευῇ συνεχεῖ καὶ δυνάμει. ὑπάρχει δ᾽ ὑμῖν χειμαδίῳ μὲν χρῆσθαι τῇ
δυνάμει Λήμνῳ καὶ Θάσῳ καὶ Σκιάθῳ καὶ ταῖς
ἐν τούτῳ τῷ τόπῳ νήσοις, ἐν αἷς καὶ λιμένες καὶ
σῖτος καὶ ἃ χρὴ στρατεύματι πάνθ᾽ ὑπάρχει· τὴν 20
δ᾽ ὥραν τοῦ ἔτους, ὅτε καὶ πρὸς τῇ γῇ γενέσθαι
ῥᾴδιον καὶ τὸ τῶν πνευμάτων ἀσφαλές, πρὸς αὐτῇ
τῇ χώρᾳ καὶ πρὸς τοῖς τῶν ἐμπορίων στόμασι
ῥᾳδίως ἔσται.

Ἃ μὲν οὖν χρήσεται καὶ πότε τῇ δυνάμει, 33
παρὰ τὸν καιρὸν ὁ τούτων κύριος καταστὰς ὑφ᾽ 26
ὑμῶν βουλεύσεται· ἃ δ᾽ ὑπάρξαι δεῖ παρ᾽ ὑμῶν,
ταῦτ᾽ ἐστίν, ἃ ᾽γὼ γέγραφα. ἂν ταῦτ᾽, ὦ ἄνδρες

Ἀθηναῖοι, πορίσητε τὰ χρήματα πρῶτον ἃ λέγω,
εἶτα καὶ τἆλλα παρασκευάσαντες, τοὺς στρατιώτας,
τὰς τριήρεις, τοὺς ἱππέας, ἐντελῆ πᾶσαν τὴν δύναμιν νόμῳ κατακλείσητ᾽ ἐπὶ τῷ πολέμῳ μένειν,
5 τῶν μὲν χρημάτων αὐτοὶ ταμίαι καὶ πορισταὶ
γιγνόμενοι, τῶν δὲ πράξεων παρὰ τοῦ στρατηγοῦ
τὸν λόγον ζητοῦντες, παύσεσθ᾽ ἀεὶ περὶ τῶν αὐτῶν
34 βουλευόμενοι καὶ πλέον οὐδὲν ποιοῦντες, καὶ ἔτι
πρὸς τούτῳ πρῶτον μέν, ὦ ἄνδρες Ἀθηναῖοι, τὸν
10 μέγιστον τῶν ἐκείνου πόρων ἀφαιρήσεσθε.
ἔστι δ᾽ οὗτος τίς; ἀπὸ τῶν ὑμετέρων ὑμῖν πολεμεῖ
συμμάχων, ἄγων καὶ φέρων τοὺς πλέοντας τὴν
θάλατταν. ἔπειτα τί πρὸς τούτῳ; τοῦ πάσχειν
αὐτοὶ κακῶς ἔξω γενήσεσθε, οὐχ ὥσπερ τὸν
15 παρελθόντα χρόνον εἰς Λῆμνον καὶ Ἴμβρον ἐμ-
βαλὼν αἰχμαλώτους πολίτας ὑμετέρους ᾤχετ᾽ ἔχων,
πρὸς τῷ Γεραιστῷ τὰ πλοῖα συλλαβὼν ἀμύθητα
χρήματ᾽ ἐξέλεξεν, τὰ τελευταῖ᾽ εἰς Μαραθῶν᾽ ἀπέβη
καὶ τὴν ἱερὰν ἀπὸ τῆς χώρας ᾤχετ᾽ ἔχων τριήρη,
20 ὑμεῖς δ᾽ οὔτε ταῦτα δύνασθε κωλύειν οὔτ᾽ εἰς
τοὺς χρόνους, οὓς ἂν προθῆσθε, βοηθεῖν.
35   Καίτοι τί δήποτ᾽, ὦ ἄνδρες Ἀθηναῖοι, νομίζετε τὴν μὲν τῶν Παναθηναίων ἑορτὴν καὶ τὴν
τῶν Διονυσίων ἀεὶ τοῦ καθήκοντος χρόνου
25 γίγνεσθαι, ἄν τε δεινοὶ λάχωσιν ἄν τ᾽ ἰδιῶται οἱ
τούτων ἑκατέρων ἐπιμελούμενοι, εἰς ἃ τοσαῦτ᾽
ἀναλίσκετε χρήματα, ὅσ᾽ οὐδ᾽ εἰς ἕνα τῶν ἀποστό-
λων, καὶ τοσοῦτον ὄχλον καὶ παρασκευήν, ὅσην
οὐκ οἶδ᾽ εἴ τι τῶν ἁπάντων ἔχει, τοὺς δ᾽ ἀποστό-

λους πάντας ὑμῖν ὑστερίζειν τῶν καιρῶν, τὸν εἰς
Μεθώνην, τὸν εἰς Παγασάς, τὸν εἰς Ποτείδαιαν; **I, 12** ³⁵⁶/⁵²
ὅτι ἐκεῖνα μὲν ἅπαντα νόμῳ τέτακται, καὶ πρόοιδεν 36
ἕκαστος ὑμῶν ἐκ πολλοῦ, τίς χορηγὸς ἢ γυμνασίαρχος τῆς φυλῆς, πότε καὶ παρὰ τοῦ καὶ τί 5
λαβόντα τί δεῖ ποιεῖν, οὐδὲν ἀνεξέταστον οὐδ᾽
ἀόριστον ἐν τούτοις ἠμέληται, ἐν δὲ τοῖς περὶ
τοῦ πολέμου καὶ τῇ τούτου παρασκευῇ ἄτακτα,
ἀδιόρθωτα, ἀόριστα ἅπαντα. τοιγαροῦν ἅμ᾽
ἀκηκόαμέν τι καὶ τριηράρχους καθίσταμεν καὶ τού- 10
τοις ἀντιδόσεις ποιούμεθα καὶ περὶ χρημάτων
πόρου σκοποῦμεν, καὶ μετὰ ταῦτ᾽ ἐμβαίνειν τοὺς
μετοίκους ἔδοξε καὶ τοὺς χωρὶς οἰκοῦντας, εἶτ᾽
αὐτοὺς πάλιν, εἶτ᾽ ἀντεμβιβάζειν, εἶτ᾽ ἐν ὅσῳ 37
ταῦτα μέλλεται, προαπόλωλε τὸ ἐφ᾽ ὃ ἂν ἐκπλέω- 15
μεν· τὸν γὰρ τοῦ πράττειν χρόνον εἰς τὸ παρασκευάζεσθαι ἀναλίσκομεν. οἱ δὲ τῶν πραγμάτων οὐ
μένουσι καιροὶ τὴν ἡμετέραν βραδυτῆτα καὶ εἰρω-
νείαν· ἃς δὲ τὸν μεταξὺ χρόνον δυνάμεις οἰόμεθ᾽
ἡμῖν ὑπάρχειν, οὐδὲν οἷαί τ᾽ οὖσαι ποιεῖν ἐπ᾽ αὐτῶν 20
τῶν καιρῶν ἐξελέγχονται. ὁ δ᾽ εἰς τοῦθ᾽ ὕβρεως
ἐλήλυθεν ὥστ᾽ ἐπιστέλλειν Εὐβοεῦσιν ἤδη τοιαύτας
ἐπιστολάς.

ΕΠΙΣΤΟΛΗ.

Τούτων, ὦ ἄνδρες Ἀθηναῖοι, τῶν ἀνεγνω- 38
σμένων ἀληθῆ μέν ἐστι τὰ πολλά, ὡς οὐκ ἔδει, οὐ 26
μὴν ἀλλ᾽ ἴσως οὐχ ἡδέ᾽ ἀκούειν. ἀλλ᾽ εἰ μέν, ὅσ᾽
ἄν τις ὑπερβῇ τῷ λόγῳ, ἵνα μὴ λυπήσῃ, καὶ τὰ
πράγμαθ᾽ ὑπερβήσεται, δεῖ πρὸς ἡδονὴν δημηγορεῖν·

εἰ δ᾿ ἡ τῶν λόγων χάρις, ἂν ᾖ μὴ προσήκουσα,
ἔργῳ ζημία γίγνεται, αἰσχρόν ἐστι φενακίζειν
ἑαυτούς, καὶ ἅπαντ᾿ ἀναβαλλομένους, ἃ ἂν ᾖ δυσ-
39 χερῆ, πάντων ὑστερεῖν τῶν ἔργων, καὶ μηδὲ τοῦτο
δύνασθαι μαθεῖν, ὅτι δεῖ τοὺς ὀρθῶς πολέμῳ
χρωμένους οὐκ ἀκολουθεῖν τοῖς πράγμασιν, ἀλλ᾿
αὐτοὺς ἔμπροσθεν εἶναι τῶν πραγμάτων,
καὶ τὸν αὐτὸν τρόπον, ὥσπερ τῶν στρατευμάτων
ἀξιώσειέ τις ἂν τὸν στρατηγὸν ἡγεῖσθαι, οὕτω καὶ
τῶν πραγμάτων τοὺς βουλευομένους, ἵν᾿, ἃ ἂν ἐκείνοις δοκῇ, ταῦτα πράττηται καὶ μὴ τὰ συμβάντ᾿
40 ἀναγκάζωνται διώκειν· ὑμεῖς δ᾿, ὦ ἄνδρες Ἀθηναῖοι,
πλείστην δύναμιν ἁπάντων ἔχοντες, τριήρεις, ὁπλί-
τας, ἱππέας, χρημάτων πρόσοδον, τούτων μὲν
μέχρι τῆς τήμερον ἡμέρας οὐδενὶ πώποτ᾿ εἰς δέον
τι κέχρησθε, οὐδὲν δ᾿ ἀπολείπετε, ὥσπερ οἱ βάρ-
βαροι πυκτεύουσιν, οὕτω πολεμεῖν Φιλίππῳ. καὶ
γὰρ ἐκείνων ὁ πληγεὶς ἀεὶ τῆς πληγῆς ἔχεται, κἂν
ἑτέρωσε πατάξῃς, ἐκεῖσ᾿ εἰσὶν αἱ χεῖρες· προβάλ-
λεσθαι δ᾿ ἢ βλέπειν ἐναντίον οὔτ᾿ οἶδεν οὔτ᾿
41 ἐθέλει. καὶ ὑμεῖς, ἂν ἐν Χερρονήσῳ πύθησθε
Φίλιππον, ἐκεῖσε βοηθεῖν ψηφίζεσθε, ἂν ἐν Πύλαις,
ἐκεῖσε, ἂν ἄλλοθί που, συμπαραθεῖτ᾿ ἄνω κάτω,
καὶ στρατηγεῖσθ᾿ ὑπ᾿ ἐκείνου, βεβούλευσθε δ᾿
οὐδὲν αὐτοὶ συμφέρον περὶ τοῦ πολέμου, οὐδὲ
πρὸ τῶν πραγμάτων προορᾶτ᾿ οὐδέν, πρὶν ἂν ἢ
γεγενημένον ἢ γιγνόμενόν τι πύθησθε. ταῦτα δ᾿
ἴσως πρότερον μὲν ἐνῆν, νῦν δ᾿ ἐπ᾿ αὐτὴν ἥκει
τὴν ἀκμήν, ὥστ᾿ οὐκέτ᾿ ἐγχωρεῖ.

Δοκεῖ δέ μοι θεῶν τις, ὦ ἄνδρες Ἀθηναῖοι, 42
τοῖς γιγνομένοις ὑπὲρ τῆς πόλεως αἰσχυνόμενος
τὴν φιλοπραγμοσύνην ταύτην ἐμβαλεῖν Φιλίππῳ.
εἰ γὰρ ἔχων, ἃ κατέστραπται καὶ προείληφεν,
ἡσυχίαν ἔχειν ἤθελεν καὶ μηδὲν ἔπραττεν ἔτι, 5
ἀποχρῆν ἐνίοις ὑμῶν ἄν μοι δοκεῖ, ἐξ ὧν αἰσχύνην
καὶ ἀνανδρίαν καὶ πάντα τὰ αἴσχιστ᾽ ὠφληκότες
ἂν ἦμεν δημοσίᾳ· νῦν δ᾽ ἐπιχειρῶν ἀεί τινι καὶ
τοῦ πλείονος ὀρεγόμενος ἴσως ἂν ἐκκαλέσαιθ᾽
ὑμᾶς, εἴπερ μὴ παντάπασιν ἀπεγνώκατε. 10
θαυμάζω δ᾽ ἔγωγε, εἰ μηδεὶς ὑμῶν μήτ᾽ ἐνθυ- 43
μεῖται μήτ᾽ ὀργίζεται, ὁρῶν, ὦ ἄνδρες Ἀθηναῖοι,
τὴν μὲν ἀρχὴν τοῦ πολέμου γεγενημένην περὶ τοῦ
τιμωρήσασθαι Φίλιππον, τὴν δὲ τελευτὴν οὖσαν
ἤδη ὑπὲρ τοῦ μὴ παθεῖν κακῶς ὑπὸ Φιλίππου. 15
ἀλλὰ μὴν ὅτι γ᾽ οὐ στήσεται, δῆλον, εἰ μή τις
κωλύσει. εἶτα τοῦτ᾽ ἀναμενοῦμεν; καὶ τριήρεις
κενὰς καὶ τὰς παρὰ τοῦ δεῖνος ἐλπίδας ἂν ἀποστεί-
λητε, πάντ᾽ ἔχειν οἴεσθε καλῶς; οὐκ ἐμβησόμεθα; 44
οὐκ ἔξιμεν αὐτοὶ μέρει γέ τινι στρατιωτῶν οἰκείων 20
νῦν, εἰ καὶ μὴ πρότερον; οὐκ ἐπὶ τὴν ἐκείνου
πλευσόμεθα; „ποῖ οὖν προσορμιούμεθα;“ ἤρετό
τις. εὑρήσει τὰ σαθρά, ὦ ἄνδρες Ἀθηναῖοι, τῶν
ἐκείνου πραγμάτων αὐτὸς ὁ πόλεμος, ἂν ἐπιχει-
ρῶμεν· ἂν μέντοι καθώμεθ᾽ οἴκοι, λοιδορουμένων 25
ἀκούοντες καὶ αἰτιωμένων ἀλλήλους τῶν λεγόντων,
οὐδέποτ᾽ οὐδὲν ἡμῖν μὴ γένηται τῶν δεόντων.
ὅποι μὲν γὰρ ἄν, οἶμαι, μέρος τι τῆς πόλεως συν- 45
αποσταλῇ, κἂν μὴ πᾶσα, καὶ τὸ τῶν θεῶν εὐμενὲς

καὶ τὸ τῆς τύχης συναγωνίζεται· ὅποι δ᾽ ἂν στρατηγὸν καὶ ψήφισμα κενὸν καὶ τὰς ἀπὸ τοῦ βήματος
ἐλπίδας ἐκπέμψητε, οὐδὲν ὑμῖν τῶν δεόντων
γίγνεται, ἀλλ᾽ οἱ μὲν ἐχθροὶ καταγελῶσιν, οἱ δὲ
5 σύμμαχοι τεθνᾶσι τῷ δέει τοὺς τοιούτους ἀποστό-
46 λους. οὐ γὰρ ἔστιν, οὐκ ἔστιν εὖ᾽ ἄνδρα δυνη-
θῆναί ποτε ταῦθ᾽ ὑμῖν πρᾶξαι πάνθ᾽ ὅσα βού-
λεσθε· ὑποσχέσθαι μέντοι καὶ φῆσαι καὶ τὸν δεῖν᾽
αἰτιάσασθαι καὶ τὸν δεῖν᾽ ἔστιν, τὰ δὲ πράγματ᾽
10 ἐκ τούτων ἀπόλωλεν. ὅταν γὰρ ἡγῆται μὲν ὁ στρατηγὸς ἀθλίων ἀπομίσθων ξένων, οἱ δ᾽, ὑπὲρ ὧν
ἂν ἐκεῖνος πράξῃ, πρὸς ὑμᾶς ψευδόμενοι ῥᾳδίως
ἐνθάδ᾽ ὦσιν, ὑμεῖς δ᾽, ἐξ ὧν ἂν ἀκούσηθ᾽, ὅ τι
ἂν τύχητε ψηφίζησθε, τί καὶ χρὴ προσδοκᾶν;
47 πῶς οὖν ταῦτα παύσεται; ὅταν ὑμεῖς, ὦ ἄνδρες
16 Ἀθηναῖοι, τοὺς αὐτοὺς ἀποδείξητε στρατιώτας καὶ
μάρτυρας τῶν στρατηγουμένων καὶ δικαστὰς οἴκαδ᾽
ἐλθόντας τῶν εὐθυνῶν, ὥστε μὴ ἀκούειν μόνον
ὑμᾶς τὰ ὑμέτερ᾽ αὐτῶν, ἀλλὰ καὶ παρόντας ὁρᾶν.
20 νῦν δ᾽ εἰς τοῦθ᾽ ἥκει τὰ πράγματ᾽ αἰσχύνης,
ὥστε τῶν στρατηγῶν ἕκαστος δὶς καὶ τρὶς κρίνεται
παρ᾽ ὑμῖν περὶ θανάτου, πρὸς δὲ τοὺς ἐχθροὺς
οὐδεὶς οὐδ᾽ ἅπαξ αὐτῶν ἀγωνίσασθαι περὶ θανάτου τολμᾷ, ἀλλὰ τὸν τῶν ἀνδραποδιστῶν καὶ
25 λωποδυτῶν θάνατον μᾶλλον αἱροῦνται τοῦ προσή-
κοντος· κακούργου μὲν γάρ ἐστι κριθέντ᾽ ἀπο-
θανεῖν, στρατηγοῦ δὲ μαχόμενον τοῖς πολεμίοις.
48   Ἡμῶν δ᾽ οἱ μὲν περιόντες μετὰ Λακεδαιμονίων φασὶ Φίλιππον πράττειν τὴν Θηβαίων

κατάλυσιν καὶ τὰς πολιτείας διασπᾶν, οἱ δ᾽ ὡς
πρέσβεις πέπομφεν ὡς βασιλέα, οἱ δ᾽ ἐν Ἰλλυριοῖς
πόλεις τειχίζειν, οἱ δὲ — λόγους πλάττοντες ἕκαστος περιερχόμεθα. ἐγὼ δ᾽ οἶμαι μέν, ὦ ἄνδρες 49
Ἀθηναῖοι, νὴ τοὺς θεοὺς ἐκεῖνον μεθύειν τῷ 5
μεγέθει τῶν πεπραγμένων καὶ πολλὰ τοιαῦτ᾽ ὀνειρο-
πολεῖν ἐν τῇ γνώμῃ, τήν τ᾽ ἐρημίαν τῶν κωλυ-
σόντων ὁρῶντα καὶ τοῖς πεπραγμένοις ἐπηρμένον,
οὐ μέντοι γε μὰ Δί᾽ οὕτω προαιρεῖσθαι πράττειν,
ὥστε τοὺς ἀνοητοτάτους τῶν παρ᾽ ἡμῖν εἰδέναι, 10
τί μέλλει ποιεῖν ἐκεῖνος· ἀνοητότατοι γάρ εἰσιν
οἱ λογοποιοῦντες. ἀλλ᾽ ἂν ἀφέντες ταῦτ᾽ ἐκεῖν᾽ 50
εἰδῶμεν, ὅτι ἐχθρὸς ἄνθρωπος καὶ τὰ ἡμέτερ᾽
ἡμᾶς ἀποστερεῖ καὶ χρόνον πολὺν ὕβρικεν, καὶ
ἄπανθ᾽, ὅσα πώποτ᾽ ἠλπίσαμέν τινα πράξειν ὑπὲρ 15
ἡμῶν, καθ᾽ ἡμῶν εὕρηται, καὶ τὰ λοιπὰ ἐν αὐτοῖς
ἡμῖν ἐστι, κἂν μὴ νῦν ἐθέλωμεν ἐκεῖ πολεμεῖν
αὐτῷ, ἐνθάδ᾽ ἴσως ἀναγκασθησόμεθα τοῦτο ποιεῖν,
ἂν ταῦτ᾽ εἰδῶμεν, καὶ τὰ δέοντ᾽ ἐσόμεθ᾽ ἐγνωκότες καὶ λόγων ματαίων ἀπηλλαγμένοι· οὐ γὰρ 20
ἅττα ποτ᾽ ἔσται δεῖ σκοπεῖν, ἀλλ᾽ ὅτι φαῦλα, ἂν
μὴ προσέχητε τὸν νοῦν καὶ τὰ προσήκοντα ποιεῖν
ἐθέλητε, εὖ εἰδέναι.

Ἐγὼ μὲν οὖν οὔτ᾽ ἄλλοτε πώποτε πρὸς χάριν 51
εἱλόμην λέγειν, ὅ τι ἂν μὴ καὶ συνοίσειν πεπει- 25
σμένος ὦ, νῦν θ᾽, ἃ γιγνώσκω, πάνθ᾽ ἁπλῶς,
οὐδὲν ὑποστειλάμενος, πεπαρρησίασμαι. ἐβουλόμην
δ᾽ ἄν, ὥσπερ ὅτι ὑμῖν συμφέρει τὰ βέλτιστ᾽

ἀκούειν οἶδα, οὕτως εἰδέναι συνοῖσον καὶ τῷ τὰ
βέλτιστ᾽ εἰπόντι· πολλῷ γὰρ ἂν ἥδιον εἶπον. νῦν
δ᾽ ἐπ᾽ ἀδήλοις οὖσι τοῖς ἀπὸ τούτων ἐμαυτῷ
γενησομένοις, ὅμως ἐπὶ τῷ, συνοίσειν ὑμῖν, ἂν
5 πράξητε ταῦτα, πεπεῖσθαι λέγειν αἱροῦμαι. νικῴη
δ᾽ ὅ τι πᾶσιν ὑμῖν μέλλει συνοίσειν. Ende April 1907

ΠΕΡΙ ΤΗΣ ΕΙΡΗΝΗΣ.

Ὁρῶ μὲν, ὦ ἄνδρες Ἀθηναῖοι, τὰ παρόντα 1
πράγματα πολλὴν δυσκολίαν ἔχοντα καὶ
ταραχήν, οὐ μόνον τῷ πολλὰ προεῖσθαι καὶ μηδὲν
εἶναι προὖργου περὶ αὐτῶν εὖ λέγειν, ἀλλὰ καὶ 5
τῷ περὶ τῶν ὑπολοίπων κατὰ ταὐτὰ μηδὲ καθ᾿
ἓν τὸ συμφέρον πάντας ἡγεῖσθαι, ἀλλὰ τοῖς μὲν
ὡδί, τοῖς δ᾿ ἑτέρως δοκεῖν· δυσκόλου δ᾿ ὄντος 2
φύσει καὶ χαλεποῦ τοῦ βουλεύεσθαι ἔτι πολλῷ
χαλεπώτερον ὑμεῖς αὐτὸ πεποιήκατε, ὦ ἄνδρες 10
Ἀθηναῖοι· οἱ μὲν γὰρ ἄλλοι πάντες ἄνθρωποι
πρὸ τῶν πραγμάτων εἰώθασι χρῆσθαι τῷ βουλεύεσθαι, ὑμεῖς δὲ μετὰ τὰ πράγματα. ἐκ δὲ
τούτου συμβαίνει παρὰ πάντα τὸν χρόνον, ὃν οἶδ᾿
ἐγώ, τὸν μὲν οἷς ἂν ἁμάρτητ᾿ ἐπιτιμῶντ᾿ εὐδο- 15
κιμεῖν καὶ δοκεῖν εὖ λέγειν, τὰ δὲ πράγματα καὶ
περὶ ὧν βουλεύεσθ᾿ ἐκφεύγειν ὑμᾶς. οὐ μὴν ἀλλὰ 3
καίπερ τούτων οὕτως ἐχόντων οἴομαι καὶ πεπεικὼς
ἐμαυτὸν ἀνέστηκα, ἂν ἐθελήσητε τοῦ θορυβεῖν καὶ
φιλονικεῖν ἀποστάντες ἀκούειν, ὡς ὑπὲρ πόλεως 20
βουλευομένοις καὶ τηλικούτων πραγμάτων προσήκει,
ἕξειν καὶ λέγειν καὶ συμβουλεύειν, δι᾿ ὧν

4*

καὶ τὰ παρόντ᾽ ἔσται βελτίω καὶ τὰ προειμένα
σωθήσεται.

4   Ἀκριβῶς δ᾽ εἰδώς, ὦ ἄνδρες Ἀθηναῖοι, τὸ
λέγειν περὶ ὧν αὐτὸς εἶπέ τις καὶ περὶ αὐτοῦ παρ᾽
5 ὑμῖν ἀεὶ τῶν πάνυ λυσιτελούντων τοῖς τολμῶσιν
ὂν, οὕτως ἡγοῦμαι φορτικὸν καὶ ἐπαχθές, ὥστ᾽
ἀνάγκην οὖσαν ὁρῶν ὅμως ἀποκνῶ. νομίζω δ᾽
ἄμεινον ἂν ὑμᾶς περὶ ὧν νῦν ἐρῶ κρῖναι, μικρὰ
τῶν πρότερόν ποτε ῥηθέντων ὑπ᾽ ἐμοῦ
5 μνημονεύσαντας. ἐγὼ γάρ, ὦ ἄνδρες Ἀθηναῖοι,
11 πρῶτον μέν, ἡνίκ᾽ ἔπειθόν τινες ὑμᾶς τῶν ἐν
Εὐβοίᾳ πραγμάτων ταραττομένων βοηθεῖν
Πλουτάρχῳ καὶ πόλεμον ἄδοξον καὶ δαπανηρὸν
ἄρασθαι, πρῶτος καὶ μόνος παρελθὼν ἀντεῖπον
15 καὶ μόνον οὐ διεσπάσθην ὑπὸ τῶν ἐπὶ μικροῖς
λήμμασι πολλὰ καὶ μεγάλ᾽ ὑμᾶς ἁμαρτάνειν πει-
348 σάντων· καὶ χρόνου βραχέος διελθόντος, μετὰ
τοῦ προσοφλεῖν αἰσχύνην καὶ παθεῖν, οἷα τῶν
ὄντων ἀνθρώπων οὐδένες πώποτε πεπόνθασιν ὑπὸ
20 τούτων, οἷς ἐβοήθησαν, πάντες ὑμεῖς ἔγνωτε τήν
τε τῶν τότε ταῦτα πεισάντων κακίαν καὶ τὰ
6 βέλτιστ᾽ εἰρηκότ᾽ ἐμέ. πάλιν τοίνυν, ὦ ἄνδρες
Ἀθηναῖοι, κατιδὼν Νεοπτόλεμον τὸν ὑποκριτὴν
τῷ μὲν τῆς τέχνης προσχήματι τυγχάνοντ᾽ ἀδείας,
25 κακὰ δ᾽ ἐργαζόμενον τὰ μέγιστα τὴν πόλιν
καὶ τὰ παρ᾽ ὑμῶν διοικοῦντα Φιλίππῳ καὶ πρυ-
τανεύοντα, παρελθὼν εἶπον εἰς ὑμᾶς, οὐδεμιᾶς
ἰδίας οὔτ᾽ ἔχθρας οὔτε συκοφαντίας ἕνεκα, ὡς ἐκ

τῶν μετὰ ταῦτ᾽ ἔργων γέγονε δῆλον. καὶ οὐκέτ᾽ 7
ἐν τούτοις αἰτιάσομαι τοὺς ὑπὲρ Νεοπτολέμου
λέγοντας (οὐδὲ εἷς γὰρ ἦν), ἀλλ᾽ αὐτοὺς ὑμᾶς· εἰ
γὰρ ἐν Διονύσου τραγῳδοὺς ἐθεάσασθε, ἀλλὰ μὴ
περὶ σωτηρίας καὶ κοινῶν πραγμάτων ἦν ὁ λόγος, 5
οὐκ ἂν οὕτως οὔτ᾽ ἐκείνου πρὸς χάριν οὔτ᾽ ἐμοῦ
πρὸς ἀπέχθειαν ἠκούσατε. καίτοι τοῦτό γ᾽ ὑμᾶς 8
οἶμαι νῦν ἅπαντας ἠσθῆσθαι, ὅτι τὴν τότ᾽ ἄφιξιν
εἰς τοὺς πολεμίους ποιησάμενος ὑπὲρ τοῦ τἀκεῖ
χρήματ᾽ ὀφειλόμενα, ὡς ἔφη, κομίσας δεῦρο λει- 10
τουργεῖν, καὶ τούτῳ τῷ λόγῳ πλείστῳ χρησάμενος,
ὡς δεινὸν εἴ τις ἐγκαλεῖ τοῖς ἐκεῖθεν ἐνθάδε τὰς
εὐπορίας ἄγουσιν, ἐπειδὴ διὰ τὴν εἰρήνην ἀδείας
ἔτυχεν, ἣν ἐνθάδ᾽ ἐκέκτητ᾽ οὐσίαν φανεράν, ταύτην
ἐξαργυρίσας πρὸς ἐκεῖνον ἀπάγων οἴχεται. δύο 9
μὲν δὴ ταῦθ᾽ ὧν προεῖπον ἐγὼ μαρτυρεῖ τοῖς 16
γεγενημένοις λόγοις ὀρθῶς καὶ δικαίως, οἷά περ
ἦν, ἀποφανθένθ᾽ ὑπ᾽ ἐμοῦ· τρίτον δ᾽, ὦ ἄνδρες
Ἀθηναῖοι (καὶ μόνον ἓν τοῦτ᾽ εἰπὼν ἔτι καὶ δὴ
περὶ ὧν παρελήλυθ᾽ ἐρῶ), ἡνίκα τοὺς ὅρκους 20
τοὺς περὶ τῆς εἰρήνης ἀπειληφότες ἥκομεν
οἱ πρέσβεις, τότε Θεσπιάς τινων καὶ Πλαταιάς **10**
ὑπισχνουμένων οἰκισθήσεσθαι, καὶ τοὺς μὲν Φωκέας ₃₄₆
τὸν Φίλιππον, ἂν γένηται κύριος, σώσειν, τὴν δὲ
Θηβαίων πόλιν διοικιεῖν, καὶ τὸν Ὠρωπὸν ὑμῖν 25
ὑπάρξειν, καὶ τὴν Εὔβοιαν ἀντ᾽ Ἀμφιπόλεως
ἀποδοθήσεσθαι, καὶ τοιαύτας ἐλπίδας καὶ φενα-
κισμούς, οἷς ἐπαχθέντες ὑμεῖς οὔτε συμφόρως οὔτ᾽
ἴσως οὔτε καλῶς προεῖσθε Φωκέας, οὐδὲν τούτων

οὔτ᾽ ἐξαπατήσας οὔτε σιγήσας ἐγὼ φανήσομαι,
ἀλλὰ προειπὼν ὑμῖν, ὡς οἶδ᾽ ὅτι μνημονεύετε,
ὅτι ταῦτ᾽ οὔτ᾽ οἶδ᾽ οὔτε προσδοκῶ, νομίζω
δὲ τὸν λέγοντα ληρεῖν.

11   Ταῦτα τοίνυν ἅπανθ᾽, ὅσα φαίνομαι βέλτιον
6 τῶν ἄλλων προορῶν, οὐδ᾽ εἰς μίαν, ὦ ἄνδρες
Ἀθηναῖοι, οὔτε δεινότητα οὔτ᾽ ἀλαζονείαν ἐπανοίσω,
οὐδὲ προσποιήσομαι δι᾽ οὐδὲν ἄλλο γιγνώσκειν
καὶ προαισθάνεσθαι, πλὴν δι᾽ ἃ ἂν ὑμῖν εἴπω δύο·
10 ἓν μέν, ὦ ἄνδρες Ἀθηναῖοι, δι᾽ εὐτυχίαν, ἣν
συμπάσης ἐγὼ τῆς ἐν ἀνθρώποις οὔσης δεινότητος
12 καὶ σοφίας ὁρῶ κρατοῦσαν· ἕτερον δέ, προῖκα
τὰ πράγματα κρίνω καὶ λογίζομαι, καὶ οὐδὲν
λῆμμ᾽ ἂν οὐδεὶς ἔχοι πρὸς οἷς ἐγὼ πεπολίτευμαι
15 καὶ λέγω δεῖξαι προσηρτημένον. ὀρθὸν οὖν, ὅ τι
ἂν ποτ᾽ ἀπ᾽ αὐτῶν ὑπάρχῃ τῶν πραγμάτων, τὸ
συμφέρον φαίνεταί μοι. ὅταν δ᾽ ἐπὶ θάτερα
ὥσπερ εἰς τρυτάνην ἀργύριον προσενέγκῃς, οἴχεται
φέρον καὶ καθείλκυκε τὸν λογισμὸν ἐφ᾽ αὑτό, καὶ
20 οὐκ ἂν ἔτ᾽ ὀρθῶς οὐδ᾽ ὑγιῶς ὁ τοῦτο ποιήσας
περὶ οὐδενὸς λογίσαιτο.

13   Ἓν μὲν οὖν ἔγωγε πρῶτον ὑπάρχειν φημὶ
δεῖν· ὅπως εἴτε συμμάχους εἴτε σύνταξιν εἴτ᾽
ἄλλο βούλεταί τις κατασκευάζειν τῇ πόλει, τὴν
25 ὑπάρχουσαν εἰρήνην μὴ λύων τοῦτο ποιήσει,
οὐχ ὡς θαυμαστὴν οὐδ᾽ ὡς ἀξίαν οὖσαν ὑμῶν·
ἀλλ᾽ ὁποία τίς ποτ᾽ ἐστὶν αὕτη, μὴ γενέσθαι
μᾶλλον εἶχε τοῖς πράγμασι καιρὸν ἢ γεγενημένη

νῦν δι᾽ ἡμᾶς λυθῆναι· πολλὰ γὰρ προείμεθα,
ὧν ὑπαρχόντων τότ᾽ ἂν ἢ νῦν ἀσφαλέστερος καὶ
ῥᾴων ἦν ἡμῖν ὁ πόλεμος. δεύτερον δ᾽ ὁρᾶν ὅπως 14
μὴ προαξόμεθα, ὦ ἄνδρες Ἀθηναῖοι, τοὺς συν-
εληλυθότας τούτους καὶ φάσκοντας Ἀμφικτύονας 5
νῦν εἶναι εἰς ἀνάγκην καὶ πρόφασιν κοινοῦ
πολέμου πρὸς ἡμᾶς. ἐγὼ γάρ, εἰ γένοιθ᾽ ἡμῖν
πρὸς Φίλιππον πάλιν πόλεμος δι᾽ Ἀμφίπολιν ἤ τι
τοιοῦτον ἔγκλημ᾽ ἴδιον, οὗ μὴ μετέχουσι Θετταλοὶ
μηδ᾽ Ἀργεῖοι μηδὲ Θηβαῖοι, οὐκ ἂν ἡμῖν οἴομαι 15
τούτων οὐδένας πολεμῆσαι, καὶ πάντων ἥκιστα 11
(καί μοι μὴ θορυβήσῃ μηδεὶς πρὶν ἀκοῦσαι)
Θηβαίους, οὐχ ὡς ἡδέως ἔχουσιν ἡμῖν, οὐδ᾽ ὡς
οὐκ ἂν χαρίζοιντο Φιλίππῳ, ἀλλ᾽ ἴσασιν ἀκριβῶς,
εἰ καὶ πάνυ φησί τις αὐτοὺς ἀναισθήτους εἶναι, 15
ὅτι, εἰ γενήσεται πόλεμος πρὸς ὑμᾶς αὐτοῖς, τὰ
μὲν κακὰ πάνθ᾽ ἕξουσιν αὐτοί, τοῖς δ᾽ ἀγαθοῖς
ἐφεδρεύων ἕτερος καθεδεῖται. οὔκουν προοῖντ᾽ ἂν
αὐτοὺς εἰς τοῦτο, μὴ κοινῆς τῆς ἀρχῆς καὶ τῆς αἰτίας
οὔσης τοῦ πολέμου. οὐδέ γ᾽ εἰ πάλιν πρὸς τοὺς 16
Θηβαίους πολεμήσαιμεν δι᾽ Ὠρωπὸν ἤ τι τῶν ἰδίων, 21
οὐδὲν ἂν ἡμᾶς παθεῖν ἡγοῦμαι· καὶ γὰρ ἡμῖν
κἀκείνοις τοὺς βοηθοῦντας ἂν οἶμαι, εἰς τὴν οἰκείαν
εἴ τις ἐμβάλοι, βοηθεῖν, οὐ συνεπιστρατεύσειν οὐδε-
τέροις. καὶ γὰρ αἱ συμμαχίαι τοῦτον ἔχουσι τὸν 25
τρόπον, ὧν καὶ φροντίσειεν ἄν τις, καὶ τὸ πρᾶγμα
φύσει τοιοῦτόν ἐστιν· οὐκ ἄχρι τῆς ἴσης ἕκαστός 17
ἐστιν εὔνους οὔθ᾽ ἡμῖν οὔτε Θηβαίοις, σῶς τ᾽ εἶναι
καὶ κρατεῖν τῶν ἄλλων, ἀλλὰ σῶς μὲν εἶναι πάντες

ἂν βούλοινθ᾿ ἕνεχ᾿ αὑτῶν, κρατήσαντας δὲ τοὺς
ἑτέρους δεσπότας ὑπάρχειν αὐτῶν οὐδὲ εἷς. τί
οὖν ἡγοῦμαι φοβερὸν καὶ τί φυλάξασθαί φημι
δεῖν ἡμᾶς; ὅπως μὴ κοινὴν πρόφασιν καὶ κοινὸν
5 ἔγκλημ᾿ ὁ μέλλων πόλεμος πρὸς ἅπαντας λάβῃ.
18 εἰ γὰρ Ἀργεῖοι μὲν καὶ Μεσσήνιοι καὶ Μεγαλοπολῖται καί τινες τῶν λοιπῶν Πελοποννησίων, ὅσοι
ταὐτὰ τούτοις φρονοῦσιν, διὰ τὴν πρὸς Λακεδαιμονίους ἡμῖν ἐπικηρυκείαν ἐχθρῶς σχήσουσι καὶ
10 τὸ δοκεῖν ἐκδέχεσθαί τι τῶν ἐκείνοις πεπραγμένων,
Θηβαῖοι δ᾿ ἔχουσι μέν, ὡς λέγουσιν, ἀπεχθῶς, ἔτι
δ᾿ ἐχθροτέρως σχήσουσιν, ὅτι τοὺς παρ᾿ ἐκείνων
φεύγοντας σῴζομεν καὶ πάντα τρόπον τὴν δυσ-
19 μένειαν ἐνδεικνύμεθ᾿ αὐτοῖς, Θετταλοὶ δ᾿, ὅτι τοὺς
15 Φωκέων φυγάδας σῴζομεν, Φίλιππος δ᾿, ὅτι
κωλύομεν αὐτὸν κοινωνεῖν τῆς ἀμφικτυονίας·
φοβοῦμαι μὴ πάντες, περὶ τῶν ἰδίων ἕκαστος,
ὀργιζόμενοι κοινὸν ἐφ᾿ ἡμᾶς ἀγάγωσι τὸν πόλεμον,
τὰ τῶν Ἀμφικτυόνων δόγματα προστησάμενοι,
20 εἶτ᾿ ἐπισπασθῶσιν ἕκαστοι πέρα τοῦ συμφέροντος
ἑαυτοῖς ἡμῖν πολεμῆσαι, ὥσπερ καὶ περὶ Φωκέας.
20 ἴστε γὰρ δήπου τοῦθ᾿, ὅτι νῦν Θηβαῖοι καὶ
Φίλιππος καὶ Θετταλοί, οὐχὶ ταῦθ᾿ ἕκαστοι μάλιστ᾿
ἐσπουδακότες, ταὐτὰ πάντες ἔπραξαν· οἷον Θηβαῖοι
25 τὸν μὲν Φίλιππον παρελθεῖν καὶ λαβεῖν τὰς
παρόδους οὐκ ἐδύναντο κωλῦσαι, οὐδέ γε τῶν
αὑτοῖς πεπονημένων ὕστατον ἐλθόντα τὴν δόξαν
21 ἔχειν· νυνὶ γὰρ Θηβαίοις πρὸς μὲν τὸ τὴν χώραν
κεκομίσθαι πέπρακταί τι, πρὸς δὲ τιμὴν καὶ δόξαν

αἴσχιστα· εἰ γὰρ μὴ παρῆλθε Φίλιππος, οὐδὲν
ἂν αὐτοῖς ἐδόκει εἶναι. ταῦτα δ᾽ οὐκ ἐβούλοντο,
ἀλλὰ τῷ τὸν Ἐρχομενὸν καὶ τὴν Κορώνειαν λαβεῖν
ἐπιθυμεῖν μὴ δύνασθαι δέ, πάντα ταῦθ᾽ ὑπέμειναν.
Φίλιππον τοίνυν τινὲς μὲν δήπου τολμῶσι λέγειν, 22
ὡς οὐδ᾽ ἐβούλετο Θηβαίοις Ἐρχομενὸν καὶ Κορώ- 6
νειαν παραδοῦναι, ἀλλ᾽ ἠναγκάσθη· ἐγὼ δὲ τούτοις
μὲν ἐρρῶσθαι λέγω, ἐκεῖνο δ᾽ οἶδ᾽, ὅτι οὐ μᾶλλόν
γε ταῦτ᾽ ἔμελεν αὐτῷ, ἢ τὰς παρόδους λαβεῖν
ἐβούλετο καὶ τὴν δόξαν τοῦ πολέμου, τοῦ δοκεῖν 10
δι᾽ αὐτὸν κρίσιν εἰληφέναι, καὶ τὰ Πύθια θεῖναι
δι᾽ αὐτοῦ· καὶ ταῦτ᾽ ἦν, ὧν μάλιστ᾽ ἐγλίχετο.
Θετταλοὶ δέ γ᾽ οὐδέτερ᾽ ἐβούλοντο τούτων, οὔτε 23
Θηβαίους οὔτε τὸν Φίλιππον μέγαν γίγνεσθαι
(ταῦτα γὰρ πάντ᾽ ἐφ᾽ ἑαυτοὺς ἡγοῦντο), τῆς πυλαίας 15
δ᾽ ἐπεθύμουν καὶ τῶν ἐν Δελφοῖς, πλεονεκτημάτων
δυοῖν, κύριοι γενέσθαι· τῷ δὲ τούτων γλίχεσθαι
τάδε συγκατέπραξαν. τῶν τοίνυν ἰδίων ἕνεχ᾽
εὑρήσεθ᾽ ἕκαστον πολλὰ προηγμένον, ὧν οὐδὲν
ἐβούλετο, πρᾶξαι. τοῦτο μέντοι, ἔτι τοῦτ᾽ ἔστι 20
φυλακτέον ἡμῖν.

„Τὰ κελευόμεν᾽ ἡμᾶς ἄρα δεῖ ποιεῖν ταῦτα 24
φοβουμένους; καὶ σὺ ταῦτα κελεύεις;“ πολλοῦ γε
καὶ δέω. ἀλλ᾽ ὡς οὔτε πράξομεν οὐδὲν ἀνάξιον
ἡμῶν αὐτῶν οὔτ᾽ ἔσται πόλεμος, νοῦν δὲ δόξομεν 25
πᾶσιν ἔχειν καὶ τὰ δίκαια λέγειν, τοῦτ᾽ οἶμαι δεῖν
ποιεῖν. πρὸς δὲ τοὺς θρασέως οὐδ᾽ ὁτιοῦν οἰομένους
ὑπομεῖναι δεῖν καὶ μὴ προορωμένους τὸν πόλεμον

ἐκεῖνα βούλομαι λογίσασθαι. ἡμεῖς Θηβαίους
ἐῶμεν ἔχειν Ὠρωπόν· καὶ εἴ τις ἔροιθ᾽ ἡμᾶς
κελεύσας εἰπεῖν τἀληθῆ, διὰ τί; „ἵνα μὴ πολεμῶμεν“,
25 φαῖμεν ἄν. καὶ Φιλίππῳ νυνὶ κατὰ τὰς συνθήκας
5 Ἀμφιπόλεως παρακεχωρήκαμεν, καὶ Καρδιανοὺς
ἐῶμεν ἔξω Χερρονησιτῶν τῶν ἄλλων τετάχθαι,
καὶ τὸν Κᾶρα τὰς νήσους καταλαμβάνειν, Χίον
καὶ Κῶν καὶ Ῥόδον, καὶ Βυζαντίους κατάγειν τὰ
πλοῖα, δῆλον ὅτι τὴν ἀπὸ τῆς εἰρήνης ἡσυχίαν
10 πλειόνων ἀγαθῶν αἰτίαν εἶναι νομίζοντες ἢ τὸ
προσκρούειν καὶ φιλονικεῖν περὶ τούτων. οὐκοῦν
εὔηθες καὶ κομιδῇ σχέτλιον, πρὸς ἑκάστους
καθ᾽ ἕν᾽ οὕτω προσενηνεγμένους περὶ τῶν
οἰκείων καὶ ἀναγκαιοτάτων, πρὸς πάντας περὶ
15 τῆς ἐν Δελφοῖς σκιᾶς νυνὶ πολεμῆσαι;

ΚΑΤΑ ΦΙΛΙΠΠΟΥ Β.

Ὅταν, ὦ ἄνδρες Ἀθηναῖοι, λόγοι γίγνωνται 1
περὶ ὧν Φίλιππος πράττει καὶ βιάζεται παρὰ τὴν
εἰρήνην, ἀεὶ τοὺς ὑπὲρ ἡμῶν λόγους καὶ δικαίους
καὶ φιλανθρώπους ὁρῶ φαινομένους, καὶ λέγειν 5
μὲν ἅπαντας ἀεὶ τὰ δέοντα δοκοῦντας τοὺς κατη-
γοροῦντας Φιλίππου, γιγνόμενον δ᾽ οὐδὲν ὡς ἔπος
εἰπεῖν τῶν δεόντων, οὐδ᾽ ὧν ἕνεκα ταῦτ᾽ ἀκούειν
ἄξιον· ἀλλ᾽ εἰς τοῦτ᾽ ἤδη προηγμένα τυγχάνει 2
πάντα τὰ πράγματα τῇ πόλει, ὥσθ᾽ ὅσῳ τις ἂν 10
μᾶλλον καὶ φανερώτερον ἐξελέγχῃ Φίλιππον καὶ
τὴν πρὸς ὑμᾶς εἰρήνην παραβαίνοντα καὶ πᾶσι
τοῖς Ἕλλησιν ἐπιβουλεύοντα, τοσούτῳ τὸ τί χρὴ
ποιεῖν συμβουλεῦσαι χαλεπώτερον. αἴτιον δὲ τούτων, 3
ὅτι πάντας, ὦ ἄνδρες Ἀθηναῖοι, τοὺς πλεονεκτεῖν 15
ζητοῦντας ἔργῳ κωλύειν καὶ πράξεσιν, οὐχὶ λόγοις
δέον, πρῶτον μὲν ἡμεῖς οἱ παριόντες τούτων μὲν
ἀφέσταμεν καὶ γράφειν καὶ συμβουλεύειν, τὴν πρὸς
ὑμᾶς ἀπέχθειαν ὀκνοῦντες, οἷα ποιεῖ δ᾽, ὡς δεινά,
καὶ τοιαῦτα διεξερχόμεθα· ἔπειθ᾽ ὑμεῖς οἱ καθή- 20
μενοι, ὡς μὲν ἂν εἴποιτε δικαίους λόγους καὶ
λέγοντος ἄλλου συνείητε, ἄμεινον Φιλίππου παρε-

σκεύασθε, ὡς δὲ κωλύσαιτ᾽ ἂν ἐκεῖνον πράττειν
ταῦτ᾽, ἐφ᾽ ὧν ἐστι νῦν, παντελῶς ἀργῶς ἔχετε.
4 συμβαίνει δὴ πρᾶγμ᾽ ἀναγκαῖον, οἶμαι, καὶ ἴσως
εἰκός· ἐν οἷς ἑκάτεροι διατρίβετε καὶ περὶ ἃ σπου-
5 δάζετε, ταῦτ᾽ ἄμεινον ἑκατέροις ἔχει, ἐκείνῳ
μὲν αἱ πράξεις, ὑμῖν δ᾽ οἱ λόγοι. εἰ μὲν οὖν
καὶ νῦν λέγειν δικαιότερ᾽ ὑμῖν ἐξαρκεῖ, ῥᾴδιον καὶ
5 πόνος οὐδεὶς πρόσεστι τῷ πράγματι· εἰ δ᾽ ὅπως τὰ
παρόντ᾽ ἐπανορθωθήσεται δεῖ σκοπεῖν καὶ μὴ
10 προελθόντ᾽ ἔτι πορρωτέρω λήσει πάνθ᾽ ἡμᾶς μηδ᾽
ἐπιστήσεται μέγεθος δυνάμεως, πρὸς ἣν οὐδ᾽ ἀντᾶραι
δυνησόμεθα, οὐχ ὁ αὐτὸς τρόπος ὅσπερ πρότερον
τοῦ βουλεύεσθαι, ἀλλὰ καὶ τοῖς λέγουσιν ἅπασιν
καὶ τοῖς ἀκούουσιν ὑμῖν τὰ βέλτιστα καὶ τὰ σώ-
15 σοντα τῶν ῥᾴστων καὶ τῶν ἡδίστων προαιρετέον.
6   Πρῶτον μέν, εἴ τις, ὦ ἄνδρες Ἀθηναῖοι,
θαρρεῖ, ὁρῶν ἡλίκος ἤδη καὶ ὅσων κύριός ἐστι
Φίλιππος, καὶ μηδέν᾽ οἴεται κίνδυνον φέρειν τοῦτο
τῇ πόλει, μηδ᾽ ἐφ᾽ ὑμᾶς πάντα παρασκευάζεσθαι,
20 θαυμάζω, καὶ δεηθῆναι πάντων ὁμοίως ὑμῶν
βούλομαι τοὺς λογισμοὺς ἀκοῦσαί μου διὰ βραχέων,
δι᾽ οὓς τἀναντί᾽ ἐμοὶ παρέστηκε προσδοκᾶν καὶ δι᾽
ὧν ἐχθρὸν ἡγοῦμαι Φίλιππον, ἵν᾽, ἐὰν μὲν
ἐγὼ δοκῶ βέλτιον προορᾶν, ἐμοὶ πεισθῆτε· ἂν δ᾽
25 οἱ θαρροῦντες καὶ πεπιστευκότες αὐτῷ, τούτοις
7 προσθήσεσθε. ἐγὼ τοίνυν, ὦ ἄνδρες Ἀθηναῖοι,
λογίζομαι, τίνων ὁ Φίλιππος κύριος πρῶτον μετὰ
τὴν εἰρήνην κατέστη; Πυλῶν καὶ τῶν ἐν Φωκεῦσι
πραγμάτων. τί οὖν; πῶς τούτοις ἐχρήσατο; ἃ

Θηβαίοις συμφέρει καὶ οὐχ ἃ τῇ πόλει, πράττειν προείλετο. τί δήποτε; ὅτι πρὸς πλεονεξίαν,
οἶμαι, καὶ τὸ πάνϑ᾽ ὑφ᾽ αὑτῷ ποιήσασϑαι τοὺς
λογισμοὺς ἐξετάζων, καὶ οὐχὶ πρὸς εἰρήνην οὐδ᾽
ἡσυχίαν οὐδὲ δίκαιον οὐδέν, εἶδε τοῦτ᾽ ὀρϑῶς, ὅτι 8
τῇ μὲν ἡμετέρᾳ πόλει καὶ τοῖς ἤϑεσι τοῖς ἡμετέροις 6
οὐδὲν ἂν ἐνδείξαιτο τοσοῦτον οὐδὲ ποιήσειεν, ὑφ᾽
οὗ πεισϑέντες ὑμεῖς τῆς ἰδίας ἕνεκ᾽ ὠφελείας τῶν
ἄλλων τινὰς Ἑλλήνων ἐκείνῳ προοῖσϑε, ἀλλὰ καὶ
τοῦ δικαίου λόγον ποιούμενοι καὶ τὴν προσοῦσαν 10
ἀδοξίαν τῷ πράγματι φεύγοντες καὶ πάνϑ᾽ ἃ προσήκει προορώμενοι ὁμοίως ἐναντιώσεσϑε, ἄν τι τοιοῦτον ἐπιχειρῇ πράττειν, ὥσπερ ἂν εἰ πολεμοῦντες
τύχοιτε· τοὺς δὲ Θηβαίους ἡγεῖτο, ὅπερ συνέβη, 9
ἀντὶ τῶν ἑαυτοῖς γιγνομένων τὰ λοιπὰ ἐάσειν 15
ὅπως βούλεται πράττειν ἑαυτόν, καὶ οὐχ ὅπως
ἀντιπράξειν καὶ διακωλύσειν, ἀλλὰ καὶ συστρατεύ-
σειν, ἂν αὐτοὺς κελεύῃ. καὶ νῦν τοὺς Μεσσηνίους
καὶ τοὺς Ἀργείους ταῦϑ᾽ ὑπειληφὼς εὖ ποιεῖ. ὃ
καὶ μέγιστόν ἐστι καϑ᾽ ὑμῶν ἐγκώμιον, ὦ ἄνδρες 20
Ἀθηναῖοι· κέκρισϑε γὰρ ἐκ τούτων τῶν ἔργων 10
μόνοι τῶν πάντων μηδενὸς ἂν. κέρδους τὰ κοινὰ
δίκαια τῶν Ἑλλήνων προέσϑαι, μηδ᾽ ἀνταλλάξασϑαι
μηδεμιᾶς χάριτος μηδ᾽ ὠφελείας τὴν εἰς τοὺς Ἕλληνας εὔνοιαν. καὶ ταῦτ᾽ εἰκότως καὶ περὶ ὑμῶν 25
οὕτως ὑπείληφεν, καὶ κατ᾽ Ἀργείων καὶ Θηβαίων
ὡς ἑτέρως, οὐ μόνον εἰς τὰ παρόνϑ᾽ ὁρῶν, ἀλλὰ
καὶ τὰ πρὸ τούτων λογιζόμενος. εὑρίσκει γάρ, 11
οἶμαι, καὶ ἀκούει τοὺς μὲν ὑμετέρους προγόνους,

ἐξὸν αὐτοῖς τῶν λοιπῶν ἄρχειν Ἑλλήνων ὥστ᾽
αὐτοὺς ὑπακούειν βασιλεῖ, οὐ μόνον οὐκ ἀνασχο-
μένους τὸν λόγον τοῦτον, ἡνίκ᾽ ἦλθεν Ἀλέξανδρος
ὁ τούτων πρόγονος περὶ τούτων κῆρυξ, ἀλλὰ καὶ
5 τὴν χώραν ἐκλιπεῖν προελομένους καὶ παθεῖν ὁτιοῦν
ὑπομείναντας, καὶ μετὰ ταῦτα πράξαντας ταῦθ᾽, ἃ
πάντες ἀεὶ γλίχονται λέγειν, ἀξίως δ᾽ οὐδεὶς εἰπεῖν
δεδύνηται, διόπερ κἀγὼ παραλείψω, δικαίως (ἔστι
γὰρ μείζω τἀκείνων ἔργα ἢ ὡς τῷ λόγῳ τις ἂν
10 εἴποι)· τοὺς δὲ Θηβαίων καὶ Ἀργείων προγόνους
τοὺς μὲν συστρατεύσαντας τῷ βαρβάρῳ, τοὺς δ᾽
12 οὐκ ἐναντιωθέντας. οἶδεν οὖν ἀμφοτέρους ἰδίᾳ
τὸ λυσιτελοῦν ἀγαπήσοντας, οὐχ ὅ τι συνοίσει κοινῇ
τοῖς Ἕλλησι σκεψομένους. ἡγεῖτ᾽ οὖν, εἰ μὲν ὑμᾶς
15 ἕλοιτο, φίλους ἐπὶ τοῖς δικαίοις αἱρήσεσθαι, εἰ δ᾽
ἐκείνοις προσθοῖτο, συνεργοὺς ἕξειν τῆς ἑαυτοῦ πλεονεξίας. διὰ ταῦτ᾽ ἐκείνους ἀνθ᾽ ὑμῶν καὶ τότε καὶ
νῦν αἱρεῖται· οὐ γὰρ δὴ τριήρεις γ᾽ ὁρᾷ πλείους
αὐτοῖς ἢ ὑμῖν οὔσας· οὐδ᾽ ἐν μὲν τῇ μεσογείᾳ
20 τιν᾽ ἀρχὴν εὕρηκεν, τῆς δ᾽ ἐπὶ τῇ θαλάττῃ καὶ
τῶν ἐμπορίων ἀφέστηκεν· οὐδ᾽ ἀμνημονεῖ τοὺς λόγους οὐδὲ τὰς ὑποσχέσεις, ἐφ᾽ αἷς τῆς εἰρήνης ἔτυχεν.
13   Ἀλλὰ νὴ Δία, εἴποι τις ἂν ὡς πάντα ταῦτ᾽
εἰδώς, οὐ πλεονεξίας ἕνεκα οὐδ᾽ ὧν ἐγὼ κατηγορῶ
25 τότε ταῦτ᾽ ἔπραξεν, ἀλλὰ τῷ δικαιότερα τοὺς
Θηβαίους ἢ ὑμᾶς ἀξιοῦν. ἀλλὰ τοῦτον καὶ
μόνον πάντων τῶν λόγων οὐκ ἔνεστιν αὐτῷ νῦν
εἰπεῖν· ὁ γὰρ Μεσσήνην Λακεδαιμονίους ἀφιέναι
κελεύων πῶς ἂν Ἐρχομενὸν καὶ Κορώνειαν τότε

Θηβαίοις παραδοὺς τῷ δίκαια νομίζειν ταῦτ᾽ εἶναι
πεποιηκέναι σκήψαιτο;

Ἀλλ᾽ ἐβιάσθη νὴ Δία (τοῦτο γάρ ἐσθ᾽ ὑπό- 14
λοιπον) καὶ παρὰ γνώμην, τῶν Θετταλῶν ἱππέων
καὶ τῶν Θηβαίων ὁπλιτῶν ἐν μέσῳ ληφθείς, συν- 5
εχώρησε ταῦτα. καλῶς. οὐκοῦν φασὶ μὲν μέλλειν
πρὸς τοὺς Θηβαίους αὐτὸν ὑπόπτως ἔχειν, καὶ
λογοποιοῦσι περιόντες τινὲς ὡς Ἐλάτειαν τειχιεῖ·
ὁ δὲ ταῦτα μὲν μέλλει καὶ μελλήσει, ὡς ἐγὼ κρίνω, 15
τοῖς Μεσσηνίοις δὲ καὶ τοῖς Ἀργείοις ἐπὶ τοὺς 10
Λακεδαιμονίους συλλαμβάνειν οὐ μέλλει, ἀλλὰ καὶ
ξένους εἰσπέμπει καὶ χρήματ᾽ ἀποστέλλει καὶ δύναμιν
μεγάλην ἔχων αὐτός ἐστι προσδόκιμος. τοὺς μὲν
οὖν ὄντας ἐχθροὺς Θηβαίων Λακεδαιμονίους ἀναιρεῖ,
οὓς δ᾽ ἀπώλεσεν αὐτὸς πρότερον Φωκέας νῦν σῴζει; 15
καὶ τίς ἂν ταῦτα πιστεύσειεν; ἐγὼ μὲν γὰρ οὐκ 16
ἂν ἡγοῦμαι Φίλιππον, οὔτ᾽ εἰ τὰ πρῶτα βιασθεὶς
ἄκων ἔπραξεν, οὔτ᾽ ἂν εἰ νῦν ἀπεγίγνωσκε Θηβαίους,
τοῖς ἐκείνων ἐχθροῖς συνεχῶς ἐναντιοῦσθαι· ἀλλ᾽
ἀφ᾽ ὧν νῦν ποιεῖ, κἀκεῖν᾽ ἐκ προαιρέσεως δῆλός 20
ἐστι ποιήσας, ἐκ πάντων δ᾽, ἄν τις ὀρθῶς θεωρῇ,
πάνθ᾽ ἃ πραγματεύεται κατὰ τῆς πόλεως συντάττων.
καὶ τοῦτ᾽ ἐξ ἀνάγκης τρόπον τιν᾽ αὐτῷ νῦν γε δὴ 17
συμβαίνει. λογίζεσθε γάρ· ἄρχειν βούλεται, τούτου δ᾽ ἀνταγωνιστὰς μόνους ὑπείληφεν ὑμᾶς. ἀδικεῖ 25
πολὺν ἤδη χρόνον, καὶ τοῦτ᾽ αὐτὸς ἄριστα σύνοιδεν
αὐτῷ· οἷς γὰρ οὖσιν ὑμετέροις ἔχει, τούτοις πάντα
τἆλλ᾽ ἀσφαλῶς κέκτηται· εἰ γὰρ Ἀμφίπολιν καὶ 18
Ποτείδαιαν προεῖτο, οὐδ᾽ ἂν οἴκοι μένειν βεβαίως

ἡγεῖτο. ἀμφότερ᾽, οὖν οἶδε, καὶ αὐτὸν ὑμῖν ἐπιβουλεύοντα καὶ ὑμᾶς αἰσθανομένους. εὖ φρονεῖν
δ᾽ ὑμᾶς ὑπολαμβάνων δικαίως αὐτὸν μισεῖν νομίζει,
καὶ παρώξυνται πείσεσθαί τι προσδοκῶν, ἂν καιρὸν
5 λάβητε, ἂν μὴ φθάσῃ ποιήσας πρότερος. διὰ ταῦτ᾽
ἐγρήγορεν, ἐφέστηκεν ἐπὶ τῇ πόλει, θεραπεύει τίνας;
Θηβαίους καὶ Πελοποννησίων τοὺς ταῦτα βουλο-
19 μένους τούτοις· οὓς διὰ μὲν πλεονεξίαν τὰ παρόντ᾽
ἀγαπήσειν οἴεται, διὰ δὲ σκαιότητα τρόπων τῶν
10 μετὰ ταῦτ᾽ οὐδὲν προόψεσθαι. καίτοι σωφρονοῦσί
γε καὶ μετρίως ἐναργῆ παραδείγματ᾽ ἔστιν ἰδεῖν,
ἃ καὶ πρὸς Μεσσηνίους καὶ πρὸς Ἀργείους ἔμοιγ᾽
344 εἰπεῖν συνέβη, βέλτιον δ᾽ ἴσως καὶ πρὸς ὑμᾶς
ἐστιν εἰρῆσθαι.

20   „Πῶς γὰρ οἴεσθε", ἔφην „ὦ ἄνδρες Μεσσήνιοι,
16 δυσχερῶς ἀκούειν Ὀλυνθίους, εἴ τίς τι λέγοι
κατὰ Φιλίππου κατ᾽ ἐκείνους τοὺς χρόνους, ὅτ᾽
Ἀνθεμοῦντα μὲν αὐτοῖς ἀφίει, ἧς πάντες οἱ πρότερον Μακεδονίας βασιλεῖς ἀντεποιοῦντο, Ποτεί-
20 δαιαν δ᾽ ἐδίδου τοὺς Ἀθηναίων ἀποίκους ἐκβαλών, καὶ τὴν μὲν ἔχθραν τὴν πρὸς ἡμᾶς αὐτὸς
ἀνῄρητο, τὴν χώραν δ᾽ ἐκείνοις ἐδεδώκει καρποῦσθαι; ἆρα ποσδοκᾶν αὐτοὺς τοιαῦτα πείσεσθαι ἢ
21 λέγοντος ἄν τινος πιστεῦσαι οἴεσθε; ἀλλ᾽ ὅμως"
25 ἔφην ἐγὼ „μικρὸν χρόνον τὴν ἀλλοτρίαν καρπω-
σάμενοι, πολὺν τῆς αὐτῶν ὑπ᾽ ἐκείνου στέρονται,
αἰσχρῶς ἐκπεσόντες, οὐ κρατηθέντες μόνον, ἀλλὰ
καὶ προδοθέντες ὑπ᾽ ἀλλήλων καὶ πραθέντες· οὐ
γὰρ ἀσφαλεῖς ταῖς πολιτείαις αἱ πρὸς τοὺς τυράν-

νους αὗται λίαν ὁμιλίαι. τί δ᾽ οἱ Θετταλοί; ἆρ᾽ 22
οἴεσθε", ἔφην „ὅτ᾽ αὐτοῖς τοὺς τυράννους ἐξέβαλλε
καὶ πάλιν Νίκαιαν καὶ Μαγνησίαν ἐδίδου, προσδοκᾶν τὴν καθεστῶσαν νῦν δεκαδαρχίαν ἔσεσθαι
παρ᾽ αὐτοῖς; ἢ τὸν τὴν πυλαίαν ἀποδόντα, τοῦτον 5
τὰς ἰδίας αὐτῶν προσόδους παραιρήσεσθαι; οὐκ ἔστι
ταῦτα. ἀλλὰ μὴν γέγονε ταῦτα καὶ πᾶσιν ἔστιν
εἰδέναι. ὑμεῖς δὲ" ἔφην ἐγὼ „διδόντα μὲν καὶ 23
ὑπισχνούμενον θεωρεῖτε Φίλιππον, ἐξηπατηκότα δ᾽
ἤδη καὶ παρακεκρουμένον ἀπεύχεσθε, εἰ σωφρονεῖτε 10
δή, ἰδεῖν. ἔστι τοίνυν νὴ Δία" ἔφην ἐγὼ „παντο-
δαπὰ εὑρημένα ταῖς πόλεσι πρὸς φυλακὴν καὶ
σωτηρίαν, οἷον χαρακώματα καὶ τείχη καὶ τάφροι
καὶ τἄλλ᾽ ὅσα τοιαῦτα. καὶ ταῦτα μέν ἐστιν ἅπαντα 24
χειροποίητα καὶ δαπάνης προσδεῖται· ἓν δέ τι κοινὸν 15
ἡ φύσις τῶν εὖ φρονούντων ἐν αὐτῇ κέκτηται
φυλακτήριον, ὃ πᾶσι μέν ἐστ᾽ ἀγαθὸν καὶ σωτήριον,
μάλιστα δὲ τοῖς πλήθεσι πρὸς τοὺς τυράννους.
τί οὖν ἐστι τοῦτο; ἀπιστία. ταύτην φυλάττετε,
ταύτης ἀντέχεσθε. ἂν ταύτην σῴζητε, οὐδὲν μὴ 20
δεινὸν πάθητε. τί ζητεῖτε;" ἔφην. „ἐλευθερίαν. 25
εἶτ᾽ οὐχ ὁρᾶτε Φίλιππον ἀλλοτριωτάτας ταύτῃ καὶ
τὰς προσηγορίας ἔχοντα; βασιλεὺς γὰρ καὶ τύραννος
ἅπας ἐχθρὸς ἐλευθερίᾳ καὶ νόμοις ἐναντίος. οὐ
φυλάξεσθ᾽ ὅπως" ἔφην „μὴ πολέμου ζητοῦντες 25
ἀπαλλαγῆναι δεσπότην εὕρητε;"

Ταῦτ᾽ ἀκούσαντες ἐκεῖνοι καὶ θορυβοῦντες, 26
ὡς ὀρθῶς λέγεται, καὶ πολλοὺς ἑτέρους λόγους παρὰ
τῶν πρέσβεων καὶ παρόντος ἐμοῦ καὶ πάλιν ὕστερον,

ὡς ἔοικεν, οὐδὲν μᾶλλον ἀποσχήσονται τῆς Φιλίππου
φιλίας οὐδ᾽ ὧν ἐπαγγέλλεται. καὶ οὐ τοῦτ᾽ ἔστιν
ἄτοπον, εἰ Μεσσήνιοι καὶ Πελοποννησίων τινὲς
παρ᾽ ἃ τῷ λογισμῷ βέλτισθ᾽ ὁρῶσί τι πράξουσιν·
27 ἀλλ᾽ ὑμεῖς οἱ καὶ συνιέντες αὐτοὶ καὶ τῶν λεγόντων
6 ἀκούοντες ἡμῶν, ὡς ἐπιβουλεύεσθε, ὡς περιστοιχί-
ζεσθε, ἐκ τοῦ μηδὲν ἤδη ποιῆσαι λήσεθ᾽, ὡς ἐμοὶ
δοκεῖ, πάνθ᾽ ὑπομείναντες. οὕτως ἡ παραυτίχ᾽
ἡδονὴ καὶ ῥᾳστώνη μεῖζον ἰσχύει τοῦ ποθ᾽ ὕστερον
10 συνοίσειν μέλλοντος.

28   Περὶ μὲν δὴ τῶν ὑμῖν πρακτέων καθ᾽ ὑμᾶς
αὐτοὺς ὕστερον βουλεύσεσθε, ἂν σωφρονῆτε· ἃ δὲ
νῦν ἀποκρινάμενοι τὰ δέοντ᾽ ἂν εἴητ᾽ ἐψηφισμένοι, ταῦτα δὴ λέξω.

15   ΑΠΟΚΡΙΣΙΣ.

Ἦν μὲν οὖν δίκαιον, ὦ ἄνδρες Ἀθηναῖοι,
τοὺς ἐνεγκόντας τὰς ὑποσχέσεις, ἐφ᾽ αἷς ἐπεί-
29 σθητε ποιήσασθαι τὴν εἰρήνην, καλεῖν· οὔτε γὰρ
αὐτὸς ἂν ποθ᾽ ὑπέμεινα πρεσβεύειν, οὔτ᾽ ἂν ὑμεῖς
20 οἶδ᾽ ὅτι ἐπαύσασθε πολεμοῦντες, εἰ τοιαῦτα πράξειν τυχόντ᾽ εἰρήνης Φίλιππον ᾤεσθε· ἀλλ᾽ ἦν
πολὺ τούτων ἀφεστηκότα τὰ τότε λεγόμενα. καὶ
πάλιν γ᾽ ἑτέρους καλεῖν· τίνας; τούς, ὅτ᾽ ἐγὼ γεγονυίας ἤδη τῆς εἰρήνης ἀπὸ τῆς ὑστέρας ἥκων
25 πρεσβείας τῆς ἐπὶ τοὺς ὅρκους, αἰσθόμενος φενακι-
ζομένην τὴν πόλιν, προὔλεγον καὶ διεμαρτυρόμην
30 καὶ οὐκ εἴων προέσθαι Πύλας οὐδὲ Φωκέας, λέγοντας

ὡς ἐγὼ μὲν ὕδωρ πίνων εἰκότως δύστροπος καὶ
δύσκολός εἰμί τις ἄνθρωπος, Φίλιππος δ᾽, ἅπερ
εὔξαισθ᾽ ἂν ὑμεῖς, ἐὰν παρέλθῃ, πράξει, καὶ Θεσπιὰς
μὲν καὶ Πλαταιὰς τειχιεῖ, Θηβαίους δὲ παύσει τῆς
ὕβρεως, Χερρόνησον δὲ τοῖς αὑτοῦ τέλεσι διορύξει, 5
Εὔβοιαν δὲ καὶ τὸν Ὠρωπὸν ἀντ᾽ Ἀμφιπόλεως
ὑμῖν ἀποδώσει· ταῦτα γὰρ ἅπαντ᾽ ἐπὶ τοῦ βήματος
ἐνταῦθα μνημονεύετ᾽ οἶδ᾽ ὅτι ῥηθέντα, καίπερ
ὄντες οὐ δεινοὶ τοὺς ἀδικοῦντας μεμνῆσθαι. καὶ 31
τὸ πάντων αἴσχιστον, καὶ τοῖς ἐκγόνοις πρὸς τὰς 10
ἐλπίδας τὴν αὐτὴν εἰρήνην εἶναι ταύτην ἐψηφίσασθε·
οὕτω τελέως ὑπήχθητε.

Τί δὴ ταῦτα νῦν λέγω καὶ καλεῖν φημι
δεῖν τούτους; ἐγὼ νὴ τοὺς θεοὺς τἀληθῆ μετὰ
παρρησίας ἐρῶ πρὸς ὑμᾶς καὶ οὐκ ἀποκρύψομαι. 15
οὐχ ἵν᾽ εἰς λοιδορίαν ἐμπεσὼν ἐμαυτῷ μὲν ἐξ ἴσου 32
λόγον παρ᾽ ὑμῖν ποιήσω, τοῖς δ᾽ ἐμοὶ προσκροῦ-
σασιν ἐξ ἀρχῆς καὶ νῦν παράσχω πρόφασιν τοῦ
πάλιν τι λαβεῖν παρὰ Φιλίππου, οὐδ᾽ ἵν᾽ ὡς
ἄλλως ἀδολεσχῶ· ἀλλ᾽ οἶμαί ποθ᾽ ὑμᾶς λυπήσειν 20
ἃ Φίλιππος πράττει μᾶλλον ἢ τὰ νυνί· τὸ γὰρ
πρᾶγμ᾽ ὁρῶ προβαῖνον, καὶ οὐχὶ βουλοίμην μὲν 33
ἂν εἰκάζειν ὀρθῶς, φοβοῦμαι δὲ μὴ λίαν ἐγγὺς
ᾖ τοῦτ᾽ ἤδη. ὅταν οὖν μηκέθ᾽ ὑμῖν ἀμελεῖν
ἐξουσία γίγνηται τῶν συμβαινόντων, μηδ᾽ ἀκούηθ᾽ 25
ὅτι ταῦτ᾽ ἐφ᾽ ὑμᾶς ἐστιν ἐμοῦ μηδὲ τοῦ δεῖνος,
ἀλλ᾽ αὐτοὶ πάντες ὁρᾶτε καὶ εὖ εἰδῆτε, ὀργίλους
καὶ τραχεῖς ὑμᾶς ἔσεσθαι νομίζω. φοβοῦμαι δὴ 34
μὴ τῶν πρέσβεων σεσιωπηκότων, ἐφ᾽ οἷς αὑτοῖς

5*

συνίσασι δεδωροδοκηκότες, τοῖς ἐπανορθοῦν τι
πειρωμένοις τῶν διὰ τούτους ἀπολωλότων τῇ παρ᾿
ὑμῶν ὀργῇ περιπεσεῖν συμβῇ· ὁρῶ γὰρ ὡς τὰ
πόλλ᾿ ἐνίους οὐκ εἰς τοὺς αἰτίους, ἀλλ᾿ εἰς τοὺς
5 ὑπὸ χεῖρα μάλιστα τὴν ὀργὴν ἀφιέντας.

35   Ἕως οὖν ἔτι μέλλει καὶ συνίσταται τὰ πράγματα καὶ κατακούομεν ἀλλήλων, ἕκαστον ὑμῶν,
καίπερ ἀκριβῶς εἰδότα, ὅμως ἐπαναμνῆσαι βούλομαι, τίς ὁ Φωκέας πείσας καὶ Πύλας ὑμᾶς προ-
10 έσθαι, ὧν καταστὰς ἐκεῖνος κύριος τῆς ἐπὶ τὴν
Ἀττικὴν ὁδοῦ καὶ τῆς εἰς Πελοπόννησον κύριος
γέγονεν, καὶ πεποίηχ᾿ ὑμῖν μὴ περὶ τῶν δικαίων
μηδ᾿ ὑπὲρ τῶν ἔξω πραγμάτων εἶναι τὴν βουλήν,
ἀλλ᾿ ὑπὲρ τῶν ἐν τῇ χώρᾳ καὶ τοῦ πρὸς τὴν
15 Ἀττικὴν πολέμου, ὃς λυπήσει μὲν ἕκαστον, ἐπειδὰν
36 παρῇ, γέγονε δ᾿ ἐν ἐκείνῃ τῇ ἡμέρᾳ. εἰ γὰρ μὴ
παρεκρούσθητε τόθ᾿ ὑμεῖς, οὐδὲν ἂν ἦν τῇ πόλει
πρᾶγμα· οὔτε γὰρ ναυσὶ δήπου κρατήσας εἰς τὴν
Ἀττικὴν ἦλθεν ἂν ποτε στόλῳ Φίλιππος, οὔτε
20 πεζῇ βαδίζων ὑπὲρ τὰς Πύλας καὶ Φωκέας, ἀλλ᾿
ἢ τὰ δίκαι᾿ ἂν ἐποίει καὶ τὴν εἰρήνην ἄγων
ἡσυχίαν εἶχεν, ἢ παραχρῆμ᾿ ἂν ἦν ἐν ὁμοίῳ
37 πολέμῳ, δι᾿ ὃν τότε τῆς εἰρήνης ἐπεθύμησεν. ταῦτ᾿
οὖν ὡς μὲν ὑπομνῆσαι νῦν ἱκανῶς εἴρηται, ὡς δ᾿
25 ἂν ἐξετασθείη μάλιστ᾿ ἀκριβῶς, μὴ γένοιτο,
ὦ πάντες θεοί· οὐδένα γὰρ βουλοίμην ἔγωγ᾿ ἄν,
οὐδ᾿ εἰ δίκαιός ἐστ᾿ ἀπολωλέναι, μετὰ τοῦ πάντων κινδύνου καὶ τῆς ζημίας δίκην ὑποσχεῖν.

(ΗΓΗΣΙΠΠΟΥ) ΠΕΡΙ ΑΛΟΝΝΗΣΟΥ.

Ὦ ἄνδρες Ἀθηναῖοι, οὐκ ἔστιν ὅπως αἱ αἰτίαι, 1
ἃς Φίλιππος αἰτιᾶται τοὺς ὑπὲρ τῶν δικαίων πρὸς
ὑμᾶς λέγοντας, κωλύσουσι συμβούλους ἡμᾶς γίγνεσθαι ὑπὲρ τῶν ὑμῖν συμφερόντων· δεινὸν γὰρ ἂν 5
εἴη, εἰ τὴν ἐπὶ τοῦ βήματος παρρησίαν αἱ παρ᾽
ἐκείνου πεμπόμεναι ἐπιστολαὶ ἀνέλοιεν. ἐγὼ δ᾽
ὑμῖν, ὦ ἄνδρες Ἀθηναῖοι, βούλομαι πρῶτον μὲν
περὶ ὧν Φίλιππος ἐπέσταλκε, περὶ τούτων διεξελ-
θεῖν· ὕστερον δέ, περὶ ὧν οἱ πρέσβεις λέγουσι, 10
καὶ ἡμεῖς λέξομεν.

Φίλιππος γὰρ ἄρχεται μὲν περὶ Ἀλοννήσου 2
λέγων ὡς ὑμῖν δίδωσιν ἑαυτοῦ οὖσαν, ὑμᾶς
δὲ οὔ φησι δικαίως αὐτὸν ἀπαιτεῖν· οὐ γὰρ ὑμετέραν οὖσαν οὔτε λαβεῖν οὔτε νῦν ἔχειν. ἔλεγε 15
δὲ καὶ πρὸς ἡμᾶς τοιούτους λόγους, ὅτε πρὸς αὐτὸν
ἐπρεσβεύσαμεν, ὡς λῃστὰς ἀφελόμενος ταύτην τὴν
νῆσον κτήσαιτο, καὶ προσήκειν αὐτὴν ἑαυτοῦ εἶναι.
τοῦτον δὲ τὸν λόγον, ὡς οὐκ ἔστι δίκαιος, οὐ 3
χαλεπόν ἐστιν αὐτοῦ ἀφελέσθαι. ἅπαντες γὰρ οἱ 20
λῃσταὶ τοὺς ἀλλοτρίους τόπους καταλαμβάνοντες
καὶ τούτους ἐχυροὺς ποιούμενοι, ἐντεῦθεν τοὺς

ἄλλους κακῶς ποιοῦσιν. ὁ δὴ τοὺς λῃστὰς τιμω-
ρησάμενος καὶ κρατήσας οὐκ ἂν δήπου εἰκότα λέγοι,
εἰ φαίη, ἃ 'κεῖνοι ἀδίκως καὶ ἀλλότρια εἶχον, ταῦθ᾽
4 ἑαυτοῦ γίγνεσθαι. εἰ γὰρ ταῦτα συγχωρήσετε, τί
5 κωλύει, καὶ εἴ τινα τῆς Ἀττικῆς λῃσταὶ τόπον
καταλάβοιεν ἢ Λήμνου ἢ Ἴμβρου ἢ Σκύρου καί
τινες τούτους τοὺς λῃστὰς ἐκκόψαιεν, εὐθὺς καὶ
τὸν τόπον τοῦτον, οὗ ἦσαν οἱ λῃσταί, τὸν ὄντα
ἡμέτερον, τῶν τιμωρησαμένων τοὺς λῃστὰς γίγνε-
5 σθαι; Φίλιππος δ᾽ οὐκ ἀγνοεῖ ταῦτ᾽ οὐ δίκαια
11 λέγων, ἀλλ᾽ εἰ καί τις ἄλλος ἐπιστάμενος, παρα-
κρουσθῆναι ἂν ὑμᾶς οἴεται ὑπὸ τῶν τἀνταῦθα
διοικήσειν, ὡς ἂν αὐτὸς ἐκεῖνος βούληται, καὶ πρὶν
ὑπεσχημένων καὶ νῦν δὲ πραττόντων. ἀλλὰ μὴν
15 οὐδ᾽ ἐκεῖνό γε λανθάνει αὐτόν, ὅτι δι᾽ ἀμφοτέρων
τῶν ὀνομάτων, ὁποτέρῳ ἂν χρῆσθε, ὑμεῖς ἕξετε
6 τὴν νῆσον, ἄν τε λάβητε ἄν τ᾽ ἀπολάβητε. τί
οὖν αὐτῷ διαφέρει, μὴ τῷ δικαίῳ ὀνόματι χρησά-
μενον ἀποδοῦναι ὑμῖν, ἀλλὰ δωρεὰν δεδωκέναι,
20 τῷ ἀδίκῳ; οὐχ ἵν᾽ εὐεργέτημά τι καταλογίσηται
πρὸς ὑμᾶς (γελοῖον γὰρ ἂν εἴη τοῦτό γ᾽ εὐεργέ-
τημα), ἀλλ᾽ ἵν᾽ ἐνδείξηται ἅπασι τοῖς Ἕλλησιν, ὅτι
Ἀθηναῖοι τὰ ἐν τῇ θαλάττῃ χωρία ἀγαπῶσι παρὰ
τοῦ Μακεδόνος λαμβάνοντες. τοῦτο δ᾽ ὑμῖν οὐ
25 ποιητέον ἐστίν, ὦ ἄνδρες Ἀθηναῖοι.
7   Ὅταν δὲ λέγῃ περὶ τούτων ὡς ἐθέλει διαδι-
κάσασθαι, οὐδὲν ἀλλ᾽ ἢ χλευάζει ὑμᾶς, πρῶτον
μὲν ἀξιῶν Ἀθηναίους ὄντας πρὸς τὸν ἐκ Πέλλης
ὁρμώμενον περὶ τῶν νήσων διαδικάζεσθαι, πότερ᾽

ὑμέτεραι ἢ 'κείνου εἰσίν. ὁπότε γὰρ ἡ μὲν δύναμις ἡ ὑμετέρα, ἡ ἐλευθερώσασα τοὺς Ἕλληνας, μὴ
δύναται ὑμῖν τὰ ἐν τῇ θαλάττῃ χωρία σώζειν, οἱ
δὲ δικασταί, οἷς ἂν ἐπιτρέψητε, οἱ κύριοι τῆς
ψήφου, οὗτοι ὑμῖν σώσουσιν, ἐὰν μὴ Φίλιππος 8
αὐτοὺς πρίηται, πῶς ὑμεῖς οὐχ ὁμολογουμένως, 6
ὅταν ταῦτα διαπράττησθε, τῶν ἐν τῇ ἠπείρῳ ἁπάντων ἀφεστήκατε, καὶ ἐπιδείκνυτε ἅπασιν ἀνθρώποις, ὅτι οὐδὲ περὶ ἑνὸς αὐτῶν διαγωνιεῖσθε, εἴγε
περὶ τῶν ἐν τῇ θαλάττῃ, οὗ φατὲ ἰσχύειν, μὴ 10
διαγωνιεῖσθε, ἀλλὰ δικάσεσθε;

Ἔτι περὶ συμβόλων φησὶ πεπομφέναι 9
πρὸς ὑμᾶς τοὺς ποιησομένους, ταῦτα δὲ
κύρια ἔσεσθαι, οὐκ ἐπειδὰν ἐν τῷ δικαστηρίῳ τῷ
παρ' ὑμῖν κυρωθῇ, ὥσπερ ὁ νόμος κελεύει, ἀλλ' 15
ἐπειδὰν ὡς ἑαυτὸν ἐπανενεχθῇ, ἐφέσιμον τὴν παρ'
ὑμῶν γενομένην γνῶσιν ὡς ἑαυτὸν ποιούμενος.
βούλεται γὰρ ὑμῶν τοῦτο προλαβεῖν καὶ ὁμολο-
γούμενον ἐν τοῖς συμβόλοις καταστῆσαι, ὅτι τῶν
περὶ Ποτείδαιαν γεγενημένων ἀδικημάτων οὐδὲν 20
ἐγκαλεῖτε αὐτῷ ὡς ἀδικούμενοι, ἀλλὰ βεβαιοῦτε
δικαίως αὐτὴν ἐκεῖνον καὶ λαβεῖν καὶ κεκτῆσθαι.
καίτοι Ἀθηναίων οἱ ἐν Ποτειδαίᾳ κατοικοῦντες, 10
οὐκ ὄντος αὐτοῖς πολέμου πρὸς Φίλιππον, ἀλλὰ
συμμαχίας, καὶ ὅρκων ὀμωμοσμένων, οὓς Φίλιππος 25
τοῖς οἰκοῦσιν ἐν Ποτειδαίᾳ ὤμοσεν, ἀφῃρέθησαν 356
ὑπ' αὐτοῦ τὰ κτήματα. ταῦτα δὴ βούλεται τἀδι-
κήματα πολλάκις πανταχόσε παρ' ὑμῖν βεβαιώσα-
σθαι, ὅτι οὔτ' ἐγκαλεῖτε οὔθ' ἡγεῖσθε ἀδικεῖσθαι·

11 ἐπεὶ ὅτι γε συμβόλων οὐδὲν δέονται Μακεδόνες
πρὸς Ἀθηναίους, ὁ παρεληλυθὼς ὑμῖν χρόνος
τεκμήριον γενέσθω· οὔτε γὰρ Ἀμύντας ὁ πατὴρ
ὁ Φιλίππου οὔθ᾽ οἱ ἄλλοι βασιλεῖς οὐδεπώποτε
5 σύμβολα ἐποιήσαντο πρὸς τὴν πόλιν τὴν ἡμετέραν.
12 καίτοι πλείους γε ἦσαν αἱ ἐπιμειξίαι τότε πρὸς
ἀλλήλους ἢ νῦν εἰσίν· ἐφ᾽ ἡμῖν γὰρ ἦν ἡ Μακεδονία καὶ φόρους ἡμῖν ἔφερον, καὶ τοῖς ἐμπορίοις
τότε μᾶλλον ἢ νῦν ἡμεῖς τε τοῖς ἐκεῖ κἀκεῖνοι
10 τοῖς παρ᾽ ἡμῖν ἐχρῶντο, καὶ ἐμπορικαὶ δίκαι οὐκ
ἦσαν, ὥσπερ νῦν, ἀκριβεῖς, αἱ κατὰ μῆνα, ποιοῦσαι
μηδὲν δεῖσθαι συμβόλων τοὺς τοσοῦτον ἀλλήλων
13 ἀπέχοντας. ἀλλ᾽ ὅμως οὐδενὸς τοιούτου ὄντος
τότε, οὐκ ἐλυσιτέλει σύμβολα ποιησαμένοις οὔτ᾽ ἐκ
15 Μακεδονίας πλεῖν Ἀθήναζε δίκας ληψομένοις, οὔθ᾽
ἡμῖν εἰς Μακεδονίαν, ἀλλ᾽ ἡμεῖς τε τοῖς ἐκεῖ νομί-
μοις ἐκεῖνοί τε τοῖς παρ᾽ ἡμῖν τὰς δίκας ἐλάμβανον.
μὴ οὖν ἀγνοεῖτε, ὅτι τὰ σύμβολα ταῦτα γίγνεται
εἰς ὑποδοχὴν τοῦ μηδ᾽ ἀμφισβητῆσαι εὐλόγως
20 ὑμᾶς ἔτι Ποτειδαίας.
14   Περὶ δὲ τῶν λῃστῶν, δίκαιόν φησιν
εἶναι κοινῇ φυλάττειν τοὺς ἐν τῇ θαλάττῃ
κακουργοῦντας ὑμᾶς τε καὶ αὐτόν, οὐδὲν ἀλλ᾽ ἢ
τοῦτ᾽ ἀξιῶν, ὑφ᾽ ὑμῶν εἰς τὴν θάλατταν καταστα-
25 θῆναι, καὶ ὁμολογῆσαι ὑμᾶς, ὡς ἄνευ Φιλίππου
οὐδὲ τὴν ἐν τῇ θαλάττῃ φυλακὴν δυνατοί ἐστε
15 φυλάττειν, ἔτι δὲ καὶ δοθῆναι αὐτῷ ταύτην τὴν
ἄδειαν, περιπλέοντι καὶ ὁρμιζομένῳ εἰς τὰς νήσους
ἐπὶ προφάσει τῇ τῶν λῃστῶν φυλακῇ διαφθείρειν

τοὺς νησιώτας καὶ ἀφιστάναι ὑμῶν, καὶ μὴ μόνον
τοὺς φυγάδας τοὺς παρ᾽ ἑαυτοῦ εἰς Θάσον κεκομι-
κέναι διὰ τῶν ὑμετέρων στρατηγῶν, ἀλλὰ καὶ τὰς
ἄλλας νήσους οἰκειώσασθαι, συμπέμπων τοὺς συμ-
πλευσομένους μετὰ τῶν στρατηγῶν τῶν ὑμετέρων, 5
ὡς κοινωνήσοντας τῆς κατὰ θάλατταν φυλακῆς.
καίτοι οὔ φασί τινες αὐτὸν προσδεῖσθαι τῆς θαλάτ- 16
της. ὁ δ᾽ οὐδὲν δεόμενος τριήρεις κατασκευάζεται
καὶ νεωσοίκους οἰκοδομεῖται καὶ ἀποστόλους ἀποστέλλειν βούλεται καὶ δαπάνας οὐ μικρὰς δαπανᾶν 10
εἰς τοὺς κατὰ θάλατταν κινδύνους, ὧν οὐδὲν προ-
τιμᾷ. Ταῦτ᾽ οἴεσθ᾽ ἂν, ὦ ἄνδρες Ἀθηναῖοι, Φίλιπ- 17
πον ἀξιῶσαι ὑμᾶς συγχωρῆσαι αὐτῷ, εἰ μὴ ὑμῶν
μὲν κατεφρόνει, οὓς δ᾽ ἐνθάδε προῄρηται φίλους
κεκτῆσθαι, τούτοις διεπίστευεν; οἳ οὐκ αἰσχύνονται 15
Φιλίππῳ ζῶντες καὶ οὐ τῇ αὑτῶν πατρίδι, καὶ
τὰς παρ᾽ ἐκείνου δωρεὰς λαμβάνοντες οἴονται
οἴκαδε λαμβάνειν, τὰ οἴκοι πωλοῦντες.

Περὶ δὲ τῆς ἐπανορθώσεως τῆς εἰρήνης, 18
ἣν ἔδοσαν ἡμῖν οἱ πρέσβεις οἱ παρ᾽ ἐκείνου πεμ- 20
φθέντες ἐπανορθώσασθαι, ὅτι ἐπηνωρθωσάμεθα,
ὃ παρὰ πᾶσιν ἀνθρώποις ὁμολογεῖται δίκαιον
εἶναι, ἑκατέρους ἔχειν τὰ ἑαυτῶν, ἀμφισβητεῖ
μὴ δεδωκέναι, μηδὲ τοὺς πρέσβεις ταῦτ᾽ εἰρηκέναι
πρὸς ὑμᾶς, οὐδὲν ἀλλ᾽ ἢ πεπεισμένος ὑπὸ τούτων, 25
οἷς χρῆται φίλοις, ὡς ὑμεῖς οὐ μνημονεύετε τὰ ἐν
τῷ δήμῳ εἰρημένα. μόνον δὲ τοῦτο οὐχ οἷόν τε 19
ὑμῖν ἐστιν ἀμνημονῆσαι· ἐν γὰρ τῇ αὐτῇ ἐκκλη-
σίᾳ καὶ οἱ πρέσβεις ὑμῖν οἱ παρ᾽ ἐκείνου ἥκοντες 343

διελέγοντο καὶ τὸ ψήφισμα ἐγράφη, ὥστ᾽ οὐχ οἷόν
τε, παραχρῆμα τῶν λόγων εἰρημένων καὶ εὐθὺς
τοῦ ψηφίσματος ἐπαναγιγνωσκομένου, τὴν κατα-
ψευδομένην γνώμην τῶν πρέσβεων, ταύτην ὑμᾶς
5 χειροτονῆσαι· ὥστε τοῦτο μὲν οὐ κατ᾽ ἐμοῦ, ἀλλὰ
καθ᾽ ὑμῶν ἐπέσταλκεν, ὡς ὑμεῖς, περὶ ὧν οὐκ
ἠκούσατε, περὶ τούτων ἀποκρινάμενοι τὴν γνώμην
20 ἀπεστείλατε. καὶ οἱ μὲν πρέσβεις αὐτοί, ὧν κατε-
ψεύδετο τὸ ψήφισμα, ὅτ᾽ ἀπεκρίνεσθε αὐτοῖς ἀνα-
10 γιγνώσκοντες καὶ ἐπὶ ξένια αὐτοὺς ἐκαλεῖτε, οὐκ
ἐτόλμησαν παρελθεῖν οὐδ᾽ εἰπεῖν ὅτι „καταψεύδεσθε
ἡμῶν, ὦ ἄνδρες Ἀθηναῖοι, καί φατε ἡμᾶς εἰρηκέναι
ἃ οὐκ εἰρήκαμεν“, ἀλλὰ σιωπῇ ἀπιόντες ᾤχοντο.
βούλομαι δ᾽ ὑμᾶς, ὦ ἄνδρες Ἀθηναῖοι, (καὶ γὰρ
15 ηὐδοκίμησεν ὁ Πύθων παρ᾽ ὑμῖν ἐν τῇ δημηγορίᾳ,
ὁ τότε πρεσβεύων) αὐτοὺς τοὺς λόγους οὓς ἔλεγεν
21 ὑπομνῆσαι· οἶδα γὰρ ὅτι μέμνησθε. παραπλήσιοι
δ᾽ ἦσαν οἷς καὶ νῦν ἐπέσταλκε Φίλιππος· ἐγκαλῶν
γὰρ ἡμῖν τοῖς διαβάλλουσι τὸν Φίλιππον καὶ ὑμῖν
20 ἐμέμφετο, ὅτι ὡρμηκότος αὐτοῦ εὖ ποιεῖν ὑμᾶς
καὶ προῃρημένου μάλιστα τῶν Ἑλλήνων φίλους
κεκτῆσθαι, αὐτοὶ κωλύετε, ἀποδεχόμενοι τοὺς λόγους
τῶν συκοφαντούντων καὶ χρήματα ἐκεῖνον αἰτούν-
των καὶ διαβαλλόντων· τοὺς γὰρ τοιούτους λόγους,
25 ὅταν ἀπαγγελλόντων ἀκούῃ, ὅτι κακῶς ἤκουεν,
ὑμεῖς δ᾽ ἀπεδέχεσθε, μεταβάλλειν αὐτοῦ τὴν γνώμην, ὅταν ἄπιστος φαίνηται τούτοις, ὧν προῄρηται
22 εὐεργέτης εἶναι. ἐκέλευεν οὖν τοὺς λέγοντας ἐν
τῷ δήμῳ τῇ μὲν εἰρήνῃ μὴ ἐπιτιμᾶν· οὐ γὰρ ἄξιον

εἶναι εἰρήνην λύειν· εἰ δέ τι μὴ καλῶς γέγραπται
ἐν τῇ εἰρήνῃ, τοῦτ᾽ ἐπανορθώσασθαι, ὡς ἅπαντα
Φίλιππον ποιήσοντα ὅσ᾽ ἂν ὑμεῖς ψηφίσησθε. ἂν
δὲ διαβάλλωσι μέν, αὐτοὶ δὲ μηδὲν γράφωσι, δι᾽
οὗ ἡ μὲν εἰρήνη ἔσται παύσεται δ᾽ ἀπιστούμενος 5
ὁ Φίλιππος, μὴ προσέχειν τὸν νοῦν τοῖς τοιούτοις ἀνθρώποις. καὶ τούτους τοὺς λόγους ὑμεῖς 23
ἀκούοντες ἀπεδέχεσθε, καὶ δίκαια ἔφατε τὸν
Πύθωνα λέγειν, καὶ ἦν δίκαια. ἔλεγε δὲ τούτους
τοὺς λόγους, οὐχ ὅπως λυθείη ἐκ τῆς εἰρήνης, ἃ 10
ἦν ἐκείνῳ συμφέροντα καὶ ὧν πολλὰ χρήματα
ἀνηλώκει ὥστε γενέσθαι, ἀλλ᾽ ὑπὸ τῶν ἐνθάδε
διδασκάλων προδεδιδαγμένος, οἳ οὐκ ᾤοντο εἶναι
τὸν γράψοντα ἐναντία τῷ Φιλοκράτους ψηφίσματι,
τῷ ἀπολλύντι Ἀμφίπολιν. ἐγὼ δέ, ὦ ἄνδρες 24
Ἀθηναῖοι, παράνομον μὲν οὐδὲν ἐτόλμησα γράψαι, 16
τῷ δὲ Φιλοκράτους ψηφίσματι οὐκ ἦν παράνομον
τἀναντία γράφειν, ὡς ἐγὼ ἐπιδείξω· τὸ γὰρ
ψήφισμα τὸ Φιλοκράτους, καθ᾽ ὃ ὑμεῖς ἀπώλλυτε
Ἀμφίπολιν, ἐναντίον ἦν τοῖς προτέροις ψηφίσμασι, 20
καθ᾽ ἃ ὑμεῖς ἐκτήσασθε ταύτην τὴν χώραν. τοῦτο 25
μὲν οὖν παράνομον ἦν τὸ ψήφισμα, τὸ τοῦ
Φιλοκράτους, καὶ οὐχ οἷόν τ᾽ ἦν τὸν τὰ ἔν-
νομα γράφοντα ταὐτὰ τῷ παρανόμῳ ψηφίσματι
γράφειν· ἐκείνοις δὲ τοῖς προτέροις ψηφίσμασι, 25
τοῖς οὖσιν ἐννόμοις καὶ σῴζουσι τὴν ὑμετέραν
χώραν, ταὐτὰ γράφων ἔννομά τ᾽ ἔγραψα καὶ
ἐξήλεγχον τὸν Φίλιππον, ὅτι ἐξηπάτα ὑμᾶς καὶ
οὐκ ἐπανορθώσασθαι ἐβούλετο τὴν εἰρήνην,

ἀλλὰ τοὺς ὑπὲρ ὑμῶν λέγοντας ἀπίστους καταστῆσαι.

26   Καὶ ὅτι μὲν δοὺς τὴν ἐπανόρθωσιν νῦν
ἔξαρνός ἐστιν, ἅπαντες ἴστε. φησὶ δ᾽ Ἀμφίπολιν
5 ἑαυτοῦ εἶναι· ὑμᾶς γὰρ ψηφίσασθαι ἐκείνου
346 εἶναι, ὅτ᾽ ἐψηφίζεσθε ἔχειν αὐτὸν ἃ εἶχεν. ὑμεῖς
δὲ τὸ μὲν ψήφισμα τοῦτ᾽ ἐψηφίσασθε, οὐ μέντοι
γ᾽ ἐκείνου εἶναι Ἀμφίπολιν. ἔστι γὰρ ἔχειν καὶ
τἀλλότρια, καὶ οὐχ ἅπαντες οἱ ἔχοντες τὰ αὑτῶν
10 ἔχουσιν, ἀλλὰ πολλοὶ καὶ τἀλλότρια κέκτηνται. ὥστε
27 τοῦτό γε τὸ σοφὸν αὐτῷ ἠλίθιόν ἐστιν. καὶ τοῦ
μὲν Φιλοκράτους ψηφίσματος μέμνηται, τῆς δ᾽
356 ἐπιστολῆς, ἣν πρὸς ὑμᾶς ἔπεμψεν ὅτ᾽ Ἀμφίπολιν
ἐπολιόρκει, ἐπιλέλησται, ἐν ᾗ ὡμολόγει τὴν Ἀμφίπολιν
15 ὑμετέραν εἶναι· ἔφη γὰρ ἐκπολιορκήσας ὑμῖν ἀπο-
δώσειν, ὡς οὖσαν ὑμετέραν καὶ οὐ τῶν ἐχόντων.
28 κἀκεῖνοι μέν, ὡς ἔοικεν, οἱ πρότερον ἐν Ἀμφιπόλει
οἰκοῦντες, πρὶν Φίλιππον λαβεῖν, τὴν Ἀθηναίων
χώραν εἶχον, ἐπειδὴ δὲ Φίλιππος αὐτὴν εἴληφεν,
20 οὐ τὴν Ἀθηναίων χώραν ἀλλὰ τὴν ἑαυτοῦ ἔχει·
οὐδ᾽ Ὄλυνθόν γε οὐδ᾽ Ἀπολλωνίαν οὐδὲ Παλλήνην,
οὐκ ἀλλοτρίας ἀλλὰ τὰς ἑαυτοῦ χώρας κέκτηται.
29 ἆρ᾽ ὑμῖν δοκεῖ πεφυλαγμένως ἅπαντα πρὸς ὑμᾶς
ἐπιστέλλειν, ὅπως ἂν φαίνηται καὶ λέγων καὶ
25 πράττων ἃ παρὰ πᾶσιν ἀνθρώποις ὁμολογεῖται
δίκαια εἶναι, ἀλλ᾽ οὐ σφόδρα καταπεφρονηκέναι,
ὃς τὴν χώραν, ἣν οἱ Ἕλληνες καὶ βασιλεὺς ὁ
Περσῶν ἐψηφίσαντο καὶ ὡμολογήκασιν ὑμετέραν
εἶναι, ταύτην φησὶν ἑαυτοῦ καὶ οὐχ ὑμετέραν εἶναι;

Περὶ δὲ τοῦ ἑτέρου ἐπανορθώματος, ὃ ὑμεῖς 30
ἐν τῇ εἰρήνῃ ἐπανορθοῦσθε, τοὺς ἄλλους Ἕλληνας, ὅσοι μὴ κοινωνοῦσι τῆς εἰρήνης, ἐλευθέρους καὶ αὐτονόμους εἶναι, καὶ ἐάν τις ἐπ᾽
αὐτοὺς στρατεύῃ, βοηθεῖν τοὺς κοινωνοῦντας τῆς 5
εἰρήνης, ἡγούμενοι καὶ δίκαιον τοῦτο καὶ φιλάν- 31
θρωπον, μὴ μόνον ἡμᾶς καὶ τοὺς συμμάχους τοὺς
ἡμετέρους καὶ Φίλιππον καὶ τοὺς συμμάχους τοὺς
ἐκείνου ἄγειν τὴν εἰρήνην, τοὺς δὲ μήθ᾽ ἡμετέρους
ὄντας μήτε Φιλίππου συμμάχους ἐν μέσῳ κεῖσθαι 10
καὶ ὑπὸ τῶν κρειττόνων ἀπόλλυσθαι, ἀλλὰ καὶ
τούτοις διὰ τὴν ὑμετέραν εἰρήνην ὑπάρχειν
σωτηρίαν, καὶ τῷ ὄντι εἰρήνην ἄγειν ἡμᾶς κατα-
θεμένους τὰ ὅπλα, τοῦτο δὲ τὸ ἐπανόρθωμα ὁμο- 32
λογῶν ἐν τῇ ἐπιστολῇ, ὡς ἀκούετε, δίκαιόν τ᾽ 15
εἶναι καὶ δέχεσθαι, Φεραίων μὲν ἀφῄρηται τὴν 344
πόλιν καὶ φρουρὰν ἐν τῇ ἀκροπόλει κατέστησεν,
ἵνα δὴ αὐτόνομοι ὦσιν, ἐπὶ δ᾽ Ἀμβρακίαν στρατεύεται, τὰς δ᾽ ἐν Κασσωπίᾳ τρεῖς πόλεις, Παν-
δοσίαν καὶ Βούχετα καὶ Ἐλάτειαν, Ἠλείων ἀποικίας, 20
κατακαύσας τὴν χώραν καὶ εἰς τὰς πόλεις βιασά-
μενος παρέδωκεν Ἀλεξάνδρῳ τῷ κηδεστῇ τῷ ἑαυτοῦ
δουλεύειν. σφόδρα γε βούλεται τοὺς Ἕλληνας
ἐλευθέρους εἶναι καὶ αὐτονόμους, ὡς δηλοῖ τὰ ἔργα.

Περὶ δὲ τῶν ὑποσχέσεων ὧν ὑμῖν διατελεῖ 33
ὑπισχνούμενος, ὡς μεγάλα ὑμᾶς εὐεργετήσων, κατα- 26
ψεύδεσθαί μέ φησιν αὐτοῦ διαβάλλοντα πρὸς τοὺς
Ἕλληνας· οὐδὲν γὰρ ὑμῖν πώποτέ φησιν
ὑπεσχῆσθαι. οὕτως ἀναιδής ἐστιν ὁ ἐν ἐπιστολῇ

γεγραφώς, ἥ ἐστι νῦν ἐν τῷ βουλευτηρίῳ, ὅσ᾽
ἐπιστομιεῖν ἡμᾶς, ἔφη, τοὺς αὐτῷ ἀντιλέγοντας,
ἐὰν ἡ εἰρήνη γένηται, τοσαῦτα ὑμᾶς ἀγαθὰ ποιήσειν·
ἃ γράφειν ἂν ἤδη, εἰ ᾔδει τὴν εἰρήνην ἐσομένην,
5 δῆλον ὡς προκεχειρισμένων καὶ ἑτοίμων ὄντων
τῶν ἀγαθῶν, ἃ ἐμέλλομεν πείσεσθαι τῆς εἰρήνης
34 γενομένης. γενομένης δὲ τῆς εἰρήνης, ἃ μὲν
ἡμεῖς ἐμέλλομεν ἀγαθὰ πείσεσθαι, ἐκποδών ἐστι,
φθορὰ δὲ τῶν Ἑλλήνων τοσαύτη γέγονεν ὅσην
10 ὑμεῖς ἴστε. ὑμῖν δ᾽ ἐν τῇ νῦν ἐπιστολῇ ὑπισχνεῖται,
ἐὰν τοῖς μὲν αὐτοῦ φίλοις καὶ ὑπὲρ αὐτοῦ λέγουσι
πιστεύητε, ἡμᾶς δὲ τοὺς διαβάλλοντας αὐτὸν πρὸς
35 ὑμᾶς τιμωρήσησθε, ὡς μεγάλα εὐεργετήσει. τὰ
μέντοι εὐεργετήματα τοιαῦτα ἔσται· οὔτε τὰ
15 ὑμέτερα ὑμῖν ἀποδώσει (αὐτοῦ γὰρ φησιν εἶναι),
οὔτ᾽ ἐν τῇ οἰκουμένῃ αἱ δωρεαὶ ἔσονται, ἵνα μὴ
διαβληθῇ πρὸς τοὺς Ἕλληνας, ἀλλ᾽ ἄλλη τις χώρα
καὶ ἄλλος ὡς ἔοικε τόπος φανήσεται, οὗ ὑμῖν αἱ
δωρεαὶ δοθήσονται.

36　　Περὶ δ᾽ ὧν ἐν τῇ εἰρήνῃ εἴληφε χωρίων,
21 ὑμῶν ἐχόντων, παρασπονδῶν καὶ λύων τὴν εἰρήνην,
ἐπειδὴ οὐκ ἔχει ὅ τι εἴπῃ, ἀλλ᾽ ἀδικῶν φανερῶς
ἐξελέγχεται, ἐπιτρέπειν φησὶ περὶ τούτων ἕτοιμος εἶναι ἴσῳ καὶ κοινῷ δικαστηρίῳ· περὶ ὧν
25 μόνων οὐδὲν δεῖ ἐπιτροπῆς, ἀλλ᾽ ἀριθμὸς ἡμερῶν
ἐστιν ὁ κρίνων. ἅπαντες γὰρ ἴσμεν, τίνι μηνὶ καὶ
37 τίνι ἡμέρᾳ ἡ εἰρήνη ἐγένετο. ὥσπερ δὲ ταῦτα ἴσμεν,
κἀκεῖνα ἴσμεν, τίνι μηνὶ καὶ τίνι ἡμέρᾳ Σέρρειον
τεῖχος καὶ Ἐργίσκη καὶ Ἱερὸν ὄρος ἑάλω. οὐ δὴ

ἀφανῆ ἐστι τὰ οὕτω πραχϑέντα, οὐδὲ κρίσεως δεό-
μενα, ἀλλὰ πᾶσι γνώριμα, πότερος πρότερος ὁ μήν
ἐστιν, ἐν ᾧ ἡ εἰρήνη ἐγένετο, ἢ ἐν ᾧ τὰ χωρία ἑάλω.

Φησὶ δὲ καὶ τοὺς αἰχμαλώτους ἡμῶν, 38
ὅσοι ἐν τῷ πολέμῳ ἑάλωσαν, ἀποδεδωκέναι· ὃς 5
τὸν μὲν Καρύστιον, τὸν πρόξενον τῆς ἡμετέρας
πόλεως, ὑπὲρ οὗ ὑμεῖς τρεῖς πρέσβεις ἐπέμψατε
ἀπαιτοῦντες, τοῦτον τὸν ἄνδρα ἐκεῖνος οὕτω σφόδρα
ὑμῖν ἐβούλετο χαρίσασθαι, ὥστ᾽ ἀπέκτεινε καὶ οὐδ᾽
ἀναίρεσιν ἔδωκεν, ἵνα ταφῇ. 10

Περὶ δὲ Χερρονήσου, ἅ τ᾽ ἐπιστέλλει 39
πρὸς ὑμᾶς ἄξιόν ἐστιν ἐξετάσαι, ἔτι δὲ καὶ ἃ
πράττει, καὶ ταῦτ᾽ εἰδέναι. τὸν μὲν γὰρ τόπον
ἅπαντα τὸν ἔξω Ἀγορᾶς ὡς ἑαυτοῦ ὄντα καὶ ὑμῖν
οὐδὲν προσήκοντα δέδωκε καρποῦσθαι Ἀπολλωνίδῃ 15
τῷ Καρδιανῷ. καίτοι Χερρονήσου οἱ ὅροι εἰσίν,
οὐκ Ἀγορά, ἀλλὰ βωμὸς τοῦ Διὸς τοῦ ὁρίου, ὅς
ἐστι μεταξὺ Πτελεοῦ καὶ Λευκῆς ἀκτῆς, ᾗ ἡ 40
διορυχὴ ἔμελλε Χερρονήσου ἔσεσθαι, ὥς γε τὸ
ἐπίγραμμα τὸ ἐπὶ τοῦ βωμοῦ τοῦ Διὸς τοῦ ὁρίου 20
δηλοῖ. ἔστι δὲ τουτί·

> Τόνδε καθιδρύσαντο θεῷ περικαλλέα βωμὸν
> Λευκῆς καὶ Πτελεοῦ μέσσον ὅρον θέμενοι
> ἐνναέται χώρης σημήϊον· ἀμμορίης δέ
>   αὐτὸς ἄναξ μακάρων ἐστὶ μέσος Κρονίδης. 25

ταύτην μέντοι τὴν χώραν τοσαύτην οὖσαν, ὅσην 41
οἱ πολλοὶ ὑμῶν ἴσασιν, ὡς ἑαυτοῦ οὖσαν τὴν μὲν
αὐτὸς καρποῦται, τὴν δ᾽ ἄλλοις δωρεὰν δέδωκε,
καὶ ἅπαντα τὰ κτήματα τὰ ὑμέτερα ὑφ᾽ αὑτῷ

ποιεῖται. καὶ οὐ μόνον τὴν ἔξω Ἀγορᾶς χώραν
σφετερίζεται, ἀλλὰ καὶ πρὸς Καρδιανούς, οἳ οἰκοῦσιν
εἴσω Ἀγορᾶς, ἐπιστέλλει ἐν τῇ νῦν ἐπιστολῇ, ὡς
δεῖ ὑμᾶς διαδικάζεσθαι πρὸς Καρδιανοὺς τοὺς
5 κατοικοῦντας ἐν τῇ ὑμετέρᾳ, εἴ τι πρὸς αὐτοὺς
42 διαφέρεσθε. διαφέρονται δὲ πρὸς ὑμᾶς, σκέψασθε
εἰ περὶ μικροῦ· ἑαυτῶν φασι τὴν χώραν οὖσαν
οἰκεῖν καὶ οὐχ ὑμετέραν, καὶ τὰ μὲν ὑμέτερα εἶναι
ἐγκτήματα ὡς ἐν ἀλλοτρίᾳ, τὰ δὲ ἑαυτῶν κτήμαθ᾽
10 ὡς ἐν οἰκείᾳ, καὶ ταῦθ᾽ ὑμέτερον πολίτην γράψαι
43 ἐν ψηφίσματι, Κάλλιππον Παιανιέα. καὶ τοῦτό
γ᾽ ἀληθῆ λέγουσιν· ἔγραψε γάρ, καὶ ἐμοῦ γ᾽
αὐτὸν γραψαμένου παρανόμων γραφὴν ὑμεῖς
ἀπεψηφίσασθε· τοιγάρτοι ἀμφισβητήσιμον ὑμῖν
15 τὴν χώραν κατεσκεύακεν. ὁπότε δὲ περὶ τούτου
τολμήσετε πρὸς Καρδιανοὺς διαδικάζεσθαι, εἴθ᾽
ὑμετέρα ἐστὶν εἴτ᾽ ἐκείνων ἡ χώρα, διὰ τί οὐ καὶ
πρὸς τοὺς ἄλλους Χερρονησίτας τὸ αὐτὸ δίκαιον
44 ἔσται; καὶ οὕτως ὑβριστικῶς ὑμῖν κέχρηται, ὥστε
20 φησίν, ἂν μὴ θέλωσι διαδικάζεσθαι οἱ Καρδιανοί,
αὐτὸς ἀναγκάσειν, ὡς ὑμῶν γ᾽ οὐκ ἂν δυναμένων
οὐδὲν ἀναγκάσαι Καρδιανοὺς ὑμῖν ποιῆσαι· ἐπειδὴ
δ᾽ ὑμεῖς οὐ δύνασθε, αὐτός φησι τοῦτ᾽ ἀναγκάσειν
αὐτοὺς ποιῆσαι. ἆρ᾽ οὐ μεγάλα φαίνεται ὑμᾶς
45 εὐεργετῶν; καὶ ταύτην τὴν ἐπιστολήν τινες εὖ
26 ἔφασαν γεγράφθαι, οἳ πολὺ ἂν δικαιότερον ὑφ᾽
ὑμῶν ἢ Φίλιππος μισοῖντο. ἐκεῖνος μέν γ᾽ ἑαυτῷ
κτώμενος δόξαν καὶ μεγάλ᾽ ἀγαθὰ ἅπαντα καθ᾽
ὑμῶν πράττει· ὅσοι δ᾽ Ἀθηναῖοι ὄντες μὴ τῇ

πατρίδι, ἀλλὰ Φιλίππῳ εὔνοιαν ἐνδείκνυνται,
προσήκει αὐτοὺς ὑφ' ὑμῶν κακοὺς κακῶς ἀπολωλέναι, εἴπερ ὑμεῖς τὸν ἐγκέφαλον ἐν τοῖς κροτάφοις
καὶ μὴ ἐν ταῖς πτέρναις καταπεπατημένον φορεῖτε.

Ὑπόλοιπόν μοί ἐστιν ἔτι, πρὸς ταύτην τὴν 46
ἐπιστολὴν τὴν εὖ ἔχουσαν καὶ τοὺς λόγους τῶν 5
πρέσβεων γράψαι τὴν ἀπόκρισιν, ἣν ἡγοῦμαι
δικαίαν τ' εἶναι καὶ συμφέρουσαν ὑμῖν.

ΠΕΡΙ ΤΩΝ ΕΝ ΧΕΡΡΟΝΗΣΩΙ.

1 Ἔδει μέν, ὦ ἄνδρες Ἀθηναῖοι, τοὺς λέγοντας
ἅπαντας μήτε πρὸς ἔχθραν ποιεῖσθαι λόγον μηδένα
μήτε πρὸς χάριν, ἀλλ᾽ ὃ βέλτιστον ἕκαστος ἡγεῖτο,
5 τοῦτ᾽ ἀποφαίνεσθαι, ἄλλως τε καὶ περὶ κοινῶν
πραγμάτων καὶ μεγάλων ὑμῶν βουλευομένων· ἐπεὶ
δ᾽ ἔνιοι τὰ μὲν φιλονικίᾳ, τὰ δ᾽ ἡτινιδήποτ᾽ αἰτίᾳ
προάγονται λέγειν, ὑμᾶς, ὦ ἄνδρες Ἀθηναῖοι, τοὺς
πολλοὺς δεῖ, πάντα τἄλλ᾽ ἀφελόντας, ἃ τῇ πόλει
10 νομίζετε συμφέρειν, ταῦτα καὶ ψηφίζεσθαι
2 καὶ πράττειν. ἡ μὲν οὖν σπουδὴ περὶ τῶν ἐν
Χερρονήσῳ πραγμάτων ἐστὶ καὶ τῆς στρατείας, ἣν
342 ἑνδέκατον μῆνα τουτονὶ Φίλιππος ἐν Θρᾴκῃ ποιεῖται,
τῶν δὲ λόγων οἱ πλεῖστοι περὶ ὧν Διοπείθης
15 πράττει καὶ μέλλει ποιεῖν, εἴρηνται. ἐγὼ δ᾽, ὅσα
μέν τις αἰτιᾶταί τινα τούτων, οὓς κατὰ τοὺς νόμους
ἐφ᾽ ὑμῖν ἐστιν, ὅταν βούλησθε, κολάζειν, κἂν ἤδη
δοκῇ κἂν ἐπισχοῦσιν περὶ αὐτῶν σκοπεῖν ἐγχωρεῖν
ἡγοῦμαι, καὶ οὐ πάνυ δεῖ περὶ τούτων οὔτ᾽ ἐμὲ
3 οὔτ᾽ ἄλλον οὐδέν᾽ ἰσχυρίζεσθαι· ὅσα δ᾽ ἐχθρὸς
21 ὑπάρχων τῇ πόλει καὶ δυνάμει πολλῇ περὶ
Ἑλλήσποντον ὢν πειρᾶται προλαβεῖν, κἂν

ἅπαξ ὑστερήσωμεν, οὐκέϑ᾽ ἕξομεν σῶσαι, περὶ
τούτων δ᾽ οἶομαι τὴν ταχίστην συμφέρειν καὶ
βεβουλεῦσθαι καὶ παρεσκευάσθαι, καὶ μὴ τοῖς περὶ
τῶν ἄλλων θορύβοις καὶ ταῖς κατηγορίαις ἀπὸ
τούτων ἀποδρᾶναι.   5

   Πολλὰ δὲ θαυμάζων τῶν εἰωθότων λέγεσθαι 4
παρ᾽ ὑμῖν, οὐδενὸς ἧττον, ὦ ἄνδρες Ἀθηναῖοι,
τεθαύμακα, ὃ καὶ πρώην τινὸς ἤκουσ᾽ εἰπόντος ἐν
τῇ βουλῇ, ὡς ἄρα δεῖ τὸν συμβουλεύοντ᾽ ἢ
πολεμεῖν ἁπλῶς ἢ τὴν εἰρήνην ἄγειν συμβου- 10
λεύειν. ἔστι δέ· εἰ μὲν ἡσυχίαν Φίλιππος ἄγει καὶ 5
μήτε τῶν ἡμετέρων ἔχει παρὰ τὴν εἰρήνην μηδὲν
μήτε συσκευάζεται πάντας ἀνθρώπους ἐφ᾽ ἡμᾶς,
οὐκέτι δεῖ λέγειν, ἀλλ᾽ ἁπλῶς εἰρήνην ἀκτέον, καὶ
τά γ᾽ ἀφ᾽ ὑμῶν ἕτοιμ᾽ ὑπάρχονθ᾽ ὁρῶ· εἰ δ᾽, ἃ μὲν 15
ὠμόσαμεν καὶ ἐφ᾽ οἷς τὴν εἰρήνην ἐποιησάμεθα,
ἔστιν ἰδεῖν καὶ γεγραμμένα κεῖται, φαίνεται δ᾽ ἀπ᾽ 6
ἀρχῆς ὁ Φίλιππος, πρὶν Διοπείθην ἐκπλεῦσαι καὶ IX, 15
τοὺς κληρούχους, οὓς νῦν αἰτιῶνται πεποιηκέναι τὸν
πόλεμον, πολλὰ μὲν τῶν ἡμετέρων ἀδίκως εἰλη- 20
φώς, ὑπὲρ ὧν ψηφίσμαθ᾽ ὑμέτερ᾽ ἐγκαλοῦντα κύρια
ταυτί, πάντα δὲ τὸν χρόνον συνεχῶς τὰ τῶν ἄλλων
Ἑλλήνων καὶ βαρβάρων λαμβάνων καὶ ἐφ᾽ ἡμᾶς
συσκευαζόμενος, τί τοῦτο λέγουσιν, ὡς πολεμεῖν ἢ
ἄγειν εἰρήνην δεῖ; οὐ γὰρ αἵρεσίς ἐστιν ἡμῖν τοῦ 7
πράγματος, ἀλλ᾽ ὑπολείπεται τὸ δικαιότατον καὶ 26
ἀναγκαιότατον τῶν ἔργων, ὃ ὑπερβαίνουσιν ἑκόντες
οὗτοι. τί οὖν ἐστι τοῦτο; ἀμύνεσθαι τὸν πρότερον

6*

πολεμοῦνϑ᾽ ἡμῖν· πλὴν εἰ τοῦτο λέγουσι νὴ Δί᾽,
ὡς, ἂν ἀπέχηται τῆς Ἀττικῆς καὶ τοῦ Πειραιῶς,
Φίλιππος οὔτ᾽ ἀδικεῖ τὴν πόλιν οὔτε ποιεῖ πόλε-
8 μον. εἰ δ᾽ ἐκ τούτων τὰ δίκαια τίϑενται καὶ τὴν
5 εἰρήνην ταύτην ὁρίζονται, ὅτι μὲν δήπουϑεν οὔϑ᾽
ὅσια οὔτ᾽ ἀνεκτὰ λέγουσιν οὔϑ᾽ ὑμῖν ἀσφαλῆ,
δῆλόν ἐστιν ἅπασιν, οὐ μὴν ἀλλ᾽ ἐναντία συμβαίνει
ταῖς κατηγορίαις, ἃς Διοπείϑους κατηγοροῦσιν, καὶ
αὐτὰ ταῦτα λέγειν αὐτούς. τί γὰρ δή ποτε τῷ
10 μὲν Φιλίππῳ πάντα τἆλλα ποιεῖν ἐξουσίαν δώσομεν,
ἂν τῆς Ἀττικῆς ἀπέχηται, τῷ Διοπείϑει δ᾽ οὐδὲ
βοηϑεῖν τοῖς Θρᾳξὶν ἐξέσται, ἢ πόλεμον ποιεῖν
9 αὐτὸν φήσομεν; ἀλλὰ νὴ Δία ταῦτα μὲν ἐξελέγχονται, δεινὰ ποιοῦσι δ᾽ οἱ ξένοι περικόπτοντες τὰν
15 Ἑλλησπόντῳ, καὶ Διοπείϑης ἀδικεῖ κατάγων τὰ
πλοῖα, καὶ δεῖ μὴ ᾽πιτρέπειν αὐτῷ. ἔστω, γιγνέσϑω
ταῦτα, οὐδὲν ἀντιλέγω. οἶμαι μέντοι δεῖν, εἴπερ
ὡς ἀληϑῶς ἐπὶ πᾶσι δικαίοις ταῦτα συμβουλεύουσιν,
10 ὥσπερ τὴν ὑπάρχουσαν τῇ πόλει δύναμιν καταλῦσαι
20 ζητοῦσι, τὸν ἐφεστηκότα καὶ πορίζοντα χρήματα
ταύτῃ διαβάλλοντες ἐν ὑμῖν, οὕτω τὴν Φιλίππου
δύναμιν δεῖξαι διαλυϑησομένην, ἂν ὑμεῖς ταῦτα
πεισϑῆτε. εἰ δὲ μή, σκοπεῖϑ᾽ ὅτι οὐδὲν ἄλλο
ποιοῦσιν ἢ καϑιστᾶσι τὴν πόλιν εἰς τὸν αὐτὸν
25 τρόπον, δι᾽ οὗ τὰ παρόντα πράγμαϑ᾽ ἅπαντ᾽
11 ἀπολώλεκεν. ἴστε γὰρ δήπου τοῦϑ᾽, ὅτι οὐδενὶ
τῶν πάντων πλέον κεκράτηκε Φίλιππος ἢ τῷ πρότερος πρὸς τοῖς πράγμασι γίγνεσϑαι. ὁ μὲν γὰρ
ἔχων δύναμιν συνεστηκυῖαν ἀεὶ περὶ αὑτὸν καὶ

προειδώς, ἃ βούλεται πρᾶξαι, ἐξαίφνης, ἐφ᾽ οὓς ἂν
αὐτῷ δόξῃ, πάρεστιν. ἡμεῖς δ᾽, ἐπειδὰν πυθώμεθά
τι. γιγνόμενον, τηνικαῦτα θορυβούμεθα καὶ παρα-
σκευαζόμεθα. εἶτ᾽, οἶμαι, συμβαίνει τῷ μέν, ἐφ᾽ 12
ἃ ἂν ἔλθῃ, ταῦτ᾽ ἔχειν κατὰ πολλὴν ἡσυχίαν, ἡμῖν 5
δ᾽ ὑστερίζειν καί, ὅσ᾽ ἂν δαπανήσωμεν, ἅπαντα
μάτην ἀνηλωκέναι, καὶ τὴν μὲν ἔχθραν καὶ τὸ
βούλεσθαι κωλύειν ἐνδεδεῖχθαι, ὑστερίζοντας δὲ
τῶν ἔργων αἰσχύνην προσοφλισκάνειν.

Μὴ τοίνυν ἀγνοεῖτ᾽, ὦ ἄνδρες Ἀθηναῖοι, ὅτι 13
καὶ τὰ νῦν τἆλλα μέν ἐστι λόγοι ταῦτα καὶ προ- 11
φάσεις, πράττεται δὲ καὶ κατασκευάζεται τοῦτο,
ὅπως ὑμῶν μὲν οἴκοι μενόντων, ἔξω δὲ μηδεμιᾶς οὔσης τῇ πόλει δυνάμεως, μετὰ πλείστης
ἡσυχίας ἅπανθ᾽ ὅσα βούλεται Φίλιππος διοι- 15
κήσεται. θεωρεῖτε γὰρ τὸ παρὸν πρῶτον, ὃ 14
γίγνεται. νυνὶ δύναμιν μεγάλην ἐκεῖνος ἔχων ἐν
Θρᾴκῃ διατρίβει καὶ μεταπέμπεται πολλήν, ὥς
φασιν οἱ παρόντες, ἀπὸ Μακεδονίας καὶ Θετταλίας.
ἐὰν οὖν περιμείνας τοὺς ἐτησίας ἐπὶ Βυζάντιον 20
ἐλθὼν πολιορκῇ, πρῶτον μὲν οἴεσθε τοὺς Βυζαντίους μενεῖν ἐπὶ τῆς ἀνοίας τῆς αὐτῆς, ὥσπερ νῦν,
καὶ οὔτε παρακαλεῖν ὑμᾶς οὔτε βοηθεῖν αὐτοῖς ἀξιώ-
σειν; ἐγὼ μὲν οὐκ οἴομαι, ἀλλὰ καὶ εἴ τισι μᾶλλον 15
ἀπιστοῦσιν ἢ ἡμῖν, καὶ τούτους εἰσφρήσεσθαι μᾶλ- 25
λον ἢ 'κείνῳ παραδώσειν τὴν πόλιν, ἄνπερ μὴ
φθάσῃ λαβὼν αὐτούς. οὐκοῦν ἡμῶν μὲν μὴ δυναμένων ἐνθένδ᾽ ἀναπλεῦσαι, ἐκεῖ δὲ μηδεμιᾶς ὑπαρχούσης ἑτοίμου βοηθείας, οὐδὲν αὐτοὺς ἀπολωλέναι

16 κωλύσει. „νὴ Δία, κακοδαιμονῶσι γὰρ ἄνθρωποι
καὶ ὑπερβάλλουσιν ἀνοίᾳ." πάνυ γε, ἀλλ᾽ ὅμως
αὐτοὺς δεῖ σῶς εἶναι· συμφέρει γὰρ τῇ πόλει. καὶ
μὴν οὐδ᾽ ἐκεῖνό γε δῆλόν ἐστιν ἡμῖν, ὡς ἐπὶ Χερρό-
5 νησον οὐχ ἥξει· ἀλλ᾽ εἰ γ᾽ ἐκ τῆς ἐπιστολῆς δεῖ
σκοπεῖν ἧς ἔπεμψε πρὸς ὑμᾶς, ἀμυνεῖσθαί φησι
17 τοὺς ἐν Χερρονήσῳ. ἂν μὲν τοίνυν ᾖ τὸ συνεστη-
κὸς στράτευμα, καὶ τῇ χώρᾳ βοηθῆσαι δυνήσεται
καὶ τῶν ἐκείνου τι κακῶς ποιῆσαι· εἰ δ᾽ ἅπαξ δια-
10 λυθήσεται, τί ποιήσομεν, ἂν ἐπὶ Χερρόνησον ἴῃ;
„κρινοῦμεν Διοπείθην νὴ Δία." καὶ τί τὰ πράγματ᾽
ἔσται βελτίω; „ἀλλ᾽ ἐνθένδ᾽ ἂν βοηθήσαιμεν αὐτοί."
ἂν δ᾽ ὑπὸ τῶν πνευμάτων μὴ δυνώμεθα; „ἀλλὰ
18 μὰ Δί᾽ οὐχ ἥξει." καὶ τίς ἐγγυητής ἐστι τούτου;
15 ἆρ᾽ ὁρᾶτε καὶ λογίζεσθε, ὦ ἄνδρες Ἀθηναῖοι, τὴν
ἐπιοῦσαν ὥραν τοῦ ἔτους, εἰς ἣν ἔρημόν τινες
οἴονται δεῖν τὸν Ἑλλήσποντον ὑμῶν ποιῆσαι καὶ
παραδοῦναι Φιλίππῳ; τί δ᾽, ἂν ἀπελθὼν ἐκ Θρά-
κης καὶ μηδὲ προσελθὼν Χερρονήσῳ μηδὲ Βυζαντίῳ
20 (καὶ γὰρ ταῦτα λογίζεσθε) ἐπὶ Χαλκίδα καὶ Μέγαρ᾽
343 ἥκῃ τὸν αὐτὸν τρόπον ὅνπερ ἐπ᾽ Ὠρεὸν πρώην,
πότερον κρεῖττον ἐνθάδ᾽ αὐτὸν ἀμύνεσθαι καὶ
προσελθεῖν τὸν πόλεμον πρὸς τὴν Ἀττικὴν ἐᾶσαι,
ἢ κατασκευάζειν ἐκεῖ τιν᾽ ἀσχολίαν αὐτῷ; ἐγὼ μὲν
25 οἴομαι τοῦτο.

19 Ταῦτα τοίνυν ἅπαντας εἰδότας καὶ λογιζομένους
χρὴ οὐ μὰ Δί᾽ οὐχ, ἣν Διοπείθης πειρᾶται τῇ
πόλει δύναμιν παρασκευάζειν, ταύτην βασκαί-
νειν καὶ διαλῦσαι πειρᾶσθαι, ἀλλ᾽ ἑτέραν αὐτοὺς

προσπαρασκευάζειν καὶ συνευποροῦντας ἐκείνῳ χρημάτων καὶ τἄλλ᾽ οἰκείως συναγωνιζομένους. εἰ 20
γάρ τις ἔροιτο Φίλιππον· „εἰπέ μοι, πότερ᾽ ἂν
βούλοιο τούτους τοὺς στρατιώτας, οὓς Διοπείθης
νῦν ἔχει, τοὺς ὁποιουστινασοῦν (οὐδὲν γὰρ ἀντι- 5
λέγω), εὐθενεῖν καὶ παρ᾽ Ἀθηναίοις εὐδοξεῖν καὶ
πλείους γίγνεσθαι τῆς πόλεως συναγωνιζομένης, ἢ
διαβαλλόντων τινῶν καὶ κατηγορούντων διασπα-
σθῆναι καὶ διαφθαρῆναι;" ταῦτ᾽ ἂν οἶμαι φήσειεν.
εἶθ᾽ ἃ Φίλιππος ἂν εὔξαιτο τοῖς θεοῖς, ταῦθ᾽ ἡμῶν 10
τινες ἐνθάδε πράττουσιν; εἶτ᾽ ἔτι ζητεῖτε, πόθεν
τὰ τῆς πόλεως ἀπόλωλεν ἅπαντα;

Βούλομαι τοίνυν ὑμᾶς μετὰ παρρησίας ἐξετά- 21
σαι τὰ παρόντα πράγματα τῇ πόλει, καὶ σκέψασθαι
τί ποιοῦμεν αὐτοὶ νῦν καὶ ὅπως χρώμεθ᾽ 15
αὐτοῖς. ἡμεῖς οὔτε χρήματ᾽ εἰσφέρειν βουλόμεθα,
οὔτ᾽ αὐτοὶ στρατεύεσθαι, οὔτε τῶν κοινῶν ἀπέ-
χεσθαι δυνάμεθα, οὔτε τὰς συντάξεις Διοπείθει
δίδομεν, οὔθ᾽ ὅσ᾽ ἂν αὐτὸς αὑτῷ πορίσηται ἐπαι- 22
νοῦμεν, ἀλλὰ βασκαίνομεν καὶ σκοποῦμεν πόθεν, 20
καὶ τί μέλλει ποιεῖν καὶ πάντα τὰ τοιαυτί, οὔτ᾽
ἐπειδήπερ οὕτως ἔχομεν, τὰ ἡμέτερ᾽ αὐτῶν πράττειν
ἐθέλομεν, ἀλλ᾽ ἐν μὲν τοῖς λόγοις τοὺς τῆς πόλεως
λέγοντας ἄξι᾽ ἐπαινοῦμεν, ἐν δὲ τοῖς ἔργοις τοῖς
ἐναντιουμένοις τούτοις συναγωνιζόμεθα. ὑμεῖς μὲν 23
τοίνυν εἰώθαθ᾽ ἑκάστοτε τὸν παριόντ᾽ ἐρωτᾶν, τί 26
οὖν χρὴ ποιεῖν; ἐγὼ δ᾽ ὑμᾶς ἐρωτῆσαι βούλομαι,
τί οὖν χρὴ λέγειν; εἰ γὰρ μήτ᾽ εἰσοίσετε, μήτ᾽ αὐτοὶ

στρατεύσεσθε, μήτε τῶν κοινῶν ἀφέξεσθε, μήτε
τὰς συντάξεις δώσετε, μήθ᾽ ὅσ᾽ ἂν αὐτῷ πορίσηται
ἐάσετε, μήτε τὰ ὑμέτερ᾽ αὐτῶν πράττειν ἐθελήσετε, οὐκ ἔχω τί λέγω. εἰ δ᾽ ἄρ᾽ ἤδη τοσαύτην
5 ἐξουσίαν τοῖς αἰτιᾶσθαι καὶ διαβάλλειν βουλομένοις δίδοτε, ὥστε καί, περὶ ὧν ἄν φασι μέλλειν
αὐτὸν ποιεῖν, καὶ περὶ τούτων προκατηγορούντων
ἀκροᾶσθαι, τί ἄν τις λέγοι;

24   Ὅ τι τοίνυν δύναται ταῦτα ποιεῖν, ἐνίους
10 μαθεῖν ὑμῶν δεῖ. λέξω δὲ μετὰ παρρησίας· καὶ
γὰρ οὐδ᾽ ἂν ἄλλως δυναίμην. πάντες ὅσοι ποτ᾽
ἐκπεπλεύκασι παρ᾽ ὑμῶν στρατηγοί (ἢ ᾽γὼ πάσχειν
ὁτιοῦν τιμῶμαι) καὶ παρὰ Χίων καὶ παρ᾽ Ἐρυ-
θραίων καὶ παρ᾽ ὧν ἂν ἕκαστοι δύνωνται, τούτων
15 τῶν τὴν Ἀσίαν οἰκούντων λέγω, χρήματα λαμβά-
25 νουσιν. λαμβάνουσι δ᾽ οἱ μὲν ἔχοντες μίαν ἢ
δύο ναῦς ἐλάττονα, οἱ δὲ μείζω δύναμιν πλείονα.
καὶ διδόασιν οἱ διδόντες οὔτε τὰ μικρὰ οὔτε τὰ
πόλλ᾽ ἀντ᾽ οὐδενός (οὐ γὰρ οὕτω μαίνονται), ἀλλ᾽
20 ὠνούμενοι μὴ ἀδικεῖσθαι τοὺς παρ᾽ αὐτῶν ἐκπλέ-
οντας ἐμπόρους, μὴ συλᾶσθαι, παραπέμπεσθαι τὰ
πλοῖα τὰ αὐτῶν, τὰ τοιαῦτα· φασὶ δ᾽ εὐνοίας
διδόναι, καὶ τοῦτο τοὔνομ᾽ ἔχει τὰ λήμματα ταῦτα.
26 καὶ δὴ καὶ νῦν τῷ Διοπείθει στράτευμ᾽ ἔχοντι
25 σαφῶς ἐστι τοῦτο δῆλον ὅτι δώσουσι χρήματα
πάντες οὗτοι. πόθεν γὰρ οἴεσθ᾽ ἄλλοθεν τὸν
μήτε λαβόντα παρ᾽ ὑμῶν μηδέν, μήτ᾽ αὐτὸν
ἔχονθ᾽ ὁπόθεν μισθοδοτήσει στρατιώτας τρέφειν;
ἐκ τοῦ οὐρανοῦ; οὐκ ἔστι ταῦτα, ἀλλ᾽ ἀφ᾽ ὧν

ἀγείρει καὶ προσαιτεῖ καὶ δανείζεται, ἀπὸ τούτων
διάγει. οὐδὲν οὖν ἄλλο ποιοῦσιν οἱ κατηγοροῦντες 27
ἐν ὑμῖν ἢ προλέγουσιν ἅπασι μηδ᾽ ὁτιοῦν
ἐκείνῳ διδόναι, ὡς καὶ τοῦ μελλῆσαι δώσοντι
δίκην, μή τι ποιήσαντί γ᾽ ἢ καταπραξαμένῳ. τοῦτ᾽ 5
εἰσὶν οἱ λόγοι „μέλλει πολιορκεῖν“, „τοὺς Ἕλληνας
ἐκδίδωσιν“. μέλει γὰρ τινι τούτων τῶν τὴν
Ἀσίαν οἰκούντων Ἑλλήνων· ἀμείνους μεντἂν εἶεν
τῶν ἄλλων ἢ τῆς πατρίδος κήδεσθαι.

Καὶ τό γ᾽ εἰς τὸν Ἑλλήσποντον εἰσπέμ- 28
πειν ἕτερον στρατηγὸν τοῦτ᾽ ἔστιν. εἰ γὰρ 11
δεινὰ ποιεῖ Διοπείθης καὶ κατάγει τὰ πλοῖα, μικρόν,
ὦ ἄνδρες Ἀθηναῖοι, μικρὸν πινάκιον ταῦτα πάντα
κωλῦσαι δύναιτ᾽ ἄν, καὶ λέγουσιν οἱ νόμοι, ταῦτα
τοὺς ἀδικοῦντας εἰσαγγέλλειν, οὐ μὰ Δία δαπάναις 15
καὶ τριήρεσι τοσαύταις ἡμᾶς αὐτοὺς φυλάττειν,
ἐπεὶ τοῦτό γ᾽ ἐστὶν ὑπερβολὴ μανίας· ἀλλ᾽ ἐπὶ 29
μὲν τοὺς ἐχθρούς, οὓς οὐκ ἔστι λαβεῖν ὑπὸ τοῖς
νόμοις, καὶ στρατιώτας τρέφειν καὶ τριήρεις ἐκπέμπειν καὶ χρήματ᾽ εἰσφέρειν δεῖ καὶ ἀναγκαῖόν 20
ἐστιν, ἐπὶ δ᾽ ἡμᾶς αὐτοὺς ψήφισμα, εἰσαγγελία,
πάραλος, ταῦτ᾽ ἔστιν. ταῦτ᾽ ἦν εὖ φρονούντων
ἀνθρώπων, ἐπηρεαζόντων δὲ καὶ διαφθειρόντων
τὰ πράγματα, ἃ νῦν οὗτοι ποιοῦσιν.

Καὶ τὸ μὲν τούτων τινὰς εἶναι τοιούτους 30
δεινὸν ὂν οὐ δεινόν ἐστιν· ἀλλ᾽ ὑμεῖς οἱ καθή- 26
μενοι οὕτως ἤδη διάκεισθε, ὥστ᾽, ἂν μέν τις εἴπῃ
παρελθών, ὅτι Διοπείθης ἐστὶ τῶν κακῶν πάντων
αἴτιος ἢ Χάρης ἢ Ἀριστοφῶν ἢ ὃν ἂν τῶν πολι-

τῶν εἴπῃ τις, εὐθέως φατὲ καὶ θορυβεῖθ', ὡς
31 ὀρθῶς λέγει· ἂν δὲ παρελθὼν λέγῃ τις τἀληθῆ,
ὅτι „ληρεῖτ', Ἀθηναῖοι· πάντων τῶν κακῶν καὶ
τῶν πραγμάτων τούτων Φίλιππός ἐστ' αἴτιος· εἰ
5 γὰρ ἐκεῖνος ἦγεν ἡσυχίαν, οὐδὲν ἂν ἦν πρᾶγμα
τῇ πόλει,“ ὡς μὲν οὐκ ἀληθῆ ταῦτ' ἐστίν, οὐκ
ἔχετ' ἀντιλέγειν, ἄχθεσθαι δέ μοι δοκεῖτε καὶ
32 ὥσπερ ἀπολλύναι τι νομίζειν. αἴτιον δὲ τούτων
(καί μοι πρὸς θεῶν, ὅταν ἕνεκα τοῦ βελτίστου
10 λέγω, ἔστω παρρησία)· παρεσκευάκασιν ὑμᾶς τῶν
πολιτευομένων ἔνιοι ἐν μὲν ταῖς ἐκκλησίαις
φοβεροὺς καὶ χαλεπούς, ἐν δὲ ταῖς παρασκευαῖς ταῖς τοῦ πολέμου ῥᾳθύμους καὶ
εὐκαταφρονήτους. ἂν μὲν οὖν τὸν αἴτιον εἴπῃ
15 τις, ὃν ἴσθ' ὅτι λήψεσθε παρ' ὑμῖν αὐτοῖς, φατὲ
καὶ βούλεσθε· ἂν δὲ τοιοῦτον λέγῃ τις, ὃν κρατήσαντας τοῖς ὅπλοις, ἄλλως δ' οὐκ ἔστιν κολάσαι,
οὐκ ἔχετ' οἶμαι τί ποιήσετε, ἐξελεγχόμενοι δ'
33 ἄχθεσθε. ἐχρῆν γάρ, ὦ ἄνδρες Ἀθηναῖοι, τοὐναν-
20 τίον ἢ νῦν ἅπαντας τοὺς πολιτευομένους ἐν μὲν
ταῖς ἐκκλησίαις πρᾴους καὶ φιλανθρώπους ὑμᾶς
ἐθίζειν εἶναι (πρὸς γὰρ ὑμᾶς αὐτοὺς καὶ τοὺς συμμάχους ἐν ταύταις ἐστὶ τὰ δίκαια), ἐν δὲ ταῖς
παρασκευαῖς ταῖς τοῦ πολέμου φοβεροὺς καὶ χαλε-
25 πούς ἐπιδεικνύναι· πρὸς γὰρ τοὺς ἐχθροὺς καὶ
34 τοὺς ἀντιπάλους ἐκείναις ἐσθ' ἀγών. νῦν δὲ
δημαγωγοῦντες ὑμᾶς καὶ χαριζόμενοι καθ' ὑπερ-
βολὴν οὕτω διατεθήκασιν, ὥστ' ἐν μὲν ταῖς ἐκκλησίαις τρυφᾶν καὶ κολακεύεσθαι πάντα πρὸς ἡδονὴν

ἀκούοντας, ἐν δὲ τοῖς πράγμασι καὶ τοῖς γιγνομένοις περὶ τῶν ἐσχάτων ἤδη κινδυνεύειν.

Φέρε γὰρ πρὸς Διός, εἰ λόγον ὑμᾶς ἀπαι-
τήσειαν οἱ Ἕλληνες ὧν νυνὶ παρείκατε καιρῶν
διὰ ῥᾳθυμίαν, καὶ ἔροινθ᾽ ὑμᾶς· „ἄνδρες Ἀθηναῖοι, 35
πέμπεθ᾽ ὡς ἡμᾶς ἑκάστοτε πρέσβεις καὶ λέγεθ᾽, 6
ὡς ἐπιβουλεύει Φίλιππος ἡμῖν καὶ πᾶσι τοῖς
Ἕλλησιν, καὶ ὡς φυλάττεσθαι δεῖ τὸν ἄνθρωπον
καὶ πάντα τὰ τοιαυτί;“ ἀνάγκη φάσκειν καὶ ὁμο-
λογεῖν· ποιοῦμεν γὰρ ταῦτα. „εἶτ᾽, ὦ πάντων 10
ἀνθρώπων φαυλότατοι, δέκα μῆνας ἀπογενομένου
τἀνθρώπου καὶ νόσῳ καὶ χειμῶνι καὶ πολέμοις
ἀποληφθέντος, ὥστε μὴ ἂν δύνασθαι ἐπανελθεῖν
οἴκαδε, οὔτε τὴν Εὔβοιαν ἠλευθερώσατε οὔτε τῶν 36
ὑμετέρων αὐτῶν οὐδὲν ἐκομίσασθε, ἀλλ᾽ ἐκεῖνος 15
μὲν ὑμῶν οἴκοι μενόντων, σχολὴν ἀγόντων, ὑγιαι-
νόντων“ (εἰ δὴ τοὺς τὰ τοιαῦτα ποιοῦντας ὑγιαί-
νειν φήσαιεν) „δύο ἐν Εὐβοίᾳ κατέστησε τυράννους,
τὸν μὲν ἀπαντικρὺ τῆς Ἀττικῆς ἐπιτειχίσας, τὸν   37
                                                 343
δ᾽ ἐπὶ Σκίαθον, ὑμεῖς δ᾽ οὐδὲ ταῦτ᾽ ἀπελύσασθε, 20
εἰ μηδὲν ἄλλ᾽ ἐβούλεσθε, ἀλλ᾽ εἰάκατε; ἀφέστατε
δῆλον ὅτι αὐτῷ, καὶ φανερὸν πεποιήκατε, ὅτι οὐδ᾽
ἂν δεκάκις ἀποθάνῃ, οὐδὲν μᾶλλον κινήσεσθε. τί
οὖν πρεσβεύετε καὶ κατηγορεῖτε καὶ πράγμαθ᾽ ἡμῖν
παρέχετε;“ ἂν ταῦτα λέγωσιν, τί ἐροῦμεν ἢ τί 25
φήσομεν, Ἀθηναῖοι; ἐγὼ μὲν γὰρ οὐχ ὁρῶ.

Εἰσὶ τοίνυν τινές, οἳ τότ᾽ ἐξελέγχειν τὸν 38
παριόντ᾽ οἴονται, ἐπειδὰν ἐρωτήσωσι, „τί οὖν χρὴ

ποιεῖν;" οἷς ἐγὼ μὲν τὸ δικαιότατον καὶ ἀληθέ-
στατον τοῦτ᾽ ἀποκρινοῦμαι, ταῦτα μὴ ποιεῖν ἃ
νυνὶ ποιεῖτε, οὐ μὴν ἀλλὰ καὶ καθ᾽ ἕκαστον ἀκριβῶς ἐρῶ. καὶ ὅπως, ὥσπερ ἐρωτῶσι προθύμως,
39 οὕτω καὶ ποιεῖν ἐθελήσουσιν. πρῶτον μέν, ὦ
6 ἄνδρες Ἀθηναῖοι, τοῦτο παρ᾽ ὑμῖν αὐτοῖς βεβαίως
γνῶναι, ὅτι τῇ πόλει Φίλιππος πολεμεῖ καὶ
τὴν εἰρήνην λέλυκεν (καὶ παύσασθε περὶ τούτου
κατηγοροῦντες ἀλλήλων) καὶ κακόνους μέν ἐστι
10 καὶ ἐχθρὸς ὅλῃ τῇ πόλει καὶ τῷ τῆς πόλεως ἐδάφει,
40 προσθήσω δὲ καὶ τοῖς ἐν τῇ πόλει πᾶσιν ἀνθρώποις, καὶ τοῖς μάλιστ᾽ οἰομένοις αὐτῷ χαρίζεσθαι
(εἰ δὲ μή, σκεψάσθωσαν Εὐθυκράτη καὶ Λασθένη
τοὺς Ὀλυνθίους, οἳ δοκοῦντες οἰκειότατ᾽ αὐτῷ δια-
15 κεῖσθαι, ἐπειδὴ τὴν πόλιν προΰδοσαν, πάντων
κάκιστ᾽ ἀπολώλασιν), οὐδενὶ μέντοι μᾶλλον ἢ τῇ
πολιτείᾳ πολεμεῖ, οὐδ᾽ ἐπιβουλεύει καὶ σκοπεῖ
μᾶλλον οὐδὲ ἓν τῶν πάντων ἢ πῶς ταύτην κατα-
41 λύσει. καὶ τοῦτ᾽ εἰκότως τρόπον τινὰ πράττει·
20 οἶδε γὰρ ἀκριβῶς, ὅτι οὐδ᾽ ἐὰν πάντων τῶν ἄλλων
γένηται κύριος, οὐδὲν ἔστ᾽ αὐτῷ βεβαίως ἔχειν,
ἕως ἂν ὑμεῖς δημοκρατῆσθε, ἀλλ᾽ ἐάν ποτε συμβῇ
τι πταῖσμα, ἃ πολλὰ γένοιτ᾽ ἂν ἀνθρώπῳ, ἥξει
πάντα τὰ νῦν συμβεβιασμένα καὶ καταφεύξεται
42 πρὸς ὑμᾶς. ἐστὲ γὰρ ὑμεῖς οὐκ αὐτοὶ πλεονεκτῆσαι
26 καὶ κατασχεῖν ἀρχὴν εὖ πεφυκότες, ἀλλ᾽ ἕτερον
λαβεῖν κωλῦσαι καὶ ἔχοντ᾽ ἀφελέσθαι δεινοί, καὶ
ὅλως ἐνοχλῆσαι τοῖς ἄρχειν βουλομένοις καὶ πάντας
ἀνθρώπους εἰς ἐλευθερίαν ἀφελέσθαι ἕτοιμοι.

οὔκουν βούλεται τοῖς ἑαυτοῦ καιροῖς τὴν παρ᾽
ὑμῶν ἐλευθερίαν ἐφεδρεύειν, οὐδὲ πολλοῦ δεῖ, οὐ
κακῶς οὐδ᾽ ἀργῶς ταῦτα λογιζόμενος.

Πρῶτον μὲν δὴ τοῦτο δεῖ, ἐχθρὸν ὑπειλη- 43
φέναι τῆς πολιτείας καὶ τῆς δημοκρατίας ἀδιάλλακ- 5
τον ἐκεῖνον· εἰ γὰρ μὴ τοῦτο πεισθήσεσθε ταῖς
ψυχαῖς, οὐκ ἐθελήσεθ᾽ ὑπὲρ τῶν πραγμάτων σπου-
δάζειν· δεύτερον δ᾽ εἰδέναι σαφῶς, ὅτι πάνθ᾽,
ὅσα πραγματεύεται καὶ κατασκευάζεται νῦν,
ἐπὶ τὴν ἡμετέραν πόλιν παρασκευάζεται, καὶ 10
ὅπου τις ἐκεῖνον ἀμύνεται, ἐνταῦθ᾽ ὑπὲρ
ὑμῶν ἀμύνεται. οὐ γὰρ οὕτω γ᾽ εὐήθης ἐστὶν 44
οὐδείς, ὃς ὑπολαμβάνει τὸν Φίλιππον τῶν μὲν ἐν
Θρᾴκῃ κακῶν (τί γὰρ ἄλλο τις ἂν εἴποι Δρογγίλον
καὶ Καβύλην καὶ Μάστειραν καὶ ἃ νῦν ἐξαιρεῖ) 15
τούτων μὲν ἐπιθυμεῖν καὶ ὑπὲρ τοῦ ταῦτα λαβεῖν
καὶ πόνους καὶ χειμῶνας καὶ τοὺς ἐσχάτους κινδύνους ὑπομένειν, τῶν δ᾽ Ἀθηναίων λιμένων καὶ 45
νεωρίων καὶ τριήρων καὶ τῶν ἔργων τῶν ἀργυ-
ρείων καὶ τοσούτων προσόδων οὐκ ἐπιθυμεῖν, 20
ἀλλὰ ταῦτα μὲν ὑμᾶς ἐάσειν ἔχειν, ὑπὲρ δὲ τῶν
μελινῶν καὶ τῶν ὀλυρῶν τῶν ἐν τοῖς Θρᾳκίοις
σιροῖς ἐν τῷ βαράθρῳ χειμάζειν. οὐκ ἔστι ταῦτα, 46
ἀλλὰ κἀκεῖν᾽ ὑπὲρ τοῦ τούτων γενέσθαι κύριος
καὶ τἆλλα πάντα πραγματεύεται. τί οὖν εὖ φρο- 25
νούντων ἀνθρώπων ἐστίν; εἰδότας ταῦτα καὶ ἐγνωκότας τὴν μὲν ὑπερβάλλουσαν καὶ ἀνείκαστον ταύτην ῥᾳθυμίαν ἀποθέσθαι, χρήματα δ᾽ εἰσφέρειν
καὶ τοὺς συμμάχους ἀξιοῦν, καὶ ὅπως τὸ συνεστη-

κὸς τοῦτο συμμενεῖ στράτευμα δρᾶν καὶ πράττειν,
ἵν᾽ ὥσπερ ἐκεῖνος ἕτοιμον ἔχει δύναμιν τὴν ἀδική-
σουσαν καὶ καταδουλωσομένην ἅπαντας τοὺς Ἕλληνας, οὕτω τὴν σώσουσαν ὑμεῖς καὶ βοηθήσουσαν
47 ἅπασιν ἕτοιμον ἔχητε. οὐ γὰρ ἔστι βοηθείαις
6 χρωμένους οὐδέποτ᾽ οὐδὲν τῶν δεόντων πρᾶξαι,
ἀλλὰ κατασκευάσαντας δεῖ δύναμιν καὶ τροφὴν
ταύτῃ πορίσαντας καὶ ταμίας καὶ δημοσίους καί,
ὅπως ἔνι τὴν τῶν χρημάτων φυλακὴν ἀκριβεστά-
10 την γενέσθαι, οὕτω ποιήσαντας τὸν μὲν τῶν χρημάτων λόγον παρὰ τούτων λαμβάνειν, τὸν δὲ τῶν
ἔργων παρὰ τοῦ στρατηγοῦ. κἂν οὕτω ποιήσητε
καὶ ταῦτ᾽ ἐθελήσηθ᾽ ὡς ἀληθῶς, ἄγειν εἰρήνην
δικαίαν καὶ μένειν ἐπὶ τῆς αὑτοῦ Φίλιππον ἀναγ-
15 κάσετε, οὗ μεῖζον οὐδὲν ἂν γένοιτ᾽ ἀγαθόν, ἢ
πολεμήσετ᾽ ἐξ ἴσου.

48   Εἰ δέ τῳ δοκεῖ ταῦτα καὶ δαπάνης μεγάλης
καὶ πόνων πολλῶν καὶ πραγματείας εἶναι, καὶ μάλ᾽
ὀρθῶς δοκεῖ· ἀλλ᾽ ἐὰν λογίζηται τὰ τῇ πόλει
20 μετὰ ταῦτα γενησόμενα, ἂν ταῦτα μὴ θέλῃ,
εὑρήσει λυσιτελοῦν τὸ ἑκόντας ποιεῖν τὰ
49 δέοντα. εἰ μὲν γάρ ἐστί τις ἐγγυητὴς (θεῶν· οὐ
γὰρ ἀνθρώπων γ᾽ οὐδεὶς ἂν γένοιτ᾽ ἀξιόχρεως
τηλικούτου πράγματος), ὡς, ἐὰν ἄγηθ᾽ ἡσυχίαν
25 καὶ ἅπαντα προῆσθε, οὐκ ἐπ᾽ αὐτοὺς ὑμᾶς τελευτῶν
ἐκεῖνος ἥξει, αἰσχρὸν μέν, νὴ τὸν Δία καὶ πάντας
τοὺς θεούς, καὶ ἀνάξιον ὑμῶν καὶ τῶν ὑπαρχόντων
τῇ πόλει καὶ πεπραγμένων τοῖς προγόνοις, τῆς
ἰδίας ἕνεκα ῥᾳθυμίας τοὺς ἄλλους πάντας Ἕλληνας

εἰς δουλείαν προέσθαι, καὶ ἔγωγ᾽ αὐτὸς μὲν
τεθνάναι μᾶλλον ἂν ἢ ταῦτ᾽ εἰρηκέναι βουλοίμην·
οὐ μὴν ἀλλ᾽ εἴ τις ἄλλος λέγει καὶ ὑμᾶς πείθει,
ἔστω, μὴ ἀμύνεσθε, ἅπαντα πρόεσθε. εἰ δὲ μηδενὶ 50
τοῦτο δοκεῖ, τοὐναντίον δὲ πρόϊσμεν ἅπαντες, ὅτι 5
ὅσῳ ἂν πλειόνων ἐάσωμεν ἐκεῖνον γενέσθαι κύριον,
τοσούτῳ χαλεπωτέρῳ καὶ ἰσχυροτέρῳ χρησόμεθ᾽
ἐχθρῷ, ποῖ ἀναδυόμεθα, ἢ τί μέλλομεν; ἢ πότε,
ὦ ἄνδρες Ἀθηναῖοι, τὰ δέοντα ποιεῖν ἐθελήσομεν;
„ὅταν νὴ Δί᾽ ἀναγκαῖον ᾖ." ἀλλ᾽ ἣν μὲν ἂν τις 51
ἐλευθέρων ἀνθρώπων ἀνάγκην εἴποι, οὐ μόνον 11
ἤδη πάρεστιν, ἀλλὰ καὶ πάλαι παρελήλυθεν, τὴν
δὲ τῶν δούλων ἀπεύχεσθαι δήπου μὴ γενέσθαι
δεῖ. διαφέρει δὲ τί; ὅτι ἐστὶν ἐλευθέρῳ μὲν ἀνθρώπῳ μεγίστη ἀνάγκη ἡ ὑπὲρ τῶν γιγνομένων 15
αἰσχύνη, καὶ μείζω ταύτης οὐκ οἶδ᾽ ἥντιν᾽ ἂν
εἴποιμεν, δούλῳ δὲ πληγαὶ καὶ ὁ τοῦ σώματος
αἰκισμός, ἃ μήτε γένοιτ᾽ οὔτε λέγειν ἄξιον.

Πάντα τοίνυν τἄλλ᾽ εἰπὼν ἂν ἡδέως καὶ 52
δείξας, ὃν τρόπον ὑμᾶς ἔνιοι καταπολιτεύον- 20
ται, τὰ μὲν ἄλλ᾽ ἐάσω· ἀλλ᾽ ἐπειδάν τι τῶν πρὸς
Φίλιππον ἐμπέσῃ, εὐθὺς ἀναστάς τις λέγει „τὸ
τὴν εἰρήνην ἄγειν ὡς ἀγαθὸν" καὶ „τὸ τρέφειν
δύναμιν μεγάλην ὡς χαλεπόν", καὶ „διαρπάζειν
τινὲς τὰ χρήματα βούλονται", καὶ τοιούτους λόγους, 25
ἐξ ὧν ἀναβάλλουσι μὲν ὑμᾶς, ἡσυχίαν δὲ
ποιοῦσιν ἐκείνῳ πράττειν ὅ τι βούλεται. ἐκ 53
δὲ τούτων περιγίγνεται ὑμῖν μὲν ἡ σχολὴ καὶ τὸ

μηδὲν ἤδη ποιεῖν, ἃ δέδοιχ᾽ ὅπως μή ποθ᾽ ἡγήσησθ᾽
ἐπὶ πολλῷ γεγενῆσθαι, τούτοις δ᾽ αἱ χάριτες καὶ
ὁ μισθὸς ὁ τούτων. ἐγὼ δ᾽ οἴομαι τὴν μὲν
εἰρήνην ἄγειν οὐχ ὑμᾶς δεῖν πείθειν, οἳ πεπει-
5 σμένοι κάθησθε, ἀλλὰ τὸν τὰ τοῦ πολέμου πράτ-
54 τοντα· ἂν γὰρ ἐκεῖνος πεισθῇ, τά γ᾽ ἀφ᾽ ὑμῶν
ὑπάρχει· νομίζειν δ᾽ εἶναι χαλεπὰ οὐχ, ὅσ᾽ ἂν
εἰς σωτηρίαν δαπανῶμεν, ἀλλ᾽ ἃ πεισόμεθα, ἂν
ταῦτα μὴ θέλωμεν ποιεῖν· καὶ τὸ „διαρπασθήσεται
10 τὰ χρήματα“ τῷ φυλακὴν εἰπεῖν, δι᾽ ἣν σωθήσεται,
κωλύειν, οὐχὶ τῷ τοῦ συμφέροντος ἀφεστάναι.
55 καίτοι ἔγωγ᾽ ἀγανακτῶ καὶ αὐτὸ τοῦτο, ὦ ἄνδρες
Ἀθηναῖοι, εἰ τὰ μὲν χρήματα λυπεῖ τινας ὑμῶν
εἰ διαρπασθήσεται, ἃ καὶ φυλάττειν καὶ κολάζειν
15 τοὺς ἀδικοῦντας ἐφ᾽ ὑμῖν ἐστι, τὴν δ᾽ Ἑλλάδα
πᾶσαν οὑτωσὶ Φίλιππος ἐφεξῆς ἁρπάζων οὐ λυπεῖ,
καὶ ταῦτ᾽ ἐφ᾽ ὑμᾶς ἁρπάζων.

56   Τί ποτ᾽ οὖν ἐστι τὸ αἴτιον, ὦ ἄνδρες Ἀθηναῖοι,
τὸ τὸν μὲν οὕτω φανερῶς στρατεύοντα, ἀδικοῦντα,
20 πόλεις καταλαμβάνοντα μηδένα τούτων πώποτ᾽
εἰπεῖν ὡς πόλεμον ποιεῖ, τοὺς δὲ μὴ ᾽πιτρέπειν
μηδὲ προΐεσθαι ταῦτα συμβουλεύοντας, τούτους
57 τὸν πόλεμον ποιήσειν αἰτιᾶσθαι; ἐγὼ διδάξω· ὅτι
τὴν ὀργήν, ἣν εἰκός ἐστι γενέσθαι παρ᾽
25 ὑμῖν, ἄν τι λυπῆσθε τῷ πολέμῳ, εἰς τοὺς
ὑπὲρ ὑμῶν λέγοντας τὰ βέλτιστα τρέψαι
βούλονται, ἵνα τούτους κρίνητε, μὴ Φίλιππον
ἀμύνησθε, καὶ κατηγορῶσιν αὐτοί, μὴ δίκην δῶσιν
ὧν ποιοῦσι νῦν. τοῦτ᾽ αὐτοῖς δύναται τὸ λέγειν,

ὡς ἄρα βούλονται πόλεμόν τινες ποιῆσαι παρ᾽ ὑμῖν,
καὶ περὶ τούτου ἡ διαδικασία αὕτη ἐστίν. ἐγὼ δ᾽ 58
οἶδ᾽ ἀκριβῶς, ὅτι οὐ γράψαντος Ἀθηναίων οὐδενός
πω πόλεμον καὶ ἄλλα πολλὰ Φίλιππος ἔχει τῶν
τῆς πόλεως καὶ νῦν εἰς Καρδίαν πέπομφε βοήθειαν. 5
εἰ μέντοι βουλόμεθ᾽ ἡμεῖς μὴ προσποιεῖσθαι
πολεμεῖν αὐτὸν ἡμῖν, ἀνοητότατος πάντων ἂν εἴη
τῶν ὄντων ἀνθρώπων, εἰ τοῦτ᾽ ἐξελέγχοι. ἀλλ᾽ 59
ἐπειδὰν ἐπ᾽ αὐτοὺς ἡμᾶς ἴῃ, τί φήσομεν; ἐκεῖνος
μὲν γὰρ οὐ πολεμεῖν, ὥσπερ οὐδ᾽ Ὠρείταις τῶν 343
στρατιωτῶν ὄντων ἐν τῇ χώρᾳ, οὐδὲ Φεραίοις 11
πρότερον πρὸς τὰ τείχη προσβάλλων αὐτῶν, οὐδ᾽ 344
Ὀλυνθίοις ἐξ ἀρχῆς, ἕως ἐν αὐτῇ τῇ χώρᾳ τὸ 349
στράτευμα παρῆν ἔχων. ἢ καὶ τότε τοὺς ἀμύνε- **IX, 11**
σθαι κελεύοντας πόλεμον ποιεῖν φήσομεν; οὐκοῦν 15
ὑπόλοιπον δουλεύειν· οὐ γὰρ ἄλλο γ᾽ οὐδέν ἐστι
μεταξὺ τοῦ μήτ᾽ ἀμύνεσθαι μήτ᾽ ἄγειν ἡσυχίαν
ἐᾶσθαι. καὶ μὴν οὐχ ὑπὲρ τῶν ἴσων ὑμῖν καὶ 60
τοῖς ἄλλοις ἔσθ᾽ ὁ κίνδυνος· οὐ γὰρ ὑφ᾽ αὑτῷ
τὴν πόλιν ποιήσασθαι βούλεται Φίλιππος, ἀλλ᾽ 20
ὅλως ἀνελεῖν. οἶδε γὰρ ἀκριβῶς, ὅτι δουλεύειν
μὲν ὑμεῖς οὔτ᾽ ἐθελήσετε, οὔτ᾽, ἂν ἐθελήσητ᾽,
ἐπιστήσεσθε (ἄρχειν γὰρ εἰώθατε), πράγματα δ᾽
αὐτῷ παρασχεῖν, ἂν καιρὸν λάβητε, πλείω τῶν
ἄλλων ἁπάντων ἀνθρώπων δυνήσεσθε. 25

Ὡς οὖν ὑπὲρ τῶν ἐσχάτων ὄντος τοῦ ἀγῶνος 61
οὕτω προσήκει γιγνώσκειν καὶ τοὺς πεπρακότας
αὑτοὺς ἐκείνῳ μισεῖν καὶ ἀποτυμπανίσαι. οὐ γὰρ
ἔστιν, οὐκ ἔστιν τῶν ἔξω τῆς πόλεως ἐχθρῶν

κρατῆσαι, πρὶν ἂν τοὺς ἐν αὐτῇ τῇ πόλει κολάσητ᾽
62 ἐχθρούς. πόθεν οἴεσθε νῦν αὐτὸν ὑβρίζειν
ὑμᾶς (οὐδὲν γὰρ ἀλλ᾽ ἔμοιγε δοκεῖ ποιεῖν ἢ τοῦτο)
καὶ τοὺς μὲν ἄλλους εὖ ποιοῦντα, εἰ μηδὲν
5 ἄλλο, ἐξαπατᾶν, ὑμῖν δ᾽ ἀπειλεῖν ἤδη; οἷον
Θετταλοὺς πολλὰ δοὺς ὑπηγάγετ᾽ εἰς τὴν νῦν
παροῦσαν δουλείαν· οὐδ᾽ ἂν εἰπεῖν δύναιτ᾽ οὐδεὶς
ὅσα τοὺς ταλαιπώρους Ὀλυνθίους πρότερον δοὺς
63 Ποτείδαιαν ἐξηπάτησε καὶ πόλλ᾽ ἕτερα· Θηβαίους
10 νῦν ὑπάγει τὴν Βοιωτίαν αὐτοῖς παραδοὺς καὶ
ἀπαλλάξας πολέμου πολλοῦ καὶ χαλεποῦ· ὥστε
καρπωσάμενοί τιν᾽ ἕκαστοι τούτων πλεονεξίαν, οἱ
μὲν ἤδη πεπόνθασιν ἃ δὴ πάντες ἴσασιν, οἱ δ᾽
ὅτι ἂν ποτε συμβῇ πείσονται. ὑμεῖς δ᾽ ὧν μὲν
15 ἀπεστέρησθε, σιωπῶ· ἀλλ᾽ ἐν αὐτῷ τῷ τὴν
εἰρήνην ποιήσασθαι πόσ᾽ ἐξηπατήθητε, πόσων
64 ἀπεστερήθητε. οὐχὶ Φωκέας, οὐ Πύλας, οὐχὶ τἀπὶ
Θρᾴκης, Δορίσκον, Σέρριον, τὸν Κερσοβλέπτην
αὐτόν, οὐ νῦν τὴν πόλιν τὴν Καρδιανῶν ἔχει καὶ
20 ὁμολογεῖ; τί ποτ᾽ οὖν ἐκείνως τοῖς ἄλλοις καὶ οὐ
τὸν αὐτὸν τρόπον ὑμῖν προσφέρεται; ὅτι ἐν μόνῃ
τῶν πασῶν πόλεων τῇ ὑμετέρᾳ ἄδει᾽ ὑπὲρ τῶν
ἐχθρῶν λέγειν δέδοται, καὶ λαβόντα χρήματ᾽ αὐτὸν
ἀσφαλές ἐστι λέγειν παρ᾽ ὑμῖν, κἂν ἀφῃρημένοι
65 τὰ ὑμέτερ᾽ αὐτῶν ἦτε. οὐκ ἦν ἀσφαλὲς λέγειν
26 ἐν Ὀλύνθῳ τὰ Φιλίππου μὴ σὺν εὖ πεπονθότων
τῶν πολλῶν Ὀλυνθίων τῷ Ποτείδαιαν καρποῦσθαι·
οὐκ ἦν ἀσφαλὲς λέγειν ἐν Θετταλίᾳ τὰ Φιλίππου
μὴ σὺν εὖ πεπονθότος τοῦ πλήθους τοῦ Θετταλῶν

τῷ τοὺς τυράννους ἐκβαλεῖν Φίλιππον αὐτοῖς καὶ
τὴν πυλαίαν ἀποδοῦναι· οὐκ ἦν ἐν Θήβαις ἀσφαλές, 66
πρὶν τὴν Βοιωτίαν ἀπέδωκε καὶ τοὺς Φωκέας
ἀνεῖλεν. ἀλλ᾽ Ἀθήνησιν οὐ μόνον Ἀμφίπολιν καὶ
τὴν Καρδιανῶν χώραν ἀπεστερηκότος Φιλίππου, 5
ἀλλὰ καὶ κατασκευάζοντος ὑμῖν ἐπιτείχισμα τὴν
Εὔβοιαν καὶ νῦν ἐπὶ Βυζάντιον παριόντος ἀσφαλές
ἐστι λέγειν ὑπὲρ Φιλίππου. καὶ γάρ τοι τούτων
μὲν ἐκ πτωχῶν ἔνιοι ταχὺ πλούσιοι γεγόνασι καὶ
ἐξ ἀνωνύμων καὶ ἀδόξων ἔνδοξοι καὶ γνώριμοι, 10
ὑμεῖς δὲ τοὐναντίον ἐκ μὲν ἐνδόξων ἄδοξοι, ἐκ δ᾽
εὐπόρων ἄποροι· πόλεως γὰρ ἔγωγε πλοῦτον
ἡγοῦμαι συμμάχους, πίστιν, εὔνοιαν, ὧν πάντων
ἔσθ᾽ ὑμεῖς ἄποροι. ἐκ δὲ τοῦ τούτων ὀλιγώρως 67
ὑμᾶς ἔχειν καὶ ἐᾶν ταῦτα φέρεσθαι ὁ μὲν εὐδαίμων 15
καὶ μέγας καὶ φοβερὸς πᾶσιν Ἕλλησι καὶ βαρβάροις,
ὑμεῖς δ᾽ ἔρημοι καὶ ταπεινοί, τῇ τῶν ὠνίων ἀφθονίᾳ
λαμπροί, τῇ δ᾽ ὧν προσῆκε παρασκευῇ κατα-
γέλαστοι.

Οὐ τὸν αὐτὸν δὲ τρόπον περὶ θ᾽ ὑμῶν καὶ 20
περὶ αὐτῶν ἐνίους τῶν λεγόντων ὁρῶ βουλευο-
μένους· ὑμᾶς μὲν γὰρ ἡσυχίαν ἄγειν φασὶ δεῖν,
κἂν τις ὑμᾶς ἀδικῇ, αὐτοὶ δ᾽ οὐ δύνανται παρ᾽
ὑμῖν ἡσυχίαν ἄγειν οὐδενὸς αὐτοὺς ἀδικοῦντος.
εἶτά φησιν ὃς ἂν τύχῃ παρελθὼν „οὐ γὰρ 68
ἐθέλεις γράφειν, οὐδὲ κινδυνεύειν, ἀλλ᾽ 26
ἄτολμος εἶ καὶ μαλακός". ἐγὼ δὲ θρασὺς μὲν
καὶ βδελυρὸς καὶ ἀναιδὴς οὔτ᾽ εἰμὶ μήτε γενοίμην,
ἀνδρειότερον μέντοι πολλῶν πάνυ τῶν ἰταμῶς

7*

69 πολιτευομένων παρ᾿ ὑμῖν ἐμαυτὸν ἡγοῦμαι. ὅστις
μὲν γάρ, ὦ ἄνδρες Ἀθηναῖοι, παριδὼν ἃ συνοίσει
τῇ πόλει, κρίνει, δημεύει, δίδωσιν, κατηγορεῖ,
οὐδεμιᾷ ταῦτ᾿ ἀνδρείᾳ ποιεῖ, ἀλλ᾿ ἔχων ἐνέχυρον
5 τῆς αὑτοῦ σωτηρίας τὸ πρὸς χάριν ὑμῖν λέγειν καὶ
πολιτεύεσθαι ἀσφαλῶς θρασύς ἐστιν· ὅστις δ᾿
ὑπὲρ τοῦ βελτίστου πολλὰ τοῖς ὑμετέροις ἐναν-
τιοῦται βουλήμασιν, καὶ μηδὲν λέγει πρὸς χάριν,
ἀλλὰ τὸ βέλτιστον ἀεί, καὶ τὴν τοιαύτην πολιτείαν
10 προαιρεῖται, ἐν ᾗ πλειόνων ἡ τύχη κυρία γίγνεται
ἢ οἱ λογισμοί, τούτων δ᾿ ἀμφοτέρων ἑαυτὸν ὑπεύ-
70 θυνον ὑμῖν παρέχει, οὗτός ἐστ᾿ ἀνδρεῖος, καὶ
χρήσιμός γε πολίτης ὁ τοιοῦτός ἐστιν, οὐχ οἱ τῆς
παρ᾿ ἡμέραν χάριτος τὰ μέγιστα τῆς πόλεως
15 ἀπολωλεκότες, οὓς ἐγὼ τοσούτου δέω ζηλοῦν ἢ
νομίζειν ἀξίους πολίτας τῆς πόλεως εἶναι, ὥστ᾿ εἴ
τις ἔροιτό με „εἰπέ μοι, σὺ δὲ τί τὴν πόλιν ἡμῖν
ἀγαθὸν πεποίηκας“; ἔχων, ὦ ἄνδρες Ἀθηναῖοι,
καὶ τριηραρχίας εἰπεῖν καὶ χορηγίας καὶ χρημάτων
20 εἰσφορὰς καὶ λύσεις αἰχμαλώτων καὶ τοιαύτας ἄλλας
71 φιλανθρωπίας, οὐδὲν ἂν τούτων εἴποιμι, ἀλλ᾿ ὅτι
τῶν τοιούτων πολιτευμάτων οὐδὲν πολιτεύομαι,
ἀλλὰ δυνάμενος ἂν ἴσως, ὥσπερ καὶ ἕτεροι, καὶ
κατηγορεῖν καὶ χαρίζεσθαι καὶ δημεύειν καὶ τἆλλ᾿,
25 ἃ ποιοῦσιν οὗτοι, ποιεῖν, οὐδ᾿ ἐφ᾿ ἓν τούτων
πώποτ᾿ ἐμαυτὸν ἔταξα οὐδὲ προήχθην οὔθ᾿ ὑπὸ
κέρδους οὔθ᾿ ὑπὸ φιλοτιμίας, ἀλλὰ διαμένω λέγων,
ἐξ ὧν ἐγὼ μὲν πολλῶν ἐλάττων εἰμὶ παρ᾿ ὑμῖν,
ὑμεῖς δ᾿, εἰ πείθεσθέ μοι, μείζους ἂν εἴητε· οὕτω

γὰρ ἂν ἴσως ἀνεπίφθονον εἰπεῖν. οὐδ' ἔμοιγε δοκεῖ 72
δικαίου τοῦτ' εἶναι πολίτου, τοιαῦτα πολιτεύμαθ'
εὑρίσκειν ἐξ ὧν ἐγὼ μὲν πρῶτος ὑμῶν ἔσομαι
εὐθέως, ὑμεῖς δὲ τῶν ἄλλων ὕστατοι· ἀλλὰ
συναυξάνεσθαι δεῖ τὴν πόλιν τοῖς τῶν ἀγαθῶν 5
πολιτῶν πολιτεύμασι, καὶ τὸ βέλτιστον ἀεί, μὴ τὸ
ῥᾷστον ἅπαντας λέγειν· ἐπ' ἐκεῖνο μὲν γὰρ ἡ
φύσις αὐτὴ βαδιεῖται, ἐπὶ τοῦτο δὲ τῷ λόγῳ δεῖ
προάγεσθαι διδάσκοντα τὸν ἀγαθὸν πολίτην.

Ἤδη τοίνυν τινὸς ἤκουσα καὶ τοιοῦτόν τι 73
λέγοντος, ὡς ἄρ' ἐγὼ λέγω μὲν ἀεὶ τὰ βέλτιστα, 11
ἔστι δ' οὐδὲν ἀλλ' ἢ λόγοι τὰ παρ' ἐμοῦ, δεῖ
δ' ἔργων τῇ πόλει καὶ πράξεώς τινος. ἐγὼ δ'
ὡς ἔχω περὶ τούτων, λέξω πρὸς ὑμᾶς καὶ οὐκ
ἀποκρύψομαι. οὐδ' εἶναι νομίζω τοῦ συμβουλεύ- 15
οντος ὑμῖν ἔργον οὐδὲν πλὴν εἰπεῖν τὰ βέλτιστα.
καὶ τοῦθ' ὅτι τοῦτον ἔχει τὸν τρόπον, ῥᾳδίως
οἶμαι δείξειν. ἴστε γὰρ δήπου τοῦθ', ὅτι Τιμόθεός 74
ποτ' ἐκεῖνος ἐν ὑμῖν ἐδημηγόρησεν ὡς δεῖ βοηθεῖν
καὶ τοὺς Εὐβοέας σῴζειν, ὅτι Θηβαῖοι κατεδου- 357
λοῦντ' αὐτούς, καὶ λέγων εἶπεν οὕτω πως· „εἰπέ 21
μοι, βουλεύεσθε“ ἔφη „Θηβαίους ἔχοντες ἐν νήσῳ,
τί χρήσεσθε καὶ τί δεῖ ποιεῖν; οὐκ ἐμπλήσετε τὴν
θάλατταν, ὦ ἄνδρες Ἀθηναῖοι, τριήρων; οὐκ ἀνα-
στάντες ἤδη πορεύσεσθ' εἰς τὸν Πειραιᾶ; οὐ καθέλ- 25
ξετε τὰς ναῦς;“ οὐκοῦν εἶπε μὲν ταῦθ' ὁ Τιμόθεος, 75
ἐποιήσατε δ' ὑμεῖς· ἐκ δὲ τούτων ἀμφοτέρων τὸ
πρᾶγμ' ἐπράχθη. εἰ δ' ὁ μὲν εἶπεν ὡς οἷόν τε
τἄριστα, ὥσπερ εἶπεν, ὑμεῖς δ' ἀπερρᾳθυμήσατε

καὶ μηδὲν ὑπηκούσατε, ἆρ᾽ ἂν ἦν γεγονός τι τῶν
τότε συμβάντων τῇ πόλει; οὐχ οἷόν τε. οὕτω
τοίνυν καί, περὶ ὧν ἂν ἐγὼ λέγω νυνὶ καὶ περὶ
ὧν ἂν ὁ δεῖν᾽ εἴπῃ, τὰ μὲν ἔργα παρ᾽ ὑμῶν αὐτῶν
5 ζητεῖτε, τὰ δὲ βέλτιστ᾽ ἐπιστήμῃ λέγειν παρὰ τοῦ
παριόντος.

76   Ἐν κεφαλαίῳ δ᾽ ἃ λέγω φράσας καταβῆναι
βούλομαι. χρήματ᾽ εἰσφέρειν φημὶ δεῖν, τὴν ὑπάρχουσαν δύναμιν συνέχειν, ἐπανορθοῦντας εἴ τι
10 δοκεῖ μὴ καλῶς ἔχειν, μὴ ὅσοις ἄν τις αἰτιάσηται
τὸ ὅλον καταλύοντας· πρέσβεις ἐκπέμπειν πανταχοῖ
τοὺς διδάξοντας, νουθετήσοντας, πράξοντας· παρὰ
πάντα ταῦτα τοὺς ἐπὶ τοῖς πράγμασι δωροδοκοῦντας
κολάζειν καὶ μισεῖν πανταχοῦ, ἵν᾽ οἱ μέτριοι καὶ
15 δικαίους αὑτοὺς παρέχοντες εὖ βεβουλεῦσθαι δοκῶσι
77 καὶ τοῖς ἄλλοις καὶ ἑαυτοῖς. ἂν οὕτω τοῖς πράγμασι
χρῆσθε καὶ παύσησθ᾽ ὀλιγωροῦντες ἁπάντων, ἴσως
ἄν, ἴσως καὶ νῦν ἔτι βελτίω γένοιτο. εἰ μέντοι
καθεδεῖσθ᾽ ἄχρι τοῦ θορυβῆσαι καὶ ἐπαινέσαι
20 σπουδάζοντες, ἐὰν δὲ δέῃ τι ποιεῖν ἀναδυόμενοι,
οὐχ ὁρῶ λόγον ὅστις ἄνευ τοῦ ποιεῖν ὑμᾶς ἃ προσήκει δυνήσεται τὴν πόλιν σῶσαι.

ΚΑΤΑ ΦΙΛΙΠΠΟΥ Γ.

Πολλῶν, ὦ ἄνδρες Ἀθηναῖοι, λόγων γιγνο- 1
μένων ὀλίγου δεῖν καθ' ἑκάστην ἐκκλησίαν περὶ
ὧν Φίλιππος, ἀφ' οὗ τὴν εἰρήνην ἐποιήσατο, οὐ
μόνον ὑμᾶς, ἀλλὰ καὶ τοὺς ἄλλους ἀδικεῖ, καὶ 5
πάντων οἶδ' ὅτι φησάντων γ' ἄν, εἰ καὶ μὴ ποιοῦσι
τοῦτο, καὶ λέγειν δεῖν καὶ πράττειν, ὅπως ἐκεῖνος
παύσεται τῆς ὕβρεως καὶ δίκην δώσει, εἰς τοῦθ'
ὑπηγμένα πάντα τὰ πράγματα καὶ προειμέν' ὁρῶ,
ὥστε δέδοικα μὴ βλάσφημον μὲν εἰπεῖν, ἀληθὲς 10
δ' ᾖ· εἰ καὶ λέγειν ἅπαντες ἐβούλονθ' οἱ παριόντες
καὶ χειροτονεῖν ὑμεῖς ἐξ ὧν ὡς φαυλότατ' ἔμελλε
τὰ πράγμαθ' ἕξειν, οὐκ ἂν ἡγοῦμαι δύνασθαι
χεῖρον ἢ νῦν διατεθῆναι. πολλὰ μὲν οὖν ἴσως 2
ἐστὶν αἴτια τούτων, καὶ οὐ παρ' ἓν οὐδὲ δύ' εἰς 15
τοῦτο τὰ πράγματ' ἀφῖκται, μάλιστα δ', ἄνπερ
ἐξετάζητ' ὀρθῶς, εὑρήσετε διὰ τοὺς χαρίζεσθαι
μᾶλλον ἢ τὰ βέλτιστα λέγειν προαιρουμένους, ὧν
τινες μέν, ὦ ἄνδρες Ἀθηναῖοι, ἐν οἷς εὐδοκιμοῦσιν
αὐτοὶ καὶ δύνανται, ταῦτα φυλάττοντες οὐδεμίαν 20
περὶ τῶν μελλόντων πρόνοιαν ἔχουσιν, ἕτεροι δὲ
τοὺς ἐπὶ τοῖς πράγμασιν ὄντας αἰτιώμενοι καὶ

διαβάλλοντες οὐδὲν ἄλλο ποιοῦσιν, ἢ ὅπως ἡ πόλις
παρ' αὐτῆς δίκην λήψεται καὶ περὶ τοῦτ' ἔσται,
Φιλίππῳ δ' ἐξέσται καὶ λέγειν καὶ πράττειν ὅ τι
3 βούλεται. αἱ δὲ τοιαῦται πολιτεῖαι συνήθεις μὲν
5 εἰσιν ὑμῖν, αἴτιαι δὲ τῶν κακῶν. ἀξιῶ δ', ὦ
ἄνδρες Ἀθηναῖοι, ἄν τι τῶν ἀληθῶν μετὰ παρρησίας λέγω, μηδεμίαν μοι διὰ τοῦτο παρ' ὑμῶν
ὀργὴν γενέσθαι. σκοπεῖτε γὰρ ὡδί· ὑμεῖς τὴν
παρρησίαν ἐπὶ μὲν τῶν ἄλλων οὕτω κοινὴν οἴεσθε
10 δεῖν εἶναι πᾶσι τοῖς ἐν τῇ πόλει, ὥστε καὶ τοῖς
ξένοις καὶ τοῖς δούλοις αὐτῆς μεταδεδώκατε (καὶ
πολλοὺς ἄν τις οἰκέτας ἴδοι παρ' ἡμῖν μετὰ πλείονος ἐξουσίας ὅ τι βούλονται λέγοντας ἢ πολίτας
ἐν ἐνίαις τῶν ἄλλων πόλεων), ἐκ δὲ τοῦ συμβου-
4 λεύειν παντάπασιν ἐξεληλάκατε. εἶθ' ὑμῖν συμβέ-
16 βηκεν ἐκ τούτου ἐν μὲν ταῖς ἐκκλησίαις τρυφᾶν
καὶ κολακεύεσθαι πάντα πρὸς ἡδονὴν ἀκούουσιν,
ἐν δὲ τοῖς πράγμασι καὶ τοῖς γιγνομένοις περὶ τῶν
ἐσχάτων ἤδη κινδυνεύειν. εἰ μὲν οὖν καὶ νῦν
20 οὕτω διάκεισθε, οὐκ ἔχω τί λέγω· εἰ δ' ἃ συμφέρει
χωρὶς κολακείας ἐθελήσετ' ἀκούειν, ἕτοιμος λέγειν.
καὶ γὰρ εἰ πάνυ φαύλως τὰ πράγματ' ἔχει καὶ
πολλὰ προεῖται, ὅμως ἔστιν, ἐὰν ὑμεῖς τὰ δέοντα
ποιεῖν βούλησθε, ἔτι πάντα ταῦτ' ἐπανορθώ-
5 σασθαι. καὶ παράδοξον μὲν ἴσως ἐστὶν ὃ μέλλω
26 λέγειν, ἀληθὲς δέ· τὸ χείριστον ἐν τοῖς παρελη-
λυθόσι, τοῦτο πρὸς τὰ μέλλοντα βέλτιστον ὑπάρχει.
τί οὖν ἐστι τοῦτο; ὅτι οὔτε μικρὸν οὔτε μέγ' οὐδὲν
τῶν δεόντων ποιούντων ὑμῶν κακῶς τὰ πράγματ'

ἔχει, ἐπεί τοι, εἰ πάνϑ᾽ ἃ προσῆκε πραττόντων
οὕτω διέκειτο, οὐδ᾽ ἂν ἐλπὶς ἦν αὐτὰ γενέσθαι
βελτίω. νῦν δὲ τῆς ῥᾳθυμίας τῆς ὑμετέρας καὶ
τῆς ἀμελείας κεκράτηκε Φίλιππος, τῆς πόλεως δ᾽
οὐ κεκράτηκεν, οὐδ᾽ ἥττησθ᾽ ὑμεῖς, ἀλλ᾽ οὐδὲ 5
κεκίνησθε.

Εἰ μὲν οὖν ἅπαντες ὡμολογοῦμεν Φίλιππον τῇ 6
πόλει πολεμεῖν καὶ τὴν εἰρήνην παραβαίνειν, οὐδὲν
ἀλλ᾽ ἔδει τὸν παριόντα λέγειν καὶ συμβουλεύειν,
ἢ ὅπως ἀσφαλέστατα καὶ ῥᾷστ᾽ αὐτὸν ἀμυνούμεθα· 10
ἐπειδὴ δ᾽ οὕτως ἀτόπως ἔνιοι διάκεινται, ὥστε
πόλεις καταλαμβάνοντος ἐκείνου καὶ πολλὰ τῶν
ὑμετέρων ἔχοντος καὶ πάντας ἀνθρώπους ἀδικοῦντος, ἀνέχεσθαί τινων ἐν ταῖς ἐκκλησίαις λεγόντων
πολλάκις, ὡς ἡμῶν τινές εἰσιν οἱ ποιοῦντες τὸν 15
πόλεμον, ἀνάγκη φυλάττεσθαι καὶ διορθοῦσθαι
περὶ τούτου· ἔστι γὰρ δέος, μήποθ᾽ ὡς ἀμυνού- 7
μεθα γράψας τις καὶ συμβουλεύσας εἰς τὴν αἰτίαν
ἐμπέσῃ τοῦ πεποιηκέναι τὸν πόλεμον. ἐγὼ δὴ τοῦτο
πρῶτον ἁπάντων λέγω καὶ διορίζομαι, εἰ ἐφ᾽ ἡμῖν 20
ἐστι τὸ βουλεύεσθαι περὶ τοῦ πότερον εἰρήνην ἄγειν ἢ πολεμεῖν δεῖ. Εἰ μὲν οὖν ἔξεστιν 8
εἰρήνην ἄγειν τῇ πόλει καὶ ἐφ᾽ ἡμῖν ἐστι τοῦτο, ἵν᾽
ἐντεῦθεν ἄρξωμαι, φήμ᾽ ἔγωγ᾽ ἄγειν ἡμᾶς δεῖν, καὶ
τὸν ταῦτα λέγοντα γράφειν καὶ πράττειν καὶ μὴ φε- 25
νακίζειν ἀξιῶ· εἰ δ᾽ ἕτερος τὰ ὅπλ᾽ ἐν ταῖς χερσὶν
ἔχων καὶ δύναμιν πολλὴν περὶ αὐτὸν τοὔνομα μὲν
τὸ τῆς εἰρήνης ὑμῖν προβάλλει, τοῖς δ᾽ ἔργοις αὐτὸς

τοῖς τοῦ πολέμου χρῆται, τί λοιπὸν ἄλλο πλὴν
ἀμύνεσθαι; φάσκειν δ᾽ εἰρήνην ἄγειν εἰ βούλεσθε,
9 ὥσπερ ἐκεῖνος, οὐ διαφέρομαι. εἰ δέ τις ταύτην
εἰρήνην ὑπολαμβάνει, ἐξ ἧς ἐκεῖνος πάντα τἆλλα
5 λαβὼν ἐφ᾽ ἡμᾶς ἥξει, πρῶτον μὲν μαίνεται, ἔπειτ᾽
ἐκείνῳ παρ᾽ ὑμῶν, οὐχ ὑμῖν παρ᾽ ἐκείνου τὴν
εἰρήνην λέγει. τοῦτο δ᾽ ἐστὶν ὃ τῶν ἀναλισκο-
μένων χρημάτων πάντων Φίλιππος ὠνεῖται, αὐτὸς
μὲν πολεμεῖν ὑμῖν, ὑφ᾽ ὑμῶν δὲ μὴ πολεμεῖσθαι.

10　　　Καὶ μὴν εἰ μέχρι τούτου περιμενοῦμεν,
11 ἕως ἂν ἡμῖν ὁμολογήσῃ πολεμεῖν, πάντων
ἐσμὲν εὐηθέστατοι· οὐδὲ γάρ, ἂν ἐπὶ τὴν Ἀττικὴν
αὐτὴν βαδίζῃ καὶ τὸν Πειραιᾶ, τοῦτ᾽ ἐρεῖ, εἴπερ
14 οἷς πρὸς τοὺς ἄλλους πεποίηκε δεῖ τεκμαίρεσθαι.
11 τοῦτο μὲν γὰρ Ὀλυνθίοις τετταράκοντ᾽ ἀπέχων
349 τῆς πόλεως στάδια εἶπεν, ὅτι δεῖ δυοῖν θάτερον,
VIII,59 ἢ ᾿κείνους ἐν Ὀλύνθῳ μὴ οἰκεῖν ἢ αὐτὸν ἐν Μακε-
δονίᾳ, πάντα τὸν ἄλλον χρόνον, εἴ τις αὐτὸν αἰτιά-
σαιτό τι τοιοῦτον, ἀγανακτῶν καὶ πρέσβεις πέμπων
346 τοὺς ἀπολογησομένους· τοῦτο δ᾽ εἰς Φωκέας ὡς
21 πρὸς συμμάχους ἐπορεύετο, καὶ πρέσβεις Φωκέων
ἦσαν, οἳ παρηκολούθουν αὐτῷ πορευομένῳ, καὶ
παρ᾽ ἡμῖν ἤριζον οἱ πολλοὶ Θηβαίοις οὐ λυσιτε-
12 λήσειν τὴν ἐκείνου πάροδον. καὶ μὴν καὶ Φερὰς
344
25 πρώην, ὡς φίλος καὶ σύμμαχος εἰς Θετταλίαν ἐλθών,
343 ἔχει καταλαβών, καὶ τὰ τελευταῖα τοῖς ταλαιπώροις
Ὠρείταις τουτοισὶ ἐπισκεψομένους ἔφη τοὺς στρατιώτας πεπομφέναι κατ᾽ εὔνοιαν· πυνθάνεσθαι γὰρ
αὐτοὺς ὡς νοσοῦσι καὶ στασιάζουσιν, συμμάχων δ᾽

εἶναι καὶ φίλων ἀληθινῶν ἐν τοῖς τοιούτοις καιροῖς
παρεῖναι. εἶτ᾽ οἴεσθ᾽ αὐτόν, οἳ ἐποίησαν μὲν οὐδὲν 13
ἂν κακόν, μὴ παθεῖν δ᾽ ἐφυλάξαντ᾽ ἂν ἴσως, τούτους μὲν ἐξαπατᾶν αἱρεῖσθαι μᾶλλον ἢ προλέγοντα
βιάζεσθαι, ὑμῖν δ᾽ ἐκ προρρήσεως πολεμήσειν, καὶ 5
ταῦθ᾽ ἕως ἂν ἑκόντες ἐξαπατᾶσθε; οὐκ ἔστι ταῦτα· 14
καὶ γὰρ ἂν ἀβελτερώτατος εἴη πάντων ἀνθρώπων,
εἰ, τῶν ἀδικουμένων ὑμῶν μηδὲν ἐγκαλούντων
αὐτῷ, ἀλλ᾽ ὑμῶν αὐτῶν τινας αἰτιωμένων, ἐκεῖνος
ἐκλύσας τὴν πρὸς ἀλλήλους ἔριν ὑμῶν καὶ φιλο- 10
νικίαν ἐφ᾽ αὑτὸν προείποι τρέπεσθαι, καὶ τῶν
παρ᾽ ἑαυτοῦ μισθοφορούντων τοὺς λόγους ἀφέλοιτο,
οἷς ἀναβάλλουσιν ὑμᾶς λέγοντες, ὡς ἐκεῖνός γ᾽ οὐ
πολεμεῖ τῇ πόλει.

Ἀλλ᾽ ἔστιν, ὦ πρὸς τοῦ Διός, ὅστις εὖ φρονῶν 15
ἐκ τῶν ὀνομάτων μᾶλλον ἢ τῶν πραγμάτων τὸν 16
ἄγοντ᾽ εἰρήνην ἢ πολεμοῦνθ᾽ ἑαυτῷ σκέψαιτ᾽ ἄν;
οὐδεὶς δήπου. ὁ τοίνυν Φίλιππος ἐξ ἀρχῆς, ἄρτι
τῆς εἰρήνης γεγονυίας, οὔπω Διοπείθους στρατη-
γοῦντος οὐδὲ τῶν ὄντων ἐν Χερρονήσῳ νῦν ἀπε- 20
σταλμένων, Σέρριον καὶ Δορίσκον ἐλάμβανεν καὶ 346
τοὺς ἐκ Σερρείου τείχους καὶ Ἱεροῦ ὄρους στρατιώτας ἐξέβαλλεν, οὓς ὁ ὑμέτερος στρατηγὸς κατέστησεν.
καίτοι ταῦτα πράττων τί ἐποίει; εἰρήνην μὲν γὰρ
ὠμωμόκει. καὶ μηδεὶς εἴπῃ, τί δὲ ταῦτ᾽ ἐστίν, ἢ 16
τί τούτων μέλει τῇ πόλει; εἰ μὲν γὰρ μικρὰ ταῦτ᾽ 26
ἢ μηδὲν ὑμῖν αὐτῶν ἔμελεν, ἄλλος ἂν εἴη λόγος
οὗτος· τὸ δ᾽ εὐσεβὲς καὶ τὸ δίκαιον ἄν τ᾽ ἐπὶ
μικροῦ τις ἄν τ᾽ ἐπὶ μείζονος παραβαίνῃ, τὴν αὐτὴν

ἔχει δύναμιν. φέρε δὴ νῦν, ἡνίκ᾽ εἰς Χερρόνησον,
ἣν βασιλεὺς καὶ πάντες οἱ Ἕλληνες ὑμετέραν ἐγνώ-
κασιν εἶναι, ξένους εἰσπέμπει καὶ βοηθεῖν ὁμο-
17 λογεῖ καὶ ἐπιστέλλει ταῦτα, τί ποιεῖ; φησὶ μὲν γὰρ
5 οὐ πολεμεῖν, ἐγὼ δὲ τοσούτου δέω ταῦτα ποιοῦντ᾽
ἐκεῖνον ἄγειν ὁμολογεῖν τὴν πρὸς ὑμᾶς εἰρήνην,
343 ὥστε καὶ Μεγάρων ἁπτόμενον καὶ ἐν Εὐβοίᾳ
τυραννίδα κατασκευάζοντα καὶ νῦν ἐπὶ Θρᾴκην
παριόντα καὶ τἀν Πελοποννήσῳ σκευωρούμενον
10 καὶ πάνθ᾽, ὅσα πράττει μετὰ τῆς δυνάμεως,
ποιοῦντα λύειν φημὶ τὴν εἰρήνην καὶ πολεμεῖν ὑμῖν, εἰ μὴ καὶ τοὺς τὰ μηχανήματ᾽ ἐφι-
στάντας εἰρήνην ἄγειν φήσετε, ἕως ἂν αὐτὰ τοῖς
τείχεσιν ἤδη προσαγάγωσιν. ἀλλ᾽ οὐ φήσετε· ὁ
15 γάρ, οἷς ἂν ἐγὼ ληφθείην, ταῦτα πράττων καὶ
κατασκευαζόμενος, οὗτος ἐμοὶ πολεμεῖ, κἂν μήπω
18 βάλλῃ μηδὲ τοξεύῃ. τίσιν οὖν ὑμεῖς κινδυνεύσαιτ᾽
ἄν, εἴ τι γένοιτο; τῷ τὸν Ἑλλήσποντον ἀλλοτριω-
θῆναι, τῷ Μεγάρων καὶ τῆς Εὐβοίας τὸν πολε-
20 μοῦνθ᾽ ὑμῖν γενέσθαι κύριον, τῷ Πελοποννησίους
τἀκείνου φρονῆσαι. εἶτα τὸν τοῦτο τὸ μηχάνημ᾽
ἐπὶ τὴν πόλιν ἱστάντα, τοῦτον εἰρήνην ἄγειν ἐγὼ φῶ
19 πρὸς ὑμᾶς; πολλοῦ γε καὶ δεῖ, ἀλλ᾽ ἀφ᾽ ἧς ἡμέρας
346 ἀνεῖλε Φωκέας, ἀπὸ ταύτης ἔγωγ᾽ αὐτὸν πολεμεῖν
25 ὁρίζομαι. ὑμᾶς δ᾽, ἐὰν ἀμύνησθ᾽ ἤδη, σωφρονή-
σειν φημί· ἐὰν δ᾽ ἐάσητε, οὐδὲ τοῦθ᾽ ὅταν βούλησθε δυνήσεσθε ποιῆσαι. καὶ τοσοῦτόν γ᾽ ἀφέ-
στηκα τῶν ἄλλων, ὦ ἄνδρες Ἀθηναῖοι, τῶν
συμβουλευόντων, ὥστ᾽ οὐδὲ δοκεῖ μοι περὶ Χερρο-

νήσου νῦν σκοπεῖν οὐδὲ Βυζαντίου, ἀλλ' ἐπαμῦναι 20
μὲν τούτοις, καὶ διατηρῆσαι μή τι πάθωσιν, καὶ
τοῖς οὖσιν ἐκεῖ νῦν στρατηγοῖς πάνθ', ὅσων ἂν
δέωνται, ἀποστεῖλαι, βουλεύεσθαι μέντοι περὶ πάντων τῶν Ἑλλήνων ὡς ἐν κινδύνῳ μεγάλῳ καθε- 5
στώτων. βούλομαι δ' εἰπεῖν πρὸς ὑμᾶς, ἐξ ὧν
ὑπὲρ τῶν πραγμάτων οὕτω φοβοῦμαι, ἵν', εἰ μὲν
ὀρθῶς λογίζομαι, μετάσχητε τῶν λογισμῶν καὶ
πρόνοιάν τιν' ὑμῶν γ' αὐτῶν, εἰ μὴ καὶ τῶν
ἄλλων ἄρα βούλεσθε, ποιήσησθε, ἐὰν δὲ ληρεῖν 10
καὶ τετυφῶσθαι δοκῶ, μήτε νῦν μήτ' αὖθις ὡς
ὑγιαίνοντί μοι προσέχητε.

Ὅτι μὲν δὴ μέγας ἐκ μικροῦ καὶ ταπεινοῦ τὸ 21
κατ' ἀρχὰς Φίλιππος ηὔξηται, καὶ ἀπίστως καὶ
στασιαστικῶς ἔχουσι πρὸς αὑτοὺς οἱ Ἕλληνες, καὶ 15
ὅτι πολλῷ παραδοξότερον ἦν τοσοῦτον αὐτὸν ἐξ
ἐκείνου γενέσθαι ἢ νῦν, ὅθ' οὕτω πολλὰ προείληφε, καὶ τὰ λοιπὰ ὑφ' αὑτῷ ποιήσασθαι, καὶ
πάνθ' ὅσα τοιαῦτ' ἂν ἔχοιμι διεξελθεῖν, παραλείψω. ἀλλ' ὁρῶ συγκεχωρηκότας ἅπαντας 22
ἀνθρώπους, ἀφ' ὑμῶν ἀρξαμένους, αὐτῷ, ὑπὲρ 21
οὗ τὸν ἄλλον ἅπαντα χρόνον πάντες οἱ πόλεμοι
γεγόνασιν οἱ Ἑλληνικοί. τί οὖν ἐστι τοῦτο; τὸ
ποιεῖν ὅ τι βούλεται καὶ καθ' ἕν' οὑτωσὶ περι-
κόπτειν καὶ λωποδυτεῖν τῶν Ἑλλήνων καὶ κατα- 25
δουλοῦσθαι τὰς πόλεις ἐπιόντα. καίτοι προστάται 23
μὲν ὑμεῖς ἑβδομήκοντ' ἔτη καὶ τρία τῶν Ἑλλήνων
ἐγένεσθε, προστάται δὲ τριάκονθ' ἑνὸς δέοντα

Λακεδαιμόνιοι· ἴσχυσαν δέ τι καὶ Θηβαῖοι τοὺς
τελευταίους τουτουσὶ χρόνους μετὰ τὴν ἐν Λεύκ-
τροις μάχην. ἀλλ᾽ ὅμως οὔθ᾽ ὑμῖν οὔτε Θηβαίοις
οὔτε Λακεδαιμονίοις οὐδεπώποτε, ὦ ἄνδρες Ἀθη-
5 ναῖοι, συνεχωρήθη τοῦθ᾽ ὑπὸ τῶν Ἑλλήνων,
24 ποιεῖν ὅ τι βούλοισθε, οὐδὲ πολλοῦ δεῖ· ἀλλὰ
τοῦτο μὲν ὑμῖν, μᾶλλον δὲ τοῖς τότ᾽ οὖσιν Ἀθηναίοις, ἐπειδή τισιν οὐ μετρίως ἐδόκουν προσφέ-
ρεσθαι, πάντες ᾤοντο δεῖν, καὶ οἱ μηδὲν ἐγκαλεῖν
10 ἔχοντες αὐτοῖς, μετὰ τῶν ἠδικημένων πολεμεῖν,
καὶ πάλιν Λακεδαιμονίοις ἄρξασι καὶ παρελθοῦσιν
εἰς τὴν αὐτὴν δυναστείαν ὑμῖν, ἐπειδὴ πλεονάζειν
ἐπεχείρουν καὶ πέρα τοῦ μετρίου τὰ καθεστηκότ᾽
ἐκίνουν, πάντες εἰς πόλεμον κατέστησαν, καὶ οἱ
25 μηδὲν ἐγκαλοῦντες αὐτοῖς. καὶ τί δεῖ τοὺς ἄλλους
16 λέγειν; ἀλλ᾽ ἡμεῖς αὐτοὶ καὶ Λακεδαιμόνιοι, οὐδὲν
ἂν εἰπεῖν ἔχοντες ἐξ ἀρχῆς, ὅ τι ἠδικούμεθ᾽ ὑπ᾽
ἀλλήλων, ὅμως, ὑπὲρ ὧν τοὺς ἄλλους ἀδικουμένους
ἑωρῶμεν, πολεμεῖν ᾠόμεθα δεῖν.

Καίτοι πάνθ᾽ ὅσ᾽ ἐξημάρτηται καὶ Λακεδαιμονίοις ἐν τοῖς τριάκοντ᾽ ἐκείνοις ἔτεσι καὶ
τοῖς ἡμετέροις προγόνοις ἐν τοῖς ἑβδομήκοντα,
ἐλάττον᾽ ἐστίν, ὦ ἄνδρες Ἀθηναῖοι, ὧν Φίλιππος
ἐν τρισὶ καὶ δέκ᾽ οὐχ ὅλοις ἔτεσιν, οἷς ἐπιπολάζει,
25 ἠδίκηκε τοὺς Ἕλληνας, μᾶλλον δ᾽ οὐδὲ μέρος
26 τούτων ἐκεῖνα. καὶ τοῦτ᾽ ἐκ βραχέος λόγου ῥᾴδιον
δεῖξαι· Ὄλυνθον μὲν δὴ καὶ Μεθώνην καὶ
353/48 Ἀπολλωνίαν καὶ δύο καὶ τριάκοντα πόλεις ἐπὶ
Θρᾴκης ἐῶ, ἃς ἁπάσας οὕτως ὠμῶς ἀνῄρηκεν, ὥστε

μηδ᾽, εἰ πώποτ᾽ ᾠκήθησαν, προσελθόντ᾽ εἶναι
ῥᾴδιον εἰπεῖν· καὶ τὸ Φωκέων ἔθνος τοσοῦτον 346
ἀνῃρημένον σιωπῶ. ἀλλὰ Θετταλία πῶς ἔχει;
οὐχὶ τὰς πολιτείας καὶ τὰς πόλεις αὐτῶν παρῄρηται 344
καὶ τετραρχίας κατέστησεν, ἵνα μὴ μόνον κατὰ 5
πόλεις, ἀλλὰ καὶ κατ᾽ ἔθνη δουλεύωσιν; αἱ δ᾽ ἐν 27
Εὐβοίᾳ πόλεις οὐκ ἤδη τυραννοῦνται, καὶ ταῦτ᾽
ἐν νήσῳ, πλησίον Θηβῶν καὶ Ἀθηνῶν; οὐ διαρρή-
δην εἰς τὰς ἐπιστολὰς γράφει „ἐμοὶ δ᾽ ἐστὶν εἰρήνη
πρὸς τοὺς ἀκούειν ἐμοῦ βουλομένους“; καὶ οὐ 10
γράφει μὲν ταῦτα, τοῖς δ᾽ ἔργοις οὐ ποιεῖ, ἀλλ᾽
ἐφ᾽ Ἑλλήσποντον οἴχεται, πρότερον ἧκεν ἐπ᾽ Ἀμβρακίαν, Ἦλιν ἔχει, τηλικαύτην πόλιν ἐν Πελοποννήσῳ,
Μεγάροις ἐπεβούλευσε πρώην, οὔθ᾽ ἡ Ἑλλὰς οὔθ᾽ 343
ἡ βάρβαρος τὴν πλεονεξίαν χωρεῖ τἀνθρώπου. καὶ 28
ταῦθ᾽ ὁρῶντες οἱ Ἕλληνες ἅπαντες καὶ ἀκούοντες οὐ 16
πέμπομεν πρέσβεις περὶ τούτων πρὸς ἀλλήλους καὶ
ἀγανακτοῦμεν, οὕτω δὲ κακῶς διακείμεθα καὶ
διορωρύγμεθα κατὰ πόλεις, ὥστ᾽ ἄχρι τῆς τήμερον
ἡμέρας οὐδὲν οὔτε τῶν συμφερόντων οὔτε τῶν 20
δεόντων πρᾶξαι δυνάμεθα, οὐδὲ συστῆναι, οὐδὲ
κοινωνίαν βοηθείας καὶ φιλίας οὐδεμίαν ποιήσα-
σθαι· ἀλλὰ μείζω γιγνόμενον τὸν ἄνθρωπον 29
περιορῶμεν, τὸν χρόνον κερδᾶναι τοῦτον, ὃν
ἄλλος ἀπόλλυται, ἕκαστος ἐγνωκώς, ὥς γ᾽ ἐμοὶ 25
δοκεῖ, οὐχ, ὅπως σωθήσεται τὰ τῶν Ἑλλήνων,
σκοπῶν οὐδὲ πράττων, ἐπεί, ὅτι γ᾽ ὥσπερ περίοδος
ἢ καταβολὴ πυρετοῦ ἢ ἄλλου τινὸς κακοῦ καὶ τῷ
πάνυ πόρρω δοκοῦντι νῦν ἀφεστάναι προσέρχεται,

30 οὐδεὶς ἀγνοεῖ δήπου. καὶ μὴν κἀκεῖνό γ᾽ ἴστε,
ὅτι ὅσα μὲν ὑπὸ Λακεδαιμονίων ἢ ὑφ᾽ ἡμῶν
ἔπασχον οἱ Ἕλληνες, ἀλλ᾽ οὖν ὑπὸ γνησίων γ᾽
ὄντων τῆς Ἑλλάδος ἠδικοῦντο, καὶ τὸν αὐτὸν τρό-
5 πον ἄν τις ὑπέλαβε τοῦθ᾽, ὥσπερ ἂν εἰ υἱὸς ἐν
οὐσίᾳ πολλῇ γεγονὼς γνήσιος διῴκει τι μὴ καλῶς
μηδ᾽ ὀρθῶς, κατ᾽ αὐτὸ μὲν τοῦτ᾽ ἄξιον μέμψεως
εἶναι καὶ κατηγορίας, ὡς δ᾽ οὐ προσήκων ἢ ὡς οὐ
κληρονόμος τούτων ὢν ταῦτ᾽ ἐποίει, οὐκ ἐνεῖναι
31 λέγειν. / εἰ δέ γε δοῦλος ἢ ὑποβολιμαῖος τὰ μὴ
11 προσήκοντ᾽ ἀπώλλυε καὶ ἐλυμαίνετο, Ἡράκλεις,
ὅσῳ μᾶλλον δεινὸν καὶ ὀργῆς ἄξιον πάντες ἂν
ἔφησαν εἶναι. ἀλλ᾽ οὐχ ὑπὲρ Φιλίππου καὶ ὧν
ἐκεῖνος πράττει νῦν, οὐχ οὕτως ἔχουσιν, οὐ μόνον
15 οὐχ Ἕλληνος ὄντος οὐδὲ προσήκοντος οὐδὲν τοῖς
Ἕλλησιν, ἀλλ᾽ οὐδὲ βαρβάρου ἐντεῦθεν ὅθεν καλὸν
εἰπεῖν, ἀλλ᾽ ὀλέθρου Μακεδόνος, ὅθεν οὐδ᾽ ἀνδρά-
ποδον σπουδαῖον οὐδὲν ἦν πρότερον πρίασθαι.

32 Καίτοι τί τῆς ἐσχάτης ὕβρεως ἀπολείπει; οὐ
20 πρὸς τῷ πόλεις ἀνῃρηκέναι τίθησι μὲν τὰ Πύθια,
τὸν κοινὸν τῶν Ἑλλήνων ἀγῶνα, κἂν αὐτὸς μὴ
παρῇ, τοὺς δούλους ἀγωνοθετήσοντας πέμπει; κύριος
δὲ Πυλῶν καὶ τῶν ἐπὶ τοὺς Ἕλληνας παρόδων
ἐστί, καὶ φρουραῖς καὶ ξένοις τοὺς τόπους τούτους
25 κατέχει; ἔχει δὲ καὶ τὴν προμαντείαν τοῦ θεοῦ,
παρώσας ἡμᾶς καὶ Θετταλοὺς καὶ Δωριέας καὶ τοὺς
ἄλλους Ἀμφικτύονας, ἧς οὐδὲ τοῖς Ἕλλησιν ἅπασι
33 μέτεστι; γράφει δὲ Θετταλοῖς ὃν χρὴ τρόπον πολιτεύεσθαι; πέμπει δὲ ξένους τοὺς μὲν εἰς Πορθ-

μόν, τὸν δῆμον ἐκβαλοῦντας τὸν Ἐρετριέων, τοὺς
δ᾽ ἐπ᾽ Ὠρεόν, τύραννον Φιλιστίδην καταστήσον-
τας; ἀλλ᾽ ὅμως ταῦθ᾽ ὁρῶντες οἱ Ἕλληνες ἀνέχον-
ται, καὶ τὸν αὐτὸν τρόπον ὥσπερ τὴν χάλαζαν
ἔμοιγε δοκοῦσι θεωρεῖν, εὐχόμενοι μὴ καθ᾽ ἑαυτοὺς 5
ἕκαστοι γενέσθαι, κωλύειν δ᾽ οὐδεὶς ἐπιχειρῶν. οὐ 34
μόνον δ᾽ ἐφ᾽ οἷς ἡ Ἑλλὰς ὑβρίζεται ὑπ᾽ αὐτοῦ,
οὐδεὶς ἀμύνεται, ἀλλ᾽ οὐδ᾽ ὑπὲρ ὧν αὐτὸς
ἕκαστος ἀδικεῖται· τοῦτο γὰρ ἤδη τοὖσχατόν
ἐστιν. οὐ Κορινθίων ἐπ᾽ Ἀμβρακίαν ἐλήλυθε 10
καὶ Λευκάδα; οὐκ Ἀχαιῶν Ναύπακτον ὀμώμοκεν 342
Αἰτωλοῖς παραδώσειν; οὐχὶ Θηβαίων Ἐχῖνον ἀφή-
ρηται; καὶ νῦν ἐπὶ Βυζαντίους πορεύεται συμμάχους
ὄντας; οὐχ ἡμῶν, ἐῶ τἆλλα, ἀλλὰ Χερρονήσου τὴν 35
μεγίστην ἔχει πόλιν Καρδίαν; ταῦτα τοίνυν 15
πάσχοντες ἅπαντες μέλλομεν καὶ μαλακιζόμεθα καὶ
πρὸς τοὺς πλησίον βλέπομεν, ἀπιστοῦντες ἀλλήλοις,
οὐ τῷ πάντας ἡμᾶς ἀδικοῦντι. καίτοι τὸν ἅπασιν
ἀσελγῶς οὕτω χρώμενον τί οἴεσθε, ἐπειδὰν καθ᾽
ἕν᾽ ἡμῶν ἑκάστου κύριος γένηται, τί ποιήσειν; 20

Τί οὖν αἴτιον τουτωνί; οὐ γὰρ ἄνευ λόγου 36
καὶ δικαίας αἰτίας οὔτε τόθ᾽ οὕτως εἶχον ἑτοίμως
πρὸς ἐλευθερίαν οἱ Ἕλληνες, οὔτε νῦν πρὸς τὸ
δουλεύειν. ἦν τι τότ᾽, ἦν, ὦ ἄνδρες Ἀθηναῖοι,
ἐν ταῖς τῶν πολλῶν διανοίαις, ὃ νῦν οὐκ ἔστιν, 25
ὃ καὶ τοῦ Περσῶν ἐκράτησε πλούτου καὶ ἐλευθέραν
ἦγε τὴν Ἑλλάδα καὶ οὔτε ναυμαχίας οὔτε πεζῆς
μάχης οὐδεμιᾶς ἡττᾶτο, νῦν δ᾽ ἀπολωλὸς ἅπαντα

λελύμανται καὶ ἄνω καὶ κάτω πεποίηκε τὰ τῶν
37 Ἑλλήνων πράγματα. τί οὖν ἦν τοῦτο; τοὺς παρὰ
τῶν ἄρχειν βουλομένων ἢ διαφθείρειν τὴν Ἑλλάδα
χρήματα λαμβάνοντας ἅπαντες ἐμίσουν, καὶ χαλεπώ-
5 τατον ἦν τὸ δωροδοκοῦντ᾽ ἐλεγχθῆναι, καὶ τιμωρίᾳ
38 μεγίστῃ τοῦτον ἐκόλαζον. τὸν οὖν καιρὸν ἑκάστου
τῶν πραγμάτων, ὃν ἡ τύχη καὶ τοῖς ἀμελοῦσι
κατὰ τῶν προσεχόντων πολλάκις παρασκευάζει,
οὐκ ἦν πρίασθαι παρὰ τῶν λεγόντων οὐδὲ τῶν
10 στρατηγούντων, οὐδὲ τὴν πρὸς ἀλλήλους ὁμόνοιαν,
οὐδὲ τὴν πρὸς τοὺς τυράννους καὶ τοὺς βαρβάρους
39 ἀπιστίαν, οὐδ᾽ ὅλως τοιοῦτον οὐδέν. νῦν δ᾽
ἅπανθ᾽ ὥσπερ ἐξ ἀγορᾶς ἐκπέπραται ταῦτα,
ἀντεισῆκται δ᾽ ἀντὶ τούτων, ὑφ᾽ ὧν ἀπόλωλε καὶ
15 νενόσηκεν ἡ Ἑλλάς. ταῦτα δ᾽ ἐστὶ τί; ζῆλος, εἴ
τις εἴληφέ τι· γέλως, ἂν ὁμολογῇ· συγγνώμη τοῖς
ἐλεγχομένοις· μῖσος, ἂν τούτοις τις ἐπιτιμᾷ· τἆλλα
40 πάνθ᾽ ὅσ᾽ ἐκ τοῦ δωροδοκεῖν ἤρτηται. ἐπεὶ
τριήρεις γε καὶ σωμάτων πλῆθος καὶ χρημάτων
20 πρόσοδοι καὶ τῆς ἄλλης κατασκευῆς ἀφθονία, καὶ
τἆλλ᾽, οἷς ἄν τις ἰσχύειν τὰς πόλεις κρίνοι, νῦν
ἅπασι καὶ πλείω καὶ μείζω ἐστὶ τῶν τότε πολλῷ.
ἀλλ᾽ ἅπαντα ταῦτ᾽ ἄχρηστα, ἄπρακτα, ἀνόνητα ὑπὸ
τῶν πωλούντων γίγνεται.

41   Ὅτι δ᾽ οὕτω ταῦτ᾽ ἔχει, τὰ μὲν νῦν ὁρᾶτε
26 δήπου καὶ οὐδὲν ἐμοῦ προσδεῖσθε μάρτυρος· τὰ
δ᾽ ἐν τοῖς ἄνωθεν χρόνοις ὅτι τἀναντί᾽ εἶχεν, ἐγὼ
δηλώσω, οὐ λόγους ἐμαυτοῦ λέγων, ἀλλὰ γράμματα τῶν προγόνων τῶν ὑμετέρων, ἃ ᾽κεῖνοι

κατέθεντ᾽ εἰς στήλην χαλκῆν γράψαντες εἰς ἀκρόπολιν, οὐχ ἵν᾽ αὐτοῖς ᾖ χρήσιμα (καὶ γὰρ ἄνευ
τούτων τῶν γραμμάτων τὰ δέοντ᾽ ἐφρόνουν), ἀλλ᾽
ἵν᾽ ὑμεῖς ἔχηθ᾽ ὑπομνήματα καὶ παραδείγματα,
ὡς ὑπὲρ τῶν τοιούτων σπουδάζειν προσήκει. τί 42
οὖν λέγει τὰ γράμματα; „Ἄρθμιος" φησὶν „Πυθώ- 6
νακτος Ζελείτης ἄτιμος καὶ πολέμιος τοῦ δήμου
τοῦ Ἀθηναίων καὶ τῶν συμμάχων αὐτὸς καὶ
γένος." εἶθ᾽ ἡ αἰτία γέγραπται, δι᾽ ἣν ταῦτ᾽
ἐγένετο, „ὅτι τὸν χρυσὸν τὸν ἐκ Μήδων εἰς 10
Πελοπόννησον ἤγαγεν". ταῦτ᾽ ἐστὶ τὰ γράμματα. 43
λογίζεσθε δὴ πρὸς θεῶν, τίς ἦν ποθ᾽ ἡ διάνοια
τῶν Ἀθηναίων τῶν τότε, ταῦτα ποιούντων, ἢ τί
τὸ ἀξίωμα· ἐκεῖνοι Ζελείτην τιν᾽ Ἄρθμιον, δοῦλον
βασιλέως (ἡ γὰρ Ζέλειά ἐστι τῆς Ἀσίας), ὅτι τῷ 15
δεσπότῃ διακονῶν χρυσίον ἤγαγεν εἰς Πελοπόννησον, οὐκ Ἀθήναζε, ἐχθρὸν αὐτῶν ἀνέγραψαν
καὶ τῶν συμμάχων, αὐτὸν καὶ γένος, καὶ ἀτίμους.
τοῦτο δ᾽ ἐστὶν οὐχ ἣν οὑτωσί τις ἂν φήσειεν
ἀτιμίαν· τί γὰρ τῷ Ζελείτῃ, τῶν Ἀθηναίων 44
κοινῶν εἰ μὴ μεθέξειν ἔμελλεν; ἀλλ᾽ ἐν τοῖς 21
φονικοῖς γέγραπται νόμοις, ὑπὲρ ὧν ἂν μὴ διδῷ
φόνου δικάσασθαι, „καὶ ἄτιμος" φησὶ „τεθνάτω".
τοῦτο δὴ λέγει, καθαρὸν τὸν τούτων τιν᾽ ἀποκτεί-
ναντ᾽ εἶναι. οὐκοῦν ἐνόμιζον ἐκεῖνοι τῆς πάντων 45
τῶν Ἑλλήνων σωτηρίας αὐτοῖς ἐπιμελητέον εἶναι· 26
οὐ γὰρ ἂν αὐτοῖς ἔμελεν, εἴ τις ἐν Πελοποννήσῳ
τινὰς ὠνεῖται καὶ διαφθείρει, μὴ τοῦθ᾽ ὑπολαμ-
βάνουσιν· ἐκόλαζον δ᾽ οὕτω καὶ ἐτιμωροῦνθ᾽,

8*

οὓς αἴσθοιντο, ὥστε καὶ στηλίτας ποιεῖν. ἐκ δὲ
τούτων εἰκότως τὰ τῶν Ἑλλήνων ἦν τῷ βαρβάρῳ
46 φοβερά, οὐχ ὁ βάρβαρος τοῖς Ἕλλησιν. ἀλλ᾽ οὐ
νῦν· οὐ γὰρ οὕτως ἔχεθ᾽ ὑμεῖς οὔτε πρὸς τὰ
5 τοιαῦτ᾽ οὔτε πρὸς τἆλλα, ἀλλὰ πῶς; εἴπω κελεύετε;
καὶ οὐκ ὀργιεῖσθε;

ΕΚ ΤΟΥ ΓΡΑΜΜΑΤΕΙΟΥ ΑΝΑΓΙΓΝΩΣΚΕΙ.

47   Ἔστι τοίνυν τις εὐήθης λόγος παρὰ τῶν
παραμυθεῖσθαι βουλομένων τὴν πόλιν, ὡς ἄρ᾽
10 οὔπω Φίλιππός ἐστι τοιοῦτος οἷοί ποτ᾽ ἦσαν Λακεδαιμόνιοι, οἳ θαλάττης μὲν ἦρχον καὶ γῆς ἁπάσης,
βασιλέα δὲ σύμμαχον εἶχον, ὑφίστατο δ᾽ οὐδὲν
αὐτούς· ἀλλ᾽ ὅμως ἠμύνατο κἀκείνους ἡ πόλις καὶ
οὐκ ἀνηρπάσθη. ἐγὼ δ᾽ ἁπάντων ὡς ἔπος εἰπεῖν
15 πολλὴν εἰληφότων ἐπίδοσιν καὶ οὐδὲν ὁμοίων
ὄντων τῶν νῦν τοῖς πρότερον, οὐδὲν ἡγοῦμαι
πλέον ἢ τὰ τοῦ πολέμου κεκινῆσθαι καὶ ἐπι-
48 δεδωκέναι. πρῶτον μὲν γὰρ ἀκούω Λακεδαιμονίους τότε καὶ πάντας τοὺς ἄλλους τέτταρας
20 μῆνας ἢ πέντε, τὴν ὡραίαν αὐτήν, ἐμβαλόντας ἂν
καὶ κακώσαντας τὴν τῶν ἀντιπάλων χώραν ὁπλίταις
καὶ πολιτικοῖς στρατεύμασιν ἀναχωρεῖν ἐπ᾽ οἴκου
πάλιν· οὕτω δ᾽ ἀρχαίως εἶχον, μᾶλλον δὲ πολιτι-
κῶς, ὥστ᾽ οὐδὲ χρημάτων ὠνεῖσθαι παρ᾽ οὐδενὸς
25 οὐδέν, ἀλλ᾽ εἶναι νόμιμόν τινα καὶ προφανῆ τὸν
49 πόλεμον. νυνὶ δ᾽ ὁρᾶτε μὲν δήπου τὰ πλεῖστα
τοὺς προδότας ἀπολωλεκότας, οὐδὲν δ᾽ ἐκ παρα-
τάξεως οὐδὲ μάχης γιγνόμενον· ἀκούετε δὲ

Φίλιππον οὐχὶ τῷ φάλαγγ᾽ ὁπλιτῶν ἄγειν βαδί-
ζονθ᾽ ὅποι βούλεται, ἀλλὰ τῷ ψιλούς, ἱππέας,
τοξότας, ξένους, τοιοῦτον ἐξηρτῆσθαι στρατόπεδον.
ἐπειδὰν δ᾽ ἐπὶ τούτοις πρὸς νοσοῦντας ἐν αὑτοῖς 50
προσπέσῃ καὶ μηδεὶς ὑπὲρ τῆς χώρας δι᾽ ἀπιστίαν 5
ἐξίῃ, μηχανήματ᾽ ἐπιστήσας πολιορκεῖ. καὶ σιωπῶ
θέρος καὶ χειμῶνα, ὡς οὐδὲν διαφέρει, οὐδ᾽ ἔστ᾽
ἐξαίρετος ὥρα τις, ἣν διαλείπει. ταῦτα μέντοι 51
πάντας εἰδότας καὶ λογιζομένους οὐ δεῖ προσέσθαι
τὸν πόλεμον εἰς τὴν χώραν, οὐδ᾽ εἰς τὴν εὐήθειαν 10
τὴν τοῦ τότε πρὸς Λακεδαιμονίους πολέμου βλέ-
ποντας ἐκτραχηλισθῆναι, ἀλλ᾽ ὡς ἐκ πλείστου
φυλάττεσθαι τοῖς πράγμασι καὶ ταῖς παρασκευαῖς,
ὅπως οἴκοθεν μὴ κινήσεται σκοποῦντας, οὐχὶ συμ-
πλακέντας διαγωνίζεσθαι. πρὸς μὲν γὰρ πόλεμον 52
πολλὰ φύσει πλεονεκτήμαθ᾽ ἡμῖν ὑπάρχει, ἄνπερ, 16
ὦ ἄνδρες Ἀθηναῖοι, ποιεῖν ἐθέλωμεν ἃ δεῖ, ἡ
φύσις τῆς ἐκείνου χώρας, ἧς ἄγειν καὶ φέρειν
ἔστι πολλὴν καὶ κακῶς ποιεῖν, ἄλλα μυρία· εἰς δ᾽
ἀγῶν᾽ ἄμεινον ἡμῶν ἐκεῖνος ἤσκηται.   20

Οὐ μόνον δὲ δεῖ ταῦτα γιγνώσκειν, οὐδὲ 53
τοῖς ἔργοις ἐκεῖνον ἀμύνεσθαι τοῖς τοῦ πολέμου,
ἀλλὰ καὶ τῷ λογισμῷ καὶ τῇ διανοίᾳ τοὺς παρ᾽
ὑμῖν ὑπὲρ αὐτοῦ λέγοντας μισῆσαι, ἐνθυμουμένους
ὅτι οὐκ ἔνεστι τῶν τῆς πόλεως ἐχθρῶν κρατῆ- 25
σαι, πρὶν ἂν τοὺς ἐν αὐτῇ τῇ πόλει κολάσηθ᾽
ὑπηρετοῦντας ἐκείνοις. ὅ, μὰ τὸν Δία καὶ 54
τοὺς ἄλλους θεούς, οὐ δυνήσεσθ᾽ ὑμεῖς ποιῆσαι,
ἀλλ᾽ εἰς τοῦτ᾽ ἀφῖχθε μωρίας ἢ παρανοίας ἢ —

οὐκ ἔχω τί λέγω (πολλάκις γὰρ ἔμοιγ᾽ ἐπελήλυθε
καὶ τοῦτο φοβεῖσθαι, μή τι δαιμόνιον τὰ πράγ-
ματ᾽ ἐλαύνῃ), ὥστε λοιδορίας, φθόνου, σκώμματος,
ἧς τινος ἂν τύχῃϑ᾽ ἕνεκ᾽ αἰτίας, ἀνθρώπους
5 μισθωτούς, ὧν οὐδ᾽ ἂν ἀρνηθεῖεν ἔνιοι ὡς οὐκ
εἰσὶ τοιοῦτοι, λέγειν κελεύετε, καὶ γελᾶτε, ἄν τισι
55 λοιδορηθῶσιν. καὶ οὐχί πω τοῦτο δεινόν, καίπερ
ὂν δεινόν· ἀλλὰ καὶ μετὰ πλείονος ἀσφαλείας
πολιτεύεσθαι δεδώκατε τούτοις ἢ τοῖς ὑπὲρ ὑμῶν
10 λέγουσιν. καίτοι θεάσασϑ᾽ ὅσας συμφορὰς παρασκευάζει τὸ τῶν τοιούτων ἐθέλειν ἀκροᾶσθαι.
λέξω δ᾽ ἔργα, ἃ πάντες εἴσεσθε.

56   Ἦσαν ἐν Ὀλύνθῳ τῶν ἐν τοῖς πράγμασι
τινὲς μὲν Φιλίππου καὶ πάνϑ᾽ ὑπηρετοῦντες
15 ἐκείνῳ, τινὲς δὲ τοῦ βελτίστου καὶ ὅπως μὴ δου-
λεύσουσιν οἱ πολῖται πράττοντες. πότεροι δὴ τὴν
πατρίδ᾽ ἐξώλεσαν; ἢ πότεροι τοὺς ἱππέας προὔδο-
348 σαν, ὧν προδοθέντων Ὄλυνθος ἀπώλετο; οἱ τὰ
Φιλίππου φρονοῦντες καί, ὅτ᾽ ἦν ἡ πόλις, τοὺς τὰ
20 βέλτιστα λέγοντας συκοφαντοῦντες καὶ διαβάλλοντες οὕτως, ὥστε τόν γ᾽ Ἀπολλωνίδην καὶ ἐκβαλεῖν
ὁ δῆμος ὁ τῶν Ὀλυνθίων ἐπείσθη.

57   Οὐ τοίνυν παρὰ τούτοις μόνον τὸ ἔθος τοῦτο
πάντα κάκ᾽ εἰργάσατο, ἄλλοθι δ᾽ οὐδαμοῦ· ἀλλ᾽
25 ἐν Ἐρετρίᾳ, ἐπειδή, ἀπαλλαγέντος Πλουτάρχου
καὶ τῶν ξένων, ὁ δῆμος εἶχε τὴν πόλιν καὶ τὸν
Πορθμόν, οἱ μὲν ἐφ᾽ ὑμᾶς ἦγον τὰ πράγματα, οἱ
δ᾽ ἐπὶ Φίλιππον. ἀκούοντες δὲ τούτων τὰ πολλὰ
μᾶλλον οἱ ταλαίπωροι καὶ δυστυχεῖς Ἐρετριεῖς

τελευτῶντες ἐπείσθησαν τοὺς ὑπὲρ αὐτῶν λέγοντας
ἐκβαλεῖν. καὶ γάρ τοι πέμψας Ἱππόνικον ὁ σύμ- 58
μαχος αὐτοῖς Φίλιππος καὶ ξένους χιλίους τὰ τείχη 343/42
περιεῖλε τοῦ Πορθμοῦ καὶ τρεῖς κατέστησε τυράννους, Ἵππαρχον, Αὐτομέδοντα, Κλείταρχον· καὶ 5
μετὰ ταῦτ᾽ ἐξελήλακεν ἐκ τῆς χώρας δίς, ἤδη βουλομένους σῴζεσθαι, τότε μὲν πέμψας τοὺς μετ᾽
Εὐρυλόχου ξένους, πάλιν δὲ τοὺς μετὰ Παρμε-
νίωνος.

     Καὶ τί δεῖ τὰ πολλὰ λέγειν; ἀλλ᾽ ἐν Ὠρεῷ 59
Φιλιστίδης μὲν ἔπραττε Φιλίππῳ καὶ Μένιππος 11
καὶ Σωκράτης καὶ Θόας καὶ Ἀγαπαῖος, οἵπερ νῦν
ἔχουσι τὴν πόλιν (καὶ ταῦτ᾽ ᾔδεσαν ἅπαντες),
Εὐφραῖος δέ τις, ἄνθρωπος καὶ παρ᾽ ἡμῖν ποτ᾽
ἐνθάδ᾽ οἰκήσας, ὅπως ἐλεύθεροι καὶ μηδενὸς δοῦλοι 15
ἔσονται. οὗτος τὰ μὲν ἄλλ᾽ ὡς ὑβρίζετο καὶ 60
προὐπηλακίζεθ᾽ ὑπὸ τοῦ δήμου, πόλλ᾽ ἂν εἴη λέ-
γειν· ἐνιαυτῷ δὲ πρότερον τῆς ἁλώσεως ἐνέδειξεν
ὡς προδότην τὸν Φιλιστίδην καὶ τοὺς μετ᾽ αὐτοῦ,
αἰσθόμενος ἃ πράττουσιν. συστραφέντες δ᾽ ἄνθρω- 20
ποι πολλοὶ καὶ χορηγὸν ἔχοντες Φίλιππον καὶ
πρυτανευόμενοι παρ᾽ ἐκείνου ἀπάγουσι τὸν Εὐφραῖον εἰς τὸ δεσμωτήριον ὡς συνταράττοντα τὴν
πόλιν. ὁρῶν δὲ ταῦθ᾽ ὁ δῆμος ὁ τῶν Ὠρειτῶν, 61
ἀντὶ τοῦ τῷ μὲν βοηθεῖν τοὺς δ᾽ ἀποτυμπανίσαι, 25
τοῖς μὲν οὐκ ὠργίζετο, τὸν δ᾽ ἐπιτήδειον ταῦτα
παθεῖν ἔφη καὶ ἐπέχαιρεν. μετὰ ταῦθ᾽ οἱ μὲν ἐπ᾽
ἐξουσίας ὁπόσης ἠβούλοντ᾽ ἔπραττον, ὅπως ἡ πόλις
ληφθήσεται, καὶ κατεσκευάζοντο τὴν πρᾶξιν· τῶν

δὲ πολλῶν εἴ τις αἴσθοιτο, ἐσίγα καὶ κατεπέπληκτο,
62 τὸν Εὐφραῖον οἷ᾽ ἔπαθεν μεμνημένοι. οὕτω δ᾽
ἀθλίως διέκειντο, ὥστ᾽ οὐ πρότερον ἐτόλμησεν
οὐδεὶς τοιούτου κακοῦ προσιόντος ῥῆξαι φωνήν,.
5 πρὶν διασκευασάμενοι πρὸς τὰ τείχη προσῄεσαν οἱ
πολέμιοι· τηνικαῦτα δ᾽ οἱ μὲν ἡμύνοντο, οἱ δὲ
προὐδίδοσαν. τῆς δὲ πόλεως οὕτως ἁλούσης αἰ-
342 σχρῶς καὶ κακῶς οἱ μὲν ἄρχουσι καὶ τυραννοῦσι,
τοὺς τότε σῴζοντας ἑαυτοὺς καὶ τὸν Εὐφραῖον
10 ἑτοίμους ὁτιοῦν ποιεῖν ὄντας, τοὺς μὲν ἐκβαλόντες,
τοὺς δ᾽ ἀποκτείναντες, ὁ δ᾽ Εὐφραῖος ἐκεῖνος ἀπέ-
σφαξεν ἑαυτόν, ἔργῳ μαρτυρήσας ὅτι καὶ δικαίως
καὶ καθαρῶς ὑπὲρ τῶν πολιτῶν ἀνθειστήκει Φιλίππῳ.

63   Τί οὖν ποτ᾽ αἴτιον, θαυμάζετ᾽ ἴσως, τὸ καὶ
16 τοὺς Ὀλυνθίους καὶ τοὺς Ἐρετριέας καὶ τοὺς Ὠρεί-
τας ἥδιον πρὸς τοὺς ὑπὲρ Φιλίππου λέγοντας ἔχειν
ἢ τοὺς ὑπὲρ αὑτῶν; ὅπερ καὶ παρ᾽ ὑμῖν, ὅτι τοῖς
μὲν ὑπὲρ τοῦ βελτίστου λέγουσιν οὐδὲ βου-
20 λομένοις ἔνεστιν ἐνίοτε πρὸς χάριν οὐδὲν
εἰπεῖν· τὰ γὰρ πράγματ᾽ ἀνάγκη σκοπεῖν ὅπως
σωθήσεται· οἱ δ᾽ ἐν αὐτοῖς οἷς χαρίζονται
64 Φιλίππῳ συμπράττουσιν. εἰσφέρειν ἐκέλευον,
οἱ δ᾽ οὐδὲν δεῖν ἔφασαν· πολεμεῖν καὶ μὴ πιστεύειν,
25 οἱ δ᾽ ἄγειν εἰρήνην ἕως ἐγκατελήφθησαν. τἆλλα
τὸν αὐτὸν τρόπον, οἶμαι, πάνθ᾽, ἵνα μὴ καθ᾽ ἕκαστα
λέγω· οἱ μὲν ἐφ᾽ οἷς χαριοῦνται ταῦτ᾽ ἔλεγον, οἱ
δ᾽ ἐξ ὧν ἔμελλον σωθήσεσθαι. πολλὰ δὲ καὶ τὰ
τελευταῖ᾽ οὐχ οὕτως πρὸς χάριν οὐδὲ δι᾽ ἄγνοιαν

οἱ πολλοὶ προσίεντο, ἀλλ᾽ ὑποκατακλινόμενοι, ἐπειδὴ
τοῖς ὅλοις ἡττᾶσθαι ἐνόμιζον. ὅ, νὴ τὸν Δία καὶ 65
τὸν Ἀπόλλω, δέδοικ᾽ ἐγὼ μὴ πάθηθ᾽ ὑμεῖς, ἐπειδὰν ἴδητ᾽ ἐκλογιζόμενοι μηδὲν ἔθ᾽ ὑμῖν ἐνόν.
καίτοι μὴ γένοιτο μέν, ὦ ἄνδρες Ἀθηναῖοι, τὰ 5
πράγματ᾽ ἐν τούτῳ· τεθνάναι δὲ μυριάκις κρεῖττον
ἢ κολακείᾳ τι ποιῆσαι Φιλίππου καὶ προέσθαι τῶν
ὑπὲρ ὑμῶν λεγόντων τινάς. καλήν γ᾽ οἱ πολλοὶ 66
νῦν ἀπειλήφασιν Ὠρειτῶν χάριν, ὅτι τοῖς Φιλίππου
φίλοις ἐπέτρεψαν αὑτούς, τὸν δ᾽ Εὐφραῖον ἐώθουν· 10
καλήν γ᾽ ὁ δῆμος ὁ Ἐρετριέων, ὅτι τοὺς μὲν ὑμετέρους πρέσβεις ἀπήλασεν, Κλειτάρχῳ δ᾽ ἐνέδωκεν
αὑτόν· δουλεύουσί γε μαστιγούμενοι καὶ σφαττό-
μενοι. καλῶς Ὀλυνθίων ἐφείσατο, τῶν τὸν μὲν
Λασθένη ἵππαρχον χειροτονησάντων, τὸν δ᾽ Ἀπολ- 15
λωνίδην ἐκβαλόντων. μωρία καὶ κακία τὰ τοιαῦτ᾽ 67
ἐλπίζειν, καὶ κακῶς βουλευομένους καὶ μηδὲν ὧν
προσήκει ποιεῖν ἐθέλοντας, ἀλλὰ τῶν ὑπὲρ τῶν
ἐχθρῶν λεγόντων ἀκροωμένους τηλικαύτην ἡγεῖσθαι
πόλιν οἰκεῖν τὸ μέγεθος, ὥστε μηδ᾽, ἂν ὁτιοῦν ᾖ, 20
δεινὸν πείσεσθαι. καὶ μὴν ἐκεῖνό γ᾽ αἰσχρόν, 68
ὕστερόν ποτ᾽ εἰπεῖν „τίς γὰρ ἂν ᾠήθη ταῦτα γενέσθαι; νὴ τὸν Δία, ἔδει γὰρ τὸ καὶ τὸ ποιῆσαι,
καὶ τὸ μὴ ποιῆσαι". πόλλ᾽ ἂν εἰπεῖν ἔχοιεν Ὀλύνθιοι νῦν, ἃ τότ᾽ εἰ προείδοντο, οὐκ ἂν ἀπώλοντο· 25
πόλλ᾽ ἂν Ὠρεῖται, πολλὰ Φωκεῖς, πολλὰ τῶν ἀπολωλότων ἕκαστοι. ἀλλὰ τί τούτων ὄφελος αὐτοῖς; 69
ἕως ἂν σῴζηται τὸ σκάφος, ἄν τε μεῖζον ἄν τ᾽
ἔλαττον ᾖ, τότε χρὴ καὶ ναύτην καὶ κυβερνήτην

καὶ πάντ᾽ ἄνδρ᾽ ἑξῆς προθύμους εἶναι, καὶ ὅπως
μήθ᾽ ἑκὼν μήτ᾽ ἄκων μηδεὶς ἀνατρέψει, τοῦτο
σκοπεῖσθαι· ἐπειδὰν δ᾽ ἡ θάλαττα ὑπέρσχῃ, μάταιος
ἡ σπουδή.

70   Καὶ ἡμεῖς τοίνυν, ὦ ἄνδρες Ἀθηναῖοι, ἕως
6 ἐσμὲν σῷοι, πόλιν μεγίστην ἔχοντες, ἀφορμὰς
πλείστας, ἀξίωμα κάλλιστον, — τί ποιῶμεν; πάλαι
τις ἡδέως ἂν ἴσως ἐρωτήσας κάθηται. ἐγὼ νὴ Δί᾽
ἐρῶ, καὶ γράψω δέ, ὥστ᾽, ἂν βούλησθε, χειροτονή-
10 σετε. αὐτοὶ πρῶτον ἀμυνόμενοι καὶ παρασκευα-
ζόμενοι, τριήρεσι καὶ χρήμασι καὶ στρατιώταις λέγω
(καὶ γάρ, ἂν ἅπαντες δήπου δουλεύειν συγχωρή-
σωσιν οἱ ἄλλοι, ἡμῖν γ᾽ ὑπὲρ τῆς ἐλευθερίας ἀγω-
71 νιστέον), ταῦτα δὴ πάντ᾽ αὐτοὶ παρεσκευασμένοι
15 καὶ ποιήσαντες φανερὰ τοὺς ἄλλους ἤδη παρακα-
λῶμεν καὶ τοὺς ταῦτα διδάξοντας ἐκπέμπωμεν
πρέσβεις πανταχοῖ, εἰς Πελοπόννησον, εἰς Ῥόδον,
εἰς Χίον, ὡς βασιλέα λέγω [οὐδὲ γὰρ τῶν ἐκείνῳ
συμφερόντων ἀφέστηκε τὸ μὴ τοῦτον ἐᾶσαι πάντα
20 καταστρέψασθαι], ἵν᾽, ἐὰν μὲν πείσητε, κοινωνοὺς
ἔχητε καὶ τῶν κινδύνων καὶ τῶν ἀναλωμάτων, ἄν τι
δέῃ, εἰ δὲ μή, χρόνους γ᾽ ἐμποιῆτε τοῖς πράγμασιν.
72 ἐπειδὴ γάρ ἐστι πρὸς ἄνδρα καὶ οὐχὶ συνεστώσης
πόλεως ἰσχὺν ὁ πόλεμος, οὐδὲ τοῦτ᾽ ἄχρηστον,
343 οὐδ᾽ αἱ πέρυσι πρεσβεῖαι περὶ τὴν Πελοπόννησον
26 ἐκεῖναι καὶ κατηγορίαι, ἃς ἐγὼ καὶ Πολύευκτος ὁ
βέλτιστος ἐκεινοσὶ καὶ Ἡγήσιππος καὶ οἱ ἄλλοι
πρέσβεις περιήλθομεν καὶ ἐποιήσαμεν ἐπισχεῖν ἐκεῖ-

νον καὶ μήτ᾽ ἐπ᾽ Ἀμβρακίαν ἐλθεῖν μήτ᾽ εἰς Πελοπόννησον ὁρμῆσαι. οὐ μέντοι λέγω μηδὲν αὐτοὺς 73
ὑπὲρ αὑτῶν ἀναγκαῖον ἐθέλοντας ποιεῖν τοὺς ἄλλους
παρακαλεῖν· καὶ γὰρ εὔηθες τὰ οἰκεῖ᾽ αὐτοὺς προϊεμένους τῶν ἀλλοτρίων φάσκειν κήδεσθαι, καὶ τὰ 5
παρόντα περιορῶντας ὑπὲρ τῶν μελλόντων τοὺς
ἄλλους φοβεῖν. οὐ λέγω ταῦτα, ἀλλὰ τοῖς μὲν
ἐν Χερρονήσῳ χρήματ᾽ ἀποστέλλειν φημὶ
δεῖν καὶ τἄλλ᾽, ὅσ᾽ ἀξιοῦσι, ποιεῖν, αὐτοὺς δὲ
παρασκευάζεσθαι, τοὺς δ᾽ ἄλλους Ἕλληνας 10
συγκαλεῖν, συνάγειν, διδάσκειν, νουθετεῖν·
ταῦτ᾽ ἐστὶ πόλεως ἀξίωμ᾽ ἐχούσης, ἡλίκον ὑμῖν
ὑπάρχει. εἰ δ᾽ οἴεσθε Χαλκιδέας τὴν Ἑλλάδα 74
σώσειν ἢ Μεγαρέας, ὑμεῖς δ᾽ ἀποδράσεσθαι τὰ
πράγματα, οὐκ ὀρθῶς οἴεσθε· ἀγαπητὸν γάρ, ἐὰν 15
αὐτοὶ σῴζωνται τούτων ἕκαστοι. ἀλλ᾽ ὑμῖν τοῦτο
πρακτέον· ὑμῖν οἱ πρόγονοι τοῦτο τὸ γέρας ἐκτή-
σαντο καὶ κατέλιπον μετὰ πολλῶν καὶ μεγάλων
κινδύνων. εἰ δ᾽ ὃ βούλεται ζητῶν ἕκαστος καθε- 75
δεῖται καὶ ὅπως μηδὲν αὐτὸς ποιήσει σκοπῶν, 20
πρῶτον μὲν οὐδὲ μή ποθ᾽ εὕρῃ τοὺς ποιήσοντας,
ἔπειτα δέδοιχ᾽ ὅπως μὴ πάνθ᾽ ἅμα, ὅσ᾽ οὐ βουλόμεθα, ποιεῖν ἡμῖν ἀνάγκη γένηται.

Ἐγὼ μὲν δὴ ταῦτα λέγω, ταῦτα γράφω· καὶ 76
οἴομαι καὶ νῦν ἔτ᾽ ἐπανορθωθῆναι ἂν τὰ πρά- 25
γματα τούτων γιγνομένων. εἰ δέ τις ἔχει τούτων
βέλτιον, λεγέτω καὶ συμβουλευέτω. ὅ τι δ᾽ ὑμῖν
δόξει, τοῦτ᾽, ὦ πάντες θεοί, συνενέγκοι.

Erklärendes Sachregister.

Ἀγαπαῖος aus Oreos auf Euboia von der makedonischen Partei IX 59.

Ἀγορά, Stadt am Ansatz des thrakischen Chersonnes VII 39, auch bei Herodot VII 58 erwähnt, an Stelle des späteren Lysimachia.

ἀγωνοθετεῖν, ein Festspiel leiten, die Kampfpreise aussetzen und verteilen IX 32.

Αἰτωλοί, sie verbünden sich um 343 mit Philippos und erhalten die Zusicherung von Naupaktos IX 34, das sie 338 auch bekommen.

ἀκρόπολις Athens III 24.

Ἀλέξανδρος a) König von Makedonien 498—54, überbrachte den Athenern die Bündnisanträge des Mardonios VI 11, b) Philippos' Schwager, Bruder der Olympias, wurde 342, nach der Entthronung des Arybbas, König von Epeiros VII 32.

Ἁλίαρτος, Stadt in Böotien, südlich des Kopaïs-Sees, wo Lysandros 395 fiel IV 17.

Ἁλόννησος, kleine Insel des ägäischen Meeres in der Nähe der Halbinsel Magnesia VII 2.

Ἀμβρακία, Stadt nahe dem ambrakischen Busen, Kolonie der Korinther IX 34, von Philippos 343 bedroht VII 32. IX 27, aber nicht genommen IX 72.

ἀμμορίη VII 40 eig. Unteilhaftigkeit, der Grenzstreifen, der keiner von zwei Nachbar-Städten zugehört.

Ἀμύντας, König von Makedonien 389—369, Vater des Philippos VII 11.

Ἀμφικτυονία. Von mehreren Staatenverbänden, die diesen Namen führen, war am berühmtesten die pyläisch-delphische A., welche den Schutz des delphischen Tempels und die

Feier der pythischen Spiele zur Aufgabe hatte, und zu
welcher zwölf Stämme mit je zwei Stimmen gehörten.
Athen führte eine der beiden Stimmen der Ionier. 346
wurden die Phoker aus dem Bunde ausgestofsen und ihre
beiden Stimmen auf Philippos und seine Nachkommen
übertragen, welcher natürlich bald in dem Verbande die
Oberhand hatte IX 32. Die Athener erkannten nach
einigem Schwanken diesen Beschlufs an V 14. 19.

Ἀμφίπολις, athenische Kolonie, am linken Strymonufer
nahe der Mündung, in einer Biegung des Flusses in
günstigster Lage. Nach seiner Thronbesteigung verzichtete
Philippos ausdrücklich auf A. Doch griff er es 357 an
mit dem Versprechen, es für Athen zu erobern II 6. VII 27,
weshalb die Athener das Hilfsgesuch der Stadt ablehnten
I 8. Die Stadt ergab sich I 5, wurde von Philippos fest-
gehalten VI 17, und Athen verzichtete darauf im philokrateischen Frieden V 25. VII 23 f. Die Bewohner *Ἀμφι-
πολῖται* I 5. 8.

ἀνδραποδιστής, Menschenräuber; wer einen Freien hinter-
listig zum Sklaven machte oder einen fremden Sklaven
raubte IV 47.

Ἀνθεμοῦς, kleine Stadt der nördlichen Chalkidike un-
gewisser Lage, von Philippos den Olynthiern überlassen
VI 20.

ἀντίδοσις, Vermögenstausch, ein Verfahren zur Verhütung
ungerechter Verteilung der Leiturgien. Beim Aufgebot der
Trierarchen setzten die Strategen einen Termin an, an
welchem der Besteuerte einen andern aufrufen durfte, der
zur Leistung mehr verpflichtet sei. Dieser letztere konnte
nun entweder die Leistung übernehmen oder auf den Vermögenstausch eingehen oder auf gerichtliche Entscheidung
über die Leistungspflicht antragen IV 36.

Ἀπολλωνία, Stadt mitten in der nördlichen Chalkidike,
von Philippos erobert VII 28 und zerstört IX 26.

Ἀπολλωνίδης a) von Kardia, Gegner Athens, von Philippos mit Land bedacht VII 39, b) von Olynthos, Gegner
der makedonischen Partei, aus der Stadt verbannt IX 56. 66.

ἀπόρρητον, Staatsgeheimnis I 4, so boten die Athener
insgeheim Philippos Pydna an, wofern er ihnen zum Besitz von Amphipolis verhelfe II 6.

ἀποτυμπανίζειν, gewaltsame und schmachvolle Todesart,
bei welcher die Verurteilten auf eine Maschine (τύμπανον)
festgebunden und dann durch einen Schlag mit der Keule
auf den Kopf getötet wurden VIII 61. IX 61.

Ἀργεῖοι, obwohl alte Freunde Athens, jetzt ihnen ent-
fremdet V 18, an den Amphiktyonenbeschlüssen beteiligt
V 14, von Philippos umworben VI 9. 15. Demosthenes'
Gesandtschaft zu ihnen VI 19, ihr Verhalten in den Perserkriegen VI 11.

Ἄρθμιος von Zeleia wird von den Athenern um die Mitte
des V. Jahrhunderts auf Kimons Antrag geächtet, weil er
mit persischem Golde nach dem Peloponnes kam IX 42.

Ἀριστείδης III 21, sein Haus III 26.

Ἀριστοφῶν von Hazenia, athenischer Staatsmann, Für-
sprecher des thebanischen Bündnisses, Freund des Chares
und Gegner des Iphikrates und Timotheos, die er 354 des
Verrats anklagte, hatte in hohem Alter in den Jahren 360—53
großen Einfluß auf die Leitung des Staates VIII 30.

Ἀρτάβαζος, persischer Satrap von Lydien und Phrygien;
im Aufstande gegen Artaxerxes III. Ochos nimmt er 356
die athenische Flotte unter Chares in seinen Dienst IV 24,
mußte jedoch zu Philippos von Makedonien flüchten, wurde
aber später vom Könige begnadigt.

Ἀρύββας, König der Molotter in Epeiros, ward 351 von
Philippos bekriegt I 13 und 342 entthront VII 32.

Αὐτομέδων, Gewalthaber in Eretria, von Philippos eingesetzt IX 58.

Ἀχαιοί, Gegner des Philippos, unterstützen die Phoker im
Bunde mit Athen IX 34.

Βοηδρόμια, attisches Fest im gleichnamigen Monat (September) zu Ehren des Schlachtenhelfers Apollon. B. πέμπειν, das Fest mit Festzug und Schmaus begehen III 31.

Βοιωτία, von den Thebanern beherrscht VIII 63. 65.

βουλευτήριον, das Rathaus am Markt von Athen, diente
auch als Staatsarchiv, bis man aus Raummangel das nahe
μητρῷον (Tempel der Kybele) dazu bestimmte VII 33.

Βούχετα, kleine Stadt in der Landschaft Kassopia in Epeiros, nördlich des ambrakischen Busens, Kolonie von Elis,
dem Alexandros unterworfen VII 32.

Βυζάντιοι, stören den Handel der Athener V 25, sind den Athenern unfreundlich gesinnt VIII 15, mit Philippos verbündet IX 34, von diesem bedroht VIII 14. 66. IX 19, wurden 340 von ihm vergeblich lange belagert und von den Athenern unter Chares und Phokion unterstützt.

Γεραιστός, Vorgebirge an der Südostspitze Euboias IV 34.
γυμνασίαρχος, die Gymnasiarchie gehörte zu den Leiturgien und war kostspielig (bis 12 Minen). Die Gymnasiarchen hatten die Teilnehmer an dem Fackelwettlauf, der bei verschiedenen Festen üblich war, zu unterhalten, sie wurden von den Phylen gestellt IV 36.

δεκαδαρχία, eine oligarchische Regierung, über die Näheres nicht bekannt ist, die Philippos 344 in Thessalien einführte VI 22.
Δελφοί. τὰ ἐν *Δελφοῖς* V 23 ist die Verwaltung des Tempelschatzes, ἡ ἐν *Δ.* σκιά ist die Amphiktyonenversammlung, insofern die Einrichtung überlebt war, mit Anspielung auf den sprichwörtlichen Streit περὶ ὄνου σκιᾶς V 25.
Δημοσθένης, des Alkisthenes Sohn, als Feldherr im peloponnesischen Kriege ausgezeichnet, aber kein Staatsmann. Er kam mit Nikias bei dem sikilischen Unternehmen um. III 21.
δημόσιοι, Staatssklaven II 19, welche auch als Unterbeamte der Finanzbehörden verwandt wurden VIII 47.
δικασταί wurden aus allen über 30 Jahre alten, im Besitz der Ehrenrechte befindlichen Männern, die sich zum Richteramte gemeldet hatten, erlost. Es waren aber in der Regel Männer in höherem Lebensalter III 35. Die Entscheidung über die Rechenschaftsablage der Strategen erfolgte in einem Gerichtshofe von 501 Richtern unter Vorsitz der Thesmotheten IV 47. Gerichtsverträge mit fremden Staaten mußten von einem Gericht genehmigt werden VII 9. Freie Schiedsgerichte gab es, wie zwischen Privatleuten, auch zwischen Staaten VII 7. 36.
Διονύσια, n. τὰ κατ᾽ ἄστυ, mehrtägiges Fest, das zu Athen im Monat Elaphebolion (März) mit Festzug, Knaben- und Dithyrambenchören und dramatischen Aufführungen unter

Leitung des Archon, dem 10 ἐπιμεληταὶ τῆς πομπῆς τῷ Διονύσῳ zur Seite standen, alljährlich gefeiert wurde IV 35.

ἐν Διονύσου n. θεάτρῳ, am Südostabhang des Burg- felsens, erst unter dem Redner Lykurgos vollendet, seit 1862 unter Leitung von Strack wieder aufgedeckt V 7.

Διοπείθης von Sunion, Führer der athenischen Kolonisten, die nach dem Frieden des Philokrates nach dem Cher- sonnes geschickt wurden, geriet in Streit mit Kardia, das von Philippos unterstützt wurde, und vertrat dort that- kräftig die Sache Athens VIII 2—30. IX 15.

διωρυχή, beabsichtigter Durchstich des thrakischen Cher- sonnes VII 40. VI 30.

Δορίσκος, Stadt in Thrakien nahe der Hebros-Mündung, wo einst Xerxes Heerschau hielt, von Philippos 346 ge- nommen VIII 64. IX 15.

Δρογγίλον, kleiner Ort im Innern Thrakiens VIII 44.

Δωριεῖς als Teilnehmer der Amphiktyonie IX 32, also als Stamm, der sowohl die aus der Metropolis wie die aus dem Peloponnes umfaſste.

εἰσαγγέλλειν, schwere Anklage durch aufserordentliche Anzeige beim Rat, gestattet bei Umsturz der Verfassung, Verrat im Kriege und gegen bestochene Staatsmänner, später jedoch vielfach gemifsbraucht VIII 28.

εἰσφέρειν, εἰσφορά ist eine aufserordentliche Vermögens- steuer, welche zu Kriegszwecken für den einzelnen Fall von der Volksversammlung beschlossen wurde I 20 u. oft; vgl. συμμορία.

Ἐλάτεια a) bedeutendste Stadt in Phokis, nördlich des Kephissos am südlichen Ausgange des wichtigsten Passes über das Knemisgebirge, daher der Schlüssel zu Mittel- Griechenland VI 14, von Philippos im Herbst 339 besetzt und befestigt, b) richtiger Ἐλάτρεια, Stadt der Landschaft Kassopia in Epeiros nördlich des ambrakischen Busens VII 32.

Ἑλλήσποντος, der Getreideschiffahrt wegen seit alters in athenischer Hand, von Philippos gefährdet VIII 3. IX 27.

ἐμπορικαὶ δίκαι, Handelsklagen, d. i. Klagen aus über- seeischen Handelsgeschäften. Zu ihrer Beschleunigung wurde um die Mitte des IV. Jahrhunderts bestimmt, daſs sie binnen Monatsfrist entschieden und der Verurteilte bis zur Bezahlung in Haft genommen würde VII 12.

ἐπιχειροτονεῖν τὰς γνώμας, zur endgiltigen Abstimmung über die der Volksversammlung vorliegenden Anträge schreiten IV 30.

Ἐργίσκη, thrakischer Küstenplatz, von Philippos 346 genommen. Die Lage ist nicht genauer bekannt VII 37.

Ἐρετρία auf Euboia, von dem Tyrannen Plutarchos beherrscht, den die Athener 348 unterstützten, der aber in demselben Jahre die Insel verlieſs IX 57. Von den beiden Parteien, die sich darauf bildeten, gewann die makedonische unter Kleitarchos die Oberhand IX 66, worauf Philippos 343/42 Söldner sandte, die Volkspartei vertrieb und drei Machthaber einsetzte IX 57.

Ἐρυθραί, bedeutende Handelsstadt auf der Halbinsel gegenüber der Insel Chios. Ἐρυθραῖοι VIII 24.

Ἐρχομενός = Ὀρχομενός, alte böotische Stadt am Einflusse des Kephissos in den Kopaïs-See, 364 von den Thebanern zerstört, dann von den Phokern besetzt und zäh verteidigt V 21, nach dem Frieden von Philippos den Thebanern übergeben V 22. VI 13.

ἐτησίαι, regelmäſsige Nordwinde, welche im Hochsommer in Griechenland gegen Ende Juli einsetzen und mit Unterbrechungen etwa vierzig Tage anhalten IV 31. VIII 14.

Εὔβοια, während der thebanischen Hegemonie in Heeresfolge der Thebaner, wurde es 357 auf des Timotheos Anregung VIII 74 durch einen kräftigen Hilfszug für das athenische Bündnis gewonnen IV 17. I 8. Schon 351 beginnt sich Philippos in die Verhältnisse der Insel zu mischen IV 37. 348 unternehmen die Athener einen Hilfszug für Plutarchos, den Tyrannen von Eretria, der höchst unheilvoll verläuft V 5, hoffen thörichterweise Euboia durch Philippos wiederzuerhalten V 10. VI 30, versäumen die Gelegenheit es wiederzunehmen VIII 36, bis Philippos sich zwei feste Plätze Oreos und Eretria durch Besatzungen und ihm ergebene Machthaber sichert VIII 66. IX 17 und dadurch Athen auf das schwerste bedroht IX 18.

Εὐθυκράτης aus Olynthos, verriet als Reiterführer die Reiterei seiner Vaterstadt an Philippos und führte dadurch den Fall der Stadt herbei VIII 40, wurde von den Athenern in die Acht erklärt, lebte aber noch 338.

εὔϑυναι, das gerichtliche Rechenschaftsverfahren, dem sich jeder Beamte nach Ablauf seines Amtes zu unterwerfen hatte I 28. IV 47.

Εὐρύλοχος, makedonischer Heerführer in Euboia IX 58.

Εὐφραῖος von Oreos, Schüler Platons, einst allmächtig am Hofe des Königs Perdikkas (365—359) zu Pella, dann in seiner Vaterstadt Gegner der makedonischen Partei, endet durch Selbstmord IX 59 f.

Ἐχῖνος, Stadt böotischer Gründung an der Nordküste des malischen Meerbusens, 342 von Philippos besetzt IX 34.

Ζέλεια, Stadt in Troas südwestlich von Kyzikos, zum attischen Seebunde gehörig IX 42 f.

Ἡγήσιππος von Sunion, Staatsmann und Redner der patriotischen Partei, betrieb 357 den Zug nach Euboia und darauf das Bündnis mit den Phokern, klagte den Kallippos erfolglos wegen Gesetzwidrigkeit an VII 43, war 343 als Gesandter bei Philippos, hielt im folgenden Jahre die Rede, die nach ihrem ersten Abschnitt περὶ Ἁλοννήσου heißst. Dann war er als Gesandter im Peloponnes IX 72. Später tritt er ganz zurück.

Ἦλις, dort gewann um 343 die aristokratische, Philippos zugewandte Partei die Oberhand IX 27. Philippos nimmt elische Pflanzstädte in Epeiros VII 32.

Ἡραῖον τεῖχος an der Nordküste der Propontis, 352 von Philippos belagert III 4.

Θάσος, Insel der thrakischen Küste, Flottenstation für Athen IV 32, thasische Verbannte werden von Philippos mit Zustimmung des Chares zurückgeführt VII 15.

Θεσπιαί, böotische Stadt westlich von Theben, um 372 von den Thebanern zerstört, erhoffte Wiederherstellung V 10. VI 30.

Θετταλοί, stehen im Rufe der Unzuverlässigkeit I 21, von Philippos durch Versprechungen getäuscht II 7 und in seiner Gewalt I 12. II 8. 14, doch noch widerwillig II 11, bevorrechtete Teilnehmer der Amphiktyonie V 14. 19. IX 32.

Sie werden nach dem phokischen Kriege zunächst belohnt, dann durch Dekadarchien niedergehalten VI 22. VIII 62. 65, sind Philippos heerespflichtig VIII 14 (ihre Reiterei war berühmt VI 14). Endlich besetzt Philippos Pherai IX 12 und beherrscht das Land durch Tetrarchien IX 26. 33.

Θηβαῖοι, stehen im Rufe geringer Klugheit V 15, ihre Hegemonie IX 23, den Athenern feindlich gesinnt I 26. III 8 wegen Oropos V 16. 24 und Euboia VIII 74. IX 27, im phokischen Kriege beschäftigt III 27. Falsche Gerüchte über Philippos' Verhältnis zu ihnen IV 48. VI 30. IX 11, der sie unterstützt VI 7 und nach dem Frieden fördert V 18. VIII 63 f., aber doch ihre Gründung Echinos wegnimmt IX 34. Der volle Umschlag erfolgte erst 339 bei dem Amphiktyonenkriege gegen Amphissa.

θεωρικά, Schaugelder, Geldspenden an das Volk an den gröfseren Festen, teils um das Eintrittsgeld in das Schauspiel zu erstatten, teils zur Bereitung einer besseren Mahlzeit, eingeführt 410 durch Kleophon, erneuert nach dem Sturz der Dreifsig durch Agyrrhios. Unter der Verwaltung des Eubulos flossen alle Überschüsse der Verwaltung in die Theorikenkasse, und dies wurde gesetzlich bestimmt III 11. 19. 31.

Θόας aus Oreos auf Euboia, Führer der makedonischen Partei IX 59.

Θρᾴκη, Philippos zieht 352 nach Thrakien und belagert Heraion Teichos I 13. III 4, legt 348 mit Olynthos 32 Städte der Chalkidike (ἐπὶ Θρᾴκης) in Trümmer IX 26, macht 346 gleich nach dem Frieden neue Eroberungen VIII 64, führt von 342 ab dort ernste Kriege VIII 2. 14. IX 17 um an sich wenig begehrenswerte Plätze VIII 44, wobei die Thraker von Diopeithes unterstützt werden VIII 8.

Ἱέραξ von Amphipolis als Gesandter in Athen I 8.

Ἱερὸν ὄρος, thrakischer Küstenplatz in der Nähe des Chersonnes, in dem 346 Kersobleptes sich Philippos ergeben mufste VII 37. IX 15.

ἱεροποιοί, Festordner, zum Teil ordentliche Jahresbeamte, ἱερ. κατ' ἐνιαυτόν, zum Teil besondere Festausschüsse, welche für die gröfseren Feste zumeist vom Rat aus seiner Mitte bestellt wurden und für die Ordnung zu sorgen hatten IV 26.

9*

Ἰλλύριοι, von Philippos 358 und 356 bekriegt und geschlagen I 13. 23. IV 48.

Ἴμβρος, Insel nahe am Hellespont, Besitz der Athener VII 4,
von Philippos geplündert IV 34.

ἱππαγωγοὶ τριήρεις wurden in Athen zuerst 430 aus
alten Trieren hergestellt, zur Aufnahme von je 30 Reitern
gebaut, sie hatten nur 60 Ruder, wahrscheinlich in gleicher
Höhe IV 16. 21.

ἵππαρχοι, 2 Reiterführer wurden jährlich aus der Gesamt-
zahl der Athener gewählt und befehligten je 5 Phylen der
Reiter. Ein dritter wurde nach Lemnos erwählt, um dort
die Reiter zu führen IV 26.

Ἵππαρχος von Eretria, durch Philippos als Machthaber
daselbst bestellt IX 58.

ἱππεῖς, die Reiter wurden aus den vermögendsten Bürgern
ausgemustert, ihre Zahl betrug 1000, sie standen unter
der Aufsicht des Rates. Befehligt wurden sie von 2 Hip-
parchen und 10 Phylarchen IV 16. 21. 28.

Ἱππόνικος, Heerführer des Philippos IX 58.

Ἰφικράτης, berühmter athenischer Feldherr, der im korinthischen Kriege mit seinen Peltasten 392 eine spartanische
Mora vernichtete IV 23.

Καβύλη, Ort im Innern Thrakiens, wahrscheinlich an der
heutigen Tundscha VIII 44.

Καλλίας, Staatssklave, später Possenreifser bei Philippos
II 19.

Κάλλιππος aus dem Gau Paiania, wurde von Hegesippos
erfolglos der Gesetzwidrigkeit angeklagt VII 42.

Καρδία, wichtige Stadt an der Westseite des thrakischen
Chersonnes, in dem Vertrage mit Kersobleptes von Thrakien 357 ausdrücklich von der Botmäfsigkeit der Athener
ausgenommen V 25, aber doch wieder von ihnen bean-
sprucht VII 41 f., von Philippos unterstützt VIII 58 und
besetzt VIII 64. IX 35.

Κᾶρες, karische Fürsten besetzen Chios, Kos und Rhodos
V 25.

Κάρυστος im südöstlichen Euboia, mit Athen verbündet.
Ein Bürger der Stadt, athenischer Geschäftsträger, von
Philippos hingerichtet VII 38.

Κασσωπία, Landschaft in Epeiros, nördlich des ambrakischen Busens VII 32.

Κερσοβλέπτης, Sohn des Kotys, König des Odrysenreiches,
erkannte 357 den Chersonnes aufser Kardia als athenisches
Besitztum an, später wiederholt im Kriege mit Philippos
und den Athenern befreundet, wurde 346 vom philokrateischen Frieden auf Philippos' Verlangen ausgeschlossen
VIII 64; 341 wurde er nach einem neuen Kriege entthront.

Κλείταρχος, Führer der makedonischen Partei in Eretria
IX 66, als Machthaber von Philippos eingesetzt IX 58.

κληροῦχοι, athenische Kolonisten, welche in einem fremden,
meist eroberten Gebiete Landlose zugewiesen erhielten,
deren Eigentum der Staat behielt. Sie blieben im Bürger-
recht und den attischen Gesetzen unterworfen, bildeten
aber eigene Gemeinwesen, in deren Verwaltung sie selb-
ständig waren VIII 6.

Κορίνθιοι, einst Athen feindlich III 20, später werden
sie in ihren Gründungen von Philippos angegriffen IX 34
und sind mit Athen verbündet. Korinthischer Krieg IV 23.

Κορώνεια, böotische Stadt, nordwestlich von Theben, wurde
um 352 von dem Phoker Onomarchos erobert, nach dem
Frieden von Philippos den Thebanern zurückgegeben V 21.
VI 13.

Κῶς, Insel des ägäischen Meeres, von den Karern bedroht V 25.

Λακεδαιμόνιοι, ihre Kriegführung im peloponnesischen
Kriege IX 48, Hegemonie IX 23, einstige Übermacht IV 3,
jetzige Ohnmacht III 27, mit Athen befreundet IV 48. V 18,
sollen Messene herausgeben VI 13. Korinthischer Krieg
IV 24.

Λάμψακος, Stadt in Troas am Hellespont, von athenischen
Söldnerführern (Chares) besetzt II 28.

Λασθένης, olynthischer Reiterführer, der seine Schar an
Philippos verriet und dadurch den Fall der Stadt herbei-
führte VIII 40. IX 66.

Λευκάς, Insel südlich des ambrakischen Busens, korinthische
Gründung, von Philippos bedroht IX 34.

Λευκὴ ἀκτή, Hafenstadt an der Propontis nördlich von
Paktye an der Grenze des Chersonnes VII 39.

Λεῦκτρα, im südlichen Böotien, Schlachtort IX 23.

Λῆμνος, Insel im Besitz Athens VII 4, von Philippos geplündert IV 34, Winterstation für die Flotte IV 32, ein
Hipparchos jährlich dahin entsandt IV 27.

λωποδύτης, Kleiderdieb, Strafsenräuber IV 47, übertragen
IX 22.

Μαγνησία, Landschaft und Halbinsel am pagasäischen Meer-
busen, bisher unter den Tyrannen von Pherai, von Philippos erobert I 13, den Thessaliern versprochen II 7. VI 22,
nicht befestigt I 22. II 11.

Μακεδονία, die makedonische Macht II 14. Verächtlich
behandelt IV 10. IX 31.

Μαραϑῶν, Ort im Osten Attikas, Raubzug des Philippos
IV 34.

Μάστειρα, sonst unbekannter Ort im Innern Thrakiens
VIII 44.

Μεγαλοπολῖται, Bewohner der von Epameinondas ge-
gründeten Hauptstadt Arkadiens, Gegner Spartas und
darum Philippos zugeneigt V 18.

Μεγαρεῖς, einst Feinde Athens III 20, dann lange neutral
und friedlich, wurden von Philippos von der Seeseite
durch einen Handstreich bedroht VIII 18. IX 17 f. 27, ihre
Ohnmacht IX 74.

Μεϑώνη, makedonische Küstenstadt nahe der Mündung des
Haliakmon, Athen verbündet IV 4, von Athen schlecht
und zu spät unterstützt I 9. IV 35, von Philippos 353
genommen und zerstört I 12. IX 26.

Μενέλαος, Stiefbruder des Philippos, befehligt als Reiterführer in athenischen Besitzungen, wahrscheinlich im Chersonnes IV 27, fiel bei der Einnahme von Olynthos in
Philippos' Hände und wurde getötet.

Μένιππος, Führer der makedonischen Partei in Oreos auf
Euboia IX 59.

Μεσσήνιοι, waren 369 von Epameinondas befreit worden,
wenn auch Sparta ihre Selbständigkeit nicht anerkannte
VI 13, den Spartanern feindlich V 18, von Philippos unterstützt VI 9. 15, von Demosthenes als Gesandtem gewarnt
VI 19, ohne Erfolg VI 26.

μέτοικοι, Beisassen in Athen, waren zu gewissen Leiturgien, zur Vermögenssteuer und zum Kriegsdienst verpflichtet,

und zwar je nach dem Einkommen als Hopliten oder auf
der Flotte IV 36.

Μῆδοι werden die Perser gern genannt, wenn von den
Perserkriegen und ihrer Zeit die Rede ist IX 42.

μηχανήματα, Belagerungsmaschinen, hauptsächlich beweg-
liche Türme, die auf Rädern liefen und außen mit rohen
Häuten bekleidet wurden, von Philippos bis 36 m hoch
gebaut IX 17. 50.

Μιλτιάδης, der Feldherr von Marathon III 26.

μυστήρια (*τὰ μεγάλα*), attisches Fest zu Ehren der De-
meter vom 14. bis gegen den 25. Boëdromion (September)
gefeiert, und zwar zuerst in Athen, am 19. wurde das
heilige Bild des Iakchos in feierlichem Aufzuge nach Eleusis
übergeführt, wo die weitere Feier stattfand III 5.

Ναύπακτος, wichtige Hafenstadt an der Nordseite des
korinthischen Busens, nahe der engsten Stelle. Die achäi-
sche Besatzung wurde von Epameinondas vorübergehend
vertrieben. 338 wurde die Stadt von Philippos den Aito-
liern zu dauerndem Besitze übergeben IX 34.

Νεοπτόλεμος von der athenischen Insel Skyros, tragischer
Schauspieler von Ruf, benutzte die der Kunst gewährte
Freiheit zu politischer Zwischenträgerei V 6.

νεώρια, Werft, Gesamtbezeichnung der für die Kriegsflotte
bestimmten Hafenräume Athens mit Schiffshäusern, Zeug-
häusern und Bauplätzen VIII 45.

νεώσοικοι, Schiffshäuser, um den Rumpf der abgetakelten
Schiffe vor der Witterung zu schützen VII 16. In Athen
gab es um 350 deren 300, von je 5½ m Breite mit einer
geneigten Steinbahn im Innern, rings an den Häfen Munichia,
Zea und Kantharos.

Νίκαια, Festung an den Thermopylen, 346 von den Phokern
an Philippos übergeben, von diesen den Thessaliern versprochen VI 22.

Νικίας, der Feldherr des sikilischen Unternehmens III 21.

νομοθέται, eine aus 500 oder 1000 heliastischen Richtern
gebildete Körperschaft, welche auf Beschluß der Volksversammlung niedergesetzt wurde, um Anträge auf Gesetzes-
änderungen zu prüfen und zwischen ihnen und den bisher
geltenden Bestimmungen zu entscheiden III 10.

ξένια in der Verbindung ἐπὶ ξένια καλεῖν bedeutet zur Speisung im Prytaneion einladen VII 20.

ξένοι, Söldner, in Griechenland zuerst im korinthischen Kriege verwandt IV 23, stehende Söldnerheere wurden gebildet von Dionysios I. von Syrakus, Iason von Pherai und Philippos II 17. IX 32. 58. Die Söldner Athens wurden sehr unregelmäfsig bezahlt IV 24. 46, Söldner unter Diopeithes VIII 9.

Ὄλυνϑος, bedeutendste Stadt der Chalkidike, im Innern des toronäischen Meerbusens, 364 von Timotheos im Bunde mit Perdikkas von Makedonien glücklich bekämpft II 14, sucht 357 Athens Freundschaft II 6, wird von Philippos durch Überlassung von Anthemus und Poteidaia gewonnen II 7. VI 20. VIII 62. 65, von Philippos bedroht IV 17, von Parteiungen gespalten IX 56, von dem Könige angegriffen VIII 59. IX 11, durch Verrat genommen VIII 40 und zerstört IX 26. 66.

ὄλυραι, geringwertige Getreideart, die in Griechenland nur als Pferdefutter, in Ägypten auch als Brotfrucht verwandt wurde, dem Spelz verwandt, wohl das Einkorn, triticum monococcum L. VIII 45.

Παγασαί, Stadt in der innersten Bucht des pagasäischen Meerbusens, von Philippos 352 belagert I 9 und genommen I 13, athenische Hilfe kommt zu spät IV 35, wird von den Thessaliern zurückgefordert I 22. II 11.

Παιανία, Gau der Phyle Pandionis, am Ostabhang des Hymettos gelegen VII 43, ihm gehörte auch Demosthenes zu.

Παίονες, Volk nördlich von Makedonien an den Quellen des Axios und Strymon, von Philippos 358 und 356 geschlagen I 13. 23.

Παλλήνη, westliche Halbinsel der Chalkidike VII 28.

Παναϑήναια, Fest zum Gedächtnis der Vereinigung der Bewohner Attikas zu einem Gesamtstaat, vom 23.—28. Hekatombaion (Juli) gefeiert, in jedem fünften Jahre mit besonderem Glanze, mit ritterlichen, gymnischen und musischen Wettkämpfen. Den Schlufs bildete die Darbringung des Peplos in feierlichem Aufzuge, welchen der Cellafries des Parthenons veranschaulicht IV 35.

Πανδοσία, bedeutende Stadt der Landschaft Kassopia in Epeiros, nördlich des ambrakischen Busens VII 32.

πάραλος, eine der beiden heiligen Trieren, welche mit Bürgern bemannt zu Theorien, Geldsendungen, Botschaften benutzt wurden VIII 29, von Philippos bei Marathon weggefangen IV 34.

Παρμενίων, Heerführer des Philippos, nach Eretria entsandt IX 58.

πεζέταιροι, das Aufgebot der freien Makedonier, welche mit der $5^1/_2$ m langen Sarisse bewaffnet das schwere Fußvolk, die Phalanx, bildeten II 17.

Πειραιεύς, der Hafen von Athen VIII 7. 74. IX 10.

Πέλλα, Stadt in Unter-Makedonien an einem See, aus dem der schiffbare Ludias fließt, seit dem Ende des peloponnesischen Krieges Hauptstadt des Landes (früher Aigai), von Philippos erheblich verschönert VII 7.

Πελοπόννησος, eine Partei ist Athen abgeneigt, Philippos zugänglich V 18. VI 18. 26. IX 18. Philippos steht der Weg dahin offen VI 35, seine Übergriffe IX 17. 27, athenische Gesandtschaften VI 19. IX 71 f. Persisches Gold im Pel. IX 42 f.

Περικλῆς, Sohn des Xanthippos, der berühmte Staatsmann Athens III 21.

Πέρσαι, von den Griechen zurückgeschlagen IX 36, der König VII 29. IX 42, Gesandtschaft von Athen zu ihm IX 71.

Πλαταιαί, Stadt am Nordfuß des Kithairon, 373 von den Thebanern durch Überfall genommen und zerstört. Erhoffte Wiederherstellung V 10. VI 30.

Πλούταρχος, Machthaber in Eretria, erbat 348 von den Athenern Hilfe und lieferte nach dem unter Phokion errungenen Siege bei Tamynai eine auf Euboia zurückgebliebene Abteilung der Athener den Gegnern in die Hände V 5, darauf verließ er Euboia IX 57.

Πολύευκτος von Sphettos, athenischer Staatsmann, als Gesandter im Peloponnes IX 72.

Πολύστρατος, mit Iphikrates zusammen als Führer der Söldner im korinthischen Kriege genannt und von den Athenern geehrt IV 23.

Πορθμός, befestigte Stadt auf Euboia, östlich von Eretria, von Philippos 342 gebrochen IX 33. 57.

πορισταί werden als athenische Beamte im peloponnesischen Kriege nach dem sikilischen Unternehmen erwähnt, mit der Aufgabe neue Einkünfte dem Staate zu erschliefsen. Das Wort steht IV 33 allgemein als „Zahler".

Ποτείδαια, wichtige Stadt an der schmalsten Stelle der Halbinsel Pallene, 364 von Timotheos erobert und bald mit attischen Kleruchen besetzt VI 20. Obwohl Philippos mit diesen ein Bündnis geschlossen VII 10, verband er sich mit Olynthos II 14, belagerte die Stadt I 9, der Athen verspätete Hilfe schickte IV 35, eroberte und zerstörte sie 356 I 12. II 7. Das Gebiet wurde den Olynthiern überlassen VI 20. VIII 62. 65. Später war es für Philippos selbst ein wichtiger Besitz VI 17.

προμαντεία, das Recht zuerst das delphische Orakel zu befragen, welches nur einmal monatlich Rede stand, ein Vorrecht, das von den Delphiern als Ehre verliehen wurde. Dann wohl auch das Recht das Orakel namens der Amphiktyonen zu befragen, welches früher im Besitz der Athener 346 auf Philippos übertragen wurde IX 32.

προστάτης (τοῦ δήμου), gewohnheitsmäfsige Bezeichnung für den leitenden Staatsmann in Athen III 27, dann auch für den leitenden Staat in Griechenland IX 23.

Πτελεόν, Ort in der Nähe von Kardia an der Grenze des Chersonnes VII 39.

Πύδνα, Stadt an der makedonischen Küste südlich von Methone, mit Athen verbündet IV 4, von Philippos 357 belagert I 9 und durch Verrat genommen I 5. 12.

Πύθια, das zweite Nationalfest der Griechen, in Delphoi im Monat Bukatios (August) im dritten Olympiadenjahr gefeiert mit musischen, gymnischen und ritterlichen Wettkämpfen V 22. IX 32.

Πύθων von Byzantion, Schüler des Isokrates, gewandter Redner, als Gesandter des Philippos in Athen VII 20 f.

Πυθώναξ von Zeleia, Vater des Arthmios IX 42.

Πύλαι, Pafs zwischen den Abhängen des Kallidromos-Gebirges und dem Meere, aus Thessalien nach Lokris führend, 352 von Philippos bedroht, aber von den Athenern gesichert IV 17. 41, seit 346 in Philippos' Besitze VI 7. VIII 64. IX 32, nachdem Demosthenes vergeblich gewarnt hatte VI 29. 35.

πυλαία, der Vorsitz in den Versammlungen der Amphiktyonen
V 23. VI 22. VIII 65.

Ρόδος, die Insel, von Karerfürsten bedroht V 25, athenische
Gesandtschaft dorthin IX 71.

Σέρριον und *Σέρρειον τεῖχος,* thrakische Küstenplätze,
von Philippos 346 gleich nach dem Frieden genommen,
ersteres VIII 64. IX 15 mit Doriskos, letzteres VII 37. IX 15
mit Hieron Oros zusammen genannt.

Σίγειον, Stadt und Vorgebirge in Troas am Eingang des
Hellespont, von Chares mit athenischen Söldnern genommen
II 28.

σιροί, Erdgruben, in denen die Thraker ihr Getreide auf-
heben VIII 45.

σιτηρέσιον, Verpflegungsgeld, welches die Soldaten im
peloponnesischen Kriege neben dem Sold erhielten, und
zwar gewöhnlich der Hoplit 2 Obolen täglich neben dem
gleichen Sold IV 28.

Σκίαθος, Insel gegenüber der Nordspitze von Euboia und
der Südspitze von Magnesia, athenische Flottenstation IV 32,
von Oreos aus durch Philippos bedroht VIII 37.

Σκῦρος, Insel des ägäischen Meeres, östlich von Euboia,
auf dem Weg von Athen zum Hellespont, Besitzung Athens
VII 4.

στηλίτην ποιεῖν τινα, jemandes Namen auf eine Schand-
säule eingraben IX 41 f.

στρατεύεσθαι. Zum Dienst aufser Landes waren die
Athener vom 20. bis 50. Jahre verpflichtet und wurden
dazu nach Jahrgängen aufgeboten III 4. IV 21, oft aber
auch aus den einzelnen Jahrgängen einzelne II 31. Befreit
vom Kriegsdienst waren Ratsherren, Beamte und Zollpächter.
Auch die Choreuten wurden auf Antrag befreit, und damit
wurde Mifsbrauch getrieben III 11.

στρατηγοί, jährlich 10 aus allen Athenern gewählt, wurden
nach dem peloponnesischen Kriege mehr und mehr Ver-
waltungsbeamte, als die Bürgerheere seltner auszogen
IV 19. 26. Die wirklichen Heerführer waren von den
Parteien und ihren Rednern abhängig II 29.

Στρατοκλῆς von Amphipolis als Gesandter in Athen I 8.

σύμβολα, Rechtsverträge, welche Staaten bei lebhaftem
Verkehr mit einander abschlossen, um die Entscheidung
von Rechtsstreitigkeiten ihrer Angehörigen zu ordnen, und
bei denen in der Regel der Prozeſs am Wohnorte des
Beklagten entschieden wurde VII 9.

συμμορίαι, Steuerabteilungen, in die die Gesamtheit der
Steuerpflichtigen so geteilt war, daſs eine jede Abteilung
einen annähernd gleichen Teil der Steuerkraft darstellte.
Jede solche Abteilung hatte ihren ἡγεμών. Zur Beschleunigung der Erhebung muſsten die 300 reichsten
Bürger (οἱ τριακόσιοι) den Steuerbetrag vorwegerlegen.
Sie zogen dann von den übrigen Bürgern den auf diese
entfallenden Teil ein, wobei es nicht ohne Willkürlichkeiten
abging II 29.

Σωκράτης, Führer der makedonischen Partei in Oreos auf
Euboia IX 59.

ταμίαι, Schatzmeister, wie sie alle Kassen in Athen hatten
IV 33. VIII 47.

ταξίαρχοι, 10 an Zahl, je einer aus der Phyle jährlich
erwählt, befehligten die Hopliten ihres Stammes IV 26.

τετραρχίαι, 342 von Philippos in Thessalien eingerichtet,
indem über die vier alten Landschaften, Thessaliotis,
Phthiotis, Pelasgiotis, Hestiaiotis je ein Machthaber, drei
davon aus dem Hause der Aleuaden, gesetzt wurde IX 26.

Τιμόθεος, Konons Sohn, athenischer Feldherr, bekämpft
364 Olynthos mit Glück II 14, ruft 357 zum Hilfszug
nach Euboia auf VIII 74, wird nach dem Bundesgenossen-
kriege 354 des Verrats angeklagt, wegen seines stolzen
Auftretens vor Gericht zu 100 Talenten verurteilt, starb
im selben Jahre zu Chalkis.

τριακόσιοι s. συμμορίαι.

τριηραρχία, schwerste der Leistungen der Bürger, bei
welcher der Staat in Demosthenes' Zeit den Schiffsrumpf
und das Gerät stellte und die Ruderer besoldete, der
Trierarch das Schiff segelfertig zu machen und zu erhalten
und Steuerleute und Matrosen zu besolden hatte. Damals
wurden schon vielfach zwei oder mehrere Bürger zu einer
Syntrierarchie verbunden II 30. IV 36.

τριήρεις ταχεῖαι, Schlachtschiffe im Gegensatze zu Transport-

schiffen (s. ἱππαγωγοί) mit 170 Ruderern bemannt, die
in drei Reihen geordnet jeder ein Ruder führten IV 22,
ἱεραί die Botenschiffe Salaminia und Paralos (s. d.), welche
letztere um 352 von Philippos bei Marathon weggefangen
wurde, als man dort zur Einsegnung der delischen Theorie
opferte IV 34.

τυραννική οἰκία in Thessalien sind die Machthaber von
Pherai, Lykophron und Peitholaos, welche 352 nach der
Niederlage der Phoker das Land räumen mußten II 14.
VI 22. VIII 65.

Φεραί, bedeutende Stadt Thessaliens, zwei Meilen westlich
der Hafenstadt Pagasai, von Philippos 352 genommen I 13,
aber wieder freigegeben VIII 59, seit 344 mit Besatzung
belegt VII 32. IX 12.

Φιλιστίδης von Oreos auf Euboia, Führer der makedonischen Partei IX 59, von Philippos als Machthaber eingesetzt IX 33.

Φιλοκράτης von Hagnus, Urheber des nach ihm benannten
Friedens VII 24 f., wird 343 von Hypereides der Bestechung
angeklagt und geht in die Verbannung.

φύλαρχοι, 10 an Zahl, je einer aus der Phyle jährlich
gewählt, befehligten die 10 Abteilungen der athenischen
Reiterei IV 26.

Φωκεῖς, ihr Krieg II 7, Geldmangel und Ohnmacht III 8.
I 26, des Philippos Eingreifen IX 11, von den Athenern
preisgegeben V 10. VI 29. 35, begehen viele Fehler IX 68,
haben ein übermächtiges Bündnis gegen sich V 19 und
werden vernichtet VI 15. IX 19. 26 zum Vorteil der Thebaner VIII 65, zum Schaden Athens VIII 64, in Philippos'
Gewalt VI 7.

Χαβρίας, athenischer Feldherr, Führer der Söldner im
korinthischen Kriege IV 23.   Er fiel 357 im Bundes-
genossenkriege als Trierarch vor Chios.

Χαλκίς, bedeutendste Stadt auf Euboia am Euripos VIII 18,
dennoch ohne Einfluß auf die Geschicke Griechenlands IX 74.

Χάρης, athenischer Feldherr, wegen seines schwelgerischen
Lebens und der Härte gegen die Bundesgenossen übel
beleumundet VIII 30.

Χαρίδημος von Oreos, ein Söldnerhauptmann, der aus dem Krieg ein Gewerbe machte, später in nähere Beziehung zu dem Odrysenkönig Kersobleptes trat und Feind der Makedonier wurde. Von den Athenern 351 nach Thrakien geschickt III 5.

Χερρόννησος, der thrakische. Die Grenze bildete sonst eine von dem älteren Miltiades erbaute (Herod. VI 36), von Derkylidas (Xen. Hell. III 2, 10) erneuerte Mauer von Kardia nach Paktye, Hegesippos jedoch will die Grenze weiter nach Norden hinausschieben VII 39. Der Ch. außer Kardia ist im Besitz der Athener IX 16, von Philippos 352 bedroht IV 17. 41. Die Absicht eines Durchstichs ist erwähnt VII 39. VI 30. Nach dem philokrateischen Frieden wurde er durch Kolonisten unter Diopeithes gesichert, die mit Kardia in Streit gerieten VIII 58.

Χίος, Insel des ägäischen Meeres, von Karerfürsten bedroht V 25, von athenischen Söldnerführern gebrandschatzt VIII 24, athenische Gesandtschaft dorthin IX 71.

χορηγοί, vermögende Leute, die von ihrer Phyle bestellt wurden, um für die Feste die dramatischen und lyrischen Chöre einzuüben, zu unterhalten und auszustatten IV 36.

χωρὶς οἰκοῦντες, Sklaven, welche von ihren Herren getrennt wohnten, für eigne Rechnung arbeiteten und an die Herren jährlich eine bestimmte Abgabe entrichteten IV 36.

Ὠρεός, Stadt an der Nordküste Euboias, von Parteiungen gespalten IX 59, von Philippos unter Freundschaftsversicherungen besetzt VIII 18. 59. IX 12, welcher Philistides als Machthaber daselbst bestellt IX 33. Die Bewohner, *Ὠρεῖται*, haben viele Fehler begangen IX 68.

Ὠρωπός, Stadt in der Nähe der Asoposmündung, beständiger Zankapfel zwischen Athen und Theben V 16, seit 366 im Besitz der Thebaner V 24, Hoffnungen der Athener auf Wiedergewinn V 10. VI 30.

Kritischer Anhang.

I 3. $\tau\varrho\acute{\epsilon}\psi\eta\tau\alpha\iota$ „in seinem Interesse wende". — 5. $\pi o \lambda \epsilon \mu o \tilde{v} \sigma \iota$, sie stehen doch schon im Kriege. — 24. $\varkappa\alpha\vartheta$' $\dot{v}\mu\tilde{\omega}\nu$ mit Harl. ist durch das folgende $\dot{\epsilon}\varphi$' $\dot{v}\mu\tilde{\alpha}\varsigma$ erfordert.

II 5. $\tau o \iota o \tilde{v} \tau o \nu$ mit Blaſs nach $\gamma\varrho$. B: $\tau o \acute{v} \tau o \iota \varsigma$. — 8. $\tilde{\eta}$ vor $\dot{\omega}\varsigma$ $o\dot{v}\varkappa$ mit Σ weggelassen. — 12. $\pi\varrho\acute{\alpha}\gamma\mu\alpha\tau\alpha$ am besten bezeugt, der gewöhnliche Gegensatz $\check{\epsilon}\varrho\gamma\alpha$ war schon vorher gebraucht. — 28. $\varkappa\alpha\grave{\iota}$ $\tilde{\alpha}$ $\check{\alpha}\nu$ Rehdantz: $'A\mu\varphi\acute{\iota}\pi o \lambda \iota \varsigma$ $\varkappa\check{\alpha}\nu$.

III 2. $\dot{\epsilon}\varkappa\epsilon\tilde{\iota}\nu o \nu$ $\tau\varrho\acute{o}\pi o \nu$ mit Voemel, $\tau\varrho\acute{o}\pi o \nu$ gehört natürlich zu $\tau\acute{\iota}\nu\alpha$. — 8. $\check{\alpha}\pi\alpha\nu\tau\epsilon\varsigma$ $\dot{\epsilon}\vartheta\varrho\acute{v}\lambda o \nu\nu$ $\tau o \tilde{v} \tau o$ mit pr. Σ und Blaſs. — 27. $\delta\grave{\epsilon}$ hinter $\dot{\epsilon}\xi\grave{o}\nu$ gestrichen mit Bekker. — 30. $\tau\acute{o}\tau\epsilon$ $\mu\grave{\epsilon}\nu$ $\pi\varrho\acute{\alpha}\tau\tau\epsilon\iota\nu$ Rehdantz: $\tau\grave{o}$ $\mu\grave{\epsilon}\nu$ $\pi\varrho\tilde{\omega}\tau o \nu$. — 35. $\mu\iota\varkappa\varrho\grave{o}\nu$ mit pr. Σ.

IV 10. $\tau\grave{\eta}\nu$ $\dot{v}\pi\grave{\epsilon}\varrho$ $\tau\tilde{\omega}\nu$ $\pi\varrho\alpha\gamma\mu\acute{\alpha}\tau\omega\nu$ $\alpha\dot{\iota}\sigma\chi\acute{v}\nu\eta\nu$. Das Treibende ist immer das Gefühl der Scham. Vgl. VIII 51. — 18 Anf. Die Interpunktion nach Weil. — 35. $o\dot{\iota}$ ... $\dot{\epsilon}\pi\iota\mu\epsilon\lambda o \acute{v}\mu\epsilon\nu o \iota$ ist Subjekt, $\lambda\acute{\alpha}\chi\omega\sigma\iota$ vertritt die Kopula. — 38. $\tau\grave{\alpha}$ $\pi\varrho\acute{\alpha}\gamma\mu\alpha\tau\alpha$ ist Subjekt. — 40. $o\dot{v}\delta\grave{\epsilon}\nu$ δ' $\dot{\alpha}\pi o \lambda\epsilon\acute{\iota}\pi\epsilon\tau\epsilon$ Dobree und Sauppe: „Ihr laſst es an nichts fehlen" ...

V 8. $\pi o \iota\eta\sigma\acute{\alpha}\mu\epsilon\nu o \varsigma$ Tournier: $\dot{\epsilon}\pi o \iota\acute{\eta}\sigma\alpha\tau o$, was in pr. Σ fehlt. — 23. $\tau o \tilde{v} \tau o$ $\mu\acute{\epsilon}\nu\tau o \iota$, $\check{\epsilon}\tau\iota$ $\tau o \tilde{v} \tau$' nach Rehdantz: $\tau o \tilde{v} \tau o$ μ. $\check{o}\tau\iota$ $\tau o \tilde{v} \tau$' pr. Σ, $\check{\epsilon}\tau\iota$, insofern gerade jetzt die Lage bedrohlich ist, wo die Amphiktyonen noch beisammen sind. — 24. $o\dot{v}\delta$' vor $\dot{o}\tau\iota o \tilde{v}\nu$ zugesetzt mit Cobet.

VI 15. $\sigma v \lambda \lambda\alpha\mu\beta\acute{\alpha}\nu\epsilon\iota\nu$ Weil: $\sigma v \mu\beta\acute{\alpha}\lambda\lambda\epsilon\iota\nu$. — 18. $\check{\alpha}\nu$ hinter $\delta\iota\varkappa\alpha\acute{\iota}\omega\varsigma$ gestrichen mit Schaefer. — $\tau\acute{\iota}\nu\alpha\varsigma$; mit Rehdantz. — 35. $\pi\epsilon\acute{\iota}\sigma\alpha\varsigma$ $\varkappa\alpha\grave{\iota}$ $\Pi\acute{v}\lambda\alpha\varsigma$ $\dot{v}\mu\tilde{\alpha}\varsigma$ nach Bekker mit einigen Hss.

VII 33. $\check{o}\sigma$' Tournier: $\check{o}\tau$'.

VIII 23. δ' $\check{\alpha}\varrho$': $\gamma\grave{\alpha}\varrho$, der Satz enthält eine Steigerung (bei Dem. nur $\epsilon\dot{\iota}$ δ' $\check{\alpha}\varrho\alpha$, $\check{\alpha}\nu$ δ' $\check{\alpha}\varrho\alpha$, daher $\epsilon\dot{\iota}$ ... $\delta\acute{\iota}\delta o \tau\epsilon$ gegen ΣL). — 33. $\dot{\epsilon}\varkappa\epsilon\acute{\iota}\nu\alpha\iota\varsigma$ mit Blaſs. — 44. Hinter $\dot{\epsilon}\xi\alpha\iota\varrho\epsilon\tilde{\iota}$ ist $\varkappa\alpha\grave{\iota}$ $\varkappa\alpha\tau\alpha\sigma\varkappa\epsilon\nu\acute{\alpha}\zeta\epsilon$-$\tau\alpha\iota$ mit Weil gestrichen. — 57. $\pi\alpha\varrho$' $\dot{v}\mu\tilde{\iota}\nu$ mit ΣL ist richtiger, so lange der Zorn noch kein Ziel hat. — 63. $\check{o}$ $\tau\iota$ $\check{\alpha}\nu$ gegen ΣL

mit X 65, weil sonst der Gegenstand des Leidens unbezeichnet bliebe. — $\dot{\varepsilon}\xi\eta\pi\alpha\tau\dot{\eta}\vartheta\eta\tau\varepsilon$ ... $\dot{\alpha}\pi\varepsilon\sigma\tau\varepsilon\varrho\dot{\eta}\vartheta\eta\tau\varepsilon$ statt des pf., um die Handlung ($\dot{\varepsilon}\nu$ $\alpha\dot{\nu}\tau\tilde{\omega}$ $\tau\tilde{\omega}$ ...) dem Zustande ($\tilde{\omega}\nu$ $\dot{\alpha}\pi\varepsilon\sigma\tau\acute{\varepsilon}\varrho\eta\sigma\vartheta\varepsilon$) entgegenzustellen.

IX 25. $o\dot{\nu}\delta\grave{\varepsilon}$ $\mu\acute{\varepsilon}\varrho o\varsigma$ mit Rehdantz ($\pi\acute{\varepsilon}\mu\pi\tau o\nu$ oder $\pi o\lambda\lambda o\sigma\tau\grave{o}\nu$ gestrichen). — Im Folgenden sind die Worte, die ΣL weglassen, zumeist beibehalten. — 65. $\check{\varepsilon}\vartheta$' $\dot{\nu}\mu\tilde{\iota}\nu$ Franke: $\dot{\varepsilon}\nu$ $\dot{\nu}\mu\tilde{\iota}\nu$ ΣL.

SMALL VOLUME

TABLESPOONS	CUPS	FLUID OUNCES
1 tablespoon = 3 teaspoons		$\frac{1}{2}$ fluid ounce
2 tablespoons	$\frac{1}{8}$ cup	1 fluid ounce
4 tablespoons	$\frac{1}{4}$ cup	2 fluid ounces
5 tablespoons + 1 teaspoon	$\frac{1}{3}$ cup	$2\frac{2}{3}$ fluid ounces
6 tablespoons	$\frac{3}{8}$ cup	3 fluid ounces
8 tablespoons	$\frac{1}{2}$ cup	4 fluid ounces
10 tablespoons + 2 teaspoons	$\frac{2}{3}$ cup	$5\frac{1}{3}$ fluid ounces
12 tablespoons	$\frac{3}{4}$ cup	6 fluid ounces
14 tablespoons	$\frac{7}{8}$ cup	7 fluid ounces
16 tablespoons	1 cup	8 fluid ounces

LARGE VOLUME

CUPS	FLUID OUNCES	PINTS/QUARTS
1 cup	8 fluid ounces	$\frac{1}{2}$ pint
2 cups	16 fluid ounces	1 pint
3 cups	24 fluid ounces	$1\frac{1}{2}$ pints = $\frac{3}{4}$ quart
4 cups	32 fluid ounces	2 pints = 1 quart
6 cups	48 fluid ounces	3 pints = $1\frac{1}{2}$ quarts
8 cups	64 fluid ounces	2 quarts = $\frac{1}{2}$ gallon
16 cups	128 fluid ounces	4 quarts = 1 gallon

Asian fish sauce, 1 tablespoon
Use 2 teaspoons soy sauce and 1 teaspoon anchovy paste.

Baking powder, 1 teaspoon
Use $\frac{1}{2}$ teaspoon cream of tartar and $\frac{1}{4}$ teaspoon baking soda (make fresh for each use).

Buttermilk, 1 cup
Place 1 tablespoon vinegar or lemon juice in cup and stir in enough milk to equal 1 cup; let stand 5 minutes to thicken. Or use 1 cup plain yogurt or sour cream, thinned with $\frac{1}{4}$ cup milk (there will be some leftover).

Cake flour, 1 cup
Place 2 tablespoons cornstarch in cup and add enough all-purpose flour to fill to overflowing; level off top; stir well before using.

Chives
Substitute green onion tops.

Chocolate, unsweetened, melted, 1 ounce
Use 3 tablespoons unsweetened cocoa plus 1 tablespoon salad oil, shortening, butter, or margarine.

Cornstarch (for thickening), 1 tablespoon
Use 2 tablespoons all-purpose flour or 2 tablespoons quick-cooking tapioca.

Light brown sugar, 1 cup
Use 1 cup granulated sugar and 1 tablespoon molasses or use dark brown sugar.

Pancetta
Substitute sliced smoked bacon. Simmer in water for three minutes, then rinse and drain.

Pepper, ground red, $\frac{1}{8}$ teaspoon
Use 4 drops hot pepper sauce.

Pine nuts
Use walnuts or almonds.

Prosciutto
Use ham, preferably Westphalian or a country ham, such as Smithfield.

Shallots
Use red onion.

Tomato sauce, 15-ounce can
Use 6-ounce can tomato paste plus $1\frac{1}{2}$ cans water.

Yeast, active dry, $\frac{1}{4}$-ounce package
Use 0.6-ounce cake, or use one-third of 2-ounce cake compressed yeast.

Vanilla extract
Use brandy or an appropriately flavored liqueur.

The Good Housekeeping Cookbook

Edited by Susan Westmoreland

FOOD DIRECTOR, GOOD HOUSEKEEPING

HEARST BOOKS
A DIVISION OF STERLING PUBLISHING CO., INC.
NEW YORK

Good Housekeeping
EDITOR-IN-CHIEF: Ellen Levine
FOOD DIRECTOR: Susan Westmoreland
ASSOCIATE FOOD DIRECTOR: Susan Deborah Goldsmith
SPECIAL PROJECTS DIRECTOR: Richard Eisenberg

The Good Housekeeping Cookbook
CULINARY CONSULTANT AND EDITOR: Deborah Mintcheff
CULINARY EDITOR, RECIPE DEVELOPMENT: Elizabeth Brainerd Burge
MANAGING EDITOR: Maryanne Bannon
WRITER: Rick Rodgers

Hearst Books
PUBLISHER: Jacqueline Deval

Book Art Direction and Design
BTDNYC: Sabrina Bowers, Erica Harrison, Kimberly Johnston, Lorie Pagnozzi, Daniel Rodney, Beth Tondreau, Mary A. Wirth

Illustrator
Alan Witschonke

Cover Design
Celia Fuller

Library of Congress Cataloging-in-Publication Data Available.

10 9 8 7 6 5 4 3 2 1

Published by Hearst Books
A Division of Sterling Publishing Co., Inc.
387 Park Avenue South, New York, NY 10016

Good Housekeeping is a trademark owned by Hearst Magazines Property, Inc., in USA, and Hearst Communications, Inc., in Canada. Hearst Books is a trademark owned by Hearst Communications, Inc.

The Good Housekeeping Cookbook Seal guarantees that the recipes in this cookbook meet the strict standards of the Good Housekeeping Institute, a source of reliable information and a consumer advocate since 1900. Every recipe has been triple-tested for ease, reliability, and great taste.

www.goodhousekeeping.com

Distributed in Canada by Sterling Publishing
c/o Canadian Manda Group, One Atlantic Avenue, Suite 105
Toronto, Ontario, Canada M6K 3E7

Distributed in Australia by Capricorn Link (Australia) Pty. Ltd.
P.O. Box 704, Windsor, NSW 2756 Australia

Printed in China

ISBN 1-58816-398-9

FOREWORD

We all need a little help in the kitchen, and there's no more reliable guidebook than the one you hold in your hands. I definitely could have used it as a young bride; we had lots of great cooking gear after the wedding but not much information on how to use it. My first big mistake was the Thanksgiving turkey. It wouldn't fit into the budget-size oven in the apartment Dick and I were renting!

Cooking was a mystery to me. I didn't have high-school home ec. I asked friends who had been married longer for help, and I approached each casserole like chemistry class, measuring ingredients carefully, in the hopes that nothing would combust. Left to my own devices, I found that that the secret to success was cooking by the book. And the clearer the recipes, the better my meals turned out.

By the time our sons, Peter and Dan, came along, I was doing dinner every night and cooking nursery food in between. (Even today, when my kids don't feel well, they long for tapioca pudding, chicken soup, and other comfort foods I made.) I started to love baking, and still do—almost as much as I love taking that first sweet bite of a homemade chocolate dessert.

I learned that pride in the the kitchen—and at the table—comes from knowing you made something yourself, and that's what this book is about. The latest in our long, venerable line of *Good Housekeeping* cookbooks (the first was published in 1903), this one, like its sisters before, is perfectly attuned to the trends and concerns of its time, from using leaner cuts of meat and less fat to cook them, to getting a tasty meal on the table quickly.

The All New Good Housekeeping Cookbook is like 10 books in one. You'll find color photos throughout, depicting ingredients, techniques, and finished dishes. We've included more veggies, grains, pasta, fruit, fish, salads and salad dressings, along with classics like meat, chicken, breads, cakes, and cookies. No question is left unanswered, no pot uncovered, whether you are a beginner or an old hand. This is your resource for everything from weeknight suppers to dinner parties—from basic baked potatoes to fancy Potatoes Anna. Every recipe, as always, has been triple-tested, all include complete nutritional information, and many are flagged as fast or low-fat. And 36 prominent chefs and authors share insider info for our quick Expert Tips.

Here at *Good Housekeeping,* we're committed to keeping America's families healthy and happy and cared for—and keeping them at the dinner table long enough to share some quality time. Although tastes have changed, the goal our great-grandmothers had at the stove is still our mission today. We cook to create warm memories, to gather loved ones close, with the scent of baking bread, the sizzle of grilled veggies, the crack-and-scramble of eggs. We draw family and friends in when and while we can, if only in brief snatches, to nourish them for the future.

As I write, our own brood is growing. More new reasons to gather round the table, break bread, stay close, and build memories. More people to hear my Thanksgiving tale, and keep it alive in the family lore.

From our kitchen to yours, happy cooking! May the book you hold in your hands take you wherever you want to go for dinner tonight and for hundreds of nights to follow.

Ellen Levine, Editor-in-Chief

CONTENTS

1 ▪ BASICS ▪ 6

2 ▪ APPETIZERS ▪ 34

3 ▪ SOUPS ▪ 56

4 ▪ MEAT ▪ 86

5 ▪ POULTRY ▪ 184

6 ▪ FISH AND SHELLFISH ▪ 250

7 ▪ EGGS ▪ 306

8 ▪ CHEESE ▪ 326

9 ▪ PASTA AND PASTA SAUCES ▪ 338

10 ▪ BEANS, RICE, AND OTHER GRAINS ▪ 370

11 ▪ VEGETABLES ▪ 400

12 ▪ FRUITS ▪ 480

13 ▪ SALADS AND SALAD DRESSINGS ▪ 520

14 ■ SAUCES, SALSAS, AND CONDIMENTS ■ 548

15 ■ QUICK BREADS ■ 564

16 ■ YEAST BREADS ■ 582

17 ■ SANDWICHES ■ 608

18 ■ DESSERTS ■ 620

19 ■ CAKES AND CAKE FROSTINGS ■ 648

20 ■ PIES AND TARTS ■ 682

21 ■ COOKIES AND CONFECTIONS ■ 710

22 ■ FROZEN DESSERTS ■ 746

23 ■ BEVERAGES ■ 760

24 ■ CANNING AND FREEZING ■ 770

INDEX ■ 802

ACKNOWLEDGMENTS ■ 832

1

BASICS

EQUIPMENT

A well-supplied kitchen is ground zero for cooking delicious meals. Start with a basic collection of reliable kitchen tools. You can accomplish a lot with a good set of knives and a few well-chosen pots and pans. Then, when you are feeling more adventurous, check out the more specialized cookware that lines the shelves of kitchenware shops. Just remember, you often get what you pay for. High-quality utensils, made from durable materials, last longer, so buy the best you can afford.

ON THE STOVE

Pots and pans can be made of many materials and are usually priced according to the metal(s) they are made of. The most common cookware metals are stainless steel, copper, cast iron, and aluminum. None of these metals is absolutely perfect as a cookware material, so many manufacturers layer the metals to create pots and pans that are good conductors of heat, easy to clean, and durable.

Stainless steel is easy to clean and not too heavy, but it isn't a very good conductor of heat; an aluminum or copper core is often added to improve its heat-conducting qualities. By contrast, copper is a superb conductor of heat and copper pots are gorgeous, but the pots must be polished and can be very heavy.

Cast iron and aluminum are inexpensive and excellent heat conductors. Unfortunately, they react to acidic ingredients, like tomatoes and wine, but they are also available enamel-coated.

Regular (not enamel-coated) cast-iron skillets and pots must be "seasoned" before being used to create a nonstick finish. Wash in hot soapy water and dry completely. Rub the entire surface, including the exterior and the lid, with a wad of paper towels soaked in vegetable oil. Heat the pan and lid upside down in a 350°F oven for one hour. Turn off the oven; leave the pan in the oven to cool completely. If at some point the cast iron rusts or the nonstick patina is removed, you must season the pan again. When washing cast iron, take special care to protect the nonstick surface. Rinse under very hot water, but do not use dishwashing detergent. Sprinkle the wet cast iron with salt; rub well with paper towels to remove any food residue. Dry immediately.

Choose pots and pans with thick bottoms to discourage scorching and with heatproof or hollow handles. Prepackaged sets of pots and pans may seem like a good investment, but you could end up with extra pans you don't need. You're better off buying just the cookware you want from open stock. Here are the pots and pans you'll need to get started:

Saucepan Three or four saucepans with lids, ranging from 1 to 4 quarts. They should be between 3½ to 4 inches deep, so you can stir without food spilling over the sides.

Basic cooking equipment: steamer, saucepans, grill pan, Dutch oven, thermometers, skillets, double boiler

Dutch oven Traditional Dutch kitchens rarely had large ovens, so cooks relied on these versatile pots for braising roasts and stews on top of the stove. A 5- to 6-quart Dutch oven is the most useful size.

Skillets You'll need at least three sizes: small (8-inch), medium (9- to 10-inch), and large (12-inch).

Saucepot This wide, deep pot can be used for soups and stews. A 5-quart saucepot with a tight-fitting lid is versatile.

Stockpot A tall, narrow 6- to 8-quart stockpot can be called into action to cook many foods, including pasta, soups, stocks, lobster, and corn on the cob.

Double boiler A saucepan topped with another saucepan; the food is gently cooked in the top section by water simmering in the bottom saucepan.

Grill pan This ridged skillet acts as a stovetop grill. Food can be cooked with little or no added fat; the ridges allow the fat to drip away. Use over high heat for the best results.

Griddle This flat metal pan can be heated on top of the stove to cook pancakes, French toast, and bacon. Electric models (some have nonstick surfaces) are also available.

IN THE OVEN

When roasting or baking, many variables come into play, including the oven temperature and the cooking time, but the pan itself is important, too.

Some of the most popular materials for bakeware include enameled cast iron (easy to clean and a good heat conductor), enameled steel (a reasonably priced, lightweight choice for roasting pans), stainless steel (moderately heavy and durable), aluminum (often laminated to create a nonstick surface), heat-resistant glass (a popular, inexpensive choice), and glass-ceramic (which can go from oven to freezer). Earthenware and stoneware are especially good for foods that require long slow baking, like stews or beans.

Cake pans that have a dull heat-absorbing finish, such as aluminum, produce the best-textured cakes. Shiny metals, such as stainless steel, reflect the heat and should not be used; also avoid dark metal pans because they absorb heat too quickly. What's bad for a cake, however, is ideal when it comes to baking bread. Choose heavy aluminum or dark metal pans for the best texture and a well-browned crust.

If you use a glass or ceramic dish for sweet baked desserts, reduce the oven temperature by twenty-five degrees so the outside isn't overdone by the time the center is cooked. (Reducing the temperature for savory foods isn't as important because these foods aren't as delicate.)

To measure a baking dish or pan, measure across the top of the dish from inside edge to inside edge. Measure the depth on the inside of the pan from the bottom to the rim.

Here is a roundup of essential bakeware:

Baking dish A large, fairly shallow oval or rectangular dish with sides about 2 inches high and usually glass or ceramic. It's good to have a variety of sizes, but 10" by 15", 13" by 9", and 11" by 7" are the most commonly used.

Baking pan Similar to a baking dish but made of metal; the sides are 1½ to 2 inches high. You'll want an 8-inch square, a 9-inch square, and a 13" by 9" pan.

Casserole Round, oval, square, or rectangular, this lidded dish can be glass, ceramic, or enameled metal.

Roasting pan A large deep pan typically made of stainless steel, enameled steel, or aluminum. A rectangular roasting pan with a rack is the most useful.

Basic baking and roasting pans: metal loaf pan, oval baking dish, jelly-roll pan, cookie sheet, roasting pan and rack, round cake pan, square baking pan, springform pan

Cake pan Layer cakes are usually baked in 8- or 9-inch round pans (you'll need two or three of each), while baking pans are used for rectangular and square cakes.

Depending on what you like to bake, you may also need the following:

Springform pan 9" by 3" and 10" by 2½" are handy.

Tube pan Comes in 9- and 10-inch diameters.

Bundt pan Sometimes called a fluted tube pan (10 inch).

Loaf pan Standard sizes are 9" by 5" and 8½" by 4½". There is a substantial volume difference between the two.

Pie plate The standard size is 9" by 1"; deep-dish pie plates are 9½" by 1½" or 9½" by 2". Glass, dark metal, and aluminum pans make crisp, nicely browned piecrusts.

Tart pan A shallow metal pan with fluted sides and a removable bottom that comes in many shapes and sizes: 9" by 1" and 11" by 1" round pans are the most common.

Cookie sheets For the best air circulation and for even browning, choose shiny heavy metal cookie sheets with one or two slightly raised sides. Double-thick insulated pans protect against overbrowning. Nonstick surfaces are another option.

Jelly-roll pan Use a standard aluminum 15½" by 10½" pan for jelly-roll cakes.

Muffin tins To bake muffins and cupcakes, use standard 2½" by 1¼" muffin-pan cups; 1¾" by 1" mini muffin-pan cups are nice to have, too.

Custard cups Purchase glass cups with a 6-ounce capacity.

MICROWAVE TALK

Microwave ovens are standard equipment in most homes. The wattage of a microwave oven determines its power: A 750-watt oven will heat food more quickly than a 500-watt oven. Some microwave ovens are capable of interspersing the microwave cooking with periods of traditional radiant heat, which browns the food. Many people only use their microwave ovens

Additional baking pans: tube pans, glass pie plate, deep-dish pie plate, square tart pan with removable bottom

for specific tasks, such as cooking vegetables, "baking" potatoes, reheating foods, and melting chocolate or butter.

When cooking in your microwave, remember that the size of the food will affect the total cooking time. Small or thin pieces of food cook faster than large or thick pieces. Avoid microwaving large cuts of bone-in meat: Bones attract microwaves, so the meat will cook unevenly. Eggs and foods with tight skin (eggplant and potatoes) should be pierced. And the dish you microwave in should be deep enough to prevent the food from boiling over.

When reheating food, cover the dish with a microwave-safe lid or use microwave-safe plastic wrap, but fold a corner or edge back, about 1 inch, to allow the steam to escape. If appropriate, stir the food to distribute the heat.

Microwave cooking has a different set of safety rules from traditional cooking. To avoid the transference of toxins to the food, only use microwave-safe plastic wrap, and never let the plastic touch the food. Don't heat paper products (including paper towels and take-out boxes) in the microwave for longer than ten minutes, or they may ignite. Don't use recycled paper, which sometimes contains metal bits capable of sparking, or dyed paper products: The dye can leach into the food.

When exposed to microwaves, most metals spark. Very few metal containers can be used in a microwave oven (certain molded aluminum take-out containers are the exception). Don't use metal twists to close plastic bags, and avoid dishes trimmed with metal. Also take care when opting to use ceramic dishes: Sometimes the glazes contain metal.

Food that has been cooked or reheated in a microwave can be very very hot. Be especially careful when opening a tight cover or removing plastic wrap, because steam often builds up. Always open a dish facing away from you, and protect your fingers. Also, watch out for sweet foods: Sugar attracts microwaves, so desserts can become extremely hot.

UTENSIL CENTRAL

In addition to pots and pans, every kitchen needs other helpful tools. Here are some we find indispensable:

Bristle brushes Use one for cleaning pots and one for scrubbing vegetables. Nylon bristles last the longest.

Colander Choose a large colander with a footed base; the more holes it has, the more quickly food can drain.

Cooling racks If you bake a lot of cookies, you should have at least two large wire racks. Convenient stackable cooling racks can be found at kitchenware stores. Bakers who like to make layer cakes should have three or four small round racks because two racks are needed to invert each layer.

Corkscrew A tool used to remove the corks from wine bottles. They are available at most kitchenware stores and range from inexpensive to costly.

Cutting boards Plastic boards are lightweight and easy to clean in the dishwasher, but wooden boards are extremely durable and don't attract or retain any more bacteria than plastic ones. See The Golden Rules of Safety (pages 14 and 15).

Grater This flat or box-shaped tool can grate (small holes), shred (large holes), or slice (large slots). Sturdy stainless steel graters are the best choice.

Measuring cups For liquids, use clear glass or plastic cups with pouring spouts. It's useful to have two sizes: a 1-cup measure for smaller amounts and a 2- or 4-cup measure for larger amounts. To measure dry ingredients accurately, it is important to use standard-size metal or plastic cups that come in nested sets of ¼ cup, ⅓ cup, ½ cup, and 1 cup.

Measuring spoons Come in nesting sets; stainless steel spoons are the most durable. Most sets include ¼ teaspoon, ½ teaspoon, 1 teaspoon, and 1 tablespoon.

Mixing bowls A set of these all-purpose bowls is invaluable. Stainless steel is the most versatile because it reacts quickly to changes in temperature. Use to quick-chill foods in ice-water baths or to act as an impromptu double boiler over a saucepan of simmering water. On the other hand, glass or ceramic bowls work well to insulate rising yeast dough.

Rolling pins Heavy pins, either hardwood or marble, work best for rolling out dough. The heavier the pin, the less pressure you need to exert.

Sieve/strainer A wire sieve can be used to sift ingredients or strain liquids. Buy a few sizes with different mesh gauges (use a fine-mesh sieve to strain the seeds from berry purees and a coarse-mesh sieve to sift dry ingredients).

Spatulas To turn food, use heatproof or metal spatulas (pancake turners). Rubber spatulas are used for mixing and folding; they're not heatproof. Silicon spatulas, somewhat new to the market, are heatproof; use instead of rubber spatulas. A long narrow metal spatula is a must for frosting cakes.

Thermometers These important tools take the guesswork out of many kitchen tasks. Meat thermometers are vital when roasting meats and poultry, and many options are available beyond the old-fashioned kind. Instant-read thermometers, which register up to 220°F, are very accurate. Probe-type thermometers give a digital reading on a unit that is placed outside of the oven. Candy thermometers register temperatures up to 400°F and can be used for candy making and deep-frying. An oven thermometer is the best way to accurately check the temperature of an oven, because the control dials and thermostats are notoriously inaccurate. Optional, but nice to have, are freezer and refrigerator thermometers.

Tongs Spring-action tongs are the best for picking up foods and for turning meats without piercing them.

Vegetable peeler Swivel-blade peelers remove less peel than fixed-blade peelers: They conform to the shape of the food.

Whisk Use the right whisk for the job. A medium-size whisk is good for sauces, vinaigrettes, and batters. Flat paddle-shaped whisks are perfect for getting into the corners of roasting pans when making pan gravies. Large balloon-shaped whisks are ideal for beating air into heavy cream or egg whites.

The following are nice-to-have extras:

Adjustable-blade slicer Use to slice, cut into matchstick strips, and waffle-cut; adjustable-blade slicers range from the classic and pricey metal mandoline to lightweight plastic models that do a great job for much less money.

Apple corer This cylindrical tool neatly cores apples as well as pears. Buy the larger size; it easily removes all the core.

Egg beater This hand-powered mixer can also be used for whipping cream. It's low-tech but useful.

Ice-cream maker Available in manual and electric models; some have insulated liners that must be frozen overnight.

Juicer Use for extracting fruit and vegetable juices. One of the most practical models is a simple ridged cone that easily juices citrus fruits. Small electric versions are great when you need a large quantity of juice.

Kitchen scissors For cutting kitchen string, snipping fresh herbs, and trimming artichoke leaves. Shears, which are larger and spring-loaded, make cutting up poultry simple. Buy sturdy models made of stainless steel.

Melon baller Besides scooping perfect globes of melon (and potatoes), this tool neatly cores apples and pears.

Mortar and pestle Use for grinding spices and herbs. You crush with the pestle (the batlike tool) in the mortar (the bowl).

Pastry bag For decorating cakes and pies, forming spritz cookies, and creating beautifully shaped pastries. Disposable plastic pastry bags don't retain odors and flavors as plastic-lined canvas bags do.

Pastry blender This tool's metal wires easily cut cold fat into flour for tart dough, pastry dough, biscuits, and scones.

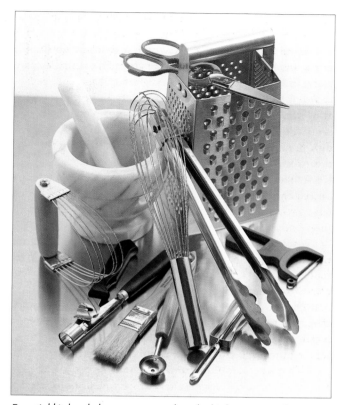

Essential kitchen helpers: mortar and pestle, kitchen scissors, box grater, vegetable peelers, tongs, whisk, melon baller, pastry brush, apple corer, zester, pastry blender

Pastry brush Use to brush dough with melted butter or beaten egg and to apply glazes; also great for dusting excess flour from dough. When buying, look for well-anchored natural bristle brushes in widths of 1 to 1½ inches.

Potato masher Perfect for potatoes and other root vegetables and for turning cooked beans into a chunky puree.

Ruler Keep a ruler in the kitchen for a multitude of uses.

Salad spinner Uses centrifugal force to dry greens, which prevents dressed salads from tasting watered down.

Skewers A must for kabobs. Always soak wooden or bamboo skewers in water before using.

Steamer The collapsible metal style easily fits into various-sized pots and pans. There is also a version that consists of a saucepan with a perforated bowl-like insert that allows the steam through. Bamboo steamers fit into woks.

Zester Pulled across the peel of citrus fruit, it removes the colorful, flavorful outer layer, leaving the bitter pith behind.

SHARPENING UP ON KNIVES

The importance of good knives cannot be overemphasized. Poorly made knives make cutting and chopping tiresome work, while good knives whip through these jobs. Take care of your fine knives, and they'll last a lifetime.

High-carbon stainless steel, an alloy that contains a large proportion of carbon, makes excellent knives that sharpen well. Some cooks prefer carbon-steel knives because they hold a very sharp edge, but they also corrode and stain easily. Knives that purport to never need sharpening have two drawbacks: The blades are finely serrated, so their ridges can tear food instead of cutting it. When the knives eventually do need sharpening, it isn't possible.

Before buying a knife, hold it in your hand to see if it feels comfortable. The best knives are made of a solid piece of metal (called the tang) that goes all the way through the handle. The extra weight of the tang gives a knife better balance.

Three knives are essential: a chef's knife (for slicing, chopping, and mincing), a paring knife (for fruits and vegetables), and a long serrated knife (for slicing breads, cakes, and thin-skinned fruits and vegetables). Useful extras are a carving knife for slicing meats (it often comes in a set with a carving fork) and a thin-bladed boning knife. A slicing knife, which has a scalloped edge (to help cut very thin slices) and a round tip (so you won't poke a hole in the roast), is good for ham and other cooked meats. A heavy cleaver comes in handy when cutting up poultry.

Sharp knives are safer and easier to use: They're less likely to slip. Hone your knives on a steel before using, and send them out once or twice a year to be professionally sharpened. Electric knife sharpeners do an excellent job and are great tools for serious cooks.

To sharpen a knife on a sharpening steel, rest the pointed end of the steel on the work surface. Position the heel of the knife (the widest part of the blade) at a 20-degree angle on the underside of the steel near the finger guard. Gradually draw the knife toward you, until you have sharpened the full length of the blade; repeat to sharpen the other side of the knife. Continue, alternating strokes, until sharp (about six strokes on each side).

MIXING IT UP

Blenders and food processors can be used for similar tasks, but they each have their own advantages. A blender makes silky-smooth soups, sauces, and smooth drinks with ease; its tall container can handle more liquid than a food processor. A food processor is good for coarser purees, chopping, shredding, and grating; it also makes pastry dough in a flash. If you want a small hand-held blender option, consider an immersion blender; it fits right into the cooking pot.

For whipping cream, beating egg whites, and mixing cake batter, an electric mixer does the best job. A hand-held mixer is light and can be easily moved, but it can stall if used for stiff doughs. A heavy-duty standing mixer easily handles large amounts of thick batter and bread dough and frees up your hands to perform other tasks. Most standing mixers come with mixing paddles, dough hooks, and balloon whisks.

COOKING BASICS

If you familiarize yourself with a few fundamental cooking skills, you will be assured success in the kitchen. Measuring ingredients may be a simple task, but if performed carelessly, it may mean the difference between success and failure. Learn how to chop, slice, and cut properly and your meal preparation time will be reduced. And remember, as with other skills, practice makes perfect.

MEASURING BASICS

Measure ingredients carefully, and you'll get consistent results each time you prepare a recipe. Every kitchen needs liquid measuring cups, dry measuring cups, and measuring spoons.

For liquids, use clear glass measuring cups with pouring spouts. Place the cup on a level surface and add the desired amount of liquid; bend down to check the accuracy of the measure at eye level (do not lift up the cup). For dry ingredients, use standard-size metal or plastic cups that can be leveled off. Nesting sets of graduated measuring spoons are used to measure both liquid and dry ingredients. We use the "spoon-and-sweep" method for measuring dry ingredients, such as flour, sugar, and cocoa. To measure flour, for example, stir it with a fork or whisk to aerate it (flour tends to pack down during storage). Lightly spoon the flour into a dry measuring cup to overflowing, then level it off with the straight edge of a knife or narrow metal spatula; don't pack the flour or shake the cup.

If a recipe calls for 1 cup sifted flour, sift the flour, then spoon it into the cup. If you need 1 cup flour, sifted, measure the flour and then sift. Do not "dip and sweep" (use the measuring cup to scoop the flour). It packs too much into the cup.

Butter and margarine come in premarked sticks, so there's no need to use a measuring cup. Use the markings on the wrapper to measure the desired amount, then cut it off. One 4-ounce (¼ pound) stick of butter or margarine equals 8 tablespoons or ½ cup.

Ingredients, such as vegetable shortening, butter, and brown sugar, should be firmly packed (pressed) into dry measuring cups or spoons and then leveled off.

Before measuring sticky ingredients, such as corn syrup, coat the measuring cup or spoon with vegetable oil or nonstick cooking spray, so it can slide out easily.

Basic measuring cups and spoons: 1-, 2-, and 4-cup glass measuring cups, set of dry measuring cups, set of measuring spoons

HIGH-ALTITUDE COOKING

The recipes in this book have been perfected for use at sea level. At higher altitudes, adjustments in the cooking time, temperature, and ingredients could be necessary.

At sea level, water boils at 212°F. With each additional five hundred feet of altitude, the boiling point drops 1°F. Even though the boiling point is lower, it takes longer to generate the heat required to cook food. Therefore, at high altitudes, foods boiled in water (such as pasta and beans) will take longer to come to a boil and will require longer cooking times than our recipes suggest. The processing times for canning foods and the blanching times for freezing vegetables will vary, too.

At high altitudes, cake recipes may need slight adjustments in the proportions of flour, leavening, liquid, eggs, etc. These adjustments will vary from recipe to recipe, and no set guidelines can be given. Many cake mixes now carry special directions on the label for high-altitude preparation.

High altitudes can also affect the rising of doughs and batters, deep-frying, candy making, and other aspects of food preparation. For complete information and special recipes for your area, call or write to the home agent at your county cooperative extension office or to the home economics department of your local utility company or state university.

If you have any doubts about the volume of a baking dish or casserole, pour a measured amount of water into the dish, right up to the top. Or double-check a baking pan's dimensions with a ruler: Even a one-inch difference can affect your baking success.

KNIFE BASICS

For the best results, use a chef's knife, and sharpen it on a steel before each use. To prevent the cutting board from slipping, place a damp towel underneath.

Hold the knife handle in your right hand near the blade. Your thumb should be on the left side of the handle and your fingers close together and wrapped around the other side of the handle.

CHOPPING AN ONION

Halve a peeled onion through the root end; place, flat side down, on a cutting board. Make horizontal cuts parallel to the board, cutting to, but not through, the root.

Make lengthwise vertical cuts, almost, but not quite through the root.

Now cut across the onion to chop into small, even pieces.

In this book, we coarsely chop, slice, cube, cut into matchstick strips, finely chop, and mince. Here's how:

Coarse chop To cut food into 1/2- to 3/4-inch irregular pieces. When chopping, the tip of the knife remains on the cutting board; the knife handle is raised and lowered in a rocking motion while the knife is moved from left to right. If necessary, tuck under the fingers of your left hand and carefully push the food toward the blade.

Chop To cut food into small irregular pieces about the size of peas. Roughly cut up the food, then move the knife through the food until the desired size.

Fine chop To chop food into very small irregular pieces, less than 1/4 inch.

Mince To cut into tiny irregular pieces, less than 1/8 inch.

Cube To cut into 1/2-inch blocks. First cut the food

lengthwise into 1/2-inch-thick slices. Stack the slices and cut into 1/2-inch-wide sticks. Then cut crosswise into 1/2-inch cubes.

Matchstick strips First, cut the food into slices 2 inches long and 1/8 inch thick. Stack the slices; cut lengthwise into 1/8-inch-wide sticks.

FOOD SAFETY AND STORAGE

Use these guidelines to help keep the food in your kitchen wholesome and safe to eat.

THE GOLDEN RULES OF FOOD SAFETY

Keep It Clean

Good old-fashioned cleanliness is the best safeguard against harmful bacteria. Keep a clean kitchen. Always wash and dry your hands before handling food. Frequently wash kitchen towels, dishcloths, and sponges. Rinse fruits and vegetables thoroughly before eating. Sterilize cutting boards once a week in a solution of 1 tablespoon bleach per 1 gallon water.

Avoid Cross-Contamination

Don't put cooked meat (or any ready-to-eat food) on a plate that has been in contact with raw meat, poultry, or fish. It's a good idea to have several cutting boards: one for raw meats, poultry, and fish, one for vegetables and cheese, and perhaps a third for fruits, nuts, and chocolate.

Cook It Right

To kill harmful bacteria that may be present in raw eggs, fish, poultry, and meat, it's essential to cook these foods thoroughly. The United States Department of Agriculture recommends cooking them to at least 160°F. At this temperature, however, food (especially meat) may be cooked beyond your preference. If you cook it less, some risk is involved, so the choice is ultimately a personal one. An instant-read thermometer is the easiest way to check for doneness. To check vi-

sually, follow these guidelines: Cook red meat to at least medium-rare, pork until the juices run clear and the meat retains just a trace of pink, poultry until the juices run clear, fish just until opaque throughout, and egg yolks and whites until thickened and set. Always cook ground meat until no pink remains. When cooking egg-based sauces, be sure the final temperature is no lower than 160°F.

Keep Hot Foods Hot and Cold Foods Cold

The safe zones for storing food are below 40°F and above 140°F. Keep food below or above these temperatures, and you'll discourage bacteria growth (bacteria love a moist, warm environment). Don't leave food out at room temperature for longer than two hours. In hot weather, protein foods, such as chicken, egg salad, or any food containing mayonnaise, should not be left out of the refrigerator for more than one hour. It's also unwise to cook food in stages. For example, don't start to cook food, stop the cooking process, then return to it later. Even when food is stored in the refrigerator between the cooking stages, safe temperatures may not be maintained and bacteria could develop.

Treat Leftovers with Respect

Refrigerate leftovers as soon as possible. Divide large amounts between smaller containers for quicker cooling. Date all leftovers so you know how long you've had them. If you have any doubt about a food's freshness, throw it out.

REFRIGERATOR KNOW-HOW

Don't take your refrigerator for granted. Help it do its job by following a few simple rules:

Be sure the temperature of your refrigerator remains between 33° and 40°F; use a refrigerator thermometer for extra insurance. To prevent spoilage, store foods on a rotating basis: Place newly stored items at the back of the shelves and move older items to the front.

Store meat, fish, and poultry on a plate to catch any drips; if you don't plan to cook them within two days, freeze them immediately. Never store eggs in the open egg compartment in the refrigerator door—it's too warm. Eggs should be kept in their original container to prevent them from absorbing the odors of other foods. For this same reason, store cheese, cream, milk, yogurt, margarine, and butter tightly closed in their containers or packaging or wrap airtight.

PANTRY STORAGE

Unless otherwise noted, these pantry staples fare best in a cool dry place. For more information on ingredients such as flour, pasta, and grains, see the chapter introductions.

Baking powder Once opened, keep well sealed; it will keep for up to six months. To test its effectiveness, add 1/2 teaspoon to 1/2 cup warm water; it should bubble vigorously.

Bread crumbs Store dried bread crumbs for up to six months or, for better flavor, refrigerate for up to two years.

Honey Lasts indefinitely; if it crystallizes, place the opened jar in a bowl of hot water. Stir until the crystals dissolve.

Hot pepper sauce Refrigerate after opening.

Olive oil Keep in a cool dark place for up to six months. Don't buy more than you can use; it can turn rancid, especially if stored in a warm place.

Pancake syrup It will keep for up to nine months (if stored longer, the syrup will thin and the flavor will weaken).

Peanut butter Unopened, it will hold for a year in your cupboard. Refrigerate after opening to avoid rancidity.

Soy sauce Unopened, it will keep for one year. Once opened, refrigerate to keep for an additional year.

Spices and dried herbs Store in opaque containers in a cool dark place (not near the stove) for up to one year. After that, herbs and spices begin to lose their flavor. It's a good idea to write the date of purchase on the label. Sniff before using: If the aroma is weak, discard and buy a new supply.

Vegetable oil Store this oil in a cool dark place for up to six months.

Vinegar Unopened, it will keep indefinitely. The sediment that sometimes appears is harmless; strain off the vinegar, if you wish. Once opened, store for up to six months. Vinegar with added flavorings, such as fruits or herbs, should be strained into a clean bottle as soon as the vinegar level drops below the top of the ingredients.

STORING FRESH HERBS

Most fresh herbs are highly perishable, so buy them in small quantities. To store for a few days, immerse the roots or stems in 2 inches of water. Cover with a plastic bag; refrigerate.

To dry fresh herbs (this works best with sturdy herbs, like rosemary and thyme), rinse lightly and pat dry with paper towels. Hang them upside down by their stems, in bunches, in a dry dark place. When the leaves become brittle (it typically takes from a few days up to one week), pick them off and discard the stems. Store the dried leaves in a tightly covered opaque container in a cool dry place.

To freeze herbs, rinse lightly, pat dry, and remove the stems; place in plastic containers or heavy-duty ziptight plastic bags. When frozen, herbs darken, but their flavor remains. There's no need to thaw frozen herbs; add them directly to the pot. Or place a few herbs (leaves only) in each section of an ice cube tray. Add enough water to cover; freeze. Unmold and store the cubes in heavy-duty ziptight plastic bags. Add the cubes to simmering soups, sauces, or stews.

TAKING FOOD ON THE ROAD

Packing a picnic or bringing food to a potluck party? Think ahead. Whenever food is removed from the refrigerator, it can easily warm to temperatures that encourage bacterial growth. But with some planning, you can avoid potential problems.

For picnics, use two small coolers rather than one large one. Use one cooler for nonperishables, such as fruit and beverages, and the other for perishable items, such as meats, poultry, salads, and cheese. Remember: A cooler cannot make foods colder than they already are, so chill foods thoroughly before placing in the cooler. To preserve the chill, don't open the lid for longer or more often than necessary.

Double-wrap meat and poultry in ziptight plastic bags so the juices don't leak out and contaminate other foods. Pack perishable items, like meat, next to the ice packs. Delicate items, such as green salads and slaws, should be stored away from the ice to prevent freezing.

Thermal carrying bags are the most convenient way to transport hot foods, but a cooler can also maintain the temperature of hot foods for a few hours. If you are bringing a hot dish to a party, heat it until piping hot. Wrap the covered dish in a thick layer of newspaper to insulate it and keep the heat in, then place in a cooler that isn't much bigger than the dish.

EATING WELL

The message is simple: Eat well to stay well. Use the Food Pyramid (opposite) to help balance your daily diet so you can get the nutrients you need without too much saturated fat, cholesterol, sugar, sodium, or calories.

DIETARY GUIDELINES FOR AMERICANS

- Eat a variety of foods to get the calories, protein, vitamins, minerals, and fiber needed.
- Balance the food you eat with enough physical activity to maintain or improve your weight.
- Choose a diet low in saturated fat and cholesterol.
- Eat plenty of vegetables, fruits, and grain products.
- Limit your consumption of sugar, salt, and alcohol .

NUTRIENTS: THE BIG THREE

Our bodies need three essential nutrients: carbohydrates, proteins, and fats. Carbohydrates are the body's major source of energy. The bulk of your carbohydrates should come from whole grains, legumes, vegetables, and fruit—not from sugary highly processed carbohydrate foods. Whole grains and legumes break down slowly thereby stabilizing blood sugar. They also lower the risk of diabetes, high blood pressure, and some types of cancer. Sugary or highy processed carbohydrates (including cookies and cake) have few nutrients but lots of calories, so their consumption should be limited. Proteins are needed to help produce new body tissue. Fats store the energy the body needs, but too much can lead to health problems, including cardiovascular disease.

Most health professionals suggest balancing your daily food intake into 50 percent complex carbohydrates, 30 percent fat, and 20 percent protein. Eating the right type of fat is more important than counting every gram. If you get a lot of exercise, you can consume more healthy fats. Keep in mind that fat is an essential nutrient, so don't cut back too much.

To calculate the amount of fat you should consume each day (30 percent limit), divide your ideal body weight by 2. For example, if your ideal body weight is 120 pounds, limit your total fat intake to 60 grams (120 lbs ÷ 2 = 60). For a diet with 20 percent fat calories, divide your ideal body weight by 3.

THE USDA FOOD PYRAMID

The Food Pyramid outlines what to eat each day. This research-based plan, developed by the United States Department of Agriculture, shows the relative importance of various foods and is meant to serve as a general guide—not a rigid prescription—to help you create a healthful diet tailored to your food preferences.

The Pyramid calls for eating a variety of foods (the five major food groups are divided into four categories) to get the carbohydrates, proteins, and fats you need, along with the right amount of calories to maintain a healthful weight. It focuses on controlling fat intake, because most American diets are too high in fat, especially saturated fat. The most servings should come from the foods shown in the two lower sections of the Pyramid, with moderate amounts of meat and dairy foods and small amounts of fats, oils, and sweets, which are located in the top section.

Each group provides some—but not all—of the nutrients needed for a balanced diet. The foods in one category can't replace those in another (and no one group is more important). For good health, you need them all.

When planning meals, choose fresh foods whenever possible. Processed foods tend to have fewer nutrients and higher amounts of fat and sodium; check the labels to make sure the fat content fits your fat budget.

Within each section of the Pyramid, the suggested range of servings is given. The number that's right for you depends on your calorie needs, which in turn depend on your age, sex, and size and on how active you are.

Bread, cereal, rice, and pasta

Grains form the base of the Pyramid. They provide complex carbohydrates, vitamins, minerals, and fiber. You need the most servings (6 to 11) of these foods each day. One serving equals: 1 slice of bread, 1 ounce ready-to-eat cereal, or ½ cup cooked rice, pasta, or cereal. The recommendation of 6 to 11 servings may seem high, but it adds up quickly. A generous bowl of cereal or pasta could easily equal 2, 3, or even 4 servings!

Starchy foods are often blamed for adding extra pounds, but high-fat toppings (butter on bread, cream sauce on pasta) are more likely the culprits. Stick with "lean" carbohydrates, like peasant bread or pita bread, instead of rich croissants and buttery crackers. Whole-grain breads and cereals offer the most fiber.

Food Pyramid

Fruits and vegetables

Eat fruits (2 to 4 servings) and vegetables (3 to 5 servings) for your daily intake of vitamins, minerals, and fiber. For the widest range of nutrients, don't eat the same fruits and vegetables day after day. Include choices high in vitamin C (citrus fruits, kiwifruit, and strawberries) and those rich in vitamin A (carrots, winter squash, spinach, kale, and cantaloupe). Research links cruciferous vegetables, such as broccoli, cabbage, cauliflower, and Brussels sprouts, with reduced risk for certain cancers, so be sure to eat them several times a week.

Meats and dairy foods

Most of the foods in this section of the Pyramid are animal based. The "meat" group includes meat, poultry, fish, dry beans, eggs, and nuts. Meat, poultry, and fish are rich in protein, B vitamins, iron, and zinc. Dry beans, eggs, and nuts provide protein along with vitamins and minerals. Dairy foods (milk, yogurt, and cheese) provide protein, bone-building calcium, and other nutrients.

Most individuals should aim for 2 to 3 servings daily from each of these groups. Many of these foods, especially meat and cheese, are high in calories, so it's easy to accidentally overdo the portion size. Weigh out the suggested portions at least once to get an idea of the amount. For example, a 2- to 3-ounce piece of lean cooked meat is approximately the size of a deck of cards. Other suggested portions are: 1 cup (whole or reduced-fat) milk or yogurt, 1½ ounces natural cheese or 2 ounces processed cheese, ½ cup cooked dry beans, 1 egg, ⅓ cup nuts, or 2 tablespoons peanut butter. Don't overdo nuts and seeds, like sesame : they're high in calories.

In general, animal products are higher in fat than plant foods, but it's not necessary to cut out all meat and dairy products to keep your fat intake low. Lowfat dairy foods, lean and well-trimmed meat, and skinless poultry provide the same amounts of vitamins and minerals as their fattier counterparts. Skinless poultry, fish, dry beans, and split peas are the "slimmest" foods in this category. By removing the skin from poultry, you reduce the fat by almost one-half. Most fish and seafood is low in fat and rich in beneficial Omega-3 oils, which lowers heart disease risk. Dry beans also provide the body with fiber, which is necessary for digestion.

You can enjoy red meat if you choose lean cuts and trim away all the visible fat. Here are some good choices:

- Beef eye round, top round, tenderloin, top sirloin, flank steak, top loin, ground beef (choose sirloin: it's 90 to 93 percent lean).
- Veal cutlets (from the leg) and loin chops
- Pork tenderloin, boneless top loin roast, loin chops, and boneless sirloin chops
- Lamb, boneless leg (shank portions), loin roast, loin chops

Vegetarians can substitute servings of dry beans and nuts for their protein needs but will also need fortified foods, extra servings of plant foods (especially grains), and/or supplements to get adequate amounts of calcium, iron, and vitamin B12.

Fats, oils, and sweets

At the top of the Pyramid are foods such as oil, cream, butter, margarine, sugar, soft drinks, candy, and desserts. To maintain a healthful weight, eat these sparingly.

It is important to understand the kind of fat you are eating. There are four types of fatty acids: saturated, monounsaturated, polyunsaturated, and trans fat. Saturated fat (found in meat, dairy products, and coconut, palm, and palm kernel oils) should be limited to 10 percent (about one-third of your total fat intake) or less; too much raises cholesterol and the risk of heart disease. Monounsaturated fat (found in olive, peanut, and canola oils) helps lower blood cholesterol. There are two types of polyunsaturated fats: Omega-6 and Omega-3. In our diets we get sufficient Omega-6 fat from corn oil, sunflower oil, cottonseed oil and from processed foods. We need more Omega-3 fat. It is sometimes called fish oil and is found in fatty fish such as salmon, mackerel, herring, sardines, and albacore tuna. Plant-based Omega-3 is found in canola oil, flaxseed, walnuts, and dark leafy greens. Omega-3 fights heart disease and may also have a role in preventing cancer and in reducing the risk of high blood pressure. Avoid foods that have "partially hydrogenated oil" in their list of ingredients. These are trans fats, which are created when vegetable oil is turned into a solid by a process called hydrogenation.

TRIMMING THE FAT

Here are some tips for trimming excess fat from your diet:

- Choose lean cuts of meat and trim all the visible fat before cooking. Remove skin from poultry before or after cooking.
- Broil meat on a rack so the fat can drip away.
- Substitute ground chicken or turkey for ground beef. Be sure the package is labeled "meat only," or it may contain skin and therefore have as much fat as ground beef.
- Substitute protein-packed dried legumes, like beans and lentils, for meat in casseroles.
- Chill soups and stews overnight so you can remove all the hardened fat from the surface.
- Be skimpy with fat. Use nonstick pans and nonstick cooking spray, or "sauté" in a small amount of broth or water.
- Lowfat and skim milk, lowfat sour cream and cheese, and nonfat yogurt provide the same amounts of calcium and protein as whole-milk varieties.
- When making dips, use nonfat yogurt instead of sour cream.
- Choose angel food cake instead of pound cake, especially when making a cake-based dessert such as a trifle.
- To reduce fat and cholesterol, you can substitute 2 egg whites for 1 whole egg in recipes, but don't substitute egg whites for all the whole eggs when baking: The dessert will have better texture and flavor if you retain a yolk or two.

THE MEDITERRANEAN DIET

For centuries, the traditional diet of the sunny Mediterranean countries has succeeded in prolonging life and preventing disease. Health experts have taken notice and suggested that the culinary habits of these countries can help Americans in their quest to cut fat and eat more nutritiously. The result is the "Mediterranean Diet," a plan not too different from the Food Pyramid. Both have a foundation in grains, vegetables, and fruits. But the Mediterranean model highlights beans and other legumes, limits red meat to a few times a month, and promotes the use of olive oil. This diet also encourages daily exercise and even a glass of wine with dinner.

What makes olive oil so great? It is predominantly a heart-healthy monounsaturated fat. When substituted for more saturated fats, it tends to lower artery-clogging LDL cholesterol while maintaining good levels of protective HDL cholesterol.

Wine with meals is traditional in Mediterranean cultures. Studies have shown that moderate drinking (defined as one drink per day for women, two for men), raises "good" cholesterol levels and may make blood less likely to form clots in arteries. But moderation is the key: One drink is a 4-ounce glass of wine, a 12-ounce serving of beer, or 1 ounce of hard liquor.

Quality of life, however, can't be overlooked as a contributing factor to health and happiness. In the Mediterranean, meals are savored along with the company of family and friends, and physical activity is a part of daily life.

USING THE NUTRITIONAL VALUES IN THIS BOOK

At the bottom of each recipe, you'll find nutritional information. To aid you in using this information, see "Nutrients: The Big Three" (page 16) and "Understanding Food Labels" (right) for the recommended daily nutrient levels. Aim to balance higher-fat recipes with leaner accompaniments. For example, serve lasagna with a green salad tossed with lowfat dressing, skim milk, and fresh fruit for dessert.

- Our nutritional calculations do not include any optional ingredients or garnishes.
- When alternative ingredients are given (such as margarine), our calculations are based on the first item listed.
- Unless otherwise noted, whole milk has been used.

UNDERSTANDING FOOD LABELS

Food labels help you make informed choices about the foods to include in your diet.

The Percent Daily Values reflect the percentage of the recommended daily amount of a nutrient in a serving (based on 2,000 calories daily). You can "budget" your intake of nutrients by adding up these percentages. For example, the label below shows a food containing 13 percent of the daily value for fat. If the next food you eat has a 10 percent daily value for fat, you've already had 23 percent of your total fat allowance for the day. When it comes to fat, saturated fat, sodium, and cholesterol, it's a good idea to keep the daily values below 100 percent. Fiber, vitamins A and C, calcium, and iron are listed because diets often fall short; aim for 100 percent of these nutrients. (Other vitamins and minerals may also appear on labels.)

The Daily Values footnote includes a chart that shows some Daily Values for diets containing 2000 and 2500 calories. Use these numbers as a guide. Your own daily values may be higher or lower, depending on your calorie needs.

Food labels are required to have an ingredients list. The ingredients are listed in descending order according to their weight. This enables you to easily discern which food products contain larger amounts of ingredients that are healthful.

Nutrition Facts

Serving Size 2 pieces (29g)
Servings Per Container 15

Amount Per Serving

Calories 150	Calories from Fat 80

	% Daily Value*
Total Fat 8g	**13%**
Saturated Fat 5g	**27%**
Cholesterol 25mg	**8%**
Sodium 115mg	**5%**
Total Carbohydrate 18g	**6%**
Dietary Fiber 0g	**0%**
Sugars 6g	
Protein 2g	

Vitamin A 0%	•	Vitamin C 0%
Calcium 2%	•	Iron 2%

* Percent Daily Values are based on a 2,000 calorie diet.

GRILLING

Grilling is hot and getting hotter. Formerly reserved for the summer months, grilling has become a way to prepare mouth-watering meals practically year-round. Whether you're grilling steak, poultry, fish, vegetables, pizza, or fruit, they all taste better when infused with the unmistakable flavor that grilling imparts. Included here is everything you'll need to know when you're ready to fire up the grill at the beach, at the park, or in your own backyard.

TYPES OF GRILLS

Kettle-type charcoal grills have tight-fitting lids and a special design that encourages good air circulation, which keeps a fire well fed with oxygen. Braziers are square-shaped and sometimes have lids. Hibachis and tabletop grills are perfect for cooking small amounts of food. Gas grills vary greatly in the amount of heat they generate (designated by the number of British Thermal Units, also called BTUs) and the amount of cooking surface. Electric grills may be convenient, but they do not get as hot as other grills, so the food takes longer to cook.

DIRECT AND INDIRECT GRILLING

There's not that much difference between grilling outdoors and cooking on a stove. When grilling, you can cook food covered or uncovered and over low, medium, or high heat. It all depends on what you are grilling and the result you want.

With direct grilling, the food is placed over the heat source. It is best for foods that take less than thirty minutes to cook, such as white meat chicken, steaks, chops, butterflied leg of lamb, fish, burgers, hot dogs, vegetables, and breads.

Indirect grilling is best reserved for foods that take more than thirty minutes to cook, including roasts and whole turkeys; it is always done in a covered grill. If using a charcoal grill, bank the briquettes on one or both sides of a flameproof drip pan on the lower rack. On a gas grill, leave one burner off and preheat the other burner(s) on high. When the coals are ready (or the gas grill is hot), place the food on the grill, centered over the drip pan. For extra moisture, you can add water, broth, or fruit juice to the drip pan. Cover the grill. You do not have to turn the food. For a standard 22½-inch grill, use twenty-five briquettes on each side of the drip pan (fifty briquettes total). For each additional hour of cooking time, add eight new briquettes to each side.

Basic grilling equipment: fish flipper, long-handled tongs, long-handled basting brush, wire-bristle grill brush, elbow-length flameproof insulated mitt, metal and bamboo skewers, hinged grill basket, grill topper

LIGHTING UP

Charcoal briquettes are a familiar, dependable fuel source for charcoal grills. Made from pulverized hardwood charcoal, mixed with binders, and pressed into pillow shapes, briquettes' uniformity provides a predictable amount of heat. Pure hardwood charcoal is another fuel choice. Usually processed from oak or mesquite, pure charcoal gives food a definable smokiness. It burns very quickly and very hot, so use it for foods that need only a short time on the grill, like steaks or chops.

When lighting up your grill, there's no need to rely on charcoal-lighter fluid (its flavor can transfer to the food). If you insist on using it, however, just remember never to add it to flames or to hot coals. The easiest way to light a grill is with a chimney charcoal starter: a metal cylinder in which briquettes are piled in the top section and crumpled newspaper is placed in the bottom section. As an alternative to a chimney starter, roll up double sheets of newspaper into tight cylinders, tie into overhand knots, and place on the bottom of the grill. Set the small charcoal grate over the newspaper and mound the briquettes in the center, forming a pyramid. Light the ends of the knots. Keep the grill uncovered while it heats up—fire needs oxygen.

Coals take twenty-five to thirty minutes to reach optimal grilling temperature. After twenty minutes, they are red-hot. It takes another five to ten minutes for the fire to die down enough so the briquettes are covered with gray ash. Before setting the grill rack in place, spread the coals in a single layer or, if cooking indirectly, bank them on either side of the drip pan.

Follow the manufacturer's directions for gas and electric grills, but keep in mind that they need to preheat for fifteen to twenty minutes to reach the proper grilling temperature.

TAMING THE FLAME

The longer coals burn, the cooler they get. To estimate the temperature of the coals, place your hand, palm side down, about six inches above the heat source. Count the seconds ("one thousand one, one thousand two," etc.) until the heat forces you to pull your hand away. If you can keep it in place for only one or two seconds, the grill is very hot. If you can hold it for three or four seconds, the grill is medium-hot. Five seconds means the heat is low.

If you need more heat, tap the ashes from the coals and push them closer together, or add fresh briquettes along the edges of the ignited coals (but give them a chance to heat up before cooking). For less heat, spread out the coals. If you have a brazier with an adjustable cooking rack, you can raise or lower the rack to bring it closer to or farther away from the coals. In a charcoal grill, the intensity of the fire can also be controlled by adjusting the air vents. Open them wide to increase the flow of oxygen: The fire will burn hotter. Close the vents and the lid, and the fire will burn at a lower, more constant temperature.

Flare-ups are caused by fat dripping onto hot coals. By trimming away the excess fat from meat, removing the skin from poultry, and reducing the amount of oil in a marinade, you will lessen the chance of flare-ups. If one does occur, move the food so it isn't directly over the coals (the perimeter of the grill is usually a good place) and cover the grill to reduce the amount of oxygen feeding the flame. You can also douse the flames with water. Punch several holes in the metal lid of a canning jar. Fill the jar with water and seal with the lid and screw band; use to sprinkle on flaming coals.

CRANKING UP THE FLAVOR

Marinating is one of the most popular ways to add flavor to grilled food. But don't marinate for too long, or the food will develop a mushy texture. Most meat and poultry need one to three hours to marinate, while seafood requires only fifteen to thirty minutes. The time also depends on the marinade ingredients. Mixtures containing acidic ingredients, such as lemon juice, vinegar, and yogurt, need less time. Marinades only penetrate about one-half inch, so they won't completely penetrate thick cuts of meat, poultry, or fish.

For smoky flavor, add some aromatic wood chips to the coals; mesquite and hickory are quite popular. More exotic choices include: alder, fruit-tree woods, oak, and grapevines. Soak about one cup of chips (or larger wood chunks) in water for thirty minutes. Drain and sprinkle over the temperature-ready coals. Many grills come with wood chip holders. Alternatively, wrap soaked and drained chips in a heavy-duty aluminum foil packet and poke a few holes in the top. Place the packet, holes side up, directly on the heat source: The foil prevents the ashes from clogging the burner jets. For the most smoky flavor, cover the grill as soon as you add the chips.

GRILLING IT EASY

Here are some tools to make outdoor grilling a snap: *Long-handled tongs* are indispensable for turning food and arranging coals. Don't turn meat or poultry with a fork, because it can pierce the flesh, releasing juices and flavor. Use a *long-handled basting brush* to apply sauce or to oil the grill rack; wash in hot soapy water after each use. A stiff *wire-bristle grill brush* makes cleaning the grill easy. When grilling, protect your hands and arms with *elbow-length flameproof insulated mitts.*

Delicate foods require special handling on the grill. For supporting delicate fish fillets when they are turned, try a *fish flipper.* Or cook the fillets on a small-hole or fine-mesh *grill topper,* which also does a great job of keeping shrimp (and vegetables) from falling through the grill. Whole fish will be easy to turn if you use a *hinged grill basket.*

Skewers enable you to grill small pieces of food with ease. Bamboo skewers must be soaked in water for thirty minutes so they don't burn; just drain them and pat dry. If you like metal skewers, you'll have the best results with skewers that are twisted or square—not round. Food tends to spin around on round skewers when you try to turn them. (Bamboo skewers aren't slippery, so they aren't a problem.)

To ensure even cooking, don't crowd food onto skewers and leave a small space between each item. Cut food into uniform pieces, and place those with similar cooking times on the same skewers. Unwieldy items, like large thick onion slices or shrimp, will be easier to handle if you thread them onto two parallel skewers.

SAFETY TIPS

Pick a safe location for your grill. The surface should be flat and level so the grill won't tip over; keep away from overhangs, fences, and shrubbery that could catch fire. To avoid a buildup of toxic fumes, position the grill in a well-ventilated location; never use a charcoal or gas grill indoors.

Grilling presents plenty of opportunities to cross-contaminate grilled food with the harmful bacteria from raw food, so take extra care. Use separate utensils for carrying raw and cooked foods. One tip: Carry raw food to the grill on an aluminum foil–lined platter. After you transfer the food to the grill, throw away the foil; the platter will still be clean and safe to use. Wash all utensils, containers, cutting boards, and work surfaces with hot soapy water once they've come in contact with uncooked food. While the flavor of many grilled foods will be enhanced by a well-browned crust, avoid a charred surface: A blackened crust is not healthful.

Dispose of coals properly. Once you've finished cooking, cover the grill, close the vents, and allow the coals to burn out completely. Let the ashes cool for at least forty-eight hours and dispose of them in a noncombustible container. If you wish to dispose of coals before they've cooled, transfer them, with long-handled tongs, to a bucket of water.

Keep your grill clean, both for health reasons and to keep off-flavors from affecting the food. There's no need to wash a grill rack after every use. Right after cooking, scrub the rack of a charcoal grill with a metal-bristle grill brush. The next time you grill, if you notice any residual food on the rack, just let it burn off, then scrub the rack with a brush. After a few months, a flaky carbon build-up will appear on the lid of the grill. Simply scrub it off with hot water and a steel-wool soap pad. To clean a gas grill, turn the heat to high and let the grill heat for ten to fifteen minutes with the lid closed. Then use a grill brush to remove any remaining cooked-on food.

ENTERTAINING

Everyone loves a party, but the trick is to ensure that the cook has a good time, too. Whether you're planning a casual backyard barbecue, an elegant dinner, or a holiday buffet, a few simple strategies will guarantee you stress-free entertaining. Sure, the menu is important, but the food is just one aspect. Setting the right mood and making guests feel at home are also vital parts of a successful party.

THINK AHEAD

All good parties are well organized. Start with a few lists: a guest list, a menu, and two shopping lists (for perishables and nonperishables). And set up a menu preparation timetable that can be checked off.

Send out invitations well in advance of the event: Most people plan their calendars two to three weeks ahead. Specify the appropriate dress, the type of food that will be served, and the expected duration of the party. Though most guests will RSVP, you may still need to make follow-up calls to get a firm head count. (While you're on the phone, inquire if the invitees have any food allergies or restrictions you need to be aware of so you can make additions or deletions to your menu.)

Simplicity is the key to a successful menu, especially when you are expecting a large number of guests. The majority of the dishes should be those you've cooked and enjoyed in the past; you could run into problems if preparing too many new recipes. Take advantage of dishes that taste even better when made ahead, such as stews and marinated vegetable salads. It's also smart to include some dishes that freeze well (pound cakes, cookies, baked pasta dishes, and pastry-type appetizers). And include some recipes whose components can be prepared ahead and assembled just before serving.

Look for food preparation time-savers. If you're making a shrimp dish, consider purchasing peeled shrimp instead of peeling them yourself (the difference in cost will be compensated by the time you save). Do as much advance preparation as you can to avoid last-minute jitters. Make croutons and hold in an airtight tin at room temperature; rinse, trim, and cut vegetables for side dishes and salads (wrap in damp paper towels and place in ziptight plastic bags in the refrigerator); make salad dressings and dessert sauces; and so on.

Let the menu reflect the time of year. Use seasonal fruits and vegetables whenever possible. They will be at their peak of flavor and reasonably priced. In the spring, serve a simple appetizer of crisp-cooked asparagus with a dipping sauce and an uncomplicated dessert of sliced strawberries drizzled with orange liqueur. During the summer, float ripe peaches, apricots, and nectarines in a bowl of ice water. It's a refreshing, healthful finish to a meal.

Be sure you have a well-stocked bar with plenty of choices for nondrinkers (tomato and fruit juices, sparkling water, soft drinks, etc.). Set out lime wedges, lemon twists, olives, and other garnishes in an interesting array of bowls. Instead of serving a wide assortment of alcoholic beverages, offer a "house drink," such as sangria. The refrigerator can be an inconvenient place to chill beverages because they take up vital space needed for food. Instead, chill beverages in an ice cooler. And get plenty of ice—even more than you think you'll need.

At least one week before the party, check your supply of chairs, glasses, serving dishes, and utensils. Rent, borrow, or buy extras, if needed. Also, check the recipes to see if you need any special items, such as wood chips for the grill. Consider the space needed to enable guests to circulate easily and, if necessary, shift or remove furniture.

If you're serving finger food, bite-size is best. The food should be small enough to be eaten in one or two bites (or easy to dip). Passed hors d'oeuvres should be reserved for your most elegant affairs, when you have extra help in the kitchen. You can dress up a plain platter with a couple of large non-toxic flowers, a bed of lemon leaves (wash and dry them first), or a generous bunch of fresh herbs. When serving olives, chicken wings, or foods on toothpicks, place small bowls next to the foods so guests can deposit the pits, bones, or toothpicks (place a pit in a bowl as a hint).

When planning a big party, don't try to do everything yourself. Ask a friend to help with the preparty shopping and cooking; it will make the time fly. At the party, delegate someone to help with the grilling, the serving of drinks, or the passing of the hors d'oeuvres tray. Or, if you wish, simply hire a bartender or wait staff.

BUFFET BASICS

Buffets are great for carefree entertaining; just put out the food and keep the bowls and platters full. But don't leave food out at room temperature for longer than two hours, and replenish the table with fresh platters you've prepared in advance rather than adding more to half-empty ones.

One of the easiest ways to entertain is to create a menu of room-temperature dishes. Serve potato or marinated vegetable salads; savory tarts and quiches; pâtés and terrines; crostini and bruschetta; cold sesame noodles; frittatas; dips and salads; sliced roast beef, turkey, or ham with rolls and condiments for making sandwiches; and cold poached chicken or fish.

Hot buffets should have one centerpiece dish, such as an elegant stuffed veal roast, a hearty pan of lasagna, or a pot of spicy chili, partnered with simple side dishes, like mixed greens and crusty bread. (Foods that don't require cutting are the most guest-friendly.) Keep desserts simple; cakes and cookies that can be eaten out of hand (with napkins) will reduce the amount of cleanup.

Avoid traffic jams at the buffet table. If possible, place the table in the center of the room, so guests can serve themselves from both sides of the table. Provide two serving utensils for each bowl or tray to reduce the serving time. Also, bundle the forks and napkins together (for easy handling) and place at both ends of the buffet. Height adds visual interest to a buffet. To create a stable surface for platters and bowls, place a couple of large baking dishes, upside down, on the table and cover with cloth napkins that complement the tablecloth. Arrange bowls and platters on top.

DINNER PARTY STRATEGIES

When planning the menu for a dinner party, it is important that the flavors, colors, textures, and richness of the food be well balanced. Follow a creamy soup with a simple roast rather than a heavily sauced main dish, and avoid repeating ingredients and flavors. For example, don't have cheese in both the first and main courses.

Also, consider the amount of time you'll need to spend in the kitchen. Soups, stews, casseroles, mousses, and sorbets can be made ahead of time. Try not to have more than two dishes that require last-minute attention.

Set a festive table with one of these suggestions:

- Accent each place setting with a miniature bouquet of fresh herbs tied with a bit of ribbon.
- Seek out one-of-a-kind linens, glasses, plates, bowls, and napkin rings at tag sales and flea markets. Don't feel that you have to set a table with just one pattern; mix and match for a whimsical look.
- Illuminate each place setting with a votive candle.
- Handwrite individual menus to place at each setting.

SETTING A PROPER TABLE

There is a proper way to set a table. To begin, place a dinner plate at each setting. If you are serving the first course family-style, you can place the plated food on top of the dinner plates; otherwise, the first course should be plated in the kitchen and brought to the table. If serving soup, place the soup bowls on top of the salad plates, which act as underliners. Set the bread plates to the left of the dinner plates above the forks.

Informal table setting: dinner plate, salad plate, salad fork, dinner fork, dinner knife, wine glass, water glass

Flatware is arranged in a common-sense way, in the order used, beginning farther away from the plate. The placement of flatware corresponds to the hand that will be used. Forks are placed on the left, while knives (cutting edge facing the plate) and spoons are on the right. The more formal the setting, the more flatware there is likely to be, but settings always follow the order-of-use rule. For example, if you are serving soup, the soup spoons are placed to the right of the knives. If you are serving salad, the salad forks are set to the left of the dinner forks. Butter knives may be placed right on the butter plates.

If you have enough flatware and room on the table, the dessert forks and spoons can be placed above the dinner plates (spoons directly above the plates, handles facing right; forks above the spoons, handles facing left). Otherwise, clear the table and set out the dessert flatware with the dessert. Also, don't forget to provide teaspoons when you serve coffee or tea.

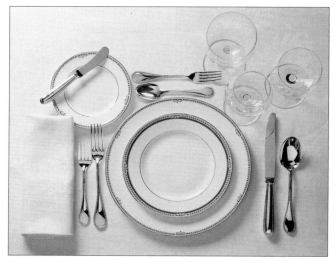

Formal table setting: dinner plate, salad plate, bread plate, salad fork, dinner fork, soup spoon, dinner knife, dessert fork, dessert spoon, butter knife, white wine glass, red wine glass, water glass

If serving only one wine, place the wine glasses slightly above the dinner knives and set the water glasses to their left. If also serving wine to accompany the first course, place those glasses to the right of the primary wine glasses.

Napkins go either to the left of the forks or in the center of the dinner plates. If you wish, roll the napkins up and tie them with ribbon (or, for a more rustic look, use raffia).

FINISHING TOUCHES

Any table looks better with a stylish centerpiece, but keep it low, so guests can easily see each other across the table; walk around the table to check it from all sides.

- Combine flowers, fruits, vegetables, and herbs: plum tomatoes with scarlet poppies; small purple and white eggplants with herbs; peaches with lemons and sage leaves.
- Line a basket with an antique cloth and fill with pears.
- Fill a favorite crystal bowl with unshelled nuts.
- Place small flowering plants in a decoratively painted box.
- In the winter, place chestnuts, pinecones, and evergreen boughs in a wide silver bowl.
- Combine small gourds and squash in a wicker basket.
- Arrange a variety of cacti in a large shallow terra-cotta saucer and surround with decorative pebbles or stones.
- Illuminate each setting with a votive candle.

Table Tips for Parties

EXPERT TIP

- When setting up a buffet table, do your guests a favor and label any possibly unfamiliar dishes, such as Cold Sesame Noodles or Zucchini Frittata, to put guests at their ease. Hand print the recipe names on large place cards in an easy-to-read type.
- Use partially cored green or red apples as candle-holders, and set one at each place or include several as part of the centerpiece.

BETTY FUSSELL
COOKBOOK AUTHOR

WINE AND BEER

When choosing a beverage to complement a meal, there's no reason to restrict yourself to wine. Though wine can be suave and elegant or simple and refreshing, when food is spicy or very robust, it can overwhelm or compete with a wine unless you choose very carefully. Beer or ale might be a better choice. Away from the dining table, wine and beer are also enjoyed on their own as thirst quenchers and can be used in cooking. Here's an overview of the most popular libations of the grape and grain.

KNOW YOUR WINES

There are two kinds of wine: red (which includes rosé) and white. The primary way a wine is described is its relative sweetness: A dry wine lacks natural sugars (but it still can be perceived as fruity), a semidry wine generally tastes sweet, and a sweet wine is very sweet. White wines range from very dry (Manzanilla sherry) to very sweet (Tokay), while red wines are usually dry (except for some kosher-type wines). In general, wines are named either for the predominant grape used in production (cabernet sauvignon) or for the region of production (Chianti). A wine is judged by three basic components: its color, aroma (bouquet), and taste. White wines range in color from pale yellow-green to straw yellow to deep gold, while red wines range from purplish red to ruby red. What is a good wine? Any wine that you enjoy drinking—it's very subjective. Let your eyes, nose, and mouth be your guides. An easy way to pair wine with food is to serve a wine from the same region or country as the food you are preparing. For example, a paella is best enjoyed with a Spanish wine, while pasta with tomato sauce is ideally matched with Chianti.

White Wines

Chardonnay One of the most popular wines, chardonnay is produced the world over. Most chardonnays are buttery, fruity, and fairly dry; they are usually aged in oak. Chardonnays that have been aged in small oak barrels (sometimes new ones) are often characterized as being "oaky," a quality that can mask a wine's lovely fruity qualities. Serve with summer foods, such as grilled salmon or chicken, as well as roasted chicken or fish.

Gewürztraminer A specialty of Alsace, France, although it's produced in other countries as well. It is a spicy wine that can be dry or semisweet. If dry, serve with fish, poultry, or spicy foods. If sweet, serve with fruit desserts.

Riesling This wine has a floral fragrance with hints of honey. Late-harvest riesling is produced from super-ripe grapes that are intensely sweet, making it one of the world's most delicious wines. German rieslings are much sweeter than Alsatian rieslings. They are excellent with Chinese food, lightly spiced food, and roast chicken. Alsatian rieslings are ideal summertime wines.

Sauvignon Blanc A refreshing, clean-flavored wine with a grassy, herbaceous aroma. It is sometimes labeled Fumé Blanc. Serve with poultry, fish, or shellfish.

Sauternes A rich, sweet French wine made from grapes that have developed a beneficial mold (*botrytis cinerea*) that causes them to shrivel and concentrates their sweetness. Serve with dessert or rich foods such as pâté, duck, or Roquefort cheese.

White wine, red wine, rosé wine, champagne

Red Wines

Beaujolais A pleasant, light-bodied, fruity French wine that goes well with meats and poultry.

Beaujolais Nouveau A light, fruity wine that is seven to nine weeks old and is released for sale on the third Thursday of November. It is an ideal wine for Thanksgiving.

Bordeaux Some of the greatest wines in the world are from the Bordeaux region in France. These wines are rich and fragrant and known for their ability to age. Goose, roast lamb, and other red meats are the perfect partners.

Burgundy Wines from the Burgundy region of France are elegant, highly prized, and some of the most expensive in the world. Burgundys, made from 100 percent pinot noir grapes, are lighter in body and color than some other red wines. They bear no resemblance to the typical California Burgundy. Enjoy with salmon, red meat, pork, poultry, and game.

Cabernet Sauvignon Produced in many countries, this well-known wine is full-bodied and can be complex, with hints of spice and ripe fruit. It complements hearty meats, poultry, and stews.

Chianti One of the most famous Italian wines, true Chianti is Tuscan. This sturdy, dry wine goes nicely with tomato-based pasta dishes, steaks, hamburgers, and pizza.

Merlot Rich, fragrant, and smooth-bodied, this wine is easy to like. Serve with robust foods such as lamb, sausages, stews, braises, and Cornish hens.

Pinot Noir This intensely flavored wine is now produced in Oregon and California—often with great success. (It is a temperamental grape to grow.) The wine can be light or full-bodied. It goes with almost any food but is especially good with salmon, poultry, pork, veal, ham, and cheese.

Zinfandel Originally grown in Europe, "Zin" has become a uniquely California wine. It has a spicy, fruity, slight raspberry flavor. It can stand up to hearty foods, such as steaks, lamb, veal chops, game birds, and hamburgers.

Other Wines

Madeira, Sherry, and Port These are all wines that have been fortified with a spirit (usually brandy) to increase their alcohol content. They are usually enjoyed after a meal, although dry sherry is often sipped before dinner.

Rosé These wines are made from red grapes: The grape skins are left on just long enough to produce the desired pink color. (Inexpensive rosés are often tinted.) Serve these light-bodied wines chilled, before dinner or with lighter foods.

Sparkling Wine These bubbly, mild-flavored wines range from slightly sweet to dry. Champagne is the most famous (even though we often use the term to mean any sparkling wine). Real champagne is produced in the Champagne region of France by the traditional *méthode champenoise,* but other countries also make fine sparklers. Sparkling wines go well with most foods, including desserts.

Serving Wine

Serve wine at the proper temperature to bring out its flavor. Red wine is often served too warm and white wine is often served too cold, which makes it difficult to fully appreciate them. Red wine should be served at cool room temperature. If it's too warm, place it in a bucket of ice water for five minutes. Some young and fruity reds, such as Beaujolais, are best when slightly chilled. White wines and sparkling wines should be served well chilled, but not so cold that their delicious flavors are hidden. To quick-chill white or sparkling wine, submerge the bottle in a bucket or pot filled with half ice and half water. Or, wrap the bottle in several thicknesses of wet paper towels and place in the freezer for twenty to thirty minutes or until chilled. (Check to make sure the wine doesn't freeze.)

Wine is traditionally served in stemmed glasses: The large flat base allows you to swirl the wine, which helps release its aroma and flavor. When drinking wine, hold the glass by the stem. This is especially important with chilled wines: It prevents the heat from your hand from warming the wine. Glasses should be filled one-half to two-thirds full, which leaves enough room for swirling.

Exposing wine to air lets it "breathe" and release its flavor, but simply uncorking the bottle doesn't do much—the wine needs to be poured. If you wish, decant it before serving. (If decanting an aged wine, leave any sediment in the bottle.)

There really aren't any strict rules when pairing wine with food. But do try to match the intensity of the flavors. For example, serve a light wine with a delicate entrée and a robust wine with a full-flavored dish. Gewürztraminer is a good match for the ginger-seasoned foods of Asian cooking, and zinfandel can stand up to the spicy flavors of Mexican food. Here are a few rules of thumb: Red wines go well with meats, roast chicken, salmon, tomato-based pasta dishes, and hard cheeses (like Parmesan). White wines are a good match for delicate-flavored fish, skillet poultry dishes, vegetable dishes, cheese-based pasta dishes, and soft and semi-soft cheeses.

Storing Wine

For long-term storage, keep wine in a cool, moist, dark place (such as a cellar). Store the bottles on their sides to prevent the corks from drying out and shrinking, which would let in the air and adversely affect the wine.

You don't need any fancy equipment to store leftover wine, though there are some inexpensive gadgets that work quite well. You can also simply refrigerate white wine or keep red wine at cool room temperature for up to forty-eight hours with the original cork in place.

KNOW YOUR BEER

Wine is fermented grape juice. The natural sugars in the fruit are converted to alcohol by yeast. Historically, people who didn't have access to grapes used sprouted grains to make alcoholic beverages. Beer, which is made from malted barley and hops, is just one example of this kind of brew. Mass-produced beer is the most common, but small-batch beers and ales from microbreweries show these refreshing beverages off to their best advantage.

Ale Any malted beverage made without hops used to be called ale. Now it refers to a brew that is heavier, darker, more flavorful and bitter than regular beer and with less carbonation. It is called "top-fermented" because it is fermented at a higher temperature than beer: The yeast rises to the top.

Beer Made from malted barley and flavored with hops (the dried flowers of a vinelike plant), which give the brew a slight bitterness. Yeasts are used as the fermenting agent. During fermentation, the yeasts sink to the bottom of the vat, so beer is called "bottom-fermented." "Light" beer is lower in calories and alcohol than regular beer. Low-alcohol and non-alcoholic beers are also available.

Bock beer A heavy dark beer that varies in style from producer to producer.

Dry beer Originally Japanese, this beer is brewed to allow the yeast to consume more sugar during fermentation, resulting in less sweetness.

Lager A clear light-bodied beer that has been stored (lagered) and aged. It is the most common American beer. Pilsner beers (named for the famous lager-producing city of Pilsen in the former Czechoslovakia) are lager-type beers.

Malt liquor This pale beverage is higher in alcohol than beer; each state regulates the alcohol content.

Stout This heavy ale gets its dark color from roasted barley. Porter is similar but less alcoholic, and it has a lighter flavor.

Wheat beer This beer, once a European specialty, is now produced by American breweries as well; wheat is its predominant grain. It is sometimes flavored with fruit, which makes it a sweet beverage.

Serving and Storing Beer

Americans prefer well-chilled beer. Any tall glass will suffice; chill it in the freezer first, if you wish. To keep foaming to a minimum, hold the glass at a slight angle and slowly pour the beer down the side of the glass, bringing the glass upright as you pour.

Keep the relative bitterness of beer in mind when matching it with food. Beer is best with salty or spicy dishes: think barbecued, Asian, and Mexican foods.

Freshness is very important with beer; check for a use-by date. Otherwise, store beer in a cool place (in the refrigerator, if you have room) and use within three months.

COOKING WITH WINE AND BEER

Use a decent wine or beer for cooking—not your absolute best but something you wouldn't hesitate to drink. If you don't have white wine, you can substitute dry vermouth (which is a white wine that has been flavored with herbs, spices, and other aromatics). When cooking with beer, unless the recipe specifies otherwise, a lager is the best choice, as any bitterness in dark beers intensify with cooking.

When adding wine or beer to a sauce or stovetop dish, let it boil down to mellow the flavor. If you prefer not to cook with alcoholic beverages, substitute ½ cup broth and 1 tablespoon lemon juice for every ½ cup of wine. If you need a substitute for beer, just use broth.

> EXPERT TIP
>
> • Think of a wine's body as its weight in the mouth. Light-bodied wines have a weight similar to skim milk, medium-bodied wines feel like whole milk, and full-bodied wines are like half-and-half.
> • A great way to discover new wines is to order different wines by the glass in restaurants. They are usually affordably priced and provide an opportunity to try an array of wines.
> • The vintage (date) is the year the grapes were harvested. Each year, a wine will be slightly different, based on the weather that year. But don't get too hung up on vintages: Today's advanced wine-making practices enable consistently good wines to be produced every year.
>
> **KAREN MACNEIL**
> *CHAIRMAN OF WINE PROGRAMS,
> CULINARY INSTITUTE OF AMERICA AT GREYSTONE*

A GLOSSARY OF COOKING TERMS

Al dente Italian for "to the tooth," describes perfectly cooked pasta: just tender and with a slight resistance.

Baste To spoon or brush a liquid over food to keep it moist during cooking. The liquid can be a sauce, marinade, broth, melted butter, or pan juices.

Beat To briskly mix or stir a mixture with a spoon, whisk, fork, or electric mixer.

Blanch To cook food (usually fruits or vegetables) briefly in boiling water, then plunge into ice water to stop the cooking. It locks in the color, texture, and flavor. Blanching is used to loosen tomato and peach skins (for peeling) and to mellow the saltiness or bitterness of certain foods.

Blend To mix ingredients until smooth or combined.

Blind bake To bake a piecrust before it's filled. To prevent the dough from puffing up during baking, the pastry dough is lined with foil and filled with pie weights or dry beans; they are removed shortly before the end of the baking time to allow the crust to color.

Boil To heat a liquid until bubbles break vigorously on the surface; water boils at 212°F. It also means to cook food, such as pasta or potatoes, in a boiling liquid.

Braise To cook food by first browning it in fat, then covered, on top of the stove or in the oven in a small amount of liquid. This slow method tenderizes tough cuts of meat by breaking down their fibers and develops their flavor.

Broth A thin, clear liquid produced by simmering vegetables in water or poultry, meat, or fish (on the bone). Broth is used as a base for soups, stews, sauces, and many other dishes. Canned broth is a convenient substitute for homemade.

Brown To cook over high heat, usually on top of the stove, to brown food.

Butterfly To split food, such as shrimp or boneless leg of lamb, horizontally, cutting almost all the way through, then opening it up (like a book) to form a butterfly shape. It exposes a more uniform surface area so food cooks evenly and quickly.

Caramelize To heat sugar until it becomes syrupy and golden to deep amber in color. Sugar-topped desserts like crème brûlée are caramelized under the broiler or with a propane torch. Onions become caramelized when slowly cooked until golden brown and very tender.

Core To remove the seeds or tough woody centers from fruits such as apples, pears, and pineapple and vegetables such as cabbage and fennel.

Cream To beat butter, margarine, or other fat until it's creamy looking or with sugar until it's fluffy and light. This technique beats in air, creating light-textured baked goods.

Crimp To decoratively pinch or press the dough edges of a single piecrust or to seal the dough edges of a double-crusted pie so the filling doesn't seep out during baking.

Curdle To coagulate or separate into solids and liquids. Egg- and milk-based mixtures can curdle if heated too quickly, overcooked, or combined with an acid, such as lemon juice.

Cut in To work a solid fat, such as shortening, butter, or margarine, into dry ingredients using a pastry blender or two knives scissor-fashion until the pieces are the desired size.

Deglaze To scrape up the flavorful browned bits from the bottom of a skillet or roasting pan in which meat or poultry has been cooked by adding water, wine, or broth and stirring while gently heating.

Devein To remove the dark intestinal vein of shrimp. The shrimp is first peeled, then a lengthwise slit is made along the back and the vein is removed.

Dollop A spoonful of soft food, such as whipped cream.

Dot To scatter bits of butter or margarine over a pie filling, casserole, or other dish before baking. It adds richness and flavor and helps promote browning.

Dredge To lightly coat with flour, cornmeal, or bread crumbs. Meats and fish are dredged before cooking to create a deliciously crisp, browned exterior.

Drippings The melted fat and juices that collect in a pan when meat or poultry is cooked. Drippings form the base for gravies and pan sauces.

Drizzle To pour melted butter, oil, syrup, melted chocolate, or other liquid back and forth over food in a fine stream.

Dust To coat lightly with confectioners' sugar or cocoa (cakes and pastries) or another powdery ingredient.

Emulsify To bind liquids that usually can't blend easily, such as oil and vinegar. The trick is to slowly add one liquid, usually the oil, to the other while mixing vigorously. Natural emulsifiers, such as egg yolks or mustard, are often added to vinaigrettes or sauces to emulsify them for a longer period.

Ferment To bring about a chemical change in foods and beverages: The change is caused by the enzymes in bacteria or yeasts. Beer, wine, yogurt, buttermilk, vinegar, cheese, and yeast breads all get their distinctive flavors from fermentation.

Flour To coat food, a surface, or a baking pan with flour.

Fold To combine a light mixture (such as beaten egg whites, whipped cream, or sifted flour) with a heavier mixture (such as a cake batter or the base of a soufflé) without deflating either. A rubber spatula is the best tool.

Fork-tender A degree of doneness for cooked vegetables and meats. When the food is pierced with a fork, there is only a very slight resistance.

Glaze To coat food by brushing with melted jelly, jam, or barbecue sauce or to brush piecrust with milk or beaten egg before baking.

Grill To cook food directly or indirectly over a source of heat (usually charcoal, briquettes, gas, or a special ridged pan). Also the name of the appliance used for grilling.

Julienne To cut food, especially vegetables, into thin, uniform matchstick strips about 2 inches long.

Knead To work dough until it's smooth and elastic, either by pressing and folding with the heel of the hand or in a heavy-duty electric mixer with a dough hook. Kneading develops the gluten in flour, an elastic protein that gives yeast breads their structure.

Leavening An agent that causes dough or batter to rise. Common leaveners include baking powder, baking soda, and yeast. Natural leaveners are air (when beaten into eggs) and steam (in popovers and cream puffs).

Marinate To flavor and/or tenderize a food by letting it sit in a liquid (such as lemon juice, wine, or yogurt) and, often, oil, herbs, or spices. When a marinade contains an acid, the marinating should be done in a nonreactive container.

Panfry To cook food in a small amount of fat in a skillet until browned and cooked through.

Parboil To partially cook food in boiling water. Carrots are often parboiled before they're added to other foods that take less time to cook.

Pare To cut away the skin or rind of a fruit or vegetable. A vegetable peeler or paring knife (a small knife with a 3- to 4-inch blade) is usually used.

Pasteurize To kill the bacteria in milk, fruit juices, or other liquids by heating to a moderately high temperature, then rapidly cooling it. All milk sold in the U.S. is pasteurized. Ultrapasteurized (UHT) milk is subjected to very high temperatures—about 300°F—and vacuum-packed for extended storage. It will keep without refrigeration for up to six months but must be refrigerated once it's opened. Ultrapasteurized cream is not vacuum-packed; it must be refrigerated.

Pinch The amount of a powdery ingredient, such as salt, pepper, or a spice, you can hold between your thumb and forefinger; about $\frac{1}{16}$ teaspoon.

Pipe To force a food, such as frosting, whipped cream, or mashed potatoes, through a pastry bag fitted with a pastry tip in a decorative manner or to shape meringues or éclairs. You can also use a plastic bag with a corner snipped off.

Poach To cook food in a gently simmering liquid; the surface should barely move. The amount and type of liquid will depend on the food being poached.

Pound To flatten to a uniform thickness using a meat mallet, meat pounder, or rolling pin. Meat and poultry is pounded to ensure even cooking. Pounding also tenderizes tough meats by breaking up hard-to-chew connective tissue.

Preheat To bring an oven or broiler to the desired temperature before cooking food.

Prick To pierce a food, usually with a fork, to prevent it from puffing up or bursting during cooking/baking.

Proof To dissolve yeast in a measured amount of warm water (105° to 115°F), sometimes with a small amount of sugar, and then to set it aside until foamy.

Punch down To deflate yeast dough after it has risen fully. It is not necessary to literally "punch" down the dough; it only needs to be gently deflated.

Puree To mash or grind food until completely smooth, usually in a food processor, blender, sieve, or food mill.

Reduce To rapidly boil a liquid, such as a sauce, wine, or stock, until it has reduced and the flavor is concentrated.

Render To slowly cook animal fat or skin until the fat separates from its connective tissue. It is strained before being used. The crisp brown bits left in the pan are called cracklings.

Roast To cook in an uncovered pan in the oven by dry heat. Roasted food develops a well-browned exterior. Tender cuts of meat, poultry, and fish are suitable for roasting, as are many vegetables.

Rolling boil A full boil that cannot be stirred down.

Sauté To cook food quickly in a small amount of hot fat in a skillet; the term derives from the French word *sauter*.

Scald To heat a liquid, such as cream or milk, just until tiny bubbles appear around the edge of the pan.

Score To make shallow cuts (usually parallel or crisscross) in the surface of food before cooking. This is done mainly to facilitate flavor absorption, as in marinated meats, chicken, and fish, but sometimes also for decorative purposes on hams. The tops of breads are often scored to enable them to rise (during baking) without bursting.

Sear To brown meat, fish, or poultry quickly by placing over very high heat.

Shred To cut, tear, or grate food into narrow strips.

Shave To cut wide paper-thin slices of food, especially Parmesan cheese or chocolate.

Shuck To remove the shells of oysters, mussels, scallops, or clams.

Sift To press ingredients, such as flour or confectioners' sugar, through a sifter or sieve. Sifting incorporates air and removes lumps, which helps ingredients to combine more easily.

Simmer To cook food in a liquid over low heat (at about 185°F). A few small bubbles should be visible on the surface.

Skim To remove fat or froth from the surface of a liquid, such as broth, boiling jelly, or soup. A skimmer, a long-handled metal utensil with a flat mesh disk or perforated bowl at one end, is the ideal tool for the job.

Soft peaks When cream or egg whites are beaten until they stand in peaks that bend over at the top.

Steam To cook food, covered, over a small amount of boiling water. The food is usually set on a rack or in a basket. Since it's not immersed in water, the food retains more nutrients, color, and flavor than with other cooking methods.

Stiff peaks When cream or egg whites are beaten until they stand in firm peaks that hold their shape.

Stir-fry To cook pieces of food quickly in a small amount of oil over high heat, stirring and tossing almost constantly. Stir-frying is used in Asian cooking; a wok is the traditional pan, although a large skillet will do just as well.

Temper To warm food gently before adding it to a hot mixture so it doesn't separate or curdle.

Tender-crisp The ideal degree of doneness for many vegetables: They're tender but retain some crunch.

Toast To brown bread, croutons, whole spices, or nuts in a dry skillet or in the oven. Toasting enhances the flavor of nuts and makes it possible to remove the skin from hazelnuts.

Toss To lift and drop pieces of food quickly and gently with two utensils, usually to coat them with a sauce (as for pasta) or a dressing (as for salad).

Whip To beat an ingredient (especially heavy or whipping cream) or mixture rapidly to incorporate air and increase the volume. You can use a whisk, egg beater, or electric mixer.

Whisk To beat ingredients (such as heavy or whipping cream, eggs, salad dressings, or sauces) with a fork or whisk to mix, blend, or incorporate air.

Zest To remove the flavorful colored part of citrus skin. Use the fine holes of a grater, a zester, or a vegetable peeler, avoiding the bitter white pith that is underneath.

INGREDIENTS GLOSSARY

This glossary defines many of the ingredients (both common and less familiar) you will find in this cookbook. Even with everyday ingredients, it's helpful to know something about them, especially when you want to make substitutions.

Almond paste A firm but pliable confection made of ground almonds and confectioners' sugar mixed with glucose, corn syrup, or egg white. Available in cans or tubes, almond paste is similar to marzipan, which is sweeter and softer. If almond paste seems hard, microwave on high for a few seconds to soften.

Amaretti cookies Hard, crisp, round Italian cookies, found at Italian grocers and specialty food stores. They often come tissue-wrapped in pairs and packed into pretty tin boxes.

Calvados A brandy distilled from apples and made in the Normandy region of France. Applejack is a good substitute.

Capers The flower buds of a bush native to parts of the Mediterranean and Asia. They are usually dried and pickled in a vinegar brine. Specialty food stores also sell them packed in salt; they have a purer flavor. Capers should be rinsed under cold water before using.

Chili powder A blend of ground dried mild chiles and ingredients such as cumin and garlic powder. Ground dried chiles without added seasonings are also available and sometimes labeled chile powder.

Chipotles en adobo Dried, smoked red jalapeño peppers canned in a thick chile puree called adobo. Handle these chiles and their sauce with care: They are very hot and can easily burn your skin. Leftover chipotles en adobo can be frozen. Freeze individual chiles with some sauce on a waxed paper–lined cookie sheet until firm, then remove from the waxed paper and store  in a heavy-duty ziptight plastic bag for up to three months. Chipotles en adobo can be found in Latino markets and many supermarkets.

Chorizo A spicy pork sausage seasoned with chiles and garlic. Spanish-style chorizo is a a firm, smoked link sausage. Do not substitute Mexican-style fresh chorizo.

Cilantro A pungent green herb, popular in Asian and Latino cooking; sometimes called fresh coriander or Chinese parsley. It is often sold with the roots still attached; the roots are sometimes chopped and used as a seasoning.

Cinnamon sticks Used to garnish hot beverages, but they can be simmered in a liquid to release their warm, spicy flavor.

Cornichons Tiny gherkinlike cucumbers that are pickled in a tart brine. Small dill pickles are an acceptable substitute if the cornichons are to be chopped and used in a sauce.

Crab boil A mix of herbs and spices (such as mustard seeds, whole allspice, peppercorns, bay leaves, and dried chiles) that is sometimes added to the water in which crab, shrimp, or lobster is cooked.

Coconut milk An unsweetened infusion of shredded coconut meat and water that is strained and canned; not interchangeable with coconut cream, which is rich, sweet, and used in desserts and tropical drinks.

Curry powder Widely used in Indian cooking; the blend of spices used and heat intensity can greatly vary. A typical curry powder can contain up to twenty different spices, including turmeric, cardamom, red chiles, black pepper, and cumin. Madras-style curry powder, available in supermarkets, is a reliable moderately spicy blend.

Durum A hard wheat used to make semolina flour.

Espresso coffee powder, instant Available at Italian grocers and many supermarkets; a convenient way to add deep-roasted coffee flavor to food and beverages.

Fish sauce An integral flavoring in Southeast Asian cooking, it is made from fermented fish. Also known as *nam pla* (Thai) and *nuoc nam* (Vietnam); the Philippine version, *pastis,* has a much milder flavor. Store at cool room temperature in a dark place; it will keep for about one year.

Five-spice powder A favorite seasoning in Chinese cooking; it is usually a blend of equal parts cinnamon, cloves, fennel, star anise, and Szechwan peppercorns.

Hoisin sauce This sweet, thick sauce is made from a base of soybeans. Refrigerate after opening. Often used in Chinese barbecue sauces for chicken and ribs.

Juniper berries Fragrant dried blue-black berries that are used as a seasoning and the main flavoring in gin. It can usually be found in spice shops and specialty food stores. If unavailable, stir 1 to 2 tablespoons of gin into the finished dish during the last five minutes of cooking.

Kirsch Also called *kirschwasser* (German for "cherry water"), a clear brandy distilled from cherry juice and pits. (This type of clear spirit made from fruit is called *eau-de-vie.*) Often used to flavor fondues and desserts.

Mango chutney A sweet and spicy condiment that is often served with curries. Major Grey's is a common brand.

Maple syrup, pure Maple sap that has been boiled down until syrupy. Pure maple syrup has a subtle and delicious flavor that is incomparable. Maple-flavored syrup is made from a liquid such as corn syrup mixed with a small amount of pure maple syrup. Pancake syrup is corn syrup with natural or artificial maple extract added.

Marsala A fortified wine, originally from Sicily but also produced in California; available sweet (best for desserts) and dry (use in savory dishes).

Miso A highly concentrated fermented soybean paste, made from a combination of soybeans and grain; widely used in Japanese cooking and made in different strengths. Red miso has the strongest flavor, golden is fairly mild, and white is mellow and slightly sweet. Look for miso in natural food stores and Asian markets.

Molasses A by-product of sugar refining, molasses is the liquid that remains after the sugar crystals are extracted. Molasses can be sulphured or unsulphured; it depends on whether sulphur was used in the refining process. Light molasses is from the first boiling (refining) and has a mild flavor. Dark molasses is from the second boiling and is darker and less sweet. Blackstrap molasses is from the third boiling and is bitter.

Mustard, Dijon This prepared mustard gets its distinctive flavor from a special blend of mustard seeds and white wine. There are many different brands, with varying heat levels, so when you find a brand you like, stick with it.

Olives The fruit of the olive tree is naturally very bitter and must be processed to make it edible. There are many olive varieties, and the finished product depends on the ripeness of the fruit and the type of processing. While each has a particular flavor, many are interchangeable. Black olives include the tiny Niçoise, the gray-black Gaeta, the vinegar-cured Kalamata (also available pitted), and the pleasantly bitter, wrinkled, oil-cured Moroccan. Picholine and manzanilla are two popular green olives. To remove the pits from olives, use an olive or cherry pitter. Or put the olives on a work surface, place the flat side of a large knife on top of one olive, and press down to lightly crush the olive; remove the pit.

Olive oil Pressing tree-ripened olives produces the prized liquid we know as olive oil. Its flavor, color, and fragrance depend on the region and the quality of the harvest. In general, extravirgin olive oil, from the first pressing, is full-flavored, bright green to green-gold in color, and best used on salads or other dishes where its taste can be most appreciated. Regular

Olive varieties: Niçoise, Gaeta, Kalamata, Moroccan, Picholine, manzanilla

olive oil (sometimes called pure olive oil) is from a subsequent pressing and has a milder, but still distinctive olive flavor; it's a good cooking oil. Light olive oil has been specially treated to remove much of the characteristic olive taste; it is not lower in fat.

Old Bay seasoning An aromatic, somewhat hot blend of ground spices, popular with cooks in the Chesapeake Bay area, especially for seafood dishes.

Pancetta An unsmoked bacon that is rolled into a cylinder and sliced to order. It is used in Italian dishes. Pancetta is available at Italian delicatessens, specialty food stores, and some supermarkets. Subsitute regular smoked bacon, if necessary.

Pepper The world's most popular spice, peppercorns are the dried berries of a perennial vine. They come in three colors: black, white, and green. Black pepper is picked just before the berry ripens; the skin turns black when dried. White pepper is the ripened berry with the skin removed; it has a milder flavor than black pepper. Green peppercorns are soft, underripe berries, usually preserved in brine. Freshly ground pepper has an incomparable flavor, so it's worth the investment to purchase a good-quality pepper grinder. Some recipes call for coarse-cracked pepper (also called butcher's grind), but it's just as easy to crush your own peppercorns in a mortar and pestle or on a work surface with a heavy skillet.

Pine nuts From the pinecones of certain pine trees, these small, elongated ivory-colored nuts are sometimes called *pignoli* or *piñon*. They turn rancid easily; store in the refrigerator for up to three months or freeze for up to nine months.

Porcini mushrooms, dried These members of *Boletus edulis* are imported from Italy and have a rich, earthy flavor; the French variety are called *cèpes* and are more expensive. They must be rehydrated in hot water before use. After soaking, rinse them under cold running water to remove any grit. Use the flavorful soaking liquid to add extra mushroom flavor. Available in specialty food stores and Italian markets.

Prosciutto A cured, aged air-dried ham with a firm texture and deliciously salty flavor. Imported Italian prosciutto, available at high-quality grocers and butchers, has a milder flavor than the domestic variety.

Salt There are so many kinds of salt available, it's easy to take this familiar ingredient for granted. Each has a different level of saltiness, so it's helpful to understand the differences. We tested our recipes with fine-grained table salt, which has additives that keep it free-flowing. Iodized salt is table salt that has been treated with iodine (which helps prevent hyperthyroidism). Kosher salt has no additives. Some cooks prefer it for its mild flavor; its coarse texture makes it easy to pick up for sprinkling. Sea salt is also less salty than common table salt. If you use kosher or sea salt in your cooking, you will need a larger quantity. Grayish rock salt is not a food-quality salt but is used in old-fashioned ice-cream makers and as a bed upon which to bake and serve stuffed oysters and clams.

Savoiardi Long, crisp Italian-style ladyfingers; usually layered with a moist filling to soften them, as in tiramisù.

Semolina A coarse, sandlike grind of durum wheat, used to make pasta and some breads.

Sesame oil, Asian Dark brown-orange in color, this oil is pressed from roasted sesame seeds. It is generally used as a seasoning, not a cooking oil.

Soy sauce Made from fermented soybeans and roasted wheat or barley, this dark, salty sauce is indispensable in Asian cooking. There are many different versions, and some can be quite salty. Use a reliable Japanese brand.

Star anise A star-shaped spice with eight points, each containing a seed. Often used in Chinese cooking, it has a delicate licorice flavor. For a change of pace, try grinding it in a coffee mill and adding $\frac{1}{2}$ teaspoon to your favorite pumpkin pie or apple pie spice mixture.

Tapenade A French olive paste seasoned with anchovies, herbs, and garlic. The Italian version is called *olivada*.

Tahini Sesame seeds ground into a thick paste; stir well to incorporate the oil that rises to the top. Available at natural food stores and most supermarkets.

Tomatoes, dried Often referred to as "sun-dried" tomatoes but rarely dried in the sun anymore, these intensely flavored dehydrated tomatoes are processed by more commerical methods. They can be purchased loose-packed or packed with oil in a jar. Loose-packed dried tomatoes should be soaked in boiling water to cover until softened, then drained.

Vinegar Bacterial activity can turn some liquids into vinegar; *vin aigre* means "sour wine." Cider vinegar, made from apple juice, is a popular vinegar. Distilled white vinegar has a strong flavor but is preferred for pickling because it doesn't darken food. Red and white wines are also made into vinegars. The more expensive vinegars are produced by an ancient process that slowly turns the wine sour, instead of innoculating it with fast-acting bacteria. Tarragon vinegar is white wine that has been infused with tarragon. Balsamic vinegar is made from semidry Trebbiano grapes, so the resulting vinegar has a sweet note. Most supermarket varieties are tasty, but they aren't true balsamic vinegars, which are aged for years in wood caskets and are quite expensive. Malt vinegar, a British favorite, is a mild vinegar made from malted barley.

Wonton wrappers Delicate thin squares of wheat noodles, they can be stuffed to make wontons or other dumplings or ravioli. Look for them in the refrigerated section of the supermarket or at Asian grocery stores. Wrap leftover wrappers in plastic wrap and heavy-duty foil and freeze for up to one month.

2

APPETIZERS

Appetizers serve two important roles: They whet one's appetite, and they set the tone for the meal that follows. A stylish sit-down dinner calls for an elegant first course that looks terrific on your best china. Mini Crab Cakes (page 51), for example, would be an excellent choice for a menu featuring a main course of meat. A casual backyard barbecue requires a different approach. Heaping bowls of fuss-free dips and chips are always popular with both guests and cooks at this kind of informal gathering. At a cocktail party, the hors d'oeuvres are the meal, so you'll want to offer a wide selection. This is the time to prepare bite-size savory pastries, such as Curried Cheddar Puffs (page 50), and finger food, such as Prosciutto-Wrapped Asparagus (page 47). Some of our favorite appetizers are simply snacks, nibbles, and munchies, meant to be served without ceremony to quell simple hunger pangs.

It is important to balance the appetizers you serve with the rest of the menu. When choosing the first course for a dinner, avoid repeating the flavors of the main course. For a party where lots of hors d'oeuvres will be served, the selection should reflect a variety of flavors, textures, shapes, and temperatures to keep guests tempted. Consider the colors of the food, too. Appetizers that are baked until golden brown are delicious, but they need to be garnished creatively and served alongside more colorful offerings. A garnish doesn't have to be

Tomato and Ricotta Salata Bruschetta

fancy. It can be as simple as a small cluster of green grapes or a few tiny apples or pears. Or take a cue from the recipe. A few clusters of fresh red and green chiles can look dramatic on a platter of Mexican-inspired goodies.

The recipes in this chapter reflect cuisines from all over the globe, including Vietnam, Indonesia, China, France, Italy, Mexico, Turkey, Greece, and Spain. While it can be fun to feature the food of a specific region when serving a variety of appetizers, it isn't necessary to stay within the culinary borders of one country or area. Simply avoid serving appetizers that are too similar. Once you've chosen something such as Easy Spicy Cheese Straws (page 46), for example, steer clear of other recipes that contain Cheddar cheese and puff pastry.

HOW TO MANAGE THE MENU

- Prepare as many appetizers in advance as possible. Among the best candidates are marinated olives and vegetables, dips, spreads, baked savory pastries, pâtés, and terrines.
- Don't select too many appetizers that demand last-minute attention. Arrange finished hors d'oeuvres in jelly-roll pans, cover, and refrigerate. If you are running short of space, invert a large roasting pan over a finished platter, then place a second platter on top of the inverted pan.
- For appetizers that require last-minute assembling, prepare and chill the separate components until serving time.

- Plan on only one or two hot appetizers. Unless you have more than one oven, it's difficult to juggle reheating more than a few items. Too many hot hors d'oeuvres also means more time spent in the kitchen than with your guests.
- Be sure to serve some appetizers, like nuts, dips, spreads, and pâtés, that require no more work than simply setting them out and checking occasionally for replenishment. A menu comprised of passed hors d'ouevres is only good if you have lots of help.
- Consider the amount of available refrigerator space when planning your menu. To save room, store dips, spreads, and marinated olives in ziptight plastic bags.
- Tea sandwiches and other miniature sandwiches make excellent appetizers, and there's quite a selection to choose from (pages 618 and 619). Make the sandwiches ahead and arrange them in jelly-roll pans. Separate the layers with damp paper towels and cover securely with plastic wrap to keep them from drying out.
- How much should you serve? Figure on about ten to twelve small appetizers per person if no meal follows. Otherwise, allow five or six pieces per guest.

DO-AHEAD STRATEGIES

- Prepare vegetables for crudités up to one day ahead. Wrap them in damp paper towels, store in ziptight plastic bags, and refrigerate. Asparagus, broccoli, green beans, and cauliflower are best when lightly cooked (blanched). Trim and cut the vegetables into the desired size or shape (flowerets, spears, or sticks) and boil them in lightly salted water just until tender-crisp (usually no longer than two minutes). Drain in a colander, rinse well with cold running water, and pat dry with paper towels. Store as directed.
- Most pâtés and terrines are best if made one to two days ahead. Wrap them tightly in foil and refrigerate. Meat pâtés freeze well when double-wrapped in foil for up to two months. Defrost overnight in the refrigerator.
- Freeze pastry appetizers, such as Empanaditas (page 48) and Greek Cheese Pastries (page 49), raw or baked, for up to one month. Layer the pastries in shallow baking pans (disposable aluminum foil pans work well), separating the layers with waxed paper. Wrap each pan tightly with a double layer of foil. To serve, unwrap the pastries and arrange them on cookie sheets. Reheat the baked pastries in a 350°F oven for about ten minutes before serving. Or bake the raw pastries straight from the freezer as the recipe directs, allowing for a little additional baking time.

SERVING WITH STYLE

- Appetizers should be easy to handle, easy to eat, and take no more than a couple of bites to finish. Set out bowls for olive pits, toothpicks, and kabob skewers. And don't forget lots of cocktail napkins.
- Arrange cut-up vegetables on a tray or in a large basket lined with plastic wrap and covered with a bed of curly endive, green or purple kale, or other leafy salad greens.
- For a change of pace, serve dips and spreads in hollowed-out loaves of bread, squash, or cabbages.
- For a buffet-style party, use flat dishes that hold a generous quantity of food. To create the most dramatic presentation, add height by placing some platters on inverted baking dishes or on boxes covered with napkins that are color-coordinated with the tablecloth.
- Store-bought crackers come in a wide assortment of shapes and flavors. Plain or mildly seasoned crackers, such as sesame or poppy, are the most versatile and can accompany a variety of savory spreads and pâtés. Herb- and garlic-flavored crackers compete with, rather than complement, aromatic spreads or strong-flavored cheeses. When serving thinly sliced bread (French baguettes work well with many dishes), store in plastic bags until the last minute to keep the bread fresh.
- Homemade toasts, from pita bread wedges or thinly sliced baguettes, are a welcome alternative to crackers and they're easy to make. Brush the bread with olive oil or melted butter and bake in a preheated 350°F oven until lightly browned, about ten minutes. Store at room temperature in an airtight container.
- For the most flavor, remove cold appetizers from the refrigerator about thirty minutes before serving, but don't let them stand at room temperature for longer than two hours.
- The microwave is ideal for reheating nonpastry appetizers, such as Chicken and Beef Saté (page 52). Appetizer pastries are best reheated in a conventional oven—microwaving makes them soggy.

Roasted Red Pepper Dip

An unusual dip with Middle Eastern flavors. If you are not familiar with roasting peppers, this is the perfect time to learn how. Once you taste them, you'll wonder why you waited so long.

Prep: 45 minutes

4	red peppers, roasted (page 448)
½	teaspoon ground cumin
½	cup walnuts, toasted
2	slices firm white bread, torn into pieces
2	tablespoons vinegar, preferably raspberry
1	tablespoon olive oil
½	teaspoon salt
⅛	teaspoon ground red pepper (cayenne)
	toasted pita bread wedges

1. Cut roasted peppers into large pieces. In small skillet, toast cumin over low heat, stirring constantly, until very fragrant, 1 to 2 minutes.

2. In food processor with knife blade attached, process walnuts until ground. Add roasted peppers, cumin, bread, vinegar, oil, salt, and ground red pepper; puree until smooth. Transfer to bowl. If not serving right away, cover and refrigerate up to 4 hours. Serve with toasted pita bread wedges. Makes about 2 cups.

Each tablespoon: About 23 calories, 0g protein, 2g carbohydrate, 2g total fat (0g saturated), 0mg cholesterol, 46mg sodium.

Roasted Red Pepper Dip

Potted Cheddar and Beer Spread

The flavors in this spread were inspired by Welsh rabbit, the ever-popular British sauce made with Cheddar cheese and beer and served over toast.

Prep: 15 minutes plus chilling and standing

1½	pounds extrasharp Cheddar cheese, shredded (6 cups)
1	can or bottle (12 ounces) beer
6	tablespoons butter or margarine, softened
1	tablespoon Dijon mustard
1	tablespoon Worcestershire sauce
⅛	teaspoon ground red pepper (cayenne)
⅛	teaspoon ground nutmeg
	assorted crackers

1. In large bowl, stir cheese and beer until mixed. Let stand until cheese has softened, about 30 minutes.

2. In food processor with knife blade attached, process cheese mixture, butter, mustard, Worcestershire, ground red pepper, and nutmeg until smooth, 3 to 5 minutes.

3. Pack cheese mixture into airtight containers and store in refrigerator up to 1 month or in freezer up to 3 months. To serve, let cheese mixture stand at room temperature until soft enough to spread, about 30 minutes. Serve with crackers. Makes 5 cups.

Each tablespoon: About 44 calories, 2g protein, 0g carbohydrate, 4g total fat (2g saturated), 11mg cholesterol, 68mg sodium.

Roasted Eggplant Dip with Herbs

The fresh flavors of lemon and mint are a perfect match for the baked eggplant in this Mediterranean-style dip.

Prep: 15 minutes plus cooling and draining   *Roast: 1 hour*

2	small eggplants (1 pound each)
2	garlic cloves, thinly sliced
2	tablespoons olive oil
4	teaspoons fresh lemon juice
1	teaspoon salt
¼	teaspoon ground black pepper
2	tablespoons chopped fresh parsley
2	tablespoons chopped fresh mint
	toasted pita bread wedges

1. Preheat oven to 400°F. With knife, cut slits all over eggplants; insert garlic slices in slits. Place eggplants in jelly-roll pan and roast until collapsed and tender, about 1 hour.

2. When cool enough to handle, cut eggplants in half. Scoop out flesh and place in colander set over bowl; discard skin. Let drain 10 minutes.

3. Transfer eggplant to food processor with knife blade attached. Add oil, lemon juice, salt, and pepper; pulse to coarsely chop. Add parsley and mint, pulsing to combine. Spoon into bowl; cover and refrigerate up to 4 hours. Serve with pita bread wedges. Makes about 2 cups.

Each tablespoon: About 14 calories, 0g protein, 2g carbohydrate, 1g total fat (0g saturated), 0mg cholesterol, 74mg sodium.

Baba Ganoush

Prepare as directed. Omit parsley and mint. Stir in ½ **teaspoon ground cumin** and ¼ **cup lowfat plain yogurt**.

Tzatziki

In Greece, this is served as a dip with pita bread or as a cold sauce to accompany grilled fish or chicken.

Prep: 20 minutes plus overnight to drain, plus chilling

1	container (16 ounces) plain lowfat yogurt
½	English (seedless) cucumber, not peeled, seeded and finely chopped plus a few very thin slices
1½	teaspoons salt
1 to 2	garlic cloves, chopped
1	tablespoon chopped fresh mint or dill plus additional sprigs
1	tablespoon extravirgin olive oil
½	teaspoon red wine vinegar
¼	teaspoon ground black pepper

1. Spoon yogurt into sieve lined with cheesecloth or coffee filter set over bowl; cover and refrigerate overnight. Transfer drained yogurt to medium bowl and discard liquid.

2. Meanwhile, in colander set over bowl, toss chopped cucumber with 1 teaspoon salt. Let drain at least 1 hour at room temperature, or cover and refrigerate up to 8 hours. In batches, wrap chopped cucumber in kitchen towel and squeeze to remove as much liquid as possible. Pat dry with paper towels, then add to bowl with yogurt.

3. With flat side of chef's knife, mash garlic to a paste with remaining ½ teaspoon salt. Add garlic, chopped mint, oil, vinegar, and pepper to yogurt and stir to combine. Cover and refrigerate at least 2 or up to 4 hours. Serve chilled or at room temperature, topped with cucumber slices and mint sprigs. Makes about 1¼ cups.

Each tablespoon: About 17 calories, 1g protein, 1g carbohydrate, 1g total fat (0g saturated), 1mg cholesterol, 182mg sodium.

Hummus

Middle Eastern dips, such as hummus, once seemed exotic, but now they're familiar old friends. Tahini is readily available at health food stores and supermarkets.

Prep: 15 minutes plus chilling

4	garlic cloves, peeled
1	large lemon
1	can (15 to 19 ounces) garbanzo beans, rinsed and drained
2	tablespoons tahini (sesame seed paste, page 33)
3	tablespoons olive oil
2	tablespoons water
½	teaspoon salt
⅛	teaspoon ground red pepper (cayenne)
½	teaspoon paprika
2	tablespoons chopped fresh cilantro (optional)
	pita bread wedges
	olives

1. In 1-quart saucepan, heat *2 cups water* to boiling over high heat. Add garlic and cook 3 minutes to blanch; drain.

2. From lemon, grate 1 teaspoon peel and squeeze 3 tablespoons juice. In food processor with knife blade attached, combine beans, tahini, garlic, lemon peel and juice, oil, water, salt, and ground red pepper. Puree until smooth. Transfer to platter; cover and refrigerate up to 4 hours. To serve, sprinkle with paprika and cilantro, if using. Serve with pita bread wedges and olives. Makes 2 cups.

Each tablespoon: About 28 calories, 1g protein, 2g carbohydrate, 2g total fat (0g saturated), 0mg cholesterol, 54mg sodium.

MEZE

Meze, little savory dishes to be nibbled before a meal or with drinks, are a tradition in Greece, Turkey, and the Middle East. Try any of the following with pita or French bread, along with feta cheese chunks, olives, radishes, sliced cucumbers, or tomato wedges: Roasted Red Pepper Dip, Tzatziki, Hummus, Roasted Eggplant Dip with Herbs, or Baba Ganoush.

Warm Layered Bean Dip

This colorful dip is always a hit. The pinto bean, Jack cheese, and salsa layers can be assembled several hours in advance, then baked just before serving.

Prep: 35 minutes   Bake: 12 minutes

2	garlic cloves, peeled
1	can (15 to 19 ounces) pinto beans, rinsed and drained
2	green onions, finely chopped
1	tablespoon tomato paste
1	tablespoon water
4	ounces Monterey Jack cheese, shredded (1 cup)
1	cup mild to medium salsa
2	avocados, each cut in half, pitted, and peeled
¼	cup chopped fresh cilantro
3	tablespoons finely chopped red onion
2	tablespoons fresh lime juice
½	teaspoon salt
1	cup sour cream
	tortilla chips

1. Preheat oven to 350°F. In 1-quart saucepan, heat *2 cups water* to boiling over high heat. Add garlic and cook 3 minutes to blanch; drain. With flat side of chef's knife, mash garlic; transfer to medium bowl and add beans, half of green onions, tomato paste, and water. Mash until well combined but still slightly chunky. Spread in bottom of 9-inch glass pie plate.

2. Sprinkle cheese over bean mixture, then spread salsa on top. Bake until piping hot, about 12 minutes.

3. Meanwhile, in medium bowl, mash avocados just until slightly chunky. Stir in cilantro, red onion, lime juice, and salt. Spoon avocado mixture over hot dip mixture and spread sour cream on top. Sprinkle with remaining green onions. Serve with tortilla chips. Makes about 5½ cups.

Each tablespoon: About 22 calories, 1g protein, 1g carbohydrate, 2g total fat (1g saturated), 3mg cholesterol, 61mg sodium.

Herbed Yogurt-Cheese Dip

Drained yogurt has a thick cheeselike consistency. Drain it the day before you intend to make the dip. The longer it drains, the thicker the "cheese" will be. If you like, substitute fresh parsley or cilantro for the basil.

Prep: 10 minutes plus overnight to drain	Cook: 5 minutes

1½	cups plain lowfat yogurt
2	garlic cloves, peeled
¾	cup finely chopped fresh basil
2	teaspoons olive oil
½	teaspoon salt
	assorted crackers or cut-up vegetables

1. Place yogurt in sieve lined with cheesecloth or coffee filter set over bowl; cover and refrigerate overnight. Transfer drained yogurt to bowl and discard liquid.

2. In 1-quart saucepan, heat *2 cups water* to boiling over high heat. Add garlic and cook 3 minutes to blanch; drain. With flat side of chef's knife, mash garlic; add to yogurt. Stir in basil, oil, and salt. Cover and refrigerate up to 4 hours. Serve with crackers or cut-up vegetables. Makes 1 cup.

Each tablespoon: About 17 calories, 1g protein, 1g carbohydrate, 1g total fat (0g saturated), 1mg cholesterol, 79mg sodium.

Easy Aïoli

Aïoli (ay-OH-lee) is a very garlicky mayonnaise from Provence. We've reduced the garlic's harshness by cooking it. Wonderful as a dip for vegetables or seafood and as a sauce for fish or lamb, it is also the traditional condiment for Bouillabaisse (page 305).

Prep: 5 minutes plus cooling	Cook: 20 minutes

1⅛	teaspoons salt
1	head garlic, separated into cloves (about 14 cloves)
½	cup mayonnaise
2	teaspoons fresh lemon juice
½	teaspoon Dijon mustard
⅛	teaspoon ground red pepper (cayenne)
¼	cup extravirgin olive oil

1. In 2-quart saucepan, combine *4 cups water* and 1 teaspoon salt; heat to boiling. Add garlic and boil until garlic has softened, about 20 minutes. Drain. When cool enough to handle, squeeze soft garlic from each clove into small bowl.

2. In blender, puree garlic, mayonnaise, lemon juice, mustard, remaining ⅛ teaspoon salt, and ground red pepper until smooth. With blender running, through hole in cover, add oil in slow, steady stream until mixture is thickened and creamy. Transfer to small bowl; cover and refrigerate up to 4 hours. Makes about ¾ cup.

Each tablespoon: About 112 calories, 0g protein, 2g carbohydrate, 12g total fat (2g saturated), 5mg cholesterol, 276mg sodium.

Black Bean Dip

Why buy bean dip when you can make it so quickly? This one is not only tasty but has the added advantage of clinging to chips and vegetables without dripping.

Prep: 10 minutes

4	garlic cloves, peeled
1	can (15 to 19 ounces) black beans, rinsed and drained
2	tablespoons tomato paste
2	tablespoons olive oil
4½	teaspoons fresh lime juice
1	tablespoon water
½	teaspoon ground cumin
½	teaspoon ground coriander
¼	teaspoon salt
⅛	teaspoon ground red pepper (cayenne)
	tortilla chips

1. In 1-quart saucepan, heat *2 cups water* to boiling over high heat. Add garlic and cook 3 minutes to blanch; drain.

2. In food processor with knife blade attached, combine beans, garlic, tomato paste, oil, lime juice, water, cumin, coriander, salt, and ground red pepper. Puree until smooth. Transfer to bowl; cover and refrigerate up to 4 hours. Serve with tortilla chips. Makes about 2 cups.

Each tablespoon: About 18 calories, 1g protein, 2g carbohydrate, 1g total fat (0g saturated), 0mg cholesterol, 50mg sodium.

Potted Shrimp

This old-fashioned recipe is a specialty in the Carolinas, where each family's rendition is cherished.

Prep: 15 minutes plus chilling	*Cook: 3 minutes*

8	tablespoons unsalted butter (1 stick), softened
1	pound medium shrimp, shelled and deveined (page 296)
¾	teaspoon salt
¼	teaspoon ground red pepper (cayenne)
2	tablespoons dry sherry
	sesame crackers or toast

1. In 10-inch skillet, melt 1 tablespoon butter over medium-high heat. Add shrimp, salt, and ground red pepper; cook, stirring frequently, until shrimp are opaque throughout, about 2 minutes. Add sherry and cook 30 seconds.

2. Transfer shrimp and pan juices to food processor with knife blade attached and pulse until shrimp is finely chopped. Cut remaining 7 tablespoons butter into pieces; add to processor and process until evenly combined.

3. Transfer shrimp mixture to serving bowl. Cover and refrigerate up to 24 hours. Let stand 30 minutes at room temperature before serving. Serve with sesame crackers or toast. Makes about 2 cups.

Each tablespoon: About 39 calories, 2g protein, 0g carbohydrate, 3g total fat (2g saturated), 25mg cholesterol, 72mg sodium.

Tapenade

This Provençal olive spread can be enjoyed on crisp toasted bread or crackers or as a condiment for fish, chicken, or pork.

Prep: 20 minutes

2	garlic cloves, peeled
1½	cups Gaeta or Kalamata olives, pitted
½	cup pimiento-stuffed olives
1	tablespoon olive oil
1	teaspoon fennel seeds
1	teaspoon freshly grated orange peel

1. In 1-quart saucepan, heat *2 cups water* to boiling over high heat. Add garlic and cook 3 minutes to blanch; drain.

2. In food processor with knife blade attached, combine Gaeta and pimiento-stuffed olives, oil, fennel seeds, orange peel, and garlic; process until chopped. Transfer to bowl; cover and refrigerate up to overnight. Makes about 1¼ cups.

Each tablespoon: About 41 calories, 0g protein, 2g carbohydrate, 4g total fat (0g saturated), 0mg cholesterol, 264mg sodium.

Tomato-Basil Cream Cheese Logs

Bursting with Italian flavor, spread this cream cheese log on thinly sliced and toasted Italian bread or crackers.

Prep: 15 minutes plus soaking and chilling

⅓	cup dried tomatoes
2	packages (8 ounces each) cream cheese, softened
⅓	cup chopped fresh basil
¼	cup freshly grated Parmesan cheese
½	teaspoon coarsely ground black pepper
½	cup pine nuts (pignoli), toasted and finely chopped

1. Soak dried tomatoes in enough *boiling water* to cover until softened, about 15 minutes. Drain tomatoes well, then finely chop.

2. In small bowl, with mixer at medium speed, beat cream cheese until light and creamy, about 1 minute. Stir in tomatoes, basil, Parmesan, and pepper.

3. On waxed paper, shape half of cheese mixture into 6-inch log; roll up in waxed paper. Repeat with remaining cheese mixture. Refrigerate until chilled and firm, at least 1 hour. Roll logs in pine nuts; wrap and chill 15 minutes longer. Makes two 6-inch logs, 12 servings each.

Each serving: About 90 calories, 3g protein, 2g carbohydrate, 8g total fat (5g saturated), 22mg cholesterol, 76mg sodium.

Hot-Pepper Nuts

Packed into pretty jars or tins, these are perfect for gift giving. If you like, use peanuts, pecans, or almonds instead of walnuts.

Prep: 5 minutes   Bake: 25 minutes

8	ounces walnuts (2 cups)
1	tablespoon butter or margarine, melted
2	teaspoons soy sauce
½ to 1	teaspoon hot pepper sauce

1. Preheat oven to 350°F. Lightly grease jelly-roll pan.
2. In prepared jelly-roll pan, toss walnuts with melted butter until coated. Bake walnuts, stirring occasionally, until well toasted, about 25 minutes. Drizzle soy sauce and hot pepper sauce over nuts, tossing until well mixed. Cool completely in pan on wire rack. Store nuts in airtight container up to 1 month. Makes about 2 cups.

Each ¼ cup: About 211 calories, 4g protein, 6g carbohydrate, 21g total fat (3g saturated), 4mg cholesterol, 116mg sodium.

Sweet-and-Spicy Nuts

Prepare nuts as directed but substitute **2 tablespoons sugar, 1½ teaspoons Worcestershire sauce, ½ teaspoon ground red pepper (cayenne),** and **¼ teaspoon salt** for soy sauce and hot pepper sauce.

Curried Nuts

Prepare nuts as directed but substitute **2 teaspoons curry powder, ½ teaspoon ground cumin,** and **½ teaspoon salt** for soy sauce and hot pepper sauce.

Chili Nuts

Prepare nuts as directed but substitute **1 tablespoon chili powder** and **½ teaspoon salt** for soy sauce and hot pepper sauce.

Tortilla Spirals

Sensational-looking spirals are easy do-ahead party fare. There are two different fillings: smoked salmon and dried tomato. Both are delicious.

Prep: 35 minutes plus chilling

	Smoked Salmon Filling (opposite)
	Dried Tomato Filling (opposite)
8	(10-inch) flour tortillas

1. Prepare fillings.
2. Spread each filling evenly over 4 tortillas. Roll each tortilla up tightly, jelly-roll fashion. Wrap each roll in plastic wrap and refrigerate until firm enough to slice, at least 4 hours or up to overnight.
3. To serve, unwrap tortilla rolls and trim ends. Cut rolls into ½-inch-thick slices. Makes about 144 appetizers.

Each appetizer with salmon filling: About 28 calories, 1g protein, 2g carbohydrate, 2g total fat (1g saturated), 6mg cholesterol, 76mg sodium.

Each appetizer with tomato filling: About 32 calories, 1g protein, 2g carbohydrate, 2g total fat (1g saturated), 6mg cholesterol, 42mg sodium.

Tortilla Spirals

Smoked Salmon Filling

In medium bowl, combine **1½ packages (8 ounces each) cream cheese,** softened, **4 ounces thinly sliced smoked salmon,** chopped, **3 tablespoons capers,** drained and chopped, and **¼ cup loosely packed fresh dill,** chopped, until blended.

Dried Tomato Filling

In medium bowl, combine **1 package (8 ounces) cream cheese,** softened, **10 dried tomato halves packed in herb-seasoned olive oil,** drained and chopped, **1 container (5.2 ounces) spreadable cheese with pepper,** and **⅓ cup packed fresh basil leaves,** chopped, until blended.

Marinated Mixed Olives

Here, an assortment of olives is marinated in extravirgin olive oil and seasoned with garlic, fennel, bay leaves, and lemon—an inviting addition to any antipasto tray.

Prep: 10 minutes plus standing and marinating   Cook: 5 minutes

¼	cup extravirgin olive oil
2	teaspoons fennel seeds, crushed
4	small bay leaves
2	pounds assorted Mediterranean olives, such as Niçoise, picholine, or Kalamata
6	strips (3" by 1" each) lemon peel
4	garlic cloves, crushed with side of chef's knife

1. In 1-quart saucepan, heat oil, fennel seeds, and bay leaves over medium heat until hot but not smoking. Remove saucepan from heat; let stand 10 minutes.

2. In large bowl, combine olives, lemon peel, garlic, and oil mixture. Cover and refrigerate, stirring occasionally, at least 24 hours or up to several days to blend flavors.

3. Store in refrigerator up to 1 month. Drain to serve. Makes about 6 cups.

Each ¼ cup: About 107 calories, 1g protein, 3g carbohydrate, 10g total fat (1g saturated), 0mg cholesterol, 680mg sodium.

Pickled Shrimp

Long a favorite in the Good Housekeeping dining room, this perfectly spiced appetizer is always made ahead: The shrimp are cooked the day before and marinated overnight. To keep them well chilled when served, set the bowl of shrimp in a larger bowl of crushed ice.

Prep: 20 minutes plus overnight to marinate   Cook: 5 minutes

¼	cup dry sherry
3	teaspoons salt
¼	teaspoon whole black peppercorns
1	bay leaf
3	pounds large shrimp, shelled and deveined (page 296), leaving tail part of shell on, if desired
⅔	cup fresh lemon juice (about 3 large lemons)
½	cup distilled white vinegar
½	cup vegetable oil
3	tablespoons pickling spices, tied in cheesecloth bag
2	teaspoons sugar
2	dill sprigs

1. In 4-quart saucepan combine *6 cups water,* sherry, 2 teaspoons salt, peppercorns, and bay leaf; heat to boiling over high heat. Add shrimp; heat to boiling. Shrimp should be opaque throughout when water returns to boil; if not, cook about 1 minute longer. Drain.

2. In large bowl, combine lemon juice, vinegar, oil, pickling spices, sugar, dill, and remaining 1 teaspoon salt. Add shrimp and toss well to coat. Spoon into ziptight plastic bags, press out excess air, and seal. Refrigerate shrimp overnight to marinate, turning bags occasionally.

3. Remove shrimp from marinade and arrange in chilled bowl. Serve with cocktail picks. Makes 24 appetizer servings.

♥ Each serving: About 69 calories, 9g protein, 1g carbohydrate, 2g total fat (0g saturated), 70mg cholesterol, 166mg sodium.

Smoked Trout Pâté

A smoky spread that is easily prepared in a food processor.

Prep: 25 minutes

3	whole smoked trout (1¼ pounds total)
1	container (8 ounces) whipped cream cheese
¼	cup lowfat mayonnaise dressing
3	tablespoons fresh lemon juice
⅛	teaspoon ground black pepper
1	tablespoon finely chopped fresh chives or green onion
	cucumber slices and assorted crackers

1. Cut head and tail from each trout; discard along with skin and bones. In food processor with knife blade attached, puree trout, cream cheese, mayonnaise dressing, lemon juice, and pepper until smooth.

2. Spoon trout mixture into medium bowl; stir in chives. Cover and refrigerate up to overnight if not serving right away. Before serving, let stand 15 minutes at room temperature to soften. Serve with cucumber slices and crackers. Makes about 3 cups.

Each tablespoon: About 32 calories, 2g protein, 1g carbohydrate, 2g total fat (1g saturated), 7mg cholesterol, 101mg sodium.

Salmon Pâté
Prepare as directed but substitute **1 can (15½ ounces) salmon,** drained and large pieces of cartilage removed, for smoked trout.

Chicken Liver Pâté

This exquisite silky-smooth pâté is seasoned the traditional way—with thyme and brandy. For the best flavor, refrigerate at least three hours before serving.

Prep: 25 minutes plus chilling	Cook: 20 minutes

2	tablespoons butter or margarine
1	small onion, finely chopped
1	garlic clove, finely chopped
1	pound chicken livers, trimmed
2	tablespoons brandy
½	cup heavy or whipping cream
½	teaspoon salt
¼	teaspoon dried thyme
¼	teaspoon ground black pepper
	assorted crackers, toast, or thinly sliced apples

1. In 10-inch skillet, melt butter over medium-high heat. Add onion and cook, stirring frequently, until tender and golden, about 10 minutes. Stir in garlic and livers and cook until livers are lightly browned but still pink inside, about 5 minutes. Stir in brandy; cook 5 minutes.

2. In blender or in food processor with knife blade attached, puree chicken-liver mixture, cream, salt, thyme, and pepper until smooth, stopping blender occasionally and scraping down side with rubber spatula.

3. Spoon mixture into small bowl; cover and refrigerate at least 3 hours or up to overnight. Let stand 30 minutes at room temperature before serving. Serve with crackers, toast, or apples. Makes about 1½ cups.

Each tablespoon: About 54 calories, 4g protein, 1g carbohydrate, 4g total fat (2g saturated), 92mg cholesterol, 75mg sodium.

Caraway-Cheese Crisps

Store these treats in an airtight container for up to three days.

Prep: 20 minutes   Bake: 10 minutes per batch

12	ounces extrasharp Cheddar cheese, shredded (3 cups)
1½	cups all-purpose flour
½	cup butter or margarine (1 stick), softened
½	teaspoon caraway seeds
¼	teaspoon salt

Preheat oven to 425°F. In large bowl, with hands, knead Cheddar, flour, butter, caraway seeds, and salt until blended. Divide dough into 3 portions. Shape 1 portion dough into ½-inch balls. Place balls 2 inches apart on ungreased cookie sheet. With fingers, flatten balls to ¼-inch thickness. Bake until lightly browned, 10 to 12 minutes. With spatula, transfer cheese crisps to wire racks to cool. Repeat with remaining dough. Makes about 54 crisps.

Each crisp: About 53 calories, 2g protein, 3g carbohydrate, 4g total fat (2g saturated), 11mg cholesterol, 67mg sodium.

Swiss Cheese Crisps

Prepare as directed but substitute **Swiss cheese** for Cheddar cheese and add ⅛ **teaspoon ground red pepper (cayenne)** to cheese mixture.

Parmesan-Pepper Sticks

These cheesy, peppery sticks get their superb flakiness from store-bought phyllo dough.

Prep: 30 minutes   Bake: 5 minutes

12	sheets (16" by 12" each) fresh or frozen (thawed) phyllo
4	tablespoons butter or margarine, melted
½	cup freshly grated Parmesan cheese
1½	teaspoons coarsely ground black pepper

1. Cover phyllo to prevent it from drying out. Place 1 sheet of phyllo on waxed paper. Brush with some melted butter. Sprinkle 2 teaspoons Parmesan and ⅛ teaspoon pepper over phyllo. Fold phyllo sheet crosswise in half. Tightly roll up phyllo, jelly-roll fashion, toward folded side. Cut roll crosswise

to make four 3-inch-long sticks. Place sticks, seam side down, on ungreased large cookie sheet; brush with melted butter.

2. Repeat with remaining phyllo sheets. If not serving right away, cover sticks with foil and refrigerate up to 4 hours.

3. To serve, preheat oven to 425°F. Bake phyllo sticks until golden brown, 5 to 8 minute. Serve hot or at room temperature. Makes 48 sticks.

Each stick: About 28 calories, 1g protein, 3g carbohydrate, 2g total fat (1g saturated), 3mg cholesterol, 52mg sodium.

Quick Quesadillas

Serve as an accompaniment to Spicy Black Bean Soup (page 64) or as the first course for a Southwest-style meal.

Prep: 10 minutes   Bake: 5 minutes

8	(7- to 8-inch) flour tortillas
1	jar (7 ounces) roasted red peppers, drained and thinly sliced
2	small green onions, thinly sliced
1	ounce Pepper Jack cheese, shredded (¼ cup)
¾	cup loosely packed fresh cilantro leaves

1. Preheat oven to 400°F. Place 4 tortillas on large cookie sheet. Sprinkle one-fourth of roasted peppers, green onions, cheese, and cilantro on each tortilla; top with remaining tortillas to make 4 quesadillas.

2. Bake quesadillas until heated through, about 5 minutes. Cut each quesadilla into 8 wedges. Serve warm. Makes 32 appetizers.

Each appetizer: About 34 calories, 1g protein, 5g carbohydrate, 1g total fat (0g saturated), 1mg cholesterol, 56mg sodium.

Tomato and Ricotta Salata Bruschetta

(pictured on page 34)

Bruschetta is toasted Italian bread that is rubbed with garlic and drizzled with olive oil. It's often topped with savory ingredients to make a simple appetizer. Here, we use ripe tomatoes and ricotta salata, a lightly salted pressed sheep's milk cheese. Ricotta salata can be found at Italian markets and specialty food stores.

Prep: 25 minutes

1	loaf (8 ounces) Italian bread, cut on diagonal into ½-inch-thick slices
8	garlic cloves, each cut in half
1	pound ripe plum tomatoes (6 medium), seeded and cut into ½-inch pieces
1	tablespoon finely chopped red onion
1	tablespoon chopped fresh basil
4	ounces ricotta salata, feta, or goat cheese, cut into ½-inch pieces
2	tablespoons extravirgin olive oil
2	teaspoons balsamic vinegar
¼	teaspoon salt
¼	teaspoon coarsely ground black pepper

1. Preheat oven to 400°F. Place bread slices on cookie sheet and bake until lightly toasted, about 5 minutes. Rub one side of each toast slice with cut side of garlic.

2. Meanwhile, in bowl, gently toss tomatoes, onion, basil, cheese, oil, vinegar, salt, and pepper until combined.

3. To serve, spoon tomato mixture on garlic-rubbed side of toast slices. Makes 16 bruschetta.

Each bruschetta: About 79 calories, 2g protein, 9g carbohydrate, 4g total fat (1g saturated), 6mg cholesterol, 236mg sodium.

Tuscan White-Bean Bruschetta

Prepare toast as directed but prepare topping as follows: In bowl, with fork, lightly mash **1 can (15½ to 19 ounces) white kidney beans (cannellini),** rinsed and drained, with **1 tablespoon fresh lemon juice.** Stir in **1 tablespoon olive oil, 2 teaspoons chopped fresh parsley, 1 teaspoon minced fresh sage, ¼ teaspoon salt,** and **⅛ teaspoon coarsely ground black pepper.** Just before serving, spoon mixture over garlic-rubbed side of toast slices. Sprinkle with **1 teaspoon chopped fresh parsley.** Makes 16 bruschetta.

♡ Each bruschetta: About 33 calories, 2g protein, 4g carbohydrate, 1g total fat (0g saturated), 0mg cholesterol, 77mg sodium.

Easy Spicy Cheese Straws

Use frozen puff pastry to make these zippy cheese straws in a flash.

Prep: 30 minutes   Bake: 20 minutes per batch

1	tablespoon paprika
½	teaspoon dried thyme
¼ to ½	teaspoon ground red pepper (cayenne)
¼	teaspoon salt
1	package (17 ¼ ounces) frozen puff-pastry sheets, thawed
1	large egg white, lightly beaten
8	ounces sharp Cheddar cheese, shredded (2 cups)

1. Grease two large cookie sheets. In small bowl, combine paprika, thyme, ground red pepper, and salt.

2. Unfold 1 puff-pastry sheet. On lightly floured surface, with floured rolling pin, roll pastry into 14-inch square. Lightly brush with egg white. Sprinkle half of paprika mixture on pastry. Sprinkle half of Cheddar on half of pastry. Fold pastry over to cover cheese, forming rectangle. With rolling pin, lightly roll over pastry to seal layers together. With pizza wheel or knife, cut pastry crosswise into ½-inch-wide strips.

3. Preheat oven to 375°F. Place strips ½ inch apart on prepared cookie sheets, twisting each strip twice to form spiral and pressing ends against cookie sheet to prevent strips from uncurling. Bake cheese straws until golden, 20 to 22 minutes. With spatula, carefully transfer to wire racks to cool.

4. Repeat with remaining puff-pastry sheet, egg white, paprika mixture, and cheese. Store in airtight container up to 1 week. Makes about 48 cheese straws.

Each straw: About 78 calories, 2g protein, 5g carbohydrate, 5g total fat (2g saturated), 5mg cholesterol, 68mg sodium.

Chorizo and Black Bean Nachos

These are serious nachos for chile lovers. Be sure to use fully cooked chorizo links, not soft bulk-style chorizo.

Prep: 20 minutes   Bake: 5 minutes per batch

36	unbroken large tortilla chips
3	large ripe plum tomatoes, cut into ¼-inch pieces
⅓	cup chopped fresh cilantro
¼	teaspoon salt
1	tablespoon vegetable oil
1	fully cooked chorizo sausage (3 ounces), finely chopped, or ¾ cup finely chopped pepperoni (3 ounces)
1	medium onion, finely chopped
1	garlic clove, finely chopped
½	teaspoon ground cumin
1	can (15 to 19 ounces) black beans, rinsed and drained
4	ounces Monterey Jack cheese, shredded (1 cup)
2	pickled jalapeño chiles, very thinly sliced

1. Preheat oven to 400°F. Arrange as many tortilla chips as will fit in single layer on two ungreased large cookie sheets. In small bowl, combine tomatoes, cilantro, and salt.

2. In 10-inch skillet, heat oil over medium heat. Add chorizo, onion, garlic, and cumin; cook, stirring, until onion is tender, about 5 minutes. Stir in beans and heat through.

3. Place 1 tablespoon bean mixture on each tortilla chip. Sprinkle cheese over beans and top each nacho with 1 slice jalapeño. Bake until cheese begins to melt, about 5 minutes.

4. Spoon about 1 teaspoon tomato mixture on each nacho. Transfer nachos to platter. Repeat with remaining chips, bean mixture, cheese, and tomato mixture. Serve warm. Makes 36 nachos.

Each nacho: About 51 calories, 2g protein, 4g carbohydrate, 3g total fat (1g saturated), 5mg cholesterol, 112mg sodium.

Prosciutto-Wrapped Asparagus

Delicate, succulent asparagus is the perfect foil for salty prosciutto. You can assemble these early in the day and bake them at the very last minute.

Prep: 25 minutes   Bake: 10 minutes

24	thick asparagus spears, trimmed and peeled
12	thin slices prosciutto (5 ounces)
½	cup freshly grated Parmesan cheese
¼	teaspoon coarsely ground black pepper

1. In 5-quart Dutch oven, heat *3 quarts water* to boiling over high heat. Add asparagus; cook 3 minutes to blanch. Drain; rinse with cold running water. Pat dry with paper towels.

2. Preheat oven to 450°F. Working in batches, spread out prosciutto on cutting board; cut each slice lengthwise in half and separate slightly. Evenly sprinkle 1 teaspoon Parmesan on each prosciutto strip. Place 1 asparagus spear at end of 1 strip; wrap prosciutto in spiral along length of asparagus (don't cover asparagus tip). Transfer to jelly-roll pan. Repeat with remaining prosciutto, Parmesan, and asparagus; sprinkle with pepper. If not serving right away, cover and refrigerate up to 6 hours.

3. Bake 10 minutes. Transfer to paper towels to drain. Arrange on platter and serve warm. Makes 24 appetizers.

Each appetizer: About 28 calories, 3g protein, 1g carbohydrate, 2g total fat (1g saturated), 6mg cholesterol, 148mg sodium.

EXPERT TIP

Classic appetizers are great, but every so often I like to add a twist.

- Serve some nice smoky ham with roasted spiced pears instead of prosciutto with melon.
- Stuff wonton wrappers with spinach, nuts, and candied ginger.
- Instead of serving raw veggies in crudités, roast them first; use cauliflower, broccoli, carrots, or fennel. Toss them with curry powder, soy sauce, or spices just before roasting.
- Make a terrine with a mix of grated cheese and chopped dried fruit.

JODY ADAMS

CHEF/OWNER, RIALTO AND RED CLAY, MASSACHUSETTS

Empanaditas

These two-bite savory pastries are stuffed with picadillo, a spiced ground-beef mixture that is sweetened with raisins.

Prep: 1 hour 15 minutes	Bake: 12 minutes per batch

Flaky Turnover Pastry (right)

2	teaspoons vegetable oil
1	small onion, finely chopped
1	large garlic clove, finely chopped
¼	teaspoon ground cinnamon
¼	teaspoon ground red pepper (cayenne)
4	ounces ground beef chuck
¼	teaspoon salt
1	cup canned tomatoes with their juice
3	tablespoons chopped golden raisins
3	tablespoons chopped pimiento-stuffed olives (salad olives)
1	large egg beaten with 2 tablespoons water

1. Prepare Flaky Turnover Pastry. Wrap in waxed paper and refrigerate while preparing filling or up to overnight.

2. In 10-inch skillet, heat oil over medium heat. Add onion and cook, stirring frequently, until tender, about 5 minutes. Stir in garlic, cinnamon, and ground red pepper; cook 30 seconds. Increase heat to medium-high; add ground beef and salt and cook, stirring frequently, until beef begins to brown, about 5 minutes. Stir in tomatoes with their juice, raisins, and olives, breaking up tomatoes with side of spoon; cook over high heat until liquid has almost evaporated, 7 to 10 minutes. Remove skillet from heat.

3. Preheat oven to 425°F. Divide dough into 4 equal pieces. On floured surface, with floured rolling pin, roll 1 piece of dough ¹⁄₁₆ inch thick. Keep remaining dough covered. With 3-inch round biscuit cutter, cut out as many rounds as possible, reserving trimmings. On one half of each dough round, place 1 level teaspoon filling. Brush edges of rounds with some egg-glaze mixture. Fold dough over to enclose filling. With fork, press edges together to seal dough; prick top. Brush turnovers lightly with some egg-glaze mixture. With spatula, lift turnovers and arrange 1 inch apart on ungreased large cookie sheet.

4. Bake turnovers until just golden, 12 to 15 minutes. Repeat with remaining dough, filling, and egg-glaze mixture. Press together dough trimmings and reroll. Serve hot or warm. Makes about 54 turnovers.

Flaky Turnover Pastry

In large bowl, combine **3 cups all-purpose flour, 1½ teaspoons baking powder,** and **¾ teaspoon salt.** With pastry blender or two knives used scissor-fashion, cut in **1 cup vegetable shortening** until mixture resembles coarse crumbs. Sprinkle with about **6 tablespoons cold water,** 1 tablespoon at a time, mixing with fork after each addition, until dough is just moist enough to hold together. Shape into ball.

Each turnover: About 72 calories, 1g protein, 6g carbohydrate, 5g total fat (1g saturated), 6mg cholesterol, 78mg sodium.

Samosas

These curried vegetable turnovers are usually deep-fried, but we like the flavorful treats best when baked.

Prep: 1 hour 20 minutes	Bake: 12 minutes per batch

Flaky Turnover Pastry (above)

1	tablespoon vegetable oil
1	medium onion, finely chopped
2	medium all-purpose potatoes, chopped (1½ cups)
1	tablespoon minced, peeled fresh ginger
1	large garlic clove, finely chopped
1	teaspoon curry powder
½	teaspoon ground cumin
¼	teaspoon ground red pepper (cayenne)
1	cup water
1	teaspoon salt
½	cup frozen baby peas
¼	cup chopped fresh cilantro
1	large egg beaten with 2 tablespoons water

1. Prepare Flaky Turnover Pastry. Wrap in waxed paper and refrigerate while preparing filling or up to overnight.

2. In 10-inch skillet, heat oil over medium heat. Add onion and cook, stirring frequently, until tender, about 5 minutes. Add potatoes and cook, stirring frequently, until onion begins to brown, about 10 minutes.

3. Stir in ginger, garlic, curry powder, cumin, and ground red pepper and cook 30 seconds. Add water and salt; heat to boiling. Reduce heat; cover and simmer until potatoes are tender, 10 to 15 minutes. Stir in frozen peas and cook, uncovered, until liquid has evaporated. Remove from heat and add cilantro, mashing potatoes coarsely with back of spoon.

4. Preheat oven to 425°F. Divide dough into 4 equal pieces. On floured surface, with floured rolling pin, roll 1 piece of dough $\frac{1}{16}$ inch thick. Keep remaining dough covered. With 3-inch round biscuit cutter, cut out as many rounds as possible, reserving trimmings. On one half of each dough round, place 1 level teaspoon filling. Brush edges of rounds with some egg-glaze mixture. Fold dough over to enclose filling. With fork, press edges together to seal dough; prick top. Brush turnovers lightly with some egg-glaze mixture. With spatula, lift turnovers and arrange 1 inch apart on ungreased large cookie sheet.

5. Bake turnovers until just golden, 12 to 15 minutes. Repeat with remaining dough, filling, and egg-glaze mixture. Serve hot or warm. Makes about 54 turnovers.

Each turnover: About 62 calories, 1g protein, 6g carbohydrate, 4g total fat (1g saturated), 4mg cholesterol, 84mg sodium.

Bite-Size Bacon Quiches

Here's a great do-ahead tip: Prepare the quiche shells, cook the bacon, and refrigerate until ready to bake.

Prep: 1 hour plus chilling	Bake: 20 minutes
Pastry Dough for 2-Crust Pie (page 686)	
1	tablespoon butter or margarine, melted
1	package (8 ounces) bacon, finely chopped
1	cup half-and-half or light cream
2	large eggs
¼	teaspoon salt
3	ounces Swiss cheese, shredded (¾ cup)

1. Prepare Pastry Dough for 2-Crust Pie. Grease and flour thirty-six 1¾-inch mini muffin-pan cups.

2. On lightly floured surface, with floured rolling pin, roll dough ⅛ inch thick. Using 3-inch round fluted cookie cutter, cut dough into 36 circles, rerolling trimmings.

3. Line muffin-pan cups with dough circles; brush lightly with melted butter. Cover and refrigerate.

4. Preheat oven to 400°F. In 12-inch skillet, cook bacon over medium heat until browned. Transfer bacon to paper towels to drain.

5. In small bowl, beat half-and-half, eggs, and salt. Divide bacon and cheese evenly among pastry cups. Spoon about 1 tablespoon egg mixture into each cup. Bake until knife in-

serted in center of quiche comes out clean, 20 to 25 minutes. Remove quiches from pan and serve hot. Makes 36 quiches.

Each quiche: About 111 calories, 3g protein, 7g carbohydrate, 8g total fat (4g saturated), 26mg cholesterol, 118mg sodium.

Greek Cheese Pastries

A peppery feta-ricotta cheese filling and store-bought phyllo are transformed into easy-to-make treats.

Prep: 1 hour 15 minutes	Bake: 15 minutes
1	package (8 ounces) feta cheese, well drained and crumbled
1	cup part-skim ricotta cheese
¼	cup chopped fresh parsley
2	large eggs
½	teaspoon coarsely ground black pepper
15	sheets (16" by 12" each) fresh or frozen (thawed) phyllo
½	cup butter or margarine (1 stick), melted

1. Grease two jelly-roll pans. In medium bowl, with fork, finely crumble feta; stir in ricotta, parsley, eggs, and pepper.

2. On surface, stack 5 phyllo sheets and cut lengthwise into 5 equal strips. Place cut phyllo on waxed paper; cover completely to prevent it from drying out. Place 1 phyllo strip on surface; brush with some melted butter. Place 1 rounded teaspoon filling at end of strip. Fold one corner of strip diagonally over filling. Continue folding over at right angles to end of strip. Repeat filling and shaping with remaining phyllo and filling, placing triangles about 1 inch apart in prepared pans. Brush with melted butter.

3. If not serving right away, cover and refrigerate up to several hours. Or to freeze, prepare as directed but do not bake. Freeze in jelly-roll pans, then store in freezer in airtight containers between layers of waxed paper up to 1 month.

4. Preheat oven to 400°F. Bake pastries until golden, 15 to 20 minutes. Makes 75 appetizers.

Each appetizer: About 37 calories, 1g protein, 2g carbohydrate, 3g total fat (1g saturated), 13mg cholesterol, 70mg sodium.

Mini Spanakopita

In 10-inch skillet, melt **2 tablespoons butter or margarine.** Add **1 jumbo onion (1 pound),** finely chopped, and cook until golden, about 15 minutes. Add to cheese filling in Step 1; stir in **3 packages (10 ounces each) frozen chopped spinach,** thawed and squeezed dry, and **½ cup chopped fresh dill.** Proceed as directed.

Curried Cheddar Puffs

If you like, bake up to one month ahead and freeze.

Prep: 20 minutes	Bake: 25 minutes
2	teaspoons curry powder
½	teaspoon ground coriander
½	teaspoon ground cumin
¼	teaspoon ground red pepper (cayenne)
6	tablespoons butter or margarine, cut into pieces
½	teaspoon salt
1	cup water
1	cup all-purpose flour
4	large eggs
4	ounces Cheddar cheese, shredded (1 cup)

1. Preheat oven to 400°F. Grease two large cookie sheets.
2. In 3-quart saucepan, combine curry powder, coriander, cumin, and ground red pepper; heat over medium heat, stirring constantly, until very fragrant, about 1 minute. Stir in butter, salt, and water; heat to boiling over high heat. Remove saucepan from heat and stir in flour all at once. Return to medium-low heat, stirring constantly with wooden spoon, until mixture forms a ball and leaves side of pan. Remove saucepan from heat.
3. Stir in eggs, one at a time, beating well after each addition, until batter is smooth and satiny; stir in cheese. Spoon batter into large pastry bag fitted with ½-inch plain tip. Pipe batter, about 1 inch apart, on cookie sheets, forming 1-inch-wide by ¾-inch-high mounds. Alternatively, drop teaspoons of dough on cookie sheet. With fingertip dipped in cool water, gently smooth peaks.
4. Bake puffs until deep golden, 25 to 30 minutes, rotating cookie sheets between oven racks halfway through baking. Transfer to wire racks to cool. Repeat with remaining batter.

5. Serve puffs at room temperature or to serve hot, reheat in 400°F oven 5 minutes. Makes about 72 puffs.

Each puff: About 20 calories, 1g protein, 1g carbohydrate, 1g total fat (1g saturated), 12mg cholesterol, 29mg sodium.

Caviar in Potato Nests

A feast for the eyes as well as the palate, these may be the most luxurious appetizers you will ever serve. The potato nests can be baked up to four hours ahead. Let stand at room temperature on a paper towel lined cookie sheet, then reheat in a 375°F oven.

Prep: 40 minutes plus chilling and cooling	Bake: 25 minutes
2	large baking potatoes (1½ pounds), not peeled, scrubbed
½	teaspoon salt
⅛	teaspoon ground black pepper
½	cup sour cream, at room temperature
1	ounce sevruga, osetra, salmon, or lumpfish caviar

1. In 3-quart saucepan, combine potatoes and enough *cold water* to cover; heat to boiling over high heat. Reduce heat; cover and simmer until tender, about 20 minutes. Drain potatoes; refrigerate until chilled, about 1 hour.
2. Preheat oven to 425°F. Grease thirty-two 1¾-inch mini muffin-pan cups. Peel and coarsely grate potatoes. Transfer to bowl and toss gently with salt and pepper.
3. Place about 1 heaping tablespoon potato mixture in each muffin-pan cup and press against bottom and up side as high as possible. Bake until edges of potato nests are golden brown, 25 to 30 minutes. Cool in pans on wire racks 10 minutes.
4. To serve, transfer warm potato nests to warm platter. Spoon 1 teaspoon sour cream into each nest and top with about ¼ teaspoon caviar. Makes 32 appetizers.

Each appetizer: About 26 calories, 1g protein, 3g carbohydrate, 1g total fat (1g saturated), 7mg cholesterol, 52mg sodium.

Mini Crab Cakes

Crab cakes are a universal favorite. These luscious morsels can be prepared ahead and refrigerated. Reheat just before serving.

Prep: 25 minutes   Bake: 16 to 18 minutes

	Lemon Sauce (right)
¼	cup mayonnaise
1	tablespoon sour cream
2	teaspoons grainy Dijon mustard
½	teaspoon freshly grated lemon peel
¼	teaspoon salt
⅛	teaspoon ground red pepper (cayenne)
1	pound lump crabmeat, picked over
1	cup fresh bread crumbs (about 2 slices bread)

1. Preheat oven to 400°F. Lightly grease large cookie sheet. Prepare Lemon Sauce; cover and refrigerate.

2. In medium bowl, stir mayonnaise, sour cream, mustard, lemon peel, salt, and ground red pepper until blended; stir in crabmeat and bread crumbs just until mixed.

3. Drop level tablespoons crab mixture on prepared cookie sheet. Bake until golden brown, 16 to 18 minutes. Top each crab cake with about ½ teaspoon lemon sauce. Serve hot. Makes 40 mini crab cakes.

Mini Crab Cakes

Lemon Sauce

In small bowl, stir together **½ cup sour cream, 1 teaspoon freshly grated lemon peel, pinch salt,** and **pinch ground red pepper (cayenne)** until blended. Makes about ½ cup.

Each crab cake with sauce: About 30 calories, 2g protein, 1g carbohydrate, 2g total fat (0g saturated), 13mg cholesterol, 70mg sodium.

Buffalo-Style Chicken Wings

Here's a broiled version of one of America's favorite appetizers. Serve with plenty of napkins!

Prep: 15 minutes   Broil: 20 minutes

4	ounces blue cheese, crumbled (1 cup)
½	cup sour cream
¼	cup mayonnaise
¼	cup milk
¼	cup chopped fresh parsley
1	tablespoon fresh lemon juice
½	teaspoon salt
3	pounds chicken wings (18 wings), tips discarded, if desired
3	tablespoons butter or margarine
¼	cup hot pepper sauce
1	medium bunch celery, cut into sticks

1. Preheat broiler. In medium bowl, combine blue cheese, sour cream, mayonnaise, milk, parsley, lemon juice, and ¼ teaspoon salt. Cover and refrigerate.

2. Arrange chicken wings on rack in broiling pan; sprinkle with remaining ¼ teaspoon salt. Broil 5 inches from heat source 10 minutes. Turn wings and broil until golden, 10 to 15 minutes longer.

3. Meanwhile, in small saucepan, melt butter with hot pepper sauce over low heat, stirring occasionally; keep hot.

4. In large bowl, toss wings with seasoned butter to coat all sides. Arrange chicken wings and celery on platter along with blue-cheese sauce and serve. Makes 18 appetizers.

Each appetizer (without wingtip): About 169 calories, 10g protein, 3g carbohydrate, 13g total fat (5g saturated), 39mg cholesterol, 349mg sodium.

Chicken and Beef Saté

These Indonesian appetizers have taken America by storm. We like them with a spicy peanut dipping sauce and a deliciously tangy cucumber salad.

Prep: 45 minutes plus marinating	*Grill: 4 minutes per batch*

1	pound chicken cutlets
1	boneless beef top sirloin steak, 1 inch thick (1¼ pounds), trimmed
2	large limes
¼	cup soy sauce
1	tablespoon grated, peeled fresh ginger
2	garlic cloves, crushed with garlic press
2	teaspoons sugar
24	(10-inch) bamboo skewers
	Spicy Peanut Sauce (opposite)
	Cucumber Salad (opposite)

1. Slice chicken cutlets lengthwise into ¾-inch-wide strips; place in medium bowl. Holding knife almost parallel to surface, cut steak crosswise into thin slices; place in separate medium bowl.

2. From limes, grate 2 teaspoons peel and squeeze 2 tablespoons juice. In small bowl, with wire whisk, mix lime peel and juice, soy sauce, ginger, garlic, and sugar. Pour half of soy-sauce mixture over chicken, tossing to coat. Pour remaining soy-sauce mixture over beef, tossing to coat. Cover and refrigerate chicken and beef 30 minutes to marinate.

3. Meanwhile prepare grill or preheat broiler. Soak bamboo skewers in water to cover 20 minutes. Prepare Spicy Peanut Sauce and Cucumber Salad.

4. Thread each chicken strip and beef strip lengthwise onto a bamboo skewer.

5. Grill chicken and beef strips in batches over medium heat or broil 4 inches from heat source, turning once, until just cooked through, 4 to 7 minutes. Serve with peanut sauce and cucumber salad. Makes 24 satés, 12 appetizer servings.

Each serving without sauce or salad: About 139 calories, 19g protein, 1g carbohydrate, 6g total fat (2g saturated), 54mg cholesterol, 304mg sodium.

Spicy Peanut Sauce

In medium bowl, with wire whisk, mix ¼ **cup creamy peanut butter**, ¼ **cup very hot water**, **4 teaspoons seasoned rice vinegar**, **1 tablespoon soy sauce**, **1 tablespoon light (mild) molasses**, and ⅛ **teaspoon crushed red pepper** until smooth. Makes about ⅔ cup.

Each tablespoon: About 46 calories, 2g protein, 3g carbohydrate, 3g total fat (1g saturated), 0mg cholesterol, 174mg sodium.

Cucumber Salad

In medium bowl, combine **1 pound kirby cucumbers (4 small)**, cut into ¼-inch pieces, **2 tablespoons chopped red onion**, ¼ **cup seasoned rice vinegar**, **1 tablespoon vegetable oil**, and ¼ **teaspoon crushed red pepper.** Makes about 2½ cups.

♥ *Each tablespoon: About 7 calories, 0g protein, 1g carbohydrate, 0g total fat (0g saturated), 0mg cholesterol, 30mg sodium.*

Chinese Dumplings

Steamed dumplings are fun to make at home. Have them for brunch: It's the way the Chinese enjoy them.

Prep: 45 minutes	*Cook: 10 minutes*

2	cups packed sliced Napa cabbage (Chinese cabbage)
8	ounces ground pork
1	green onion, finely chopped
1½	teaspoons minced, peeled fresh ginger
2	tablespoons soy sauce
1	tablespoon dry sherry
2	teaspoons cornstarch
36	wonton wrappers (9 ounces)
1	large egg white, beaten
	Soy Dipping Sauce (opposite)

1. Prepare filling: In 2-quart saucepan, heat *1 inch water* to boiling over high heat. Add cabbage and heat to boiling. Cook 1 minute; drain. Immediately rinse with cold running water to stop cooking. With hands, squeeze out as much water from cabbage as possible. Finely chop cabbage. Squeeze out any remaining water from cabbage; place in medium bowl. Stir in pork, green onion, ginger, soy sauce, sherry, and cornstarch until well blended.

2. Arrange half of wonton wrappers on waxed paper. With pastry brush, brush each wrapper lightly with egg white. Spoon 1 rounded teaspoon filling in center of each wrapper. Bring two opposite corners of each wonton wrapper together over filling; pinch and pleat edges together to seal in filling. Repeat with remaining wrappers, egg white, and filling.

3. In deep nonstick 12-inch skillet, heat *½ inch water* to boiling over high heat. Place all dumplings, pleated edges up, in one layer in skillet. With spatula, move dumplings gently to prevent them from sticking to bottom of skillet. Heat to boiling. Reduce heat; cover and simmer until dumplings are cooked through, about 5 minutes.

4. Meanwhile, prepare Soy Dipping Sauce.

Chinese Dumplings

5. With slotted spoon, transfer dumplings to platter. Serve with dipping sauce. Makes 36 dumplings.

♥ Each dumpling without sauce: About 40 calories, 2g protein, 5g carbohydrate, 1g total fat (1g saturated), 5mg cholesterol, 103g sodium.

Soy Dipping Sauce

In small serving bowl, stir **¼ cup soy sauce, ¼ cup seasoned rice vinegar or white wine vinegar,** and **2 tablespoons peeled fresh ginger,** cut into very thin slivers, until blended. Makes about ½ cup.

♥ Each teaspoon: About 4 calories, 0g protein, 1g carbohydrate, 0g total fat (0g saturated), 0mg cholesterol, 221mg sodium.

Prosciutto with Melon

The marriage of sweet ripe melon and slightly salty prosciutto is a classic combination. Imported prosciutto di Parma, available at Italian grocers and specialty food markets, is much milder than the domestic varieties of this ham. It's worth seeking out.

Prep: 10 minutes

1	small honeydew melon or 1 medium cantaloupe, chilled
4	ounces prosciutto, thinly sliced
	freshly ground black pepper

1. Cut melon in half through stem end and remove seeds. Cut each half into 4 wedges; cut off rind.

2. Arrange 2 melon wedges on each of four plates; arrange prosciutto to side of melon. Sprinkle pepper on each serving. Makes 4 first-course servings.

♥ Each serving: About 150 calories, 9g protein, 22g carbohydrate, 4g total fat (1g saturated), 23mg cholesterol, 548mg sodium.

Prosciutto with Other Fruit

Prepare as directed but substitute **8 large green or black figs,** each cut in half, or **2 medium papayas,** peeled, seeded, and sliced, for melon.

Gravlax

This classic Scandinavian salt-and-dill-cured salmon is a great make-ahead dish for brunch or supper. Serve with thinly sliced cucumbers and pumpernickel bread, so guests can make their own open-faced sandwiches.

Prep: 30 minutes plus 24 to 36 hours to marinate
2 pieces salmon fillet (1 pound each) with skin
3 tablespoons salt
2 tablespoons sugar
1 tablespoon cracked black pepper
2 tablespoons brandy or aquavit
1 bunch fresh dill
Mustard Sauce (right)
lemon wedges

1. With tweezers, remove any small bones from salmon fillets. In small bowl, combine salt, sugar, and pepper. Gently rub salt mixture on all sides of salmon; sprinkle with brandy.

2. Divide dill into 3 portions. Line bottom of medium baking dish with one-third of dill. Place 1 salmon fillet, skin side down, on dill; top with another one-third of dill. Place remaining fillet, skin side up, on dill; top with remaining dill.

3. Cover salmon with plastic wrap and set heavy plate (larger than salmon) on top; place two or three heavy cans on plate to weight down salmon. Refrigerate at least 24 hours but preferably 36 hours, turning salmon and dill over halfway through marinating.

4. Prepare Mustard Sauce.

5. Scrape dill and pepper from salmon and discard. Holding knife almost parallel to surface, cut salmon into very thin slices. Transfer to platter or individual plates. Place lemon wedges around salmon and serve with mustard sauce. Makes about 16 first-course servings.

Each serving without sauce: About 101 calories, 10g protein, 1g carbohydrate, 6g total fat (1g saturated), 30mg cholesterol, 466mg sodium.

Mustard Sauce

In small bowl, with wire whisk, blend **½ cup Dijon mustard, ½ cup vegetable oil, ¼ cup white wine vinegar, ¼ cup sugar,** and **⅛ teaspoon salt** until smooth. Stir in **¼ cup chopped fresh dill.** Makes 1½ cups.

Each tablespoon: About 54 calories, 0g protein, 2g carbohydrate, 5g total fat (1g saturated), 0mg cholesterol, 132mg sodium.

Shrimp Cocktail

Everyone loves to dip shrimp into sauce. So, here are two sauces that are very different but equally delicious.

Prep: 25 minutes plus chilling   Cook: 17 minutes
1 lemon, thinly sliced
4 bay leaves
20 whole black peppercorns
10 whole allspice berries
2 teaspoons salt
24 extra-large shrimp (1 pound), shelled and deveined (page 296)
Southwestern-Style Cocktail Sauce (opposite)
Mustard Dipping Sauce (opposite)
12 small romaine lettuce leaves
24 (7-inch) bamboo skewers

1. In 5-quart Dutch oven, combine *2 quarts water,* lemon, bay leaves, peppercorns, allspice berries, and salt; heat to boiling. Cover and boil 15 minutes.

2. Add shrimp and cook just until opaque throughout, 1 to 2 minutes. Drain and rinse with cold running water to stop cooking. Cover and refrigerate shrimp up to 24 hours.

3. Prepare Southwestern-Style Cocktail Sauce and/or Mustard Dipping Sauce.

4. Just before serving, place bowls of sauces in center of platter; arrange romaine leaves around bowls, leaf tips facing out. Thread each shrimp on a bamboo skewer and arrange skewers on romaine. Makes 8 first-course servings.

♥ Each serving without sauce: About 51 calories, 10g protein, 1g carbohydrate, 1g total fat (0g saturated), 70mg cholesterol, 141mg sodium.

Southwestern-Style Cocktail Sauce

In bowl, stir **1 cup bottled cocktail sauce, 2 tablespoons chopped fresh cilantro, 2 teaspoons minced jalapeño chile,** and **2 teaspoons fresh lime juice** until well combined. Cover and refrigerate up to 24 hours. Makes about 1 cup.

♥ Each tablespoon: About 18 calories, 0g protein, 4g carbohydrate, 0g total fat (0g saturated), 0mg cholesterol, 191mg sodium.

Mustard Dipping Sauce

In small serving bowl, stir **1 cup reduced-fat sour cream, 3 tablespoons grainy Dijon mustard, 3 tablespoons chopped fresh parsley, ¼ teaspoon freshly grated lemon peel, ¼ teaspoon salt,** and **⅛ teaspoon coarsely ground black pepper** until well combined. Cover and refrigerate up to 24 hours. Makes about 1 cup.

Each tablespoon: About 28 calories, 1g protein, 1g carbohydrate, 2g total fat (1g saturated), 5mg cholesterol, 111mg sodium.

Oysters Rockefeller

A classic that is worth having again and again.

Prep: 30 minutes	Bake: 10 minutes
1	dozen oysters, shucked, bottom shells reserved
	kosher or rock salt (optional)
1	bunch spinach (10 to 12 ounces),
	tough stems trimmed, washed, and dried very well
1	tablespoon plus 2 teaspoons butter or margarine
2	tablespoons finely chopped onion
	pinch ground red pepper (cayenne)
¼	cup heavy or whipping cream
1	tablespoon Pernod or other anise-flavored liqueur
	pinch salt
2	tablespoons plain dried bread crumbs

1. Preheat oven to 425°F. Arrange oysters in shells in jelly-roll pan, lined with ½-inch layer of kosher salt to keep them flat, if desired; refrigerate.

2. In 2-quart saucepan, cook spinach over high heat until wilted. Drain. Rinse with cold running water; drain well. Finely chop spinach. Wipe saucepan dry with paper towels.

3. In same saucepan, melt 1 tablespoon butter over medium heat. Add onion; cook until tender, about 3 minutes.

Stir in ground red pepper. Stir in chopped spinach, cream, Pernod, and salt. Cook over high heat, stirring, until liquid has reduced and thickened. Remove from heat.

4. In small saucepan, melt remaining 2 teaspoons butter over low heat; remove from heat and stir in bread crumbs.

5. Spoon spinach mixture evenly on top of oysters. Sprinkle with buttered bread crumbs. Bake until edges of oysters curl, about 10 minutes. Makes 4 first-course servings.

Each serving: About 166 calories, 6g protein, 9g carbohydrate, 12g total fat (7g saturated), 57mg cholesterol, 228mg sodium.

Clams Casino

Bacon and bell peppers make a flavorful topping for clams.

Prep: 30 minutes	Bake: 10 minutes
3	slices bacon
1	tablespoon olive oil
½	red pepper, very finely chopped
½	green pepper, very finely chopped
¼	teaspoon coarsely ground black pepper
1	garlic clove, finely chopped
1	cup fresh bread crumbs (about 2 slices bread)
2	dozen littleneck clams,
	scrubbed and shucked (page 286), bottom shells reserved
	kosher or rock salt (optional)

1. Preheat oven to 425°F. Arrange clams in shells in jelly-roll pan, lined with ½-inch layer of kosher salt to keep them flat, if desired; refrigerate.

2. In 10-inch skillet, cook bacon over medium heat until browned; transfer to paper towels to drain. Discard fat from skillet. Add oil, red and green peppers, and black pepper to skillet; cook, stirring occasionally, until peppers are tender, about 5 minutes. Stir in garlic and cook 30 seconds; remove from heat.

3. Finely chop bacon; stir bacon and bread crumbs into pepper mixture in skillet. Spoon crumb mixture evenly over clams. Bake until topping is lightly golden, about 10 minutes. Makes 6 first-course servings.

Each serving: About 107 calories, 9g protein, 6g carbohydrate, 5g total fat (1g saturated), 23mg cholesterol, 122mg sodium.

3

SOUPS

Soups and stocks are the very essence of food in a pot. There are few foods more comforting and satisfying. Infinite in variety, a soup can be a light and elegant first course, a substantial rib-sticking meal-in-a-pot, or a refreshing cooler on a summer's day. The soups in this chapter range from suave and sophisticated Shrimp Bisque (page 75) to homey Chicken Soup with Rice (page 78) to earthy Mushroom and Wild Rice Soup (page 71). And of course, one of soup's best qualities is that it can be made ahead. In fact, soup should be made in quantity to allow for tasty leftovers.

The best homemade soups rely on good stock or broth for incomparable flavor. (For most cooking purposes here, the terms *stock* and *broth* are interchangeable.) Whether making stock or broth, there is one steadfast rule: Be patient. It takes time to draw all the flavor out of the ingredients. To make a high-quality stock, skim off all the foam that rises to the surface as the liquid is being brought to a boil. Once the liquid begins to boil, reduce the heat to very low and continue cooking at a bare simmer. Otherwise, the stock becomes cloudy and tastes greasy.

One of the glories of a well-made stock is the creation of a crystal-clear consommé. A consommé begins with a very full flavored stock, since some flavor will be lost during the clarifi-

Minestrone with Pesto

cation process. It is strained, cooled, and then refrigerated to solidify the fat that rises to the surface. (Use this handy trick to remove the fat from any homemade stock—it's easier than skimming fat off hot stock.) To make a proper consommé, every trace of fat must be removed—it should be absolutely fat-free. Then, in a clean soup pot, for every four cups of stock, the white and crumbled shell of one egg are stirred in. The stock is brought to a simmer over low heat and gently stirred occasionally. As the egg whites cook, they rise to the surface and solidify, bringing the shell and all the tiny bits and pieces of meat and vegetables still floating in the stock with them. From this point on, the liquid is never allowed to boil. Lastly, it is ladled through a cheesecloth-lined sieve. The finished consommé is then served either hot or cold. Hot consommé can be garnished with vegetables that have been cut into matchstick-thin sticks or into tiny dice and blanched. When consommé is refrigerated, it gels. So to be served cold, it is finely chopped, then spooned into soup cups and sprinkled with any favorite chopped fresh herb (chives are especially nice).

Homemade stock is a wonderful ingredient to have on hand (a freezer full of stock is a real culinary treasure trove), but don't underestimate the convenience and quality of canned broth—it supplies flavor in a flash. Supermarkets carry an assortment of canned broths, including chicken, beef, and vegetable, not to mention reduced-sodium, no-salt-added, and fat-free. In our test kitchens, we will sometimes dilute one 14½-ounce can of broth (about 1¾ cups) with ¾ cup water. This step is entirely optional and a matter of personal taste, but we think it softens the intense flavor of canned broth.

Low-sodium and no-salt-added broths are recommended in recipes when regular canned broth would oversalt the finished dish. This is especially true in dishes where the cooking liquid evaporates substantially. When using homemade broth or stock instead of canned, just add salt to taste.

Fat-free broth is healthful, but it's just as easy to remove the fat from canned broth yourself. Simply freeze the unopened can of broth for one or two hours to solidify the thin layer of surface fat. Open the can, lift off the fat, and discard. Bouillon cubes and powders have a less natural flavor than homemade or canned broths, so while cubes and powders are convenient, broth has the flavor edge. When making fish soup, bottled clam juice is a handy substitute for homemade fish stock. It is quite salty though, so use only a minimum of salt (if any) when seasoning.

SOUP SAVVY

Here are some of the most popular types of soups:

Bisque A classic French soup with a rich, creamy texture. It is usually made from shellfish and thickened with rice.

Broth A flavorful liquid made from simmered meat, fish, or poultry and/or vegetables. Broth can be a light soup on its own and is an excellent base for most other soups.

Chowder Hearty and chunky, this soup is chock-full of fish, shellfish, and/or vegetables. Clam chowder has been popular in New England since colonial times.

Consommé Broth that has been clarified into a crystal-clear liquid.

Gumbo One of the signature dishes of Cajun cooking, gumbo is a thick soup that can contain chicken, duck, seafood, or ham and vegetables such as tomatoes, onion, bell peppers, and celery. It is thickened with a roux (a browned butter and flour mixture), okra, and/or filé (ground sassafras leaves) and is served over white rice.

Stock Similar to broth but made from simmered bones, water, and/or vegetables.

STORING SOUPS AND STOCKS

- Soup and stock should be quickly cooled before storing in the refrigerator or freezer. To cool down a pot of soup or stock, place the pot in a sink filled with ice water and let stand, stirring until tepid. Or pour the soup into small containers and cool for thirty minutes, then refrigerate.
- Stocks and most soups freeze well in airtight containers for up to three months. Be sure to leave enough headspace to allow for expansion. Freezing may diminish some of a soup's flavor, so be sure to taste the soup and adjust the seasoning before serving.
- Soup enriched with cream, yogurt, or eggs cannot be frozen because it will curdle when reheated; the soup base can be frozen, however. Prepare the soup just up to the point of adding the cream, yogurt, or eggs. Freeze like any other soup, then thaw and reheat, adding the enrichment at the last minute—just long enough to heat through. Do not allow the soup to boil, or it may curdle.

GARNISHING SOUPS

As delicious as soup is, almost any bowl of soup will be enhanced by an added splash of color or a bit of extra flavor. Chopped fresh herbs are the simplest of all garnishes. Choose an herb that complements the soup's flavor and color. For example, Summertime Corn Chowder (page 65) is topped with basil, contrasting with its soft ivory hue and also contributing an aromatic touch. Spicy Black Bean Soup (page 64) is finished with a sprinkling of chopped cilantro, an ideal flavor match. For the best results, chop or snip fresh herbs just before using so they don't darken.

Pureed soups can accommodate other kinds of garnishes. The smooth texture of a pureed bean or tomato soup calls out for a sprinkling of freshly grated Parmesan cheese, crunchy homemade croutons, or crumbled crisp bacon. Pureed vegetable soups are often topped with a drizzle of heavy cream. For a dramatic touch, the tip of a sharp knife can be pulled through the cream to create a marbleized effect. If the flavor of a vegetable soup, such as asparagus, would benefit from a hint of acidity, top with a dollop of sour cream, which will slowly melt into the soup, giving it a subtle tangy note.

French Onion Soup

Onions, slowly cooked until deep brown and caramelized, give this welcome classic its distinctive flavor. Great for a party, this recipe is easily doubled; simply cook the onions in two skillets.

Prep: 10 minutes   Cook/Bake: 2 hours

4	tablespoons butter or margarine
6	medium onions, thinly sliced
¼	teaspoon salt
4	cups water
1	can (14½ ounces) beef broth
	or 1¾ cups Brown Beef Stock (page 83)
¼	teaspoon dried thyme
4	diagonal slices (½ inch thick) French bread
4	ounces Gruyère or Swiss cheese, shredded (1 cup)

1. In nonstick 12-inch skillet, melt butter over medium-low heat. Add onions and salt and cook, stirring occasionally, until onions are very tender and begin to caramelize, about 45 minutes. Reduce heat to low and cook, stirring frequently, until onions are deep golden brown, about 15 minutes longer.

2. Transfer onions to 5-quart Dutch oven. Add ½ cup water to same skillet and heat to boiling, stirring until browned bits are loosened from bottom of skillet. Add to onions in Dutch oven. Add remaining 3½ cups water, broth, and thyme to onions and heat to boiling over high heat. Reduce heat and simmer 30 minutes.

3. Preheat oven to 450°F. Arrange bread slices on cookie sheet and bake until lightly toasted, about 5 minutes. Place four ovenproof bowls in jelly-roll pan for easier handling. Spoon soup evenly into bowls and top with toasted bread, slightly pressing bread into soup. Sprinkle Gruyère evenly on top. Bake until cheese has melted and begins to brown, 12 to 15 minutes. Makes about 5 cups or 4 first-course servings.

Each serving: About 402 calories, 15g protein, 37g carbohydrate, 22g total fat (13g saturated), 64mg cholesterol, 887mg sodium.

Cream of Mushroom Soup

This mushroom-laden soup is very versatile. Use one variety or a mix of favorites. Alter the soup's flavor by varying the mushrooms. Some flavorful possibilities are cremini, shiitake, and portobello.

Prep: 20 minutes   Cook: 35 minutes

3	tablespoons butter or margarine
1	pound mushrooms, trimmed and thinly sliced
1	medium onion, thinly sliced
2	tablespoons all-purpose flour
2	cups water
1	can (14½ ounces) chicken broth
	or 1¾ cups Chicken Broth (page 84)
½	teaspoon fresh thyme or ¼ teaspoon dried thyme
½	teaspoon salt
⅛	teaspoon ground black pepper
½	cup heavy or whipping cream

1. In 5-quart Dutch oven, melt 2 tablespoons butter over medium-high heat. Add mushrooms and cook, stirring occasionally, until mushrooms are tender and begin to brown, about 15 minutes. Transfer to bowl.

2. In same Dutch oven, melt remaining 1 tablespoon butter over medium heat. Add onion and cook until tender and golden, about 10 minutes.

3. Stir in flour until blended; cook 1 minute. Gradually stir in water, broth, thyme, salt, pepper, and half of mushrooms; heat to boiling, stirring constantly.

4. Spoon half of mushroom mixture into blender; cover, with center part of cover removed to let steam escape, and puree until smooth. Pour puree into bowl. Repeat with remaining mixture.

5. Return puree to clean Dutch oven; stir in cream and remaining mushrooms with their juice. Heat through (do not boil). Makes about 6 cups or 6 first-course servings.

Each serving: About 167 calories, 3g protein, 9g carbohydrate, 14g total fat (8g saturated), 43mg cholesterol, 548mg sodium.

Butternut-Apple Soup

Elegant and autumnal, this silky-smooth golden soup is the perfect beginning for a holiday meal.

Prep: 15 minutes	Cook: 40 to 45 minutes

2	tablespoons vegetable oil
1	small onion, chopped
2	medium butternut squash (1¾ pounds each), peeled, seeded, and cut into ¾-inch pieces
¾	pound Golden Delicious apples (2 medium), peeled, cored, and coarsely chopped
1	can (14½ ounces) vegetable broth or 1¾ cups Vegetable Broth (page 83)
1½	cups water
1	teaspoon fresh thyme or ¼ teaspoon dried thyme
1	teaspoon salt
⅛	teaspoon coarsely ground black pepper
1	cup half-and-half or light cream

1. In 4-quart saucepan, heat oil over medium heat. Add onion and cook until tender and golden, about 10 minutes. Stir in squash, apples, broth, water, thyme, salt, and pepper; heat to boiling over high heat. Reduce heat; cover and simmer, stirring often, until squash is very tender, 20 to 25 minutes.

2. Spoon one-third of squash mixture into blender; cover, with center part of cover removed to let steam escape, and puree until smooth. Pour puree into bowl. Repeat with remaining mixture.

3. Return puree to saucepan; stir in half-and-half. Heat through over medium heat, stirring occasionally (do not boil). Makes about 9 cups or 8 first-course servings.

Each serving: About 175 calories, 3g protein, 28g carbohydrate, 7mg total fat (3mg saturated), 11mg cholesterol, 525mg sodium.

Butternut-Apple Soup

Spicy Curried Carrot Soup

Use a good-quality mild Madras-style curry powder for spice without heat. Briefly sautéing the curry powder releases all its complex flavors.

Prep: 25 minutes	Cook: 45 minutes

2	tablespoons olive oil
1	jumbo onion (1 pound), chopped
4	teaspoons curry powder
1	tablespoon grated, peeled fresh ginger
3	bags (16 ounces each) carrots, peeled and coarsely chopped
2	cans (14½ ounces each) chicken broth or 3½ cups Chicken Broth (page 84)
6	cups water
1½	teaspoons salt
1	cup half-and-half or light cream

1. In 5-quart Dutch oven, heat oil over medium heat. Add onion; cook until tender and golden, 10 to 15 minutes.

2. Add curry powder and ginger; cook, stirring constantly, 1 minute. Add carrots, broth, 2 cups water, and salt; heat to boiling. Reduce heat; cover and simmer until carrots are very tender, about 20 minutes. Cool slightly.

3. Spoon one-fourth of carrot mixture into blender; cover, with center part of cover removed to let steam escape, and puree until smooth. Pour puree into bowl. Repeat with remaining mixture.

4. Return puree to Dutch oven; stir in half-and-half and remaining 4 cups water. Heat through over medium heat, stirring frequently (do not boil). Makes about 13 cups or 12 first-course servings.

Each serving: About 115 calories, 3g protein, 15g carbohydrate, 5g total fat (2g saturated), 7mg cholesterol, 621mg sodium.

Sorrel Soup

Delicate, lemony-tart sorrel is always a sign of spring. When cooked, it tints this soup a lovely pale green.

Prep: 20 minutes	Cook: 25 minutes
8	ounces fresh sorrel, stems removed
1	tablespoon butter or margarine
1	medium onion, chopped
3	tablespoons all-purpose flour
1	can (14½ ounces) chicken broth or 1¾ cups Chicken Broth (page 84)
2	cups water
⅛	teaspoon salt
	pinch ground black pepper
½	cup heavy or whipping cream

1. Roll up several sorrel leaves together, cigar fashion, and thinly slice (about 4¼ cups). Reserve ¼ cup sliced leaves.

2. In 3-quart saucepan, melt butter over medium heat. Add onion and cook, stirring frequently, until tender, about 5 minutes. Stir in 4 cups sliced sorrel and cook, stirring frequently, until completely wilted. Add flour and cook, stirring, 1 minute.

3. Gradually stir in broth, water, salt, and pepper. Heat to boiling over high heat. Reduce heat and simmer 5 minutes.

4. Spoon one-fourth of sorrel mixture into blender; cover, with center part of cover removed to let steam escape, and puree until smooth. Pour puree into bowl. Repeat with remaining mixture.

5. Return puree to clean saucepan; stir in cream and heat through (do not boil). Sprinkle with reserved sliced sorrel to serve. Makes about 4⅔ cups or 4 first-course servings.

Each serving: About 187 calories, 3g protein, 11g carbohydrate, 15g total fat (9g saturated), 49mg cholesterol, 545mg sodium.

Caldo Verde

In Portugal, this delicious soup gets its rich green color from finely shredded Galician cabbage that is sold in the outdoor markets. Kale, readily available in supermarkets, makes a fine substitute. If you like, sprinkle the soup with one-half cup finely chopped fully cooked spicy smoked sausage, such as linguiça or chorizo.

Prep: 15 minutes	Cook: 40 to 45 minutes
2	tablespoons olive oil
1	large onion (12 ounces), chopped
3	garlic cloves, finely chopped
2½	pounds all-purpose potatoes (8 medium), peeled and cut into 2-inch pieces
2	cans (14½ ounces each) chicken broth or 3½ cups Chicken Broth (page 84)
3	cups water
1	teaspoon salt
¼	teaspoon coarsely ground black pepper
1	pound kale, tough stems and veins trimmed and leaves very thinly sliced

1. In 5-quart Dutch oven, heat oil over medium heat. Add onion and garlic; cook until onion is golden, about 10 minutes. Add potatoes, broth, water, salt, and pepper; heat to boiling over high heat. Reduce heat; cover and simmer until potatoes are tender, about 20 minutes.

2. Mash potatoes in broth, keeping potatoes lumpy.

3. Stir in kale; simmer, uncovered, until kale is tender, 5 to 8 minutes. Makes about 10 cups or 5 main-dish servings.

Each serving: About 251 calories, 7g protein, 41g carbohydrate, 7g total fat (1g saturated), 0mg cholesterol, 1,187mg sodium.

Soups should be seasonal, taking advantage of the many vegetables that are both inexpensive and in ample supply. A little cheating can be done by cooking tomatoes, peppers, and other vegetables when they are at their flavorful peak, then pureeing and freezing them for delicious soups in the winter.

BARBARA KAFKA
COOKBOOK AUTHOR

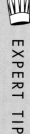

Cream of Asparagus Soup

For the most flavor, choose the thickest asparagus you can find for this creamy soup. If you wish, garnish each serving with a sprinkling of chopped fresh chives, tarragon, or parsley.

Prep: 10 minutes Cook: 25 to 30 minutes

2	tablespoons butter or margarine
1	medium onion, chopped
12	ounces asparagus, trimmed and cut into 1-inch pieces (3 cups)
3	tablespoons all-purpose flour
¼	teaspoon salt
⅛	teaspoon ground black pepper
1	can (14½ ounces) chicken or vegetable broth or 1¾ cups Chicken Broth (page 84) or Vegetable Broth (page 83)
1	cup half-and-half or light cream

1. In 3-quart saucepan, melt butter over medium heat; add onion and cook, stirring frequently, until tender and golden, about 10 minutes. Add asparagus; cook 1 minute.

2. Stir in flour, salt, and pepper until blended. Gradually stir in broth; heat to boiling, stirring constantly. Reduce heat; cover and simmer until asparagus is tender, 5 to 10 minutes.

3. Spoon half of mixture into blender; cover, with center part of cover removed to let steam escape, and puree until smooth. Pour into bowl. Repeat with remaining mixture.

4. Return puree to saucepan; stir in half-and-half. Heat through (do not boil). Serve soup hot, or cover and refrigerate to serve chilled later. If chilled soup is too thick, stir in some milk. Makes about 5 cups or 4 first-course servings.

Each serving: About 194 calories, 6g protein, 14g carbohydrate, 14g total fat (8g saturated), 38mg cholesterol, 657mg sodium.

Cream of Broccoli Soup

Prepare as directed but substitute **3 cups small broccoli flowerets** for asparagus. Makes about 4½ cups or 4 first-course servings.

Cream of Cauliflower Soup

Prepare as directed but substitute **3 cups small cauliflower flowerets** for asparagus, use **1¼ cups half-and-half or light cream,** and add **dash of ground red pepper.** If desired, stir in

4 ounces sharp Cheddar cheese, shredded (1 cup) and **½ teaspoon Dijon mustard** when heating through. Makes about 5 cups or 4 first-course servings.

Cream of Spinach Soup

Prepare as directed but substitute **2 packages (10 ounces each) frozen chopped spinach,** thawed for asparagus and omit the 5 to 10 minutes of cooking time in Step 2. Makes about 4½ cups or 4 first-course servings.

Quick Cream of Broccoli Soup

Frozen vegetables are picked and processed so quickly they often retain more nutrients than fresh. Here, frozen broccoli is easily transformed into a satisfying soup.

Prep: 5 minutes Cook: 20 minutes

1	tablespoon butter or margarine
1	medium onion, chopped
1	package (10 ounces) frozen chopped broccoli
1	can (14½ ounces) chicken broth or 1¾ cups Chicken Broth (page 84)
¼	teaspoon dried thyme
⅛	teaspoon salt
⅛	teaspoon ground black pepper
	pinch ground nutmeg
	pinch ground red pepper (cayenne; optional)
1½	cups milk
2	teaspoons fresh lemon juice

1. In 3-quart saucepan, melt butter over medium heat. Add onion and cook, stirring occasionally, until tender, about 5 minutes. Add frozen broccoli, broth, thyme, salt, pepper, nutmeg, and ground red pepper, if using; heat to boiling over high heat. Reduce heat and simmer 10 minutes.

2. Spoon half of mixture into blender; cover, with center part of cover removed to let steam escape, and puree until smooth. Pour into bowl. Repeat with remaining mixture.

3. Return puree to saucepan; stir in milk. Heat through, stirring often (do not boil). Remove from heat and stir in lemon juice. Makes about 3¾ cups or 4 first-course servings.

Each serving: About 130 calories, 6g protein, 12g carbohydrate, 7g total fat (4g saturated), 21mg cholesterol, 594mg sodium.

Quick Cream of Pea Soup

Prepare as directed but substitute **1 package (10 ounces) frozen peas** for broccoli; if you like, add **¼ teaspoon dried mint leaves** with broth.

Quick Cream of Asparagus Soup

Prepare as directed but substitute **1 package (10 ounces) frozen asparagus** for broccoli; if you like, add **¼ teaspoon dried tarragon** with broth.

Quick Cream of Squash Soup

Prepare as directed but substitute **1 package (10 ounces) frozen cooked winter squash** for broccoli; if you like, add **¼ teaspoon pumpkin-pie spice** after cooking onion and cook 30 seconds before adding broth.

Quick Cream of Corn Soup

Prepare as directed but substitute **1 package (10 ounces) frozen whole-kernel corn** for broccoli; if you like, add **¾ teaspoon chili powder** after cooking onion and cook 30 seconds before adding broth.

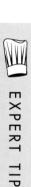

Good-quality vegetable stocks are not generally available, but they are easy to make. Some of the easiest and most flavorful are those prepared using a juicer. Centrifugal-style juicers are the best because they give you juice with just a tiny bit of pulp which adds body; it is great for making quick, delicious soups and sauces. I have my favorite vegetable blends, such as carrot, red bell pepper, and fennel with a little fresh ginger thrown in. It's fun to experiment and come up with your own combinations. Also, remember to save the cooking liquid from potatoes and beans. It makes a flavorful base stock to which you can add fresh herbs, chiles, or vegetable juices.

JOHN ASH
CULINARY DIRECTOR,
FETZER VINEYARDS, CALIFORNIA

EXPERT TIP

Italian White Bean and Spinach Soup

A touch of fresh lemon juice, stirred in just before serving, gives this robust soup a light citrus note.

Prep: 20 minutes	Cook: 30 minutes
1	tablespoon vegetable oil
1	medium onion, chopped
1	stalk celery, chopped
1	garlic clove, finely chopped
2	cans (15 to 19 ounces each) white kidney beans (cannellini), rinsed and drained
2	cups water
1	can (14½ ounces) chicken broth or 1¾ cups Chicken Broth (page 84)
¼	teaspoon coarsely ground black pepper
⅛	teaspoon dried thyme
1	bunch (10 to 12 ounces) spinach, tough stems trimmed
1	tablespoon fresh lemon juice
	freshly grated Parmesan cheese (optional)

1. In 3-quart saucepan, heat oil over medium heat. Add onion and celery; cook, stirring, until celery is tender, 5 to 8 minutes. Stir in garlic and cook 30 seconds. Add beans, water, broth, pepper, and thyme; heat to boiling over high heat. Reduce heat and simmer 15 minutes.

2. Roll up several spinach leaves together, cigar fashion, and thinly slice. Repeat with remaining spinach.

3. With slotted spoon, remove 2 cups beans from soup mixture and reserve. Spoon one-fourth of mixture into blender; cover, with center part of cover removed to let steam escape, and puree until smooth. Pour into bowl. Repeat with remaining mixture.

4. Return puree and reserved beans to saucepan; heat to boiling over medium-high heat. Stir in spinach and cook just until wilted, about 1 minute. Remove from heat and stir in lemon juice. Serve with Parmesan, if you like. Makes about 7½ cups or 6 first-course servings.

♥ Each serving: About 170 calories, 11g protein, 24g carbohydrate, 4g total fat (1g saturated), 0mg cholesterol, 539mg sodium.

Spicy Black Bean Soup

Canned beans make this soup a snap to prepare, while just the right blend of spices gives it a Tex-Mex wallop of flavor.

Prep: 10 minutes   Cook: 30 minutes

1	tablespoon vegetable oil
1	medium onion, chopped
2	garlic cloves, finely chopped
2	teaspoons chili powder
1	teaspoon ground cumin
1/4	teaspoon crushed red pepper
2	cans (15 to 19 ounces each) black beans, rinsed and drained
2	cups water
1	can (14 1/2 ounces) chicken broth or 1 3/4 cups Chicken Broth (page 84)
1/4	cup coarsely chopped fresh cilantro lime wedges

1. In 3-quart saucepan, heat oil over medium heat. Add onion and cook, stirring occasionally, until tender, 5 to 8 minutes. Stir in garlic, chili powder, cumin, and crushed red pepper; cook 30 seconds. Stir in beans, water, and broth; heat to boiling over high heat. Reduce heat and simmer 15 minutes.

2. Spoon one-fourth of mixture into blender; cover, with center part of cover removed to let steam escape, and puree until smooth. Pour puree into bowl. Repeat with remaining mixture. Sprinkle with cilantro and serve with wedges of lime. Makes about 6 2/3 cups or 6 first-course servings.

♥ Each serving: About 137 calories, 7g protein, 19g carbohydrate, 4g total fat (0g saturated), 0mg cholesterol, 563mg sodium.

Garden Vegetable Chowder

Use your favorite vegetable broth instead of water for more depth of flavor in this tempting chock-full-of-vegetables soup.

Prep: 20 minutes   Cook: 30 minutes

2	medium leeks (12 ounces)
1	tablespoon butter or margarine
2	carrots, peeled and cut into 1/4-inch-thick slices
1	stalk celery, cut into 1/4-inch-thick slices
1	pound red potatoes (6 medium), cut into 1/2-inch pieces
1	can (14 1/2 ounces) chicken or vegetable broth or 1 3/4 cups Chicken Broth (page 84) or Vegetable Broth (page 83)
1	cup water
3/4	teaspoon salt
1/8	teaspoon dried thyme
1/8	teaspoon ground black pepper
2	ounces green or wax beans, trimmed and cut into 1/2-inch pieces
1	large zucchini (10 ounces), cut into 1/2-inch pieces
1	cup half-and-half or light cream
1	tablespoon chopped fresh dill

1. Cut off roots and trim dark green tops from leeks; cut each leek lengthwise in half, then crosswise into 1/4-inch pieces. Rinse leeks in large bowl of cold water, swishing to remove all sand; transfer to colander to drain, leaving sand in bottom of bowl.

2. In 3-quart saucepan, melt butter over medium heat. Stir in leeks, carrots, and celery; cover and cook, stirring occasionally, until vegetables are tender, about 10 minutes.

3. Stir in potatoes, broth, water, salt, thyme, and pepper. Heat to boiling; cook, uncovered, 5 minutes. Stir in beans and cook 5 minutes. Stir in zucchini and cook 5 minutes longer.

4. Stir in half-and-half and heat through (do not boil). Remove from heat and stir in dill. Makes about 6 1/2 cups or 4 first-course servings.

Each serving: About 263 calories, 7g protein, 36g carbohydrate, 11g total fat (6g saturated), 30mg cholesterol, 959mg sodium.

Summertime Corn Chowder

Summertime Corn Chowder

A basket of warm Buttermilk Biscuits (page 568) and thickly sliced ham are all that's needed to complete the menu for a real summertime treat.

Prep: 25 minutes   Cook: 35 to 40 minutes

6	medium ears corn, husks and silk removed
4	slices bacon, cut into ½-inch pieces
1	medium red onion, chopped
1	jalapeño chile, seeded and finely chopped
1	garlic clove, finely chopped
2	tablespoons all-purpose flour
½	teaspoon salt
⅛	teaspoon ground black pepper
1	pound red potatoes (6 medium), cut into ½-inch pieces
2	cans (14½ ounces each) chicken broth or 3½ cups Chicken Broth (page 84)
2	cups half-and-half or light cream
2	small ripe tomatoes (8 ounces), peeled, seeded, and chopped
	thinly sliced basil leaves

1. Cut kernels from corncobs (about 3 cups), reserving 3 corncobs; discard remaining corncobs.

2. In 5-quart Dutch oven, cook bacon over medium heat until browned. With slotted spoon, transfer bacon to paper towels to drain; crumble.

3. To bacon drippings in Dutch oven, add onion and jalapeño and cook, stirring, until onion is tender, about 5 minutes. Add garlic; cook 1 minute longer. Stir in flour, salt, and pepper; cook, stirring, 1 minute.

4. Stir in potatoes, corncobs, broth, and half-and-half; heat to boiling over high heat. Reduce heat; cover and simmer until potatoes are tender, 10 to 15 minutes.

5. Discard corncobs; stir in corn kernels and heat through. Transfer chowder to warm tureen. Stir in tomatoes and sprinkle with bacon and basil. Makes about 9½ cups or 8 first-course servings.

Each serving: About 272 calories, 7g protein, 29g carbohydrate, 15g total fat (7g saturated), 30mg cholesterol, 693mg sodium.

Vichyssoise

This luxurious soup, traditionally served cold, is just as delicious hot (just call it cream of potato and leek soup). Either way, serve in small cups and garnish with freshly chopped chives.

Prep: 20 minutes plus chilling   Cook: 55 minutes

4	medium leeks (1¼ pounds)
2	tablespoons butter or margarine
1	pound all-purpose potatoes (3 medium), peeled and thinly sliced
2	cans (14½ ounces each) chicken broth or 3½ cups Chicken Broth (page 84)
½	cup water
1	teaspoon salt
¼	teaspoon ground black pepper
1	cup milk
½	cup heavy or whipping cream

1. Cut off roots and trim dark green tops from leeks; cut each leek lengthwise in half. Cut enough of white and pale green parts crosswise into ¼-inch pieces to equal 4½ cups. (Reserve any leftover leeks for another use.) Rinse leeks in large bowl of cold water, swishing to remove sand; transfer to colander to drain, leaving sand in bottom of bowl.

2. In 4-quart saucepan, melt butter over medium heat; add leeks and cook, stirring occasionally, 8 to 10 minutes. Add potatoes, broth, water, salt, and pepper; heat to boiling over high heat. Reduce heat; cover and simmer 30 minutes.

3. Spoon half of mixture into blender; cover, with center part of cover removed to let steam escape, and puree until smooth. Pour into bowl. Repeat with remaining mixture.

4. Stir milk and cream into puree. To serve hot, return soup to same clean saucepan and heat through over low heat (do not boil). To serve cold, cover and refrigerate at least 4 hours or until very cold. Makes about 8 cups or 8 first-course servings.

Each serving: About 161 calories, 4g protein, 14g carbohydrate, 10g total fat (6g saturated), 32mg cholesterol, 778mg sodium.

Gazpacho with Cilantro Cream

Recipes for this chilled Spanish soup abound—ours is topped with a dollop of cilantro-spiked sour cream.

Prep: 30 minutes plus chilling

2	medium cucumbers (8 ounces each), peeled
1	yellow pepper
¼	small red onion
2	pounds ripe tomatoes (5 medium), peeled, seeded, and chopped
½ to 1	small jalapeño chile, seeded
3	tablespoons fresh lime juice
2	tablespoons extravirgin olive oil
¾ plus ⅛	teaspoon salt
¼	cup reduced-fat sour cream or plain lowfat yogurt
1	tablespoon milk
4	teaspoons chopped fresh cilantro

1. Chop half of 1 cucumber, half of yellow pepper, and all of onion into ¼-inch pieces; set aside. Cut remaining cucumbers and yellow pepper into large pieces.

2. In blender or in food processor with knife blade attached, puree large pieces of cucumber and yellow pepper, tomatoes, jalapeño, lime juice, oil, and ¾ teaspoon salt until smooth. Pour puree into bowl; add cut-up cucumber, yellow pepper, and onion. Cover and refrigerate until well chilled, at least 6 hours or up to overnight.

3. Prepare cilantro cream: In small bowl, stir sour cream, milk, cilantro, and remaining ⅛ teaspoon salt until smooth. Cover and refrigerate.

4. To serve, top soup with dollops of cilantro cream. Makes about 5 cups or 4 first-course servings.

Each serving: About 156 calories, 4g protein, 17g carbohydrate, 10g total fat (2g saturated), 6mg cholesterol, 545mg sodium.

Cool Cucumber Soup

A blender whirls up this tangy no-cook soup in no time flat.

Prep: 10 minutes

1	pound cucumbers (2 medium), peeled, seeded, and coarsely chopped
1	container (16 ounces) plain lowfat yogurt
½	cup cold water
1	tablespoon fresh lemon juice
¾	teaspoon salt
¼	teaspoon coarsely ground black pepper
1	cup ice cubes
¼	cup coarsely chopped fresh mint

In blender, puree cucumbers, yogurt, water, lemon juice, salt, and pepper until almost smooth. With motor on and center part of cover removed, add ice cubes, one at a time. Add mint and process 5 seconds to blend. Makes about 4 cups or 4 first-course servings.

Each serving: About 91 calories, 7g protein, 12g carbohydrate, 2g total fat (1g saturated), 7mg cholesterol, 524mg sodium.

Split Pea Soup with Ham

On a wintry day, nothing satisfies more than an old-fashioned favorite like split pea soup.

Prep: 10 minutes   Cook: 1 hour 15 minutes

2	tablespoons vegetable oil
2	white turnips (6 ounces each), peeled and chopped (optional)
2	carrots, peeled and finely chopped
2	stalks celery, finely chopped
1	medium onion, finely chopped
1	package (16 ounces) dry split peas, rinsed and picked through
2	smoked ham hocks (1½ pounds)
8	cups water
1	bay leaf
1	teaspoon salt
¼	teaspoon ground allspice

1. In 5-quart Dutch oven, heat oil over medium-high heat. Add turnips if using, carrots, celery, and onion; cook, stirring frequently, until carrots are tender-crisp, about 10 minutes. Add split peas, ham hocks, water, bay leaf, salt, and allspice; heat to boiling over high heat. Reduce heat; cover and simmer 45 minutes.

2. Discard bay leaf. Transfer ham hocks to cutting board; discard skin and bones. Finely chop meat. Return meat to soup. Heat through. Makes 11 cups or 6 main-dish servings.

Each serving: About 343 calories, 21g protein, 52g carbohydrate, 7g total fat (1g saturated), 3mg cholesterol, 1,174mg sodium.

Pasta e Piselli

Here is a quick weeknight version of pasta e fagiole. In season, use fresh peas (piselli). Cook them in the broth until tender before adding the pasta.

Prep: 10 minutes plus cooking pasta   Cook: 20 minutes

2	tablespoons olive oil
3	garlic cloves, crushed with side of chef's knife
1	can (14½ ounces) diced tomatoes
2	cans (14½ ounces each) chicken broth or 3½ cups Chicken Broth (page 84)
½	cup water
¼	cup loosely packed fresh basil leaves, coarsely chopped
8	ounces mixed pasta, such as penne, bow ties, or elbow macaroni (2 cups), cooked as label directs
1	package (10 ounces) frozen peas, thawed
	freshly grated Parmesan cheese

1. In nonreactive 4-quart saucepan, heat oil over medium heat. Add garlic; cook, stirring frequently, until golden, about 2 minutes.

2. Add tomatoes with their juice, broth, water, and basil; heat to boiling. Reduce heat; cover and simmer 5 minutes. Discard garlic.

3. Stir in pasta and peas; heat through. Serve with Parmesan. Makes about 10 cups or 5 main-dish servings.

Each serving without Parmesan: About 317 calories, 12g protein, 51g carbohydrate, 8g total fat (1g saturated), 0mg cholesterol, 1,044mg sodium.

Curried Lentil Soup

Based on an Indian classic, this thick and hearty soup is bound to become a staple in your soup repertoire. Lentils, unlike other dried legumes, don't require presoaking, so this can be prepared in less time than most bean soups.

Prep: 30 minutes   Cook: 1 hour to 1 hour 10 minutes

2	tablespoons olive oil
4	carrots, peeled and finely chopped
2	large stalks celery, finely chopped
1	large onion (12 ounces), finely chopped
1	medium Granny Smith apple, peeled, cored, and finely chopped
1	tablespoon grated, peeled fresh ginger
1	large garlic clove, crushed with garlic press
2	teaspoons curry powder
¾	teaspoon ground cumin
¾	teaspoon ground coriander
1	package (16 ounces) lentils, rinsed and picked through
5	cups water
2	cans (14½ ounces each) vegetable or chicken broth or 3½ cups Vegetable Broth (page 83) or Chicken Broth (page 84)
¼	cup chopped fresh cilantro
½	teaspoon salt
	plain lowfat yogurt

1. In 5-quart Dutch oven, heat oil over medium-high heat. Add carrots, celery, onion, and apple; cook, stirring occasionally, until lightly browned, 10 to 15 minutes.

2. Add ginger, garlic, curry powder, cumin, and coriander; cook, stirring, 1 minute.

3. Add lentils, water, and broth; heat to boiling over high heat. Reduce heat; cover and simmer, stirring occasionally, until lentils are tender, 45 to 55 minutes. Stir in cilantro and salt. To serve, top soup with dollops of yogurt. Makes about 10 cups or 5 main-dish servings.

♥ Each serving without yogurt: About 434 calories, 27g protein, 69g carbohydrate, 7g total fat (1g saturated), 0mg cholesterol, 966mg sodium.

German Lentil Soup

German cooks like to add a meaty ham hock and some chopped bacon to their lentil soups to lend a smoky note.

Prep: 25 minutes   Cook: 1 hour 30 to 35 minutes

4	slices bacon, cut into ½-inch pieces
2	medium onions, chopped
2	carrots, peeled and chopped
1	large stalk celery, chopped
1	package (16 ounces) lentils, rinsed and picked through
1	smoked ham hock (1 pound)
8	cups water
1	bay leaf
1	teaspoon salt
½	teaspoon dried thyme
½	teaspoon ground black pepper
2	tablespoons fresh lemon juice

1. In 5-quart Dutch oven, cook bacon over medium-low heat until lightly browned. Add onions, carrots, and celery; cook over medium heat until vegetables are tender, 15 to 20 minutes. Add lentils, ham hock, water, bay leaf, salt, thyme, and pepper; heat to boiling over high heat. Reduce heat; cover and simmer until lentils are tender, 50 to 60 minutes. Remove and discard bay leaf.

2. Transfer ham hock to cutting board; cut off meat and discard skin and bone. Cut meat into bite-size pieces and return to soup. Heat through. Stir in lemon juice. Makes about 11 cups or 6 main-dish servings.

♥ Each serving: About 390 calories, 25g protein, 52g carbohydrate, 10g total fat (3g saturated), 13mg cholesterol, 1,027mg sodium.

Minestrone with Pesto

(pictured on page 56)

Freshly made pesto adds body and richness to this soup.

Prep: 20 minutes plus soaking beans   Cook: 1 hour

8	ounces dry Great Northern beans (1⅓ cups), soaked and drained (page 372)
2	tablespoons olive oil
3	carrots, peeled and cut into ¼-inch-thick slices
2	stalks celery, cut into ¼-inch-thick slices
1	large onion (12 ounces), finely chopped
2	ounces pancetta or bacon, finely chopped
1	pound all-purpose potatoes (3 medium), peeled and chopped
2	medium zucchini (8 ounces each), each cut lengthwise into quarters, then crosswise into ¼-inch-thick slices
½	medium head savoy cabbage (1 pound), thinly sliced
1	large garlic clove, crushed with garlic press
1	can (14½ ounces) diced tomatoes
2	cans (14½ ounces each) chicken broth or 3½ cups Chicken Broth (page 84)
1	cup water
	Pesto (right) or ½ cup store-bought pesto
½	teaspoon salt

1. In 4-quart saucepan, combine beans and enough *water to cover by 2 inches;* heat to boiling over high heat. Reduce heat; cover and simmer, stirring occasionally, until beans are tender, 40 minutes to 1 hour. Drain beans.

2. Meanwhile, in nonreactive 5-quart Dutch oven, heat oil over medium-high heat. Add carrots, celery, onion, and pancetta; cook, stirring occasionally, until onions begin to brown, about 10 minutes. Add potatoes, zucchini, cabbage, and garlic; cook, stirring constantly, until cabbage has wilted. Add tomatoes with their juice, broth, and water; heat to boiling over high heat. Reduce heat; cover and simmer until vegetables are tender, about 30 minutes.

3. Meanwhile, prepare Pesto.

4. In blender or in food processor with knife blade attached, puree ½ cup beans with 1 cup soup mixture until smooth. Stir puree, remaining beans, and salt into soup; heat to boiling. Reduce heat; cover and simmer 10 minutes. Garnish with dollops of pesto. Makes about 13 cups or 6 main-dish servings.

Pesto

In blender, puree **⅔ cup packed fresh basil leaves, ¼ cup freshly grated Parmesan cheese, ¼ cup olive oil, 1 tablespoon water,** and ¼ **teaspoon salt** until smooth.

Each serving with pesto: About 444 calories, 18g protein, 53g carbohydrate, 20g total fat (4g saturated), 9mg cholesterol, 1,204mg sodium.

Miso Soup

Miso, a highly concentrated paste made from soybeans and a grain such as rice or barley, is often used as a base for Japanese-style soups. This is one of the best.

Prep: 20 minutes   Cook: 35 minutes

1	tablespoon vegetable oil
2	large carrots, peeled and thinly sliced
1	small onion, finely chopped
2	garlic cloves, finely chopped
1	tablespoon grated, peeled fresh ginger
½	small head napa cabbage (Chinese cabbage; 8 ounces), cored and cut crosswise into ½-inch-thick slices (4 cups)
6¼	cups water
1	tablespoon seasoned rice vinegar
¼	teaspoon coarsely ground black pepper
¼	cup red miso
1	package (16 ounces) firm tofu, drained and cut into ½-inch cubes
2	green onions, thinly sliced

1. In 5-quart Dutch oven, heat oil over medium heat. Add carrots, onion, garlic, and ginger; cook, stirring occasionally, until onion is lightly browned, about 10 minutes.

2. Add cabbage, 6 cups water, vinegar, and pepper; heat to boiling over high heat. Reduce heat; cover and simmer until vegetables are tender, about 20 minutes. In small bowl, beat miso with remaining ¼ cup water until smooth.

3. Stir tofu and miso into soup; heat through. Sprinkle with green onions to serve. Makes about 9½ cups or 6 main-dish servings.

Each serving: About 187 calories, 14g protein, 14g carbohydrate, 10g total fat (1g saturated), 0mg cholesterol, 495mg sodium.

Tuscan Vegetable Soup

Classic Italian ingredients make this a thick, soul-satisfying soup. We think serving it with Parmesan cheese is a must!

Prep: 45 minutes plus soaking beans
Cook: 1 hour 10 to 25 minutes

5	carrots, peeled
1	jumbo onion (1 pound), peeled
8	ounces dry Great Northern beans (1⅓ cups), soaked and drained (page 372)
1	bay leaf
3	tablespoons olive oil
4	ounces pancetta or cooked ham, finely chopped
3	large stalks celery, coarsely chopped
1	small fennel bulb (1 pound), trimmed and coarsely chopped
2	garlic cloves, finely chopped
1	pound all-purpose potatoes (3 medium), peeled and cut into ½-inch pieces
1	medium head escarole (12 ounces), cut crosswise into ¼-inch-thick strips
2	cans (14½ ounces each) chicken broth or 3½ cups Chicken Broth (page 84)
½	teaspoon salt
	freshly grated Parmesan cheese (optional)

1. Cut 1 carrot crosswise in half. Coarsely chop remaining carrots. Cut onion into 4 wedges. Leave 1 wedge whole; coarsely chop remaining 3 wedges.

2. In 4-quart saucepan, combine beans, halved carrot, onion wedge, bay leaf, and enough *water to cover by 2 inches;* heat to boiling over high heat. Reduce heat; cover and simmer, stirring occasionally, until beans are tender, 40 minutes to 1 hour. Drain beans and vegetables, reserving 3 cups cooking liquid. Discard carrot halves, onion wedge, and bay leaf.

3. Meanwhile, in 5-quart Dutch oven, heat oil over medium-high heat. Add pancetta, celery, fennel, chopped carrots, and chopped onion; cook, stirring, until vegetables begin to brown, about 15 minutes. Add garlic; cook 1 minute.

4. Stir in beans, potatoes, escarole, broth, and reserved cooking liquid; heat to boiling over high heat. Reduce heat; cover and simmer until vegetables are very tender, 15 to 20 minutes. Stir in salt. Serve with Parmesan, if you like. Makes about 14 cups or 6 main-dish servings.

Each serving: About 391 calories, 16g protein, 51g carbohydrate, 15g total fat (4g saturated), 11mg cholesterol, 1,086mg sodium.

Hearty Mushroom-Barley Soup

A real rib-sticker. Get a head start by cooking the barley the day before, then cool and refrigerate.

Prep: 20 minutes   Cook: 1 hour

¾	cup pearl barley
8	cups water
2	tablespoons olive oil
3	stalks celery, cut into ¼-inch-thick slices
1	large onion (12 ounces), chopped
1½	pounds mushrooms, trimmed and thickly sliced
2	tablespoons tomato paste
5	carrots, each peeled and cut lengthwise in half, then crosswise into ¼-inch-thick slices
2	cans (14½ ounces each) beef broth or 3½ cups Brown Beef Stock (page 83)
¼	cup dry sherry
1½	teaspoons salt

1. In 3-quart saucepan, combine barley and 4 cups water; heat to boiling over high heat. Reduce heat; cover and simmer 30 minutes. Drain.

2. Meanwhile, in 5-quart Dutch oven, heat oil over medium-high heat. Add celery and onion; cook, stirring until golden, about 10 minutes. Increase heat to high; add mushrooms and cook, stirring occasionally, until liquid has evaporated and mushrooms are lightly browned, 10 to 12 minutes.

3. Reduce heat to medium-high; add tomato paste and cook, stirring, 2 minutes. Add barley, carrots, broth, sherry, salt, and remaining 4 cups water; heat to boiling. Reduce heat; cover and simmer until carrots and barley are tender, 20 to 25 minutes. Makes about 12 cups or 10 first-course servings.

♥ Each serving: About 133 calories, 5g protein, 21g carbohydrate, 4g total fat (1g saturated), 1mg cholesterol, 684mg sodium.

Mushroom and Wild Rice Soup

Wild rice is really a grass, not a grain. Its deep earthy flavor is a perfect match for the woodsy taste of mushrooms.

Prep: 15 minutes   Cook: 1 hour 30 minutes

½	cup wild rice
4½	cups water
1	package (½ ounce) dried mushrooms
2	tablespoons olive oil
2	stalks celery, finely chopped
1	large onion (12 ounces), finely chopped
10	ounces mushrooms, trimmed and cut into ¼-inch-thick slices
2	cans (14½ ounces each) chicken broth or 3½ cups Chicken Broth (page 84)
1	tablespoon soy sauce
½	teaspoon dried thyme
¼	teaspoon coarsely ground black pepper
¼	cup cream sherry

Mushroom and Wild Rice Soup

1. In 3-quart saucepan, combine wild rice and 2½ cups water; heat to boiling over high heat. Reduce heat; cover and simmer until rice is tender and most of water has been absorbed, about 45 minutes.

2. Meanwhile, heat remaining 2 cups water to boiling over high heat. In small bowl, pour boiling water over dried mushrooms; let stand 20 minutes. With slotted spoon, remove dried mushrooms. Rinse mushrooms to remove any grit, then chop. Strain mushroom liquid through sieve lined with paper towels. Reserve.

3. In nonstick 12-inch skillet, heat 1 tablespoon oil over medium-high heat. Add celery and onion; cook until vegetables are tender and lightly browned, about 10 minutes. Transfer to 4-quart saucepan.

4. In same skillet, heat remaining 1 tablespoon oil. Add fresh mushrooms; cook until mushrooms are tender and lightly browned, about 10 minutes. Add to celery mixture.

5. Add wild rice and any cooking liquid, dried mushrooms and mushroom liquid, broth, soy sauce, thyme, and pepper to celery mixture; heat to boiling over high heat. Reduce heat; cover and simmer 5 minutes. Stir in sherry. Makes about 9½ cups or 8 first-course servings.

Each serving: About 118 calories, 4g protein, 15g carbohydrate, 5g total fat (1g saturated), 0mg cholesterol, 570mg sodium.

Classic Black Bean Soup

Ham and dry sherry add rich flavor to this classic soup—a perfect choice for Sunday supper.

Prep: 20 minutes plus soaking beans   Cook: 2 hours 30 minutes

3	tablespoons olive oil
3	large carrots, peeled and chopped
3	medium onions, chopped
3	stalks celery with leaves, chopped
4	garlic cloves, peeled
2	bay leaves
½	teaspoon dried thyme
1	pound dry black beans, soaked and drained (page 372)
2	smoked ham hocks (1½ pounds)
10	cups water
1	teaspoon coarsely ground black pepper
½	cup chopped fresh parsley
3	tablespoons dry sherry
2	teaspoons salt
12	paper-thin lemon slices

1. In 5-quart Dutch oven, heat oil over medium heat. Add carrots, onions, and celery and cook, stirring occasionally, until vegetables are tender, about 10 minutes. Add garlic, bay leaves, and thyme; cook 1 minute.

2. Add beans, ham hocks, water, and pepper to Dutch oven; heat to boiling over high heat. Reduce heat and simmer until beans are very tender, about 2 hours. Discard ham hocks and bay leaves.

3. Spoon one-fourth of bean mixture into blender; cover, with center part of cover removed to let steam escape, and puree until very smooth. Pour puree into bowl. Repeat with remaining mixture. Return puree to Dutch oven and stir in all but 2 tablespoons parsley, sherry, and salt. Cook 5 minutes.

4. To serve, ladle soup into bowls, garnish with lemon slices, and sprinkle with remaining 2 tablespoons parsley. Makes about 13 cups or 12 first-course servings.

♥ Each serving: About 207 calories, 10g protein, 32g carbohydrate, 5g total fat (1g saturated), 2mg cholesterol, 788mg sodium.

Caribbean-Flavored Black Bean Soup

An unusual black bean soup inspired by the kitchens of Jamaica. Cilantro, ginger, allspice, thyme, and fresh chiles all contribute to its vibrant flavor.

Prep: 25 minutes plus soaking beans   Cook: 2 hours 30 minutes

3	tablespoons vegetable oil
2	medium red onions, chopped
4	jalapeño chiles, seeded and finely chopped
2	tablespoons minced, peeled fresh ginger
4	garlic cloves, finely chopped
½	teaspoon ground allspice
½	teaspoon dried thyme
1	pound dry black beans, soaked and drained (page 372)
12	cups water
1½	pounds sweet potatoes (2 medium), peeled and cut into ¾-inch pieces
1	tablespoon brown sugar
2	teaspoons salt
6	green onions, finely chopped
½	cup chopped fresh cilantro
	lime wedges

1. In 5-quart Dutch oven, heat oil over medium heat. Add onions and cook, stirring occasionally, until tender, about 5 minutes. Add jalapeños, ginger, garlic, allspice, and thyme; cook, stirring, 3 minutes.

2. Add beans and water to Dutch oven; heat to boiling over high heat. Reduce heat and simmer 1 hour 30 minutes. Add sweet potatoes, brown sugar, and salt and cook 30 minutes. Add green onions and cook 3 minutes longer.

3. Transfer 1 cup mixture to blender; cover, with center part of cover removed to let steam escape, and puree until smooth. Return puree to Dutch oven and stir in cilantro. Serve with lime wedges. Makes about 10 cups or 10 first-course servings.

♥ Each serving: About 270 calories, 12g protein, 47g carbohydrate, 5g total fat (1g saturated), 0mg cholesterol, 481mg sodium.

New England Clam Chowder

Clam chowder, New England's signature seafood dish, derives its name from chaudière, *the French word for cauldron. The saltiness of clams and salt pork varies; taste to season before serving.*

	Prep: 20 minutes plus cooling Cook: 45 minutes
1	cup water
1½	dozen chowder or cherrystone clams, scrubbed (page 286)
2	ounces salt pork or bacon, chopped
1	medium onion, finely chopped
1	tablespoon all-purpose flour
⅛	teaspoon ground black pepper
1	pound all-purpose potatoes (3 medium), peeled and chopped
4	cups half-and-half or light cream
½	teaspoon salt

1. In 4-quart saucepan, heat water to boiling over high heat. Add clams; heat to boiling. Reduce heat; cover and simmer until clams open, 5 to 10 minutes, transferring clams to bowl as they open. Discard any clams that have not opened.

2. When cool enough to handle, remove clams from their shells and coarsely chop. Discard shells. Strain clam broth through sieve lined with paper towels into measuring cup; if necessary add enough *water* to equal 2 cups.

3. In same clean saucepan, cook salt pork over medium heat until lightly browned. With slotted spoon, remove salt pork and discard. Add onion to drippings in pan; cook, stirring occasionally, until tender, about 5 minutes. Stir in flour and pepper until blended; cook 1 minute. Gradually stir in clam broth until smooth. Add potatoes; heat to boiling. Reduce heat; cover and simmer until potatoes are tender, about 15 minutes. Stir in half-and-half and clams; heat through (do not boil). Taste for seasoning; add salt as needed. Makes about 9 cups or 8 first-course servings.

Each serving: About 227 calories, 7g protein, 16g carbohydrate, 15g total fat (9g saturated), 52mg cholesterol, 232mg sodium.

Manhattan Clam Chowder

Chowder clams, sometimes called quahogs, are flavorful, but they are also tough and must be chopped after cooking. Substitute cherrystone clams, if you like—there's no need to chop them.

	Prep: 30 minutes plus cooling Cook: 50 minutes
5	cups water
3	dozen chowder or cherrystone clams, scrubbed (page 286)
5	slices bacon, finely chopped
1	large onion (12 ounces), finely chopped
2	large carrots, peeled and finely chopped
2	stalks celery, finely chopped
1	pound all-purpose potatoes (3 medium), peeled and finely chopped
½	bay leaf
1¼	teaspoons dried thyme
¼	teaspoon ground black pepper
1	can (28 ounces) plum tomatoes
2	tablespoons chopped fresh parsley
¾	teaspoon salt

1. In nonreactive 8-quart saucepot, heat 1 cup water to boiling over high heat. Add clams; heat to boiling. Reduce heat; cover and simmer until clams open, 5 to 10 minutes, transferring clams to bowl as they open. Discard any clams that have not opened.

2. When cool enough to handle, remove clams from shells and coarsely chop. Discard shells. Strain clam broth through sieve lined with paper towels into bowl.

3. In same clean saucepot, cook bacon over medium heat until browned; add onion and cook until tender, about 5 minutes. Add carrots and celery; cook 5 minutes.

4. Add clam broth to bacon mixture in saucepot. Add potatoes, remaining 4 cups water, bay leaf, thyme, and pepper; heat to boiling. Reduce heat; cover and simmer 10 minutes. Add tomatoes with their liquid, breaking them up with side of spoon. Simmer 10 minutes longer.

5. Stir in chopped clams and heat through. Discard bay leaf and sprinkle with parsley. Taste for seasoning; add salt as needed. Makes about 12 cups or 12 first-course servings.

Each serving: About 117 calories, 5g protein, 12g carbohydrate, 6g total fat (2g saturated), 12mg cholesterol, 342mg sodium.

Mussels in Saffron-Tomato Broth

Serve steaming bowls of these mussels with hunks of country-style bread to sop up all of the savory juices.

Prep: 20 minutes   Cook: 30 minutes

3	tablespoons olive oil
2	garlic cloves, crushed with side of chef's knife
1	small bay leaf
1/2	teaspoon loosely packed saffron threads
1/8 to 1/4	teaspoon crushed red pepper
1	can (14 1/2 ounces) diced tomatoes
1	bottle (8 ounces) clam juice
1/2	cup dry white wine
5	dozen medium mussels, scrubbed and debearded (page 291)

1. In nonreactive 8-quart saucepot, heat oil over medium heat. Add garlic and cook until golden. Add bay leaf, saffron, and crushed red pepper; cook, stirring, 1 minute.

2. Add tomatoes with their liquid, clam juice, and wine; heat to boiling over high heat. Reduce heat; cover and simmer 20 minutes.

3. Add mussels; heat to boiling over high heat. Reduce heat to medium; cover and simmer until mussels open, about 5 minutes, transferring mussels to bowl as they open. Discard bay leaf and any mussels that have not opened. To serve, transfer mussels and broth to large soup bowls. Makes 4 main-dish servings.

Each serving: About 219 calories, 16g protein, 10g carbohydrate, 13g total fat (2g saturated), 34mg cholesterol, 642mg sodium.

A piece of flavorful cheese rind, such as Parmesan or Romano, adds rich flavor to homemade minestrone soup, while a ham bone or a piece of bacon is ideal in bean soup.

BARBARA KAFKA
COOKBOOK AUTHOR

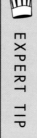

EXPERT TIP

Yankee Cod Chowder

Potatoes, fennel, and carrots accompany chunks of cod in this creamy winter soup.

Prep: 20 minutes   Cook: 40 minutes

4	slices bacon
3	carrots, each peeled and cut lengthwise in half, then crosswise into 1/4-inch-thick slices
1	medium fennel bulb (1 pound) or 3 stalks celery, finely chopped
1	medium onion, finely chopped
1	pound all-purpose potatoes (3 medium), peeled and chopped
3	bottles (8 ounces each) clam juice
1	can (14 1/2 ounces) chicken broth or 1 3/4 cups Chicken Broth (page 84)
1	bay leaf
1	pound cod fillet, cut into 1 1/2-inch pieces
1	cup half-and-half or light cream
1/4	teaspoon ground black pepper

1. In 5-quart Dutch oven, cook bacon over medium heat until browned. Using slotted spoon, transfer to paper towels to drain; crumble.

2. Discard all but 2 tablespoons bacon drippings from Dutch oven. Add carrots, fennel, and onion and cook, stirring occasionally, until lightly browned, 12 to 15 minutes. Add potatoes, clam juice, broth, and bay leaf; heat to boiling. Reduce heat; cover and simmer until vegetables are tender, about 15 minutes.

3. Add cod; cover and cook until fish is just opaque throughout, 2 to 5 minutes. Carefully stir in half-and-half and pepper; heat through (do not boil). Discard bay leaf. Sprinkle soup with crumbled bacon. Makes about 10 cups or 5 main-dish servings.

Each serving: About 316 calories, 24g protein, 25g carbohydrate, 14g total fat (6g saturated), 65mg cholesterol, 930mg sodium.

Shrimp Bisque

A quick stock made with the shrimp shells contributes a surprising amount of flavor. A sprinkling of chopped fresh chives or parsley provides the color counterpoint.

Prep: 20 minutes   Cook: 1 hour 20 minutes

3	tablespoons butter or margarine
1	pound medium shrimp, shelled and deveined (page 296), shells reserved
2	cans (14½ ounces each) low-sodium chicken broth or 3½ cups Chicken Broth (page 84)
1	cup dry white wine
½	cup water
1	large onion (12 ounces), chopped
2	carrots, peeled and chopped
2	stalks celery, chopped
2	tablespoons regular long-grain rice
1	bay leaf
1¼	teaspoons salt
⅛ to ¼	teaspoon ground red pepper (cayenne)
1	can (14½ ounces) diced tomatoes
1	cup half-and-half or light cream
2	tablespoons brandy or dry sherry

1. In nonreactive 5-quart Dutch oven, melt 1 tablespoon butter over medium heat. Add shrimp shells and cook, stirring frequently, 5 minutes. Add broth, wine, and water; heat to boiling. Reduce heat; cover and simmer 15 minutes. Strain broth mixture through sieve into bowl, pressing on shells with spoon to extract any remaining liquid. Discard shells.

2. In same clean Dutch oven, melt remaining 2 tablespoons butter over medium-high heat. Add shrimp and cook until opaque throughout, about 3 minutes. With slotted spoon, transfer shrimp to separate bowl. Add onion, carrots, and celery to Dutch oven and cook until celery is tender, about 10 minutes. Add shrimp broth, rice, bay leaf, salt, and ground red pepper; heat to boiling over high heat. Reduce heat; cover and simmer until rice is tender, about 20 minutes. Add tomatoes with their juice and cook 10 minutes longer. Remove from heat and discard bay leaf. Stir in shrimp.

3. Spoon one-fourth of shrimp mixture into blender; cover, with center part of cover removed to let steam escape, and puree until very smooth. Pour puree into bowl. Repeat with remaining mixture.

4. Return puree to Dutch oven; stir in half-and-half and brandy. Heat through over medium heat (do not boil). Makes about 10 cups or 10 first-course servings.

Each serving: About 149 calories, 10g protein, 9g carbohydrate, 7g total fat (4g saturated), 74mg cholesterol, 667mg sodium.

Oyster-Corn Chowder

Serve this quintessential oyster soup as the prelude to your family's Thanksgiving feast.

Prep: 15 minutes   Cook: 15 minutes

1	pint shucked oysters (2 dozen), with their liquid
1	pound all-purpose potatoes (3 medium), peeled and cut into ¼-inch pieces
2	bottles (8 ounces each) clam juice
1	cup half-and-half or light cream
1	can (15 to 16 ounces) whole-kernel corn, drained
2	cups milk
¼	teaspoon coarsely ground black pepper
	chopped fresh chives or parsley
1	teaspoon salt

1. Drain oysters, reserving ⅔ cup oyster liquid. (If necessary, add enough *water* to equal ⅔ cup.)

2. In 4-quart saucepan, combine potatoes, clam juice, and oyster liquid; heat to boiling over high heat. Reduce heat; cover and simmer until potatoes are tender, about 10 minutes. Remove from heat.

3. With slotted spoon, remove 1 cup potatoes. In blender, puree potatoes with half-and-half until smooth.

4. Return puree to saucepan; stir in corn, milk, and pepper. Heat mixture just to boiling over medium-high heat. Add oysters and cook, stirring frequently, until oyster edges curl and centers are firm, about 5 minutes. Sprinkle with chives or parsley. Taste for seasoning; add salt as needed. Makes about 9 cups or 8 first-course servings.

Each serving: About 194 calories, 10g protein, 23g carbohydrate, 7g total fat (4g saturated), 54mg cholesterol, 616mg sodium.

Billi-Bi

Supposedly this soup was created by a French chef for a customer who wanted mussel soup without any mussels in it. Nowadays, Billi-Bi is often made with the addition of whole mussels.

Prep: 20 minutes plus cooling   Cook: 20 minutes

2	pounds mussels, scrubbed and debearded (page 291)
1	large onion (12 ounces), thinly sliced
1	cup dry white wine
1	cup water
5	sprigs plus 1 tablespoon chopped fresh parsley
	pinch dried thyme
2	tablespoons all-purpose flour
½	cup heavy or whipping cream
	pinch ground red pepper
	salt (optional)

1. In nonreactive 5-quart Dutch oven, combine mussels, onion, wine, water, parsley sprigs, and thyme. Cover and heat to boiling over high heat. Reduce heat to medium; cook until mussels open, about 5 minutes, transferring mussels with slotted spoon to bowl as they open. Discard any mussels that have not opened.

2. When cool enough to handle, remove mussels from shells and discard shells. Strain mussel broth through sieve lined with paper towels into nonreactive 3-quart saucepan.

3. Heat mussel broth to boiling over high heat. In cup, with wire whisk, mix flour into cream until smooth; gradually whisk into broth and heat to boiling, whisking. Add ground red pepper; reduce heat and simmer, whisking occasionally, 2 minutes. Stir in mussels and heat through; do not overcook, or mussels will become tough. Taste for seasoning; add salt if necessary. Stir in chopped parsley. Makes about 3⅓ cups or 4 first-course servings.

Each serving without salt: About 236 calories, 10g protein, 12g carbohydrate, 13g total fat (7g saturated), 59mg cholesterol, 205mg sodium.

Greek-Style Lemon Soup

Called avgolemono *in Greece, this chicken and lemon soup is thickened slightly with eggs and rice. It is best when freshly made; the eggs may curdle if reheated.*

Prep: 15 minutes   Cook: 50 minutes

1	large skinless, boneless chicken breast half (6 ounces)
1	small onion, peeled and studded with 2 whole cloves
1	carrot, peeled and cut into 2-inch pieces
1	stalk celery, cut into 2-inch pieces
2	cans (14½ ounces each) chicken broth or 3½ cups Chicken Broth (page 84)
2½	cups water
⅔	cup regular long-grain rice
3	large eggs
⅓	cup fresh lemon juice (about 2 large lemons)
1	tablespoon butter or margarine, cut into pieces

1. In nonreactive 3-quart saucepan, combine chicken, onion, carrot, celery, broth, and water; heat to boiling over high heat. Reduce heat; cover and simmer 10 minutes.

2. With slotted spoon, remove chicken and vegetables from saucepan; discard vegetables. When cool enough to handle, shred chicken into thin strips.

3. Meanwhile, add rice to simmering broth; heat to boiling over high heat. Reduce heat; cover and simmer until rice is tender, 15 to 20 minutes.

4. In large bowl, with wire whisk, mix eggs and lemon juice until combined.

5. Slowly whisk 2 cups simmering broth into bowl with egg mixture, whisking constantly. Return broth mixture to saucepan; heat just to simmering, whisking constantly, until broth has slightly thickened, about 5 minutes (do not  boil). Remove from heat and stir in shredded chicken and butter. Makes about 7 cups or 6 first-course servings.

♥ *Each serving: About 185 calories, 12g protein, 19g carbohydrate, 6g total fat (2g saturated), 128mg cholesterol, 644mg sodium.*

Chicken and Coconut Milk Soup

Now you can make one of the glories of Thai cuisine at home.

	Prep: 25 minutes Cook: 45 minutes
2	cans (14½ ounces each) low-sodium chicken broth or 3½ cups Chicken Broth (page 84)
1	tablespoon Thai green curry paste
4	garlic cloves, finely chopped
1	tablespoon minced, peeled fresh ginger
1	cup water
½	cup chopped fresh cilantro plus ½ cup loosely packed leaves
1	teaspoon coriander seeds
½	teaspoon whole black peppercorns
⅛	teaspoon cumin seeds
1	cup well-stirred unsweetened coconut milk (not cream of coconut)
1	cup thinly sliced shallots (5 medium)
1	teaspoon brown sugar
1	small skinless, boneless chicken breast half (4 ounces), cut into 2" by ¼" strips
2	tablespoons Asian fish sauce (nam pla, page 31)
1	tablespoon fresh lime juice
1 or 2	jalapeño chiles, seeded, if desired, and minced

1. In a 5-quart Dutch oven, combine ½ cup broth, curry paste, garlic, and ginger; heat to boiling. Reduce heat; cover and simmer until ginger has softened, about 15 minutes. Add remaining 3 cups broth, water, chopped cilantro, coriander seeds, peppercorns, and cumin seeds; heat to boiling. Reduce heat; partially cover and simmer 15 minutes. Strain broth through sieve into bowl; discard solids.

2. Pour ½ cup coconut milk into same clean Dutch oven and heat to boiling. Add shallots and brown sugar; cook over medium-high heat, stirring constantly, until shallots are tender and liquid has evaporated, about 3 minutes. Reduce heat to medium; add chicken and cook, stirring frequently, until chicken loses its pink color throughout, 1 to 2 minutes.

3. Stir in strained broth, remaining ½ cup coconut milk, fish sauce, and lime juice. Cook, stirring, until heated through. Sprinkle soup with cilantro leaves and jalapeños. Makes about 7 cups or 6 first-course servings.

Each serving: About 159 calories, 8g protein, 9g carbohydrate, 10g total fat (8g saturated), 11mg cholesterol, 763mg sodium.

Vietnamese Noodle Soup

Although Vietnamese soup is traditionally served with thinly sliced beef, our variation suggests chicken. The flat, wide rice noodles (bahn pho) can be purchased in the Asian section of some grocery stores or in Asian markets.

	Prep: 20 minutes Cook: 25 minutes
4	ounces flat dried rice noodles or linguine
3	green onions, thinly sliced on diagonal
2	garlic cloves, peeled
6	basil sprigs
6	sprigs plus 2 tablespoons chopped fresh cilantro
4	cans (14½ ounces each) low-sodium chicken broth or 7 cups Chicken Broth (page 84)
1	teaspoon coriander seeds
1	cinnamon stick (3 inches)
2	large skinless, boneless chicken breast halves (1 pound)
4	medium mushrooms, trimmed and sliced
	mint sprigs
	lime wedges (optional)

1. In large bowl, soak rice noodles in enough *warm water* to cover 20 minutes, or cook linguine as label directs. Drain.

2. Meanwhile, in 3-quart saucepan, combine one-third of green onions, garlic, basil and cilantro sprigs, broth, coriander seeds, and cinnamon stick; heat to boiling over high heat. Reduce heat; cover and simmer 10 minutes. Strain through sieve set over bowl; discard solids. Return broth to saucepan.

3. Cut chicken breast halves on diagonal into thin strips. Stir chicken, drained noodles, mushrooms, and remaining green onions into broth; heat to boiling over high heat. Reduce heat; cover and simmer until chicken loses its pink color throughout, about 3 minutes. Sprinkle with chopped cilantro and top with mint sprigs. Serve with lime wedges, if you like. Makes about 9 cups or 4 main-dish servings.

♥ Each serving: About 269 calories, 30g protein, 27g carbohydrate, 2g total fat (0g saturated), 66mg cholesterol, 1,107mg sodium.

Chicken Soup with Rice

For an Italian touch, add thinly sliced spinach leaves and sprinkle each serving with freshly grated Parmesan cheese.

Prep: 10 minutes plus making broth	Cook: 30 minutes

5 cups Chicken Broth (page 84)
  or 3 cans (14½ ounces each) low-sodium chicken broth
3 carrots, peeled and cut into ¼-inch pieces
1 stalk celery, cut into ¼-inch pieces
1 teaspoon salt
2 cups cooked chicken, cut into bite-size pieces
1 cup regular long-grain rice or ¾ cup small pasta shapes, such as tubettini, alphabets, stars, or orzo, cooked as label directs

1. Remove and discard fat from broth.

2. In 3-quart saucepan, combine carrots, celery, broth, and salt; heat to boiling over high heat. Reduce heat and simmer until vegetables are very tender, about 15 minutes. Stir in chicken and rice; heat through. Makes about 6½ cups or 6 first-course servings.

♥ Each serving: About 203 calories, 18g protein, 22g carbohydrate, 5g total fat (2g saturated), 44mg cholesterol, 523mg sodium.

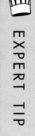

When peeling ginger, save the peel in a ziptight plastic bag in the refrigerator for up to one week or in a heavy-duty ziptight plastic bag in the freezer for up to two months. It's terrific added to homemade stock and gives instant flavor and zing to canned broth.

BARBARA TROPP
COOKBOOK AUTHOR

EXPERT TIP

South-of-the-Border Chicken Soup

This popular Latino soup is topped with ripe avocado and crisp tortilla chips.

Prep: 25 minutes	Cook: 1 hour

8 medium all-purpose potatoes (2½ pounds)
1 chicken (4 pounds), cut into 8 pieces
3 large stalks celery, each cut into thirds
3 carrots, peeled and each cut into thirds
2 medium onions, not peeled, each cut into quarters
10 cups water
10 sprigs plus ¼ cup chopped fresh cilantro
2 bay leaves
1 teaspoon whole black peppercorns
1 can (15¼ to 16 ounces) whole-kernel corn, drained
2 teaspoons salt
¼ cup fresh lime juice (about 2 large limes)
2 ripe medium avocados, cut into ½-inch pieces
  tortilla chips
  lime wedges

1. Peel 3 potatoes. In 8-quart Dutch oven, combine chicken, peeled potatoes, celery, carrots, onions, water, cilantro sprigs, bay leaves, and peppercorns; heat to boiling over high heat. Reduce heat; cover and simmer until chicken loses its pink color throughout and vegetables are tender, 35 to 45 minutes. Transfer chicken and potatoes to separate bowls.

2. Strain broth through sieve into large bowl; discard vegetables. Skim and discard fat from broth; return broth to same clean Dutch oven. Mash cooked potatoes with 1 cup broth; stir mashed-potato mixture into broth in Dutch oven.

3. Peel and chop remaining 5 potatoes. Add potatoes to broth; heat to boiling over high heat. Reduce heat; cover and simmer until potatoes are tender, about 10 minutes.

4. Meanwhile, discard skin and bones from chicken; cut chicken into bite-size pieces. Stir chicken, corn, and salt into broth; heat through.

5. Just before serving, stir lime juice and chopped cilantro into soup. Serve with avocado, tortilla chips, and lime wedges. Makes about 16 cups or 8 main-dish servings.

Each serving without garnishes: About 344 calories, 28g protein, 34g carbohydrate, 12g total fat (2g saturated), 76mg cholesterol, 772mg sodium.

South-of-the-Border Chicken Soup

Turkey Soup

What's the Friday after Thanksgiving without turkey soup? Use your favorite vegetables to personalize the recipe.

Prep: 15 minutes plus overnight to chill   Cook: 5 hours

6	carrots, peeled
3	stalks celery
	roasted turkey carcass, plus 2 cups cooked turkey meat, finely chopped
2	medium onions, each cut into quarters
5	parsley sprigs
1	garlic clove, peeled
1/4	teaspoon dried thyme
1/2	bay leaf
	about 6 quarts water
1 1/4	teaspoons salt
1	cup regular long-grain rice, cooked as label directs
2	tablespoons fresh lemon juice or 1 tablespoon dry sherry

1. Cut 2 carrots and 1 stalk celery into 2-inch pieces. In 12-quart stockpot, combine turkey carcass, carrot and celery pieces, onions, parsley sprigs, garlic, thyme, bay leaf, and 6 quarts water or enough water to cover; heat to boiling over high heat. Skim foam from surface. Reduce heat and simmer, skimming occasionally, 4 hours.

2. Strain broth through colander set over large bowl; discard solids. Strain again through sieve into several containers; cool. Cover and refrigerate overnight.

3. Remove and discard fat from surface of broth; measure broth and pour into 5-quart saucepot. If necessary, boil broth over high heat until reduced to 10 cups to concentrate flavor. Cut remaining 4 carrots and remaining 2 stalks celery into 1/2-inch pieces; add to broth with salt. Heat soup to boiling. Reduce heat and simmer until vegetables are tender, about 15 minutes. Stir in cooked rice and turkey; heat through, about 5 minutes. Remove from heat and stir in lemon juice. Makes about 13 cups or 12 first-course servings.

♥ Each serving: About 113 calories, 10g protein, 12g carbohydrate, 2g total fat (1g saturated), 21mg cholesterol, 355mg sodium.

Hearty Borscht

Beets, beef, and plenty of vegetables make a robust borscht.

Prep: 45 minutes   Cook: 2 hours 15 minutes

1	pound lean boneless beef chuck, trimmed and cut into 3/4-inch pieces
2	tablespoons vegetable oil
1	large onion (12 ounces), chopped
2	garlic cloves, finely chopped
1	cinnamon stick (3 inches)
1/2	teaspoon ground allspice
1	can (14 to 16 ounces) tomatoes
2	bunches beets with tops (1 pound), trimmed, peeled, and coarsely shredded
1	small bulb celery root (celeriac; 8 ounces), peeled and coarsely shredded
4	cups water
2	cans (14 1/2 ounces each) beef broth or 3 1/2 cups Brown Beef Stock (page 83)
1	bay leaf
1 1/2	teaspoons salt
1	small head green cabbage (1 pound), cored and chopped
3	large carrots, peeled and cut into 1/2-inch pieces
12	ounces all-purpose potatoes (2 medium), peeled and cut into 1/2-inch pieces
10	ounces parsnips (2 medium), peeled and cut into 1/2-inch pieces
1/4	cup red wine vinegar
	sour cream (optional)
1/3	cup chopped fresh dill or parsley

1. Pat beef dry with paper towels. In nonreactive 8-quart saucepot, heat 1 tablespoon oil over medium-high heat until very hot. Add half of beef and cook until well browned, using slotted spoon to transfer meat to bowl as it is browned. Repeat with remaining 1 tablespoon oil and remaining beef.

2. Reduce heat to medium. Add onion to saucepot and cook, stirring occasionally, until tender and golden, about 10 minutes. Add garlic, cinnamon stick, and allspice; cook 30 seconds. Add tomatoes with their juice and cook 5 minutes, breaking up tomatoes with side of spoon.

3. Return beef to saucepot. Stir in beets, celery root, water, broth, bay leaf, and salt; heat to boiling over high heat. Reduce heat; cover and simmer 1 hour.

4. Stir in cabbage, carrots, potatoes, and parsnips; heat to boiling over high heat. Reduce heat; cover and simmer until vegetables and beef are tender, about 30 minutes. Stir in vinegar; remove from heat. Discard cinnamon stick and bay leaf.

5. Spoon into bowls. Top with dollops of sour cream, if you like, and sprinkle with dill. Makes about 15 cups or 7 main-dish servings.

Each serving: About 279 calories, 18g protein, 32g carbohydrate, 10g total fat (3g saturated), 44mg cholesterol, 1,139mg sodium.

Beef-Vegetable Soup

An old-fashioned soup to feed a crowd. It can be made a day ahead, but for the most vibrant color, stir in the peas just before serving. You'll have plenty of soup here—the leftovers freeze well.

Prep: 30 minutes plus soaking beans	Cook: 1 hour 45 minutes
1	tablespoon vegetable oil
2	pounds bone-in beef shank cross cuts, each 2 inches thick, trimmed
2	medium onions, chopped
3	garlic cloves, finely chopped
1/8	teaspoon ground cloves
4	large carrots, peeled and chopped
2	stalks celery, chopped
1/2	small head green cabbage (8 ounces), cored and chopped (5 cups)
4	cups water
1	can (14½ ounces) beef broth or 1¾ cups Brown Beef Stock (page 83)
2	teaspoons salt
1/2	teaspoon dried thyme
1/2	teaspoon ground black pepper
8	ounces dry large lima beans (1¼ cups), soaked and drained (page 372)
1	pound all-purpose potatoes (3 medium), peeled and cut into 1-inch pieces
1	can (14 to 16 ounces) tomatoes, chopped
1	cup frozen whole-kernel corn
1	cup frozen peas
1/4	cup chopped fresh parsley

1. In nonreactive 8-quart saucepot, heat oil over medium-high heat until very hot. Add beef, in batches, and cook until well browned, transferring meat to bowl as it is browned. Reduce heat to medium; add onions and cook, stirring, until tender, about 5 minutes. Stir in garlic and cloves and cook 30 seconds. Return beef to saucepot; add carrots, celery, cabbage, water, broth; salt, thyme, and pepper; heat to boiling. Reduce heat; cover and simmer until beef is tender, about 1 hour.

2. Meanwhile, in 4-quart saucepan, combine beans and enough *water to cover by 2 inches;* heat to boiling over high heat. Reduce heat; cover and simmer until beans are just tender, about 30 minutes; drain.

3. Add potatoes and beans to saucepot; heat to boiling. Cover and simmer 5 minutes. Stir in tomatoes with their juice; cover and simmer until potatoes are tender, about 10 minutes longer.

4. With slotted spoon, transfer beef to cutting board. Cut beef into ½-inch pieces, discarding bones and gristle. Return beef to saucepot and add frozen corn and peas; heat through. Spoon into bowls and sprinkle with parsley. Makes about 15½ cups or 8 main-dish servings.

Each serving: About 278 calories, 24g protein, 35g carbohydrate, 6g total fat (1g saturated), 30mg cholesterol, 955mg sodium.

Soup can be informally served in mugs. Cut all the ingredients into small pieces so the soup can be eaten without a spoon.

BARBARA KAFKA
COOKBOOK AUTHOR

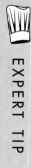

EXPERT TIP

Pasta e Fagioli with Sausage

Pasta e fagioli, Italian pasta and bean soup, becomes a meal-in-a-pot with the addition of sweet sausage and fresh spinach.

| Prep: 15 minutes plus soaking beans | Cook: 1 hour 45 minutes |

1½ cups dry Great Northern beans,
    soaked and drained (page 372)

1   pound sweet Italian-sausage links, casings removed

1   tablespoon olive oil

2   medium onions, chopped

2   garlic cloves, crushed with garlic press

1   can (28 ounces) plum tomatoes

2   cans (14½ ounces each) chicken broth
    or 3½ cups Chicken Broth (page 84)

2   cups water

½   teaspoon salt

6   ounces ditalini or tubetti pasta (1 rounded cup)

5   ounces spinach, washed and dried very well,
    tough stems trimmed, and leaves cut into 1-inch-wide strips
    freshly grated Parmesan cheese (optional)

Pasta e Fagioli with Sausage

1. In 4-quart saucepan, combine beans and enough *water to cover by 2 inches*; heat to boiling over high heat. Reduce heat; cover and simmer, stirring occasionally, until beans are tender, 40 minutes to 1 hour. Drain; set aside.

2. Meanwhile, heat nonreactive 5-quart Dutch oven over medium-high heat until very hot. Add sausage and cook until well browned, breaking up sausage with side of spoon. Transfer sausage to bowl.

3. Reduce heat to medium; add oil to Dutch oven. Add onions and cook until tender and golden, about 10 minutes. Add garlic; cook 1 minute. Add tomatoes with their juice, breaking them up with side of spoon.

4. Add beans, broth, water, and salt; heat to boiling over high heat. Reduce heat; cover and simmer 30 minutes. Add sausage and heat through.

5. Meanwhile, in clean 4-quart saucepan, cook pasta as label directs, but do not add salt to water; drain.

6. Just before serving, stir spinach and cooked pasta into soup. Serve with Parmesan, if you like. Makes about 16 cups or 8 main-dish servings.

Each serving: About 460 calories, 21g protein, 47g carbohydrate, 21g total fat (7g saturated), 43mg cholesterol, 1,171mg sodium

Pasta e Fagioli with Canned Beans

Substitute **3 cans (15 to 19 ounces each) Great Northern or white kidney (cannellini) beans,** rinsed and drained, for dry beans and omit Step 1. Continue as directed but in Step 4 omit salt, adding only broth and water. Cover and simmer 15 minutes, then add canned beans. Heat to boiling; cover and simmer 15 minutes longer. Add sausage and heat through. Continue as directed.

Vegetable Broth

This broth is delicious, nutritious, and great in soups, risottos, and sauces. The optional fennel and parsnip lend a natural sweetness and an additional depth of flavor. For an Asian-flavored broth, add minced lemongrass, minced fresh ginger, or chopped fresh cilantro.

	Prep: 25 minutes Cook: 2 hours
4	large leeks
2 to 4	garlic cloves, not peeled
13	cups water
	salt
1	large all-purpose potato, peeled, cut lengthwise in half, and thinly sliced
1	small fennel bulb, trimmed and chopped (optional)
3	parsnips, peeled and thinly sliced (optional)
2	large carrots, peeled and thinly sliced
3	stalks celery with leaves, thinly sliced
4	ounces mushrooms, trimmed and thinly sliced
10	parsley sprigs
4	thyme sprigs
2	bay leaves
1	teaspoon whole black peppercorns
	ground black pepper

1. Cut off roots and trim dark green tops from leeks; thinly slice leeks. Rinse leeks in large bowl of cold water, swishing to remove sand; transfer to colander to drain, leaving sand in bottom of bowl.

2. In 6-quart saucepot, combine leeks, garlic, 1 cup water, and pinch salt; heat to boiling. Reduce heat to medium; cover and cook until leeks are tender, about 15 minutes.

3. Add potato, fennel if using, parsnips if using, carrots, celery, mushrooms, parsley and thyme sprigs, bay leaves, peppercorns, and remaining 12 cups water. Heat to boiling; reduce heat and simmer, uncovered, at least 1 hour 30 minutes.

4. Taste and continue cooking if flavor is not concentrated enough. Season with salt and pepper to taste. Strain broth through fine-mesh sieve into containers, pressing on solids with back of wooden spoon to extract liquid; cool. Cover and refrigerate to use within 3 days, or freeze up to 4 months. Makes about 6 cups.

♥ Each cup: About 19 calories, 1g protein, 4g carbohydrate, 0g total fat (0g saturated), 0mg cholesterol, 9mg sodium.

Brown Beef Stock

For a richer, meatier flavor, use four pounds of beef bones and one pound of oxtails.

	Prep: 5 minutes Cook: 7 hours 30 minutes
5	pounds beef bones, cut into 3-inch pieces
2	medium onions, each cut in half
3	carrots, peeled and each cut in half
2	stalks celery, each cut in half
13	cups water
1	small bunch parsley
1	bay leaf
½	teaspoon dried thyme

1. Preheat oven to 450°F. Spread beef bones, onions, carrots, and celery in large roasting pan (17½" by 11½"). Roast, stirring every 15 minutes, until well browned, about 1 hour.

2. With tongs, transfer browned bones and vegetables to 6-quart saucepot. Carefully pour off fat from roasting pan. Add 1 cup water to roasting pan and heat to boiling, stirring until browned bits are loosened from bottom of pan; add to pot. Add remaining 12 cups water, parsley, bay leaf, and thyme to pot. Heat to boiling over high heat, skimming foam from surface. Reduce heat and simmer, skimming foam occasionally, 6 hours.

3. Strain broth through colander into large bowl; discard solids. Strain again through fine-mesh sieve into containers. Cool. Cover and refrigerate to use within 3 days, or freeze up to 4 months.

4. To use, skim and discard fat from surface of stock. Makes about 5 cups.

♥ Each cup: About 39 calories, 5g protein, 5g carbohydrate, 0g total fat (0g saturated), 0mg cholesterol, 73mg sodium.

Chicken Broth

Nothing beats the flavor of homemade chicken broth. Make it in large batches and freeze in sturdy containers for up to three months. Our recipe has an added bonus: The cooked chicken can be used in casseroles and salads.

Prep: 10 minutes plus cooling	*Cook: 4 hours 30 minutes*
1	chicken (3 to 3½ pounds), including neck (giblets reserved for another use)
2	carrots, peeled and cut into 2-inch pieces
1	stalk celery, cut into 2-inch pieces
1	medium onion, cut into quarters
5	parsley sprigs
1	garlic clove
½	teaspoon dried thyme
½	bay leaf
	about 3 quarts water

1. In 6-quart saucepot, combine chicken, chicken neck, carrots, celery, onion, parsley, garlic, thyme, bay leaf, and 3 quarts water or enough water to cover; heat to boiling over high heat. Skim foam from surface. Reduce heat and simmer 1 hour, turning chicken once and skimming.

2. Remove from heat; transfer chicken to large bowl. When cool enough to handle, remove skin and bones from chicken. (Reserve chicken for another use.) Return skin and bones to Dutch oven and heat to boiling. Skim foam; reduce heat and simmer 3 hours.

3. Strain broth through colander into large bowl; discard solids. Strain again through sieve into containers; cool. Cover and refrigerate to use within 3 days, or freeze up to 4 months.

4. To use, skim and discard fat from surface of broth. Makes about 5 cups.

♥ Each cup: About 36 calories, 3g protein, 4g carbohydrate, 1g total fat (1g saturated), 3mg cholesterol, 91mg sodium.

Pressure Cooker Chicken Broth

In 6-quart pressure cooker, place all ingredients for Chicken Broth but use only **4 cups water.** Following manufacturer's directions, cover pressure cooker and bring up to high pressure (15 pounds). Cook 15 minutes. Remove cooker from heat and allow pressure to drop 5 minutes, then follow manufacturer's directions for quick release of pressure. Strain broth through colander into large bowl; discard solids. Strain again through sieve into containers; cool. Meanwhile, remove skin and bones from chicken; discard. (Reserve chicken for another use.) Cover broth and refrigerate to use within 3 days, or freeze up to 4 months. To use, skim and discard fat from surface of broth. Makes about 5½ cups or 6 first-course servings.

Peachy Melon Soup

Be sure to use the ripest, most fragrant melon you can find. The soup is also scrumptious garnished with slivers of prosciutto.

	Prep: 15 minutes plus chilling
1	large cantaloupe (2½ pounds), chilled
1	cup peach or apricot nectar
1	tablespoon fresh lime juice
	lime slices

1. Cut cantaloupe in half. Scoop out and discard seeds. Cut away rind, then cut cantaloupe into bite-size pieces.

2. In blender, puree cantaloupe, peach nectar, and lime juice until smooth. Increase speed to high; blend 1 minute. If not serving right away, pour soup into bowl and refrigerate. To serve, garnish with lime slices. Makes 5 first-course or dessert servings.

♥ Each serving: About 67 calories, 1g protein, 17g carbohydrate, 0g total fat, 0mg cholesterol, 14mg sodium.

Tart Cherry Soup

When the weather turns hot, offer this refreshing chilled soup for dessert, as a first course, or for a light lunch. Tart cherries, also called pie cherries, are available frozen and canned. In season, use two pounds of pitted fresh tart cherries instead.

Prep: 5 minutes plus standing and chilling   Cook: 15 minutes

2½	cups riesling or other semidry white wine
2	cans (16 ounces each) or 1 jar (32 ounces) pitted tart (sour) cherries, drained, liquid reserved
⅓	cup sugar
1½	teaspoons quick-cooking tapioca
6	strips (3" by ½" each) orange peel
1	cinnamon stick (3 inches)
1	vanilla bean, split, or ½ teaspoon vanilla extract
6	whole allspice berries
6	whole black peppercorns
½	cup sour cream

1. In nonreactive 2-quart saucepan, combine wine, ⅓ cup reserved cherry liquid, sugar, tapioca, orange peel, cinnamon stick, vanilla bean, allspice berries, and peppercorns. Heat to boiling over medium heat. Reduce heat; cover and simmer 7 minutes. Remove from heat and let stand 20 minutes. Strain through fine-mesh sieve set over bowl, pressing with back of spoon to push tapioca through; discard spices and peel. (You can rinse vanilla bean, let it dry, and use it to flavor sugar in a canister.) Add vanilla extract, if using.

2. Stir in cherries. Transfer soup to blender and puree until smooth. Pour soup into bowl and, with wire whisk, mix in sour cream until smooth. Cover and refrigerate about 4 hours or until cold. Makes 4 first-course servings.

♥ Each serving: About 317 calories, 3g protein, 41g carbohydrate, 6g total fat (4g saturated), 13mg cholesterol, 45mg sodium.

Pear and Red Wine Soup

Serve this chilled soup before a hearty main course. As with all fruit soups, make it with fully ripened fruit at its peak of flavor.

Prep: 10 minutes plus chilling   Cook: 20 to 25 minutes

1	cup dry red wine
1	cup water
½	cup sugar
1	lemon
1½	pounds ripe pears, peeled, cored, and cut into quarters

1. In nonreactive 2-quart saucepan, combine wine, water, and sugar; heat to boiling over high heat, stirring frequently, until sugar has dissolved.

2. Meanwhile, with vegetable peeler, from lemon, remove two 3-inch strips peel; squeeze 1 tablespoon juice.

3. Add pears and lemon peel to saucepan; heat to boiling over high heat. Reduce heat and simmer until pears are very tender, 10 to 15 minutes.

4. Spoon one-fourth of pear mixture into blender. Cover, with center part of cover removed to let steam escape, and puree until smooth. Pour puree into bowl. Repeat with remaining mixture. Stir in lemon juice. Cover soup and refrigerate at least 4 hours or until very cold. Makes about 3½ cups or 4 first-course servings.

♥ Each serving: About 234 calories, 1g protein, 50g carbohydrate, 1g total fat (0g saturated), 0mg cholesterol, 3mg sodium.

Use chicken stock in place of some or all of the oil in a salad dressing or substitute for some or all of the cream in an au gratin potato dish.

STEVEN RAICHLEN
COOKBOOK AUTHOR

EXPERT TIP

MEAT

Meat is the major source of protein in the American diet, so it is important to know how to choose it and cook it properly. It is true that chicken, fish, and vegetable main courses are served more frequently now than in the past, but we are still a nation of meat eaters. And while beef, lamb, pork, and veal all have different flavors, they are prepared in similar ways. No matter what kind of meat you cook, however, remember that it is usually the cut that dictates the cooking method.

BUYING MEAT

All meat in the U.S. is inspected by the United States Department of Agriculture to ensure that it is safe to eat and free of disease, although some diseases, such as *E. coli* and salmonella, cannot be detected by the naked eye.

Grading, unlike inspection, is a voluntary procedure, and the grade given to any particular piece of meat reflects its tenderness. In other words, the higher the grade, the more tender the meat. There are different criteria for grading beef, lamb, and veal. In general, meat is graded according to age (the older the animal, the tougher the flesh) and the amount of marbling (streaks or flecks of fat within the flesh). The internal fat melts during the cooking process, moistening and flavoring the meat. The external fat that surrounds meat, such

Herb-Crusted Rib Roast

as chops or steaks, can be trimmed away, reducing the amount of fat consumed.

The meat available to consumers is graded prime, choice, and select or good. Lesser grades, such as standard, commercial, utility, cutter, and canner are processed into such products as canned meats, soups, hot dogs, and dog food. Beef has the largest number of grading levels because the degree of tenderness varies so much from cut to cut. Lamb is also graded but veal only occasionally. Pork is rarely graded because only the highest grade is sold to consumers. If a meat label contains a term you are unfamiliar with, ask the butcher for its equivalent USDA grade. Prime meat is found only at the best butchers. Even then, some cuts may have to be ordered ahead of time. One good bit of advice: Always buy the highest grade of meat you can afford.

Because the cut of meat is directly related to its tenderness, it helps to understand the primal cuts. These cuts are the large sections of the carcass that are sold to wholesalers, which in turn are sold to retail butchers. The butcher then separates each primal cut into steaks, chops, roasts, and so on. While the primal cuts for beef, veal, lamb, and pork are somewhat different, there are similarities. In general, the less exercise a muscle gets, the tenderer it will be. Muscles along the back (the rib, loin, and sirloin) are the tenderest. Cuts from the arm or leg (the round, chuck, rump, and ham) and the underside (the flank, brisket, and belly) are tougher. These tougher cuts also have a high proportion of chewy tendons, gristle, and sinew, which are mainly collagen, a protein that softens with slow, moist cooking.

Beyond USDA inspections and voluntary grading, a consumer has other choices when buying meat. Some are based on religious considerations. *Kosher* meat is processed according to Jewish dietary laws. Only certain cuts of meat from certain animals can be consumed, and the animal must be specially bled. The kosher stamp is a guarantee of freshness, since the meat must be eaten within seventy-two hours of slaughter. Because it is not aged, however, kosher meat is not especially tender or flavorful. Muslim communities have *Halal* butchers, who butcher beef, goat, and lamb (never pork) according to Islamic law, which determines how the animal is killed and how the carcass is bled. Halal meat is no more than two days old and is never frozen.

Some consumers are understandably concerned about the possibility of residual chemicals or drugs in their meat and prefer meat raised in a manner that supports the environment. The USDA regularly tests for chemical and drug contamination, and it reports that violations are rare. Health food stores and some supermarkets sell meat labeled *natural* or *organic*. Natural meat has been processed without artificial color, flavor, or preservatives. Under this definition, however, just about any fresh meat is natural. The term *organic* is not recognized by the USDA, but some states, such as California, have passed laws that define organic meat as that from animals raised without antibiotics, pesticides, or steroids and in a way that will minimally affect the environment. And though they are not regulated by law, national organic food associations exist, and many producers follow their standards, as indicated by an association stamp on meat packaging.

When shopping, look for evenly colored meat with creamy white fat. When buying chops or steaks, make sure the external fat has been well trimmed. Also check that the bones are cut cleanly with no obvious splintering. Keep in mind that vacuum-packed meat has a longer shelf life, and always note the sell-by date on the label.

If a recipe calls for a cut to be prepared in an unfamiliar manner, such as butterflied, boned, or frenched, just ask the butcher to do it for you. But because supermarket butchers are often less skilled than private butchers, it is worth your while to find the best butcher in your area for any special needs.

As for how much to serve, for boneless cuts and ground meat, figure on 4 to 5 ounces per serving. For cuts with some bone, such as chops, allow 5 to 8 ounces, and for bony cuts, such as ribs, allow 12 to 16 ounces per serving.

In supermarkets, you will also find a large selection of cured beef and pork products, from sausages and hams to cold cuts. During the curing process, the meat is salted, which draws out the juices that would otherwise cause it to spoil. Salt also inhibits bacteria growth and seasons the meat.

STORING MEAT

Store raw meat in the coldest part of the refrigerator (usually the bottom shelf), away from cooked and ready-to-eat foods. Place the meat on a plate or tray to catch any drips. Refrigerate uncooked meats up to two days or freeze up to six months. Ground meat can be refrigerated for one or two days or frozen for up to three months. Veal cutlets and variety meats, such as the kidneys, brains, and thymus gland (sweetbreads), should be used on the day of purchase.

For short-term storage (for up to two days in the refrigerator or up to two weeks in the freezer), leave the raw meat in its original wrapping. For longer freezing, or if the wrapping is torn, carefully rewrap the meat in freezer wrap or heavy-duty foil, pressing out all the air. Stack steaks, chops, and patties between sheets of freezer paper before wrapping. Label each package with the name of the cut, the number of servings, and the date.

Thaw frozen meat, on a plate to catch drips, overnight in the refrigerator—never at room temperature. Do not refreeze uncooked meat, or the texture will suffer. And for the best results, do not freeze meat, raw or cooked, for longer than three months. Large roasts, however, can be frozen for up to one year.

COOKING TECHNIQUES

The USDA recommends that all meat be cooked to well-done (160°F) to kill any bacteria that could cause illness. We sometimes recommend cooking temperatures that are below this figure because some meat tastes best cooked medium-rare or medium. Food-borne illnesses are relatively rare and usually only affect infants, the elderly, or people with weak immune systems. The degree to which you cook meat is a matter of personal taste, but also keep in mind who you are cooking for.

Tender cuts are usually cooked by dry-heat cooking methods, such as grilling, sautéing, or roasting. Tough cuts are best prepared by moist-heat methods, such as stewing or braising, where long, slow, moist cooking tenderizes muscles that would not be softened by dry-heat cooking.

Roasting

There is only one way to guarantee that meat is roasted to the desired doneness: Use a meat thermometer. Insert the thermometer into the center or thickest part of the roast without touching any bones or fatty sections, since they are heat conductors and would give an inaccurate reading. If you use an instant-read thermometer, which gives a fast reading, be sure to remove it from the meat once you get a reading.

Most roasts are tied to help them keep their shape during roasting. Tying is not necessary with bone-in rib or loin roasts, but boned meat needs to be tied to hold the meat together. Boneless cuts, such as beef tenderloin, are tied to give them a neat shape. When roasting boneless cuts, you may want to place the meat on a rack in the roasting pan. That way, the heat can circulate under the meat and prevent it from simmering in its juices. Not all boneless roasts need to be cooked on racks, however. Tenderloin and some loin roasts cook so quickly they don't have time to create juices. Rib roasts and other bone-in cuts come with their own natural built-in racks.

Remove a roast from the oven when it reaches 5° to 10°F less than the desired temperature: The temperature will continue to rise as the meat stands. Do not cover the meat. The density of the hot roast will keep it from cooling too quickly, and a foil cover would trap the steam and soften the roast's delicious crusty exterior.

Panfrying and Sautéing

These fastest of cooking methods yield quick, tasty results. The browned bits that accumulate in the bottom of the skillet and are often used to create flavorful pan sauces in minutes.

Before sautéing, pat the meat dry with paper towels so it can brown easily. Use a heavy-bottomed skillet so the heat is conducted evenly. A nonstick skillet is not necessary. In fact, its slick surface will inhibit the formation of a good crust. Do not crowd the meat in the pan, or it will steam, hindering the browning process. Cook the meat over medium-high to high heat to sear it. If the meat begins to burn, simply reduce the heat a bit. This searing process adds great flavor to the meat.

Braising and Stewing

Few dishes satisfy as much as a long-simmered stew or braised pot roast, heady with fragrant herbs and brimming with chunky vegetables. Be patient when simmering tough meat cuts: They need lots of time to become tender. The key word here is "simmering." Do not allow the cooking liquid to boil, or the meat will dry out and toughen.

Use a heavy-bottomed pan with a tight-fitting lid to prevent scorching and to keep in the steam. Braises and stews can be cooked over medium-low heat on top of the stove (use a flame diffuser if necessary, to keep the liquid at a simmer, and stir occasionally to discourage scorching) or in a 325°F oven. To test the meat for doneness, pierce it with a fork; the fork should slip in and out easily.

If you are making a stew, cut the meat into cubes of equal size so they cook in the same amount of time, and pat them dry with paper towels before browning. Many stews taste even better when cooked a day ahead and refrigerated overnight to allow the flavors to meld. Scrape off and discard any hardened surface fat before reheating. If the recipe includes fragile vegetables like peas, you may want to add them to the stew during the last few minutes of reheating to avoid overcooking. Taste the stew and season again, if needed, just before serving.

Broiling and Grilling

Is there any sound more appetizing than the sizzle of steaks or chops on the grill? Not only is grilling outdoors fun, but it guarantees incomparable smoky flavor. You can get similar results from indoor broiling, but without the lovely infusion of smoke. So when broiling indoors, use a flavorful marinade or dry rub to add lots of flavor.

In either case, allow enough time for the heat source to preheat and reach the proper temperature. On an outdoor grill, the coals should burn until covered with a thin layer of gray ash (this is referred to as being *ashed over*). This will take twenty to thirty minutes. Coals are at their hottest as soon as they become covered with ash; they cool down as they burn.

Preheat a gas grill or broiler on high for about ten minutes. Stoves with separate broiling units have adjustable broiler racks that allow them to be positioned as close to or as far away from the heating element as desired. Electric ovens that double as broilers are problematic. There is usually only one upper rack position that is close to the heating element, but it is sometimes farther away than the ideal distance. This makes preheating especially important.

Thin cuts should be quickly grilled or broiled. Avoid piercing the meat, which would release the flavorful juices, and when possible, use tongs rather than a fork to turn the meat. On an outdoor grill, put the meat on the cooking rack just as soon as the coals are ready. You should be able to hold your hand at the cooking grid level for one or two seconds. For indoor broiling, the ideal position for most meats is about six inches from the heat source. To prevent flare-ups, do not line the rack with foil. The fat must be able to drip through the rack. If you like, however, line the broiler pan with foil.

Grilled meat should have a nicely browned crust, but avoid charring: It creates carbon, a known carcinogen. It may not seem like a problem, but now that gas grills have made grilling a year-round activity, it is easier than you think to consume large amounts of charred meat.

CARVING

Steaks and roasts benefit from a resting period before serving. This allows the juices to be redistributed throughout the meat, enriching the flavor and firming the meat for easier carving. Steaks should be transferred to a warm platter to keep them from cooling off, but they only need to stand for a minute or two before being served. Average-size roasts (about three pounds) should stand for ten minutes, and larger roasts for up to fifteen minutes.

For safety's sake, it's a good idea to place a towel under the cutting board to prevent it from slipping. Always carve with a sharp thin-bladed knife and use a two-tine meat fork to steady the roast. Carve across the grain, not parallel to the fibers of the meat: This produces shorter fibers, making the meat more tender.

FOOD SAFETY

When handling any raw meat, keep it well separated from other ingredients until ready to combine. If the meat comes in contact with the work surface, the surface should be thoroughly washed, along with your hands, knives, and any other utensils, in hot soapy water.

Do not allow raw meat to stand at room temperature longer than one hour. Some cookbooks suggest letting meat stand out until it reaches room temperature so the meat will roast more evenly. We don't agree, and all of our recipes are cooked with refrigerator-temperature meat. If you are serving

GAME

Not too long ago, the only way to obtain game was to know a hunter. Now, many varieties of game are raised on farms and supplied to upscale supermarkets and fine butchers. Farm raised game is full of flavor, but it is leaner than traditional farmed meats like beef. Be careful not to overcook it, or it will dry out. Tougher cuts, like stew meat, can be long-simmered. While not absolutely necessary, game often benefits from a soak in a marinade, which adds moisture and depth of flavor.

VENISON In America, most commercial venison is the Cervena variety that is imported from New Zealand. Never overcook venison, or it will be dry and tough. Steaks and chops should be cooked by dry-heat methods to no more than medium-rare doneness. Roasts are best when slow-cooked in a 325°F oven.

BUFFALO Also called bison, these huge animals are being raised in many states of the union. The tenderest cuts of buffalo meat are very expensive because most of the carcass meat is tough and only good for ground meat or stews.

BEEFALO A cross between American buffalo and domestic cattle. Both beefalo and buffalo are becoming popular with cooks who want lowfat red meat. Both can substitute for beef in recipes, but, as with venison, do not overcook.

GOAT Goat is found in ethnic markets that cater to Caribbean, Greek, and Italian cooks. It is often spit-roasted whole as a sumptuous main course for special occasions. Goat shoulder, usually cubed and bone-in, is a delicious substitute for lamb in recipes that call for braising.

cooked meat as part of a buffet, do not let it stand at room temperature longer than two hours, and keep replenishments refrigerated until ready to use.

BEEF

Beef deserves its popularity as America's favorite meat. No matter how it is cooked, whether you're enjoying a grilled steak, a juicy burger, or a savory stew, its deep, hearty flavor comes through. Our love for beef is traditional. The vast plains of the West have always provided enough grass and grain to feed huge herds of cattle. In countries without an enormous expanse of fertile land, beef remains costly.

BUYING AND STORING BEEF

Consumers demanded leaner meat and the beef industry has responded. Beef is now about 30 percent leaner than in the past, and butchers trim away much of the external fat before meat is sold. If you are looking for especially lean cuts, look for the words "round" or "loin" on the label: Top round and tenderloin are good examples.

Beef has eight primal cuts: the chuck, ribs, short loin, sirloin, round, flank, plate, and foreleg (brisket). Ground beef can be made from chuck, round, sirloin, or a combination of these cuts. Beef is graded by the USDA (page 87). There are eight grades of beef, but the average consumer only has access to three: prime, choice, and select.

Prime beef has the most marbling and is usually sold to restaurants and high-quality butchers. It is expensive but worth seeking for a special occasion. Even though we often use the term "prime rib" to describe any beef rib roast, most are not really prime grade, which makes up only about 2 percent of beef production. Choice beef has moderate marbling and represents 45 percent of all the beef sold. It is the grade found most often in supermarkets. Select beef is the least expensive. It comprises 21 percent of the graded beef sold, has the least marbling, and is often sold as a store's house brand.

ROASTING TIMES

This roasting chart gives guidelines for cooking a variety of cuts from medium-rare to well-done when cooking without a recipe. Start with meat at refrigerator temperature. Remove a roast from the oven when it reaches 5° to 10°F below desired doneness; temperature will continue to rise as it stands.

Cut	Oven Temperature	Weight	Approximate Cooking Time (minutes per pound)		
			MEDIUM-RARE (135°-140°F)	MEDIUM (145°-155°F)	WELL-DONE (OVER 160°F)
Rib roast (chine bone removed)	325°F	4 to 6 pounds	24 to 30 minutes	30 to 36 minutes	34 to 38 minutes
		6 to 8 pounds	15 to 20 minutes	22 to 26 minutes	27 to 30 minutes
Rib-eye roast	350°F	4 to 6 pounds	15 to 20 minutes	18 to 22 minutes	20 to 24 minutes
Whole tenderloin	450°F	4 to 5 pounds	40 to 60 minutes *(total time)*		
Half tenderloin	450°F	2 to 3 pounds	40 to to 50 minutes *(total time)*		
Round tip roast	325°F	3 to 4 pounds	25 to 30 minutes	30 to 35 minutes	35 to 38 minutes
		6 to 8 pounds	22 to 25 minutes	26 to 32 minutes	30 to 35 minutes
Eye round roast	325°F	2 to 3 pounds	20 to 25 minutes	25 to 30 minutes	30 to 35 minutes

Remember that grading is a voluntary procedure, and while it rates the degree of tenderness, it doesn't rate wholesomeness or sanitary conditions, although all meat is processed according to strict sanitary regulations. Lots of ungraded beef is sold to consumers. The butcher often gives this meat an ambiguous and misleading name like "butcher's choice" or "special select," terms that mean nothing except that they are neither prime nor choice. When meat is a bargain, it is usually because it hasn't been USDA graded.

Once the primal cuts have been separated into individual cuts of meat, the meat is aged to improve its texture and flavor. Traditional "dry-aging" can take up to six weeks. Dry-aged beef is generally found at fancy butcher shops and upscale restaurants, where it is stored in special refrigerators that expose the meat to the air. The surface of the meat dries out and is then trimmed away before being sold, which decreases the amount of saleable meat, making dry-aged beef quite expensive but with a flavor that justifies the price. Most supermarket meats are "wet-aged" in vacuum-sealed packages for a week or so. Sometimes larger cuts of meat, such as whole beef tenderloin, are sold in their vacuum packaging. When opened, these meats tend to have an unpleasant smell, which is due to the lack of oxygen in the package, but the odor dissipates once the meat is exposed to the air.

When buying beef, look for bright to deep red meat; any fat should be creamy white. As with all meat, color is a good indicator of quality. Cut edges should look freshly cut and moist—never wet. Vacuum-packed beef is darker and often looks more purple than red. Lastly, remember that the names of steaks and roasts often vary from state to state: A strip steak in California is known as a shell steak in New York.

COOKING BEEF

The goal of most cooks is to serve a tender piece of beef. The key is to correctly match the cut of meat to an appropriate cooking technique, although the grade and age of the beef also come into play. With the right cooking method, any cut of beef can be tender.

Broiling, Grilling, and Panfrying Lean, tender, thin cuts are best when employing these quick-cooking methods. When broiling or grilling steaks that are at least one inch thick, position them a little farther from the heat source than usual so the outside doesn't char before the steak is done.

Best Bets Porterhouse steak, T-bone steak, London broil (top round), top loin, rib-eye, sirloin steak, tenderloin, flank steak, skirt steak, cube steak, minute steak, and ground beef.

Braising and Stewing Tougher cuts of beef become deliciously tender when slowly simmered in a flavorful liquid. These cuts are less expensive, too.

Best Bets Chuck roast, brisket, short ribs, shin (shank cross cuts), and oxtails. Cubes for stew are usually cut from boneless chuck or bottom round, but chuck gives the moistest results. Bone-in cuts add flavor and body to stews.

Roasting Large, tender cuts with some internal fat make the best roasts.

Best Bets Standing rib roast, tenderloin, rib-eye, eye round, and tri-tip.

CURED BEEF

Today, cured beef is appreciated for its taste rather than as a form of meat preservation. Curing became unnecessary when refrigeration allowed fresh meat to be stored for a longer period of time without going bad. Nevertheless, because cured meat is so delicious and different tasting, the process has remained popular. Some cured meats are also smoked. Here are some of the most popular cured beef products.

CORNED BEEF Beef, usually brisket or round, is first cured in a spiced brine (or injected with brine and coated with spices), then simmered in water until tender. Because corning was the preferred method of beef preservation in Ireland, it is still the traditional meal for St. Patrick's Day.

PASTRAMI One of the glories of the delicatessen, pastrami is a cut of beef (brisket, plate, or round) that is cured with a rub of salt and spices, which can include garlic, peppercorns, red pepper flakes, cinnamon, cloves, and/or coriander. After curing, the meat is smoked, then cooked.

BRESAOLA A delicacy of Northern Italy and Switzerland, bresaola is dried, salted beef fillet that has been aged for two months. It is usually thinly sliced and served as an appetizer.

JERKY Enjoyed as a chewy snack, jerky is made from thin strips of beef that have been marinated and dried (traditionally in the sun, but now in ovens).

POPULAR BEEF CUTS

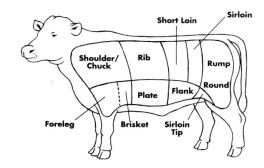

Beef rib roast small end

(roast). Also called standing rib roast.

Beef rib-eye roast

(roast). Large center muscle of rib with bones and seam fat removed.

Beef bottom round roast

(braise, roast). Also called beef bottom round pot roast; suitable for roasting if high quality.

Beef chuck shoulder pot roast, boneless

(braise). Also called boneless cross-rib pot roast.

Beef chuck 7-bone steak

(braise). Named for blade bone which resembles number 7; also called center chuck steak.

Beef chuck short ribs

(braise). Also called flanken short ribs.

Beef shank cross cuts

(braise). Crosswise cuts from foreshank or hindshank.

Beef top loin steak

(broil, grill, panfry). Also called shell, strip, New York, club, and Delmonico steak. Also available boneless.

Beef loin porterhouse steak *(broil, grill, panfry).* Includes tenderloin at least 1¼ inches in diameter.

Beef rib-eye steak

(broil, panfry). Boneless steak also called fillet or Spencer steak; cut from beef rib-eye roast. Also available bone-in.

Beef round top round steak

(broil, grill). Also known as London broil. Best when marinated.

Beef loin tenderloin roast

(roast). Cut from tenderloin muscle; very tender, boneless, with very little (or no) fat covering. Also called beef tenderloin.

Oxtails

(braise). Excellent as a rich and delicious substitute for beef stewing meat; skim fat from surface of cooking liquid before serving.

Herb-Crusted Rib Roast

(Pictured on page 86)

If you like, reserve the fat from the pan drippings to make Yorkshire Pudding (opposite), then prepare an au jus sauce. Add two cups of homemade Brown Beef Stock (page 83) to the pan drippings and bring to a boil, scraping up all the flavorful browned bits.

Prep: 15 minutes   Roast: 2 hours 30 minutes
1 (3-rib) beef rib roast from small end (5½ pounds), trimmed and chine bone removed
1 teaspoon salt
½ teaspoon dried rosemary, crumbled
¼ teaspoon ground black pepper
1 lemon
1½ cups fresh bread crumbs (about 3 slices bread)
½ cup chopped fresh parsley
2 garlic cloves, finely chopped
1 tablespoon olive oil
2 tablespoons Dijon mustard

1. Preheat oven to 325°F. In medium roasting pan (14" by 10"), place rib roast, fat side up. In small bowl, combine salt, rosemary, and pepper. Use to rub on roast.

2. Roast beef until meat thermometer inserted in thickest part of meat (not touching bone) reaches 140°F, about 2 hours 30 minutes. Internal temperature of meat will rise to 145°F (medium) upon standing. Or roast until desired degree of doneness.

3. About 1 hour before roast is done, prepare bread coating: From lemon, grate ½ teaspoon peel and squeeze 1 tablespoon juice. In small bowl, combine lemon peel and juice, bread crumbs, parsley, garlic, and oil. Remove roast from oven; evenly spread mustard on top of roast. Press breadcrumb mixture onto mustard-coated roast. Roast 1 hour longer or until desired doneness.

4. When roast is done, transfer to warm large platter and let stand 15 minutes to set juices for easier carving. Makes 8 main-dish servings.

Each serving: About 352 calories, 39g protein, 5g carbohydrate, 18g total fat (7g saturated), 112mg cholesterol, 508mg sodium.

Yorkshire Pudding

Preheat oven to 450°F. In medium bowl, with wire whisk, combine **1½ cups all-purpose flour** and **¾ teaspoon salt.** Add **1½ cups milk** and **3 large eggs,** beaten. Beat until smooth. Pour **3 tablespoons drippings** from roast beef pan into small metal baking pan (13" by 9"); bake 2 minutes. Remove pan from oven and pour batter over drippings. Bake until puffed and lightly browned, about 25 minutes. Cut into squares. Makes 8 accompaniment servings.

Each serving: About 183 calories, 6g protein, 20g carbohydrate, 8g total fat (4g saturated), 90mg cholesterol, 246mg sodium.

CARVING A RIB ROAST

The chine bone should be removed by your butcher so you can carve the roast between the rib bones. Carving will be easier and the meat will be juicier if the roast stands at least 15 minutes after you have removed it from the oven.

Place the roast, rib side down, on cutting board. With a carving knife, make a vertical cut toward the ribs, cutting a slice about ¼ inch thick.

Release the slice by cutting horizontally along the top of the rib bone. Transfer the slice to a warm platter.

Repeat to cut more slices. As each rib bone is exposed, cut it away from the roast and add to the platter. This will make it easier to carve the remaining meat.

Beef Rib Roast with Creamy Horseradish Sauce

There aren't enough pan drippings from a rib roast to make gravy for ten, so we suggest a zesty horseradish sauce instead.

	Prep: 25 minutes Roast: 3 hours
1	(4-rib) beef rib roast from small end (7 pounds), trimmed and chine bone removed
3	tablespoons whole tricolor peppercorns (red, green, and black)
1	teaspoon salt
	Creamy Horseradish Sauce (below)

1. Preheat oven to 325°F. In medium roasting pan (14" by 10"), place rib roast, fat side up. In mortar, with pestle, crush peppercorns with salt. Use to rub on fat side of roast.

2. Roast beef until meat thermometer inserted in thickest part of meat (not touching bone) reaches 140°F, about 3 hours. Internal temperature of meat will rise to 145°F (medium) upon standing. Or roast until desired doneness.

3. When roast is done, transfer to warm large platter and let stand 15 minutes to set juices for easier carving. Meanwhile, prepare Creamy Horseradish Sauce. Makes 10 main-dish servings.

Each serving without sauce: About 317 calories, 39g protein, 1g carbohydrate, 16g total fat (7g saturated), 113mg cholesterol, 322mg sodium.

Creamy Horseradish Sauce

In small bowl, combine **1 jar (6 ounces) white horseradish, drained, ½ cup mayonnaise, 1 teaspoon sugar,** and **½ teaspoon salt.** Whip **½ cup heavy or whipping cream;** fold into horseradish mixture. Makes about 1⅔ cups.

Each tablespoon: About 49 calories, 0g protein, 1g carbohydrate, 5g total fat (2 g saturated), 9mg cholesterol, 74mg sodium

Beef Eye Round au Jus

Roast some herbed new potatoes at the same time. And for the tenderest results, do not roast this cut to more than medium-rare.

	Prep: 30 minutes Roast: 1 hour 10 minutes
1	beef eye round roast (4½ pounds), trimmed
1½	teaspoons salt
½	teaspoon dried thyme
¼	teaspoon ground black pepper
2	tablespoons olive oil
1	bag (16 ounces) carrots, peeled and cut into 2" by ¼" matchstick strips
1	pound leeks (3 medium), white and light green parts, cut into 2" by ¼" matchstick strips
4	garlic cloves, thinly sliced
1¼	cups dry red wine
½	cup water
1	bay leaf

1. Preheat oven to 450°F. In small bowl, combine salt, thyme, and pepper. Use to rub on roast. In 10-inch skillet, heat oil over medium-high heat until very hot. Add beef and cook until browned, about 10 minutes. Transfer beef to nonreactive medium roasting pan (14" by 10").

2. Add carrots, leeks, and garlic to skillet and cook, stirring occasionally, until carrots are tender, about 7 minutes. Arrange vegetable mixture around beef.

3. Roast beef 25 minutes. Add wine, water, and bay leaf to roasting pan. Turn oven control to 325°F and roast until meat thermometer inserted in center of roast reaches 140°F, about 45 minutes longer. Internal temperature of meat will rise to 145°F (medium) upon standing. Or roast until desired doneness. Remove and discard bay leaf.

4. When roast is done, transfer to warm large platter and let stand 15 minutes to set juices for easier slicing. To serve, cut roast into thin slices and serve with vegetables. Makes 12 main-dish servings.

Each serving: About 232 calories, 33g protein, 6g carbohydrate, 8g total fat (2g saturated), 76mg cholesterol, 358mg sodium.

Stuffed Beef Tenderloin with Mushroom Gravy

A real showstopper. We gild the lily by dressing up this already exquisite roast with a melt-in-your-mouth stuffing.

Prep: 45 minutes	Roast/Cook: 1 hour

	Spinach-Mushroom Stuffing (right)
2	teaspoons chopped fresh thyme
1	teaspoon salt
1	teaspoon coarsely ground black pepper
1	whole beef tenderloin, trimmed (4 pounds)
2	tablespoons butter or margarine
¼	cup plain dried bread crumbs
1	can (14½ ounces) chicken broth
	or 1¾ cups Chicken Broth (page 84)
2	tablespoons dry vermouth
8	ounces mushrooms, trimmed and sliced
2	tablespoons all-purpose flour

1. Prepare Spinach-Mushroom Stuffing; set aside.

2. Preheat oven to 425°F. In small bowl, combine thyme, salt, and pepper; use to rub on tenderloin. Turn thinner end of meat under tenderloin to make meat an even thickness. With sharp knife, cut 1½-inch-deep slit in tenderloin, beginning 2 inches from thicker end of meat and ending 2 inches from opposite end.

3. Spoon Spinach-Mushroom Stuffing into slit in tenderloin. With string, tie tenderloin at 2-inch intervals to help hold its shape. Place stuffed tenderloin on rack in large roasting pan (17" by 11½"); roast tenderloin 30 minutes.

4. Meanwhile, in 1-quart saucepan, melt 1 tablespoon butter over low heat. Remove saucepan from heat; stir in bread crumbs.

5. Remove tenderloin from oven; sprinkle bread-crumb topping on stuffing. Roast tenderloin until meat thermometer inserted in center of meat reaches 140°F, about 10 minutes longer. Internal temperature of meat will rise to 145°F (medium) upon standing. Or roast until desired doneness. Transfer tenderloin to warm platter and let stand 10 minutes to set juices for easier slicing.

6. Meanwhile, prepare mushroom gravy: Add ½ cup broth and vermouth to drippings in roasting pan; stir over low heat until browned bits are loosened from bottom of pan. Pour drippings mixture into 4-cup measuring cup; let stand until fat separates from meat juice. Skim and discard fat from meat-juice mixture. Add remaining broth and enough *water* to equal 2½ cups; set aside.

7. In 12-inch skillet, melt remaining 1 tablespoon butter over medium-high heat. Add mushrooms and cook until golden and liquid has evaporated, about 12 minutes. Stir in flour. Gradually stir meat-juice mixture into mushrooms and cook, stirring constantly, until gravy has thickened slightly and boils; boil 1 minute.

8. To serve, remove string and cut tenderloin into slices. Serve with mushroom gravy. Makes 10 main-dish servings.

Each serving with gravy: About 371 calories, 35g protein, 8g carbohydrate, 21g total fat (10g saturated), 114mg cholesterol, 679mg sodium.

Spinach-Mushroom Stuffing

In 12-inch skillet, melt **4 tablespoons butter or margarine** over medium-high heat; add **1 pound mushrooms,** coarsely chopped, and cook until golden and liquid has evaporated, 12 to 15 minutes. Stir in **2 tablespoons dry vermouth;** cook 1 minute longer. Remove skillet from heat; stir in **1 package (10 ounces) frozen chopped spinach,** thawed and squeezed dry, **2 tablespoons freshly grated Parmesan cheese, 2 tablespoons plain dried bread crumbs, 1 teaspoon chopped fresh thyme,** ¼ **teaspoon salt,** and ½ **teaspoon coarsely ground black pepper.** Cool.

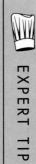

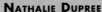

The easiest thing to do when entertaining is to cook a large piece of meat. With a method such as slow roasting, the meat will take a long—but unattended—time to cook, therefore allowing you time for your family or guests.

NATHALIE DUPREE
COOKBOOK AUTHOR/TELEVISION HOST

EXPERT TIP

Roasted Beef Tenderloin

Beef tenderloin can be brushed with a spice mixture of your choice. Served hot or at room temperature, it's perfect party fare.

Prep: 5 minutes	Roast: 50 minutes
2	tablespoons butter or margarine, melted
2	teaspoons Worcestershire sauce
1	teaspoon salt
1	teaspoon coarsely ground black pepper
1	whole beef tenderloin (5 pounds), trimmed and tied

1. Preheat oven to 450°F. In small bowl, combine butter, Worcestershire, salt, and pepper. Brush mixture on tenderloin.

2. Place tenderloin in 15½" by 10½" jelly-roll pan and roast until meat thermometer inserted in center of meat reaches 140°F, about 50 minutes. Internal temperature of meat will rise to 145°F (medium) upon standing. Or roast until desired doneness.

3. Transfer tenderloin to warm platter and let stand 10 minutes to set juices for easier slicing. Makes 12 main-dish servings.

Each serving: About 251 calories, 29g protein, 0g carbohydrate, 14g total fat (6g saturated), 92mg cholesterol, 276mg sodium.

Southwestern-Flavored Tenderloin

In small bowl, combine **1 tablespoon vegetable oil, 1 teaspoon honey, 1 tablespoon chili powder, 2 teaspoons ground cumin, 1 teaspoon salt,** and **¼ teaspoon dried oregano,** crumbled. Brush mixture on tenderloin instead of butter mixture; roast as directed.

Asian-Flavored Tenderloin

In small bowl, combine **2 teaspoons soy sauce, 2 teaspoons Asian sesame oil, 1 teaspoon honey, 1 teaspoon Chinese five-spice powder, ¼ teaspoon ground ginger,** and **⅛ teaspoon ground red pepper (cayenne).** Brush mixture on tenderloin instead of butter mixture; roast as directed.

SAUCES FOR BEEF TENDERLOIN

Any of the following is perfect with roasted beef tenderloin: Béarnaise Sauce (page 551); Roasted Garlic Sauce (page 553); or Roasted Red Pepper Sauce (page 553). Cilantro Sauce (page 554) is a good choice for the Asian-Flavored Tenderloin. For the Southwestern-Flavored variation, try either the Cilantro Sauce or Tomato Salsa (page 556) or Orange-Fennel Salsa (page 555).

Deviled Short Ribs

Short ribs have a succulence that can only come from slow, patient cooking. Save this recipe for a leisurely weekend and indulge.

Prep: 10 minutes plus marinating	Roast: 2 hours 45 minutes
6	tablespoons spicy brown mustard
2	tablespoons cider vinegar
2	tablespoons green jalapeño chile sauce
2	teaspoons Worcestershire sauce
4	pounds beef chuck short ribs
¾	teaspoon ground black pepper
1½	cups fresh bread crumbs (about 3 slices bread)

1. In small bowl, combine 3 tablespoons mustard, vinegar, 1 tablespoon jalapeño sauce, and Worcestershire; with wire whisk, whisk until blended. Transfer to ziptight plastic bag; add short ribs, turning to coat. Seal bag, pressing out as much air as possible. Refrigerate ribs at least 1 hour or up to 24 hours to marinate.

2. Preheat oven to 425°F. Arrange ribs on rack in medium roasting pan (14" by 10"), brushing with remaining marinade from bag; roast 40 minutes. Turn oven control to 325°F and roast 1 hour 20 minutes longer.

3. In small bowl, combine remaining 3 tablespoons mustard, remaining 1 tablespoon jalapeño sauce, and black pepper. Brush on top of ribs. Press bread crumbs onto coated ribs; roast until crumbs are crisp and lightly browned, about 45 minutes longer. Makes 6 main-dish servings.

Each serving: About 762 calories, 34g protein, 6g carbohydrate, 64g total fat (27g saturated), 143mg cholesterol, 400mg sodium.

Beef Stroganoff

This classic dish never goes out of style. Imported Hungarian paprika makes the flavor authentic.

Prep: 15 minutes	Cook: 30 minutes
1	pound beef tenderloin, trimmed
2	tablespoons butter or margarine
1	medium onion, thinly sliced
¾	cup chicken broth
1	teaspoon sweet Hungarian paprika
4	ounces mushrooms, trimmed and sliced
1	tablespoon fresh lemon juice
1	tablespoon brandy
½	teaspoon dried tarragon, crumbled
½	teaspoon salt
⅛	teaspoon ground black pepper
½	cup sour cream
3	teaspoons chopped fresh dill or flat-leaf parsley

1. Cut tenderloin into ⅜-inch-thick slices, then cut into 1½" by ⅜" strips.

2. In 12-inch skillet, melt butter over medium heat. Add half of beef (do not crowd) and cook until browned, using slotted spoon to transfer meat to bowl as it is browned. Repeat with remaining beef.

3. Reduce heat to medium-low; stir in onion and cook until tender. Add ¼ cup broth and paprika and cook, stirring, until onion is very tender, about 5 minutes.

4. Add mushrooms, lemon juice, brandy, tarragon, salt, and pepper and cook, stirring, until mushrooms are tender and almost all liquid has evaporated, about 8 minutes.

5. Stir in beef, remaining ½ cup broth, sour cream, and 2 teaspoons dill. Cook until heated through (do not boil), about 2 minutes. To serve, sprinkle with remaining 1 teaspoon dill. Makes 4 main-dish servings.

Each serving: About 336 calories, 26g protein, 7g carbohydrate, 21g total fat (11g saturated), 99mg cholesterol, 599mg sodium.

Provençal Beef Stew (Daube)

In Provence, in Southern France, the food is richly flavored with tomatoes, olives, garlic, orange peel, fresh herbs, and even lavender. Serve our robust rendition with boiled potatoes and crusty French bread to soak up the luscious sauce.

Prep: 15 minutes	Cook: 2 hours 30 minutes to 3 hours
2	pounds lean boneless beef chuck, trimmed and cut into 2-inch pieces
4	teaspoons olive oil
1	large onion (12 ounces), chopped
2	carrots, peeled and chopped
2	garlic cloves, finely chopped
1	can (14 to 16 ounces) tomatoes
2	cups dry red wine
4	strips (3" by ¾" each) orange peel
3	whole cloves
1	teaspoon salt
¼	teaspoon ground black pepper
¼	teaspoon dried thyme
1	bay leaf
2	tablespoons chopped fresh parsley

1. Pat beef dry with paper towels. In nonreactive 5-quart Dutch oven, heat 2 teaspoons oil over medium-high heat until very hot. Add half of beef and cook until well browned, using slotted spoon to transfer meat to bowl as it is browned. Repeat with remaining 2 teaspoons oil and remaining beef.

2. Reduce heat to medium. Add onion and carrots to Dutch oven and cook, stirring occasionally, until tender, about 5 minutes. Stir in garlic and cook until very fragrant, about 30 seconds. Stir in tomatoes with their juice, breaking them up with side of spoon. Add wine, orange peel, cloves, salt, pepper, thyme, bay leaf, and beef; heat to boiling over high heat.

3. Reduce heat; cover and simmer 2 hours to 2 hours 30 minutes, until meat is very tender. With slotted spoon, transfer meat to serving bowl and keep warm. Skim and discard fat from stew liquid.

4. Increase heat to medium-high and boil liquid 10 minutes to concentrate flavors. Discard bay leaf and spoon liquid over meat. Sprinkle with parsley. Makes 6 main-dish servings.

Each serving: About 292 calories, 30g protein, 11g carbohydrate, 14g total fat (4g saturated), 95mg cholesterol, 601mg sodium.

Boeuf Bourguignon

Another French classic that has become an American favorite.

Prep: 30 minutes   Cook: 2 hours 45 minutes

2	slices bacon, chopped
2	pounds lean boneless beef chuck, trimmed and cut into 1½-inch pieces
2	teaspoons vegetable oil
1	large onion (12 ounces), chopped
2	carrots, peeled and chopped
2	garlic cloves, finely chopped
2	tablespoons all-purpose flour
2	teaspoons tomato paste
2	cups dry red wine
½	bay leaf
1	teaspoon plus pinch salt
¼	teaspoon plus pinch ground black pepper
1	pound small white onions, peeled
3	tablespoons butter or margarine
1	teaspoon sugar
1	cup water
1	pound mushrooms, trimmed and cut into quarters if large

1. In nonreactive 5-quart Dutch oven, cook bacon over medium heat until just beginning to brown. With slotted spoon, transfer bacon to medium bowl.

2. Pat beef dry with paper towels. Add 1 teaspoon oil to Dutch oven and increase heat to medium-high. Add beef, in batches, to bacon drippings and cook until well browned, using slotted spoon to transfer beef as it is browned to bowl with bacon. Add remaining 1 teaspoon oil if necessary.

3. Reduce heat to medium. Add chopped onion, carrots, and garlic to Dutch oven; cook until onion and carrots are tender, about 8 minutes. Stir in flour; cook 1 minute. Stir in tomato paste; cook 1 minute. Add wine, bay leaf, 1 teaspoon salt, and ¼ teaspoon pepper, stirring until browned bits are loosened. Return beef and bacon to Dutch oven; heat to boiling. Reduce heat; cover and simmer until beef is very tender, about 1 hour 30 minutes. Remove bay leaf. Skim and discard fat.

4. Meanwhile, in 10-inch skillet, combine small white onions, 1 tablespoon butter, sugar, and water. Heat to boiling; cover and simmer until onions are just tender, about 10 minutes. Remove cover and cook over medium-high heat, swirling pan occasionally, until water has evaporated and onions are golden. Transfer to bowl; keep warm.

5. In same skillet, melt remaining 2 tablespoons butter over medium-high heat. Add mushrooms and remaining pinch each salt and pepper; cook, stirring, until mushrooms are tender and liquid has evaporated. Stir onions and mushrooms into stew. Makes 6 main-dish servings.

Each serving: About 415 calories, 33g protein, 20g carbohydrate, 23g total fat (9g saturated), 116mg cholesterol, 261mg sodium.

Chili

Hot Mexican chili powder will make this chili even better.

Prep: 15 minutes   Cook: 3 hours

2	pounds lean boneless beef chuck, trimmed and cut into 1-inch pieces
1	tablespoon olive oil
1	large onion (12 ounces), chopped
1	large green pepper, cut into 1-inch pieces
3	garlic cloves, finely chopped
2	tablespoons chili powder
1	teaspoon ground cumin
1	teaspoon ground coriander
½	teaspoon dried oregano, crumbled
½	teaspoon salt
1	can (28 ounces) plum tomatoes in puree, chopped
1	can (15 to 19 ounces) red kidney beans, rinsed and drained

1. Pat beef dry with paper towels. In nonreactive 5-quart Dutch oven, heat oil over medium heat until very hot. Add half of beef and cook until browned, using slotted spoon to transfer meat to bowl as it is browned. Repeat with remaining beef.

2. Add onion, green pepper, and garlic to Dutch oven and cook, stirring occasionally, until onion is tender, about 5 minutes. Stir in chili powder, cumin, coriander, oregano, and salt; cook 1 minute. Add tomatoes with their puree and heat to boiling. Reduce heat; cover and simmer until meat is tender, about 2 hours 30 minutes. Stir in beans and cook until heated through, about 15 minutes longer. Skim and discard fat from chili liquid. Makes 6 main-dish servings.

Each serving: About 368 calories, 36g protein, 24g carbohydrate, 15g total fat (5g saturated), 98mg cholesterol, 647mg sodium.

Carbonnades à la Flamande

This Belgian classic should be prepared with a full-flavored dark beer to complement the caramelized onions. In a pinch, use lager.

Prep: 45 minutes   Bake: 2 hours 30 minutes

3	tablespoons olive or vegetable oil
2	pounds onions, thinly sliced
4	slices bacon, chopped
3	pounds lean boneless beef chuck, trimmed and cut into 2-inch pieces
½	teaspoon salt
¼	teaspoon ground black pepper
3	tablespoons all-purpose flour
1	can (14½ ounces) beef broth or 1¾ cups Brown Beef Stock (page 83)
1	bottle (12 ounces) dark beer (not stout)
½	teaspoon dried thyme
1	bay leaf

1. Preheat oven to 350° F. In 5-quart Dutch oven, heat 2 tablespoons oil over medium-high heat. Add onions and cook until tender and browned, 20 to 25 minutes. Transfer onions to large bowl.

2. In Dutch oven, cook bacon over medium heat until browned; with slotted spoon, transfer to bowl with onions.

3. Pat beef dry with paper towels; sprinkle with salt and pepper. Add half of beef to bacon drippings in Dutch oven and cook over high heat until well browned, using slotted spoon to transfer beef as it is browned to bowl with bacon. Repeat with remaining beef.

4. Reduce heat to medium-high. Add remaining 1 tablespoon oil to Dutch oven. Stir in flour until well blended and cook, stirring constantly until flour browns. Gradually stir in broth and beer. Cook, stirring constantly, until sauce has thickened and boils.

5. Return beef mixture to Dutch oven; add thyme and bay leaf. Cover and place in oven. Bake until meat is tender, about 2 hours 30 minutes. Skim and discard fat from stew liquid; discard bay leaf. Makes 8 main-dish servings.

Each serving: About 369 calories, 29g protein, 14g carbohydrate, 22g total fat (7g saturated), 93mg cholesterol, 574mg sodium.

Pot Roast with Root Vegetables

Sweet spices give this stew an inviting aroma and accentuate the natural sweetness of the turnips, parsnips, carrots, and rutabaga.

Prep: 30 minutes   Bake: 4 hours

1	boneless beef chuck roast (6 pounds), trimmed and tied or 2 chuck steaks (3 pounds each)
1½	teaspoons salt
1	teaspoon coarsely ground black pepper
¾	teaspoon ground cinnamon
¾	teaspoon ground ginger
¼	teaspoon ground cloves
¼	teaspoon ground nutmeg
1	tablespoon vegetable oil
1	pound small onions, cut into quarters
2	cans (14½ ounces each) beef broth or 3½ cups Brown Beef Stock (page 83)
½	cup dry red wine
1	tablespoon Worcestershire sauce
1	bay leaf
1	rutabaga (2 pounds), peeled and cut into 1½-inch pieces
10	small red potatoes, each cut into quarters
2	large turnips (8 ounces each), peeled and cut into 1½-inch pieces
3	carrots, peeled and cut into 1½-inch pieces
2	small parsnips (4 ounces each), peeled and cut into 1½-inch pieces

1. Preheat oven to 350°F. In cup, combine salt, pepper, cinnamon, ginger, cloves, and nutmeg. Use to rub on roast.

2. In 8-quart Dutch oven, heat oil over medium-high heat until very hot. Add roast and cook until well browned. Transfer roast to plate. Add onions to Dutch oven and cook, stirring occasionally, until golden.

3. Stir in broth, wine, Worcestershire, and bay leaf; heat to boiling. Return roast to pot; cover and place in oven. Bake 2 hours 30 minutes.

4. After roast has baked 2 hours 30 minutes, stir in rutabaga, potatoes, turnips, carrots, and parsnips. Bake until meat and vegetables are very tender, about 1 hour 30 minutes longer.

Pot Roast with Root Vegetables

5. Transfer roast to warm platter. With slotted spoon, remove vegetables from pot. Place 2 cups of vegetables in food processor fitted with knife blade and puree. Skim and discard fat from pot liquid. With food processor running, pour liquid into pureed vegetables. Spoon remaining vegetables around roast and serve with sauce. Makes 12 main-dish servings.

Each serving: About 421 calories, 38g protein, 33g carbohydrate, 15g total fat (5g saturated), 114mg cholesterol, 799mg sodium.

EXPERT TIP

Meat should be salted before it is cooked. Contrary to popular belief, salting meat right before cooking does not dry it out or cause it to lose juices. Instead, presalting brings out the taste of the meat and rounds out the savory flavors associated with properly browned meat. Meat that is salted after cooking simply tastes of salt layered on top of the more complex flavors produced from browning.

BRUCE AIDELLS

COOKBOOK AUTHOR

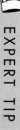

Country Pot Roast

This is blue-ribbon country cooking. To give the home-style sauce a bit more body, we puree half of the vegetables.

Prep: 25 minutes   Bake: 3 hours

1	tablespoon vegetable oil
1	boneless beef chuck cross-rib pot roast or boneless chuck eye roast (4 pounds), trimmed
1	large onion (12 ounces), coarsely chopped
1	carrot, peeled and coarsely chopped
1	stalk celery, coarsely chopped
2	garlic cloves, finely chopped
1	can (15 ounces) crushed tomatoes
½	cup chicken broth
1	teaspoon salt
½	teaspoon dried thyme, crumbled
¼	teaspoon ground black pepper
1	bay leaf

1. Preheat oven to 350°F. In nonreactive 5-quart Dutch oven, heat oil over high heat until very hot. Add roast and cook until browned. Transfer roast to plate.

2. Add onion, carrot, and celery to Dutch oven and cook over medium-high heat until lightly browned. Add garlic; cook, stirring, until fragrant, about 20 seconds. Return roast to Dutch oven; add tomatoes, broth, salt, thyme, pepper, and bay leaf; heat to boiling. Cover and place in oven. Bake, turning roast once, until roast is tender, about 3 hours.

3. When roast is done, transfer to large platter and keep warm. Discard bay leaf. Skim and discard fat from liquid in Dutch oven. Transfer half of vegetables and liquid to blender; cover, with center part of cover removed to let steam escape, and puree until smooth. Pour pureed mixture back into Dutch oven and stir until combined; heat to boiling. Cut meat into thin slices and serve with vegetables and sauce. Makes 8 main-dish servings.

Each serving: About 304 calories, 35g protein, 6g carbohydrate, 15g total fat (5g saturated), 114mg cholesterol, 573mg sodium.

Braised Oxtails

Like other bony cuts of meat, oxtails add richness to the braising liquid. The sweet-hot combination of ginger, allspice, and cayenne contributes exotic flavor. Pass the mashed potatoes, please.

Prep: 25 minutes   Bake: 2 hours

1	tablespoon olive oil
3½	pounds oxtails
1	medium onion, chopped
4	garlic cloves, finely chopped
4	carrots, peeled and cut on diagonal into ½-inch pieces
1	can (14 to 16 ounces) tomatoes, chopped
¾	cup chicken broth
1½	teaspoons ground ginger
¾	teaspoon salt
¼	teaspoon ground red pepper (cayenne)
⅛	teaspoon ground allspice

1. In nonreactive 5-quart Dutch oven, heat oil over medium heat until very hot. Cook oxtails, in batches, until browned, about 5 minutes per batch, using slotted spoon to transfer oxtails to bowl as they are browned.

2. Add onion and garlic to drippings in pan; cook until onion is tender, about 7 minutes. Stir in carrots. Add tomatoes with their juice. Stir in broth, ginger, salt, ground red pepper, and allspice; heat to boiling. Stir in oxtails; cover and place in oven. Bake until meat is tender, about 2 hours.

3. With slotted spoon, transfer oxtails to warm platter. Skim and discard fat from pot liquid; pour juice over meat and serve. Makes 4 main-dish servings.

Each serving: About 327 calories, 17g protein, 17g carbohydrate, 21g total fat (8g saturated), 61mg cholesterol, 881mg sodium.

Braciole

Serve these Italian beef rolls with a side of pasta, topped with a sprinkling of Parmesan cheese.

Prep: 30 minutes	Cook: 40 minutes
1½	cups fresh bread crumbs (about 3 slices bread)
⅓	cup freshly grated Parmesan cheese
⅓	cup chopped fresh basil
3	tablespoons dried currants
¾	teaspoon salt
8	thin slices beef top round (1 pound)
1	tablespoon olive oil
3	garlic cloves, crushed with side of chef's knife
2	cups chopped canned tomatoes with their juice
⅓	cup chicken broth
3	strips (3" by ½" each) orange peel

1. In medium bowl, combine bread crumbs, Parmesan, basil, currants, and ¼ teaspoon salt.

2. With meat mallet, or between two sheets of plastic wrap or waxed paper with rolling pin, pound beef slices to ⅛-inch thickness. Sprinkle one side of slices with remaining ½ teaspoon salt. Spoon bread-crumb mixture on top, pressing so it adheres to meat. From one short end, roll up each meat slice jelly-roll fashion. Secure each roll with toothpicks.

3. In nonstick 10-inch skillet, heat oil over medium heat until very hot. Add beef and cook, turning rolls, until browned, about 5 minutes. Add garlic and cook 30 seconds. Add tomatoes with their juice, broth, and orange peel; heat to boiling. Reduce heat; cover and simmer until meat is tender, about 30 minutes. Remove and discard orange peel and toothpicks before serving braciole with pan sauce. Makes 4 main-dish servings.

Each serving: About 310 calories, 33g protein, 20g carbohydrate, 11g total fat (3g saturated), 72mg cholesterol, 984mg sodium.

Grillades

This New Orleans–style smothered steak is often served with grits for breakfast. We like it for lunch and dinner, too.

Prep: 15 minutes	Cook: 1 hour
4	beef minute steaks (6 ounces each)
½	teaspoon salt
¼	teaspoon ground black pepper
3	teaspoons vegetable oil
1	medium onion, chopped
1	green pepper, chopped
1	stalk celery, chopped
2	garlic cloves, finely chopped
1	can (14 to 16 ounces) tomatoes in puree
1	cup beef broth
1	teaspoon Worcestershire sauce
2	bay leaves
1	tablespoon red wine vinegar

1. Sprinkle beef with salt and black pepper. In nonstick 12-inch skillet, heat 1 teaspoon oil over medium-high heat until very hot. Add steaks and cook until browned, about 2 minutes per side, transferring to plate as they are browned.

2. Add remaining 2 teaspoons oil to skillet; reduce heat to medium. Add onion and cook, stirring, 5 minutes. Add green pepper, celery, and garlic; cook, stirring, 3 minutes longer. Add tomatoes with their puree, breaking them up with side of spoon. Stir in broth, Worcestershire, and bay leaves. Increase heat to high; heat to boiling.

3. Return steaks to skillet and reduce heat. Cover and simmer 40 minutes. Transfer steaks to platter; keep warm. Increase heat to high; stir in vinegar and heat to boiling. Boil until sauce has thickened, about 5 minutes. Discard bay leaves from sauce. To serve, spoon sauce over steaks. Makes 4 main-dish servings.

Each serving: About 437 calories, 37g protein, 13g carbohydrate, 26g total fat (9g saturated), 107mg cholesterol, 772mg sodium.

Ropa Vieja

In Spanish, ropa vieja *means "old clothes." In Mexico, this dish originated as a way to use leftover meat and vegetables to fill tacos. The stew is simmered a long time so the meat can be shredded into thin strips resembling tattered fabric.*

Prep: 45 minutes   Cook: 3 hours to 3 hours 30 minutes

1	beef flank steak (1¾ pounds)
1	medium onion, coarsely chopped
1	carrot, peeled and coarsely chopped
1	bay leaf
2	teaspoons salt
5	cups water
4	teaspoons olive oil
1	large onion (12 ounces), sliced
1	red pepper, cut into ½-inch-wide strips
1	yellow pepper, cut into ½-inch-wide strips
1	green pepper, cut into ½-inch-wide strips
3	garlic cloves, crushed with garlic press
3	serrano or jalapeño chiles, seeded and finely chopped
¼	teaspoon ground cinnamon
1	can (14 to 16 ounces) tomatoes
	capers

1. Cut flank steak crosswise into thirds. In nonreactive 5-quart Dutch oven, combine flank steak, chopped onion, carrot, bay leaf, 1 teaspoon salt, and water; heat to boiling over high heat. Reduce heat; cover and simmer until meat is very tender, 2 hours 30 minutes to 3 hours. Remove Dutch oven from heat. Remove cover and let flank steak stand 30 minutes.

2. In 12-inch skillet, heat oil over medium-high heat. Add sliced onion, red, yellow, and green peppers, and remaining 1 teaspoon salt; cook, stirring often, until vegetables are tender, about 15 minutes. Stir in garlic, serrano chiles, and cinnamon; cook 30 seconds. Stir in tomatoes with their juice, breaking them up with side of spoon, and cook 5 minutes.

3. With slotted spoon, transfer beef to bowl; strain broth. Set aside 2 cups broth (reserve remaining broth for another use). Using two forks, shred beef into fine strips.

4. Stir 2 cups broth and shredded meat into pepper mixture and simmer, stirring occasionally, 10 minutes. Sprinkle with capers to serve. Makes 6 main-dish servings.

Each serving: About 246 calories, 25g protein, 10g carbohydrate, 12g total fat (4g saturated), 57mg cholesterol, 779mg sodium.

Brisket with Mushrooms

Humble beef brisket becomes a company dish when combined with a heady combination of fresh and dried mushrooms and served with a rich red wine sauce.

Prep: 1 hour 30 minutes   Bake: 2 hours 30 minutes

¾	cup boiling water
½	ounce dried porcini mushrooms (½ cup)
8	ounces small shiitake mushrooms, stems removed
8	ounces white mushrooms, trimmed
¼	cup vegetable oil
1	fresh beef brisket (4 pounds), well trimmed
4	medium red onions, sliced
2	garlic cloves, sliced
3	tablespoons all-purpose flour
1	can (14½ ounces) beef broth or 1¾ cups Brown Beef Stock (page 83)
1	cup dry red wine
¼	cup brandy
4	large fresh sage leaves
1	bay leaf
1½	teaspoons fresh thyme
½	teaspoon salt
¼	teaspoon coarsely ground black pepper
¼	cup chopped fresh parsley

1. In small bowl, pour boiling water over porcini mushrooms; let stand 30 minutes.

2. With slotted spoon, remove porcini, reserving mushroom liquid. Rinse mushrooms to remove any grit, then chop. Strain liquid through sieve lined with paper towels; set aside.

3. Preheat oven to 325°F. In 8-quart Dutch oven, heat oil over medium-high heat until very hot. Add brisket and cook until browned, about 10 minutes. Transfer brisket to platter; set aside. Add onions to Dutch oven and cook over medium heat, stirring occasionally, until lightly browned, about 15 minutes. Stir in garlic and cook 30 seconds. Stir in flour and cook, stirring until golden brown, about 2 minutes.

4. Return brisket to Dutch oven. Stir in porcini mushrooms, mushroom liquid, shiitake and white mushrooms, broth, wine, brandy, sage leaves, bay leaf, thyme, salt, pepper, and 2 tablespoons parsley. Heat to boiling over high heat. Cover and place in oven. Bake until brisket is tender, about 2 hours 30 minutes.

5. Transfer meat from Dutch oven to warm platter; let stand 15 minutes. Skim and discard fat from liquid in Dutch oven. Discard sage leaves and bay leaf. Heat liquid in pot to boiling over high heat. Reduce heat to medium; cook, uncovered, until thickened, about 15minutes.

6. Slice brisket thinly across the grain. Stir remaining 2 tablespoons parsley into brisket liquid. Spoon some over meat; pass remaining separately. Makes 10 main-dish servings.

Each serving: About 333 calories, 34g protein, 12g carbohydrate, 16g total fat (4g saturated), 90mg cholesterol, 447mg sodium.

LONDON BROIL

The original London broil was a marinated, grilled, and thinly sliced flank steak. Now it can mean just about any less tender cut that is grilled or broiled. Some butchers even label parts of the chuck or sirloin as London broil. Flank, hanger, and skirt steaks all come from the underside of the beef. They are very tasty and the best examples of how good this kind of steak can be. Top round is often cut into 1- to 2-inch-thick steaks but it must be marinated well to become sufficiently moist. No matter what cut you use, London broil should never be grilled beyond medium-rare, or it will dry out.

Two techniques, marinating and slicing thinly, help turn these cuts into tender, juicy steaks. Use an acid-based (wine, vinegar, or lemon juice) marinade. Two possibilities are the marinades for Oregano–Red Wine Vinegar Kebabs (page 116) and Sesame-Ginger Kebabs (page 116). Place the steak in a ziptight plastic bag with the marinade and refrigerate for at least two hours or up to twenty-four hours, turning the bag occasionally.

For more tender slices, London broil must be sliced against the grain: The grain is the direction of the meat's muscle pattern; it looks somewhat like wood grain. On flank steak, the grain is very visible; on top round, less so. Before slicing, let the meat stand for 3 to 5 minutes so the juices can redistribute themselves. Holding a sharp thin-bladed knife at a slight angle (to cut slices with a larger face), cut the steak into ⅛-inch-thick slices.

Oven-Barbecued Beef Brisket with Mop Sauce

Stirring a bit of coffee into beef stew is an old cowboy secret. The sauce is traditionally prepared in such large quantities for Texas barbecues that it is brushed on with a mop.

Prep: 10 minutes	Bake: 3 hours
½	cup water
¼	cup dark corn syrup
¼	cup ketchup
¼	cup cider vinegar
2	tablespoons Worcestershire sauce
2	tablespoons vegetable oil
2	tablespoons spicy brown mustard
2	teaspoons instant-coffee granules
1	teaspoon salt
⅛	teaspoon hot pepper sauce
1	fresh beef brisket (3 pounds), well trimmed

1. Preheat oven to 325°F. Prepare mop sauce: In nonreactive 1-quart saucepan, combine water, corn syrup, ketchup, vinegar, Worcestershire, oil, mustard, coffee granules, salt, and hot pepper sauce; heat to boiling over medium-high heat. Cook, stirring, 5 minutes. Remove from heat.

2. Place brisket in 13" by 9" baking dish. Pour mop sauce over brisket. Cover baking dish with foil and bake 3 hours, or until brisket is tender, turning brisket halfway through baking.

3. Transfer brisket to cutting board and let stand 10 minutes. Cut meat across the grain into thin slices. Skim and discard fat from sauce and serve alongside brisket. Makes 8 main-dish servings.

Each serving: About 285 calories, 26g protein, 11g carbohydrate, 15g total fat (4g saturated), 81mg cholesterol, 549mg sodium.

New England Boiled Dinner

Gently simmering the meat in this hearty winter favorite for hours creates its melt-in-your-mouth quality. If you like, substitute turnips or parsnips for the rutabaga, or add a few additional potatoes so you can make Corned Beef Hash (page 118) with the tasty leftovers.

Prep: 15 minutes   Cook: 3 hours 30 minutes to 4 hours

1	corned beef brisket (4 to 4½ pounds)
1	medium onion studded with 4 whole cloves
8	cups water
8	medium all-purpose potatoes (2½ pounds), peeled and each cut in half
8	carrots, peeled and each cut in half
1	small rutabaga (2 pounds), peeled and cut in half, each half cut into 8 wedges
1	small green cabbage (2 pounds), cut into 8 wedges
2	tablespoons chopped fresh parsley
	Dijon mustard
	bottled white horseradish

1. In 8-quart Dutch oven, place brisket, clove-studded onion, and water and heat to boiling over high heat. With slotted spoon, skim and discard foam from surface. Reduce heat; cover and simmer until brisket is tender, 2 hours 30 minutes to 3 hours.

2. Add potatoes, carrots, and rutabaga to Dutch oven; heat to boiling over high heat. Reduce heat; cover and simmer until vegetables are tender, about 30 minutes.

3. With slotted spoon, transfer brisket and vegetables to deep large platter; keep warm.

4. Heat liquid remaining in Dutch oven to boiling over high heat. Add cabbage; heat to boiling. Cover and boil until cabbage is tender, about 5 minutes.

5. Slice brisket very thinly across the grain. Transfer sliced meat to platter with vegetables. Place cabbage wedges on platter, sprinkle parsley on vegetables, and serve mustard and horseradish alongside. Makes 8 main-dish servings.

Each serving: About 587 calories, 35g protein, 43g carbohydrate, 31g total fat (10g saturated), 157mg cholesterol, 1,887mg sodium.

Filet Mignon with Mustard-Caper Sauce

A well-browned exterior is the key to maximum flavor with sautéed beef. Be sure to cook it over high heat.

Prep: 5 minutes   Cook: 20 minutes

4	beef tenderloin steaks (filet mignon), 1½ inches thick (6 ounces each)
½	teaspoon salt
¼	teaspoon coarsely ground black pepper
1	tablespoon olive oil
3	tablespoons finely chopped shallots
⅓	cup dry white wine
⅓	cup beef broth
⅓	cup heavy or whipping cream
3	tablespoons capers, drained
1	tablespoon Dijon mustard
¼	cup chopped watercress leaves plus (optional) additional leaves

1. Sprinkle steaks with salt and pepper. In nonstick 12-inch skillet, heat oil over high heat until very hot. Add steaks and cook, without turning, until browned, about 7 minutes. Turn steaks and cook 7 minutes longer for medium-rare or until desired doneness. Transfer to plates; keep warm.

2. Add shallots to drippings in skillet; cook 30 seconds. Stir in wine; cook, stirring, until browned bits are loosened from bottom of skillet. Stir in broth and boil 1 minute. Stir in cream; boil 1 minute longer. Stir in capers, mustard, and chopped watercress, if using.

3. To serve, spoon sauce over meat and garnish with watercress, if desired. Makes 4 main-dish servings.

Each serving: About 334 calories, 27g protein, 3g carbohydrate, 22g total fat (9g saturated), 105mg cholesterol, 799mg sodium.

New England Boiled Dinner

Steak au Poivre

Here's the classic version of this very popular bistro dish. It can be prepared in very little time, which is why it is featured on so many restaurant menus.

Prep: 5 minutes   Cook: 12 minutes

2	tablespoons whole black peppercorns, crushed
½	teaspoon salt
4	beef rib-eye steaks, ¾ inch thick (10 ounces each), trimmed
1	tablespoon butter or margarine
1	tablespoon vegetable oil
¼	cup dry white wine
2	tablespoons brandy
½	cup heavy or whipping cream
1	tablespoon chopped fresh parsley (optional)

1. In cup, combine crushed peppercorns and salt; use to rub on steaks.

2. In nonstick 12-inch skillet, melt butter with oil over medium-high heat. Add steaks and cook 4 to 5 minutes per side for medium-rare or until desired doneness. Transfer to plates; keep warm.

3. Increase heat to high. Add wine and brandy. Heat to boiling, stirring until browned bits are loosened from bottom of skillet. Add cream and boil until sauce has thickened, about 3 minutes. Pour sauce over steaks and sprinkle with parsley, if desired. Makes 4 main-dish servings.

Each serving: About 468 calories, 35g protein, 3g carbohydrate, 31g total fat (15g saturated), 149mg cholesterol, 439mg sodium.

Chicken-Fried Steak

Serve this old-fashioned dish, prized for its crispy exterior and creamy gravy, with plenty of mashed potatoes.

Prep: 10 minutes   Cook: 20 minutes

¾	cup all-purpose flour
1½	teaspoons salt
1	teaspoon paprika
1	teaspoon coarsely ground black pepper
⅛	teaspoon ground red pepper (cayenne)
6	beef cubed steaks (6 ounces each)
½	cup vegetable oil
½	cup beef broth
2	cups milk

1. Preheat oven to 200°F. Line jelly-roll pan with paper towels. On waxed paper, combine flour, salt, paprika, black pepper, and ground red pepper. Reserve 3 tablespoons seasoned-flour mixture. Coat cubed steaks with remaining mixture, shaking off excess.

2. In 12-inch skillet, heat oil to 375° F. Cook steaks, two at a time, 2 minutes; turn and cook 1 minute longer. Transfer steaks to prepared jelly-roll pan to drain and place in oven. Repeat with remaining steaks, transferring each batch to jelly-roll pan in oven after cooking.

3. Discard all but 2 tablespoons oil from skillet. Reduce heat to medium-high. Stir in reserved flour mixture and cook, stirring, 1 minute. With wire whisk, whisk in broth until browned bits are loosened from bottom of skillet; boil 1 minute. Whisk in milk and heat to boiling; boil 2 minutes. (Makes 2 cups.)

4. Place steaks on warm platter and serve with gravy. Makes 6 main-dish servings.

Each serving with gravy: About 385 calories, 38g protein, 16g carbohydrate, 18g total fat (5g saturated), 103mg cholesterol, 757mg sodium.

Steak Pizzaiola

Made with ingredients typically found at neighborhood pizzerias, this is perfect fare for a midweek supper. If you like, serve over grilled Italian bread.

Prep: 15 minutes   Cook: 15 minutes

2	tablespoons olive oil
1	large onion (12 ounces), thinly sliced
2	garlic cloves, finely chopped
1	large red pepper, thinly sliced
1	large yellow pepper, thinly sliced
4	ounces mushrooms, trimmed and thickly sliced
1	can (15 ounces) crushed tomatoes
¾	teaspoon salt
8	beef minute steaks (2 ounces each)

1. In nonreactive 12-inch skillet, heat 1 tablespoon oil over medium heat. Add onion and garlic and cook, stirring frequently, until onion is tender-crisp, about 2 minutes.

2. Add red and yellow peppers and mushrooms and cook, stirring frequently, until peppers are tender-crisp, about 2 minutes longer. Add tomatoes with their juice and ¼ teaspoon salt; cook just until sauce has slightly thickened, about 2 minutes longer. Transfer to medium bowl; keep warm.

3. Wipe skillet with paper towels, then heat remaining 1 tablespoon oil over medium-high heat until very hot. Sprinkle beef with remaining ½ teaspoon salt; cook steaks, in batches, until just cooked through, about 2 minutes per side. Transfer steaks to warm platter as they are cooked. Spoon sauce over steaks. Makes 4 main-dish servings.

Each serving: About 355 calories, 26g protein, 14g carbohydrate, 22g total fat (7g saturated), 72mg cholesterol, 668mg sodium

Flank Steak with Red Onion Marmalade

This juicy panfried steak, topped with a sweet and tangy red onion mixture, is an easy weeknight put-together.

Prep: 10 minutes   Cook: 35 minutes

3	tablespoons butter or margarine
2	medium red onions (1 pound), thinly sliced
3	tablespoons distilled white vinegar
3	tablespoons sugar
1	teaspoon salt
1	beef flank steak (1½ pounds)
¼	teaspoon coarsely ground pepper

1. In nonstick 12-inch skillet, melt 2 tablespoons butter over medium heat. Add onions and cook, stirring occasionally, until tender, about 15 minutes. Stir in vinegar, sugar, and ½ teaspoon salt. Reduce heat and simmer 5 minutes. Spoon red onion marmalade into small bowl; keep warm.

2. Wash skillet and wipe dry. Sprinkle steak with pepper and remaining ½ teaspoon salt. In skillet over medium-high heat, melt remaining 1 tablespoon butter. Add steak and cook 6 to 8 minutes per side for medium-rare or until desired doneness.

3. Slice steak and serve with red onion marmalade. Makes 6 main-dish servings.

Each serving: About 281 calories, 24g protein, 14g carbohydrate, 14g total fat (7g saturated), 72mg cholesterol, 150mg sodium.

Steak Pizzaiola

Tuscan Pan-Seared Strip Steak

Tuscan cooks know that a squeeze of fresh lemon juice is the perfect flavor accent for a rich cut of beef.

Prep: 5 minutes   Cook: 12 minutes

4	boneless beef strip (shell) steaks, 1 inch thick (8 ounces each)
2	teaspoons olive oil
1	teaspoon dried rosemary, crumbled
1	teaspoon salt
1	teaspoon coarsely ground black pepper
4	lemon wedges

1. Heat 12-inch skillet over high heat until very hot. Brush steaks with olive oil. In small bowl, combine rosemary, salt, and pepper. Use to rub on steaks.

2. Place steaks in skillet; reduce heat to medium-high. Cook steaks 7 minutes; turn and cook 5 minutes longer for medium-rare or 7 minutes longer for medium. Serve with lemon wedges. Makes 4 main-dish servings.

Each serving: About 375 calories, 49g protein, 1g carbohydrate, 18g total fat (6g saturated), 129mg cholesterol, 699mg sodium.

Steak with Red Wine Sauce

Try this simple sauce with any panfried beef, from burgers to filet mignon. It is thickened with a little butter at the end, a French cooking technique that often comes in handy. (Do not use margarine: It will not thicken the sauce.)

Prep: 5 minutes   Cook: 20 minutes

2	teaspoons vegetable oil
4	boneless beef strip (shell) steaks, 1 inch thick (8 ounces each)
½	teaspoon salt
¼	teaspoon ground black pepper
¼	cup finely chopped shallots
1	cup dry red wine
	pinch dried thyme, crumbled
2	tablespoons butter, cut into pieces
2	teaspoons chopped fresh tarragon or flat-leaf parsley

1. In nonstick 12-inch skillet, heat oil over medium-high heat until very hot. Sprinkle steaks with salt and pepper. Cook 5 to 6 minutes per side for medium-rare or until desired doneness. Transfer steaks to warm platter.

2. Discard drippings from skillet. Add shallots to pan and cook, stirring, until tender, about 1 minute. Add wine and thyme; heat to boiling over high heat. Boil until sauce has reduced to ⅓ cup, about 5 minutes. Remove pan from heat; stir in butter, stirring just until incorporated.

3. Cut steaks into thin slices. Transfer to warm platter; pour sauce on top and sprinkle with tarragon. Makes 4 main-dish servings.

Each serving: About 436 calories, 49g protein, 3g carbohydrate, 24g total fat (10g saturated), 145mg cholesterol, 179mg sodium.

Cajun Steaks

A heavy cast-iron skillet is best for cooking these spicy steaks. If you don't have one, use your heaviest skillet. We've used shell (boneless strip) steaks; you can use any favorite cut.

Prep: 5 minutes   Cook: 10 minutes

1	teaspoon dried thyme, crumbled
1	teaspoon onion powder (not onion salt)
½	teaspoon salt
½	teaspoon ground black pepper
¼	teaspoon ground red pepper (cayenne)
¼	teaspoon sugar
4	boneless beef strip (shell) steaks, 1 inch thick (8 ounces each)
2	teaspoons olive oil

1. In bowl, combine thyme, onion powder, salt, black pepper, ground red pepper, and sugar. Use to rub on steaks.

2. In cast-iron 12-inch skillet, heat oil over medium-high heat until very hot. Add steaks and cook 5 to 6 minutes per side for medium-rare or until desired doneness. Makes 4 main-dish servings.

Each serving: About 293 calories, 37g protein, 1g carbohydrate, 14g total fat (5g saturated), 98mg cholesterol, 362mg sodium.

Thai Beef with Basil

Simple and fresh-tasting, this easy but exotic stir-fry is seasoned with fish sauce, one of the fundamental flavors of Thai cooking.

Prep: 15 minutes plus marinating	Cook: 6 minutes

3	tablespoons Asian fish sauce (nuoc nam, page 31)
1	tablespoon soy sauce
1	tablespoon brown sugar
1	beef top round steak (1 pound)
1	tablespoon plus 1 teaspoon vegetable oil
1	jumbo sweet onion (1 pound), cut into ¼-inch-thick slices
3	long red chiles or serrano chiles, seeded and thinly sliced
3	garlic cloves, cut into long thin slices
2	teaspoons minced, peeled fresh ginger
1	cup loosely packed basil leaves

1. In medium bowl, combine fish sauce, soy sauce, and brown sugar. Cut round steak lengthwise in half, then cut into ⅛-inch-thick slices across the grain. Add beef to fish-sauce mixture, tossing to coat well; cover and refrigerate beef 30 minutes to marinate.

Thai Beef with Basil

2. In 12-inch skillet, heat 1 tablespoon oil over high heat until very hot. Add beef mixture and cook, stirring frequently (stir-frying), just until beef is no longer pink, about 1 minute. Transfer beef to bowl.

3. Add remaining 1 teaspoon oil to skillet. Add onion and cook, stir-frying, until tender-crisp, about 3 minutes. Stir in chiles, garlic, and ginger; cook 30 seconds.

4. Return beef to skillet and add basil; heat through. Makes 4 main-dish servings.

Each serving: About 291 calories, 31g protein, 20g carbohydrate, 10g total fat (2g saturated), 65mg cholesterol, 779mg sodium

Sesame Steak

Marinating the beef as well as the thickly sliced onions in a heady Asian-style marinade gives this dish its full-flavored taste.

Prep: 20 minutes plus marinating	Broil: 20 minutes

½	cup soy sauce
¼	cup fresh lemon juice
1	tablespoon Asian sesame oil
1	tablespoon sugar
2	garlic cloves, crushed with side of chef's knife
¼	teaspoon cracked black pepper
1	boneless beef top sirloin steak, 1½ inches thick (2½ pounds), trimmed
4	medium onions, cut into 1-inch-thick slices

1. Prepare marinade: In 13" by 9" baking dish, combine soy sauce, lemon juice, sesame oil, sugar, garlic, and pepper.

2. Place steak and onions in marinade, turning to coat both sides of steak. Cover and let stand 20 minutes at room temperature to marinate, turning occasionally.

3. Preheat broiler. Place steak and onions on rack in broiling pan. Broil steak 6 inches from heat source 10 to 12 minutes per side for medium-rare or until desired doneness, brushing steak often with marinade and stirring onions frequently to prevent burning. Keep onions warm. Let steak stand 10 minutes. Cut steak into thin slices across the grain and serve with onions. Makes 8 main-dish servings.

♥ Each serving: About 283 calories, 36g protein, 12g carbohydrate, 9g total fat (3g saturated), 99mg cholesterol, 763mg sodium.

Spicy Tangerine Beef

Here's a home-cooked version of this ever-popular takeout food.

Prep: 25 minutes   Cook: 25 minutes

4	tangerines or 3 medium navel oranges
1	large bunch broccoli (1½ pounds)
3	tablespoons vegetable oil
1	boneless beef top sirloin steak (12 ounces), thinly sliced crosswise
2	tablespoons plus ½ teaspoon cornstarch
2	tablespoons water
3	green onions, cut on diagonal into 2-inch pieces
1	red pepper, thinly sliced
3	garlic cloves, finely chopped
1	tablespoon minced, peeled fresh ginger
3	tablespoons soy sauce
¼	teaspoon crushed red pepper

1. Cut peel and white pith from 1 tangerine. Holding tangerine over small bowl to catch juice, cut on either side of membranes to release each section, allowing fruit and juice to drop into bowl; set aside. With vegetable peeler, remove 8 strips (3" by ¾" each) peel from remaining tangerines. With knife, remove any remaining white pith from peel. Squeeze ¾ cup juice; set aside.

2. Cut broccoli into small flowerets. With vegetable peeler, peel broccoli stems; cut into ¼-inch-thick slices.

3. In 12-inch skillet, heat 2 tablespoons oil over high heat until very hot. Add strips of peel and cook until lightly browned, about 3 minutes. Transfer peel to large bowl.

4. On waxed paper, toss beef slices with 2 tablespoons cornstarch, coating evenly. Add half of beef to skillet and cook, stirring frequently (stir-frying), until crisp and lightly browned on both sides, about 5 minutes, using slotted spoon to transfer beef as it is browned to bowl with peel. Repeat with remaining 1 tablespoon oil and remaining beef.

5. Add broccoli and water to skillet. Reduce heat to medium; cover and cook 2 minutes. Increase heat to high. Remove cover and add green onions and red pepper; cook, stir-frying, 2 minutes. Add garlic and ginger; stir-fry 1 minute.

6. Meanwhile, in cup, combine tangerine juice, soy sauce, crushed red pepper, and remaining ½ teaspoon cornstarch and

stir until blended. Stir cornstarch mixture into skillet. Stir fry until sauce has thickened and boils.

7. Return beef mixture to skillet. Add citrus sections and juice in bowl; toss to combine. Makes 4 main-dish servings.

Each serving: About 300 calories, 23g protein, 21g carbohydrate, 15g total fat (3g saturated), 52mg cholesterol, 853mg sodium.

Fajitas

Fajitas are ideal party fare. Serve with your favorite salsa.

Prep: 15 minutes plus marinating   Cook/Broil: 20 minutes

3	tablespoons fresh lime juice
3	tablespoons fresh orange juice
¾	teaspoon salt
½	teaspoon dried oregano, crumbled
1	beef skirt steak (1¾ pounds)
1	tablespoon olive oil
2	medium onions, thinly sliced
2	garlic cloves, thinly sliced
3	large red peppers, cut into ½-inch-thick strips
1	large green pepper, cut into ½-inch-thick strips
2	teaspoons finely chopped pickled jalapeño chile
12	(6-inch) flour tortillas

1. In cup, combine lime and orange juices, ½ teaspoon salt, and oregano. Transfer to ziptight plastic bag; add meat, turning to coat. Seal bag, pressing out as much air as possible. Refrigerate beef 1 hour to marinate, turning bag once.

2. Preheat broiler. Meanwhile, in 12-inch skillet, heat oil over medium heat. Add onions and garlic and cook, stirring frequently, until onions are tender, about 5 minutes. Add red and green peppers, jalapeño, and remaining ¼ teaspoon salt; cook, stirring frequently, until red and green peppers are tender, about 7 minutes.

3. Remove meat from marinade and place on rack in broiling pan. Broil steak 6 inches from heat source 3 to 4 minutes per side for medium-rare or until desired doneness. Cut meat into thin slices across the grain and serve with tortillas and pepper mixture. Makes 6 main-dish servings.

Each serving: About 418 calories, 30g protein, 34g carbohydrate, 17g total fat (6g saturated), 66mg cholesterol, 531mg sodium.

Spicy Tangerine Beef

Flank Steak with Chimichurri Sauce

Chimichurri is a thick green herb sauce that is served with grilled meats in Argentina. It can be prepared ahead and refrigerated up to two days. Bring it to room temperature before serving.

Prep: 15 minutes   Broil: 9 minutes

1½	cups loosely packed fresh parsley leaves, chopped
1½	cups loosely packed fresh cilantro leaves, chopped
¼	cup olive oil
3	tablespoons red wine vinegar
1	garlic clove, crushed with garlic press
¾	teaspoon salt
¼	teaspoon ground black pepper
	pinch crushed red pepper
½	teaspoon chili powder
½	teaspoon sugar
¼	teaspoon ground coriander
¼	teaspoon ground cumin
1	beef flank steak (1½ pounds)

1. Preheat broiler. Prepare chimichurri sauce: In small bowl, combine parsley, cilantro, oil, vinegar, garlic, ¼ teaspoon salt, black pepper, and crushed red pepper; set aside.

2. In cup, combine chili powder, sugar, coriander, cumin, and remaining ½ teaspoon salt; rub on flank steak.

3. Place flank steak on rack in broiling pan. Broil 6 inches from heat source about 4½ minutes per side for medium-rare or until desired doneness. Holding knife in slanting position, almost parallel to cutting board, slice steak thinly across the grain. Serve with sauce. Makes 4 main-dish servings.

Each serving with 1 tablespoon sauce: About 239 calories, 25g protein, 2g carbohydrate, 14g total fat (5g saturated), 62mg cholesterol, 497mg sodium.

Stir-Fried Beef and Broccoli

If you wish, marinate the beef up to ten hours before cooking.

Prep: 15 minutes plus marinating   Cook: 15 minutes

2	tablespoons soy sauce
5	teaspoons vegetable oil
3	teaspoons cornstarch
1	teaspoon honey
1	beef flank steak (1 pound)
1	medium bunch broccoli (1 to 1¼ pounds)
¾	cup plus 1 tablespoon water
1½	teaspoons grated, peeled fresh ginger
1	garlic clove, finely chopped
	pinch crushed red pepper
2	tablespoons oyster sauce

1. In large bowl, combine soy sauce, 1 teaspoon oil, 2 teaspoons cornstarch, and honey.

2. Cut flank steak lengthwise in half. With knife held in slanting position, almost parallel to cutting surface, cut each half of steak crosswise into ⅛-inch-thick slices. Add meat to soy mixture; toss to coat. Cover and refrigerate 30 minutes.

3. Cut broccoli into small flowerets. With vegetable peeler, peel broccoli stems; cut into ⅛-inch-thick slices.

4. In nonstick 12-inch skillet, heat 1 teaspoon oil over high heat. Add broccoli flowerets and stems and cook, stirring frequently (stir-frying), 1 minute. Add ¼ cup water. Cover and cook 2 minutes; remove cover and cook, stir-frying, until water has evaporated, about 2 minutes longer. Transfer to large bowl; keep warm. Wipe skillet clean with paper towels.

5. In skillet, heat 1 teaspoon oil over high heat until very hot. Add half of beef and stir-fry until browned, about 3 minutes, transferring meat as it is browned to bowl with broccoli. Repeat with 1 teaspoon oil and remaining beef.

6. In small bowl, blend remaining 1 teaspoon cornstarch and 1 tablespoon water until smooth; set aside. Heat remaining 1 teaspoon oil in skillet over high heat until hot. Add ginger, garlic, and crushed red pepper; cook 30 seconds. Stir in remaining ½ cup water and oyster sauce; heat to boiling. Stir in cornstarch mixture. Stir-fry until sauce has thickened and boils. Stir beef and broccoli into sauce in pan; heat through. Transfer to warm platter. Makes 4 main-dish servings.

Each serving: About 274 calories, 26g protein, 9g carbohydrate, 14g total fat (4g saturated), 57mg cholesterol, 973mg sodium.

Beef with Snow Peas and Carrots
Prepare as directed but omit broccoli. Stir-fry **8 ounces snow peas** and **8 ounces carrots,** sliced, in **½ teaspoon oil.**

Spice-Rubbed Beef Tenderloin

You can grill the meat right after seasoning it, or refrigerate for up to twenty-four hours for even greater depth of flavor.

Prep: 5 minutes	Grill: 30 to 40 minutes
1	tablespoon fennel seeds, crushed
2	teaspoons salt
½	teaspoon ground ginger
½	teaspoon crushed red pepper
1	center-cut beef tenderloin roast (2½ pounds), trimmed and tied

1. Prepare grill. In cup, combine fennel seeds, salt, ginger, and crushed red pepper. Use to rub on beef tenderloin.

2. Place tenderloin on grill over medium heat. Cook beef, turning occasionally, until meat thermometer inserted in center of meat reaches 140°F, 30 to 40 minutes. Internal temperature of meat will rise to 145°F (medium) upon standing. Or cook until desired doneness. Transfer roast to cutting board and let stand 10 minutes to set juices for easier slicing. Cut into thin slices and serve. Makes 8 main-dish servings.

Each serving: About 177 calories, 22g protein, 1g carbohydrates, 9g total fat (3g saturated), 65mg cholesterol, 631mg sodium.

Orange-Glazed Steak

We marinate round steak in a soy-and-garlic mixture, then brush it with orange marmalade for a tasty finish. Serve with Peach Salsa (page 556).

Prep: 5 minutes plus marinating	Grill: 25 minutes
¼	cup soy sauce
2	garlic cloves, crushed with garlic press
1	teaspoon coarsely ground black pepper
1	beef top round steak, 1¼ inches thick (2 pounds), trimmed
⅓	cup orange marmalade

1. In 13" by 9" baking dish, combine soy sauce, garlic, and pepper. Add steak to soy-sauce mixture, turning to coat. Cover and refrigerate 30 minutes to marinate, turning once.

2. Prepare grill. Place steak on grill over medium heat. Cook steak 25 minutes for medium-rare or until desired doneness, brushing steak with orange marmalade during last 10 minutes of cooking and turning occasionally. Transfer steak to cutting board and let stand 10 minutes to set juices for easier slicing. Cut into thin slices across the grain. Makes 6 main-dish servings.

♥ Each serving: About 202 calories, 28g protein, 12g carbohydrate, 4g total fat (1g saturated), 72mg cholesterol, 419mg sodium.

Anise Beef Kabobs

When company calls during grilling season, kabobs often come to mind. Here are three sure-fire pleasers.

Prep: 10 minutes plus marinating	Grill: 8 minutes
4	wooden skewers, 10 to 12 inches long
2	teaspoons olive oil
1	teaspoon anise seeds or fennel seeds, crushed
½	teaspoon salt
¼	teaspoon coarsely ground black pepper
	pinch crushed red pepper (optional)
1	boneless beef top sirloin steak, 1 inch thick (1 pound), cut into 1¼-inch pieces

1. In medium bowl, combine oil, anise seeds, salt, black pepper, and crushed red pepper, if using. Add beef, tossing until well coated. Cover and let beef stand 20 minutes at room temperature to marinate. Meanwhile, prepare grill. Soak wooden skewers in water 15 minutes.

2. Loosely thread meat onto skewers. Grill over medium heat 8 to 10 minutes for medium-rare or until desired doneness, turning occasionally. Makes 4 main-dish servings.

Each serving: About 186 calories, 26g protein, 0g carbohydrate, 8g total fat (3g saturated), 75mg cholesterol, 329mg sodium.

Oregano–Red Wine Vinegar Kabobs

Marinate beef in **1 tablespoon red wine vinegar, 2 teaspoons olive oil, 1 garlic clove,** crushed with garlic press, **½ teaspoon dried oregano,** crumbled, **½ teaspoon salt,** and **¼ teaspoon coarsely ground black pepper.** Let stand 20 minutes at room temperature; thread on skewers and grill.

Sesame-Ginger Kabobs

Toss beef with **1 tablespoon soy sauce, 2 teaspoons Asian sesame oil, 2 teaspoons rice vinegar, 1 teaspoon grated, peeled fresh ginger, ½ teaspoon honey,** and **⅛ teaspoon coarsely ground black pepper.** Do not marinate. Thread meat on skewers and grill.

Barbecued Beef Ribs

Usually found in Texas, where everything is BIG, these generously sized ribs are sometimes labeled "beef ribs for barbecue."

Prep: 20 minutes   Grill: 20 minutes

1	bottle (12 ounces) chili sauce
⅓	cup bottled white horseradish
⅓	cup firmly packed brown sugar
¼	cup spicy brown mustard
1	tablespoon Worcestershire sauce
1	tablespoon red wine vinegar
½	teaspoon hot pepper sauce
2	chipotle chiles in adobo (page 31), finely chopped, or ½ teaspoon liquid smoke
1	tablespoon paprika
2	teaspoons chili powder
1	teaspoon ground cumin
½	teaspoon coarsely ground black pepper
⅛	teaspoon ground red pepper (cayenne)
6	pounds beef back ribs, cut into 1-rib portions

1. Prepare grill. In medium bowl, combine chili sauce, horseradish, brown sugar, mustard, Worcestershire, vinegar, hot pepper sauce, and chipotle chiles; set aside.

2. In small bowl, combine paprika, chili powder, cumin, black pepper, and ground red pepper. Use to rub on ribs.

3. Place ribs on grill over medium heat; grill, turning frequently, until cooked through, about 10 minutes. Brush ribs

with sauce; grill 10 minutes longer, turning ribs frequently and brushing with sauce. Makes 6 main-dish servings.

Each serving: About 746 calories, 49g protein, 30g carbohydrate, 46g total fat (18g saturated), 184mg cholesterol, 1,099mg sodium.

Korean-Style Sesame Short Ribs

Marinating these meaty ribs overnight makes them irresistible.

Prep: 15 minutes plus overnight to marinate
Grill: 20 minutes

4	pounds beef chuck short ribs, cut into 2-inch pieces
½	cup reduced-sodium soy sauce
4	teaspoons minced, peeled fresh ginger
3	large garlic cloves, finely chopped
2	teaspoons Asian sesame oil

Korean-Style Sesame Short Ribs

1. With sharp knife, cut ¼-inch-deep slashes in meaty side of short ribs at ½-inch intervals.

2. In ziptight plastic bags, combine soy sauce, ginger, garlic, and sesame oil. Add ribs, turning to coat. Seal bags, pressing out as much air as possible. Place bags in 13" by 9" baking dish and refrigerate overnight to marinate, turning bags several times.

3. Prepare grill. Place ribs on grill over medium heat and brush with remaining marinade. Grill 20 to 25 minutes for medium-rare or until desired doneness, turning ribs occasionally. Makes 8 appetizer servings.

Each serving: About 546 calories, 25g protein, 1g carbohydrate, 48g total fat (20g saturated), 107mg cholesterol, 357mg sodium.

Brisket with Chunky BBQ Sauce

A great do-ahead main dish for a summer picnic. You can slow-cook the brisket on the stovetop up to several days ahead. Then, twenty minutes before serving, brush it with sauce and grill until heated through.

Prep: 15 minutes   Cook/Grill: 3 hours 35 minutes

Brisket

1	fresh beef brisket (4½ pounds), well trimmed
1	medium onion, cut into quarters
1	large carrot, peeled and cut into 1½-inch pieces
1	bay leaf
1	teaspoon whole black peppercorns
¼	teaspoon whole allspice

Chunky BBQ Sauce

1	tablespoon vegetable oil
1	large onion (12 ounces), finely chopped
3	garlic cloves, finely chopped
2	tablespoons minced, peeled fresh ginger
1	teaspoon ground cumin
1	can (14½ ounces) tomatoes in puree, chopped
1	bottle (12 ounces) chili sauce
⅓	cup cider vinegar
2	tablespoons light (mild) molasses
2	tablespoons brown sugar
2	teaspoons dry mustard
1	tablespoon cornstarch
2	tablespoons water

1. Prepare brisket: In 8-quart Dutch oven, place brisket, onion, carrot, bay leaf, peppercorns, allspice, and enough *water* to cover; heat to boiling over high heat. Reduce heat; cover and simmer until meat is tender, about 3 hours.

2. Meanwhile, prepare Chunky BBQ Sauce: In nonstick 12-inch skillet, heat oil over medium heat. Add onion and cook, stirring occasionally, until tender, about 10 minutes. Add garlic and ginger and cook, stirring, 1 minute. Stir in cumin and cook 1 minute longer.

3. Stir in chopped tomatoes with their puree, chili sauce, vinegar, molasses, brown sugar, and dry mustard; heat to boiling over high heat. Reduce heat and simmer, stirring occasionally, 5 minutes.

4. In cup, blend cornstarch and water until smooth. After sauce has simmered 5 minutes, stir in cornstarch mixture. Heat to boiling, stirring; boil 1 minute. Cover and refrigerate sauce if not using right away. Makes about 4 cups.

5. When brisket is done, transfer to platter. If not serving right away, cover and refrigerate until ready to serve.

6. Prepare grill. Place brisket on grill (preferably one with a cover) over medium heat and cook 10 minutes. Turn brisket and cook 5 minutes longer. Spoon 1 cup barbecue sauce on top of brisket and cook until brisket is heated through, about 5 minutes longer. (Do not turn brisket after topping with sauce.) Reheat remaining sauce in small saucepan on grill. Slice brisket thinly across the grain and serve with sauce. Makes 12 main-dish servings.

Each serving: About 241 calories, 26g protein, 6g carbohydrate, 11g total fat (4g saturated), 81mg cholesterol, 174mg sodium.

Each ¼ cup sauce: About 61 calories, 1g protein, 13g carbohydrate, 1g total fat (0g saturated), 0mg cholesterol, 328mg sodium.

Short ribs undoubtedly make the best stew meat of all. Simply remove the bones and cut the meat into two-inch chunks. Since this cut tends to be a little fatty, you may want to trim away some of the external fat.

BRUCE AIDELLS
COOKBOOK AUTHOR

EXPERT TIP

Corned Beef Hash

A breakfast tradition, especially with a freshly poached egg on top. By adding chopped cooked beets to the mixture, you get Red Flannel Hash, a Yankee classic. Purchase cooked corned beef or use leftovers from New England Boiled Dinner (page 107).

Prep: 15 minutes   Cook: 25 minutes

3	tablespoons butter or margarine
1	large onion (12 ounces), chopped
2	cups chopped lean cooked corned beef
2	cups chopped cooked all-purpose potatoes
¼	teaspoon coarsely ground pepper
1	tablespoon chopped fresh parsley

1. In 10-inch skillet, melt butter over medium heat. Add onion and cook, stirring often, until tender, about 5 minutes.

2. Stir in corned beef, potatoes, and pepper until well combined. Cook, pressing hash down firmly with spatula, until bottom of hash has browned, about 15 minutes.

3. With spatula, turn hash over one small section at a time. Press down with spatula and cook until second side has browned, 5 to 10 minutes longer. Sprinkle with parsley. Makes 4 main-dish servings.

Each serving: About 337 calories, 23g protein, 21g carbohydrate, 18g total fat (9g saturated), 89mg cholesterol, 947mg sodium.

Red Flannel Hash

Prepare as directed, adding **1 cup finely chopped cooked beets** with corned beef, potatoes, and pepper.

GROUND BEEF

Some of America's favorite dishes start with ground beef: meat loaf, meatballs, burgers, chili, and casseroles, and that's just the beginning. There are many reasons why ground beef shows up so often on the dinner table. Foremost is cost—few meats are more economical, and it can be combined with other reasonably priced ingredients to stretch it even further. But ground beef delivers in the flavor department, too.

BUYING AND STORING

The label on ground beef often denotes the percentage of lean meat to fat, but sometimes the cut of meat is also listed. You can buy ground chuck, which is about 80 percent lean; ground sirloin, which is 90 to 95 percent extra-lean; and ground round, which at 85 percent lean, is juicy, flavorful, and the most popular cut. If the meat is simply labeled "ground beef," it comes from a combination of cuts and is only 70 percent lean.

The amount of fat in ground beef affects the moistness and texture of the cooked dish, so you will get different results when using ground chuck, ground round, or ground sirloin. For example, a burger made from these three main types of ground beef will be as follows: A chuck burger will be the juiciest but will also shrink a good deal as the fat melts away. Ground round will make a firmer burger that is still quite juicy, and sirloin will make a burger that has lots of beef flavor but is fairly dry and crumbly.

Many supermarkets also carry a ground meat-loaf mixture, which includes beef, pork, and veal. This combination makes a meat loaf with the hearty flavor of beef, the binding properties of veal, and the moistness of pork.

Ground beef should be cherry red. Don't worry if the meat in the center looks darker than the meat on the exterior. The darker color comes from a lack of oxygen. When exposed to the air, this darker meat will become redder.

E. coli, a strain of potentially deadly bacteria, has been found in mass-produced meat patties. To guard against this bacteria, always purchase ground beef from a reliable source and shape your own burgers. Because *E. coli* is most easily spread in unsanitary conditions, the level of cleanliness at your local butcher is more important now than ever.

COOKING GROUND BEEF

Disease-causing bacteria like *E. coli* contaminate the outer surface of food. Thus, the inside of a roast or steak will not be affected. The bacteria is killed when the outside of the food is exposed to high temperatures, when sautéing and roasting, for example. When beef is ground, any outer surface contamination is mixed throughout the meat. The bacteria on the surface of a grilled burger may be killed, but unless the interior of the meat is cooked to 160°F, dangerous bacteria can still be present. To eliminate this danger, always cook ground beef until well-done. When pressed in the center, a burger or patty should feel firm and spring back.

Classic Hamburgers

What could be more satisfying than a classic burger? Here's the way to do it right.

Prep: 5 minutes   Cook: 8 minutes

1 ¼	pounds ground beef chuck
½	teaspoon salt
¼	teaspoon ground black pepper

1. Shape ground beef into 4 patties, each ¾ inch thick, handling meat as little as possible. Sprinkle patties with salt and pepper.

2. Heat 12-inch skillet over high heat until hot. Add patties and cook about 4 minutes per side for medium or until desired doneness. Makes 4 burgers.

Each burger: About 243 calories, 29g protein, 0g carbohydrate, 14g total fat (6g saturated), 88mg cholesterol, 391mg sodium.

Grilled Hamburgers

Prepare outdoor grill. Shape patties as directed. Place patties on grill over medium heat and cook about 4 minutes per side for medium or until desired doneness.

Tex-Mex Burgers

Before shaping into patties, combine **2 tablespoons finely chopped onion, 2 tablespoons bottled salsa, 1 teaspoon salt,** and **1 teaspoon chili powder** with ground beef just until well blended but not overmixed. Panfry or grill as directed.

Each burger: About 249 calories, 29g protein, 1g carbohydrate, 14g total fat (6g saturated), 88mg cholesterol, 771mg sodium.

Greek Burgers

Before shaping into patties, combine **¼ cup chopped fresh parsley, 1 teaspoon dried mint,** crumbled, **1 teaspoon salt,** and **¼ teaspoon ground black pepper** with ground beef just until well blended but not overmixed. Panfry or grill as directed.

Each burger: About 245 calories, 29g protein, 0g carbohydrate, 14g total fat (6g saturated), 88mg cholesterol, 686mg sodium.

Roquefort Burgers

Before shaping into patties, combine **1 tablespoon Worcestershire sauce** and **½ teaspoon coarsely ground black pep-** per with ground beef just until well blended but not overmixed. Shape mixture into 4 balls. Make indentation in center of each ball; place **½ ounce crumbled Roquefort or blue cheese** into each indentation. Shape ground-beef mixture around cheese; flatten each into ¾-inch-thick patty. Panfry or grill as directed.

Each burger: About 299 calories, 32g protein, 1g carbohydrate, 19g total fat (8g saturated), 101mg cholesterol, 399mg sodium.

Teriyaki Burgers

Before shaping into patties, combine **¼ cup chopped green onions, 2 tablespoons soy sauce, 1 tablespoon brown sugar,** and **¼ teaspoon ground red pepper (cayenne)** with ground beef just until well blended but not overmixed. Panfry or grill as directed, but during last 2 minutes of cooking, brush burgers on each side with a mixture of **2 tablespoons apple jelly, 2 teaspoons minced, peeled fresh ginger,** and **1 teaspoon soy sauce.**

Each burger: About 290 calories, 29g protein, 12g carbohydrate, 14g total fat (6g saturated), 88mg cholesterol, 708mg sodium.

Tex-Mex Burgers

Danish Meatballs

These tender meatballs have a creamy sauce just made for spooning over noodles or rice. If you wish, serve the meatballs as they do in Denmark, with a dollop of lingonberry preserves.

Prep: 25 minutes   Cook: 15 minutes

1½	pounds ground beef chuck or ground meat for meat loaf (beef, pork, and veal)
½	cup plain dried bread crumbs
1	large egg
¼	cup chopped fresh flat-leaf parsley
2	tablespoons chopped fresh dill
1	tablespoon grated onion
1	teaspoon salt
¼	teaspoon ground black pepper
⅛	teaspoon ground nutmeg
2	tablespoons butter or margarine
2	tablespoons all-purpose flour
1½	cups milk
1	cup low-sodium chicken broth
	lingonberry preserves (optional)

1. In large bowl, combine ground beef, bread crumbs, egg, parsley, dill, onion, salt, pepper, and nutmeg just until well blended but not overmixed. Shape mixture into 24 meatballs, handling meat as little as possible.

2. In 12-inch skillet, melt butter over medium-high heat. Add meatballs and cook until browned, using slotted spoon to transfer meatballs to bowl as they are browned. Discard all but 2 tablespoons drippings from skillet.

3. Stir flour into drippings in skillet; cook over medium heat, stirring, 1 minute. Gradually add milk and broth; cook, stirring constantly, until mixture has thickened and boils.

4. Add meatballs to skillet; heat to boiling. Reduce heat; cover and simmer 10 minutes. Serve with lingonberry preserves, if desired. Makes 6 main-dish servings.

Each serving: About 330 calories, 28g protein, 12g carbohydrate, 19g total fat (9g saturated), 125mg cholesterol, 991mg sodium.

Mexican Meatballs

If chipotle chiles are hard to find, substitute one seeded and minced jalapeño chile and one-quarter teaspoon liquid smoke.

Prep: 30 minutes   Cook: 45 minutes

1½	pounds ground beef chuck
¾	cup plain dried bread crumbs
1	large egg
3	garlic cloves, finely chopped
1	teaspoon salt
½	teaspoon ground black pepper
¼	cup water
1	can (28 ounces) tomatoes
1	chipotle chile in adobo (page 31)
2	teaspoons vegetable oil
1	small onion, finely chopped
1	teaspoon ground cumin
1	cup chicken broth
¼	cup chopped fresh cilantro

1. In large bowl, combine ground beef, bread crumbs, egg, one-third of garlic, salt, pepper, and water just until well blended but not overmixed. Shape mixture into 1-inch meatballs, handling meat as little as possible.

2. In blender, puree tomatoes with their juice and chipotle chile until smooth.

3. In nonreactive 5-quart Dutch oven, heat oil over medium heat. Add onion and cook, stirring often, until tender, about 5 minutes. Stir in cumin and remaining garlic; cook 30 seconds. Stir in tomato mixture and broth; heat to boiling over high heat.

4. Add meatballs; heat to boiling. Reduce heat and simmer 30 minutes. To serve, sprinkle with cilantro. Makes 6 main-dish servings.

Each serving: About 318 calories, 28g protein, 18g carbohydrate, 15g total fat (5g saturated), 106mg cholesterol, 1,001mg sodium.

Greek Meatballs

These baked meatballs are prepared with a combination of beef and lamb, a touch of mint, and some feta cheese. They are usually served plain, but offer some marinara sauce alongside, if you like.

	Prep: 20 minutes Bake: 20 minutes
1	pound ground beef chuck
1	pound lean ground lamb
1	cup fresh bread crumbs (about 2 slices bread)
2	large eggs
4	ounces feta cheese, finely crumbled (1 cup)
3	bunches green onions, finely chopped (1 cup)
¼	cup chopped fresh flat-leaf parsley
2	garlic cloves, finely chopped
1	tablespoon dried mint, crumbled
2	tablespoons olive oil
1	tablespoon red wine vinegar
½	teaspoon salt
¼	teaspoon ground black pepper

1. Preheat oven to 425°F. In large bowl, combine ground beef, ground lamb, bread crumbs, eggs, feta, green onions, parsley, garlic, mint, oil, vinegar, salt, and pepper just until well blended but not overmixed.

2. Shape mixture into scant ¼-cup meatballs, handling meat as little as possible. Place 1 inch apart in two jelly-roll pans. Bake until cooked through, 20 to 25 minutes. Makes 6 main-dish servings.

Each serving: About 487 calories, 34g protein, 7g carbohydrate, 36g total fat (15g saturated), 190mg cholesterol, 566mg sodium.

"Susan's" Meat Loaf

This delicious basic meat loaf is from the "Susan, Our Teenage Cook" series, which ran in Good Housekeeping *for decades. Ground chuck makes it tender and tasty.*

	Prep: 15 minutes Bake: 1 hour
2	pounds ground beef chuck
2	large eggs
2	cups fresh bread crumbs (about 4 slices bread)
2	green onions, finely chopped
1	medium onion, finely chopped
¾	cup ketchup
¼	cup milk
2	tablespoons bottled white horseradish
1½	teaspoons salt
1	teaspoon dry mustard

1. Preheat oven to 400°F. In large bowl, combine ground beef, eggs, bread crumbs, green onions, onion, ¼ cup ketchup, milk, horseradish, salt, and dry mustard just until well blended but not overmixed.

2. Spoon mixture into 9" by 5" metal loaf pan, pressing firmly. Spread remaining ½ cup ketchup on top of loaf. Bake 1 hour. Let stand 10 minutes to set juices for easier slicing. Makes 8 main-dish servings.

Each serving: About 283 calories, 27g protein, 15g carbohydrate, 13g total fat (5g saturated), 125mg cholesterol, 845mg sodium.

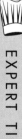

This terrific tip comes from barbecue champion John Willingham. To ensure that your burgers are thoroughly cooked in the center, with clean hands, form a hole the size of a quarter in the center of each burger. The burgers will cook in half the time because they are cooking both from the center and the edges, and you will have moister, more evenly cooked burgers.

SHIRLEY O. CORRIHER
COOKBOOK AUTHOR

EXPERT TIP

Cajun Meat Loaf

Cajun Meat Loaf

This colorful meat loaf is for those who like a bit of kick in their comfort food.

Prep: 20 minutes   Bake: 1 hour 15 minutes

2	tablespoons butter or margarine
2	carrots, peeled and finely chopped
1	large onion (12 ounces), chopped
1	large stalk celery, chopped
1	small green pepper, finely chopped
2	garlic cloves, crushed with garlic press
2	pounds ground meat for meat loaf (beef, pork, and veal)
2	large eggs
1	cup fresh bread crumbs (about 2 slices bread)
½	cup plus 2 tablespoons ketchup
¼	cup milk
1	tablespoon Worcestershire sauce
2	teaspoons salt
1	teaspoon ground cumin
½	teaspoon dried thyme
½	teaspoon ground nutmeg
½	teaspoon ground red pepper (cayenne)
½	teaspoon coarsely ground black pepper

1. In nonstick 12-inch skillet, melt butter over medium heat. Add carrots, onion, celery, and green pepper and cook, stirring occasionally, until vegetables are tender, about 15 minutes. Add garlic and cook 1 minute longer. Set aside to cool slightly.

2. Preheat oven to 375°F. In large bowl, combine ground meat, eggs, bread crumbs, ½ cup ketchup, milk, Worcestershire, salt, cumin, thyme, nutmeg, ground red pepper, black pepper, and cooked vegetable mixture just until well blended but not overmixed.

3. In 13" by 9" baking pan, shape mixture into 10" by 5" loaf, pressing firmly. Brush remaining 2 tablespoons ketchup on top of loaf. Bake 1 hour 15 minutes. Let stand 10 minutes to set juices for easier slicing. Makes 8 main-dish servings.

Each serving: About 364 calories, 24g protein, 14g carbohydrate, 23g total fat (10g saturated), 149mg cholesterol, 961mg sodium.

Sausage and Pepper Meat Loaf

Sausage and peppers are old friends that work as well in meat loaf as they do in other dishes.

Prep: 30 minutes   Bake: 1 hour 10 minutes

1	tablespoon olive oil
2	red peppers, chopped
1	large onion (12 ounces), chopped
1	large garlic clove, crushed with garlic press
1	pound sweet Italian-sausage links, casings removed
1	pound ground beef chuck
2	large eggs
1½	cups fresh bread crumbs (about 3 slices bread)
⅓	cup freshly grated Parmesan cheese
1	can (8 ounces) tomato sauce
½	teaspoon salt

1. In nonstick 12-inch skillet, heat oil over medium heat. Add red peppers and onion and cook until vegetables are tender and lightly browned, 10 to 15 minutes. Add garlic; cook 1 minute. Set vegetables aside to cool.

2. Preheat oven to 375°F. In large bowl, combine sausage meat, ground beef, eggs, bread crumbs, Parmesan, tomato sauce, salt, and cooked vegetables just until well blended but not overmixed.

3. In 13" by 9" baking pan, shape mixture into 9" by 5" loaf, pressing firmly. Bake meat loaf 1 hour 10 minutes. Let stand 10 minutes to set juices for easier slicing. Makes 8 main-dish servings.

Each serving: About 390 calories, 24g protein, 11g carbohydrate, 28g total fat (10g saturated), 134mg cholesterol, 884mg sodium.

Italian Stuffed Cabbage

Stuffed cabbage freezes well, so prepare a large batch.

Prep: 25 minutes   Bake: 1 hour 20 minutes

1	medium head cabbage (2½ pounds)
12	ounces sweet Italian-sausage links, casings removed
4	ounces ground beef chuck
⅓	cup uncooked regular long-grain rice
¼	cup freshly grated Parmesan cheese
2	tablespoons chopped fresh parsley
½	teaspoon fennel seeds, crushed
¼	teaspoon ground black pepper
½	cup water
1	teaspoon vegetable oil
2	garlic cloves, crushed with garlic press
1	can (14½ ounces) diced tomatoes
1	tablespoon tomato paste
½	cup chicken broth

1. In 5-quart saucepot, heat *4 quarts water* to boiling over high heat. Add cabbage to water; cover and cook 10 minutes. Transfer cabbage to colander. When cool enough to handle, peel off tender outer leaves. Repeat, if necessary, to obtain 12 large leaves. Trim thick ribs from base of leaves.

2. Meanwhile, in large bowl, combine sausage meat, ground beef, rice, Parmesan, parsley, fennel seeds, pepper, and water. Mix until well blended but not overmixed.

3. Preheat oven to 350°F. In oven-safe 12-inch skillet (if skillet is not oven-safe, wrap handle with double layer of foil), heat oil over medium heat. Add garlic and cook 30 seconds. Stir in tomatoes with their juice, tomato paste, and broth; heat to boiling. Reduce heat and simmer 5 minutes.

4. Place cabbage leaf in ⅓-cup measuring cup and stuff with ¼ cup meat filling. Fold leaf edges over filling, trimming overhang if necessary. Repeat with remaining cabbage leaves and filling.

5. Arrange cabbage packages seam side down in tomato sauce in skillet. Cover and bake until cooked through, about 1 hour 20 minutes. Makes 12 cabbage rolls.

Each cabbage roll: About 170 calories, 9g protein, 7g carbohydrate, 12g total fat (4g saturated), 31mg cholesterol, 403mg sodium.

Two-Alarm Chili

If you like really hot chili, increase the pickled jalapeño and ground red pepper to your taste. Here, cocoa is the secret ingredient that balances the seasonings.

Prep: 20 minutes   Cook: 35 minutes

1	tablespoon olive oil
1	medium onion, chopped
2	garlic cloves, finely chopped
2	green peppers, chopped
2	pounds ground beef chuck
3	pickled jalapeño chiles, seeded and finely chopped (2 tablespoons)
3	tablespoons chili powder
2	teaspoons unsweetened cocoa
1¼	teaspoons salt
¾	teaspoon ground coriander
½	teaspoon dried oregano
¼	teaspoon ground red pepper (cayenne)
1	can (14 to 16 ounces) tomatoes, chopped

1. In nonstick 12-inch skillet, heat oil over medium heat. Add onion and garlic and cook, stirring occasionally, until onion is tender, about 5 minutes. Add green peppers and cook, stirring, until tender-crisp, about 5 minutes longer.

2. Add ground beef and cook, breaking up meat with side of spoon, until meat is no longer pink. Stir in pickled jalapeños, chili powder, cocoa, salt, coriander, oregano, and ground red pepper; cook 1 minute. Add tomatoes with their juice and heat to boiling. Reduce heat and simmer, stirring occasionally, until slightly thickened, 15 to 20 minutes longer. Makes 6 main-dish servings.

Each serving: About 326 calories, 33g protein, 10g carbohydrate, 18g total fat (6g saturated), 94mg cholesterol, 758mg sodium.

Cincinnati Chili

This dish is served many ways in chili restaurants all over Cincinnati. A "three-way" is over spaghetti with shredded Cheddar on top. Add chopped onion and it becomes a "four-way." For a "five-way," add cooked red kidney beans.

Prep: 25 minutes   Cook: 3 hours

2	teaspoons vegetable oil
2	medium onions, chopped
2	teaspoons finely chopped garlic
2	pounds ground beef chuck
2	tablespoons chili powder
1	tablespoon ground cumin
1	teaspoon ground cinnamon
1	teaspoon salt
½	teaspoon dried oregano
½	teaspoon ground red pepper (cayenne)
2	cans (16 ounces each) tomatoes
1	can (14½ ounces) beef broth or 1¾ cups Brown Beef Stock (page 83)
1½	cups water
½	square (½ ounce) unsweetened chocolate, chopped
1	package (16 ounces) spaghetti or linguine, cooked as label directs

1. In nonreactive 5-quart Dutch oven, heat oil over medium heat. Add onions and cook, stirring occasionally, until tender, about 5 minutes. Transfer to small bowl; set aside. Add garlic to Dutch oven; cook 1 minute longer. Transfer to bowl with onions.

2. In same Dutch oven, cook ground beef over high heat, breaking up meat with side of spoon, until meat is browned. Discard fat. Stir in chili powder, cumin, cinnamon, salt, oregano, and ground red pepper; cook 1 minute longer.

3. Add tomatoes with their juice to Dutch oven, breaking them up with side of spoon. Stir in broth, water, chocolate, browned beef, and onion-garlic mixture; heat to boiling. Reduce heat; cover and simmer 2 hours 30 minutes. Remove cover and simmer until thickened, about 30 minutes longer.

4. Meanwhile, in large saucepot, cook pasta as label directs. Drain. Serve chili over pasta. Makes 8 main-dish servings.

Each serving without spaghetti: About 270 calories, 26g protein, 12g carbohydrate, 14g total fat (5g saturated), 71mg cholesterol, 756mg sodium.

Picadillo

Serve this intriguingly seasoned ground beef stew with a bowl of rice and a crisp green salad. If you like, cook the picadillo a little longer, until almost all the liquid has evaporated, and use it as a filling for empanadas or turnovers.

Prep: 10 minutes   Cook: 25 minutes

4	teaspoons olive oil
1	medium onion, finely chopped
4	garlic cloves, finely chopped
2	pounds ground beef chuck
1	can (15 ounces) crushed tomatoes
½	cup pimiento-stuffed olives (salad olives), coarsely chopped
⅓	cup dark seedless raisins
3	tablespoons tomato paste
1	tablespoon red wine vinegar
1	teaspoon unsweetened cocoa
1	teaspoon ground cumin
½	teaspoon salt
¼	cup slivered almonds, toasted

1. In 10-inch skillet, heat oil over medium heat. Add onion and garlic and cook until onion is tender, about 5 minutes. Stir in ground beef and cook, breaking up meat with side of spoon, until meat is no longer pink, about 5 minutes.

2. Add tomatoes, olives, raisins, tomato paste, vinegar, cocoa, cumin, and salt and heat to boiling. Reduce heat and simmer until slightly thickened, about 5 minutes. Stir in almonds and serve. Makes 6 main-dish servings.

Each serving: About 397 calories, 34g protein, 17g carbohydrate, 23g total fat (7g saturated), 94mg cholesterol, 743mg sodium.

Tamale Pie

This tamale pie has a velvety soft cornmeal top and bottom crust. If you prefer firm slices, be sure to let it rest for at least twenty-five minutes before serving.

Prep: 25 minutes   Bake: 45 minutes

2	teaspoons vegetable oil
1	medium onion, chopped
1	pound ground beef chuck
1	tablespoon chili powder
1	teaspoon ground cumin
1	cup medium-hot salsa
1	can (15¼ to 16 ounces) whole-kernel corn, drained
4	cups water
1	cup cornmeal
1	teaspoon salt
2	ounces Cheddar cheese, shredded (½ cup)

1. Preheat oven to 350°F. In nonstick 12-inch skillet, heat oil over medium-high heat; add onion and cook until tender and golden, about 5 minutes. Stir in ground beef and cook, breaking up meat with side of spoon, until meat is browned, about 5 minutes. Skim and discard any fat. Stir in chili powder and cumin and cook 2 minutes longer. Remove from heat and stir in salsa and corn.

2. In 2-quart saucepan, heat water to boiling. With wire whisk, gradually whisk in cornmeal and salt. Cook over medium heat, whisking frequently, 5 minutes.

3. Pour half of cornmeal mixture into shallow 2-quart casserole. Spoon beef mixture over cornmeal; spoon remaining cornmeal over beef and sprinkle Cheddar on top. Bake 45 minutes. Remove casserole from oven and let stand 15 to 25 minutes before serving. Makes 6 main-dish servings.

Each serving: About 334 calories, 21g protein, 33g carbohydrate, 13g total fat (5g saturated), 57mg cholesterol, 1,026mg sodium.

Sloppy Joes

Fun to eat and easy to make, this dish is guaranteed to be a hit with kids and adults alike.

Prep: 20 minutes   Cook: 30 minutes

4	teaspoons olive oil
1	medium onion, chopped
2	garlic cloves, finely chopped
1	medium red pepper, chopped
1	small green pepper, chopped
1	stalk celery, chopped
2	pounds ground beef chuck
1	can (28 ounces) whole tomatoes in puree, chopped
2	tablespoons light (mild) molasses
1	tablespoon cider vinegar
1	teaspoon salt
¼	teaspoon ground black pepper
6	hamburger buns, split

1. In nonstick 12-inch skillet, heat oil over medium heat. Add onion and garlic and cook until onion is tender, about 5 minutes.

2. Add red and green peppers and celery and cook until tender, about 5 minutes. Stir in ground beef and cook, breaking up meat with side of spoon, until meat is longer pink, about 5 minutes. Stir in tomatoes with their puree, molasses, vinegar, salt, and black pepper and heat to boiling. Reduce heat and simmer until sauce has slightly thickened, about 10 minutes.

3. Place split buns on plates and top with Sloppy Joe mixture. Makes 6 main-dish servings.

Each serving: About 481 calories, 36g protein, 39g carbohydrate, 20g total fat (7g saturated), 94mg cholesterol, 936mg sodium.

VEAL

Veal has always been regarded as one of the finest meats and is associated with some of Europe's most elegant dishes. This lean, delicate meat resembles poultry more than beef, and it has a versatility that lends itself to a variety of seasonings and cooking techniques. But remember, veal requires a bit of extra attention to keep it from becoming overcooked and dried out.

BUYING AND STORING VEAL

Veal calves are raised for eight to sixteen weeks. In order to maintain the meat's delicate texture, the calves are never subjected to excessive movement. The finest and most expensive veal is milk-fed: either their mother's milk or a special milk formula. Milk-fed veal is rarely labeled as such but can be recognized by its light pink, almost white color.

"Grain-fed veal" comes from older calves raised on a diet of grain or grass. It has a deep rosy pink color and a slightly stronger flavor than milk-fed veal. This veal is sometimes labeled "calf," but more often it is just labeled "veal."

The best source for high-quality veal is a specialty butcher. Italian neighborhoods are especially reliable places to find excellent milk-fed meat. Large roasts may have to be special ordered, but you will be well rewarded at the dinner table.

Veal is sold to retailers in six primal cuts: the shoulder (which includes the neck), rib, loin, hind leg, breast, and front leg. Ground veal can be seasoned just like ground beef and turned into patties or meatballs. It is especially good when combined with beef for meat loaf; its high gelatin content makes the cooked meat loaf very easy to slice.

When buying veal at the supermarket, let your eye be the judge of both quality and value for the price asked. Look for meat that is fine-textured and pale. While marbled fat in beef is desirable, veal should have very little marbling, and what fat there is should be firm and very white. The bones of milk-fed veal have reddish marrow. Prime veal is usually milk-fed, whereas grain-fed veal is usually graded choice. Veal marketed under brand names is rarely graded.

Veal cutlets are readily available but vary in quality. Depending on where you live, they can be called veal scallopini, veal scallops, or even schnitzel. The cutlets are ideally cut from a single muscle, usually the top or bottom round. This is important because some butchers make cutlets that contain two or three muscles, which cause the cutlets to curl when cooked. Veal cutlets are usually cut about ¼ inch thick. Some

POPULAR VEAL CUTS

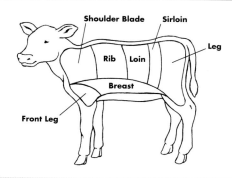

Veal shoulder roast, boneless

(braise, roast). Shoulder cut with bones removed; rolled and tied to keep its shape.

Veal breast

(braise, roast). Also called breast of veal. Contains lower ribs, lean meat, and layers of fat, making it juicy and flavorful.

Veal breast riblets

(braise). Also called veal riblets; long, narrow cuts containing rib bones with thin fat covering.

Veal shoulder blade steak

(braise, panfry). Also called veal shoulder steak or veal shoulder chop.

Veal rib chops

(braise, panfry, grill, broil). Contain big rib-eye muscle. Expensive and tasty.

Veal loin chops

(braise, panfry, grill, broil). Muscles include top loin and tenderloin.

Veal top loin chops

(braise, panfry, grill, broil). Same as veal loin chops except does not contain tenderloin.

Veal cutlets

(braise, panfry). Very lean, thin, boneless slices from leg that are pounded thinly. Also called scallopini.

Veal shank cross cuts

(braise). Cut crosswise from hindshank, usually 1 to 2½ inches thick. Also called osso buco.

recipes require the cutlets to be pounded so they cook more quickly. Unless you purchase cutlets from a high-quality butcher who will pound them for you, they will need to be pounded at home. To pound veal cutlets, with meat mallet, or between two sheets of plastic wrap or waxed paper with rolling pin, pound cutlets to 1/8-inch thickness. (The meat will spread out as it is pounded, so leave some space between the cutlets.)

Because veal is a moist meat, it is fairly perishable. Large cuts and stew meat will only keep for two days, tightly wrapped, in the refrigerator. Use veal cutlets the day of purchase.

COOKING VEAL

When cooking veal, remember that it is very lean and can dry out easily if overcooked. Most cuts can be cooked by dry-heat methods, but tough cuts from the breast, front leg (shank and osso buco), and neck must be braised. Roasts should not be cooked to a final internal temperature of more than 160°F.

ROASTING TIMES
(OVEN TEMPERATURE OF 325°F)

Start with meat at refrigerator temperature. Remove roast from oven when it reaches 5°F below desired doneness; temperature will continue to rise as roast stands.

CUT	MEAT THERMOMETER READING	APPROXIMATE COOKING TIME (MINUTES PER POUND)
Boneless shoulder roast	160°F	35 to 40 minutes
Leg rump or round roast (boneless)	160°F	35 to 40 minutes
Boneless leg roast	160°F	25 to 30 minutes
Rib roast	160°F	30 to 35 minutes

Broiling, Grilling, and Panfrying Choose fairly thick chops and steaks; cuts that are too thin will dry out. Veal cutlets are usually panfried. They cook very quickly, so keep a close watch. And don't crowd them in the pan, or they will steam instead of brown. If necessary, sauté in batches and set aside on a warm plate, loosely covered with foil, until ready to serve.

Best Bets Arm (shoulder) or blade steaks, loin chops, rib chops, ground veal, and cutlets.

Braising and Stewing Bone-in pieces are especially suited to long cooking because the bones add extra flavor to the liquid. Veal shanks have meaty-tasting marrow in the center, which helps enrich stews. But don't ignore boneless veal stew meat, cut from the neck or shoulder, which is readily available and delicious. When cooked, braised or stewed veal should be nice and tender. One other cut that is moist-cooked is veal breast. Its layers of fat and connective tissue can only be dissolved by this type of cooking.

Best Bets Shanks, shank cross cuts (osso buco), arm (shoulder) or blade steak, breast, and shoulder.

Roasting Many large cuts of veal roast nicely. Since veal roasts are generally very lean, you'll get juicier results by cooking them to only 155°F, since the temperature will rise as it stands. Veal breast and shoulder roasts should be cooked until well-done and tender.

Best Bets Rib roast, loin roast, round, shoulder roast, and breast.

Stuffed Veal Roast

Pancetta, unsmoked Italian bacon, lends rich flavor to this roast. If you can't find it, use the mildest regular bacon available.

Prep: 15 minutes   Roast: 1 hour 20 minutes

3	ounces pancetta, chopped
1	shallot, finely chopped
1/4	cup water
1	package (10 ounces) frozen chopped spinach, thawed and squeezed dry
3	ounces Fontina cheese, chopped (3/4 cup)
1	boneless veal shoulder roast (3 pounds)
1/2	cup dry white wine
2	tablespoons heavy or whipping cream
3/4	cup chicken broth
3/4	teaspoon cornstarch
1	tablespoon water

1. Preheat oven to 425°F. In 10-inch skillet, combine pancetta, shallot, and water; heat to boiling over medium heat. Reduce heat and simmer until pancetta is cooked through and shallot is soft, about 5 minutes. Stir in spinach until well combined. Transfer spinach mixture to medium bowl and stir in Fontina until combined.

2. Using sharp knife, cut roast lengthwise three-quarters of the way through, being careful not to cut all the way through. Open and spread flat like a book. Spoon spinach mixture on roast, leaving ½-inch border all around. Roll up roast from one long side to enclose filling; tie with string at 1-inch intervals to secure.

3. Place roast in small roasting pan (13" by 9") and roast 30 minutes. Turn oven control to 350°F and roast until meat thermometer inserted in center of roast reaches 155°F, about 50 minutes longer. Internal temperature of meat will rise to 160°F (medium) upon standing. Transfer roast to warm large platter and let stand 15 minutes to set juices for easier slicing.

4. Meanwhile, skim and discard fat from roasting pan. Add wine and heat to boiling, stirring until browned bits are loosened from bottom of pan. Pour into 1-quart saucepan and heat to boiling. Add cream and heat to boiling; boil until liquid has reduced by half. Add broth and heat to boiling again. In small bowl, blend cornstarch with water until smooth. Stir cornstarch mixture into saucepan. Heat to boiling over high heat, stirring. Spoon sauce over meat and serve. Makes 8 main-dish servings.

Each serving: About 329 calories, 39g protein, 2g carbohydrate, 17g total fat (7g saturated), 173mg cholesterol, 446mg sodium.

Veal Rib Roast

This is company fare at its best. Serve with roasted new potatoes and steamed asparagus.

Prep: 10 minutes	Roast: 2 hours
1¼	teaspoons salt
½	teaspoon dried sage
¼	teaspoon dried thyme, crumbled
1	tablespoon olive oil
1	veal rib roast (5 pounds), trimmed and chine bone removed
4	garlic cloves, not peeled
½	cup white wine
1½	cups chicken broth
1½	teaspoons cornstarch
1	tablespoon water
2	tablespoons fresh lemon juice
1	tablespoon cold butter or margarine

1. Preheat oven to 450°F. In small bowl, combine salt, sage, thyme, and oil. Use to rub on roast. Place veal and garlic in medium roasting pan (14" by 10"). Roast 1 hour.

2. Pour wine into roasting pan, cover veal with loose tent of foil, and turn oven control to 350°F. Roast veal until meat thermometer inserted in thickest part of roast (not touching bone) reaches 155°F, about 1 hour longer. Internal temperature of meat will rise to 160°F (medium) upon standing. Transfer roast to cutting board and let stand 15 minutes to set juices for easier carving.

3. Skim and discard fat from roasting pan; pour any pan drippings into 2-quart saucepan. Pour broth into roasting pan and heat to boiling, stirring until browned bits are loosened from bottom of pan; add to saucepan. Heat to boiling over medium heat. In small bowl, blend cornstarch with water until smooth. Stir cornstarch mixture into saucepan and heat to boiling over high heat, stirring; boil 1 minute. Remove from heat; stir in lemon juice and swirl in butter. Slice veal and serve with sauce. Makes 8 main-dish servings.

Each serving: About 277 calories, 35g protein, 2g carbohydrate, 13g total fat (4g saturated), 159mg cholesterol, 696mg sodium.

Fruit-Stuffed Veal Roast

Fruit is frequently included in pork stuffings, but many fruits also complement the mild flavor of veal. If you like, only use one type of dried fruit, such as apples, pears, or prunes.

Prep: 35 minutes   Roast: 1 hour 20 minutes

2	slices firm white bread, cut into ½-inch cubes
4	teaspoons olive oil
2	shallots, finely chopped
1	garlic clove, finely chopped
½	cup mixed dried fruit, coarsely chopped
2	teaspoons Dijon mustard
¾	teaspoon salt
½	teaspoon dried rosemary, crumbled
1	boneless veal shoulder roast (2½ pounds)
½	cup chicken broth
1	Golden Delicious apple, peeled, cored, and chopped
¼	cup applejack brandy or Calvados
½	cup heavy or whipping cream

1. Preheat oven to 375°F. Place bread cubes on cookie sheet and bake until lightly browned, about 5 minutes. Transfer to medium bowl. Turn oven control to 425°F.

2. In 1-quart saucepan, heat 2 teaspoons oil over medium heat. Add half of shallots and garlic and cook, stirring until shallot is tender, about 4 minutes; add to bowl with croutons. Add dried fruit, mustard, ¼ teaspoon salt, and ¼ teaspoon rosemary; toss to combine.

3. Using sharp knife, cut roast lengthwise three-quarters of the way through, being careful not to cut all the way through. Open and spread flat like a book. Spoon fruit mixture on roast, leaving 1-inch border all around. Roll up roast from one long side to enclose filling; tie with string at 1-inch intervals to secure. Rub ¼ teaspoon of salt and remaining ¼ teaspoon rosemary on veal. Place roast in small roasting pan (13" by 9") and roast until lightly browned, about 30 minutes. Turn oven control to 375°F and roast until meat thermometer inserted in center of roast reaches 155°F, about 50 minutes longer. Internal temperature of meat will rise to 160°F (medium) upon standing. Transfer roast to warm platter and let stand 10 minutes to set juices for easier slicing.

4. Meanwhile, skim and discard fat from roasting pan. Add broth and heat to boiling, stirring until browned bits are loosened from bottom of pan. Heat remaining 2 teaspoons oil in skillet over medium heat. Add remaining shallots and cook, stirring frequently, until tender, about 4 minutes. Add apple and cook, stirring frequently, until tender-crisp, about 4 minutes. Remove from heat and add applejack. Return to heat and cook until liquid has evaporated. Add broth from roasting pan and heat to boiling; boil 3 minutes. Add cream and boil until sauce has slightly thickened, about 5 minutes. Stir in remaining ¼ teaspoon salt.

5. Slice veal and serve with applejack sauce. Makes 8 main-dish servings.

Each serving: About 323 calories, 30g protein, 13g carbohydrate, 15g total fat (7g saturated), 145mg cholesterol, 463mg sodium.

Stuffed Breast of Veal

This cut of meat can always be counted on for being moist, flavorful, and easy on the wallet. Here, it is filled with the classic Sicilian combination of spinach and golden raisins. Serve it hot or at room temperature; either way, it will be equally delicious.

Prep: 25 minutes plus cooling   Bake: 2 hours 15 minutes

1	tablespoon olive oil
1	small onion, chopped
3	garlic cloves, finely chopped
2	packages (10 ounces each) frozen chopped spinach, thawed and squeezed dry
1	lemon
⅓	cup golden raisins
¾	teaspoon salt
1	bone-in veal breast (4 pounds), with pocket for stuffing
1	cup chicken broth

1. Preheat oven to 425°F. In 12-inch skillet, heat oil over medium-low heat. Add onion and garlic and cook, stirring frequently, until onion is tender, about 5 minutes. Add spinach and cook, stirring frequently, until liquid has evaporated, about 2 minutes. Remove from heat.

2. From lemon, grate ¾ teaspoon peel and squeeze 2 tablespoons juice; set juice aside. Add raisins, ½ teaspoon salt, and lemon peel to spinach. Cool to room temperature. Spoon spinach mixture into pocket of veal.

3. Place breast, meat side up, in medium roasting pan

(14" by 10"). Sprinkle remaining ¼ teaspoon salt on meat side (not rib side) of veal and roast 1 hour. Turn veal, rib side up, and pour broth and lemon juice into bottom of roasting pan. Cover veal with loose tent of foil and bake until tender, about 1 hour and 15 minutes longer.

4. Transfer veal to cutting board, rib side down, and let stand 10 minutes to set juices for easier carving. Skim and discard fat from drippings in pan. Carve veal by slicing down along one rib bone. Cut away rib bone and discard, then continue carving. Transfer slices to warm platter and serve with pan juices. Makes 6 main-dish servings.

Each serving: About 425 calories, 51g protein, 13g carbohydrate, 18g total fat (6g saturated), 183mg cholesterol, 637mg sodium.

Braised Veal Chops with Tomatoes and Peas

The bones in the shoulder chops contribute extra flavor and body to the sauce. Two large chops will easily feed four people.

Prep: 10 minutes Cook: 1 hour 15 minutes	
2	veal shoulder blade chops, 1 inch thick (1 pound each)
1	slice bacon, chopped
¼	teaspoon salt
⅛	teaspoon ground black pepper
1	medium onion, chopped
2	garlic cloves, finely chopped
1	can (14½ ounces) tomatoes in puree
1	cup chicken broth
½	cup dry white wine
¼	teaspoon dried sage, crumbled
1	cup frozen peas

1. In nonstick 12-inch skillet, cook bacon over medium-high heat until browned. With slotted spoon, transfer bacon to paper towels to drain; reserve. Pat veal dry with paper towels. Sprinkle chops with salt and pepper. Cook chops in drippings in skillet over medium-high heat until browned, about 5 minutes per side. Transfer veal to plate.

2. Add onion to skillet and cook over medium heat, stirring occasionally, until lightly browned, about 5 minutes. Stir in garlic and cook 1 minute longer. Stir in tomatoes with their puree, broth, wine, and sage and heat to boiling, breaking up tomatoes with side of spoon.

3. Return chops to skillet; cover and simmer over medium-low heat until veal is tender, about 45 minutes. Transfer to platter; keep warm. Add peas to skillet and cook 5 minutes. To serve, cut veal into serving portions, spoon sauce over veal, and sprinkle bacon on top. Makes 4 main-dish servings.

♥ Each serving: About 289 calories, 35g protein, 16g carbohydrate, 9g total fat (3g saturated), 139mg cholesterol, 782mg sodium.

Veal and Mushroom Stew

Here, veal simmers slowly in its own juices until meltingly tender.

Prep: 30 minutes Bake: 1 hour 15 minutes	
1½	pounds boneless veal shoulder, cut into 1½-inch pieces
¾	teaspoon salt
¼	teaspoon ground black pepper
3	tablespoons vegetable oil
1	pound white mushrooms, trimmed and cut in half
¼	pound shiitake mushrooms, stems removed
½	cup water
⅓	cup dry Marsala wine
1	package (10 ounces) frozen peas, thawed

1. Preheat oven to 350°F. Pat veal dry with paper towels. Sprinkle veal with salt and pepper. In nonreactive 5-quart Dutch oven, heat 2 tablespoons oil over medium-high heat until very hot. Add half of veal and cook until browned, using slotted spoon to transfer meat to bowl as it is browned. Repeat with remaining veal (without additional oil).

2. In Dutch oven, heat remaining 1 tablespoon oil over medium-high heat. Add white and shiitake mushrooms and cook, stirring occasionally, until lightly browned.

3. Return veal to Dutch oven; stir in water and Marsala, stirring until brown bits are loosened from bottom of pan. Heat veal mixture to boiling.

4. Cover Dutch oven and bake, stirring occasionally, until veal is tender, 1 hour to 1 hour 15 minutes. Stir in peas and heat through. Makes 6 main-dish servings.

Each serving: About 249 calories, 26g protein, 12g carbohydrate, 11g total fat (2g saturated), 94mg cholesterol, 448mg sodium.

Osso Buco with Gremolata

This aromatic recipe from Northern Italy is especially wonderful when served with Creamy Polenta (page 394).

Prep: 40 minutes   Bake: 2 hours

4	meaty veal shank cross cuts (osso buco), each about 2 inches thick (1 pound each)
1/2	teaspoon salt
1/4	teaspoon ground black pepper
1	tablespoon olive oil
2	medium onions, chopped
3	carrots, peeled and chopped
2	stalks celery, chopped
4	garlic cloves, finely chopped
1	can (14 1/2 to 16 ounces) tomatoes in puree
1	cup dry white wine
1	cup chicken broth
1	bay leaf
2	tablespoons chopped fresh parsley
1/2	teaspoon freshly grated lemon peel

1. Preheat oven to 350°F. Sprinkle shanks with salt and pepper. In nonreactive 5-quart Dutch oven, heat oil over medium-high heat until very hot. Add shanks and cook until browned, about 10 minutes, transferring shanks to plate as they are browned. Add onions to Dutch oven and cook over medium heat, stirring occasionally, until slightly browned, about 5 minutes. Add carrots, celery, and three-fourths of garlic; cook 2 minutes longer.

2. Return veal to Dutch oven. Stir in tomatoes with their puree, wine, broth, and bay leaf. Heat to boiling over high heat. Cover and place in oven. Bake until veal is tender when pierced with fork, about 2 hours.

3. Meanwhile, prepare gremolata: In small bowl, mix parsley, lemon peel, and remaining garlic. Cover and refrigerate until ready to serve.

4. Transfer veal to platter. Heat sauce in Dutch oven to boiling over high heat; boil until it has reduced to 4 cups, about 10 minutes. Pour sauce over veal and sprinkle with gremolata. Makes 4 main-dish servings.

♥ Each serving: About 374 calories, 53g protein, 20g carbohydrate, 8g total fat (2g saturated), 183mg cholesterol, 874mg sodium.

Osso Buco with Gremolata

Veal Stew with Gremolata

Use **2 1/2 pounds boneless veal shoulder,** cut into 1 1/2-inch pieces. Proceed as in Step 1 but brown veal in batches, transferring meat to bowl as it is browned. Continue as directed but bake only 1 1/2 hours. Makes 6 main-dish servings.

Creamy Veal Stew

Known in France as Blanquette de Veau, *this velvety stew is perfect just the way it is. It can, however, be accented with two tablespoons chopped fresh tarragon and two tablespoons fresh lemon juice, stirred in with the cream.*

Prep: 35 minutes   Bake: 1 hour 15 minutes

2	pounds boneless veal shoulder, cut into 1 1/2-inch pieces
1/4	cup all-purpose flour
1	teaspoon salt
1/4	teaspoon ground black pepper
2	tablespoons plus 2 teaspoons vegetable oil
1	cup dry white wine
2	medium onions, chopped
1	cup chicken broth
1	bay leaf
1/4	teaspoon dried thyme
1/4	cup heavy or whipping cream

1. Preheat oven to 350°F. Pat veal dry with paper towels. On waxed paper, combine flour, salt, and pepper. Coat veal with seasoned flour, shaking off excess. In nonstick 12-inch skillet, heat 1 tablespoon oil over medium-high heat until very hot. Add half of veal and cook until browned, using slotted spoon to transfer meat to bowl as it is browned. Repeat with 1 tablespoon oil and remaining veal. Add wine to skillet and heat to boiling, stirring until browned bits are loosened from bottom of skillet; remove from heat.

2. In nonreactive 5-quart Dutch oven, heat remaining 2 teaspoons oil over medium heat. Add onions and cook until tender, about 5 minutes. Stir in veal, broth, bay leaf, thyme, and pan-juice mixture from skillet. Heat to boiling; cover and bake until veal is tender, about 1 hour 15 minutes. Stir in heavy cream. Makes 6 main-dish servings.

Each serving: About 285 calories, 31g protein, 10g carbohydrate, 13g total fat (4g saturated), 139mg cholesterol, 696mg sodium.

Vitello Tonnato

Serve this delicious cold buffet dish with bowls of roasted red peppers, potato salad, and a variety of olives. The creamy tuna sauce can also be served over cold poached chicken.

Prep: 20 minutes plus cooling and chilling
Cook: 1 hour 50 minutes

1	rolled boneless veal shoulder roast (2¾ to 3 pounds), trimmed and tied
10	anchovy fillets
2	garlic cloves, thinly sliced
3	cups water
1	can (14½ ounces) chicken broth or 1¾ cups Chicken Broth (page 84)
1	cup dry white wine
1	medium onion, thinly sliced
2	carrots, peeled and thinly sliced
1	can (6 ounces) tuna packed in oil, undrained
½	cup mayonnaise
½	cup heavy or whipping cream
1	tablespoon fresh lemon juice
½	teaspoon salt
¼	teaspoon dried sage
2	tablespoons chopped fresh parsley

1. With sharp knife, make slits all over veal. Coarsely chop 2 anchovies; insert chopped anchovies and garlic into slits.

2. In nonreactive 5-quart Dutch oven, combine water, broth, wine, onion, and carrots and heat to boiling over medium heat. Add roast to Dutch oven. Reduce heat; cover and simmer until veal is tender, about 1 hour and 45 minutes.

3. Remove from heat; let veal cool in broth 1 hour, then transfer veal to plate and refrigerate to cool completely. Strain broth, reserving ¾ cup; discard remaining broth. Transfer reserved broth to food processor fitted with knife blade. Add tuna, mayonnaise, cream, lemon juice, salt, sage, and remaining 8 anchovies; puree. Cut veal into thin slices and transfer to deep platter or shallow casserole large enough to hold veal in one or two layers. Pour sauce over veal; cover and refrigerate at least 1 hour or up to 24 hours. Serve chilled or at room temperature, sprinkled with parsley. Makes 8 main-dish servings.

Each serving: About 401 calories, 37g protein, 3g carbohydrate, 26g total fat (7g saturated), 172mg cholesterol, 801mg sodium.

Wiener Schnitzel

Travelers to Vienna rarely leave without enjoying at least one meal of these thin, tender breaded veal cutlets.

Prep: 15 minutes   Cook: 20 minutes

6	veal cutlets (1½ pounds)
2	large eggs
⅓	cup all-purpose flour
1	teaspoon salt
½	teaspoon coarsely ground black pepper
⅓	cup all-purpose flour
1½	cups plain dried bread crumbs
4	tablespoons butter or margarine
6	anchovy fillets (optional)
2	tablespoons capers, drained
2	tablespoons chopped fresh parsley
2	lemons, each cut into 6 wedges

1. With meat mallet, or between two sheets of plastic wrap or waxed paper with rolling pin, pound cutlets to ⅛-inch thickness.

2. In pie plate, beat eggs; on waxed paper combine flour, salt, and pepper. Place bread crumbs on separate sheet of waxed paper. Coat cutlets in seasoned flour, dip in eggs, and then coat evenly with bread crumbs.

3. In nonstick 12-inch skillet, melt 2 tablespoons butter over medium-high heat. Add cutlets, a few at a time, and cook until browned, 3 to 4 minutes per side, adding remaining 2 tablespoons butter as needed. With slotted spatula, transfer cutlets to warm platter as they are browned.

4. To serve, top cutlets with anchovies, if using, and capers; sprinkle with parsley and garnish with lemon wedges. Makes 6 main-dish servings.

Each serving: About 348 calories, 30g protein, 25g carbohydrate, 13g total fat (6g saturated), 180mg cholesterol, 920mg sodium.

Schnitzel à la Holstein
Prepare Wiener Schnitzel as directed but serve each cutlet topped with **1 fried egg.**

Veal Scallopini Marsala

This sensational dish takes only minutes to prepare.

Prep: 10 minutes   Cook: 15 minutes

1	pound veal cutlets
¼	cup all-purpose flour
¼	teaspoon salt
⅛	teaspoon coarsely ground pepper
3	tablespoons butter or margarine
½	cup dry Marsala wine
½	cup chicken broth
1	tablespoon chopped fresh parsley

1. With meat mallet, or between two sheets of plastic wrap or waxed paper with rolling pin, pound cutlets to ⅛-inch thickness. Cut cutlets into 3" by 3" pieces. On waxed paper, combine flour, salt, and pepper; coat veal with seasoned flour, shaking off excess.

2. In nonstick 10-inch skillet, melt butter over medium-high heat. Cook veal, in batches, until lightly browned, 45 to 60 seconds per side, using slotted spatula to transfer pieces to warm platter as they are browned; keep warm.

3. Stir Marsala and broth into veal drippings in pan; cook until syrupy, 4 to 5 minutes, stirring until browned bits are loosened from bottom of skillet. Pour sauce over veal and sprinkle with parsley. Makes 6 main-dish servings.

Each serving: About 179 calories, 17g protein, 5g carbohydrate, 7g total fat (4g saturated), 75mg cholesterol, 288mg sodium.

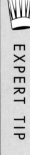

Did You Know?

- Veal flank steak is excellent for grilling—ask your butcher.
- Veal shoulder is a flavorful, inexpensive cut that is ideal for roasting.
- Lobster and veal are a delicious flavor match.
- Veal sweetbreads can be poached, separated into nuggets, then skewered and grilled.

CHRIS SCHLESINGER

CHEF/OWNER, EAST COAST GRILL, MASSACHUSETTS

EXPERT TIP

Veal Parmigiana

Smothered in marinara sauce and topped with mozzarella cheese, this Italian-restaurant favorite is easy to make at home.

Prep: 30 minutes   Cook: 25 minutes

2	cups Marinara Sauce (page 343) or bottled marinara sauce
1	cup plain dried bread crumbs
½	teaspoon salt
⅛	teaspoon ground black pepper
1	large egg
2	tablespoons water
6	veal cutlets (1½ pounds)
3	tablespoons butter or margarine
¼	cup freshly grated Parmesan cheese
4	ounces part-skim mozzarella cheese, shredded (1 cup)

1. Prepare Marinara Sauce, if using.

2. On waxed paper, combine bread crumbs, salt, and pepper. In pie plate, beat egg and water. Dip cutlets in egg mixture, then in bread crumbs; repeat to coat each cutlet twice.

3. In 12-inch skillet, melt butter over medium heat. Add cutlets, a few at a time, and cook until browned, about 5 minutes per side, using slotted spatula to transfer cutlets to platter as they are browned.

4. Return cutlets to skillet. Spoon sauce evenly over cutlets. Sprinkle with Parmesan and top with mozzarella. Reduce heat to low; cover and cook just until cheese has melted, about 5 minutes. Makes 6 main-dish servings

Each serving: About 367 calories, 35g protein, 19g carbohydrate, 17g total fat (8g saturated), 154mg cholesterol, 913mg sodium.

Chicken Parmigiana

Substitute **1½ pounds skinless, boneless chicken breast halves** for veal and prepare as directed.

Veal with Tomato and Arugula Salad

Crispy veal cutlets topped with a zesty salad offer a mouthwatering combination of contrasting colors, flavors, and textures.

🕐 **Prep:** 20 minutes   **Cook:** 10 minutes

2	teaspoons fresh lemon juice
6	tablespoons olive oil
1	teaspoon salt
¾	teaspoon ground black pepper
1	large tomato (12 ounces), coarsely chopped
1	cup loosely packed basil leaves
¼	cup coarsely chopped red onion
1	pound veal cutlets
2	large eggs
½	cup all-purpose flour
1	cup plain dried bread crumbs
1	bunch arugula (10 ounces), trimmed

1. In medium bowl, combine lemon juice, 2 tablespoons oil, ½ teaspoon salt, and ¼ teaspoon pepper. Stir in tomato, basil, and onion; set aside.

2. With meat mallet, or between two sheets of plastic wrap or waxed paper with rolling pin, pound cutlets to ⅛-inch thickness. In pie plate, beat eggs with remaining ½ teaspoon each salt and pepper. Place flour on waxed paper; place bread crumbs on separate waxed paper. Dip cutlets in flour, then in egg mixture, then in bread crumbs.

3. In nonstick 12-inch skillet, heat 2 tablespoons oil over medium-high heat until very hot. Add half of cutlets and cook about 3 minutes per side. Transfer to platter large enough to hold cutlets in single layer; keep warm. Repeat with remaining 2 tablespoons oil and remaining veal.

4. Add arugula to tomato mixture and toss to combine. Spoon on top of hot veal. Makes 4 main-dish servings.

Each serving: About 538 calories, 35g protein, 39g carbohydrate, 27g total fat (5g saturated), 195mg cholesterol, 939mg sodium.

Veal with Tomato and Arugula Salad

Veal Piccata

This piquant dish depends on real dairy butter for its success. Do not use margarine—the sauce will not thicken properly.

🕐 **Prep:** 10 minutes   **Cook:** 15 minutes

¼	cup all-purpose flour
½	teaspoon salt
¼	teaspoon ground black pepper
1	pound veal cutlets
4	teaspoons olive or vegetable oil
⅓	cup dry white wine
1	cup chicken broth
2	tablespoons fresh lemon juice
1	tablespoon butter
1	tablespoon chopped fresh flat-leaf parsley

1. With meat mallet, or between two sheets of plastic wrap or waxed paper with rolling pin, pound cutlets to ¼-inch thickness. On waxed paper, combine flour, salt, and pepper. Coat cutlets with seasoned flour, shaking off excess.

2. In nonstick 12-inch skillet, heat 2 teaspoons oil over medium-high heat until very hot. Add half of cutlets and cook until browned, about 2 minutes. Turn cutlets and cook 1 minute longer. Transfer cutlets to platter; keep warm. Repeat with remaining 2 teaspoons oil and remaining veal.

3. Increase heat to high and add wine to skillet, stirring to loosen browned bits from bottom of skillet. Add broth and heat to boiling; boil until sauce has reduced to ½ cup, 4 to 6 minutes. Stir in lemon juice, butter, and parsley. When butter has melted, pour sauce over veal. Makes 4 main-dish servings.

Each serving: About 226 calories, 26g protein, 7g carbohydrate, 10g total fat (3g saturated), 96mg cholesterol, 643mg sodium.

Veal Stuffed with Fontina, Prosciutto, and Basil

A simple, flavorful stuffing makes these chops great for grilling, as well. To keep them moist and tender, avoid overcooking.

Prep: 15 minutes	Broil: 10 minutes
2	ounces Fontina cheese, shredded (½ cup)
1	ounce prosciutto, chopped (¼ cup)
¼	cup chopped fresh basil
¼	teaspoon salt
⅛	plus ¼ teaspoon ground black pepper
4	veal loin chops, 1 inch thick (8 ounces each)
1	teaspoon olive oil

1. Preheat broiler. In small bowl, toss Fontina, prosciutto, basil, and ⅛ teaspoon pepper until evenly combined.

2. Pat veal dry with paper towels. Holding knife parallel to surface, cut a horizontal pocket in each chop. Stuff one-fourth of cheese mixture into pocket of each chop. Rub chops with oil, then sprinkle with salt and remaining ¼ teaspoon pepper.

3. Place chops on rack in broiling pan. Place pan in broiler at position closest to heat source. Broil chops 5 to 6 minutes per side for medium-rare or until desired doneness. Makes 4 main-dish servings.

Each serving: About 266 calories, 33g protein, 1g carbohydrate, 14g total fat (6g saturated), 133mg cholesterol, 488mg sodium.

Grilled Veal Chops

Often the least complicated recipes are the best. It is especially true here, since grilling imparts such scrumptious smoky flavor.

Prep: 5 minutes plus marinating	Cook: 20 minutes
4	veal rib chops, 1½ inches thick (12 ounces each)
¼	cup balsamic vinegar
2	teaspoons olive or vegetable oil
1	teaspoon dried rosemary, crumbled
½	teaspoon salt
½	teaspoon coarsely ground pepper

1. Prepare grill. In ziptight plastic bag, combine chops and vinegar, turning to coat. Seal bag, pressing out as much air as possible. Let veal stand 20 minutes at room temperature to marinate.

2. Drain chops and brush with oil; sprinkle with rosemary, salt, and pepper. Grill 10 minutes per side over medium to medium-low heat until cooked to desired doneness. Makes 4 main-dish servings.

Each serving: About 308 calories, 42g protein, 1g carbohydrate, 14g total fat (4g saturated), 185mg cholesterol, 446mg sodium.

No-Frills Veal Chops
Omit balsamic-vinegar marinade, brush chops with oil, and grill as directed.

Veal Nuggets with Sour Cream–Dill Sauce

These tender nuggets are smothered in a sour cream sauce that is great with egg noodles.

Prep:15 minutes   Cook: 25 minutes

2	tablespoons butter or margarine
1	small onion, finely chopped
1½	pounds ground veal
1	cup fresh bread crumbs (about 2 slices bread)
1	large egg
1	cup milk
1¼	teaspoons salt
1	tablespoon all-purpose flour
¾	cup water
½	cup reduced-fat sour cream
¼	cup chopped fresh dill

1. In nonstick 12-inch skillet, melt 1 tablespoon butter over medium heat. Add onion and cook, stirring occasionally, until tender. Transfer to large bowl and cool slightly.

2. To onion in bowl, add ground veal, bread crumbs, egg, ⅓ cup milk, and 1 teaspoon salt, mixing just until well blended but not overmixed. Shape mixture into 1-inch meatballs, handling meat as little as possible. Flatten each meatball to ½-inch thickness.

3. In same skillet, melt remaining 1 tablespoon butter over medium-high heat. Add flattened meatballs, half at a time; cook until browned, about 2 minutes per side, using slotted spatula to transfer them to bowl as they are browned.

4. Reduce heat to medium. Add flour and remaining ¼ teaspoon salt to drippings in skillet, stirring until blended. Gradually stir in water and remaining ⅔ cup milk, stirring until browned bits are loosened from bottom of skillet. Cook, stirring constantly, until mixture has thickened and boils.

5. Return veal to skillet; simmer, stirring occasionally, 10 minutes. Gently stir in sour cream and dill; heat through (do not boil). Makes 6 main-dish servings.

Each serving: About 301 calories, 27g protein, 10g carbohydrate, 17g total fat (8g saturated), 151mg cholesterol, 695mg sodium.

PORK

From breakfast bacon to a pork chop supper, from holiday ham to grilled sausage, there are many ways to enjoy pork. It is interesting to note, however, that only one-third of American pork is served fresh: The rest is smoked, salted, cured, or made into sausage.

BUYING AND STORING PORK

Modern breeding methods have standardized pork to the degree that the cuts are no longer graded according to their quality—the amount of fat doesn't vary much from pig to pig. Simply check the label for the cut you need. And since pork is slaughtered at an early age, it is naturally tender.

The pig is divided into four primal cuts: the ham, loin, shoulder, and belly. The ham is the hind leg. The back (loin) is cut into three portions: the sirloin, center-cut, and blade end. The shoulder consists of two sections: The top part is called Boston butt or Boston shoulder roast, and the bottom part is called picnic. The belly area includes the spareribs and bacon.

Miscellaneous pork parts, like ears and tails, can be found at ethnic markets, and supermarkets often carry pig's feet. Ham hocks, from the middle section of the front shank, are sold fresh and smoked (smoked ham hocks are a flavorful substitute for ham bones in split pea soup). Fresh pork fat, from the back of the pig (fatback), is also available. When the fat has been rendered and cooled until solid again, it is called lard. Even though it is highly saturated, lard is prized by many cooks as a flavorful cooking fat, and pastry made with lard is wonderfully flaky. During the holidays, ethnic markets often sell whole suckling pigs. They are processed when six to eight weeks old and have juicy, tender meat.

Fresh pork has not been salted, brined, smoked, or cured in any way. A fresh ham is simply an uncured hind leg of pork. Cured pork is traditionally prepared by salting it with a dry rub. Pork can also be cured by soaking it in brine or injecting it with a brine solution. Sodium nitrate, which keeps pork pink, is often added during the curing process. Smoked pork is generally processed after curing to impart a smoky flavor.

There are many cured and smoked pork products available. Smoked ham is from the hind leg of pork, whereas picnic ham comes from the shoulder. These hams are labeled either "partially cooked" or "fully cooked." In either case, be sure to follow the label's instructions. Partially cooked ham must be cooked to 155°F before eating. While fully cooked ham is

POPULAR PORK CUTS

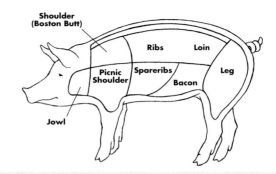

Shoulder (Boston Butt) · Ribs · Loin · Leg · Spareribs · Bacon · Picnic Shoulder · Jowl

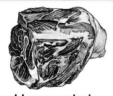

Pork shoulder arm picnic

(roast). Also called picnic or whole fresh picnic.

Pork shoulder arm roast

(roast). Also called pork arm roast.

Pork leg roast, boneless

(roast). Also called rolled fresh ham.

Pork loin center rib roast

(roast). Contains loin eye muscle and rib bones; also called pork loin roast and center cut pork roast.

Pork loin tenderloin

(roast, broil, panfry, grill). Very tender and lean; cut into slices for panfrying or stir-frying. Also called pork tenderloin.

Pork spareribs

(roast, bake, braise, broil, grill). Contains long rib bones with thin covering of meat on outside of and between ribs.

Pork loin country-style ribs

(roast, bake, braise, broil, grill). Actually blade end loin chops that have been split. Also called country-style spareribs.

Pork loin rib chops

(braise, panfry, broil, grill). Contain loin eye muscle and backbone. Also called center cut chops.

Pork loin chops

(braise, panfry, broil, grill). Contain eye muscle and tenderloin separated by T-shaped bone. Also called loin end chops.

Pork loin sirloin chops

(braise, panfry, broil, grill). From sirloin end of loin. Also called sirloin pork chops or sirloin pork steaks.

Pork loin sirloin cutlets

(braise, panfry, broil, grill). Boneless, tender slices cut from sirloin end of loin.

Pork loin blade chops

(braise, panfry, broil, grill). From blade end of loin. Also called pork loin blade steaks.

ready to serve, its flavor is much improved by heating it to an internal temperature of 130° to 140°F. Ham is available bone-in (whole, shank, or butt portions), semiboneless (the aitch and shank bones have been removed; only the leg bone remains), and boneless (rolled and shaped, or formed). For easy serving, purchase spiral-sliced ham, where the ham has been cut in one long continuous slice. Canned ham is cured but not always smoked. Boneless smoked pork shoulder (rolled and wrapped in a mesh stockingette that must be removed before serving) is much smaller than ham. It's a great way to serve smoked pork when you're not expecting a crowd. The term "water added" means that the meat has absorbed extra water during the curing process or was injected with water by the manufacturer. Smoked pork loin or loin chops are fine, tasty alternatives to their unsmoked counterparts.

Country hams, such as Smithfield and Virginia, are heavily salted and smoked. They should be soaked in cold water for twenty-four to thirty-six hours to remove the excess salt, then thoroughly cooked. Prosciutto is cured, air-dried ham that has not been smoked. Freshly sliced imported or domestic prosciutto can be purchased from specialty food stores. Prosciutto is sometimes added to dishes to heighten the flavor of mild-tasting meats or poultry.

Bacon is made from the pork belly; it is cured and then usually smoked. Italian *pancetta* is a type of unsmoked bacon that is shaped like a jelly roll and sliced to order. Salt pork, like bacon, is from the pork belly. Look for pieces that are streaked with meat. It is salt-cured but not smoked and is fattier than regular bacon. Salt pork lends rich flavor to dishes such as baked beans and fish chowder. Don't confuse it with salt fatback, however, which doesn't contain any meat at all. Canadian bacon is closer in flavor and texture to ham than to bacon. It is cut from the loin and is, therefore, very lean.

Sausage is a favorite way to enjoy pork. Fresh sausage is seasoned ground pork that has been stuffed into casings or formed into patties; it must be cooked. Cured and smoked sausages usually, but not always, require further cooking. Andouille, a spicy smoked sausage, is an important ingredient in Cajun cooking. Kielbasa, also known as Polish sausage, is a good substitute for andouille and is delicious grilled. Chorizo is a smoked hard sausage that is heavily seasoned with chiles and plays a big role in Southwestern and Mexican cooking. Many German-style sausages, such as bratwurst (a combination of pork and veal), are fresh sausages and must be cooked. Dried and cured sausages, such as salami and pepperoni, are usually presliced and don't require cooking.

SMOKED MEAT CUTS

Smoked ham rump portion
(roast, bake). Also called ham butt end.

Smoked ham shank portion
(roast, bake). Cured and smoked shank half of pork leg.

Smoked pork shoulder roll
(roast, bake, braise). Also called smoked shoulder butt.

Smoked whole pork shoulder picnic
(roast, bake, braise). Also called smoked picnic or smoked picnic shoulder.

Smoked ham center slice
(broil, panfry, roast, bake). Cut from center portion of cured, smoked ham.

Like other meats, today's pork is much leaner than in the past. Recipes used to require pork to be cooked to 170°F. This was done not just for the sake of tenderness. It was to prevent any possible infection from trichinosis, a disease that could be passed to humans through undercooked pork. Not only has trichinosis been eradicated from pork products, but the parasite that carries the disease is killed at 137°F. Regardless of what your grandmother taught you or what the marking on your meat thermometer says, for the best results, today's pork should not be cooked to above 160°F. Large cuts like fresh ham, however, should be cooked to 170°F. When carved, they will have just a hint of pink at the center (with a deeper pink color near the bone), but the juices will run clear. Cook ground pork just until no trace of pink remains in the center.

To keep pork chops juicy, cook only until the meat is just opaque at the bone.

Look for fresh pork that's pinkish white to grayish pink (leg and shoulder cuts tend to be darker than the loin cuts). The flesh should be firm to the touch. The amount of marbled fat should be minimal, and any external fat should be white, firm, and well trimmed. Cured and smoked pork products are darker in color due to the curing process.

Fresh pork can be refrigerated, tightly wrapped, for up to two days after purchase. Cured and smoked products, if unsliced and sealed in their original packaging, will last two weeks or longer, but only one week after being opened. Do not store according to the "purchase by" date on the package, as supermarket refrigerators are colder than those at home.

ROASTING TIMES
(OVEN TEMPERATURE OF 350°F)

Start with meat at refrigerator temperature. Remove roast from oven when it reaches 5°F below desired doneness; temperature will continue to rise as roast stands.

CUT	WEIGHT	MEAT THERMOMETER READING	APPROXIMATE COOKING TIME (MINUTES PER POUND)
FRESH PORK (WITH BONE)			
Crown roast	6 to 10 pounds	160°F	25 to 30 minutes
Center loin roast	3 to 5 pounds	160°F	25 to 30 minutes
Boneless top loin roast	2 to 4 pounds	160°F	25 to 30 minutes
Whole leg (fresh ham)	10 to 14 pounds	160° to 170°F	25 to 30 minutes
Leg half, shank or butt portion	3 to 5 pounds	160° to 170°F	40 minutes
Boston butt	3 to 6 pounds	160° to 170°F	45 minutes
Tenderloin (roast at 425° to 450°F)	½ to 1½ pounds	160°F	25 to 35 minutes total
SMOKED, COOK BEFORE EATING (HEAT AT 325°F)			
Whole ham	14 to 16 pounds	160°F	15 to 18 minutes
SMOKED FULLY COOKED PORK			
Whole ham	14 to 16 pounds	130° to 140°F	1 to 1¾ hours total
Half ham	6 to 8 pounds	130° to 140°F	1 hour total

COOKING PORK

Since pork is usually tender, many cuts are equally suitable for dry-heat and moist-heat cooking methods. Just take care not to overcook the leaner cuts of pork.

Broiling, Grilling, Panfrying, and Stir-frying A wide range of lean pork cuts lend themselves to these methods.

Best Bets Tenderloin, loin, rib chops, loin chops, sirloin chops, sirloin cutlets, blade chops, and sausages. After precooking, spareribs, baby back ribs, and meaty country-style ribs are good broiled or grilled.

Braising and Stewing Many cuts of pork stand up well to long slow cooking in liquid. Well-marbled cuts are especially succulent when braised or stewed. Avoid using very lean cuts, such as tenderloin, which only toughen from long cooking.

Best Bets Sirloin chops, blade chops, pork or ham hocks, spareribs, back ribs, and country-style ribs. Pork cubes for stew are usually cut from the shoulder or leg. Pork neck, which is sawed into pieces with the bone still attached, can also be stewed, but the bones make it difficult to eat.

Roasting Use tender cuts from the loin (the back of the pig from shoulder to hip), such as the leg or shoulder.

Best Bets Rib crown roast, shoulder arm roast, arm picnic roast, bone-in leg (fresh ham), whole boneless tenderloin, bone-in loin, boneless loin, spareribs, and country-style ribs.

EXPERT TIP

Lean cuts of pork, such as the loin and tenderloin, can be made juicy by brining, which also imparts flavor. A brine is a solution of water and salt. For flavor, a sweetener (sugar, maple syrup, etc.) is often added, as well as flavorings, such as pepper, mustard, chili powder, juniper berries, lemon peel, herbs, or garlic. And instead of water, you can use beer or apple cider. For a basic brine, dissolve ½ cup salt and ½ cup sugar in 8 cups hot water. Add 2 teaspoons vanilla extract and 2 tablespoons freshly cracked pepper; refrigerate until chilled. Add up to 6 pounds of loin or tenderloins to the brine. Pork loin should be refrigerated in the brine for 2 days, whereas pork tenderloin needs only 6 to 8 hours. Remove the meat and proceed with any roasting or grilling recipe.

BRUCE AIDELLS
COOKBOOK AUTHOR

Pork Crown Roast with Apple Stuffing

An elegant crown roast always makes a dramatic centerpiece for an important occasion. Be sure to order your roast ahead of time from your butcher. The savory apple stuffing is also good with turkey or goose.

Prep: 20 minutes   Roast: 3 hours 30 minutes

1	pork rib crown roast (7 pounds)
2½	teaspoons salt
½	plus ⅛ teaspoon ground black pepper
6	tablespoons butter or margarine
4	stalks celery, chopped
1	large onion (12 ounces), chopped
1	pound Golden Delicious apples (3 medium), peeled, cored, and chopped
8	cups fresh bread cubes (10 to 12 slices firm white bread)
½	cup apple juice
1	large egg, lightly beaten
1	teaspoon poultry seasoning
¼	cup Calvados, applejack brandy, or water
3	tablespoons all-purpose flour
1	can (14½ ounces) chicken broth or 1¾ cups Chicken Broth (page 84)

1. Preheat oven to 325°F. Rub roast with 1 teaspoon salt and ¼ teaspoon pepper. Place roast, rib ends down, in large roasting pan (17" by 11½"). Roast 1 hour.

2. Meanwhile, in 5-quart Dutch oven, melt butter over medium heat. Add celery and onion and cook, stirring, until tender, about 5 minutes. Add apples and cook until tender, 6 to 8 minutes longer. Remove Dutch oven from heat. Stir in bread cubes, apple juice, egg, poultry seasoning, 1 teaspoon salt, and ¼ teaspoon pepper. Toss until well combined.

3. Remove roast from oven and turn rib ends up. Fill cavity of roast with stuffing. (Place any leftover stuffing into greased 1½-quart casserole. Bake leftover stuffing, uncovered, during last 30 minutes of roasting time.)

4. Return pork to oven and continue roasting until meat thermometer inserted in thickest part of roast (not touching bone) reaches 155°F, about 2 hours 30 minutes. Internal temperature of pork will rise to 160°F upon standing. If stuffing browns too quickly, cover it with foil.

Pork Crown Roast with Apple Stuffing

5. When roast is done, transfer to warm platter and let stand 15 minutes to set juices for easier carving.

6. Meanwhile, prepare gravy: Pour pan drippings into 2-cup measuring cup or medium bowl (set roasting pan aside); let stand until fat separates from meat juice. Skim off 3 tablespoons fat from drippings; if necessary, add enough melted *butter* to equal 3 tablespoons. Pour into 2-quart saucepan. Skim and discard any remaining fat from meat juice. Add Calvados to roasting pan; heat over medium heat, stirring until brown bits are loosened from bottom of pan. Add to meat juice in cup.

7. Into fat in saucepan, with wire whisk, whisk flour, remaining ½ teaspoon salt, and remaining ⅛ teaspoon pepper until blended; cook over medium heat 1 minute. Gradually whisk in meat-juice mixture and broth. Heat to boiling, stirring constantly; boil 1 minute. Serve roast warm with gravy and stuffing. Makes 14 main-dish servings.

Each serving: About 406 calories, 32g protein, 19g carbohydrate, 21g total fat (9g saturated), 104mg cholesterol, 716mg sodium.

Fresh Ham with Spiced Apple Glaze

A whole ham will provide enough meat for your grandest dinner party. A fragrant blend of cinnamon, cloves, and nutmeg—ideal with pork—is rubbed on before roasting. Serve with Dried Pear Chutney (page 559) and several kinds of mustard.

Prep: 15 minutes   Bake: 5 hours

1	whole pork leg (fresh ham, 15 pounds), trimmed
2	teaspoons dried thyme
2	teaspoons ground cinnamon
2	teaspoons salt
1	teaspoon coarsely ground black pepper
½	teaspoon ground nutmeg
½	teaspoon ground cloves
1	jar (10 ounces) apple jelly
¼	cup balsamic vinegar

1. Preheat oven to 350°F. With knife, remove skin and trim excess fat from pork leg, leaving only a thin layer of fat.

2. In cup, combine thyme, cinnamon, salt, pepper, nutmeg, and cloves. Use to rub on pork. Place pork, fat side up, on rack in large roasting pan (17" by 11½"). Roast pork 3 hours. Cover pork loosely with tent of foil. Continue roasting until meat thermometer inserted into thickest part of pork (not touching bone) registers 150°F, about 1 hour.

3. Meanwhile, in 1-quart saucepan, heat apple jelly and vinegar to boiling over high heat; boil 2 minutes. Set aside.

4. When pork has reached 150°F, remove foil and brush pork with glaze. Continue roasting pork, brushing occasionally with remaining glaze, until meat thermometer registers 165°. (Meat near bone will be slightly pink.) Internal temperature of pork will rise to 170° upon standing.

5. When roast is done, transfer to warm large platter; let stand 20 minutes to set juices for easier carving. Makes 24 main-dish servings.

Each serving: About 298 calories, 38g protein, 6g carbohydrate, 12g total fat (4g saturated), 123mg cholesterol, 232mg sodium.

Pork Roast with Fennel and Garlic

Fennel, with its licoricelike flavor, marries well with pork.

Prep: 10 minutes   Roast: 1 hour 30 minutes

4	garlic cloves, finely chopped
2½	teaspoons fennel seeds, crushed
1¼	teaspoons salt
2	teaspoons olive oil
1	bone-in pork loin roast (4 pounds), trimmed

1. Preheat oven to 450°F. In cup, combine garlic, fennel seeds, salt, and oil to make paste.

2. Place roast in small roasting pan (13" by 9") and rub fennel paste on outside of pork and between bones. Roast pork 45 minutes. Turn oven control to 350°F, cover meat loosely with tent of foil, and roast until meat thermometer inserted in thickest part of roast (not touching bone) reaches 155°F, about 45 minutes longer. Internal temperature of meat will rise to 160°F upon standing. When roast is done, transfer to warm platter and let stand 15 minutes to set juices for easier carving. Makes 8 main-dish servings.

Each serving: About 270 calories, 35g protein, 1g carbohydrate, 13g total fat (4g saturated), 99mg cholesterol, 427mg sodium.

Pork Roast with Fresh Sage

Our flavorful secret is a fresh-herb paste. For greater flavor absorption, rub the meat ahead of time and refrigerate for up to twenty-four hours. Bone-in cuts, such as this one, take a little longer to cook but are the most flavorful.

Prep: 15 minutes   Roast: 2 hours to 2 hours 15 minutes

¼	cup chopped fresh parsley
2	tablespoons chopped fresh sage
2	garlic cloves, finely chopped
½	teaspoon dried thyme
1	teaspoon salt
½	teaspoon ground black pepper
1	bone-in pork loin roast (4 pounds), trimmed
⅓	cup dry white wine
⅔	cup chicken broth

1. Preheat oven to 350°F. On cutting board, chop parsley, sage, garlic, thyme, salt, and pepper together, occasionally crushing mixture with side of chef's knife, to make thick paste.

2. Place roast in small roasting pan (13" by 9") and rub herb paste on pork. Roast pork until meat thermometer inserted in thickest part of roast (not touching bone) reaches 155°F, 2 hours to 2 hours 15 minutes. Internal temperature of meat will rise to 160°F upon standing.

3. When roast is done, transfer to warm platter and let stand 15 minutes to set juices for easier carving. Meanwhile, add wine to roasting pan and heat to boiling over high heat, stirring until browned bits are loosened from bottom of pan. Add broth and heat to boiling. Remove from heat and skim and discard fat. Serve sauce with roast. Makes 8 main-dish servings.

Each serving: About 268 calories, 35g protein, 1g carbohydrate, 12g total fat (4g saturated), 99mg cholesterol, 440mg sodium.

Pork Roast with Caraway Seeds

A simple but elegant roast loin of pork, dressed with an unusual crushed-caraway-seed-and-herb coating. Serve with applesauce or the more robust Horseradish Applesauce (page 483).

Prep: 10 minutes	Roast: 2 hours 30 minutes
2	tablespoons caraway seeds, crushed
1	teaspoon salt
1	teaspoon dry mustard
½	teaspoon dried thyme
½	teaspoon dried oregano
1	tablespoon vegetable oil
1	bone-in pork loin roast (6 pounds), trimmed
3	tablespoons all-purpose flour

1. Preheat oven to 325°F. In cup, combine caraway seeds, salt, dry mustard, thyme, oregano, and oil. Use to rub on fat side of roast.

2. Place roast, fat side up, on rack in large roasting pan (17" by 11½"). Roast until meat thermometer inserted in thickest part of roast (not touching bone) reaches 155°F, about 2 hours 30 minutes. Internal temperature of meat will rise to 160°F upon standing.

3. When roast is done, transfer to warm platter and let stand 15 minutes to set juices for easier carving. Makes 10 main-dish servings.

Each serving: About 334 calories, 43g protein, 3g carbohydrate, 16g total fat (5g saturated), 119mg cholesterol, 310mg sodium.

French Roast Pork

The spice mixture rubbed onto the pork is a classic French combination known as quatre épices, *which means "four spices." We've taken the liberty of adding a few more spices for good measure. Once the pork begins roasting, the scent of warm spices will fill your kitchen.*

Prep: 5 minutes	Roast: 1 hour
1	boneless pork loin roast (2 pounds), trimmed
1	teaspoon salt
¾	teaspoon dried thyme
½	teaspoon ground cinnamon
½	teaspoon ground black pepper
⅛	teaspoon ground nutmeg
⅛	teaspoon ground cloves
⅓	cup dry white wine
⅔	cup chicken broth
	applesauce

1. Preheat oven to 350°F. Pat pork dry with paper towels.

2. In cup, combine salt, thyme, cinnamon, pepper, nutmeg, and cloves. Use to rub on pork.

3. Place roast on rack in small roasting pan (13" by 9"). Roast pork until meat thermometer inserted in center of roast reaches 155°F, about 1 hour. Internal temperature of meat will rise to 160°F upon standing.

4. When roast is done, transfer to warm platter and let stand 15 minutes to set juices for easier slicing. Meanwhile, add wine to roasting pan and heat to boiling over high heat, stirring until browned bits are loosened from bottom of pan. Add broth and heat to boiling; boil 2 minutes. Remove from heat and skim and discard fat. Serve pan juices and applesauce with pork. Makes 6 main-dish servings.

Each serving: About 254 calories, 33g protein, 1g carbohydrate, 11g total fat (4g saturated), 93mg cholesterol, 561mg sodium.

Caribbean Pork Roast

The seasonings that give this dish its Caribbean flavor are similar to those used in jerk cooking. The piquant sauce would also go well with grilled chicken or fish.

Prep: 10 minutes   Roast: 1 hour 20 minutes

1	boneless pork shoulder blade roast (fresh pork butt, 2½ pounds), trimmed
1½	teaspoons salt
1¼	teaspoons sugar
¾	teaspoon ground ginger
½	teaspoon ground allspice
½	teaspoon ground black pepper
3	teaspoons Dijon mustard
⅔	cup mango chutney, chopped
6	tablespoons fresh lime juice
2	tablespoons water

1. Preheat oven to 425°F. Using sharp knife, cut roast lengthwise almost in half, being careful not to cut all the way through. Open and spread flat like a book. In cup, combine salt, sugar, ginger, allspice, and pepper. Brush cut side of pork with 2 teaspoons mustard and sprinkle with half of seasoning mixture. Close pork "book" and rub remaining seasoning mixture on outside of pork. Tie roast with string at 1-inch intervals. Place roast on rack in small roasting pan (13" by 9").

2. Roast pork 1 hour. Turn oven control to 350°F and roast until meat thermometer inserted in center of roast reaches 155°F, about 20 minutes longer. Internal temperature of meat will rise to 160°F upon standing. Let stand 10 minutes to set juices for easier slicing.

3. Meanwhile, in small bowl, combine chutney, lime juice, water, and remaining 1 teaspoon mustard. Serve sauce with sliced pork. Makes 6 main-dish servings.

Each serving: About 417 calories, 35g protein, 28g carbohydrate, 17g total fat (6g saturated), 124mg cholesterol, 1,050mg sodium.

Carribbean Pork Roast

Oven-Barbecued Spareribs

These sweet and sticky ribs are worth getting your fingers dirty for!

Prep: 10 minutes   Roast: 1 hour 30 minutes

6	pounds pork spareribs, cut into 1-rib portions
1	can (6 ounces) tomato paste
¼	cup packed brown sugar
½	cup water
¼	cup honey
¼	cup cider vinegar
2	tablespoons vegetable oil
1	tablespoon grated onion
2	teaspoons chili powder
2	teaspoons salt

1. Preheat oven to 325°F. Arrange spareribs in single layer in large roasting pan (17" by 11½"). Roast spareribs 1 hour.

2. Meanwhile, prepare glaze: In medium bowl, combine tomato paste with brown sugar, water, honey, vinegar, oil, onion, chili powder, and salt until well blended.

3. Brush ribs with glaze. Roast ribs, brushing frequently with glaze, until ribs are tender, about 30 minutes longer. Makes 6 main-dish servings.

Each serving: About 849 calories, 53g protein, 27g carbohydrate, 59g total fat (20g saturated), 214mg cholesterol, 1,178mg sodium.

CARVING A WHOLE HAM

Place cooked ham on a cutting board. Using a carving fork to steady the ham, cut a few slices from the thin side of ham. Turn the ham over. Cut a few slices from the meaty end.

Cut out a small wedge of meat at the shank end of the ham.

Cut even slices along the ham, cutting through to the bone. Release the meat by cutting horizontally along the top of the bone. Transfer the slices to a warm platter.

Pineapple-Glazed Ham

Here's our recipe for this time-honored classic, along with a few delicious alternatives.

Prep: 15 minutes   Bake: 2 hours 10 minutes

1	fully cooked smoked bone-in ham (14 pounds)
1	can (20 ounces) crushed pineapple, drained
1	cup packed dark brown sugar
1	tablespoon Dijon mustard

1. Preheat oven to 325°F. With sharp knife, remove skin and trim fat from ham, leaving about ¼-inch-thick layer of fat. Place ham on rack in large roasting pan (17" by 11½"). Bake ham 1 hour 45 minutes.

2. Meanwhile, prepare pineapple glaze: In medium bowl, combine pineapple, brown sugar, and mustard until blended. Remove ham from oven. Brush pineapple mixture on ham. Bake until meat thermometer inserted in thickest part of ham (not touching bone) reaches 135°F, 25 to 30 minutes longer. Internal temperature of ham will rise to 140°F upon standing. Transfer ham to warm platter and let stand 15 minutes to set juices for easier slicing. Makes 20 main-dish servings.

♥ Each serving: About 193 calories, 21g protein, 15g carbohydrate, 5g total fat (2g saturated), 47mg cholesterol, 1,151mg sodium.

FAVORITE BAKED HAM GLAZES

Prepare one of the glazes below and substitute for the pineapple glaze in Step 2 of Pineapple Glazed Ham. During the last thirty minutes of roasting time, brush the glaze over the ham two or three times.

MELBA GLAZE
⅔ cup peach preserves
½ cup red raspberry jelly or jam

In small saucepan, heat peach preserves and raspberry jelly until melted and smooth. Makes about 1 cup.

TOMATO AND ONION GLAZE
1 tablespoon butter or margarine
2 tablespoons finely chopped onion
1 can (8 ounces) tomato sauce
2 tablespoons brown sugar
1 teaspoon Worcestershire sauce

In small saucepan, melt butter over medium heat. Add onion and cook until tender. Stir in tomato sauce, brown sugar, and Worcestershire; heat to boiling. Reduce heat; simmer until glaze thickens, about 5 minutes. Makes about 1 cup.

Whole Smithfield Ham

To qualify as a "genuine" Smithfield ham, the ham must be dry salt–cured and aged for a minimum of six months. Generic country hams are generally aged for about three months, resulting in a milder-tasting ham.

Prep: 10 minutes plus 24 to 36 hours soaking and cooling
Cook/Bake: 4 hours 30 minutes

1	cook-before-eating Smithfield or country-style ham (15 pounds)
½	cup dark corn syrup

1. Prepare ham as label directs, or prepare as follows: Place ham, skin side down, in saucepot large enough to hold whole ham; add enough *water* to cover ham completely. Let ham soak in water in cool place at least 24 hours or up to 36 hours, changing water frequently.

2. About 6 hours before serving or early in day, drain ham. With vegetable brush, scrub and rinse ham well with cool running water.

3. In same saucepot, cover ham with *water*; heat to boiling over high heat. Reduce heat; cover and simmer until bone on small end of ham (shank bone) pokes out about 1 inch and feels loose, about 3 hours 30 minutes.

4. Transfer ham to rack in large roasting pan (17" by 11½"); cool until easy to handle.

5. Preheat oven to 325°F. With sharp knife, remove skin and trim fat from ham, leaving about ¼-inch layer of fat. Brush ham with corn syrup. Bake until well glazed, about 15 minutes. Serve ham warm, or refrigerate to serve cold later. Cut into very thin slices. Makes about 35 main-dish servings.

♥ Each serving: About 117 calories, 14g protein, 5g carbohydrate, 3g total fat (2g saturated), 45mg cholesterol, 1,639mg sodium.

MORE WAYS TO ENJOY HAM

Here are just a few ways to add the rich smoky flavor of ham to your meals.

ZESTY SANDWICH SPREAD
In food processor, grind enough ham to equal 2 cups. Transfer to medium bowl and stir in ½ cup sweet pickle relish, ½ cup finely chopped celery, and 1 package (3 ounces) cream cheese, softened. Serve as sandwich spread or with unsalted crackers.

EGGS BENEDICT
Serve thinly sliced ham on a toasted English muffin, topped with poached egg and Hollandaise Sauce (page 550).

HEARTY SOUPS
Use ham bone in split-pea soup, bean soup, or German Lentil Soup (page 68).

OPEN-FACED GRILLED SANDWICHES
Brown slices of ham and pineapple in butter or margarine. Place on toasted kaiser roll halves, top with Cheddar cheese, and broil until cheese melts.

FLAVORFUL SAUCE
Add some minced ham to Béchamel (White Sauce, page 550), and serve over chicken or vegetables.

MAIN-DISH SALADS
Toss some chopped ham into macaroni, potato, or rice salad for a tasty main dish. Or add ¼ cup chopped ham to Creamy Potato Salad (page 533).

HAM AND MELON
Arrange thinly sliced ham on thinly sliced melon wedges or other fruit to serve for breakfast, lunch, or as a first-course.

HAM BISCUITS
Make biscuits (page 567). Split, spread with butter and top with thinly sliced ham.

Oven-Baked Pepper Bacon

The perfect way to make bacon for a crowd—in the oven! This method works best when using lean bacon, but if the bacon renders an excessive amount of fat, pour it off before switching racks.

Prep: 10 minutes	Bake: 25 minutes
1½	pounds sliced lean bacon
2½	teaspoons coarsely ground black pepper

1. Preheat oven to 400°F. Arrange bacon slices in two jelly-roll or roasting pans, overlapping the lean edge of each bacon slice with fat edge of the next.

2. Sprinkle pepper evenly over bacon. Bake until bacon is golden brown and crisp, about 25 minutes, rotating baking pans between upper and lower oven racks halfway through baking. Transfer bacon to paper towels to drain; keep warm until ready to serve. Makes 12 accompaniment servings.

Each serving: About 93 calories, 5g protein, 0g carbohydrate, 8g total fat (3g saturated), 13mg cholesterol, 254mg sodium.

EXPERT TIP

Pork shoulder butt, also called Boston shoulder butt, Boston butt, or pork butt, is one of the most versatile and least appreciated pork cuts. Because it has sufficient marbling, it is the best cut to use in moist-cooked dishes, such as stews and braises. It is also tender enough to roast, and when cooked slowly in a covered grill, it can be pulled apart to produce the best pulled pork barbecue you've ever tasted. No one knows pork or pork cookery better than the Chinese, and this is the cut they prefer for both taste and versatility. Often sold in boneless pieces, weighing from two to four pounds, it is very inexpensive if not downright cheap when purchased on sale. It also freezes well.

BRUCE AIDELLS
COOKBOOK AUTHOR

Sicilian Stuffed Pork Chops

Golden raisins lend the stuffing a slightly sweet note. If you can't find chard, spinach works equally well.

Prep: 20 minutes	Cook: 1 hour 10 minutes
12	ounces Swiss chard, thinly sliced (4 cups)
4	teaspoons olive oil
1	garlic clove, minced
¼	cup golden raisins
2	tablespoons pine nuts (pignoli), toasted and chopped
¾	teaspoon salt
4	pork loin chops, 1½ inches thick (10 ounces each)
¼	teaspoon ground black pepper
1	cup chicken broth
⅓	cup dry white wine

1. In 2-quart saucepan, combine Swiss chard and *1 inch water*. Bring to boil over high heat; cover and cook 5 minutes. Transfer to sieve; rinse with cold running water until cool. Press hard to remove excess liquid from Swiss chard.

2. In same saucepan, heat 1 teaspoon oil over medium heat. Add garlic and cook 30 seconds. Remove pan from heat; stir in Swiss chard, raisins, pine nuts, and ¼ teaspoon salt until well combined.

3. Pat pork dry with paper towels. Holding knife parallel to surface, cut a horizontal pocket in each chop. Fill pockets with chard mixture. Gently press pockets closed to seal in stuffing; secure with toothpicks. Sprinkle chops with remaining ½ teaspoon salt and pepper.

4. In nonstick 12-inch skillet, heat remaining 3 teaspoons oil over medium-high heat until very hot. Add chops and cook until well browned, about 4 minutes per side. Add broth and wine to skillet; heat to boiling. Reduce heat; cover and simmer until chops are tender, about 1 hour.

5. Transfer chops to platter; keep warm. Increase heat to high and heat pan juices to boiling; boil juices until reduced to ¾ cup. Skim and discard fat from juices and serve with chops. Makes 4 main-dish servings.

Each serving: About 400 calories, 46g protein, 12g carbohydrate, 19g total fat (5g saturated), 117mg cholesterol, 973mg sodium.

Mexican-Style Spareribs

A heady blend of tequila, orange juice, lime juice, and jalapeño pepper gives these pork ribs their personality. If you wish, the ribs can be marinated for as long as overnight.

Prep: 15 minutes   Roast: 1 hour 50 minutes

1	cup firmly packed fresh cilantro leaves and stems
½	small onion, thinly sliced
4	garlic cloves, crushed with garlic press
1	pickled jalapeño chile
½	cup fresh lime juice
¼	cup fresh orange juice
¼	cup tequila
1	tablespoon olive oil
2	tablespoons sugar
½	teaspoon dried oregano
3	pounds pork spareribs

1. Preheat oven to 350°F.

2. In blender, combine cilantro, onion, garlic, pickled jalapeño, lime and orange juices, tequila, oil, sugar, and oregano and puree until smooth.

3. Place spareribs in nonreactive roasting pan just large enough to hold them in single layer. Pour cilantro mixture over ribs, turning to coat well. Roast, turning ribs twice, 1 hour 30 minutes. Turn oven control to 450°F and roast ribs until very tender and richly colored, about 20 minutes longer.

4. Transfer ribs to warm platter. Skim and discard fat from sauce remaining in pan and spoon sauce over ribs. Makes 4 main-dish servings.

Each serving: About 610 calories, 40g protein, 13g carbohydrate, 44g total fat (15g saturated), 161mg cholesterol, 183mg sodium.

Hungarian Pork Goulash

Old-world recipes for goulash always include some sauerkraut. Look for plastic bags of fresh sauerkraut in the refrigerated section of the supermarket. Do not use the canned variety—it's too sour. Serve with egg noodles to sop up all the delectable sauce.

Prep: 20 minutes   Bake: 1 hour 30 minutes

2	tablespoons vegetable oil
2	large onions (12 ounces each), chopped
1	garlic clove, finely chopped
¼	cup paprika, preferably sweet Hungarian
2	pounds boneless pork shoulder blade roast (fresh pork butt), trimmed and cut into 1½-inch pieces
1	bag (16 ounces) sauerkraut, rinsed and drained
1	can (14½ ounces) diced tomatoes
1	can (14½ ounces) beef broth or 1¾ cups Brown Beef Stock (page 83)
½	teaspoon salt
¼	teaspoon ground black pepper
1	container (8 ounces) sour cream

1. Preheat oven to 325°F. In nonreactive 5-quart Dutch oven, heat oil over medium heat. Add onions and cook, stirring frequently, 10 minutes. Stir in garlic; cook until onions are very tender, about 5 minutes longer.

2. Add paprika to onions, stirring well. Cook 1 minute. Add pork, sauerkraut, tomatoes with their juice, broth, salt, and pepper; heat to boiling over high heat. Cover and place in oven. Bake until pork is tender, about 1 hour 30 minutes. Remove stew from oven.

3. Stir in sour cream. Heat through over medium heat (do not boil). Makes 6 main-dish servings.

Each serving: About 450 calories, 33g protein, 17g carbohydrate, 28g total fat (11g saturated), 120mg cholesterol, 1,135mg sodium.

Adobo-Style Chili

Adobo is a dark red chile sauce that is popular in Mexico, where it is often combined with pork and turned into a stewlike dish. The flavor is kicked up with a splash of vinegar.

Prep: 20 minutes	*Cook: 2 hours 30 minutes*

2	pounds boneless pork shoulder, trimmed and cut into 1½-inch pieces
2	teaspoons vegetable oil
1	large onion (12 ounces), chopped
4	garlic cloves, crushed with garlic press
3	tablespoons chili powder
1	tablespoon ground cumin
¼	teaspoon ground cinnamon
¼	teaspoon ground red pepper (cayenne)
⅛	teaspoon ground cloves
1	can (28 ounces) tomatoes
¼	cup cider vinegar
¾	teaspoon salt
½	teaspoon dried oregano
1	bay leaf
2	tablespoons chopped fresh cilantro
	warm corn tortillas (optional)

1. Pat pork dry with paper towels. In nonreactive 5-quart Dutch oven, heat 1 teaspoon oil over medium-high heat until very hot. Add half of pork and cook until browned, using slotted spoon to transfer meat to bowl as it is browned. Repeat with remaining oil and remaining pork.

2. Reduce heat to medium. Add onion and cook until tender, about 10 minutes. Stir in garlic, chili powder, cumin, cinnamon, ground red pepper, and cloves; cook 1 minute. Return pork to Dutch oven. Add tomatoes with their juice, vinegar, salt, oregano, and bay leaf. Heat to boiling over high heat, breaking up tomatoes with side of spoon. Reduce heat; cover and simmer until pork is very tender, about 2 hours.

3. Discard bay leaf. Skim and discard fat. Sprinkle pork with cilantro and serve with warm tortillas, if you like. Makes 6 main-dish servings.

Each serving: About 325 calories, 31g protein, 13g carbohydrate, 17g total fat (5g saturated), 103mg cholesterol, 654mg sodium.

New Mexican Green Chili

At New Mexico's chili stands, green chili is as popular as red chili. Tomatillos, which resemble small, hard green tomatoes and are covered with papery husks, are sold fresh and canned. Dark green poblano chiles are sometimes called fresh ancho chiles, but don't confuse them with dried anchos.

Prep: 30 minutes	*Bake: 2 hours 30 minutes to 3 hours*

1	bunch cilantro
3	garlic cloves, finely chopped
1½	teaspoons salt
2	pounds boneless pork shoulder, trimmed and cut into ¾-inch pieces
2	medium onions, chopped
3	serrano or jalapeño chiles, seeded and finely chopped
1	teaspoon ground cumin
¼	teaspoon ground red pepper (cayenne)
2	pounds tomatillos, husked, rinsed, and cut into quarters
4	poblano chiles or 2 green peppers, roasted (page 448), seeded, and cut into 1-inch pieces
1	can (15¼ to 16 ounces) whole-kernel corn, drained
	sour cream (optional)
	warm flour tortillas (optional)

1. Preheat oven to 325°F. Chop enough cilantro leaves and stems to equal ¼ cup; chop and reserve another ¼ cup cilantro leaves for garnish. With side of chef's knife, mash garlic and salt to paste; transfer to 5-quart Dutch oven. Add pork, onions, serranos, cilantro leaves and stems, cumin, and ground red pepper; toss to combine. Cover and bake 1 hour.

2. Stir in tomatillos and roasted poblanos. Cover and bake until pork is very tender, 1 hour 30 minutes to 2 hours longer. Skim and discard fat. Stir in corn and heat through. Sprinkle with reserved cilantro and serve with sour cream and tortillas, if you like. Makes 6 main-dish servings.

Each serving: About 378 calories, 34g protein, 27g carbohydrate, 16g total fat (5g saturated), 103mg cholesterol, 802mg sodium.

Pulled Pork Barbecue

This easy indoor pork barbecue is so tender it can be pulled apart. For authentic smoky flavor, brown the pork on the grill.

Prep: 10 minutes plus cooling   Cook: 2 hours 45 minutes

3	pounds boneless pork shoulder blade roast, trimmed and tied
1/2	teaspoon salt
1/4	teaspoon ground black pepper
1	tablespoon vegetable oil
2	cups water
1	cup ketchup
1/4	cup distilled white vinegar
1/4	cup Worcestershire sauce
1/3	cup packed brown sugar
1	tablespoon dry mustard
1/4 to 1/2	teaspoon crushed red pepper
10	hamburger buns, split

1. Pat pork dry with paper towels. Sprinkle roast with salt and pepper. In nonreactive 5-quart Dutch oven, heat oil over medium-high heat until very hot. Add roast and cook until browned, about 5 minutes. Transfer pork to plate; discard drippings from pan.

2. Combine water, ketchup, vinegar, Worcestershire, brown sugar, dry mustard, and crushed red pepper in Dutch oven. Add pork and heat to boiling over high heat. Reduce heat; cover and simmer, turning roast every 30 minutes, 2 hours 30 minutes.

3. Transfer roast to plate and cool. Boil pot liquid until it has reduced and thickened, about 5 minutes.

4. When roast is cool enough to handle, discard strings. Separate meat into chunks, removing as much fat as possible. With hands or fork, shred meat into bite-size pieces. Return pork to Dutch oven, stirring; heat through. Serve pulled pork on hamburger buns. Makes 10 main-dish servings.

Each serving: About 408 calories, 31g protein, 37g carbohydrate, 15g total fat (4g saturated), 93mg cholesterol, 806mg sodium.

Orange-Glazed Pork Rolls

When you want smoky pork flavor but don't want to serve ham, roast a smoked pork shoulder roll. Its neat shape makes for easy serving, so it's no trouble to prepare several.

Prep: 5 minutes   Cook/Bake: 1 hour 50 minutes

2	smoked pork shoulder rolls (3 pounds each)
1/4	teaspoon whole black peppercorns
1	bay leaf
1	jar (10 to 12 ounces) orange marmalade
2	tablespoons bottled white horseradish

1. Remove stockinette casing (if any) from pork rolls, if directed on label. In 8-quart saucepot, place shoulder rolls, peppercorns, bay leaf, and enough *water* to cover meat; heat to boiling over high heat. Reduce heat; cover and simmer until rolls are tender, about 1 hour 30 minutes.

2. Preheat oven to 350°F. In small bowl, combine orange marmalade and horseradish.

3. When shoulder rolls are done, remove casings, if any. Arrange pork in 13" by 9" baking pan; bake, brushing occasionally with marmalade mixture, 20 minutes.

4. To serve, cut rolls into slices and arrange on warm platter. Makes 12 main-dish servings.

Each serving: About 605 calories, 33g protein, 18g carbohydrate, 44g total fat (16g saturated), 126mg cholesterol, 1,847mg sodium.

Breaded Pork Tenderloin

This recipe shows just how quickly pork tenderloin can be transformed into a delicious meal. Serve with your favorite salsa or with lemon wedges.

Prep: 20 minutes   Cook: 10 minutes

1	pork tenderloin (12 ounces), trimmed
1	large egg
2	tablespoons water
1/2	teaspoon salt
1/4	teaspoon dried rosemary, crumbled
3/4	cup plain dried bread crumbs
3	tablespoons vegetable oil

1. Using sharp knife, cut tenderloin lengthwise almost in half, being careful not to cut all the way through. Open and spread flat like a book. With meat mallet, or between two sheets of plastic wrap or waxed paper with rolling pin, pound pork to ¼-inch thickness; cut crosswise into 4 equal pieces.

2. In pie plate, with fork, lightly beat egg, water, salt, and rosemary. Place bread crumbs on waxed paper. Using tongs, dip pork in egg mixture, then in bread crumbs. Repeat to coat each piece of pork twice.

3. In 12-inch skillet, heat oil over medium-high heat until very hot. Add pork and cook until browned and cooked through, about 5 minutes per side. Makes 4 main-dish servings.

Each serving: About 291 calories, 22g protein, 15g carbohydrate, 15g total fat (3g saturated), 108mg cholesterol, 522mg sodium.

Choucroute Garni

For sauerkraut lovers! Serve this filling, homey dish, best made during the cold winter months, with boiled potatoes, a pot of good-quality mustard, and a loaf of crusty bread.

Prep: 20 minutes   Cook: 50 minutes

4	slices bacon, cut into 1-inch pieces
¼	cup water
1	large onion (12 ounces), thinly sliced
2	McIntosh apples, each peeled, cut into quarters, and thinly sliced
2	bags (16 ounces each) sauerkraut, rinsed and drained
1½	cups fruity white wine, such as riesling
6	juniper berries, crushed
1	bay leaf
6	smoked pork chops, ½ inch thick (4 ounces each)
1	pound kielbasa (smoked Polish sausage), cut into 1½-inch pieces

1. In nonreactive 5-quart Dutch oven, combine bacon and water; cook over medium-low heat until bacon is lightly crisped, about 4 minutes. Add onion and cook, stirring frequently, until onion is tender and golden, about 7 minutes.

Choucroute Garni

2. Add apples and cook until tender, about 3 minutes. Stir in sauerkraut, wine, juniper berries, and bay leaf and heat to boiling. Reduce heat; cover and simmer 15 minutes.

3. Nestle pork chops and kielbasa into cabbage mixture; cover and cook until pork is heated through and sauerkraut is tender, about 20 minutes; remove bay leaf and serve. Makes 6 main-dish servings.

Each serving: About 524 calories, 27g protein, 19g carbohydrate, 37g total fat (13g saturated), 106mg cholesterol, 3,151mg sodium.

Orange-Ginger Pork Medallions

Medallions are simply small round pieces of meat. They make a neat presentation.

Prep: 10 minutes   Cook: 15 minutes

1	pork tenderloin (1 pound), trimmed
2	medium oranges
3	teaspoons vegetable oil
¼	teaspoon salt
3	green onions, thinly sliced
1	tablespoon grated, peeled fresh ginger

1. Pat pork dry with paper towels. Cut tenderloin crosswise into ¾-inch-thick slices. With meat mallet, or between two sheets of plastic wrap or waxed paper with rolling pin, pound each slice of pork into ½-inch-thick medallion.

2. From 1 orange, grate peel and squeeze ½ cup juice. Cut remaining unpeeled orange into ½-inch-thick slices. Cut each slice crosswise in half; set aside.

3. In nonstick 12-inch skillet, heat 2 teaspoons oil over medium-high heat until very hot. Add medallions and sprinkle with salt. Cook until pork just loses its pink color throughout, about 2½ minutes per side. Transfer medallions to platter; keep warm.

4. In same skillet, heat remaining 1 teaspoon oil. Add green onions, ginger, and grated orange peel; cook until green onions are lightly browned and tender, 2 to 3 minutes. Add orange slices and juice to skillet; cook 1 minute. Return medallions to skillet; heat through. Makes 4 main-dish servings.

Each serving: About 203 calories, 25g protein, 9g carbohydrate, 7g total fat (2g saturated), 74mg cholesterol, 202mg sodium.

Sweet and Savory Pork

Salty olives and capers interplay with sweet prunes to make the mouthwatering sauce for this dish.

Prep: 15 minutes   Cook: 10 minutes

1	pork tenderloin (1 pound), trimmed and cut crosswise into 1-inch-thick slices
2	tablespoons brown sugar
3	garlic cloves, crushed with garlic press
¾	teaspoon salt
¼	teaspoon ground black pepper
2	teaspoons olive oil
½	cup dry white wine
2	tablespoons red wine vinegar
1	teaspoon cornstarch
¼	teaspoon dried oregano
½	cup pitted prunes, coarsely chopped
¼	cup pitted green olives, coarsely chopped
2	tablespoons capers, drained

1. Pat pork dry with paper towels. On waxed paper, combine brown sugar, garlic, salt, and pepper; use to coat pork.

2. In nonstick 12-inch skillet, heat oil over medium-high heat until very hot. Add pork and cook until slices are lightly browned and lose their pink color throughout, about 3 minutes per side. Transfer pork to plate.

3. In 1-cup measuring cup, blend wine, vinegar, cornstarch, and oregano until combined. Stir cornstarch mixture into skillet. Heat to boiling, stirring constantly. Return pork to skillet. Add prunes, olives, and capers; heat through. Makes 4 main-dish servings.

Each serving: About 270 calories, 25g protein, 22g carbohydrate, 7g total fat (2g saturated), 74mg cholesterol, 892mg sodium.

Balsamic-Glazed Pork Chops

Balsamic vinegar is very versatile; it's not just for salad dressing. Here it's turned into a sweet-tart sauce just made for tender pork.

Prep: 5 minutes   Cook: 10 minutes

8	boneless pork loin chops, ½ inch thick (3 ounces each), trimmed
½	teaspoon salt
¼	teaspoon ground black pepper
1	tablespoon olive oil
3	tablespoons finely chopped shallot or onion
⅓	cup balsamic vinegar
¼	cup packed brown sugar

1. Pat pork dry with paper towels. Sprinkle chops with salt and pepper. In nonstick 12-inch skillet, heat oil over medium-high heat until hot. Cook pork 4 minutes on one side; turn and cook 3 minutes on second side. Transfer pork to platter; keep warm.

2. Increase heat to high. Stir shallot into pan juices; cook 1 minute. Stir in vinegar and sugar and cook 1 minute longer. Pour sauce over pork. Makes 4 main-dish servings.

Each serving: About 275 calories, 28g protein, 15g carbohydrate, 11g total fat (3g saturated), 76mg cholesterol, 364mg sodium.

You don't need a special smoker to do stovetop smoking. Line a wok with foil and put about 1 tablespoon of sawdust in the bottom. Place a round wire rack on top and arrange 1 to 1½ pounds meat (burgers, chops, boneless chicken breast, for example) on the rack. Cover the wok tightly and smoke over medium heat for about 18 minutes.

STEVE RAICHLEN
COOKBOOK AUTHOR

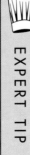

EXPERT TIP

Stuffed Pork Chops

The aroma of this dish will remind you of childhood trips to your grandparents for Sunday supper. If you don't have rye bread for the stuffing, use whole wheat.

Prep: 20 minutes   Cook: 30 minutes

4	teaspoons vegetable oil
1	small onion, chopped
1	Golden Delicious apple, peeled, cored, and chopped
½	teaspoon caraway seeds
	pinch dried thyme
2	slices rye bread, toasted and cut into ¼-inch pieces
2	tablespoons plus ½ cup chicken broth
1	tablespoon spicy brown mustard
4	pork loin chops, 1 inch thick (8 ounces each)
¼	teaspoon salt

1. In 10-inch skillet, heat 2 teaspoons oil over medium heat. Add onion and cook until tender, about 5 minutes. Add apple, caraway seeds, and thyme and cook 3 minutes longer. Transfer apple mixture to medium bowl. Wipe skillet clean.

2. Stir bread pieces, 2 tablespoons broth, and mustard into apple mixture. Pat pork dry with paper towels. Holding knife parallel to surface, cut a horizontal pocket in each chop. Stuff apple mixture into pocket of each chop and secure with toothpicks. Sprinkle with salt.

3. In 12-inch skillet, heat remaining 2 teaspoons oil over medium heat until hot. Cook chops until they just lose their pink color throughout, about 7 minutes per side.

4. Transfer chops to warm platter. Increase heat to high. Add remaining ½ cup broth to skillet and heat to boiling. Boil broth until reduced to ¼ cup, 3 to 5 minutes. Pour sauce over chops. Makes 4 main-dish servings.

Each serving: About 367 calories, 39g protein, 15g carbohydrate, 15g total fat (4g saturated), 102mg cholesterol, 540mg sodium.

Ham Steak with Apple Chutney

This freshly made chutney is perfect with ham steak. You can also serve the chutney with grilled pork or chicken.

Prep: 10 minutes   Cook: 35 minutes

2	teaspoons vegetable oil
1	medium onion, chopped
2	Golden Delicious apples, peeled, cored, and chopped
1	teaspoon minced, peeled fresh ginger
¾	cup apple juice
1	tablespoon cider vinegar
¼	cup golden raisins
½	teaspoon freshly grated orange peel
¼	teaspoon salt
1	fully cooked smoked-ham center slice, 1 inch thick (2 pounds)

1. In 2-quart saucepan, heat oil over medium heat. Add onion and cook, stirring occasionally, 5 minutes. Stir in apples and ginger and cook 3 minutes longer. Stir in apple juice, vinegar, raisins, orange peel, and salt; heat to boiling. Reduce heat and simmer 10 minutes. (Makes 2⅔ cups chutney.)

2. Meanwhile, heat 10-inch skillet over medium heat until hot. Add ham steak and cook until heated through and lightly browned, 8 to 10 minutes per side. Serve with chutney. Makes 6 main-dish servings.

♥ Each serving: About 257 calories, 29g protein, 17g carbohydrate, 8g total fat (2g saturated), 65mg cholesterol, 1,922mg sodium.

Ham and Grits with Red-Eye Gravy

A Southern-style breakfast that is hard to beat. The reddish gravy gets its name from the circle of liquid fat (the "eye") that forms on the surface.

Prep: 5 minutes   Cook: 30 minutes

4	cups water
1	cup white hominy grits
½	teaspoon salt
3	tablespoons butter or margarine
1	tablespoon vegetable oil
6	slices country ham, ¼ inch thick (2 ounces each)
½	cup brewed coffee
½	cup water
¼	teaspoon sugar

1. In 2-quart saucepan, heat water to boiling; slowly stir in grits and salt. Reduce heat to low; cover and cook, stirring occasionally, until thickened, 15 to 20 minutes. Remove from heat. Stir in butter and keep warm.

2. Meanwhile, in 12-inch skillet, heat oil over medium heat until very hot. Cook country ham, 3 slices at a time, turning once, until browned; transfer to platter and keep warm.

3. Add coffee, water, and sugar to drippings in skillet. Heat to boiling over medium heat, stirring until browned bits are loosened from bottom of skillet. Cook, stirring occasionally, 5 minutes. Serve gravy over ham and grits. Make 6 main-dish servings.

Each serving: About 279 calories, 18g protein, 21g carbohydrate, 13g total fat (5g saturated), 55mg cholesterol, 1,780mg sodium.

Spicy Shredded Pork in Lettuce Cups

This is Chinese-style finger food at its best. If you can find snow peas that are already trimmed, you will be rewarded with a quick entrée that puts most take-out food to shame.

Prep: 30 minutes   Cook: 12 minutes

1	boneless pork loin roast (1 pound), trimmed
2	tablespoons soy sauce
1	teaspoon cornstarch
¼	teaspoon sugar
2	tablespoons vegetable oil
1	tablespoon minced, peeled fresh ginger
1	garlic clove, finely chopped
¼	teaspoon ground red pepper (cayenne)
1	medium onion, thinly sliced
1	carrot, peeled and cut into 2" by ¼" matchstick strips
8	ounces snow peas, strings removed
4	large Boston or iceberg lettuce leaves

1. Pat pork dry with paper towels. With knife held in slanting position, almost parallel to surface, cut loin crosswise into ⅛-inch-thick slices; cut slices into thin strips.

2. In cup, blend soy sauce, cornstarch, and sugar until combined; set aside.

3. In 12-inch skillet, heat 1 tablespoon oil over high heat until very hot. Add pork, ginger, garlic, and ground red pepper and cook, stirring frequently (stir-frying), until browned, about 5 minutes, using slotted spoon to transfer pork strips to bowl as they are browned.

4. Add remaining 1 tablespoon oil to skillet. Add onion and carrot and stir-fry until tender-crisp. Add snow peas and stir-fry until snow peas are tender-crisp. Add pork to skillet. Stir cornstarch mixture; stir into skillet and stir-fry until sauce has thickened and boils. Spoon some pork mixture onto each lettuce leaf and serve. Makes 4 main-dish servings.

Each serving: About 283 calories, 27g protein, 12g carbohydrate, 13g total fat (3g saturated), 67mg cholesterol, 585mg sodium.

Pork Tenderloin Cutlets with Plum Glaze

The cutlets and glaze can be prepped in advance—up to several hours ahead. The grilling takes only minutes. Serve with ginger iced tea and scallion pancakes.

Prep: 10 minutes   Grill: 6 minutes

1	pork tenderloin (1 pound), trimmed
¾	teaspoon salt
¼	teaspoon coarsely ground black pepper
½	cup plum jam or preserves
1	tablespoon brown sugar
1	tablespoon grated, peeled fresh ginger
2	garlic cloves, crushed with garlic press
1	tablespoon fresh lemon juice
½	teaspoon ground cinnamon
4	large plums (1 pound), each pitted and cut in half

1. Prepare grill. Using sharp knife, cut tenderloin lengthwise almost in half, being careful not to cut all the way through. Open and spread flat like a book. With meat mallet or between two sheets of plastic wrap or waxed paper with rolling pin, pound meat to ¼-inch thickness. Cut crosswise into 4 equal pieces; sprinkle cutlets with salt and pepper.

2. In small bowl, combine plum jam, brown sugar, ginger, garlic, lemon juice, and cinnamon. Brush one side of each cutlet and cut side of each plum half with plum glaze. Place cutlets and plums on grill over medium heat, glaze side down, and cook 3 minutes. Brush cutlets and plums with remaining plum glaze; turn pork and plums over and cook until cutlets are lightly browned on both sides and just lose their pink color throughout and plums are hot, about 3 minutes longer. Makes 4 main-dish servings.

Each serving: About 333 calories, 27g protein, 44g carbohydrate, 6g total fat (2g saturated), 80mg cholesterol, 509mg sodium.

Pork Tenderloin Cutlets with Plum Glaze

Spice-Rubbed Pork Tenderloin

A quick curry rub adds great flavor to juicy, lean pork tenderloin. Serve with a colorful vegetable stir-fry and jasmine rice.

Prep: 5 minutes   Broil: 15 minutes

1	tablespoon curry powder
1	teaspoon ground cumin
¾	teaspoon salt
¼	teaspoon ground cinnamon
2	teaspoons vegetable oil
1	pork tenderloin (1 pound), trimmed

1. Preheat broiler. In cup, combine curry powder, cumin, salt, cinnamon, and oil; use to rub on tenderloin.

2. Place tenderloin on rack in broiling pan. Place pan in broiler 5 to 7 inches from heat source. Broil tenderloin, turning once, until meat thermometer inserted in center of pork reaches 155°F, 15 to 20 minutes. Internal temperature will rise to 160°F upon standing.

3. Place meat on cutting board. Let stand 5 minutes to set juices for easier slicing. With knife held in slanting position, almost parallel to board, cut tenderloin into ¼-inch-thick slices. Makes 4 main-dish servings.

Each serving: About 187 calories, 26g protein, 1g carbohydrate, 8g total fat (2g saturated), 80mg cholesterol, 493mg sodium.

Maple-Glazed Pork Tenderloins

Plan on leftovers and look forward to a sandwich treat of thinly sliced pork topped with sharp Cheddar cheese and slices of apple.

Prep: 10 minutes plus refrigerating   Grill: 20 minutes

2	pork tenderloins (12 ounces each), trimmed
½	teaspoon salt
¼	teaspoon ground black pepper
8	wooden toothpicks
6	slices bacon
½	cup maple or maple-flavored syrup

1. Sprinkle tenderloins with salt and pepper. Place pork in bowl; cover and refrigerate 30 minutes.

2. Meanwhile, soak toothpicks in water for 30 minutes. Prepare grill.

3. Wrap 3 bacon slices around each tenderloin and secure with toothpicks. Place tenderloins on grill and cook over medium heat, brushing frequently with syrup and turning occasionally, until meat thermometer inserted in center of pork reaches 155°F, 20 to 25 minutes. Internal temperature will rise to 160°F upon standing. Let pork stand 5 minutes to set juices for easier slicing. Makes 6 main-dish servings.

Each serving: About 265 calories, 28g protein, 18g carbohydrate, 9g total fat (3g saturated), 86mg cholesterol, 352mg sodium.

Teriyaki Pork Chops with Grilled Pineapple Slices

Many fruits go well with pork, but pineapple certainly tops the list.

Prep: 15 minutes plus marinating   Grill: 20 minutes

⅓	cup soy sauce
2	tablespoons plus ¼ cup packed brown sugar
2	green onions, chopped
2	tablespoons grated, peeled fresh ginger
4	pork loin chops, ¾ inch thick (6 to 8 ounces each)
1	small pineapple

1. Prepare grill. In 13" by 9" baking dish, combine soy sauce, 2 tablespoons brown sugar, green onions, and ginger. Add chops, turning to coat. Let stand 20 minutes at room temperature to marinate.

2. Meanwhile, cut off rind from pineapple, then cut pineapple crosswise into ½-inch-thick slices. Sprinkle pineapple slices with remaining ¼ cup brown sugar.

3. Place pineapple on grill and cook over medium heat, turning slices occasionally, until browned on both sides, 15 to 20 minutes. After pineapple has cooked 10 minutes, place chops on grill and cook 10 minutes or until chops are lightly browned on both sides and juices run clear when center of

chop is pierced with tip of knife, turning chops occasionally and brushing with remaining teriyaki mixture halfway through cooking. Serve chops with grilled pineapple slices. Makes 4 main-dish servings.

♥ Each serving: About 399 calories, 30g protein, 48g carbohydrate, 11g total fat (4g saturated), 78mg cholesterol, 1,433mg sodium.

Lemon-Grilled Pork Chops

This full-flavored marinade does its job in just twenty minutes.

Prep: 5 minutes plus marinating	Grill: 15 minutes
3	tablespoons fresh lemon juice
1	tablespoon olive oil
2	tablespoons finely chopped fresh parsley
1/2	teaspoon dried oregano
1/4	teaspoon salt
1/4	teaspoon ground black pepper
6	pork rib or loin chops, 1 inch thick (8 to 10 ounces each)
6	lemon wedges

1. Prepare grill. In ziptight plastic bag, combine lemon juice, oil, parsley, oregano, salt, and pepper. Add chops, turning to coat. Seal bag, pressing out as much air as possible. Let stand 20 minutes at room temperature, turning once.

2. Remove chops from bag; discard marinade. Place chops on grill and cook over medium heat until cooked through and juices run clear when center of chop is pierced with tip of knife, about 7 minutes per side. Serve with lemon wedges. Makes 6 main-dish servings.

Each serving: About 262 calories, 34g protein, 2g carbohydrate, 13g total fat (4g saturated), 93mg cholesterol, 125mg sodium.

Fennel-Orange Pork Chops

Crushing fennel seeds releases their flavor.

Prep: 15 minutes	Grill: 12 minutes
1	teaspoon freshly grated orange peel
1	teaspoon fennel seeds, crushed
3/4	teaspoon salt
1/2	teaspoon dried thyme, crumbled
1/4	teaspoon coarsely ground black pepper
4	pork rib or loin chops, 3/4 inch thick (6 to 8 ounces each)
1	tablespoon olive oil
1	tablespoon balsamic vinegar
1	large round head radicchio (8 ounces), cut into 8 wedges
2	large heads Belgian endive, each cut lengthwise into quarters

1. Prepare grill. In small bowl, combine orange peel, fennel seeds, 1/2 teaspoon salt, thyme, and pepper until well blended. Use to rub on chops.

2. In medium bowl, combine oil, vinegar, and remaining 1/4 teaspoon salt. Add radicchio and endive to bowl, gently tossing to coat.

3. Place chops on grill and cook over medium heat 6 to 7 minutes. Turn chops and place vegetables on grill. Cook until juices run clear when center of chop is pierced with tip of knife and vegetables are browned, 6 to 7 minutes longer. Serve chops with grilled vegetables. Makes 4 main-dish servings.

Each serving: About 321 calories, 31g protein, 5g carbohydrate, 19g total fat (6g saturated), 96mg cholesterol, 523mg sodium.

Apply sweet barbecue sauces during the last five minutes of grilling. If you apply them any sooner, the sugar in the sauce will burn.

STEVE RAICHLEN
COOKBOOK AUTHOR

EXPERT TIP

Barbecued Pork Spareribs

Plain spareribs? Of course not! It's the sauces that makes these special. Here are three of our favorites.

Prep: 1 hour 20 minutes	Grill: 20 minutes
4	pounds pork spareribs, cut into 1- or 2-rib portions
	choice of sauce (below)

1. Early in day or 1 day ahead, precook spareribs: In 8-quart Dutch oven, combine ribs and enough *water* to cover and heat to boiling over high heat. Reduce heat; cover and simmer until spareribs are tender, about 1 hour. Transfer spareribs to platter; cover and refrigerate.

2. Prepare desired barbecue sauce. Prepare grill.

3. To grill: Place cooked spareribs on grill and cook over medium heat, turning ribs frequently and brushing with barbecue sauce often, until heated through, about 20 minutes.

To broil: Preheat broiler. Place ribs on rack in broiling pan 8 to 10 inches from heat source and broil, turning ribs occasionally and brushing with sauce often, until heated through, about 20 minutes. Makes 8 main-dish servings.

Balsamic-Rosemary Sauce

In 1-quart saucepan, combine ⅔ **cup balsamic vinegar, 2 tablespoons brown sugar, 1 teaspoon salt,** and ½ **teaspoon pepper** and heat to boiling over medium heat. Cook until sauce has reduced to ⅓ cup, 15 minutes. Stir in **1 teaspoon dried rosemary,** crumbled.

Each serving with Balsamic-Rosemary Sauce: About 368 calories, 26g protein, 4g carbohydrate, 27g total fat (10g saturated), 107mg cholesterol, 376mg sodium.

Orange-Dijon Sauce

In cup, combine **1 cup sweet orange marmalade,** ¼ **cup Dijon mustard,** ¼ **cup packed brown sugar, 1 teaspoon freshly grated orange peel,** and 1½ **teaspoons salt.**

Each serving with Orange-Dijon Sauce: About 483 calories, 26g protein, 33g carbohydrate, 27g total fat (10g saturated), 107mg cholesterol, 723mg sodium.

Asian Barbecue Sauce

In 1-quart saucepan, heat **1 tablespoon vegetable oil** over medium heat; add **2 green onions,** finely chopped, and cook until tender, about 5 minutes. Add **2 teaspoons grated, peeled fresh ginger** and **1 garlic clove,** crushed with garlic press; cook, stirring frequently, 1 minute longer. Stir in ⅔ **cup packed brown sugar,** ¼ **cup soy sauce,** ¼ **cup dry sherry, 1 tablespoon cornstarch,** and ½ **teaspoon salt.** Heat to boiling over medium-high heat, stirring, until mixture has thickened and boils. Stir in **1 teaspoon Asian sesame oil.**

Each serving with Asian Barbecue Sauce: About 453 calories, 26g protein, 20g carbohydrate, 29g total fat (10g saturated), 107mg cholesterol, 750mg sodium.

Southwestern Ham Steak

Serve with one of our fresh salsas (pages 555-557).

Prep: 5 minutes	Grill: 8 minutes
2	teaspoons chili powder
½	teaspoon ground cumin
¼	teaspoon ground coriander
¼	teaspoon ground red pepper (cayenne)
¼	teaspoon sugar
1	fully cooked smoked-ham center slice, ½ inch thick (1¼ pounds)

1. Prepare grill. In small bowl, combine chili powder, cumin, coriander, ground red pepper, and sugar. Use to rub on ham steak.

2. Place ham steak on grill and cook over medium heat until heated through and lightly browned, about 4 minutes per side. Makes 4 main-dish servings.

Each serving: About 171 calories, 27g protein, 1g carbohydrate, 6g total fat (2g saturated), 61mg cholesterol, 1,727mg sodium.

Barbecued Pork Spareribs

Stuffed Cabbage with Dill

If you come from an Eastern European background, our version of stuffed cabbage will bring back fond memories.

	Prep: 40 minutes Bake: 1 hour
1	large head green cabbage (3 pounds), cored
½	cup regular long-grain rice
2	tablespoons butter or margarine
2	medium onions, chopped
1	pound ground pork
¼	cup chopped fresh dill plus additional sprigs
1¼	teaspoons salt
⅜	teaspoon ground black pepper
¼	teaspoon ground nutmeg
1	can (28 ounces) tomatoes
1	teaspoon sugar

1. In 8-quart Dutch oven, heat *6 quarts water* to boiling over high heat. Add cabbage to water; cover and cook 10 minutes. Transfer cabbage to colander. When cabbage is cool enough to handle, peel off tender outer cabbage leaves. Repeat, if necessary, to obtain 12  large leaves. (Reserve remaining cabbage for another use). Trim thick ribs from base of leaves.

2. Meanwhile, cook rice as package directs. In nonstick 10-inch skillet, melt 1 tablespoon butter over medium heat. Add half of onions and cook, stirring frequently, until tender, about 5 minutes. Transfer to medium bowl. Add cooked rice, ground pork, dill, ¾ teaspoon salt, ¼ teaspoon pepper, and nutmeg and stir until combined.

3. Preheat oven to 375°F. Spread cabbage leaves on work surface. Place about ¼ cup rice filling on each leaf; roll leaf up around filling, tucking in sides, and arrange, seam side down, in shallow 2-quart casserole.

4. In same clean skillet, melt remaining 1 tablespoon butter. Add remaining onions and cook over medium heat, stirring frequently, until tender, about 5 minutes. Add tomatoes with their juice, sugar, remaining ½ teaspoon salt, and remaining ⅛ teaspoon pepper and heat to boiling, breaking up tomatoes with side of spoon. Pour sauce evenly over cabbage rolls; cover casserole with foil and bake 1 hour. Remove cover and garnish with dill sprigs. Makes 4 main-dish servings.

Each serving: About 552 calories, 26g protein, 45g carbohydrate, 31g total fat (13g saturated), 97mg cholesterol, 1,206mg sodium.

Beer-Braised Bratwurst Dinner

No need to make any side dishes—this can be the entire meal.

	Prep: 10 minutes Cook: 50 minutes
1	tablespoon vegetable oil
1½	pounds bratwurst
1	large onion (12 ounces), thinly sliced
½	teaspoon caraway seeds
1	small head green cabbage (1½ pounds), thinly sliced
1	pound red potatoes, cut into quarters
1	can or bottle (12 ounces) beer
¼	cup chicken broth
½	teaspoon salt
¼	teaspoon ground black pepper

1. In 12-inch skillet, heat oil over medium-high heat until very hot. Add bratwurst and cook, turning frequently, until browned. With tongs, transfer sausages to paper towels to drain.

2. Add onion and caraway seeds to skillet and cook over medium heat until onion is golden brown, about 15 minutes.

3. Add cabbage, potatoes, sausages, beer, broth, salt, and pepper to skillet; heat to boiling over high heat. Reduce heat; cover and simmer until potatoes are tender, about 25 minutes. Makes 6 main-dish servings.

Each serving: About 476 calories, 20g protein, 28g carbohydrate, 32g total fat (11g saturated), 68mg cholesterol, 897mg sodium.

Kielbasa and Red Cabbage

It's worth a trip to a Polish butcher for homemade kielbasa to make this rib-sticking skillet meal.

Prep: 15 minutes   Cook: 40 minutes

2	tablespoons butter or margarine
1	small onion, chopped
1	small head red cabbage (1½ pounds), thinly sliced
2	Golden Delicious apples, peeled, cored, and thinly sliced
½	cup apple juice
3	tablespoons red wine vinegar
1	tablespoon sugar
1	teaspoon salt
1	pound kielbasa (smoked Polish sausage), cut crosswise into 2-inch pieces

1. In nonstick 10-inch skillet, melt butter over medium heat. Add onion and cook, stirring, until tender. Add cabbage, apples, apple juice, vinegar, sugar, and salt; heat to boiling. Reduce heat to low; cover and simmer 15 minutes.

2. Add kielbasa to cabbage mixture; heat to boiling over high heat. Reduce heat; cover and simmer 15 minutes. Makes 4 main-dish servings.

Each serving: About 524 calories, 18g protein, 32g carbohydrate, 37g total fat (15g saturated), 92mg cholesterol, 1,883mg sodium.

Kielbasa and Red Cabbage

Breakfast Patties

Make a double batch of these patties and store them in your freezer so you can have them anytime.

Prep: 25 minutes   Cook: 25 minutes per batch

3	pounds boneless pork shoulder blade roast (fresh pork butt), trimmed and cut into 1-inch pieces
⅓	cup chopped fresh parsley
1	tablespoon dried sage, crumbled
2	teaspoons salt
1	teaspoon cracked black pepper

1. With meat grinder, using coarse cutting disk, grind pork into large bowl; or, in small batches, use food processor with knife blade attached and pulse until coarsely ground. Add parsley, sage, salt, and pepper; combine just until well blended but not overmixed. Shape mixture into twenty 4-inch patties, handling meat as little as possible. Cover and refrigerate patties until ready to cook.

2. In 12-inch skillet, over medium-low heat, cook patties, in batches, turning occasionally, until browned and cooked through, about 25 minutes. With slotted spatula, transfer patties to platter lined with paper towels to drain. Makes 20 breakfast patties.

Each patty: About 176 calories, 11g protein, 0g carbohydrate, 14g total fat (5g saturated), 43mg cholesterol, 268mg sodium.

Polenta and Sausage Casserole

Layers of creamy polenta, cheese, and a tomato-sausage sauce make this a terrific casserole for a potluck party, buffet, or brunch.

Prep: 1 hour   Bake: 35 minutes

8	ounces sweet Italian-sausage links, casings removed
8	ounces hot Italian-sausage links, casings removed
1	tablespoon olive oil
1	large onion (12 ounces), chopped
1	large stalk celery, chopped
1	carrot, peeled and chopped
1	can (28 ounces) plum tomatoes in puree
2	cups yellow cornmeal
1	can (14½-ounces) chicken broth or 1¾ cups Chicken Broth (page 84)
¾	teaspoon salt
4½	cups boiling water
½	cup freshly grated Parmesan cheese
8	ounces Fontina or mozzarella cheese, shredded (2 cups)

1. Prepare tomato-sausage sauce: In nonreactive 5-quart Dutch oven, cook sweet and hot sausage meat over medium-high heat, breaking up meat with side of spoon, until browned. With slotted spoon, transfer meat to bowl. Discard fat from Dutch oven.

2. Add oil to Dutch oven. Add onion, celery, and carrot and cook over medium-high heat until browned. Stir in sausage and tomatoes with their puree, breaking up tomatoes with side of spoon. Heat to boiling over high heat. Reduce heat; cover and simmer 10 minutes. Remove cover and simmer 10 minutes longer.

3. Preheat oven to 350°F. Prepare polenta: In 4-quart saucepan with wire whisk, mix cornmeal, broth, and salt. Over medium-high heat, add boiling water and cook, whisking constantly, until mixture has thickened, about 5 minutes. Whisk in Parmesan.

4. Grease 13" by 9" baking dish. Evenly spread half of polenta mixture in baking dish; top with half of tomato-sausage sauce, then half of Fontina. Repeat with remaining polenta mixture and sauce.

5. Bake casserole 15 minutes. Sprinkle with remaining Fontina; bake until mixture is bubbling and cheese is golden, about 20 minutes longer. Let stand 15 minutes for easier serving. Makes 8 main-dish servings.

Each serving: About 466 calories, 23g protein, 38g carbohydrate, 25g total fat (11g saturated), 70mg cholesterol, 1,323mg sodium.

Italian Sausage and Broccoli Rabe

In this rustic classic, sweet sausage balances the appealing bitterness of broccoli rabe. Fans of this bitter green may want to double the amount used.

Prep: 5 minutes   Cook: 30 minutes

1	bunch broccoli rabe (1 pound), tough ends trimmed
2	teaspoons salt
1	pound sweet Italian-sausage links, pricked with fork
¼	cup water
1	tablespoon olive oil
1	large garlic clove, finely chopped
⅛	teaspoon crushed red pepper

1. In 5-quart saucepot, heat *4 quarts water* to boiling. Add broccoli rabe and salt. Cook just until stems are tender, about 5 minutes; drain. When cool enough to handle, coarsely chop broccoli rabe.

2. Meanwhile, in 10-inch skillet, heat sausage links and water to boiling over medium heat. Cover and cook 5 minutes. Remove cover and cook, turning sausages frequently, until water has evaporated and sausages are well browned, about 20 minutes longer. With tongs, transfer sausages to paper towels to drain; cut each sausage on diagonal in half.

3. Discard fat from skillet but do not wipe clean. To drippings in skillet, add oil, garlic, and crushed red pepper. Cook, stirring, until very fragrant, about 15 seconds. Add broccoli rabe and cook, stirring, until well coated and heated through, about 2 minutes. Stir in sausages and remove from heat. Makes 4 main-dish servings.

Each serving: About 325 calories, 19g protein, 6g carbohydrate, 25g total fat (8g saturated), 65mg cholesterol, and 1,079mg sodium.

Polenta and Sausage Casserole

Italian Sausage and Peppers

For this old-fashioned Italian favorite, use sweet or hot sausage, green or red peppers, or a combination.

Prep: 10 minutes	Cook: 30 minutes
1½	pounds hot or sweet Italian-sausage links, pricked with fork
¼	cup water
2	large green or red peppers, cut into ¾-inch-wide strips
2	large onions (12 ounces each), cut into ½-inch-thick slices
1	garlic clove, finely chopped
¼	teaspoon salt

1. In 12-inch skillet, heat sausage links and water to boiling over medium heat. Cover and cook 5 minutes. Remove cover and cook, turning sausages frequently, until water has evaporated and sausages are well browned, about 20 minutes longer. With tongs, transfer sausages to paper towels to drain.

2. Pour off all but 1 tablespoon fat from skillet. Add green peppers, onions, garlic, and salt; cook over medium heat, stirring frequently, until vegetables are tender.

3. Add cooked sausage links to peppers and onions; heat through. Makes 6 main-dish servings.

Each serving: About 322 calories, 18g protein, 10g carbohydrate, 23g total fat (8g saturated), 66mg cholesterol, 874mg sodium.

LAMB

The unique, relatively mild flavor of lamb pairs well with bold seasonings like garlic, rosemary, and wine, making it the favored meat of the Mediterranean. Lamb shish kebab is popular with cooks from Greece to Turkey and beyond. In North Africa and India, lamb dishes are prepared with intriguing combinations of assertive, exotic spices and sweet fruits. In the spring, when Easter and Passover are celebrated, roast lamb makes its annual appearance at many family gatherings. And recently, the luscious, melting texture of braised lamb shanks has helped this inexpensive cut gain popularity, while our appreciation for a hearty ground lamb casserole hasn't waned.

BUYING AND STORING LAMB

Americans generally prefer the mild taste of young lamb, and the good news is that most supermarket lamb is from animals from six to twelve months of age. Baby lamb (milk-fed lamb) is less than two months old and has a delicate flavor and pale pink color. Even though it is raised year-round, so-called spring lamb (Easter lamb) comes from slightly older sheep, up to five months old. Both of these younger lambs are specialty items that are most easily found during the holiday season at ethnic butchers. Meat from sheep from one to two years old is sold as yearling lamb, and the meat from sheep over two years old is mutton. These older meats have a gamier flavor than younger lambs and can occasionally be found in ethnic markets. It should be well trimmed, as the fat is especially strong tasting. Lamb imported from Australia and New Zealand can also be found in supermarkets and butcher shops. The cuts are noticeably smaller since they come from smaller—not younger—animals.

The primal cuts for lamb are the shoulder (including the neck), foreleg (including the breast), rib, loin, and leg. There are four grades: prime, choice, good, and utility. Prime lamb, which is scarce and expensive, is graded based on the shape of the muscle, not the amount of marbled fat. Almost all supermarket lamb is choice.

Ground lamb, often prepared from lamb shoulder, can be found at some ethnic markets, but be sure it doesn't look too fatty. It is sometimes best to ask the butcher to grind trimmed boneless leg of lamb to order, or simply grind it at home in a food processor.

When shopping for lamb, look for meat that is pinkish red. Darker meat indicates an older animal, and it will have a stronger flavor. The fat should look white, firm, and waxy. The bones should be porous and unsplintered, with a reddish tinge at the cut end. If you buy a large cut of lamb, such as a whole leg, be sure the fell (the thin membrane covering the fat) has been removed. If necessary, peel it off with the help of a sharp knife. In any case, the fat should be trimmed away so only a thin covering remains—lamb fat isn't very tasty.

Lamb chops, stew meat, and roasts can be stored for up to two days in the refrigerator. Ground lamb is quite perishable, so it should be used within one day of purchase.

COOKING LAMB

When cooking a tender cut of lamb by any of the dry-heat methods, keep in mind that it can dry out quickly if overcooked. So unless you prefer well-done meat, for the best results, cook lamb medium-rare.

Broiling, Grilling, and Panfrying Tender cuts of lamb work best here. Marinades add moisture and extra flavor and discourage overcooking.

Best Bets Rib chops, loin chops, sirloin, arm (shoulder) and blade chops, leg steaks, butterflied leg, and cubed leg of lamb (kabob meat).

Braising and Stewing These moist-heat methods are best reserved for the less tender, economical cuts. If you want to use bone-in stew meat rather than boneless, buy one-third to one-half more to compensate for the weight of the bones. Simmer gently and skim off the fat from the surface before serving.

Best Bets Neck slices, arm (shoulder) chops, boneless shoulder roast, blade chops, shanks, breast, and breast riblets. Boneless lamb cubes for stew are usually cut from the shoulder, but bone-in neck and shoulder pieces are sometimes available.

Roasting Many tender cuts of lamb are good for roasting, but the leg and rib sections are the most popular. Place lamb roasts, fat side up, on a rack in a roasting pan: The melting fat keeps the meat moist and flavorful. Follow the chart below when roasting lamb without a recipe.

Best Bets Whole leg of lamb, leg shank half, rack (rib roast), crown roast, saddle, loin, and boneless shoulder roast.

ROASTING TIMES
(OVEN TEMPERATURE OF 350°F)

Start with meat at refrigerator temperature. Remove roast from the oven when it reaches 5°F below desired doneness; temperature will continue to rise as roast stands.

CUT	WEIGHT	APPROXIMATE COOKING TIME (MINUTES PER POUND)		
		MEDIUM-RARE (135°-140°F)	MEDIUM (145°-155°F)	WELL-DONE (OVER 160°F)
Whole leg	5 to 7 pounds	15 minutes	15 to 18 minutes	20 minutes
	7 to 9 pounds	20 minutes	20 to 23 minutes	25 minutes
Leg shank half	3 to 4 pounds	20 to 25 minutes	30 minutes	35 to 40 minutes
Leg sirloin half	3 to 4 pounds	20 to 23 minutes	25 to 30 minutes	35 minutes
Leg roast (boneless)	4 to 7 pounds	15 to 18 minutes	20 to 23 minutes	25 minutes
Rib roast or rack (roast at 375°F)	1½ to 2½ pounds	20 to 25 minutes	30 minutes	35 minutes
Crown roast, unstuffed (roast at 375°F)	2 to 3 pounds	20 minutes	25 minutes	30 minutes
Shoulder roast	4 to 6 pounds	20 minutes	25 minutes	30 minutes
Shoulder roast (Boneless)	3½ to 6 pounds	35 minutes	40 minutes	45 minutes

POPULAR LAMB CUTS

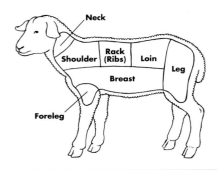

Neck

Shoulder | Rack (Ribs) | Loin

Breast

Leg

Foreleg

Lamb rib roast

(roast). Elegant and expensive. Also called rack of lamb.

Lamb shoulder neck slices

(braise). Cross cuts of neck. Also called neck of lamb and bone-in lamb for stew.

Lamb rib chops

(broil, grill, panfry, roast, bake). Also called rack lamb chops.

Lamb loin chops

(broil, grill, panfry). Meaty area has both rib-eye muscle and tenderloin.

Lamb leg sirloin chop

(broil, grill, panfry). Includes three different muscles. Also called lamb sirloin steak.

Lamb shoulder arm chops

(braise, broil, grill). Cut from arm portion of shoulder. Also called arm cut chops, round bone chops, or shoulder chops.

Lamb shoulder blade chops

(braise, broil, grill, panfry). From the blade portion of the shoulder. Also called lamb shoulder chops or blade cut chops.

Lamb shanks

(braise). Cut from the arm of the shoulder.

Lamb leg whole

(roast). Also called leg of lamb; available bone-in and boneless.

Lamb leg shank half

(roast). Sirloin half removed. Lower half of leg and round leg bone included.

Lamb breast riblets

(braise). Cut from breast, contains long and narrow ribs with layers of meat and fat.

Lamb breast

(braise, roast). Also called breast of lamb. Part of forequarter, containing row of ribs.

Roasted Leg of Lamb with Pistachio-Mint Crust

To prevent the nut crust from burning, don't spread it over the roast until after it has cooked for one hour. Some Indian markets sell shelled pistachios, or simply shell your own.

Prep: 30 minutes	Roast: 2 hours 15 to 30 minutes

- 1 whole bone-in lamb leg (7 pounds), trimmed
- 2 large garlic cloves, sliced
- 1½ teaspoons salt
- 2 tablespoons butter or margarine
- 1 small onion, chopped
- 1½ slices firm white bread, torn into ¼-inch pieces
- ½ cup pistachios, finely chopped
- 2 tablespoons coarsely chopped fresh mint
- ¼ teaspoon coarsely ground black pepper
- ½ cup port wine
- 3 tablespoons all-purpose flour
- 1 can (14½ ounces) chicken broth or 1¾ cups Chicken Broth (page 84)

1. Preheat oven to 325°F. Cut about a dozen ½-inch-long slits in lamb and insert slice of garlic in each. Sprinkle lamb with 1 teaspoon salt. Place lamb, fat side up, on rack in large roasting pan (17" by 11½"). Roast lamb 1 hour.

2. Meanwhile, in 10-inch skillet, melt butter over medium heat. Add onion and cook until lightly browned and tender, about 10 minutes; remove from heat. Stir in bread, pistachios, mint, remaining ½ teaspoon salt, and pepper. After lamb has roasted 1 hour, carefully pat mixture onto lamb.

3. Roast lamb 1 hour 15 to 30 minutes longer, until meat thermometer inserted in thickest part of lamb (not touching bone) reaches 140°F. Internal temperature of meat will rise to 145°F (medium) upon standing. Or roast until desired doneness. When lamb is done, transfer to warm platter and let stand 15 minutes to set juices for easier carving.

4. Meanwhile, prepare gravy: Remove rack from roasting pan; pour pan drippings into 2-cup measuring cup. Add port to pan, stirring until browned bits are loosened from bottom of pan. Pour into drippings in cup; let stand until fat separates out. Skim 2 tablespoons fat from drippings; return to roasting pan. Discard any remaining fat.

5. With wire whisk, whisk flour into fat in roasting pan over medium-high heat until well blended. Gradually whisk in meat juice and broth and bring to boil, stirring constantly; boil 1 minute. Pour gravy into gravy boat and serve with lamb. Makes 10 main-dish servings.

Each serving: About 404 calories, 46g protein, 8g carbohydrate, 18g total fat (7g saturated), 144mg cholesterol, 680mg sodium.

Rosemary Leg of Lamb

The French often roast lamb that has first been rubbed with a mix of fragrant dried herbs. We like to do it, too.

Prep: 5 minutes	Roast: 1 hour 45 minutes to 2 hours

- 1 whole bone-in lamb leg (7½ pounds), trimmed
- ½ teaspoon dried rosemary, crumbled
- ½ teaspoon dried thyme, crumbled
- ½ teaspoon salt
- ¼ teaspoon ground black pepper

1. Preheat oven to 450°F. Place lamb in large roasting pan (17" by 11½"). In cup, combine rosemary, thyme, salt, and pepper. Use to rub on lamb.

2. Roast lamb 15 minutes. Turn oven control to 350°F and roast, basting every 15 minutes with pan juices, until meat thermometer inserted in thickest part of lamb (not touching bone) reaches 140°F, 1 hour 30 to 45 minutes longer.  Internal temperature of meat will rise to 145°F (medium) upon standing. Or roast until desired doneness.

3. When lamb is done, transfer to cutting board and let stand 15 minutes to set juices for easier carving.

4. Carve lamb into slices and arrange on warm platter. Makes 10 main-dish servings.

Each serving: About 312 calories, 46g protein, 0g carbohydrate, 13g total fat (5g saturated), 145mg cholesterol, 227mg sodium.

Herbed Lamb Rib Roast

When you feel like showing off a bit, few dishes do it more elegantly than a classic rack of lamb. For easier carving, ask the butcher to loosen the backbone from the ribs.

Prep: 10 minutes   Roast: 1 hour 5 minutes

2	lamb rib roasts (racks of lamb), 8 ribs each (2½ pounds each), trimmed
½	teaspoon salt
3	tablespoons butter or margarine
2	cups fine fresh bread crumbs (about 4 slices firm white bread)
2	teaspoons dried rosemary, crumbled
¼	teaspoon ground black pepper
2	tablespoons chopped fresh parsley
2	tablespoons Dijon mustard

1. Preheat oven to 375°F. In large roasting pan (17" by 11½"), place roasts rib side down; sprinkle with salt. Roast lamb 50 minutes.

2. Meanwhile, in 10-inch skillet, melt butter over medium heat. Add bread crumbs, rosemary, and pepper and cook, stirring frequently, until crumbs are golden brown. Stir in parsley.

3. Spread mustard on tops of roasts. Press bread-crumb mixture onto mustard and pat so it adheres. Roast lamb until meat thermometer inserted in center of lamb (not touching bone) reaches 140°F, 15 to 20 minutes longer. Internal temperature of meat will rise to 145°F (medium) upon standing. Or roast to desired doneness.

4. When roasts are done, transfer to cutting board and let stand 10 minutes to set juices for easier carving. Cut off backbone from ribs. Transfer roasts to warm platter. To serve, with sharp knife, cut lamb between bones to separate chops. Makes 8 main-dish servings.

Each serving: About 311 calories, 27g protein, 7g carbohydrate, 18g total fat (8g saturated), 99mg cholesterol, 436mg sodium.

CARVING A LEG OF LAMB

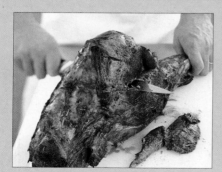

Cut a slice from the thin side of the leg so it can lie flat for easier carving; turn the leg cut side down. Holding the meat steady with a carving fork, make a vertical cut to the bone about 1 inch from the shank. Holding the knife horizontally, cut along the top of the bone about halfway down its length.

Holding the leg steady by grasping the bone or by inserting a carving fork into the lamb, slice the meat that has been released from the bone. Make a second horizontal cut almost to the end of the leg, then slice the remaining lamb.

Turn the leg over. With the knife blade almost flat and working away from you, cut long slices following the line of the bone.

Moroccan-Style Lamb with Couscous

This sweet but slightly spicy stew is served on a bed of couscous, a grain-shaped semolina pasta.

Prep: 20 minutes   Cook: 1 hour 45 minutes

2	pounds boneless lamb shoulder, trimmed and cut into 1¼-inch pieces
2	tablespoons olive oil
2	garlic cloves, finely chopped
1½	teaspoons ground cumin
1½	teaspoons ground coriander
1	large onion (12 ounces), cut into 8 wedges
1	can (14½ to 16 ounces) stewed tomatoes
1	cinnamon stick (3 inches)
1¼	teaspoons salt
¼	teaspoon ground red pepper (cayenne)
1	cup water
2	pounds sweet potatoes (3 large), peeled and cut into 2-inch pieces
2	cups couscous (Moroccan pasta)
1	can (15 to 19 ounces) garbanzo beans, rinsed and drained
1	cup dark seedless raisins
¼	cup chopped fresh cilantro

1. Pat lamb dry with paper towels. In nonreactive 5-quart Dutch oven, heat 1 tablespoon oil over medium-high heat until very hot. Add half of lamb and cook until browned, using slotted spoon to transfer meat to bowl as it is browned. Repeat with remaining 1 tablespoon oil and remaining lamb.

2. To drippings in Dutch oven, add garlic, cumin, and coriander; cook 30 seconds. Return lamb to Dutch oven. Stir in onion, tomatoes, cinnamon stick, salt, ground red pepper, and water; heat to boiling over high heat. Reduce heat; cover and simmer, stirring occasionally, 45 minutes. Stir in sweet potatoes; cover and simmer 30 minutes longer.

3. Meanwhile, prepare couscous as label directs.

4. Add garbanzo beans and raisins to Dutch oven. Cover and cook, stirring once or twice, until lamb and vegetables are tender, about 5 minutes longer.

5. Just before serving, stir cilantro into stew. Serve lamb stew on couscous. Makes 8 main-dish servings.

♥ Each serving: About 570 calories, 33g protein, 81g carbohydrate, 13g total fat (3g saturated), 75mg cholesterol, 651mg sodium.

Moroccan-Style Lamb with Couscous

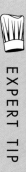

Never buy precut meat labeled "stew meat." You will pay more and won't know what cut(s) of meat it is. (This is also true for meat labeled "kabobs"). Often, the butcher is trying to sell a less desirable cut, such as the bottom round, which cooks up dry and stringy. Instead, purchase a piece of boneless chuck, and cut it up yourself or ask the butcher to cut it for you. Be sure to tell him to cut the meat into two-inch chunks. Many butchers cut stew meat into pieces that are much too small and therefore get overcooked and fall apart.

BRUCE AIDELLS

COOKBOOK AUTHOR

EXPERT TIP

Braised Lamb Shanks with White Beans and Vegetables

Here the meat of succulent braised lamb shanks is stirred into a toothsome bean mixture, turning it into a hearty stew.

Prep: 20 minutes plus soaking beans and cooling   Cook: 3 hours

2	lamb shanks (1 to 1¼ pounds each), trimmed
3	tablespoons olive oil
1	large onion (12 ounces), chopped
1	can (14½ ounces) diced tomatoes, drained
2	jalapeño chiles, seeded and chopped
6	garlic cloves, finely chopped
6	thyme sprigs or ¼ teaspoon dried thyme
2	bay leaves
1	teaspoon ground cumin
	pinch ground cloves
	pinch ground allspice
1	cup dry white beans, such as Great Northern or navy, soaked (page 372)
3	cups hot water
¼	cup plus 1 tablespoon chopped fresh parsley
2	red peppers, roasted (page 448), seeded, and chopped
1	tablespoon red wine vinegar
½	teaspoon salt
¼	teaspoon ground black pepper

1. Pat lamb dry with paper towels. In nonreactive 5-quart Dutch oven, heat oil over medium heat until hot. Add onion and cook, stirring, until lightly browned, about 15 minutes. Add shanks and cook, turning, until browned, about 15 minutes. Stir in tomatoes, jalapeños, garlic, thyme, bay leaves, cumin, cloves, and allspice and cook 5 minutes.

2. Stir in beans and hot water; heat to boiling. Reduce heat; cover and simmer gently, stirring occasionally, until lamb is very tender, about 2 hours, adding more hot water if beans are dry or sticking on bottom. With tongs, transfer shanks to plate. Remove Dutch oven from heat.

3. When shanks are cool enough to handle, remove and shred meat. With tip of knife, remove marrow from bones, if possible. Add meat and marrow to Dutch oven with ¼ cup parsley, roasted peppers, vinegar, salt, and pepper. Remove

Braised Lamb Shanks with White Beans and Vegetables

cover and simmer, stirring occasionally, 30 minutes longer, adding more water, if necessary, to prevent beans from sticking. Garnish with remaining 1 tablespoon parsley. Makes 4 main-dish servings.

Each serving: About 502 calories, 44g protein, 42g carbohydrate, 18g total fat (4g saturated), 100mg cholesterol, 404mg sodium.

Lamb Steak with Red Pepper Relish

Lamb steak, an often overlooked cut, is simply a thick crosswise slice of leg of lamb that is every bit as delicious as you'd expect.

Prep: 30 minutes   Broil: 10 minutes

⅓	cup cider vinegar
¼	cup sugar
1¼	teaspoons salt
	pinch dried thyme, crumbled
	pinch fennel seeds, crushed
2	small red peppers, chopped
1	medium Golden Delicious apple, peeled, cored, and chopped
2	jalapeño chiles, seeded and finely chopped
1	center-cut lamb steak, 1-inch thick (1½ pounds), or 8 lamb loin chops, 1-inch thick (4 ounces each)

1. In 2-quart saucepan, combine vinegar, sugar, 1 teaspoon salt, thyme, and fennel seeds; heat to boiling over high heat. Add red peppers, apple, and jalapeños; heat to boiling. Reduce heat and simmer, stirring occasionally, until liquid has evaporated, 15 to 20 minutes. Keep warm.

2. Meanwhile, preheat broiler. Sprinkle lamb with remaining ¼ teaspoon salt. Place lamb on rack in broiling pan. Place pan at closest position to heat source and broil lamb 5 minutes. Turn lamb and broil 5 minutes longer for medium-rare or until desired doneness. Serve lamb with warm red pepper relish. Makes 4 main-dish servings.

♥ Each serving: About 267 calories, 26g protein, 21g carbohydrate, 9g total fat (3g saturated), 82mg cholesterol, 799mg sodium.

Irish Stew

There's something special about Irish stew: It is so perfectly simple, delicious, and satisfying—a complete meal in a bowl.

Prep: 20 minutes   Cook: 2 hours

3	leeks
2	pounds boneless lamb shoulder, trimmed and cut into 1-inch pieces
2	tablespoons vegetable oil
¼	teaspoon salt
⅛	teaspoon dried thyme
⅛	teaspoon ground black pepper
1	can (14½ ounces) beef broth or 1¾ cups Brown Beef Stock (page 83)
1¾	cups water
6	sprigs plus 3 tablespoons chopped fresh parsley
8	small red potatoes (1 pound), each cut in half
1¼	cups peeled baby carrots
1	large turnip (8 ounces), cut into ¾-inch wedges

1. Cut off roots and trim dark green tops from leeks; cut each leek crosswise into thin slices. Rinse leeks in large bowl of cold water, swishing to remove sand; transfer to colander to drain, leaving sand in bottom of bowl.

2. Pat lamb dry with paper towels. In 5-quart Dutch oven, heat oil over medium heat until very hot. Cook lamb, in batches, until browned, using slotted spoon to transfer meat to bowl as it is browned. Add leeks, salt, thyme, and pepper to Dutch oven and cook, stirring, until leeks are lightly browned, about 15 minutes.

3. Return lamb to Dutch oven and add broth, water, and parsley sprigs; heat to boiling over high heat. Reduce heat; partially cover and simmer 30 minutes. Add potatoes, carrots, and turnip and heat to boiling over high heat. Reduce heat; partially cover and simmer, stirring occasionally, until meat and vegetables are very tender, about 1 hour longer. Discard parsley sprigs; transfer stew to serving bowl and stir in chopped parsley. Makes 6 main-dish servings.

Each serving: About 381 calories, 33g protein, 27g carbohydrate, 16g total fat (4g saturated), 100mg cholesterol, 526mg sodium.

Greek-Style Lamb Shanks

A savory dish that combines four favorite Greek flavors: lamb, lemon, dill, and parsley. The addition of potatoes and green beans makes it a warming winter meal.

Prep: 30 minutes   Bake: 2 hours 45 minutes

4	small lamb shanks (1 pound each), trimmed
1	tablespoon vegetable oil
2	medium onions, chopped
1	large carrot, peeled and chopped
2	garlic cloves, finely chopped
1	can (14½ ounces) diced tomatoes
1	cup chicken broth
½	teaspoon salt
4	medium all-purpose potatoes (1¾ pounds), peeled and each cut into quarters
12	ounces green beans, cut into 2-inch pieces
2	medium lemons
2	tablespoons chopped fresh dill
2	tablespoons chopped fresh parsley

1. Pat lamb dry with paper towels. In nonreactive 8-quart Dutch oven, heat oil over medium-high heat until very hot. Cook 2 shanks, turning, until browned, transferring shanks to plate as they are browned. Repeat with remaining 2 shanks.

2. Preheat oven to 350°F. Add onions and carrot to drippings in Dutch oven and cook until tender and lightly browned, about 10 minutes. Add garlic; cook 2 minutes.

3. Return shanks to Dutch oven. Add tomatoes with their juice, broth, and salt; heat to boiling over high heat. Cover and place in oven. Bake 1 hour 30 minutes. Turn shanks over; add potatoes and green beans to Dutch oven. Cover and bake until lamb and potatoes are tender, about 1 hour 15 minutes.

4. Meanwhile, from lemons, grate 1 tablespoon peel and squeeze 2 tablespoons juice; set aside.

5. When shanks are done, skim and discard fat from pot liquid. Stir in lemon peel and juice, dill, and parsley. Makes 4 main-dish servings.

♥ *Each serving: About 672 calories, 73g protein, 55g carbohydrate, 18g total fat (5g saturated), 200mg cholesterol, 930mg sodium.*

Lamb Navarin

Lots of herbs and fresh asparagus make this French ragout especially tempting for a springtime celebration.

Prep: 20 minutes   Cook: 2 hours

3	pounds boneless lamb shoulder, trimmed and cut into 1-inch pieces
2	tablespoons butter or margarine
2	small onions, each cut into quarters, then crosswise into slices
1½	cups dry white wine
1½	cups chicken broth
1	cup water
6	sprigs plus 2 tablespoons chopped fresh parsley
2	thyme sprigs or ¼ teaspoon dried thyme
2	bay leaves
4	garlic cloves, finely chopped
½	teaspoon salt
¼	teaspoon ground black pepper
8	ounces peeled baby carrots (1⅓ cups)
2	small turnips (4 ounces each), peeled and cut into ¾-inch pieces
8	ounces pearl onions, peeled (1 cup)
1½	pounds asparagus, trimmed and cut into 2-inch lengths
2	teaspoons sugar

1. Pat lamb dry with paper towels. In nonreactive 5-quart Dutch oven, melt butter over medium heat. Cook lamb, in batches, until well browned, using slotted spoon to transfer meat to bowl as it is browned. Add onions to Dutch oven and cook, stirring, until tender, about 5 minutes. Add wine, broth, water, parsley sprigs, thyme sprigs, bay leaves, and lamb to pot; heat to boiling over high heat. Reduce heat; cover and simmer 15 minutes. Add garlic, salt, and pepper and simmer 30 minutes longer.

2. Add carrots, turnips, and pearl onions to Dutch oven; partially cover and cook until lamb is tender, about 30 minutes longer. Stir in asparagus and cook until vegetables are tender, 5 to 10 minutes longer.

3. With slotted spoon, transfer meat and vegetables to deep dish and keep warm. Boil stew liquid over medium-high heat until it has reduced and thickened, about 10 minutes. Discard parsley and thyme sprigs and bay leaves. Stir in sugar.

Taste for seasoning; add salt as needed. Spoon stew liquid over meat and sprinkle with parsley. Makes 8 main-dish servings.

Each serving: About 312 calories, 39g protein, 14g carbohydrate, 11g total fat (5g saturated), 117mg cholesterol, 500mg sodium.

Glazed Rosemary Lamb Chops

These rosemary-scented lamb chops are broiled with an apple-jelly-and-balsamic-vinegar glaze. Keep this glaze in mind for pork, too.

Prep: 10 minutes   Broil: 10 minutes

8	lamb loin chops, 1 inch thick (4 ounces each)
1	large garlic clove, cut in half
2	teaspoons chopped fresh rosemary or ½ teaspoon dried rosemary, crumbled
¼	teaspoon salt
¼	teaspoon coarsely ground black pepper
¼	cup apple jelly
1	tablespoon balsamic vinegar

1. Preheat broiler. Rub both sides of chops with cut side of garlic; sprinkle with rosemary, salt, and pepper. In cup, combine apple jelly and vinegar.

2. Place chops on rack in broiling pan. Place pan in broiler at closest position to heat source; broil chops 4 minutes. Brush chops with half of apple-jelly mixture; broil 1 minute. Turn chops and broil 4 minutes longer. Brush chops with remaining jelly mixture and broil 1 minute longer for medium-rare or until desired doneness.

3. Transfer lamb to warm platter. Skim and discard fat from drippings in pan. Serve chops with pan juices, or drizzle with additional balsamic vinegar. Makes 4 main-dish servings.

Each serving: About 240 calories, 26g protein, 14g carbohydrate, 8g total fat (3g saturated), 82mg cholesterol, 223mg sodium.

Aromatic Leg of Lamb

Once your butcher has boned out a leg of lamb for you, ask for the lamb bone. Take it home and use it to cook up some flavorful lamb broth for an especially tasty stew.

	Prep: 20 minutes Grill: 15 to 25 minutes
3	pounds boneless lamb leg, butterflied and trimmed
3	garlic cloves, each cut in half and crushed with side of chef's knife
1	tablespoon olive oil
2	teaspoons fennel seeds, crushed
2	teaspoons cumin seeds, crushed
2	teaspoons coriander seeds, crushed
1½	teaspoons salt
	lemon wedges

1. Prepare grill. Rub both sides of lamb with cut sides of garlic cloves; discard garlic.

2. In small bowl, combine oil, fennel seeds, cumin seeds, coriander seeds, and salt. Use to rub on lamb.

3. Place lamb on grill over medium heat. Cook 15 to 25 minutes for medium-rare or until desired doneness, turning lamb occasionally. Thickness of butterflied lamb will vary throughout; cut off sections of lamb as they are done and place on cutting board. Let stand 10 minutes to set juices for easier slicing. Cut into thin slices and serve lamb with lemon wedges. Makes 8 main-dish servings.

Each serving: About 265 calories, 36g protein, 1g carbohydrate, 12g total fat (4g saturated), 114mg cholesterol, 525mg sodium.

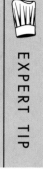

Turn your meat—don't stab it. Use tongs, not a barbecue fork, for turning steaks. The tines poke holes in the meat, draining the flavorful juices onto the coals.

STEVE RAICHLEN
COOKBOOK AUTHOR

EXPERT TIP

Grilled Leg of Lamb with Mint and Oregano

Lemon and fresh herbs imbue this grilled lamb with the taste of the sun-drenched Aegean countryside. For a simple feast, serve the lamb with rice and sliced summer tomatoes.

	Prep: 25 minutes plus overnight to marinate Grill: 15 to 25 minutes
1	large bunch fresh mint
1	large bunch fresh oregano
3	tablespoons plus ¼ cup olive oil
3	tablespoons plus ¼ cup fresh lemon juice
1	garlic clove, finely chopped
1½	teaspoons salt
¾	teaspoon ground black pepper
3	pounds boneless lamb leg, butterflied and trimmed

1. Measure ¼ cup each mint and oregano leaves and chop, reserving remainder for sauce. In 13" by 9" baking dish, combine chopped mint and oregano, 3 tablespoons each oil and lemon juice, garlic, 1 teaspoon salt, and ½ teaspoon pepper. Add lamb, turning to coat. Cover with plastic wrap and refrigerate lamb overnight to marinate.

2. Prepare grill. For sauce, chop 2 tablespoons each mint and oregano leaves. In small bowl, combine mint and oregano with remaining ¼ cup each oil and lemon juice, remaining ½ teaspoon salt, and remaining ¼ teaspoon pepper.

3. Remove lamb from marinade and grill over medium heat, turning occasionally, 15 to 25 minutes for medium-rare or until desired doneness. Thickness of butterflied lamb will vary throughout; cut off sections of lamb as they are done and place on cutting board. Let stand 10 minutes to set juices for easier slicing. Cut into thin slices and spoon herb sauce on top. Makes 8 main-dish servings.

Each serving: About 266 calories, 22g protein, 2g carbohydrate, 19g total fat (4g saturated), 69mg cholesterol, 491mg sodium.

Rosemary Lamb Kabobs

The fresh, clean flavors of orange and rosemary are wonderful with lamb. Serve alongside skewers of grilled cherry tomatoes and a bowl of yellow rice.

Prep: 30 minutes plus marinating	Grill/Broil: 10 minutes
3	oranges
1	tablespoon olive oil
1	tablespoon chopped fresh rosemary
	or 1½ teaspoons dried rosemary, crumbled
2	garlic cloves, each cut in half
¼	teaspoon salt
¼	teaspoon ground red pepper (cayenne)
1	pound boneless lamb leg, cut into 1½-inch pieces
8	metal skewers
1	red pepper, cut into 1½-inch squares
1	yellow pepper, cut into 1½-inch squares
1	orange pepper, cut into 1½-inch squares
1	pint cherry tomatoes
6	green onions, cut into 2-inch pieces
10	ounces small mushrooms, trimmed

1. Prepare grill or preheat broiler. From oranges, grate 1 teaspoon peel and squeeze 1 cup juice. In large bowl, combine orange peel and juice, oil, rosemary, garlic, salt, and ground red pepper. Add lamb, turning to coat, and let stand 10 minutes at room temperature, stirring occasionally.

2. Skewer lamb on four metal skewers and skewer vegetables on remaining four skewers, alternating vegetables.

3. Grill or broil lamb and vegetable skewers, turning once, 10 to 12 minutes for medium-rare or until desired doneness. Arrange on platter. Makes 4 main-dish servings.

Each serving: About 245 calories, 28g protein, 12g carbohydrate, 10g total fat (3g saturated), 81mg cholesterol, 118mg sodium.

Grilled Lamb Chops with Spice Rub

Grilling chops that have been seasoned with a rub is the easiest way to guarantee lots of flavor.

Prep: 5 minutes	Grill: 10 minutes
4	lamb shoulder chops, ¾ inch thick (8 ounces each)
	choice of dry rub (below)

1. Prepare grill. In small bowl, combine rub ingredients; use to rub on lamb chops.

2. Grill chops over medium heat about 5 minutes per side for medium-rare or until desired doneness. Makes 4 main-dish servings.

Each serving: About 454 calories, 57g protein, 2g carbohydrate, 22g total fat (8g saturated), 196mg cholesterol, 470mg sodium.

Curry Rub
Combine **2 tablespoons brown sugar, 1 tablespoon curry powder, ½ teaspoon salt,** and **¼ teaspoon ground black pepper.**

Southwestern Rub
Combine **2 teaspoons chili powder, ½ teaspoon salt, ¼ teaspoon ground cumin, ¼ teaspoon coriander, ¼ teaspoon ground red pepper (cayenne),** and **¼ teaspoon ground black pepper.**

Middle Eastern Rub
Combine **1 tablespoon dried mint,** crumbled, **1 teaspoon ground cumin, ½ teaspoon salt,** and **¼ teaspoon ground black pepper.**

Herbes de Provence Rub
Combine **1½ teaspoons dried thyme,** crumbled, **1 teaspoon dried rosemary,** crumbled, **½ teaspoon dried marjoram,** crumbled, **½ teaspoon salt,** and **¼ teaspoon ground black pepper.**

Eggplant and Lamb Casserole

Our version of moussaka uses roasted rather than sautéed eggplant, so the dish is lighter than usual. If you like, substitute ground beef for the lamb.

Prep: 55 minutes   Bake: 35 minutes

2	small eggplants (about 1¼ pounds each), cut lengthwise into ½-inch-thick slices
3	tablespoons olive oil
2	pounds ground lamb
1	large onion (12 ounces), chopped
2	garlic cloves, finely chopped
1½	teaspoons salt
1	teaspoon ground cumin
½	teaspoon ground cinnamon
½	teaspoon coarsely ground black pepper
1	can (28 ounces) plum tomatoes in puree
4	large eggs
⅓	cup all-purpose flour
3	cups milk
¼	teaspoon ground nutmeg

1. Preheat oven to 450°F. Grease two small cookie sheets. Place eggplant slices on cookie sheets; brush with 2 tablespoons oil. Bake eggplant until soft and browned, about 20 minutes, rotating cookie sheets between upper and lower oven racks halfway through baking time. Remove eggplant from oven; turn oven control to 375°F.

2. Meanwhile, in nonstick 12-inch skillet at least 2 inches deep, combine ground lamb, onion, and garlic and cook over medium-high heat, stirring, until lamb is browned, about 15 minutes. Skim and discard fat. Stir in 1 teaspoon salt, cumin, cinnamon, and ¼ teaspoon pepper; cook 1 minute longer. Remove skillet from heat; add tomatoes with their puree, breaking them up with side of spoon.

3. Break eggs into small bowl and, with wire whisk, lightly beat; set aside. In 3-quart saucepan, heat remaining 1 tablespoon oil over medium heat. Whisk in flour and cook, whisking, 1 minute (mixture will appear dry and crumbly). Gradually whisk in milk. Heat to boiling; cook until mixture has thickened, about 8 minutes. Remove from heat. Gradually beat one-fourth of milk mixture into eggs. Return egg mixture to saucepan, beating to combine. Stir in nutmeg, remaining ½ teaspoon salt, and remaining ¼ teaspoon pepper.

4. In shallow 4-quart casserole or 13" by 9" baking dish, arrange half of eggplant slices, overlapping slices to fit if necessary; top with half of meat mixture. Repeat with remaining eggplant slices and meat mixture. Pour egg mixture over top. Bake until top is puffed and golden and casserole is heated through, 35 to 40 minutes. Makes 10 main-dish servings.

Each serving: About 375 calories, 23g protein, 21g carbohydrate, 22g total fat (8g saturated), 157mg cholesterol, 593mg sodium.

Shepherd's Pie

Traditional shepherd's pie is made with lamb. If you use beef instead, it's really "Cottage Pie." Either way, it's real comfort food.

Prep: 40 minutes   Bake: 20 minutes

2	pounds all-purpose potatoes, peeled and cut into quarters
½	cup milk
3	tablespoons butter or margarine
¼	cup plus 1 tablespoon freshly grated Parmesan cheese
1	teaspoon salt
¼	plus ⅛ teaspoon ground black pepper
1	medium onion, chopped
2	carrots, peeled and chopped
1	pound ground lamb
2	tablespoons tomato paste
2	tablespoons all-purpose flour
¼	cup dry red wine
1	cup chicken broth
¼	teaspoon dried thyme
1	cup frozen peas

1. Preheat oven to 425°F. In 4-quart saucepan, combine potatoes and enough *water* to cover; heat to boiling. Boil until potatoes are tender, about 20 minutes; drain and return to saucepan. With potato masher, mash potatoes with milk and 2 tablespoons butter. Stir in ¼ cup Parmesan, ½ teaspoon salt, and ¼ teaspoon pepper; set aside.

2. Meanwhile, in nonstick 10-inch skillet, melt remaining 1 tablespoon butter over medium heat. Add onion and carrots; cook until vegetables are tender, about 5 minutes. Add ground lamb and cook over medium-high heat, stirring and breaking up meat with spoon, until lamb is no longer pink, about 5 minutes. Skim and discard fat. Add tomato paste and cook, stirring, 1 minute. Add flour and cook, stirring, 1 minute longer. Stir in wine and cook until wine has evapo-

rated. Add broth, thyme, remaining ½ teaspoon salt, and remaining ⅛ teaspoon pepper, stirring until browned bits are loosened from bottom of skillet. Heat to boiling; stir in peas.

3. Transfer lamb mixture to 9-inch deep-dish pie plate. Spoon mashed potatoes evenly on top and sprinkle with remaining 1 tablespoon Parmesan. Place on foil-lined cookie sheet and bake until slightly browned, about 20 minutes. Makes 4 main-dish servings.

Each serving: About 599 calories, 31g protein, 50g carbohydrate, 31g total fat (15g saturated), 113mg cholesterol, 1,272mg sodium.

VARIETY MEATS

Economical and tasty, variety meats (offal) are the organs of an animal. These cuts are becoming better known as cooks experiment with different cuisines or try old family recipes. When possible, buy variety meats at ethnic markets that have an appreciative clientele, to ensure fast turnover. Variety meats have a short shelf life and must be cooked within twenty-four hours of purchase. While each cut retains a certain amount of that animal's flavor, you can usually substitute the same cut from a different animal. Simply adjust the recipe to allow for any size difference. Plan ahead: Variety meats always need some advance preparation to remove tough tissues and excess blood.

Brains

Veal, lamb, pork, and beef brains are readily available. Cooked brains have a delectably creamy texture. Place the brains in a bowl of cold water. Refrigerate and soak, occasionally changing the water, until the water is clear, about one and one-half hours. Peel off the clear membrane surrounding the lobes.

Liver

Delicate in flavor and texture, calf's liver is highly appreciated but is usually expensive. Beef and pork livers are less costly and also delicious. Their somewhat stronger flavor can be mellowed with a one-hour soak in milk. Before cooking, peel off the membrane surrounding the liver. If you purchase sliced liver, check that the butcher has removed the membrane. If necessary, remove it yourself.

Chicken livers lend themselves to a variety of preparations, from quick sautés to smooth pâtés. Rinse the chicken livers with cold running water. Pat dry with paper towels; they'll brown better without any surface moisture. Trim away any membranes and greenish areas.

Kidneys

Most cooks prefer veal kidneys, which have the best texture and flavor; pork kidneys are similar in size. Beef and lamb kidneys are much larger and are usually sliced before cooking. To reduce their strong flavor and aroma, soak whole beef or lamb kidneys in cold water to cover for two hours in the refrigerator. Do not soak veal or pork kidneys, which are more delicate and have a tendency to soak up water. All kidneys need to be trimmed of any fat and the surrounding membrane. Cut beef and veal kidneys lengthwise in half and trim out the fatty core, but leave the core fat intact in lamb and pork kidneys.

Sweetbreads

These are either the thymus glands or the pancreas of a calf. Sweetbreads are prized for their tenderness and delicate flavor. To prepare, refrigerate the sweetbreads in cold water to cover, occasionally changing the water, until the water is clear, about one and one-half hours. If you want the sweetbreads to be creamy white, add the juice of one lemon to each change of water. Drain them well. To precook, place the sweetbreads in a saucepan and cover with cold water. Bring to a boil over medium heat, then reduce the heat to low and simmer, uncovered, for about five minutes. Drain and rinse under cold water. Peel off the membrane, fat, and tubes from each sweetbread. To firm the sweetbreads and give them a compact shape, place them between two plates or baking dishes. Place about two pounds of cans on top to help press out the excess water. Refrigerate until chilled and firm, two to three hours. The sweetbreads are now ready for their final cooking.

Tongue

Especially appreciated by sandwich lovers, tongue is usually sliced and served on rye bread. It can be fresh or corned (cured in salt and spices) and beef, veal, lamb, or pork. Choose the smallest tongue available for the tenderest results. Blanch tongue in boiling water for ten minutes to remove any excess blood or saltiness, then simmer until very tender; from about forty-five minutes for a small veal, pork, or lamb tongue to about two and one-half hours for a beef tongue. Remove from the pot and let cool. (If serving the tongue hot, save the cooking liquid.) Make a lengthwise incision on the underside of the tongue. Peel off the thick skin and discard any fat, gristle, and small bones. If desired, reheat in the cooking liquid, or cover and chill to serve cold.

VARIETY MEAT CUTS

Calf's Liver
(panfry, broil, grill). Pork and beef liver also available.

Chicken liver
(panfry, broil, grill on skewers). Duck liver is available in some Asian markets.

Foie gras
(panfry, or bake as a terrine). Goose or duck liver.

Beef kidney
(panfry). Veal, pork, and lamb kidneys also available.

Fresh Foie Gras

Foie gras (FWAH-grah), the buttery, rich liver of a fattened duck or goose, is a traditional luxury in France and has been produced here since the early 1980s. This delicacy takes only a moment to cook, so organize your ingredients and serving plates for a fast assembly line. Fresh foie gras can be ordered from specialty markets and fancy butchers.

Prep: 40 minutes plus making sauce	*Cook: 5 minutes*

1	fresh duck foie gras (1¼ pounds)
2	cups or more milk
	choice of sauce (opposite)
1	bunch watercress, tough stems trimmed
	salt
	ground black pepper

1. In large bowl, combine foie gras with just enough milk to cover. Cover bowl and refrigerate 30 minutes. Meanwhile, prepare desired sauce.

2. Drain foie gras and pat dry with paper towels. Gently separate the two lobes. With knife held at 45° angle, cut foie gras into ½-inch-thick slices; arrange in single layer in jelly-roll pan. With tip of paring knife, remove any blood spots or veins, wiping knife clean on paper towels between cuts. Refrigerate foie gras until ready to cook.

3. Arrange watercress on one side of plates. Sprinkle foie gras with salt and pepper. Heat 10-inch skillet over medium-high heat until very hot (foie gras should sizzle when it touches skillet). Cook foie gras, a few slices at a time, just until lightly browned, 20 to 30 seconds per side. (Foie gras will melt as it cooks; do not overcook.) Arrange on plates next to watercress. Spoon desired sauce on top and next to foie gras and watercress. Makes 8 appetizer servings.

Each serving without sauce: About 233 calories, 6g protein, 3g carbohydrate, 22g total fat (7g saturated), 75mg cholesterol, 355mg sodium.

Pear-Balsamic Sauce

In nonreactive 1-quart saucepan, combine **1 cup balsamic vinegar, ¼ cup packed brown sugar, ¼ cup finely chopped shallots,** and **¼ teaspoon coarsely ground black pepper** and heat to boiling over high heat. Reduce heat to medium-high and boil until liquid has reduced to ½ cup. Stir in **1 fully ripe pear,** such as Bosc, peeled, cored, and cut into ½-inch pieces; reduce heat and simmer until tender, about 5 minutes. Makes about ¾ cup.

Each tablespoon: About 30 calories, 0g protein, 8g carbohydrate, 0g total fat (0g saturated), 0mg cholesterol, 3mg sodium.

Port Sauce with Prunes

In nonreactive 2-quart saucepan, combine **1 cup port wine, 1 cup dry red wine, 1 cup pitted prunes,** coarsely chopped, **2 tablespoons sugar, 2 strips (3" by 1" each) orange peel,** and **¼ teaspoon coarsely ground black pepper** and heat to boiling over high heat. Reduce heat; simmer, stirring occasionally, until sauce has reduced to 1¼ cups, about 25 minutes. Discard orange peel. Makes about 1¼ cups.

Each tablespoon: About 31 calories, 0g protein, 8g carbohydrate, 0g total fat (0g saturated), 0mg cholesterol, 2mg sodium.

Chicken Livers Marsala

In this classic preparation, Marsala wine mellows and sweetens the chicken livers. Serve with rice or noodles to soak up the juices.

Prep: 15 minutes   Cook: 15 minutes

1	pound chicken livers, trimmed and cut in half
3	tablespoons butter or margarine
¾	teaspoon salt
1	medium onion, chopped
8	ounces mushrooms, trimmed and cut in half
¼	teaspoon ground black pepper
¼	cup dry Marsala wine
1	tablespoon chopped fresh parsley

1. Pat livers dry with paper towels. In 10-inch skillet, melt 1 tablespoon butter over medium-high heat. Add livers, sprinkle with ½ teaspoon salt, and cook, stirring often, until livers are browned but still pink in center, 3 to 4 minutes. Or cook until desired doneness. Transfer livers to bowl.

2. Add remaining 2 tablespoons butter to skillet. Add onion and cook until tender, about 5 minutes. Add mushrooms, pepper, and remaining ¼ teaspoon salt and cook until mushrooms are tender. Stir in Marsala and heat to boiling. Add livers and heat through. Sprinkle with parsley. Makes 4 main-dish servings.

Each serving: About 272 calories, 22g protein, 12g carbohydrate, 13g total fat (7g saturated), 522mg cholesterol, 619mg sodium.

Chicken Livers with Mushrooms and Onions

This serves four as a main course or six as an appetizer. If you like, serve over toast or pasta. If you have any leftovers, transfer to a food processor and puree until smooth for a quick pâté.

Prep: 10 minutes   Cook: 15 minutes

2	tablespoons olive oil
1	medium onion, chopped
12	ounces mushrooms, trimmed and thinly sliced
1	pound chicken livers, trimmed
¾	teaspoon salt
¼	teaspoon ground black pepper
¼	cup port wine

1. In 12-inch skillet, heat 1 tablespoon oil over medium heat. Add onion and cook, stirring frequently, until tender, about 5 minutes. Add mushrooms and cook, stirring, until tender, about 4 minutes.

2. Add livers and remaining 1 tablespoon oil to skillet. Sprinkle livers with salt and pepper and cook, stirring frequently, until livers are browned but still slightly pink in center, about 3 minutes. Or cook until desired doneness. Add port to skillet and heat to boiling. Boil just until slightly reduced, about 2 minutes. Makes 4 main-dish servings.

Each serving: About 262 calories, 23g protein, 13g carbohydrate, 12g total fat (2g saturated), 498mg cholesterol, 532mg sodium.

Panfried Calf's Liver and Bacon

A classic combination of crispy bacon and panfried liver.

🕐 *Prep: 10 minutes   Cook: 8 minutes*

4	slices bacon
3	tablespoons all-purpose flour
4	slices calf's liver, ½ inch thick (1 pound)
¼	teaspoon salt
	chopped fresh parsley
1	small lemon, cut into 4 wedges

1. In 12-inch skillet, cook bacon over medium-high heat until browned. With slotted spoon, transfer bacon to paper towels to drain; keep warm.

2. Place flour on waxed paper. Coat liver with flour, shaking off excess.

3. Discard all but 1 tablespoon bacon drippings from skillet. Add liver slices to hot drippings in skillet and cook over medium-high heat until crisp and browned but slightly pink inside, about 1½ to 2 minutes per side. (Don't overcook, or liver will be tough.) Sprinkle with salt.

4. Place liver and bacon on warm platter; sprinkle with parsley and serve with lemon wedges. Makes 4 main-dish servings.

Each serving: About 233 calories, 23g protein, 10g carbohydrate, 11g total fat (4g saturated), 358mg cholesterol, 331mg sodium.

Venetian-Style Calf's Liver

Sweet onions, cooked until meltingly tender and golden brown, complement the liver. If you prefer, cut the liver into ½-inch-thick slices, cook, and then cut into strips.

Prep: 10 minutes   Cook: 22 minutes

2	tablespoons olive oil
3	large onions (12 ounces each), thinly sliced (5 cups)
3	tablespoons all-purpose flour
1	pound calf's liver, cut into 1-inch-wide strips
½	teaspoon salt

1. In 12-inch skillet, heat 1 tablespoon oil over medium-low heat. Add onions and cook, stirring frequently, until golden brown and tender, about 20 minutes. Transfer to plate and keep warm.

2. Add remaining 1 tablespoon oil to skillet; increase heat to medium-high. Place flour on waxed paper. Coat liver with flour, shaking off excess. Add liver to skillet and cook, stirring constantly, until lightly browned, about 2 minutes. Transfer liver to warm platter, sprinkle with salt, and top with onions. Makes 4 main-dish servings.

Each serving: About 309 calories, 23g protein, 27g carbohydrate, 12g total fat (3g saturated), 351mg cholesterol, 366mg sodium.

Smoked Tongue

The leftovers make wonderful sandwiches on rye or pumpernickel.

Prep: 10 minutes   Cook: 3 hours

1	smoked beef tongue (3¼ pounds)
1	small carrot, peeled and coarsely chopped
1	small onion, sliced
2	teaspoons salt
½	teaspoon whole black peppercorns
3	whole cloves
	Creamy Horseradish Sauce (page 95)

1. In 5-quart Dutch oven, combine tongue, carrot, onion, salt, peppercorns, cloves, and enough *water* to cover; heat to boiling over high heat. Reduce heat; cover and simmer until tongue is tender, about 2 hours 45 minutes. Drain.

2. Prepare Creamy Horseradish Sauce.

3. When tongue is cool enough to handle, slit skin on underside from thick end to tip, then loosen skin all around thick end and pull it off. With sharp knife, trim all bones and

gristle from thick end of tongue. Cut tongue crosswise into thin slices. Serve with horseradish sauce. Makes 10 main-dish servings.

Each serving without sauce: About 240 calories, 19g protein, 1g carbohydrate, 17g total fat (8g saturated), 90mg cholesterol, 1,004mg sodium.

Sweetbreads Braised with Madeira

Steamed spinach is the perfect accompaniment to rich, delicate sweetbreads. After blanching, sweetbreads are often weighted down to create a slightly firmer texture; skip this step if you prefer your sweetbreads softer.

Prep: 35 minutes plus soaking and chilling   Cook: 55 minutes

1	pair veal sweetbreads (1 pound)
1	tablespoon distilled white vinegar
1/4	cup all-purpose flour
2	tablespoons butter or margarine
1	small onion, finely chopped
1	carrot, peeled and finely chopped
1/2	stalk celery, finely chopped
1/4	cup finely chopped smoked ham
1	garlic clove, finely chopped
1	tablespoon tomato paste
2/3	cup chicken broth
1/3	cup Madeira wine
1/8	teaspoon dried thyme
1/8	teaspoon salt
1/8	teaspoon ground black pepper
1	tablespoon chopped fresh parsley

1. In bowl, soak sweetbreads in *cold water* 1 hour; drain. In 4-quart sauce-pan, combine sweetbreads, vinegar, and *2 quarts water;* heat to boiling over high heat. Reduce heat and simmer 5 minutes; drain. In same saucepan filled with *cold water,* cool sweetbreads 5 minutes. Peel off outer membranes from sweetbreads.

2. Transfer sweetbreads to plate; cover with plastic wrap. Weight with second plate and two pounds cans; refrigerate 1 hour. (If you like, remove top plate and cans; refrigerate up to 24 hours.)

3. Holding knife at a 45° angle, cut sweetbreads into 1/2-inch-thick slices. Place flour on waxed paper. Coat sweetbread slices with flour, shaking off excess. In 10-inch skillet, melt butter over medium-high heat. Add sweetbreads and cook until golden brown, about 4 minutes per side; transfer sweetbreads to clean plate.

4. Reduce heat to medium. Add onion, carrot, celery, and ham to skillet; cook, stirring often, until vegetables are tender, 5 to 8 minutes. Stir in garlic and cook 15 seconds. Add tomato paste, stirring until blended. Stir in broth, Madeira, thyme, salt, and pepper; heat to boiling. Return sweetbreads to skillet. Reduce heat; cover and simmer 30 minutes.

5. With slotted spoon, transfer sweetbreads to warm platter. Increase heat to high and boil until sauce has been reduced and thickens, about 3 minutes. Spoon sauce over sweetbreads and sprinkle with parsley. Makes 4 main-dish servings.

Each serving: About 242 calories, 24g protein, 14g carbohydrate, 9g total fat (4g saturated), 324mg cholesterol, 566mg sodium.

Sautéed Veal Kidneys with Mustard

Don't overcook the kidneys, or they will become tough.

Prep: 5 minutes   Cook: 15 minutes

1	tablespoon olive oil
2	veal kidneys (12 ounces each), well trimmed
3	shallots, chopped
1 1/2	cups chicken broth
1/4	cup heavy or whipping cream
2	tablespoons Dijon mustard
1/4	teaspoon salt
1/4	teaspoon ground black pepper
2	tablespoons chopped fresh parsley

1. In 10-inch skillet, heat oil over medium-high heat until very hot. Add kidneys and cook until browned, about 3 minutes per side. Transfer to plate.

2. Reduce heat to low; add shallots and cook, stirring frequently, until tender, about 4 minutes. Add broth, increase heat to high, and cook until liquid has reduced by one-third. Add cream, mustard, salt, and pepper and heat to boiling.

3. Cut kidneys crosswise into 1/2-inch-wide strips and return to skillet. Cook just until heated through or longer if you prefer kidneys well-done. Stir in parsley and serve. Makes 4 main-dish servings.

Each serving: About 274 calories, 28g protein, 4g carbohydrate, 15g total fat (6g saturated), 640mg cholesterol, 1,008mg sodium.

5

POULTRY

All around the globe, poultry has found its way into just about every kitchen, in simple and exotic incarnations alike. It is prized for its versatility and for the ease with which it can be combined with a vast range of ingredients. Everyone has heard the phrase "a chicken in every pot," but the creator of this famous phrase probably never imagined how true it would turn out to be. Whether you are preparing a creole chicken gumbo to be served over steamed rice, a succulent and juicy golden brown holiday turkey to grace the Thanksgiving table, boldly spiced tandoori chicken, or a classic like chicken cacciatore—these are dishes guaranteed to satisfy family and friends alike. Keep in mind that chicken, duck, goose, turkey, Cornish hen, and quail all fall under the heading of poultry. (Rabbit is also included because its lean meat is similar to poultry.) Here is a primer on how to buy, store, and prepare poultry, the favorite of cooks and diners alike.

BUYING

The United States Department of Agriculture inspection sticker (or tag) guarantees that the poultry was raised and processed under strict conditions according to government guidelines. Grade A birds, the most common variety in supermarkets, are the highest quality and are indicated by a shield-

Apple and Thyme Roast Chicken

shaped label. More than 90 percent of all broiler-fryers (chickens that range from about 2½ to 4 pounds) are marketed under a brand name, a further assurance of quality.

Choose fresh, whole birds that appear plump and have meaty breasts. (Meatier birds are a better buy, because you're paying for less bone per pound.) Chicken parts should also look plump. Poultry skin should be smooth and moist and free of bruises and pinfeathers. The color of the skin can range from creamy white to yellow. It simply depends on the bird's feed and breed and is not an indication of flavor or quality. Generally, tenderness depends on the age of the bird. Broiler-fryers are tender young birds and can be roasted, fried, sautéed, grilled, or broiled. Roasting chickens are bred to be large (about 5 to 7 pounds) but are still relatively tender and are best when roasted. Tough older birds, called fowl or stewing hens, are available in some markets and must be braised or stewed in liquid to become tender.

The term *organic* is not recognized by the USDA, so it cannot appear on labels. It can be used, however, to promote poultry on store posters, for example. Generally, organic poultry has been raised on organically grown, antibiotic-free feed, which some cooks believe gives the meat richer flavor. *Free-range* poultry has been raised in a relatively spacious environment that provides access to open spaces but not necessarily an open farmyard. This free movement allows it to develop more muscle, which also contributes to fuller-flavored meat. Organic and free-range birds are more expensive. If your poultry is labeled *all-natural*, it means it has been minimally processed, but its feed was not necessarily organic and could have included antibiotics to protect the bird from disease. All poultry is free of hormones and growth stimulants, which is not true of mass-produced beef.

Kosher poultry has been processed according to Kosher dietary laws under the strict supervision of a rabbi. The procedure includes salting, a process that draws out the blood and seasons the meat. If you live in an area that has a Muslim community, you may also see *Halal* poultry, which has been slaughtered by a butcher of the Muslim faith.

Have you ever bought a fresh bird only to find that the giblets were frozen? Labeling laws have only recently been changed to clarify the meaning of the words "fresh" and "frozen." In the past, because of the high demand for fresh poultry, birds could be stored at 0°F and still be called fresh. The law has been changed. It now states that only poultry that has never been chilled below 26°F can be called fresh. (Poultry freezes solid at 6°F lower than water.) If a bird is chilled below 0°F, it must be labeled frozen. If the label says neither fresh nor frozen, assume the poultry was stored at a temperature between 0° and 26°F, then thawed before sale, which explains those frozen giblets. Lastly, the ends of the bones of fresh poultry should be pinkish white. Red bone tips indicate the bird was frozen.

Buy fresh poultry according to the "sell-by" date on the package. Remember that the store's refrigerator is much colder than yours, so once you get the bird home, cook it within two days. When you open the package, the chicken may have an unpleasant odor. This is caused by oxidation and should disappear once the bird is rinsed with cold running water. If the poultry still smells unpleasant, return it to the market. Avoid packages with leaks or tears.

If you buy frozen poultry, be sure the meat is rock-hard and without any signs of freezer burn. The quick commercial freezing process should guarantee the poultry hasn't absorbed any water, but check by making sure there are no ice crystals. The packaging should be tightly sealed and intact. Frozen liquid in the bottom can mean the bird was thawed and refrozen.

POULTRY SENSE

POULTRY	READY-TO-COOK WEIGHT	SERVINGS	STUFFING
Broiler-fryer	2½ to 4½ pounds	2 to 4	1 to 3 cups
Roasting chicken	5 to 7 pounds	5 to 7	3 to 6 cups
Capon	6 to 8 pounds	6 to 8	3 to 6 cups
Cornish hens	1 to 2 pounds	1 to 2	¾ to 1½ cups
Turkey	8 to 12 pounds	6 to 8	6 to 9 cups
	12 to 16 pounds	12 to 16	9 to 12 cups
	16 to 20 pounds	16 to 20	12 to 15 cups
	20 to 24 pounds	20 to 24	15 to 18 cups
Turkey breast	4 to 6 pounds	5 to 8	—
Turkey breast (boneless)	4 to 6 pounds	5 to 8	—
Duck	4 to 5 pounds	4	3 to 4 cups
Goose	10 to 12 pounds	6 to 8	6 to 9 cups

HANDLING AND STORAGE

Store raw poultry in its original wrapping on a plate to contain any leaks or drips. If wrapped in butcher paper, remove the paper and place the bird in a large plastic bag. Keep poultry in the coldest part of the refrigerator (usually the bottom shelf), away from cooked or ready-to-eat foods. Before cooking, pat whole poultry dry inside and out with paper towels. (Drying the skin helps it brown during cooking.) Don't discard the giblets! They can be turned into an easy broth or cooked, chopped, and added to gravy. See Giblet Gravy (page 231) for general instructions. Store uncooked giblets separately in the refrigerator and use within a day, or wrap and freeze for up to one month.

Be sure to wash your hands, the cutting board, and any utensils that have come in contact with raw poultry with hot water and soap. To destroy germs, bleach your cutting board once a week or so with a solution of one tablespoon chlorine bleach to one gallon warm water.

Freeze raw whole poultry or parts for up to six months. Ground poultry will keep in the refrigerator for one day, or in the freezer for up to three months. Cool cooked poultry as quickly as possible, then cover and refrigerate for two to three days, or wrap and freeze for up to three months.

Thawing

For safety's sake, it's important to thaw poultry in one of two ways: in the refrigerator or by immersion in cold water. Never thaw poultry on the kitchen counter, because bacteria can multiply rapidly at room temperature. Here are some tips for successful thawing:

- Frozen poultry should be thawed completely before being cooked, so allow sufficient time, especially for large birds.
- Remove giblets as soon as possible during thawing, then wrap and refrigerate to use in stock or gravy, if desired.
- If the ice crystals have disappeared from the body cavity and the meat is soft and the joints are flexible, the bird has thawed.
- Once thawed, cook the bird within twelve hours. Wipe out the body and neck cavities with paper towels, and pat the skin dry.
- For reasons of texture, not safety, do not refreeze poultry once it has been thawed.

Thawing in the refrigerator: This is the preferred method. Leave the bird in its original wrapper, and place it on a tray to catch any drips. Thawing time will depend on both the size of the bird and the temperature of the refrigerator (ideally 35° to 40°F). As a general rule, allow about six hours per pound. For example, a twenty-four-pound turkey will take approximately four days to thaw completely.

Thawing in cold water: If there's no time to thaw the bird in the refrigerator, use this method, which takes less time but requires more attention. Place the bird (in its original wrapper or in a watertight plastic bag) in a large pan or in the sink with enough cold water to cover. (Warm water thaws poultry too quickly and can encourage bacteria growth.) Change the water every thirty minutes to maintain the temperature. Allow about thirty minutes of thawing time per pound, then add one hour to that total.

THE WHITE AND DARK OF IT

The breast is the tenderest part of the bird—and the leanest. A 3½-ounce portion of breast meat without skin has about 4 grams of fat. The same amount of skinless dark meat has about 10 grams of fat. Removing poultry skin slashes the amount of fat almost in half. You may prefer, however, to cook poultry with the skin on to keep the moisture in. Then simply remove the skin before eating. The fat reduction is practically the same.

White meat is ideal for stir-frying, pan-frying, and other quick, moist-cooking methods like poaching. It also takes well to dry-heat methods, such as broiling or grilling, but because white meat dries out quickly, care must be taken not to over-cook it. (This is especially true of turkey breast.) Dark meat, moister and more deeply flavored than white, really comes into its own in long-simmered casseroles and stews, where it remains succulent and tasty. Boneless thighs and breasts are convenient and also cook quickly. While it's true that poultry cooked on the bone has the best flavor and tends to be juicier, creative seasoning and marinades can add flavor and moisture to these boneless cuts.

ROASTING A PERFECT BIRD

Everyone loves a gorgeous turkey, roasted until golden brown and bursting with flavorful juices. Use our chart (below) to estimate the roasting time for whole birds. The indicated roasting time, especially for large birds like turkey and goose, are only an estimate, as there are many variables that affect the total cooking time: the temperature of the bird when removed from the refrigerator, the shape of the bird, and the true oven temperature.

Roast poultry on a rack in the roasting pan to allow the heat to circulate under the bird. If you like, occasionally baste with the pan drippings. Basting doesn't make meat moister, but it does help to crisp and brown the skin. If the skin begins to brown too quickly, cover the bird with a loose tent of foil.

When roasting fatty birds, such as duck or goose, prick the skin all over with a two-tine fork so the fat can drain away. Prick the skin with the fork tines facing up so you don't pierce the meat. Rendered duck and goose fat is prized in French kitchens, where it is used to add delicious flavor to dishes, such as sautéed potatoes and braised cabbage. As the fat renders and collects in the roasting pan, spoon it off (or use a bulb baster) and transfer to a bowl. Skim off the clear yellow fat that rises to the top, transfer to a clean bowl, and return any dark brown juices to the pan. Cover and refrigerate the rendered fat for up to one month or freeze in covered containers for up to four months.

To be sure a whole bird is fully cooked, always use a meat thermometer. (Don't trust the pop-up thermometers that come with some turkeys because the roasting juices can inadvertently "glue" the mechanism shut.) Insert the meat thermometer into the thickest part of the thigh just under the

ROASTING TIMES

POULTRY	READY-TO-COOK WEIGHT	COOKING TIME (UNSTUFFED)	COOKING TIME (STUFFED)
Chicken (at 350°F)	2½ to 3 pounds	1¼ to 1½ hours	1¼ to 1½ hours
	3 to 4½ pounds	1½ to 1¾ hours	1½ to 1¾ hours
	5 to 7 pounds	2 to 2¼ hours	2 to 2¼ hours
Capon (at 325°F)	5 to 6 pounds	2 to 2½ hours	2½ to 3 hours
	6 to 8 pounds	2½ to 3½ hours	3 to 4 hours
Cornish hen (at 350°F)	1 to 2 pounds	1 to 1¼ hours	1 to 1¼ hours
Turkey (at 325°F)	Variations in roasting conditions could increase indicated roasting times up to 30 minutes.		
	8 to 12 pounds	2¾ to 3 hours	3 to 3½ hours
	12 to 14 pounds	3 to 3¾ hours	3½ to 4 hours
	14 to 18 pounds	3¾ to 4¼ hours	4 to 4¼ hours
	18 to 20 pounds	4¼ to 4½ hours	4¼ to 4¾ hours
	20 to 24 pounds	4½ to 5 hours	4¾ to 5½ hours
Duck (at 350°F)	4 to 5 pounds	2½ to 2¾ hours	2½ to 2¾ hours
Goose (at 350°F)	10 to 12 pounds	2¾ to 3¼ hours	3 to 3½ hours

drumstick, pointing toward the body. Do not let the thermometer touch any bone. This would give an inaccurate reading, since bone conducts heat. If you have a standard meat thermometer, insert it before cooking. If you have an instant-read thermometer, use it to test the temperature during the last quarter of the estimated roasting time, removing and washing it after each test. As a second criteria for doneness, insert a small knife into the thickest part of the thigh. The juices should run clear with no trace of pink (if you wish, catch the juice in a white saucer to better gauge the color). Also check that the legs move easily: Do not cook the bird until the

drumsticks "jiggle," or it will be overcooked. Transfer the bird to a warm platter and let the pan juices stand for a minute, then spoon off most or all of the fat from the top. The degreased juices can be used to make gravy or can be spooned over each serving as a simple but delicious sauce.

CARVING TIPS

Letting the bird rest after roasting results in firmer, juicier meat that is easier to carve. Poultry should stand at least ten minutes before carving so the simmering juices can relax back into the meat. Large turkeys will remain hot for at least thirty minutes, freeing up the oven for the heating of side dishes such as extra stuffing. When carving, use a sharp thin-bladed knife that is long enough to slice off the breast of large birds like turkey or long-bodied birds such as duck or goose.

CARVING A ROAST CHICKEN

To remove the breast meat, using a thin sharp knife, start along one side of the breastbone, cutting down along the rib cage (scraping against the bones as you go), cutting off the breast meat in one piece. Repeat on the other side.

To carve the breast meat, holding the knife at a slight angle, cut the meat crosswise into even slices.

To remove a chicken leg, force it away from the body with a carving fork until it pops out of its socket. Separate the thigh from the body by cutting through the joint. If you like, separate the drumstick from the thigh by cutting through the center joint. Repeat on the other side. To remove the wings, cut through the joints where the wings meet the body.

Apple and Thyme Roast Chicken

(pictured on page 184)

Your kitchen will be filled with the fragrance of apples, herbs, and spices.

Prep: 20 minutes   Roast: 1 hour

1	chicken (3½ pounds)
2	sprigs plus 1 tablespooon chopped fresh thyme
¾	teaspoon salt
¼	teaspoon coarsely ground black pepper
⅛	teaspoon ground allspice
1	jumbo onion (1 pound), cut into 12 wedges
¼	cup water
2	teaspoons olive oil
2	large Granny Smith apples, each cored and cut into quarters
2	tablespoons applejack brandy or Calvados
½	cup chicken broth

1. Preheat oven to 450°F. Remove giblets and neck from chicken; reserve for another use. Rinse chicken inside and out with cold running water; Drain. Pat chicken dry with paper towels.

2. With fingertips, gently separate skin from meat on chicken breast. Place 1 thyme sprig under skin of each breast half. In cup, combine chopped thyme, salt, pepper, and allspice.

3. With chicken breast side up, lift wings up toward neck,

then fold wing tips under back of chicken so wings stay in place. Tie legs together with string.

4. In medium roasting pan (14" by 10"), toss onion, chopped-thyme mixture, water, and oil. Push onion mixture to sides of pan. Place chicken, breast side up, on small rack in center of roasting pan.

5. Roast chicken and onion mixture 40 minutes. Add apples to pan; roast about 20 minutes longer. Chicken is done when temperature on meat thermometer inserted in thickest part of thigh, next to body, reaches 175° to 180°F and juices run clear when thigh is pierced with tip of knife.

6. Transfer chicken to warm platter; let stand 10 minutes to set juices for easier carving.

7. Meanwhile, remove rack from roasting pan. With slotted spoon, transfer onion mixture to platter with chicken. Skim and discard fat from drippings in pan. Add apple-jack to pan drippings; cook 1 minute over medium heat, stirring constantly. Add broth; heat to boiling. Serve pan-juice mixture with chicken. Remove skin from chicken

before eating, if desired. Makes 4 main-dish servings.

Each serving with skin: About 589 calories, 49g protein, 22g carbohydrate, 33g total fat (9g saturated), 159mg cholesterol, 708mg sodium.

Each serving without skin: About 441 calories, 43g protein, 22g carbohydrate, 20g total fat (5g saturated), 132mg cholesterol, 686mg sodium.

Roast Chicken with Forty Cloves of Garlic

Slow roasting mellows garlic to a sweet nuttiness. Serve with lots of crusty bread for spreading the extra garlic.

Prep: 15 minutes   Roast: 1 hour

1	chicken (3½ pounds)
6	thyme sprigs
½	teaspoon salt
¼	teaspoon coarsely ground black pepper
40	garlic cloves (2 heads), loose papery skin discarded but not peeled
1	cup chicken broth

1. Preheat oven to 450°F. Remove giblets and neck from chicken; reserve for another use. Rinse chicken inside and out with cold running water; drain. Pat dry with paper towels.

2. With fingertips, gently separate skin from meat on chicken breast. Place 2 thyme sprigs under skin of each breast half. Place remaining 2 sprigs inside cavity of chicken. Sprinkle salt and pepper on outside of chicken.

3. With chicken breast side up, lift wings up toward neck, then fold wing tips under back of chicken so wings stay in place. Tie legs together with string. Place chicken, breast side up, on rack in small roasting pan (13" by 9").

4. Roast chicken 30 minutes. Add garlic cloves to pan; roast about 30 minutes longer. Chicken is done when temperature on meat thermometer inserted in thickest part of thigh, next to body, reaches 175° to 180°F and juices run clear when thigh is pierced with tip of knife. Transfer chicken to warm platter; let stand 10 minutes to set juices for easier carving.

5. Meanwhile, remove rack from roasting pan. With slotted spoon, transfer garlic cloves to small bowl. Skim and discard fat from drippings in pan. Remove and discard skin from 6 garlic cloves; return peeled garlic to roasting pan and add broth. Heat broth mixture to boiling over medium heat, stirring to loosen browned bits from bottom of pan and mashing garlic with back of spoon until well blended. Serve chicken with pan juices and remaining garlic cloves. Remove skin from chicken before eating, if desired. Makes 4 main-dish servings.

Each serving with skin: About 501 calories, 50g protein, 11g carbohydrate, 28g total fat (8g saturated), 157mg cholesterol, 688mg sodium.

Each serving without skin: About 352 calories, 44g protein, 10g carbohydrate, 14g total fat (4g saturated), 129mg cholesterol, 667mg sodium.

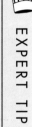
Roast Chicken with Herb Butter

For an aromatic and extramoist chicken, blend fresh chives and parsley with softened butter and spread under the skin.

Prep: 10 minutes Roast: 1 hour	
1	chicken (3½ pounds)
3	tablespoons butter or margarine, softened
2	tablespoons chopped fresh chives
1	tablespoon chopped fresh parsley
¼	teaspoon salt
¼	teaspoon coarsely ground black pepper

1. Preheat oven to 450°F. Remove giblets and neck from chicken; reserve for another use. Rinse chicken inside and out with cold running water; drain. Pat dry with paper towels.

2. In cup, combine butter, chives, and parsley until well blended. With fingertips, gently separate skin from meat on chicken breast and thighs. Rub herb mixture on meat under skin. Sprinkle salt and pepper on outside of chicken.

3. With chicken breast side up, lift wings up toward neck, then fold wing tips under back of chicken so wings stay in place. Tie legs together with string. Place chicken, breast side up, on rack in small roasting pan (13" by 9").

4. Roast chicken about 1 hour. Chicken is done when temperature on meat thermometer inserted in thickest part of thigh, next to body, reaches 175° to 180°F and juices run clear when thigh is pierced with tip of knife.

5. Transfer chicken to warm platter; let stand 10 minutes to set juices for easier carving. Remove skin from chicken before eating, if desired. Makes 4 main-dish servings.

Each serving with skin: About 495 calories, 48g protein, 0g carbohydrate, 32g total fat (12g saturated), 177mg cholesterol, 375mg sodium.

Each serving without skin: About 347 calories, 41g protein, 0g carbohydrate, 19g total fat (8g saturated), 150mg cholesterol, 353mg sodium.

Tarragon Roast Chicken
Prepare as directed, replacing chives with **2 tablespoons chopped fresh tarragon.**

Roast Peking Chicken

Peking duck is an elaborate Chinese dish where in a bicycle pump is used to force air between the skin and meat to produce the crispest skin imaginable. Our twist employs pouring boiling water over chicken for a tender, juicy bird with very crisp skin.

Prep: 20 minutes   Roast: 1 hour

1	chicken (3½ pounds)
2	tablespoons honey
2	tablespoons soy sauce
1	teaspoon seasoned rice vinegar
1	tablespoon minced, peeled fresh ginger
2	garlic cloves, crushed with garlic press
⅛	teaspoon ground red pepper (cayenne)
8	(8-inch) flour tortillas
¼	cup chicken broth
2	tablespoons water
¼	cup hoisin sauce
2	green onions, each cut crosswise into thirds and sliced lengthwise into thin strips

1. Preheat oven to 450°F. Remove giblets and neck from chicken; reserve for another use. Rinse chicken inside and out with cold running water; drain. Pat dry with paper towels.

2. With chicken breast side up, lift wings up toward neck, then fold wing tips under back of chicken so wings stay in place. Tie legs together with string.

3. Place chicken on rack in sink. With chicken breast side up, slowly pour *1 quart boiling water* over chicken; turn chicken over. Slowly pour additional *1 quart boiling water* over back of chicken. (This process allows fat to render easily from chicken and helps crisp skin during roasting.)

4. Place chicken, breast side up, on rack in small roasting pan (13" by 9"). Roast chicken 50 minutes.

5. Meanwhile, in small bowl, combine honey, soy sauce, vinegar, ginger, garlic, and ground red pepper.

6. After chicken has roasted 50 minutes, brush with half of honey glaze; roast 5 minutes. Brush with remaining glaze; roast about 5 minutes longer. Chicken is done when temperature on meat thermometer inserted in thickest part of thigh, next to body, reaches 175° to 180°F and juices run clear when thigh is pierced with tip of knife.

7. Transfer chicken to warm platter; let stand 10 minutes to set juices for easier carving.

8. Meanwhile, warm tortillas as label directs. Remove rack from roasting pan. Skim and discard fat from drippings in pan. Add broth and water to pan drippings; heat to boiling over medium heat, stirring until browned bits are loosened from bottom of pan. Stir in hoisin sauce.

9. To serve, slice chicken and wrap in tortillas with hoisin-sauce mixture and green onions. Makes 4 main-dish servings.

Each serving with skin: About 739 calories, 55g protein, 59g carbohydrate, 29g total fat (7g saturated), 154mg cholesterol, 1,401mg sodium.

Fennel-Rubbed Roast Chicken

Fennel and orange, an enticing combination that is both savory and sweet, becomes a special rub for chicken. Roasted with fennel, new potatoes, and onion wedges, it makes a fine one-dish meal.

Prep: 20 minutes   Roast: 1 hour

1	chicken (3½ pounds)
1	tablespoon fennel seeds, crushed
1	teaspoon freshly grated orange peel
1	teaspoon salt
½	teaspoon coarsely ground black pepper
1	large fennel bulb (1½ pounds), trimmed and cut into 8 wedges
1½	pounds medium red potatoes, cut into 1-inch pieces
1	large red onion (12 ounces), cut into 8 wedges
2	teaspoons olive oil

1. Preheat oven to 450°F. Remove giblets and neck from chicken; reserve for another use. Rinse chicken inside and out with cold running water; drain. Pat dry with paper towels.

2. In cup, combine fennel seeds, orange peel, ½ teaspoon salt, and ¼ teaspoon pepper. With fingertips, gently separate skin from meat on chicken breast and thighs. Rub half of spice mixture on meat under skin. Rub remaining spice mixture on outside of chicken.

3. With chicken breast side up, lift wings up toward neck, then fold wing tips under back of chicken so wings stay in place. Tie legs together with string.

4. In large roasting pan (17" by 11½"), toss fennel, potatoes, and red onion with oil and remaining ½ teaspoon salt and remaining ¼ teaspoon pepper. Push vegetable mixture to sides of pan. Place chicken, breast side up, on rack in center of roasting pan.

5. Roast chicken and vegetables about 1 hour. Chicken is done when temperature on meat thermometer inserted in thickest part of thigh, next to body, reaches 175° to 180°F and juices run clear when thigh is pierced with tip of knife.

6. Transfer chicken to warm platter; let stand 10 minutes to set juices for easier carving.

7. Meanwhile, remove rack from roasting pan. Skim and discard fat from drippings in pan. With slotted spoon, transfer vegetables to platter with chicken. Serve with pan juices. Remove skin from chicken before eating, if desired. Makes 4 main-dish servings.

Each serving with skin: About 695 calories, 54g protein, 43g carbohydrate, 33g total fat, (9g saturated), 159mg cholesterol, 739mg sodium.

Each serving without skin: About 485 calories, 48g protein, 43g carbohydrate, 14g total fat (4g saturated), 130mg cholesterol, 745mg sodium.

Roast Chicken with Green Olives and Sherry

Green olive paste spread under the skin and dry sherry in the sauce give this chicken Spanish flair.

Prep: 15 minutes Roast: 1 hour	
1	chicken (3½ pounds)
12	green olives, such as manzanilla, pitted and finely chopped
1	tablespoon chopped fresh parsley
1	small shallot, minced
1	garlic clove, minced
½	teaspoon freshly grated lemon peel
1	tablespoon extravirgin olive oil
¼	teaspoon salt
¼	teaspoon coarsely ground black pepper
¾	cup chicken broth
3	tablespoons dry sherry

1. Preheat oven to 450°F. Remove giblets and neck from chicken; reserve for another use. Rinse chicken inside and out with cold running water; drain. Pat dry with paper towels.

2. In small bowl, combine olives, parsley, shallot, garlic, lemon peel, oil, salt, and pepper until well blended. With fin-gertips, gently separate skin from meat on chicken breast and thighs. Rub olive mixture on meat under skin.

3. With chicken breast side up, lift wings up toward neck, then fold wing tips under back of chicken so wings stay in place. Tie legs together with string. Place chicken, breast side up, on rack in small roasting pan (13" by 9").

4. Roast chicken about 1 hour. Chicken is done when temperature on meat thermometer inserted in thickest part of thigh, next to body, reaches 175° to 180°F and juices run clear when thigh is pierced with tip of knife.

5. Transfer chicken to warm platter; let stand 10 minutes to set juices for easier carving.

6. Meanwhile, remove rack from roasting pan. Skim and discard fat from drippings in pan. Add broth and sherry; heat to boiling over medium heat, stirring until browned bits are loosened from bottom of pan. Serve chicken with pan-juice mixture. Remove skin from chicken before eating, if desired. Makes 4 main-dish servings.

Each serving with skin: About 494 calories, 48g protein, 2g carbohydrate, 30g total fat (7g saturated), 154mg cholesterol, 712mg sodium.

Each serving without skin: About 347 calories, 42g protein, 2g carbohydrate, 17g total fat (4g saturated), 126mg cholesterol, 691mg sodium.

CAPONS

Capons, castrated young male chickens, which usually range from 7 to 10 pounds, are large enough to become the centerpiece of a holiday meal. They have been fed a special milk diet that results in especially firm, full-flavored white flesh.

Mahogany Roast Chicken

Give your roast chicken a deep amber glaze by brushing it with a simple mix of balsamic vinegar, brown sugar, and dry vermouth.

Prep: 10 minutes	Roast: 1 hour 15 minutes
1	chicken (3½ pounds)
¾	teaspoon salt
½	teaspoon coarsely ground black pepper
2	tablespoons dark brown sugar
2	tablespoons balsamic vinegar
2	tablespoons dry vermouth
¼	cup water

1. Preheat oven to 375°F. Remove giblets and neck from chicken; reserve for another use. Rinse chicken inside and out with cold running water; drain. Pat dry with paper towels. Sprinkle salt and pepper on outside of chicken.

2. With chicken breast side up, lift wings up toward neck, then fold wing tips under back of chicken so wings stay in place. Tie legs together with string. Place chicken, breast side up, on rack in small roasting pan (13" by 9"). Roast chicken 45 minutes.

3. Meanwhile, prepare glaze: In small bowl, stir brown sugar, vinegar, and vermouth until sugar has dissolved.

4. After chicken has roasted 45 minutes, brush with some glaze. Turn oven control to 400°F and roast chicken, brushing with glaze twice more during roasting, until chicken is deep brown, about 30 minutes longer. Chicken is done when temperature on meat thermometer inserted in thickest part of thigh, next to body, reaches 175° to 180°F and juices run clear when thigh is pierced with tip of knife.

5. Transfer chicken to warm platter; let stand 10 minutes to set juices for easier carving.

6. Meanwhile, remove rack from roasting pan. Skim and discard fat from drippings in pan. Add water to pan; heat to boiling over medium heat, stirring until browned bits are loosened from bottom of pan. Serve chicken with pan juices. Makes 4 main-dish servings.

Each serving with skin: About 446 calories, 48g protein, 7g carbohydrate, 24g total fat (7g saturated), 154mg cholesterol, 583mg sodium.

Roast Lemon Chicken

Roasting an extralarge chicken is an easy way to serve a crowd.

Prep: 10 minutes	Roast: 1 hour 30 minutes to 2 hours
1	roasting chicken or capon (7 pounds)
2	lemons
1	bunch thyme
2	garlic cloves
¾	teaspoon salt
½	teaspoon ground black pepper
1¼	cups chicken broth
2	teaspoons cornstarch
1	tablespoon cold water

1. Preheat oven to 375°F. Remove giblets and neck from chicken; reserve for another use. Rinse chicken inside and out with cold running water; drain. Pat dry with paper towels.

2. From 1 lemon, cut 4 thin slices. Cut remainder of lemon and second lemon into quarters. With fingertips, gently separate skin from meat on chicken breast. Place 2 lemon slices under skin of each breast half. Set aside several thyme sprigs for garnish. Place garlic cloves, lemon quarters, and remaining thyme sprigs inside cavity of chicken. Sprinkle chicken with ½ teaspoon salt and ¼ teaspoon pepper.

3. With chicken breast side up, lift wings up toward neck, then fold wing tips under back of chicken so wings stay in place. Tie legs together with string. Place chicken, breast side up, on rack in medium roasting pan (14" by 10").

4. Roast chicken, basting occasionally with pan drippings, 1 hour 30 minutes to 2 hours. When chicken turns golden brown, cover loosely with tent of foil to prevent overbrowning. Chicken is done when temperature on meat thermometer inserted in thickest part of thigh, next to body, reaches 175° to 180°F and juices run clear when thigh is pierced with tip of knife.

5. Transfer chicken to warm platter; let stand 15 minutes to set juices for easier carving.

6. Meanwhile, prepare gravy: Remove rack from roasting pan. Skim and discard fat from drippings. Add broth to pan, stirring until browned bits are loosened from bottom of pan. In cup, blend cornstarch and water until smooth. Stir cornstarch mixture into broth; add remaining ¼ teaspoon each salt and pepper. Heat to boiling over high heat, stirring; boil 1 minute.

7. Garnish chicken with reserved thyme sprigs. Serve with gravy. Remove skin from chicken before eating, if desired. Makes 8 main-dish servings.

Each serving with skin: About 469 calories, 50g protein, 3g carbohydrate, 28g total fat (8g saturated), 156mg cholesterol, 525mg sodium.

Each serving without skin: About 291 calories, 42g protein, 3g carbohydrate, 11g total fat (3g saturated), 125mg cholesterol, 500mg sodium.

Lemon-Roasted Chicken for a Crowd

When you need a special dish for a big party but you don't have time to fuss, turn to this crowd-pleasing recipe.

Prep: 20 minutes   Roast: 1 hour 30 minutes

1½	cups fresh lemon juice (7 large lemons)
¼	cup vegetable oil
1	large onion (12 ounces), finely chopped
2	large garlic cloves, crushed with garlic press
1	tablespoon plus 2 teaspoons salt
1	tablespoon dried thyme
2	teaspoons ground black pepper
5	chickens (3 pounds each), each cut into quarters

1. Preheat oven to 375°F. In medium bowl, combine lemon juice, oil, onion, garlic, salt, thyme, and pepper. In two large roasting pans (17" by 11½"), arrange chicken, skin side up. Pour lemon-juice mixture over chicken.

2. Roast chicken, basting occasionally with pan juices, until juices run clear when thickest part of chicken is pierced with tip of knife, about 1 hour 30 minutes.

3. Transfer chicken to warm platters. Skim and discard fat from drippings in pan; pour pan drippings into medium bowl. Spoon some pan juices over chicken and serve chicken with remaining juices. Makes 20 main-dish servings.

Each serving: About 381 calories, 41g protein, 3g carbohydrate, 22g total fat (6g saturated), 132mg cholesterol, 706mg sodium.

CUTTING UP A RAW CHICKEN

To remove a leg, cut down between the thigh and the body. Bend the leg portion back; twist to crack the hip joint. Cut through the joint. Repeat for the other leg.

To separate the leg from the thigh, place the leg skin side down and cut through the center joint. Repeat with the other leg.

To remove a wing, pull the wing away from the body, then cut between the wing joint and the breast. Repeat with the other wing.

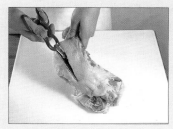

Using kitchen shears, cut through the rib cage along one side of the backbone from the tail to the neck. Repeat on the other side to remove the backbone in one piece.

Place the breast skin side down and cut in half by placing a heavy knife lengthwise along the center of the breastbone. Press the knife down to cut through the bone and meat.

Rosemary-Apricot Chicken

A great buffet dish that is hard to beat. Served hot or cold, it has a delicious, tangy-sweet flavor that everyone will love.

Prep: 20 minutes plus marinating	*Roast: 45 minutes*

- 4 garlic cloves, crushed with garlic press
- 2 teaspoons salt
- 1 teaspoon dried rosemary, crumbled
- ½ teaspoon ground black pepper
- 3 chickens (3 pounds each), each cut into quarters and skin removed from all but wings
- ½ cup apricot preserves
- 2 tablespoons fresh lemon juice
- 2 teaspoons Dijon mustard

1. In cup, combine garlic, salt, rosemary, and pepper; rub mixture on chicken. Place chicken in large bowl or ziptight plastic bags; cover bowl or seal bags and refrigerate chicken 2 hours to marinate.

2. Preheat oven to 350°F. Arrange chicken, skin side up, in two large roasting pans (17" by 11½") or two jelly-roll pans (15½" by 10½"). Roast chicken 25 minutes, rotating pans between upper and lower oven racks halfway through roasting.

3. Meanwhile, in small bowl, with fork, mix apricot preserves, lemon juice, and mustard. Brush apricot mixture over chicken; roast until juices run clear when thickest part of chicken is pierced with tip of knife, about 20 minutes longer, rotating pans after 10 minutes. Serve chicken hot, or cover and refrigerate to serve cold. Makes 12 main-dish servings.

♥ Each serving: About 267 calories, 35g protein, 9g carbohydrate, 9g total fat (2g saturated), 108mg cholesterol, 519mg sodium.

Thyme-Roasted Chicken and Vegetables

In just over an hour, you can have a one-dish meal of roasted chicken with fennel, potatoes, and onion ready to serve.

Prep: 20 minutes	*Roast: 50 minutes*

- 1 chicken (3½ pounds), cut into 8 pieces and skin removed from all but wings
- 1 pound all-purpose potatoes (3 medium), not peeled, cut into 2-inch pieces
- 1 large fennel bulb (1½ pounds), trimmed and cut into 8 wedges
- 1 large red onion, cut into 8 wedges
- 1 tablespoon chopped fresh thyme or 1 teaspoon dried thyme
- 1 teaspoon salt
- ½ teaspoon ground black pepper
- 2 tablespoons olive oil
- ⅓ cup water

1. Preheat oven to 450°F. In large roasting pan (17" by 11½"), arrange chicken, skin side up, and place potatoes, fennel, and onion around it. Sprinkle chicken with thyme, salt, and pepper. Drizzle oil over chicken and vegetables.

2. Roast chicken and vegetables 20 minutes; baste with drippings in pan. Roast, basting once more, until juices run clear when chicken breasts are pierced with tip of knife, about 20 minutes longer. Transfer chicken to platter; keep warm.

3. Continue roasting remaining chicken pieces until juices run clear when thickest part of chicken is pierced with tip of knife and vegetables are fork-tender, about 10 minutes longer. Transfer chicken and vegetables to platter with breasts; keep warm.

4. Skim and discard fat from drippings in pan. To drippings, add water; heat to boiling over medium heat, stirring until brown bits are loosened from bottom. Spoon pan juices over chicken and vegetables. Makes 4 main-dish servings.

♥ Each serving: About 401 calories, 43g protein, 28g carbohydrate, 13g total fat (2g saturated), 124mg cholesterol, 870mg sodium.

Thyme-Roasted Chicken and Vegetables

Baked Lime Chicken

Besides a zesty topping of grated lime peel and brown sugar, this easy dish has a luscious sweet-and-sour sauce.

Prep: 10 minutes   **Bake:** 50 minutes

2	small limes
1	chicken (3½ pounds), cut into 8 pieces and skin removed from all but wings
¼	cup all-purpose flour
½	teaspoon salt
½	teaspoon ground black pepper
3	tablespoons butter or margarine, melted
2	tablespoons brown sugar
1	can (14½ ounces) chicken broth or 1¾ cups Chicken Broth (page 84)

1. Preheat oven to 400°F. From limes, grate 2 teaspoons peel and squeeze 2 tablespoons juice. Set peel aside. In large bowl, toss chicken pieces with lime juice, coating evenly.

2. On waxed paper, combine flour, salt, and pepper. Coat chicken with flour mixture, shaking off excess. Arrange chicken in 15½" by 10½" jelly-roll pan. Drizzle with melted butter.

3. In cup, combine lime peel and brown sugar; sprinkle on chicken pieces.

4. Pour broth into roasting pan and bake, basting chicken with pan juices occasionally, until juices run clear when chicken is pierced with tip of knife, about 50 minutes.

5. Transfer chicken to warm platter. Skim and discard fat from drippings in pan. Spoon pan juices over chicken. Makes 4 main-dish servings.

Each serving: About 389 calories, 42g protein, 14g carbohydrate, 17g total fat (7g saturated), 142mg cholesterol, 924mg sodium.

Herb Chicken

Fresh herbs add delicate flavor to a chicken that is fabulous hot or cold. If you like, garnish with sprigs of thyme and rosemary. And if your herb garden is plentiful, serve the chicken on a bed of herbs for a dramatic and fragrant presentation.

Prep: 10 minutes   **Bake:** 40 minutes

1	tablespoon olive oil
2	teaspoons chopped fresh thyme
2	teaspoons chopped fresh rosemary
1½	teaspoons salt
1	teaspoon coarsely ground black pepper
2	chickens (3½ pounds each), each cut into 8 pieces

1. Preheat oven to 425°F. In small bowl, combine oil, thyme, rosemary, salt, and pepper. Rub herb mixture on chicken pieces.

2. Arrange chicken, skin side up, on rack in large roasting pan (17" by 11½").

3. Bake chicken (do not turn), until golden brown and juices run clear when thickest part of chicken is pierced with tip of knife, about 40 minutes.

4. Transfer chicken to warm large platter. Makes 8 main-dish servings.

Each serving: About 434 calories, 48g protein, 0g carbohydrate, 25g total fat (7g saturated), 154mg cholesterol, 579mg sodium.

Baked "Fried" Chicken

For this healthier version of fried chicken, skinless chicken pieces are dipped in a spicy bread-crumb coating and baked until crispy and golden brown. You won't miss the calories.

Prep: 15 minutes   **Bake:** 35 minutes

	olive oil nonstick cooking spray
½	cup plain dried bread crumbs
¼	cup freshly grated Parmesan cheese
2	tablespoons cornmeal
½	teaspoon ground red pepper (cayenne)
1	large egg white
½	teaspoon salt
1	chicken (3½ pounds), cut into 8 pieces and skin removed from all but wings

1. Preheat oven to 425°F. Grease 15½" by 10½" jelly-roll pan with cooking spray.

2. On waxed paper, combine bread crumbs, Parmesan, cornmeal, and ground red pepper. In pie plate, beat egg white and salt.

3. Dip each piece of chicken in egg-white mixture, then coat with crumb mixture, firmly pressing so mixture adheres. Arrange chicken in prepared pan; lightly coat chicken with cooking spray.

4. Bake chicken until coating is crisp and golden brown and juices run clear when thickest part of chicken is pierced with tip of knife, about 35 minutes. Makes 4 main-dish servings.

Each serving: About 329 calories, 46g protein, 14g carbohydrate, 9g fat (3g saturated), 137mg cholesterol, 660mg sodium.

Southwest Chicken

The skinless chicken has a crunchy cornmeal crust and the dish is a cinch to prepare.

Prep: 5 minutes	*Bake: 40 minutes*
1	can (4 to 4½ ounces) chopped mild green chiles
¼	cup Dijon mustard
2	teaspoons fresh lime juice
¼	teaspoon ground black pepper
⅓	cup plain dried bread crumbs
⅓	cup cornmeal
1	tablespoon coarsely chopped fresh cilantro
2	teaspoons paprika
½	teaspoon dried oregano
¼	teaspoon salt
1	chicken (3 pounds), cut into 8 pieces and skin removed from all but wings
1	tablespoon olive or vegetable oil

1. Preheat oven to 425°F. In small bowl, combine chiles, mustard, lime juice, and pepper until well blended. On waxed paper, combine bread crumbs, cornmeal, cilantro, paprika, oregano, and salt.

2. Evenly brush mustard mixture on chicken, then coat with crumb mixture, firmly pressing so mixture adheres.

3. Lightly grease large roasting pan (17" by 11½"). Arrange chicken in pan. Lightly brush oil on chicken.

4. Bake chicken (do not turn) until coating is crisp and golden brown and juices run clear when thickest part of chicken is pierced with tip of knife, 40 to 45 minutes. Makes 4 main-dish servings.

Each serving: About 364 calories, 38g protein, 18g carbohydrate, 13g total fat (3g saturated), 108mg cholesterol, 858mg sodium.

Roasted Tandoori-Style Chicken Breasts

Plain yogurt tenderizes the chicken, while the exotic spices add lots of flavor.

Prep: 10 minutes plus marinating	*Roast: 30 minutes*
2	limes
1	container (8 ounces) plain lowfat yogurt
½	small onion, chopped
1	tablespoon minced, peeled fresh ginger
1	tablespoon paprika
1	teaspoon ground cumin
1	teaspoon ground coriander
¾	teaspoon salt
¼	teaspoon ground red pepper (cayenne)
	pinch ground cloves
6	medium bone-in chicken breast halves (3 pounds), skin removed

1. From 1 lime, squeeze 2 tablespoons juice. Cut remaining lime into 6 wedges; set aside for garnish. In blender, puree lime juice, yogurt, onion, ginger, paprika, cumin, coriander, salt, ground red pepper, and cloves until smooth. Place chicken and yogurt marinade in medium bowl or in ziptight plastic bag, turning to coat chicken. Cover bowl or seal bag and refrigerate chicken 30 minutes to marinate.

2. Preheat oven to 450°F. Arrange chicken on rack in medium roasting pan (14" by 10"). Spoon half of marinade over chicken; discard remaining marinade.

3. Roast chicken until juices run clear when thickest part of chicken is pierced with tip of knife, about 30 minutes.

4. Transfer chicken to warm platter; garnish with lime wedges to serve. Makes 6 main-dish servings.

Each serving: About 197 calories, 36g protein, 5g carbohydrate, 3g total fat (1g saturated), 88mg cholesterol, 415mg sodium.

Chicken Breasts Stuffed with Dried Tomatoes and Basil

A blend of dried tomatoes, Parmesan, and basil, tucked under the chicken skin, gives this dish Mediterranean gusto.

Prep: 15 minutes   Bake: 35 minutes

¼	cup chopped fresh basil plus additional leaves
2	tablespoons coarsely chopped oil-packed dried tomatoes plus 1 tablespoon oil from dried tomatoes
3	tablespoons freshly grated Parmesan cheese
½	teaspoon coarsely ground black pepper
4	medium bone-in chicken breast halves (2 pounds)
½	teaspoon salt

1. Preheat oven to 425°F. In small bowl, combine chopped basil, dried tomatoes, Parmesan, and ¼ teaspoon pepper until well blended.

2. Carefully push fingertips between skin and meat of each chicken breast half to form pocket; place some basil mixture in each pocket. Arrange chicken, skin side up, in small roasting pan (13" by 9"). Brush with dried-tomato oil; sprinkle with salt and remaining ¼ teaspoon pepper.

3. Bake chicken, basting occasionally with pan drippings, until juices run clear when thickest part of chicken is pierced with tip of knife, 35 to 40 minutes.

4. Transfer chicken to warm platter; garnish with basil leaves to serve. Makes 4 main-dish servings.

Each serving: About 312 calories, 39g protein, 3g carbohydrate, 15g total fat (4g saturated), 107mg cholesterol, 492mg sodium.

Apricot-Glazed Chicken

A quick and easy four-ingredient glaze is how we season up this winning recipe.

Prep: 5 minutes   Bake: 25 minutes

⅓	cup apricot preserves
1	tablespoon chili sauce
2	teaspoons Dijon mustard
½	teaspoon salt
4	large bone-in chicken breast halves (2½ pounds), skin removed

1. Preheat oven to 425°F. In a small bowl, combine apricot preserves, chili sauce, mustard, and salt. Arrange chicken in 13" by 9" baking dish; brush with apricot glaze.

REMOVING SKIN FROM RAW CHICKEN

To remove the skin from a chicken thigh, grasp the skin tightly and pull it off in one piece. If you like, grasp the skin with a piece of paper towel or dip your fingers into a little coarse salt to get a better grip.

To remove the skin from a drumstick, grasp the skin at the meaty end of the drumstick; pull the skin down and off the end of the drumstick. (If necessary, use a sharp knife to cut the skin off.)

To remove the skin from a breast, grasp the skin at the thin end of breast and pull it off. (It is difficult to remove the skin from chicken wings—don't bother.)

2. Bake, brushing occasionally with glaze, until chicken is tender and juices run clear when thickest part of chicken is pierced with tip of knife, 25 to 30 minutes. Transfer to warm platter. Makes 4 main-dish servings.

♥ Each serving: About 338 calories, 43g protein, 35g carbohydrate, 2g total fat (1g saturated), 107mg cholesterol, 548mg sodium.

Picnic Chicken with Three Sauces

This walnut-crusted baked chicken is delicious hot or cold, especially when dipped into one of our easy sauces.

Prep: 30 minutes   Bake: 30 minutes
olive oil nonstick cooking spray
1¾ cups walnuts (about 8 ounces)
1 cup plain dried bread crumbs
1½ teaspoons salt
¼ to ½ teaspoon ground red pepper (cayenne)
2 large eggs
8 medium bone-in chicken breast halves (4 pounds), skin removed
8 medium chicken drumsticks (1¾ pounds), skin removed
choice of sauce (below)

1. Preheat oven to 425°F. Grease two 15½" by 10½" jelly-roll pans with cooking spray.
2. In food processor with knife blade attached, process walnuts with ¼ cup bread crumbs until walnuts are finely ground. In medium bowl, place nut mixture, salt, ground red pepper, and remaining ¾ cup bread crumbs; stir to mix well.
3. In pie plate, beat eggs.
4. Cut each chicken breast half crosswise into two pieces. One at a time, dip breast pieces and drumsticks in beaten egg, then into walnut mixture to coat evenly, firmly pressing so mixture adheres. Arrange chicken on jelly-roll pans. Coat chicken with cooking spray.
5. Bake chicken until golden brown and juices run clear when thickest part of chicken is pierced with tip of knife, 30 to 35 minutes, rotating pans between upper and lower oven racks halfway through baking.
6. Meanwhile, prepare sauce. Cover and refrigerate sauce if not serving right away.

7. Serve chicken hot with dipping sauce, or cool chicken slightly, cover, and refrigerate to serve cold later with sauce. Makes 12 main-dish servings.

Each serving without sauce: About 311 calories, 32g protein, 10g carbohydrate, 16g total fat (2g saturated), 113mg cholesterol, 468mg sodium.

Blue-Cheese Sauce
In medium bowl, combine **4 ounces blue cheese,** crumbled (1 cup), **½ cup mayonnaise, ½ cup plain lowfat yogurt, ½ teaspoon hot pepper sauce,** and **¼ teaspoon coarsely ground black pepper** until blended. Makes about 1½ cups sauce.

Each tablespoon: About 53 calories, 1g protein, 1g carbohydrate, 5g total fat (1g saturated), 7mg cholesterol, 98mg sodium.

Creamy Honey-Mustard Sauce
In medium bowl, combine ⅔ **cup Dijon mustard, ¼ cup sour cream, ¼ cup honey,** and **¾ teaspoon Worcestershire sauce** until well blended. Makes about 1¼ cups sauce.

Each tablespoon: About 27 calories, 0g protein, 4g carbohydrate, 1g total fat (0g saturated), 1mg cholesterol, 197mg sodium.

Apricot-Balsamic Sauce
In medium bowl, combine **1 jar (12 ounces) apricot preserves, 2 tablespoons balsamic vinegar, 1 tablespoon soy sauce,** and **¼ teaspoon freshly grated orange peel** until well blended. Makes about 1¼ cups sauce.

♥ Each tablespoon: About 42 calories, 0g protein, 11g carbohydrate, 0g total fat (0g saturated), 0mg cholesterol, 58mg sodium.

Chicken Roulades

Butterflying is a cutting technique in which food is cut horizontally almost in half, then opened flat, resembling a butterfly.

Prep: 30 minutes   Cook: 20 minutes

4	medium skinless, boneless chicken breast halves (1¼ pounds)
½	7-ounce jar roasted red peppers, drained and sliced
2	ounces herb-and-garlic goat cheese
½	cup loosely packed basil leaves plus additional leaves
¼	teaspoon salt
¼	teaspoon coarsely ground black pepper
1	tablespoon olive oil

1. Holding knife parallel to cutting surface and against one long side of a chicken breast half, cut chicken almost in half, making sure not to cut all the way through. Open chicken breast half and spread flat like a book. With meat mallet, or between two sheets of plastic wrap or waxed paper with rolling pin, pound chicken breast half to ¼-inch thickness. Repeat with remaining chicken.

2. Place one-fourth each red pepper slices, goat cheese, and basil leaves on each breast half. Starting from one long side, roll each breast half jelly-roll fashion; secure with toothpicks. Sprinkle chicken roulades with salt and pepper.

3. Heat oil in nonstick 12-inch skillet over medium-high heat until very hot. Add chicken and cook until golden on all sides. Reduce heat to medium; cover and cook until chicken loses its pink color throughout, 12 to 15 minutes longer.

4. Transfer chicken to cutting board; discard toothpicks. Cut chicken roulades crosswise on diagonal into ½-inch-thick slices. Transfer chicken to platter and garnish with additional basil leaves. Makes 4 main-dish servings.

Each serving: About 203 calories, 29g protein, 3g carbohydrate, 8g total fat (3g saturated), 81mg cholesterol, 341mg sodium.

Chicken Roulades

Coq au Vin

This well-known dish, basically chicken stewed in a red-wine sauce, is a specialty of the Burgundy region of France. If possible, use a moderately priced California or Oregon Pinot Noir, which is made from the same grape as more expensive French Burgundy.

Prep: 45 minutes   Bake: 45 minutes

4	slices bacon, cut into ¾-inch pieces
4	tablespoons butter or margarine
¼	teaspoon salt
⅛	teaspoon ground black pepper
1	chicken (3½ pounds), cut into 8 pieces and skin removed from all but wings
1	small onion, finely chopped
1	carrot, peeled and finely chopped
18	pearl onions (generous 1 cup), peeled

10	ounces mushrooms, trimmed
1/3	cup all-purpose flour
2	cups dry red wine
1 1/3	cups chicken broth
2	tablespoons tomato paste
1	stalk celery
12	sprigs plus 3 tablespoons chopped fresh parsley
2	bay leaves

1. Preheat oven to 325°F. In 5-quart Dutch oven, cook bacon over medium-high heat until crisp. With slotted spoon, transfer to paper towels to drain. Reduce heat to medium and add butter to drippings in pot. Sprinkle chicken with salt and pepper. Add chicken to Dutch oven, in batches if necessary, and cook until golden brown, about 5 minutes per side. With slotted spoon, transfer chicken pieces to bowl as they are browned.

2. Add chopped onion and carrot to Dutch oven and cook until lightly browned, about 5 minutes. With slotted spoon, transfer to bowl with chicken. Add pearl onions to Dutch oven and cook, stirring, until browned, about 6 minutes; transfer to bowl. Add mushrooms to pot and cook, stirring, until browned, about 6 minutes; transfer to bowl.

3. Add flour to Dutch oven and cook, stirring, 2 minutes. With wire whisk, whisk in 1/2 cup wine until smooth. Add remaining 1 1/2 cups wine, broth, and tomato paste. Heat to boiling, whisking constantly; boil 2 minutes. Return chicken, vegetables, and three-fourths of bacon to Dutch oven. With string, tie together celery, parsley sprigs, and bay leaves; add to Dutch oven. Cover and place in oven. Bake, stirring occasionally, 45 minutes.

4. At end of cooking time, skim fat and discard celery bundle. Sprinkle coq au vin with remaining bacon and chopped parsley. Makes 6 main-dish servings.

Each serving: About 414 calories, 32g protein, 17g carbohydrate, 24g total fat (10g saturated), 115mg cholesterol, 645mg sodium.

Chicken Mole

Mole (MO-lay) is a thick, rich, dark brown Mexican sauce traditionally made with dried chiles, spices, seeds such as pumpkin, nuts, and a small amount of unsweetened chocolate. Here's our version, which should be served over rice to soak up the spicy mole and with crisp tortillas.

Prep: 10 minutes   Cook: 45 minutes

1	can (14 1/2 ounces) diced tomatoes
1	can (4 to 4 1/2 ounces) chopped mild green chiles
1/2	cup whole blanched almonds
1/2	small onion, coarsely chopped
1	small garlic clove, peeled
1	tablespoon chili powder
1	teaspoon ground cumin
1	teaspoon ground coriander
3/4	teaspoon ground cinnamon
3/4	teaspoon salt
1/2	teaspoon sugar
1	tablespoon olive oil
3	pounds bone-in chicken parts, skin removed from all but wings
1/2	square (1/2 ounce) unsweetened chocolate, chopped
1/4	cup water
2	tablespoons chopped fresh cilantro

1. Prepare mole sauce: In blender or in food processor with knife blade attached, puree tomatoes, chiles, almonds, onion, garlic, chili powder, cumin, coriander, cinnamon, salt, and sugar until smooth.

2. In nonstick 12-inch skillet, heat oil over medium-high heat until very hot. Add chicken and cook until golden brown, about 5 minutes per side; transfer chicken pieces to large bowl as they are browned.

3. Add mole sauce, chocolate, and water to skillet; cook, stirring, until chocolate melts. Return chicken to skillet; heat to boiling. Reduce heat; cover and simmer until chicken juices run clear when chicken thigh is pierced with tip of knife, 30 to 35 minutes. Sprinkle with cilantro to serve. Makes 6 main-dish servings.

Each serving: About 263 calories, 27g protein, 9g carbohydrate, 14g total fat (3g saturated), 76mg cholesterol, 617mg sodium.

Country Captain Casserole

Though the exact origin of this well-known dish is often debated, its great flavor is never in dispute.

Prep: 30 minutes   Bake: 1 hour

2	tablespoons plus 1 teaspoon vegetable oil
2	chickens (3½ pounds each), each cut into 8 pieces and skin removed from all but wings
2	medium onions, chopped
1	large Granny Smith apple, peeled, cored, and chopped
1	large green pepper, chopped
3	large garlic cloves, finely chopped
1	tablespoon grated, peeled fresh ginger
3	tablespoons curry powder
½	teaspoon coarsely ground black pepper
¼	teaspoon ground cumin
1	can (28 ounces) plum tomatoes in puree
1	can (14½ ounces) chicken broth or 1¾ cups Chicken Broth (page 84)
½	cup dark seedless raisins
1	teaspoon salt
¼	cup chopped fresh parsley

1. In nonreactive 8-quart Dutch oven, heat 2 tablespoons oil over medium-high heat until very hot. Add chicken, in batches, and cook until golden brown, about 5 minutes per side. With slotted spoon, transfer chicken pieces to bowl as they are browned.

2. Preheat oven to 350°F. In same Dutch oven, heat remaining 1 teaspoon oil over medium-high heat. Add onions, apple, green pepper, garlic, and ginger; cook, stirring frequently, 2 minutes. Reduce heat to medium; cover and cook 5 minutes longer.

3. Stir in curry powder, black pepper, and cumin; cook 1 minute. Add tomatoes with their puree, broth, raisins, salt, and chicken pieces. Heat to boiling over high heat; boil 1 minute. Cover and place in oven. Bake 1 hour. Sprinkle with parsley. Makes 8 main-dish servings.

♥ Each serving: About 347 calories, 43g protein, 19g carbohydrate, 11g total fat (2g saturated), 133mg cholesterol, 825mg sodium.

Country Captain Casserole

Arroz con Pollo

From Santiago to Miami to Madrid, different versions of this comforting chicken-and-rice dish are served almost anywhere Spanish is spoken.

Prep: 15 minutes   Cook: 40 minutes

1	tablespoon vegetable oil
6	medium bone-in chicken thighs (1½ pounds), skin and fat removed
1	medium onion, finely chopped
1	red pepper, chopped
1	garlic clove, finely chopped
⅛	teaspoon ground red pepper (cayenne)
1	cup regular long-grain rice
1	can (14½ ounces) chicken broth or 1¾ cups Chicken Broth (page 84)
¼	cup water
1	strip (3" by ½") lemon peel
¼	teaspoon dried oregano
¼	teaspoon salt
1	cup frozen peas
¼	cup chopped pimiento-stuffed olives (salad olives)
¼	cup chopped fresh cilantro
	lemon wedges

1. In 5-quart Dutch oven, heat oil over medium-high heat until very hot. Add chicken and cook until golden brown, about 5 minutes per side. With slotted spoon, transfer chicken pieces to bowl as they are browned.

2. Reduce heat to medium. Add onion and red pepper to Dutch oven and cook until tender, about 5 minutes. Stir in garlic and ground red pepper and cook 30 seconds. Add rice and cook, stirring, 1 minute. Stir in broth, water, lemon peel, oregano, salt, and chicken; heat to boiling. Reduce heat; cover and simmer until juices run clear when thickest part of chicken is pierced with tip of knife, about 20 minutes.

3. Stir in peas; cover and heat through. Remove from heat and let stand 5 minutes.

4. Transfer chicken to serving bowl. Sprinkle with olives and cilantro; serve with lemon wedges. Makes 4 main-dish servings.

Each serving: About 387 calories, 26g protein, 48g carbohydrate, 9g total fat (2g saturated), 81mg cholesterol, 927mg sodium.

Chicken Cacciatore

Food prepared alla cacciatore, *"hunter-style," includes mushrooms in the sauce. This is the kind of home cooking that found its way first into Italian restaurants and then into American kitchens. Serve over wide, flat noodles.*

Prep: 15 minutes   Cook: 40 minutes

2	tablespoons olive oil
1	chicken (3½ pounds), cut into 8 pieces and skin removed from all but wings
3	tablespoons all-purpose flour
1	medium onion, finely chopped
4	garlic cloves, crushed with garlic press
8	ounces mushrooms, trimmed and thickly sliced
1	can (14 to 16 ounces) tomatoes
½	teaspoon salt
½	teaspoon dried oregano, crumbled
¼	teaspoon dried sage
⅛	teaspoon ground red pepper (cayenne)

1. In nonstick 12-inch skillet, heat oil over medium-high heat until very hot. On waxed paper, coat chicken with flour, shaking off excess. Add chicken to skillet and cook until golden brown, about 3 minutes per side. With slotted spoon, transfer chicken pieces to bowl as they are browned.

2. Add onion and garlic to skillet. Reduce heat to medium-low and cook, stirring occasionally, until onion is tender, about 5 minutes. Add mushrooms and cook, stirring frequently, until just tender, about 3 minutes.

3. Add tomatoes with their juice, breaking them up with side of spoon. Add salt, oregano, sage, ground red pepper, and chicken and heat to boiling over high heat. Reduce heat; cover and simmer until juices run clear when thickest part of chicken is pierced with tip of knife, about 25 minutes.

4. Transfer chicken to serving bowl. Spoon sauce over chicken. Makes 4 main-dish servings.

Each serving: About 371 calories, 44g protein, 18g carbohydrate, 13g total fat (3g saturated), 133mg cholesterol, 608mg sodium.

Chicken Curry

Serve curry over rice with an array of condiments—the more, the merrier. Chopped cilantro, chopped peanuts, shredded coconut, golden raisins, cucumber sticks, mango chutney, toasted slivered almonds, and sliced bananas are the most popular items but by no means the only possibilities.

	Prep: 15 minutes plus cooling Cook: 1 hour 15 minutes
1	chicken (3½ pounds), cut into 8 pieces
4	medium onions, finely chopped
2	carrots, peeled and finely chopped
2	stalks celery with leaves, finely chopped
8	parsley sprigs
1	lime
4	tablespoons butter or margarine
2	Granny Smith apples, peeled, cored, and chopped
3	garlic cloves, finely chopped
1	tablespoon curry powder
3	tablespoons all-purpose flour
½	cup half-and-half or light cream
⅓	cup golden raisins
2	tablespoons mango chutney, chopped
2	teaspoons minced, peeled fresh ginger
½	teaspoon salt
	pinch ground red pepper (cayenne)

1. In 5-quart Dutch oven, combine chicken, one-fourth onions, carrots, celery, and parsley sprigs with just enough *water* to cover. Heat to boiling over high heat. Reduce heat; partially cover and simmer, turning once, until chicken loses its pink color throughout, 25 to 30 minutes. With slotted spoon, transfer chicken to bowl. When cool enough to handle, remove and discard skin and bones; with hands, shred chicken.

2. Meanwhile, strain broth through sieve, discarding vegetables. Return broth to Dutch oven; heat to boiling and boil until reduced to 2 cups. Skim and discard fat from broth; reserve broth.

3. From lime, grate ½ teaspoon peel and squeeze 5 teaspoons juice; reserve.

4. In 12-inch skillet, melt butter over medium heat. Add remaining three-fourths onions, apples, garlic, and curry powder and cook, stirring, until apples are tender, about 10 minutes. Sprinkle with flour, stirring to blend. Gradually add 2 cups reserved broth, stirring constantly until broth has thick-

ened and boils. Stir in reserved lime peel and juice, half-and-half, raisins, chutney, ginger, salt, and ground red pepper. Reduce heat and simmer, stirring occasionally, 5 minutes. Add chicken and heat through. Makes 6 main-dish servings.

Each serving: About 379 calories, 30g protein, 33g carbohydrate, 14g total fat (7g saturated), 117mg cholesterol, 449mg sodium.

Chicken with Rosemary Dumplings

It doesn't takes hours to make a stew when you're using chicken breasts. And the tender dumplings will melt in your mouth.

	Prep: 15 minutes Cook: 1 hour
2	tablespoons vegetable oil
6	large bone-in chicken breast halves (3¼ pounds), skin removed
4	large carrots, peeled and cut into 1-inch pieces
2	large stalks celery, cut into ¼-inch-thick slices
1	medium onion, finely chopped
1	cup plus 2 tablespoons all-purpose flour
2	teaspoons baking powder
1½	teaspoons chopped fresh rosemary or ½ teaspoon dried rosemary, crumbled
1	teaspoon salt
1	large egg
1½	cups milk
2	cups water
1	can (14½ ounces) low-sodium chicken broth or 1¾ cups Chicken Broth (page 84)
¼	teaspoon ground black pepper
1	package (10 ounces) frozen peas

1. In 8-quart Dutch oven, heat 1 tablespoon oil over medium-high heat until very hot. Add 3 chicken breast halves; cook until golden brown, about 5 minutes per side. With slotted spoon, transfer chicken pieces to bowl as they are browned. Repeat with remaining chicken.

2. Add remaining 1 tablespoon oil to drippings in Dutch oven. Add carrots, celery, and onion and cook, stirring frequently, until vegetables are golden brown and tender, about 10 minutes.

3. Meanwhile, prepare dumplings: In small bowl, combine 1 cup flour, baking powder, rosemary, and ½ teaspoon salt. In cup, with fork, beat egg with ½ cup milk. Stir egg mixture into flour mixture until just blended.

4. Return chicken to Dutch oven; add water, broth, pepper, and remaining ½ teaspoon salt. Heat to boiling over high heat. Drop dumpling mixture by rounded tablespoons on top of chicken and vegetables to make 12 dumplings. Reduce heat; cover and simmer 15 minutes.

5. With slotted spoon, transfer dumplings, chicken, and vegetables to serving bowl; keep warm. Reserve broth in Dutch oven.

6. In cup, blend remaining 2 tablespoons flour with remaining 1 cup milk until smooth; stir into broth mixture. Heat to boiling over high heat; boil 1 minute to thicken slightly. Add peas and heat through. Pour sauce over chicken and dumplings. Makes 6 main-dish servings.

♥ Each serving: About 437 calories, 46g protein, 38g carbohydrate, 10g total fat (3g saturated), 137mg cholesterol, 951mg sodium

When making chicken or turkey meatballs or burgers, try to chill the shaped mixture a couple of hours before cooking. They will hold together better.
ANNE ROSENZWEIG
CHEF/OWNER, THE LOBSTER CLUB, NEW YORK CITY

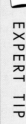
EXPERT TIP

Spicy Peanut Chicken

This exotic dish is based on the cuisines of Southeast Asia. A crisp cucumber salad and jasmine or basmati rice, now available in most supermarkets, are the usual accompaniments.

Prep: 15 minutes	Cook: 1 hour 10 minutes
1	teaspoon ground cumin
¼	teaspoon ground cinnamon
4	medium chicken leg quarters (2¼ pounds), skin and fat removed
1	tablespoon vegetable oil
1	medium onion, thinly sliced
1	can (28 ounces) plum tomatoes, drained, coarsely chopped, and juice reserved
¼	cup creamy peanut butter
¼	cup packed fresh cilantro leaves plus additional sprigs
2	garlic cloves, peeled
½	teaspoon salt
¼	teaspoon crushed red pepper

1. In cup, combine cumin and cinnamon; rub on chicken.

2. In nonstick 12-inch skillet, heat oil over medium-high heat until very hot. Add chicken and cook until golden brown, about 5 minutes per side. Add onion and cook until golden, about 5 minutes.

3. Meanwhile, in blender or in food processor with knife blade attached, puree reserved tomato juice, peanut butter, cilantro, garlic, salt, and crushed red pepper until smooth.

4. Pour peanut-butter mixture and chopped tomatoes over chicken; heat to boiling. Reduce heat; cover and simmer until juices run clear when thickest part of chicken is pierced with tip of knife, about 40 minutes. Garnish with cilantro sprigs. Makes 4 main-dish servings.

Each serving: About 361 calories, 36g protein, 16g carbohydrate, 18g fat (3g saturated), 116mg cholesterol, 817mg sodium.

Chicken Bouillabaisse

Serve in oversized soup bowls with a dollop of garlic mayonnaise and thickly sliced French bread toasts.

Prep: 1 hour   Bake: 30 minutes

1	tablespoon olive oil
8	large bone-in chicken thighs (2½ pounds), skin and fat removed
2	large carrots, peeled and finely chopped
1	medium onion, finely chopped
1	large fennel bulb (1½ pounds), cut into ¼-inch-thick slices
½	cup water
3	garlic cloves, finely chopped
1	can (14½ ounces) diced tomatoes
1	can (14½ ounces) chicken broth or 1¾ cups Chicken Broth (page 84)
½	cup dry white wine
2	tablespoons anisette (anise-flavored liqueur; optional)
¼	teaspoon dried thyme
¼	teaspoon salt
⅛	teaspoon ground red pepper (cayenne)
1	bay leaf
	pinch saffron threads

1. In 5-quart Dutch oven, heat oil over medium-high heat until very hot. Add chicken, in batches, and cook until golden brown, about 5 minutes per side. With slotted spoon, transfer chicken pieces to bowl as they are browned.

2. Add carrots and onion to Dutch oven and cook over medium heat, stirring occasionally, until tender and golden, about 10 minutes. Transfer to bowl with chicken.

3. Preheat oven to 350°F. Add fennel and water to Dutch oven, stirring to loosen browned bits. Cook over medium heat, stirring occasionally, until fennel is tender and browned, about 7 minutes. Add garlic and cook 3 minutes.

4. Return chicken and carrot mixture to Dutch oven; add tomatoes with their juice, broth, wine, anisette, if using, thyme, salt, ground red pepper, bay leaf, and saffron. Heat to boiling. Cover and place in oven. Bake until juices run clear when thickest part of chicken is pierced with tip of knife, about 30 minutes. Discard bay leaf. Makes 4 main-dish servings.

Each serving: About 317 calories, 36g protein, 18g carbohydrate, 11g total fat (2g saturated), 135mg cholesterol, 1,036mg sodium.

Chicken Couscous

It's surprising how the addition of a few poultry spices transforms basic ingredients into a special meal.

Prep: 20 minutes   Cook: 50 minutes

6	large bone-in chicken thighs (1¾ pounds), fat removed
¼	teaspoon salt
¼	teaspoon ground red pepper (cayenne)
2	tablespoons butter or margarine
1	medium red onion, thinly sliced
5	carrots, peeled and cut into 1-inch pieces
3	small turnips, each peeled, cut in half, and cut into 6 wedges
1	jalapeño chile, seeded and finely chopped
1	teaspoon ground coriander
½	teaspoon ground cumin
¼	teaspoon ground ginger
1	can (15 to 19 ounces) garbanzo beans, rinsed and drained
⅓	cup golden raisins
2	cups chicken broth
3	tablespoons chopped fresh cilantro or parsley
2	cups couscous, cooked (page 393)

1. Sprinkle chicken with salt and ground red pepper. In 12-inch skillet, melt butter over medium heat. Add chicken to skillet and cook until golden brown, about 5 minutes per side. With slotted spoon, transfer chicken pieces to medium bowl as they are browned.

2. Increase heat to medium-high; add onion and cook until lightly browned, about 5 minutes. With slotted spoon, transfer onion to bowl with chicken. To skillet, add carrots, turnips, jalapeño, coriander, cumin, and ginger; cook, stirring, 5 minutes.

3. Reduce heat to medium; stir in beans, raisins, and broth and cook 1 minute. Return chicken and onion to skillet and heat to boiling. Reduce heat; cover and simmer 20 minutes. Remove cover and simmer until juices run clear when thickest part of chicken is pierced with tip of knife, about 10 minutes longer. Sprinkle with chopped cilantro; serve over couscous. Makes 6 main-dish servings.

Each serving without couscous: About 393 calories, 23g protein, 26g carbohydrate, 22g total fat (7g saturated), 98mg cholesterol, 685mg sodium.

Creole Chicken Gumbo

Gumbo gets much of its rich flavor from a deeply browned roux made with a generous amount of fat. Here, the flour is browned in the oven, which results in the same flavor and color without the fat. This makes a big batch—leftovers can be frozen.

Prep: 1 hour 10 minutes plus cooling   Cook: 1 hour 30 minutes

2/3	cup all-purpose flour
12	large bone-in chicken thighs (about 3½ pounds), fat removed
12	ounces fully cooked andouille or kielbasa sausage, cut into ½-inch-thick slices
6	cups chicken broth
1	can (6 ounces) tomato paste
2	cups water
2	medium onions, thinly sliced
12	ounces okra, sliced, or 1 package (10 ounces) frozen cut okra, thawed
1	large yellow pepper, chopped
4	stalks celery with leaves, cut into ¼-inch-thick slices
¾	cup chopped fresh parsley
4	garlic cloves, thinly sliced
2	bay leaves
1½	teaspoons salt
1	teaspoon dried thyme
1	teaspoon ground red pepper (cayenne)
1	teaspoon ground black pepper
½	teaspoon ground allspice
1	can (14 to 16 ounces) tomatoes, drained and chopped
½	cup finely chopped green-onion tops
2	tablespoons distilled white vinegar
3	cups regular long-grain rice, cooked as label directs

1. Preheat oven to 375°F. Place flour in oven-safe 12-inch skillet (if skillet is not oven-safe, wrap handle with double layer of foil). Bake until flour begins to brown, about 25 minutes. Stir with wooden spoon, breaking up any lumps. Bake, stirring flour every 10 minutes, until it turns nut brown, about 35 minutes longer. Remove flour from oven and let cool. Strain flour through sieve to remove any lumps.

Creole Chicken Gumbo

2. Heat nonreactive 8-quart Dutch oven over medium-high heat until very hot. Cook chicken, skin side down first, in batches, until golden brown, about 5 minutes per side. Transfer chicken pieces to large bowl as they are browned. Add sausage to Dutch oven and cook over medium heat, stirring constantly, until lightly browned, about 5 minutes. With slotted spoon, transfer sausage to bowl with chicken.

3. Reduce heat to medium-low. Gradually stir in browned flour, about 3 tablespoons at a time, and cook, stirring constantly, 2 minutes.

4. Immediately add broth, stirring until browned bits are loosened from bottom of pan. Blend tomato paste with water and add to Dutch oven. Stir in onions, okra, yellow pepper, celery, ¼ cup parsley, garlic, bay leaves, salt, thyme, ground red pepper, black pepper, and allspice. Add sausage, chicken, and tomatoes. Heat to boiling over high heat. Reduce heat and simmer until liquid has thickened, about 1 hour.

5. Add remaining ½ cup parsley, green onions, and vinegar; heat through. Remove from heat; cover and let stand 10 minutes. Discard bay leaves. Serve gumbo in bowls over rice. Makes 18 cups, or 12 main-dish servings.

Each serving: About 447 calories, 27g protein, 28g carbohydrate, 25g total fat (8g saturated), 107mg cholesterol, 1,357mg sodium.

Chicken Thighs Provençal

The combination of thyme, basil, fennel, and orange is quintes-sentially Provençal and makes sensational chicken.

Prep: 30 minutes   Cook: 1 hour 15 minutes

2	pounds skinless, boneless chicken thighs, fat removed and cut into quarters
¾	teaspoon salt
3	teaspoons olive oil
2	red peppers, cut into ¼-inch-wide strips
1	yellow pepper, cut into ¼-inch-wide strips
1	jumbo onion (1 pound), thinly sliced
3	garlic cloves, crushed with garlic press
1	can (28 ounces) plum tomatoes
¼	teaspoon dried thyme
¼	teaspoon fennel seeds, crushed
3	strips (3" by 1" each) orange peel
½	cup loosely packed fresh basil leaves, chopped

1. Sprinkle chicken with ½ teaspoon salt. In nonreactive 5-quart Dutch oven, heat 1 teaspoon oil over medium-high heat until very hot. Add half of chicken and cook until golden brown, about 5 minutes per side. With slotted spoon, transfer chicken pieces to bowl as they are browned. Repeat with 1 teaspoon oil and remaining chicken.

2. Reduce heat to medium. To drippings in Dutch oven, add remaining 1 teaspoon oil; cook red and yellow peppers and onion with remaining ¼ teaspoon salt, stirring frequently, until vegetables are tender and lightly browned, about 20 minutes. Add garlic; cook 1 minute longer.

3. Return chicken to Dutch oven. Add tomatoes with their juice, thyme, fennel seeds, and orange peel; heat to boiling, breaking up tomatoes with side of spoon. Reduce heat; cover and simmer until chicken loses its pink color throughout, about 15 minutes.

4. Transfer to serving bowl and sprinkle with basil to serve. Makes 8 main-dish servings.

Each serving: About 204 calories, 24g protein, 12g carbohydrate, 7g total fat (1g saturated), 94mg cholesterol, 480mg sodium.

Poule au Pot with Tarragon

Stewed chicken and vegetables is a favorite Sunday supper in France. Use the leftover broth as the base for a soup.

Prep: 15 minutes   Cook: 1 hour

3	medium leeks (about 1 pound)
1	chicken (3½ pounds), cut into 8 pieces
1	pound small red potatoes
1	bag (16 ounces) carrots, peeled and cut into 3-inch pieces
4	cups water
1	can (14½ ounces) chicken broth or 1¾ cups Chicken Broth (page 84)
½	teaspoon salt
¼	teaspoon dried thyme
¼	teaspoon ground black pepper
1	large sprig plus 1 tablespoon chopped fresh tarragon

1. Cut off roots and trim dark green tops from leeks; cut each leek lengthwise in half, then crosswise into 3-inch pieces. Rinse in large bowl of cold water, swishing to remove sand; transfer to colander to drain, leaving sand in bottom of bowl.

2. In 6- to 8-quart Dutch oven, combine leeks, chicken, potatoes, carrots, water, broth, salt, thyme, pepper, and tarragon sprig. Heat to boiling over high heat. Reduce heat; cover and simmer until chicken loses its pink color throughout, about 45 minutes.

3. With slotted spoon, transfer chicken and vegetables to serving bowl. Remove and discard skin from chicken. Skim and discard fat from broth. Pour 1 cup broth over chicken (refrigerate remaining broth for another use). To serve, sprinkle chopped tarragon on top. Makes 4 main-dish servings.

♥ Each serving: About 472 calories, 47g protein, 44g carbohydrate, 11g total fat (3g saturated), 127mg cholesterol, 859mg sodium.

Turkish Chicken in Walnut Sauce

This chilled dish is a perfect do-ahead dinner for a hot summer night. Serve with sliced ripe tomatoes and a crisp green salad.

Prep: 20 minutes plus cooling and standing
Cook: 30 minutes

4	large bone-in chicken breast halves (2½ pounds)
1	can (14½ ounces) chicken broth
	or 1¾ cups Chicken Broth (page 84)
1	cup water
3	sprigs plus 1 tablespoon chopped fresh parsley
1¼	cups walnuts (5 ounces), toasted
3	slices firm white bread, torn
1	small garlic clove, minced
¾	teaspoon salt
½	teaspoon paprika
⅛	teaspoon ground red pepper (cayenne)

1. In 4-quart saucepan, combine chicken, broth, water, and parsley sprigs. Heat to boiling over high heat. Reduce heat; cover and simmer until chicken loses its pink color throughout, 20 to 25 minutes. Remove saucepan from heat and cool chicken in broth 30 minutes.

2. With slotted spoon, transfer chicken to bowl. Remove and discard skin and bones from chicken; cut chicken into ½-inch-wide strips. Strain broth through sieve; skim and discard fat from broth. Reserve broth.

3. In food processor with knife blade attached, process walnuts and bread until walnuts are finely ground. Add 1 cup reserved broth (cool and refrigerate remaining broth for another use), garlic, salt, paprika, and ground red pepper; process until well combined.

4. Stir half of walnut sauce into chicken until combined. Spoon onto serving platter. Pour remaining sauce on top. Cover with plastic wrap and let stand 30 minutes, or refrigerate up to 8 hours.

5. To serve, sprinkle chopped parsley over chicken. Makes 6 main-dish servings.

Each serving: About 349 calories, 33g protein, 11g carbohydrate, 19g total fat (2g saturated), 77mg cholesterol, 594mg sodium.

Chicken Breasts Tonnato

We use chicken instead of veal for this tasty variation of vitello tonnato, *a Piedmontese specialty that features thinly sliced veal blanketed in a tuna-and-mayonnaise sauce. For the best results, use Italian tuna packed in olive oil.*

Prep: 5 minutes plus chilling   Cook: 15 minutes

6	small skinless, boneless chicken breast halves (1½ pounds)
1	medium onion, thinly sliced
2	cups water
1	can (6½ ounces) white tuna in oil
4	anchovy fillets
2	tablespoons plus 2 teaspoons capers, drained
¼	cup olive oil
¼	cup fresh lemon juice
¼	teaspoon salt
1	bunch arugula (10 ounces) or lettuce leaves
	lemon slices

1. In 12-inch skillet, combine chicken, onion, and water. Heat to boiling over high heat. Reduce heat; cover and simmer, turning chicken once, until chicken loses its pink color throughout, 8 to 10 minutes. With slotted spoon, transfer chicken to plate; cover loosely and refrigerate until chilled. Strain poaching liquid through sieve; skim and discard fat. Reserve ¼ cup poaching liquid.

2. In blender or in food processor with knife blade attached, blend tuna with its oil, anchovies, 2 tablespoons capers, olive oil, lemon juice, salt, and reserved poaching liquid until smooth.

3. Line platter with arugula. Dip each cold chicken breast half into tuna sauce to coat; arrange on arugula. Pour any remaining sauce over chicken. Garnish with lemon slices and remaining 2 teaspoons capers. Makes 6 main-dish servings.

Each serving: About 286 calories, 36g protein, 2g carbohydrate, 14g total fat (2g saturated), 76mg cholesterol, 519mg sodium.

Chicken Breasts with Mushrooms and Tarragon

Fast and flavorful, this delicious blend of mushrooms and herbs makes chicken cutlets festive enough for special dinner guests.

Prep: 20 minutes   Cook: 25 minutes

2	tablespoons olive oil
1	pound assorted mushrooms (white and cremini, trimmed and sliced; shiitake, stems removed and caps sliced)
1	large shallot, finely chopped
3	tablespoons all-purpose flour
2	tablespoons chopped fresh tarragon or 1 teaspoon dried tarragon
½	teaspoon salt
¼	teaspoon ground black pepper
6	small skinless, boneless chicken breast halves (1½ pounds)
1	cup chicken broth
¼	cup dry white wine

1. In 12-inch skillet, heat 1 tablespoon oil over medium-high heat. Add mushrooms and shallot and cook, stirring occasionally, until mushrooms are golden brown and any liquid has evaporated, 12 to 15 minutes. Transfer mushroom mixture to bowl.

2. On waxed paper, combine flour, 1 tablespoon chopped tarragon, salt, and pepper; use flour mixture to coat chicken, shaking off excess.

3. In same skillet, heat remaining 1 tablespoon oil over medium-high heat until very hot. Add chicken and cook until chicken is golden brown and loses its pink color throughout, about 4 minutes per side. Transfer chicken to warm platter.

4. Add broth, wine, remaining 1 tablespoon chopped tarragon, and mushroom mixture to skillet; cook 1 minute, stirring until browned bits are loosened from bottom of skillet. Pour sauce over chicken. Makes 6 main-dish servings.

♥ Each serving: About 212 calories, 29g protein, 7g carbohydrate, 7g total fat (1g saturated), 66mg cholesterol, 437mg sodium.

Chicken Breasts with Pecan Crust

These irresistibly crisp chicken breasts deliver real maple flavor and plenty of pecan crunch in every bite.

Prep: 15 minutes   Cook: 10 minutes

4	medium skinless, boneless chicken breast halves (1¼ pounds)
2	tablespoons maple or maple-flavored syrup
½	cup pecans, finely chopped
½	cup plain dried bread crumbs
¾	teaspoon salt
1	tablespoon butter or margarine
2	tablespoons vegetable oil

1. Brush chicken on both sides with maple syrup. On waxed paper, combine chopped pecans, bread crumbs, and salt; use to coat chicken, firmly pressing so mixture adheres.

2. In nonstick 12-inch skillet, melt butter with oil over medium-high heat. Add chicken and cook until chicken is golden brown and loses its pink color throughout, about 4 minutes per side. Makes 4 main-dish servings.

Each serving: About 411 calories, 36g protein, 19g carbohydrate, 21g total fat (4g saturated), 90mg cholesterol, 675mg sodium.

SKINNING AND BONING CHICKEN BREASTS

To remove the skin from a chicken breast, grasp the skin at the thickest end of the breast and pull it away from the meat.

To bone a chicken breast, hold a knife as close as possible to the bone; move the blade along the rib bones, gently pulling the meat away from the bones with the other hand. Cut away the white tendon from the underside of the breast.

Chicken Breasts with Green Peppercorns

Green peppercorns have a mild bite that adds a moderate level of heat. Refrigerate leftover peppercorns for up to one week.

Prep: 10 minutes   Cook: 10 minutes

1¼	pounds skinless, boneless chicken breast halves
2	tablespoons all-purpose flour
2	tablespoons butter or margarine
1	green onion, finely chopped
½	cup water
¼	cup dry white wine
1	tablespoon water-packed green peppercorns, drained
2	teaspoons Dijon mustard
½	teaspoon salt
½	teaspoon sugar

1. With meat mallets, or between two sheets of plastic wrap or waxed paper with rolling pin, pound chicken breast halves to ¼-inch thickness. Place flour on waxed paper; use to coat chicken, shaking off excess.

2. In 12-inch skillet, melt butter over medium-high heat. Add chicken and cook until golden brown and chicken loses its pink color throughout, 1 to 1½ minutes per side. Transfer to platter; keep warm.

3. Reduce heat to medium. To drippings in skillet, add green onion and cook, stirring occasionally, until tender, about 1 minute. Add water, wine, green peppercorns, mustard, salt, and sugar, stirring until browned bits are loosened from bottom of skillet. Heat to boiling over high heat; immediately remove from heat. Spoon sauce over chicken. Makes 4 main-dish servings.

Each serving: About 237 calories, 33g protein, 4g carbohydrate, 8g total fat (4g saturated), 98mg cholesterol, 577mg sodium.

Chicken Breasts with Lemon-Caper Sauce

Preparing chicken alla Francese *reverses the order in which chicken is ordinarily coated. Here, the chicken is first dredged in flour and then dipped into beaten egg. The result is deep golden chicken with a delicate, puffy coating.*

Prep: 15 minutes   Cook: 20 minutes

4	medium skinless, boneless chicken breast halves (1¼ pounds)
2	tablespoons plus 1½ teaspoons all-purpose flour
½	teaspoon salt
1	large egg
2	teaspoons olive oil
2	tablespoons butter or margarine
2	lemons, each cut in half
3	garlic cloves, crushed with side of chef's knife
½	cup chicken broth
¼	cup dry white wine
2	tablespoons capers, drained
1	tablespoon chopped fresh parsley

1. With meat mallet, or between two sheets of plastic wrap or waxed paper with rolling pin, pound chicken breast halves to ½-inch thickness. On waxed paper, combine 2 tablespoons flour and salt. In pie plate, beat egg. Coat chicken with flour mixture, then dip in egg.

2. In nonstick 12-inch skillet, heat oil over medium-high heat until very hot. Stir in 1 tablespoon butter until melted. Add chicken; cook 5 minutes. Reduce heat to medium, turn chicken, and cook until chicken loses its pink color throughout, 8 to 10 minutes longer. Transfer to platter; keep warm.

3. From ½ lemon, cut thin slices; from remaining 1½ lemons, squeeze 2 tablespoons juice. To drippings in skillet, add lemon slices and garlic; cook, stirring, until garlic is golden. In small bowl, blend broth, wine, lemon juice, and remaining 1½ teaspoons flour until smooth; stir into mixture in skillet. Heat sauce to boiling; boil 1 minute. Stir in capers and remaining 1 tablespoon butter until butter melts. Discard garlic. Arrange lemon slices over and between chicken breasts. Pour sauce over chicken; sprinkle with chopped parsley. Makes 4 main-dish servings.

Each serving: About 287 calories, 35g protein, 7g carbohydrate, 11g total fat (5g saturated), 151mg cholesterol, 773mg sodium.

Balsamic Chicken and Pears

Balsamic vinegar has a unique sweet-and-sour flavor; use sparingly. Look for the word tradizionale *on the label.*

Prep: 10 minutes   Cook: 20 minutes

2	teaspoons vegetable oil
4	small skinless, boneless chicken breast halves (1 pound)
2	Bosc pears, not peeled, each cut in half, cored, and cut into 8 wedges
1	cup chicken broth
3	tablespoons balsamic vinegar
2	teaspoons cornstarch
1½	teaspoons sugar
¼	cup dried cherries or raisins

1. In nonstick 12-inch skillet, heat 1 teaspoon oil over medium-high heat until very hot. Add chicken and cook until chicken is golden brown and loses its pink color throughout, 4 to 5 minutes per side. Transfer chicken to plate; keep warm.

2. In same skillet, heat remaining 1 teaspoon oil. Add pears and cook until tender and golden brown.

3. In cup, blend broth, vinegar, cornstarch, and sugar. Stir broth mixture and dried cherries into skillet with pears. Heat to boiling, stirring; boil 1 minute. Return chicken to skillet; heat through. Makes 4 main-dish servings.

♥ Each serving: About 235 calories, 27g protein, 22g carbohydrate, 4g total fat (1g saturated), 66mg cholesterol, 325mg sodium.

Chicken Breasts with Six Quick Sauces

A choice of easy sauces makes this recipe one for the file.

Prep: 2 minutes plus making sauce   Cook: 10 minutes

1	teaspoon vegetable oil
4	small skinless, boneless chicken breast halves (1 pound)
	choice of sauce (right)

1. In nonstick 12-inch skillet, heat oil over medium-high heat until very hot. Add chicken and cook until chicken is golden brown and loses its pink color throughout, 4 to 5 minutes per side. Transfer chicken to platter; keep warm.

2. Prepare sauce and serve. Makes 4 main-dish servings.

Apple-Curry Sauce

After removing chicken, reduce heat to medium. Add **2 teaspoons vegetable oil** to skillet. Add **1 Golden Delicious apple,** peeled, cored, and chopped, and **1 small onion,** chopped. Cook, stirring, until tender. Stir in **1½ teaspoons curry powder** and **¼ teaspoon salt;** cook 1 minute. Stir in **½ cup mango chutney, ½ cup frozen peas,** and **½ cup water.** Heat to boiling; boil 1 minute. Spoon over chicken.

♥ Each serving with chicken: About 352 calories, 34g protein, 38g carbohydrate, 5g total fat (1g saturated), 82mg cholesterol, 596mg sodium.

Black Bean Salsa

After removing chicken, reduce heat to medium. Add **1 can (15 to 19 ounces) black beans,** rinsed and drained, **1 jar (10 ounces) thick-and-chunky salsa, 1 can (8¾ ounces) whole-kernel corn,** drained, **2 tablespoons chopped fresh cilantro,** and **¼ cup water** to skillet. Cook, stirring, until heated through, about 1 minute. Spoon over chicken.

♥ Each serving with chicken: About 282 calories, 38g protein, 22g carbohydrate, 4g total fat (1g saturated), 82mg cholesterol, 1,086mg sodium.

Chinese Ginger Sauce

After removing chicken, reduce heat to medium. Add **1 teaspoon vegetable oil** to skillet. Add **1 red pepper,** thinly sliced, and cook until tender-crisp. Add **½ cup water, 2 tablespoons soy sauce, 2 tablespoons seasoned rice vinegar,** and **1 tablespoon grated, peeled fresh ginger.** Heat to boiling; boil 1 minute. Sprinkle with **2 green onions,** chopped. Spoon over chicken.

♥ Each serving with chicken: About 195 calories, 34g protein, 4g carbohydrate, 4g total fat (1g saturated), 82mg cholesterol, 757mg sodium.

Provençal Sauce

After removing chicken, reduce heat to medium. Add **1 teaspoon olive or vegetable oil** to skillet. Add **1 medium onion,** chopped, and cook, stirring, until tender. Stir in **1 can (14½ ounces) Italian-style stewed tomatoes, ½ cup pitted ripe olives,** each cut in half, **1 tablespoon drained capers,** and **¼ cup water.** Cook, stirring, until heated through, about 1 minute. Spoon over chicken.

♥ Each serving with chicken: About 253 calories, 35g protein, 11g carbohydrate, 7g total fat (1g saturated), 82mg cholesterol, 785mg sodium.

Creamy Mushroom Sauce

After removing chicken, add **1 teaspoon vegetable oil** to skillet. Add **10 ounces mushrooms,** trimmed and sliced, **1 medium onion,** thinly sliced, and **¾ teaspoon salt.** Cook, stirring, until vegetables are golden brown and tender. Reduce heat to low; stir in **½ cup light sour cream** and **¼ cup water;** heat through (do not boil). Spoon over chicken.

❤ Each serving with chicken: About 260 calories, 37g protein, 9g carbohydrate, 8g total fat (3g saturated), 92mg cholesterol, 548mg sodium.

Dijon Sauce

After removing chicken, add **½ cup half-and-half or light cream, 2 tablespoons Dijon mustard with seeds,** and **¾ cup seedless red or green grapes,** each cut in half, to skillet. Cook over low heat, stirring to blend flavors, until sauce has thickened, about 1 minute. Spoon over chicken.

❤ Each serving with chicken: About 234 calories, 34g protein, 7g carbohydrate, 7g total fat (3g saturated), 93mg cholesterol, 285mg sodium.

New Chicken Cordon Bleu

A zesty balsamic pan sauce adds a quick flavor boost.

🕐 Prep: 10 minutes   Cook: 20 minutes

1	tablespoon butter or margarine
4	small skinless, boneless chicken breast halves (1 pound)
½	cup chicken broth
2	tablespoons balsamic vinegar
⅛	teaspoon coarsely ground black pepper
4	thin slices cooked ham (2 ounces)
4	thin slices part-skim mozzarella cheese (2 ounces)
1	bag (5 to 6 ounces) prewashed baby spinach

1. In nonstick 12-inch skillet, melt butter over medium-high heat. Add chicken and cook until golden brown, about 6 minutes. Turn chicken over and reduce heat to medium; cover and cook until chicken loses its pink color throughout, about 6 minutes longer.

2. Increase heat to medium-high. Stir in broth, vinegar, and pepper; cook, uncovered, 1 minute. Remove skillet from heat; top each breast half with ham slice, then cheese slice. Cover skillet until cheese melts, about 3 minutes.

3. Arrange spinach on warm platter. With spatula, arrange chicken on top of spinach; drizzle with balsamic mixture. Makes 4 main-dish servings.

Each serving: About 224 calories, 34g protein, 2g carbohydrate, 8g total fat (4g saturated), 90mg cholesterol, 535mg sodium.

Szechwan Chicken

Serve this stir-fry over rice or Asian rice noodles.

🕐 Prep: 20 minutes   Cook: 10 minutes

1	pound skinless, boneless chicken breast halves
2	tablespoons soy sauce
2	tablespoons dry sherry
2	teaspoons cornstarch
2	teaspoons grated, peeled fresh ginger
¼	teaspoon sugar
¼	teaspoon crushed red pepper
2	tablespoons vegetable oil
6	green onions, cut into 2-inch pieces
1	green pepper, cut into ½-inch pieces
1	red pepper, cut into ½-inch pieces
¼	cup dry-roasted unsalted peanuts

1. With knife held in slanting position, almost parallel to cutting surface, cut each chicken breast half crosswise into ⅛-inch-thick slices. In medium bowl, combine soy sauce, sherry, cornstarch, ginger, sugar, and crushed red pepper; add chicken, tossing to coat.

2. In 12-inch skillet, heat 1 tablespoon oil over medium-high heat until very hot. Add green onions and red and green peppers and cook, stirring frequently (stir-frying), until vegetables are tender-crisp, 2 to 3 minutes. With slotted spoon, transfer vegetables to bowl.

3. Increase heat to high and add remaining 1 tablespoon oil to skillet; heat until very hot. Add chicken mixture and stir-fry until chicken loses its pink color throughout, 2 to 3 minutes. Return vegetables to skillet; heat through. To serve, transfer chicken and vegetables to warm platter and sprinkle with peanuts. Makes 4 main-dish servings.

Each serving: About 277 calories, 30g protein, 9g carbohydrate, 13g total fat (2g saturated), 66mg cholesterol, 594mg sodium.

Thai Chicken with Basil

The essence of Thai cooking, the blending of cool and hot flavors, such as cilantro, basil, ginger, garlic, and chiles, lends an exotic touch to this stir-fry.

Prep: 20 minutes plus marinating **Cook: 10 minutes**

1	pound skinless, boneless chicken breast halves
3	tablespoons Asian fish sauce (nuoc nam, page 31)
1	tablespoon soy sauce
1	tablespoon brown sugar
2	teaspoons vegetable oil
1	large onion (12 ounces), cut into ¼-inch-thick slices
2	red or green chiles (serrano or jalapeño), seeded and cut into matchstick strips
2	teaspoons minced, peeled fresh ginger
2	garlic cloves, crushed with garlic press
1½	cups loosely packed fresh basil leaves

1. With knife held in slanting position, almost parallel to cutting surface, cut each chicken breast half crosswise into ¼-inch-thick slices. In medium bowl, combine fish sauce, soy sauce, and brown sugar; add chicken slices, tossing to coat. Let marinate 5 minutes.

2. In nonstick 12-inch skillet, heat oil over medium-high heat until very hot. Add chicken with marinade and cook, stirring frequently (stir-frying), until chicken loses its pink color throughout, 3 to 4 minutes. With slotted spoon, transfer chicken to bowl.

3. Add onion to marinade remaining in skillet and cook, stir-frying, until tender-crisp, about 4 minutes. Stir in chiles, ginger, and garlic; cook 1 minute longer.

4. Return chicken to skillet; heat through. Stir in basil leaves just before serving. Makes 4 main-dish servings.

♥ Each serving: About 238 calories, 31g protein, 16g carbohydrate, 5g total fat (1g saturated), 66mg cholesterol, 784mg sodium.

Thai Chicken with Basil

Southern Fried Chicken

Here it is—our favorite recipe for this all-time classic. Mashed potatoes or biscuits are a must.

Prep: 15 minutes
Cook: 20 minutes per batch plus 8 minutes for gravy

4	cups vegetable oil
1½	cups milk
2	cups all-purpose flour
1¾	teaspoons salt
1	teaspoon baking powder
¾	teaspoon ground black pepper
2	chickens (3 pounds each), each cut into 8 pieces
1	can (14½ ounces) chicken broth or 1¾ cups Chicken Broth (page 84)

1. In 12-inch skillet, heat oil over medium heat to 350°F on deep-fat thermometer. Meanwhile, pour ½ cup milk into pie plate; on waxed paper, combine 1¾ cups flour, 1 teaspoon salt, baking powder, and ½ teaspoon pepper. Dip chicken in milk, then coat well with flour mixture. Repeat, dipping and coating chicken twice.

2. Carefully place one-third of chicken pieces, skin side up, in hot oil. Cook until underside of chicken is golden brown, about 5 minutes. Reduce heat to low and cook 5 minutes longer. With spatula, loosen chicken from skillet bottom. Turn chicken skin side down. Increase heat to medium-high and cook until skin side of chicken is golden brown, about 5 minutes. Reduce heat to low and cook until juices run clear when thickest part of chicken is pierced with tip of knife, about 5 minutes longer. With spatula, transfer chicken pieces, skin side up, to paper towels to drain; keep warm. Repeat with remaining chicken.

3. Prepare gravy: Spoon 2 tablespoons oil from skillet into 2-quart saucepan. Over medium heat, with wooden spoon, stir remaining ¼ cup flour into oil until blended. Cook, stirring constantly, until flour is lightly browned. Gradually stir in remaining 1 cup milk, broth, remaining ¾ teaspoon salt, and remaining ¼ teaspoon pepper; continue cooking, stirring constantly, until gravy has thickened and boils. (Makes 2⅔ cups gravy.) Serve gravy with chicken. Makes 8 main-dish servings.

Each serving: About 657 calories, 46g protein, 26g carbohydrate, 40g total fat (9g saturated), 138mg cholesterol, 942mg sodium.

Broiled Chicken Teriyaki

Just brush our fresh orange-ginger teriyaki sauce over the chicken as it broils, then sit back and accept the compliments.

Prep: 15 minutes   Broil: 45 minutes

⅓	cup reduced-sodium soy sauce
2	tablespoons vegetable oil
1	tablespoon dry sherry
1	tablespoon minced, peeled fresh ginger
2	teaspoons freshly grated orange peel
1	small garlic clove, finely chopped
¼	teaspoon crushed red pepper
1	chicken (3 pounds), cut into quarters
1	large green onion, finely chopped

1. Preheat broiler. In small bowl, combine soy sauce, oil, sherry, ginger, orange peel, garlic, and crushed red pepper.

2. Place chicken, skin side down, in greased broiling pan without rack. Brush top of chicken with some soy-sauce mixture. Place pan in broiler 8 to 10 inches from heat source; broil chicken 25 minutes.

3. Turn chicken skin side up. Broil, brushing with remaining soy-sauce mixture during last 10 minutes of broiling, until juices run clear when thickest part of chicken is pierced with tip of knife, 20 to 25 minutes. Sprinkle chicken with green onion before serving. Makes 4 main-dish servings.

Each serving: About 436 calories, 42g protein, 3g carbohydrate, 27g total fat (7g saturated), 132mg cholesterol, 916mg sodium.

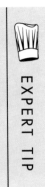

Whenever you prepare poultry (chicken, duck, quail, etc.), cut off the wing tips. Place them in a heavy-duty ziptight plastic bag and freeze, adding more wing tips as you get them. This way you'll always have the ingredients for a quick stock.

ANNE ROSENZWEIG
CHEF/OWNER, THE LOBSTER CLUB, NEW YORK CITY

EXPERT TIP

Jamaican Jerk Chicken Kabobs

Originally, jerk seasoning was only used to season pork shoulder, which was "jerked" apart into shreds before serving. Nowadays, this very popular power-packed seasoning rub is enjoyed on fish and chicken as well.

Prep: 15 minutes plus marinating	*Broil: 10 minutes*

2	green onions, chopped
1	jalapeño chile, seeded and minced
1	tablespoon minced, peeled fresh ginger
2	tablespoons white wine vinegar
2	tablespoons Worcestershire sauce
3	teaspoons vegetable oil
1	teaspoon ground allspice
1	teaspoon dried thyme
1/2	teaspoon plus 1/8 teaspoon salt
1	pound skinless, boneless chicken breast halves, cut into 12 pieces
1	red pepper, cut into 1-inch pieces
1	green pepper, cut into 1-inch pieces

1. In blender or in food processor with knife blade attached, process green onions, jalapeño, ginger, vinegar, Worcestershire, 2 teaspoons oil, allspice, thyme, and 1/2 teaspoon salt until paste forms.

2. Place chicken in small bowl or in ziptight plastic bag and add green-onion mixture, turning to coat chicken. Cover bowl or seal bag and refrigerate chicken 1 hour to marinate.

3. Meanwhile, in small bowl, toss red and green peppers with remaining 1 teaspoon oil and remaining 1/8 teaspoon salt.

4. Preheat broiler. On four metal skewers, alternately thread chicken and pepper pieces.

5. Place kabobs on rack in broiling pan. Brush kabobs with any remaining marinade. Place pan in broiler at closest position to heat source. Broil kabobs 5 minutes; turn and broil until chicken loses its pink color throughout, about 5 minutes longer. Makes 4 main-dish servings.

♥ Each serving: About 181 calories, 27g protein, 6g carbohydrate, 5g total fat (1g saturated), 66mg cholesterol, 525mg sodium.

Jamaican Jerk Chicken Kabobs

Citrus-Sage Chicken

Sage makes an excellent addition to a garden or window box. It doesn't require much attention and grows more lush and beautiful each year. At summer's end, hang it upside down in bunches in a cool dark place to dry.

Prep: 25 minutes plus marinating	*Grill: 30 minutes*

2	large oranges
2	large lemons
1/4	cup chopped fresh sage plus additional leaves
2	tablespoons olive oil
2	teaspoons salt
3/4	teaspoon coarsely ground black pepper
2	chickens (3 1/2 pounds each), each cut into 8 pieces and skin removed from all but wings

1. From oranges, grate 1 tablespoon peel and squeeze 3 tablespoons juice. From lemons, grate 1 tablespoon peel and squeeze 3 tablespoons juice.

2. In large bowl, with wire whisk, combine orange and lemon peels and juices, chopped sage, oil, salt, and pepper. Add chicken, turning to coat. Cover and refrigerate chicken 2 hours to marinate, turning 3 or 4 times.

3. Prepare grill. Arrange chicken, meat side down, on grill over medium heat and grill 20 minutes. Turn chicken and grill until juices run clear when thickest part of chicken is pierced with tip of knife, 10 to 15 minutes longer.

4. To serve, arrange chicken on warm platter; garnish with sage leaves. Makes 8 main-dish servings.

Each serving: About 307 calories, 41g protein, 2g carbohydrate, 14g total fat (3g saturated), 127mg cholesterol, 705mg sodium.

Tarragon Broiled Chicken

Prized for its delicate licoricelike aroma and flavor, tarragon raises broiled chicken to new heights.

Prep: 5 minutes	Broil: 40 minutes
¾	teaspoon dried tarragon, crushed
¾	teaspoon salt
⅛	teaspoon coarsely ground black pepper
1	chicken (3 pounds), cut into quarters
1	tablespoon butter or margarine, melted
1	tablespoon fresh lemon juice

1. Preheat broiler. In cup, combine tarragon, salt, and pepper; sprinkle on chicken.

2. Place chicken, skin side down, in broiling pan without rack. Brush chicken with melted butter and sprinkle with lemon juice. Place pan in broiler 8 to 10 inches from heat source; broil chicken 5 minutes. Baste with melted butter in broiling pan; broil 15 minutes longer. Turn chicken skin side up; broil, basting occasionally with pan drippings, until juices run clear when thickest part of chicken is pierced with tip of knife, 20 to 25 minutes. Makes 4 main-dish servings.

Each serving: About 326 calories, 34g protein, 1g carbohydrate, 20g total fat (7g saturated), 118mg cholesterol, 568mg sodium.

All-American Barbecued Chicken

Our traditional-style barbecue sauce is perfect with grilled chicken, beef, or spareribs. We like to remove the skin from the chicken: It reduces the chance of flareups.

Prep: 1 hour	Grill: 40 minutes
2	tablespoons olive oil
1	large onion (12 ounces), chopped
2	cans (15 ounces each) tomato sauce
1	cup red wine vinegar
½	cup light (mild) molasses
¼	cup Worcestershire sauce
⅓	cup packed brown sugar
¾	teaspoon ground red pepper (cayenne)
2	chickens (3½ pounds each), each cut into quarters and skin removed from all but wings, if desired

1. In nonstick 10-inch skillet, heat oil over medium heat. Add onion and cook until tender, about 5 minutes. Stir in tomato sauce, vinegar, molasses, Worcestershire, brown sugar, and ground red pepper; heat to boiling over high heat. Reduce heat to medium-low and cook, stirring occasionally, until sauce has thickened slightly, about 45 minutes. (Makes about 3½ cups sauce.) If not using sauce right away, cover and refrigerate to use within 2 weeks.

2. Prepare grill. Reserve 1½ cups of sauce to serve with chicken. Arrange chicken on grill over medium heat and grill, turning once, 20 to 25 minutes. Generously brush chicken with some of remaining barbecue sauce and grill, brushing frequently with sauce and turning chicken often, until juices run clear when thickest part of chicken is pierced with tip of knife, about 20 minutes longer. Serve with reserved sauce. Makes 8 main-dish servings.

Each serving without additional sauce, with skin: About 518 calories, 49g protein, 21g carbohydrate, 26g total fat (7g saturated), 154mg cholesterol, 564mg sodium.

Each serving without additional sauce, without skin: About 370 calories, 42g protein, 21g carbohydrate, 13g total fat (3g saturated), 127mg cholesterol, 543mg sodium.

Each ¼ cup sauce: About 99 calories, 1g protein, 20g carbohydrate, 2g total fat (0g saturated), 0mg cholesterol, 422mg sodium.

Ginger-Grilled Chicken for a Crowd

When you have a crowd to feed at a backyard bash, try this honey-and-ginger party pleaser.

Prep: 10 minutes plus overnight to marinate
Grill/Broil: 35 minutes

1¼	cups soy sauce
¾	cup honey
¼	cup fresh lemon juice
2	tablespoons vegetable oil
2	tablespoons minced, peeled fresh ginger
2	garlic cloves, crushed with garlic press
3	chickens (3 pounds each), each cut into quarters

1. In small bowl, combine soy sauce, honey, lemon juice, oil, ginger, and garlic until well blended. Divide chicken and marinade among three ziptight plastic bags, turning to coat chicken. Seal bags, pressing out as much air as possible. Refrigerate chicken overnight to marinate.

2. Next day, prepare grill. Remove chicken from marinade; discard marinade. Arrange chicken on grill over medium heat and grill until golden brown, about 5 minutes per side. Arrange chicken around perimeter of grill (where it is cooler); cover and grill until juices run clear when thickest part of chicken is pierced with tip of knife, about 25 minutes longer.

To broil in oven: Marinate chicken as in Step 1. Preheat broiler. Place chicken, skin side down, on rack in large broiling pan. (Chicken may have to be broiled in batches.) Place pan in broiler about 8 to 10 inches from heat source. Broil chicken until golden brown, about 20 minutes. Turn chicken skin side up; broil chicken, brushing occasionally with marinade, until juices run clear when thickest part of chicken is pierced with tip of knife, about 20 minutes longer. Makes 12 main-dish servings.

Each serving: About 410 calories, 42g protein, 10g carbohydrate, 22g total fat (6g saturated), 132mg cholesterol, 988mg sodium.

Tandoori-Style Grilled Chicken

The appealingly spicy yogurt marinade keeps skinless chicken moist and succulent and provides lots of flavor without extra fat.

Prep: 10 minutes plus marinating   Grill: 20 minutes

1	tablespoon paprika, preferably sweet Hungarian
½	teaspoon ground cinnamon
½	teaspoon ground coriander
½	teaspoon ground cumin
¼	teaspoon ground cardamom
1	container (8 ounces) plain lowfat yogurt
2	tablespoons fresh lemon juice
1	tablespoon olive oil
½	small onion, cut into quarters
2	garlic cloves
1	tablespoon sliced pickled jalapeño chile or diced fresh jalapeño chile with seeds
1	tablespoon sliced, peeled fresh ginger
½	teaspoon salt
1	chicken (3½ pounds), cut into 8 pieces and skin removed from all but wings
	lemon wedges (optional)

1. In 6-inch skillet, heat paprika, cinnamon, coriander, cumin, and cardamom over low heat until very fragrant, about 3 minutes. Transfer to blender with yogurt, lemon juice, oil, onion, garlic, jalapeño, ginger, and salt; puree until smooth.

2. Make several ¼-inch-deep slashes in each chicken piece. Place chicken in ziptight plastic bag, pour in yogurt mixture and turn to coat the chicken. Seal bag, pressing out as much air as possible. Refrigerate chicken 1 to 3 hours to marinate, turning once or twice.

3. Lightly grease grill rack. Prepare grill. Arrange chicken on grill over medium heat and grill, turning chicken every 5 minutes, until juices run clear when thickest part of chicken is pierced with tip of knife, 20 to 25 minutes. Transfer to warm platter and serve with lemon wedges, if desired. Makes 4 main-dish servings.

♥ *Each serving: About 301 calories, 44g protein, 7g carbohydrate, 10g total fat (2g saturated), 136mg cholesterol, 466mg sodium.*

Lemon-Rosemary Chicken Breasts

This quick, lowfat grilled chicken has plenty of flavor. Grill some zucchini, onions, and red peppers alongside, if desired.

Prep: 10 minutes   Grill: 10 minutes

2	lemons
1	tablespoon chopped fresh rosemary or $\frac{1}{2}$ teaspoon dried rosemary
1	garlic clove, finely chopped
2	teaspoons olive oil
$\frac{1}{2}$	teaspoon salt
$\frac{1}{4}$	teaspoon coarsely ground black pepper
4	small skinless, boneless chicken breast halves (1 pound)

1. Prepare grill. From 1 lemon, grate 2 teaspoons peel. From $\frac{1}{2}$ lemon, cut thin slices; reserve for garnish. Squeeze juice from remaining 3 lemon halves into medium bowl. Stir in lemon peel, rosemary, garlic, oil, salt, and pepper.

2. Add chicken breast halves to bowl, turning to coat with lemon-juice mixture.

3. Arrange chicken on grill over medium heat and grill, brushing with remaining lemon-juice mixture in bowl, 5 minutes. Turn chicken and grill until chicken loses its pink color throughout, about 5 minutes longer. Garnish with lemon slices. Makes 4 main-dish servings.

♥ Each serving: About 153 calories, 26g protein, 3g carbohydrate, 4g total fat (1g saturated), 66mg cholesterol, 364mg sodium.

Spicy Buttermilk-Grilled Chicken

Buttermilk is a welcome addition to marinades. Its natural acidity tenderizes and adds tangy flavor to meat and poultry. Best of all, it turns grilled food a luscious golden brown.

Prep: 5 minutes plus marinating   Grill: 20 minutes

$\frac{1}{2}$	cup buttermilk
1	tablespoon hot pepper sauce
1	teaspoon paprika
$\frac{1}{2}$	teaspoon salt
1	chicken ($3\frac{1}{2}$ pounds), cut into 8 pieces and skin removed from all but wings

1. In ziptight plastic bag, combine buttermilk, hot pepper sauce, paprika, and salt. Add chicken, turning to coat. Seal bag, pressing out as much air as possible. Refrigerate chicken 1 hour to marinate, turning once.

2. Prepare grill. Remove chicken from bag; discard marinade. Arrange chicken on grill over medium heat and grill, turning occasionally, until juices run clear when thickest part of chicken is pierced with tip of knife, about 20 to 25 minutes. Makes 4 main-dish servings.

♥ Each serving: About 222 calories, 39g protein, 1g carbohydrate, 6g total fat (2g saturated), 125mg cholesterol, 454mg sodium.

Grilled Chicken Breasts with Cumin, Coriander, and Lime

A Mexican-inspired blend of spices and fresh lime juice adds bold flavor to boneless chicken.

Prep: 10 minutes   Grill: 10 minutes

3	tablespoons fresh lime juice
2	tablespoons olive oil
1	teaspoon ground cumin
1	teaspoon ground coriander
1	teaspoon sugar
1	teaspoon salt
$\frac{1}{8}$	teaspoon ground red pepper (cayenne)
4	medium skinless, boneless chicken breast halves ($1\frac{1}{4}$ pounds)
1	tablespoon chopped fresh cilantro leaves

1. Prepare grill. In large bowl, combine lime juice, oil, cumin, coriander, sugar, salt, and ground red pepper. Add chicken, turning to coat.

2. Arrange chicken on grill over medium heat and grill 5 to 6 minutes per side, brushing with any remaining cumin mixture halfway through cooking, until chicken loses its pink color throughout.

3. Transfer chicken to warm platter and sprinkle with cilantro. Makes 4 main-dish servings.

Each serving: About 225 calories, 33g protein, 2g carbohydrate, 9g total fat (1g saturated), 82mg cholesterol, 676mg sodium.

North Carolina–Style Barbecued Chicken

In North Carolina, where barbecue is taken very seriously, the sauce you prepare depends upon your locale. In the northeastern part of the state, the sauce is made with vinegar and pepper flakes. In the south, a vinegar-and-mustard-based sauce is a must, and in the west, a tangy, tomato-based blend is what the locals revere.

Prep: 15 minutes   Grill: 25 minutes

1	can (15 ounces) tomato sauce
1/3	cup cider vinegar
3	tablespoons honey
2	tablespoons olive oil
1	teaspoon dry mustard
3/4	teaspoon salt
3/4	teaspoon ground black pepper
1/4	teaspoon liquid smoke
1	chicken (3 1/2 pounds), cut into 8 pieces and skin removed from all but wings

1. Prepare grill. In nonreactive 2-quart saucepan, heat tomato sauce, vinegar, honey, oil, dry mustard, 1/2 teaspoon salt, 1/2 teaspoon pepper, and liquid smoke over medium heat to boiling. Boil 2 minutes. Remove from heat. (Makes about 2 cups sauce.) Reserve 1 cup sauce to serve with chicken.

2. Sprinkle chicken with remaining 1/4 teaspoon each salt and pepper. Arrange chicken on grill over medium heat and grill, turning occasionally, 15 minutes. Continue to grill, turning and brushing chicken every 2 minutes with barbecue sauce, until juices run clear when thickest part of chicken is pierced with tip of knife, 10 to 15 minutes longer. Serve with reserved barbecue sauce. Makes 4 main-dish servings.

Each serving without extra sauce: About 491 calories, 49g protein, 11g carbohydrate, 27g total fat (7g saturated), 154mg cholesterol, 685mg sodium.

Each 1/4 cup sauce: About 73 calories, 1g protein, 11g carbohydrate, 4g total fat (0g saturated), 0mg cholesterol, 540mg sodium.

Portuguese Mixed Grill

Here's a colorful and tasty summertime grill. In Portuguese cooking, a vinegar marinade is used to tenderize tough cuts of meat and poultry. We like it for its deliciously zesty flavor, since our chicken rarely needs tenderizing.

Prep: 30 minutes plus marinating   Grill: 25 minutes

1/4	cup red wine vinegar
2	tablespoons olive oil
2	tablespoons chopped fresh oregano or 1 teaspoon dried oregano
1	teaspoon salt
1/2	teaspoon coarsely ground black pepper
8	medium bone-in skinless chicken thighs (1 3/4 pounds), fat removed
3	medium red onions, each cut into 6 wedges
12	ounces fully cooked chorizo sausage links, each cut crosswise in half
2/3	cup assorted olives such as Kalamata, cracked green, and picholine

1. In bowl, combine vinegar, 1 tablespoon oil, 1 tablespoon oregano, salt, and pepper. Add chicken, turning to coat. Cover and refrigerate 30 minutes to marinate, no longer.

2. Meanwhile, thread onion wedges onto three long metal skewers.

3. Prepare grill. Place onion skewers on grill over medium heat; brush with remaining 1 tablespoon oil and grill 5 minutes. Arrange chicken on grill and grill, turning onions and chicken once, until onions are tender and juices run clear when thickest part of chicken is pierced with tip of knife, about 20 minutes longer.

4. About 10 minutes before onions and chicken are done, place chorizo pieces on grill and cook, turning chorizo occasionally, until lightly browned and heated through.

5. To serve, remove onion wedges from skewers and arrange on warm platter with chicken and chorizo. Scatter olives on top and sprinkle with remaining 1 tablespoon oregano. Makes 6 main-dish servings.

Each serving: About 482 calories, 34g protein, 11g carbohydrate, 33g total fat (10g saturated), 130mg cholesterol, 1,495mg sodium.

Chicken with Tomato-Olive Relish

Puttanesca, a piquant Italian pasta sauce, is the concept behind grilled chicken breasts topped with a no-cook tomato relish.

Prep: 15 minutes   Grill: 10 minutes

2	medium tomatoes, chopped
¼	cup Kalamata olives, pitted and coarsely chopped plus additional whole olives
2	tablespoons finely chopped red onion
2	tablespoons capers, drained
3	teaspoons olive oil
1	teaspoon red wine vinegar
4	small skinless, boneless chicken breast halves (1 pound)
¼	teaspoon salt
¼	teaspoon coarsely ground black pepper

1. Prepare grill. In small bowl, combine tomatoes, chopped olives, red onion, capers, 1 teaspoon oil, and vinegar.

2. In medium bowl, sprinkle chicken with salt and pepper and drizzle with remaining 2 teaspoons oil.

3. Arrange chicken on grill over medium heat and grill until chicken loses its pink color throughout, 5 to 6 minutes per side. Serve chicken topped with tomato-olive relish and garnished with whole olives. Makes 4 main-dish servings.

Each serving: About 198 calories, 27g protein, 5g carbohydrate, 7g total fat (1g saturated), 66mg cholesterol, 565mg sodium.

Grilled Chicken Breasts Saltimbocca

In Italian, saltimbocca *means "jump in your mouth" and these irresistible prosciutto-and-sage-topped chicken breasts will do just that. One note of caution: Don't slice the prosciutto paper-thin, or it could burn.*

Prep: 5 minutes   Grill: 10 minutes

4	medium skinless, boneless chicken breast halves (1¼ pounds)
⅛	teaspoon salt
⅛	teaspoon ground black pepper
12	fresh sage leaves
4	large slices prosciutto (4 ounces)

1. Prepare grill. Sprinkle chicken with salt and pepper. Place 3 sage leaves on each breast half. Place 1 prosciutto slice on top of each breast half, tucking in edges if necessary; secure with toothpicks.

2. Arrange chicken, prosciutto side down, on grill over medium heat and grill 5 to 6 minutes. Turn and grill until chicken loses its pink color throughout, 5 to 6 minutes longer. Makes 4 main-dish servings.

Each serving: About 223 calories, 41g protein, 0g carbohydrate, 6g total fat (1g saturated), 105mg cholesterol, 690mg sodium.

Grilled Chicken Breasts Saltimbocca

Apricot-Ginger Chicken

Grill up a batch of these people pleasers and serve with your favorite potato salad and lots of creamy cole slaw.

Prep: 15 minutes	Grill: 35 minutes
2	green onions, chopped
1/2	cup apricot preserves
1/3	cup ketchup
2	tablespoons cider vinegar
1	tablespoon plus 1 teaspoon soy sauce
1	tablespoon plus 1 teaspoon grated, peeled fresh ginger
6	large chicken leg quarters (about 3¾ pounds)

1. Prepare grill. In small bowl, combine green onions, apricot preserves, ketchup, vinegar, soy sauce, and ginger.

2. Arrange chicken on grill over medium heat; grill until golden brown, about 5 minutes per side. Arrange chicken around perimeter of grill (where it is cooler); cover and grill until juices run clear when thickest part of chicken is pierced with knife, 25 to 30 minutes longer. During last 10 minutes, brush with apricot mixture. Makes 6 main-dish servings.

Each serving: About 408 calories, 37g protein, 22g carbohydrate, 19g total fat (5g saturated), 129mg cholesterol, 518mg sodium.

GROUND CHICKEN AND GROUND TURKEY

To answer the public's demand for reduced-fat ground meats, poultry producers now offer both ground turkey and ground chicken. Each type of ground poultry has a different fat content, and since fat provides moisture and flavor, expect different results when cooking with different varieties. For example, lean ground turkey breast works well when cooked in a liquid (think along the lines of turkey meatballs in tomato sauce), but it is less successful when made into turkey burgers, where its lack of fat may make the burgers dry.

- Ground chicken: Made from white and dark chicken meat with skin, its fat content is about 10 percent. It is an excellent all-purpose ground poultry, but any recipe prepared using this product will have a slightly softer texture than the same dish prepared with ground turkey.
- Ground turkey breast meat: 99 percent lean; this is simply white turkey breast meat, ground without any skin or fat.
- Ground turkey: White and dark turkey meat; ground with the skin, which adds moisture. It has about 7 percent fat, which is similar to the fat content of ground beef sirloin.
- Ground turkey dark meat: Usually found in the frozen section of the supermarket, packed in plastic tubes. It contains about 15 percent fat. Ground dark turkey meat may be less expensive, but it has the same fat content as ground beef round, so it doesn't offer much in the way of fat reduction.

Chicken Shepherd's Pie

Shepherd's pie was originally created as a way to utilize Sunday supper leftovers. We've lightened the ingredients and topped it off with a mantle of creamy smooth, chive-flecked potatoes.

Prep: 45 minutes	Bake: 20 minutes
2	pounds all-purpose potatoes (6 medium), peeled and cut into 1-inch pieces
2	tablespoons vegetable oil
2	carrots, peeled and finely chopped
1	large onion (12 ounces), finely chopped
1	large red pepper, finely chopped
2	tablespoons butter or margarine
1	teaspoon salt
3/4	cup milk
2	tablespoons chopped fresh chives or green-onion tops
10	ounces mushrooms, trimmed and thickly sliced
1¼	cups chicken broth
1	tablespoon all-purpose flour
1½	pounds ground chicken meat
1/4	teaspoon coarsely ground black pepper
1/4	teaspoon dried thyme
2	tablespoons ketchup
1	tablespoon Worcestershire sauce

1. In 3-quart saucepan, combine potatoes and enough *water* to cover; heat to boiling over high heat. Reduce heat; cover and simmer until potatoes are tender, about 15 minutes.

2. Meanwhile, in 12-inch skillet, heat 1 tablespoon oil over medium-high heat. Add carrots and cook 5 minutes. Add onion and red pepper and cook, stirring occasionally, until vegetables are tender and lightly browned, about 10 minutes longer. With slotted spoon, transfer vegetables to bowl.

Chicken Shepherd's Pie

3. When potatoes are tender, drain. Mash potatoes in saucepan with butter and ½ teaspoon salt. Gradually add milk; mash until mixture is smooth and well blended. Stir in chives; set aside.

4. In same skillet, heat remaining 1 tablespoon oil over medium-high heat. Add mushrooms and cook until well browned, about 10 minutes. Transfer to bowl with vegetables.

5. In 2-cup measuring cup, blend broth and flour until smooth; set aside.

6. Preheat oven to 400°F. In same skillet, cook ground chicken, black pepper, thyme, and remaining ½ teaspoon salt over high heat, stirring occasionally, until chicken is lightly browned and any liquid in skillet has evaporated, 7 to 10 minutes. Stir in ketchup, Worcestershire, cooked vegetables, and broth mixture. Cook, stirring constantly, until liquid has thickened and boils, 3 to 5 minutes.

7. Spoon chicken mixture into shallow 2-quart casserole; top with mashed potatoes. Place casserole on foil-lined cookie sheet to catch any overflow during baking. Bake until potato topping is lightly browned, 20 to 25 minutes. Makes 6 main-dish servings.

Each serving: About 415 calories, 26g protein, 33g carbohydrate, 20g total fat (6g saturated), 109mg cholesterol, 848mg sodium.

Texas Chicken Burgers

The addition of grated zucchini and carrots makes these lowfat chicken burgers light and moist.

Prep: 15 minutes   Cook: 12 minutes

1	pound ground chicken meat
2	green onions, chopped
1	small zucchini, grated
1	carrot, peeled and grated
1	tablespoon chili powder
¾	teaspoon salt
¼	teaspoon ground cumin
⅛	teaspoon ground red pepper (cayenne)
	nonstick cooking spray

1. In medium bowl, with hands, combine ground chicken, green onions, zucchini, carrot, chili powder, salt, cumin, and ground red pepper just until well blended but not overmixed.

2. On waxed paper, shape ground chicken mixture into four 3½-inch patties, handling meat as little as possible.

3. Grease 12-inch skillet with cooking spray. Heat over medium-high heat until very hot. With spatula, transfer patties to skillet. Cook 6 minutes; turn patties and cook until no longer pink inside, about 6 minutes longer. Makes 4 main-dish servings.

Each serving: About 198 calories, 21g protein, 4g carbohydrate, 11g total fat (3g saturated), 94mg cholesterol, 556mg sodium.

Leaner Meatballs

Enjoy some of these tasty Italian-style meatballs with your favorite pasta and sauce, and freeze the rest. Let them cool in the pan on a wire rack, then transfer the meatballs to a jelly-roll pan and place in the freezer until frozen. Transfer them to large ziptight plastic bags and freeze for up to one month.

Prep: 25 minutes   Bake: 15 minutes

1/3	cup water
1 1/2	cups fresh bread crumbs (about 3 slices firm white bread)
1	pound lean ground beef
1	pound lean ground turkey meat
2	large egg whites
1/3	cup freshly grated Romano or Parmesan cheese
3	tablespoons grated onion
2	tablespoons chopped fresh parsley
1	garlic clove, minced
1	teaspoon salt
1/4	teaspoon coarsely ground black pepper

1. Preheat oven to 425°F. Line 15½" by 10½" jelly-roll pan with foil and lightly grease.

2. In large bowl, pour water over bread crumbs. With hands, toss until bread is evenly moistened. Add ground beef, ground turkey, egg whites, Romano, onion, parsley, garlic, salt, and pepper; with hands, combine just until well blended but not overmixed.

3. Shape mixture into twenty-four 2-inch meatballs (for easier shaping, use slightly wet hands), handling meat as little as possible. Arrange meatballs in prepared pan and bake until lightly browned and cooked through, 15 to 20 minutes. Makes 24 meatballs.

Each meatball: About 80 calories, 8g protein, 2g carbohydrate, 4g total fat (1g saturated), 44mg cholesterol, 166mg sodium.

Turkey Meat Loaf

Thickly slice any leftover meat loaf and place between slices of hearty bread that have been spread with mango chutney for the best brown-bag lunch ever.

Prep: 15 minutes   Bake: 1 hour

1	tablespoon olive oil
1	medium onion, finely chopped
2	garlic cloves, finely chopped
2	pounds ground turkey meat
2	large eggs
1	cup fresh bread crumbs (about 2 slices firm white bread)
1/4	cup milk
1/4	cup mango chutney, chopped
2	tablespoons ketchup
1 1/4	teaspoons salt
1/2	teaspoon dried sage

1. Preheat oven to 350°F. In 6-inch skillet, heat oil over medium heat. Add onion and garlic and cook, stirring frequently, until tender, about 5 minutes. Transfer to medium bowl; cool to room temperature.

2. Add ground turkey, eggs, bread crumbs, milk, chutney, ketchup, salt, and sage to bowl; combine just until well blended but not overmixed. Spoon mixture into 9" by 5" metal loaf pan; press down gently. Cover with foil and bake until meat thermometer inserted in center of meat loaf registers 170°F, about 1 hour. Cool in pan 10 minutes; turn out onto warm platter and slice. Makes 8 main-dish servings.

Each serving: About 261 calories, 23g protein, 14g carbohydrate, 12g total fat (3g saturated), 137mg cholesterol, 657mg sodium.

CORNISH HENS

These small birds, a crossbreed of the White Plymouth and Cornish chicken strains, weigh between 1½ and 1¾ pounds and yield two servings. For a bird small enough for a single serving, look for *poussin* at specialty butchers. Pronounced "poose-ahn," these small chickens weigh about 1 pound each. You can substitute *poussin* for Cornish hens in most recipes, but reduce the cooking time by about one-third.

Cornish Hens with Wild Rice and Mushroom Stuffing

With the tasty mushroom and wild rice mixture stuffed under the skin, these crispy little birds make a great company dinner. Serve with steamed or creamed spinach.

Prep: 1 hour	Roast: 50 minutes
	Wild Rice and Mushroom Stuffing (below)
4	Cornish hens (1½ pounds each)
¼	cup honey
2	tablespoons fresh lemon juice
2	tablespoons dry vermouth
½	teaspoon salt
¼	teaspoon dried thyme

1. Prepare Wild Rice and Mushroom Stuffing; set aside.

2. Preheat oven to 400°F. Remove giblets and necks from hens; reserve for another use. With poultry shears, cut each hen lengthwise in half. Rinse hen halves with cold running water; pat dry with paper towels.

3. With fingertips, carefully separate skin from meat on each hen half to form pocket; spoon some stuffing into each pocket. Place hens, skin side up, in two large roasting pans (17" by 11½").

4. In small bowl, combine honey, lemon juice, vermouth, salt, and thyme. Brush hens with some honey mixture. Roast hens, basting occasionally with remaining honey mixture and drippings in pan, until juices run clear when thickest part of thigh is pierced with tip of knife, about 50 minutes, rotating pans between upper and lower oven racks halfway through roasting. Makes 8 main-dish servings.

Each serving: About 521 calories, 37g protein, 30g carbohydrate, 28g total fat (8g saturated), 191mg cholesterol, 554mg sodium.

Wild Rice and Mushroom Stuffing

In 3-quart saucepan, melt **1 tablespoon butter or margarine** over medium heat; add **1 small onion,** finely chopped, and cook until tender, about 5 minutes. Add **1 pound mushrooms,** trimmed and chopped, and cook, stirring occasionally, until tender, about 10 minutes. Meanwhile, rinse **1 cup (6 ounces) wild rice;** drain. To mixture in saucepan, add wild rice, **1 can (14½ ounces) chicken broth or 1¾ cups Chicken Broth (page 84),** and ¼ **teaspoon salt;** heat to boiling over high heat. Reduce heat; cover and simmer until rice is tender and all liquid has been absorbed, 45 to 50 minutes. Stir in ¼ **cup chopped fresh parsley.** Makes 4 cups stuffing.

Molasses-Glazed Cornish Hens

During the sugar refining process, the juice extracted from the sugar is boiled until syrupy—the result is molasses. Light (mild) molasses has the lightest flavor and color.

Prep: 5 minutes plus marinating	Roast: 1 hour
2	Cornish hens (1½ pounds each)
1	teaspoon ground allspice
1	teaspoon dried thyme
½	teaspoon ground red pepper (cayenne)
¼	teaspoon ground ginger
¼	teaspoon salt
2	tablespoons light (mild) molasses

1. Remove giblets and necks from hens; reserve for another use. Rinse hens inside and out with cold running water and drain well; pat dry with paper towels.

2. In large bowl, combine allspice, thyme, ground red pepper, ginger, and salt. Add hens, turning to coat. Cover and refrigerate hens 2 hours to marinate.

3. Preheat oven to 375°F. With hens breast side up, lift wings up toward neck, then fold wing tips under back of hens so wings stay in place. Tie legs together with string.

4. Place hens, breast side up, on rack in small roasting pan (13" by 9") and roast 40 minutes. Brush with molasses and roast, basting twice, until hens are tender and juices run clear when thickest part of thigh is pierced with tip of knife, about 20 minutes longer. To serve, cut each hen lengthwise in half. Makes 4 main-dish servings.

Each serving: About 402 calories, 32g protein, 8g carbohydrate, 26g total fat (7g saturated), 187mg cholesterol, 239mg sodium.

Cornish Hens Milanese

Italians call the mix of lemon peel, garlic, and parsley gremolata.

Prep: 5 minutes   Roast: 50 minutes

2	Cornish hens (1½ pounds each)
3	tablespoons chopped fresh parsley
1	teaspoon extravirgin olive oil
¼	teaspoon salt
⅛	teaspoon ground black pepper
1	small garlic clove, minced
½	teaspoon freshly grated lemon peel

1. Preheat oven to 375°F. Remove giblets and necks from hens; reserve for another use. With poultry shears, cut each hen lengthwise in half. Rinse hen halves with cold running water; pat dry with paper towels.

2. In small bowl, combine 2 tablespoons parsley, oil, salt, and pepper. With fingertips, carefully separate skin from meat on each hen half; spread parsley mixture under skin. Place hens, skin side up, in large roasting pan (17" by 11½").

3. Roast hens, basting with drippings 3 times, until juices run clear when thickest part of thigh is pierced with tip of knife, about 50 minutes.

4. Arrange hens warm on platter. In cup, combine remaining 1 tablespoon parsley, garlic, and lemon peel; sprinkle over hens. Makes 4 main-dish servings.

Each serving: About 384 calories, 32g protein, 0g carbohydrate, 27g total fat (7g saturated), 187mg cholesterol, 236mg sodium.

Cornish Hens with Anise-Orange Glaze

Frequent basting gives these hens a lustrous sheen.

Prep: 10 minutes   Grill/Broil: 35 minutes

2	Cornish hens (1½ pounds each)
⅓	cup packed light brown sugar
⅓	cup red wine vinegar
3	tablespoons soy sauce
1	tablespoon vegetable oil
1	teaspoon anise seeds, crushed
½	teaspoon freshly grated orange peel

Cornish Hens Milanese

1. Prepare grill. Remove giblets and necks from hens; reserve for another use. With poultry shears, cut each hen lengthwise in half. Rinse hen halves with cold running water; pat dry with paper towels.

2. In small bowl, combine brown sugar, vinegar, soy sauce, oil, anise seeds, and orange peel. Arrange hens on grill over medium heat and grill, brushing frequently with glaze and turning hens often, until juices run clear when thickest part of thigh is pierced with tip of knife, 35 to 40 minutes.

To broil in oven: Preheat broiler. Prepare hens and glaze as above. Arrange hens, skin side down, on rack in broiling pan; broil, about 8 to 10 inches from heat source, until golden brown, about 20 minutes. Brush generously with some glaze; broil 2 to 3 minutes longer. Turn hens skin side up; broil, brushing frequently with glaze, until juices run clear when thickest part of thigh is pierced with tip of knife, about 15 minutes longer. Makes 4 main-dish servings.

Each serving: About 482 calories, 33g protein, 20g carbohydrate, 30g total fat (8g saturated), 187mg cholesterol, 870mg sodium.

TURKEY

Choose your turkey by size—there is no difference in flavor or texture between a tom (male) and a hen (female). Fresh birds are especially delicious, but if you choose to buy a frozen bird, be sure to allow enough time for thorough thawing. Farm-raised wild turkeys, found in specialty butcher shops, have a mildly gamy flavor and are never as big or as meaty as the supermarket variety.

Turkey Parts

Turkey parts are readily available and can be prepared in as many ways as chicken. Whole turkey breast is a good way to feed a crowd and makes tasty leftovers for sandwiches. Turkey drumsticks, both economical and tasty, are an excellent choice for a weeknight meal. Lean turkey cutlets (boneless sliced turkey breast) cook quickly and look elegant, but take care not to overcook them, or they will toughen and dry out.

Traditional Roast Turkey with Giblet Gravy

Here it is—the traditional Thanksgiving centerpiece. The chart on page 188 will tell you, in a flash, how much time you'll need to roast the perfect bird, no matter how small or how large.

Prep: 1 hour (not including stuffing)
Roast: 3 hours 45 minutes

	choice of stuffing (pages 244 to 248)
1	turkey (14 pounds)
1½	teaspoons salt
½	teaspoon coarsely ground black pepper
	Giblet Gravy (page 231)

1. Prepare desired stuffing; set aside.
2. Preheat oven to 325°F. Remove giblets and neck from turkey; reserve for making Giblet Gravy. Rinse turkey inside and out with cold running water and drain well; pat dry with paper towels.

3. Loosely spoon some stuffing into neck cavity. Fold neck skin over stuffing; fasten neck skin to turkey back with one or two skewers.

4. Loosely spoon remaining stuffing into body cavity (bake any leftover stuffing in small covered casserole during last 30 minutes of roasting time). Fold skin over cavity opening; skewer closed, if necessary. Tie legs and tail together with string, push drumsticks under band of skin, or use stuffing clamp. Secure wings to body with string, if desired.

5. Place turkey, breast side up, on rack in large roasting pan (17" by 11½"). Sprinkle salt and pepper on outside of turkey. Cover with loose tent of foil.

6. Roast about 3 hours 45 minutes. Start checking for doneness during last hour of roasting.

7. To brown turkey, remove foil during last hour of roasting and baste occasionally with pan drippings. Turkey is done when temperature on meat thermometer inserted in thickest part of thigh, next to body, reaches 180° to 185°F and juices run clear when thickest part of thigh is pierced with tip of knife. (Breast temperature should be 170° to 175°F, stuffing temperature 160° to 165°F.)

8. While turkey is roasting, prepare giblets and neck to use in Giblet Gravy.

9. Transfer turkey to large platter; keep warm. Let stand at least 15 minutes to set juices for easier carving. Prepare Giblet Gravy.

10. Serve turkey with stuffing and gravy. Makes 14 main-dish servings.

♥ Each serving without skin, stuffing, or gravy: About 143 calories, 25g protein, 0g carbohydrate, 4g total fat (1g saturated), 65mg cholesterol, 146mg sodium.

Giblet Gravy

Prepare giblets and neck: In 3-quart saucepan, combine **gizzard, heart, neck,** and enough **water** to cover; heat to boiling over high heat. Reduce heat; cover and simmer 45 minutes. Add **liver** and cook 15 minutes longer. Strain giblet broth through sieve into large bowl. Pull meat from neck; discard bones. Coarsely chop neck meat and giblets. Cover and refrigerate meat and broth separately.

To make gravy, remove rack from roasting pan. Strain **pan drippings** through sieve into 4-cup measuring cup or medium bowl. Add **1 cup giblet broth** to hot roasting pan and heat to boiling, stirring until browned bits are loosened from bottom of pan; add to drippings in measuring cup. Let stand 1 minute, or until fat separates from meat juice. Spoon **2 tablespoons fat** from drippings into 2-quart saucepan; skim and discard any remaining fat. Add **remaining giblet broth** and enough **water** to meat juice in cup to equal 3½ cups.

Heat fat in saucepan over medium heat; stir in **2 tablespoons all-purpose flour** and ½ **teaspoon salt.** Cook, stirring, until flour turns golden brown. With wire whisk, gradually whisk in **meat-juice mixture** and cook, whisking, until gravy has thickened slightly and boils; boil 1 minute. Stir in reserved giblets and neck meat; heat through. Pour gravy into gravy boat. Makes about 3½ cups gravy.

Each ¼ cup gravy: About 128 calories, 17g protein, 1g carbohydrate, 5g total fat (2g saturated), 153mg cholesterol, 152mg sodium.

GIBLETS

Giblets are poultry organs that can be cooked and eaten and include the liver, heart, and gizzard. They are usually used to enrich gravy or to create a quick broth. Giblets are usually found, separately wrapped, inside the poultry cavity along with the neck, but the content varies with each poultry producer. If you really want giblet gravy for your holiday turkey, it might be a good idea to purchase the giblets separately just to be sure of what you're getting.

CARVING A ROAST TURKEY

Cut through the skin where the leg is attached. To remove the leg, force it away from the body with a carving fork until it pops out of the socket. Separate the thigh from the body by cutting through the joint. If you like, separate the drumstick from the thigh by cutting through the center joint. To carve the leg, slice the thigh and drumstick meat, cutting parallel to the bones. Repeat on the other side.

To carve the breast, make a horizontal cut above the wing joint along the length of the bird, making sure to cut down to the bone.

With the knife parallel to the rib cage, cut the breast meat into thin slices. Cut off the wing. Repeat on the other side.

Traditional Roast Turkey with Giblet Gravy

Rosemary Roast Turkey Breast

When a whole turkey is too much, just use the breast. It will make white meat fans very happy.

Prep: 20 minutes Roast: 2 hours 15 to 30 minutes	
1	bone-in turkey breast (6 to 7 pounds)
1½	teaspoons dried rosemary, crumbled
1	teaspoon salt
¾	teaspoon coarsely ground black pepper
1	cup chicken broth

1. Preheat oven to 350°F. Rinse turkey breast with cold running water and drain well; pat dry with paper towels. In cup, combine rosemary, salt, and pepper. Rub rosemary mixture on inside and outside of turkey breast.

2. Place turkey, skin side up, on rack in small roasting pan (13" by 9"). Cover turkey with loose tent of foil.

3. Roast turkey 1 hour 30 minutes. Remove foil. Roast 45 to 60 minutes longer, occasionally basting with pan drippings. Start checking for doneness during last 30 minutes of cooking. Turkey breast is done when temperature on meat thermometer inserted into thickest part of breast (not touching bone) reaches 170°F and juices run clear when thickest part of breast is pierced with tip of knife.

4. Transfer turkey to warm platter. Let stand 15 minutes to set juices for easier carving.

5. Meanwhile, pour broth into drippings in hot roasting pan; heat to boiling, stirring until browned bits are loosened from bottom of pan. Strain pan-juice mixture through sieve into 1-quart saucepan; let stand 1 minute. Skim and discard fat. Heat pan-juice mixture over medium heat until hot; serve with turkey. Remove skin before eating. Makes 10 main-dish servings.

♥ Each serving without skin and with pan juices: About 251 calories, 55g protein, 0g carbohydrate, 2g total fat (0g saturated), 152mg cholesterol, 428mg sodium.

Roast Turkey Breast with Caramelized Shallots

Richly caramelized shallots add color, flavor, and moistness to roasted turkey breast.

Prep: 40 minutes Roast: 2 hours 30 minutes to 3 hours	
1	tablespoon olive oil
8	ounces shallots or red onion, thinly sliced (2 cups)
4	garlic cloves, thinly sliced
2	tablespoons brown sugar
2	tablespoons plus ½ cup water
1	tablespoon balsamic vinegar
½	teaspoon salt
¼	teaspoon coarsely ground black pepper
1	bone-in turkey breast (6 to 7 pounds)
½	cup dry red wine
1	cup chicken broth
1	tablespoon cornstarch

1. In nonstick 10-inch skillet, heat oil over medium-high heat. Add shallots and cook, stirring occasionally, until tender and golden, about 5 minutes. Add garlic and cook 1 minute longer. Stir in brown sugar, 1 tablespoon water, vinegar, salt, and pepper; cook 1 minute. Transfer to small bowl and cool to room temperature.

2. Preheat oven to 325°F. Rinse turkey breast with cold running water and drain well; pat dry with paper towels. With fingertips, gently separate skin from meat on turkey breast. Spread cooled shallot mixture on meat under skin.

3. Place turkey, skin side up, on rack in medium roasting pan (14" by 10"). Cover turkey with loose tent of foil.

4. Roast turkey 1 hour 30 minutes. Remove foil. Roast 1 to 1 hour 30 minutes longer, occasionally basting with pan drippings. Turkey breast is done when temperature on meat thermometer inserted in thickest part of breast (not touching bone) reaches 170°F and juices run clear when thickest part of breast is pierced with tip of knife.

5. Transfer turkey to warm platter. Let stand 15 minutes to set juices for easier carving.

6. Meanwhile, prepare sauce: Remove rack from roasting pan. Skim and discard fat from drippings in pan. In 2-quart saucepan, heat wine to boiling over medium heat; boil 2 minutes. Stir in broth, ½ cup water, and pan drippings; heat to boiling. In cup, blend cornstarch with remaining 1 tablespoon

water until smooth. With wire whisk, whisk into sauce and boil 1 minute, stirring. Strain through sieve into gravy boat. Serve with turkey. Makes 10 main-dish servings.

Each serving with skin and sauce: About 400 calories, 53g protein, 8g carbohydrate, 15g total fat (4g saturated), 136mg cholesterol, 336mg sodium.

Rolled Turkey Breast with Basil Mayonnaise

Here's a dramatic-looking party entrée that takes very little effort.

Prep: 45 minutes	Roast: 1 hour 15 minutes
1	boneless turkey breast (4½ to 5 pounds), cut in half
2	teaspoons salt
1	teaspoon coarsely ground black pepper
1	jar (12 ounces) roasted red peppers, drained
1½	cups loosely packed fresh basil leaves plus additional sprigs
1	tablespoon olive oil
	Basil Mayonnaise (page 234)

1. To butterfly breast halves, place 1 breast half, skinned side up, on cutting board. With sharp knife held parallel to surface, and starting at one long side, horizontally cut turkey breast half three-quarters of the way through and open like a book. With meat mallet, or between two sheets of plastic wrap or waxed paper with rolling pin, pound turkey breast half to about ¼-inch thickness. Repeat with second breast half.

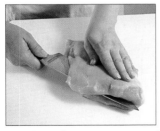 

2. Preheat oven to 350°F. Sprinkle ½ teaspoon salt and ¼ teaspoon black pepper on each breast half. Arrange roasted red peppers evenly over breast halves, leaving 2-inch border around edges; top with basil leaves. Starting at one narrow end, roll each breast half jelly-roll fashion. Tie each turkey roll with string at 2-inch intervals; brush with oil and sprinkle with remaining 1 teaspoon salt and remaining ½ teaspoon pepper.

Rolled Turkey Breast with Basil Mayonnaise

3. Place turkey rolls, seam side down, on rack in large roasting pan (17" by 11½"). Roast turkey rolls about 1 hour 15 minutes. Turkey is done when temperature on meat thermometer inserted in center of roll reaches 160°F. Internal temperature of turkey will rise to 165°F upon standing.

4. When turkey rolls are done, place on warm platter. Let stand 10 minutes to set juices for easier slicing if serving warm. If not serving right away, cool turkey 1 hour; wrap in plastic wrap and refrigerate up to 24 hours to serve cold later.

5. To serve, remove strings. Thinly slice turkey, garnish with basil sprigs, and serve with Basil Mayonnaise. Makes 10 main-dish servings.

♥ Each serving without Basil Mayonnaise: About 268 calories, 53g protein, 5g carbohydrate, 3g total fat (1g saturated), 133mg cholesterol, 638mg sodium.

Basil Mayonnaise

In blender or in food processor with knife blade attached, puree **2 cups loosely packed fresh basil leaves, 1 cup light mayonnaise, 1 cup reduced-fat sour cream, 2 teaspoons fresh lemon juice,** and **¼ teaspoon salt** until smooth. Cover and refrigerate until ready to use. Makes 2 cups mayonnaise.

Each tablespoon: About 40 calories, 1g protein, 1g carbohydrate, 4g total fat (1g saturated), 5mg cholesterol, 80mg sodium.

Sautéed Turkey Cutlets

This tender cut cooks in just five minutes. Take your pick of the three easy, delicious sauces for spooning over the top.

Prep: 15 minutes plus making sauce	Cook: 15 minutes
1	pound turkey cutlets
¼	teaspoon salt
¼	teaspoon coarsely ground black pepper
2	teaspoons olive oil
	choice of sauce (below)

1. With meat mallet, or between two sheets of plastic wrap or waxed paper with rolling pin, pound turkey cutlets to ¼-inch thickness. Sprinkle salt and pepper on cutlets. In nonstick 12-inch skillet, heat oil over medium-high heat until very hot. Add turkey cutlets, a few at a time, and cook until cutlets are golden brown and lose their pink color throughout, about 2 minutes per side. Transfer cutlets to platter as they are done; keep warm.

2. In same skillet, prepare one of the sauces. Spoon sauce over turkey cutlets. Makes 4 main-dish servings.

Tomato-Olive Sauce

To drippings in skillet, add **2 teaspoons olive oil** and **1 small onion,** finely chopped; cook over medium heat until tender, about 5 minutes. Add **1 garlic clove,** finely chopped; cook 1 minute. Stir in **1 can (14½ ounces) diced tomatoes** with their juice. Sprinkle with **2 tablespoons coarsely chopped pitted Kalamata olives.**

Each serving with turkey: About 211 calories, 29g protein, 8g carbohydrate, 7g total fat (1g saturated), 70mg cholesterol, 443mg sodium.

Mushroom Sauce

To drippings in skillet, add **2 teaspoons olive oil** and **1 garlic clove,** crushed with garlic press; cook over medium heat 10 seconds. Add **1 pound mushrooms,** trimmed and sliced, and **¼ teaspoon dried thyme;** cook until mushrooms are golden brown and liquid has evaporated, about 10 minutes. In cup, blend **1 cup chicken broth** and **1 teaspoon cornstarch** until smooth. Stir broth mixture into skillet; heat to boiling, stirring. Boil 1 minute.

Each serving with turkey: About 206 calories, 31g protein, 6g carbohydrate, 6g total fat (1g saturated), 70mg cholesterol, 453mg sodium.

Curry-Apricot Sauce

To drippings in skillet, add **2 teaspoons olive oil** and **1 small onion,** chopped; cook over medium heat, stirring occasionally, until onion is golden and tender, 6 to 8 minutes. Increase heat to medium-high. Add **1 teaspoon curry powder** and **½ teaspoon ground coriander;** cook, stirring, 1 minute. In cup, blend **1 cup chicken broth** and **1 teaspoon cornstarch** until smooth. Stir broth mixture and **½ cup dried apricots,** coarsely chopped, into skillet; heat to boiling, stirring. Boil 1 minute.

Each serving with turkey: About 259 calories, 36g protein, 13g carbohydrate, 6g total fat (0g saturated), 88mg cholesterol, 465mg sodium.

Turkey Marsala with Mushrooms

Turkey cutlets are an excellent and economical substitute for veal scallopini, and this recipe proves it.

Prep: 15 minutes	Cook: 15 minutes
2	tablespoons butter or margarine
10	ounces mushrooms, trimmed and sliced
¾	teaspoon salt
1	pound turkey cutlets, large pieces cut in half
3	tablespoons all-purpose flour
¼	teaspoon ground black pepper
1	tablespoon olive oil
½	cup dry Marsala wine
¼	cup water

1. In nonstick 12-inch skillet, melt 1 tablespoon butter over medium-high heat. Add mushrooms and ¼ teaspoon salt; cook until mushrooms are golden brown and liquid has evaporated, about 7 minutes. With slotted spoon, transfer mushrooms to medium bowl.

2. Meanwhile, with meat mallet or between two sheets of plastic wrap or waxed paper with rolling pin, pound turkey cutlets to ¼-inch thickness. On waxed paper, combine flour, pepper, and remaining ½ teaspoon salt; use to coat cutlets, shaking off excess.

3. In same skillet, melt remaining 1 tablespoon butter with oil over medium-high heat. Add half of cutlets and cook until cutlets are golden brown and lose their pink color throughout, 1 to 2 minutes per side. Transfer cutlets to bowl with mushrooms; keep warm. Repeat with remaining cutlets.

4. To skillet, add Marsala and water; cook 1 minute. Stir in turkey cutlets and mushrooms, turning to coat with sauce. Makes 4 main-dish servings.

Each serving: About 284 calories, 30g protein, 9g carbohydrate, 10g total fat (4g saturated), 86mg cholesterol, 556mg sodium.

Turkey Cutlets with Chopped Salad

Crisp turkey cutlets served over arugula and tomato salad warm the vegetables just enough to bring out all their flavor.

Prep: 15 minutes   Cook: 12 minutes

1	green onion, thinly sliced
2	tablespoons freshly grated Parmesan cheese
4	tablespoons olive oil
1	tablespoon red wine vinegar
½	teaspoon Dijon mustard
¼	teaspoon salt
¼	teaspoon coarsely ground black pepper
1	pound turkey cutlets
⅓	cup seasoned dried bread crumbs
1	pound plum tomatoes (4 large), cut into ¾-inch pieces
2	small bunches arugula (6 to 8 ounces), coarsely chopped

1. Prepare dressing: In medium bowl, with fork, mix green onion, Parmesan, 2 tablespoons oil, vinegar, mustard, salt, and pepper; set aside.

2. With meat mallet, or between two sheets of plastic wrap with rolling pin, pound turkey cutlets to ¼-inch thickness. On waxed paper, coat cutlets with bread crumbs.

3. In nonstick 12-inch skillet, heat remaining 2 tablespoons oil over medium-high heat until very hot. Add turkey cutlets, a few at a time, and cook until cutlets are golden brown and lose their pink color throughout, about 2½ minutes per side. Transfer cutlets to warm dish as they are done.

4. Add tomatoes and arugula to reserved dressing; gently toss to mix well. Pile salad on platter and top with turkey cutlets. Makes 4 main-dish servings.

Each serving: About 336 calories, 33g protein, 15g carbohydrate, 16g total fat (3g saturated), 73mg cholesterol, 559mg sodium.

Turkey Cutlets with Chopped Salad

Herbed Turkey Cutlets

Fragrant and fresh, lemon and sage complement turkey perfectly. Use a grill pan if you don't have an outdoor grill.

Prep: 5 minutes   Grill: 5 minutes

2	lemons plus lemon slices
1	tablespoon vegetable oil
1	tablespoon chopped fresh sage plus additional leaves
1	garlic clove, crushed with garlic press
1/2	teaspoon salt
1/4	teaspoon coarsely ground black pepper
1	pound turkey cutlets

1. Prepare grill. From lemons, grate 2 teaspoons peel and squeeze 2 tablespoons juice. In small bowl, combine lemon peel and juice, oil, sage, garlic, salt, and pepper.

2. With meat mallet, or between two sheets of plastic wrap or waxed paper with rolling pin, pound turkey cutlets to 1/4-inch thickness. Arrange turkey cutlets on grill over medium-high heat and grill, brushing with lemon mixture, until cutlets lose their pink color throughout, 2 1/2 to 3 1/2 minutes per side.

3. Arrange turkey cutlets on warm platter; garnish with lemon slices and sage leaves. Makes 4 main-dish servings.

Each serving: About 161 calories, 28g protein, 2g carbohydrate, 4g total fat (1g saturated), 70mg cholesterol, 345mg sodium.

For a juicy and perfectly seasoned turkey, try brining it. For a 12 pound turkey, in a large pot, dissolve 2 cups kosher salt in 2 gallons cold water. Add the turkey and refrigerate for 12 hours. Remove the turkey from the brine and roast using your favorite recipe.

ANNE ROSENZWEIG
CHEF/OWNER, THE LOBSTER CLUB, NEW YORK CITY

EXPERT TIP

Charcoal-Grilled Whole Turkey

Grilled turkey is becoming so popular that some cooks serve it for Thanksgiving. A twelve-pound bird is the largest size that will comfortably fit on a grill. Don't be concerned about the pink color of the meat under the skin—this is caused by the smoke.

Prep: 15 minutes   Grill: 2 hours 15 minutes to 3 hours

1	turkey (12 pounds)
2	tablespoons vegetable oil
2	teaspoons dried sage
2	teaspoons dried thyme
2	teaspoons salt
1/2	teaspoon ground black pepper

1. Prepare grill: In bottom of covered charcoal grill, with vents open and grill uncovered, ignite 60 charcoal briquettes (not self-starting). Allow to burn until all coals are covered with thin coat of gray ash, about 30 minutes. With tongs, move hot briquettes to two opposite sides of grill and arrange in two piles. Place sturdy disposable foil pan (13" by 9" by 2") in center of grill between piles of coals to catch drips.

2. Remove giblets and neck from turkey; reserve for another use. Rinse turkey inside and out with cold running water and drain well; pat dry with paper towels.

3. Fasten neck skin to turkey back with one or two skewers. Tie legs and tail together with string, push drumsticks under band of skin, or use stuffing clamp. Secure wings to body with string, if desired. In cup, combine oil, sage, thyme, salt, and pepper; rub mixture on outside of turkey.

4. Place turkey, breast side up, on rack directly over foil pan. Cover grill and grill 2 hours 15 minutes to 3 hours, adding eight or nine briquettes to each side of grill every hour to maintain grill temperature of 325°F on oven or grill thermometer. Turkey is done when temperature on meat thermometer inserted in thickest part of thigh, next to body, reaches 180° to 185°F and juices run clear when thickest part of thigh is pierced with tip of knife.

5. When turkey is done, place on warm platter; let stand 15 minutes to set juices for easier carving. If you like, skim and discard fat from drippings in bottom of pan; serve drippings with turkey. Makes 12 main-dish servings.

Each serving: About 524 calories, 73g protein, 0g carbohydrate, 23g total fat (7g saturated), 212mg cholesterol, 575mg sodium.

Grilled Turkey with Chili-Cumin Rub

Prepare as directed but substitute **2 tablespoons chili powder** and **2 teaspoons ground cumin** for sage and thyme.

Turkey Thighs Osso Buco–Style

Cooked in a manner usually reserved for veal shanks, turkey thighs make an excellent stew. Serve with soft polenta or rice pilaf.

Prep: 20 minutes   Bake: 1 hour 30 minutes

¼	teaspoon salt
¼	teaspoon ground black pepper
2	turkey thighs (1¼ pounds each), skin removed
2	teaspoons vegetable oil
2	medium onions, finely chopped
4	carrots, peeled and cut into ¾-inch pieces
2	stalks celery, cut into ½-inch pieces
4	garlic cloves, finely chopped
1	can (14½ ounces) tomatoes in puree
½	cup dry red wine
1	bay leaf
¼	teaspoon dried thyme

1. Preheat oven to 350°F. Sprinkle salt and pepper on turkey. In nonreactive 5-quart Dutch oven, heat oil over medium-high heat until very hot. Add 1 turkey thigh and cook, turning occasionally, until golden brown, about 5 minutes. Transfer thigh to plate; repeat with second thigh. Discard all but 1 tablespoon fat from Dutch oven.

2. Reduce heat to medium. Add onions to Dutch oven and cook, stirring occasionally, 5 minutes. Add carrots, celery, and garlic; cook, stirring frequently, 2 minutes longer.

3. Stir in tomatoes with puree, wine, bay leaf, and thyme, breaking up tomatoes with side of spoon. Heat to boiling; add browned turkey. Cover and place in oven. Bake until turkey is tender, about 1 hour 30 minutes. Discard bay leaf. Remove turkey meat from bones and cut into bite-size pieces; return meat to Dutch oven and stir well. Makes 4 main-dish servings.

♥ Each serving: About 323 calories, 36g protein, 24g carbohydrate, 9g total fat (3g saturated), 122mg cholesterol, 483mg sodium.

White Turkey Chili

If you prefer, substitute skinless, boneless chicken breast for the turkey. The chili will be just as tasty.

Prep: 20 minutes   Cook: 25 minutes

2	tablespoons olive oil
2	pounds skinless, boneless turkey breast, cut into ¾-inch pieces
1	large onion (12 ounces), finely chopped
3	garlic cloves, finely chopped
1	can (19 ounces) white kidney beans (cannellini), rinsed and drained
1	can (4 to 4½ ounces) chopped mild green chiles
1½	cups chicken broth
1½	teaspoons chili powder
¾	teaspoon ground cumin
¾	teaspoon ground coriander
¼	teaspoon salt
¼	teaspoon ground black pepper
1	package (10 ounces) frozen whole-kernel corn
½	cup chopped fresh cilantro
2	tablespoons fresh lime juice

1. In 5-quart Dutch oven, heat oil over medium-high heat until very hot. Add turkey, in batches, and cook until golden brown, about 4 minutes per batch. With slotted spoon, transfer turkey to large bowl.

2. To Dutch oven, add onion and garlic. Reduce heat to medium and cook, stirring frequently, until onion is tender, about 5 minutes. Add beans, chiles, broth, chili powder, cumin, coriander, salt, and pepper; heat to boiling over high heat. Reduce heat; cover and simmer until flavors have blended, about 7 minutes. Add corn, cilantro, and turkey; cook until corn is hot and turkey has lost its pink color throughout, about 3 minutes longer. Stir in lime juice and serve. Makes 8 cups or 6 main-dish servings.

♥ Each serving: About 341 calories, 44g protein, 25g carbohydrate, 7g total fat (1g saturated), 94mg cholesterol, 656mg sodium.

Turkey Potpie with Cornmeal Crust

Chock-filled with turkey and vegetables, this potpie is the last word in comfort food.

Prep: 30 minutes   Bake: 35 minutes

1	tablespoon vegetable oil
1	medium rutabaga (1 pound), peeled and cut into ½-inch pieces
3	carrots, peeled and cut into ½-inch pieces
1	large onion (12 ounces), chopped
1	pound all-purpose potatoes (3 medium), peeled and cut into ½-inch pieces
2	large stalks celery, chopped
¾	teaspoon salt
1	pound cooked turkey or chicken, cut into ½-inch pieces (4 cups)
1	package (10 ounces) frozen peas
1	can (14½ ounces) chicken broth or 1¾ cups Chicken Broth (page 84)
1	cup milk
¼	cup all-purpose flour
¼	teaspoon ground black pepper
⅛	teaspoon dried thyme
	Cornmeal Crust (right)
1	large egg, beaten

1. Prepare potpie filling: In nonstick 12-inch skillet, heat oil over medium-high heat; add rutabaga, carrots, and onion and cook 10 minutes. Stir in potatoes, celery, and ½ teaspoon salt; cook, stirring frequently, until rutabaga is tender-crisp, about 10 minutes longer. Spoon into 13" by 9" baking dish; add turkey and peas.

2. In 2-quart saucepan, heat broth to boiling. Meanwhile, in small bowl, blend milk and flour until smooth. Stir milk mixture into broth; add pepper, thyme, and remaining ¼ teaspoon salt. Heat to boiling over high heat, stirring. Stir sauce into chicken-vegetable mixture in baking dish.

3. Prepare Cornmeal Crust. Preheat oven to 425°F.

4. On lightly floured surface, with floured rolling pin, roll dough into rectangle 4 inches larger than top of baking dish. Arrange dough rectangle over filling; trim edge, leaving 1-inch overhang. Fold overhang under; flute. Brush crust with some egg. If desired, reroll trimmings; cut into decorative shapes to garnish top of pie. Brush dough cutouts with egg. Cut several slits in crust to allow steam to escape during baking.

5. Place potpie on foil-lined cookie sheet to catch any overflow during baking. Bake potpie until crust is golden brown and filling is hot and bubbling, 35 to 40 minutes. During last 10 minutes of baking, cover edges of crust with foil to prevent overbrowning. Makes 10 main-dish servings.

Each serving: About 416 calories, 21g protein, 42g carbohydrate, 18g total fat (5g saturated), 60mg cholesterol, 644mg sodium.

Cornmeal Crust

In large bowl, combine **1½ cups all purpose-flour, ¼ cup cornmeal,** and **¾ teaspoon salt.** With pastry blender or two knives used scissor-fashion, cut in **⅔ cup vegetable shortening** until mixture resembles coarse crumbs. Sprinkle **6 to 7 tablespoons cold water,** 1 tablespoon at a time, over flour mixture, mixing with fork after each addition until dough is just moist enough to hold together.

Turkey Potpie with Cornmeal Crust

Chicken Enchiladas

These enchiladas in green chile sauce are so tempting you may find yourself roasting a big bird just to have enough leftovers to make them.

Prep: 15 minutes   Bake: 20 minutes

1	can (4 to 4½ ounces) chopped mild green chiles, undrained
¾	cup loosely packed fresh cilantro leaves and stems
3	green onions, sliced
2	tablespoons sliced pickled jalapeño chiles
2	tablespoons fresh lime juice
¼	teaspoon salt
⅓	cup water
4	(8-inch) flour tortillas
8	ounces cooked chicken or turkey, shredded (2 cups)
¼	cup heavy or whipping cream
3	ounces Monterey Jack cheese, shredded (¾ cup)

1. Preheat oven to 350°F. Grease 11" by 7" baking dish.

2. In blender, combine chiles, cilantro, green onions, pickled jalapeños, lime juice, salt, and water; puree until smooth. Transfer to 8-inch skillet and heat to boiling over medium heat; boil 2 minutes. Dip one side of each tortilla in sauce; spread 1 tablespoon sauce over other (dry) side of tortilla and top with chicken. Roll up tortilla and place, seam side down, in prepared baking dish.

3. Stir cream into remaining sauce in skillet; spoon over filled tortillas. Cover with foil and bake 15 minutes. Remove foil; sprinkle with cheese and bake until cheese has melted, about 5 minutes longer. Makes 4 main-dish servings.

Each serving: About 402 calories, 30g protein, 23g carbohydrate, 21g total fat (9g saturated), 106mg cholesterol, 713mg sodium.

Turkey Tetrazzini

The original Chicken Tetrazzini was named in honor of the Italian opera star Luisa Tetrazzini. It's just about the best way to use up Thanksgiving turkey leftovers.

Prep: 30 minutes   Bake: 30 minutes

4	tablespoons butter or margarine
¼	cup all-purpose flour
2¾	cups chicken broth
¼	cup dry white wine
¼	teaspoon dried thyme
	pinch ground nutmeg
½	cup heavy or whipping cream
1	small onion, chopped
10	ounces mushrooms, trimmed and cut into quarters
8	ounces linguine, cooked as label directs
12	ounces cooked turkey, coarsely chopped (3 cups)
3	tablespoons freshly grated Parmesan cheese

1. Preheat oven to 400°F. In 2-quart saucepan, melt 3 tablespoons butter over medium heat. Stir in flour and cook 3 minutes. With wire whisk, whisk in broth, wine, thyme, and nutmeg until smooth. Heat to boiling, whisking constantly. Reduce heat and simmer, whisking frequently, 5 minutes. Stir in cream; set sauce aside.

2. In 10-inch skillet, melt remaining 1 tablespoon butter over medium heat. Add onion and cook until tender, about 5 minutes. Add mushrooms and cook, stirring occasionally, 10 minutes longer.

3. In 2- to 2½-quart shallow casserole, combine cooked linguine, mushroom mixture, and turkey. Stir in sauce and sprinkle with Parmesan. Bake until bubbly, about 30 minutes. Makes 6 main-dish servings.

Each serving: About 458 calories, 30g protein, 37g carbohydrate, 21g total fat (11g saturated), 104mg cholesterol, 648mg sodium.

Old-Fashioned Creamed Turkey

This old-time favorite, sometimes called turkey hash, deserves a place in the comfort food Hall of Fame. You can stir in leftover cooked vegetables along with the turkey—carrots, peas, and potatoes are all good. Spoon over noodles, mashed potatoes, or rice.

Prep: 10 minutes   Cook: 20 minutes

2	tablespoons butter or margarine
1	small onion, finely chopped
3	tablespoons all-purpose flour
2	cups milk
½	teaspoon salt
⅛	teaspoon ground black pepper
	pinch ground nutmeg
8	ounces cooked turkey or chicken, cut into ½-inch pieces (2 cups)
2	tablespoons chopped fresh parsley

1. In 3-quart saucepan, melt butter over medium heat. Add onion and cook, stirring, until tender, about 5 minutes. Stir in flour and cook, stirring constantly, 1 minute. With wire whisk, gradually whisk in milk, salt, pepper, and nutmeg. Heat to boiling over medium-high heat, whisking. Reduce heat and simmer, whisking occasionally, 5 minutes.

2. Stir turkey into sauce and heat through. Stir in parsley and serve. Makes 4 main-dish servings.

Each serving: About 277 calories, 26g protein, 13g carbohydrate, 13g total fat (7g saturated), 87mg cholesterol, 462mg sodium.

DUCK

Most supermarket ducks are of the Pekin (Long Island) breed. While the meat is flavorful, it can also be fatty. Cutting a duck into quarters helps render the excess fat. Specialty butchers often carry Moulard or Muscovy ducks, which are leaner and meatier than the Pekin variety but also much more expensive.

Spiced Duck

Marinating duck overnight gives it flavor that's hard to match.

Prep: 10 minutes plus overnight to marinate   Roast: 2 hours

2	green onions, cut into 2-inch pieces
2	teaspoons salt
1	teaspoon crushed red pepper
1	teaspoon fennel seeds, crushed
¼	teaspoon ground cloves
¼	teaspoon ground ginger
1	duck (4½ pounds), cut into quarters, fat removed
1	tablespoon soy sauce
2	tablespoons honey

1. Crush green onions with side of chef's knife. In small bowl, combine salt, crushed red pepper, fennel seeds, cloves, and ginger.

2. Pat duck dry with paper towels. With two-tine fork, prick skin in several places.

3. Rub duck quarters with crushed green onions; discard green onions. Rub duck with spice mixture. Place duck in large bowl; cover and refrigerate overnight to marinate.

4. Preheat oven to 350°F. Place duck, skin side up, on rack in large (17" by 11½") roasting pan. Roast 2 hours.

5. About 15 minutes before duck is done, brush with soy sauce, then with honey; continue roasting until golden brown and tender. Makes 4 main-dish servings.

Each serving: About 695 calories, 37g protein, 10g carbohydrate, 55g total fat (19g saturated), 163mg cholesterol, 1,539mg sodium.

FEATHERED GAME

QUAIL Tiny birds that weigh about eight ounces and have pale, juicy flesh. They are often sold with the breastbones removed, which makes them easier to stuff and to eat.

PHEASANT Wild pheasant has become so scarce that almost all the pheasant sold is farm raised. Pheasant is a relatively small bird with a delicate chickenlike flavor. One bird will feed two to three people.

SQUAB These birds, especially loved by Chinese cooks, have rich dark meat. Squabs are actually baby pigeons (they aren't called pigeons until they have flown), harvested four weeks before they begin to fly. Squab is usually served medium-rare to keep it from tasting liverish.

Ginger-Glazed Duck

To ensure crisp, flavorful skin, this glazed duck is roasted at high heat during the last ten minutes.

Prep: 10 minutes   Roast: 2 hours 10 minutes

1	duck (4½ pounds), cut into quarters, fat removed
3	teaspoons grated, peeled fresh ginger
½	teaspoon salt
¼	teaspoon ground black pepper
2	tablespoons honey
1	tablespoon soy sauce

1. Preheat oven to 350°F. Pat duck dry with paper towels. With two-tine fork, prick skin in several places.

2. In cup, combine 1 teaspoon ginger, salt, and pepper; rub on meat side of duck quarters. Place duck, skin side up, on rack in large (17" by 11½") foil-lined roasting pan. Roast 2 hours, using spoon or bulb baster to remove fat from pan occasionally.

3. Meanwhile, in cup, combine honey, soy sauce, and remaining 2 teaspoons ginger.

4. Turn oven control to 450°F. Remove duck from oven and brush all over with ginger glaze. Return to oven and roast 10 minutes longer. Makes 4 main-dish servings.

Each serving: About 690 calories, 37g protein, 9g carbohydrate, 55g total fat (19g saturated), 163mg cholesterol, 662mg sodium.

Chipotle-Glazed Duck

Prepare as directed but omit ginger, honey, and soy sauce. While duck roasts, press **2 tablespoons chopped canned chipotle chiles in adobo** (page 31) through sieve into small bowl; discard skin and seeds. Stir **2 tablespoons light (mild) molasses** into chipotle chiles. Proceed as in Step 4.

Red-Cooked Duck

Chinese "red-cooked" food is simmered in a soy-sauce mixture, which turns the food a dark reddish brown.

Prep: 25 minutes   Bake: 2 hours

4	green onions
1	duck (4½ pounds), cut into 8 pieces, fat removed
1	tablespoon olive oil
¼	cup soy sauce
2	tablespoons dry sherry
1	tablespoon minced, peeled fresh ginger
3	garlic cloves, each cut in half
1	tablespoon brown sugar
2	whole star anise or ½ teaspoon anise seeds
¼	teaspoon ground red pepper (cayenne)
¾	cup water

1. Preheat oven to 350°F. Cut green onions on diagonal into 1½-inch pieces.

2. Pat duck dry with paper towels.

3. In 8-quart Dutch oven, heat oil over high heat until very hot. Cook duck, in batches, until golden brown, about 8 minutes; transfer duck pieces to large bowl as they are browned. Discard all but 1 tablespoon fat from Dutch oven. Add green onions and cook, stirring, until lightly browned, about 5 minutes.

4. Stir in soy sauce, sherry, ginger, garlic, brown sugar, star anise, ground red pepper, and water. Heat to boiling over high heat, stirring until browned bits are loosened from bottom of Dutch oven.

5. Return duck to Dutch oven. Cover and place in oven. Bake 2 hours, basting duck several times with pan liquid.

6. With slotted spoon, transfer duck to large deep platter. Strain sauce through sieve; skim and discard fat. Serve duck topped with sauce. Makes 4 main-dish servings.

Each serving: About 721 calories, 38g protein, 8g carbohydrate, 59g total fat (19g saturated), 163mg cholesterol, 1,293mg sodium.

Breast of Duck with Mango Chutney Sauce

Magret refers to the duck breast of the Moulard, a variety fat-tened to produce the enlarged livers required for foie gras. Magret is much larger and meatier than the common Pekin (Long Island) duck and easily feeds four. It is usually eaten medium-rare. You can find it at specialty butchers.

Prep: 15 minutes   Cook: 35 minutes

1	magret (whole boneless Moulard duck breast; 1¾ pounds)
2	tablespoons butter or margarine
2	large shallots, finely chopped
¼	teaspoon salt
⅛	teaspoon ground black pepper
½	cup cider vinegar
1½	cups chicken broth
¼	cup mango chutney, chopped
2	tablespoons brown sugar
1	tablespoon chopped fresh parsley

1. Remove skin and fat from magret. Split magret length-wise into 2 breast halves.

2. In 10-inch skillet, melt butter over medium-high heat. Add magret and cook until golden brown, 2 to 3 minutes per side. Transfer magret to plate; set aside.

3. To same skillet, add shallots, salt, and pepper and cook, stirring, until shallots are golden brown, about 3 min-utes. Increase heat to high; stir in vinegar and cook until al-most all liquid has evaporated, about 3 minutes.

4. Add broth, chutney, and brown sugar and heat to boil-ing. Reduce heat to low and return magret to skillet. Slowly simmer magret, turning once with tongs, about 12 minutes for medium-rare or until desired doneness. Transfer magret to plate and keep warm.

5. Boil sauce over high heat until slightly thickened, about 10 minutes.

6. Place magret on cutting surface. Holding knife at 45° angle to cutting board, cut magret crosswise into thin slices. Fan slices onto plates, spoon sauce on top, and sprinkle with parsley. Makes 4 main-dish servings.

♥ Each serving: About 242 calories, 18g protein, 26g carbohydrate, 7g total fat (4g saturated), 105mg cholesterol, 840mg sodium.

Pan-Roasted Quail

To serve as an entrée, allow two quail per person, omit the greens and serve over Creamy Polenta (page 394).

Prep: 15 minutes   Cook: 45 minutes

8	quail (2¾ pounds)
6	garlic cloves, peeled
¼	teaspoon salt
¼	teaspoon ground black pepper
2	tablespoons olive oil
2	slices bacon, cut into ¼-inch pieces
1	large red onion, finely chopped
1	can (14½ ounces) chicken broth or 1¾ cups Chicken Broth (page 84)
¼	cup brandy
¼	cup dry white wine
4	tablespoons chopped fresh parsley plus additional sprigs
8	ounces mixed baby greens

1. Trim and discard dark skin around necks and body cavities of quail. Rinse quail inside and out with cold running water and drain well; pat dry with paper towels. Cut 4 garlic cloves in half and place 1 garlic half in cavity of each quail. Sprinkle salt and pepper on outside of quail.

2. In 12-inch skillet, heat oil over medium heat until very hot. Cook quail, wing sides down first, in batches, turning them with long-handled cooking spoons, until golden brown, about 12 minutes. Transfer quail to platter; keep warm. To same skillet, add bacon and onion and cook over medium heat, stirring, until onion is golden, about 5 minutes.

3. Very thinly slice remaining 2 garlic cloves. Add ¾ cup broth, brandy, wine, and garlic to skillet. Increase heat to high; cook, stirring until browned bits are loosened from bot-tom of skillet. Reduce heat to medium-low; add 3 tablespoons parsley. Return quail to skillet; cover and cook until a leg moves easily when lifted, about 20 minutes.

4. Place quail on large platter and keep warm. Add remaining broth to skillet and heat to boiling over high heat; boil until sauce has reduced to 1 cup, about 4 minutes.

5. To serve, arrange greens on plates and top with quail. Spoon sauce over quail; sprinkle with remaining 1 tablespoon parsley. Makes 8 first-course servings.

Each serving with sauce: About 355 calories, 29g protein, 5g carbohydrate, 24g total fat (6g saturated), 109mg cholesterol, 417mg sodium.

GOOSE

Goose is the holiday bird of choice for many families. It has dark, deep-flavored, firm-textured flesh, and when roasted properly, sports an irresistible crisp, golden skin. A goose is a large bird, but it isn't very meaty. The meat is fairly rich and is usually served in small portions accompanied by generous helpings of stuffing.

Crispy Roasted Goose with Orange Sauce

Piercing the skin of goose helps drain off the large amount of fat and also crisps the skin. Serve with one of our homemade cranberry sauces (pages 557 to 559) or chutneys (pages 559 to 560). Pour all the flavorful fat through a fine sieve and freeze for up to four months. Use for browning potatoes.

Prep: 30 minutes	Roast: 4 hours 25 minutes
1	goose (12 pounds)
5	navel oranges, each cut in half
1	bunch thyme
4	bay leaves
½	teaspoon dried thyme
1¼	teaspoons salt
½	teaspoon coarsely ground black pepper
3	tablespoons orange-flavored liqueur
2	tablespoons cornstarch
½	cup orange marmalade

1. Preheat oven to 400°F. Remove giblets and neck from goose; reserve for another use. Trim and discard fat from body cavity and any excess skin. Rinse goose inside and out with cold running water and drain well; pat dry with paper towels. With goose breast side up, lift wings up toward neck, then fold wing tips under back of goose so wings stay in place. Place 6 orange halves, thyme sprigs, and bay leaves in body cavity. Tie legs and tail together with string. Fold neck skin over back. With two-tine fork, prick skin in several places to drain fat during roasting.

2. Place goose, breast side up, on rack in large roasting pan (17" by 11½"). In cup, combine dried thyme, 1 teaspoon salt, and pepper; rub mixture over goose. Cover goose and roasting pan with foil. Roast 1 hour 30 minutes; turn oven control to 325°F and roast 2 hours longer.

3. Meanwhile, in small bowl, from remaining 4 orange halves, squeeze ¾ cup juice. Stir in 1 tablespoon liqueur, cornstarch, and remaining ¼ teaspoon salt; set aside. In cup, mix orange marmalade with remaining 2 tablespoons liqueur.

4. With spoon or bulb baster, remove as much fat from roasting pan as possible. Remove foil and roast goose 45 minutes longer. Remove goose from oven and turn oven control to 450°F. Brush marmalade mixture over goose. Roast goose until skin is golden brown and crisp, about 10 minutes longer. Transfer goose to warm platter; let stand at least 15 minutes for juices to set for easier carving.

5. Prepare sauce: Remove rack from roasting pan. Strain pan drippings through sieve into 8-cup measuring cup or large bowl. Let stand until fat separates from meat juice; skim and reserve fat for another use (there should be about 5 cups fat). Measure meat juice; if necessary, add enough water to meat juice to equal 1 cup. Return meat juice to pan and add reserved orange-juice mixture. Heat sauce to boiling over medium heat, stirring; boil 1 minute. (Makes about 1¾ cups.) Serve sauce with goose. Remove skin before eating, if desired. Makes 10 main-dish servings.

Each serving with skin: About 810 calories, 66g protein, 5g carbohydrate, 57g total fat (18g saturated), 235mg cholesterol, 472mg sodium.

Each serving without skin: About 488 calories, 57g protein, 5g carbohydrate, 25g total fat (9g saturated), 188mg cholesterol, 440mg sodium.

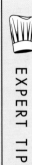

Ducks cook up crisper if they are boiled for five minutes before roasting.

ANNE ROSENZWEIG
CHEF/OWNER, THE LOBSTER CLUB, NEW YORK CITY

EXPERT TIP

STUFFING POULTRY

Tradition often dictates a stuffed bird (especially the holiday turkey), so the juices of the bird can moisten the stuffing. But some cooks prefer their birds unstuffed and heat the stuffing in a separate baking dish. If you prefer your poultry stuffed, here are some pointers on how to do it safely.

- One important rule of thumb: Remember that the stuffing is only being heated through while inside the bird and does not actually cook. Therefore, it is important that the ingredients are thoroughly cooked before being combined.
- To save time, cut up the raw stuffing ingredients the night before, then cover and refrigerate. If you wish, you can cook the vegetables and meat, then cool, cover, and refrigerate. When you're ready to put the stuffing together, reheat the cooked ingredients in a large skillet before proceeding with the recipe.
- Stuff the bird just before roasting—never in advance—and roast immediately. Use warm cooked ingredients and hot broth or stock to make your stuffing. A warm stuffing will reach the safe temperature of 160°F more quickly. At this safe temperature, bacteria, including salmonella, are killed.
- Lightly stuff the body and neck cavities; do not pack. Stuffing needs room to expand during cooking. You will rarely be able to fit all of the stuffing inside the bird, so bake the extra stuffing in a covered buttered baking dish for about thirty minutes or until heated through.
- After cooking, the stuffing temperature should have reached 160°F to be safe. Check the temperature with a meat thermometer inserted deep into the stuffing. If the poultry has reached temperature but the stuffing hasn't, transfer the stuffing to a buttered baking dish and continue baking until 160°F is reached.
- Any leftover stuffing should be promptly removed from the bird (to avoid potential bacterial growth). Transfer the stuffing to a covered container and use within three days, or freeze up to one month.

Southwestern Corn Bread Stuffing

This old-style stuffing starts with moist homemade Monterey Jack corn bread. Crumble the corn bread, drizzle with chicken broth, and you've got stuffing!

Prep: 20 minutes plus cooling	*Bake: 1 hour 45 minutes*

2	cups yellow cornmeal
2	teaspoons baking powder
1	teaspoon baking soda
1	teaspoon salt
2	cups buttermilk
½	cup butter or margarine (1 stick), melted and cooled
1	can (14¾ ounces) cream-style corn
2	cans (4 to 4½ ounces each) chopped mild green chiles
8	ounces Monterey Jack cheese, shredded (2 cups)
4	large eggs, lightly beaten
½	cup chicken broth

1. Prepare corn bread: Preheat oven to 350°F. Grease 13" by 9" baking pan or deep oven-safe 12-inch skillet (if skillet is not oven-safe, wrap handle with double layer of foil).

2. In large bowl, with spoon, mix cornmeal, baking powder, baking soda, and salt. Stir in buttermilk, melted butter, corn, chiles, cheese, and eggs and mix until thoroughly blended. Pour batter into baking pan.

3. Bake corn bread until top is browned and toothpick inserted in center comes out clean, 60 to 65 minutes. Cool corn bread in pan on wire rack. (The cornbread can be used after cooling to make stuffing, but it will make a firmer stuffing if allowed to stale slightly. If desired, cover and reserve corn bread up to 2 days.)

4. Prepare stuffing: Crumble corn bread into large bowl. Drizzle with broth; toss to mix well. Use to stuff 12- to 16-pound turkey, or serve in baking dish alongside poultry or ham: Spoon stuffing into greased 13" by 9" baking dish; cover with foil and bake in preheated 325°F oven until heated through, about 45 minutes. Makes about 11 cups stuffing.

Each ½ cup stuffing: About 161 calories, 6g protein, 15g carbohydrate, 9g total fat (5g saturated), 62mg cholesterol, 481mg sodium.

Country Sausage and Corn Bread Stuffing

It's hard to resist this all-time favorite stuffing of pecans, sausage, and store-bought stuffing mix.

Prep: 45 minutes   Bake: 45 minutes

1	pound pork sausage meat
4	tablespoons butter or margarine
3	stalks celery, coarsely chopped
1	large onion (12 ounces), coarsely chopped
1	red pepper, coarsely chopped
1	can (14½ ounces) chicken broth or 1¾ cups Chicken Broth (page 84)
½	teaspoon coarsely ground black pepper
¾	cup water
1	package (14 to 16 ounces) corn bread stuffing mix
1½	cups pecans (6 ounces), toasted and coarsely chopped
¼	cup chopped fresh parsley

1. Heat 12-inch skillet over medium-high heat until very hot. Add sausage meat and cook, breaking up sausage with side of spoon until browned, about 10 minutes. With slotted spoon, transfer sausage to large bowl.

2. Discard all but 2 tablespoons sausage drippings. Add butter, celery, onion, and red pepper to skillet; cook, stirring occasionally, until vegetables are golden brown and tender. Stir in broth, black pepper, and water; heat to boiling, stirring until browned bits are loosened from bottom of skillet.

3. Add vegetable mixture, stuffing mix, pecans, and parsley to sausage; stir to combine well. Use to stuff 12- to 16-pound turkey, or serve in baking dish alongside poultry or ham: Spoon stuffing into greased 13" by 9" baking dish; cover with foil and bake in preheated 325°F oven until heated through, about 45 minutes. Makes about 12 cups stuffing.

Each ½ cup stuffing: About 174 calories, 4g protein, 15g carbohydrate, 11g total fat (3g saturated), 13mg cholesterol, 407mg sodium.

Chestnut and Apple Stuffing

It's easiest to peel chestnuts while they're warm. Peel only a few at a time—keep the rest hot.

Prep: 1 hour   Bake: 45 minutes

2	pounds fresh chestnuts
10	cups ½-inch cubes day-old French bread (one 16-ounce loaf)
6	tablespoons butter or margarine
2	stalks celery, sliced
1	medium onion, coarsely chopped
1¾	pounds Rome Beauty or Crispin apples (3 large), peeled, cored, and coarsely chopped
2	teaspoons poultry seasoning
1	can (14½ ounces) chicken broth or 1¾ cups Chicken Broth (page 84)
1	cup water
1	teaspoon salt

1. Preheat oven to 400°F. With sharp knife, slash shell of each chestnut. Place in jelly-roll pan and roast until shells burst open, about 20 minutes. When cool enough to handle, with paring knife, peel chestnuts. Chop chestnut meat; place in large bowl. Add bread cubes to bowl with chestnuts and toss to combine.

2. In 3-quart saucepan, melt butter over medium-high heat. Add celery and onion and cook until golden brown and tender, about 10 minutes. Add apples and poultry seasoning; cook, stirring occasionally, 2 minutes longer. Stir in broth, water, and salt; heat to boiling over high heat.

3. Pour hot vegetable mixture over chestnut mixture; stir to combine well. Use to stuff 12- to 16-pound turkey, or serve in baking dish alongside poultry or ham: Spoon stuffing into greased 13" by 9" baking dish; cover with foil and bake in preheated 325°F oven until heated through, about 45 minutes. Makes about 12 cups stuffing.

♥ Each ½ cup stuffing: About 158 calories, 3g protein, 28g carbohydrate, 4g total fat (2g saturated), 8mg cholesterol, 321mg sodium.

Northwest Fruit Stuffing

The sour cherry orchards of the Northwest are celebrated in this fruit-studded stuffing.

Prep: 40 minutes   Bake: 45 minutes

½	cup butter or margarine (1 stick)
1	large red onion, coarsely chopped
1	medium fennel bulb (1¼ pounds), trimmed and coarsely chopped
2	large pears, peeled, cored, and coarsely chopped
1	large Granny Smith apple, peeled, cored, and coarsely chopped
1½	loaves (16 ounces each) sliced firm white bread, cut into ¾-inch cubes and lightly toasted
1	cup chicken broth
⅔	cup dried tart cherries
½	cup golden raisins
⅓	cup chopped fresh parsley
2	teaspoons chopped fresh thyme
1	teaspoon chopped fresh sage
1	teaspoon salt
½	teaspoon coarsely ground black pepper

1. In 12-inch skillet, melt butter over medium-high heat. Add onion and fennel and cook, stirring occasionally, until vegetables are golden brown and tender, 10 to 12 minutes. Add pears and apple and cook 5 minutes longer. Transfer to large bowl.

2. Add bread cubes, broth, cherries, raisins, parsley, thyme, sage, salt, and pepper to bowl with pears and apple; toss to combine well. Use to stuff 12- to 16-pound turkey, or serve in baking dish alongside poultry or ham: Spoon stuffing into greased 13" by 9" baking dish; cover with foil and bake in preheated 325°F oven until heated through, about 45 minutes. Makes about 12 cups stuffing.

♥ Each ½ cup stuffing: About 151 calories, 3g protein, 24g carbohydrate, 5g total fat (3g saturated), 11mg cholesterol, 351mg sodium.

Moist Bread Stuffing

This is the traditional stuffing recipe most of us grew up with. For the best results, use firm white bread. If you wish, let the bread cubes become stale by setting them out overnight.

Prep: 25 minutes   Bake: 45 minutes

½	cup butter or margarine (1 stick)
5	stalks celery, finely chopped
1	medium onion, finely chopped
2	loaves (16 ounces each) sliced firm white bread, cut into ¾-inch cubes
1	can (14½ ounces) chicken broth or 1¾ cups Chicken Broth (page 84)
¼	cup chopped fresh parsley
1	teaspoon dried thyme
¾	teaspoon salt
½	teaspoon ground black pepper
½	teaspoon dried sage

1. In 5-quart Dutch oven, melt butter over medium heat. Add celery and onion and cook, stirring occasionally until tender, about 15 minutes.

2. Remove Dutch oven from heat. Add bread cubes, broth, parsley, thyme, salt, pepper, and sage; toss to combine well. Use to stuff 12- to 16-pound turkey, or serve in baking dish alongside poultry or ham: Spoon stuffing into greased 13" by 9" baking dish; cover with foil and bake in preheated 325°F oven until heated through, about 45 minutes. Makes about 10 cups stuffing.

Each ½ cup stuffing: About 170 calories, 4g protein, 24g carbohydrate, 6g total fat (3g saturated), 13mg cholesterol, 473mg sodium.

Wild Rice and Vegetable Stuffing

A jewel-like blend that is a nice flavor change from familiar bread stuffing.

Prep: 15 minutes   Cook: 1 hour

2/3	cup wild rice (4 ounces)
2	cans (14½ ounces each) chicken broth or 3½ cups Chicken Broth (page 84)
1½	cups water
2	teaspoons fresh thyme or ½ teaspoon dried thyme
1	teaspoon salt
2	tablespoons vegetable oil
4	carrots, peeled and sliced
2	stalks celery, sliced
1	medium onion, chopped
10	ounces mushrooms, trimmed and sliced
1½	cups regular long-grain rice
¼	cup chopped fresh parsley

1. In 4-quart saucepan, combine wild rice, broth, water, thyme, and salt; heat to boiling over high heat. Reduce heat; cover and simmer 35 minutes.

2. Meanwhile, in nonstick 10-inch skillet, heat 1 tablespoon oil over medium heat. Add carrots, celery, and onion and cook, stirring occasionally, until vegetables are tender. With slotted spoon, transfer vegetables to medium bowl.

3. Add remaining 1 tablespoon oil and mushrooms to skillet; cook until mushrooms are golden brown and all liquid has evaporated.

4. Stir long-grain rice, vegetable mixture, and mushrooms into wild rice. Increase heat to high and heat to boiling. Reduce heat; cover and simmer until rice is tender and all liquid has been absorbed, about 20 minutes longer. Stir in parsley. Use to stuff 12- to 16-pound turkey. Or, spoon stuffing into serving bowl; keep warm until ready to serve. Makes about 8 cups stuffing.

♥ Each ½ cup stuffing: About 126 calories, 3g protein, 23g carbohydrate, 2g total fat (0g saturated), 0mg cholesterol, 385mg sodium.

Rice and Escarole Stuffing

Italian-style stuffing sweetened with a touch of raisins is ideal for a large roasting chicken.

Prep: 10 minutes   Cook: 25 minutes

1⅓	cups chicken broth
½	cup regular long-grain rice
2	tablespoons olive oil
1	medium onion, chopped
1	large stalk celery, chopped
1	small head escarole (about 12 ounces), coarsely chopped
¼	cup dark seedless raisins, coarsely chopped
¼	teaspoon dried sage
¼	teaspoon salt
¼	teaspoon coarsely ground black pepper

1. In 1-quart saucepan, heat broth to boiling over high heat; stir in rice. Reduce heat; cover and simmer until rice is tender and all liquid has been absorbed, about 20 minutes.

2. Meanwhile, in 12-inch skillet, heat oil over medium-high heat until hot. Add onion and celery; cook, stirring occasionally, until vegetables are golden brown and tender, 6 to 8 minutes. Add escarole; cook, stirring, until escarole just wilts.

3. Remove skillet from heat; stir in rice, raisins, sage, salt, and pepper. Use to stuff 6- to 8-pound roasting chicken. Or, spoon into serving bowl; keep warm until ready to serve. Makes 3 cups stuffing.

♥ Each ⅓ cup stuffing: About 95 calories, 2g protein, 15g carbohydrate, 3g total fat (0g saturated), 0mg cholesterol, 226mg sodium.

Parsnips, Swiss Chard, and Bacon Stuffing

With its smoky flavor, this deliciously different stuffing would be right at home at an Arkansas farmhouse Thanksgiving dinner.

Prep: 45 minutes   Bake: 45 minutes

8	ounces sliced bacon, cut into ½-inch pieces
1	pound parsnips, peeled and coarsely chopped
3	stalks celery, coarsely chopped
1	large onion (12 ounces), coarsely chopped
1½	pounds Swiss chard, tough stems trimmed and leaves cut into 2-inch pieces
1	can (14½ ounces) chicken broth or 1¾ cups Chicken Broth (page 84)
½	teaspoon coarsely ground black pepper
2	packages (8 ounces each) herb-seasoned stuffing mix

1. In 12-inch skillet, cook bacon over medium-low heat until browned. With slotted spoon, transfer to large bowl.

2. Discard all but ¼ cup bacon drippings from skillet. Increase heat to medium-high; add parsnips, celery, and onion and cook, stirring occasionally, until vegetables are golden and tender, about 15 minutes. Add Swiss chard; cook, stirring frequently, until chard wilts, about 2 minutes. Stir in broth and pepper.

3. Add vegetable mixture and stuffing mix to bacon in bowl; toss to combine well. Use to stuff 12- to 16-pound turkey, or serve in baking dish alongside poultry or ham: Spoon stuffing into greased 13" by 9" baking dish; cover with foil and bake in preheated 325°F oven until stuffing is heated through, about 45 minutes. Makes about 14 cups stuffing.

♥ Each ½ cup stuffing: About 112 calories, 3g protein, 17g carbohydrate, 3g total fat (1g saturated), 3mg cholesterol, 390mg sodium.

RABBIT

Rabbit, like chicken and veal, has a neutral flavor that can act as a canvas for a range of ingredients and cooking methods. But be careful not to overcook it, or its lean meat will dry out.

Rabbit Braised in Red Wine

A hint of spice, a little bacon, and some red wine make a most heavenly sauce for rabbit. If you like, add one-half cup coarsely chopped prunes along with the wine—it adds a rich sweet-and-savory note. Ask the butcher to cut up the rabbit into two forequarters, two hindquarters, two saddle pieces, and two loin pieces.

Prep: 15 minutes   Cook: 1 hour 30 minutes

1	rabbit (3 pounds), cut into 8 pieces
¼	cup all-purpose flour
4	teaspoons vegetable oil
1	medium onion, finely chopped
1	carrot, finely chopped
2	slices bacon, finely chopped
1	garlic clove, finely chopped
2	tablespoons tomato paste
2	cups dry red wine
¾	teaspoon salt
¼	teaspoon dried thyme
⅛	teaspoon ground ginger
⅛	teaspoon ground allspice
	pinch ground cinnamon
	pinch ground red pepper (cayenne)
1	small bay leaf
1	tablespoon chopped fresh parsley

1. On waxed paper, coat rabbit with flour, shaking off excess. In nonreactive 5-quart Dutch oven, heat 2 teaspoons oil over medium-high heat until very hot. Add half of rabbit pieces and cook until golden, 2 to 3 minutes per side; transfer rabbit pieces to bowl as they are browned. Repeat with remaining 2 teaspoons oil and remaining rabbit.

2. Reduce heat to medium. Add onion, carrot, and bacon to Dutch oven and cook, stirring frequently, until tender, about 5 minutes. Stir in garlic and cook until fragrant, about 30 seconds. Stir in tomato paste until blended. Add wine, salt, thyme, ginger, allspice, cinnamon, ground red pepper, bay

leaf, and rabbit; heat to boiling over high heat. Reduce heat; cover and simmer until rabbit is tender, about 1 hour.

3. With slotted spoon, transfer rabbit to platter and keep warm. Increase heat to high and heat sauce to boiling; boil until sauce has been reduced and thickened, about 5 minutes. Discard bay leaf. To serve, spoon sauce over rabbit and sprinkle with parsley. Makes 4 main-dish servings.

Each serving: About 526 calories, 55g protein, 16g carbohydrate, 26g total fat (7g saturated), 155mg cholesterol, 699mg sodium.

Rabbit Niçoise

A sprinkling of orange peel, cloves, and fresh basil finishes this dish with flair. If you like, substitute chicken for rabbit (remove the skin first and simmer the chicken forty-five to sixty minutes).

Rabbit Niçoise

Prep: 20 minutes Cook: 1 hour 30 minutes	
1	rabbit (3 pounds), cut into 8 pieces
¼	cup all-purpose flour
6	teaspoons vegetable oil
2	medium onions, thinly sliced
2	garlic cloves, finely chopped
	pinch crushed red pepper
1	can (28 ounces) tomatoes
½	cup dry white wine
¾	teaspoon salt
¼	teaspoon ground black pepper
¼	teaspoon dried thyme
½	bay leaf
1	orange
¼	cup Kalamata olives, pitted and chopped
⅓	cup chopped fresh basil

1. On waxed paper, coat rabbit with flour, shaking off excess. In nonreactive 5-quart Dutch oven, heat 2 teaspoons oil over medium-high heat until very hot. Add half of rabbit pieces and cook until golden, 2 to 3 minutes per side; transfer rabbit pieces to bowl as they are browned. Repeat with 2 more teaspoons oil and remaining rabbit.

2. Reduce heat to medium; add remaining 2 teaspoons oil to Dutch oven. Add onions and cook, stirring frequently, until tender and golden brown. Stir in garlic and crushed red pepper and cook 30 seconds. Add tomatoes with their juice, wine, salt, pepper, thyme, and bay leaf, breaking up tomatoes with side of spoon. From orange, with vegetable peeler, remove 3 strips (3" by 1" each) peel and add to Dutch oven. Add rabbit, stirring to coat; heat to boiling over high heat. Reduce heat; cover and simmer until rabbit is tender, 1 hour to 1 hour 15 minutes.

3. Meanwhile, from orange, with vegetable peeler, remove and finely chop 2 teaspoons orange peel. In small bowl, combine orange peel with olives and basil.

4. When rabbit is done, with slotted spoon, transfer rabbit to platter and keep warm. Increase heat to high and heat sauce to boiling; boil until sauce has been reduced and thickened, about 5 minutes. Discard bay leaf. Spoon sauce over rabbit and sprinkle with orange-peel mixture. Makes 4 main-dish servings.

Each serving: About 547 calories, 56g protein, 25g carbohydrate, 24g total fat (6g saturated), 148mg cholesterol, 1,022mg sodium.

6

FISH AND SHELLFISH

The growing popularity of fish and shellfish is hardly a surprise. The pristine flavor of well-prepared seafood is undeniably delicious, but other attributes are drawing cooks to the fish counter, too. First, there is the health aspect: Seafood is a rich source of protein, vitamins, and minerals and is low in fat. Even oily fish, such as salmon and tuna, are high in Omega-3 fatty acids, which can lower blood cholesterol levels, and they have much less fat than red meat or poultry. And, because seafood must be cooked quickly to retain its moisture and texture, it is perfect for cooks with busy lifestyles.

It wasn't too long ago that fish lovers didn't have much choice at their local markets, but that is quickly changing because of customer demand and improved shipping practices. You are as likely to be eating Norwegian salmon, Thai shrimp, or Chilean sea bass as you are seafood from local waters. And it is all delicious.

BUYING FISH AND SHELLFISH

Because it is highly perishable, purchase fish and shellfish carefully. When you find a purveyor you like, be it at a supermar-

Chinese-Style Steamed Fish

ket or private store, let them know you appreciate their commitment to quality. A good fish counter will be spotlessly clean and have a fresh sea aroma. Avoid stores with an unpleasant fishy or ammonia smell.

The USDA does not have an inspection program for fish. It is an unfortunate reality that some fish live in tainted waters, and they can pass on pollutants to the consumer. Unlike bacterial pathogens found in food, some of these contaminants aren't destroyed by heat. With fish, however, this is only a danger if you live in an area with polluted waters and you eat fish from those waters day after day. The fish in your supermarket is much more likely to be global in origin. So pay more attention to the benefits of eating fish and don't be unduly alarmed.

Clams, oysters, and mussels are subject to a government inspection program that guarantees that the waters they come from are clean. These shellfish must be sold with an inspection sticker attached to each wholesale unit. For this reason, it is not a good idea to buy shellfish right off the trucks of local fishermen unless they can demonstrate that their wares have been inspected—see the sticker, or don't buy there.

When purchasing fish, let your eyes and nose be your guides. Firm flesh that bounces back when lightly pressed is a good sign of freshness, but no fish store will allow you to touch the fish, for obvious health reasons. The surface of a whole fish should glisten but not look slimy. Ask the fishmonger to show you the gills; they should be bright red with no tinge of brown. Take a sniff; the gills should smell appetizingly fresh. The eyes should not be sunken, but don't worry if they are clouded over, because the eyes of some fish lose their shine soon after they are caught.

Fish fillets and steaks are often sold in plastic-wrapped trays, which prevent you from applying the sniff test. Look for fish that appear moist and have no gaps in the flesh. The flesh should feel firm through the plastic. The meat of dark fish, such as tuna, should not contain any rainbow streaks.

Mollusks (shellfish with hard shells and soft bodies, such as clams, mussels, and oysters) must be purchased alive because their viscera deteriorate quickly once dead. Tightly closed shells indicate the mollusks are alive, but if you tap a gaping shell and it closes, it's also fine. Don't buy mollusks with broken shells. And if a clam or mussel feels especially heavy compared to the others in the batch, it may be filled with mud; discard it. Mollusks sold out of their shells, like scallops and squid, should be as sweet smelling as an ocean breeze. The siphons of soft-shell clams should retract slightly when touched.

Live crustaceans (which have long bodies and jointed shells), such as crabs and lobsters, should be purchased from a store with a large turnover and be lively: If the crustaceans have been held in a water tank for more than two weeks, they will be lethargic and tasteless. Fresh shrimp should also be subjected to the sniff test, and black spots on the shell mean the shrimp are over the hill.

STORING FISH AND SHELLFISH

Keep fish and shellfish as cold as possible. The higher above 32°F the storage temperature is, the faster fish deteriorates. Have the seafood you purchase packed in ice, or place it in the same bag as your frozen food. During hot weather, you may want to take a cooler with you to the market.

Fresh fish should be cooked within one day of purchase. Store in the coldest part of the refrigerator, where the temperature should be between 35° and 40°F. If your refrigerator is not this cold, store the fish on ice. Most fish is wrapped in plastic or in paper and a plastic bag. Fill a deep baking dish with ice cubes and place the wrapped seafood on the ice; re-

plenish the ice as it melts. You can also cover frozen artificial ice packets with a kitchen towel and place the fish on top (the towel will prevent the fish from getting too cold and freezing).

It is especially important to keep oily fish, such as mackerel and bluefish, as cold as possible. Their high fat content means they go rancid quickly at warmer-than-ideal temperatures.

If you have a surplus of leftover fresh fish, don't try to freeze it. Home freezers rarely freeze below 0°F, so the moisture in the fish freezes slowly and forms large crystals. When thawed, the flavor and texture suffers. If you must freeze seafood, be sure it is very fresh, and wrap it tightly in plastic wrap and then in heavy-duty foil. Freeze the fish for up to three months.

Shellfish also keeps best in the coldest part of the refrigerator. Do not store on ice, though, or it may freeze and die. Live clams, mussels, oysters, lobsters, and crabs need to breathe; never store them in plastic bags (and avoid buying mollusks wrapped in plastic). Store them in a large bowl covered with a wet towel. Although mollusks will stay fresh for two to three days, it is preferable to cook them sooner. Refrigerate crabs in a tightly closed heavy-duty paper bag poked with a few airholes; cook within twenty-four hours after purchase, preferably the same day. Lobsters should be cooked on the day of purchase because they don't last long once out of water. Keep them wrapped in a wet cloth or several layers of newspaper and store in the refrigerator.

Cooked crab and lobster should be eaten within one day of purchase. Shucked oysters and crabmeat are often pasteurized, which extends their shelf life but decreases their flavor. Always pay close attention to the use-by date on the package.

BUYING AND STORING FROZEN FISH AND SHELLFISH

Much of the so-called "fresh" seafood we buy is flash-frozen at temperatures below 20°F while the fishing boats are far out to sea. The difference in quality between fresh and flash-frozen seafood is unnoticeable, because the ice crystals that form are so tiny that when the fish is thawed, the original texture and flavor are maintained. Flash-freezing is actually advisable for fish that will be consumed rare or as sushi, because the procedure kills parasites.

If purchasing frozen fish fillets, be sure the fish is tightly wrapped in moisture- and vapor-proof material. Avoid fish with dry-looking white or discolored portions, which may indicate freezer burn or deterioration, and be sure there is no detectable odor. Store frozen fish no longer than three months.

Never thaw frozen fish at room temperature, where bacteria can multiply rapidly. Place the fish in its original package on a plate and refrigerate overnight. If you're in a hurry, place the wrapped fish under cold running water. Do not refreeze.

Frozen shrimp, available at Asian markets, wholesale food clubs, and larger supermarkets, is a bargain. Sometimes the shrimp is individually frozen and sold in bags, but more often it is sold in blocks. Put the individually frozen shrimp in a colander and place under cold running water until thawed. For block-frozen shrimp, place under cold running water, and pull off the amount of shrimp you need as they thaw; return the remaining block of shrimp to the freezer.

COOKING SUCCESS

Here's the secret to cooking fish successfully: Don't overcook it. Fish and shellfish toughen and lose flavor when cooked too long. Cook just until the flesh is no longer translucent and is opaque all the way through. Remember, it will continue to cook after it has been removed from the heat.

Before cooking fillets, especially thick ones such as salmon or cod, run your fingers over the flesh to feel for any stray bones. Use tweezers to remove them. If you cook fish often, keep a separate pair of tweezers in your kitchen. If using tweezers from your medicine cabinet, wash them well, then sterilize over an open flame before using.

A small sharp knife is the best tool when it comes to testing whether or not fish is properly cooked. To check fish fillets or steaks for doneness, use the tip of the knife to separate the flesh in the thickest part—it should be uniformly opaque. Do not follow the old adage that fish should flake when done—it will be overcooked. (Besides, not all fish become flaky.) To check whole fish, make an incision at the backbone to see if the flesh is opaque, or insert an instant-read thermometer in the thickest part near the backbone; it should read 135° to 140°F. It is stylish to cook certain fish, such as tuna, salmon, and swordfish, until medium-rare, but this is a matter of personal taste. The ultimate goal is to serve fish when it is perfectly moist and absolutely delicious.

When cooking hard-shelled mollusks, such as clams, mussels, and oysters, scrub the shells well under cold running water to remove any surface sand and grit. This step is very important, especially in recipes where the mollusks are steamed in liquid—a little bit of sand can spoil the pleasure of eating a bowl of clams.

Any clams or mussels that remain unopened after cooking may have been dead before they went into the pot; they are unsafe to eat and should be discarded. On the other hand, sometimes they are just stubborn. You can return them to the pot and cook them for another couple of minutes. If they still remain clamped shut, throw them out.

KNOW YOUR FISH

Fish is categorized two ways—by shape (round or flat) and by fat content (lean to oily). It is also helpful to be familiar with the bony structure of fish, especially if you fillet fish yourself (before or after cooking), so you know where the bones are. More important, however, is to have some knowledge of the fat content, flavor, and texture of various fish, especially when substituting one fish for another.

Round fish have a plump, cylindrical shape and eyes that lie on each side of the head. The backbone runs down the center of the fish, separating the two thick fillets. Round fish are generally filleted or cut into steaks but can also be cooked whole. Common round fish include salmon, red snapper, sea bass, monkfish, and catfish.

Flatfish have wide, thin bodies—in fact, they almost look two-dimensional. Both eyes are on the same side of the head. The backbone runs down the center of the fish, with two lines of bones fanning out on either side, separating the top and bottom fillets. Flatfish are usually filleted. Very large and relatively thick flatfish, such as halibut, can also be cut into steaks. The most common flatfish are sole and flounder.

The fat content of a fish is a good indicator of the flavor you can expect. In general, the higher the fat content, the darker the flesh and the richer the flavor. Feel free to substitute one type of fish within a category for another; this will add variety to your menu and allow you to take advantage of whichever fish look good in the market. But keep the texture of the fish in mind as well. A fragile, flaky fillet is not a good substitute for a thick, meaty fish steak unless you take great care not to overcook it.

Lean fish, with a fat content of 2.5 percent or less, make up the majority of fish. They have the blandest flavor and most delicate texture. Moderately oily fish have a slightly higher fat content (about 6 percent), a pleasant texture, and mild flavor. Some fish, such as tuna, can be categorized as either moderately oily or oily, depending on the species. Oily fish average 12 percent fat content; their flesh is strong-tasting, firm, and meaty. They are high in Omega-3 fatty acids. These fatty acids are polyunsaturated fats and do not clog arteries, unlike the saturated fats found in meat and poultry.

Today, many fish that were once caught only in their natural habitats, such as striped bass, trout, and salmon, are farm-raised. This has made them less expensive and more widely available, but farm-raised fish lack the full flavor of their wild cousins. In season, high-quality fish stores often carry the wild varieties. Buy them when you see them.

Here is a glossary of the fish you are most likely to find in your market. We have included recipes for most of these fish. Use the chart on page 256 to guide you when substituting one fish for another.

Anchovy Occasionally found fresh in ethnic fish markets, this small fish is delicious when tossed in olive oil and grilled. It is most often filleted and canned. Anchovy is used sparingly as a flavoring in Mediterranean dishes.

Arctic char Very similar to salmon and usually farm-raised. Also known as *salmon trout.*

Bluefish A dark-fleshed, strong-flavored, oily fish that is very popular with sport fishermen. The fresher the fish, the milder the flavor.

Catfish A beloved freshwater fish of the American South. Wild catfish sometimes have a slightly muddy flavor that you either love or hate. Farm-raised catfish are readily available.

Cod This saltwater fish, found in both Atlantic and Pacific waters, is known for its mild flavor and white, flaky flesh, making it one of the most popular and ubiquitous fish in the world. Small cod are called *scrod.* Cod can also be preserved by salting and is then known as *salt cod.*

Flounder One of America's favorite fish. White-fleshed and with a delicate texture and mild flavor, the fillets are often stuffed, rolled, and baked or sautéed. Whole flounder is also delicious grilled. On the West Coast, small flounderlike fish called *dabs* are quite popular.

Grouper Has firm, meaty, white flesh and is sold whole or filleted. There are many species: One is marketed as *Chilean sea bass,* even though it is really a type of grouper.

Haddock Very closely related to cod, it is almost always sold with the skin on.

Halibut A large flatfish with firm, flavorful flesh. Often sold as fillets, but one of the few flatfish thick enough to be cut into steaks.

Mackerel An oily fish with a pronounced fish flavor. This fish can turn rancid quickly, so keep well refrigerated. When large, it is called *Spanish mackerel.*

Monkfish A favored fish of French Provençal cooks, monkfish has firm flesh and a lobsterlike flavor. The meaty flesh is removed from the large tail in two thick fillets and then usually cut into steaks. If a thin gray membrane covers the fillets, remove it before cooking.

Ocean perch On the West Coast, this fish is called *rock cod* or *rockfish.* It has delicately textured pinkish flesh and a flavor similar to red snapper.

Orange roughy A very mild flavored fish, usually shipped frozen from the southern Pacific. Use as you would any flaky white fish.

Pike A large freshwater game fish available worldwide and especially popular in the northern lakes of the U.S. because of its mildly flavored, firm white flesh.

Pollock A mild white-fleshed fish similar to cod but with a smaller flake. Atlantic pollock is sometimes called *Boston bluefish,* although it doesn't resemble that full-flavored oily fish at all. Pacific pollock is often processed into *surimi,* a crab-meat substitute.

Pompano This is the fish's Atlantic Coast name; Pacific pompano is called *yellowtail.* It is either left whole or filleted and is a popular fish for grilling. It has somewhat oily flesh and a firm texture.

Red snapper An excellent all-purpose fish and one of the few fillets firm enough to be grilled. Be careful when buying snapper because there are many species. Although others are acceptable, not all have the same fine flavor and texture as true red snapper. These "impostors" include yellow snapper and Pacific red snapper, which is really a red rockfish that is similar to ocean perch.

Salmon Much of the salmon in our markets is farm-raised, even when labeled "Atlantic" or "Norwegian." It is consistently excellent, but true wild salmon, such as *coho, king,* and *sockeye,* have superior flavor. Wild salmon are available in limited quantities from the spring through the fall.

Shad A bony fish with firm white flesh and delicious flavor. It is available in the spring. Remove as many bones as possible before cooking. Shad roe (the egg sac from the females) is a delicacy; cook it gently to maintain its creamy texture.

Skate Actually a ray with a complicated cartilage structure. Let the fishmonger fillet the wings for you. A favorite of restaurant chefs, it has firm, flaky flesh.

Smelts Tiny fish, either freshwater or saltwater, that are cooked whole and eaten off the bone. Smelts are usually sold gutted and headless. If you can only buy head-on smelts, make an incision along the belly of each fish and pull off the head; the guts and gills will come out at the same time. They are sometimes called *whitebait*.

Sole True sole is a flatfish with firm white flesh and a distinctively delicious flavor. *Dover sole*, from the English Channel and North Sea, is highly prized. *English, petrale, lemon,* and *sand soles* are excellent choices but not in the same league as Dover sole.

Striped bass Fishing fans and their friends have long appreciated the meaty (but not oily) flavor of wild striped bass. Most of the striped bass in today's markets is a farm-raised hybrid of striped bass and white bass. The farm-raised variety has a less distinctive flavor but is still a very good eating fish and is readily available.

Swordfish The firm and meaty texture of swordfish makes it a good choice for various cooking techniques as well as for marinades. The skin is very tough and inedible; remove it before or after cooking.

Tilapia A farm-raised fish that is easily found at supermarkets but one that lacks depth of flavor. It is best served with full-flavored sauces.

Tilefish An Atlantic Coast fish with a codlike flavor but with a firmer, meatier texture, which flakes into large pieces; excellent baked or broiled.

Trout When referring to trout, most cooks think of the small *rainbow* or *brook* varieties that are about twelve ounces each and served one to a diner rather than large trout, such as Atlantic char, that are served in portions. These smaller trout were once game fish but are now usually farm-raised.

Tuna A huge fish with plenty of muscle and flavor. The most common varieties are *bluefin* (expensive and rare), *yellowfin* (most readily available and very good), *albacore* (pale pink flesh and slightly milder flavor), and *skipjack*. Tuna is also known as *ahi* and *bonito*.

Turbot A large flatfish resembling halibut. European turbot (always pricey) has the best flavor and texture.

Whiting A very delicate white-fleshed fish; also known as *hake* or *merluzzo*. Whiting often look dull and limp even though they're perfectly fresh.

KNOW YOUR SHELLFISH

Mollusks have soft bodies that are protected by shells consisting of one or more parts. This glossary lists the most popular.

Clams Hard-shell clams, the most common Atlantic Coast variety, are categorized by size. *Littlenecks* are the smallest (less than two inches in diameter), *cherrystones* are medium, and *chowder clams* (with meat so tough it is usually chopped) are the largest. *Manila clams*, imported from tropical Pacific waters, are small and have gorgeous striped shells.

Soft-shell clams have delicate shells that don't completely close because of the long necklike siphon that protrudes from the two halves of the shell. On the East Coast, they are usually called *steamers*, because they are best prepared by steaming. West Coast soft-shell clams include the huge *geoduck* (GOO-ee-duck) and the long *razor clam*, whose shell resembles a straight-edged razor.

When buying hard-shell clams, be sure the shells are tightly closed and not broken. If slightly open, they should snap shut when tapped; discard any that don't. To check soft-shell clams, touch the siphon; it should retract slightly.

As they eat, soft-shell clams often collect grit in their bodies. You will want them to expel it before cooking. To help remove the grit, soak the clams in a large bowl filled with well-salted cold water in the refrigerator for about two hours, then drain. Hard-shell clams should be scrubbed well under cold running water before shucking (page 286), which should always be done just before serving.

Mussels Most markets carry *blue mussels*. They have bluish black shells and are harvested wild or cultivated. *New Zealand green mussels*, which are slightly larger and have a bright green shell, can also be found at some fish markets.

Buy mussels with undamaged tightly closed shells or with shells that snap shut when tapped. Discard any that remain open. Avoid mussels that feel heavy (they may be full of mud) or any that feel light and loose (they may be dead).

Just before cooking, scrub the mussels under cold water and scrape away any barnacles. Pull off the beards (the hairlike cord attached to each mussel) as shown on page 291. Cultivated (farm-raised) mussels may not have beards. Once the beards have been removed, cook the mussels immediately, because they will soon die and spoil.

Oysters Oysters are usually named for the location of their beds. Some of the most famous are *Wellfleet, Chincoteague,* and *Apalachicola* on the East Coast and *Westcott Bay,*

Tomales Bay, and the tiny *Olympia* on the West Coast. They are best during the fall and winter months, because most species spawn in the summer. Since spawning leaves them tired and not as plump as usual, some oyster fans choose not to eat them in the months that don't have an "r" in their names (May, June, July, and August).

Purchase oysters with undamaged, tightly closed shells. If you buy shucked oysters, the packing liquid should be clear, not cloudy. Clean fresh oysters by scrubbing them with a stiff brush under cold running water to remove any sand. Shuck oysters just before serving, discarding any whose shells are open or damaged.

Scallops Unshucked scallops with their orange roe still attached are sometimes available at high-quality fish stores, but shucked scallops are much more common. The part of the scallop we eat is called the adductor muscle. The scallop uses this muscle to slam its shells together and to create a strong jet of water to propel itself.

The three most common types of scallops are *sea, bay,* and *calico.* Sea scallops are gathered year round and are relatively large. If more than two inches in diameter, cut them in half or into quarters before cooking. Small bay scallops are only available in the fall and winter. While they are expensive, their sweet flavor is worth the price. Calico scallops are very small, but because they have been shucked by a commercial steaming method that parcooks them, they have the least flavor and the toughest texture.

Scallops are highly perishable and are usually shucked right on the boat. Many scallops are soaked in a preservative solution to keep them from spoiling. Avoid scallops that are shiny and look just a bit too plump and white; they could develop an odd flavor and expel a lot of liquid when cooked. The best scallops look almost dry (in fact, fishmongers call unsoaked scallops "dry"). For the best results, cook scallops just until they turn opaque throughout; overcooking makes them tough.

Squid Sometimes called by its Italian name, *calamari,* squid is economical and delicious, especially when deep-fried.

Cleaned squid is pretty easy to find, but if you have to clean your own, see page 302. Buy small squid with bright white flesh, clear eyes, and a fresh ocean aroma. Refrigerate for no longer than a day or two in a tightly covered container. Frozen squid is very good, but it usually comes in large two- to three-pound boxes; defrost under cold running water.

THE FISH EXCHANGE

Lean	Moderate	Oily
Cod, Scrod	Bluefish	Bluefin tuna
Flounder	Catfish	Butterfish
Grouper	Mahi-mahi	Herring
Haddock	Rainbow trout	Lake trout
Halibut	Striped bass	Mackerel
Monkfish	Swordfish	Pompano
Ocean perch	Yellowfin tuna	Salmon
Orange roughy		Shad
Pike		Whitefish
Pollock		
Red snapper		
Rockfish		
Sea bass		
Sole		
Tilefish		
Turbot		
Whiting		

CRUSTACEANS

Crustaceans have elongated bodies covered by jointed shells. Their sweet, succulent meat is one of the true eating pleasures.

Crab Crab is available in many forms: cooked or live, and fresh or frozen. The meat is sometimes removed from the shell and sold separately.

On the West Coast (and in high-quality fish stores in the rest of the country), look for the large, deliciously sweet *Dungeness crab.* Its season runs from October to April. *King crab,* usually from Alaska, provides the large legs that are sold fresh or frozen.

Small *blue crabs* are found along the East and Gulf Coasts. Their meat is usually cooked, picked from the shells, and packaged. The large pieces of meat from the body are sold as *lump, jumbo,* or *backfin crabmeat.* Smaller pieces from the body or claw, called *flaked crabmeat*, are usually sold with a piece of the claw shell still attached, which makes a natural holder. Be sure to pick carefully through crabmeat to remove any stray bits of cartilage or shell. Crabmeat is usually pasteurized to prolong its shelf life, but unpasteurized crabmeat, when you can find it, has a richer flavor. If you choose to buy artificial crabmeat, sometimes called *surimi*, be prepared to sacrifice a lot of quality for the lower price.

Soft-shell crabs are blue crabs caught during the short period after they have shed their hard shells and before their new soft shells have hardened. They are available fresh from May to September. (They require a special cleaning technique; see page 289.) It is best to buy soft-shell crabs fresh; clean them just before cooking. If the fish market cleans them for you, cook the crabs within a few hours.

Stone crabs are popular in Florida. The claws are harvested, and the rest of the crab is tossed back into the water so new claws can regenerate.

Lobster There are two types of lobster: *American (Maine) lobster,* from the North Atlantic coast, which is the most popular, and *rock (spiny) lobster.* Rock lobster, which is commercially harvested off Florida, California, Australia, and New Zealand, has no claws. It is usually sold as frozen lobster tail.

When buying a live lobster, pick it up near its head; the tail should curl under and the lobster should feel heavy for its size. If it's too light, the meat has begun to dry out, and if it doesn't put up a good fight, it is tired and won't taste good. Also, check that both claws are intact. One-clawed lobsters, called *culls*, are sometimes available at a reduced price.

When buying whole lobsters, allow a 1¼- to 1½-pound lobster for each serving. Larger lobsters make a good visual impression, but their meat can be tough. If buying tails, allow one 6- to 8-ounce tail or two or three smaller tails per serving.

Shrimp After canned tuna, shrimp is the most popular seafood in America. Although we think of shrimp as being fresh, more than 95 percent of it has been previously frozen. Fresh shrimp usually ends up in restaurants, where it is often given a special name such as *dayboat shrimp* (so-called because the shrimp boat returns on the same day it goes out).

There are thousands of shrimp varieties, but only a few hundred have any commercial value. The two major types available are *warm-water shrimp* and *cold-water shrimp.* Warm-water shrimp live in tropical waters and are usually categorized by the color of their shell: pink, white, blue, or black tiger; the color distinctions are not always visible to the naked eye. When shrimp are cooked, they turn red or orange. Cold-water shrimp, from the frigid waters of the Pacific Northwest, Maine, and Scandinavia, are the tiny pink shrimp used in salads and sandwiches in restaurants and food stores.

Shrimp is also sorted by size. Some regions use a size description such as extra-large, whereas other areas use the number of shrimp in a pound (extra-large would correspond to 26 to 30 shrimp per pound). In any case, these denominations are somewhat arbitrary, so common sense has to come into play. We like to cook with large shrimp (about 30 shrimp per pound) or medium shrimp (about 35 shrimp per pound). Very large shrimp are often called *prawns,* but in California, any shrimp can be called a prawn regardless of size.

Select shrimp with firm-looking meat and shiny shells that look and feel full. Avoid shrimp with black spots, which are a sign of aging. Shrimp are usually sold without their heads; if not, gently pull the head away from the body before shelling. Cooked shrimp should be plump with white flesh and a mild, sweet, appetizing aroma.

When buying shrimp in their shells, buy about 25 percent more than you think you will need to account for the weight of the shells. For example, 1¼ pounds of shrimp will yield 1 pound after shelling and deveining. Shrimp can be shelled either before or after cooking. However, if the cooked shrimp is to be used in a salad, cook it with the shell on for the most flavor. Deveining small and medium shrimp is optional; the vein in large shrimp should be removed. See page 296 for instructions on how to shell and devein shrimp.

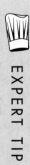

When it comes to lobsters, don't buy any amputees, and don't accept lobsters with short antennae. It means they've been in the tank for a long time and have had their antennae eaten by another lobster.

To be sure lobster is of good quality, turn it over and stick your finger inside the first ring of the belly. The skin should be taut and you should be able to feel the lumpy meat underneath.

ERIC RIPERT
EXECUTIVE CHEF, LE BERNARDIN, NEW YORK CITY

EXPERT TIP

ANCHOVIES These tiny salted fish are an important seasoning in Mediterranean cooking. They are most commonly found filleted, salt-cured, and canned in oil. Because most recipes only call for a few fillets, you will often have leftover anchovies; cover the can tightly with plastic wrap and use within one week. Anchovy paste is a convenient product because there is no waste. About ½ teaspoon of anchovy paste equals one fillet. Italian markets often carry salted anchovy fillets in bulk. These are larger and meatier than the canned fillets and should be rinsed well before using to remove any salt.

CAVIAR Real caviar is the salted roe of sturgeon. You may see lumpfish and salmon "caviar," but they are not really caviar—they're just fish eggs. Caviar is food fit for kings; it is rare, costly, and uniquely delicious. There are three categories: Beluga (large dark gray eggs), osetra (medium eggs that range in color from yellow to brown), and sevruga (smaller eggs that are light gray). Some caviar is also graded as *malossol*, which means "little salt." It is not a type of caviar.

SALT COD Cod that has been salted and dried. Salt cod is especially popular in Mediterranean cooking. It can be purchased in specialty food stores (where it is sometimes vacuum-packed). Buy thick white pieces: Salt cod turns gray as it ages. Salt cod is always soaked before cooking to remove the salt.

SMOKED SALMON Once a culinary icon of New York City's Jewish population, smoked salmon can now be found all over the country (just like the bagel). Nova is named after the true Nova Scotia salmon, which is rarely seen in our markets. It has been cured in brine and then smoked. Lox is salmon that has been pickled in a spiced brine but is not always smoked.

Grilled Whole Flounder

Make sure your grill is good and hot when you cook this deliciously simple fish. It's a perfect quick dinner for two. If you have a hinged fish grilling basket, use it here. Simply oil the basket before enclosing the fish.

Prep: 5 minutes   Grill: 14 minutes

1	whole flounder (1½ pounds), cleaned and scaled
1	teaspoon vegetable oil
½	teaspoon salt
	lemon wedges

1. Prepare grill. Rinse flounder inside and out with cold running water; pat dry with paper towels. Rub oil all over flounder; sprinkle with salt. Grill flounder over medium-high heat until just opaque throughout when knife is inserted at backbone, about 7 minutes per side.

2. To serve, slide cake server under front section of top fillet and lift off fillet; transfer to platter. Slide server under backbone and lift it away from bottom fillet; discard. Slide cake server between bottom fillet and skin and transfer fillet to platter. Serve with lemon wedges. Makes 2 main-dish servings.

Each serving: About 161 calories, 29g protein, 0g carbohydrate, 4g total fat (1g saturated), 74mg cholesterol, 704mg sodium.

Fish live in cold water, so their enzymes work at cold temperatures. Fish lose quality fast—even in the refrigerator. Try to buy fish on the day you are cooking it, but if you have to keep it even overnight, place it in a large strainer set over a bowl, pile ice on top of the fish, and refrigerate. The melting ice will rinse away any bacteria and keep the fish in better condition.

SHIRLEY O. CORRIHER

COOKBOOK AUTHOR

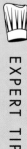

EXPERT TIP

Poached Whole Salmon

This classic buffet dish is very beautiful but not at all difficult to prepare. Try other sauces, too, such as Salsa Verde (page 554) or Tzatziki (page 38).

Prep: 30 minutes plus chilling   Cook: 40 minutes

10	cups water
2	cups dry white wine or dry vermouth
2	stalks celery, sliced
1	medium onion, cut into quarters
1	large carrot, peeled and sliced
1	lemon, sliced
4½	teaspoons salt
½	teaspoon whole black peppercorns
1	whole salmon (7 to 8 pounds), cleaned and scaled
	double recipe Basil Mayonnaise (page 234)
¼	cup prepared mayonnaise
1	English (seedless) cucumber

1. In 26-inch fish poacher, combine water, wine, celery, onion, carrot, lemon, salt, and peppercorns; heat to boiling over high heat; cover and cook 10 minutes.

2. Rinse salmon inside and out with cold running water. Place salmon on rack in fish poacher; heat poaching liquid to boiling. Reduce heat; cover and simmer until fish is just opaque when knife is inserted at backbone, about 30 minutes. Lift out poaching rack and, using two wide spatulas, transfer salmon to large platter. Cover fish and refrigerate until well chilled, about 2 hours 30 minutes.

3. Meanwhile, prepare Basil Mayonnaise.

4. Carefully peel off skin from top of salmon; discard. Spread prepared mayonnaise evenly over fish. Thinly slice cucumber; arrange slices, overlapping slightly, on salmon to resemble scales. To serve, slide cake server under front section of top fillet and lift off fillet; transfer to separate platter. Slide server under backbone and lift it away from bottom fillet; discard. Slide cake server between bottom fillet and skin and transfer fillet to platter. Serve with Basil Mayonnaise. Makes 16 main-dish servings.

Each serving without mayonnaise: About 281 calories, 28g protein, 1g carbohydrate, 18g total fat (3g saturated), 84mg cholesterol, 247mg sodium.

Tarragon-Roasted Salmon

No fish poacher? Roast a whole salmon in the oven!

Prep: 10 minutes   Roast: 40 minutes

2	large lemons, thinly sliced
1	whole salmon (5½ pounds), cleaned and scaled
2	tablespoons olive oil
½	teaspoon salt
½	teaspoon coarsely ground black pepper
1	large bunch tarragon
1	small bunch parsley
	Caper Sauce (page 260)
	lemon wedges

1. Preheat oven to 450°F. Line jelly-roll pan with foil.

2. Place one-third of lemon slices in row down center of pan. Rinse salmon inside and out with cold running water; pat dry with paper towels. Rub outside of salmon with oil. Place salmon on top of lemon slices. Sprinkle cavity with salt and pepper. Place tarragon and parsley sprigs and half of remaining lemon slices in cavity. Arrange remaining lemon slices on top of fish.

3. Roast salmon until just opaque throughout when knife is inserted at backbone, about 40 minutes.

4. Meanwhile, prepare Caper Sauce.

5. Carefully remove lemon slices and peel off skin from top of salmon; discard. Using two wide spatulas, transfer salmon to cutting board.

6. To serve, slide cake server under front section of top fillet and lift off fillet; transfer to warm large platter. Slide server under backbone and lift it away from bottom fillet; discard. Slide cake server between bottom fillet and skin and transfer fillet to platter. Serve with lemon wedges and caper sauce. Makes 10 main-dish servings.

Each serving without sauce: About 325 calories, 33g protein, 1g carbohydrate, 20g total fat (4g saturated), 96mg cholesterol, 213mg sodium.

Caper Sauce

In medium bowl, mix ¾ **cup sour cream,** ½ **cup mayonnaise,** ¼ **cup milk, 3 tablespoons capers,** drained and chopped, **2 tablespoons chopped fresh tarragon,** ½ **teaspoon freshly grated lemon peel,** and ⅛ **teaspoon coarsely ground black pepper** until blended. Cover and refrigerate until ready to serve, up to 2 days. Makes about 1⅔ cups.

Each tablespoon: About 58 calories, 0g protein, 1g carbohydrate, 6g total fat (2g saturated), 7mg cholesterol, 90mg sodium.

Chinese-Style Steamed Fish

(Pictured on page 250)

This is one of the easiest, most foolproof, and flavorful ways to cook a whole fish. A large wok with a wire rack makes an ideal steamer, but you can also use a heat-safe plate set on a rack in a large Dutch oven.

 Prep: 10 minutes plus marinating   Cook: 10 minutes

1	whole sea bass or red snapper (2½ to 3 pounds), cleaned and scaled
	1½-inch piece fresh ginger, peeled and cut into 1½" by ¼" matchstick strips
2	green onions, cut into 1½" by ¼" matchstick strips
2	tablespoons vegetable oil
2	tablespoons soy sauce
2	teaspoons Asian sesame oil
1½	teaspoons seasoned rice vinegar
¼	teaspoon salt
	pinch ground red pepper (cayenne)

1. Rinse bass inside and out with cold running water; pat dry with paper towels. Make three diagonal slashes on each side of fish, cutting almost to bone. Place fish on lightly oiled heat-safe deep plate that will fit into wok (if necessary, trim head and tail of fish to fit). Place ginger and half of green onions in cavity of fish.

2. In cup, with fork, beat vegetable oil, soy sauce, sesame oil, vinegar, salt, and ground red pepper until blended. Drizzle half of soy-sauce mixture in fish cavity and drizzle remaining mixture on top of fish, rubbing mixture into skin and slashes. Let fish stand 20 minutes at room temperature.

3. Place 1-inch-high wire rack in wok. Add enough *water* to come up to rack. Set plate with fish on rack. Heat water to boiling, then cover and steam over medium heat until fish is just opaque when knife is inserted at backbone, allowing 10 to 12 minutes per inch of fish (measuring at thickest part). Carefully remove cover and let steam escape. Carefully lift out plate with fish. To serve, use two wide slotted spatulas to transfer fish to large platter. Sprinkle with remaining green onions. Makes 4 main-dish servings.

Each serving: About 209 calories, 23g protein, 2g carbohydrate, 12g total fat (2g saturated), 50mg cholesterol, 779mg sodium.

Grilled Whole Sea Bass with Lemon and Herbs

The firm white flesh of sea bass holds up well on the grill. If you can't get whole sea bass, substitute red snapper or striped bass.

 Prep: 5 minutes   Grill: 15 minutes

2	whole sea bass (1½ pounds each), cleaned and scaled
1½	teaspoons salt
4	thin lemon slices, each cut in half
8	oregano or rosemary sprigs
1	tablespoon olive oil

1. Prepare grill. Rinse bass inside and out with cold running water; pat dry with paper towels. Make three diagonal slashes on each side of fish, cutting almost to bone. Sprinkle fish inside and out with salt. Place lemon slices and oregano sprigs in fish cavities. Rub oil all over bass. Grill bass over medium-high heat until just opaque when knife is inserted at backbone, about 8 minutes per side.

2. To serve, slide cake server under front section of top fillet of each fish and lift off fillet; transfer to platter. Slide server under backbone and lift it away from bottom fillet; discard. Slide cake server between bottom fillet and skin and transfer fillet to platter. Makes 4 main-dish servings.

Each serving: About 162 calories, 25g protein, 1g carbohydrate, 6g total fat (1g saturated), 54mg cholesterol, 673mg sodium.

Fried Smelts

Available from September through May, these small fish are especially delicious when coated with bread crumbs and fried.

Prep: 10 minutes   Cook: 10 minutes

8	smelts (4 ounces each), cleaned and scaled
½	cup plain dried bread crumbs
1	teaspoon salt
¼	teaspoon ground black pepper
2	large eggs
2	tablespoons water
4	tablespoons vegetable oil
	lemon wedges

1. Rinse smelts inside and out with cold running water; pat dry with paper towels. On waxed paper, combine bread crumbs, salt, and pepper. In pie plate, lightly beat eggs and water. Dip fish, one at a time, into eggs, then into bread crumbs, patting crumbs to evenly cover. Place fish on separate sheet of waxed paper.

2. In 12-inch skillet, heat 2 tablespoons oil over medium-high heat until hot. Fry 4 smelts until just opaque throughout, about 2 minutes per side. Transfer to paper towels to drain. Repeat with remaining oil and remaining fish. Serve smelts with lemon wedges. Makes 4 main-dish servings.

Each serving: About 339 calories, 27g protein, 14g carbohydrate, 20g total fat (3g saturated), 194mg cholesterol, 806 mg sodium.

Salt-Baked Fish

Baking a whole fish in a crust of kosher salt seals in the juices and guarantees exquisitely moist (and surprisingly unsalty) flesh.

Prep: 5 minutes   Bake: 30 minutes

4	cups kosher salt
1	whole red snapper, striped bass, or porgy (1½ pounds), cleaned and scaled
1	lemon
3	rosemary or thyme sprigs

1. Preheat oven to 450°F. Line 13" by 9" baking pan with foil; spread 2 cups salt in bottom of pan.

2. Rinse snapper inside and out with cold running water; pat dry with paper towels. From lemon, cut 3 slices. Cut remaining lemon into wedges. Place lemon slices and rosemary in cavity of fish. Place snapper on bed of salt; cover with remaining 2 cups salt. Bake until fish is just opaque throughout when knife is inserted at backbone, about 30 minutes.

3. To serve, tap salt crust to release from top of fish; discard. Slide cake server under front section of top fillet and lift off fillet; transfer to platter. Slide server under backbone and lift it away from bottom fillet; discard. Slide cake server between bottom fillet and skin and transfer fillet to platter. Serve with reserved lemon wedges. Makes 2 main-dish servings.

Each serving: About 188 calories, 37g protein, 6g carbohydrate, 3g total fat (1g saturated), 66mg cholesterol, 800mg sodium.

Roasted Striped Bass

Serve this dramatic-looking entrée with an herb sauce such as Salsa Verde (page 554), Chimichurri (page 554), or Salmoriglio (page 554), or with lemon wedges.

Prep: 5 minutes   Roast: 30 minutes

1	whole striped bass (2¼ pounds), cleaned and scaled
3	thin slices lemon
3	rosemary sprigs (optional)

1. Preheat oven to 450°F. Rinse bass inside and out with cold running water; pat dry with paper towels. Place lemon slices and rosemary, if using, in cavity. Make diagonal slashes on each side of fish at 1-inch intervals, about ¼ inch deep. Place bass in medium roasting pan (14" by 10"). Roast until fish is just opaque throughout when knife is inserted at backbone, about 30 minutes.

2. To serve, slide cake server under front section of top fillet and lift off fillet; transfer to platter. Slide server under backbone and lift it away from bottom fillet; discard. Slide cake server between bottom fillet and skin and transfer fillet to platter. Makes 4 main-dish servings.

Each serving: About 117 calories, 20g protein, 0g carbohydrate, 4g total fat (1g saturated), 88mg cholesterol, 76mg sodium.

Trout Meunière

Here's a basic recipe for sautéed trout and three mouthwatering variations. One trout per person makes a generous serving.

Prep: *10 minutes plus standing*   **Cook:** *20 minutes*

4	brook or rainbow trout (10 to 12 ounces each), cleaned and scaled
1	cup milk
¼	cup all-purpose flour
½	teaspoon salt
4	tablespoons vegetable oil
¼	cup fresh lemon juice
4	tablespoons butter or margarine
¼	cup chopped fresh parsley

1. Rinse trout inside and out with cold running water; pat dry with paper towels. Soak fish in milk 10 minutes. On waxed paper, combine flour and salt. Remove trout from milk and coat with flour mixture, shaking off excess.

2. In 12-inch skillet, heat 2 tablespoons oil over medium heat until very hot. Add 2 trout and cook until just opaque throughout when knife is inserted in backbone, 4 to 5 minutes per side. Transfer to platter and keep warm. Repeat with remaining oil and remaining fish.

3. Pour off any fat remaining in skillet and wipe skillet clean with paper towels. Return skillet to heat; add lemon juice and cook 15 seconds. Add butter; cook until foamy, about 2 minutes. Stir in parsley and pour butter sauce over fish. Makes 4 main-dish servings.

Each serving: About 493 calories, 41g protein, 8g carbohydrate, 32g total fat (10g saturated), 143mg cholesterol, 468mg sodium.

Trout Meunière

Trout with Brown Butter and Sage

Prepare as directed through Step 2. Omit parsley. Add **2 tablespoons chopped fresh sage** to skillet with butter and cook until butter is lightly browned, about 3 minutes. Add **1 teaspoon fresh lemon juice** and pour sauce over fish.

Trout Amandine

Prepare as directed through Step 2. Omit parsley. Add **¼ cup sliced almonds** to skillet with butter and cook until almonds are golden, 2 to 3 minutes. Add **1 teaspoon fresh lemon juice** and pour sauce over fish.

Trout Grenobloise

Prepare as directed through Step 2. Omit lemon juice. From **1 lemon,** remove peel and white pith. Cut lemon into ¼-inch-thick slices; discard seeds. Cut slices into ½-inch pieces. After cooking butter until foamy, add lemon pieces, **4 teaspoons capers,** and **1 tablespoon chopped fresh parsley.** Spoon sauce over fish.

Trout with Cornmeal and Bacon

Dipped in a crunchy cornmeal coating and topped with crisp bacon, this trout is a real down-home treat.

Prep: 5 minutes plus standing	Cook: 25 minutes
4	brook or rainbow trout (10 to 12 ounces each), cleaned and scaled
1	cup milk
⅓	cup cornmeal
½	teaspoon salt
¼	teaspoon ground black pepper
4	slices bacon
	vegetable oil for frying

1. Rinse trout inside and out with cold running water; pat dry with paper towels. Soak fish in milk 10 minutes. On waxed paper, combine cornmeal, salt, and pepper. Remove trout from milk and coat evenly with cornmeal mixture, shaking off excess.

2. Meanwhile, in 12-inch skillet, cook bacon over medium heat until browned. With slotted spoon, transfer bacon to paper towels to drain; crumble.

3. Transfer all but 2 tablespoons bacon drippings to small bowl and reserve. Heat drippings in skillet over medium heat until very hot. Add 2 trout and cook until just opaque throughout when knife is inserted at backbone, 4 to 5 minutes per side. Transfer to platter and keep warm. Repeat with reserved bacon drippings, adding enough vegetable oil to equal 2 tablespoons, if necessary, and remaining fish. To serve, sprinkle bacon over fish. Makes 4 main-dish servings.

Each serving: About 408 calories, 43g protein, 10g carbohydrate, 21g total fat (6g saturated), 127mg cholesterol, 515mg sodium.

Cold Poached Salmon Steaks with Watercress Sauce

One of the best warm-weather entrées around. Fast and easy, and you don't have to turn on the oven.

Prep: 15 minutes plus cooling	Cook: 10 minutes
1	medium lemon
4	salmon steaks, 1 inch thick (6 ounces each)
¾	teaspoon salt
½	teaspoon coarsely ground black pepper
1	medium onion, thinly sliced
	Watercress Sauce (page 264)

1. From lemon, squeeze juice; reserve for Watercress Sauce. Set lemon shell aside. Rub salmon steaks evenly with salt and pepper.

2. In 12-inch skillet, heat *½ inch water* to boiling over high heat. Add salmon, onion, and lemon shell; heat to boiling. Reduce heat; cover and simmer until fish is just opaque throughout, 5 to 8 minutes. With slotted spatula, transfer fish to platter. Let cool 30 minutes, or cover and refrigerate to serve later.

3. Meanwhile, prepare Watercress Sauce.

4. Remove skin and bones from salmon, if you like. Serve with watercress sauce. Makes 4 main-dish servings.

Each serving without sauce: About 274 calories, 30g protein, 0g carbohydrate, 16g total fat (3g saturated), 88mg cholesterol, 231mg sodium.

Watercress Sauce

In blender or in food processor with knife blade attached, puree ½ **bunch watercress,** tough stems trimmed (1 cup), **½ cup sour cream, 1 tablespoon fresh lemon juice, 1 teaspoon chopped fresh tarragon or ⅛ teaspoon dried tarragon, 1½ teaspoons sugar,** and **1 teaspoon salt** until smooth. Cover and refrigerate. Makes about ½ cup sauce.

Each tablespoon: About 35 calories, 1g protein, 2g carbohydrate, 3g total fat (2g saturated), 6mg cholesterol, 301mg sodium.

Grilled Spiced Salmon Steaks

Rich salmon steaks marry well with our fragrant spice blend.

Prep: 5 minutes   Grill: 8 minutes

1	tablespoon chili powder
2	teaspoons brown sugar
1	teaspoon ground cumin
1	teaspoon dried thyme
1	teaspoon salt
2	teaspoons olive oil
4	salmon steaks, ¾ inch thick (8 ounces each)
	lemon wedges

1. Prepare grill. In cup, combine chili powder, brown sugar, cumin, thyme, salt, and oil. Use to rub on both sides of salmon steaks.

2. Grill salmon over medium heat until just opaque throughout, about 4 minutes per side. Serve with lemon wedges. Makes 4 main-dish servings.

Each serving: About 403 calories, 40g protein, 4g carbohydrate, 24g total fat (5g saturated), 118mg cholesterol, 721mg sodium.

Broiled Salmon Steaks

A quick way to get healthful salmon steaks onto the dinner table.

Prep: 3 minutes   Broil: 10 minutes

4	salmon steaks, 1 inch thick (6 ounces each)
1	teaspoon vegetable oil
	pinch salt
	pinch ground black pepper

Preheat broiler. Rub both sides of salmon steaks with oil and sprinkle with salt and pepper. Place salmon on rack in broiling pan. Place pan in broiler, 4 inches from heat source. Broil salmon 5 minutes, then turn and broil until fish is just opaque throughout, about 5 minutes longer. Makes 4 main-dish servings.

Each serving: About 284 calories, 30g protein, 0g carbohydrate, 17g total fat (3g saturated), 88mg cholesterol, 123mg sodium.

Salmon Steaks Teriyaki

This dish is a time-honored classic in Japanese restaurants. The sauce also works well with swordfish, tuna, and catfish.

Prep: 10 minutes   Broil: 10 minutes

6	tablespoons soy sauce
½	teaspoon Asian sesame oil
3	tablespoons brown sugar
1	garlic clove, finely chopped
1	teaspoon minced, peeled fresh ginger
4	salmon steaks, 1 inch thick (6 ounces each)
2	green onions, cut on diagonal into thin slices

1. In small saucepan, combine soy sauce, sesame oil, brown sugar, garlic, and ginger; heat to boiling over medium-high heat. Boil until mixture has thickened slightly, about 3 minutes. Strain through fine sieve; discard solids.

2. Preheat broiler. Place salmon on rack in broiling pan. Place pan in broiler, 4 inches from heat source. Broil salmon 3 minutes; brush generously with teriyaki sauce and broil 2 minutes longer. Turn fish and broil 3 minutes. Brush with remaining teriyaki sauce and broil until fish is just opaque throughout, 2 to 3 minutes longer. Sprinkle with green onions and serve. Makes 4 main-dish servings.

Each serving: About 336 calories, 31g protein, 13g carbohydrate, 17g total fat (3g saturated), 88mg cholesterol, 1,637mg sodium.

Swordfish Steaks Broiled with Maître d'Hôtel Butter

Terrific with the classic lemon-and-herb butter, but any of the other flavored butters (page 563) would be just as inviting. If you like, top each steak with a tablespoon of the herbed butter.

Prep: 15 minutes   Broil: 8 minutes

4	teaspoons Maître d'Hôtel Butter (page 563)
4	swordfish steaks, 1 inch thick (6 ounces each)

1. Prepare Maître d'Hôtel Butter.

2. Preheat broiler. Place swordfish on rack in broiling pan. Spread ½ teaspoon maître d'hôtel butter on each side of each fish steak. Place pan in broiler, 4 inches from heat source. Broil swordfish, without turning, until just opaque throughout, 8 to 10 minutes. Spoon pan juices over fish to serve. Makes 4 main-dish servings.

Each serving: About 217 calories, 30g protein, 0g carbohydrate, 10g total fat (4g saturated), 69mg cholesterol, 175mg sodium.

Swordfish Steaks Broiled with Maître d'Hôtel Butter

Swordfish Kabobs

A favorite along the coasts of Turkey, serve with steamed rice.

Prep: 25 minutes plus marinating   Grill: 5 minutes

1	pound boneless swordfish steak, 1 inch thick
½	cup chicken or vegetable broth
3	tablespoons fresh lemon juice
1	tablespoon olive oil
1	very small onion, thinly sliced
2	garlic cloves, thinly sliced
14	large bay leaves
½	teaspoon salt
½	teaspoon paprika
¼	teaspoon ground coriander
⅛	teaspoon ground black pepper
12	(7-inch) bamboo skewers
12	thin lemon slices, seeded and each cut in half
1	tablespoon chopped fresh parsley

1. Discard swordfish skin. Cut fish into 1-inch cubes.

2. In medium bowl, combine broth, lemon juice, oil, onion, garlic, 2 bay leaves, salt, paprika, coriander, and pepper. Add swordfish and toss to coat. Cover and refrigerate fish 3 hours to marinate, tossing occasionally.

3. Meanwhile, soak remaining 12 bay leaves and bamboo skewers 1 hour in enough *boiling water* to cover. Drain. With kitchen shears, snip each bay leaf crosswise in half.

4. Prepare grill or preheat broiler. Remove swordfish from marinade, reserving marinade. Thread each skewer as follows: ½ bay leaf, cube swordfish, ½ lemon slice, cube swordfish; then repeat once, gently pressing bay leaves, lemon slices, and fish together.

5. Grill kabobs over medium-high heat, turning kabobs and brushing with marinade during first half of cooking, until fish is just opaque throughout, 5 to 8 minutes. Or broil 3 to 4 inches from heat source, turning kabobs and brushing with marinade, until just opaque throughout, 5 to 8 minutes.

6. Meanwhile, strain remaining marinade into small saucepan and heat to boiling; boil 3 minutes. Strain marinade, if desired. Arrange kabobs on platter, drizzle with hot marinade, and sprinkle with parsley. Makes 4 main-dish servings.

Each serving: About 189 calories, 22g protein, 7g carbohydrate, 8g total fat (2g saturated), 42mg cholesterol, 514mg sodium.

Swordfish with Balsamic Glaze

Balsamic vinegar, blended with brown sugar and reduced to a syrup, makes a rich, winelike glaze that is perfect with meaty swordfish. For a delicious variation, serve the fish atop a salad.

Prep: 15 minutes   Grill: 7 minutes

2	teaspoons olive oil
¼	cup finely chopped shallots
½	cup balsamic vinegar
2	teaspoons brown sugar
2	teaspoons tomato paste
¼	teaspoon dried thyme
¼	teaspoon salt
¼	teaspoon ground black pepper
4	swordfish steaks, 1 inch thick (6 ounces each)

1. Prepare grill. In 10-inch skillet, heat oil over medium-low heat. Add shallots and cook, stirring occasionally, until tender, about 4 minutes. Add vinegar and brown sugar; increase heat to high and boil until liquid has thickened and is syrupy, about 5 minutes. Remove from heat and stir in tomato paste until blended.

2. Sprinkle thyme, salt, and pepper on swordfish. Grill over medium-high heat 4 minutes. Turn swordfish and brush with glaze; grill until just opaque throughout, 3 to 4 minutes longer. Makes 4 main-dish servings.

Each serving: About 226 calories, 30g protein, 5g carbohydrate, 8g total fat (2g saturated), 59mg cholesterol, 305mg sodium.

Balsamic-Glazed Swordfish with Greens

In large bowl, whisk together **2 tablespoons balsamic vinegar, 2 tablespoons extravirgin olive oil,** and **⅛ teaspoon salt.** Add **2 cups each washed, dried, and torn Bibb and Boston lettuce** and **2 cups sliced Belgian endive;** toss to coat. Place on plates. Prepare fish as directed and serve over greens.

Each serving: About 299 calories, 31g protein, 8g carbohydrate, 16g total fat (3g saturated), 59mg cholesterol, 388mg sodium.

Sicilian Tuna

A robust sauce of tomatoes, Kalamata olives, capers, and chopped fresh basil complements the flavor of the marinated tuna steaks.

Prep: 25 minutes plus marinating   Broil: 6 minutes

6	tablespoons olive oil
5	tablespoons fresh lemon juice
4	anchovy fillets, chopped
1	garlic clove, finely chopped
¼	teaspoon dried thyme
⅛	teaspoon ground black pepper
8	tuna steaks, ¾ inch thick (5 ounces each)
1	large stalk celery, chopped
3	ripe medium plum tomatoes, chopped
2	green onions, sliced
¼	cup pitted Kalamata or Niçoise olives, coarsely chopped
2	tablespoons capers, drained
¼	cup chopped fresh basil

1. In 13" by 9" baking dish, combine 3 tablespoons oil, 3 tablespoons lemon juice, anchovies, garlic, thyme, and pepper. Add tuna, turning to coat. Cover and refrigerate fish at least 45 minutes or up to 2 hours to marinate, turning once.

2. Meanwhile, in 2-quart saucepan, heat remaining 3 tablespoons oil over medium heat; add celery and cook 5 minutes. Stir in tomatoes, green onions, olives, and capers; cook until mixture has thickened slightly, about 5 minutes. Stir in basil and remaining 2 tablespoons lemon juice; keep warm.

3. Preheat broiler. Place tuna on rack in broiling pan. Place pan in broiler at closest position to heat source. Broil tuna until pale pink in center (medium), about 3 minutes per side or until desired doneness. Serve tuna with sauce. Makes 8 main-dish servings.

Each serving: About 239 calories, 24g protein, 3g carbohydrate, 14g total fat (2g saturated), 39mg cholesterol, 291mg sodium.

Pan-Seared Tuna

This is a great way to cook tuna steaks: Get the oil in the pan very hot and sear the fish very quickly. The oil in the marinade moistens the fish but hardly adds any fat at all.

Prep: 10 minutes plus marinating   Cook: 6 minutes
4 large lemons
6 tablespoons olive oil
6 tablespoons chopped fresh parsley
½ teaspoon salt
¼ teaspoon ground black pepper
4 tuna steaks, ¾ inch thick (5 ounces each)

1. From lemons, grate 1 teaspoon peel and squeeze ⅔ cup juice. In 9-inch square baking dish, with wire whisk, whisk lemon peel and juice, 3 tablespoons oil, 5 tablespoons parsley, salt, and pepper until mixed. Add tuna, turning to coat. Cover and refrigerate 45 minutes to marinate, turning occasionally.

2. In 10-inch cast-iron skillet or other heavy skillet, heat remaining 3 tablespoons oil over medium-high heat until hot. Add tuna and cook until pale pink in center (medium), about 3 minutes per side or until desired doneness. Transfer to plates and sprinkle with remaining 1 tablespoon parsley. Makes 4 main-dish servings.

Each serving: About 246 calories, 30g protein, 1g carbohydrate, 13g total fat (2g saturated), 48mg cholesterol, 341mg sodium.

Do not buy cubed fish or already-skewered fish for kabobs. Some markets use this ploy to sell otherwise unwanted bellies. And the bellies, especially on swordfish, can have more parasites than other parts of the fish.

JASPER WHITE
COOKBOOK AUTHOR

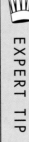

EXPERT TIP

Halibut Braised in Red Wine

Red wine does go with fish! Here, the slight acidity of the wine accents the mild halibut. Salmon and monkfish also work well.

Prep: 10 minutes   Cook: 30 minutes
2 tablespoons butter or margarine
½ cup finely chopped shallots (3 large)
1 garlic clove, finely chopped
1 carrot, peeled and thinly sliced
2 cups dry red wine
¾ cup chicken broth
½ teaspoon salt
¼ teaspoon dried thyme
4 skinless, boneless halibut steaks, 1 inch thick (6 ounces each)
2 tablespoons chopped fresh parsley

1. In nonstick 12-inch skillet, melt 1 tablespoon butter over low heat. Add shallots and garlic and cook, stirring occasionally, until shallots are tender, about 4 minutes. Add carrot and cook 4 minutes longer. Add wine and heat to boiling over high heat; boil 2 minutes. Add broth, salt, and thyme. Slip in halibut and reduce heat to low. Cover and cook until fish is just opaque throughout, about 8 minutes. With slotted spatula, transfer fish to platter and keep warm.

2. Increase heat to high and boil wine mixture until it has reduced by half, 7 to 10 minutes. Remove from heat and swirl in remaining 1 tablespoon butter until melted. Strain sauce through fine-mesh sieve. To serve, spoon sauce over fish and sprinkle with parsley. Makes 4 main-dish servings.

Each serving: About 277 calories, 37g protein, 8g carbohydrate, 10g total fat (4g saturated), 70mg cholesterol, 643mg sodium.

Greek-Style Grilled Halibut

Greek cooks have long favored the clean, simple flavors of fresh lemon and oregano with fish.

Prep: 10 minutes plus marinating   Grill: 6 minutes

1	lemon
3	tablespoons olive oil
2	garlic cloves, finely chopped
2	teaspoons chopped fresh oregano
½	teaspoon salt
4	halibut steaks, ¾ inch thick (6 ounces each)

1. From lemon, grate 1 teaspoon peel and squeeze 2 tablespoons juice. In large bowl, with wire whisk, whisk lemon peel and juice, oil, garlic, oregano, and salt until mixed. Add halibut, turning to coat. Cover and refrigerate fish 1 hour to marinate, turning once or twice.

2. Meanwhile, prepare grill. Remove halibut from marinade. Grill halibut over high heat, brushing with marinade during first half of grilling, until halibut is just opaque throughout, 3 to 4 minutes per side. Makes 4 main-dish servings.

Each serving: About 199 calories, 29g protein, 1g carbohydrate, 8g total fat (1g saturated), 44mg cholesterol, 218mg sodium.

Greek-Style Grilled Halibut

Cod Veracruz

This is fish, Mexican-style. Chile aficionados may want to add a little more cayenne pepper or use hot chili powder.

Prep: 15 minutes   Cook: 35 minutes

4	tablespoons vegetable oil
1	yellow pepper, cut into thin strips
1	medium onion, thinly sliced
1	jalapeño chile, seeded and finely chopped
1	garlic clove, thinly sliced
¾	teaspoon chili powder
½	teaspoon salt
1	can (14½ to 16 ounces) tomatoes in puree
½	teaspoon ground coriander
¼	teaspoon ground cumin
⅛	teaspoon ground red pepper (cayenne)
4	cod steaks, ¾ inch thick (4 ounces each)

1. In nonstick 12-inch skillet, heat 2 tablespoons oil over medium heat. Add yellow pepper and onion and cook, stirring, until tender and golden, 15 minutes. Add jalapeño, garlic, ½ teaspoon chili powder, and ¼ teaspoon salt and cook, stirring, 3 minutes.

2. Add tomatoes with their puree and cook, breaking up tomatoes with side of spoon, until mixture has slightly reduced, about 10 minutes.

3. In cup, combine coriander, cumin, remaining ¼ teaspoon each chili powder and salt, and ground red pepper. Sprinkle both sides of cod steaks with spice mixture.

4. In 10-inch skillet, heat remaining 2 tablespoons oil until hot. Add cod and cook until just opaque throughout and nicely browned, 3 to 4 minutes per side. To serve, arrange fish on platter and top with warm tomato sauce. Makes 4 main-dish servings.

Each serving: About 254 calories, 19g protein, 12g carbohydrate, 14g total fat (2g saturated), 43mg cholesterol, 508mg sodium.

Broiled Cod Steaks Montauk

A flavored mayonnaise topping is a quick way to add punch to grilled fish.

🕐 Prep: 5 minutes   Broil: 6 minutes

¼	cup mayonnaise
½	teaspoon Dijon mustard
⅛	teaspoon salt
⅛	teaspoon ground black pepper
4	cod steaks, ½ inch thick (6 ounces each)

1. Preheat broiler. In small bowl, combine mayonnaise, mustard, salt, and pepper.

2. Lightly oil rack in broiling pan. Place cod on rack in broiling pan. Place pan in broiler, 4 inches from heat source. Broil cod until just opaque throughout, 5 to 7 minutes. Remove broiling pan from broiler. Brush mayonnaise mixture on fish. Return pan to broiler; broil until mayonnaise mixture is lightly browned and bubbling, 1 to 2 minutes longer. Makes 4 main-dish servings.

Each serving: About 222 calories, 27g protein, 0g carbohydrate, 12g total fat (2g saturated), 72mg cholesterol, 247mg sodium.

Lemon Topping

Prepare as directed but substitute ½ **teaspoon freshly grated lemon peel** for Dijon mustard.

Horseradish Topping

Prepare as directed but substitute **1 teaspoon bottled white horseradish** for Dijon mustard.

Dill-Pepper Topping

Prepare as directed but substitute **2 tablespoons chopped fresh dill** for Dijon mustard and ¼ **teaspoon coarsely ground black pepper** for ground black pepper.

Lime-Jalapeño Topping

Prepare as directed but substitute ½ **teaspoon freshly grated lime peel** for Dijon mustard and add **1 small jalapeño chile**, seeded and minced.

Parmesan Topping

Prepare as directed but substitute **2 tablespoons freshly grated Parmesan cheese** for Dijon mustard.

Dried Tomato Topping

Prepare as directed but substitute **1 dried tomato,** finely chopped, for Dijon mustard.

Fennel-Crusted Bluefish

If you prefer to grill, rub the bluefish with olive oil, then with the fennel mixture. Serve with lemon wedges.

🕐 Prep: 5 minutes   Cook: 8 minutes

2	teaspoons fennel seeds, crushed
½	teaspoon whole black peppercorns, crushed
½	teaspoon salt
4	pieces bluefish fillet (6 ounces each)
1	tablespoon butter or margarine
1	teaspoon olive oil

1. In cup, combine fennel seeds, peppercorns, and salt. Use to rub on both sides of bluefish fillets.

2. In nonstick 12-inch skillet, melt butter with oil over medium-high heat. Add bluefish and cook until fish is just opaque throughout, 4 to 6 minutes per side. Makes 4 main-dish servings.

Each serving: About 247 calories, 34g protein, 0g carbohydrate, 11g total fat (3g saturated), 108mg cholesterol, 422mg sodium.

Fried Catfish

Before frying, let the coated fish fillets stand for a few minutes to set the crust: It will stay on better and fry to crispy perfection.

Prep: 15 minutes plus standing   Cook: 20 minutes

¾	cup cornmeal
2	tablespoons all-purpose flour
½	teaspoon salt
¼	teaspoon ground black pepper
¼	cup milk
6	catfish fillets (6 ounces each)
4	tablespoons vegetable oil
	lemon wedges

1. In ziptight plastic bag, combine cornmeal, flour, salt, and pepper. Pour milk into pie plate. Dip catfish fillets, one at a time, into milk to coat well, then into cornmeal mixture, shaking bag to coat fish. Place coated catfish on wire rack set over waxed paper; set aside to dry 20 minutes.

2. In 10-inch skillet, heat 2 tablespoons oil over medium-high heat until hot. Add 3 catfish fillets to skillet and fry until just opaque throughout and golden, 4 to 5 minutes per side. Transfer to paper towels to drain. Repeat with remaining 2 tablespoons oil and remaining catfish. Serve with lemon wedges. Makes 6 main-dish servings.

Each serving: About 377 calories, 28g protein, 16g carbohydrate, 22g total fat (4g saturated), 58mg cholesterol, 255mg sodium.

Jerk Catfish with Grilled Pineapple

This Jamaican-style fish is flavored with a spicy jerk seasoning and served with grilled brown sugar-glazed pineapple wedges.

Prep: 15 minutes   Grill: 10 minutes

2	green onions, chopped
1	jalapeño chile, seeded and minced
1	tablespoon minced, peeled fresh ginger
2	tablespoons white wine vinegar
2	tablespoons Worcestershire sauce
1	tablespoon vegetable oil
1¼	teaspoons dried thyme
1	teaspoon ground allspice
¼	teaspoon salt
4	catfish fillets (5 ounces each)
2	tablespoons brown sugar
1	small pineapple, cut lengthwise into 4 wedges

1. Prepare grill. In medium bowl, combine green onions, jalapeño, ginger, vinegar, Worcestershire, oil, thyme, allspice, and salt. Add catfish, turning to coat. Let stand 5 minutes.

2. Meanwhile, rub brown sugar on flesh of pineapple.

3. Place pineapple and catfish on grill over medium-high heat. Brush half of jerk mixture in bowl on catfish. Grill 5 minutes. Turn pineapple and catfish. Brush remaining jerk mixture on fillets and cook until fish is just opaque throughout and pineapple is golden brown, 5 to 7 minutes longer. Makes 4 main-dish servings.

Each serving: About 351 calories, 23g protein, 35g carbohydrate, 14g total fat (3g saturated), 47mg cholesterol, 279mg sodium.

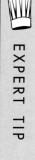

Any of the many fish or crab cakes in this book can be turned into delicious hors d'oeuvres by rolling the mixtures into small balls and deep-frying them. You may need to tighten the mixture with bread crumbs, if too loose.

JASPER WHITE
COOKBOOK AUTHOR

EXPERT TIP

Barbecued Catfish

Fish fillets glazed with a slightly sweet sauce are sure to be a hit with adults and kids alike. Serve with coleslaw and corn on the cob.

Prep: 5 minutes   Broil: 8 minutes

¼	cup ketchup
2	tablespoons light (mild) molasses
2	teaspoons red wine vinegar
¼	teaspoon Worcestershire sauce
4	catfish fillets (6 ounces each)

Preheat broiler. In small bowl, combine ketchup, molasses, vinegar, and Worcestershire. Place catfish fillets, skinned side up, on rack in broiling pan. Brush half of sauce on catfish. Place pan in broiler, about 6 inches from heat source. Broil catfish 4 minutes. Brush remaining sauce on fillets (do not turn) and broil until fish is just opaque throughout, about 4 minutes longer. Makes 4 main-dish servings.

Each serving: About 261 calories, 26g protein, 11g carbohydrate, 12g total fat (3g saturated), 56mg cholesterol, 241mg sodium.

TURNING FILLETS IN FRYING PAN

To turn fish fillets so they don't fall apart, use a wide spatula, supporting the fillet with your fingers as you turn it.

Codfish Cakes

Crisp but tender fish cakes are a great weekend supper; serve with homemade Tartar Sauce (page 552).

Prep: 30 minutes plus chilling   Cook: 10 minutes

3	tablespoons vegetable oil
2	large stalks celery, chopped
1	small onion, chopped
1½	cups fresh bread crumbs (about 3 slices bread)
1	pound cod fillet
1	large egg, lightly beaten
2	tablespoons light mayonnaise
1	tablespoon chopped fresh parsley
1	teaspoon fresh lemon juice
¼	teaspoon hot pepper sauce
½	teaspoon salt
	lemon wedges

1. In 12-inch skillet, heat 1 tablespoon oil over medium heat. Add celery and onion and cook, stirring occasionally, until onion is tender and lightly browned, about 10 minutes. Remove from heat.

2. Place two-thirds of bread crumbs on waxed paper. Place remaining crumbs in medium bowl. With tweezers, remove any bones from cod. With large chef's knife, finely chop fish; add to bowl with bread crumbs. Stir in celery-onion mixture, egg, mayonnnaise, parsley, lemon juice, pepper sauce, and salt until well combined.

3. Shape fish mixture into four 3-inch patties (mixture will be very soft and moist). Refrigerate patties until firm, at least 30 minutes. Wipe skillet clean.

4. Use bread crumbs on waxed paper to coat patties, patting crumbs to cover. In same skillet, heat remaining 2 tablespoons oil over medium-low heat until hot. Add patties to skillet and cook until browned and cooked through, 5 to 6 minutes per side. Serve with lemon wedges. Makes 4 main-dish servings.

Each serving: About 298 calories, 24g protein, 15g carbohydrate, 16g total fat (2g saturated), 105mg cholesterol, 565mg sodium.

Mexican Fish Cakes

These creatively spiced fish cakes have just a hint of heat. Serve with parslied rice and a steamed green vegetable or thickly sliced summer tomatoes.

Prep: 35 minutes   Cook: 12 minutes

2	tablespoons vegetable oil
1	medium onion, chopped
1	large garlic clove, finely chopped
¼	teaspoon ground cinnamon
¼	teaspoon ground cumin
	pinch ground cloves
1½	cups fresh bread crumbs (about 3 slices bread)
1	pound cod fillet
1	large egg, lightly beaten
1	tablespoon fresh lime juice
1	jalapeño chile, seeded and minced
3	tablespoons chopped fresh cilantro
½	teaspoon salt
1	tablespoon butter or margarine
	lime wedges

1. In 12-inch skillet, heat 1 tablespoon oil over medium heat. Add onion and cook, stirring frequently, until tender, about 5 minutes. Stir in garlic, cinnamon, cumin, and cloves; cook 30 seconds. Transfer to medium bowl; wipe skillet clean.

2. Place two-thirds of bread crumbs on waxed paper. Add remaining crumbs to onion mixture in bowl.

3. With tweezers, remove any bones from cod. With large chef's knife, finely chop fish; add to bowl with bread crumbs. Stir in egg, lime juice, jalapeño, 2 tablespoons cilantro, and salt. Shape fish mixture into four 3-inch patties.

4. Toss remaining 1 tablespoon cilantro with crumbs on waxed paper; use to coat patties, patting crumbs to cover. In same skillet, melt butter with remaining 1 tablespoon oil over medium-low heat until hot. Add patties and cook until browned and cooked through, 6 to 8 minutes per side. Serve with lime wedges. Makes 4 main-dish servings.

Each serving: About 275 calories, 24g protein, 16g carbohydrate, 13g total fat (3g saturated), 110mg cholesterol, 512mg sodium.

Old-Fashioned Fish Cakes

Don't let last night's supper go to waste! Make these fish cakes with leftover cooked fish and mashed potatoes.

Prep: 15 minutes   Cook: 6 minutes

¼	cup plain dried bread crumbs
½	teaspoon salt
⅛	teaspoon ground black pepper
1	cup flaked cooked white fish
⅔	cup mashed potatoes
1	large egg, lightly beaten
1	green onion, finely chopped
2	tablespoons chopped fresh parsley
2	tablespoons butter or margarine
	lemon wedges

1. On waxed paper, combine bread crumbs, salt, and pepper. In large bowl, combine fish, potatoes, egg, green onion, and parsley. Shape into four 3½-inch patties. Use bread-crumb mixture to coat patties, patting crumbs to cover.

2. In 12-inch skillet, melt butter over medium-high heat until hot. Add patties and cook until golden and heated through, 3 minutes per side. Serve with lemon wedges. Makes 4 main-dish servings.

Each serving: About 180 calories, 13g protein, 11g carbohydrate, 9g total fat (4g saturated), 93mg cholesterol, 560mg sodium.

Baked Scrod with Fennel and Potatoes

A simple dish that only needs a green salad to a be complete meal.

Prep: 15 minutes   Bake: 55 minutes

1½	pounds red potatoes (4 large), not peeled, thinly sliced
1	medium fennel bulb (1 pound), trimmed and thinly sliced, feathery tops reserved
1	garlic clove, finely chopped
2	tablespoons olive oil
¾	plus ⅛ teaspoon salt
½	teaspoon coarsely ground black pepper
4	pieces scrod fillet (5 ounces each)
1	large ripe tomato (8 ounces), seeded and chopped

1. Preheat oven to 425°F. In shallow 2½-quart baking dish, toss potatoes, fennel, garlic, oil, ¾ teaspoon salt, and ¼ teaspoon pepper until well combined; spread evenly in baking dish. Bake, stirring once, until vegetables are tender and lightly browned, about 45 minutes.

2. With tweezers, remove any bones from scrod. Sprinkle scrod with remaining ⅛ teaspoon salt and remaining ¼ teaspoon pepper. Arrange on top of potato mixture. Bake until fish is just opaque throughout, 10 to 15 minutes. Sprinkle with tomato and garnish with reserved fennel tops. Makes 4 main-dish servings.

♥ Each serving: About 335 calories, 30g protein, 35g carbohydrate, 8g total fat (1g saturated), 61mg cholesterol, 679mg sodium.

Scrod with Lemon-Garlic Bread Crumbs

An easy way to bake flaky scrod fillets: Top with garlicky crumbs.

Prep: 20 minutes   Bake: 10 minutes

2	tablespoons butter or margarine
1	garlic clove, finely chopped
1	cup fresh bread crumbs (about 2 slices bread)
4	pieces scrod or cod fillet (6 ounces each)
2	tablespoons fresh lemon juice
½	teaspoon salt
1	tablespoon chopped fresh parsley
	lemon wedges

1. Preheat oven to 450°F. In 10-inch skillet, melt butter over medium heat. Add garlic; cook until golden. Add bread crumbs and cook, stirring frequently, until lightly toasted. Remove skillet from heat.

2. With tweezers, remove any bones from scrod. In 13" by 9" baking dish, arrange fillets; sprinkle with lemon juice and salt. Press bread-crumb mixture onto fillets. Bake until fish is just opaque throughout, 10 to 15 minutes.

3. To serve, sprinkle scrod with parsley and serve with lemon wedges. Makes 4 main-dish servings.

♥ Each serving: About 231 calories, 32g protein, 8g carbohydrate, 7g total fat (4g saturated), 89mg cholesterol, 517mg sodium.

Cod, Cabbage, and Bacon in Parchment

You might find cod prepared this way in a French restaurant, but it's simple enough to make at home. Curly savoy cabbage is more delicate than plain green cabbage and goes especially well with the subtle flavor of cod.

Prep: 20 minutes   Bake: 20 minutes

2	slices bacon, chopped
2	teaspoons vegetable oil
½	head (¾ pound) savoy cabbage, thinly sliced (6 cups)
½	plus ⅛ teaspoon salt
¼	plus ⅛ teaspoon ground black pepper
	pinch dried thyme
4	thick pieces cod fillet (6 ounces each)
4	squares (12 inches each) cooking parchment or foil
1	tablespoon butter or margarine, cut into pieces

1. Preheat oven to 400°F.

2. In 12-inch skillet, cook bacon over medium-low heat until browned. Transfer to paper towels to drain. Discard drippings from skillet; wipe skillet clean.

3. Heat oil in same skillet. Add cabbage, ½ teaspoon salt, ¼ teaspoon pepper, and thyme; cook over high heat, stirring frequently, until cabbage is tender. Stir in bacon.

4. With tweezers, remove any bones from cod. Place one-fourth cabbage mixture on one half of each parchment square to create bed for fish. Place fillets on top of cabbage. Sprinkle fillets with remaining ⅛ teaspoon each salt and pepper and evenly dot with butter.

5. Fold unfilled half of parchment over cod. To seal packets, beginning at a corner where parchment is folded, make small ½-inch-wide folds, with each new fold overlapping previous one, until packet is completely sealed. Packet will resemble half circle. Place packets in jelly-roll  pan. Bake 20 minutes (packets will puff up and brown). Cut packets open to serve. Makes 4 main-dish servings.

Each serving: About 232 calories, 33g protein, 7g carbohydrate, 8g total fat (3g saturated), 84mg cholesterol, 567mg sodium.

Lemon-Thyme Cod

Lemon peel and thyme add zest to these panfried cod fillets.

🕐 *Prep: 5 minutes   Cook: 10 minutes*

2	large lemons
2	tablespoons all-purpose flour
2	teaspoons chopped fresh thyme or ½ teaspoon dried thyme
½	teaspoon salt
¼	teaspoon coarsely ground black pepper
4	pieces cod fillet (5 ounces each)
2	tablespoons butter or margarine

1. From 1 lemon, grate peel; cut remaining lemon into thick wedges.

2. On waxed paper, combine flour, lemon peel, thyme, salt, and pepper. With tweezers, remove any bones from cod. Coat fillets with seasoned flour, shaking off excess.

3. In nonstick 12-inch skillet, melt butter over medium-high heat until hot. Add cod and cook until just opaque throughout, about 5 minutes per side. Serve with lemon wedges. Makes 4 main-dish servings.

Each serving: About 190 calories, 26g protein, 7g carbohydrate, 7g total fat (4g saturated), 77mg cholesterol, 426mg sodium.

Roasted Scrod with Tomato Relish

A sweet-and-sour relish is just the thing to perk up scrod fillets.

Prep: 15 minutes   Cook/Roast: 40 minutes

1	can (28 ounces) plum tomatoes
3	teaspoons vegetable oil
1	small onion, chopped
2	tablespoons water
¼	cup red wine vinegar
2	tablespoons brown sugar
½	teaspoon salt
4	pieces scrod fillet (6 ounces each)
¼	teaspoon coarsely ground black pepper

1. Preheat oven to 450°F. Drain tomatoes; cut each tomato into quarters.

2. In 2-quart saucepan, heat 2 teaspoons oil over medium heat. Add onion and water and cook until tender and golden, about 10 minutes. Stir in tomatoes, vinegar, brown sugar, and ¼ teaspoon salt; heat to boiling over high heat. Continue cooking over high heat, stirring frequently, until relish has thickened, about 15 minutes.

3. Meanwhile, with tweezers, remove any bones from scrod. Arrange fillets in 9-inch square baking dish; sprinkle with remaining 1 teaspoon oil, pepper, and remaining ¼ teaspoon salt. Roast scrod until just opaque throughout, 12 to 15 minutes. To serve, transfer fish to plates and spoon tomato relish on top. Makes 4 main-dish servings.

♥ Each serving: About 248 calories, 32g protein, 18g carbohydrate, 5g total fat (1g saturated), 73mg cholesterol, 708mg sodium.

Oven-Fried Fish

Here's a reduced-fat way to get crispy fish without lots of oil. To keep the fat profile low, serve with Tartar Sauce (page 552), made with lowfat mayonnaise or simply sprinkle the fish with malt vinegar. For fish and chips, serve with crisp Oven Fries (page 452) and malt vinegar.

🕐 *Prep: 10 minutes   Bake: 12 minutes*

2	teaspoons vegetable oil
¼	cup all-purpose flour
½	teaspoon salt
¼	teaspoon ground red pepper (cayenne)
2	large egg whites
1	cup plain dried bread crumbs
1	pound flounder or sole fillets, cut on diagonal into 1-inch-wide strips

1. Preheat oven to 450°F. Grease cookie sheet with oil.

2. On waxed paper, combine flour, salt, and ground red pepper. In shallow bowl, beat egg whites just until foamy. On separate sheet of waxed paper, place bread crumbs. Coat flounder strips with seasoned flour, shaking off excess. Dip into egg white, then coat in bread crumbs, patting crumbs to cover. Arrange fish strips on prepared cookie sheet.

3. Place cookie sheet on lowest oven rack and bake fish 6 minutes. With wide spatula, turn fish. Bake until just opaque throughout and golden, about 6 minutes longer. Makes 4 main-dish servings.

♥ Each serving: About 267 calories, 27g protein, 26g carbohydrate, 5g total fat (1g saturated), 54mg cholesterol, 642mg sodium.

Baked Flounder with Savory Crumb Topping

Need a fast midweek supper? This tasty flounder is just the ticket.

Prep: 15 minutes   Bake: 10 minutes

1½	cups fresh bread crumbs (about 3 slices bread)
2	tablespoons chopped fresh parsley
¼	cup dry white wine
4	flounder fillets (5 ounces each)
¼	teaspoon salt
¼	cup mayonnaise

1. Preheat oven to 400°F. In 10-inch skillet, toast bread crumbs over medium heat, stirring frequently, until golden, about 10 minutes. Remove from heat and stir in parsley.
2. Pour wine into 13" by 9" baking dish; add flounder fillets, turning to coat. Arrange fillets, skinned side up, in dish, tucking thin ends under. Sprinkle with salt and spread mayonnaise on top. Gently pat bread-crumb mixture over mayonnaise. Bake until fish is just opaque throughout and topping has crisped, about 10 minutes. Makes 4 main-dish servings.

Each serving: About 295 calories, 29g protein, 11g carbohydrate, 13g total fat (2g saturated), 76mg cholesterol, 452mg sodium.

Crispy Flounder

Here's another basic fish recipe with a couple of delicious variations to suit any mood.

Prep: 15 minutes   Cook: 8 minutes

1	cup plain dried bread crumbs
2	tablespoons chopped fresh parsley (optional)
¾	teaspoon salt
4	flounder or sole fillets (4 ounces each)
2	tablespoons butter or margarine

1. On waxed paper, combine bread crumbs, parsley if using, and salt. Use bread-crumb mixture to coat flounder fillets, patting crumbs to cover.
2. In 12-inch skillet, melt 1 tablespoon butter over medium-high heat until hot. Add 2 fillets and cook until just opaque throughout and golden, 2 to 3 minutes per side. Transfer to platter; keep warm. With paper towels, wipe pan clean; melt remaining 1 tablespoon butter and cook remaining fillets. Makes 4 main-dish servings.

Each serving: About 261 calories, 25g protein, 20g carbohydrate, 9g total fat (4g saturated), 70mg cholesterol, 819mg sodium.

Parmesan Cheese Fillets
Prepare as directed but only use ⅔ cup plain dried bread crumbs and add ⅓ cup freshly grated Parmesan cheese to bread-crumb mixture.

Sesame Seed Fillets
Prepare as directed but only use ¾ cup plain dried bread crumbs and add ¼ cup sesame seeds to bread-crumb mixture.

Asian-Style Flounder Baked in Parchment

Baking in parchment packets seals in the juices and the flavor. Substitute foil for the parchment paper, if necessary.

Prep: 15 minutes   Bake: 8 minutes

2	large green onions
2	tablespoons soy sauce
2	tablespoons seasoned rice vinegar
4	flounder fillets (6 ounces each)
4	sheets (12" by 15" each) cooking parchment or foil
2	teaspoons grated, peeled fresh ginger

1. Cut green onion tops into 2" by ¼" matchstick strips; reserve for garnish. Thinly slice white part of green onions.

2. In small bowl, combine soy sauce and vinegar.

3. Preheat oven to 425°F. Place 1 flounder fillet on one half of each parchment sheet. Sprinkle with ginger and sliced green onions; drizzle with soy-sauce mixture. Fold unfilled half of parchment over fish. To seal packets, beginning at a corner where parchment is folded, make small ½-inch-wide folds, with each new fold overlapping previous one, until packet is completely sealed. Packet will resemble half-circle. Place packets in jelly-roll pan. Bake 8 minutes (packets will puff up and brown).

4. To serve, cut packets open and garnish fish with reserved green-onion strips. Makes 4 main-dish servings.

Each serving: About 170 calories, 33g protein, 3g carbohydrate, 2g total fat (0g saturated), 82mg cholesterol, 802mg sodium.

Rolled Sole Stuffed with Crab

For a fuss-free dinner party, roll up the fish and refrigerate up to four hours before baking; the sauce can also be prepared ahead and reheated just before serving.

Prep: 20 minutes   Bake: 25 minutes

2	tablespoons butter or margarine
4	tablespoons finely chopped shallots
8	ounces lump crabmeat, picked over
½	cup fresh bread crumbs (about 1 slice bread)
1	tablespoon chopped fresh parsley
2	teaspoons fresh lemon juice
½	plus ⅛ teaspoon salt
⅛	teaspoon plus pinch ground black pepper
6	sole or flounder fillets (6 ounces each)
1	can (14 to 16 ounces) tomatoes, drained
¼	cup heavy or whipping cream
1	teaspoon chopped fresh tarragon or parsley

Rolled Sole Stuffed with Crab

1. Preheat oven to 400°F. Grease 13" by 9" baking dish.

2. In nonstick 10-inch skillet, melt 1 tablespoon butter over medium heat. Add 2 tablespoons shallots and cook until tender, about 2 minutes. Transfer to medium bowl. Add crabmeat, bread crumbs, parsley, lemon juice, $\frac{1}{4}$ teaspoon salt, and $\frac{1}{8}$ teaspoon pepper; toss with fork until evenly combined.

3. Sprinkle skinned side of sole fillets with $\frac{1}{4}$ teaspoon salt. Spoon crabmeat mixture evenly over fillets. Roll up fillets and place, seam side down, in prepared baking dish. Bake until just opaque throughout, about 25 minutes.

4. Meanwhile, in blender, puree tomatoes until smooth. In same 10-inch skillet, melt remaining 1 tablespoon butter over medium heat. Add remaining 2 tablespoons shallots and cook until tender, about 2 minutes. Add pureed tomatoes, remaining $\frac{1}{8}$ teaspoon salt, and remaining pinch pepper; increase heat to high and cook, stirring frequently, until liquid has almost evaporated, about 5 minutes. Stir in cream and heat to boiling. Remove from heat and stir in tarragon.

5. With wide slotted spatula, transfer fish to warm platter. Stir any juices in baking dish into tomato sauce; spoon sauce over fish. Makes 6 main-dish servings.

Each serving: About 298 calories, 41g protein, 7g carbohydrate, 11g total fat (5g saturated), 144mg cholesterol, 665mg sodium.

SAUCES FOR FISH

Unlike meat and poultry dishes, where pan sauces are often created from the cooking juices, most fish sauces are separate recipes. For a Mediterranean touch, try Salmoriglio Sauce (page 553) or Salsa Verde (page 554). Some favorite mayonnaise-based sauces include Tartar Sauce (page 552), Sauce Gribiche (page 553), and Easy Aïoli (page 40). Salsas, such as Orange-Fennel or Olive and Lemon (page 555), are excellent condiments for grilled fish, or top fish with a pat of Pesto Butter or Herb Butter (page 563).

Portuguese-Style Monkfish

Here, chunks of firm monkfish are cooked in a spicy sausage-tomato sauce until deliciously tender. Serve over rice or pasta.

Prep: 25 minutes	Cook: 40 minutes

1	tablespoon olive oil
1	medium onion, chopped
3	garlic cloves, finely chopped
1	fully cooked chorizo sausage (3 ounces), cut lengthwise into quarters, then crosswise into thin slices
1	red pepper, chopped
$\frac{2}{3}$	cup chicken broth
1	can (14 to 16 ounces) tomatoes, chopped
$\frac{1}{4}$	teaspoon salt
$\frac{1}{4}$	teaspoon crushed red pepper
$1\frac{1}{2}$	pounds monkfish, dark membrane removed, cut into 1-inch pieces
$\frac{1}{4}$	cup chopped fresh parsley

1. In nonstick 10-inch skillet, heat oil over medium-low heat. Add onion and garlic and cook, stirring frequently, until onion is tender, about 5 minutes.

2. Add chorizo and chopped red pepper and cook, stirring frequently, until pepper is tender, about 5 minutes. Add broth and heat to boiling. Stir in tomatoes with their juice, salt, and crushed red pepper; heat to boiling.

3. Add monkfish to skillet. Reduce heat; cover and simmer until monkfish is tender, about 10 minutes. With slotted spoon, transfer monkfish to bowl. Increase heat to high and boil liquid until sauce has reduced and is thickened, about 5 minutes. Return fish to skillet and stir in parsley. Makes 4 main-dish servings.

Each serving: About 308 calories, 32g protein, 11g carbohydrate, 15g total fat (4g saturated), 61mg cholesterol, 781mg sodium.

Salmon Burgers

Not for ginger lovers only, these Asian-style burgers are topped with home-pickled ginger. A V-shape food slicer or mandoline makes quick work of slicing the ginger.

Prep: 45 minutes	*Cook: 10 minutes*
	Pickled Ginger (below)
1	pound salmon fillet, skin removed
2	green onions, thinly sliced
1	teaspoon grated, peeled fresh ginger
2	tablespoons soy sauce
1/4	teaspoon ground black pepper
1/4	cup plain dried bread crumbs
2	tablespoons sesame seeds
1	tablespoon vegetable oil

1. Prepare Pickled Ginger.

2. Meanwhile, with tweezers, remove any bones from salmon. Using large chef's knife, finely chop fish. Place in medium bowl and stir in green onions, ginger, soy sauce, and pepper. Shape into four 3-inch patties. On waxed paper, combine bread crumbs and sesame seeds; use to coat patties, patting crumbs to cover.

3. In nonstick 10-inch skillet, heat oil over medium heat until hot. Add patties and cook until golden and cooked through, about 5 minutes per side. Top with Pickled Ginger. Makes 4 main-dish servings.

Each serving with Pickled Ginger: About 341 calories, 23g protein, 22g carbohydrate, 18g total fat (3g saturated), 63mg cholesterol, 638mg sodium.

Pickled Ginger

In 1-quart saucepan, combine **1 cup water, 1/2 cup distilled white vinegar,** and **1/4 cup sugar;** heat to boiling over high heat. Add **1/4 cup thinly sliced, peeled fresh ginger;** reduce heat and simmer until tender, about 30 minutes. Drain.

Salmon and Lentils

This nicely herbed dish features a sprightly lemon dressing, spooned over flavorful salmon and lentils. Serve a green vegetable or salad on the side.

Prep: 10 minutes	*Cook/Bake: 50 minutes*
1	cup lentils, rinsed and picked through
2 1/4	cups water
3/4	plus 1/8 teaspoon salt
4	pieces salmon fillet with skin (6 ounces each)
1	teaspoon plus 2 tablespoons olive oil
1/8	plus 1/4 teaspoon coarsely ground pepper
1	lemon
1	teaspoon Dijon mustard
4	teaspoons chopped fresh tarragon
1	tablespoon butter or margarine
1/4	cup finely chopped shallots
1/4	cup chopped fresh parsley

1. Preheat oven to 400°F. In 2-quart saucepan, combine lentils, water, and 1/2 teaspoon salt; heat to boiling over high heat. Reduce heat; cover and simmer until lentils are tender, 20 to 30 minutes. Drain.

2. Meanwhile, grease 13" by 9" baking dish. With tweezers, remove any bones from salmon. Arrange fillets in prepared baking dish. Rub with 1 teaspoon oil and sprinkle with 1/8 teaspoon each salt and pepper. Bake until fish is just opaque throughout, 15 to 20 minutes.

3. While salmon is baking, prepare dressing: From lemon, grate 1/2 teaspoon peel and squeeze 2 tablespoons juice. In small bowl, with wire whisk, whisk together lemon juice, mustard, and remaining 1/4 teaspoon salt. Gradually whisk in remaining 2 tablespoons oil, then stir in 2 teaspoons tarragon.

4. In 10-inch skillet, melt butter over medium heat. Add shallots and cook, stirring, 2 minutes. Stir in lentils, lemon peel, and remaining 1/4 teaspoon pepper. Remove from heat and stir in parsley and remaining 2 teaspoons tarragon. Spread lentil mixture on platter. Arrange salmon on top of lentils and spoon dressing over. Makes 4 main-dish servings.

Each serving: About 582 calories, 48g protein, 30g carbohydrate, 30g total fat (7g saturated), 108mg cholesterol, 604mg sodium.

Salmon and Lentils

Five-Spice Salmon Fillets

Chinese five-spice powder adds an intriguing hint of licorice to rich salmon.

🕐 Prep: 5 minutes   Cook: 8 minutes

4	pieces salmon fillet (4 ounces each), skin removed
2	teaspoons Chinese five-spice powder
1	teaspoon all-purpose flour
½	teaspoon salt
¼	teaspoon cracked black pepper
2	teaspoons vegetable oil

1. With tweezers, remove any bones from salmon fillets. On waxed paper, combine five-spice powder, flour, salt, and pepper. Use to rub on both sides of fillets.

2. In nonstick 10-inch skillet, heat oil over medium heat until hot. Add salmon; cook until just opaque throughout, 4 to 5 minutes per side. Makes 4 main-dish servings.

Each serving: About 222 calories, 21g protein, 2g carbohydrate, 14g total fat (3g saturated), 63mg cholesterol, 353mg sodium.

Baked Salmon Fillets

Thick center-cut pieces of salmon bake in about twenty minutes. If using thinner pieces cut nearer the tail, check after fifteen minutes. There are many sauces that go well with baked salmon; try Salmoriglio Sauce (page 553) or a fruit salsa (pages 555 to 556).

🕐 Prep: 5 minutes   Bake: 15 minutes

4	pieces salmon fillet with skin (6 ounces each)
1	teaspoon olive oil
⅛	teaspoon salt
⅛	teaspoon ground black pepper

Preheat oven to 400°F. Grease 13" by 9" baking dish. With tweezers, remove any bones from salmon fillets. Arrange fillets in prepared baking dish; rub with oil and sprinkle with salt and pepper. Bake until salmon is just opaque throughout, 15 to 20 minutes. Makes 4 main-dish servings.

Each serving: About 331 calories, 34g protein, 0g carbohydrate, 21g total fat (4g saturated), 100mg cholesterol, 174mg sodium.

Salmon Cakes

These flavorful, lowfat fish cakes can be served with any one of our cucumber salads (page 530) or burger-style on a bun with shredded lettuce and chili sauce. Economical canned salmon makes this a fast meal.

🕐 Prep: 10 minutes   Cook: 10 minutes

1	can (14¾ ounces) red or pink salmon, drained and flaked
1	green onion, sliced
3	tablespoons bottled white horseradish
2	tablespoons plain dried bread crumbs
1	teaspoon soy sauce
¼	teaspoon coarsely ground black pepper
1	tablespoon vegetable oil

1. In medium bowl, gently combine salmon, green onion, horseradish, bread crumbs, soy sauce, and pepper. Shape mixture into four 3-inch patties.

2. In nonstick 12-inch skillet, heat oil over medium heat until hot. Add salmon cakes; cook until salmon cakes are golden and heated through, about 5 minutes per side. Makes 4 main-dish servings.

Each serving: About 172 calories, 19g protein, 4g carbohydrate, 8g total fat (2g saturated), 34mg cholesterol, 549mg sodium.

Broiled Shad

Shad, with its delicate flesh and roe, is a seasonal delight. Serve with steamed asparagus and boiled new potatoes for an elegant springtime meal.

🕐 Prep: 5 minutes   Broil: 8 minutes

4	pieces shad fillet with skin (6 ounces each)
1	tablespoon butter or margarine
2	tablespoons fresh lemon juice
½	teaspoon salt
1	tablespoon chopped fresh parsley
	lemon wedges

1. Preheat broiler. Lightly oil broiling pan rack.

2. In small saucepan, melt butter over medium heat; stir in lemon juice and salt. Place shad fillets, skin side down, on rack in broiling pan. Place pan in broiler, about 4 inches from

heat source. Brush lemon butter on fish. Broil shad, without turning, until just opaque throughout, 8 to 10 minutes. Sprinkle shad with parsley and serve with lemon wedges. Makes 4 main-dish servings.

Each serving: About 363 calories, 29g protein, 1g carbohydrate, 26g total fat (2g saturated), 8mg cholesterol, 406mg sodium.

Broiled Shad with Roe

Prepare shad as directed but also place **shad roe** on rack of pan and brush with butter mixture; broil.

Each serving: About 432 calories, 40g protein, 1g carbohydrate, 29g total fat (3g saturated), 193mg cholesterol, 406mg sodium.

Skate with Brown Butter, Lemon, and Capers

Skate fillets come from the "wings" of a ray, so they look quite different from other fish. Nonetheless, they are one of the most delicious white-fleshed fish you can buy.

Prep: 15 minutes   Cook: 8 minutes

1	tablespoon vegetable oil
2	skinless skate wings (10 ounces each), filleted
½	teaspoon salt
¼	cup all-purpose flour
3	tablespoons butter or margarine
¼	cup fresh lemon juice
3	tablespoons chopped fresh parsley
2	tablespoons capers, rinsed and drained

1. In nonstick 12-inch skillet, heat oil over medium-high heat until hot. Sprinkle skate fillets with salt, then coat with flour, shaking off excess. Add skate to skillet and cook until just opaque throughout and golden brown, about 2 minutes per side. Transfer to platter; keep warm.

2. Add butter to skillet and cook until it begins to foam and turn light brown. Add lemon juice, parsley, and capers and swirl to combine. Pour over skate and serve. Makes 4 main-dish servings.

Each serving: About 212 calories, 16g protein, 8g carbohydrate, 13g total fat (6g saturated), 63mg cholesterol, 619mg sodium.

Red Snapper in Parchment with Tomatoes and Basil

The snapper juices mingle with the tomatoes and basil in a parchment packet to create a fabulous sauce.

Prep: 25 minutes   Bake: 15 minutes

1	tablespoon butter or margarine
1	large garlic clove, finely chopped
1	pound ripe plum tomatoes, seeded and chopped (2 cups)
¼	plus ⅛ teaspoon salt
¼	teaspoon ground black pepper
⅓	cup chopped fresh basil
4	red snapper fillets (6 ounces each), skin removed
4	squares (12 inches each) cooking parchment or foil

1. Preheat oven to 400°F.

2. In 12-inch skillet, melt butter over medium-high heat. Add garlic and cook 30 seconds. Add tomatoes, ¼ teaspoon salt, and ⅛ teaspoon pepper. Cook, stirring frequently, until liquid has almost evaporated, about 5 minutes. Remove from heat and stir in basil.

3. With tweezers, remove any bones from snapper fillets. Place 1 fillet, skinned side down, on one half of each parchment square. Sprinkle with remaining ⅛ teaspoon each salt and pepper; top with tomato mixture.

4. Fold unfilled half of parchment over fish. To seal packets, beginning at a corner where parchment is folded, make small ½-inch-wide folds, with each new fold overlapping previous one, until packet is completely sealed. Packet will resemble half-circle. Place packets in jelly-roll pan. Bake 15 minutes (packets will puff up and brown). Cut packets open to serve. Makes 4 main-dish servings.

Each serving: About 207 calories, 33g protein, 6g carbohydrate, 5g total fat (2g saturated), 65mg cholesterol, 359mg sodium.

Grilled Thai Snapper Packets

Grilling snapper fillets in foil packets keeps the meat intact, and Thai seasonings give the fish a distinctive Asian flavor.

	Prep: 25 minutes Grill: 8 minutes
3	tablespoons fresh lime juice
1	tablespoon Asian fish sauce (nuoc nam, page 31)
1	tablespoon olive oil
1	teaspoon grated, peeled fresh ginger
1	small garlic clove, finely chopped
1/2	teaspoon sugar
4	red snapper fillets (6 ounces each)
1	large carrot, peeled and cut into 2 1/4" by 1/4" matchstick strips
1	large green onion, thinly sliced
1/4	cup tightly packed fresh cilantro

1. Prepare grill. In small bowl, with wire whisk, whisk lime juice, fish sauce, oil, ginger, garlic, and sugar. With tweezers, remove any bones from snapper fillets.

2. From roll of foil, cut four 16" by 12" sheets. Fold each sheet crosswise in half, then open up like a book.

3. With tweezers, remove any bones from snapper fillets. Place 1 fillet, skin side down, on one half of each piece of foil. Evenly sprinkle fillets with carrot, green onion, and cilantro; spoon lime-juice mixture on top. Fold unfilled half of foil over fish. To seal, fold and crimp edges of foil all around.

4. Place packets on grill over medium heat; cook 8 minutes. To serve, cut packets open. Makes 4 main-dish servings.

♥ Each serving: About 228 calories, 36g protein, 5g carbohydrate, 6g total fat (1g saturated), 63mg cholesterol, 268mg sodium.

Tunisian Snapper Fillets

Try a fruit salsa (pages 555 to 556) with this spice-crusted fish. Crush the seeds with a mortar and pestle or under the weight of a heavy skillet on a work surface, but let the spices retain some of their texture.

	Prep: 5 minutes Cook: 6 minutes
4	red snapper fillets (6 ounces each)
1/2	teaspoon salt
1/4	teaspoon cumin seeds, crushed
1/4	teaspoon coriander seeds, crushed
1/4	teaspoon fennel seeds, crushed
1/4	teaspoon crushed red pepper
2	teaspoons vegetable oil
	lemon wedges

1. With tweezers, remove any bones from snapper fillets.

2. On waxed paper, combine salt, cumin, coriander, and fennel seeds, and crushed red pepper. Use to rub on flesh side of fillets.

3. In nonstick 12-inch skillet, heat oil over medium-high heat until hot. Add fillets and cook until just opaque throughout, 3 to 4 minutes per side. Serve with lemon wedges. Makes 4 main-dish servings.

♥ Each serving: About 192 calories, 35g protein, 0g carbohydrate, 5g total fat (1g saturated), 63mg cholesterol, 399mg sodium.

Snapper Livornese

Vibrant with olives, capers, and basil, this preparation works beautifully with any lean white fish.

	Prep: 10 minutes Cook: 25 minutes
1	tablespoon olive oil
1	garlic clove, finely chopped
1	can (14 to 16 ounces) tomatoes
1/8	teaspoon salt
1/8	teaspoon ground black pepper
4	red snapper fillets (6 ounces each)
1/4	cup chopped fresh basil
1/4	cup Kalamata or Gaeta olives, pitted and chopped
2	teaspoons capers, drained

Snapper Livornese

1. In nonstick 10-inch skillet, heat oil over medium heat. Add garlic and cook just until very fragrant, about 30 seconds. Stir in tomatoes with their juice, salt, and pepper, breaking up tomatoes with side of spoon. Heat to boiling; reduce heat and simmer 10 minutes.

2. With tweezers, remove any bones from snapper fillets. Place fillets, skin side down, in skillet. Cover and simmer until fish is just opaque throughout, about 10 minutes. With wide slotted spatula, transfer fish to warm platter. Stir basil, olives, and capers into tomato sauce and spoon over snapper. Makes 4 main-dish servings.

💙 Each serving: About 250 calories, 36g protein, 6g carbohydrate, 8g total fat (1g saturated), 63mg cholesterol, 571mg sodium.

Red Snapper with Bacon and Apples

The flavors and textures of apples and bacon are wonderful with fish. If you like, add two or three tablespoons of heavy cream at the end to enrich the sauce.

	Prep: 15 minutes Cook: 30 minutes
2	slices bacon, chopped
1	small red onion, cut into quarters and thinly sliced
2	Granny Smith apples, peeled, cored, and cut into 2" by ¼" matchstick strips
1	cup apple cider or juice
2	teaspoons cider vinegar
4	red snapper fillets (6 ounces each)
½	teaspoon salt
⅛	teaspoon ground black pepper
1	tablespoon butter or margarine
1	tablespoon chopped fresh chives or parsley

1. In nonstick 12-inch skillet, cook bacon over medium heat until browned. With slotted spoon, transfer bacon to paper towels to drain. Add onion to drippings in skillet and cook, stirring, until tender, about 5 minutes.

2. Add apples, cider, and vinegar to skillet. Cook over high heat, stirring, until apples are tender, about 5 minutes. With slotted spoon, transfer apples and onions to bowl. Boil liquid in skillet until very thick and brown, about 3 minutes. Pour sauce into bowl with apples. Wipe skillet clean.

3. With tweezers, remove any bones from snapper fillets; season fillets with salt and pepper. In same skillet, melt butter over medium heat until hot. Add snapper and cook until just opaque throughout, 4 to 6 minutes per side. Transfer fish to platter and keep warm. Return apple mixture to skillet and cook over medium-high heat just until heated through. To serve, spoon apple mixture over fish and sprinkle with bacon and chives. Makes 4 main-dish servings.

Each serving: About 336 calories, 36g protein, 20g carbohydrate, 12g total fat (5g saturated), 78mg cholesterol, 510mg sodium.

Sautéed Shad Roe

To ensure that the roe is evenly cooked, keep the skillet covered. Shad roe is glorious on its own, but crisp bacon is a lovely way to gild the lily.

	Prep: 5 minutes Cook: 6 minutes
2	pairs shad roe
¼	cup all-purpose flour
2	tablespoons butter
¼	teaspoon salt
	pinch ground black pepper
4	slices bacon, cooked and crumbled
	lemon wedges

Coat shad roe with flour, shaking off excess. In 10-inch skillet, melt butter over medium heat until hot. Add roe; cover and cook until roe just loses its pink color, 3 to 4 minutes per side. Sprinkle with salt and pepper; top with bacon and serve with lemon wedges. Makes 4 main-dish servings.

Each serving: About 255 calories, 25g protein, 7g carbohydrate, 15g total fat (6g saturated), 392mg cholesterol, 303mg sodium.

Kedgeree

A traditional British breakfast dish, kedgeree is also delicious for brunch or supper.

	Prep: 35 minutes Bake: 30 minutes
1	tablespoon butter or margarine
1	small onion, chopped
¾	teaspoon curry powder
1½	cups regular long-grain rice
3	cups water
1	teaspoon salt
¼	teaspoon coarsely ground pepper
1	pound smoked haddock fillet (finnan haddie)
1	lemon
4	large eggs, hard-cooked and coarsely chopped
¼	cup chopped fresh parsley
½	cup heavy or whipping cream

1. In 2-quart saucepan, melt butter over medium heat. Add onion and cook until tender, about 5 minutes. Stir in

curry powder and rice. Add water, salt, and pepper; heat to boiling. Reduce heat; cover and simmer, without stirring or lifting lid, until rice is tender and all liquid has been absorbed, about 20 minutes. Transfer to large bowl.

2. Meanwhile, in 10-inch skillet, combine smoked haddock fillet with enough *water* to cover; heat to boiling. Reduce heat and simmer just until haddock begins to flake, 5 to 10 minutes. Drain and cool slightly.

3. Preheat oven to 350°F. From lemon, grate ½ teaspoon peel and squeeze 1 tablespoon juice; add lemon peel and juice to rice, fluffing with fork. Flake haddock, discarding any skin or bones. Add fish, eggs, and parsley to rice, tossing gently. Spread in 13" by 9" baking dish; drizzle cream on top. Cover with foil and bake 30 minutes. Makes 6 main-dish servings.

Each serving: About 406 calories, 27g protein, 42g carbohydrate, 14g total fat (7g saturated), 232mg cholesterol, sodium n/a.

Brandade

A little of this flavorful, velvety Provençal hors d'oeuvre goes a long way. Spread on thin slices of toasted bread.

Prep: 20 minutes plus 24 to 36 hours to soak cod
Cook: 20 minutes

1	pound salt cod fillets
1	large baking potato (12 ounces), peeled and thinly sliced
3	garlic cloves, peeled
1	cup heavy or whipping cream
	pinch ground nutmeg
2	tablespoons extravirgin olive oil
	thinly sliced French bread, toasted

1. In medium bowl, combine salt cod fillets and enough *cold water* to cover generously. Cover and refrigerate, changing water several times, 24 to 36 hours. Drain and rinse well.

2. In 3-quart saucepan, combine potato, garlic, and *3 cups water*; heat to boiling over high heat. Reduce heat and simmer until potato is tender, 12 to 15 minutes. Drain, reserving 1 cup water. Mash potato and garlic until almost smooth.

3. Meanwhile, in 3-quart saucepan, combine cod and enough *water* to cover; heat to boiling. Reduce heat and simmer until fish can be flaked with fork, 5 to 10 minutes; drain. When cool enough to handle, discard any skin or bones.

Transfer cod to food processor with knife blade attached and pulse until flaked.

4. In clean 3-quart saucepan, heat cream over low heat. With wooden spoon, stir in cod, potato mixture, reserved potato water, and nutmeg; stir until well combined. With wire whisk, gradually whisk in oil. Serve with toast. Makes 4 cups or 12 first-course servings.

Each ¼ cup without toast: About 216 calories, 25g protein, 5g carbohydrate, 11g total fat (5g saturated), 85mg cholesterol, sodium n/a.

Salt Cod Salad

The saltiness of the cod will vary with the thickness of the fillets and the length of the soaking time.

Prep: 15 minutes plus 24 to 36 hours to soak cod plus standing
Cook: 15 minutes

1	pound salt cod fillets
⅓	cup fresh lemon juice
3	tablespoons extravirgin olive oil
¼	teaspoon coarsely ground black pepper
1	cup fresh flat-leaf parsley leaves
1	very small red onion, very thinly sliced
1	pound ripe tomatoes (3 medium), cut into ½-inch pieces
	olives, such as Niçoise, Kalamata, or Gaeta (optional)

1. In medium bowl, combine salt cod fillets and enough cold water to cover generously. Cover and refrigerate, changing water several times, 24 to 36 hours. Drain and rinse well.

2. In 3-quart saucepan, combine cod and enough *water* to cover; heat to boiling. Reduce heat and simmer until fish can be flaked with fork, 5 to 10 minutes; drain.

3. Meanwhile, in medium bowl, whisk together lemon juice, oil, and pepper. When cod is cool enough to handle, discard any skin or bones and, with fingers, flake cod into dressing in bowl. Add parsley and onion, tossing to combine; gently stir in tomatoes. Cover and let stand 30 minutes to blend flavors. Spoon cod mixture onto platter and top with olives, if desired. Makes 6 first-course servings.

Each serving: About 298 calories, 48g protein, 4g carbohydrate, 9g total fat (1g saturated), 115mg cholesterol, sodium n/a.

SCRUBBING AND SHUCKING CLAMS

Scrub the clams well with cold running water to remove all the grit.

Protecting your hand with a folded towel, hold the clam with the "hinge" facing you; wedge the thin edge of the clam knife between the shells.

Slide the knife around to separate the shells.

Open the shell. Cut the clam meat away from the top shell; discard the top shell.

Slide the knife underneath the meat in the bottom shell to release it.

Salt Cod Portuguese-Style

They say that the Portuguese have 365 ways to cook salt cod. This is certainly one of the best—layered with tomatoes and potatoes.

Prep: 35 minutes plus 24 to 36 hours to soak cod
Cook/Bake: 1 hour 20 minutes

1	pound salt cod fillets
1	pound (5 small) all-purpose potatoes
1/4	cup olive oil, preferably extravirgin
3	small onions, thinly sliced
2	garlic cloves, thinly sliced
1	can (28 ounces) tomatoes, drained and chopped
1/4	cup plus 1 tablespoon chopped fresh parsley
1/4	teaspoon salt
1/4	teaspoon ground black pepper
2	large hard-cooked eggs, each cut lengthwise into quarters
16	oil-cured black olives, pitted
2	teaspoons capers, drained

1. In medium bowl, combine salt cod fillets and enough cold water to cover generously. Cover and refrigerate, changing water several times, 24 to 36 hours. Drain and rinse well.

2. In 3-quart saucepan, combine cod and enough *water* to cover; heat to boiling. Reduce heat and simmer until fish can be flaked with fork, 5 to 10 minutes; drain. When cool enough to handle, discard any skin or bones and coarsely flake cod.

3. Meanwhile, in 10-inch skillet, heat oil over medium heat. Add onions and garlic and cook, stirring, until very tender and golden, about 10 minutes. With slotted spoon, transfer onions to bowl. Pour oil in skillet into cup; reserve.

4. In 5-quart Dutch oven, combine potatoes and enough *salted cold water* to cover; heat to boiling. Cook just until potatoes are tender when pierced with fork, about 20 minutes. When cool enough to handle, peel potatoes and cut into thin slices.

5. Preheat oven to 350°F. Lightly oil 8-inch square baking dish. In dish, layer potatoes, tomatoes, 1/4 cup parsley, half of onions, cod, and remaining onions, lightly sprinkling each layer with salt and pepper. Bake until golden and heated through, about 35 minutes. Drizzle with reserved oil. Arrange eggs on top and sprinkle with olives, capers, and remaining 1 tablespoon parsley. Makes 4 main-dish servings.

Each serving: About 697 calories, 80g protein, 39g carbohydrate, 25g total fat (4g saturated), 279mg cholesterol, sodium n/a.

Steamed Soft-Shell Clams

A great appetizer or main dish to have with an ice-cold beer on a hot summer day!

 Prep: 5 minutes   Cook: 10 minutes

6	dozen steamer (soft-shell) clams
	melted butter or margarine (optional)

1. In very large bowl or in kitchen sink, place clams and enough cold water to cover. Drain. Repeat rinsing and draining until sand no longer falls to bottom of bowl.

2. In steamer or 8-quart saucepot fitted with rack, heat enough *water* to cover pan bottom to boiling over high heat. Place clams on rack in steamer. Reduce heat; cover and steam until clams open, 5 to 10 minutes, transferring clams to bowl as they open. Discard any clams that have not opened.

3. Strain clam broth through sieve lined with paper towels and pour into 6 soup cups or mugs.

4. To eat, with fingers, pull clams from shells by neck; peel off and discard black sheath that covers neck. Dip clams first in broth to remove any sand, then into melted butter, if you like. When sand has settled to bottom, broth can be sipped, if desired. Makes 6 first-course servings.

 Each serving without butter: About 76 calories, 13g protein, 3g carbohydrate, 1g total fat (0g saturated), 35mg cholesterol, 57mg sodium.

Chinese Steamed Clams

Serve this flavorful dish with white rice.

 Prep: 10 minutes   Cook: 10 minutes

1	tablespoon vegetable oil
2	green onions, finely chopped
1	tablespoon minced, peeled fresh ginger
1	garlic clove, finely chopped
2	dozen cherrystone or littleneck clams, scrubbed (opposite), or mussels, scrubbed and debearded (page 291)
½	cup water
3	tablespoons dry sherry
2	tablespoons soy sauce
2	tablespoons chopped fresh cilantro

In 8-quart saucepot, heat oil over high heat. Add green onions, ginger, and garlic; cook until green onions are tender, about 1 minute. Add clams, water, sherry, and soy sauce; heat to boiling. Reduce heat; cover and simmer 5 to 10 minutes, transferring clams to large platter as they open. Discard any clams that have not opened. Pour broth over clams on platter and sprinkle with cilantro. Makes 4 first-course servings.

 Each serving: About 131 calories, 14g protein, 5g carbohydrate, 4g total fat (1g saturated), 36mg cholesterol, 576mg sodium.

Always buy live crabs. They should be energetic and robust, not wobbling around feebly. Each crab should feel heavy and have a clean shell. Purchase female crabs; they contain the tasty roe. You can easily tell the males and females apart: The apron on the underside of the male crab is thin and pointed, while on the female it is rounded.

ERIC RIPERT
EXECUTIVE CHEF, LE BERNARDIN, NEW YORK CITY

EXPERT TIP

Panfried Soft-Shell Crabs

Here's the classic way to prepare soft-shell crabs so they're crispy outside and moist inside.

Prep: 30 minutes	Cook: 12 minutes
½	cup all-purpose flour
¾	teaspoon salt
½	teaspoon ground black pepper
8	live soft-shell crabs (6 ounces each), cleaned (opposite)
4	tablespoons butter or margarine
	lemon wedges

1. On waxed paper, combine flour, salt, and pepper. Coat crabs evenly with seasoned flour, shaking off excess.

2. In 12-inch skillet, melt 2 tablespoons butter over medium heat until hot; add 4 crabs and cook until golden, 3 to 4 minutes per side. Transfer crabs to platter and keep warm. Repeat with remaining butter and remaining crabs. Serve with lemon wedges. Makes 4 main-dish servings.

Each serving: About 256 calories, 19g protein, 12g carbohydrate, 15g total fat (8g saturated), 188mg cholesterol, 1,207mg sodium.

Panfried Soft-Shell Crabs

Soft-Shell Crabs with Lemon-Caper Sauce

A versatile dish that can be served as an appetizer or main course.

Prep: 35 minutes	Cook: 8 minutes
1	small lemon
2	tablespoons chopped fresh parsley
2	tablespoons capers, drained
4	live large soft-shell crabs (6 ounces each), cleaned (opposite)
¼	cup all-purpose flour
2	tablespoons plus 2 teaspoons butter or margarine
½	teaspoon salt
¼	teaspoon ground black pepper
¼	cup finely chopped shallots

1. With small knife, cut off ends from lemon. Stand lemon upright on cutting board; with small knife, cut peel and white pith from lemon. Cut lemon into ¼-inch-thick slices, discarding seeds; finely chop. In cup, combine lemon, parsley, and capers. Set aside.

2. On waxed paper, coat crabs evenly with flour, shaking off excess. In nonstick 10-inch skillet, melt 2 tablespoons butter over medium heat until hot. Add crabs to skillet and sprinkle with salt and pepper; cook until golden, 3 to 4 minutes per side. Transfer crabs to platter and keep warm.

3. Add remaining 2 teaspoons butter and shallots to same skillet; cook 1 minute. Stir in reserved lemon mixture and heat through. Spoon lemon sauce over crabs. Makes 4 first-course or 2 main-dish servings.

Each first-course serving: About 201 calories, 17g protein, 10g carbohydrate, 11g total fat (6g saturated), 168mg cholesterol, 1,171mg sodium.

Crab Boil

A big pot of spiced boiled crabs, a Chesapeake Bay tradition, is a delicious but messy affair. Cover the table with newspaper and have lots of big napkins on hand. Serve with coleslaw and rolls. (If you want to cook crab so you can pick the meat for another recipe, omit the crab boil seasoning and red pepper.)

Prep: 5 minutes	Cook: 40 minutes
2	medium onions, coarsely chopped
1	carrot, peeled and coarsely chopped
1	stalk celery, coarsely chopped
1	lemon, sliced
½	cup crab boil seasoning
1	tablespoon crushed red pepper
1	tablespoon salt
1	gallon (16 cups) water
1	can or bottle (12 ounces) beer
2	dozen live hard-shell blue crabs, rinsed

1. In 12-quart stockpot, combine onions, carrot, celery, lemon, crab boil seasoning, crushed red pepper, salt, water, and beer. Heat to boiling over high heat; cook 15 minutes.

2. Using tongs, transfer crabs to stockpot. Cover and heat to boiling. Boil 5 minutes (crabs will turn red). With tongs, transfer crabs to colander to drain, then place on platter.

3. To eat crab, twist off claws and legs, then crack shell to remove meat. Break off flat pointed apron from underside of crab; remove top shell. Discard feathery gills. With kitchen shears or hands, break body in half down center. With fingers or lobster pick, remove meat. Makes 4 main-dish servings.

♥ Each serving: About 123 calories, 24g protein, 0g carbohydrate, 2g total fat (0g saturated), 119mg cholesterol, 1,410mg sodium.

Crab Cakes

Homey yet luxurious, crab cakes never fail to please.

Prep: 15 minutes	Cook: 10 minutes
2	large eggs
1	tablespoon dry sherry
1	tablespoon finely chopped onion
¼	teaspoon salt
1	container (16 ounces) lump crabmeat, picked over
½	cup coarsely crumbled saltine crackers
3	tablespoons butter or margarine

1. In medium bowl, stir eggs, sherry, onion, and salt until blended; add crabmeat and crumbled crackers, stirring just until mixed.

2. In 12-inch skillet, melt butter over medium heat. Drop crab mixture into skillet, forming 4 equal mounds; with wide spatula, press mounds into 3½-inch round cakes. Cook crab cakes until browned and heated through, about 5 minutes per side. Makes 4 main-dish servings.

Each serving: About 272 calories, 27g protein, 7g carbohydrate, 14g total fat (7g saturated), 243mg cholesterol, 693mg sodium.

CLEANING SOFT-SHELL CRABS

Soft-shell crabs are sometimes available already cleaned, but it is better to do it yourself at home, because crabs begin to spoil once their viscera are removed. To clean, with kitchen shears, cut across each crab ¼ inch behind the eyes; discard front portion. Cut off the flat pointed "apron" on the underside. Bend back the top shell on each side and snip off the spongy gills. Rinse with cold running water; pat dry with paper towels.

Crab Cakes Rémoulade

In 10-inch skillet, melt **2 tablespoons butter or margarine** over medium heat. Add **1 onion,** finely chopped, **½ red pepper,** finely chopped, **1 stalk celery,** finely chopped, and **⅛ teaspoon ground red pepper (cayenne);** cook, stirring frequently, until vegetables are tender, about 10 minutes. Prepare crab cakes as directed but substitute cooked vegetable mixture for onion and add **1 tablespoon mayonnaise.** Makes 4 main-dish servings.

Each serving: About 368 calories, 28g protein, 11g carbohydrate, 23g total fat (11g saturated), 260mg cholesterol, 781mg sodium.

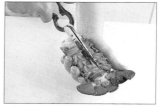

Each serving with butter: About 340 calories, 29g protein, 2g carbohydrate, 24g total fat (15g saturated), 162mg cholesterol, 760mg sodium.

Steamed Lobster

Quite simply, a seafood lover's dream.

Prep: 5 minutes   Cook: 20 minutes

2	live lobsters (1¼ to 1½ pounds each)
4	tablespoons butter or margarine, melted
2	teaspoons fresh lemon juice

1. In 12-quart stockpot, heat *1½ inches water* to boiling over high heat. Plunge lobsters, headfirst, into boiling water. Cover and heat to boiling; steam 12 minutes. With tongs, transfer lobsters to colander to drain, then place on platter.

2. Combine melted butter and lemon juice; transfer to small cups for dipping lobster.

3. To eat lobster, twist off claws and legs. With lobster cracker, nut cracker, or hammer, crack large claws; remove meat. Separate legs at joints; push out meat. Twist to separate tail from body. Reserve any red roe (coral) and greenish liver (tomalley) separately, if desired. With kitchen shears, cut

down along center of underside of tail; gently remove meat. Lift bony portion behind small legs from shell; with lobster pick or fork, remove small nuggets of meat. Dip lobster into lemon butter. Makes 2 main-dish servings.

Lobster Bisque

When you serve lobster, save the shells and cooking liquid, if desired, and make this splendid soup the next day.

Prep: 15 minutes   Cook: 1 hour 15 minutes

2	tablespoons butter or margarine
1	medium onion, chopped
1	carrot, peeled and chopped
1	stalk celery, chopped
1	garlic clove, finely chopped
3	tablespoons tomato paste
	leftover shells and heads from 4 steamed lobsters
2	tablespoons cognac or brandy
6	cups water
2	bottles (8 ounces each) clam juice or 2 cups cooking liquid from steaming lobsters
3	parsley sprigs
⅛	teaspoon dried thyme
	pinch ground nutmeg
	pinch ground red pepper (cayenne)
3	tablespoons all-purpose flour
¾	cup heavy or whipping cream

1. In 12-quart stockpot, melt butter over medium heat. Add onion, carrot, celery, and garlic and cook until onion is tender, about 5 minutes. Stir in tomato paste.

2. Increase heat to high and add lobster shells; cook, stirring occasionally, 5 minutes. Stir in cognac and cook until liquid has evaporated. Add water, clam juice, parsley, thyme, nutmeg, and ground red pepper; heat to boiling. Reduce heat; cover and simmer 30 minutes.

3. Strain soup through sieve into 4-quart saucepan; discard solids. Heat to boiling over high heat; boil until reduced to 5 cups, 10 to 15 minutes.

4. In small bowl, with wire whisk, whisk flour into cream until blended and smooth. Gradually whisk cream mixture into soup; heat just to boiling, whisking constantly. Reduce heat and simmer 2 minutes. Makes about 5½ cups or 4 first-course servings.

Each serving: About 258 calories, 3g protein, 12g carbohydrate, 22g total fat (14g saturated), 77mg cholesterol, 441mg sodium.

Mussels with Tomatoes and White Wine

This saucy dish should be served with plenty of good crusty bread for dipping.

Prep: 20 minutes   Cook: 25 minutes

1	tablespoon olive or vegetable oil
1	small onion, chopped
2	garlic cloves, finely chopped
¼	teaspoon crushed red pepper
1	can (14 to 16 ounces) tomatoes
¾	cup dry white wine
4	pounds large mussels, scrubbed and debearded (right)
2	tablespoons chopped fresh parsley

1. In nonreactive 5-quart Dutch oven, heat oil over medium heat. Add onion and cook until tender and golden, 6 to 8 minutes. Add garlic and crushed red pepper and cook 30 seconds longer. Stir in tomatoes with their juice and wine, breaking up tomatoes with side of spoon. Heat to boiling; boil 3 minutes.

2. Add mussels; heat to boiling. Reduce heat; cover and simmer until mussels open, about 5 minutes, transferring mussels to large bowl as they open. Discard any mussels that have not opened. Pour mussel broth over mussels and sprinkle with parsley. Makes 8 first-course or 4 main-dish servings.

Each first-course serving: About 104 calories, 9g protein, 6g carbohydrate, 3g total fat (1g saturated), 18mg cholesterol, 277mg sodium.

Mussels with Tomatoes and White Wine

SCRUBBING AND DEBEARDING MUSSELS

Scrub mussels well with cold running water. To debeard, grasp the hairlike beard with your thumb and forefinger and pull it away, or scrape it off with a knife. (Cultivated mussels usually do not have beards.)

Moules à la Marinière

The way French cooks usually serve mussels. Use a crisp white wine, such as sauvignon blanc or dry vermouth, which adds extra flavor because of the herbs used in the distillation process.

Prep: 20 minutes   Cook: 15 minutes

1½	cups dry white wine or dry vermouth
⅓	cup finely chopped shallots or red onion
2	garlic cloves, finely chopped
1	tablespoon butter or olive oil
½	teaspoon salt
	pinch ground black pepper
4	pounds mussels, preferably cultivated, scrubbed and debearded (page 291)
¼	cup chopped fresh parsley

1. In nonreactive 5-quart Dutch oven, combine wine, shallots, garlic, butter, salt, and pepper; heat to boiling over high heat. Boil 2 minutes.

2. Add mussels; heat to boiling. Reduce heat; cover and simmer until mussels open, about 5 minutes, transferring mussels to large bowl as they open. Discard any mussels that have not opened. Pour mussel broth over mussels and sprinkle with parsley. Makes 4 main-dish servings.

♥ Each serving: About 212 calories, 16g protein, 9g carbohydrate, 6g total fat (2g saturated), 45mg cholesterol, 703mg sodium.

Scalloped Oysters

Bake these crumb-topped oysters in individual ramekins, if you have them, or in a shallow two-and-one-half-quart baking dish. The baking time will depend on the depth of the dish.

Prep: 40 minutes   Bake: 15 minutes

10	slices firm white bread, torn into 1-inch pieces
4	tablespoons butter or margarine, melted
1½	pints shucked oysters with their liquid
¾	cup heavy or whipping cream
¼	teaspoon salt
⅛	teaspoon coarsely ground black pepper
2	tablespoons chopped fresh parsley

1. Preheat oven to 400°F. Place bread pieces in jelly-roll pan and drizzle with melted butter, tossing to coat evenly. Toast bread, stirring occasionally, until crisp and golden, about 25 minutes.

2. Meanwhile, drain oysters, reserving liquid, and refrigerate. In 1-quart saucepan, heat oyster liquid to boiling over high heat. Reduce heat to medium and cook until oyster liquid has reduced to 3 tablespoons, about 5 minutes. Add cream, salt, and pepper; heat to boiling. Remove saucepan from heat.

3. In large bowl, gently combine toasted bread pieces, oysters, and parsley. Spoon mixture into eight 12-ounce ramekins, dividing it evenly; pour about 2 tablespoons cream mixture over each. Bake just until edges of oysters begin to curl, about 15 minutes. Makes 8 first-course servings.

Each serving: About 288 calories, 10g protein, 22g carbohydrate, 18g total fat (10g saturated), 99mg cholesterol, 436mg sodium.

Panfried Oysters

Large plump oysters work best in this seaside favorite.

Prep: 15 minutes   Cook: 10 minutes

1	pint shucked oysters, drained
⅔	cup finely crushed saltine crackers
2	tablespoons butter or margarine
2	tablespoons vegetable oil
	lemon wedges

1. Gently pat oysters dry with paper towels. Place cracker crumbs on waxed paper and coat oysters with crumbs.

2. In 10-inch skillet, heat 1 tablespoon butter and 1 tablespoon oil over medium-high heat until hot. Add half of oysters to skillet and cook until golden brown, 2 to 3 minutes per side. Repeat with remaining butter, oil, and oysters. Serve with lemon wedges. Makes 4 first-course servings.

Each serving: About 249 calories, 10g protein, 13g carbohydrate, 17g total fat (5g saturated), 85mg cholesterol, 353mg sodium.

Oyster Pan Roast

Modeled after the Oyster Pan Roast served at the Oyster Bar in Grand Central Station in New York City, this hearty treat is perfect for cold winter evenings.

Prep: 10 minutes   Cook: 10 minutes

2	tablespoons butter or margarine
1/3	cup finely chopped shallots or onion
1/2	teaspoon paprika
1/2	teaspoon salt
1/4	teaspoon celery salt (optional)
1/4	cup dry white wine or dry vermouth
2	cups half-and-half or light cream
1	tablespoon tomato paste
1	teaspoon Worcestershire sauce
1	pint shucked oysters with their liquid
2	tablespoons chopped fresh parsley
6	dashes hot pepper sauce or to taste
6	slices firm white bread, toasted and each cut on diagonal in half

1. In 3-quart saucepan, melt butter over medium heat. Add shallots, paprika, salt, and celery salt, if using, and cook, stirring, 3 minutes. Increase heat to high; add wine and boil until liquid has evaporated, about 3 minutes.

2. Reduce heat to medium; stir in half-and-half, tomato paste, and Worcestershire. Heat to boiling; add oysters with their liquid, 1 tablespoon parsley, and hot pepper sauce. Cook just until edges of oysters begin to curl, 3 to 4 minutes.

3. To serve, place toast slices in 6 shallow soup bowls, top with oyster mixture, and sprinkle with remaining 1 tablespoon parsley. Makes 6 first-course servings.

Each serving: About 289 calories, 11g protein, 23g carbohydrate, 16g total fat (9g saturated), 87mg cholesterol, 553mg sodium.

Scallop Pan Roast

Prepare as directed but substitute **1 pound bay or sea scallops** for oysters. If scallops are large, cut in half or into quarters.

Each serving: About 297 calories, 18g protein, 22g carbohydrate, 15g total fat (8g saturated), 65mg cholesterol, 580mg sodium.

Scallops Provençal

A hint of orange peel gives this tomato sauce a Southern French flavor. If you wish, make the sauce in advance and reheat at serving time. You can substitute bay scallops for the sea scallops.

Prep: 20 minutes   Cook: 20 minutes

1	large leek (8 ounces)
2	tablespoons olive oil
2	garlic cloves, finely chopped
1	can (14 to 16 ounces) tomatoes, chopped
1	teaspoon salt
1/2	teaspoon freshly grated orange peel
	pinch ground red pepper (cayenne)
1	pound sea scallops
1/4	cup all-purpose flour

1. Cut off roots and trim dark green tops from leek; cut lengthwise in half, then crosswise into thin slices. Rinse in large bowl of cold water, swishing to remove sand; transfer to colander to drain, leaving sand in bottom of bowl.

2. In nonstick 10-inch skillet, heat 1 tablespoon oil over medium heat. Add leek and garlic and cook, stirring frequently, until leek is tender, about 7 minutes. Add tomatoes with their juice, 1/2 teaspoon salt, orange peel, and ground red pepper; heat to boiling. Reduce heat and simmer until sauce has thickened slightly, about 5 minutes.

3. Meanwhile, pull off and discard tough crescent-shaped muscle from each scallop. Pat scallops dry with paper towels. Cut each scallop horizontally in half if large.

4. In 12-inch skillet, heat remaining 1 tablespoon oil over medium-high heat until hot. Place flour on waxed paper and coat scallops with flour, shaking off excess. Sprinkle remaining 1/2 teaspoon salt on scallops. Add scallops to skillet and cook, stirring, until just opaque throughout and lightly golden, about 4 minutes. Stir in sauce and heat through. Makes 4 main-dish servings.

Each serving: About 227 calories, 21g protein, 17g carbohydrate, 8g total fat (1g saturated), 37mg cholesterol, 944mg sodium.

Scallop and Asparagus Stir-Fry

Tossing this dish with chopped basil just before serving adds a pleasing touch of fresh flavor. With steamed rice, you have a complete meal.

Prep: 20 minutes   Cook: 15 minutes

1	pound sea scallops
2	tablespoons reduced-sodium soy sauce
1	tablespoon minced, peeled fresh ginger
2	tablespoons vegetable oil
2	garlic cloves, thinly sliced
1½	pounds asparagus, trimmed and cut into 2-inch pieces
¼	teaspoon crushed red pepper
½	cup loosely packed fresh basil leaves, chopped, plus additional leaves

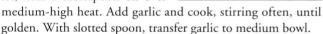

1. Pull off and discard tough crescent-shaped muscle from each scallop. In bowl, toss scallops with 1 tablespoon soy sauce and ginger.

2. In nonstick 12-inch skillet, heat 1 tablespoon oil over medium-high heat. Add garlic and cook, stirring often, until golden. With slotted spoon, transfer garlic to medium bowl.

3. Add asparagus and crushed red pepper to skillet and cook, stirring frequently (stir-frying), until asparagus is tender-crisp, about 7 minutes. Transfer asparagus to bowl with garlic.

4. Add remaining 1 tablespoon oil to skillet; add scallop mixture and stir-fry until scallops are just opaque throughout, 3 to 5 minutes.

5. Return asparagus and garlic to skillet, along with remaining 1 tablespoon soy sauce; heat through. Add chopped basil, tossing to combine. Spoon mixture onto platter and top with basil leaves. Makes 4 main-dish servings.

Each serving: About 204 calories, 24g protein, 10g carbohydrate, 8g total fat (1g saturated), 37mg cholesterol, 487mg sodium.

Scallop and Asparagus Stir-Fry

Scallops with Leeks and Cream

Leeks cooked with wine and cream make a melt-in-your-mouth base for tender scallops. If you like, prepare the leek mixture one hour ahead, then reheat to cook the scallops at the last minute.

Prep: 15 minutes   Cook: 20 minutes

3	leeks (1½ pounds)
1	tablespoon butter or margarine
½	teaspoon salt
	pinch ground black pepper
1	pound sea scallops
¼	cup dry white wine
½	cup heavy or whipping cream

1. Cut off roots and trim dark green tops from leeks; cut each leek lengthwise in half, then crosswise into 1-inch pieces.

Rinse leeks in large bowl of cold water, swishing to remove sand; transfer to colander to drain, leaving sand in bowl.

2. In 3-quart saucepan, melt butter over medium heat. Add leeks, salt, and pepper; cook, stirring occasionally, until tender, about 15 minutes (do not let leeks brown).

3. Meanwhile, pull off and discard tough crescent-shaped muscle from each scallop. Cut each scallop horizontally in half; set aside.

4. Add wine to leeks in saucepan; heat to boiling over high heat and boil 1 minute. Stir in cream; heat to boiling and boil 1 minute. Stir in scallops. Cover and cook over high heat, stirring occasionally, until scallops are just opaque throughout, about 3 minutes. Spoon into 6 shallow bowls or cups. Makes 6 first-course servings.

Each serving: About 189 calories, 14g protein, 9g carbohydrate, 10g total fat (6g saturated), 57mg cholesterol, 352mg sodium.

Scallops with Bacon and Cream

The cream and apple juice accentuate the natural sweetness of the scallops. Serve over rice, mashed potatoes, or warm toast.

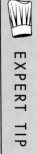 Prep: 10 minutes   Cook: 20 minutes

2	slices bacon, chopped
1	pound sea scallops
2/3	cup apple juice
1/3	cup heavy or whipping cream
1/4	teaspoon salt
1/8	teaspoon ground black pepper
3	teaspoons chopped fresh chives

1. In nonstick 12-inch skillet, cook bacon over medium heat until browned. With slotted spoon, transfer bacon to paper towels to drain. Meanwhile, pull off and discard tough crescent-shaped muscle from each scallop. Pat scallops dry with paper towels.

2. Increase heat to high. Add scallops to drippings in skillet and cook, turning once, until just opaque throughout and browned, about 4 minutes. Transfer scallops to platter and keep warm.

3. Add apple juice, cream, salt, and pepper to skillet. Heat to boiling over high heat; boil until sauce has thickened slightly, about 7 minutes.

4. Pour sauce over scallops and toss with 2 teaspoons chives. To serve, sprinkle with bacon and remaining chives. Makes 4 main-dish servings.

Each serving: About 251 calories, 20g protein, 8g carbohydrate, 15g total fat (7g saturated), 72mg cholesterol, 412mg sodium.

Panfried Scallops

Try these during the fall and winter months, when small bay scallops are in season. Otherwise, substitute sea scallops and increase the cooking time accordingly. This simple preparation makes for a quick midweek meal.

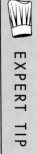 Prep: 5 minutes   Cook: 5 minutes

2	tablespoons olive oil
1	pound bay scallops
1/2	teaspoon salt
2	tablespoons chopped fresh parsley
4	lemon wedges

Pat scallops dry with paper towels. In 12-inch skillet, heat oil over medium-high heat until hot. Add scallops to skillet and sprinkle with salt. Cook, stirring, until just opaque throughout, about 4 minutes. Add parsley and toss. Serve with lemon wedges. Makes 4 main-dish servings.

Each serving: About 160 calories, 19g protein, 3g carbohydrate, 8g total fat (1g saturated), 37mg cholesterol, 473mg sodium.

With kitchen shears or a small knife, cut the shrimp shell along the outer curve, just deep enough into flesh to expose the dark vein.

Peel back the shell from the cut and gently separate the shell from the shrimp. Discard the shell (or use to make fish stock).

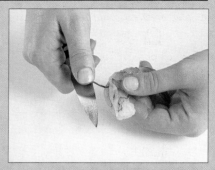

Remove the vein with the tip of a small knife; discard. Rinse the shrimp with cold running water.

Shrimp Curry

This is a mildly seasoned curry prepared in the French style with cream. Serve over rice, if you like.

Prep: 20 minutes   Cook: 12 minutes

2	tablespoons butter or margarine
2	garlic cloves, finely chopped
2	teaspoons minced, peeled fresh ginger
2	teaspoons curry powder
½	teaspoon ground coriander
½	teaspoon ground cumin
¾	cup heavy or whipping cream
1	teaspoon salt
1	medium zucchini (8 ounces), cut lengthwise in half, then crosswise into thin slices
1	pound medium shrimp, shelled and deveined (above)
½	teaspoon ground black pepper
2	tablespoons chopped fresh cilantro

1. In 2-quart saucepan, melt 1 tablespoon butter over medium heat. Add garlic, ginger, curry powder, coriander, and cumin; cook, stirring, 1 minute. Stir in cream and ½ teaspoon salt; increase heat to high and boil until curry sauce has thickened, about 5 minutes.

2. In 10-inch skillet, melt remaining 1 tablespoon butter over medium-high heat. Add zucchini and cook, stirring, until zucchini begins to brown, 2 to 3 minutes. Stir in shrimp, pepper, and remaining ½ teaspoon salt; cook, stirring, until shrimp are just opaque throughout, about 2 minutes. Stir shrimp and zucchini into curry sauce; sprinkle with cilantro. Makes 4 main-dish servings.

Each serving: About 318 calories, 21g protein, 5g carbohydrate, 24g total fat (14g saturated), 216mg cholesterol, 797mg sodium.

Beer-Batter Fried Shrimp

Beer makes this batter light and fluffy. Serve with Tartar Sauce (page 552) or cocktail sauce, or with juicy lemon wedges.

🕐 *Prep: 15 minutes   Cook: 12 minutes*

½	cup all-purpose flour
½	cup beer
½	teaspoon salt
	vegetable oil for frying
1½	pounds medium shrimp, shelled and deveined (opposite)

1. In small bowl, with wire whisk, mix flour, beer, and salt until smooth batter forms.

2. In 2-quart saucepan, heat 2 inches vegetable oil until temperature reaches 375°F on deep-fat thermometer.

3. Pat shrimp dry with paper towels. Dip shrimp, one at a time, into batter and carefully drop into hot oil. Fry 6 shrimp at a time, turning once, until golden, about 1 minute per batch. Using slotted spoon, transfer shrimp to paper towels to drain. Makes 6 first-course servings.

Each serving: About 199 calories, 20g protein, 10g carbohydrate, 9g total fat (1g saturated), 140mg cholesterol, 331mg sodium.

BUTTERFLYING SHRIMP

Shell the shrimp, leaving the tail segment in place. With kitchen shears or a small knife, cut the shrimp along the outer curve, about three-fourths of the way through the flesh.

Spread the flesh open and remove the dark vein with the tip of the knife. Rinse the butterflied shrimp with cold running water.

Shrimp and Potatoes in Feta-Tomato Sauce

Feta cheese gives this Greek-style dish a tangy finish.

Prep: 20 minutes   Cook: 50 minutes

1	tablespoon olive oil
2	medium onions, chopped
1½	pounds all-purpose potatoes, peeled and cut into 1-inch pieces
1	large garlic clove, finely chopped
	pinch ground red pepper (cayenne)
¾	cup water
½	teaspoon salt
1	can (14 to 16 ounces) tomatoes
1	pound medium shrimp, shelled and deveined (opposite)
4	ounces feta cheese, crumbled (1 cup)
¼	cup chopped fresh dill

1. In nonstick 10-inch skillet, heat oil over medium heat. Add onions and cook, stirring frequently, until tender and golden, about 10 minutes.

2. Add potatoes and cook, stirring, until potatoes begin to brown, about 10 minutes. Stir in garlic and ground red pepper and cook 30 seconds. Stir in water and salt; cover and cook until potatoes are almost tender, about 10 minutes.

3. Add tomatoes with their juice, breaking up tomatoes with side of spoon. Cook, uncovered, until liquid has thickened slightly, about 10 minutes.

4. Stir in shrimp and feta. Cover and cook until shrimp are opaque throughout, 3 to 5 minutes. Remove from heat and stir in dill. Makes 4 main-dish servings.

Each serving: About 359 calories, 27g protein, 37g carbohydrate, 11g total fat (5g saturated), 165mg cholesterol, 926mg sodium.

Shrimp Étouffée

Étouffée means "smothered" in Cajun French, and that's just what these shrimp are—in a scrumptious sauce loaded with vegetables and plenty of flavor.

Prep: 30 minutes   Cook: 1 hour

4	tablespoons butter or margarine
¼	cup all-purpose flour
1	yellow pepper, chopped
2	medium onions, chopped
2	stalks celery with some leaves, chopped
2	garlic cloves, finely chopped
3	cups water
3	tablespoons tomato paste
2	bay leaves
1½	teaspoons salt
¾	teaspoon chili powder
¼	teaspoon dried thyme
¼	teaspoon ground black pepper
1½	pounds medium shrimp, shelled and deveined (page 296)
1	cup chopped green onions (5 medium)
¼	cup plus 2 tablespoons chopped fresh parsley
1	cup regular long-grain rice, cooked as label directs

1. In 4-quart Dutch oven, melt butter over medium heat. With wooden spoon, gradually stir in flour until blended and cook, stirring constantly, until flour mixture is color of peanut butter; do not let burn. Add yellow pepper, onions, celery, and garlic. Cook, stirring frequently, until onions are tender, about 5 minutes. Stir in water and tomato paste and heat to boiling. Add bay leaves, salt, chili powder, thyme, and black pepper; reduce heat and simmer 30 minutes.

2. Stir in shrimp, green onions, and ¼ cup parsley. Return to simmer and cook 3 minutes. Remove from heat, cover, and let stand 10 minutes. Discard bay leaves and sprinkle étouffée with remaining 2 tablespoons parsley. Serve with hot rice. Makes about 6 main-dish servings.

Each serving without rice: About 229 calories, 21g protein, 15g carbohydrate, 10g total fat (5g saturated), 161mg cholesterol, 882mg sodium.

Crawfish Étouffée

Prepare as directed but substitute **1 pound fresh or frozen cooked crawfish tail meat** for shrimp.

Each serving without rice: About 217 calories, 20g protein, 14g carbohydrate, 9g total fat (5g saturated), 155mg cholesterol, 797mg sodium.

Thai Shrimp

To serve, spoon the chunky shrimp-and-vegetable mixture over fragrant jasmine rice.

Prep: 30 minutes   Cook: 15 minutes

2	medium limes
3	teaspoons vegetable oil
1	small onion, finely chopped
1	small red pepper, thinly sliced
2	teaspoons grated, peeled fresh ginger
⅛	to ¼ teaspoon ground red pepper (cayenne)
4	ounces medium mushrooms, cut into quarters
½	teaspoon salt
1	can (13¾ to 15 ounces) light coconut milk (not cream of coconut)
1	pound large shrimp, shelled and deveined (page 236)
2	ounces snow peas, strings removed and cut into 2" by ¼" matchstick strips
⅓	cup loosely packed fresh cilantro leaves

1. From limes, with vegetable peeler, peel six 1" by ¾" strips of peel; squeeze 2 tablespoons juice. Set aside.

2. In nonstick 12-inch skillet, heat 2 teaspoons oil over medium heat. Add onion and cook until tender, about 5 minutes. Add sliced red pepper and cook 1 minute. Stir in ginger and ground red pepper; cook 1 minute. Transfer onion mixture to small bowl.

3. In same skillet, heat remaining 1 teaspoon oil over medium-high heat. Add mushrooms and salt and cook until tender and lightly browned, about 3 minutes. Stir in coconut milk, lime peel and juice, and onion mixture and heat to boiling. Add shrimp and cook until shrimp are opaque throughout, about 2 minutes. Stir in snow peas and cilantro. Makes 4 main-dish servings.

Each serving: About 222 calories, 20g protein, 11g carbohydrate, 11g total fat (4g saturated), 140mg cholesterol, 456mg sodium.

Stir-Fried Shrimp with Bok Choy

You don't have to be a Chinese chef to make this dish. Hoisin sauce, ginger, and garlic give it authentic flavor.

Prep: 25 minutes   Cook: 10 minutes

4	tablespoons water
2	tablespoons hoisin sauce
2	tablespoons rice vinegar
½	teaspoon minced, peeled fresh ginger
1	teaspoon brown sugar
½	teaspoon cornstarch
⅛	teaspoon crushed red pepper
2	pounds bok choy
3	tablespoons vegetable oil
1	pound medium shrimp, shelled and deveined (page 296)
1	garlic clove, finely chopped
6	green onions, cut on diagonal into 1-inch pieces

1. In small bowl, combine 2 tablespoons water, hoisin sauce, vinegar, ginger, brown sugar, cornstarch, and crushed red pepper.

2. Trim and core bok choy. Separate leaves from stems, then cut each stem lengthwise in half. Cut stems and leaves crosswise into 2-inch pieces; wash and drain.

3. In nonstick 12-inch skillet, heat 1 tablespoon oil over medium-high heat until hot. Add bok choy and remaining 2 tablespoons water; cook, stirring frequently (stir-frying), until bok choy stems are just tender, 4 to 6 minutes. Transfer to platter and keep warm.

4. Heat remaining 2 tablespoons oil in skillet until hot. Add shrimp and garlic and stir-fry 2 minutes. Add green onions and reserved hoisin-sauce mixture; stir-fry until sauce has thickened and shrimp are opaque throughout, about 3 minutes. To serve, spoon shrimp and sauce on top of bok choy. Makes 4 main-dish servings.

Each serving: About 250 calories, 22g protein, 13g carbohydrate, 12g total fat (2g saturated), 140mg cholesterol, 428mg sodium.

Shrimp Tempura

Shrimp tempura waits for no one—it gets soggy quickly. Serve as soon as shrimp are lifted out of the pot.

Prep: 25 minutes   Cook: 15 minutes

	vegetable oil for frying
⅓	cup chicken broth
3	tablespoons soy sauce
2	tablespoons water
1	tablespoon plus 1 teaspoon seasoned rice vinegar
2	teaspoons sugar
1	teaspoon minced, peeled fresh ginger
¾	cup ice-cold water
1	cup cake flour (not self-rising)
1	teaspoon baking powder
¼	teaspoon salt
1	pound large shrimp, shelled, deveined, and butterflied (pages 296 and 297)

1. In 5-quart Dutch oven, heat 2½ inches vegetable oil until temperature reaches 400°F on deep-fat thermometer.

2. Meanwhile, in small saucepan, combine broth, soy sauce, 2 tablespoons water, vinegar, sugar, and ginger; heat to boiling over high heat. Boil 2 minutes. Strain through sieve into small bowl and keep dipping sauce warm.

3. Pour ice-cold water into medium bowl; sift flour, baking powder, and salt into water. With fork, stir just until barely incorporated; a few lumps may remain.

4. Dip 4 shrimp at a time into batter to coat lightly, allowing excess to drip off. Add shrimp to hot oil and fry, turning once or twice, until coating is very pale golden, 1 to 2 minutes. With slotted spoon, transfer shrimp to paper towels to drain. Serve immediately with warm dipping sauce. Makes 4 main-dish servings.

Each serving: About 309 calories, 22g protein, 27g carbohydrate, 12g total fat (2g saturated), 140mg cholesterol, 1,355mg sodium.

Sausage and Shrimp Gumbo

As they say in New Orleans, "Bon temps rouler!" (Let the good times roll!) This gumbo gets its characteristic full-bodied texture from a flour-and-oil roux and okra.

Prep: 20 minutes   Cook: 40 minutes

1	pound hot Italian-sausage links, pricked with fork
3	tablespoons vegetable oil
1/4	cup all-purpose flour
2	stalks celery, chopped
1	green pepper, chopped
1	medium onion, chopped
1	can (14 1/2 ounces) chicken broth or 1 3/4 cups Chicken Broth (page 84)
1/2	cup water
1	package (10 ounces) frozen whole okra
2	teaspoons hot pepper sauce
1/4	teaspoon dried thyme
1/4	teaspoon dried oregano
1	bay leaf
1	pound large shrimp, shelled and deveined (page 296)
1	cup regular long-grain rice, cooked as label directs

1. Heat 5-quart Dutch oven over medium-high heat until hot. Add sausages and cook, turning frequently, until well browned, about 10 minutes. Transfer sausages to plate to cool slightly. Cut each sausage into 3 pieces.

2. Discard all but 1 tablespoon drippings from Dutch oven. Add oil and heat over medium heat. With wooden spoon, gradually stir in flour until blended and cook, stirring constantly, until flour mixture (roux) is brown; do not let burn. Add celery, green pepper, and onion and cook, stirring occasionally, until vegetables are tender, 8 to 10 minutes. Return sausage to Dutch oven. Gradually stir in broth, water, frozen okra, hot pepper sauce, thyme, oregano, and bay leaf; heat to boiling over high heat. Reduce heat; cover and simmer 15 minutes. Add shrimp and cook, uncovered, until shrimp are opaque throughout, about 2 minutes. Discard bay leaf. Serve gumbo in large bowls with scoop of hot rice in center. Makes 6 main-dish servings.

Each serving: About 491 calories, 28g protein, 37g carbohydrate, 25g total fat (7g saturated), 138mg cholesterol, 956mg sodium.

Sausage and Shrimp Gumbo

Fried Calamari Fra Diavolo

Crispy golden-fried squid served with a tomato dipping sauce that is often as spicy as the devil (fra diavolo means "brother devil"). Or simply serve with lemon wedges.

Prep: 10 minutes   Cook: 25 minutes

1	tablespoon olive oil
2	garlic cloves, crushed with side of chef's knife
1/8 to 1/4	teaspoon crushed red pepper
1	can (14 to 16 ounces) tomatoes
3/4	teaspoon salt
1	pound cleaned squid
2/3	cup all-purpose flour
1	cup water
	vegetable oil for frying

1. In nonreactive 1-quart saucepan, heat olive oil over medium heat. Add garlic and crushed red pepper; cook until garlic is golden, about 30 seconds. Add tomatoes with their juice and 1/2 teaspoon salt, breaking up tomatoes with side of spoon; heat to boiling. Reduce heat; cover and simmer 10 minutes. Keep warm.

2. Rinse squid with cold running water and gently pat dry with paper towels. Slice squid bodies crosswise into 3/4-inch rings. Cut tentacles into pieces if large.

3. In small bowl, with fork, mix flour and water until smooth. In 10-inch skillet, heat 1/2 inch vegetable oil over medium heat until very hot. (A small piece of bread dropped into oil should sink, then rise to top and begin bubbling.) In small batches, drop squid into batter, allowing excess to drip off, then add to hot oil. Fry, turning to brown on all sides, until golden, about 2 minutes. With slotted spoon, transfer squid to paper towels to drain; sprinkle with remaining 1/4 teaspoon salt. Serve with tomato sauce for dipping. Makes 4 first-course servings.

Each serving: About 325 calories, 21g protein, 25g carbohydrate, 16g total fat (2g saturated), 264mg cholesterol, 660mg sodium.

Grilled Squid

For tender grilled squid, you need a very hot grill and just a few seconds of cooking.

Prep: 15 minutes   Grill: 2 minutes

1	pound cleaned squid
1	tablespoon extravirgin olive oil
1	tablespoon fresh lemon juice
1/4	teaspoon salt
1/8	teaspoon ground black pepper
	metal skewers
1	tablespoon chopped fresh parsley
	lemon wedges

1. Prepare grill. Rinse squid with cold running water and pat dry with paper towels. Cut squid bodies lengthwise down one side and open flat. Cut tentacles in half if large. In bowl, combine oil, lemon juice, salt, and pepper. Add squid bodies and tentacles, tossing to coat.

2. Thread squid bodies lengthwise onto skewers so they lie flat; thread tentacles onto separate skewers. Grill over high heat, turning once, until just opaque throughout, 1 to 2 minutes. Remove squid from skewers and pile on platter. Sprinkle with parsley and serve with lemon wedges. Makes 4 first-course servings.

Each serving: About 136 calories, 18g protein, 4g carbohydrate, 5g total fat (1g saturated), 264mg cholesterol, 193mg sodium.

CLEANING SQUID

Although cleaned and ready-to-use squid is widely available at fish markets, it's easy and more economical to clean your own. Hold the body of a squid in one hand and grip the head and tentacles in the other. Gently pull to remove all the innards. Pull out the clear plasticlike quill from the body and discard. Cut off the tentacles just below the eyes; reserve the tentacles. Remove and discard the beak from the center of the tentacles. Discard the head and ink sac. Rub or scrape off the purple skin from the body; discard the skin. Rinse the body well inside and out with cold running water; rinse the tentacles.

Stuffed Squid

Use part of a loaf of French or Italian bread in the stuffing, and serve the remainder with the squid to soak up all the savory juices.

Prep: 30 minutes   Cook: 1 hour 5 minutes

2	tablespoons plus 1 teaspoon olive oil
2	garlic cloves, finely chopped
2	cups fresh bread crumbs (about 1/4 French or Italian bread)
1/4	cup chopped fresh parsley
1/4	cup freshly grated Pecorino Romano cheese
1/2	teaspoon salt
1/2	teaspoon coarsely ground black pepper
1 1/2	pounds cleaned squid
1	can (14 to 16 ounces) tomatoes

1. In nonstick 10-inch skillet, heat 2 tablespoons oil over medium heat. Add half of garlic and cook, stirring frequently, until very fragrant but not browned. Remove skillet from heat and stir in bread crumbs, parsley, Pecorino, and 1/4 teaspoon each salt and pepper.

2. Rinse squid with cold running water and pat dry with paper towels. Spoon stuffing loosely into each squid body (stuffing will expand when cooked). With toothpicks, close each squid body at top.

3. Wipe skillet clean. Add remaining 1 teaspoon oil and remaining garlic to skillet; cook over medium heat until very fragrant. Stir in tomatoes with their juice and remaining 1/4 teaspoon each salt and pepper, breaking up tomatoes with side of spoon; heat to boiling. Add squid tentacles and squid bodies. Reduce heat; cover and simmer until squid are very tender, about 1 hour. To serve, remove toothpicks. Makes 4 main-dish servings.

Each serving: About 333 calories, 32g protein, 22g carbohydrate, 13g total fat (3g saturated), 403mg cholesterol, 711mg sodium.

California Cioppino

This classic seafood stew from San Francisco doesn't take a lot of time; much of the preparation of the seafood can be done while the vegetables are cooking. If you're lucky enough to find Dungeness crab, cut one or two cooked crabs (still in the shell) into serving-size pieces and use instead of shrimp.

Prep: 35 minutes   Cook: 20 minutes

1/3	cup olive oil
2	medium red onions, thinly sliced
4	green onions, thinly sliced
3	strips (3" by 3/4" each) lemon peel
3	garlic cloves, thinly sliced
1	yellow pepper, chopped
3/4	cup dry vermouth or dry white wine
1	can (28 ounces) tomatoes, chopped
1	cup water
1/2	teaspoon salt
	pinch crushed red pepper
1 1/2	pounds striped bass or red snapper fillets, cut into 2-inch pieces
1	pound medium shrimp, shelled and deveined (page 296)
3/4	cup chopped fresh parsley
2	tablespoons chopped fresh basil

1. In nonreactive 5-quart Dutch oven, heat oil over medium-high heat. Add red and green onions, lemon peel, and garlic and cook, stirring, until red onions are very tender, about 10 minutes. Add yellow pepper and vermouth and cook, stirring, 5 minutes.

2. Increase heat to high; stir in tomatoes with their juice, water, salt, and crushed red pepper; heat to boiling. Add bass, shrimp, and 1/2 cup parsley; cover and simmer until fish and shrimp are just opaque throughout, about 5 minutes.

3. Remove from heat and stir in remaining 1/4 cup parsley and basil. Makes about 8 cups or 6 main-dish servings.

Each serving: About 379 calories, 36g protein, 16g carbohydrate, 16g total fat (2g saturated), 184mg cholesterol, 644mg sodium.

Shrimp and Scallop Kabobs

One word of advice: Don't soak the shellfish in the soy and rice vinegar mixture. The vinegar will firm and "cook" the flesh.

Prep: 20 minutes   Grill: 6 minutes

1	pound large shrimp, shelled and deveined (page 296), leaving tail part of shell on, if you like
12	ounces large sea scallops
3	tablespoons soy sauce
3	tablespoons seasoned rice vinegar
1	tablespoon Asian sesame oil
2	tablespoons grated, peeled fresh ginger
2	garlic cloves, crushed with garlic press
1	tablespoon brown sugar
1	bunch green onions, cut on diagonal into 3-inch pieces
12	cherry tomatoes
6	long metal skewers

1. Prepare grill. Pull off and discard tough crescent-shaped muscle from each scallop. Pat shrimp and scallops dry with paper towels.

2. In large bowl, combine soy sauce, vinegar, sesame oil, ginger, garlic, and brown sugar. Add shrimp and scallops, tossing to coat.

3. Alternately thread shrimp, scallops, green-onion pieces, and cherry tomatoes onto skewers. Grill over medium heat, turning skewers occasionally and brushing shrimp and scallops with any remaining soy-sauce mixture during first half of cooking, until shrimp and scallops are just opaque throughout, 6 to 8 minutes. Makes 6 main-dish servings.

Each serving: About 168 calories, 23g protein, 9g carbohydrate, 4g total fat (1g saturated), 112mg cholesterol, 851mg sodium.

Seafood Paella

This festive dish is party fare at its finest. You can prepare the shrimp stock in advance and cook the paella through Step Two. If you purchase already-cleaned shrimp, substitute chicken broth for the shrimp stock and reduce the salt. Try to use medium-grain rice: It will give the paella an authentic slightly sticky texture.

Prep: 30 minutes   Cook: 1 hour 45 minutes

1	pound medium shrimp, shelled and deveined (page 296), shells reserved
4	cups water
1	pound cleaned squid
2	tablespoons olive oil
1	medium onion, chopped
3	garlic cloves, thinly sliced
1	red pepper, cut into thin strips
1	cup canned tomatoes, with their juice, chopped
1½	teaspoons salt
2	cups medium-grain rice
⅛	teaspoon ground saffron
1	pound sea scallops
1	cup frozen peas

1. Make shrimp stock: In 3-quart saucepan, combine shrimp shells and water. Heat to boiling; reduce heat, partially cover, and simmer 30 minutes. Strain broth through sieve; discard shells. There should be about 3 cups shrimp broth.

2. Rinse squid with cold running water and pat dry with paper towels. Slice squid bodies crosswise into ½-inch rings. Cut tentacles into 1-inch pieces. In deep nonstick 12-inch skillet, heat oil over medium-low heat. Add onion and garlic and cook, stirring frequently, until onion is tender, about 7 minutes. Add red pepper and cook 4 minutes. Add squid and cook 2 minutes.

3. Add tomatoes with their juice, ½ cup shrimp broth, and ¼ teaspoon salt; heat to boiling. Reduce heat; cover and simmer 30 minutes. Stir in rice, saffron, remaining 2½ cups shrimp stock, and remaining 1¼ teaspoons salt. Heat to boiling over high heat. Reduce heat; cover and simmer until squid is tender and rice is cooked through, about 20 minutes.

4. Pull off and discard tough crescent-shaped muscle from each scallop. Cut scallops horizontally in half if large. Stir scallops, shrimp, and frozen peas into rice mixture in skillet; cover and cook until scallops and shrimp are just opaque throughout, about 9 minutes longer. Makes 6 main-dish servings.

💙 Each serving: About 518 calories, 43g protein, 65g carbohydrate, 8g total fat (1g saturated), 294mg cholesterol, 921mg sodium.

Peruvian Seafood Soup

This cilantro and lime scented soup is an opportunity to enjoy one of the classic dishes of Peru.

Prep: 30 minutes   Cook: 25 minutes

1	tablespoon vegetable oil
1	medium onion, chopped
2	garlic cloves, finely chopped
2	serrano or jalapeño chiles, seeded and finely chopped
1	pound red potatoes, cut into ¾-inch pieces
3	bottles (8 ounces each) clam juice
2	cups water
¾	teaspoon salt
⅛	teaspoon dried thyme
1	lime
1	pound monkfish, dark membrane removed, cut into 1-inch pieces
1	pound medium shrimp, shelled and deveined (page 296), leaving tail part of shell on, if you like
¼	cup chopped fresh cilantro

1. In 4-quart saucepan, heat oil over medium heat. Add onion and cook, stirring frequently, until tender and golden, about 10 minutes. Stir in garlic and chiles and cook 30 seconds. Add potatoes, clam juice, water, salt, and thyme; heat to boiling over high heat. Reduce heat to medium; cook until potatoes are just tender, about 10 minutes.

2. Cut lime in half; cut one half into wedges and set aside. Add remaining lime half and monkfish to soup; cover and cook 5 minutes. Stir in shrimp and cook until shrimp are just opaque throughout and monkfish is tender, 3 to 5 minutes.

3. With tongs, remove lime half, squeezing juice into soup. Sprinkle soup with cilantro and serve with lime wedges. Makes about 11 cups or 6 main-dish servings.

💙 Each serving: About 222 calories, 26g protein, 18g carbohydrate, 5g total fat (0g saturated), 112mg cholesterol, 660mg sodium.

Bouillabaisse

Ask Provençal cooks how to make bouillabaisse and you'll get a different and passionate response every time. When preparing this classic fisherman's stew, use at least three different kinds of fish, with textures ranging from firm to flaky; add the most fragile fish to the pot last. Serve with bread toasts and generous dollops of the aïoli. Magnifique!

Prep: 1 hour   Cook: 1 hour

3	leeks (1 pound)
2	tablespoons olive oil
1	large fennel bulb (1½ pounds), trimmed and thinly sliced
1	medium onion, chopped
2	garlic cloves, finely chopped
	pinch ground red pepper (cayenne)
1	cup dry white wine
2	bottles (8 ounces each) clam juice
1	can (14 to 16 ounces) tomatoes
1	cup water
3	strips (3" by 1" each) orange peel
½	bay leaf
¾	teaspoon salt
¼	teaspoon dried thyme
⅛	teaspoon ground black pepper
	Easy Aïoli (page 40)
1	pound monkfish, dark membrane removed, cut into 1-inch pieces
1	dozen medium mussels, scrubbed and debearded (page 291)
1	pound cod fillet, cut into 1-inch pieces
1	pound medium shrimp, shelled and deveined (page 296)
2	tablespoons chopped fresh parsley
1	loaf French bread, thinly sliced and lightly toasted

1. Cut off roots and trim dark green tops from leeks; cut each leek lengthwise in half, then crosswise into thin slices. Rinse leeks in large bowl of cold water, swishing to remove sand; transfer to colander to drain, leaving sand in bottom.

2. In nonreactive 5-quart Dutch oven, heat oil over medium heat. Stir in leeks, fennel, and onion; cook, stirring occasionally, until vegetables are tender, about 15 minutes. Add garlic and ground red pepper and cook 30 seconds.

3. Add wine and heat to boiling; boil 1 minute. Stir in clam juice, tomatoes with their juice, water, orange peel, bay leaf, salt, thyme, and black pepper, breaking up tomatoes with side of spoon; heat to boiling. Reduce heat and simmer 20 minutes. Discard bay leaf.

4. Meanwhile, prepare Easy Aïoli.

5. Increase heat to medium-high. Stir in monkfish; cover and cook 3 minutes. Stir in mussels; cover and cook 1 minute. Stir in cod and shrimp; cover and cook until mussels open and fish and shrimp are just opaque throughout, 2 to 3 minutes longer. Discard any mussels that have not opened.

6. To serve, ladle bouillabaisse into large shallow soup bowls; sprinkle with parsley. Spoon aïoli onto toasted French bread and float in bouillabaisse. Makes 11 cups or 6 main-dish servings.

♥ Each serving without toast or Easy Aïoli: About 312 calories, 42g protein, 17g carbohydrate, 8g total fat (1g saturated), 149mg cholesterol, 835mg sodium.

7

EGGS

There is an old saying that "The egg is to cuisine what the article is to speech." Like the little words that string a sentence together, the humble egg is taken for granted. Without eggs, cakes would be tough and flat, custards wouldn't set, a meringue would be just a pile of sugar, soufflés wouldn't puff, mayonnaise wouldn't thicken, meat loaves would crumble, and breakfast just wouldn't be the same. The egg is an indispensable, invaluable ingredient that no kitchen can do entirely without. Eggs are a complete food, meant to nourish chicks while still in the shell. They are a good source of protein, iron, and vitamins. And while whole eggs and egg yolks are relatively high in fat and cholesterol, egg whites are completely fat- and cholesterol-free.

SALMONELLA AND EGGS

Raw eggs pose a health concern because they can be contaminated with *salmonella,* a bacterium that can cause food poisoning. Salmonella is killed at 160°F, so be sure to cook eggs to at least that temperature—easily reached with scrambled eggs, "over hard" fried eggs, custards, and other favorite egg dishes. Certain people, such as the elderly, infants, pregnant women, and those with compromised immune systems, are especially

Italian Sausage and Mozzarella Frittata

susceptible to infection and should not eat undercooked eggs. After handling raw eggs, thoroughly wash your hands and any utensils that have come in contact with the eggs with soap and hot water.

Pasteurized eggs, which are newly available in the dairy case, are free from salmonella, E. coli, and listeria. Cook them the way you would any other eggs.

Egg substitutes, which are pasteurized and salmonella-free, are used by people with special dietary needs. Liquid egg substitute (colored egg whites) can substitute for whole eggs, but don't expect the same rich flavor real eggs deliver. Dehydrated egg whites and meringue powder are a good substitute for fresh egg whites in meringue recipes. Just follow the reconstituting directions on the package.

CHOOSING EGGS

Eggs are sold by size and grade as defined by the United States Department of Agriculture. The grade is based on many factors, including the appearance of the shell, the quality of the interior of the egg, and the size of the air pocket at the top of the egg (usually determined by candling, a process in which the egg is held against a strong light to illuminate its interior). Grade AA eggs have firm, high yolks and thick whites; they are best for frying, poaching, and cooking in the shell. Grade A eggs have thinner whites and are fine all-purpose eggs that are good for baking. Grade B eggs, which have the thinnest whites, are rarely available to the consumer; they are usually sold to food manufacturers. The chalaza, the thin white cord that attaches the yolk to the shell, is especially prominent in a very fresh egg and disappears as an egg ages. (When making a custard, you may want to strain the custard to remove the chalazae, which tends to become hard when cooked.) The size of an egg is determined by its weight. Eggs are graded jumbo, extra large, large, medium, and small. *All of the recipes in this book use large eggs unless otherwise noted.* Using the right size egg is important, especially in recipes that call for a large number.

An eggshell's color is determined solely by the breed of hen. Cooks in the Northeast often prefer brown eggs, but they are no different from the white variety. It is important, however, that the eggshells be clean and uncracked; never buy cracked eggs. Before purchasing eggs, move them in the carton to make sure they haven't cracked and stuck.

STORING EGGS

Eggs should be stored in their carton in a cool part of the refrigerator. The open egg compartment on the refrigerator door is not the ideal place, because it is exposed to warm air every time the door is opened. Also, keep eggs away from strong-smelling foods, such as cheese or onions. Aromas and flavors can easily pass through an egg's thin shell, which is another good reason to keep eggs in their protective carton. To keep the yolks centered, store eggs pointed end down. If stored at around 40°F, eggs will keep for about one month.

If you forget to mark your hard-cooked eggs and can't tell them apart from your uncooked eggs, spin the eggs on a flat surface. Hard-cooked eggs spin easily and smoothly, but raw eggs spin slowly and awkwardly.

Keep eggs refrigerated until ready to use, because they deteriorate quickly at room temperature. As fresh eggs age, their thick translucent whites thin out and their round firm yolks flatten. For poaching and frying, use very fresh eggs, because they hold their shape the best. The carton "sell-by" date is the easiest way to tell how old eggs are: It can never be more than thirty days past the packing date. Some states show the packing date in Julian numbers, which run from 001 (January 1) to 365 (December 31).

If you don't have the egg carton and want to check for freshness, all you need is a glass of water. As an egg ages, its liquid begins to evaporate, making the air space at the top of the egg bigger and the egg increasingly buoyant. When placed in a glass of water, a fresh egg will sink to the bottom, a slightly older egg will stand upright, and an old egg will float. As a last resort, there's always the smell test. Break the egg into a saucer and give it a sniff. An egg should have no odor at all or smell absolutely clean and slightly sweet. There's no mistaking the aroma of a bad egg.

The color of an egg yolk can range from yellow to orange. It is determined solely by the hen's diet and is not an indication of taste or freshness. You will sometimes see a small blood spot on an egg yolk. This is caused by a ruptured blood vessel and does not denote freshness. If desired, it can easily be removed with the tip of a knife.

COOKING EGGS

Scrambled For each serving, whisk 2 eggs, 2 tablespoons milk, and salt and pepper to taste just until blended. In an 8-inch skillet, melt 2 teaspoons butter or margarine over medium heat. Add the eggs, and as they begin to set, with a heat-proof rubber spatula or a wooden spatula, push the egg mixture to form large soft curds. Continue cooking until the eggs have thickened and set.

Poached In a skillet, heat 1½ inches water to boiling. (For additional flavor, use broth, tomato juice, dry red wine, or milk instead of water.) Reduce the heat so the water gently simmers. For the best-shaped poached eggs, use cold fresh eggs. Break the eggs, one at a time, into a cup. Holding the cup close to the water, slip in the egg. Cook for three to five minutes, until the whites are set and the yolks begin to thicken. With a slotted spoon, lift out an egg and drain it, still held in the spoon, on paper towels. Repeat with the remaining eggs. If desired, trim away any uneven edges of white to give the eggs a neater appearance.

Fried In an 8-inch skillet, melt 1 tablespoon butter or margarine over medium heat. Break 2 eggs into the pan; reduce the heat to low. For "sunny-side up" eggs, cover and slowly cook until the whites are set and the yolks have thickened. For "over easy" eggs, carefully turn the eggs and cook on the second side.

Cooked in shell Place the eggs in a saucepan with enough cold water to cover by at least 1 inch. Heat just to boiling; remove from the heat and cover. Let the eggs stand for four to five minutes for soft-cooked eggs or fifteen minutes for hard-cooked eggs. To avoid an unattractive greenish ring around the yolks, do not boil or overcook the eggs. Carefully pour off the water and rinse the eggs with cold running water to cool them and stop the cooking. To peel, gently tap a cooled hard-cooked egg against a hard surface until the shell is cracked all over. Starting at the rounder end (where the air space makes peeling easier), peel the egg under cold running water. Unpeeled eggs keep in the refrigerator for up to one week.

Baked Preheat oven to 350°F. Generously butter a round baking dish or ramekin. Break 2 eggs into the dish. Top with 1 tablespoon milk or heavy cream and season with salt and pepper. Bake until the eggs are set to the desired doneness, fifteen to twenty minutes. Serve the eggs in the baking dish.

SEPARATING EGGS

Many recipes call for egg whites or egg yolks, which means the eggs must be separated. Eggs separate most easily when cold. You can use an egg separator, but the half-shell method works just as well.

To separate an egg, on the side of a bowl, sharply tap the eggshell along its middle to make a crosswise crack. With your thumbs, gently pull open the shell along the crack, letting some of the white run into the bowl. Slowly transfer the yolk back and forth from one half-shell to the other, being careful not to break the yolk on any sharp shell edges, until all the white has run into the bowl. The smallest trace of fat from the yolks will keep the whites from foaming properly when beaten, so be very careful. If any yolk does get into the whites, it can sometimes be removed with a small spoon or the edge of an eggshell, but be sure to remove it all.

Cover leftover unbroken egg yolks with cold water (to prevent a skin from forming on the surface) and refrigerate for up to two days; drain before using. Store egg whites for up to five days in an airtight container in the refrigerator.

BEATING EGG WHITES

When beating egg whites, keep in mind that their volume will increase six to nine times, so be sure to use a large enough bowl. The bowl and the beaters must be absolutely clean, because even the tiniest bit of fat will prevent peaks from forming. Stainless steel or glass bowls do the best job—plastic bowls retain grease no matter how clean they are. And while it is true that egg whites beaten in a copper bowl form especially stable peaks that are hard to overbeat, a copper bowl isn't really necessary. A little cream of tartar will also stabilize egg whites. The addition of salt to egg whites does not help; in fact, it actually discourages foaming.

Room-temperature egg whites beat to the fullest volume. Let chilled whites stand for thirty minutes to warm up. Or, place the bowl of egg whites into a separate bowl of hot water and stir for one or two minutes.

If a recipe says to beat egg whites until "foamy" or "frothy," beat them until they form a mass of tiny clear bubbles. For "soft peaks," beat until the whites form soft rounded peaks that droop when the beaters are lifted.

For "stiff glossy peaks," beat until the whites form peaks that hold their shape when the beaters are lifted but are still moist. Overbeaten whites look lumpy and watery—there is no way to salvage them. Simply begin again with new whites.

How and when sugar is added to egg whites is crucial. Sugar should always be added gradually so it has time to dissolve. First, beat the egg whites to the soft peak stage, then begin adding the sugar, about 2 tablespoons at a time, beating until the whites are stiff and glossy.

Basic Omelets

A well-made omelet can be a quick supper or a satisfying break-fast. Mix up a batch of eggs, prepare your fillings, and you're ready for quick assembly-line production. For lower-fat omelets, use four large eggs and eight egg whites.

 Prep: 5 minutes plus preparing filling
Cook: 2 minutes per omelet

	choice of filling (right)
8	large eggs
½	cup water
½	teaspoon salt
4	teaspoons butter or margarine

1. Prepare filling. In medium bowl, with wire whisk, beat eggs, water, and salt.

2. In nonstick 10-inch skillet, melt 1 teaspoon butter over medium-high heat. Pour ½ cup egg mixture into skillet. Cook, gently lifting edge of eggs with heat-safe rubber spatula and tilting pan to allow uncooked eggs to run underneath, until eggs are set, about 1 minute. Spoon one-fourth of

filling over half of omelet. Fold unfilled half of omelet over filling and slide onto warm plate. Repeat with remaining butter, egg mixture, and filling. If desired, keep omelets warm in 200°F oven until all omelets are cooked. Makes 4 main-dish servings.

Each omelet without filling: About 183 calories, 13g protein, 1g carbohydrate, 14g total fat (5g saturated), 435mg cholesterol, 455mg sodium.

Basic Omelet with Garden-Vegetable Filling

Creamy Mushroom Filling

In nonstick 10-inch skillet, melt **1 tablespoon butter or margarine** over medium-high heat. Add **1 medium onion,** finely chopped; cook until tender, about 5 minutes. Stir in **8 ounces mushrooms,** trimmed and thinly sliced, ¼ **teaspoon salt,** and ⅛ **teaspoon ground black pepper;** cook until liquid has evaporated. Stir in ¼ **cup heavy cream;** boil until thickened, about 3 minutes. Stir in **2 tablespoons chopped fresh parsley.** Use one-fourth mushroom mixture for each omelet.

Each filled omelet: About 291 calories, 15g protein, 8g carbohydrate, 23g total fat (11g saturated), 463mg cholesterol, 637mg sodium.

Black Bean and Salsa Filling

In nonstick 10-inch skillet, cook **1 cup canned black beans,** rinsed and drained, and **1 cup medium-hot salsa** over medium-high heat, stirring frequently, until liquid has evaporated. Divide black-bean mixture, **1 ripe medium avocado,** peeled and chopped, and ¼ **cup sour cream** among omelets.

Each filled omelet: About 365 calories, 17g protein, 18g carbohydrate, 25g total fat (9g saturated), 442mg cholesterol, 1,307mg sodium.

Garden-Vegetable Filling

In nonstick 10-inch skillet, heat **1 tablespoon olive oil** over medium heat. Add **1 small onion,** chopped, **1 small zucchini (6 ounces),** chopped, **1 small yellow pepper,** chopped, **½ teaspoon salt,** and **⅛ teaspoon ground black pepper;** cook until vegetables are tender, about 10 minutes. Stir in **2 ripe plum tomatoes,** chopped, and **¼ cup chopped fresh basil;** heat through. Use one-fourth mixture for each omelet.

Each filled omelet: About 239 calories, 14g protein, 7g carbohydrate, 17g total fat (6g saturated), 435mg cholesterol, 749mg sodium.

Spinach, Cheddar, and Bacon Filling

In 3-quart saucepan, cook **1 bunch (10 to 12 ounces) spinach,** washed, dried very well, and tough stems trimmed, over high heat just until wilted; drain. When cool enough to handle, squeeze out excess liquid from spinach and coarsely chop. Divide chopped spinach, **4 ounces Cheddar cheese,** shredded (1 cup), and **4 slices bacon,** cooked and crumbled, among omelets.

Each filled omelet: About 346 calories, 23g protein, 4g carbohydrate, 27g total fat (13g saturated), 471mg cholesterol, 776mg sodium.

Red Pepper and Goat Cheese Filling

In nonstick 10-inch skillet, melt **2 teaspoons butter or margarine** over medium-high heat. Add **1 red pepper,** thinly sliced, and **¼ teaspoon salt;** cook until tender and lightly browned. Add **1 garlic clove,** finely chopped; cook 1 minute. Divide red pepper, **2 ounces goat cheese,** and **½ cup loosely packed trimmed and torn arugula** among omelets.

Each filled omelet: About 257 calories, 16g protein, 3g carbohydrate, 20g total fat (10g saturated), 452mg cholesterol, 692mg sodium.

Western Filling

In nonstick 10-inch skillet, heat **1 tablespoon olive oil** over medium heat. Add **1 small onion,** chopped, **1 green pepper,** chopped, **8 ounces mushrooms,** trimmed and thinly sliced, and **¼ teaspoon salt;** cook until vegetables are tender and liquid has evaporated, about 10 minutes. Add **4 ounces sliced ham,** finely chopped (1 cup), and heat through. Use one-fourth filling for each omelet.

Each filled omelet: About 294 calories, 19g protein, 8g carbohydrate, 21g total fat (7g saturated), 452mg cholesterol, 974mg sodium.

HOW MANY? HOW MUCH?

If you are measuring eggs by volume, use these amounts:

- 1 large egg white = about 2 tablespoons
- 1 large egg yolk = about 1 tablespoon
- 5 large eggs = about 1 cup
- 8 large egg whites = about 1 cup

Egg White Omelet

When you crave an omelet but are watching your fat intake, this is the perfect one. Skim milk and flour keep the omelet soft and tender, while turmeric tints the whites pale yellow to give the illusion of egg yolks. Choose a nonfat filling, such as chopped tomatoes and herbs.

Prep: 5 minutes plus preparing filling	Cook: 3 minutes

	choice of filling (optional)
2	tablespoons skim milk
1	tablespoon all-purpose flour
4	large egg whites
½	teaspoon salt
½	teaspoon ground tumeric (optional)
2	teaspoons olive oil

1. Prepare filling, if desired. In medium bowl, with wire whisk, blend milk and flour until smooth. Whisk in egg whites, salt, and tumeric, if using.

2. In nonstick 6-inch skillet, heat oil over medium heat. Add egg-white mixture and cook, gently lifting edge of eggs with heat-safe rubber spatula and tilting pan to allow uncooked eggs to run underneath, until just set, about 2 minutes. Spoon filling, if using, over half of omelet; fold unfilled half of omelet over filling and slide onto warm plate. Makes 1 main-dish serving.

Each omelet without filling: About 186 calories, 16g protein, 9g carbohydrate, 9g total fat (1g saturated), 1mg cholesterol, 1,393mg sodium.

Basic Fluffy Omelet

Beaten egg whites give this oven-baked omelet extra lift. For a cheese omelet, sprinkle with your favorite shredded cheese during the last minute of baking.

Prep: 10 minutes   Cook/Bake: 15 minutes

4	large eggs, separated
2	tablespoons water
1/8	teaspoon salt
1	tablespoon butter or margarine

1. Preheat oven to 350°F. In medium bowl, with mixer at high speed, beat egg whites until stiff peaks form when beaters are lifted. In large bowl, with mixer at high speed, beat egg yolks, water, and salt until egg-yolk mixture has thickened. With rubber spatula, gently fold one-third of beaten egg whites into egg-yolk mixture. Fold in remaining egg whites until just blended.

2. In oven-safe nonstick 10-inch skillet (if skillet is not oven-safe, wrap handle with double layer of foil), melt butter over medium-low heat. Add egg mixture and cook until top has puffed and underside is golden, about 3 minutes.

3. Place skillet in oven. Bake until top of omelet is golden and center springs back when lightly touched with finger, about 10 minutes.

QUICK NO-COOK FILLINGS FOR OMELETS

In the mood for a deliciously different omelet? Try one of these flavorful combinations.

Mango chutney and sour cream • diced avocado, salsa, and sour cream • chopped tomato and pesto • chopped smoked salmon, cubed cream cheese, and capers • chopped smoked turkey, thinly sliced red onion, and cubed Brie cheese • chopped tomato, crumbled feta cheese, and dill • diced ham, chopped green onions, and shredded Pepper Jack cheese • caponata and grated Parmesan cheese • ricotta cheese, berries, and confectioners' sugar • crumbled goat cheese, jalapeño jelly, and sour cream • chopped fresh herbs, green onions, and sour cream.

4. To serve, loosen omelet from skillet and slide onto warm platter. Makes 2 main-dish servings.

Each serving: About 200 calories, 13g protein, 1g carbohydrate, 16g total fat (7g saturated), 441mg cholesterol, 331mg sodium.

Potato-Salsa Frittata

Frittatas are delicious at just about any temperature. This one is topped with salsa just before serving.

Prep: 10 minutes   Cook/Bake: 20 minutes

1	teaspoon olive oil
12	ounces red potatoes (2 large), cut into 1/2-inch pieces
6	large eggs
1	jar (11 to 12 ounces) medium-hot salsa, chopped if chunks are large
1/2	teaspoon salt
1/4	teaspoon coarsely ground black pepper
1	ounce sharp Cheddar cheese, shredded (1/4 cup)
1	ripe medium tomato (8 ounces), chopped

1. Preheat oven to 425°F. In oven-safe nonstick 10-inch skillet (if skillet is not oven-safe, wrap handle with double layer of foil), heat oil over medium-high heat. Add potatoes; cover and cook, stirring occasionally, until potatoes are tender and golden brown, about 10 minutes.

2. Meanwhile, in medium bowl, with wire whisk, beat eggs, 1/4 cup salsa, salt, and pepper until well blended. Stir in Cheddar cheese.

3. Stir egg mixture into potatoes in skillet; cover and cook over medium heat until egg mixture begins to set around edge, about 3 minutes. Remove cover and place skillet in oven; bake until frittata is set, 4 to 6 minutes.

4. Meanwhile, stir tomato into remaining salsa. To serve, loosen frittata from skillet and slide onto warm platter. Cut into 4 wedges and top with salsa. Makes 4 main-dish servings.

Each serving: About 252 calories, 13g protein, 23g carbohydrate, 11g total fat (4g saturated), 326mg cholesterol, 1,279mg sodium.

Chive and Goat Cheese Frittata

This frittata is packed with the delicious flavors of tangy goat cheese, ripe tomato, and fresh chives.

Prep: 15 minutes   Cook/Bake: 15 minutes

8	large eggs
½	cup milk
½	teaspoon salt
⅛	teaspoon coarsely ground black pepper
1	ripe medium tomato (6 ounces), chopped
2	tablespoons chopped fresh chives
2	teaspoons butter or margarine
1	package (3½ ounces) goat cheese

1. Preheat oven to 375°F. In medium bowl, with wire whisk, beat eggs, milk, salt, and pepper until well blended. Stir in tomato and chives.

2. In oven-safe nonstick 10-inch skillet (if skillet is not oven-safe, wrap handle with double layer of foil), melt butter over medium heat. Pour in egg mixture; drop tablespoons of goat cheese on top of egg mixture. Cook until egg mixture begins to set around edge, 3 to 4 minutes.

3. Place skillet in oven; bake until frittata is set, 8 to 10 minutes. To serve, loosen frittata from skillet and slide onto warm platter; cut into 4 wedges. Makes 4 main-dish servings.

Each serving: About 279 calories, 19g protein, 5g carbohydrate, 20g total fat (10g saturated), 454mg cholesterol, 581mg sodium.

USING LEFTOVER EGG WHITES AND EGG YOLKS

There are many uses for leftover egg whites and egg yolks. Dessert possibilities for leftover whites include Angel Food Cake (page 666), Fresh Apple Soufflé or one of its many variations (page 623), and Miniature Meringue Shells (page 626). Egg whites can also replace some of the whole eggs in the Basic Omelet (page 310). The thickening power of egg yolks is also put to good use in many sauces; Hollandaise and Béarnaise (pages 550 and 551) are classic savory examples. Egg yolks are also essential in many sweet dishes, including custards and Custard Sauce (page 562).

Potato and Ham Frittata

While the frittata bakes, whip up a salad of baby spinach and red onion, dressed with your favorite vinaigrette.

Prep: 10 minutes   Cook/Bake: 45 minutes

10	ounces all-purpose potatoes (2 medium), peeled, cut lengthwise in half, then crosswise into thin slices (2 cups)
1¼	teaspoons salt
3	tablespoons vegetable oil
1	piece cooked ham (4 ounces), cut into ½-inch pieces (1 cup)
1	medium onion, thinly sliced
8	large eggs
¼	cup water
¼	teaspoon coarsely ground black pepper
	pinch dried thyme

1. Preheat oven to 425°F. In 2-quart saucepan, combine potatoes, *3 cups cold water*, and 1 teaspoon salt; heat to boiling over high heat. Cook until tender, about 10 minutes; drain.

2. In oven-safe nonstick 10-inch skillet (if skillet is not oven-safe, wrap handle with double layer of foil), heat 1 tablespoon oil over medium-high heat. Add ham and cook, stirring occasionally, until lightly browned, about 3 minutes. With slotted spoon, transfer ham to plate.

3. Add 1 tablespoon oil to skillet; add onion and cook, stirring occasionally, until tender and golden, about 10 minutes. Transfer onion to plate with ham.

4. In large bowl, with wire whisk, beat eggs, water, remaining ¼ teaspoon salt, pepper, and thyme until well blended. Stir in potatoes, ham, and onion. Heat remaining 1 tablespoon oil in skillet over medium heat. Pour in egg mixture; cover and cook until egg mixture begins to set around edge, about 3 minutes. Remove cover and place skillet in oven; bake until frittata is set, 8 to 10 minutes.

5. To serve, loosen frittata from skillet and slide onto warm platter; cut into 6 wedges. Makes 6 main-dish servings.

Each serving: About 232 calories, 14g protein, 10g carbohydrate, 15g total fat (4g saturated), 294mg cholesterol, 663mg sodium.

Spaghetti Frittata

This is a great way to use up leftover pasta, even if the pasta is coated with tomato sauce. (You'll need about three cups.)

Prep: 20 minutes   Cook/Broil: 10 minutes

6	large eggs
¼	cup milk
⅓	cup freshly grated Parmesan cheese
¼	cup chopped fresh basil
½	teaspoon salt
¼	teaspoon ground black pepper
6	ounces thin spaghetti, broken in half and cooked as label directs
1	tablespoon olive oil

1. Preheat broiler. In large bowl, with wire whisk, beat eggs, milk, Parmesan, basil, salt, and pepper until well blended. Add pasta and toss to combine.

2. In oven-safe nonstick 10-inch skillet (if skillet is not oven-safe, wrap handle with double layer of foil), heat oil over medium-low heat. Add pasta-egg mixture, pressing lightly with spatula to flatten. Cook until mixture is almost set in center, about 10 minutes. Place skillet in broiler 6 inches from heat source. Broil until frittata is set, about 1 minute.

3. To serve, loosen frittata from skillet and slide onto warm platter; cut into 4 wedges. Makes 4 main-dish servings.

Each serving: About 347 calories, 19g protein, 34g carbohydrate, 14g total fat (5g saturated), 327mg cholesterol, 545mg sodium.

When poaching eggs, set the timer when you add the first egg to the skillet, positioning the egg at the top of the pan (at the 12 o'clock position). Add the remaining eggs in clockwise order. When the timer goes off, remove the egg at 12 o'clock first, then remove the remaining eggs in clockwise order (the order in which they were added to the pan).

MARIE SIMMONS
COOKBOOK AUTHOR

EXPERT TIP

Italian Sausage and Mozzarella Frittata

(pictured on page 306)

The hearty flavor of this frittata makes it ideal for brunch on a cold winter day.

Prep: 20 minutes   Cook/Bake: 35 minutes

6	ounces sweet Italian-sausage links, casings removed
2	yellow peppers, cut into 2" by ¼" matchstick strips
1	large red onion (12 ounces), thinly sliced
½	cup water
8	large eggs
¼	cup chopped fresh parsley
¾	teaspoon salt
¼	teaspoon ground black pepper
4	ounces mozzarella cheese, preferably fresh, shredded (1 cup)

1. Preheat oven to 350°F. In oven-safe nonstick 10-inch skillet (if skillet is not oven-safe, wrap handle with double layer of foil), cook sausage over medium heat, breaking up sausage with side of spoon, until well browned and cooked through, about 5 minutes. With slotted spoon, transfer sausage to paper towels to drain.

2. Add yellow peppers, onion, and water to drippings in skillet and cook, stirring occasionally, until peppers are tender and water has evaporated, about 12 minutes.

3. In medium bowl, with wire whisk, beat eggs, parsley, salt, and pepper until well blended; stir in mozzarella and sausage. Pour egg mixture over vegetables in skillet. Cook over medium heat until egg mixture begins to set around edge, about 3 minutes. Place skillet in oven and bake until frittata is set, about 12 minutes.

4. To serve, loosen frittata from skillet and slide onto warm platter; cut into 6 wedges. Makes 6 main-dish servings.

Each serving: About 274 calories, 17g protein, 7g carbohydrate, 20g total fat (5g saturated), 318mg cholesterol, 601mg sodium.

Classic Cheese Soufflé

An all-American soufflé made with sharp Cheddar cheese. For the most height, don't overfold the cheese mixture before pouring it into the soufflé dish.

Prep: 20 minutes	Bake: 55 minutes

2	tablespoons plain dried bread crumbs or freshly grated Parmesan cheese
4	tablespoons butter or margarine
¼	cup all-purpose flour
1½	cups milk, warmed
8	ounces sharp Cheddar cheese, shredded (2 cups)
¼	teaspoon salt
⅛	teaspoon ground red pepper (cayenne)
5	large eggs, separated
1	large egg white

1. Preheat oven to 325°F. Grease 2-quart soufflé dish; sprinkle evenly with bread crumbs.

2. Prepare cheese sauce: In heavy 2-quart saucepan, melt butter over low heat. Add flour and cook, stirring, 1 minute. With wire whisk, gradually whisk in warm milk. Cook over medium heat, stirring constantly with wooden spoon, until sauce has thickened and boils. Reduce heat and simmer, stirring frequently, 3 minutes. Stir in Cheddar, salt, and ground red pepper; cook, stirring, just until cheese has melted and sauce is smooth. Remove saucepan from heat.

3. In bowl, with wire whisk, lightly beat egg yolks; gradually whisk in ½ cup hot cheese sauce. Gradually whisk egg-yolk mixture into cheese sauce in saucepan, stirring rapidly to prevent curdling. Pour cheese mixture back into bowl.

4. In large bowl, with mixer at high speed, beat 6 egg whites until stiff peaks form when beaters are lifted. With rubber spatula, gently fold one-third of beaten egg whites into cheese mixture. Fold in remaining whites just until blended.

5. Pour mixture into prepared soufflé dish. If desired, to create top-hat effect (center will rise higher than edge), with back of spoon, make 1-inch-deep indentation all around top of soufflé about 1 inch from edge of dish. Bake until soufflé has puffed and is golden brown and knife inserted 1 inch from edge comes out clean, 55 to 60 minutes. Serve hot. Makes 6 main-dish servings.

Each serving: About 356 calories, 18g protein, 9g carbohydrate, 27g total fat (15g saturated), 246mg cholesterol, 519mg sodium.

Gruyère-Spinach Soufflé

Prepare as directed but substitute **8 ounces Gruyère cheese** for Cheddar and stir **1 package (10 ounces) frozen chopped spinach,** thawed and squeezed dry, into cheese mixture before folding in beaten egg whites. Substitute **pinch of ground nutmeg** for ground red pepper.

Each serving: About 372 calories, 21g protein, 11g carbohydrate, 27g total fat (15g saturated), 248mg cholesterol, 446mg sodium.

Southwestern Soufflé

Prepare as directed but substitute **8 ounces Monterey Jack cheese** for Cheddar and stir **½ cup chopped cooked ham** into cheese mixture before folding in beaten egg whites.

Each serving: About 366 calories, 21g protein, 9g carbohydrate, 27g total fat (15g saturated), 253mg cholesterol, 662mg sodium.

Southwestern Soufflé

Sweet Onion Tart with Herbs

Our caramelized onion tart will easily serve a crowd. When cut into bite-size pieces, it makes a tasty appetizer.

Prep: 1 hour   Bake: 55 minutes

3	cups all-purpose flour
2	teaspoons salt
½	cup vegetable shortening
½	cup (1 stick) plus 3 tablespoons butter or margarine
7 to 8 tablespoons cold water	
2	pounds onions (about 3 large), thinly sliced
5	large eggs
2½	cups milk
¾	cup freshly grated Parmesan cheese
1	tablespoon chopped fresh parsley
2	teaspoons chopped fresh thyme
	or ¼ teaspoon dried thyme
½	teaspoon coarsely ground black pepper

1. Prepare pastry dough: In large bowl, combine flour and 1 teaspoon salt. With pastry blender or two knives used scissor-fashion, cut in shortening and ½ cup butter until mixture resembles coarse crumbs. Sprinkle water, 1 tablespoon at a time, over flour mixture, mixing lightly with fork after each addition, until mixture is just moist enough to hold together. With hands, shape dough into disk.

2. On floured surface, with floured rolling pin, roll dough into rectangle approximately 18" by 13". Fold rectangle into fourths; lift and transfer to ungreased 15½" by 10½" jelly-roll pan. Unfold dough. Lightly press onto bottom and against sides of pan. Trim dough, leaving ½-inch overhang. Fold overhang under and pinch to form decorative edge level with rim of pan. Cover and refrigerate crust about 30 minutes.

3. Meanwhile, in 12-inch skillet, melt remaining 3 tablespoons butter over medium-high heat. Add onions and cook, stirring frequently, until golden brown, 25 to 30 minutes. Remove skillet from heat and let onions cool.

4. Preheat oven to 425°F. Line tart shell with foil and fill with pie weights or dry beans. Bake 20 minutes. Remove foil with weights; bake until golden, about 10 minutes longer. Turn oven control to 400°F.

5. Meanwhile, in medium bowl, with wire whisk, beat eggs, milk, Parmesan, parsley, thyme, remaining 1 teaspoon salt, and pepper until well blended. Spread cooled onions evenly in tart shell; pour egg mixture over onions.

6. Bake tart until egg mixture is set and tart shell is golden brown, about 25 minutes. Cool on wire rack 15 minutes. Serve hot or at room temperature. Makes 12 main-dish servings.

Each main-dish serving: About 398 calories, 11g protein, 34g carbohydrate, 25g total fat (11g saturated), 128mg cholesterol, 649mg sodium.

Quiche Lorraine

This is the cheese and bacon quiche we all fell in love with. Gruyère is traditional, but domestic Swiss cheese can easily be substituted.

Prep: 35 minutes   Bake: 55 minutes

Pastry Dough for 1-Crust Pie (page 687)	
4	slices bacon, chopped
4	large eggs
2	cups half-and-half or light cream
½	teaspoon salt
⅛	teaspoon ground black pepper
	pinch ground nutmeg
4	ounces Gruyère or Swiss cheese, shredded (1 cup)

1. Prepare Pastry Dough for 1-Crust Pie. Preheat oven to 425°F. Use dough to line 9-inch pie plate. Line pie shell with foil and fill with pie weights or dry beans. Bake 10 minutes. Remove foil with weights; bake until golden, 5 to 10 minutes longer. Cool on wire rack. Turn oven control to 350°F.

2. Meanwhile, in 10-inch skillet, cook bacon over medium-low heat until browned. Transfer to paper towels to drain well.

3. In medium bowl, with wire whisk, beat eggs, half-and-half, salt, pepper, and nutmeg until well blended. Sprinkle bacon and Gruyère over bottom of crust; pour egg mixture over bacon and cheese.

4. Place pie plate on foil-lined cookie sheet to catch any overflow. Bake until knife inserted in center comes out clean, 55 to 60 minutes. Cool on wire rack 15 minutes. Serve hot or at room temperature. Makes 8 main-dish servings.

Each serving: About 342 calories, 12g protein, 18g carbohydrate, 25g total fat (13g saturated), 162mg cholesterol, 429mg sodium.

Sherried Crab Quiche

Prepare and bake Pastry Dough for 1-Crust Pie. Prepare egg mixture as directed but omit bacon and Gruyère. In 1-quart saucepan, melt **1 tablespoon butter or margarine** over medium heat; add **2 tablespoons chopped green onions.** Cook until tender, about 5 minutes. Stir **8 ounces crabmeat,** picked over, green onions, **2 tablespoons dry sherry,** ¼ **teaspoon salt,** and ⅛ **teaspoon ground red pepper (cayenne)** into egg mixture. Pour into piecrust. Proceed with Step 4.

Each serving: About 313 calories, 13g protein, 18g carbohydrate, 20g total fat (10g saturated), 176mg cholesterol, 497mg sodium.

Mushroom Quiche

Prepare and bake Pastry Dough for 1-Crust Pie. Prepare egg mixture as directed but omit bacon and Gruyère. In 10-inch skillet, melt **2 tablespoons butter or margarine** over medium-high heat; add **8 ounces mushrooms,** trimmed and very thinly sliced, **2 tablespoons finely chopped onion,** ¼ **teaspoon salt,** ⅛ **teaspoon coarsely ground black pepper,** and **pinch dried thyme.** Cook, stirring frequently, until mushrooms are tender and liquid has evaporated, about 10 minutes. Add to egg mixture, stirring to mix. Pour into piecrust. Proceed with Step 4, but reduce baking time to 45 to 50 minutes.

Each serving: About 299 calories, 8g protein, 19g carbohydrate, 22g total fat (11g saturated), 152mg cholesterol, 433mg sodium.

Asparagus Quiche

Prepare and bake Pastry Dough for 1-Crust Pie. Prepare egg mixture as directed but omit bacon. Trim **1 pound asparagus** and cut into ¾-inch pieces (2½ cups). In 2-quart saucepan, heat *4 cups water* to boiling over high heat. Add asparagus and cook until tender, 6 to 8 minutes; drain. Rinse asparagus with cold running water; drain. Spread asparagus over bottom of crust and sprinkle with Gruyère; pour egg mixture over. Proceed with Step 4, but reduce baking time to 40 to 45 minutes.

Each serving: About 334 calories, 13g protein, 20g carbohydrate, 23g total fat (12g saturated), 160mg cholesterol, 380mg sodium.

Huevos Rancheros

Hungry ranchers know that this Mexican country-style egg dish is an excellent source of energy before a long, hard day.

Prep: 10 minutes   Cook/Bake: 20 minutes

2	tablespoons vegetable oil
1	medium onion, coarsely chopped
1	garlic clove, finely chopped
1	jalapeño chile, seeded and finely chopped
1	can (14 to 16 ounces) tomatoes
¼	teaspoon salt
4	(6-inch) corn or flour tortillas
3	tablespoons butter or margarine
4	large eggs
2	tablespoons sour cream
1	tablespoon chopped fresh cilantro
1	ripe medium avocado, pitted, peeled, and cut crosswise into thin slices

1. Preheat oven to 350°F. In nonreactive 2-quart saucepan, heat 1 tablespoon oil over medium-high heat. Add onion, garlic, and jalapeño and cook, stirring occasionally, until onion is tender, about 5 minutes. Stir in tomatoes with their juice and salt; heat to boiling over high heat, breaking up tomatoes with side of spoon. Reduce heat; cover and simmer, stirring occasionally, 5 minutes.

2. Wrap tortillas in foil; place in oven until heated through, about 10 minutes.

3. Meanwhile, in 10-inch skillet, melt butter over medium heat. Break 1 egg into small cup and, holding cup close to skillet, slip egg into skillet; repeat with remaining eggs. Reduce heat to low; cook slowly, spooning butter over eggs to baste them and turning eggs to cook on both sides, until egg whites are completely set and egg yolks begin to thicken but are not hard.

4. Place tortillas on warm plates; place 1 fried egg on each tortilla and spoon 2 tablespoons tomato sauce over each. Top with some sour cream and sprinkle with cilantro; garnish with avocado slices. Serve with remaining tomato sauce. Makes 4 main-dish servings.

Each serving: About 403 calories, 11g protein, 25g carbohydrate, 31g total fat (10g saturated), 239mg cholesterol, 521mg sodium.

Basic Crepes

These delicate pancakes can be stuffed with one of our fillings, or rolled up with some jam. The crepes can be prepared up to one day ahead; wrap a stack tightly in plastic wrap and refrigerate.

Prep: 5 minutes plus chilling   Cook: 25 minutes

3	large eggs
1½	cups milk
4	tablespoons butter or margarine, melted
⅔	cup all-purpose flour
½	teaspoon salt

1. In blender, blend eggs, milk, 2 tablespoons butter, flour, and salt until smooth, scraping down sides of blender. Transfer batter to medium bowl; cover and refrigerate at least 1 hour or up to overnight to allow flour to absorb liquid.

2. Heat nonstick 10-inch skillet over medium-high heat. Brush bottom of skillet lightly with some remaining butter. With wire whisk, throughly mix batter to blend well. Pour scant ¼ cup batter into skillet; tilt pan to coat bottom completely with batter. Cook crepe until top is set and underside is lightly browned, about 1½ minutes.

3. With heat-safe rubber spatula, loosen edge of crepe; turn. Cook until second side has browned, about 30 seconds. Slip crepe onto waxed paper. Repeat with remaining batter, brushing pan lightly with butter before cooking each crepe and stacking crepes between layers of waxed paper. Makes about 12 crepes.

Each crepe: About 97 calories, 3g protein, 7g carbohydrate, 6g total fat (3g saturated), 68mg cholesterol, 166mg sodium.

Crepes with Pipérade Filling

In the Basque region, which straddles the Spanish-French border, pipérade is a favorite component of egg dishes.

Prep: 45 minutes   Cook/Bake: 45 minutes

	Basic Crepes (left)
1	tablespoon olive oil
1	medium onion, thinly sliced
1	red pepper, thinly sliced
1	yellow or green pepper, thinly sliced
¾	teaspoon salt
1	garlic clove, finely chopped
⅛	teaspoon ground red pepper (cayenne)
1	can (14 to 16 ounces) tomatoes
3	ounces Gruyère cheese, shredded (¾ cup)
1	tablespoon chopped parsley

1. Prepare Basic Crepes. Set aside 8 crepes. (Reserve remaining crepes for another use.) Preheat oven to 400°F.

2. In 10-inch skillet, heat oil over medium heat. Add onion, red and yellow peppers, and salt; cover and cook until vegetables are tender, about 15 minutes. Stir in garlic and ground red pepper; cook 30 seconds. Add tomatoes with their juice, breaking them up with side of spoon. Cook, uncovered, until juices have thickened, about 15 minutes.

3. Place crepes on surface; sprinkle one-fourth of Gruyère over each crepe, leaving 1-inch border. Spread generous ¼ cup filling down center of each crepe. Roll up crepes and place, seam side down, in shallow 2-quart baking dish. Bake until heated through, about 15 minutes. Sprinkle with parsley. Makes 4 main-dish servings.

Each serving: About 360 calories, 15g protein, 25g carbohydrate, 23g total fat (11g saturated), 159mg cholesterol, 1,019mg sodium.

Crepes with Chicken, Spinach, and Mushroom Filling

The assembled crepes can be covered and refrigerated for up to eight hours. Allow ten minutes extra baking time to heat through.

Prep: 1 hour 15 minutes	*Cook/Bake: 50 minutes*

	Basic Crepes (opposite)
	double recipe Mornay Sauce (page 550)
1	pound skinless, boneless chicken breast halves
¾	teaspoon salt
1	tablespoon butter or margarine
1	small onion, chopped
8	ounces mushrooms, trimmed and sliced
¼	teaspoon ground black pepper
1	package (10 ounces) frozen chopped spinach, thawed and squeezed dry

1. Prepare Basic Crepes and double batch Mornay Sauce.

2. In 10-inch skillet, combine chicken, enough *water* to cover, and ½ teaspoon salt; heat to boiling over medium-high heat. Reduce heat; cover and simmer gently 8 minutes. Remove from heat and let stand 15 minutes; chicken will lose its pink color throughout. Drain. When cool enough to handle, cut chicken into ½-inch pieces.

3. Meanwhile, in 3-quart saucepan, melt butter over medium heat. Add onion and cook, stirring frequently, until tender, about 5 minutes. Stir in mushrooms, remaining ¼ teaspoon salt, and pepper; cook, stirring frequently, until mushrooms are tender and liquid has evaporated, about 10 minutes. Stir in spinach and remove from heat. Stir in chicken and half of mornay sauce.

4. Preheat oven to 400°F. Lightly grease 13" by 9" baking dish. Place crepes on surface. Spread ⅓ cup chicken mixture down center of each crepe. Roll up crepes and place, seam side down, in prepared baking dish. Spoon remaining mornay sauce over tops of crepes. Bake until sauce is bubbling, 20 to 25 minutes. Makes 6 main-dish servings.

Each serving: About 536 calories, 35g protein, 27g carbohydrate, 32g total fat (18g saturated), 237mg cholesterol, 1,297mg sodium.

Crepes Filled with Apples and Gruyère

Apples and Gruyère, a match made in heaven, are an easy but delicious crepe filling.

Prep: 45 minutes	*Cook/Bake: 10 minutes*

	Basic Crepes (opposite)
1	tablespoon butter or margarine
2	Golden Delicious apples, each peeled, cored, and cut into 16 wedges
4	ounces Gruyère cheese, shredded (1 cup)

1. Prepare Basic Crepes. Set aside 8 crepes. (Reserve remaining crepes for another use.) Preheat oven to 400°F. Grease large cookie sheet.

2. In nonstick 10-inch skillet, melt butter over medium-high heat. Add apples and cook, stirring frequently, until tender and beginning to brown, about 5 minutes.

3. Place crepes on surface; sprinkle one-fourth of Gruyère over half of each crepe. Place one-fourth of apples over Gruyère. Fold over crepes to enclose filling; place on prepared cookie sheet. Bake until cheese melts, about 5 minutes. Makes 4 main-dish servings.

Each serving: About 372 calories, 15g protein, 23g carbohydrate, 25g total fat (14g saturated), 174mg cholesterol, 457mg sodium.

To avoid any mishaps when separating eggs, use three small bowls. Separate an egg, holding it over one of the bowls. Empty the shell, dropping the yolk into the second bowl and the white into the remaining bowl. Repeat; always separating each egg over the empty bowl. Then if one yolk breaks, you won't ruin all the whites.

MARIE SIMMONS
COOKBOOK AUTHOR

EXPERT TIP

Cheese Blintzes

This is our updated version of blintzes: There are no eggs in the filling. The pancakes can be made up to two months ahead. Wrap in heavy-duty foil and freeze.

Prep: 25 minutes plus standing   Cook: 6 minutes per batch

2	large eggs
½	cup all-purpose flour
¼	teaspoon salt
¾	cup plus 2 tablespoons milk
3	tablespoons butter or margarine, melted
1	package (7½ ounces) farmer cheese
1	package (3 ounces) cream cheese, softened
¼	cup sugar
½	teaspoon freshly grated orange peel

1. In bowl, with wire whisk, beat eggs, flour, and salt until smooth; gradually whisk in milk and 1 tablespoon butter until well blended. Let stand 20 minutes at room temperature.

2. Meanwhile, in small bowl, with mixer at medium speed, beat farmer cheese, cream cheese, sugar, and orange peel until smooth.

3. Lightly grease nonstick 8-inch skillet and heat over medium heat. Pour about 2 tablespoons batter into skillet; tilt pan to coat bottom completely with batter. Cook pancake until top is set and underside is lightly browned, about 1 minute. Slip pancake, browned side up, onto waxed paper.

4. Repeat with remaining batter, stacking pancakes between layers of waxed paper and greasing skillet as needed. Cool to room temperature. Place 12 pancakes, browned side up, on surface. Spoon 2 tablespoons cheese mixture onto center of each pancake. Fold two opposite sides over to enclose filling. Fold sides in.

5. In 10-inch skillet, heat remaining 2 tablespoons butter over medium heat. In batches, place blintzes, seam side down, in pan and cook, turning once, until lightly browned, 6 to 10 minutes. Serve hot. Makes 4 main-dish servings.

Each serving: About 419 calories, 18g protein, 28g carbohydrate, 25g total fat (15g saturated), 179mg cholesterol, 577mg sodium.

Scrambled Eggs with Cream Cheese

These rich and creamy scrambled eggs are not everyday fare. This is a great large-batch recipe for brunch—but it is easily halved.

Prep: 10 minutes   Cook: 10 minutes

14	large eggs
¼	teaspoon ground black pepper
3	tablespoons butter or margarine
2	packages (3 ounces each) cream cheese, cut into 1-inch cubes

1. In large bowl, with wire whisk, beat eggs and pepper until well blended. In nonstick 12-inch skillet, melt butter over medium heat; add eggs. With heat-safe rubber spatula, gently push egg mixture as it begins to set to form soft curds.

2. When eggs are partially cooked, top with cream cheese. Continue cooking, stirring occasionally, until eggs have thickened and no visible liquid egg remains. Serve on warm platter. Makes 8 main-dish servings.

Each serving: About 243 calories, 13g protein, 2g carbohydrate, 20g total fat (10g saturated), 407mg cholesterol, 217mg sodium.

Scrambled Eggs with Cream Cheese and Salmon

Prepare as directed but sprinkle **4 ounces smoked salmon,** chopped (¾ cup), over eggs with cream cheese. To serve, top with ¼ **cup chopped green onions.**

Each serving: About 260 calories, 15g protein, 2g carbohydrate, 21g total fat (10g saturated), 410mg cholesterol, 501mg sodium.

Eggs Benedict

This brunch classic serves eight, allowing one egg and one muffin half per diner (although if you're serving friends or family with large appetites, it will serve four.)

Prep: 25 minutes   Cook: 10 minutes

	Hollandaise Sauce (page 550)
8	slices Canadian bacon
4	English muffins, split and toasted
8	large eggs

1. Prepare Hollandaise Sauce; keep warm.

2. In jelly-roll pan, arrange toasted English muffins and top each with slice of Canadian bacon; keep warm.

3. Poach eggs: In 12-inch skillet, heat *1½ inches water* to boiling. Reduce heat to medium-low. Break 1 egg into small cup; holding cup close to surface of water, slip into simmering water. Repeat with remaining eggs. Cook until egg whites have set and egg yolks begin to thicken but are not hard, 3 to 5 minutes.

4. Place jelly-roll pan with bacon-topped English muffins next to poaching eggs. With slotted spoon, carefully remove eggs, one at a time, from water and very briefly drain (still held in spoon) on paper towels; set 1 egg on top of each slice of Canadian bacon. Spoon hollandaise sauce over. Serve hot. Makes 8 main-dish servings.

Each serving: About 311 calories, 15g protein, 15g carbohydrate, 21g total fat (10g saturated), 337mg cholesterol, 786mg sodium.

Puffy Pancake

This baked pancake, which is really popover batter cooked in a skillet, is a tasty brunch-time treat. If you like, fill it with fresh berries and bananas, or serve with jam. Use a skillet made of heavy aluminum or cast iron for best results.

Prep: 5 minutes   Bake: 15 minutes

4	large eggs
1	cup milk
1	cup all-purpose flour
2	tablespoons granulated sugar
¼	teaspoon salt
2	tablespoons butter or margarine
	confectioners' sugar

1. Preheat oven to 425°F. In blender or in food processor with knife blade attached, blend eggs, milk, flour, granulated sugar, and salt until smooth.

2. In oven-safe 12-inch skillet (if skillet is not oven-safe, wrap handle with double layer of foil), melt butter in oven. Pour batter into skillet; return to oven and bake until pancake has puffed and is golden, about 15 minutes. Dust with confectioners' sugar and serve hot. Makes 6 main-dish servings.

Each serving: About 200 calories, 8g protein, 22g carbohydrate, 9g total fat (4g saturated), 158mg cholesterol, 197mg sodium.

Puffy Apple Pancake

Caramelized apples are an easy and delicious way to enhance our basic puffy pancake.

Prep: 15 minutes   Cook/Bake: 30 minutes

2	tablespoons butter or margarine
½	cup plus 2 tablespoons sugar
¼	cup water
6	medium Granny Smith or Newtown Pippin apples (2 pounds), each peeled, cored, and cut into 8 wedges
3	large eggs
¾	cup milk
¾	cup all-purpose flour
¼	teaspoon salt

1. Preheat oven to 425°F. In oven-safe 12-inch skillet (if skillet is not oven-safe, wrap handle with double layer of foil), combine butter, ½ cup sugar, and water; heat to boiling over medium-high heat. Add apples. Cook, stirring occasionally, until apples are golden and sugar mixture begins to caramelize, about 15 minutes.

2. Meanwhile, in blender or in food processor with knife blade attached, blend eggs, milk, flour, remaining 2 tablespoons sugar, and salt until smooth.

3. Pour batter over apples. Place skillet in oven and bake until pancake has puffed and is golden, about 15 minutes. Serve hot. Makes 6 main-dish servings.

Each serving: About 301 calories, 6g protein, 54g carbohydrate, 8g total fat (4g saturated), 121mg cholesterol, 181mg sodium.

French Toast

If you like, try adding a pinch of cinnamon, nutmeg, orange peel, and/or vanilla extract to the basic egg mixture.

🕐 *Prep: 5 minutes   Cook: 15 minutes*

3	large eggs
¾	cup milk
⅛	teaspoon salt
4	tablespoons butter or margarine
8	slices (½ inch thick) sourdough or other firm white bread
	softened butter or margarine, maple syrup, or honey

1. In pie plate, with wire whisk, beat eggs, milk, and salt until well blended. In nonstick 12-inch skillet, melt 2 tablespoons butter over medium-high heat.

2. Dip 4 bread slices, one at a time, in beaten egg mixture to coat both sides well. Place in skillet and cook until browned, about 4 minutes per side. Transfer to cookie sheet; keep warm. Repeat with remaining 2 tablespoons butter and remaining 4 bread slices. Serve hot with butter, maple syrup, or honey. Makes 4 main-dish servings.

Each serving without butter, syrup, or honey: About 341 calories, 11g protein, 32g carbohydrate, 18g total fat (10g saturated), 197mg cholesterol, 605mg sodium.

Overnight Baked French Toast

With its glorious brown sugar crust, this French toast tastes just like sticky buns, but it's made with very little effort.

Prep: 10 minutes plus overnight to chill   Bake: 1 hour

12	slices firm white bread
6	large eggs
2	cups milk
1	teaspoon vanilla extract
¼	teaspoon ground cinnamon
¼	teaspoon ground nutmeg
	pinch salt
½	cup packed brown sugar
4	tablespoons butter or margarine, softened
1	tablespoon maple syrup

1. Arrange bread slices in four stacks in 8-inch square baking dish.

2. In medium bowl, with wire whisk, beat eggs, milk, vanilla, cinnamon, nutmeg, and salt until well blended. Slowly pour egg mixture over bread slices; press bread down to absorb egg mixture, spooning egg mixture over any uncoated bread. Cover and refrigerate overnight.

3. Preheat oven to 350°F. In small bowl, stir brown sugar, butter, and maple syrup until combined. Spread evenly over top of each stack of bread. Bake until knife inserted 1 inch from center comes out clean, about 1 hour. Let stand 15 minutes before serving. Makes 8 main-dish servings.

Each serving: About 318 calories, 10g protein, 39g carbohydrate, 13g total fat (6g saturated), 184mg cholesterol, 388mg sodium.

Spinach Roulade with Mushrooms

Spinach gives this roll its attractive green color. Serve with sautéed cherry tomatoes.

Prep: 25 minutes   Bake: 15 minutes

1	tablespoon butter or margarine
2	green onions, thinly sliced
8	ounces white mushrooms, trimmed and coarsely chopped
8	ounces shiitake mushrooms, stems removed and caps thinly sliced
½	teaspoon salt
¼	teaspoon ground black pepper
1	package (10 ounces) frozen chopped spinach, thawed and squeezed dry
6	large eggs
⅔	cup milk
½	cup freshly grated Parmesan cheese
6	ounces mild or sharp Cheddar cheese, shredded (1½ cups)

1. Preheat oven to 350°F. Line 15½" by 10½" jelly-roll pan with foil, leaving 2-inch overhang at each short end; grease foil.

2. In nonstick 12-inch skillet, melt butter over medium heat. Add green onions and cook until wilted, about 1 minute. Add white and shiitake mushrooms, salt, and pepper; cook,

Spinach Roulade with Mushrooms

stirring frequently, until mushrooms are tender and liquid has evaporated, about 7 minutes. Remove from heat.

3. In blender, puree spinach, eggs, milk, and Parmesan until smooth. Pour into prepared pan, smoothing top with rubber spatula. Bake just until spinach mixture is set, 8 to 10 minutes. Lift foil with spinach mixture and place on surface. Sprinkle with Cheddar and spread mushroom mixture on top.

Roll up from one long end, using foil to help roll and place, seam side down, in jelly-roll pan. Bake until Cheddar melts, about 5 minutes longer. To serve, using serrated knife, cut into 8 thick slices. Makes 8 main-dish servings.

Each serving: About 217 calories, 15g protein, 6g carbohydrate, 15g total fat (8g saturated), 193mg cholesterol, 490mg sodium.

Lemon-and-Parsley-Baked Eggs

Baked eggs are sometimes known as shirred eggs; the French call them oeufs en cocotte. *Serve with buttered toast or croissants.*

Prep: 5 minutes   Bake: 14 minutes

½	cup heavy or whipping cream
1	tablespoon chopped fresh parsley
1½	teaspoons freshly grated lemon peel
¼	teaspoon ground coriander
¼	teaspoon salt
⅛	teaspoon ground black pepper
4	large eggs

1. Preheat oven to 325°F. Lightly grease four 6-ounce custard cups or four 4-ounce ramekins.

2. In small bowl, combine cream, parsley, lemon peel, coriander, salt, and pepper. Spoon 1 tablespoon cream mixture into each custard cup; break 1 egg into each cup. Drizzle evenly with remaining cream mixture.

3. Place custard cups in jelly-roll pan for easier handling and place in oven. Bake until eggs are set, 14 to 16 minutes. Serve hot. Makes 4 main-dish servings.

Each serving: About 188 calories, 7g protein, 2g carbohydrate, 17g total fat (9g saturated), 253mg cholesterol, 218mg sodium.

Spinach Strata

This strata is best when assembled the night before, then baked the next day. For a real treat, use fresh mozzarella.

Prep: 15 minutes plus chilling   Bake: 1 hour

8	slices firm white bread
4	ounces mozzarella cheese, shredded (1 cup)
1	package (10 ounces) frozen chopped spinach, thawed and squeezed dry
1	tablespoon butter or margarine
6	large eggs
2	cups milk
½	teaspoon salt
¼	teaspoon ground black pepper

1. Lightly grease 8-inch square baking dish. Arrange 4 bread slices in bottom of dish. Sprinkle with ½ cup moz-

zarella and top with spinach; sprinkle with remaining ½ cup mozzarella. Spread butter on one side of remaining 4 bread slices and arrange, butter side up, over mozzarella.

2. In large bowl, with wire whisk, beat eggs, milk, salt, and pepper until well blended. Slowly pour egg mixture over bread slices; press bread down to absorb egg mixture, spooning egg mixture over any uncoated bread. Cover and refrigerate at least 4 hours or up to overnight.

3. Preheat oven to 350°F. Remove cover and bake strata until golden and knife inserted in center comes out clean, about 1 hour. Let stand about 15 minutes before serving. Makes 6 main-dish servings.

Each serving: About 313 calories, 17g protein, 25g carbohydrate, 16g total fat (7g saturated), 244mg cholesterol, 624mg sodium.

Stuffed Eggs

Stuffed eggs are make-ahead appetizers that work just as well with large or small groups.

Prep: 30 minutes   Cook: 10 minutes plus standing

6	large eggs
¼	cup mayonnaise
1	tablespoon milk
⅛	teaspoon salt

1. In 3-quart saucepan, place eggs and enough *cold water* to cover by at least 1 inch; heat to boiling over high heat. Immediately remove saucepan from heat and cover tightly; let stand 15 minutes. Pour off hot water and run cold water over eggs to cool. Peel eggs.

2. Slice eggs lengthwise in half. Gently remove yolks and place in medium bowl; with fork, finely mash yolks. Stir in mayonnaise, milk, and salt until evenly blended. Egg-yolk mixture and egg whites can be covered separately and refrigerated up to 24 hours.

3. Place egg whites in jelly-roll pan lined with paper towels (to prevent eggs from rolling). Spoon egg-yolk mixture into pastry bag fitted with star tip or ziptight plastic bag with one corner cut off. Pipe about 1 tablespoon yolk mixture into each egg-white half, or simply spoon mixture. Cover eggs and refrigerate up to 4 hours. Makes 12 appetizers.

Each appetizer: About 72 calories, 3g protein, 0g carbohydrate, 6g total fat (1g saturated), 109mg cholesterol, 82mg sodium.

Bacon-Horseradish Stuffed Eggs

Prepare as directed but add **2 tablespoons crumbled crisp-cooked bacon** and **1 tablespoon bottled white horseradish** to yolk mixture. If not serving right away, sprinkle crumbled bacon on top of stuffed eggs instead of adding to yolk mixture.

Each appetizer: About 80 calories, 4g protein, 1g carbohydrate, 7g total fat (2g saturated), 110mg cholesterol, 102mg sodium.

Dried Tomato–Caper Stuffed Eggs

Prepare as directed but add **1 tablespoon plus 2 teaspoons chopped dried tomatoes packed in oil and herbs, 1 tablespoon plus 2 teaspoons chopped drained capers,** and **⅛ teaspoon coarsely ground black pepper** to yolk mixture.

Each appetizer: About 78 calories, 3g protein, 1g carbohydrate, 7g total fat (1g saturated), 109mg cholesterol, 143mg sodium.

Lemon-Basil Stuffed Eggs

Prepare as directed but add **1 tablespoon chopped fresh basil, ¼ teaspoon freshly grated lemon peel,** and **¼ teaspoon coarsely ground black pepper** to yolk mixture.

Each appetizer: About 73 calories, 3g protein, 0g carbohydrate, 6g total fat (1g saturated), 109mg cholesterol, 82mg sodium.

Lemon-Basil Stuffed Eggs

Pimiento-Studded Stuffed Eggs

Prepare as directed but add **2 tablespoons chopped pimientos, 2 teaspoons Dijon mustard,** and **⅛ teaspoon ground red pepper (cayenne)** to yolk mixture.

Each appetizer: About 74 calories, 3g protein, 1g carbohydrate, 6g total fat (1g saturated), 109mg cholesterol, 102mg sodium.

Pickled Eggs

Pickled eggs, an old-fashioned picnic favorite, can be served with cold meats, as part of a relish tray, or simply accompanied by ice-cold beer.

Prep: 20 minutes plus overnight to chill

12	medium eggs
2	cups distilled white vinegar
¼	cup sugar
1	tablespoon pickling spices
1	teaspoon salt
1	bay leaf

1. In 4-quart saucepan, place eggs and enough *cold water* to cover by at least 1 inch; heat to boiling over high heat. Immediately remove saucepan from heat and cover tightly; let stand 15 minutes. Pour off hot water; run cold water over eggs to cool. Peel eggs.

2. Meanwhile, in 1-quart saucepan, combine vinegar, sugar, pickling spices, salt, and bay leaf; heat to boiling over high heat. Remove from heat.

3. Place eggs in 1-quart jar; add vinegar mixture. Cover and refrigerate overnight or up to 1 week. Remove with slotted spoon to serve. Makes 12 eggs.

Each egg: About 87 calories, 5g protein, 7g carbohydrate, 4g total fat (1g saturated), 187mg cholesterol, 250mg sodium.

8

CHEESE

No matter how you slice it, cheese is simply coagulated milk curd. The final product depends on many variables. What kind of milk was used? Cow's is the most common, but many cheeses use sheep's or goat's milk. How long was the cheese aged? In general, the older the cheese, the harder the texture. Was any special bacteria, yeast, or mold added to the cheese to give it distinction? Penicillin molds give blue cheeses their unique taste and veined appearance. Brie is treated with a mold that forms an edible rind, which cures the cheese from the outside in. Whether you appreciate cheese by itself as an appetizer or dessert course or use it in casseroles, pizzas, salads, or other dishes, this delicious food delivers a lot of flavor, even in small amounts.

Cheese is made by combining milk with a starter: a bacterial culture that curdles the milk to form curds (solids) and whey (liquid). The whey is then drained off. For some fresh cheeses, the curds are served in their soft state (cottage cheese, for example), but for most cheeses, the curds are further coagulated. This is usually accomplished by adding an animal product called rennet. The cheese is then cured by pressing (which removes more whey and makes the cheese harder), cooking, or by adding bacterial agents.

Classic Swiss Fondue

Cheese is often categorized by its texture. Hard cheeses, such as Parmigiano-Reggiano and Romano, can be grated. Sliceable cheeses, such as Monterey Jack and Gouda, are considered semihard. Semisoft cheeses, such as Camembert and triple-crèmes, are spreadable. Fresh cheeses, such as cottage cheese and mascarpone, are soft and usually quite perishable. Blue cheeses and goat cheeses have distinctive flavors, which put them in their own separate categories. They can be creamy or crumbly, very sharp or quite mild. Processed cheese is made from pasteurized cheese that has been combined with emulsifiers and other ingredients to create a moister, more uniform product. Since processed cheese only has to contain 51 percent actual cheese, its flavor is much milder than that of natural cheese.

BUYING CHEESE

Cheese is a living organism and needs to be treated with respect and a certain amount of care. To buy the best cheese, find a cheese or specialty food store that prides itself on the quality of its merchandise. Some cheeses, such as Camembert, ripen and change texture as they age, becoming softer and runnier. It is important to know what stage a cheese is at so it can be served at its peak. A cheese seller will be able to recommend cheeses that are ripe and ready to eat, as well as those that should be served at a later date. A good cheese store will be happy to provide samples, too.

Avoid cheese that has an ammonia odor. Also, do not buy any hard or semihard cheese with beads of moisture on the surface or with dry, cracked rinds. semisoft cheeses should yield to gentle pressure. Any powdery "bloom" on the rind should be evenly colored and slightly moist. Try to purchase cheese that is freshly cut from a block rather than a piece that is precut and packaged.

STORING CHEESE

Store cheese in the refrigerator, tightly wrapped to prevent it from drying out. Leave the original wrapping intact, or rewrap in waxed paper and then in foil. To prolong the life of a cheese, change the wrapping every few days. Strong-smelling cheese should be stored in an airtight container so its aroma doesn't affect other foods.

In general, the harder a cheese, the longer it will keep. Soft cheese, especially goat cheese, should be eaten as soon as possible. semihard cheeses will keep for a few weeks if wrapped tightly. If a cheese (like Cheddar) dries out, grate it and use in cooked dishes. Hard grating cheeses, such as Romano and Parmesan, can be stored for up to several months.

If a hard cheese develops a moldy spot, cut it away; the remaining cheese is fine to eat. Discard any soft cheese that has developed mold, because it could have permeated the cheese.

If absolutely necessary, you can freeze hard or semihard cheese, but when thawed, the cheese will lose moisture and become crumbly. Use it for cooking, not eating. To freeze, wrap the cheese airtight in moisture-proof wrapping and freeze for up to three months.

COOKING WITH CHEESE

Do not overcook cheese, or it will become stringy, rubbery, and oily. (Processed cheese can tolerate higher temperatures without getting stringy.) When adding cheese to a sauce, stir it in at the end of the cooking and heat just until melted and blended. For skillet dishes, sprinkle the cheese over and cover; the heat of the food will melt it.

Grate or shred cheese for even melting. Freshly grated cheese is a must for pasta; grate hard cheese, such as Parmigiano-Reggiano or Romano, on the small holes of a grater.

Cheese that is coarsely shredded on the large holes of a grater will melt evenly and smoothly. The cheese should be cold when grated; firm up soft cheese, such as mozzarella, by freezing it for thirty minutes. Cheese curls add an interesting texture to salads and pasta dishes. To make them, peel curls from a wedge of hard grating cheese with a vegetable peeler.

If substituting one cheese for another in a recipe, use one with a similar moisture content. For example, Monterey Jack can easily stand in for Gouda, but not for a soft goat cheese. Take care with reduced-fat cheese. It quickly turns tough and rubbery when overcooked.

SERVING CHEESE

For the best flavor, most cheeses should stand at room temperature for about one hour before serving. Fresh cheeses, such as cottage or ricotta, should be eaten chilled.

A well-executed cheese board can be a palate-teasing appetizer or an intriguing dessert. The key to success is variety. Choose at least three different types of cheeses varying in flavor from mild to sharp, with crumbly to firm textures. A tangy and crumbly Roquefort, a smooth young goat cheese, and a firm Cheddar would be an ideal combination.

Cheese and bread were made for each other, but take care when matching them. Crusty French or Italian bread is always a good choice. Some strong-flavored cheeses have an affinity for coarse dark bread, such as pumpernickel or rye. Neutrally flavored plain or seeded crackers are the most versatile. Only use flavored crackers with cheeses that would benefit from the added seasoning (for example, garlic-flavored crackers would enhance plain goat cheese).

Most cheese boards are finished off with a selection of fruit. Add apples or pears, fresh figs, or small clusters of seedless grapes. Dried fruits (figs, pears, or apricots) work as well as fresh, and shelled walnuts are always welcome. Some cheeses can be served with vegetables. Crisp sticks of fennel are a fine match for a piquant Italian cheese such as Taleggio, and celery is the classic partner for Stilton.

A CHEESE GLOSSARY

Appenzeller semihard cheese with a sharp flavor. A favorite in Swiss cheese dishes, such as fondue, where it is often mixed with Gruyère and Emmental and it is used as a substitute for raclette cheese.

Asiago A sharp cow's milk cheese made in Northern Italy since the 16th century. The most readily available version is a domestic hard grating cheese.

Blue cheese An entire category of cheese with blue green veins (created by inoculating the milk with Penicillium mold) that give the cheese a tart, sharp flavor and aroma. These cheeses are usually referred to by their individual names, although American, Canadian, and Danish varieties are simply called "blue cheese." Danish blue cheese is especially good; its hearty flavor works well in salad dressings. French *Roquefort* is considered the king of blue cheeses; made with sheep's milk, it is crumbly and sharp, with distinct blue veining. Italian Gorgonzola is made from cow's milk and has a creamier texture and milder flavor. Young *dolce Gorgonzola* has the softest texture and mildest flavor (although it is still quite tangy), while aged *naturale Gorgonzola* is firmer and more assertive. British *Stilton*, with its inedible thick rind, is another highly regarded cow's milk blue cheese. (There are American imitations of both Gorgonzola and Stilton, but they aren't as distinctively flavored as the originals.) *Cambozola* is a factory-made German cheese that has the characteristics of both Brie and Gorgonzola.

Soft-ripened cheeses: Brie, Camembert, Explorateur

Brie A French classic with many American imitators, Brie is a semisoft cheese with an edible white rind. When purchased, it should have a soft, not runny, consistency. Once cut, it will not ripen further (a hard underripe Brie will stay that way).

Camembert A perfectly ripe Camembert has a creamy, runny center and rich buttery flavor; avoid any with an ammonia aroma. This semisoft cheese has a "bloomed" (velvety looking) edible rind. It's originally French, but there are good domestic versions available.

Cheddar A semihard cheese that ranges in flavor from mild to extrasharp and in color from ivory to orange. It is named after the British village that specializes in its production, but it has become an American classic. Cheddar has been produced domestically since 1890, most notably in Vermont and New York. *Colby* is a mild Cheddar-type cheese from Wisconsin.

Cream cheese A soft fresh cheese made from cow's milk and cream; available in rectangular blocks, plain or flavored, or whipped; it has a mild flavor with a gentle tang. American *Neufchâtel* is a reduced-fat cream cheese.

Edam A mild-flavored Dutch cheese made from partially skimmed cow's milk and shaped into a flattened ball. If destined for export, Edam from Holland is coated with red paraffin and wrapped in red cellophane. American-made Edam is just coated in red paraffin.

Blue cheeses: Maytag Blue, Roquefort, Stilton, Danish Blue, Gorgonzola

Fresh cheeses: Cream cheese, farmer cheese, large curd cottage cheese, ricotta, mascarpone

Farmer cheese True farmer cheese is a soft fresh curd cheese that is firm enough to slice; it has a mild, tangy flavor. The term is sometimes incorrectly used to describe any spoonable fresh cheese such as cottage cheese.

Semifirm cheeses: Jarlsberg, Emmental, Colby, fontina

Feta An important cheese in Eastern Mediterranean cuisines. Depending on its country of origin and the type of milk used, the flavor of feta varies. It is always stored in brine, which contributes an inherent saltiness. If you wish, rinse the cheese briefly under cold running water to remove some of the salt. Imported European feta cheese is usually made from sheep's milk. Greek feta is crumbly, salty, and sharp. Bulgarian feta has a more delicate taste and a creamier texture, and French feta is milder still. American feta is made in the Greek style but is usually made from cow's or goat's milk.

Fontina The classic *Fontina d'Aosta,* smooth-textured and mildly pungent, is one of the great cheeses of Italy. There are also tasty American, Danish, and Swedish versions that are good but not as complex.

Goat's and sheep's milk cheeses: Classic ash-coated log, buttons, pyramid, ricotta salata, Bûcheron, feta

Goat cheese Sharp, tangy, and brilliant white, this cheese is sometimes referred to by its French name, *chèvre.* It can be young and soft (the perfect appetizer or dessert cheese) or aged and hard (grate and use on pizzas, pastas, and salads). Some are coated in herbs, spices, or wood ash, wrapped in leaves, or soaked in olive oil. It can be round, button-shaped, or resemble a pyramid; many have rinds. French chèvres are highly revered, but there are excellent American goat cheeses that

Firm cheeses: Cheddar, Dry Jack, provolone

compare favorably. For most cooking, choose a rindless, semi-soft, unseasoned goat cheese such as *Montrachet.*

Gouda   Similar in flavor and appearance to Edam, but made from whole cow's milk. Aged Gouda is sharp-tasting and butterscotch in color; it is a delicious grating cheese.

Gruyère   See Swiss cheese.

Havarti   Danish Havarti is a brick-shaped cheese, dotted throughout with tiny holes; there is also a domestic version. Its mild flavor and soft texture is reminiscent of Monterey Jack.

Limburger   A highly aromatic (store in an airtight container), soft-textured cheese with a thin, inedible rind. Originally only produced in Belgium, it is now made in Wisconsin and also imported from Germany.

Manchego   In America, this golden yellow Spanish sheep's milk cheese is available in two stages of ripeness: one-year-old *curado* and two-year-old *añejo.* Some liken its sharp flavor and dry, crumbly texture to fine Cheddar cheese.

Mascarpone   This mild clotted cream (the ingredient that gives tiramisù its luscious richness) has a creamy yogurtlike consistency. Both the Italian and (recently available) American versions are excellent.

Monterey Jack   An American original developed by Scotsman David Jacks near Monterey, California in the 1890s. Soft-textured, with a mild acidic bite, true Monterey Jack has tiny holes running through it; Jacks from other states may lack

this characteristic. Jack cheese is sometimes flavored with jalapeño peppers. *Dry Jack* is a very hard, aged cheese that is used primarily for grating.

Mozzarella   Mozzarella is one of the best melting cheeses; it develops appealingly chewy strings when heated. In Southern Italy, the original cheese was made from *bufala* (water buffalo) milk and hand formed into balls. Domestically, the version found most often is factory-produced from whole or partially skimmed cow's milk. Some stores also carry fresh mozzarella, which is hand-formed the old-fashioned way, and smoked mozzarella which has with a light brown exterior. Small balls of fresh mozzarella called *bocconcini* are also available.

Muenster   American Muenster is a brick-shaped, paprika-sprinkled cheese with a mild flavor and smooth texture; it is a good melting cheese. There are French, Danish, and German *Munsters* (note the different spelling), but they are much stronger than the American version; the French version smells much like Limburger cheese.

Parmesan   There are many Parmesan cheeses, but only one authentic *Parmigiano-Reggiano.* Serve this delicious cheese in chunks or grate over food. Protected by Italian law, Parmigiano-Reggiano can only be made in a geographically defined area around Parma, Italy. It is aged for at least fourteen months and has its name repeatedly stamped on the rind. Whenever possible, buy Parmigiano by the wedge and grate it

Soft cheeses: Mozzarella, Monterey Jack, Muenster

Hard (grating) cheeses: Pecorino Romano, Parmigiano-Reggiano

Ricotta Its name literally means "recooked." The traditional version of this soft fresh Italian cheese is prepared from whey collected after making other cheeses; the whey is cooked a second time with curdling agents to produce this mild, granular cheese. The ricotta cheese in American supermarkets is usually a blend of whey and cow's milk, either partially skimmed or whole. Some Italian grocers and cheese shops make their own fresh ricotta that is similar to the Italian classic.

Ricotta Salata No relation to soft ricotta, this is a pressed, lightly salted Sicilian sheep's milk cheese with a slightly crumbly, firm texture.

Romano A hard grating cheese that is often substituted for Parmesan. Romano has a slightly salty, more piquant taste that goes beautifully with the robust tomato sauces and vegetable dishes of Southern Italy. Italian Pecorino Romano is made from sheep's milk; Locatelli is a common brand. Many supermarkets carry grated Romano but, like Parmesan, it is best when freshly grated.

String cheese Strips of a mozzarella-type cheese pressed together into braids. To eat, the "strings" of the cheese are pulled apart. Great as a snack or on toast.

Swiss cheese Americans refer to any cheese with holes as Swiss cheese, but there are distinct types. Generic Swiss cheese is American-made, usually in California or Wisconsin. There are two classic Swiss-made cheeses that are indispensable in fondue: Gruyère and Emmental. As they age, their characteristic holes are formed by carbon dioxide trapped in the cheese. *Gruyère* has pea-size holes and full, rich flavor. The French version is called *Comté. Emmental* has holes of various shapes and a nutty edge. *Jarlsberg,* one of the most popular of all imported cheeses, is a Norwegian version of Emmental, but with larger holes and a softer texture.

Taleggio This cow's milk cheese has a soft interior, with flavor that can range from tart and salty to rich and buttery. Its reddish brown crust should be dry and uncracked. It is made in Lombardy, a region of Northern Italy.

Triple-crème cheese A category of cheeses made with cow's milk and enriched with cream, resulting in buttery rich texture and flavor. *Brilleat-Savarin, St.-Andre,* and *Explorateur* are three of the best-known triple-crème cheeses.

just before serving, because it loses moisture as soon as it's grated. Generic Parmesan cheese can be American (some Wisconsin brands compare well to the original), Argentinean, or Uruguayan.

Port-Salut Formerly made by French Trappist monks, this cheese is now factory-produced. It has a mild flavor, semisoft texture, and an edible orange-colored rind.

Provolone The somewhat soft, mild provolone found in most supermarkets is the American version. It comes in a variety of shapes, from balls to cylinders, but it is always bound with rope to maintain its form. Italian provolone is often aged until sharp and firm.

Queso blanco A popular cheese in Latino cooking, it is pressed into firm blocks; when sliced and heated, it will melt. It is often confused with *queso fresco,* which has a dry texture and does not melt. Crumble and use as a topping for tacos, enchiladas, or other Mexican dishes.

Raclette A semisoft cheese from Switzerland with excellent melting qualities.

Reduced-fat cheese Some cheeses, such as Swiss and mozzarella, are made in reduced-fat versions. Their flavors are much milder than the traditional versions, and they don't melt very well.

Raclette

Raclette is a traditional après-ski delicacy in the Alps. Its name is derived from the French verb racler, *meaning "to scrape off." Classically, the melted cheese is scraped from a slab heated in front of a fireplace by those partaking in this treat.*

Prep: 25 minutes plus cooling	Bake: 6 minutes per batch

- 8 small all-purpose potatoes (1½ pounds)
- 1 pound raclette cheese
- ¼ teaspoon ground black pepper
- cornichons or chopped sour pickle
- cocktail onions

1. Preheat oven to 375°F. In 3-quart saucepan, combine potatoes and enough *water* to cover; heat to boiling over high heat. Reduce heat and simmer until tender, about 10 minutes. Drain. When just cool enough to handle, cut potatoes into thin slices.

2. Cut rind from raclette; cut cheese into thin slices. In shallow baking dish, arrange some cheese in single layer, overlapping slices slightly. Bake just until cheese has melted and is smooth, 6 to 8 minutes. Sprinkle with pepper.

3. Meanwhile, arrange warm potatoes, pickles, and onions around edges of plates. With flat serving spoon, transfer portion of cheese into center of each plate. To eat, scoop cheese onto potatoes. Repeat melting with remaining cheese. Makes 4 main-dish servings.

Each serving: About 539 calories, 31g protein, 25g carbohydrate, 35g total fat (22g saturated), 132mg cholesterol, 914mg sodium.

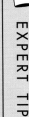

It is always better to buy cheese on the day you will be serving it, and purchase only the amount you think you will need.

MAX McCALMAN

MAÎTRE FROMAGER, PICHOLINE, NEW YORK CITY

EXPERT TIP

Classic Swiss Fondue

(pictured on page 326)

Eating fondue, Switzerland's most famous cheese dish, is a social occasion, best saved for small groups. It is important to use a dry, slightly acidic wine, such as sauvignon blanc, or the cheese won't melt smoothly.

Prep: 15 minutes	Cook: 15 minutes

- 1 garlic clove, cut in half
- 1½ cups dry white wine
- 1 tablespoon kirsch or brandy
- 8 ounces Swiss or Emmental cheese, shredded (2 cups)
- 8 ounces Gruyère cheese, shredded (2 cups)
- 3 tablespoons all-purpose flour
- ⅛ teaspoon ground black pepper
- pinch ground nutmeg
- 1 loaf (16 ounces) French bread, cut into 1-inch cubes

1. Rub inside of fondue pot or heavy nonreactive 2-quart saucepan with garlic; discard garlic. Pour wine into fondue pot. Heat over medium-low heat until very hot but not boiling; stir in kirsch.

2. Meanwhile, in medium bowl, toss Swiss cheese, Gruyère, and flour until mixed. Add cheese mixture, one handful at a time, to wine, stirring constantly and vigorously until cheese has melted and mixture is thick and smooth. If mixture separates, increase heat to medium, stirring just until smooth. Stir in pepper and nutmeg.

3. Transfer fondue to table; place over tabletop heater to keep hot, if you like. To eat, spear cubes of French bread onto long-handled fondue forks and dip into cheese mixture. Makes 6 first-course servings.

Each serving: About 567 calories, 29g protein, 45g carbohydrate, 25g total fat (14g saturated), 76mg cholesterol, 689mg sodium.

Cottage Cheese and Bacon Puffs

A homey type of soufflé that is perfect for a cozy supper.

Prep: 30 minutes   Bake: 35 minutes

6	slices bacon, chopped
3	tablespoons butter or margarine
3	tablespoons all-purpose flour
¼	cup milk
4	large eggs, separated
1	container (8 ounces) cottage cheese

1. Preheat oven to 325°F. Grease four 15-ounce soufflé dishes or a 2-quart soufflé dish. In 10-inch skillet, cook bacon over medium heat until browned. Transfer bacon to paper towels to drain.

2. In 2-quart saucepan, melt butter over low heat. Add flour and cook, stirring, 1 minute. With wire whisk, gradually whisk in milk. Cook over medium heat, stirring constantly, until mixture has thickened and boils. Reduce heat and simmer, stirring frequently, 1 minute.

3. In large bowl, lightly beat egg yolks. With wire whisk, stir in small amount of hot milk mixture. Slowly pour egg-yolk mixture into milk mixture, whisking rapidly to prevent curdling. Stir in cottage cheese and bacon.

4. In separate large bowl, with mixer at high speed, beat egg whites until stiff peaks form when beaters are lifted. With rubber spatula, fold one-third beaten egg whites into cheese mixture. Gently fold in remaining egg whites until just blended. Pour into prepared dishes.

5. Bake until golden and knife inserted 1 inch from edge comes out clean, about 35 minutes for 15-ounce dishes or about 45 minutes for 2-quart dish. Serve immediately. Makes 4 main-dish servings.

Each serving: About 313 calories, 17g protein, 7g carbohydrate, 24g total fat (11g saturated), 254mg cholesterol, 540mg sodium.

Old-Fashioned Cheese Mold with Fresh Fruit

For easier unmolding, dip the mold into warm water just to the rim for about ten seconds. Be careful not to let the gelatin melt.

Prep: 20 minutes plus chilling

1	envelope unflavored gelatin
¾	cup cold water
1	container (16 ounces) cottage cheese
1	package (8 ounces) cream cheese, softened
2	tablespoons confectioners' sugar
¾	teaspoon freshly grated lemon peel
⅛	teaspoon salt
	honeydew melon wedges, strawberries, blueberries, and seedless green grapes
	honey (optional)

1. In small saucepan, evenly sprinkle gelatin over cold water; let stand 2 minutes to soften gelatin slightly. Cook over medium-low heat, stirring constantly, until gelatin has completely dissolved. Remove saucepan from heat.

2. Press cottage cheese through sieve into large bowl. Add cream cheese, confectioners' sugar, lemon peel, salt, and gelatin mixture. With mixer at medium speed, beat mixture until smooth; pour into 4-cup mold or bowl. Cover and refrigerate until set, about 4 hours.

3. To serve, unmold onto chilled large platter and arrange fresh fruits around. If you like, drizzle mold with honey. Makes 6 main-dish servings.

Each serving: About 224 calories, 13g protein, 6g carbohydrate, 17g total fat (10g saturated), 53mg cholesterol, 469mg sodium.

Mozzarella in Carrozza

Mozzarella in carrozza, *"mozzarella in a carriage,"* is usually deep-fried, but we panfry ours. It is served with a buttery anchovy sauce, which can be drizzled over each serving.

🕐 Prep: 20 minutes   Cook: 5 minutes

8	ounces part-skim mozzarella cheese
8	slices firm white bread, crusts removed
2	large eggs, well beaten
¼	cup milk
¼	cup all-purpose flour
½	teaspoon salt
¼	teaspoon ground black pepper
½	cup plain dried bread crumbs
3	tablespoons vegetable oil
4	tablespoons butter or margarine
8	anchovy fillets, drained
1	tablespoon chopped fresh parsley
1	teaspoon capers, drained
1	teaspoon fresh lemon juice

1. Stand mozzarella on its side and cut lengthwise into 4 equal slices. Place 1 slice cheese between 2 slices bread to form sandwich. Repeat with remaining cheese and bread.

2. Preheat oven to 200°F. In pie plate, with wire whisk, beat eggs and milk. On waxed paper, combine flour, salt, and pepper; spread bread crumbs on separate sheet of waxed paper. Dip sandwiches, one at a time, in flour mixture, shaking off excess, then in egg mixture, and finally in bread crumbs, shaking off excess.

3. In nonstick 12-inch skillet, heat oil over medium heat until hot. Add sandwiches; cook until golden brown, about 1½ minutes per side. Cut each sandwich on diagonal in half. Arrange on platter in single layer. Keep warm in oven.

4. In same skillet, melt butter; add anchovies and cook, stirring constantly, 1 minute. Add parsley, capers, and lemon juice; cook 30 seconds longer. Transfer sauce to small bowl. Serve sauce with sandwiches. Makes 8 appetizer servings.

Each serving: About 309 calories, 13g protein, 22g carbohydrate, 19g total fat (8g saturated), 89mg cholesterol, 713mg sodium.

Mozzarella in Carrozza

Welsh Rabbit

Whether you call it rarebit or rabbit (perhaps named by an unsuccessful hunter), this is classic comfort food. If you top it with bacon, it becomes Yorkshire rabbit.

Prep: 10 minutes   Cook: 10 minutes

2	tablespoons butter or margarine
¼	cup all-purpose flour
1	cup milk, warmed
⅔	cup beer
8	ounces sharp Cheddar cheese, shredded (2 cups)
1	teaspoon Dijon mustard
½	teaspoon Worcestershire sauce
⅛	teaspoon ground red pepper (cayenne)
9	slices white bread, toasted

1. In 2-quart saucepan, melt butter over medium heat. With wooden spoon, stir in flour. With wire whisk, gradually whisk in warm milk until smooth. Whisk in beer and heat to boiling, whisking constantly. Reduce heat and simmer 1 minute. Stir in Cheddar, mustard, Worcestershire, and ground red pepper; remove from heat. Stir until smooth.

2. Cut toast slices on diagonal in half. Arrange 3 toast halves on each plate and spoon cheese mixture over. Makes 6 main-dish servings.

Each serving: About 342 calories, 14g protein, 26g carbohydrate, 19g total fat (11g saturated), 56mg cholesterol, 521mg sodium.

Lacy Parmesan Crisps

Called frico *in Italy, these delicious wafers are simply spoonfuls of grated cheese that are baked and cooled. Reusable nonstick bakeware liners, available at most kitchenware stores and bakery suppliers, give the best results and are easy to use, but you can use a nonstick cookie sheet instead.*

Prep: 20 minutes   Bake: 6 minutes per batch

6	ounces Parmesan cheese, coarsely grated (1½ cups)

1. Preheat oven to 375°F. Line large cookie sheet with reusable nonstick bakeware liner. Drop level tablespoons Parmesan 3 inches apart onto cookie sheet; spread to form 2-inch rounds.

2. Bake Parmesan rounds until edges just begin to color, 6 to 7 minutes. Transfer crisps, still on bakeware liner, to wire rack; cool 2 minutes. Transfer to paper towels to drain. Repeat with remaining Parmesan. Makes about 24 crisps.

Each crisp: About 28 calories, 3g protein, 0g carbohydrate, 2g total fat (1g saturated), 5mg cholesterol, 114mg sodium.

Cheddar Crisps

Prepare as directed but substitute **6 ounces sharp Cheddar cheese,** coarsely shredded (1½ cups) for Parmesan. Bake until bubbling but not browned, 6 to 7 minutes per batch.

Lacy Parmesan Crisps

Savory Ricotta Cheesecake

This basil-scented cheesecake can be served warm or cool with a salad of baby greens or tomatoes and crusty bread.

Prep: 15 minutes   Bake: 1 hour 10 minutes

2	garlic cloves, peeled
1	cup loosely packed fresh basil leaves
1	container (32 ounces) part-skim ricotta cheese
1	package (8 ounces) cream cheese
1/3	cup freshly grated Parmesan cheese
4	large eggs
3	tablespoons all-purpose flour
3/4	teaspoon freshly grated orange peel
1/2	teaspoon salt
1/4	teaspoon ground black pepper

1. Preheat oven to 350°F. Lightly grease 9-inch springform pan. Place on cookie sheet.

2. In 1-quart saucepan, heat *2 cups water* to boiling over high heat. Add garlic and cook 3 minutes to blanch. Drain. In food processor with knife blade attached, process garlic and basil until chopped. Add ricotta, cream cheese, Parmesan, eggs, flour, orange peel, salt, and pepper; puree until smooth and well combined. Pour into prepared pan.

3. Bake until cake is just set and toothpick inserted in center comes out clean, about 1 hour 10 minutes. Cool in pan on wire rack for 10 minutes. With small knife, carefully loosen cheesecake from side of pan; remove side of pan. To serve, cut into wedges. Makes 12 first-course servings.

Each serving: About 222 calories, 14g protein, 7g carbohydrate, 15g total fat (9g saturated), 117mg cholesterol, 319mg sodium.

Mozzarella with Dried Tomatoes

Serve flavorful dried tomatoes and creamy fresh mozzarella as a first course or as part of an antipasto platter. You'll find fresh mozzarella at Italian grocers and specialty food stores.

Prep: 20 minutes plus standing

4	dried tomato halves
2	tablespoons extravirgin olive oil
1/4	teaspoon crushed red pepper
12	ounces fresh mozzarella cheese, thinly sliced

1. In 1-quart saucepan, combine dried tomatoes and enough *water* to cover; heat to boiling over high heat. Remove from heat and let stand 10 minutes. Drain tomatoes and pat dry with paper towels; chop tomatoes.

2. In medium bowl, combine tomatoes, oil, and crushed red pepper. Add mozzarella and toss to coat evenly. Let stand 20 minutes at room temperature or cover and refrigerate up to overnight. Makes 6 first-course servings.

Each serving: About 207 calories, 10g protein, 3g carbohydrate, 17g total fat (1g saturated), 40mg cholesterol, 42mg sodium.

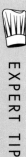

Even if other foods are being served, I recommend setting out more than one type of cheese, such as a cow's milk cheese, a goat cheese, and a sheep's milk cheese. You can also present one soft cheese, one hard cheese, and one blue cheese, or try a grouping of cheeses from different countries, such as the United States, Italy, and France, which can make for a much more interesting display.

MAX MCCALMAN

MAÎTRE FROMAGER, PICHOLINE, NEW YORK CITY

EXPERT TIP

PASTA AND PASTA SAUCES

Pasta has become the favorite weeknight meal for many cooks: It's nutritious, easy to prepare, and absolutely delicious. And best of all, pasta is extremely versatile. It can be rich and satisfying when combined with meat, light and luscious with vegetables or seafood, fast and easy when topped with a no-cook sauce, or appetizingly layered and baked until bubbling.

In the last few years, American cooks have changed the way they view pasta. It was assumed the best pasta sauces took hours to cook. While those time-honored sauces are wonderful, there are many fine sauces that better fit into today's lifestyles, where time is of the essence when mealtime rolls around. Like other recipes in this chapter, Pasta with Squash and Mint (page 348) can be prepared in the time it takes for pasta water to boil. The sauce for Bow Ties with Tomatoes and Lemon (page 346) isn't cooked at all. No-cook sauces are especially handy during the hot summer months for quick tasty meals that keep the kitchen cool.

In this book, with a few exceptions, we use dried Italian-style pasta, which is available everywhere and easy to turn into a quick meal. For special occasions, however, homemade or prepared fresh pasta is an excellent alternative. Made with eggs, fresh pasta has a silky surface and a delicate texture that work best with creamy or light-bodied sauces. Dried pasta, made from flour and water, is more economical, lower in fat, and a good match for robust, highly flavored sauces.

BUYING AND STORING

For the best taste and texture, buy dried pasta made from durum wheat flour or from semolina flour, which is coarsely ground durum wheat flour. It's natural to gravitate to imported Italian pastas, but there are many excellent American brands, too. Store dried pasta in a cool, dry, dark place for up to one year and whole-wheat pasta for up to six months. Don't store pasta in clear containers: Exposing it to light destroys riboflavin, a key nutrient in pasta. Buy pasta in cardboard boxes, which keep out light, rather than in clear packaging.

Store commercially made fresh pasta in the refrigerator according to the package directions for up to one week, or freeze for up to one month. Homemade pasta can be refrigerated for up to three days or frozen for up to one month. For the best results, don't thaw frozen pasta before cooking.

Pasta Primavera

A PASTA GLOSSARY

Here are some of the most popular Italian- and American-made pastas, categorized by shape. (One helpful hint: If the label says "rigate" after the pasta name, it means that the pasta is ribbed or grooved.)

Long Strands (Spaghetti Family)

Bucatini   Long thick tubes resembling hollow spaghetti.

Capellini   Also called *capelli d' angelo* or "angel hair." Very thin, delicate strands; take care not to overcook.

Fusilli   Usually long strands resembling a telephone cord, but also the name for short spiral pasta.

Spaghetti   "Lengths of cord."

Vermicelli   "Little strings" or "little worms." Very thin spaghetti.

Flat Ribbons (Fettuccine Family)

Egg noodles   American-style noodles, enriched with egg yolks; yolk-free versions also available.

Fettuccine   "Small ribbons." Flat noodles ¼ inch wide.

Lasagna   Very wide flat pasta. Often layered with sauce and cheese, then baked. Also available in a no-boil version.

Linguine   "Little tongues." Ribbons of pasta ⅛ inch wide.

Mafalde   Wide pasta ribbons with one long ruffled edge.

Pappardelle   Ribbons about 1 inch wide.

Tagliatelle   Slightly wider than fettuccine.

Tubular Pastas (Macaroni Family)

Elbow macaroni   Small curved tubular pasta.

Mostaccioli   "Little mustaches." About 2 inches long; available plain and ribbed.

Penne   "Quills." Tubular pasta with ends cut on the diagonal, resembling a quill pen.

Rigatoni   Large ribbed tubes.

Ziti   "Bridegrooms." Medium tubes about 1 inch long.

Small Pastas (Soup or Accompaniment Pastas)

Alphabets   Tiny letter-shaped pasta.

Acini di pepe   "Peppercorns." Tiny pasta stubs.

Ditalini   "Little thimbles." Very short macaroni.

Orzo   Although rice-shaped, its name translates as "barley." Usually served as an accompaniment pasta.

Pastina   "Tiny dough." Very, very small pasta flakes.

Tubetti   Short tubes of pasta, slightly smaller than ditalini.

Miscellaneous Shapes

Cavatelli   Small elongated ridged pasta.

Conchiglie   "Shells." Medium shells for saucing.

Creste di gallo   Curly medium ribbed pasta that looks like a rooster's crest.

Farfalle   Literally "butterflies," but also known by Americans as bow ties. Also made in a very small version.

Gemelli   "Twins." Two short spaghettilike strands that are twisted together.

Manicotti   "Small muffs." Large tubes of pasta for stuffing.

Orecchiette   Plump disks of pasta that resemble "small ears."

Radiatori   Small deeply ribbed pasta resembling little "radiators."

Rotini   Corkscrew pasta. Also called "fusilli" or "rotelle."

Ruote   Wagon wheel–shaped pasta.

Asian Noodles

Cellophane noodles   Also called bean threads or *mai fun*.

Chinese-style egg noodles   Made from wheat flour, these tender strands, sometimes dyed bright yellow, are similar to egg linguine, a good substitute.

Rice sticks   Very thin rice stick noodles, also called *mai fun* or rice vermicelli. Are cooked by soaking or deep-fried and served as a puffed, crispy garnish for Asian salads.

Soba   Thin brownish gray noodles made from buckwheat flour; served hot in broth or cold with a dipping sauce.

Udon noodles   Long, thick, chewy Japanese wheat noodles.

KNOW YOUR PASTA

Pasta is available in a wide variety of shapes and sizes as well as many colors and flavors. Each has its own texture and cooking time. Some pastas share the same name—a corkscrew shape can be called *fusilli* by one manufacturer and *rotini* by another. You can interchange pastas of similar sizes and shapes, but measure by weight, not by cup volume.

Choose the right sauce for your pasta. Thin pastas are crushed under the weight of heavy sauces, and a too-delicate sauce will be overpowered by a hearty pasta. While personal taste comes into play, here are some tried-and-true guidelines.

• Thin pastas, such as capellini and vermicelli, should be dressed with delicate, light sauces. Meat sauces tend to slip off the skinny strands and end up at the bottom of the bowl.

• Fettuccine and linguine are excellent with light-bodied meat, vegetable, seafood, cheese, and cream sauces.

Cavatelli

Conchiglie

Manicotti

Rotini

Stelline

Gemelli

Linguine

Orecchiette

Ruote

Creste di gallo

Radiatori

Farfalle

Orzo

- Tubular pastas are great with meat sauces: The nuggets of meat nestle right inside the tubes. Chunky vegetable or olive sauces are also a good match for macaroni-type pastas, as well as for baked dishes.
- Tiny pastas are best saved for soups or combined with other ingredients.

PASTA PERFECT

In most of our recipes, pasta is prepared according to the package directions, since the cooking time varies from brand to brand. To cook pasta perfectly, however, here are a few tips.

How Much Should I Make?

Most packages list a two-ounce serving size, but a more generous main-dish measure is four ounces dried pasta or three ounces fresh pasta per person. The cooked yield of each type of pasta depends on its shape: Four ounces of tube-shaped pasta like penne, ziti, or corkscrew equals two and one-half cups cooked; four ounces of long-strand pasta like fettuccine, spaghetti, or linguine equals two cups cooked; four ounces of egg noodles equals three cups cooked. In addition, you may get more servings from richer pasta preparations.

Cook Pasta in Plenty of Water

Use at least four quarts of water for each pound of pasta. Cover the pot, bring the water to a rapid boil over high heat, then salt the water. Adding salt sooner will increase the time it takes for the water to boil. Stir in the pasta. If the water stops boiling, cover the pot until the water begins to boil.

Use Salted Water

Pasta doesn't contain salt, so it needs to be cooked in salted water to be seasoned properly. If you are concerned about the amount of sodium in your diet, rest assured that only 10 percent of the salt in the cooking water is absorbed by the pasta—the rest is drained away. The nutritional analyses for our recipes are based on pasta cooked in salted water. The basic proportion is two teaspoons of salt per pound of pasta.

Stir Frequently

Stirring ensures even cooking and keeps pasta from clumping together and sticking to the bottom of the pot. It is not necessary to add oil to the cooking water. Oil only coats the pasta, which keeps the sauce from clinging properly.

Don't Overcook

The cooking time on pasta packages is only a guide, so start checking for doneness before the suggested time, and check often. The only way to test pasta is to remove a piece from the boiling water, rinse it briefly under warm water, and bite into it. When pasta is perfectly cooked, it should be, as the Italians say, *al dente,* or "to the tooth" with no raw flour taste and a tiny chalk white center. After it's drained, the pasta will continue to cook from the residual heat and from the hot sauce with which it's tossed. If the pasta is to be baked, undercook it slightly, since it will continue to cook in the oven.

Drain Well and Don't Rinse

Drain the pasta in a colander, shaking to remove the excess water. Unless indicated in the recipe, don't rinse pasta. Rinsing cools down pasta and removes both the surface starch that keeps it firm and its essential nutrients. Only lasagna noodles and pasta for salad should be rinsed.

Serve It Hot

When pasta stands, it gets cold and unappetizingly gummy. So call everyone to the table while you're tossing the pasta. To keep it as hot as possible, return the drained pasta to the cooking pot, which will still be warm, and combine it with the sauce there. Or warm the serving bowl and the individual bowls: Place the bowls into a preheated 200°F oven for five minutes, or fill the bowls with hot water, let stand briefly, and then drain and dry. Toss the pasta with the sauce in the warm serving bowl.

Keep your pantry stocked with a variety of pasta shapes and staples, such as jarred olives, capers, canned tomatoes, tuna, anchovies, and beans. You'll be able to put together a delicious, impromptu pasta dinner in no time.

MICHELE SCICOLONE
COOKBOOK AUTHOR

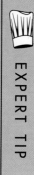

EXPERT TIP

Big-Batch Tomato Sauce

This recipe makes ten cups of mildly seasoned sauce. Freeze it in small batches so it's on hand for a quick and delicious dinner.

	Prep: 15 minutes Cook: 1 hour
3	tablespoons olive oil
3	carrots, peeled and finely chopped
1	large onion (12 ounces), chopped
2	garlic cloves, finely chopped
3	cans (28 ounces each) plum tomatoes in puree
1	bay leaf
¾	teaspoon salt
¼	teaspoon coarsely ground black pepper

1. In nonreactive 5-quart Dutch oven, heat oil over medium heat. Add carrots and onion and cook, stirring occasionally, until vegetables are very tender, about 20 minutes. Add garlic; cook, stirring, 2 minutes.

2. Add tomatoes with their puree, bay leaf, salt, and pepper to Dutch oven; heat to boiling over high heat, breaking up tomatoes with side of spoon. Reduce heat; cover and simmer 15 minutes. Remove cover and simmer until sauce has thickened slightly, about 20 minutes longer. Discard bay leaf. Use 3 cups sauce to coat 1 pound pasta for 4 main-dish servings. Makes about 10 cups.

Each ¼ cup: About 29 calories, 1g protein, 5g carbohydrate, 1g total fat (0g saturated), 0mg cholesterol, 140mg sodium.

Arrabbiata Sauce

Arrabbiatta means "angry" in Italian. True to its name, this recipe makes a hefty pot of hot-tempered sauce, generously spiced with crushed red pepper. Freeze in small containers for up to two months.

	Prep: 5 minutes Cook: 1 hour
½	cup olive oil
6	garlic cloves, crushed with side of chef's knife
5	cans (28 ounces each) plum tomatoes
1	tablespoon salt
1 to 1½	teaspoons crushed red pepper

1. In nonreactive 8-quart saucepot, heat oil over medium heat. Add garlic and cook, stirring, 2 minutes (do not brown). Stir in tomatoes with their juice, salt, and crushed red pepper; heat to boiling over high heat. Reduce heat; simmer, stirring occasionally and breaking up tomatoes with side of spoon, until sauce has thickened slightly, about 40 minutes.

2. If smooth rather than chunky texture is preferred, press sauce through food mill. Use 3 cups sauce to coat 1 pound pasta for 4 main-dish servings. Makes about 14 cups.

Each ¼ cup: About 32 calories, 1g protein, 3g carbohydrate, 2g total fat (0g saturated), 0mg cholesterol, 240mg sodium.

Marinara Sauce

This sauce is very versatile—we use it in recipes throughout the book. For a toothsome alternative, stir eight ounces of sweet or hot Italian-sausage links, cooked and crumbled, into the sauce. Or top each serving with a spoonful of ricotta cheese for a creamy treat.

	Prep: 5 minutes Cook: 30 minutes
2	tablespoons olive oil
1	small onion, chopped
1	garlic clove, finely chopped
1	can (28 ounces) plum tomatoes
2	tablespoons tomato paste
2	tablespoons chopped fresh basil or parsley (optional)
½	teaspoon salt

1. In nonreactive 3-quart saucepan, heat oil over medium heat; add onion and garlic and cook, stirring, until onion is tender, about 5 minutes.

2. Stir in tomatoes with their juice, tomato paste, basil if using, and salt. Heat to boiling, breaking up tomatoes with side of spoon. Reduce heat; partially cover and simmer, stirring occasionally, until sauce has thickened slightly, about 20 minutes. Use to coat 1 pound pasta for 4 main-dish servings. Makes 3½ cups.

Each ½ cup: About 67 calories, 1g protein, 7g carbohydrate, 4g total fat (1g saturated), 0mg cholesterol, 388mg sodium.

Penne with Tomato Cream

This restaurant favorite is a cinch to prepare at home. Don't hesitate to add the vodka. You won't taste it: It just melds the flavors.

Prep: 15 minutes   Cook: 30 minutes

1	tablespoon olive oil
1	small onion, chopped
1	garlic clove, finely chopped
1/8 to 1/4	teaspoon crushed red pepper
1	can (28 ounces) tomatoes in puree, coarsely chopped
3	tablespoons vodka (optional)
1/2	teaspoon salt
1/2	cup heavy or whipping cream
1	cup frozen peas, thawed
1	package (16 ounces) penne or rotini
1/2	cup loosely packed fresh basil leaves, thinly sliced

1. In nonstick 12-inch skillet, heat oil over medium heat. Add onion and cook until tender, about 5 minutes. Add garlic and crushed red pepper; cook until garlic is golden, about 30 seconds longer. Stir in tomatoes with their puree, vodka if using, and salt; heat to boiling over high heat. Reduce heat and simmer until sauce has thickened, 15 to 20 minutes. Stir in cream and peas; heat to boiling.

2. Meanwhile, in large saucepot, cook pasta as label directs. Drain. In warm serving bowl, toss pasta with sauce and sprinkle with basil. Makes 4 main-dish servings.

♥ Each serving: About 652 calories, 20g protein, 107g carbohydrate, 17g total fat (8g saturated), 41mg cholesterol, 763mg sodium.

Penne with Tomato Cream

1. Prepare Marinara Sauce.

2. In nonreactive 12-inch skillet, heat wine to boiling over high heat. Add clams; cover and cook until clams open, 5 to 10 minutes, transferring clams to bowl as they open. Discard any clams that have not opened. Strain clam broth through sieve lined with paper towels; reserve 1/4 cup. When cool enough to handle, remove clams from shells and coarsely chop. Discard shells.

3. Meanwhile, in large saucepot, cook the pasta as label directs. Drain.

4. In same clean 12-inch skillet, combine marinara sauce, reserved clam broth, and clams; cook over low heat until heated through. In warm serving bowl, toss pasta with sauce and butter, if using. Sprinkle with parsley and serve. Makes 6 main-dish servings.

♥ Each serving: About 429 calories, 20g protein, 67g carbohydrate, 9g total fat (2g saturated), 29mg cholesterol, 582mg sodium.

Linguine with Red Clam Sauce

If you wish, substitute two cans (ten ounces each) of whole baby clams plus one-fourth of the clam liquid for the littlenecks.

Prep: 20 minutes   Cook: 1 hour

	Marinara Sauce (page 343)
1/2	cup dry white wine
2	dozen littleneck clams, scrubbed (page 286)
1	package (16 ounces) linguine
1	tablespoon butter or margarine, cut into pieces (optional)
1/4	cup chopped fresh parsley

Linguine with Fresh Tomato Sauce

If the ripe summer tomatoes you use taste a bit acidic, simply add one teaspoon sugar to the sauce. If using juicy beefsteak tomatoes instead of meaty plum tomatoes, simmer the sauce uncovered for about twenty minutes to allow the excess juices to evaporate.

Prep: 15 minutes   Cook: 30 minutes

1	tablespoon olive oil
1	small onion, chopped
2	pounds ripe plum tomatoes or beefsteak tomatoes, peeled and coarsely chopped
½	teaspoon salt
3	tablespoons butter, cut into pieces, or olive oil
2	tablespoons chopped fresh sage or ½ cup chopped fresh basil
1	package (16 ounces) linguine or penne

1. In nonstick 10-inch skillet, heat oil over medium heat. Add onion and cook until tender and golden, about 10 minutes. Add tomatoes with their juice and salt; heat to boiling over high heat. Reduce heat; cover and simmer, stirring and breaking up tomatoes with side of spoon, until sauce has thickened, 15 to 20 minutes. Stir in butter and sage.

2. Meanwhile, in large saucepot, cook pasta as label directs. Drain. In warm serving bowl, toss pasta with sauce. Makes 6 main-dish servings.

♥ Each serving: About 388 calories, 11g protein, 65g carbohydrate, 10g total fat (4g saturated), 16mg cholesterol, 334mg sodium.

Spaghetti with Roasted Tomatoes

Oven-roasted tomatoes have a sweet, intense flavor that is hard to resist. They make a terrific pasta sauce.

Prep: 10 minutes plus cooling   Roast/Cook: 1 hour

2	tablespoons olive oil
3	pounds ripe plum tomatoes (16 medium), cut lengthwise in half
6	garlic cloves, not peeled
1	package (16 ounces) spaghetti or linguine
¾	teaspoon salt
¼	teaspoon coarsely ground black pepper
	freshly grated Pecorino Romano cheese (optional)

1. Preheat oven to 450°F. Brush jelly-roll pan with 1 tablespoon oil. Arrange tomatoes, cut side down, in pan; add garlic. Roast tomatoes and garlic until tomatoes are well browned and garlic has softened, 50 to 60 minutes.

2. When cool enough to handle, peel tomatoes over medium bowl to catch any juices. Place tomatoes in bowl; discard skins. Squeeze garlic to separate pulp from skins. Add garlic to tomatoes.

3. Meanwhile, in large saucepot, cook the pasta as label directs. Drain.

4. With back of spoon, crush tomatoes and garlic. Stir in salt, pepper, and remaining 1 tablespoon oil. Serve sauce at room temperature or transfer to saucepan and heat through over low heat. In warm serving bowl, toss pasta with sauce. Serve with Pecorino, if you like. Makes 4 main-dish servings.

♥ Each serving: About 552 calories, 17g protein, 101g carbohydrate, 10g total fat (1g saturated), 0mg cholesterol, 570mg sodium.

Always save a little of the cooking water when preparing pasta. Just before draining it, scoop some of the water into a large cup. Then, when you toss the pasta and sauce together, you can use the water to thin the sauce if it is too dry without adding extra fat or additional ingredients.

MICHELE SCICOLONE
COOKBOOK AUTHOR

EXPERT TIP

Radiatori with Arugula, Cherry Tomatoes, and Pancetta

No need to cook the arugula in this easy dish; it quickly wilts when tossed with the hot pasta and sauce.

Prep: 15 minutes   Cook: 25 minutes

4	ounces sliced pancetta or bacon, chopped
1	garlic clove, crushed with garlic press
1	pound cherry tomatoes, cut into quarters
1/2	teaspoon salt
1/4	teaspoon coarsely ground black pepper
1	package (16 ounces) radiatori or rotini
2	bunches arugula (10 ounces each), trimmed
1/4	cup freshly grated Parmesan cheese

1. In nonstick 10-inch skillet, cook pancetta over medium heat until lightly browned. (If cooking bacon, discard all but 1 tablespoon bacon drippings.) Add garlic and cook, stirring, 30 seconds. Add tomatoes, salt, and pepper and cook until tomatoes are warmed through, 1 to 2 minutes longer.

2. Meanwhile, in large saucepot, cook pasta as label directs. Drain. In warm serving bowl, toss pasta with pancetta mixture, arugula, and Parmesan. Makes 4 main-dish servings.

♥ Each serving: About 557 calories, 22g protein, 93g carbohydrate, 11g total fat (4g saturated), 14mg cholesterol, 676mg sodium.

Penne with No-Cook Tomato Sauce

Enjoy this sauce at the height of summer with flavorful peak-of-the-season tomatoes. Try making it with equal amounts of red and yellow tomatoes for a jewel-like effect.

Prep: 20 minutes plus standing   Cook: 25 minutes

2	pounds ripe tomatoes (6 medium), chopped
1	cup loosely packed fresh basil leaves, thinly sliced
8	ounces fresh mozzarella cheese, cut into 1/2-inch cubes
2	tablespoons olive oil
1	tablespoon red wine vinegar
1	teaspoon salt
1/4	teaspoon coarsely ground black pepper
1	package (16 ounces) penne or rotini

1. In medium bowl, combine tomatoes, basil, mozzarella, oil, vinegar, salt, and pepper, tossing gently to mix. Let sauce stand at least 15 minutes or up to 1 hour at room temperature to blend flavors.

2. Meanwhile, in large saucepot, cook pasta as label directs. Drain. In warm serving bowl, toss pasta with sauce. Makes 4 main-dish servings.

♥ Each serving: About 698 calories, 27g protein, 99g carbohydrate, 21g total fat (1g saturated), 40mg cholesterol, 749mg sodium.

Bow Ties with Tomatoes and Lemon

A quick and easy summery sauce that "cooks" from the heat of the drained pasta. Here, mint provides a light, refreshing note.

Prep: 15 minutes plus standing   Cook: 25 minutes

2	pounds ripe tomatoes (6 medium), chopped
1/4	cup loosely packed fresh mint leaves, chopped
1/4	cup loosely packed fresh basil leaves, chopped
1	garlic clove, crushed with garlic press
1	teaspoon freshly grated lemon peel
2	tablespoons olive oil
1	teaspoon salt
1/4	teaspoon ground black pepper
1	package (16 ounces) bow ties or ziti

1. In serving bowl, combine tomatoes, mint, basil, garlic, lemon peel, oil, salt, and pepper. Let stand at least 15 minutes or up to 1 hour at room temperature to blend flavors.

2. Meanwhile, in large saucepot, cook pasta as label directs. Drain. Add pasta to tomato mixture and toss well. Makes 4 main-dish servings.

♥ Each serving: About 536 calories, 17g protein, 97g carbohydrate, 9g total fat (1g saturated), 0mg cholesterol, 711mg sodium.

Spaghetti with Oil and Garlic

The classic combination of garlic and oil gives this simple pasta its heady flavor. Serve with lots of freshly grated Parmesan cheese.

Prep: 5 minutes   Cook: 25 minutes

1	package (16 ounces) spaghetti or linguine
1/4	cup olive oil
1	large garlic clove, finely chopped
1/8	teaspoon crushed red pepper (optional)
3/4	teaspoon salt
1/4	teaspoon coarsely ground black pepper
2	tablespoons chopped fresh parsley

1. In large saucepot, cook pasta as label directs. Drain.

2. Meanwhile, in 1-quart saucepan, heat oil over medium heat. Add garlic and cook just until golden, about 1 minute; add crushed red pepper, if using, and cook 30 seconds longer. Remove saucepan from heat; stir in salt and black pepper. In warm serving bowl, toss pasta with sauce and parsley. Makes 6 main-dish servings.

♥ Each serving: About 362 calories, 10g protein, 57g carbohydrate, 10g total fat (1g saturated), 0mg cholesterol, 361mg sodium.

THINGS TO ADD TO OIL AND GARLIC SAUCE

Spaghetti with Oil and Garlic is just the starting point for many delicious possibilities.

- Add 4 to 6 coarsely chopped anchovy fillets in oil, drained (or 1 to 1 1/2 teaspoons anchovy paste) and 2 tablespoons capers, drained, to garlic-oil mixture; reduce heat and stir until anchovies break up, about 30 seconds.
- Add 1/2 cup Gaeta, Kalamata, or green Sicilian olives, pitted and chopped, to cooked garlic and oil mixture; reduce heat and stir until olives are heated through, about 1 minute.
- Add 2 to 3 ounces crumbled firm goat cheese (chèvre) to tossed pasta; toss again.
- Add 1/3 cup chopped dried tomatoes to pasta with garlic-oil mixture and parsley; toss.
- Substitute 2 to 4 tablespoons chopped fresh basil, oregano, chives, or tarragon for parsley.

Spaghetti with Pesto

Pesto is the perfect way to make good use of all that fresh summer basil. If you don't plan to serve the pesto with pasta, omit the water in Step Two. To store pesto, spoon into half-pint containers and top with a few tablespoons of olive oil. Cover and refrigerate up to one week.

Prep: 10 minutes   Cook: 25 minutes

1	package (16 ounces) spaghetti or linguine
2	cups firmly packed fresh basil leaves
1	garlic clove, crushed with garlic press
2	tablespoons pine nuts (pignoli) or walnuts
1/4	cup olive oil
1	teaspoon salt
1/4	teaspoon coarsely ground black pepper
1/2	cup freshly grated Parmesan cheese

1. In large saucepot, cook pasta as label directs. Drain, reserving 1/4 cup pasta water. Return pasta to pot; keep warm.

2. Meanwhile, in blender or in food processor with knife blade attached, puree basil, pine nuts, oil, reserved pasta water, salt, and pepper until smooth. Add Parmesan and blend until combined. Add pesto to pasta in saucepot; toss to combine. Makes about 3/4 cup sauce or 4 main-dish servings.

♥ Each serving: About 655 calories, 24g protein, 92g carbohydrate, 22g total fat (5g saturated), 10mg cholesterol, 920mg sodium.

Bow Ties with a Trio of Peas

Snow peas, sugar snap peas, and green peas are combined in a lemon broth to make this simple yet elegant pasta dish.

Prep: 15 minutes   Cook: 25 minutes

1	package (16 ounces) bow ties or rotini
1	tablespoon butter or margarine
1	tablespoon olive oil
4	ounces snow peas, strings removed
4	ounces sugar snap peas, strings removed
1	garlic clove, crushed with garlic press
1	cup frozen baby peas
½	cup low-sodium chicken broth
¾	teaspoon salt
¼	teaspoon coarsely ground black pepper
½	teaspoon freshly grated lemon peel

1. In large saucepot, cook pasta as label directs. Drain.

2. Meanwhile, in 10-inch skillet, melt butter with oil over medium-high heat. Add snow peas and sugar snap peas and cook, stirring, until tender-crisp, 1 to 2 minutes. Stir in garlic and cook 30 seconds. Add frozen baby peas, broth, salt, and pepper; heat to boiling. Stir in lemon peel. In warm serving bowl, toss pasta with vegetable mixture until combined. Makes 4 main-dish servings.

Each serving: About 536 calories, 19g protein, 95g carbohydrate, 8g total fat (3g saturated), 8mg cholesterol, 704mg sodium.

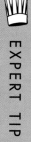

Even when there is nothing else in the house to eat, I always seem to have the ingredients to make Spaghetti with Walnuts. Cook 2 peeled and crushed garlic cloves in ¼ cup olive oil until golden. Remove the garlic and add 1 cup finely chopped walnuts and a pinch of salt. Cook until toasted, about 5 minutes. Toss the walnuts and oil with 1 pound cooked and drained spaghetti, ¼ cup grated Parmesan, and freshly ground black pepper. If available, add 2 tablespoons chopped fresh parsley or basil. Add a little of the cooking water if the pasta seems dry.

EXPERT TIP

MICHELE SCICOLONE
COOKBOOK AUTHOR

Pasta with Squash and Mint

Colorful, easy, and imbued with the cool flavor of mint, this dish is guaranteed to become a favorite for no-fuss weeknight meals.

Prep: 15 minutes   Cook: 30 minutes

1	package (16 ounces) bow ties or penne
1	tablespoon butter or margarine
1	tablespoon olive oil
3	medium yellow summer squash (8 ounces each), cut lengthwise in half, then crosswise into ¼-inch-thick slices
3	medium zucchini (8 ounces each), cut lengthwise in half, then crosswise into ¼-inch-thick slices
½	cup chopped fresh mint leaves
2	garlic cloves, crushed with garlic press
¾	teaspoon salt
¼	teaspoon coarsely ground black pepper
1	cup low-sodium chicken broth
¼	cup freshly grated Parmesan cheese plus (optional) additional cheese

1. In large saucepot, cook pasta as label directs. Drain.

2. Meanwhile, in 12-inch skillet, melt butter with oil over high heat. Add squash, zucchini, ¼ cup mint, garlic, salt, and pepper. Cook, stirring frequently, until vegetables are just tender, about 10 minutes.

3. Add broth and ¼ cup Parmesan to vegetable mixture; heat to boiling over high heat. Boil 1 minute.

4. In warm serving bowl, toss pasta with vegetable mixture and remaining ¼ cup mint. Serve with additional Parmesan, if you like. Makes 4 main-dish servings.

Each serving: About 572 calories, 22g protein, 98g carbohydrate, 11g total fat (4g saturated), 13mg cholesterol, 836mg sodium.

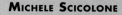

Penne with Spinach and Raisins

Golden raisins are a classic flavor addition to many Sicilian dishes, where they add an unexpected touch of sweetness.

Prep: 15 minutes	*Cook: 20 minutes*

3	tablespoons olive oil
4	garlic cloves, crushed with side of chef's knife
1	bunch (10 to 12 ounces) spinach, tough stems trimmed, washed and dried very well
1	can (15 to 19 ounces) garbanzo beans, rinsed and drained
½	cup golden raisins
½	teaspoon salt
¼	teaspoon crushed red pepper
½	cup chicken broth
1	package (16 ounces) penne or bow ties

1. In 12-inch skillet, heat oil over medium heat. Add garlic and cook until golden. Increase heat to medium-high. Add spinach, beans, raisins, salt, and crushed red pepper; cook, stirring frequently, just until spinach wilts. Stir in broth and heat through.

2. Meanwhile, in large saucepot, cook pasta as label directs. Drain. In warm serving bowl, toss pasta with spinach mixture. Makes 6 main-dish servings.

♥ Each serving: About 445 calories, 14g protein, 76g carbohydrate, 10g total fat (1g saturated), 0mg cholesterol, 466mg sodium.

Linguine with Broccoli Rabe and Anchovies

This pasta sings with the bold flavors of broccoli rabe and anchovies. Use good-quality olive oil: It will show the dish off to its best advantage.

Prep: 10 minutes	*Cook: 25 minutes*

2	bunches broccoli rabe (1 pound each), trimmed and cut into 2-inch pieces
2	teaspoons salt
1	package (16 ounces) linguine or spaghetti
3	tablespoons olive oil
3	garlic cloves, crushed with side of chef's knife
1	can (2 ounces) anchovy fillets, drained
¼	teaspoon crushed red pepper
½	cup golden raisins

1. In 6-quart saucepot, heat *4 quarts water* to boiling over high heat. Add broccoli rabe and salt; cover and heat to boiling. Boil 5 minutes. With tongs, transfer broccoli rabe to bowl. Add pasta to saucepot and cook as label directs. Drain, reserving ¼ cup pasta water. Return pasta to pot; keep warm.

2. Meanwhile, in 12-inch skillet, heat oil over medium heat. Add garlic and cook until golden. Add anchovies and crushed red pepper; cook, stirring, just until anchovies begin to dissolve. Add broccoli rabe and raisins to anchovy mixture. Cook, stirring occasionally, until broccoli rabe is heated through and well coated with oil, about 5 minutes.

3. Add broccoli rabe mixture and reserved pasta water to pasta in saucepot; toss to combine thoroughly. Makes 4 main-dish servings.

♥ Each serving: About 625 calories, 23g protein, 106g carbohydrate, 13g total fat (2g saturated), 6mg cholesterol, 695mg sodium.

Ziti with Roasted Asparagus

Ziti with Roasted Asparagus

Toasted pecans make this easy dish luxurious.

	Prep: 15 minutes Roast/Cook: 30 minutes
2	tablespoons olive oil
¼	teaspoon dried rosemary
2	pounds asparagus,
	trimmed and cut into 1-inch pieces (6 cups)
1	package (16 ounces) ziti
1	cup half-and-half or light cream
¾	teaspoon freshly grated lemon peel
½	teaspoon salt
¼	teaspoon ground black pepper
⅓	cup toasted pecans, coarsely chopped

1. Preheat oven to 400°F. Combine oil and rosemary in 13" by 9" baking pan. Place pan in oven until oil is hot, about 4 minutes. Add asparagus; toss to coat with oil. Roast asparagus, tossing occasionally, until tender, about 15 minutes.

2. Meanwhile, in large saucepot, cook the pasta as label directs. Drain.

3. In 12-inch skillet, heat half-and-half to boiling over medium heat; cook 5 minutes. Stir in lemon peel, salt, and pepper. Add pasta and asparagus; toss to coat. Transfer to warm serving bowls and sprinkle with pecans. Makes 6 main-dish servings.

♥ Each serving: About 410 calories, 15g protein, 63g carbohydrate, 12g total fat (4g saturated), 15mg cholesterol, 282mg sodium.

Linguine with Broccoli

With just a few pantry ingredients and a head of broccoli, you can make a fast and flavorful pasta sauce.

	Prep: 15 minutes Cook: 30 minutes
2½	teaspoons salt
1	large bunch broccoli (1¾ pounds), cut into small flowerets
1	package (16 ounces) linguine or spaghetti
¼	cup olive oil
1	large garlic clove, finely chopped
⅛	teaspoon crushed red pepper (optional)
¾	teaspoon coarsely ground black pepper
2	tablespoons chopped fresh parsley

1. In 6-quart saucepot, heat *4 quarts water* to boiling over high heat. Add 2 teaspoons salt and broccoli; heat to boiling. Cook until broccoli is tender, 4 to 6 minutes. With slotted spoon, transfer broccoli to colander; rinse with cold running water. Heat water in saucepot to boiling; add pasta and cook as label directs. Drain and return pasta to saucepot. Keep warm.

2. Meanwhile, in 10-inch skillet, heat oil over medium heat; add garlic and cook just until golden, about 1 minute. Add crushed red pepper, if using, and cook 30 seconds longer. Remove from heat and stir in remaining ½ teaspoon salt and black pepper. Add broccoli; cook, stirring, until broccoli is coated with oil, 2 to 3 minutes.

3. Add broccoli mixture and parsley to pasta in pot; toss to combine. Makes 4 main-dish servings.

♥ Each serving: About 577 calories, 18g protein, 92g carbohydrate, 16g total fat (2g saturated), 0mg cholesterol, 575mg sodium.

Linguine with Mushroom Sauce

The combination of dried porcini and fresh shiitake mushrooms gives this sauce a deep, earthy flavor.

Prep: 20 minutes plus standing	Cook: 25 minutes

½	cup boiling water
1	package (.35 ounce) dried porcini mushrooms
2	tablespoons olive oil
1	medium onion, chopped
2	garlic cloves, finely chopped
8	ounces shiitake mushrooms, stems removed and caps thinly sliced
12	ounces white mushrooms, trimmed and thinly sliced
½	teaspoon salt
¼	teaspoon freshly ground black pepper
1¼	cups chicken broth
1	package (16 ounces) linguine
2	tablespoons butter, cut into pieces (optional)
¼	cup chopped fresh parsley

1. In small bowl, pour boiling water over porcini mushrooms; let stand about 30 minutes. With slotted spoon, remove porcini. Rinse mushrooms to remove any grit, then chop. Strain mushroom liquid through sieve lined with paper towels; set aside.

2. In 12-inch skillet, heat 1 tablespoon oil over low heat. Add onion and garlic and cook, stirring frequently, until onion is tender. Add shiitake mushrooms and cook, stirring, 5 minutes. Add remaining 1 tablespoon oil, white and porcini mushrooms, salt, and pepper; cook until mushrooms are tender, about 7 minutes. Add reserved mushroom liquid and cook, stirring frequently, until liquid has evaporated, about 2 minutes. Add broth and heat to boiling; cook until broth has reduced by one-third.

3. Meanwhile, in large saucepot, cook pasta as label directs. Drain. In warm serving bowl, toss pasta with mushroom sauce, butter if using, and parsley. Makes 6 main-dish servings.

♥ Each serving without butter: About 366 calories, 13g protein, 64g carbohydrate, 6g total fat (1g saturated), 0mg cholesterol, 475mg sodium.

Pasta Primavera

(pictured on page 338)

A dish to celebrate spring and the arrival of the first asparagus of the season.

Prep: 15 minutes	Cook: 25 minutes

½	cup heavy or whipping cream
3	tablespoons butter or margarine
4	ounces shiitake mushrooms, stems removed and caps thinly sliced
2	very small yellow squash or zucchini (4 ounces each), cut into 2" by ¼" matchstick strips
4	green onions, thinly sliced
1	tablespoon chopped fresh parsley
1	package (16 ounces) fettuccine
1	pound asparagus, trimmed and cut on diagonal into 1½-inch pieces
4	ounces sugar snap peas, strings removed
¾	cup freshly grated Parmesan cheese
¼	teaspoon salt

1. In 1-quart saucepan, heat cream to boiling and boil 1 minute. Remove from heat and set aside.

2. In nonstick 10-inch skillet, melt butter over medium heat. Add mushrooms and cook, stirring, 1 minute. Add squash and cook, stirring, until vegetables are tender, about 3 minutes. Remove from heat; stir in green onions and parsley. Keep warm.

3. Meanwhile, in large saucepot, cook pasta as label directs. After pasta has cooked 7 minutes, add asparagus and sugar snap peas to pasta water. Cook until pasta and vegetables are tender, 3 to 5 minutes longer. Drain pasta and vegetables, reserving ½ cup pasta water.

4. In warm serving bowl, toss pasta and vegetables with reserved pasta water, Parmesan, and salt. Stir in cream and mushroom mixture. Makes 6 main-dish servings.

Each serving: About 491 calories, 18g protein, 64g carbohydrate, 18g total fat (11g saturated), 52mg cholesterol, 462mg sodium.

Fettuccine Alfredo

Roman restaurateur Alfred di Lello created this luscious, creamy dish in the early 1900s, and its popularity has never waned. Be sure to use only freshly grated Parmesan cheese (preferably Italian Parmigiano-Reggiano) when making this indulgent pasta.

Prep: 10 minutes   Cook: 25 minutes

1	package (16 ounces) fettuccine
1½	cups heavy or whipping cream
1	tablespoon butter or margarine
½	teaspoon salt
¼	teaspoon coarsely ground black pepper
¾	cup freshly grated Parmesan cheese
	chopped fresh parsley

1. In large saucepot, cook pasta as label directs. Drain.

2. Meanwhile, in 2-quart saucepan, heat cream, butter, salt, and pepper to boiling over medium-high heat. Boil until sauce has thickened slightly, 2 to 3 minutes. In warm serving bowl, toss pasta with sauce and Parmesan. Sprinkle with parsley. Makes 6 accompaniment servings.

Each serving: About 558 calories, 16g protein, 59g carbohydrate, 29g total fat (17g saturated), 96mg cholesterol, 532mg sodium.

Light Fettuccine Alfredo

To reduce the fat in traditional Alfredo sauce, we've used skim milk and chicken broth instead of heavy cream. Broccoli adds crunch, color, and flavor.

Prep: 15 minutes   Cook: 20 minutes

2	teaspoons vegetable oil
1	small onion, finely chopped
1	large garlic clove, crushed with garlic press
2	cups skim milk
1	cup chicken broth
3	tablespoons all-purpose flour
½	teaspoon salt
¼	teaspoon coarsely ground black pepper
½	cup freshly grated Parmesan cheese
1	package (16 ounces) fettuccine
1	package (16 ounces) broccoli flowerets

1. In nonstick 12-inch skillet, heat oil over medium heat. Add onion and garlic and cook until onion is golden, about 8 minutes. In bowl, with wire whisk, whisk milk, broth, flour, salt, and pepper until smooth. Add to onion mixture and cook, stirring, until sauce has thickened and boils; boil 1 minute. Stir in Parmesan.

2. Meanwhile, in large saucepot, cook pasta as label directs. After pasta has cooked 7 minutes, add broccoli to pasta water. Cook until pasta and broccoli are done, 3 to 5 minutes longer. Drain pasta and broccoli.

3. In warm serving bowl, toss pasta and broccoli with sauce. Makes 4 main-dish servings.

♥ Each serving: About 613 calories, 29g protein, 104g carbohydrate, 9g total fat (3g saturated), 12mg cholesterol, 981mg sodium.

Farfalle with Gorgonzola Sauce

Farfalle, which means "butterflies" in Italian, are commonly called bow ties. We've combined them with a creamy blue-cheese sauce and a sprinkling of toasted walnuts.

Prep: 10 minutes   Cook: 25 minutes

1	package (16 ounces) bow ties or penne
1	cup half-and-half or light cream
¾	cup chicken broth
4	ounces Gorgonzola or blue cheese, crumbled
¼	teaspoon coarsely ground black pepper
1	cup frozen peas, thawed
½	cup chopped walnuts, toasted

1. In large saucepot, cook pasta as label directs. Drain.

2. Meanwhile, in 2-quart saucepan, heat half-and-half and broth just to boiling over medium-high heat. Reduce heat to medium; cook 5 minutes. Add Gorgonzola and pepper, stirring constantly until cheese has melted and sauce is smooth. Stir in peas. In warm serving bowl, toss pasta with sauce; sprinkle with walnuts. Makes 6 main-dish servings.

Each serving: About 486 calories, 18g protein, 63g carbohydrate, 18g total fat (8g saturated), 31mg cholesterol, 499mg sodium.

Pasta with Bacon and Peas

You probably already have most of the ingredients for this dish on hand. The sauce is quickly prepared while the pasta is cooking.

Prep: 10 minutes   Cook: 20 minutes

1	package (16 ounces) thin spaghetti or vermicelli
1	package (10 ounces) frozen peas
4	slices bacon
1	medium onion, chopped
1	container (15 ounces) part-skim ricotta cheese
½	cup freshly grated Pecorino Romano cheese
½	teaspoon salt
¼	teaspoon coarsely ground black pepper

1. In large saucepot, cook pasta as label directs. After pasta has cooked 6 minutes, add frozen peas to pasta water. Cook until pasta is done, about 2 minutes longer. Drain, reserving 1 cup pasta water. Return pasta and peas to saucepot.

2. Meanwhile, in 12-inch skillet, cook bacon over medium heat until browned. With slotted spoon, transfer bacon to paper towels to drain. Discard all but 1 tablespoon bacon drippings from skillet. Add onion and cook until tender and golden, about 10 minutes.

3. Add reserved pasta water, onion, ricotta, Pecorino, salt, and pepper to pasta and peas in saucepot; toss to combine. Crumble in bacon; toss again. Makes 4 main-dish servings.

Each serving: About 738 calories, 37mg protein, 104mg carbohydrate, 19g fat (9g saturated), 51mg cholesterol, 845mg sodium.

Pasta with Tuna Puttanesca

This tomato-less, no-cook version of puttanesca sauce is simply mouthwatering. The unusual mix of greens, shallots, capers, and lemon hits the spot. For the most authentic Italian flavor, use tuna packed in olive oil.

Prep: 15 minutes   Cook: 25 minutes

1	package (16 ounces) rotini or medium shells
3	tablespoons capers, drained and chopped
3	tablespoons finely chopped shallots
½	teaspoon freshly grated lemon peel
2	tablespoons red wine vinegar
1	tablespoon olive oil
½	teaspoon salt
¼	teaspoon coarsely ground black pepper
1	can (6 ounces) light tuna in olive oil
2	bunches watercress (4 to 6 ounces each), tough stems removed
½	cup loosely packed fresh basil leaves, chopped

1. In large saucepot, cook pasta as label directs. Drain, reserving ½ cup pasta water.

2. Meanwhile, in large bowl, with fork, mix capers, shallots, lemon peel, vinegar, oil, salt, and pepper until well combined. Add undrained tuna and watercress; toss.

3. In pasta saucepot, toss pasta, basil, tuna mixture, and reserved pasta water. Makes 6 main-dish servings.

Each serving: About 374 calories, 18g protein, 59g carbohydrate, 7g total fat (1g saturated), 11mg cholesterol, 630mg sodium.

Penne with Salmon and Asparagus

A white-wine-and-tarragon-infused broth is a luscious match for the salmon in this ever-popular seafood-and-vegetable combination.

Prep: 15 minutes	Cook: 30 minutes

1	package (16 ounces) penne rigate or bow ties
3	teaspoons olive oil
1	pound asparagus, trimmed and cut into 2-inch pieces
½	teaspoon salt
¼	teaspoon coarsely ground black pepper
1	large shallot, finely chopped (¼ cup)
⅓	cup dry white wine
1	cup low-sodium chicken broth
1	skinless salmon fillet (1 pound), cut crosswise into thirds, then lengthwise into ¼-inch-thick slices
1	tablespoon chopped fresh tarragon

1. In large saucepot, cook pasta as label directs. Drain.

2. Meanwhile, in nonstick 12-inch skillet, heat 2 teaspoons oil over medium-high heat. Add asparagus, salt, and pepper and cook until asparagus is almost tender-crisp, about 5 minutes. Add shallot and remaining 1 teaspoon oil; cook, stirring constantly, 2 minutes longer. Add wine; heat to boiling over high heat. Stir in broth and heat to boiling. Arrange salmon slices in skillet; cover and cook until just opaque throughout, 2 to 3 minutes. Remove skillet from heat; stir in tarragon. In warm serving bowl, toss pasta with asparagus mixture. Makes 6 main-dish servings.

♥ Each serving: About 470 calories, 27g protein, 60g carbohydrate, 12g total fat (2g saturated), 45mg cholesterol, 404mg sodium.

Pad Thai

Pad Thai

Authentic Pad Thai is made with rice noodles (use the ⅛-inch-wide ones) that are available at Asian markets. If you can't find them, use angel hair pasta or linguine (cooked according to the package directions). It will still be delicious.

Prep: 25 minutes plus soaking noodles	Cook: 5 minutes

1	package (7 to 8 ounces) rice stick noodles (rice vermicelli), or 8 ounces angel hair pasta
¼	cup fresh lime juice
¼	cup Asian fish sauce (nam pla, page 31)
2	tablespoons sugar
1	tablespoon vegetable oil
8	ounces medium shrimp, shelled and deveined (page 296), then cut lengthwise in half
2	garlic cloves, finely chopped
¼	teaspoon crushed red pepper
3	large eggs, lightly beaten
6	ounces bean sprouts (2 cups), rinsed and drained
⅓	cup unsalted roasted peanuts, coarsely chopped
3	green onions, thinly sliced
½	cup loosely packed fresh cilantro leaves
	lime wedges

1. In large bowl, soak rice stick noodles, if using, in enough *hot water* to cover for 20 minutes. Drain. With kitchen shears, cut noodles into 4-inch lengths. If using angel hair pasta, break in half, cook in large saucepot as label directs, drain, and rinse with cold running water.

2. Meanwhile, in small bowl, combine lime juice, fish sauce, and sugar. Assemble all remaining ingredients and place next to stove.

3. In 12-inch skillet, heat oil over high heat until hot. Add shrimp, garlic, and crushed red pepper; cook, stirring, 1 minute. Add eggs and cook, stirring, until just set, about 20 seconds. Add drained noodles and cook, stirring, 2 minutes. Add fish-sauce mixture, half of bean sprouts, half of peanuts, and half of green onions; cook, stirring, 1 minute.

4. Transfer Pad Thai to warm platter or serving bowl. Top with remaining bean sprouts and sprinkle with remaining peanuts, remaining green onions, and cilantro. Serve with lime wedges. Makes 4 main-dish servings.

♥ Each serving: About 472 calories, 21g protein, 63g carbohydrate, 16g total fat (3g saturated), 230mg cholesterol, 811mg sodium.

Quick White Clam Sauce

Try this speedy version of white clam sauce.

Prep: 10 minutes	Cook: 25 minutes
2	cans (10 ounces each) whole baby clams
2	tablespoons olive or vegetable oil
2	tablespoons butter or margarine
1	garlic clove, finely chopped
¼	teaspoon crushed red pepper
¼	cup dry white wine
¼	cup chopped fresh parsley
½	teaspoon salt
¼	teaspoon coarsely ground black pepper
1	package (16 ounces) linguine or spaghetti

1. Drain clams, reserving liquid. In nonreactive 2-quart saucepan, heat oil and butter over medium heat. Add garlic and crushed red pepper; cook until garlic is golden. Add wine and cook until liquid has reduced slightly, about 2 minutes. Add reserved clam liquid; heat to boiling. Reduce heat; cover and simmer 10 minutes to blend flavors. Add clams and cook, stirring occasionally, until heated through, 2 to 3 minutes. Stir in parsley, salt, and pepper.

2. Meanwhile, in large saucepot, cook pasta as label directs. Drain. In warm serving bowl, toss pasta with sauce. Makes 6 main-dish servings.

♥ Each serving: About 436 calories, 23g protein, 59g carbohydrate, 10g total fat (3g saturated), 43mg cholesterol, 359mg sodium.

Linguine with White Clam Sauce

Start with fresh clams and add a few ingredients to cook up one of the best of all pasta dishes. Don't overcook the clams or they will become tough.

Prep: 15 minutes	Cook: 30 minutes
½	cup dry white wine
2	dozen littleneck clams, scrubbed (page 286)
1	package (16 ounces) linguine or spaghetti
¼	cup olive oil
1	large garlic clove, finely chopped
¼	teaspoon crushed red pepper
¼	cup chopped fresh parsley

1. In nonreactive 5-quart Dutch oven, heat wine to boiling over high heat. Add clams; cook until clams open, 5 to 10 minutes, transferring clams to bowl as they open. Discard any clams that have not opened.

2. Strain clam broth through sieve lined with paper towels; set aside. When cool enough to handle, remove clams from shells and coarsely chop. Discard shells.

3. Meanwhile, in large saucepot, cook the pasta as label directs. Drain.

4. Add oil, garlic, and crushed red pepper to same clean Dutch oven. Cook over medium heat, stirring occasionally, just until garlic turns golden. Stir in parsley, clams, and clam broth; heat just to simmering. Add pasta to Dutch oven and toss until combined. Makes 6 main-dish servings.

♥ Each serving: About 427 calories, 19g protein, 59g carbohydrate, 11g total fat (1g saturated), 24mg cholesterol, 111mg sodium.

Seafood Fra Diavolo

Shrimp and mussels adorn this festive pasta, while rings of tender squid provide extra flavor.

Prep: 25 minutes   Cook: 1 hour

8	ounces cleaned squid
1	tablespoon olive oil
1	large garlic clove, finely chopped
¼	teaspoon crushed red pepper
1	can (28 ounces) plum tomatoes
½	teaspoon salt
1	dozen mussels, scrubbed and debearded (page 291)
8	ounces medium shrimp, shelled and deveined (page 296)
1	package (16 ounces) linguine or spaghetti
¼	cup chopped fresh parsley

1. Rinse squid and pat dry with paper towels. Slice squid bodies crosswise into ¼-inch rings. Cut tentacles into several pieces if they are large.

2. In non-reactive 4-quart saucepan, heat oil over medium heat. Add garlic and crushed red pepper; cook just until fragrant, about 30 seconds. Stir in tomatoes with their juice and salt, breaking up tomatoes with side of spoon. Heat to boiling over high heat. Add squid and heat to boiling. Reduce heat; cover and simmer 30 minutes. Remove cover and simmer 15 minutes longer. Increase heat to high. Add mussels; cover and cook 3 minutes. Stir in shrimp; cover and cook until mussels open and shrimp are opaque throughout, about 2 minutes longer. Discard any mussels that have not opened.

3. Meanwhile, in large saucepot, cook pasta as label directs. Drain. In warm serving bowl, toss pasta with seafood mixture and parsley. Makes 6 main-dish servings.

♥ Each serving: About 410 calories, 25g protein, 65g carbohydrate, 5g total fat (1g saturated), 140mg cholesterol, 588mg sodium.

Spaghetti and Meatballs

These large meatballs are all cooked at the same time in one skillet. If you prefer smaller meatballs, you'll need to cook them in two skillets or in batches, or simply bake them in a jelly-roll pan. If you like, substitute Leaner Meatballs (page 226).

Prep: 20 minutes   Cook: 1 hour

	Marinara Sauce (page 343)
1½	pounds ground meat for meat loaf (beef, pork, and/or veal) or ground beef chuck
1	cup fresh bread crumbs (about 2 slices bread)
1	large egg
¼	cup freshly grated Pecorino Romano or Parmesan cheese
¼	cup chopped fresh parsley
1	garlic clove, finely chopped
1	teaspoon salt
¼	teaspoon ground black pepper
2	teaspoons olive oil
1	package (16 ounces) spaghetti

1. Prepare Marinara Sauce.

2. Meanwhile, prepare meatballs: In large bowl, combine ground meat, bread crumbs, egg, Pecorino, parsley, garlic, salt, and pepper just until blended but not overmixed. Shape into twelve 2-inch meatballs, handling meat as little as possible.

3. In nonstick 10-inch skillet, heat oil over medium heat until hot. Add meatballs and cook, gently turning, until browned and just cooked through, about 20 minutes. Stir sauce into meatballs and heat to boiling, stirring to loosen browned bits from bottom of skillet.

4. Meanwhile, in large saucepot, cook pasta as label directs. Drain. In warm serving bowl, gently toss pasta with meatballs and sauce. Makes 6 main-dish servings.

Each serving: About 692 calories, 34g protein, 69g carbohydrate, 30g total fat (10g saturated), 129mg cholesterol, 1,077mg sodium.

Seafood Fra Diavolo

Classic Bolognese Sauce

A staple in Bologna, Italy, this tomato-based meat sauce, enriched with cream and mellowed by long simmering, is well worth the time. Freeze leftovers in small batches.

Prep: 10 minutes Cook: 1 hour 25 minutes

2	tablespoons olive oil
1	medium onion, chopped
1	carrot, peeled and finely chopped
1	stalk celery, finely chopped
1½	pounds ground meat for meat loaf (beef, pork, and/or veal) or ground beef chuck
½	cup dry red wine
1	can (28 ounces) plum tomatoes, chopped
2	teaspoons salt
¼	teaspoon ground black pepper
⅛	teaspoon ground nutmeg
¼	cup heavy or whipping cream

1. In nonreactive 5-quart Dutch oven, heat oil over medium heat. Add onion, carrot, and celery and cook, stirring occasionally, until tender, about 10 minutes.

2. Add ground meat and cook, breaking up meat with side of spoon, until no longer pink. Stir in wine and heat to boiling. Stir in tomatoes with their juice, salt, pepper, and nutmeg. Heat to boiling over high heat. Reduce heat and simmer, stirring occasionally, 1 hour.

3. Stir in cream and heat through, stirring constantly. Use 2½ cups sauce to coat 1 pound pasta for 6 main-dish servings. Makes 5 cups.

Each serving: About 678 calories, 32g protein, 68g carbohydrate, 30g total fat (11g saturated), 104mg cholesterol, 1,210mg sodium.

Rigatoni with "Sausage" Sauce

Fennel seeds and crushed red pepper give lean ground beef a rich sausagelike flavor that belies its lowfat profile. It's fast and easy, too.

Prep: 5 minutes Cook: 25 minutes

12	ounces extralean ground beef
1	medium onion, chopped
1	teaspoon fennel seeds, crushed
¾	teaspoon salt
¼	teaspoon crushed red pepper
1	package (16 ounces) rigatoni or ziti
2	cans (14½ ounces each) Italian-style stewed tomatoes

1. In nonstick 12-inch skillet (at least 2 inches deep), cook ground beef, onion, fennel seeds, salt, and crushed red pepper over medium-high heat, breaking up meat with side of spoon, until pan juices have evaporated and meat is well browned.

2. Meanwhile, in large saucepot, cook the pasta as label directs. Drain.

3. Stir in tomatoes; heat to boiling over high heat. Reduce heat; cover and simmer 10 minutes. In warm serving bowl, toss pasta with sauce. Makes 4 main-dish servings.

Each serving: About 686 calories, 33g protein, 102g carbohydrate, 16g total fat (6g saturated), 59mg cholesterol, 1,498mg sodium.

Penne with Sausage

This simple dish proves that a pasta sauce doesn't have to cook forever to be flavorful.

Prep: 15 minutes Cook: 30 minutes

8	ounces sweet Italian-sausage links, casings removed
2	garlic cloves, finely chopped
1	pound mushrooms, trimmed and sliced
1	can (28 ounces) plum tomatoes
1	teaspoon sugar
¾	teaspoon salt
1	package (16 ounces) penne or rotini

1. In nonstick 12-inch skillet, cook sausage and garlic over medium-high heat, breaking up sausage with side of spoon, until sausage is browned, about 5 minutes. Add mushrooms and cook over high heat, stirring, until all liquid has evaporated and mushrooms are browned. Stir in tomatoes with their juice, sugar, and salt, breaking up tomatoes with side of spoon; heat to boiling. Reduce heat and simmer until thickened, 5 to 8 minutes.

2. Meanwhile, in large saucepot, cook pasta as label directs. Drain. In warm serving bowl, toss pasta with sauce. Makes 4 main-dish servings.

♥ Each serving: About 690 calories, 27g protein, 100g carbohydrate, 20g total fat (7g saturated), 43mg cholesterol, 1,283mg sodium.

Spaghetti all'Amatriciana

Named for the town of Amatrice, near Rome, this sauce gets its distinctive character from the pancetta and chiles .

Prep: 10 minutes	Cook: 45 minutes
1	tablespoon olive oil
4	ounces sliced pancetta, chopped
1	small onion, chopped
1	garlic clove, finely chopped
¼	teaspoon crushed red pepper
1	can (28 ounces) plum tomatoes
½	teaspoon salt
1	package (16 ounces) spaghetti or rigatoni
¼	cup chopped fresh parsley

1. In nonreactive 5-quart Dutch oven, heat oil over medium heat. Add pancetta and cook, stirring, until lightly browned, about 5 minutes. Stir in onion and cook until tender, about 3 minutes. Stir in garlic and crushed red pepper; cook 15 seconds. Add tomatoes with their juice and salt; heat to boiling, breaking up tomatoes with side of spoon. Reduce heat and simmer, stirring occasionally, 30 minutes.

2. Meanwhile, in large saucepot, cook pasta as label directs. Drain. In warm serving bowl, toss pasta with sauce and parsley. Makes 4 main-dish servings.

♥ Each serving: About 605 calories, 21g protein, 96g carbohydrate, 15g total fat (4g saturated), 17mg cholesterol, 1,017mg sodium.

Neapolitan Pasta Sauce

This is the kind of old-time pasta sauce that simmers for hours, filling the kitchen with enticing aromas. It makes a big batch, enough to coat about five pounds of pasta, so plan to freeze the leftovers. Serve with a sturdy pasta such as rigatoni.

Prep: 15 minutes	Cook: 4 hours 15 minutes
2	pounds boneless pork shoulder blade roast (fresh pork butt), trimmed
1	garlic clove, thinly sliced
1	tablespoon olive oil
1	pound sweet Italian-sausage links
8	ounces hot Italian-sausage links
2	large onions (12 ounces each), finely chopped
4	garlic cloves, finely chopped
4	cans (28 ounces each) plum tomatoes
1	can (28 ounces) tomato puree
1	tablespoon sugar
½	teaspoon salt

1. With small knife, make several slits in pork shoulder and insert garlic slices. In nonreactive 12-quart saucepot, heat oil over medium heat until very hot. Cook pork and sweet and hot sausages in batches until lightly browned, using slotted spoon to transfer meat to bowl as it is browned.

2. Add onions and chopped garlic to saucepot; cook until onion is tender, about 5 minutes. Add tomatoes with their juice, tomato puree, sugar, and salt; heat to boiling, breaking up tomatoes with side of spoon.

3. Return pork to saucepot. Reduce heat; partially cover and simmer 3 hours. Add sausage and cook until pork is very tender, about 45 minutes longer. Remove pork and cut into bite-size pieces; return to saucepot (keep sausages whole). Use 3 cups sauce to coat 1 pound pasta for 6 main-dish servings. Makes 16 cups.

Each ½ cup: About 139 calories, 9g protein, 5g carbohydrate, 9g total fat (3g saturated), 35mg cholesterol, 318mg sodium.

PASTA—THREE WAYS

Start with 6 ounces orzo (1 cup) or mini bow tie pasta (1¾ cups) and cooked as the label directs to make any of the delicious side dishes below.

Prep: 10 minutes   Cook: 25 minutes

CONFETTI PASTA

In 10-inch skillet, heat **2 teaspoons olive oil** over medium heat. Add **2 carrots,** shredded, **1 medium zucchini (8 ounces),** shredded, **1 garlic clove,** crushed with garlic press, **¾ teaspoon salt,** and **¼ teaspoon coarsely ground black pepper** and cook 5 minutes. Stir in cooked **pasta;** heat through. Makes 4 accompaniment servings.

♥ Each serving: About 203 calories, 7g protein, 37g carbohydrate, 3g total fat (0g saturated), 0mg cholesterol, 490mg sodium.

ORANGE-FENNEL PASTA

In 10-inch skillet, heat **2 teaspoons olive oil** over medium heat. Add **1 garlic clove,** crushed with garlic press, **¾ teaspoon salt,** and **¼ teaspoon coarsely ground black pepper** and cook 30 seconds. Stir in **1 teaspoon freshly grated orange peel** and **½ teaspoon fennel seeds,** crushed. Stir in cooked **pasta** and **2 tablespoons chopped fresh parsley;** heat through. Makes 4 accompaniment servings.

♥ Each serving: About 181 calories, 6g protein, 32g carbohydrate, 3g total fat (0g saturated), 0mg cholesterol, 477mg sodium.

PASTA WITH PEAS AND ONION

In 10-inch skillet, heat **2 teaspoons olive oil** over medium heat. Add **1 small onion,** chopped, and **2 tablespoons water** and cook until onion is tender and golden, about 10 minutes. Stir in cooked **pasta** and **1 cup frozen peas,** thawed, and heat through. Makes 4 accompaniment servings.

♥ Each serving: About 216 calories, 8g protein, 39g carbohydrate, 3g total fat (0g saturated), 0mg cholesterol, 81mg sodium.

Buttered Noodles with Herbs

This is comfort food of the first order. Serve with garlic chicken, pork roast, or your favorite meat loaf.

Prep: 10 minutes   Cook: 25 minutes

12	ounces wide egg noodles
¼	cup chopped fresh parsley
1	teaspoon chopped fresh rosemary, thyme, oregano, or sage
2	tablespoons butter or margarine, cut into pieces
½	teaspoon salt
¼	teaspoon coarsely ground black pepper

1. In large saucepot, cook noodles as label directs. Drain.

2. In same saucepot, combine parsley, rosemary, butter, salt, and pepper, stirring until butter has melted. Return cooked noodles to saucepot, tossing to coat well with herb mixture. Makes 6 accompaniment servings.

♥ Each serving: About 251 calories, 8g protein, 41g carbohydrate, 6g total fat (3g saturated), 64mg cholesterol, 293mg sodium.

Tubetti with Lemon and Cream

This dish takes very little effort and is great with broiled chicken or veal chops.

Prep: 5 minutes   Cook: 25 minutes

1½	cups tubetti (7 ounces)
¼	cup plus 2 tablespoons heavy or whipping cream
½	teaspoon freshly grated lemon peel
¼	teaspoon salt
	pinch ground black pepper
2	tablespoons chopped fresh parsley

1. In medium saucepot, cook pasta as label directs. Drain.

2. Meanwhile, in 2-quart saucepan, combine cream, lemon peel, salt, and pepper; heat to boiling over medium-high heat. Boil 1 minute. Remove from heat and keep warm.

3. Add pasta and 1 tablespoon parsley to cream in saucepan. Cook over medium heat, stirring constantly,

1 minute. Transfer to warm serving bowl and sprinkle with remaining 1 tablespoon parsley. Makes 6 accompaniment servings.

Each serving: About 175 calories, 5g protein, 25g carbohydrate, 6g total fat (3g saturated), 20mg cholesterol, 132mg sodium.

Pasta with Browned Butter and Sage

Browned butter and sage is a classic combination. Only two tablespoons gives this dish a surprising amount of flavor.

Prep: 5 minutes   Cook: 25 minutes

1½	cups tiny bow ties or ditalini (7 ounces)
2	tablespoons butter
½	teaspoon chopped fresh sage plus additional sprigs
¼	teaspoon salt
	pinch ground black pepper

1. In medium saucepot, cook pasta as label directs. Drain.

2. Meanwhile, in 2-quart saucepan, melt butter over medium heat. Cook, stirring, until butter turns golden brown (if butter gets too dark, it will be bitter). Remove from heat and add chopped sage, salt, and pepper; keep warm.

3. Add pasta to sage-butter mixture in saucepan. Cook over medium heat, stirring, 1 minute. Transfer to warm serving bowl and garnish with sage sprigs. Makes 6 accompaniment servings.

Each serving: About 157 calories, 4g protein, 25g carbohydrate, 4g total fat (2g saturated), 10mg cholesterol, 165mg sodium.

Northern-Style Lasagna

The dairy-rich regions of Northern Italy are where you'll find lasagna layered with creamy béchamel sauce.

Prep: 2 hours   Bake: 40 minutes

	Classic Bolognese Sauce (page 358)
12	lasagna noodles (10 ounces)
4	tablespoons butter or margarine
¼	cup all-purpose flour
3	cups milk, warmed
¼	teaspoon salt
⅛	teaspoon ground black pepper
	pinch ground nutmeg
¾	cup freshly grated Parmesan cheese

1. Prepare Classic Bolognese Sauce but omit cream.

2. Meanwhile, in large saucepot, cook lasagna noodles as label directs. Drain and rinse with cold running water. Return noodles to saucepot with enough *cold water* to cover.

3. Prepare white sauce: In heavy 3-quart saucepan, melt butter over low heat. Add flour and cook, stirring, 1 minute. With wire whisk, gradually whisk in warm milk. Cook over medium heat, stirring constantly with wooden spoon, until sauce has thickened and boils. Reduce heat and simmer, stirring frequently, 5 minutes. Stir in salt, pepper, and nutmeg; remove from heat.

4. Preheat oven to 375°F. Drain noodles on clean kitchen towels. In 13" by 9" baking dish, evenly spread 1¼ cups Bolognese sauce. Arrange 4 lasagna noodles over sauce, overlapping to fit. Spoon 1¼ cups Bolognese sauce over noodles and top with one-third of white sauce; sprinkle with ¼ cup Parmesan. Repeat layering 2 more times with noodles, Bolognese sauce, white sauce, and Parmesan.

5. Cover lasagna with foil and bake 30 minutes. Remove foil and bake until heated through and bubbling, about 10 minutes longer. Let stand 15 minutes for easier serving. Makes 12 main-dish servings.

Each serving: About 384 calories, 19g protein, 30g carbohydrate, 21g total fat (9g saturated), 69mg cholesterol, 822mg sodium.

Vegetable Lasagna

You'll never miss the meat in this lasagna chock-full of vegetables and cheese.

Prep: 1 hour	**Bake: 40 minutes**

Marinara Sauce (page 343)

12	lasagna noodles (10 ounces)
2	medium zucchini (8 ounces each), cut into ¼-inch-thick slices
2	tablespoons olive oil
¾	teaspoon salt
¼	teaspoon ground black pepper
1	garlic clove, finely chopped
⅛	teaspoon crushed red pepper
2	tablespoons all-purpose flour
⅔	cup milk, warmed
2	packages (10 ounces each) frozen chopped spinach, thawed and squeezed dry
2	tablespoons plus ¼ cup freshly grated Parmesan cheese
1	container (15 ounces) part-skim ricotta cheese
2	tablespoons chopped fresh parsley
4	ounces mozzarella cheese, shredded (1 cup)

1. Prepare Marinara Sauce.

2. Meanwhile, in large saucepot, cook lasagna noodles as label directs. Drain and rinse with cold running water. Return noodles to saucepot with enough *cold water* to cover.

3. Preheat oven to 450°F. In large bowl, toss zucchini with 1 tablespoon oil, ¼ teaspoon salt, and ⅛ teaspoon black pepper. Arrange zucchini slices on large cookie sheet and bake, turning once, until tender, about 12 minutes.

4. Meanwhile, in nonstick 12-inch skillet, heat remaining 1 tablespoon oil over medium heat. Add garlic and crushed red pepper; cook until garlic is golden. Stir in flour until blended. With wire whisk, gradually whisk in warm milk with wooden spoon. Cook, stirring constantly, until sauce has thickened and boils, about 2 minutes. Remove from heat and stir in spinach, 2 tablespoons Parmesan, and ¼ teaspoon salt.

5. In medium bowl, stir ricotta, parsley, remaining ¼ cup Parmesan, remaining ¼ teaspoon salt, and remaining ⅛ teaspoon black pepper until combined.

6. Turn oven control to 350°F. Drain lasagna noodles on clean kitchen towels.

7. In 13" by 9" baking dish, spread about 1 cup marinara sauce. Arrange 4 lasagna noodles over sauce, overlapping to fit. Spread ricotta mixture on top of noodles. Arrange 4 more noodles over ricotta and top with all of zucchini, overlapping slices to fit. Spread with 1 cup sauce and sprinkle with half of mozzarella; top with all of spinach mixture. Arrange remaining 4 noodles on top and spread with remaining marinara sauce. Sprinkle with remaining mozzarella.

8. Cover lasagna with foil and bake 30 minutes. Remove foil and bake until cheese is lightly golden, about 10 minutes longer. Let stand 15 minutes for easier serving. Makes 10 main-dish servings.

Each serving: About 219 calories, 13g protein, 14g carbohydrate, 13g total fat (5g saturated), 27mg cholesterol, 687mg sodium.

Beef and Sausage Lasagna

Always let lasagna stand for a good fifteen minutes after baking so the ingredients have time to settle—it makes for easier cutting.

Prep: 1 hour	**Bake: 45 minutes**

8	ounces hot Italian-sausage links, casings removed
8	ounces ground beef chuck
1	medium onion, chopped
1	can (28 ounces) plum tomatoes
2	tablespoons tomato paste
1¼	teaspoons salt
12	lasagna noodles (10 ounces)
1	container (15 ounces) part-skim ricotta cheese
1	large egg
¼	cup chopped fresh parsley
⅛	teaspoon coarsely ground pepper
8	ounces part-skim mozzarella cheese, shredded (2 cups)

1. Prepare meat sauce: In 4-quart saucepan, cook sausage, ground beef, and onion over high heat, breaking up sausage and meat with side of spoon, until meat is well browned. Discard fat. Add tomatoes with their juice, tomato paste, and 1 teaspoon salt. Heat to boiling, breaking up tomatoes with side of spoon. Reduce heat; cover and simmer, stirring occasionally, 30 minutes.

2. Meanwhile, in large saucepot, cook lasagna noodles as label directs but do not add salt to water. Drain and rinse with

Beef and Sausage Lasagna

cold running water. Return to saucepot with enough *cold water* to cover.

3. Preheat oven to 375°F. In medium bowl, stir ricotta, egg, parsley, remaining ¼ teaspoon salt, and pepper until well combined.

4. Drain noodles on clean kitchen towels. In 13" by 9" baking dish, arrange 6 lasagna noodles, overlapping to fit. Spread with all of ricotta mixture and sprinkle with half of mozzarella; top with half of meat sauce. Cover with remaining 6 noodles and spread with remaining meat sauce. Sprinkle with remaining mozzarella.

5. Cover lasagna with foil and bake 30 minutes. Remove foil and bake until sauce is bubbling and top has lightly browned, about 15 minutes longer. Let stand 15 minutes for easier serving. Makes 10 main-dish servings.

Each serving: About 363 calories, 23g protein, 31g carbohydrate, 16g total fat (7g saturated), 74mg cholesterol, 780mg sodium.

Lasagna Rolls

To avoid last-minute preparation, you can assemble this dish in advance and refrigerate. Since it will be cold, allow for some extra baking time.

Prep: 35 minutes   Bake: 55 minutes

	Marinara Sauce (page 343)
9	lasagna noodles (8 ounces)
1	tablespoon olive oil
1	small onion, chopped
2	garlic cloves, finely chopped
1	package (10 ounces) frozen chopped spinach, thawed and squeezed dry
1	container (15 ounces) part-skim ricotta cheese
1/3	cup freshly grated Parmesan cheese
1	large egg, lightly beaten
1/2	teaspoon salt
1/4	teaspoon ground black pepper

1. Prepare Marinara Sauce.

2. Meanwhile, in large saucepot, cook lasagna noodles as label directs. Drain and rinse with cold running water. Return noodles to saucepot with enough *cold water* to cover.

3. Preheat oven to 375°F. In 10-inch skillet, heat oil over medium heat. Add onion and garlic and cook, stirring frequently, until onion is tender and golden, about 8 minutes. Add spinach and cook until tender, about 4 minutes. Transfer to medium bowl; stir in ricotta, then add Parmesan, egg, salt, and pepper.

4. Drain lasagna noodles on clean kitchen towels. Spread about 1/3 cup spinach mixture on each noodle. Roll up from a short end. Place filled noodles, seam side down, in 11" by 7" baking dish and spoon marinara sauce on top.

5. Cover lasagna rolls with foil and bake until piping hot, about 30 minutes. To serve, cut each roll crosswise in half; serve each person 3 slices. Makes 6 main-dish servings.

Each serving: About 394 calories, 19g protein, 45g carbohydrate, 16g total fat (6g saturated), 62mg cholesterol, 915mg sodium.

Curly Mac 'n' Cheese

Kids will absolutely love the curly corkscrew pasta in this ever-popular supper dish.

Prep: 30 minutes   Bake: 25 minutes

1	package (16 ounces) rotini
6	cups milk
3	tablespoons cornstarch
3/4	teaspoon salt
1/8	teaspoon ground nutmeg
1/2	cup freshly grated Parmesan cheese
8	ounces sharp Cheddar cheese, shredded (2 cups)

1. Preheat oven to 375°F. In large saucepot, cook pasta as label directs. Drain. Meanwhile, in 4-quart saucepan, with wire whisk, mix milk, cornstarch, salt, and nutmeg until smooth. Cook over medium heat, whisking frequently, until mixture has thickened slightly and boils. Boil, whisking constantly, 1 minute.

PASTA FOR LASAGNA

When you're shopping for lasagna noodles, you are faced with several options. Domestic pasta is on the thick side, while imported pasta is thinner and more delicate. Choosing one over the other is just a matter of personal choice. (Break leftover pasta into manageable pieces, cook, and serve with a hearty tomato sauce.)

No-boil pasta, a relatively new product, eliminates the need for boiling the pasta before assembling lasagna. The pasta has been precooked, then dried: During baking it soaks up liquid from the other ingredients and softens. If you follow the recipe on the package, you are guaranteed the proper cooking of the no-boil noodles. If you use your own recipe, stir about 1 cup of additional water or tomato juice into your finished sauce so it contains more liquid. Or use your recipe without any changes, but reconstitute the sheets of pasta before using: Let them soak in enough warm water to cover until supple, 5 to 10 minutes, then drain the noodles and assemble the lasagna.

2. Remove from heat. Gradually whisk in Parmesan until cheese has melted and sauce is smooth.

3. Spoon pasta into shallow 3½-quart or 13" by 9" baking dish. Pour sauce over pasta and stir to thoroughly mix. Sprinkle Cheddar over top. Bake until Cheddar has melted and mixture is hot and bubbling, about 25 minutes. Makes 8 main-dish servings.

Each serving: About 476 calories, 23g protein, 54g carbohydrate, 18g total fat (11g saturated), 60mg cholesterol, 650mg sodium.

Reduced-Fat Macaroni and Cheese

They'll never know we took out ten grams of fat per serving, because this macaroni and cheese is as good as—even better than—the old-fashioned recipe.

Prep: 20 minutes	Bake/Broil: 22 minutes
8	ounces elbow macaroni twists
1	container (16 ounces) lowfat (1%) cottage cheese
2	tablespoons all-purpose flour
2	cups skim milk
4	ounces sharp Cheddar cheese, shredded (1 cup)
1	teaspoon salt
¼	teaspoon ground black pepper
	pinch ground nutmeg
¼	cup freshly grated Parmesan cheese

1. Preheat oven to 375°F. Grease broiler-safe shallow 2½-quart casserole. In medium saucepot, cook macaroni as label directs, but do not add salt to water. Drain.

2. In food processor with knife blade attached, puree cottage cheese until smooth. (Or, in blender, puree cottage cheese with ¼ cup of milk in recipe until smooth.)

3. In 2-quart saucepan, blend flour with ¼ cup milk until smooth. With wire whisk, slowly stir in remaining milk until blended. Cook over medium heat, stirring, until mixture has thickened slightly and boils. Remove from heat; stir in cottage cheese, Cheddar, salt, pepper, and nutmeg.

4. Spoon macaroni into prepared casserole and cover with cheese sauce. Bake 20 minutes. Remove from oven; sprinkle with Parmesan. Turn oven control to broil.

5. Place casserole in broiler at closest position to heat source; broil until top is golden brown, 2 to 3 minutes. Makes 8 accompaniment or 4 main-dish servings.

Each accompaniment serving: About 251 calories, 18g protein, 28g carbohydrate, 7g total fat (4g saturated), 21mg cholesterol, 724mg sodium.

Baked Ziti

Always a hit with kids, guests, and the cook. For variety, add one-half cup chopped fresh basil or eight ounces sweet Italian-sausage meat, cooked and crumbled, to the ricotta layer.

Prep: 40 minutes	Bake: 30 minutes
	Marinara Sauce (page 343)
1	package (16 ounces) ziti
1	container (15 ounces) part-skim ricotta cheese
¼	cup freshly grated Parmesan cheese
¼	teaspoon salt
8	ounces part-skim mozzarella cheese, shredded (2 cups)

1. Prepare Marinara Sauce.

2. Meanwhile, in large saucepot, cook the pasta as label directs. Drain.

3. Preheat oven to 350°F. In large bowl, combine pasta and marinara sauce, stirring to coat. In medium bowl, combine ricotta, Parmesan, and salt. Spoon half of pasta into 13" by 9" baking dish. Spread evenly with ricotta mixture and top with remaining pasta.

4. Cover ziti with foil and bake 20 minutes. Remove foil and sprinkle with mozzarella. Bake until cheese has melted, about 10 minutes longer. Makes 8 main-dish servings.

Each serving: About 429 calories, 23g protein, 52g carbohydrate, 14g total fat (7g saturated), 35mg cholesterol, 719mg sodium.

Baked Rigatoni and Peas

This is a terrific dish for a big party. Place one dish on the buffet table, and keep the other warm in the oven. To make a day ahead, prepare through the making of the topping in Step Four. Cover and refrigerate the rigatoni and topping separately. To serve, sprinkle the topping over the rigatoni and bake, allowing for some extra baking time since the rigatoni will be cold.

Prep: 45 minutes   Bake: 30 minutes

14	tablespoons butter or margarine (1¾ sticks)
½	cup all-purpose flour
7	cups milk, warmed
2	cups freshly grated Parmesan cheese
2	teaspoons plus 1 tablespoon salt
2	packages (16 ounces each) rigatoni or ziti
1	bag (20 ounces) frozen peas, thawed
2	cans (14½ ounces each) diced tomatoes
1	cup loosely packed fresh basil leaves, thinly sliced
½	cup plain dried bread crumbs

1. Prepare cheese sauce: In heavy 4-quart saucepan, melt 10 tablespoons butter over low heat. Add flour and cook, stirring, 2 minutes. With wire whisk, gradually whisk in warm milk. Cook over medium heat, stirring constantly with wooden spoon, until sauce has thickened and boils. Reduce heat and simmer, stirring frequently, about 5 minutes. Stir in 1½ cups Parmesan and 2 teaspoons salt. Remove from heat.

2. Meanwhile, in 12-quart saucepot, cook pasta as label directs, adding remaining 1 tablespoon salt to water; drain. Return rigatoni to saucepot.

3. Preheat oven to 350°F. Pour cheese sauce over rigatoni in saucepot, stirring to combine. Stir in peas, tomatoes with their juice, and basil. Spoon pasta mixture into two shallow 3½- to 4-quart casseroles or two 13" by 9" baking dishes.

4. In small saucepan, melt remaining 4 tablespoons butter over low heat. Remove from heat and stir in bread crumbs and remaining ½ cup Parmesan. Sprinkle topping over pasta. Bake until hot and bubbling and topping is golden, 30 to 35 minutes. Makes 20 main-dish servings.

Each serving: About 390 calories, 15g protein, 48g carbohydrate, 15g total fat (9g saturated), 41mg cholesterol, 703mg sodium.

Dried Fruit Kugel

This heavenly lowfat version of sweet noodle pudding is studded with prunes. If you prefer an even sweeter dessert, use dates.

Prep: 20 minutes   Bake: 35 minutes

8	ounces wide egg noodles
1	container (8 ounces) lowfat (1%) cottage cheese
1	container (8 ounces) reduced-fat sour cream
¼	cup packed brown sugar
1	large egg
⅓	cup water
1	teaspoon vanilla extract
1	cup chopped prunes or dates

1. Preheat oven to 350°F. In medium saucepot, cook noodles as label directs. Drain.

2. In large bowl, with wire whisk, mix cottage cheese, sour cream, brown sugar, egg, water, and vanilla. Add prunes and noodles and toss well. Spoon mixture into 9-inch square baking dish. Bake until golden brown, about 35 minutes. Serve warm or at room temperature. Makes 6 dessert servings.

♥ Each serving: About 347 calories, 14g protein, 56g carbohydrate, 8g total fat (3g saturated), 85mg cholesterol, 229mg sodium.

Homemade Pasta Dough

This is a basic recipe for pasta dough; use it to prepare any of the pasta shapes or Jumbo Cheese Ravioli (page 368).

Prep: 25 minutes plus standing   Cook: 18 minutes

2	cups all-purpose flour
2½	teaspoons salt
3	large eggs, lightly beaten

1. In large bowl, with fork, stir flour and ½ teaspoon salt until well combined. With hand, make a well in center of flour; pour in eggs. Using fork, gradually draw in flour from side of bowl to make a stiff  dough, mixing gently in only one direction to prevent air pockets from forming.

2. On well-floured surface, knead dough until smooth, about 10 minutes. Cover dough with inverted bowl or plastic wrap and let rest for 30 minutes. Cut as directed. If not cooking immediately, cover with plastic wrap and refrigerate up to 3 days.

3. To cook pasta, in 6-quart saucepot, heat *4 quarts water* to boiling over high heat. Add remaining 2 teaspoons salt and pasta, stirring gently to separate pasta strips. Heat to boiling; cook pasta until tender but firm, 2 to 3 minutes. Makes about 1 pound pasta or 4 main-dish servings.

♥ Each serving without sauce: About 283 calories, 11g protein, 48g carbohydrate, 4g total fat (1g saturated), 159mg cholesterol, 1,503mg sodium.

Fettuccine

Prepare Homemade Pasta Dough; divide dough into 6 equal pieces. Work with one piece at a time, keeping remaining pieces covered to prevent them from drying out. Follow pasta machine directions and roll dough to thinnest setting. Cut with fettuccine attachment. Or, if your machine does not have fettuccine attachment, fold dough lengthwise in half. With sharp knife, cut folded dough crosswise into ¼-inch-wide strips. Unfold strips. Sprinkle strips with flour to prevent them from sticking, then place in jelly-roll pans lined with lightly floured clean kitchen towels. Cook as directed above.

Pappardelle

Prepare Homemade Pasta Dough. Follow instructions for making fettuccine but cut folded dough crosswise into 1-inch-wide strips. Cook as directed left.

Herb Pasta Squares

Prepare Homemade Pasta Dough. Divide dough into 6 equal pieces. Work with one piece of dough at a time, keeping remaining pieces covered to prevent them from drying out. Follow pasta machine directions and roll each piece of dough to thinnest setting. Cut each piece crosswise in half to form two 16-inch-long strips. Cover surface of one dough strip with fresh parsley, dill, or tarragon leaves. Cover with second strip of dough. Use machine at thinnest setting and roll dough through one more time. Repeat with remaining pasta. With sharp knife, cut dough into 2-inch squares, sprinkling squares with flour to prevent sticking. Place pasta squares in single layers in jelly-roll pans lined with lightly floured clean kitchen towels. Cook as directed left.

Jumbo Cheese Ravioli

These ravioli are luscious when topped with our Marinara Sauce (page 343) or tossed with butter, Parmesan, and parsley for a decadent delight.

Prep: 1 hour 30 minutes plus standing   Cook: 18 minutes

	Homemade Pasta Dough (page 367)
3	cups ricotta cheese
⅓	cup freshly grated Parmesan cheese
¼	cup chopped fresh parsley
2¼	teaspoons salt
⅛	teaspoon ground black pepper
1	large egg white
1	teaspoon water

1. Prepare Homemade Pasta Dough.

2. In large bowl, combine ricotta, Parmesan, parsley, ¼ teaspoon salt, and pepper. Cover and refrigerate until ready to use.

3. Divide pasta dough into 6 equal pieces. Work with one piece at a time, keeping remaining pieces covered to prevent drying out. Follow pasta machine directions and roll dough to thinnest setting. Cut each piece crosswise in half to form two 16-inch-long strips.

4. In small bowl, lightly beat egg white and water. Drop mounds of ricotta filling, using 2 rounded tablespoons per mound, 2 inches apart, in one row, down center of one dough strip. With pastry brush, paint dough around each mound with egg-white mixture. Place second dough strip on top. With fingertips, press down firmly around each mound to seal ravioli, pushing out any  trapped air. Using fluted pastry wheel or sharp knife, cut pasta into squares to form ravioli, cutting along egg-white seam. Trim edges if needed. (If ravioli are not thoroughly sealed, filling may escape during cooking.) Repeat with remaining dough strips and filling.

5. Place ravioli in jelly-roll pans lined with lightly floured clean kitchen towels. Let ravioli dry about 30 minutes, turning occasionally to dry evenly.

6. In 5-quart saucepot, heat *4 quarts water* to boiling over high heat. Add remaining 2 teaspoons salt and ravioli; heat to boiling. Cook, stirring gently to separate ravioli, until tender and cooked through, 3 to 5 minutes. Drain. Makes about 24 ravioli or 6 main-dish servings.

Each serving without sauce: About 431 calories, 24g protein, 36g carbohydrate, 20g total fat (12g saturated), 173mg cholesterol, 1,375mg sodium.

Easy Wonton Ravioli

Substitute **1 package (50) wonton wrappers** for pasta dough. Prepare filling as in Step 2. Lightly beat egg white and water. Place 1 wrapper on surface. With pastry brush, brush egg-white mixture along edges; place 1 rounded tablespoon ricotta mixture in one corner, keeping filling away from edges. Fold opposite corner over fill-  ing to form triangle; press with fingertips to seal. Continue with Step 5. Makes about 48 ravioli or 6 main-dish servings.

Each serving without sauce: About 436 calories, 23g protein, 43g carbohydrate, 19g total fat (11g saturated), 73mg cholesterol, 690mg sodium.

Gnocchi

Usually served as a first course, these Italian potato dumplings will be perfect with your favorite sauce (we're partial to our Marinara Sauce, page 343). Or drizzle with butter, top with Parmesan cheese, and broil just until it is melted.

Prep: 1 hour   Cook: 30 minutes

5	all-purpose potatoes (1½ pounds)
1	teaspoon salt
1½	cups all-purpose flour

1. In 4-quart saucepan, heat potatoes and enough *water* to cover to boiling over high heat. Reduce heat; cover and simmer until potatoes are tender, 20 to 25 minutes. Drain. When cool enough to handle, peel potatoes.

2. Press warm potatoes through food mill or ricer. With wooden spoon, stir in salt and flour until dough begins to come together. Gently press dough into a ball; divide in half.

3. On floured surface, with floured hands, knead each dough half until smooth. Divide each half into 6 equal pieces.

On lightly floured surface, roll one piece of dough at a time into rope about ¾ inch thick. Cut rope into ¾-inch lengths.

4. Place one piece of dough on inside curve of fork tines, gently pressing on dough with thumb as you roll dough along tines. Allow dough to drop off fork, slightly curling in on itself, forming an oval. One side of gnocchi will have ridges and opposite side will have an indentation. Repeat rolling, cutting, and shaping with remaining dough. (Gnocchi can be made up to 4 hours ahead to this point. Arrange in floured jelly-roll pan; cover and refrigerate.)

5. In 5-quart saucepot, heat *4 quarts water* to boiling over high heat. Add one-third of gnocchi to boiling water. When gnocchi float to surface, cook 30 seconds. With slotted spoon, transfer gnocchi to warm shallow serving bowl. Repeat with remaining gnocchi. Makes 8 first-course servings.

♥ Each serving without sauce: About 160 calories, 4g protein, 35g carbohydrate, 0g total fat (0g saturated), 0mg cholesterol, 295mg sodium.

Ricotta Gnocchi with Browned Butter and Sage

Most cooks don't consider gnocchi everyday fare, but these are so easy to whip up, they may become a weekly staple at your house.

Prep: 1 hour   Cook: 17 minutes
3 tablespoons butter
1 teaspoon chopped fresh sage
¾ teaspoon salt
¼ teaspoon ground pepper
1 container (15 ounces) ricotta cheese
6 tablespoons freshly grated Parmesan cheese
¾ cup chopped fresh parsley
¾ cup all-purpose flour or as needed

Ricotta Gnocchi with Browned Butter and Sage

1. In 2-quart saucepan, melt butter over medium heat. Continue to cook, stirring, until butter turns golden brown. (If butter gets too dark, it will be bitter). Remove from heat and add sage, ¼ teaspoon salt, and pepper; set aside.

2. In medium bowl, combine ricotta, Parmesan, parsley, and remaining ½ teaspoon salt. Sprinkle flour over ricotta mixture and, with your hands, work mixture into soft, smooth dough. If dough is sticky, add some flour. Work dough just until flour is incorporated into cheese mixture; do not overwork.

3. Break off piece of dough; on lightly floured surface, roll into ¾-inch-thick rope. (If rope doesn't hold together, return to bowl with remaining dough and work in more flour.) Cut dough rope into ¾-inch lengths. Place one piece of dough on inside curve of fork tines, gently pressing on dough with thumb as you roll dough along tines. Allow dough to drop off fork, slightly curling in on itself, forming an oval. One side of gnocchi will have ridges and opposite side will have an indentation. Repeat rolling, cutting, and shaping with remaining dough. (Gnocchi can be made up to 4 hours ahead to this point. Arrange in floured jelly-roll pan; cover and refrigerate.)

4. In 5-quart saucepot, heat *4 quarts water* to boiling over high heat. Add half of gnocchi and cook until gnocchi float to surface, 2 to 3 minutes. With slotted spoon, transfer gnocchi to warm shallow serving bowl. Repeat with remaining gnocchi. To serve, toss gnocchi with sage butter. Makes 8 first-course servings.

Each serving: About 196 calories, 9g protein, 11g carbohydrate, 13g total fat (8g saturated), 42mg cholesterol, 394mg sodium.

10

BEANS, RICE, AND OTHER GRAINS

Many cultures use beans and grains as their major source of protein. Although this lowfat, high-fiber dynamic duo also provides a healthy amount of minerals and vitamins in one's diet, the protein in beans or grains alone is incomplete. When a protein is incomplete, it lacks at least one of the essential amino acids, which are the indispensable chemicals our bodies use to perform a wide range of functions. Luckily, the amino acids missing from beans can be found in grains, and vice versa, so when served together, they create a complete protein source similar to the protein found in animal products. Beans or grains can also be served along with small amounts of meat or dairy foods, such as cheese, milk, or eggs, to complete the protein. And, of course, we rely on grain flours for bread and other baked goods. Cooking with beans and grains is an inexpensive way to bring tasty, healthful food that will please every palate to the table.

BUYING AND STORING BEANS

As a food category, dried beans encompass a large variety of legumes, including split peas and lentils. Because tofu is made

Paella

from soybeans (actually soy milk), it is included in this chapter, too. Fresh shell beans are a welcome summertime treat; look for them in farmers' markets. But, because their availability is somewhat limited, most cooks rely on the convenience of dried and canned beans.

Dried beans keep for about one year, but they become less flavorful and drier as time passes, and older beans take longer to cook. Beans are not stamped with a "sell-by" date, so purchase them from a grocer with a high turnover—ethnic markets are a good bet. Buy them in small quantities and use within six months. Avoid packages with any hint of dust or mold, and store in an airtight container in a cool dry place.

Canned beans are a boon to the busy cook because they don't require soaking or further cooking, and some people find them easier to digest than freshly cooked dried beans. Different brands vary greatly in texture and saltiness, however, so take note of your favorite label. Canned beans should be rinsed and drained under cold water before being used. This quick rinse freshens their flavor and removes some of the sodium added during the canning process. One can of beans (15 to 19 ounces) equals about two cups drained beans.

SOAKING DRIED BEANS

Before soaking, sort through the beans to remove tiny stones or debris. Place the beans in a colander and rinse well with cold water, running your fingers through the beans to reveal any bits of dirt. Transfer the beans to a large bowl. (Dried beans rehydrate to at least double their size, so use a large bowl.) Add enough cold water to cover the beans by two inches. The standard overnight (or about eight hours) soaking time is really for the cook's convenience. The job is done when the beans have swelled to about double their size, which takes about four hours, but beans can be soaked for up to twenty-four hours. In hot weather, to prevent the beans from fermenting, refrigerate them while they soak. If you want to reduce the soaking time by about half, cover the beans with boiling water. Just before cooking, drain the soaked beans and rinse them again. Discard the soaking water and cook the beans in fresh water.

When time is of the essence, use this quick-soak technique: Combine the beans and water in a pot and heat to boiling; cook for three minutes. Remove from the heat, cover tightly, and set aside for one hour; drain and rinse the beans. Although this process saves time, quick-soaked beans tend to break up during cooking. In a chili or bean stew, a few broken beans are not a problem. But if you want the beans to remain whole, for a bean salad, for example, use the long-soak method.

COOKING DRIED BEANS

There are two reasons to soak dried beans in water before they're cooked. First, soaking returns moisture to the beans and softens them, reducing the cooking time. Second, soaking allows some of the gas-causing *oligosaccharides* (complex sugars the human body cannot digest) to dissolve in the water, which makes digestion easier.

There is an enormous range of cooking times for dried beans. Use the directions on the package as a guide, then taste often to check for doneness, because their age and relative dryness will affect the exact time.

Dried beans should always be cooked in soft water, or they will be tough. If you live in an area with hard water, add a pinch of baking soda to the cooking water. Because water boils at a lower temperature at high altitudes, beans will take longer to cook at high altitudes; be sure they are well soaked and softened before cooking. Adding salt to beans at the be-

ginning of cooking toughens the skins and increases the cooking time. However, beans usually taste better when seasoned early, so we often use a minimal amount of salt when the cooking begins, then add the remainder at the end. Acidic ingredients, such as tomatoes, sugar, and wine, also lengthen the cooking time, but they are worth the trade-off when it comes to flavor.

Although the volume changes slightly with each bean variety, one cup dried beans averages two cups cooked beans. Large beans, like limas, yield about two and one-half cups, whereas small beans, such as black beans, yield just under two cups. Cooked beans keep well, so it's a good idea to make more than you will need for one meal to provide leftovers for salads or side dishes. Cover leftover cooked beans with some of their cooking liquid in containers and refrigerate for four or five days, or freeze for up to six months.

KNOW YOUR BEANS AND BEAN PRODUCTS

Adzuki These small dark red beans are a member of the mung bean family and have a sweet flavor. They are used to make the red bean paste that flavors many Asian desserts.

Anasazi Named for the Native American tribe that cultivated them, these can be used in place of red kidney beans.

Black Also called *turtle beans,* these are a staple in Latin America and the Caribbean. They're prized as a base for black bean soup, for mixing with rice, and as a burrito filling.

Black-eyed peas Beige beans with a black circular "eye," they are also called *cowpeas.* Used to make Hoppin' John, a Southern specialty, they have a mealy texture and an earthy taste.

Black-eyed peas, garbanzo beans, red beans

Cranberry These beautiful plump beans, also called *shell beans,* are cream colored and have red streaks that disappear during cooking. They have a delicious nutty flavor.

Fava Also known as *broad beans,* these flat light brown beans resemble large limas. They have a tough skin that should be removed by blanching before cooking.

Flageolets In France, these white beans are traditionally served as a side dish with roasted lamb. They hold their shape well after cooking, so they are especially good in salads.

Garbanzo Also called *chickpeas,* they're best known as the base for hummus, the Middle Eastern dip. Their cooking time is unpredictable, so check often for tenderness.

Great Northern These white beans have a delicate flavor. Popular in soups and baked-bean dishes, they can be substituted for other white beans in most recipes.

Heirloom Bean varieties that almost became extinct as farmers came to rely on newer, easy-to-grow strains, but they are now cultivated in small quantities by innovative farmers. These colorful beans have equally colorful

Great Northern beans, white kidney beans, pink beans

names, such as *rattlesnake, appaloosa,* and *scarlet runner.* They can be found at specialty food stores and farmers' markets.

Lima Also called *butter beans,* these large oval cream-colored beans hold their shape well when cooked.

Miso Used in Japanese cooking, this is a salty paste made from fermented soybeans. Available in many varieties: the lighter the color, the milder the flavor.

Mung Small beans that play a big role in Asian cooking. They are green, black, or brown and are most commonly used in their sprouted form. Mung bean flour is used to make clear cellophane noodles.

Navy (pea) Small white beans, also called *Yankee*

Baby lima beans, flageolets, black beans

beans. They're most often used for pork and beans, soups, and Boston baked beans.

Pigeon peas Also called *gandules,* these beans are used in Caribbean stews and soups. Look for them at Latino markets.

Pink Smooth reddish brown beans that are popular in the Southwest, where they're used to make refried beans and chili. They are interchangeable with pinto beans.

Pinto Named for the Spanish word for "speckled," these pale pink beans are splotched with reddish brown streaks. Grown in the Southwest and prized in most Spanish-speaking countries, they are used for making refried beans and in soups and stews.

Red Small red beans that are well known as the main ingredient in red beans and rice. They are sometimes called *chili* or *Mexican red beans.*

Red kidney Good all-purpose beans that have a firm, burgundy-colored skin, pale flesh, a sweet flavor, and a slightly mealy texture.

Pinto beans, navy beans, red kidney beans

Soybeans Not usually served as a food, but processed into products, such as oil, soy milk, or tofu. Dried soybeans can be sprouted and added to stir-fries.

Split peas (yellow or green) Dried peas that have been peeled and split in half.

Tofu Soy milk that has been coagulated (usually by a calcium compound) and pressed into cubes. Depending on the amount of liquid pressed out of the curd, tofu can be extra-firm, firm, or soft. This type of tofu, which is usually stored in buckets of water at Asian markets or found in individual boxes at supermarkets, is best for stir-fries. Silken tofu, sold in aseptic boxes, has not been pressed. Available soft or firm, this smooth-textured tofu is more delicate than regular tofu and works well in recipes that call for pureed tofu.

Tempeh Fermented soybean cakes with a yeasty, mushroomlike flavor. Tempeh is a popular meat substitute in vegetarian cooking.

White kidney (cannellini) These beans have a creamier texture and a milder flavor than the red variety. White kidney beans are common in Italian cooking, where they're used in soups, pastas, and salads.

KNOW YOUR LENTILS

Protein-packed lentils, one of our oldest cultivated crops, can be cooked into countless savory dishes including hearty stews and satisfying salads. They don't need to be presoaked and they cook faster than other dried beans.

Black beluga lentils These tiny lentils are named for their caviarlike appearance. They're best in salads and side dishes.

Brown lentils The most common variety. They have a firm texture and a mild, nutty flavor.

Green lentils Popular in European cooking, they have a firm texture and a nutty, earthy taste.

Red lentils A smaller round variety, they become yellow and soft when cooked; often used in Indian dals.

Small green French lentils (Puy) These tiny plump lentils are grown in central France in the Auvergne region. Considered to have superior flavor, they cook quickly, hold their shape, and have a nutty taste.

Black beluga lentils, green lentils

Red lentils, French green lentils

Hoppin' John

This moist and delicious rice-and-pea mixture is traditionally served in the South on New Year's Day for good luck: The peas represent coins, ensuring a prosperous year.

	Prep: 15 minutes Cook: 1 hour
1	tablespoon vegetable oil
2	stalks celery, chopped
1	large onion (12 ounces), chopped
1	red pepper, chopped
2	garlic cloves, finely chopped
1	package (16 ounces) dry black-eyed peas, rinsed and picked through
1	large smoked ham hock (12 ounces)
4	cups water
2	cans (14½ ounces each) chicken broth or 3½ cups Chicken Broth (page 84)
2	teaspoons salt
¼	teaspoon crushed red pepper
1	bay leaf
2	cups regular long-grain rice

1. In 4-quart saucepan, heat oil over medium heat; add celery, onion, and chopped red pepper. Cook, stirring frequently, until onion is golden, about 10 minutes. Add garlic; cook 2 minutes longer.

2. Add black-eyed peas, ham hock, water, broth, 1 teaspoon salt, crushed red pepper, and bay leaf to celery mixture; heat to boiling over high heat. Reduce heat; cover and simmer, stirring occasionally, until black-eyed peas are tender, about 40 minutes. Discard bay leaf.

3. Meanwhile, prepare rice as label directs, adding remaining 1 teaspoon salt. (Do not add butter or margarine.)

4. In large bowl, gently combine black-eyed–pea mixture and rice. Makes 14 cups or 18 accompaniment servings.

♥ Each serving: About 188 calories, 9g protein, 33g carbohydrate, 2g total fat (0g saturated), 3mg cholesterol, 549mg sodium.

Three-Bean Vegetarian Chili

Hearty and colorful, this chili gets an extra wallop of flavor from a chipotle (smoked jalapeño) chile. If you can't find chipotles, add one or two additional fresh jalapeños with seeds for more heat. Vary the beans according to what you have on hand.

Prep: 25 minutes plus soaking beans   Cook: 1 hour 45 minutes

1	cup dry white kidney beans (cannellini), soaked and drained (page 372)
1	cup dry red kidney beans, soaked and drained (page 372)
1	cup dry black beans, soaked and drained (page 372)
1	tablespoon olive or vegetable oil
2	medium onions, chopped
3	carrots, peeled and chopped
1	stalk celery, chopped
1	red pepper, chopped
3	garlic cloves, finely chopped
1	jalapeño chile, finely chopped
2	teaspoons ground cumin
½	teaspoon ground coriander
⅛	teaspoon ground cinnamon
⅛	teaspoon ground red pepper (cayenne)
1	can (28 ounces) tomatoes in puree
1	chipotle chile in adobo (page 31), finely chopped
2	teaspoons salt
¼	teaspoon dried oregano
2	cups water
1	package (10 ounces) frozen whole-kernel corn, thawed
½	cup chopped fresh cilantro

Three-Bean Vegetarian Chili

1. In nonreactive 5-quart Dutch oven, combine white kidney, red kidney, and black beans and enough *water to cover by 2 inches;* heat to boiling over high heat. Reduce heat; cover and simmer until beans are tender, about 1 hour. Drain beans and return to Dutch oven.

2. Meanwhile, in nonstick 10-inch skillet, heat oil over medium heat. Add onions, carrots, celery, and red pepper. Cook, stirring frequently, until carrots are tender, about 10 minutes. Stir in garlic, jalapeño, cumin, coriander, cinnamon, and ground red pepper; cook 30 seconds. Stir in tomatoes with their puree, chipotle chile, salt, and oregano, breaking up tomatoes with side of spoon. Heat to boiling; reduce heat and simmer 10 minutes, stirring several times.

3. Add tomato mixture and water to beans in Dutch oven; heat to boiling over medium-high heat. Reduce heat; cover and simmer, stirring occasionally, 15 minutes. Stir in corn and cook 5 minutes longer. Remove from heat and stir in ¼ cup cilantro. Spoon into bowls and sprinkle with remaining ¼ cup cilantro. Makes about 10 cups or 6 main-dish servings.

♥ Each serving: About 461 calories, 25g protein, 86g carbohydrate, 4g total fat (1g saturated), 0mg cholesterol, 1,048mg sodium.

Old-Fashioned Baked Beans

An heirloom recipe for not-too-sweet baked beans. This makes a big enough batch for a July 4th bash or a winter pot-luck party.

Prep: 15 minutes plus soaking beans
Bake: 3 hours 30 minutes to 4 hours

2	packages (16 ounces each) dry navy (pea) beans, soaked and drained (page 372)
7½	cups water
4	slices bacon, cut into 1-inch pieces, or 4 ounces salt pork, finely chopped
2	medium onions, chopped
½	cup dark molasses
⅓	cup packed brown sugar, preferably dark
5	teaspoons salt
4	teaspoons dry mustard

Preheat oven to 350°F. In 8-quart Dutch oven, combine beans and water; heat to boiling over high heat. Cover and place in oven. Bake 1 hour. Stir in bacon, onions, molasses, brown sugar, salt, and dry mustard. Cover and bake, stirring occasionally, 1 hour. Remove cover and bake until thickened and soupy, 1 hour 30 minutes to 2 hours longer. Makes about 11 cups or 14 accompaniment servings.

♥ Each serving: About 312 calories, 15g protein, 54g carbohydrate, 5g total fat (2g saturated), 4mg cholesterol, 895mg sodium.

Tuscan White Beans with Sage

Leave it to the Italians to give us flawlessly flavored beans. These are perfect with Pork Roast with Fennel and Garlic (page 144).

Prep: 15 minutes plus soaking beans   Bake: 45 to 60 minutes

1	package (16 ounces) white kidney beans (cannellini), soaked and drained (page 372)
3	slices bacon
2	small onions, very thinly sliced
4	garlic cloves, crushed with side of chef's knife
2	sprigs plus 2 teaspoons thinly sliced fresh sage leaves
1	bay leaf
3	tablespoons olive oil
2	teaspoons salt
½	teaspoon ground black pepper

1. Preheat oven to 325°F. In 5-quart Dutch oven, combine beans, bacon, onions, garlic, sage sprigs, bay leaf, oil, and enough *water to cover by 2 inches;* heat to boiling over high heat. Cover and place in oven. Bake until beans are tender but still retain their shape, 45 to 60 minutes.

2. Drain beans, reserving cooking liquid. Discard bacon, sage sprigs, and bay leaf. Return beans to pot and stir in sliced sage, salt, pepper, and ½ cup to 1 cup bean cooking liquid until desired consistency. Spoon into serving bowl and serve hot, warm, or at room temperature. Makes about 6 cups or 8 accompaniment servings.

♥ Each serving: About 263 calories, 14g protein, 37g carbohydrate, 7g total fat (1g saturated), 2mg cholesterol, 617mg sodium.

White Beans, French-Style

In French homes and bistros, white beans are the traditional accompaniment to roasted leg of lamb. Add leftovers to soups, or top them with buttered fresh bread crumbs and reheat in a shallow casserole.

Prep: 10 minutes plus soaking beans
Cook: 1 hour 20 minutes

1	package (16 ounces) dry Great Northern beans, soaked and drained (page 372)
2	medium onions, 1 peeled and studded with 2 whole cloves
1	bay leaf
2	tablespoons butter or olive oil
1	garlic clove, finely chopped
1	can (14 to 16 ounces) tomatoes
2	teaspoons salt
¼	teaspoon ground black pepper
¼	cup chopped fresh parsley

1. In 5-quart Dutch oven, combine beans, clove-studded onion, bay leaf, and enough *water to cover by 2 inches;* heat to boiling over high heat. Reduce heat; cover and simmer until beans are tender, about 1 hour. Drain beans, discarding onion and bay leaf; return beans to Dutch oven.

2. Meanwhile, finely chop remaining onion. In nonstick 10-inch skillet, melt butter over medium heat. Add onion and cook until tender, about 5 minutes. Stir in garlic and cook 30 seconds. Add tomatoes with their juice, salt, and pepper; heat

to boiling over high heat, breaking up tomatoes with side of spoon. Reduce heat and simmer, stirring occasionally, until almost all liquid has evaporated, 10 to 15 minutes.

3. Gently stir tomato mixture and parsley into beans. Makes about 6½ cups or 8 accompaniment servings.

♥ Each serving: About 246 calories, 13g protein, 42g carbohydrate, 4g total fat (2g saturated), 8mg cholesterol, 709mg sodium.

Indian-Style Lentils

Fresh ginger and cumin give lentils an Indian-flavor twist, while diced sweet potatoes add dulcet flavor and color.

Prep: 20 minutes	Cook: 45 minutes
1	tablespoon vegetable oil
1	medium onion, chopped
1	tablespoon minced, peeled fresh ginger
1	large garlic clove, finely chopped
1½	teaspoons cumin seeds
⅛	teaspoon ground red pepper (cayenne)
1	pound sweet potatoes, peeled and cut into ¾-inch pieces (3 cups)
1	cup brown lentils, rinsed and picked through
1	can (14½ ounces) chicken or vegetable broth or 1¾ cups Chicken Broth (page 84) or Vegetable Broth (page 83)
1	cup water
¼	teaspoon salt
1	container (8 ounces) plain lowfat yogurt
¼	cup chopped fresh mint or cilantro

1. In 3-quart saucepan, heat oil over medium heat. Add onion and cook, stirring, until tender, about 5 minutes. Stir in ginger, garlic, cumin seeds, and ground red pepper; cook 30 seconds. Stir in sweet potatoes, lentils, broth, water, and salt; heat to boiling over high heat. Reduce heat; cover and simmer, stirring, until lentils are just tender, about 30 minutes. Transfer to serving bowl.

2. In small bowl, combine yogurt and mint. Serve with lentils. Makes 6 accompaniment servings.

♥ Each serving: About 234 calories, 13g protein, 38g carbohydrate, 4g total fat (1g saturated), 2mg cholesterol, 421mg sodium.

French Lentils with Shallots and Brandy

Tiny green lentils (sometimes labeled lentilles vertes du Puy*) can be found at specialty food stores. They cook faster than brown lentils, retain their shape, and have superb flavor. Serve with roasted chicken or grilled salmon.*

Prep: 10 minutes	Cook: 35 to 40 minutes
1	cup green French lentils, rinsed and picked through
¾	teaspoon salt
2	tablespoons butter or margarine
⅓	cup finely chopped shallots
2	tablespoons brandy
¼	teaspoon ground black pepper
¼	cup chopped fresh parsley

1. In 2-quart saucepan, combine lentils, ½ teaspoon salt, and enough *water to cover by 2 inches;* heat to boiling over high heat. Reduce heat; cover and simmer until lentils are just tender, 20 to 25 minutes. Drain.

2. In same clean saucepan, melt butter over medium heat. Add shallots and cook until tender, about 3 minutes. Stir in brandy and cook until almost all liquid has evaporated, about 1 minute longer. Stir in lentils, remaining ¼ teaspoon salt, and pepper and heat through. Stir in parsley. Transfer to serving bowl. Makes 6 accompaniment servings.

♥ Each serving: About 162 calories, 9g protein, 20g carbohydrate, 4g total fat (2g saturated), 10mg cholesterol, 335mg sodium.

Quick "Baked" Beans

With store-bought ingredients, you can have authentic-tasting baked beans on the table in only twenty minutes.

Prep: 10 minutes   Cook: 15 minutes

2	teaspoons olive oil
1	small onion, chopped
1	cup ketchup
½	cup water
3	tablespoons light (mild) molasses
1	tablespoon Dijon mustard
½	teaspoon Worcestershire sauce
¼	teaspoon salt
	pinch ground cloves
1	can (15 to 19 ounces) black beans, rinsed and drained
1	can (15 to 19 ounces) red kidney beans, rinsed and drained
1	can (15 to 19 ounces) pink beans, rinsed and drained
1	can (15 to 19 ounces) white beans, such as Great Northern, rinsed and drained

1. In 4-quart saucepan, heat oil over medium-low heat. Add onion and cook until tender and golden, 5 to 8 minutes.

2. Stir in ketchup, water, molasses, mustard, Worcestershire, salt, and cloves until blended. Add black, red kidney, pink, and white beans; heat to boiling over high heat. Reduce heat; cover and simmer 5 minutes. Makes about 6 cups or 8 accompaniment servings.

Each serving: About 233 calories, 12g protein, 43g carbohydrate, 2g total fat (0g saturated), 0mg cholesterol, 709mg sodium.

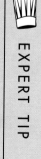

Leftover cooked beans make an excellent puree to serve with bread instead of butter. Discard any herb sprigs. Transfer the beans into a food processor with the knife blade attached and process until smooth, drizzling in some extravirgin olive oil. If desired, stir in some olive paste, pesto, or chopped fresh herbs. Transfer to a bowl and serve.

LIDIA BASTIANICH
TELEVISION HOST OF LIDIA'S ITALIAN TABLE

EXPERT TIP

Black Bean Cakes

Serve these as a first course with a lettuce and tomato salad or as "burgers" on toasted sesame buns for a tasty vegetarian lunch.

Prep: 10 minutes   Cook: 7 minutes

1	can (15 to 19 ounces) black beans, rinsed and drained
2	tablespoons mayonnaise
¼	cup chopped fresh cilantro
1	tablespoon plain dried bread crumbs
½	teaspoon ground cumin
	pinch dried oregano, crumbled
¼	teaspoon hot pepper sauce
2	tablespoons olive oil
2	tablespoons all-purpose flour
¼	cup mild or medium salsa
8	teaspoons sour cream

1. In large bowl, with potato masher, mash beans and mayonnaise until almost smooth, leaving some lumps. Stir in cilantro, bread crumbs, cumin, oregano, and hot pepper sauce. With lightly floured hands, shape into four 3-inch patties.

2. In 10-inch skillet, heat oil over medium heat. Dust patties with flour, shaking off excess. Cook patties until crusty and lightly browned, about 3 minutes per side. Transfer to plates; top each patty with 1 tablespoon salsa and 2 teaspoons sour cream. Makes 4 first-course servings.

Each serving: About 223 calories, 5g protein, 17g carbohydrate, 15g total fat (3g saturated), 8mg cholesterol, 422mg sodium.

Refried Beans

As a Mexican-style side dish, refried beans are hard to beat. Lard is the traditional cooking medium, but we prefer the smoky flavor of bacon.

Prep: 10 minutes   Cook: 22 minutes

3	slices bacon, coarsely chopped
2	tablespoons water
1	medium onion, chopped
3	garlic cloves, finely chopped
2	cans (15 to 19 ounces each) pinto beans, rinsed and drained
¾	cup chicken broth

1. In 12-inch skillet, cook bacon with water over medium heat until browned. With slotted spoon, transfer bacon to paper towels to drain.

2. Add onion and garlic to drippings in skillet; cook, stirring frequently, until onion is tender, about 7 minutes. Add beans and 1/4 cup broth. With potato masher or wooden spoon, mash beans. Continue cooking beans until liquid has been absorbed, about 3 minutes. Add 1/4 cup broth and stir until beans are piping hot and almost all liquid has been absorbed, about 3 minutes. Add remaining 1/4 cup broth and heat to boiling. Spoon onto platter and sprinkle with bacon. Makes 4 cups or 4 accompaniment servings.

Each serving: About 241 calories, 11g protein, 25g carbohydrate, 11g total fat (4g saturated), 11mg cholesterol, 661mg sodium.

Winter Vegetable Chili

Serve this black bean chili with a stack of warmed tortillas.

Prep: 15 minutes   Cook: 1 hour 15 minutes

4	teaspoons olive oil
1	medium butternut squash (1 3/4 pounds), peeled and cut into 3/4-inch pieces
2	carrots, peeled and chopped
1	medium onion, chopped
3	tablespoons chili powder
1	can (28 ounces) plum tomatoes
1	can (4 to 4 1/2 ounces) chopped mild green chiles
1	cup vegetable broth
1/4	teaspoon salt
2	cans (15 to 19 ounces each) black beans, rinsed and drained
1/4	cup chopped fresh cilantro
	sour cream or yogurt (optional)

1. In nonreactive 5-quart Dutch oven, heat 2 teaspoons oil over medium-high heat. Add squash; cook until golden. Transfer to bowl.

2. In same Dutch oven, heat remaining 2 teaspoons oil. Add carrots and onion; cook, stirring occasionally, until well browned. Stir in chili powder; cook, stirring, 1 minute. Add tomatoes with their juice, chiles with their liquid, broth, and salt. Heat to boiling over high heat, breaking up tomatoes with side of spoon. Reduce heat; cover and simmer 30 minutes.

3. Stir in beans and squash; heat to boiling over high heat. Reduce heat; cover and simmer until squash is tender and chili has thickened, about 15 minutes. Stir in cilantro. Serve with sour cream, if you like. Makes 9 cups or 6 main-dish servings.

Each serving: About 233 calories, 9g protein, 42g carbohydrate, 5g total fat (1g saturated), 0mg cholesterol, 911mg sodium.

Red Beans and Rice

Creole cooks traditionally made this dish on wash day (Monday) because it could simmer unattended all day long. Here's our quick, lowfat version that can be served whenever the mood strikes.

Prep: 10 minutes   Cook: 20 minutes

1	tablespoon vegetable oil
2	stalks celery with leaves, sliced
1	medium red onion, coarsely chopped
2	garlic cloves, finely chopped
1/2	teaspoon dried thyme
1	bay leaf
2	cans (15 to 19 ounces each) red kidney beans, rinsed and drained
1	package (6 ounces) sliced Canadian bacon, cut into thin strips
1	cup low-sodium chicken broth
5	tablespoons chopped fresh parsley
1	teaspoon Worcestershire sauce
1/8 to 1/4	teaspoon hot pepper sauce
1	cup regular long-grain rice, cooked as label directs

1. In 4-quart saucepan, heat oil over medium heat. Add celery, onion, garlic, thyme, and bay leaf; cook, stirring occasionally, until vegetables are tender and lightly browned, about 10 minutes.

2. Stir in beans, Canadian bacon, broth, 4 tablespoons parsley, Worcestershire, and hot pepper sauce. Cook, stirring occasionally, until heated through. Discard bay leaf.

3. To serve, spoon hot rice, then bean mixture into large soup bowls. Sprinkle with remaining 1 tablespoon parsley. Serve with additional hot pepper sauce, if you like. Makes 4 main-dish servings.

Each serving: About 468 calories, 26g protein, 71g carbohydrate, 8g total fat (2g saturated), 21mg cholesterol, 1,085mg sodium.

Falafel

Falafel is a staple in the Middle East and can be found at sandwich stands in many large American cities. Here, instead of small deep-fried falafel, we've made large shallow-fried patties. If you have the time, roasted eggplant strips are a wonderful addition.

Prep: 15 minutes plus chilling   Cook: 10 minutes

4	green onions, chopped
½	cup tightly packed fresh flat-leaf parsley leaves
2 to 4	garlic cloves, peeled and each cut in half
2	teaspoons dried mint leaves
1	can (15 to 19 ounces) garbanzo beans, rinsed and drained
½	cup plain dried bread crumbs
1	teaspoon baking powder
1	teaspoon ground coriander
1	teaspoon ground cumin
½	teaspoon salt
¼	teaspoon ground red pepper (cayenne)
¼	teaspoon ground allspice
½	cup vegetable or light olive oil
4	(6-to 7-inch) pitas
	Tzatziki (page 38; optional)
	thinly sliced Romaine lettuce, roasted pepper strips, chopped tomatoes, sliced red onion, sliced cucumbers

1. To food processor with knife blade attached, with motor running, add green onions, parsley, garlic, and mint through feed tube, processing until finely chopped. Add beans, bread crumbs, baking powder, coriander, cumin, salt, ground red pepper, and allspice, processing to a coarse puree. Transfer falafel mixture to bowl; cover and refrigerate at least 30 minutes or up to several hours.

2. Shape falafel mixture into 8 patties. Prepare Tzatziki, if using.

3. In nonstick 12-inch skillet, heat oil over medium-high heat until hot. Add patties and cook, turning once, until dark golden brown, about 8 minutes (patties will be fragile). Using wide spatula, transfer patties to paper towels to drain. Serve warm falafel in pita bread with tzatziki, if you like, and toppings of your choice. Makes 4 main-dish servings.

Each serving: About 475 calories, 12g protein, 59g carbohydrate, 21g total fat (3g saturated), 0mg cholesterol, 993mg sodium.

RICE AND OTHER GRAINS

BUYING AND STORING GRAINS

When we cook grains, we are actually using the fruits of grasses, which are called *kernels*. Whole kernels are also known as *berries* or *groats;* finely cracked groats are called *grits*. The kernels can then be coarsely ground into *meal* or finely ground into *flour.*

Each kernel has three components: the bran, the endosperm, and the germ. The bulk of the kernel is the endosperm. The bran is the fiber-rich outer coating of the kernel, and the germ is the seed. Some grains also have an inedible husk, which is always removed. A grain that has the bran, endosperm, and germ intact is called a *whole grain* because it contains all the grain's nutrients and vitamins. Grains often have their bran and germ removed and, in the process, the fiber and some of the vitamins are lost. These processed grains are often enriched with selected vitamins to replace some that were lost.

Freshness is an important factor when buying grains, because the oils found in the bran and germ can turn rancid quickly. Purchase grains at a store that has a high turnover. Store uncooked grains in an airtight container at cool room temperature or in the refrigerator for up to one month, or freeze for up to three months.

Cooked grains can be refrigerated in a tightly covered container for up to two days. To reheat, add a few tablespoons of water or broth and cook, covered, over low heat.

COOKING GRAINS

Before cooking, whole grains should be washed in cold water to remove any dust, chaff, or natural coatings that may impart a bitter taste. To do this, place the grains in a sieve, then swish the sieve back and forth in a large bowl of cold water. Lift out the sieve, pour out the water, and repeat the process until the water looks relatively clear. Lastly, rinse the grains briefly with cold running water, then drain thoroughly.

Whole berries such as wheat or rye, and even brown rice, cook more quickly if presoaked. At least eight or up to twenty-four hours before cooking, place the rinsed grain berries in a large bowl of cold water and let stand at room temperature. (In hot weather, place in the refrigerator.) Drain well before cooking. Presoaking gives berries a softer texture, so do not presoak if preparing a salad, since a resilient texture is desirable.

Some grains benefit from toasting before cooking. (*Toasting* refers to a light precooking of the grain, not to giving it a brownish color.) This is usually done to enhance the grain's aroma and flavor, but there are specific instances where toasting is imperative. Millet is toasted to bring out its flavor and texture. Kasha is coated with beaten egg and then toasted to keep the grains separate. In rice pilaf, the rice is toasted in the saucepan to firm up the outside layer, making the cooked rice firmer. Risotto is always prepared with a high-starch rice like Arborio. The starch thickens the cooking liquid to a creamy consistency, so the rice is first toasted to seal in the starch and to keep it from being released too quickly.

To toast whole grains, place them in a heavy skillet or saucepan over medium heat. (Add 1 or 2 tablespoons of oil, butter, or margarine to the pan first, if you wish.) Cook, stirring almost constantly, until the grains are fragrant, usually 3 to 5 minutes. Be careful not to scorch the grains.

Grains are usually cooked in measured amounts of water or broth in a covered saucepan until tender. The rule of thumb is two cups of liquid to one cup of grain. If the cooking liquid is absorbed before the grain is tender, simply add more hot liquid. Or, if the grain is tender and some liquid remains, simply drain it off. Grains can also be cooked in a large amount of water, like pasta, but some of the nutrients will then be drained away. Follow the instructions on the package for exact liquid measurements and estimated cooking times.

Like beans, the outer coating of some whole grains, like whole-wheat berries and amaranth, toughens and prohibits the proper absorption of liquid if salt is present. When in doubt, cook the grains in unsalted water and season when they are almost tender.

KNOW YOUR GRAINS

Amaranth Actually a seed but treated like a grain; when cooked, it has a crunchy porridgelike consistency.

Barley An ancient grain used for cereals, breads, salads, and soups. Pearl barley has been polished (milled) to remove the outer hull. Quick-cooking pearl barley has been presteamed.

Buckwheat A grain with an earthy flavor. Buckwheat groats are cooked like rice. Kasha is roasted buckwheat kernels.

Bulgur Wheat kernels that have been steamed, dried, and crushed. A staple in Middle Eastern cuisine, bulgur has a satisfying chewy yet tender texture. It is available fine, medium, and coarse.

Wheat berries, bulgur, barley, kasha

Cornmeal Dried corn kernels (yellow, white, or blue) ground to a fine, medium, or coarse texture. Stoneground cornmeal has not been degerminated (the process that removes the germ of the grain) and has the best flavor.

Couscous (Moroccan pasta) Not a grain but actually tiny pellets of semolina pasta. Most couscous is precooked and needs only a soaking in hot liquid to soften. Authentic couscous is not precooked and needs to be steamed in a special two-part pot called a *couscousière*.

Hominy Corn kernels that have been soaked in a lime or lye solution to remove the hulls and germ, then dried. This process gives hominy a chewy texture. Hominy is finely cracked to make *hominy grits*.

Millet Another seed (commonly known as bird seed) that is eaten like a grain. It should be toasted, without butter or oil, before cooking.

Quinoa (KEEN-wah) A staple grain of the ancient Incas, quinoa is rich in protein and vital nutrients. The tiny seeds cook quickly: They have a slightly earthy taste, a resilient texture, and a translucent appearance.

Rye An important grain in cold-weather European countries where wheat cannot grow. Cooked rye berries are

Cornmeal, quinoa, grits, couscous

softer than wheat berries and have a slightly tangy flavor.

Triticale A laboratory-engineered hybrid, a cross between wheat and rye. Toasting brings out its subtle rye flavor.

Wheat Cooked wheat berries are often served in pilafs and salads. The most common type of wheat is red winter wheat. Three other varieties that are now becoming available are *kamut, spelt,* and Italian *farro.*

BUYING AND STORING RICE

The USDA divides rice into three categories: long-, medium-, and short-grain. In general, shorter grains contain the most starch, resulting in soft, sticky cooked rice. Most Americans are familiar with long-grain white rice, which has had the hull and bran removed. Brown rice retains its bran layer, as do other whole-grain rice varieties that are covered with a black or red bran layer. Although many cooks prefer fluffy long-grain white rice, because of the influence of foreign cuisines, exotic rice varieties are now available. Recipes often call for a specific rice. For example, for authentic taste and texture, paella is best when made with a short- or medium-grain rice, and risotto will lack its classic creaminess unless prepared with Arborio or a similar starchy variety.

Store rice in a cool, dry, insect-free area in its own package so it can "breathe." White rice will keep for up to two years, brown rice for up to one year. For longer storage, keep in the refrigerator.

COOKING RICE

There's no need to rinse most domestic rice before cooking. The rice was cleaned before milling, and you'll rinse away the starchy coating on enriched rice that contains nutrients such as thiamin, niacin, and iron. You should, however, rinse wild rice and imported varieties such as basmati or jasmine, which may be dirty or dusty. Brown rice and sticky (glutinous) rice will cook more quickly if presoaked overnight, but do not soak any other kinds of rice.

There are two methods for cooking rice: immersion and absorption. The immersion method is fine when you are in a hurry and don't want to bother with measuring. The rice is boiled like pasta in a large amount of salted water until tender, then drained. The disadvantage is that the nutrients are drained away with the cooking water. For the absorption method (our recommendation), rice is cooked in a measured quantity of liquid, all of which is absorbed, thus conserving nutrients. (Rice cookers use the absorption method and have a built-in timer; some also double as steamers for other foods). The cooking time and amount of liquid will depend on the variety of rice.

KNOW YOUR RICE

Long-Grain Rice

Aromatic Some rice varieties become fragrant when cooked. The best-known is *basmati,* a rice native to India that is valued for its perfumed scent, delicate taste, and fluffy texture. When cooked, the slender grains swell lengthwise, resulting in thin dry grains perfect for pilafs. Similar fragrant rice varieties include *jasmine* (popular in Southeast Asian cooking) and *popcorn* (a favorite of Louisiana cooks).

Instant Rice that has been partially or fully cooked, then dehydrated. It cooks quickly, in just a few minutes, but remains dry and chewy.

Parboiled (also called *converted*) Rice that has been steamed, pressure treated, and dehydrated; the grains remain firm and separate after cooking.

COOKING RICE

In all cases, for 1 cup of rice, combine the rice, cooking liquid (you can use water, but broth adds flavor), optional salt, and butter or margarine in a 2- to 3-quart saucepan. Heat to boiling. Reduce heat; cover and simmer until done. Do not uncover the saucepan to check on the rice's progress until the last 5 minutes of cooking. When the rice is tender, remove from heat and let stand, covered, for 5 minutes. This short waiting period ensures a better texture. Fluff the rice with a fork before serving.

RICE VARIETY (1 CUP)	AMOUNT OF LIQUID	COOKING TIME	YIELD
Regular long-grain	1¾ to 2 cups	18 to 20 minutes	3 cups
Medium- or short-grain	1½ to 1¾ cups	18 to 20 minutes	3 cups
Brown	2 to 2½ cups	45 to 50 minutes	3 to 4 cups
Wild	2 to 2½ cups	45 to 60 minutes	2⅔ cups

Regular Slender, polished, elongated white grains; it cooks into dry grains that separate easily.

Medium-Grain Rice

Arborio The traditional rice for Italian risotto; this plump roundish medium-grain rice has a high starch content and yields a moist, creamy texture. *Vialone Nano* and *Carnaroli* rice varieties can also be used to make risotto. They have a higher starch content than Arborio, which some cooks find preferable. Previously, only imported Arborio was available, now domestic varieties of Arborio are cultivated. Some imported brands are simply labeled "short-grain" because the Italian government has only two rice categories—long and short.

Brown, regular, converted rices

Aborio, basmati, sushi rices

Japanese (sushi) rice Starchy medium-grain rice that clings together after cooking, making it the perfect rice for sushi.

Paella (Valencia) The preferred rice in Spanish cooking, found at Latino markets and specialty food stores. Excellent in many savory Latino dishes, it is also delicious in puddings where its creamy, slightly sticky texture is an asset.

Short-Grain Rice

Sticky Also called *glutinous* or *sweet rice.* An opaque white short-grain rice with a slightly sweet taste and a soft, sticky texture. In Thai cooking, it is an all-purpose rice, but in Chinese cooking, it is used mostly for desserts. To accentuate its texture, sticky rice is usually soaked, drained, and then steamed over boiling water.

Brown and Black Rice

Brown The least processed form of rice. The outer hull has been removed, but the nutritious, high-fiber bran layers that give this rice its light tan color, nutty flavor, and chewy texture remain. Brown rice can be long-, medium- or short-grain. Other varieties include *Wehani,* a new designer brown rice, and *red rice,* which has a red bran layer.

Black There are many varieties of this hulled rice with its black bran, including *Thai black sticky* and *Chinese black rice,* which are available at some Southeast Asian markets. And many natural food stores carry a domestic black rice that isn't sticky at all.

Wild Rice

Wild rice Not truly a rice but the seed of a water grass. The hand-harvested variety of wild rice, *manohmin,* is gathered the traditional way, in canoes. The rice grains vary in both length and color, and have a slightly smoky, earthy flavor and a chewy texture. It is available in specialty food stores. Commercially cultivated wild rice is uniform in size and color, less expensive than the true wild variety, and available in large supermarkets.

Hot Fluffy Rice

For drier rice, use only one and three-quarter cups water; for extratender rice, use two and one-third cups water and cook four to five minutes longer.

Prep: 5 minutes Cook: 25 minutes

2	cups water
1	cup regular long-grain rice
1	tablespoon butter or margarine (optional)
1	teaspoon salt

In 3-quart saucepan, heat water to boiling over high heat. Stir in rice, butter if using, and salt; heat to boiling. Reduce heat; cover and simmer, without stirring or lifting lid, until rice is tender and all liquid has been absorbed, 18 to 20 minutes. Remove from heat and let stand 5 minutes. Fluff rice with fork. Makes about 3 cups or 4 accompaniment servings.

♥ Each serving: About 169 calories, 3g protein, 37g carbohydrate, 0g total fat (0g saturated), 0mg cholesterol, 585mg sodium.

Brown Rice
Use **2½ cups water, 1 cup brown rice,** and **1 teaspoon salt.** Prepare as directed for Hot Fluffy Rice but simmer 45 to 50 minutes. Or prepare as label directs. Makes about 4 cups or 6 accompaniment servings.

♥ Each serving: About 114 calories, 2g protein, 24g carbohydrate, 1g total fat (0g saturated), 0mg cholesterol, 391mg sodium.

Aromatic Rice

Follow these basic directions to cook up fluffy rice, then add the desired flavoring for one of the six options below.

Prep: 5 minutes Cook: 25 minutes

1	cup chicken broth
¾	cup water
1	cup regular long-grain rice
¼	teaspoon salt
	seasonings (below)

In 3-quart saucepan, heat broth and water to boiling over high heat. Stir in rice and salt; heat to boiling. Reduce heat; cover and simmer, without stirring or lifting lid, until rice is tender and all liquid has been absorbed, 18 to 20 minutes. Remove from heat and let stand 5 minutes. Fluff rice with fork and stir in seasonings. Makes about 3 cups or 4 accompaniment servings.

♥ Each serving: About 176 calories, 4g protein, 37g carbohydrate, 1g total fat (0g saturated), 0mg cholesterol, 395mg sodium.

Lemon-Parsley Rice
Cook as directed. Stir in **2 tablespoons chopped fresh parsley** and **1 teaspoon freshly grated lemon peel.**

Asian Rice
Cook as directed but omit salt. Stir in **2 green onions,** chopped, **2 teaspoons soy sauce,** and **¼ teaspoon Asian sesame oil.**

Lemon-Parmesan Rice
Cook as directed. Stir in **¼ cup freshly grated Parmesan cheese, 1 teaspoon freshly grated lemon peel,** and **¼ teaspoon ground black pepper.**

Pepper Jack Rice
Cook as directed. Stir in **2 ounces Monterey Jack cheese with jalapeño chiles,** shredded (½ cup), and **3 green onions,** thinly sliced.

Coconut Rice
Cook as directed. Stir in **½ cup unsweetened coconut milk, ½ teaspoon freshly grated lime peel,** and **pinch ground red pepper (cayenne).**

Green Rice

Cook as directed but after the rice has cooked 15 minutes, stir in **1 package (10 ounces) frozen chopped spinach,** thawed; cover and cook 5 minutes longer. Stir in **2 ounces feta cheese,** finely crumbled (½ cup).

Mexican Red Rice

A hint of tomato lends color to this south-of-the-border pilaf.

Prep: 10 minutes	Cook: 35 minutes
½	cup canned tomatoes with their juice
1	tablespoon vegetable oil
1	medium onion, finely chopped
1	cup regular long-grain rice
1	garlic clove, finely chopped
1	cup chicken broth
1	cup water
¼	teaspoon salt
½	cup frozen peas (optional)
¼	cup chopped fresh cilantro

1. In blender or in food processor with knife blade attached, puree tomatoes with their juice until smooth. In nonreactive 3-quart saucepan, heat oil over medium heat. Add onion and cook until tender, about 5 minutes. Add rice; cook, stirring occasionally, until onion is lightly browned, about 5 minutes longer. Stir in garlic and cook 30 seconds. Add pureed tomatoes; cook, stirring frequently, until almost all liquid has been absorbed.

2. Stir in broth, water, and salt; heat to boiling. Reduce heat; cover and simmer, without stirring or lifting lid, 15 minutes. Stir in frozen peas, if using. Cook 5 minutes longer. Remove from heat and let stand 5 minutes. Fluff rice gently with fork and sprinkle with cilantro. Makes 4 cups or 4 accompaniment servings.

💙 Each serving: About 230 calories, 5g protein, 42g carbohydrate, 4g total fat (1g saturated), 0mg cholesterol, 446mg sodium.

Baked Rice

Here's an alternative to rice cooked on the stove. Substitute chicken or beef broth for the water, if you wish, but delete the salt.

Prep: 5 minutes	Bake: 30 minutes
2	cups boiling water
1	cup regular long-grain rice
1	tablespoon butter or margarine, cut into pieces
½	teaspoon salt

Preheat oven to 350°F. Grease shallow 1½-quart casserole or 8-inch square baking dish. In casserole, combine boiling water, rice, butter, and salt. Cover and bake until rice is tender and all liquid has been absorbed, 30 to 35 minutes. Makes about 3 cups or 4 accompaniment servings.

💙 Each serving: About 194 calories, 3g protein, 37g carbohydrate, 3g total fat (2g saturated), 8mg cholesterol, 321mg sodium.

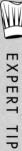

Since short-grain rice is 97 percent starch, always add a splash of dry white wine to the saucepan after toasting the rice, and allow the wine to be completely absorbed. The wine will provide a nice acidic balance for the rice.

LIDIA BASTIANICH

TELEVISION HOST OF LIDIA'S ITALIAN TABLE

EXPERT TIP

Persian Rice Pilaf

Sweet currants and a touch of spice create heavenly aromatic rice. Try it with grilled chicken or butterflied leg of lamb.

Prep: 10 minutes   Cook: 30 minutes

1	tablespoon butter or margarine
1	small onion, finely chopped
1	cup regular long-grain rice
1	can (14½ ounces) chicken or vegetable broth or 1¾ cups Chicken Broth (page 84) or Vegetable Broth (page 83)
¼	cup water
¼	cup dried currants
⅛	teaspoon ground black pepper
	pinch ground cinnamon
½	teaspoon freshly grated orange peel
¼	cup pine nuts (pignoli), toasted
¼	cup chopped fresh parsley

1. In 2-quart saucepan, melt butter over medium heat. Add onion and cook, stirring, until tender, about 4 minutes. Add rice; cook, stirring, 1 minute. Stir in broth, water, currants, pepper, and cinnamon; heat to boiling. Reduce heat; cover and simmer, without stirring or lifting lid, until rice is tender and all liquid has been absorbed, 18 to 20 minutes.

2. Remove rice from heat; let stand 5 minutes. Add orange peel, fluffing rice with fork until combined. Stir in pine nuts and parsley. Makes 4 cups or 4 accompaniment servings.

♥ *Each serving: About 291 calories, 7g protein, 48g carbohydrate, 9g total fat (3g saturated), 8mg cholesterol, 463mg sodium.*

Rice Pilaf with Vermicelli

Browned vermicelli pasta, onions, and pine nuts add delicious texture and flavor to rice.

Prep: 10 minutes   Cook: 50 minutes

3	tablespoons butter or margarine
½	cup vermicelli or spaghettini, broken into small pieces
1	medium onion, finely chopped
1	cup regular long-grain rice
1	cup chicken broth
1	cup water
¼	teaspoon salt
¼	cup pine nuts (pignoli), toasted

1. In 3-quart saucepan, melt butter over medium heat. Add vermicelli; cook, stirring, until browned, about 4 minutes. Add onion and cook until tender, about 4 minutes.

2. Add rice, broth, water, and salt to pan; heat to boiling over high heat. Cover and simmer, without stirring or lifting lid, until rice is tender and all liquid has been absorbed, 18 to 20 minutes. Remove from heat and let stand 5 minutes. Sprinkle pilaf with pine nuts. Makes about 4 cups or 4 accompaniment servings.

Each serving: About 368 calories, 8g protein, 53g carbohydrate, 14g total fat (6g saturated), 23mg cholesterol, 486mg sodium.

Indian-Spiced Rice

Whole spices are toasted in oil for maximum flavor in this delicately scented pilaf. Be sure to tell your guests not to eat the hard spices (whole peppercorns and cardamom pods).

Prep: 2 minutes   Cook: 25 minutes

1	tablespoon vegetable oil
1	cinnamon stick (3 inches)
10	whole black peppercorns
6	whole cardamom pods
4	whole cloves
1	cup regular long-grain rice
2	cups water
½	teaspoon salt

1. In 2-quart saucepan, heat oil over medium heat. Add cinnamon stick, peppercorns, cardamom pods, and cloves; cook just until spices begin to darken and pop. Add rice and cook, stirring, 1 minute. Stir in water and salt; heat to boiling over high heat.

2. Reduce heat; cover and simmer, without stirring or lifting lid, until rice is tender and all liquid has been absorbed, 18 to 20 minutes. Remove from heat and let stand 5 minutes. Remove cinnamon stick and fluff rice with fork. Makes 3 cups or 4 accompaniment servings.

♥ Each serving: About 201 calories, 3g protein, 37g carbohydrate, 4g total fat (1g saturated), 0mg cholesterol, 292mg sodium.

Cumin Rice with Black Beans

The time-honored combination of rice and beans is found throughout Latin America and the Caribbean. Serve as a side dish for a juicy grilled steak.

Prep: 10 minutes Cook: 30 minutes	
1	tablespoon vegetable oil
1	medium onion, finely chopped
1	garlic clove, finely chopped
2	teaspoons cumin seeds
1½	cups regular long-grain rice
1	can (14½ ounces) chicken or vegetable broth or 1¾ cups Chicken Broth (page 84) or Vegetable Broth (page 83)
1¼	cups water
¼	teaspoon salt
1	can (15 to 19 ounces) black beans, rinsed and drained
2	tablespoons chopped fresh cilantro
	lime wedges

1. In 3-quart saucepan, heat oil over medium heat. Add onion and cook until tender, about 5 minutes. Stir in garlic and cumin seeds; cook, stirring, until fragrant. Add rice and cook, stirring, 1 minute. Add broth, water, and salt; heat to boiling over high heat. Reduce heat; cover and simmer, without stirring or lifting lid, until rice is tender and most of liquid has been absorbed, about 15 minutes.

2. Stir beans into rice. Cover and cook 5 minutes longer. Remove from heat and let stand 5 minutes. Spoon into serving bowl and sprinkle with cilantro. Serve with lime wedges. Makes about 6 cups or 6 accompaniment servings.

♥ Each serving: About 256 calories, 7g protein, 48g carbohydrate, 4g total fat (1g saturated), 0mg cholesterol, 515mg sodium.

Brown Rice and Vegetable Pilaf

Fragrant herbs and a variety of fresh vegetables complement the nutty flavor of brown rice in this flavorful vegetarian dish. Serve as an accompaniment or main course.

Prep: 15 minutes Cook: 1 hour 10 minutes	
1	tablespoon olive or vegetable oil
1	medium onion, finely chopped
1	stalk celery, finely chopped
8	ounces mushrooms, trimmed and sliced
1	garlic clove, finely chopped
1	cup long-grain brown rice
2¼	cups water
2	carrots, peeled and chopped
1¼	teaspoons salt
⅛	teaspoon dried thyme
⅛	teaspoon ground black pepper
	pinch dried sage

In 10-inch skillet, heat oil over medium heat. Add onion and celery; cook, stirring frequently, until onion is tender, about 5 minutes. Stir in mushrooms; increase heat to medium-high and cook until mushrooms begin to brown and liquid has evaporated. Stir in garlic. Add rice; cook, stirring, 30 seconds. Stir in water, carrots, salt, thyme, pepper, and sage; heat to boiling. Reduce heat; cover and simmer until rice is tender and all liquid has been absorbed, about 45 minutes. Makes about 4½ cups or 6 accompaniment servings.

♥ Each serving: About 167 calories, 4g protein, 31g carbohydrate, 3g total fat (0g saturated), 0mg cholesterol, 503mg sodium.

Ginger Fried Rice

Fried rice is an excellent way to use leftover rice. The rice must be completely cooled (preferably chilled), or it will clump in the skillet.

Prep: 30 minutes   Cook: 20 minutes

2	tablespoons vegetable oil
2	teaspoons minced, peeled fresh ginger
2	garlic cloves, finely chopped
12	very thin asparagus spears, trimmed and cut on diagonal into 2-inch pieces
1	cup small broccoli flowerets
1	carrot, peeled and cut into thin diagonal slices
½	cup chicken broth
6	medium shiitake mushrooms, stems removed and caps thinly sliced
1	small yellow pepper, finely chopped
2	large eggs, lightly beaten
1	cup regular long-grain rice, cooked as label directs, cooled or chilled
12	ounces medium shrimp, shelled, deveined, and cooked (page 296)
2	ounces lean ham, cut into 2" by ¼" matchstick strips (½ cup)
½	cup frozen peas, thawed
2	green onions, finely chopped
2	tablespoons soy sauce
1½	teaspoons Asian sesame oil
¼	cup chopped fresh cilantro

1. In nonstick 12-inch skillet, heat 1 tablespoon oil over medium heat. Add ginger and garlic and cook, stirring frequently (stir-frying), 2 minutes. Add asparagus, broccoli, carrot, and ¼ cup broth; stir-fry until vegetables are tender-crisp, about 8 minutes. Add mushrooms and yellow pepper and stir-fry 1 minute. Transfer vegetables to bowl.

2. Heat remaining 1 tablespoon oil in skillet; add eggs. Cook, stirring, until eggs are softly scrambled, about 1 minute. Add rice, remaining ¼ cup broth, shrimp, ham, peas, green onions, soy sauce, and sesame oil. Stir-fry, breaking up any clumps of rice, about 5 minutes. Add vegetables and stir-fry until heated through. Sprinkle with cilantro. Makes 4 main-dish servings.

Each serving: About 427 calories, 31g protein, 44g carbohydrate, 14g total fat (3g saturated), 279mg cholesterol, 1,108mg sodium.

Jambalaya

A Cajun favorite, jambalaya is a rice dish with countless variations. The two constants, however, are pork and shellfish.

Prep: 20 minutes plus cooling   Cook: 55 minutes

8	ounces hot Italian-sausage links, pricked with fork
1	medium onion, finely chopped
1	green pepper, chopped
1	stalk celery, chopped
1	garlic clove, finely chopped
⅛	teaspoon ground red pepper
1½	cups regular long-grain rice
1	can (14½ ounces) chicken broth or 1¾ cups Chicken Broth (page 84)
1¼	cups water
¼	teaspoon salt
⅛	teaspoon dried thyme
1	can (14 to 16 ounces) tomatoes, drained and chopped
1	pound medium shrimp, shelled and deveined (page 296)
2	green onions, thinly sliced
	hot pepper sauce (optional)

1. In nonreactive 5-quart Dutch oven, cook sausages over medium heat until browned, about 10 minutes. With slotted spoon, transfer sausages to paper towels to drain. When cool enough to handle, cut sausages into ½-inch pieces.

2. To drippings in Dutch oven, add onion, green pepper, and celery; cook until tender, about 10 minutes. Stir in garlic and ground red pepper and cook 30 seconds. Add rice and cook, stirring, 1 minute. Stir in sausages, broth, water, salt, and thyme; heat to boiling over high heat. Reduce heat; cover and simmer 15 minutes.

3. Stir in tomatoes; cover and cook 5 minutes. Stir in shrimp; cover and cook until shrimp are opaque throughout, about 5 minutes longer. Transfer to serving bowl and sprinkle with green onions. Serve with hot pepper sauce, if you like. Makes 6 main-dish servings.

Each serving: About 405 calories, 23g protein, 45g carbohydrate, 14g total fat (5g saturated), 122mg cholesterol, 873mg sodium.

Paella

(pictured on page 370)

Every Spanish cook has his or her own version of paella, which may include a wide range of ingredients. The crucial ingredient in every paella is a medium-grain rice, such as Spanish Valencia or Italian Arborio, because of their texture and the way the grains cling together when cooked. (Long-grain rice, which cooks up fluffy, can be substituted in a pinch.)

Prep: 30 minutes   Cook: 1 hour

1	tablespoon olive oil
1½	pounds skinless, boneless chicken thighs, cut into 2-inch pieces
2	chorizo sausages (3 ounces each)
1	medium onion, finely chopped
1	red pepper, finely chopped
2	garlic cloves, finely chopped
¼	teaspoon ground red pepper (cayenne)
½	cup canned tomatoes in puree
½	cup dry white wine
2	cups medium-grain rice
4	ounces green beans, cut into 1-inch pieces
2½	cups water
1	can (14½ ounces) chicken broth or 1¾ cups Chicken Broth (page 84)
1½	teaspoons salt
¼	teaspoon loosely packed saffron threads, crumbled
⅛	teaspoon dried thyme
½	bay leaf
1	pound mussels, scrubbed and debearded (page 291)
12	ounces medium shrimp, shelled and deveined (page 296)
¼	cup chopped fresh parsley
	lemon wedges

1. In deep nonreactive 12-inch skillet, heat oil over medium-high heat until very hot. Add chicken and chorizo; cook until browned, about 10 minutes. With slotted spoon, transfer chicken and chorizo to bowl.

2. Reduce heat to medium. Add onion and chopped red pepper to skillet; cook, stirring frequently, until onion is tender, about 5 minutes. Stir in garlic and ground red pepper; cook 30 seconds. Add tomatoes with their puree and wine; cook, breaking up tomatoes with side of spoon, until liquid has evaporated.

3. Stir rice, green beans, water, broth, salt, saffron, thyme, and bay leaf into skillet. Thinly slice chorizo; return chorizo and chicken to skillet. Heat to boiling over high heat. Reduce heat; cover and simmer 20 minutes.

4. Tuck mussels into paella; cover and cook 3 minutes. Tuck shrimp into paella; cover and cook just until mussels have opened and shrimp are opaque throughout, about 3 minutes longer. Remove from heat and let stand 5 minutes. Discard bay leaf and any mussels that have not opened. Sprinkle paella with parsley and serve with lemon wedges. Makes 8 main-dish servings.

Each serving: About 467 calories, 35g protein, 45g carbohydrate, 15g total fat (4g saturated), 146mg cholesterol, 1,110mg sodium.

To flavor beans with an herb, such as sage or rosemary, begin cooking the beans with a small amount of coarse sea salt and enough water to cover by about 1 inch. As the beans cook, check the level of the water. When the beans are almost tender, the liquid should form a saucy consistency. Season with additional salt and drizzle with some flavorful olive oil. Add some herb sprigs or leaves and set aside until the beans to come to room temperature, gently stirring occasionally (the beans will absorb the flavor of the herbs). Discard the herb sprigs, if using, and serve.

LIDIA BASTIANICH

TELEVISION HOST OF LIDIA'S ITALIAN TABLE

EXPERT TIP

Shrimp Risotto with Baby Peas

Making a quick stock with the shrimp shells gives this pretty risotto a more complex shellfish flavor.

Prep: 35 minutes   Cook: 55 minutes

4	cups water
1	can (14½ ounces) chicken or vegetable broth or 1¾ cups Chicken Broth (page 84) or Vegetable Broth (page 83)
1	pound medium shrimp, shelled and deveined (page 296), shells reserved
1	tablespoon butter or margarine
1½	teaspoons salt
⅛	teaspoon ground black pepper
1	tablespoon olive oil
1	small onion, finely chopped
2	cups Arborio rice (Italian short-grain rice) or medium-grain rice
½	cup dry white wine
1	cup frozen baby peas
¼	cup chopped fresh parsley

1. In 3-quart saucepan, combine water, broth, and shrimp shells. Heat to boiling over high heat. Reduce heat; simmer 20 minutes. Strain broth through sieve into bowl and measure. If needed, add *water* to equal 5½ cups. Return broth to same clean saucepan; heat to boiling. Reduce heat to maintain simmer; cover.

2. In 4-quart saucepan, melt butter over medium-high heat. Add shrimp, ½ teaspoon salt, and pepper; cook, stirring, just until shrimp are opaque throughout, about 2 minutes. Transfer to bowl.

3. In same saucepan, heat oil over medium heat. Add onion and cook until tender, about 5 minutes. Add rice and remaining 1 teaspoon salt; cook, stirring frequently, until rice grains are opaque. Add wine; cook until wine has been absorbed. Add about ½ cup simmering broth to rice, stirring until liquid has been absorbed. Continue cooking, adding remaining broth ½ cup at a time and stirring after each addition, until all liquid has been absorbed and

rice is tender but still firm, about 25 minutes (risotto should have a creamy consistency). Stir in frozen peas and shrimp and heat through. Stir in parsley. Makes 4 main-dish servings.

💗 Each serving: About 511 calories, 28g protein, 76g carbohydrate, 10g total fat (3g saturated), 148mg cholesterol, 1,532mg sodium.

Risotto Milanese

Saffron-infused Risotto Milanese is the traditional accompaniment to Osso Buco (page 133). It is also delicious as a first course or as a meatless main course when followed by a generous mixed greens salad.

Prep: 10 minutes   Cook: 45 minutes

3½	cups water
1	can (14½ ounces) chicken broth or 1¾ cups Chicken Broth (page 84)
2	tablespoons butter or olive oil
1	small onion, finely chopped
2	cups Arborio rice (Italian short-grain rice) or medium-grain rice
1	teaspoon salt
½	cup dry white wine
¼	teaspoon loosely packed saffron threads
½	cup freshly grated Parmesan cheese

1. In 2-quart saucepan, heat water and broth to boiling over high heat. Reduce heat to maintain simmer; cover.

2. Meanwhile, in 4-quart saucepan, melt butter over medium heat. Add onion and cook, stirring occasionally, until tender, about 5 minutes. Add rice and salt and cook, stirring frequently, until rice grains are opaque. Add wine; cook until wine has been absorbed.

3. Add about ½ cup simmering broth to rice, stirring until liquid has been absorbed. Continue cooking, adding broth ½ cup at a time and stirring after each addition. After cooking 10 minutes, crumble saffron into rice. Continue cooking, adding remaining broth ½ cup at a time and stirring, until all liquid has been absorbed and rice is tender but still firm, about 25 minutes longer (risotto should have a creamy consistency). Remove risotto from heat; stir in Parmesan. Makes about 6½ cups or 8 accompaniment servings.

💗 Each serving: About 216 calories, 6g protein, 35g carbohydrate, 6g total fat (3g saturated), 13mg cholesterol, 649mg sodium.

Shrimp Risotto with Baby Peas

Mushroom Risotto

Just a few dried porcini mushrooms add deep earthy flavor to ordinary white mushrooms. The flavorful soaking liquid is used, too;, so don't throw it out.

	Prep: 20 minutes plus standing Cook: 45 minutes
½	cup boiling water
½	ounce dried porcini mushrooms
3¼	cups water
1	can (14½ ounces) chicken or vegetable broth or 1¾ cups Chicken Broth (page 84) or Vegetable Broth (page 83)
2	tablespoons butter or margarine
1	pound white mushrooms, trimmed and sliced
1¼	teaspoons salt
¼	teaspoon ground black pepper
	pinch dried thyme
1	tablespoon olive oil
1	small onion, finely chopped
2	cups Arborio rice (Italian short-grain rice) or medium-grain rice
½	cup dry white wine
½	cup freshly grated Parmesan cheese
2	tablespoons chopped fresh parsley

1. In small bowl, pour boiling water over porcini mushrooms; let stand 30 minutes. With slotted spoon, remove porcini. Rinse mushrooms to remove any grit, then chop. Strain mushroom liquid through sieve lined with paper towels into separate small bowl.

2. In 2-quart saucepan, heat water, broth, and mushroom liquid to boiling over high heat. Reduce heat to maintain simmer; cover.

3. Meanwhile, in 4-quart saucepan, melt butter over medium heat. Add white mushrooms, ½ teaspoon salt, pepper, and thyme. Cook, stirring occasionally, until mushrooms are tender and liquid has evaporated, about 10 minutes. Stir in chopped porcini. Transfer to bowl.

4. In same saucepan, heat oil over medium heat. Add onion and cook until tender, about 5 minutes. Add rice and remaining ¾ teaspoon salt and cook, stirring frequently, until rice grains are opaque. Add wine; cook until wine has been absorbed. Add about ½ cup simmering broth to rice, stirring until liquid has been absorbed. Continue cooking, adding remaining broth ½ cup at a time and stirring after each addition, until all liquid has been absorbed and rice is tender but still firm, about 25 minutes (risotto should have a creamy consistency). Stir in mushroom mixture, Parmesan, and parsley; heat through. Makes 4 main-dish servings.

♥ Each serving: About 504 calories, 16g protein, 77g carbohydrate, 15g total fat (7g saturated), 25mg cholesterol, 1,447mg sodium.

Wild Rice with Mushrooms

Here's a great way to clean mushrooms quickly and easily: Fill a ziptight plastic bag halfway with water and add one-third cup flour; shake to mix. Add the mushrooms and shake again. Remove the mushrooms, leaving all the grit behind.

	Prep: 5 minutes Cook: 1 hour to 1 hour 15 minutes
1	cup wild rice
1	cup water
1	cup chicken broth
¼	teaspoon salt
2	tablespoons butter or margarine
1	tablespoon chopped shallots
8	ounces mushrooms, trimmed and sliced
2	tablespoons chopped fresh parsley

1. Rinse wild rice; drain. In 2-quart saucepan, combine wild rice, water, broth, and salt; heat to boiling over high heat. Reduce heat; cover and simmer until wild rice is tender and some grains have popped, 45 to 60 minutes. Drain if necessary; keep warm.

2. Meanwhile, in 10-inch skillet, melt butter over medium-high heat. Add shallots and cook until tender, about 2 minutes. Add mushrooms; cook, stirring occasionally, until mushrooms are tender and liquid has evaporated.

3. Stir mushrooms and parsley into wild rice. Makes about 4 cups or 6 accompaniment servings.

Each serving: About 145 calories, 5g protein, 22g carbohydrate, 5g total fat (3g saturated), 10mg cholesterol, 305mg sodium.

Wild Rice Pilaf with Dried Cranberries

A mélange of sautéed vegetables and dried cranberries adds flavor and color to this savory wild-and-white-rice mixture.

Prep: 20 minutes   Cook: 1 hour to 1 hour 15 minutes

1	cup wild rice
4	cups water
¾	cup dried cranberries
4	tablespoons butter or margarine
3	carrots, peeled and chopped
1	stalk celery, chopped
½	small fennel bulb (8 ounces), trimmed and chopped
1	medium onion, chopped
1½	teaspoons chopped fresh thyme or ¼ teaspoon dried thyme
2	cups regular long-grain rice
1	can (14½ ounces) chicken broth or 1¾ cups Chicken Broth (page 84)
¾	teaspoon salt
¼	teaspoon coarsely ground black pepper

1. Rinse wild rice; drain. In 3-quart saucepan, combine wild rice and 2 cups water; heat to boiling over high heat. Reduce heat; cover and simmer until wild rice is tender and some grains have popped, 45 to 60 minutes. Stir in dried cranberries; heat 1 minute. Drain, if necessary.

2. Meanwhile, in 5-quart Dutch oven, melt butter over medium-high heat. Add carrots, celery, fennel, and onion; cook, stirring, until vegetables are tender and lightly browned, about 20 minutes. Stir in thyme; cook 1 minute. Transfer vegetables to medium bowl.

3. In same 5-quart Dutch oven, combine white rice, broth, and remaining 2 cups water; heat to boiling over high heat. Reduce heat; cover and simmer, without stirring or lifting lid, until rice is tender and all liquid has been absorbed, 18 to 20 minutes. Stir in salt, pepper, wild-rice mixture, and vegetable mixture; heat through. Makes about 12 cups or 12 accompaniment servings.

♥ Each serving: About 240 calories, 5g protein, 44g carbohydrate, 5g total fat (3g saturated), 10mg cholesterol, 354mg sodium.

Couscous

Couscous is not a grain, but a tiny pasta made from semolina flour. Here's a basic recipe and some mouthwatering variations.

Prep: 5 minutes   Cook: 5 minutes

1¼	cups water
¼	cup dark seedless raisins or dried currants (optional)
1	tablespoon butter or margarine
¾	teaspoon salt
1	cup couscous (Moroccan pasta)

In 3-quart saucepan, combine water, raisins if using, butter, and salt; heat to boiling over high heat. Stir in couscous. Remove from heat; cover and let stand 5 minutes. Makes about 3 cups or 4 accompaniment servings.

♥ Each serving: About 226 calories, 6g protein, 43g carbohydrate, 3g total fat (2g saturated), 8mg cholesterol, 471mg sodium.

Lime Couscous
Prepare couscous as directed but omit raisins and add **1 tablespoon fresh lime juice** and **½ teaspoon freshly grated lime peel** to water.

Moroccan Couscous
Prepare couscous as directed but add **¼ teaspoon ground cinnamon, ¼ teaspoon ground turmeric (optional), and ¼ teaspoon ground cumin** to water.

Dried Tomato and Green Onion Couscous
Prepare couscous as directed but omit raisins and add **1 green onion,** sliced, and **5 dried tomato halves,** chopped, to water.

Dried-Cherry Couscous
Prepare couscous as directed but substitute ¼ **cup dried tart cherries** for raisins.

Creamy Polenta

Polenta has long been a popular staple in Northern Italy and now Americans love it, too. Our method ensures lump-free results. Serve with your favorite roasted or grilled bird.

Prep: 5 minutes   Cook: 30 minutes

2	cups cold water
1	teaspoon salt
1½	cups yellow cornmeal
4½	cups boiling water
½	cup freshly grated Parmesan cheese
4	tablespoons butter or margarine, cut into pieces

1. In 5-quart Dutch oven, combine cold water and salt. With wire whisk, gradually beat in cornmeal until smooth. Whisk in boiling water. Heat to boiling over high heat. Reduce heat to medium-low and cook, stirring frequently with wooden spoon, until mixture is very thick, 20 to 25 minutes.

2. Stir Parmesan and butter into polenta until butter has melted. Serve immediately. Makes 8 accompaniment servings.

Each serving: About 173 calories, 5g protein, 20g carbohydrate, 8g total fat (5g saturated), 20mg cholesterol, 464mg sodium.

Broiled Polenta Wedges

Line 13" by 9" baking pan with foil, extending foil over rim. Prepare Creamy Polenta as directed but use only **3½ cups boiling water** and cook until mixture is very thick and indentation remains when a spoon is dragged through polenta, 30 to 35 minutes. Stir in Parmesan and butter as directed. Spoon mixture into prepared pan, smoothing top. Refrigerate until very firm, at least 1 hour. Preheat broiler. Lift foil with polenta from baking pan; place on cookie sheet. Cut polenta into 16 triangles; separate triangles. Brush **1 tablespoon melted butter or margarine** on polenta wedges. Broil about 5 to 7 inches from heat source until lightly browned and heated through, about 10 minutes.

Each serving: About 186 calories, 5g protein, 20g carbohydrate, 9g total fat (6g saturated), 24mg cholesterol, 479mg sodium.

Rosemary Polenta Wedges

Prepare Broiled Polenta Wedges as directed but add ½ **teaspoon chopped fresh rosemary** or ¼ **teaspoon dried rosemary,** crumbled, to melted butter.

Puffy Cheddar Grits

Serve this cheese-filled casserole for brunch along with bacon and sausages or as a side dish for dinner. If you wish, refrigerate the cooked grits overnight and bake them the next morning for brunch; just add twenty minutes to the baking time.

Prep: 20 minutes   Bake: 45 minutes

3½	cups milk
2	cups water
2	tablespoons butter or margarine
1	teaspoon salt
1¼	cups quick-cooking grits
8	ounces Cheddar cheese, shredded (2 cups)
5	large eggs
1	teaspoon hot pepper sauce
¼	teaspoon ground black pepper

1. Preheat oven to 325°F. Grease shallow 2½-quart casserole. In 3-quart saucepan, combine 1½ cups milk, water, butter, and salt; heat to boiling over medium-high heat. With wire whisk, gradually stir in grits, beating constantly to prevent lumps. Reduce heat; cover and cook, stirring occasionally with wooden spoon, 5 minutes (grits will be very stiff). Remove from heat; stir in Cheddar.

2. In large bowl, with wire whisk, mix eggs, remaining 2 cups milk, hot pepper sauce, and pepper until blended. Gradually stir grits mixture into egg mixture.

3. Pour grits mixture into prepared casserole. Bake until knife inserted in center comes out clean, about 45 minutes. Makes 8 main-dish servings.

Each serving: About 338 calories, 16g protein, 24g carbohydrate, 20g total fat (11g saturated), 185mg cholesterol, 604mg sodium.

Creamy Polenta with Sausage and Mushrooms

Creamy Polenta with Sausage and Mushrooms

To keep its texture creamy, prepare the polenta just before serving.

	Prep: 25 minutes Cook: 40 minutes
1	pound sweet Italian-sausage links, casings removed
1	pound mushrooms, trimmed and sliced
1	medium onion, chopped
2	garlic cloves, finely chopped
¼	teaspoon coarsely ground black pepper
1	can (28 ounces) plum tomatoes in puree
	Creamy Polenta (opposite)
2	tablespoons chopped fresh parsley

1. Heat 12-inch skillet over medium-high heat until hot. Add sausage; cook, stirring frequently to break up sausage, until browned, about 10 minutes. With slotted spoon, transfer sausage to bowl.

2. Discard all but 1 tablespoon drippings from skillet. Add mushrooms, onion, garlic, and pepper. Cook, stirring occasionally, until vegetables are golden and mushroom liquid has evaporated, about 10 minutes. Stir in tomatoes with their puree; heat to boiling over high heat, breaking up tomatoes with side of spoon. Return sausage to skillet. Reduce heat; cover and simmer 10 minutes.

3. Meanwhile, prepare Creamy Polenta as directed. Serve polenta topped with sausage mixture and sprinkled with parsley. Makes 4 main-dish servings.

Each serving: About 737 calories, 31g protein, 64g carbohydrate, 40g total fat (18g saturated), 108mg cholesterol, 2,031mg sodium.

Spoonbread

Soft enough to eat with a spoon, this Southern classic is a cross between a bread and a soufflé.

	Prep: 15 minutes plus standing Bake: 40 minutes
3	cups milk
1/2	teaspoon salt
1/4	teaspoon ground black pepper
1	cup cornmeal
4	tablespoons butter or margarine, cut into pieces
3	large eggs, separated

1. Preheat oven to 400°F. Generously grease shallow 1½-quart baking dish.

2. In 4-quart saucepan, combine milk, salt, and pepper; heat to boiling over medium-high heat. Remove from heat; with wire whisk, whisk in cornmeal. Add butter, stirring until melted. Let stand 5 minutes.

3. Whisk egg yolks into cornmeal mixture, one at a time, until blended. In small bowl, with mixer at high speed, beat egg whites just until soft peaks form when beaters are lifted. Gently fold egg whites, one-half at a time, into cornmeal mixture. Pour evenly into prepared baking dish. Bake until spoonbread is set, about 40 minutes. Serve immediately. Makes 8 accompaniment servings.

Each serving: About 203 calories, 7g protein, 18g carbohydrate, 11g total fat (6g saturated), 108mg cholesterol, 272mg sodium.

Spoonbread

Mushroom-Barley Pilaf

Serve barley instead of rice for a flavorful change of pace.

	Prep: 15 minutes Cook: 55 minutes
1	cup pearl barley
2	tablespoons butter or margarine
1	medium onion, chopped
2	stalks celery, cut into 1/4-inch-thick slices
12	ounces mushrooms, trimmed and sliced
1	can (14½ ounces) chicken or vegetable broth or 1¾ cups Chicken Broth (page 84) or Vegetable Broth (page 83)
3/4	cup water
1/2	teaspoon salt
1/8	teaspoon dried thyme
1/8	teaspoon ground black pepper
1/4	cup chopped fresh parsley

1. In 3-quart saucepan, toast barley over medium heat, shaking pan occasionally, until barley begins to brown, about 4 minutes. Transfer to bowl.

2. In same saucepan, melt butter over medium heat. Add onion and celery; cook until onion is tender, about 5 minutes. Stir in mushrooms; cook until mushrooms are tender and liquid has evaporated. Stir in barley, broth, water, salt, thyme, and pepper. Heat to boiling over high heat. Reduce heat; cover and simmer until barley is tender, about 30 minutes. Stir in parsley. Makes 4 cups or 6 accompaniment servings.

♥ Each serving: About 187 calories, 6g protein, 32g carbohydrate, 5g total fat (3g saturated), 10mg cholesterol, 536mg sodium.

Kasha with Mushrooms

Sautéed onion, red pepper, and mushrooms pair ideally with kasha's earthy flavor. The egg helps keep the kasha grains separate; if you prefer, use two egg whites instead of the whole egg.

Prep: 10 minutes   Cook: 20 minutes

3	tablespoons butter or margarine
4	ounces mushrooms, trimmed and sliced
1	small red pepper, chopped
1	small onion, finely chopped
1	large egg
1	cup medium-grain kasha
2	cups boiling water
1	teaspoon salt

1. In 10-inch skillet, melt 2 tablespoons butter over medium heat. Add mushrooms, red pepper, and onion; cook, stirring occasionally, until onion is tender, about 5 minutes.

2. Meanwhile, in small bowl, lightly beat egg. Add kasha and stir until grains are well coated.

3. Push vegetables to one side of skillet. Add remaining 1 tablespoon butter to other side of skillet. Add kasha and cook, stirring constantly, until grains have become separate and dry, about 2 minutes. Stir in boiling water and salt; heat to boiling over high heat. Reduce heat; cover and simmer until kasha is tender, 10 to 12 minutes. Makes about 5 cups or 8 accompaniment servings.

Each serving: About 147 calories, 5g protein, 21g carbohydrate, 6g total fat (3g saturated), 38mg cholesterol, 347mg sodium.

Basic Bulgur

Bulgur takes only minutes to prepare. It's nutritious and has a pleasant nutty flavor.

Prep: 2 minutes   Cook: 20 minutes

1	can (14½ ounces) chicken broth or 1¾ cups Chicken Broth (page 84)
¼	cup water
¼	teaspoon dried thyme
	pinch ground nutmeg
1	cup bulgur wheat

In 2-quart saucepan, combine broth, water, thyme, and nutmeg; heat to boiling over high heat. Stir in bulgur. Reduce heat; cover and simmer until liquid has been absorbed, 10 to 15 minutes. Makes 3 cups or 4 accompaniment servings.

Each serving: About 133 calories, 5g protein, 27g carbohydrate, 1g total fat (0g saturated), 0mg cholesterol, 434mg sodium.

Bulgur Pilaf with Apricots

A taste of the Middle East—perfect with lamb or chicken or as part of a vegetarian feast.

Prep: 15 minutes   Cook: 30 minutes

2	tablespoons butter or margarine
1	medium onion, chopped
1	cup bulgur wheat
1	can (15 to 19 ounces) garbanzo beans, rinsed and drained
⅓	cup chopped dried apricots
1	can (14½ ounces) chicken or vegetable broth or 1¾ cups Chicken Broth (page 84) or Vegetable Broth (page 83)
1	cinnamon stick (3 inches)
¼	teaspoon salt
⅛	teaspoon ground black pepper
¼	cup chopped fresh parsley

1. In 3-quart saucepan, melt butter over medium heat. Add onion and cook, stirring frequently, until tender, about 5 minutes. Add bulgur and cook, stirring, 2 minutes longer.

2. Stir in beans, apricots, broth, cinnamon stick, salt, and pepper; heat to boiling over high heat. Reduce heat; cover and simmer 15 minutes. Remove from heat and let stand 15 minutes. With fork, stir in parsley and fluff. Discard cinnamon stick. Makes 3 cups or 6 accompaniment servings.

Each serving: About 206 calories, 7g protein, 33g carbohydrate, 6g total fat (3g saturated), 10mg cholesterol, 515mg sodium.

Quinoa

Quinoa, (KEEN-wah) is the tiniest grain known. It should be rinsed in a fine-mesh sieve before cooking to remove its natural coating, saponin, which is slightly bitter.

Prep: 10 minutes   Cook: 25 minutes

1	cup quinoa
1¾	cups water
¾	teaspoon salt
3	ears corn, husks and silk removed
1	tablespoon butter or margarine
4	green onions, sliced
¼	teaspoon black pepper
½	teaspoon freshly grated lemon peel

1. In sieve, rinse quinoa with cold running water. In 2-quart saucepan, combine water, quinoa, and ½ teaspoon salt; heat to boiling over high heat. Reduce heat; cover and simmer until water has been absorbed, about 15 minutes.

2. Meanwhile, cut corn kernels from cobs. In 10-inch skillet, melt butter over medium-high heat. Add corn, green onions, remaining ¼ teaspoon salt, and pepper. Cook, stirring frequently, until corn is tender-crisp, about 3 minutes. Stir in lemon peel. Add quinoa and cook, stirring, until evenly combined. Makes about 5 cups or 6 accompaniment servings.

♥ Each serving: About 188 calories, 6g protein, 34g carbohydrate, 4g total fat (1g saturated), 5mg cholesterol, 340mg sodium.

Wheat Berries with Brown Butter and Pecans

Wheat berries have an appealing chewy texture. Combining them with pecans and brown butter brings out the grain's nutty flavor.

Prep: 10 minutes plus overnight to soak   Cook: 1 hour 20 minutes

1	cup wheat berries (whole-grain wheat)
2	tablespoons butter or margarine
1	medium onion, chopped
½	cup pecans, coarsely chopped
½	teaspoon salt
⅛	teaspoon ground black pepper
1	tablespoon water
2	tablespoons chopped fresh parsley

1. In medium bowl, soak wheat berries overnight in enough *water to cover by 2 inches*. Drain.

2. In 3-quart saucepan, combine wheat berries and *3 cups water*; heat to boiling over high heat. Reduce heat; cover and simmer until wheat berries are tender but still firm to the bite, about 1 hour. Drain.

3. In same clean saucepan, melt butter over medium heat. Add onion and cook, stirring frequently, until tender, about 5 minutes. Stir in pecans, salt, and pepper. Cook, stirring, until pecans are lightly toasted and butter begins to brown, about 3 minutes. Stir in wheat berries and water; heat through. Stir in parsley. Makes 3½ cups or 6 accompaniment servings.

Each serving: About 212 calories, 5g protein, 27g carbohydrate, 11g total fat (3g saturated), 10mg cholesterol, 233mg sodium.

Hazelnut-Honey Granola

Eat this granola as a snack, or serve as a breakfast cereal.

Prep: 20 minutes   Bake: 30 to 35 minutes

3	cups old-fashioned oats, uncooked
¾	cup honey
4	tablespoons butter or margarine, melted
1½	teaspoons vanilla extract
1	cup hazelnuts (filberts) and/or whole natural almonds, coarsely chopped
½	cup toasted wheat germ
½	cup sesame seeds
1	cup dried tart cherries (4 ounces) or dark seedless raisins
½	cup dried apricots (3 ounces), thinly sliced
½	cup golden raisins

1. Preheat oven to 350°F. In two jelly-roll pans, bake oats, stirring twice, until lightly toasted, about 15 minutes.

2. In large bowl, combine honey, butter, and vanilla. Add toasted oats, hazelnuts, wheat germ, and sesame seeds, stirring to coat. Spread mixture evenly in same jelly-roll pans.

3. Bake, stirring every 5 minutes, until mixture is dark golden brown, 15 to 20 minutes. Cool granola in pans on wire racks. Transfer granola to bowl and stir in cherries, apricots, and raisins. Store in airtight container. Makes 9 cups.

Each ¼ cup: About 118 calories, 2g protein, 18g carbohydrate, 5g total fat (1g saturated), 3mg cholesterol, 15mg sodium.

Stir-Fried Tofu with Vegetables

Here is a great way to show what a super meat substitute firm tofu is. If you wish, vary the vegetables. Small broccoli flowerets or zucchini strips can stand in for the carrots and mushrooms.

Prep: 25 minutes   Cook: 15 minutes

1	cup chicken or vegetable broth
1	tablespoon soy sauce
1	tablespoon brown sugar
2	teaspoons cornstarch
½	teaspoon salt
2	teaspoons vegetable oil
2	teaspoons Asian sesame oil
1	package (16 ounces) firm tofu, drained and cut cut into 1" by ½" pieces
1	large carrot, peeled and thinly sliced
1	red pepper, cut into 1-inch pieces
3	green onions, thinly sliced
2	garlic cloves, finely chopped
1	tablespoon minced, peeled fresh ginger
8	ounces mushrooms, trimmed and thinly sliced

1. In 2-cup measuring cup, combine broth, soy sauce, brown sugar, cornstarch, and salt until well blended.

2. In nonstick 12-inch skillet, heat vegetable and sesame oils over medium-high heat. Add tofu and cook, stirring frequently (stir-frying), until heated through and lightly browned, about 4 minutes. Transfer to bowl. Add carrot, red pepper, green onions, garlic, and ginger to skillet and stir-fry until vegetables are tender-crisp, about 3 minutes longer.

3. Add mushrooms and stir-fry 3 minutes. Add broth mixture and tofu and stir-fry until sauce has thickened slightly and boils, about 3 minutes. Makes 4 main-dish servings.

Each serving: About 269 calories, 20g protein, 18g carbohydrate, 15g total fat (2g saturated), 0mg cholesterol, 828mg sodium.

Stir-Fried Tofu with Vegetables

Tofu "Egg Salad"

The familiar egg-salad seasonings lend themselves well to tofu. Serve in pita breads with lettuce and tomatoes for a light lunch.

Prep: 15 minutes

1	package (16 ounces) firm tofu, drained
1	stalk celery, chopped
½	small red pepper, finely chopped
1	green onion, chopped
¼	cup lowfat mayonnaise dressing
½	teaspoon salt
⅛	teaspoon turmeric

In medium bowl, with fork, mash tofu until it resembles scrambled eggs; stir in celery, red pepper, green onion, mayonnaise, salt, and turmeric. Cover and refrigerate up to 1 day if not serving right away. Makes 4 main-dish servings.

Each serving: About 195 calories, 18g protein, 10g carbohydrate, 11g total fat (1g saturated), 0mg cholesterol, 455mg sodium.

11

VEGETABLES

In kitchens across America, vegetables no longer play second fiddle at the dinner table. Cooks are preparing lighter meals and looking for ways to serve more vegetables as part of a well-balanced, healthful diet. While this chapter concentrates on vegetables as accompaniments to meat, poultry, and fish, you'll also find a selection of delicious vegetable main dishes and appetizers. And there are many other examples of vegetables as primary ingredients in other chapters, too.

Vegetables that were once considered exotic are now everyday fare. And what was old is new again, as farmers' markets offer intriguing and delicious heirloom vegetables: flavorful old varieties grown from old seeds that have never been hybridized. We offer recipes for an interesting array of vegetables, but we know that we're only scratching the surface. If you shop at an ethnic market, you will see even more vegetables than we have room to discuss here. A knowledgeable clerk can help you identify any unfamiliar varieties and perhaps even offer a recipe or two.

Vegetables are often grouped according to their family: onions, leafy greens, cruciferous (cabbage, broccoli, and cauliflower), fruits with seeds that aren't sweet and are therefore treated like vegetables (eggplants, peppers, and tomatoes), roots (carrots, turnips, and the like), stalks (such as asparagus

Baked Artichokes with Parmesan Stuffing

and celery), tubers (starchy potatoes and sweet potatoes), and mushrooms. To make them easy for you to locate, the vegetables in this chapter are listed alphabetically.

BUYING AND STORING VEGETABLES

When buying vegetables, appearance is usually the best indication of freshness. Avoid bruised vegetables or those with soft spots. Leafy tops should be crisp and fresh looking. Prepackaged vegetables in bags aren't always a good choice because you can't inspect them thoroughly. And some vegetables are covered with a thin edible wax coating that seals in their moisture and gives them a fake sheen.

Organic produce is available at natural food stores and, increasingly, at supermarkets. These vegetables and fruits have been grown without the use of chemical fertilizers or pesticides. They are not only healthier to eat, they often taste better. As with organic meat, there are no federal regulations, and the agricultural standards vary from state to state. Because organic farming is labor-intensive and the yields are usually relatively low, organic vegetables and fruits are more expensive than those grown by high-production methods.

Refrigeration is the key to keeping most vegetables in prime condition, because they deteriorate rapidly at room temperature. Store them in the coolest part of the refrigerator (usually the bottom shelf) or the crisper drawer. Don't store vegetables in airtight plastic bags: Condensation forms in the bags and encourages their rapid decay. The exception is leafy greens: They wilt in the presence of oxygen. To store greens, wrap them loosely in paper towels and enclose in a plastic bag, pressing out all the air. Mushrooms should be kept in a brown paper bag so they can breathe. It is best to store potatoes, onions, garlic, and winter squash in a dark well-ventilated place at cool room temperature.

PREPARING VEGETABLES

Wash vegetables briefly just before using. Vegetables should not be soaked: They will get waterlogged and their nutrients will leach out into the water. Usually a quick rinse under cold running water is all that is needed. If necessary, a gentle scrub with a soft vegetable brush will remove any surface dirt that is difficult to detect. When washing leafy greens, use several changes of cool water (which loosens any dirt hiding in crevices better than cold water).

Cut or peel vegetables as close to serving time as possible. Once the skin on vegetables is broken, they begin to lose valuable nutrients. Use a stainless steel knife: Carbon steel discolors many vegetables. Some vegetables, such as artichokes and cardoons, discolor when exposed to air. To prevent discoloration, rub the cut surfaces with the cut half of a lemon: The acid in the juice counteracts browning. Peeled potatoes can be held in cold water to cover for up to several hours.

Not all vegetables require peeling. But you may want to peel certain vegetables if their peel is tough or unpleasant-tasting. It is important to remove as thin a layer of peel as possible; a vegetable peeler is the best choice. Knives often remove more of the vegetable than is desirable.

Vegetables should be cut into uniform pieces to ensure even cooking. If you are making soup or preparing a recipe for which evenly cut pieces aren't important, use a food processor. But food processors aren't good for every vegetable. Onions, for example, release too much juice when processed.

COOKING VEGETABLES

Roasting, stir-frying, microwaving, and grilling: These are just a few of the many ways to prepare vegetables. In this chapter, we have used the cooking method that best suits each recipe. To help you along, here is some basic information about the most popular cooking techniques.

The most common way to cook vegetables is in boiling water, which yields the brightest color, best texture, and freshest flavor. Be sure to use a minimum amount of water so the vitamins and minerals aren't released into the cooking water. We do not always salt the water. Salt can draw out the juices, affecting the texture, and some vegetables contain enough natural sodium to make additional salting unnecessary. Time the vegetables from the moment the water returns to a full boil. Cover the pot to speed up the process. While vegetables can be cooked to any degree of doneness you like, remember that overcooking destroys nutrients. We recommend cooking most vegetables until tender-crisp. Drain the vegetables well; reserve the cooking liquid for soups, sauces, stocks, or stews.

If you are cooking vegetables ahead of time, drain and then rinse them under cold running water to stop the cooking and set the color. Pat the vegetables dry with paper towels, and store in ziptight plastic bags in the refrigerator for up to one day. To reheat, heat 1 to 2 tablespoons of butter, margarine, or olive oil in a large skillet over medium-high heat. Add the vegetables and cook, stirring occasionally, just until heated through. Season with salt and pepper and, if you wish, sprinkle with chopped fresh herbs: Dill, tarragon, parsley, and basil are just some of your choices.

Microwave-cooked vegetables are cooked in a very small amount of liquid, resulting in vibrant color and great flavor. To microwave vegetables, cut them into uniform pieces and spread in a single layer in a microwave-safe dish. Add 3 to 4 tablespoons of lightly salted water, broth, or stock. Cover with plastic wrap or a lid, leaving a corner vented. The exact cooking time will depend on the wattage of your microwave oven—the higher the wattage, the shorter the time. Cook on high, turning the dish occasionally (unless your microwave has a self-turning carousel), until the vegetables are tender-crisp. When you begin to smell the vegetables, start checking for doneness, but be very careful of the released steam.

When vegetables are roasted, their colors intensify: The high temperature and dry heat encourage their natural sugars to caramelize. Firm vegetables, such as asparagus and winter squash, are ideal candidates, though many other vegetables can be roasted with great success. Preheat the oven to 450°F. In one or two large shallow baking dishes or heavy roasting pans, toss the vegetables with 1 to 2 tablespoons of olive oil and season with salt and pepper. Roast the vegetables, stirring occasionally, until lightly browned and tender. Depending on the vegetable, this can take anywhere from fifteen minutes to one hour or longer. If roasting both soft and hard vegetables, roast the hard vegetables first, then add the soft ones later.

Grilling is another cooking technique that exposes vegetables to direct heat, bringing out their sweet flavor in the process. When grilling vegetables, use medium heat, or the vegetables may scorch before they are cooked through. The vegetables should be tossed with oil before cooking or brushed with oil during cooking. In any case, oil the grill rack well so the vegetables don't stick.

Stir-frying is an ideal way to cook vegetables and is also speedy. The proper cooking vessel is important: If there isn't enough room, the ingredients will steam rather than fry. Use a very large skillet (at least 12 inches) or wok; if you use a non-stick pan, you will need less oil. There are two key elements to successful stir-frying: Each ingredient should be cut into small uniform pieces so they all cook in the same amount of time, and the pan should be as hot as possible without smoking so the cooking is fast. In the skillet, heat 1 tablespoon of vegetable oil over medium-high heat until very hot, but not smoking. If you wish, add some chopped garlic and/or ginger to the pan to add an Asian flavor; stir-fry until fragrant. Add the vegetables and stir-fry for one minute. Add ¼ to ½ cup water (depending on the amount of vegetables) and cook, stirring almost constantly, until the water has evaporated and the vegetables are tender-crisp. (If the vegetables are done before the water has evaporated, drain them before serving.)

ARTICHOKES

Availability
Year round

Peak Season
March, April, and May

Buying Tips
Buy compact, plump artichokes that are heavy for their size. The leaves should be thick, tightly closed, and evenly colored. Don't worry about brown spots or streaks: They are usually caused by frost. Avoid artichokes with dry, spreading, or hard-tipped leaves. An artichoke's size depends on where it grows on the plant. *Baby artichokes,* which are entirely edible, grow near the base between the leaves and the stalk, while larger ones grow higher up on the stalk.

To Store
Refrigerate in the crisper drawer up to three days.

To Prepare
Rinse the artichokes. Bend back the outer green leaves from around the base of an artichoke and snap them off. With kitchen shears, trim the thorny tops from the remaining outer leaves, rubbing all the cut surfaces with a lemon half to prevent browning. Lay the artichoke on its side and cut off the stem level with the bottom of the artichoke. Cut 1 inch off the top of the artichoke, then place in a bowl containing cold water and the juice of the remaining lemon half. Repeat with the remaining artichokes.

To Cook
Artichokes are often steamed or boiled, then served with a dip such as lemon butter. To steam artichokes, in a nonreactive 5-quart saucepot, heat 1 inch of water and 1 tablespoon lemon juice to boiling over high heat. Stand artichokes in boiling water. Reduce heat; cover and simmer until a knife inserted in bottom of an artichoke goes in easily, 30 to 40 minutes. Drain and cool. Cooked artichokes (remove the center leaves and choke) can also be stuffed and baked.

To Eat

With your fingers, starting at the bottom, pluck off the leaves one by one until you reach leaves that are too thin to eat. Dip the base of each leaf in a dip or sauce, if using, then pull the leaf through your teeth, scraping off the pulp. Place the discarded leaves in a pile on your plate. Pull out all the remaining thin leaves from the artichoke to reveal the fuzzy choke. With the tip of a teaspoon, scrape out the choke and discard. Cut the solid heart into chunks and enjoy.

Braised Baby Artichokes with Olives

An Italian-inspired way to cook baby artichokes—accented with garlic and olives.

Prep: 20 minutes   Cook: 15 minutes

2	pounds baby artichokes (about 16)
1	lemon, cut in half
¼	cup olive oil
3	garlic cloves, sliced
1	cup water
½	teaspoon salt
½	teaspoon coarsely ground black pepper
⅓	cup oil-cured olives, pitted and coarsely chopped

1. Trim artichokes: Bend back outer green leaves and snap off at base until remaining leaves are green on top and yellow on bottom. Cut off stems level with bottom of artichoke. Cut off top half of each artichoke and discard. Rub cut surfaces with lemon half to prevent browning. Cut each artichoke lengthwise in half or into quarters if large, dropping them into bowl of cold water and juice of remaining lemon half.

2. In nonstick 12-inch skillet, heat *1 inch water* to boiling over high heat. Drain artichokes and add to skillet; cook 5 minutes; drain. Wipe skillet dry with paper towels.

3. In same skillet, heat oil over medium-high heat. Add garlic and cook until golden. Add artichokes; cook until lightly browned, about 2 minutes. Stir in water, salt, and pepper; cover and cook until knife inserted in bottom of artichoke goes in easily, about 5 minutes longer. Stir in olives and heat through. Makes 8 first-course servings.

Each serving: About 103 calories, 2g protein, 6g carbohydrate, 9g total fat (1g saturated), 0mg cholesterol, 383mg sodium.

Baked Artichokes with Parmesan Stuffing

(pictured on page 400)

The simple bread stuffing, seasoned with Parmesan cheese, anchovies, and pine nuts is a classic match for artichokes. If serving as a first course, use six small artichokes.

Prep: 1 hour   Bake: 15 minutes

4	large artichokes
1	lemon, cut in half
2	tablespoons fresh lemon juice
4	slices firm white bread, coarsely grated (opposite)
2	tablespoons olive oil
2	large garlic cloves, finely chopped
4	anchovy fillets, chopped
½	cup pine nuts (pignoli), lightly toasted, or walnuts, toasted and chopped
⅓	cup freshly grated Parmesan cheese
2	tablespoons chopped fresh parsley
¼	teaspoon salt
¾	cup chicken broth

1. Trim artichokes: Bend back outer green leaves from around base of artichoke and snap off. With kitchen shears, trim thorny tops from remaining outer leaves, rubbing all cut surfaces with lemon half to prevent browning. Lay artichoke on its side and cut off stem level with bottom of artichoke.

Peel stem; place in bowl of cold water and juice of remaining lemon half. Cut 1 inch off top of artichoke; add artichoke to lemon water. Repeat with remaining artichokes.

2. In nonreactive 5-quart saucepot, heat *1 inch water* and 1 tablespoon lemon juice to boiling over high heat. Stand artichokes in boiling water; add stems and heat to boiling. Reduce heat; cover and simmer until knife inserted in bottom of artichoke goes in easily, 30 to 40 minutes. Drain. When cool

enough to handle, pull out prickly center leaves from each artichoke and, with teaspoon, scrape out fuzzy choke (without cutting into heart) and discard. Finely chop stems.

3. Meanwhile, preheat oven to 400°F. Spread grated bread in jelly-roll pan. Place in oven and toast until golden, about 5 minutes.

4. In 1-quart saucepan, heat oil over medium heat. Add garlic and cook 1 minute. Add anchovies and cook, stirring, until garlic is golden and anchovies have almost dissolved.

5. In medium bowl, combine toasted bread, pine nuts, Parmesan, parsley, chopped artichoke stems, garlic mixture, salt, ¼ cup broth, and remaining 1 tablespoon lemon juice.

6. Pour remaining ½ cup broth into 13" by 9" baking dish; stand artichokes in dish. Spoon bread mixture between artichoke leaves and into center cavities. Bake until stuffing is golden and artichokes are heated through, 15 to 20 minutes. Makes 4 main-dish servings.

Each serving: About 359 calories, 17g protein, 35g carbohydrate, 20g total fat (4g saturated), 9mg cholesterol, 934mg sodium.

GRATING FRESH BREAD CRUMBS

Grate firm day-old Italian or French bread on the large holes of a box grater. Or process the bread in a food processor with the knife blade attached to form coarse crumbs. One slice of bread yields about ½ cup crumbs.

Artichokes with Roasted-Red-Pepper-and-Basil Sauce

This dish is great party food. It can be prepared in advance, it's colorful, and it's easy to eat with your fingers.

Prep: 25 minutes	Cook: 35 to 45 minutes
4	medium artichokes
1	lemon, cut in half
2	tablespoons fresh lemon juice
1	jar (7 ounces) roasted red peppers, drained
½	cup light mayonnaise
1	teaspoon sugar
¾	teaspoon salt
½	teaspoon hot pepper sauce
½	cup chopped fresh basil or parsley
	thinly sliced fresh basil leaves (optional)

1. Trim artichokes: Bend back outer green leaves from around base of artichoke and snap off. With kitchen shears, trim thorny tops from outer leaves, rubbing all cut surfaces with lemon half to prevent browning. Lay artichoke on its side and cut off stem level with bottom of artichoke. Cut 1 inch off top of artichoke, then place in bowl of cold water and juice of remaining lemon half. Repeat with remaining artichokes.

2. In nonreactive 5-quart saucepot, heat *1 inch water* and 1 tablespoon lemon juice to boiling over high heat. Stand artichokes in boiling water; heat to boiling. Reduce heat; cover and simmer until knife inserted in bottom of artichoke goes in easily, 30 to 40 minutes. Drain.

3. Meanwhile, in blender or in food processor with knife blade attached, combine roasted red peppers, mayonnaise, remaining 1 tablespoon lemon juice, sugar, salt, and hot pepper sauce and puree until smooth. Spoon red pepper sauce into bowl; stir in chopped basil. Cover and refrigerate. (Makes 1½ cups sauce.)

4. When cool enough to handle, cut each artichoke into 4 wedges. Pull out prickly center leaves and, with teaspoon, scrape out fuzzy choke (without cutting into heart); discard. Serve warm, or cover and refrigerate up to 6 hours. To serve on platter, arrange artichoke wedges around bowl of red pepper sauce. Sprinkle with sliced basil, if desired. Makes 8 first-course or accompaniment servings.

Each serving: About 90 calories, 2g protein, 11g carbohydrate, 5g total fat (1g saturated), 5mg cholesterol, 434mg sodium.

ASPARAGUS

Availability
Almost Year round

Peak Season
March, April, and May

Buying Tips
Look for bright green, firm, crisp stalks with compact tips and no trace of brown or rust. Buy evenly sized stalks for uniform cooking. White asparagus, imported from Europe, is an expensive delicacy.

To Store
Asparagus is very perishable. Stand the stalks in ½ inch of cold water in a container. Refrigerate up to two days.

To Prepare
Hold the base of each asparagus spear in one hand and bend back the stalk; the end will break off at the spot where the stalk becomes too tough to eat. Discard the tough stem. Rinse well to remove any sand. Some cooks like to peel asparagus, but this is a matter of personal choice. Leave asparagus whole or cut diagonally into 1- to 2-inch pieces.

To Cook
Asparagus can be boiled, steamed, stir-fried, roasted, or grilled. Serve hot, room temperature, or cold. To boil, in a 12-inch skillet, heat 1 inch of water to boiling over high heat. Add asparagus and ½ teaspoon salt; heat to boiling. Reduce heat to medium-high and cook, uncovered, until barely tender, 5 to 10 minutes (depending on the thickness of asparagus); drain. If serving cold, rinse under cold running water to stop cooking; drain again.

Asparagus with Lemon-Caper Vinaigrette

Delicious served cold or at room temperature.

Prep: 10 minutes   Cook: 10 minutes

3	pounds asparagus, trimmed
¾	teaspoon salt
1	large lemon
2	tablespoons capers, drained and chopped
2	teaspoons Dijon mustard
1	teaspoon sugar
¼	teaspoon coarsely ground black pepper
3	tablespoons olive oil

1. In 12-inch skillet, heat *1 inch water* to boiling over high heat. Add asparagus and ½ teaspoon salt; heat to boiling. Reduce heat and simmer until tender, 5 to 10 minutes. Drain and rinse with cold running water. Drain.

2. Meanwhile, prepare vinaigrette: From lemon, with vegetable peeler, remove 3 strips (3" by 1" each) peel. Cut strips lengthwise into slivers. From lemon, squeeze 2 tablespoons juice. In bowl, with wire whisk, mix lemon juice, capers, mustard, sugar, remaining ¼ teaspoon salt, and pepper until blended. In thin, steady stream, whisk in oil until blended.

3. Place asparagus on platter. Pour vinaigrette over asparagus; toss to coat. Sprinkle lemon peel slivers over top. Serve at room temperature, or cover and refrigerate up to 3 hours. Makes 10 accompaniment servings.

Each serving: About 64 calories, 3g protein, 5g carbohydrate, 4g total fat (1g saturated), 0mg cholesterol, 218mg sodium.

Sesame Stir-Fried Asparagus

Thin asparagus, which cooks quickly and requires little advance preparation, is the ideal candidate for stir-frying.

Prep: 15 minutes   Cook: 5 minutes

1	tablespoon vegetable oil
½	teaspoon Asian sesame oil
1	pound thin asparagus, trimmed and cut on diagonal into 1-inch pieces
¼	teaspoon salt
1	tablespoon sesame seeds, toasted

In 10-inch skillet, heat vegetable and sesame oils over high heat until hot. Add asparagus and sprinkle with salt; cook, stirring frequently, until tender-crisp, about 5 minutes. Transfer to serving bowl and sprinkle with toasted sesame seeds. Makes 4 accompaniment servings.

Each serving: About 68 calories, 3g protein, 4g carbohydrate, 5g total fat (1g saturated), 0mg cholesterol, 145mg sodium.

Roasted Asparagus

This could easily become your favorite way to prepare asparagus.

Prep: 12 minutes   Roast: 20 minutes

2	pounds asparagus, trimmed
1	tablespoon olive oil
½	teaspoon salt
¼	teaspoon coarsely ground black pepper
	freshly grated lemon peel (optional)
	lemon wedges

1. Preheat oven to 450°F.
2. In large roasting pan (17" by 11½"), toss asparagus, oil, salt, and pepper until coated.
3. Roast asparagus, shaking pan occasionally, until tender and lightly browned, about 20 minutes. Sprinkle with grated lemon peel, if you like, and serve with lemon wedges. Makes 6 accompaniment servings.

Each serving: About 47 calories, 4g protein, 5g carbohydrate, 3g total fat (0g saturated), 0mg cholesterol, 195mg sodium.

AVOCADOS

Availability
Year round, but less plentiful in early winter

Buying Tips
The avocado is really a fruit, but because it isn't sweet, we treat it like a vegetable. Avocados must be ripened until they yield to gentle pressure, or they will be flavorless. Buy avocados that are heavy for their size and free of bruises and soft spots. Don't buy very soft avocados—they are overripe. The most common avocado is the *Hass* variety: It has thick pebbled skin that turns dark purple when ripe. The *Fuerte* (also called Florida) avocado is somewhat larger than the Hass and has shiny green skin that doesn't change color when ripe.

To Store
Ripen firm avocados at room temperature. If desired, place in a closed paper bag (this traps the gases given off by the avocado and speeds up the ripening). Ripe avocados can be refrigerated up to three or four days.

To Prepare
Cut the avocado lengthwise in half, cutting around the seed. Twist the two halves to separate. To remove the seed, give it a whack with the blade of a knife, so it is slightly embedded in the seed. Twist and lift out. With your fingers, gently peel away the skin from the avocado and discard. Slice or cut up the avocado, depending on its use. Avocado flesh darkens quickly when exposed to air; toss with lemon or lime juice to discourage discoloration, or press plastic wrap onto the cut surfaces. Avocados lose their flavor when cooked, so they are almost always served raw.

Guacamole

Guacamole is usually served as a dip, but it is also a great accompaniment for fajitas or tacos. For the best results, use Hass avocados. Their buttery, nutty flavor is incomparable.

🕐 *Prep: 20 minutes*

2	ripe avocados, pitted
1	tablespoon fresh lime juice
1	large ripe tomato (10 ounces), chopped
¼	cup chopped green onions
¼	cup chopped fresh cilantro
1 to 2	jalapeño chiles, seeded and minced
¾	teaspoon salt
	tortilla chips or cut-up vegetables

With spoon, scoop out avocado and place in medium bowl. Mash avocado with lime juice; stir in tomato, green onions, cilantro, jalapeños, and salt. Spoon guacamole into serving bowl; cover and refrigerate up to 2 hours. Serve with tortilla chips or cut-up vegetables. Makes about 2 cups.

Each tablespoon: About 22 calories, 0g protein, 1g carbohydrate, 2g total fat (0g saturated), 0mg cholesterol, 57mg sodium.

BEANS, GREEN AND WAX

Availability
Year round

Peak Season
June, July, and August

Buying Tips
The term *bean* refers to an enormous category of plants with edible seeds, but in some cases the pods are edible, too. When

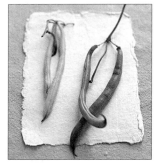

buying fresh *green beans* or *wax beans*, look for crisp, firm pods without any brown spots. You can use the old-fashioned test of breaking a bean in half; it should snap, and beads of moisture should appear at the break. Look for uniformly green or yellow beans. *Purple wax beans* turn green when cooked. Small, thin *haricots verts* aren't as firm as regular green beans, so they cook quickly. Flat *Italian (Romano)* beans are larger and take a bit longer to cook.

To Store
Refrigerate in the crisper drawer up to two or three days.

To Prepare
Rinse the beans under cold running water. Snap off or trim the ends. Leave the beans whole or cut into bite-size pieces.

To Cook
Green and wax beans are most often steamed or boiled, but they can also be roasted or stir-fried. To steam, in a 12-inch skillet, heat 1 inch of water and 1 teaspoon salt to boiling over medium-high heat. Add beans; cover and cook until tender-crisp, 5 to 10 minutes; drain.

Wax and Green Beans with Lemon and Mint

Here, summer garden favorites, wax beans and green beans, are tossed in a piquant lemon dressing

🕐 *Prep: 15 minutes   Cook: 10 minutes*

1¼	teaspoons salt
8	ounces wax beans, trimmed
8	ounces green beans, trimmed
1	lemon
1	tablespoon olive oil
⅛	teaspoon ground coriander
⅛	teaspoon ground black pepper
3	tablespoons chopped fresh mint

1. In 12-inch skillet, heat *1 inch water* and 1 teaspoon salt to boiling over high heat. Add wax and green beans; heat to boiling. Cover and cook until tender-crisp, 6 to 8 minutes.

2. Meanwhile, from lemon, grate ½ teaspoon peel and squeeze 2 teaspoons juice.

3. Drain beans; transfer to serving bowl. While green beans are hot, add oil, remaining ¼ teaspoon salt, coriander, and pepper, tossing to coat. Cool slightly.

4. To serve, add mint and lemon peel and juice, tossing until mixed. Makes 6 accompaniment servings.

Each serving: About 42 calories, 1g protein, 5g carbohydrate, 2g total fat (0g saturated), 0mg cholesterol, 296mg sodium.

Roasted Green Beans with Dill Vinaigrette

Green beans take well to roasting and to our dilled dressing.

Prep: 20 minutes   Roast: 20 to 30 minutes

2	pounds green beans, trimmed
3	tablespoons olive oil
¾	teaspoon salt
2	tablespoons white wine vinegar
1½	teaspoons Dijon mustard
½	teaspoon sugar
½	teaspoon coarsely ground black pepper
2	tablespoons chopped fresh dill

1. Preheat oven to 450°F. In large roasting pan (17" by 11½"), toss green beans, 1 tablespoon oil, and ½ teaspoon salt until coated. Roast, stirring twice, until tender and lightly browned, 20 to 30 minutes.

2. Meanwhile, prepare vinaigrette: In large bowl, with wire whisk, mix vinegar, mustard, sugar, remaining ¼ teaspoon salt, and pepper until blended. In thin, steady stream, whisk in remaining 2 tablespoons oil until blended; stir in dill.

3. When green beans are done, transfer to serving bowl. Drizzle vinaigrette over green beans; toss until coated. Makes 8 accompaniment servings.

Each serving: About 79 calories, 2g protein, 8g carbohydrate, 5g total fat (1g saturated), 0mg cholesterol, 247mg sodium.

Green Beans with Hazelnuts

Green beans are always popular at large holiday get-togethers. Here's a special way to serve them: with a hint of lemon and lots of crunchy toasted nuts.

Prep: 20 minutes   Cook: 15 minutes

1½	teaspoons salt
2	pounds green beans, trimmed
4	tablespoons butter or margarine
⅔	cup hazelnuts (filberts), toasted and skinned (page 729), chopped
1	teaspoon freshly grated lemon peel
¼	teaspoon ground black pepper

1. In 12-inch skillet, heat *1 inch water* and 1 teaspoon salt to boiling over high heat. Add green beans and heat to boiling. Cover and cook until tender-crisp, 6 to 8 minutes. Drain; wipe skillet dry with paper towels.

2. In same skillet, melt butter over medium heat. Add hazelnuts and cook, stirring, until butter just begins to brown, about 3 minutes. Add green beans, lemon peel, remaining ½ teaspoon salt, and pepper. Cook, stirring, until heated through, about 5 minutes. Makes 8 accompaniment servings.

Each serving: About 143 calories, 3g protein, 9g carbohydrate, 12g total fat (4g saturated), 16mg cholesterol, 356mg sodium.

Green Beans Amandine
Prepare as directed but substitute ⅔ **cup slivered almonds,** toasted, for hazelnuts.

Sesame Green Beans

These Asian-inspired green beans are served hot, but they are also delicious at room temperature.

Prep: 15 minutes   Cook: 20 minutes

1	teaspoon salt
1	pound green beans, trimmed
1	tablespoon soy sauce
½	teaspoon Asian sesame oil
1½	teaspoons minced, peeled fresh ginger or ¾ teaspoon ground ginger
1½	teaspoons sesame seeds, toasted

1. In 4-quart saucepan, combine *7 cups water* and salt; heat to boiling over high heat. Add green beans; heat to boiling. Cover and cook until just tender-crisp, 6 to 8 minutes. Drain; return green beans to saucepan.

2. Add soy sauce, sesame oil, and ginger to green beans in saucepan. Cook over low heat, stirring occasionally, until flavors have blended, about 3 minutes. Transfer to serving bowl and sprinkle with sesame seeds. Makes 4 accompaniment servings.

♥ *Each serving: About 45 calories, 2g protein, 8g carbohydrate, 1g total fat (0g saturated), 0mg cholesterol, 553mg sodium.*

BEANS, SHELL

Availability

Limas and other shell beans, August and September; fava beans, late April through July

Buying Tips

The pods of shell beans are discarded; only the plump inner beans are eaten. (The beans of many varieties are also dried.) The most common fresh shell bean varieties include *lima* (pale ivory with a creamy texture; frozen lima beans are a convenient and very good product), *cranberry* (pink- and white-striped beans that are excellent in soups), and *fava* (sometimes called broad beans; pale green, full-flavored beans protected by thick, furry green pods). Look for tender, well-filled pods that contain plump beans. Allow 1 pound of beans (in the shell) for every 2 or 3 servings (2 to 2½ cups) of shelled beans. For fava beans, allow 1 pound of beans (in the shell) for each 1 cup shelled beans.

To Store

Refrigerate shell beans (in their pods) in the crisper drawer up to two days.

To Prepare

Snap off one end of the pod and split the pod open to remove the beans.

To Cook

Shelled fava beans must be individually peeled before cooking (unless the beans are very young and small) because the thin inner skins are tough. Blanch beans in boiling water for 30 to 60 seconds; drain and rinse under cold running water. Pinch beans to squeeze them out of their skins. To steam shelled beans, in a 3-quart saucepan, heat 1 inch of water to boiling over high heat; add beans and heat to boiling. Reduce heat to medium-high and cook until tender, 20 to 30 minutes; drain. Cook fava beans in boiling water until tender, 1 to 3 minutes.

Sautéed Lima Beans with Bacon

You can substitute one and one-half pounds of fresh lima beans or any other shell bean in season for the frozen. Just be sure to shell and cook them first.

Prep: 5 minutes   Cook: 20 minutes

4	slices bacon
1	package (10 ounces) frozen baby lima beans
2	stalks celery, thinly sliced
¼	teaspoon salt
⅛	teaspoon ground black pepper
⅓	cup water

1. In 10-inch skillet, cook bacon over medium heat until browned. With slotted spoon, transfer bacon to paper towels to drain; crumble. Discard all but 1 tablespoon bacon drippings from skillet.

2. To drippings in skillet, add frozen lima beans, celery, salt, and pepper. Cook over medium heat, stirring frequently, until vegetables are tender, about 5 minutes.

3. Add water to skillet; heat to boiling over high heat. Reduce heat and simmer, 5 minutes. Spoon lima bean mixture into serving bowl; sprinkle with crumbled bacon. Makes 4 accompaniment servings.

Each serving: About 156 calories, 7g protein, 19g carbohydrate, 6g total fat (2g saturated), 8mg cholesterol, 314mg sodium.

Peas and Fava Beans

If you make this with fresh fava beans and peas, you'll have an extraordinary dish, but the frozen vegetables are almost as tasty.

Prep: 30 minutes plus cooling   Cook: 12 minutes

4½	pounds fresh fava beans or 2 packages (10 ounces each) frozen baby lima beans
2	ounces pancetta or 2 slices bacon, chopped
1	garlic clove, thinly sliced
1	package (10 ounces) frozen baby peas, thawed
2	tablespoons chopped fresh parsley
¼	teaspoon salt
⅛	teaspoon ground black pepper

Peas and Fava Beans

1. Remove fava beans from shells and place in colander in sink. Meanwhile, in 4-quart saucepan, heat *8 cups water* to boiling over high heat. Pour boiling water over beans. When cool enough to handle, remove outer skins from fava beans. (If using lima beans, cook as label directs.)

2. In 10-inch skillet, cook pancetta and garlic over medium heat, stirring, until pancetta crisps, about 8 minutes.

3. Add peas, parsley, salt, and pepper and cook, stirring, 2 minutes. Add fava beans and cook, stirring, 2 minutes longer. Makes 6 accompaniment servings.

♥ Each serving: About 149 calories, 10g protein, 19g carbohydrate, 4g total fat (1g saturated), 6mg cholesterol, 312mg sodium.

BEETS

Availability
Year round

Peak Season
June through October

Buying Tips
Choose smooth, deeply colored beets without ridges and blemishes; soft spots indicate decay. Buy evenly sized beets for uniform cooking. The green tops, if attached, should be fresh-looking. (They can be cooked separately like other greens; see Stir-Frying 101, page 436.) In addition to the familiar crimson-colored beets, *golden beets* and *striped beets* are often available at specialty food stores and farmers' markets.

To Store
If the tops are attached, trim them, leaving about 1 inch of stem attached (this prevents the beets from "bleeding" and losing color). Place the tops and beets in separate plastic bags. Refrigerate in the the crisper drawer: beets up to one week, tops up to two days (they wilt quickly).

To Prepare
Wash beet tops under cool running water to remove any hidden grit. Scrub beets well under cold running water.

To Cook
Beets can be boiled, but roasting enhances their natural sweetness. Cook beets unpeeled and uncut to retain their color.

When it comes to picking out vegetables, a good rule of thumb is that they feel heavy for their size and are moist (but not wet or sticky). Because vegetables are largely composed of water, this applies to all vegetables, even those as little and light as mushrooms. As their moisture evaporates, vegetables become lighter and drier, losing flavor, weight, and succulence. If you're surprised at how light something is when you pick it up, you may well be holding a vegetable with a hollow center or dryish flesh.

DEBORAH MADISON
COOKBOOK AUTHOR

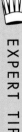

Roasted Beets and Onions

Roasted beets have a deep purple color and virtually burst with sweetness. The balsamic vinegar sauce enhances their naturally rich flavor.

Prep: 20 minutes plus cooling	Roast/Cook: 1 hour 40 minutes
2	bunches beets with tops (2 pounds)
3	small red onions (1 pound), not peeled
2	tablespoons extravirgin olive oil
1/3	cup chicken broth
1/4	cup balsamic vinegar
1	teaspoon brown sugar
1	teaspoon fresh thyme
1/4	teaspoon salt
1/4	teaspoon coarsely ground black pepper
1	tablespoon chopped fresh parsley

1. Preheat oven to 400°F.

2. Trim all but 1 inch of stems from beets. Place beets and onions in nonstick oven-safe 10-inch skillet (if skillet is not oven-safe, wrap handle with double layer of foil) or in 13" by 9" baking pan; drizzle with oil. Roast, shaking skillet occasionally, until onions have softened and beets are tender, about 1 hour 30 minutes, transferring vegetables to plate as they are done.

3. In same skillet, combine broth, vinegar, brown sugar, and thyme; heat to boiling over high heat. Boil, stirring and scraping bottom of skillet, until vinegar mixture is dark brown and syrupy and has reduced to about 1/4 cup, 5 to 7 minutes; stir in salt and pepper. Remove from heat.

4. When cool enough to handle, peel beets and onions. Cut beets into 1/4-inch-wide matchstick strips and onions into thin rounds; place in bowl. Pour vinegar mixture over vegetables and toss until coated. Sprinkle with parsley. Makes 6 accompaniment servings.

Each serving: About 103 calories, 2g protein, 14g carbohydrate, 5g total fat (1g saturated), 0mg cholesterol, 203mg sodium.

Harvard Beets

This classic sweet-and-sour dish is a tried-and-true way to add beets to your vegetable repertoire.

Prep: 15 minutes plus cooling	Cook: 45 to 55 minutes
1	bunch beets with tops (1 pound)
1/3	cup cider vinegar
1/4	cup sugar
1	tablespoon cornstarch
1/2	teaspoon salt
1	tablespoon butter or margarine, cut into pieces

1. Trim all but 1 inch of stems from beets. In 4-quart saucepan, combine beets and enough *water* to cover; heat to boiling over high heat. Reduce heat; cover and simmer until tender, 20 to 30 minutes. Drain, reserving 1/3 cup beet liquid. When cool enough to handle, peel beets and cut into 1/4-inch-thick slices.

2. In nonreactive 2-quart saucepan, blend reserved beet liquid, vinegar, sugar, cornstarch, and salt until smoth. Add butter; heat to boiling over medium heat, stirring until sauce has thickened and boils. Reduce heat and simmer 1 minute. Add beets; cook until heated through. Makes 4 accompaniment servings.

♥ *Each serving: About 104 calories, 1g protein, 20g carbohydrate, 3g total fat (2g saturated), 8mg cholesterol, 352mg sodium.*

Pickled Beets

Sweet pickled beets are right at home at a summer barbecue. The cooking time will vary depending on the size of the beets.

Prep: 20 minutes plus overnight to chill	Cook: 45 minutes
2	bunches beets with tops (2 pounds)
3/4	cup cider vinegar
1/2	cup sugar
1	tablespoon pickling spices

1. Trim all but 1 inch of stems from beets. In 5-quart Dutch oven, combine beets and enough *water* to cover; heat to boiling over high heat. Reduce heat; cover and simmer until tender, 20 to 30 minutes. Drain, reserving 2 cups beet liquid. When cool enough to handle, peel beets and cut into 1/4-inch-thick slices. Place in medium bowl.

2. In nonreactive 1-quart saucepan, heat reserved beet liquid, vinegar, sugar, and pickling spices over medium heat, stirring frequently, just until sugar has dissolved; pour over beets. Stir gently to combine, then cool to room temperature. Cover and refrigerate overnight or up to 1 week. Makes 8 accompaniment servings.

 Each serving: About 71 calories, 1g protein, 18g carbohydrate, 0g total fat (0g saturated), 0mg cholesterol, 33mg sodium.

BOK CHOY

Availability
Year round

Buying Tips
Look for bok choy in Asian markets and large supermarkets. Select heads with crisp white stalks and bright green leaves, which may be slightly wilted. Avoid bok choy that has any brown spots.

To Store
Refrigerate in the the crisper drawer up to three days.

To Prepare
Separate the stalks and tops; cut into ½-inch-thick slices.

To Cook
Bok choy is almost always stir-fried with Asian seasonings to enhance its mild flavor. Cook the stems first, then add the tender tops at the end.

When preparing sautéed or baked vegetables, toss in a clove of peeled garlic and a sprig or two of fresh thyme or half a sprig of rosemary. Just remember to discard the garlic and herbs before serving.

DANIEL BOULUD
CHEF/OWNER, DANIEL AND CAFÉ BOULUD,
NEW YORK CITY

EXPERT TIP

Stir-Fried Bok Choy

This is the classic Chinese preparation, and it is as delicious as it is simple.

 Prep: 10 minutes   Cook: 10 minutes

1	head bok choy (2 pounds)
1	tablespoon vegetable oil
1	garlic clove, crushed with side of chef's knife
2	tablespoons soy sauce

1. Cut bok choy stalks from leaves; cut stalks and leaves, separately, into ½-inch-thick slices.

2. In 10-inch skillet, heat oil over medium-high heat. Add garlic and cook until golden. Add bok choy stalks and cook, stirring frequently (stir-frying), until just tender, about 4 minutes. Add bok choy leaves and stir-fry until wilted, about 2 minutes longer. Stir in soy sauce and remove from heat. Makes 4 accompaniment servings.

Each serving: About 62 calories, 3g protein, 5g carbohydrate, 4g total fat (0g saturated), 0mg cholesterol, 644mg sodium.

BROCCOFLOWER

Availability
October through February

Buying Tips
Even though its fluorescent-green color is reminiscent of broccoli, this brightly colored vegetable is related to cauliflower. Look for firm heads with tightly packed flowerets and no browning. The leaves should look crisp.

To Store
Place in a plastic bag with a few holes poked in it. Refrigerate in the crisper drawer up to two days.

To Prepare
Discard the leaves; cut into bite-size flowerets or keep whole.

To Cook
Cook like cauliflower (boil, steam, or roast), keeping in mind that, when cooked, broccoflower turns deep green.

BROCCOLI

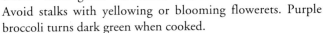

Availability
Year round

Peak Season
October through February

Buying Tips
Look for firm stalks with tightly closed dark green flowerets. Avoid stalks with yellowing or blooming flowerets. Purple broccoli turns dark green when cooked.

To Store
Place in a plastic bag with a few holes poked in it. Refrigerate in the crisper drawer up to two days.

To Prepare
Remove the large leaves and trim the ends of the stalks if woody. Cut the broccoli tops into 2-inch flowerets. Peel the stalks and cut into ¼- to ½-inch-thick slices.

To Cook
Broccoli can be stir-fried, but it is often boiled and served with a sauce or butter and lemon. To cook, in a skillet, heat 1 inch of water to boiling over high heat; add broccoli stalks and heat to boiling. Cook 1 minute. Add flowerets and heat to boiling. Reduce heat to medium-low; cover and cook until broccoli is tender-crisp, about 5 minutes. Drain.

Stir-Fried Broccoli

The heat is high and the cooking fast in this flavorful stir-fry, so measure out all the ingredients beforehand.

 Prep: 10 minutes   Cook: 6 minutes

1	medium bunch broccoli (1 pound)
1	tablespoon vegetable oil
1	teaspoon minced, peeled fresh ginger
1	garlic clove, finely chopped
⅛	teaspoon crushed red pepper
¼	teaspoon salt
⅓	cup water

1. Cut broccoli into 2-inch flowerets; peel stalks and cut into ¼-inch-thick slices.

2. In 12-inch skillet, heat oil over high heat until hot. Stir in ginger, garlic, and crushed red pepper; cook until very fragrant, about 10 seconds. Add broccoli and salt; cook, stirring frequently (stir-frying), until broccoli is well coated with oil, about 1 minute. Add water and stir-fry until broccoli is tender-crisp and water has evaporated (if water evaporates before broccoli is done, add a little water), about 4 minutes longer. Makes 4 accompaniment servings.

Each serving: About 55 calories, 2g protein, 5g carbohydrate, 4g total fat (0g saturated), 0mg cholesterol, 165mg sodium.

BROCCOLI RABE

Availability
Year round

Buying Tips
This slightly bitter green is also called *broccoli raab, broccoli rabe,* and *broccoli di rape.* The leaves should be perky, with thin green stalks and small bud clusters. Avoid stalks with yellowish leaves.

To Store
Place in a plastic bag with a few holes poked in it. Refrigerate in the crisper drawer up to two days.

To Prepare
Trim stems and discard any tough leaves. Wash in several changes of cold water to remove any grit.

To Cook
Broccoli rabe is cooked like other leafy greens. In a large skillet, heat ½ inch of water to boiling; add broccoli rabe and heat to boiling. Reduce heat to medium-high and cook until stems are almost tender, about 5 minutes; drain well. Wipe skillet dry. In same skillet, cook some chopped garlic in olive oil until golden. Stir in broccoli rabe; cook, stirring, until heated through. Season with salt and pepper.

Broccoli Rabe with Garbanzo Beans

For a quick main course, toss this combination of pleasantly bitter greens and garbanzo beans with your favorite pasta.

Prep: 10 minutes	Cook: 18 minutes
2	bunches broccoli rabe (1¼ pounds each), trimmed
2½	teaspoons salt
2	tablespoons olive oil
3	garlic cloves, crushed with side of chef's knife
¼	teaspoon crushed red pepper
1	can (15 to 19 ounces) garbanzo beans, rinsed and drained

1. In 8-quart saucepot, heat *4 quarts water* to boiling over high heat. Add broccoli rabe and 2 teaspoons salt; heat to boiling. Cook until thickest part of stems is tender, about 3 minutes. Drain, reserving ¼ cup cooking water. Cool slightly, then cut into 1½-inch pieces.

2. Wipe saucepot dry with paper towels; add oil and heat over medium heat. Add garlic and cook until golden. Add crushed red pepper and cook 15 seconds. Add broccoli rabe, garbanzo beans, reserved cooking water, and remaining ½ teaspoon salt. Cook, stirring, until heated through, about 3 minutes. Makes 8 accompaniment servings.

Each serving: About 93 calories, 5g protein, 10g carbohydrate, 4g total fat (0g saturated), 0mg cholesterol, 378mg sodium.

BRUSSELS SPROUTS

Availability
Year round, except June and July

Peak Season
October through January

Buying Tips
Purchase firm, bright green sprouts with tight outer leaves.

Avoid soft sprouts or any with black spots. Brussels sprouts are usually available in 10-ounce boxes, but some farmers' markets sell them still attached to their long stalks.

To Store
Refrigerate in the crisper drawer up to two days.

To Prepare
Trim off any yellow or wilted leaves, and trim the stem end. Cut a shallow X in the stem end to shorten the cooking time. Rinse well under cold running water.

To Cook
Brussels sprouts are usually boiled, but for a delicious change of pace, thinly slice and sauté until tender. For steamed Brussels sprouts with the freshest flavor, cook the sprouts just until tender-crisp; long cooking brings out their strong flavor and unappealing sulfurous aroma. In a large saucepan, heat 1 inch of water to boiling over high heat; add Brussels sprouts and heat to boiling. Reduce heat to medium-high. Cover and cook until tender-crisp, about 10 minutes (or a little longer if you prefer very tender sprouts); drain.

Sautéed Brussels Sprouts

In this simple dish, the cabbagelike flavor of Brussels sprouts is tempered by plenty of butter.

Prep: 25 minutes	Cook: 12 minutes
4	tablespoons butter or margarine
3	containers (10 ounces each) Brussels sprouts, trimmed and cut lengthwise into very thin slices
½	teaspoon salt

In 12-inch skillet, melt butter over medium-high heat. Add Brussels sprouts; sprinkle with salt and cook, stirring, until tender-crisp and beginning to brown, 10 to 12 minutes. Makes 10 accompaniment servings.

Each serving: About 74 calories, 3g protein, 7g carbohydrate, 5g total fat (3g saturated), 12mg cholesterol, 182mg sodium.

Brussels Sprouts with Bacon

For many families, Brussels sprouts are a given at the Thanksgiving table. If you wish, prepare ahead through step two, then spend five minutes finishing the cooking.

Prep: 15 minutes	Cook: 25 minutes
3	containers (10 ounces each) Brussels sprouts, trimmed and cut lengthwise in half
6	slices bacon
1	tablespoon olive oil
2	garlic cloves, finely chopped
½	teaspoon salt
¼	teaspoon coarsely ground black pepper
¼	cup pine nuts (pignoli), toasted

1. In 4-quart saucepan, heat *8 cups water* to boiling over high heat. Add Brussels sprouts and heat to boiling. Cook until tender-crisp, about 5 minutes; drain.

2. In 12-inch skillet, cook bacon over medium heat until browned. With slotted spoon, transfer bacon to paper towels to drain; crumble.

3. Discard all but 1 tablespoon bacon drippings from skillet. Add oil and heat over medium-high heat. Add Brussels sprouts, garlic, salt, and pepper. Cook, stirring frequently, until Brussels sprouts are lightly browned, about 5 minutes. To serve, sprinkle with pine nuts and bacon. Makes 10 accompaniment servings.

Each serving: About 96 calories, 5g protein, 8g carbohydrate, 6g total fat (1g saturated), 4mg cholesterol, 202mg sodium.

Brussels Sprouts with Bacon and Chestnuts
Prepare as directed but use **Roasted Chestnuts** (page 426) instead of pine nuts. Cut chestnuts into quarters and add to Brussels sprouts along with garlic, salt, and pepper.

NAPA (CHINESE) CABBAGE

Availability
Year round

Buying Tips
Although Chinese cabbage is cylindrical and napa cabbage is roundish, they are interchangeable in most recipes. Buy crisp, fresh-looking cabbage, free from blemishes. Tiny brown freckles are to be expected.

To Store
Place in a plastic bag with a few holes poked in it. Refrigerate in the crisper drawer up to three days.

To Prepare
Remove any wilted leaves and cut the cabbage lengthwise in half or into quarters. Rinse well. Cut out most of the core and thinly slice or prepare as directed.

Pickled Chinese Cabbage

A cooling dish to serve with spicy Asian-style food.

Prep: 10 minutes plus chilling and overnight to marinate
1	large head napa (Chinese) cabbage (3 pounds)
5	teaspoons salt
1	tablespoon sugar
2	tablespoons distilled white vinegar

1. Trim both ends of cabbage. Cut crosswise into thirds. Cut portion of cabbage containing core lengthwise into quarters; remove core. Wash cabbage and drain. In large bowl, toss cabbage and salt until combined; cover and refrigerate about 3 hours.

2. Drain liquid from cabbage. Add sugar and vinegar to cabbage; toss to mix. Cover and refrigerate overnight, tossing occasionally. Makes 8 accompaniment servings.

Each serving: About 19 calories, 1g protein, 4g carbohydrate, 0g total fat (0g saturated), 0mg cholesterol, 298mg sodium.

Napa Cabbage Stir-Fry

This dish cooks quickly. Don't be fooled by the amount of raw napa cabbage—it shrinks considerably when cooked.

Prep: 20 minutes   Cook: 7 minutes

2	tablespoons vegetable oil
	2-inch piece fresh ginger, peeled and cut into 2" by ⅛" matchstick strips
4	garlic cloves, thinly sliced
1	small head napa (Chinese) cabbage (1 pound), trimmed, cored, and thinly sliced
1	cup shredded carrots (about 2)
½	teaspoon salt
⅛	teaspoon ground red pepper (cayenne)
6	green onions, chopped
1	tablespoon seasoned rice vinegar

In nonstick 12-inch skillet, heat oil over medium-high heat. Add ginger and garlic and cook, stirring frequently (stir-frying), 2 minutes. Add cabbage, carrots, salt, and ground red pepper and stir-fry until cabbage has wilted and softened, about 4 minutes. Stir in green onions and vinegar and stir-fry 1 minute longer. Makes 4 accompaniment servings.

Each serving: About 106 calories, 2g protein, 10g carbohydrate, 7g total fat (1g saturated), 0mg cholesterol, 387mg sodium.

GREEN AND RED CABBAGE

Availability
Year round

Buying Tips
Buy heavy, firm, blemish free heads with tightly packed leaves; the outer leaves of summer-harvested cabbage will be loosely packed and should be crisp and brightly colored. Savoy cabbage is considered the best-tasting green variety; it has crinkly leaves.

To Store
Place in a plastic bag with a few holes poked in it. Refrigerate in the crisper drawer up to one week.

To Prepare
Discard any tough outer leaves. Cut the head into wedges and cut away most of the tough core from each wedge, leaving just enough to hold the cabbage together. With a large knife, thinly slice, or shred in a food processor with the knife blade attached.

To Cook
Cabbage can be boiled, stir-fried, sautéed, braised, or served raw. To retain the color of red cabbage, add a little vinegar or lemon juice while it is cooking.

Braised Sweet-and-Sour Red Cabbage

Here, red cabbage is flavored with apple juice, allspice, and bay leaves—flavors it has a natural affinity for.

Prep: 20 minutes   Cook: 1 hour 30 minutes

3	tablespoons vegetable oil
2	medium onions, chopped
1	pear, peeled, cored, and chopped
2	medium heads red cabbage (2 pounds each), cut into quarters, cored, and thinly sliced
1	can (14½ ounces) beef broth or 1¾ cups Brown Beef Stock (page 83)
1	cup apple juice
⅓	cup cider vinegar
¼	cup packed brown sugar
2	small bay leaves
¾	teaspoon salt
¼	teaspoon coarsely ground black pepper
⅛	teaspoon ground allspice

1. In nonreactive 8-quart saucepot, heat oil over medium heat. Add onions and pear; cook until tender, 10 minutes.

2. Stir in cabbage, broth, apple juice, vinegar, brown sugar, bay leaves, salt, pepper, and allspice; heat to boiling over high heat. Reduce heat; cover and simmer, stirring occasionally, until cabbage is very tender, about 1 hour. Remove cover and cook over medium-high heat, stirring occasionally, until most of liquid has evaporated, about 15 minutes longer. Makes 10 accompaniment servings.

Each serving: About 136 calories, 3g protein, 23g carbohydrate, 5g total fat (1g saturated), 1mg cholesterol, 335mg sodium.

Southern-Style Cabbage

Slowly cooking cabbage makes it tender and sweet.

Prep: 10 minutes   Cook: 40 minutes

4	slices bacon, cut into 1-inch pieces
1	medium head green cabbage (2 pounds), cored and thickly sliced
1	small onion, thinly sliced
½	teaspoon salt
½	cup water

In 5-quart Dutch oven, cook bacon over medium heat until browned. Add cabbage, onion, and salt to bacon in pot; stir to coat cabbage evenly with bacon drippings. Add water and reduce heat to medium-low; cover and cook, stirring occasionally, until cabbage is very tender, 35 to 40 minutes. Makes 6 accompaniment servings.

Each serving: About 120 calories, 3g protein, 8g carbohydrate, 9g total fat (3g saturated), 10mg cholesterol, 319mg sodium.

Hot Slaw with Poppy Seed Dressing

Ham or roast pork will seem even more delicious when served with a helping of this slaw.

Prep: 10 minutes   Cook: 8 minutes

2	tablespoons vegetable oil
½	small head green cabbage (12 ounces), cored and thinly sliced
1	large carrot, peeled and shredded
1	small onion, chopped
2	tablespoons cider vinegar
4	teaspoons sugar
2	teaspoons poppy seeds
½	teaspoon salt

1. In 5-quart Dutch oven, heat oil over medium-high heat. Add cabbage, carrot, and onion and cook, stirring occasionally, until cabbage is tender-crisp, about 5 minutes.

2. Stir in vinegar, sugar, poppy seeds, and salt; cook 2 minutes longer. Makes 4 accompaniment servings.

Each serving: About 123 calories, 2g protein, 14g carbohydrate, 8g total fat (1g saturated), 0mg cholesterol, 312mg sodium.

Cabbage with Ginger and Cumin

Ginger adds a spicy nuance to braised cabbage.

Prep: 10 minutes   Cook: 20 minutes

1	tablespoon butter or margarine
1	tablespoon vegetable oil
1	medium onion, chopped
2	tablespoons minced, peeled fresh ginger
2	garlic cloves, finely chopped
1	medium head green cabbage (2 pounds), cut into quarters, cored, and very thinly sliced
½	teaspoon cumin seeds, crushed
½	teaspoon salt
1	cup water

In 12-inch skillet, melt butter with oil over medium heat. Add onion and cook until tender, about 5 minutes. Stir in ginger and garlic; cook 30 seconds. Stir in cabbage, cumin seeds, and salt; increase heat to medium-high and cook, stirring frequently, until cabbage begins to wilt, about 5 minutes (do not let garlic burn). Add water and cook, stirring occasionally, until cabbage is very tender and water has evaporated, about 10 minutes. Makes 6 accompaniment servings.

Each serving: About 80 calories, 2g protein, 10g carbohydrate, 4g total fat (1g saturated), 5mg cholesterol, 236mg sodium.

Tuscan Cabbage and Beans

Tuscan "grandmother" food—a hearty and satisfying dish that an Italian nonna *might serve.*

Prep: 20 minutes   Cook: 40 minutes

1	tablespoon olive oil
2	small onions, thinly sliced
2	garlic cloves, thinly sliced
1	medium head green cabbage (2 pounds), cored and very thinly sliced
1	can (14½ ounces) diced tomatoes
1	cup water
¾	teaspoon salt
¼	teaspoon ground black pepper
1	can (15 to 19 ounces) white kidney beans (cannellini), rinsed and drained
⅓	cup chopped fresh parsley

In nonstick 12-inch skillet, heat oil over medium heat. Add onions and garlic and cook, stirring, until onions are tender, about 5 minutes. Add cabbage, tomatoes with their juice, water, salt, and pepper; cover and cook, stirring occasionally, until cabbage is very tender, about 30 minutes. Add white kidney beans and all but 1 tablespoon parsley; cook 2 minutes. Transfer to serving bowl and sprinkle with remaining 1 tablespoon parsley. Make 6 accompaniment servings.

♥ Each serving: About 136 calories, 7g protein, 22g carbohydrate, 3g total fat (0g saturated), 0mg cholesterol, 527mg sodium.

CARDOON

Availability
October through February

Buying Tips
Also called *cardoni*. Look for cardoons in Italian markets, especially around Christmas. Buy large, thick, ivory-colored stalks with prickly leaves.

To Store
Refrigerate in the crisper drawer up to five days.

To Prepare
Cardoons discolor when their cut surfaces are exposed to air. To discourage browning, rub the cut surfaces with lemon halves (but even if the surfaces brown, they will turn grayish white when cooked). Separate the stalks, discarding the tough outer ones. Using a vegetable peeler, remove the outer strings.

To Cook
Cardoons are always eaten cooked. In a medium saucepan, heat 1 inch of water to boiling over high heat; add cardoons and heat to boiling. Reduce heat to medium-high and cook until tender, about 20 minutes; drain.

Sautéed Cardoons with Parsley

The unique look and flavor of cardoons make them a treat: They look like stalks of prehistoric celery and taste like artichoke hearts.

Prep: 20 minutes	Cook: 28 minutes
2	lemons, each cut in half
3	pounds cardoons
2	tablespoons salt
2	tablespoons butter or margarine
1	tablespoon chopped fresh parsley

1. Fill large bowl with cold water. Add 3 lemon halves, squeezing juice into water.

2. Remove leaves along edges of cardoon stalks. Remove strings and tough membranes (as you would with celery) and rub stalks as they are cut with remaining lemon half to prevent browning. Cut stalks into 2-inch pieces and place in lemon water to prevent browning.

3. In 8-quart saucepot, combine *4 quarts water* and salt; heat to boiling over high heat. Drain cardoons and add to saucepot. Cook until tender, 15 to 20 minutes. Drain and pat dry with paper towels.

4. In nonstick 12-inch skillet, melt butter over medium heat. Add cardoons and cook, stirring, until heated through and coated with butter, about 2 minutes.

5. To serve, transfer cardoons to serving bowl and sprinkle with parsley. Makes 8 accompaniment servings.

Each serving: About 43 calories, 1g protein, 4g carbohydrate, 3g total fat (2g saturated), 8mg cholesterol, 463mg sodium.

CARROTS

Availability
Year round

Buying Tips
Buy firm, well-formed, bright-colored carrots. Avoid any with yellowish greens or signs of sprouting on the carrots. *Baby carrots* are often available in bunches. *Baby-cut carrots,* sold in plastic bags, should show no sign of moisture.

To Store
Cut off the greens, leaving about 2 inches of stem. Place in a plastic bag. Refrigerate in the crisper drawer up to five days.

To Prepare
Scrub under cold running water or peel. Leave carrots whole or slice, shred, or cut them into pieces.

To Cook
No longer are carrots simply boiled: They are glazed, candied, stir-fried, roasted, shredded, or served as slaw. To serve them the simple old-fashioned way, in a saucepan, heat 1 inch of water to boiling over high heat; add carrots and heat to boiling. Reduce heat to medium-high; cover and cook until tender-crisp, whole carrots about 15 minutes, cut-up carrots, 5 to 10 minutes.

Candied Carrots

This dish is so sweet and delicious, that it will get children of all ages to eat their vegetables.

Prep: 15 minutes   Cook: 25 minutes

1	bag (16 ounces) carrots, peeled
1	lemon
2	tablespoons butter or margarine
3	tablespoons brown sugar

1. Cut each carrot crosswise in half. Cut thick portion of carrots lengthwise in half. In 4-quart saucepan, heat *1 inch water* to boiling over medium heat. Add carrots and heat to boiling. Cover and simmer until tender, about 15 minutes. Drain and return to saucepan.

2. Meanwhile, from lemon, grate ½ teaspoon peel and squeeze 1 teaspoon juice.

3. Add butter, brown sugar, and lemon juice to carrots; cook over medium heat, stirring gently, until sugar has dissolved and carrots are glazed, about 5 minutes.

4. Stir in lemon peel. Makes 4 accompaniment servings.

Each serving: About 133 calories, 1g protein, 20g carbohydrate, 6g total fat (4g saturated), 16mg cholesterol, 98mg sodium.

Ginger Candied Carrots
Prepare as directed but add **1 teaspoon grated, peeled fresh ginger** with butter.

Candied Parsnips
Prepare as directed but substitute **1 pound parsnips,** peeled, for carrots.

Shredded Carrots

The fastest way to cook carrots and also one of the best. Add a pinch each of cloves and ginger for a spicier dish, if you like.

Prep: 5 minutes   Cook: 5 minutes

4	carrots, peeled and shredded (2 cups)
2	tablespoons water
2	tablespoons butter or margarine
1	teaspoon sugar
½	teaspoon salt

In small saucepan, combine carrots, water, butter, sugar, and salt; heat to boiling over high heat. Reduce heat; cover and simmer, stirring occasionally, until carrots are tender, 3 to 4 minutes. Makes 4 accompaniment servings.

Each serving: About 78 calories, 1g protein, 7g carbohydrate, 6g total fat (4g saturated), 16mg cholesterol, 367mg sodium.

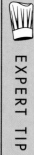

An easy low-calorie vegetable sauce can be made by pureeing boiled vegetables (artichoke hearts, fennel, carrots, celery, pumpkin, or peppers) with a bit of their cooking liquid, some extravirgin olive oil, and salt and pepper until smooth.

DANIEL BOULUD
*CHEF/OWNER, DANIEL AND CAFÉ BOULUD,
NEW YORK CITY*

EXPERT TIP

Hot-and-Sour Carrots

Feel free to add red pepper to your own taste, but do be a little generous—after all, this is called hot-and-sour carrots.

Prep: 15 minutes	Cook: 18 minutes	
1	tablespoon vegetable oil	
1	tablespoon minced, peeled fresh ginger	
2	packages (10 ounces each) shredded carrots (7 cups)	
½	cup rice vinegar	
1	tablespoon sugar	
¼ to ½	teaspoon ground red pepper (cayenne)	
⅛	teaspoon salt	
2	tablespoons chopped fresh cilantro (optional)	

In nonstick 12-inch skillet, heat oil over medium heat. Add ginger and cook, stirring, 3 minutes. Increase heat to medium-high and add carrots, vinegar, sugar, ground red pepper, and salt. Cover and cook until carrots are tender-crisp, about 8 minutes. Remove cover and cook until liquid has evaporated, about 5 minutes longer. Sprinkle with cilantro, if desired. Makes 4 accompaniment servings.

Each serving: About 105 calories, 2g protein, 18g carbohydrate, 4g total fat (0g saturated), 0mg cholesterol, 123mg sodium.

CAULIFLOWER

Availability
Year round

Peak Season
October through January

Buying Tips
Heads should be firm and creamy white with granular-looking flowerets. The leaves should be fresh-looking. Do not buy heads with brown spots or flowering buds. Purple or green cauliflower occasionally shows up at farmers' markets.

To Store
Place in a plastic bag with a few holes poked in it. Refrigerate in the crisper drawer up to five days.

To Prepare
Remove the leaves and cut out the core. Separate the head into flowerets or leave whole. Rinse under cold running water.

To Cook
Cauliflower is frequently boiled, but it's also delicious roasted (see Roasted Cauliflower, page 422). To boil, in a large saucepan, heat 1 inch of water to boiling over high heat; add cauliflower and heat to boiling. Reduce heat to medium-high. Cover and cook whole cauliflower until tender, 10 to 15 minutes, or flowerets until tender-crisp, about 5 minutes; drain well.

Cauliflower Polonaise

This classic dish, a whole head of cauliflower under a buttery crumb topping, has withstood the test of time.

Prep: 30 minutes	Cook: 20 minutes	
1	large head cauliflower (2½ pounds)	
3	tablespoons butter or margarine	
2	slices firm white bread, coarsely grated (page 405)	
2	large eggs, hard-cooked, peeled, and chopped	
2	tablespoons chopped fresh parsley	
½	teaspoon freshly grated lemon peel	
½	teaspoon salt	

1. Remove outer leaves and core of cauliflower, keeping head whole. In 5-quart saucepot, heat *1 inch water* to boiling over high heat; add cauliflower. Reduce heat; cover and simmer until tender, 10 to 15 minutes; drain. Transfer to platter and keep warm.

2. In 10-inch skillet, melt butter over medium heat. Add grated bread and cook, stirring, until golden. Stir in eggs, parsley, lemon peel, and salt.

3. To serve, sprinkle bread mixture over cauliflower. Makes 8 accompaniment servings.

Each serving: About 92 calories, 4g protein, 7g carbohydrate, 6g total fat (3g saturated), 65mg cholesterol, 253mg sodium.

Roasted Cauliflower

Cauliflower becomes lightly browned and tender-crisp when roasted. It's a delicious change from the familiar boiled version.

Prep: 10 minutes   Roast: 23 minutes

1	medium head cauliflower (2 pounds), cut into 1½" flowerets
1	tablespoon olive oil
½	teaspoon salt
¼	teaspoon coarsely ground black pepper
2	tablespoons chopped fresh parsley
1	garlic clove, finely chopped

1. Preheat oven to 450°F. In jelly-roll pan, toss cauliflower, oil, salt, and pepper until evenly coated. Roast until cauliflower is tender, about 20 minutes, stirring halfway through roasting.

2. In small cup, combine parsley and garlic. Sprinkle over cauliflower and stir to mix evenly. Roast 3 minutes longer. Spoon into serving dish. Makes 6 accompaniment servings.

Each serving: About 35 calories, 1g protein, 3g carbohydrate, 2g total fat (0g saturated), 0mg cholesterol, 202mg sodium.

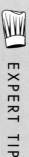

EXPERT TIP

Recently, wild vegetables and weeds that are entirely edible and delicious have been rediscovered. Two of my favorite "weeds," which are showing up in nifty restaurants, are purslane and dandelion. In fact, both are now being cultivated. Purslane grows almost everywhere. Its leaves and stems are juicy and succulent and have a lovely lemon-herb flavor. In Italy, they serve the tender raw leaves sprinkled over salads and crisp-cooked vegetables. And in Mexico, purslane is quickly sautéed with tomatoes, tomatillos, chiles, and the like. Mustard and dandelion greens have become even more mainstream. They're wonderful quickly sautéed with a little bacon and a few drops of a good vinegar. Don't be afraid to ask for or to try some of these former weeds. It's just like back to the future!

JOHN ASH

*CULINARY DIRECTOR,
FETZER VINEYARDS, CALIFORNIA*

Curry-Roasted Cauliflower

*Prepare as directed but substitute **2 tablespoons chopped fresh cilantro** for parsley and add **1 teaspoon curry powder** to garlic mixture.*

Cauliflower with Golden Raisins and Pine Nuts

This Sicilian-inspired side dish has just a touch of anchovy for authentic flavor. If you prefer to omit the anchovy, add a little more salt.

Prep: 20 minutes   Cook: 18 minutes

1	large head cauliflower (2½ pounds), cut into 1½" flowerets
2¼	teaspoons salt
2	tablespoons olive oil
2	garlic cloves, crushed with side of chef's knife
1	teaspoon anchovy paste (optional)
¼	teaspoon crushed red pepper
¼	cup golden raisins
2	tablespoons pine nuts (pignoli), lightly toasted
1	tablespoon chopped fresh parsley

1. In 5-quart Dutch oven, heat *8 cups water* to boiling over high heat. Add cauliflower and 2 teaspoons salt; heat to boiling. Cook until tender, 5 to 7 minutes; drain. Wipe Dutch oven dry.

2. In same Dutch oven, heat oil over medium heat. Add garlic and cook until golden. Add anchovy paste, if using, and crushed red pepper; cook 15 seconds. Add cauliflower, raisins, pine nuts, and remaining ¼ teaspoon salt; cook, stirring, until heated through, about 2 minutes. To serve, sprinkle with parsley. Makes 6 accompaniment servings.

Each serving: About 93 calories, 2g protein, 9g carbohydrate, 6g total fat (1g saturated), 0mg cholesterol, 401mg sodium.

Curried Cauliflower with Potatoes and Peas

Ginger, garlic, cumin, and curry powder give this vegetable medley complex aroma and flavor.

Prep: 25 minutes   Cook: 30 minutes

1	tablespoon vegetable oil
1	large onion (12 ounces), finely chopped
12	ounces all-purpose potatoes (2 medium), peeled and cut into ½-inch pieces
1	tablespoon minced, peeled fresh ginger
2	garlic cloves, finely chopped
1	teaspoon curry powder
¼	teaspoon ground cumin
1½	cups water
1	teaspoon salt
1	medium head cauliflower (2 pounds), cut into small flowerets
1	cup frozen peas
¼	cup chopped fresh cilantro

Curried Cauliflower with Potatoes and Peas

1. In 10-inch skillet, heat oil over medium heat. Add onion and cook until tender, about 5 minutes. Add potatoes, ginger, garlic, curry powder, and cumin; cook, stirring, 2 minutes. Add water and salt; heat to boiling. Reduce heat to medium; cover and cook 10 minutes.

2. Stir in cauliflower; cover and cook until cauliflower is tender, about 10 minutes longer. Stir in frozen peas and cook, uncovered, until most of liquid has evaporated. Stir in cilantro and serve. Makes 8 accompaniment servings.

Each serving: About 83 calories, 3g protein, 14g carbohydrate, 2g total fat (0g saturated), 0mg cholesterol, 322mg sodium.

CELERY

Availability
Year round

Buying Tips
Choose a compact bunch of light-colored, crisp stalks with fresh-looking leaves. (Stalks that are thin and dark-colored can be bitter and stringy.)

To Store
Refrigerate in the crisper drawer up to five days.

To Prepare
Remove the leaves (use in soups or stews) and trim the root end. Rinse the stalks under cold running water. Use the outer stalks for cooking or cut up for salads. Serve the tender inner stalks raw in salads or with dips.

To Cook
To braise as a side dish, cut stalks into 4- to 6-inch pieces and place in shallow baking dish. Add enough chicken broth to come halfway up celery; sprinkle with pepper. Bake at 375°F, basting frequently, until very tender, about 30 minutes.

Braised Celery

This richly flavored, old-fashioned dish will convert even skeptics into celery lovers. It makes a good accompaniment to roast chicken or meat.

Prep: 20 minutes	Cook: 50 minutes
1	bunch celery
1	tablespoon butter or margarine
2	slices bacon, finely chopped
1	small onion, finely chopped
1	small carrot, peeled and finely chopped
1	garlic clove, finely chopped
1	tablespoon tomato paste
½	cup chicken broth
½	cup water
	pinch ground black pepper

1. Trim celery stalks. With knife, remove tough strings from stalks. Cut each stalk crosswise in half.

2. In 12-inch skillet, melt butter with bacon over medium heat. Stir in onion and carrot and cook until vegetables are tender, about 5 minutes. Stir in garlic and cook 30 seconds. Add tomato paste and cook, stirring, 1 minute longer. Stir in broth, water, and pepper; heat to boiling. Stir in celery, spooning vegetable mixture over it; heat to boiling. Reduce heat; cover and simmer until celery is very tender and most of liquid has evaporated, 35 to 40 minutes. Makes 6 accompaniment servings.

Each serving: About 100 calories, 2g protein, 9g carbohydrate, 7g total fat (3g saturated), 10mg cholesterol, 312mg sodium.

Butter-Braised Celery

Here, celery is transformed into a delectable side dish that has a clean and delicate flavor.

Prep: 10 minutes	Cook: 25 minutes
1	bunch celery
½	cup water
2	tablespoons butter or margarine, cut into pieces

1. Trim celery stalks. With knife, remove tough strings from stalks. Cut each stalk lengthwise in half, then cut into ½-inch pieces.

2. In 10-inch skillet, combine celery, water, and butter; heat to boiling over high heat. Reduce heat; cover and simmer until tender, about 15 minutes. Remove cover; increase heat to medium-high and boil just until liquid has evaporated, about 5 minutes. Makes 6 accompaniment servings.

Each serving: About 58 calories, 1g protein, 6g carbohydrate, 4g total fat (2g saturated), 10mg cholesterol, 171mg sodium.

CELERY ROOT (CELERIAC)

Availability
Year round

Peak Season
October through March

Buying Tips
Choose firm, small (less than 4 inches in diameter) celery root knobs that are well shaped (the smoother the knob, the easier it is to peel). If only large celery root is available, remove the center if soft and woody.

To Store
Refrigerate in the crisper drawer up to five days.

To Prepare
Scrub under cold running water. Use a small knife to cut away the peel and root end. Cut as directed. The flesh of celery root discolors when exposed to air. If preparing ahead, place the cut celery root in a bowl containing 4 cups cold water and 2 tablespoons lemon juice or vinegar; set aside until ready to cook. Drain well.

To Cook
Celery root can be served raw (as a salad), boiled, mashed (alone or with potatoes), or braised.

Celery Root Rémoulade

Matchstick strips of celery root wilt and mellow in the mustardy mayonnaise in this classic bistro dish.

Prep: 25 minutes plus chilling

2	tablespoons fresh lemon juice
1½	pounds celery root (celeriac), trimmed and peeled
½	cup mayonnaise
2	tablespoons Dijon mustard
1	tablespoon chopped fresh parsley
¼	teaspoon ground black pepper

1. Pour lemon juice into large bowl. With adjustable-blade slicer or very sharp knife, cut celery root into ⅛-inch-thick matchstick strips. Immediately place celery root in lemon juice as it is cut, tossing to coat completely to prevent celery root from browning.

2. In small bowl, combine mayonnaise, mustard, parsley, and pepper. Add to celery root in bowl and toss to coat. Cover and refrigerate at least 1 hour to blend flavors or up to overnight. Makes 6 accompaniment servings.

Each serving: About 176 calories, 2g protein, 10g carbohydrate, 15g total fat (2g saturated), 11mg cholesterol, 322mg sodium.

Celery Root with Mashed Potatoes

Here, celery root lends its unique celery-parsley flavor to mashed potatoes: One taste, and you'll be hooked.

Prep: 25 minutes   Cook: 25 minutes

2	pounds all-purpose potatoes (6 medium), peeled and cut into 1-inch pieces
2	pounds celery root (celeriac), trimmed, peeled, and cut into ½-inch pieces
4	tablespoons butter or margarine, cut into pieces
1	teaspoon salt
1	cup milk, warmed
2	tablespoons chopped fresh parsley

1. In 4-quart saucepan, combine potatoes, celery root, and enough *water* to cover; heat to boiling over high heat. Reduce heat; cover and simmer until vegetables are tender, about 15 minutes. Drain.

2. Return potatoes and celery root to saucepan. Add butter and salt; mash vegetables, gradually adding warm milk. Mash until mixture is smooth and well blended. Sprinkle with parsley before serving. Makes 8 accompaniment servings.

Each serving: About 175 calories, 4g protein, 26g carbohydrate, 7g total fat (4g saturated), 20mg cholesterol, 468mg sodium.

CHAYOTE

Availability
Year round

Buying Tips
Also called mirliton and christophene, this ridged, pear-shaped dark green squash tastes like summer squash. When buying, choose firm chayote.

To Store
Refrigerate in the crisper drawer up to one week.

To Prepare
Small chayotes have thin skins that do not require peeling. Otherwise, remove the peel with a vegetable peeler or knife. Cut in half and discard the hard central seed; cut as directed.

To Cook
Chayote can be steamed, sautéed, or braised just like summer squash. To roast, brush the cut sides of chayote halves with some fruity olive oil and bake in a preheated 375°F oven until tender, 30 to 40 minutes.

Sautéed Chayote

To retain the chayote's crisp-tender texture and sweet flavor, we give it a quick sauté.

Prep: 10 minutes   Cook: 12 minutes

2	chayotes
1	tablespoon vegetable oil
¼	teaspoon salt
1	garlic clove, finely chopped (optional)
	pinch ground red pepper (cayenne)

1. Peel chayotes and cut each lengthwise in half; remove seeds, if you like. Cut chayotes crosswise into very thin slices.

2. In 10-inch skillet, heat oil over medium heat. Add chayotes and salt. Cook, stirring frequently, until tender and lightly browned, about 10 minutes. Stir in garlic, if using, and ground red pepper; cook, stirring constantly, until fragrant, about 30 seconds longer. Makes 4 accompaniment servings.

Each serving: About 55 calories, 1g protein, 5g carbohydrate, 4g total fat (0g saturated), 0mg cholesterol, 147mg sodium.

CHESTNUTS

Availability
November through January, but most plentiful in November

Buying Tips
Chestnuts are always imported (usually from Italy), so buy them from a store with good turnover to ensure freshness. Buy chestnuts with firm, shiny shells; avoid any with tiny holes. Vacuum-packed chestnuts are acceptable in stuffings, but canned chestnuts don't have much flavor. One pound of fresh chestnuts yields about 2 cups peeled.

To Store
Refrigerate in a brown paper bag up to two weeks.

To Prepare
Chestnuts are always cooked and peeled before eating. The following recipe is the traditional method.

Roasted Chestnuts

Chestnuts are an integral part of cold-weather cooking and can be presented in many guises: in almost any stuffing, added to your favorite vegetable medley, or pureed with sugar and vanilla and served with softly whipped cream for a special dessert.

Prep: 30 minutes   Roast: 20 minutes

1	pound fresh chestnuts

1. Preheat oven to 400°F. With sharp knife, cut an X in flat side of shell of each chestnut. Place in jelly-roll pan and roast chestnuts until shells open, about 20 minutes.

2. Cover chestnuts. When cool enough to handle, with paring knife, peel hot chestnuts, keeping unpeeled chestnuts warm for easier peeling. Makes 2 cups.

Each ½ cup: About 179 calories, 2g protein, 38g carbohydrate, 2g total fat (0g saturated), 0mg cholesterol, 3mg sodium.

CHICORY

Availability
Year round

Buying Tips
Chicory is sometimes called curly endive. Buy heads with curly, spiky, fresh-looking leaves that have dark green tops and pale green ribs.

To Store
Wrap loosely in paper towels and place in a plastic bag. Refrigerate in the crisper drawer up to five days.

To Prepare
Trim the stems. Wash leaves well in several changes of cold water to remove any grit. Tear into bite-size pieces.

To Cook
Serve raw in salads combined with sweet-tasting greens, or cook like other bitter greens.

CORN

Availability
Year round

Peak Season
July through September

Buying Tips
Buy ears that are firm and well shaped under fresh-looking husks with shiny, moist silk. (Unshucked corn stays fresh longer.) Pick ears that look plump, with kernels running to the tops of the ears. Tiny kernels indicate immaturity, but very large deep yellow kernels can be chewy. The fresher the corn, the sweeter the kernels: With age, the sugar in corn converts to starch. Frozen and canned corn kernels are good substitutes for fresh in many recipes, including corn puddings and fritters. Canned baby corn is used in Asian stir-fries. One medium ear of corn yields about ½ cup corn kernels.

To Store
Cook and eat corn as soon as possible after picking. If you must, refrigerate in the crisper drawer up to one or two days.

To Prepare
Shuck the corn and remove the silk just before cooking. (An exception is corn grilled with the husks intact.) To remove the kernels, trim the stalk so you can stand the ear on its end. With a sharp knife, slice down to cut off the kernels, cutting close to the cob.

To Cook
Corn is one of the most versatile vegetables. Sauté the kernels alone or with other vegetables; stir into puddings, fritters, or other batters; or roast or boil on the cob. To boil, in a large saucepot, heat 3 inches of water to boiling over high heat; add shucked corn and heat to boiling. Do not add salt; it toughens corn. Reduce heat to low. Cover and simmer 5 minutes; drain.

Creamy Corn Pudding

This custardy corn dish is perfect with baked ham.

Prep: 30 minutes	Bake: 1 hour 15 minutes
2	tablespoons butter or margarine
1	small onion, chopped
¼	cup all-purpose flour
2	cups half-and-half or light cream, warmed
1	cup milk, warmed
1	package (10 ounces) frozen whole-kernel corn, thawed
4	large eggs
1	teaspoon salt
¼	teaspoon coarsely ground black pepper

1. Preheat oven to 325°F. In 2-quart saucepan, melt butter over medium heat. Add onion and cook until tender and golden, about 10 minutes. Add flour and cook, stirring, 1 minute. With wire whisk, gradually whisk in half-and-half and warm milk; heat to boiling, whisking constantly. Reduce heat and simmer, stirring occasionally, until sauce has thickened and boils, about 5 minutes. Remove from heat; stir in corn, salt, and pepper.

2. In 2-quart casserole, beat eggs lightly. Slowly add corn mixture, beating constantly.

3. Set casserole in 13" by 9" baking pan; place pan on oven rack. Pour enough *boiling water* into pan to come halfway up sides of casserole. Bake until knife inserted in center comes out clean, about 1 hour 15 minutes. Makes 10 accompaniment servings.

Each serving: About 168 calories, 6g protein, 13g carbohydrate, 11g total fat (6g saturated), 112mg cholesterol, 315mg sodium.

Louisiana Maquechoux

This Cajun classic is a colorful mix of corn, red pepper, and onion, with just a touch of cream for a smooth finish.

Prep: 20 minutes   Cook: 45 minutes

1	tablespoon vegetable oil
1	large onion (12 ounces), chopped
1	large red pepper, chopped
5	cups corn kernels cut from cobs (about 8 ears) or 3 packages (10 ounces each) frozen whole-kernel corn
1	can (14½ ounces) diced tomatoes, drained
1½	teaspoons salt
½	teaspoon sugar
	pinch to ¼ teaspoon ground red pepper (cayenne)
¼	cup half-and-half or light cream
	chopped fresh parsley (optional)

1. In nonstick 12-inch skillet, heat oil over medium-high heat. Add onion and red pepper; cook, stirring, until vegetables are tender and well browned, about 15 minutes.

2. Add corn, tomatoes, salt, sugar, and ground red pepper to onion mixture, stirring to mix. Heat to boiling over high heat. Reduce heat; cover and simmer, stirring occasionally, until corn is tender, about 20 minutes (10 minutes if using frozen corn).

3. Stir in half-and-half; heat through. Sprinkle with parsley, if you like. Makes 8 accompaniment servings.

♥ Each serving: About 133 calories, 4g protein, 24g carbohydrate, 4g total fat (1g saturated), 3mg cholesterol, 539mg sodium.

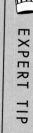

When grilling vegetables, you can never grill too many! The leftovers have many uses. They can be added to a salad or turned into one with the addition of fresh herbs, olive oil, and vinegar. If you have just a few leftover vegetables, dress them with a vinaigrette and some capers and pile on crusty bread or toss with spaghetti for a light meal. Or turn them into a delicately smoky vegetable soup.

DEBORAH MADISON
COOKBOOK AUTHOR

EXPERT TIP

West Texas Creamed Corn

This mildly spiced version of creamed corn is loaded with flavor and is terrific made with either fresh or canned corn.

Prep: 20 minutes   Cook: 20 minutes

3	tablespoons butter or margarine
1	large onion (12 ounces), finely chopped
1	jalapeño chile, seeded and finely chopped
1	garlic clove, finely chopped
2	tablespoons all-purpose flour
¾	teaspoon ground coriander
¾	teaspoon ground cumin
¼	teaspoon salt
⅛	teaspoon ground red pepper (cayenne)
1	cup milk, warmed
4	cups corn kernels cut from cobs (about 6 ears) or 2 cans (15¼ to 16 ounces each) whole-kernel corn, drained
3	ounces Monterey Jack cheese, shredded (¾ cup)
2	tablespoons chopped fresh cilantro plus additional leaves

1. In 3-quart saucepan, melt butter over medium heat. Add onion and jalapeño; cook, stirring occasionally, until tender, about 5 minutes. Add garlic; cook 1 minute. Add flour, coriander, cumin, salt, and ground red pepper and cook, stirring, 1 minute. With wire whisk, gradually whisk in warm milk; heat to boiling, whisking constantly. Add corn; reduce heat and simmer, stirring occasionally, until sauce has thickened and boils, about 5 minutes. Remove saucepan from heat.

2. Add Monterey Jack and all but 1 teaspoon chopped cilantro; stir until cheese has melted. Sprinkle with remaining 1 teaspoon cilantro and garnish with cilantro leaves. Makes 8 accompaniment servings.

Each serving: About 188 calories, 7g protein, 22g carbohydrate, 10g total fat (5g saturated), 27mg cholesterol, 201mg sodium.

Grilled Sweet Corn

Corn is especially tasty when grilled with fresh herbs tucked in.

Prep: 20 minutes plus soaking   Grill: 30 to 40 minutes

8	ears corn, with husks and silk
3	tablespoons olive oil
	basil, rosemary, sage, and/or thyme sprigs

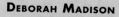

1. Prepare grill. In 8-quart saucepot, place unhusked corn and enough *water* to cover; soak 15 minutes.

2. Remove corn from water and drain. Gently pull husks back three-fourths of way; remove silk. With pastry brush, brush each ear with some oil. Rewrap corn with husks, tucking in several herb sprigs between corn and husk on each ear. Remove thin strip of husk from each ear and use to tie tops of husks together.

3. Place corn on grill over medium heat. Grill, turning corn occasionally, until tender, 30 to 40 minutes. Makes 8 accompaniment servings.

Each serving: About 164 calories, 5g protein, 27g carbohydrate, 6g total fat (1g saturated), 0mg cholesterol, 22mg sodium.

Sautéed Fresh Corn

While this is a fine way to cook raw corn, it's also a very clever way to heat up the kernels cut from leftover corn on the cob.

Prep: 15 minutes   Cook: 5 minutes

2	tablespoons butter or margarine
4	cups corn kernels cut from cobs (about 6 ears)
½	teaspoon salt
¼	teaspoon coarsely ground pepper
¼	cup chopped fresh chives or thinly sliced green onions

In 10-inch skillet, melt butter over medium-high heat. Add corn, salt, and pepper and cook, stirring frequently, until tender, about 4 minutes. Remove from heat and stir in chives. Makes 4 accompaniment servings.

Each serving: About 238 calories, 7g protein, 41g carbohydrate, 8g total fat (4g saturated), 16mg cholesterol, 381mg sodium.

CUCUMBERS

Availability
Year round

Peak Season
June through September

Buying Tips
Pick firm, uniformly slender cucumbers. Overmature cucumbers, which are generally seedy, are dull or yellowish and have an overgrown, puffy look. Smaller varieties, such as *Kirbys*, are preferred for pickling. *English (seedless) cucumbers* are long and slender and have very small seeds that do not have to be removed.

To Store:
Refrigerate in the crisper drawer up to one week.

To Prepare
Rinse cukes under cold running water; scrub Kirbys with a vegetable brush. If the skin is tender and unwaxed (Kirbys and seedless varieties), cucumbers do not have to be peeled. Simply trim the ends and cut the cucumber as desired. To remove the seeds, cut the cucumber lengthwise in half and scoop out the seeds with spoon.

To Cook
Cucumbers are well known as a salad ingredient, but they can also be sautéed alone or with other vegetables. When cooked, they have a mild squashlike flavor.

Sautéed Cucumbers with Dill

Cooked cucumbers are an excellent match for fish.

Prep: 10 minutes   Cook: 10 minutes

3	medium cucumbers (8 ounces each)
1	tablespoon butter or margarine
½	teaspoon salt
1	tablespoon chopped fresh dill, parsley, or mint
¼	teaspoon coarsely ground black pepper

1. Peel cucumbers; cut each lengthwise in half and remove seeds. Cut crosswise into ½-inch-thick slices.

2. In 10-inch skillet, melt butter over medium-high heat. Add cucumbers and salt; cook, stirring frequently, just until cucumbers begin to brown, about 8 minutes. Remove from heat. Sprinkle with dill and pepper and stir to combine. Makes 6 accompaniment servings.

Each serving: About 33 calories, 1g protein, 4g carbohydrate, 2g total fat (1g saturated), 5mg cholesterol, 219mg sodium.

Stir-Fried Cucumbers and Radishes

With just one taste of this unusual stir-fry, you'll be hooked. Chinese hoisin sauce is an easy way to add lots of flavor and is readily found in supermarkets.

Prep: 10 minutes plus standing	Cook: 8 minutes

1	large English (seedless) cucumber, thinly sliced
1¼	teaspoons salt
1	tablespoon vegetable oil
4	large radishes, each trimmed, cut in half, and thinly sliced
2	bunches watercress (4 ounces each), tough stems trimmed
1	tablespoon hoisin sauce
⅛	teaspoon ground red pepper (cayenne)

1. In colander over bowl, toss cucumber and 1 teaspoon salt; let stand 20 minutes at room temperature. Discard liquid in bowl. Pat cucumber dry with paper towels.

2. In 12-inch skillet, heat oil over medium heat. Add cucumber and radishes and cook, stirring frequently (stir-frying), until tender, about 4 minutes. Add watercress, hoisin sauce, remaining ¼ teaspoon salt, and ground red pepper and stir-fry until watercress has wilted, about 2 minutes. Serve hot. Makes 6 accompaniment servings.

Each serving: About 44 calories, 2g protein, 4g carbohydrate, 2g total fat (0g saturated), 0mg cholesterol, 466mg sodium.

EGGPLANT

Availability
Year round

Peak Season
July through October

Buying Tips
Eggplant should be firm and shiny with a bright green cap and no scars, cuts, or bruises. It should feel heavy for its size. Varieties include the familiar plump oval dark purple *Mediterranean*, the slender light purple *Japanese*, and the round green *Thai* eggplant.

To Store
Refrigerate in the crisper drawer up to one week.

To Prepare
Rinse under cold running water. Do not peel eggplant unless the skin seems tough. Some recipes call for salting eggplant, which draws out the water and any bitter juices. Slice or cut eggplant as desired just before cooking; it discolors quickly.

To Cook
Braise, grill, bake, sauté, or roast eggplant. It is often combined with tomato, zucchini, or roasted peppers.

Caponata

Caponata (which gets its name from the capers in the dish) has an intriguing sweet-and-sour flavor. Serve it as part of a cold antipasto, spread it on bruschetta, or offer it as a first course.

Prep: 30 minutes plus cooling	Roast/Cook: 45 minutes

2	small eggplants (1 pound each), ends trimmed and cut into ¾-inch pieces
½	cup extravirgin olive oil
¼	teaspoon salt
3	small red onions, thinly sliced
1½	pounds ripe tomatoes (4 medium), peeled, seeded, and chopped
1	cup olives, such as Gaeta, green Sicilian, or Kalamata, pitted and chopped
3	tablespoons capers, drained
3	tablespoons golden raisins
¼	teaspoon coarsely ground black pepper
4	stalks celery with leaves, thinly sliced
⅓	cup red wine vinegar
2	teaspoons sugar
¼	cup chopped fresh flat-leaf parsley

1. Preheat oven to 450°F. In two jelly-roll pans, place eggplant, dividing evenly. Drizzle with ¼ cup oil and sprinkle with salt, tossing to coat. Roast eggplant 10 minutes, stir, and then roast until browned, about 10 minutes longer.

2. Meanwhile, in nonstick 12-inch skillet, heat remaining ¼ cup oil over medium heat. Add onions and cook, stirring, until tender and golden, about 10 minutes. Add tomatoes, olives, capers, raisins, and pepper. Reduce heat; cover and simmer 15 minutes.

3. Add eggplant and celery to skillet and cook over medium heat, stirring, until celery is just tender, 8 to 10 minutes. Stir in vinegar and sugar and cook 1 minute longer. Cool to room temperature, or cover and refrigerate up to overnight. To serve, sprinkle with parsley. Makes about 5 cups.

Each 1/4 cup: About 106 calories, 1g protein, 9g carbohydrate, 8g total fat (1g saturated), 0mg cholesterol, 336mg sodium.

Glazed Japanese Eggplant

The deliciously fragrant and zesty glaze will inspire even the most finicky eaters to clean their plates. Only buy Japanese eggplants for this dish.

Prep: 15 minutes   Cook: 22 minutes
5   medium Japanese eggplants (5 ounces each), each cut lengthwise in half
1   tablespoon minced, peeled fresh ginger
3   garlic cloves, crushed with garlic press
1   tablespoon brown sugar
1/4   teaspoon cornstarch
3   tablespoons soy sauce
1   tablespoon seasoned rice vinegar
1/2   teaspoon Asian sesame oil
2   tablespoons vegetable oil
1/2   cup plus 2 tablespoons water

1. With knife, lightly score cut side of eggplants in crisscross pattern, about 3/4 inch apart, being careful not to cut all the way to edge.

2. In small bowl, combine ginger, garlic, brown sugar, cornstarch, soy sauce, vinegar, and sesame oil until mixed.

3. In nonstick 12-inch skillet, heat 1 tablespoon vegetable oil over medium-high heat. Arrange half of eggplant, cut side down, in skillet; add 1/4 cup water. Cover and cook until tender and lightly browned, 7 to 10 minutes. Transfer eggplant to plate; keep warm. Repeat with remaining 1 tablespoon vegetable oil, remaining eggplant, and 1/4 cup water.

4. Reduce heat to medium. Add soy-sauce mixture and remaining 2 tablespoons water to skillet. Heat to boiling, stirring until sauce has thickened; boil 1 minute. Pour sauce over eggplant. Makes 5 accompaniment servings.

Each serving: About 111 calories, 2g protein, 14g carbohydrate, 6g total fat (1g saturated), 0mg cholesterol, 684mg sodium.

Roasted Eggplant Parmesan

Eggplant Parmesan usually requires lots of frying—but not our streamlined recipe.

Prep: 35 minutes   Roast/Cook: 45 minutes
2   small eggplants (1 1/4 pounds each), cut into 1/2-inch-thick slices
1/4   cup olive oil
1/2   teaspoon salt
1   can (28 ounces) plum tomatoes, drained and chopped
1/4   teaspoon ground black pepper
1/3   cup chopped fresh parsley
4   ounces mozzarella cheese, shredded (1 cup)
1/2   cup freshly grated Parmesan cheese

1. Preheat oven to 450°F. Place eggplant on two large cookie sheets. Brush oil on both sides of eggplant and sprinkle with 1/4 teaspoon salt. Roast 15 minutes; turn slices and roast until eggplant has browned and is tender, 20 to 25 minutes.

2. Meanwhile, in nonstick 12-inch skillet, combine tomatoes, remaining 1/4 teaspoon salt, and pepper; cook over low heat, stirring occasionally, until tomatoes have thickened, about 20 minutes. Stir in parsley.

3. Turn oven control to 400°F. In shallow 2 1/2-quart casserole, layer half of eggplant and top with half of tomato sauce; sprinkle with half of mozzarella. Repeat layers; top with grated Parmesan.

4. Cover loosely with foil. Bake until bubbling, about 10 minutes. Remove casserole from oven and let stand at least 10 minutes before serving. Serve hot or at room temperature. Makes 6 main-dish servings.

Each serving: About 248 calories, 11g protein, 19g carbohydrate, 16g total fat (5g saturated), 21mg cholesterol, 693mg sodium.

BELGIAN ENDIVE

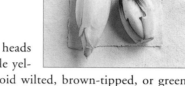

Availability
Year round

Peak Season
September through May

Buying Tips
Choose small compact heads with white leaves and pale yellow or deep red tips. Avoid wilted, brown-tipped, or green outer leaves or heads that are totally pale green. (Belgian endive is grown in the dark; light turns the leaves green and bitter.)

To Store
Wrap in paper towels. Refrigerate in the crisper drawer up to one week.

To Prepare
Trim away any bruised leaves. Rinse briefly under cold running water; Belgian endive is usually quite clean. If using for salad, cut out the tough inner core.

To Cook
Serve Belgian endive raw in salads, with dips, or braise.

Butter-Braised Belgian Endive

Deliciously luxurious is the best way to describe this meltingly tender braised endive.

 Prep: 5 minutes   Cook: 25 minutes

4	tablespoons butter or margarine
½	teaspoon sugar
¼	teaspoon salt
6	large heads Belgian endive, each cut lengthwise in half

In 12-inch skillet, melt butter with sugar and salt over medium-low heat. Arrange endive in skillet in one layer. Cover and cook, turning occasionally, until tender and lightly browned, about 15 minutes. Remove cover; cook until half of liquid has evaporated, about 5 minutes longer. Makes 6 accompaniment servings.

Each serving: About 79 calories, 1g protein, 2g carbohydrate, 8g total fat (5g saturated), 21mg cholesterol, 178mg sodium.

ESCAROLE

Availability
Year round

Peak of Season
October through April

Buying Tips
Like chicory and Belgian endive, escarole's bitterness is its attraction. Look for broad heads of escarole with dark green leaves. If the leaves have white ribs, it indicates that the heads were blanched during cultivation, which is similar to the technique used to keep endive white.

To Store
Refrigerate in open plastic bag up to five days.

To Prepare
Trim stems. Wash well in several changes of cool water to remove any grit. Tear into bite-size pieces.

To Cook
Serve raw in salad combined with sweet-tasting greens, or cook like other bitter greens (See Stir-Frying 101, on page 436).

Escarole with Raisins and Pignoli

Sweet raisins round out the flavor of slightly bitter escarole.

Prep: 10 minutes   Cook: 20 minutes

1	tablespoon olive oil
1	garlic clove, finely chopped
1	large head escarole (1 pound), coarsely chopped
¼	cup golden raisins
¼	teaspoon salt
2	tablespoons pine nuts (pignoli), toasted

In 5-quart Dutch oven, heat oil over medium heat. Stir in garlic and cook just until golden, about 30 seconds. Stir in escarole, raisins, and salt. Cover and cook 5 minutes. Remove cover and cook until escarole is tender and liquid has evaporated, about 10 minutes longer. Stir in pine nuts and remove from heat. Makes 4 accompaniment servings.

Each serving: About 101 calories, 3g protein, 12g carbohydrate, 6g total fat (1g saturated), 0mg cholesterol, 169mg sodium.

FENNEL

Availability
September through April

Buying Tips
Fennel is also called *finocchio*. Buy firm, compact, unblemished bulbs. The fronds, if attached, should be bright green and sprightly.

To Store
Refrigerate in the crisper drawer up to three or four days.

To Prepare
Trim off the fronds, if attached. Rinse fennel under cold running water. Trim the root end and remove the stalks. Cut the bulb lengthwise into wedges or slices; trim the central core.

To Cook
The mild licorice flavor and celerylike texture of fennel is accentuated by roasting. Layer with potatoes in a gratin, or braise (see Braised Celery, page 424).

Roasted Fennel

This side dish can't be beat as the perfect partner for grilled fish. Try it with trout or salmon for pure eating pleasure.

Prep: 10 minutes   Roast: 1 hour
3 medium fennel bulbs (1¼ pounds each), each trimmed and cut into 6 wedges
1 tablespoon olive oil
½ teaspoon salt
¼ teaspoon ground black pepper

1. Preheat oven to 425°F. In jelly-roll pan, toss fennel, oil, salt, and pepper to coat.

2. Roast until fennel is tender and has browned at edges, about 1 hour. Makes 6 accompaniment servings.

Each serving: About 58 calories, 3g protein, 7g carbohydrate, 3g total fat (0g saturated), 0mg cholesterol, 420mg sodium.

Fennel and Potato Gratin

A gratin is simply a dish topped with cheese or bread crumbs, then baked or broiled until crispy. This versatile rendition complements main courses from the simple to the magnificent.

Prep: 20 minutes   Bake: 1 hour 20 minutes
1 medium fennel bulb (1¼ pounds), trimmed and cut lengthwise into very thin slices
1½ pounds all-purpose potatoes (about 4 medium), peeled and very thinly sliced (3½ cups)
1 teaspoon salt
¼ teaspoon ground black pepper
1 cup heavy or whipping cream
1 garlic clove, crushed with side of chef's knife
pinch ground nutmeg
¼ cup freshly grated Parmesan cheese

1. Preheat oven to 400°F. In large bowl, toss fennel, potatoes, salt, and pepper until combined. Spread evenly in shallow 2-quart baking dish. Cover with foil and bake 1 hour.

2. Meanwhile, in 1-quart saucepan, combine cream, garlic, and nutmeg; heat to boiling over high heat. Discard garlic. Pour evenly over fennel-potato mixture; sprinkle with Parmesan. Bake, uncovered, until golden, about 20 minutes longer. Makes 8 accompaniment servings.

Each serving: About 177 calories, 4g protein, 14g carbohydrate, 12g total fat (7g saturated), 43mg cholesterol, 420mg sodium.

Braised Fennel with Parmesan

Easy enough for a weeknight, yet elegant enough for company.

Prep: 15 minutes   Bake: 1 hour

1	wedge Parmesan cheese
3	medium fennel bulbs (1 pound each), trimmed and cut lengthwise into ½-inch-thick slices
⅔	cup chicken broth
⅓	cup water
1	tablespoon butter or margarine, cut into pieces
⅛	teaspoon coarsely ground black pepper

1. Preheat oven to 425°F. With vegetable peeler, remove enough shavings from wedge of Parmesan to measure ½ cup, loosely packed (about 1 ounce).

2. Place fennel in 13" by 9" baking dish. Pour broth and water over fennel and top with butter. Cover with foil.

3. Bake 15 minutes. Remove foil; turn fennel and bake, uncovered, until very tender and liquid has almost been absorbed, 40 to 45 minutes.

4. Arrange Parmesan shavings over fennel and sprinkle with pepper. Bake until Parmesan melts, about 5 minutes longer. Makes 6 accompaniment servings.

Each serving: About 106 calories, 8g protein, 6g carbohydrate, 6g total fat (4g saturated), 15mg cholesterol, 540mg sodium.

GARLIC

Availability
Year round

Buying Tips
A garlic head should be firm, heavy for its size, and enclosed in dry, papery layers. Do not buy heads that have soft spots or are sprouting. Store-bought chopped garlic is a nice convenience, but nothing beats the flavor of freshly chopped garlic.

To Store
Store at cool room temperature in a well-ventilated area; it will keep for several months. Do not refrigerate.

To Prepare
Separate the garlic cloves from the head as needed. To peel, place a clove on the work surface and place the flat side of a large knife on top. Press down on the knife to lightly crush the garlic; remove the peel. See below for roasting whole garlic heads.

To Cook
Garlic is an indispensable seasoning, enhancing everything from soups to sauces. It is often used raw. Whole peeled garlic cloves can also be cooked in oil until golden and then removed, once their flavor has permeated the oil. When cooking garlic, take care not to let it brown, or it could turn bitter. Roasting a whole head of garlic mellows its flavor.

Roasted Garlic

When garlic is roasted, it turns into a soft, spreadable paste with a tantalizingly sweet, mellow flavor. Try it the classic way—spread on grilled or toasted country-style bread. Or, do as chefs do: Toss some of the garlic with cooked vegetables or hot pasta; stir into soups, mashed potatoes or rice; or spread on grilled meat, poultry, or seafood.

Prep: 10 minutes plus cooling   Roast: 1 hour

4	heads garlic
2	tablespoons extravirgin olive oil
⅛	teaspoon salt
⅛	teaspoon coarsely ground black pepper
4	fresh thyme sprigs

1. Preheat oven to 350°F. Remove any loose papery skin from garlic, leaving heads intact. Place garlic on sheet of heavy-duty foil; drizzle with oil and sprinkle with salt and pepper. Place 1 thyme sprig on top of each head.

2. Loosely wrap foil around garlic, folding foil edges securely to keep in oil. Roast until garlic has softened, about 1 hour. Transfer packet to plate. Open carefully and discard foil and herb sprigs.

3. When cool enough to handle, separate garlic into cloves. Squeeze soft garlic from each clove into small bowl. Makes about 1¼ cups.

Each tablespoon: About 25 calories, 1g protein, 3g carbohydrate, 1g total fat (0g saturated), 0mg cholesterol, 16mg sodium.

GREENS

Availability
Year round

Buying Tips
Buy clean, crisp (or tender) leaves, free of decay and dirt. Coarse stems or bruised, dried, or yellowing leaves indicate poor quality. Some greens are quite strongly flavored, even spicy. Popular greens for cooking include the following:

Collard greens Wide dark green leaves with thick stems and a pronounced spiciness.

Dandelion greens Spiky green leaves with a slight lemon flavor. Sometimes served raw in salads.

Kale Curly dark green leaves with a mildly bitter taste. Some purple or variegated kales are grown as ornamentals, but they are edible and have a milder flavor than regular kale. Varieties include *Tuscan kale* and *black kale* (*cavolo nero*).

Mustard greens Spicy and bitter, with large coarse leaves.

Swiss chard Delicately flavored greens with wide curly leaves. The stems are edible and should be cut off and prepared separately. Red Swiss chard has thin red stems and veins.

Also see beet greens (page 411), bok choy (page 413), broccoli rabe (page 414), chicory (page 426), escarole (page 432), napa (Chinese) cabbage (page 416), and spinach (page 459).

To Store
Wrap loosely in paper towels and place in a plastic bag. Refrigerate in the crisper drawer up to two days.

To Prepare
Rinse in several changes of cool water to remove all the grit. Drain, but do not shake dry. Trim tough stems or ribs. Leave whole, or stack and cut into ½- to 1-inch-wide slices.

To Cook
See Stir-Frying 101, page 436.

Southern-Style Greens

This classic recipe makes a big batch, but it can easily be halved. Be traditional amd do what Southerners do—drink the flavorful cooking liquid (pot liquor) or dunk chunks of corn bread into it.

Prep: 30 minutes	Cook: 1 hour 15 minutes
5	pounds assorted greens, such as kale, collard greens, or mustard greens
1½	pounds smoked ham hocks
1	medium onion
8	cups water
1	teaspoon salt
	hot pepper sauce

1. Remove stems and tough ribs from greens; rinse well with cool running water. Cut into ½-inch pieces.

2. In 8-quart saucepot, combine ham hocks, onion, and water; heat to boiling over high heat. Add greens in batches, stirring to wilt. Heat to boiling. Reduce heat; cover and simmer until very tender, about 1 hour. Discard ham hocks. Serve with hot pepper sauce. Makes 10 accompaniment servings.

Each serving: About 82 calories, 5g protein, 13g carbohydrate, 3g total fat (1g saturated), 2mg cholesterol, 560mg sodium.

STIR-FRYING 101

One of the best ways to serve nutritious greens is to stir-fry them, which cooks them just enough to mellow their flavor but retain their bright color. Tough, bitter greens, such as broccoli rabe and collard greens, should first be blanched to tenderize them and to remove some of their bitterness.

PREPARATION

Discard discolored leaves and trim thick stem ends; slice or tear leaves, if necessary. To blanch (if recommended), add greens to *6 quarts boiling water*; cook, uncovered, as directed (begin timing as soon as greens are added), then drain. Now you're ready to let things sizzle.

STIR-FRYING

In nonstick 12-inch skillet or wok, heat *1 tablespoon olive oil* over high heat until hot. Add *2 garlic cloves*, crushed with flat side of chef's knife. Cook, stirring frequently (stir-frying), until golden. Add *1/8 teaspoon salt* and cook, stir-frying as directed below. Discard garlic, if desired.

TYPE OF GREENS (1 POUND)	PREPARE	BLANCH	STIR-FRY
Beet greens	Wash.	No	5 minutes
Bok choy (pak choi, pak choy, Chinese mustard cabbage)	Wash and thinly slice stems. Cut leaves into 1-inch-wide slices.	No	5 minutes
Broccoli rabe (rape, rapini, broccoli di rape)	Wash; trim stems.	5 minutes	5 minutes
Chicory (curly endive)	Wash; tear leaves into bite-size pieces.	No	5 minutes
Collard greens	Wash. Discard stems; cut leaves into 1-inch pieces.	3 minutes	5 minutes
Dandelion greens	Wash.	3 minutes	5 minutes
Escarole (broad-leaf endive)	Wash; tear leaves.	No	5 minutes
Kale, dinosaur kale (lacinato kale, Tuscan kale, black kale)	Wash; discard stems and center ribs. Cut leaves into 1-inch-wide slices.	5 minutes	5 minutes
Mustard greens	Wash.	5 minutes	5 minutes
Napa (Chinese) cabbage, celery cabbage	Wash and thinly slice.	No	3 minutes
Spinach	Wash thoroughly.	No	3 minutes
Swiss chard	Wash and thinly slice stems. Cut leaves into 1-inch-wide slices.	No	3 minutes
Watercress	Wash.	No	3 minutes

JICAMA

Availability
Year round

Buying Tips
Turnip-shaped jicama has thin brown skin and white flesh. It tastes like water chestnuts and ranges in size from one to six pounds. Choose smaller jicama to avoid any woodiness.

To Store
Refrigerate jicama in the crisper drawer up to two weeks.

To Prepare
Scrub under cold running water. Peel and slice to serve raw in salads or with dips, or cut into bite-size pieces; substitute for water chestnuts in stir-fries.

KOHLRABI

Availability
Year round

Peak Season
May and June

Buying Tips
Bulbs should be pale green or purple, smooth and unblemished, with fresh-looking tops and tender skin.

To Store
Discard leafy tops. Refrigerate bulbs in the crisper drawer up to one week.

To Prepare
Cut off the stems, then peel the bulb with a vegetable peeler or small knife, being sure to remove the fibrous layer just under the skin. Slice, quarter, shred, or cut into matchstick strips.

To Cook
Kohlrabi can be sautéed or served raw in salads. It can also be simmered. In a medium saucepan, heat 1 inch of water to boiling over high heat; add sliced kohlrabi and heat to boiling. Reduce heat to medium-low; cover and cook until tender, 15 to 30 minutes; drain. Toss with butter.

Sautéed Kohlrabi

Kohlrabi, which has a delicate cabbage flavor, takes only minutes to cook when shredded.

 Prep: 10 minutes   Cook: 6 minutes

1	tablespoon butter or margarine
3	medium kohlrabi (8 ounces each), peeled and coarsely shredded
¼	teaspoon salt
⅛	teaspoon ground black pepper
1	tablespoon chopped fresh parsley

In 10-inch skillet, melt butter over medium heat. Add kohlrabi, salt, and pepper. Increase heat to medium-high and cook, stirring frequently, until just tender, about 5 minutes. Sprinkle with parsley. Makes 4 accompaniment servings.

Each serving: About 47 calories, 1g protein, 5g carbohydrate, 3g total fat (2g saturated), 8mg cholesterol, 188mg sodium.

LEEKS

Availability
Year round

Peak Season
April through September

Buying Tips
Buy leeks that are straight, with firm white roots and leafy green tops. Avoid leeks with wilted or yellowish tops or cracked roots.

To Store
Refrigerate in the crisper drawer up to three days.

To Prepare
Cut off the roots and trim the dark green tops, leaving about 1 inch of the pale green area. Leeks have sand hidden between their layers and should be washed carefully. Cut the leeks lengthwise, almost halfway through, leaving 2 to 3 inches of the root ends uncut. Rinse the leeks in a large bowl of cold water, swishing to remove all the sand. Or chop the trimmed leeks and swish in a bowl of cold water. With a slotted spoon, transfer to a colander to drain.

Braised Leeks

Chopped leeks braised with a bit of butter make a divine side dish to serve with any mild-flavored fish of your choice.

Prep: 10 minutes   **Cook:** 15 minutes

1	bunch leeks (about 1½ pounds)
1	tablespoon butter or margarine
⅛	teaspoon salt
¼	cup water

1. Cut off roots and trim dark green tops from leeks; cut each leek lengthwise in half, then crosswise into ½-inch-thick slices. Rinse leeks in large bowl of cold water, swishing to remove sand; transfer to colander to drain, leaving sand in bottom of bowl.

2. In 2-quart saucepan, combine leeks, butter, salt, and water; heat to boiling over high heat. Reduce heat; cover and simmer until just tender, about 5 minutes. Remove cover; cook until water has evaporated, about 5 minutes longer. Makes 4 accompaniment servings.

Each serving: About 68 calories, 1g protein, 10g carbohydrate, 3g total fat (2g saturated), 8mg cholesterol, 116mg sodium.

Leeks Vinaigrette

If you can only find large leeks, use just four; cook until tender (they'll take a bit longer), then cut lengthwise in half.

Prep: 25 minutes   **Cook:** 10 minutes

8	slender leeks (2½ pounds)
2⅛	teaspoons salt
1	tablespoon red wine vinegar
1	teaspoon Dijon mustard
	pinch ground black pepper
2	tablespoons olive oil
1	tablespoon chopped fresh parsley

1. In 5-quart Dutch oven, heat *12 cups water* to boiling over high heat. Meanwhile, cut off roots from leeks and trim leeks to 6 inches; discard green tops. Beginning at green end, make 4-inch-long slit in each leek, cutting almost halfway through, leaving 2 inches of root end of leeks uncut. Rinse leeks in large bowl of cold water, swishing to remove sand; transfer to colander to drain, leaving sand in bottom of bowl.

2. Add leeks and 2 teaspoons salt to boiling water in Dutch oven; cook until tender, about 10 minutes. Transfer leeks to colander; rinse with cold running water. Drain; pat dry.

3. In small bowl, with wire whisk, mix vinegar, mustard, remaining ⅛ teaspoon salt, and pepper until blended. In thin, steady stream, whisk in oil until blended, then whisk in parsley.

Leeks Vinaigrette

4. Arrange leeks on serving plate in single layer. Spoon dressing over. Makes 4 first-course servings.

Each serving: About 146 calories, 2g protein, 20g carbohydrate, 7g total fat (1g saturated), 0mg cholesterol, 424mg sodium.

MUSHROOMS

Availability
Year round

Buying Tips
Mushrooms generally fall into three categories: common, wild, and exotic. Common mushrooms are the familiar *white button* variety. Wild mushrooms are foraged from forests and are strictly seasonal: They include the *chanterelle, morel,* and *porcini.* Wild mushrooms are always expensive. Exotic mushrooms are sometimes called wild mushrooms, but they are really just unusual cultivated varieties. Some exotic mushrooms include *shiitake* (meaty-tasting and often used in stir-fries), *oyster* (mild-flavored and smooth-textured), *enoki* (long thin white stems with tiny caps), *portobello* (very large with somewhat flat caps and a rich meaty flavor), and *cremini* (small portobellos with dark brown caps). Buy firm mushrooms with tightly closed gills (dark undersides). Mushrooms should never be withered, wrinkled, or show any sign of moisture.

To Store
Place mushrooms (unwashed) in a brown paper bag. Refrigerate up to three days.

To Prepare
Do not peel mushrooms. Rinse them briefly under cold running water and drain well on paper towels. The tough stems of shiitake mushrooms must be removed; trim the stem ends of other varieties. Leave mushrooms whole or prepare as the recipe directs.

Grilled Portobello Mushroom Salad

Hearty portobellos are perfect for grilling. Baby greens make a good substitute for arugula.

 Prep: 20 minutes   Grill: 9 minutes

1	wedge Parmesan cheese
2	small bunches arugula (4 ounces each), trimmed
2	tablespoons balsamic vinegar
2	tablespoons olive oil
2	tablespoons minced shallots
2	tablespoons chopped fresh parsley
¼	teaspoon salt
⅛	teaspoon ground black pepper
1	pound portobello mushrooms, stems removed

1. Prepare grill or preheat broiler. With vegetable peeler, remove enough shavings from wedge of Parmesan to measure ½ cup, loosely packed (about 1 ounce). Arrange arugula on serving platter.

2. In small bowl, with wire whisk, mix vinegar, oil, shallots, parsley, salt, and pepper until blended. Place mushrooms, stem side down, on grill or on rack in broiling pan at closest position to heat source. Brush mushrooms with 1 tablespoon dressing. Grill or broil 4 minutes. Turn; brush mushrooms with 1 more tablespoon dressing. Grill or broil until tender, about 5 minutes longer.

3. Thinly slice mushrooms and arrange on arugula. Spoon remaining dressing over; top with Parmesan shavings. Makes 4 first-course servings.

Each serving: About 139 calories, 7g protein, 9g carbohydrate, 10g total fat (2g saturated), 5mg cholesterol, 285mg sodium.

Sautéed Mixed Mushrooms

This classic French preparation brings out the meaty texture and woodsy flavor of mushrooms. Use just one variety, if you prefer.

🕐 *Prep: 15 minutes   Cook: 10 minutes*

2	tablespoons butter or margarine
¼	cup minced shallots
8	ounces white mushrooms, trimmed and cut into quarters
4	ounces shiitake mushrooms, stems removed and caps cut into 1-inch-thick wedges
4	ounces oyster mushrooms, cut in half if large
¼	teaspoon salt
⅛	teaspoon ground black pepper
⅛	teaspoon dried thyme
1	small garlic clove, finely chopped
1	tablespoon chopped fresh parsley

In 12-inch skillet, melt butter over medium-high heat. Add shallots and cook, 1 minute. Stir in white, shiitake, and oyster mushrooms. Sprinkle with salt, pepper, and thyme and cook, stirring, until mushrooms are tender and liquid has evaporated, about 8 minutes longer. Stir in garlic and parsley and cook 1 minute longer. Makes 4 accompaniment servings.

Each serving: About 86 calories, 3g protein, 7g carbohydrate, 6g total fat (4g saturated), 16mg cholesterol, 207mg sodium.

Lemon-Marinated Mushrooms

The clean flavors of this simple dish go well with almost any menu.

Prep: 15 minutes plus standing

1	pound small mushrooms, trimmed and cut into quarters
¼	cup minced shallots
¼	cup chopped fresh parsley
5	tablespoons olive oil
1	tablespoon plus 1 teaspoon fresh lemon juice
½	teaspoon salt
¼	teaspoon ground black pepper

In bowl, combine mushrooms, shallots, parsley, oil, lemon juice, salt, and pepper until mixed. Let stand at room temperature 1 hour, stirring occasionally. Serve, or refrigerate up to 6 hours. Makes 6 accompaniment servings.

Each serving: About 124 calories, 2g protein, 5g carbohydrate, 12g total fat (2g saturated), 0mg cholesterol, 198mg sodium.

OKRA

Availability
Year round

Peak Season
July through September

Buying Tips
Buy tender, young pods less than 4½ inches long, without any brown spots.

To Store
Place in a brown paper bag. Refrigerate in the crisper drawer up to two days.

To Prepare
Rinse okra under cold running water and cut off the stem ends. Leave whole or slice.

Fried Okra

In this down-home favorite, okra gets a crunchy cornmeal coating.

🕐 *Prep: 15 minutes   Cook: 2 minutes per batch*

1	large egg
12	ounces okra, cut into 1-inch pieces
½	cup cornmeal
½	teaspoon salt
⅛	teaspoon ground red pepper (cayenne)
	vegetable oil for frying

1. In medium bowl, lightly beat egg; add okra and toss to coat. On waxed paper, combine cornmeal, salt, and ground red pepper. Add okra and toss to coat.

2. Meanwhile, in heavy 10-inch skillet, heat ¼ inch oil over medium-high heat until hot. In small batches, fry okra until golden, 2 to 3 minutes. With slotted spoon, transfer to paper towels to drain. Makes 4 accompaniment servings.

Each serving: About 205 calories, 5g protein, 20g carbohydrate, 12g total fat (2g saturated), 53mg cholesterol, 313mg sodium.

Okra with Tomatoes

Okra and tomatoes are a classic combo in cuisines from the Mediterranean to India. Here's a favorite from the American South—okra braised with tomatoes, onion, and celery.

Prep: 20 minutes   Cook: 35 minutes

2	tablespoons olive oil
1	medium onion, chopped
1	small green pepper, chopped
1	stalk celery with leaves, chopped
2	garlic cloves, finely chopped
½	cup water
½	teaspoon all-purpose flour
1	can (14½ ounces) diced tomatoes
1	tablespoon chopped fresh parsley
	or 1 teaspoon chopped fresh oregano
½	teaspoon salt
¼	teaspoon coarsely ground black pepper
12	ounces okra

1. In 10-inch skillet, heat oil over medium heat. Add onion, green pepper, celery, and garlic; cook, stirring occasionally, until vegetables are tender, about 15 minutes.

2. In small cup, blend water and flour until smooth.

3. Stir tomatoes with their juice, parsley, salt, black pepper, and flour mixture into vegetables in skillet. Add okra and heat to boiling. Reduce heat; cover and simmer, stirring occasionally, until okra is tender, about 15 minutes. Makes 4 accompaniment servings.

Each serving: About 138 calories, 3g protein, 17g carbohydrate, 7g total fat (1g saturated), 0mg cholesterol, 475mg sodium.

ONIONS

Availability
Year round

Buying Tips
Onions should be firm and clean, with dry, papery skin. Do not buy onions that have sprouted. Yellow *cooking onions* (also called Spanish onions) range from small to very large and have a sharp flavor that sweetens and mellows when cooked. *Red onions* have a stronger flavor than yellow onions, and although some people like to cook with them, they are probably best

when sliced and served raw in salads. *White onions* are quite mild; they are the preferred cooking onion of many Latino cooks. Sweet onions, often named for the location of their harvest, are the ultimate salad onion: *Maui, Walla Walla,* and *Vidalia* are three of the most well known. Most are available in the late spring. Small white onions are often called *boiling onions;* they are braised until tender and often mixed with cream sauce. *Pearl onions* are smaller than boiling onions and can be red, white, or yellow.

To Store
Store onions in a cool (60°F or below) dark place (or in the refrigerator) in a container with good air circulation for up to several weeks.

To Prepare
To peel cooking, red, and sweet onions, trim the roots and blossom ends, cutting off as little flesh as possible. With a small knife, peel off all the skin, along with the first layer of onion and the slippery membrane. To loosen the skins of

small white boiling or pearl onions to make them easier to peel, in a large saucepan, heat 2 inches of water to boiling. Add onions and cook for 1 minute. Drain and rinse under cold running water.

Caramelized Onions

Sweet glazed onions are perfect with a holiday roast.

Prep: 15 minutes   Cook: 38 minutes

2	pounds small white onions
3	tablespoons butter or margarine
2	tablespoons sugar
½	teaspoon salt

1. Peel onions, leaving a little of root end attached to help onions hold their shape.

2. In 12-inch skillet, combine onions and *3 cups water*; heat to boiling over high heat. Reduce heat; cover and simmer until tender, 10 to 15 minutes. Drain well.

3. In same skillet, melt butter over medium heat. Add onions, sugar, and salt; cook, shaking skillet occasionally, until onions have browned, about 15 minutes. Makes 10 accompaniment servings.

Each serving: About 71 calories, 1g protein, 10g carbohydrate, 4g total fat (2g saturated), 9mg cholesterol, 159mg sodium.

Caramelized Onions with Raisins
Prepare as directed but add ½ **cup golden raisins** at end of cooking; heat through.

Caramelized Shallots
Prepare as directed but substitute **shallots** for onions.

Creamed Pearl Onions

A traditional Thanksgiving side dish that is great Year round.

Prep: 20 minutes   Cook: 20 minutes

2	baskets (10 ounces each) pearl onions
3	tablespoons butter or margarine
3	tablespoons all-purpose flour
2	cups milk, warmed
¼	teaspoon salt
⅛	teaspoon ground black pepper
	pinch ground nutmeg

1. In 10-inch skillet, heat *1 inch water* to boiling over high heat. Add onions; heat to boiling. Reduce heat; cover and simmer until tender, 10 to 15 minutes. Drain.

2. When cool enough to handle, peel onions, leaving a little of root end attached to help onions hold their shape.

3. Meanwhile, prepare white sauce: In heavy 2-quart saucepan, melt butter over low heat. Add flour and cook, stirring, 1 minute. With wire whisk, gradually whisk in hot milk. Cook over medium heat, stirring constantly with wooden spoon, until mixture has thickened and boils. Reduce heat and simmer, stirring frequently, 3 minutes. Stir in salt, pepper, and nutmeg; remove from heat.

4. Return onions to skillet. Add sauce and cook, stirring, until heated through. Makes 10 accompaniment servings.

Each serving: About 87 calories, 2g protein, 8g carbohydrate, 5g total fat (3g saturated), 16mg cholesterol, 121mg sodium.

Creamed Onions and Peas
Prepare as directed but add **1 package (10 ounces) frozen peas,** thawed, to onions with sauce.

Oven-Roasted Onions

These delectable onions complement steak, roast beef, or burgers equally well.

Prep: 15 minutes	Roast: 1 hour 20 minutes
5	tablespoons olive or vegetable oil
5	jumbo red or white onions (1¼ pounds each), cut into ¾-inch-thick rounds
½	teaspoon salt
2	tablespoons brown sugar
1	tablespoon cider vinegar

1. Preheat oven to 400°F. Grease two jelly-roll pans with 2 tablespoons oil.

2. Arrange onions in single layer in prepared pans. Brush with 2 tablespoons oil, then sprinkle with ¼ teaspoon salt. Place pans on separate oven racks and roast 45 minutes.

3. Turn onions; brush with remaining 1 tablespoon oil, then sprinkle with remaining ¼ teaspoon salt. Rotate pans between upper and lower racks and roast until tender and golden, about 30 minutes longer.

4. In cup, combine brown sugar and vinegar. Brush onions with vinegar mixture and roast 5 minutes longer. Makes 12 accompaniment servings.

Each serving: About 93 calories, 1g protein, 10g carbohydrate, 6g total fat (1g saturated), 0mg cholesterol, 106mg sodium.

Crumb-Topped Onions

Prepare as directed but omit vinegar mixture. In small bowl, combine **1 cup fresh bread crumbs** (about 2 slices bread), **¼ cup chopped fresh parsley**, and **1 tablespoon vegetable oil**. Top each onion slice with rounded tablespoon of crumb mixture. Roast until crisp, about 10 minutes longer.

French-Fried Onion Rings

Onion rings are wonderfully versatile; pile them on your favorite grilled meat—they'll add a whole new dimension.

Prep: 10 minutes	Cook: 5 minutes per batch
1	jumbo onion (1 pound), cut into ¼-inch-thick slices
	vegetable oil for frying
¼	cup milk
1	cup all-purpose flour
½	teaspoon salt

1. Separate onion slices into rings. In 4-quart saucepan, heat 2 inches oil over medium heat until temperature reaches 370°F on deep-fat thermometer.

2. Pour milk into large bowl. In ziptight plastic bag, mix flour and salt. Dip one-fourth of onion rings in milk. With tongs, transfer to flour mixture; shake to coat.

3. Drop coated onion rings into hot oil; fry until golden brown, 5 to 7 minutes. With slotted spoon, transfer to paper towels to drain. Repeat dipping, coating, and frying with remaining onion rings. Serve immediately. Makes 4 accompaniment servings.

Each serving: About 487 calories, 4g protein, 26g carbohydrate, 42g total fat (5g saturated), 1mg cholesterol, 298mg sodium.

GREEN ONIONS, SCALLIONS, RAMPS, AND SHALLOTS

Availability
Green onions, scallions, and shallots, Year round; ramps, late March, April, and May

Buying Tips
Green onions are the shoots of any onion before the bulb has formed. *Scallions* are the shoots of white onions, although in some parts of the United States, the word scallion is used to mean any green onion. *Ramps* are tender wild onions that shoot up in the forests of West

Virginia; they are very strong and should be used judiciously. *Shallots* are made up of bulbs containing two or three cloves each (similar to garlic). They have a complex flavor and are an integral part of French cooking.

Sautéed Green Onions

Here, green onions are quickly turned into a light side dish. Add some thinly sliced radishes for a nice color contrast.

Prep: 15 minutes   Cook: 8 minutes

1	tablespoon vegetable oil
5	bunches green onions, cut into 2-inch pieces (2½ cups)
½	teaspoon freshly grated lemon peel
¼	teaspoon salt
⅛	teaspoon coarsely ground black pepper
½	cup water
2	radishes, each cut in half and thinly sliced (optional)

In 12-inch skillet, heat oil over medium-high heat. Add green onions, lemon peel, salt, and pepper and cook, stirring frequently, 2 minutes. Add water and cook, stirring, until green onions are tender and lightly browned and liquid has evaporated, 5 to 7 minutes longer. Toss with radishes, if you like. Makes 4 accompaniment servings.

Each serving: About 52 calories, 1g protein, 5g carbohydrate, 4g total fat (0g saturated), 0mg cholesterol, 154mg sodium.

PARSNIPS

Availability
Year round, but less plentiful in April, May, and September

Buying tips
Look for smooth, firm, well-shaped medium parsnips. Avoid large coarse roots and gray or soft spots.

To Store
Place in a plastic bag with a few holes poked in it. Refrigerate in the crisper drawer up to two weeks.

To Prepare
Scrub under cold running water. Trim the ends and peel. Leave whole, slice, cut lengthwise in half, or cut into quarters.

Pureed Parsnips

Parsnips are one of the sweetest of all the root vegetables and easily mash into a smooth puree.

Prep: 15 minutes   Cook: 25 minutes

2½	pounds parsnips, peeled and cut into 1-inch pieces
1	cup milk, warmed
4	tablespoons butter or margarine, softened
1	teaspoon salt
2	tablespoons chopped fresh parsley (optional)

1. In 4-quart saucepan, combine parsnips and enough *water* to cover; heat to boiling over high heat. Reduce heat; cover and simmer until tender, about 15 minutes. Drain.

2. In food processor with knife blade attached, combine parsnips, warm milk, butter, and salt and puree until smooth. Serve hot, sprinkled with parsley, if desired. Makes 8 accompaniment servings.

Each serving: About 166 calories, 3g protein, 23g carbohydrate, 7g total fat (4g saturated), 20mg cholesterol, 377mg sodium.

Roasted Parsnips

Roasted parsnips can be served with almost any meat or poultry dish. They are at their peak of flavor in the autumn, just in time for the holidays.

Prep: 10 minutes   Roast: 45 minutes

2½	pounds parsnips, peeled and cut into 1-inch pieces
1	tablespoon olive oil
¼	teaspoon salt
	pinch ground black pepper
1	tablespoon chopped fresh parsley (optional)

1. Preheat oven to 425°F. In jelly-roll pan, toss parsnips, oil, salt, and pepper to coat.

2. Roast 25 minutes. Turn parsnips; roast, turning every 5 minutes, until tender and golden, about 20 minutes longer.

Serve hot, sprinkled with parsley, if desired. Makes 6 accompaniment servings.

♥ Each serving: About 148 calories, 2g protein, 29g carbohydrate, 3g total fat (0g saturated), 0mg cholesterol, 111mg sodium.

PEAS

Availability
Year round

Peak Season
April, May, and June

Buying Tips
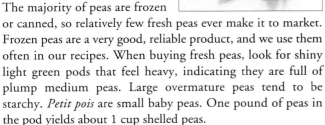
The majority of peas are frozen or canned, so relatively few fresh peas ever make it to market. Frozen peas are a very good, reliable product, and we use them often in our recipes. When buying fresh peas, look for shiny light green pods that feel heavy, indicating they are full of plump medium peas. Large overmature peas tend to be starchy. *Petit pois* are small baby peas. One pound of peas in the pod yields about 1 cup shelled peas.

To Store
Place peas in their pods in a plastic bag. Refrigerate in the crisper drawer up to two days.

To Prepare
Remove the stem and string from each pod. Run your thumb along the length of the "seam" to open the pod and release the peas.

To Cook
To cook fresh peas, in a saucepan, heat 1 inch of water and 1 teaspoon salt to boiling over high heat; add peas and heat to boiling. Reduce heat to medium-high; cover saucepan and cook just until tender, 3 to 5 minutes; drain.

Peas with Mushrooms

An old-fashioned and comforting combination.

 Prep: 10 minutes   Cook: 12 minutes

2	tablespoons butter or margarine
8	ounces mushrooms, trimmed and sliced
¼	teaspoon salt
⅛	teaspoon coarsely ground black pepper
1	package (10 ounces) frozen baby peas, thawed
½	teaspoon chopped fresh thyme or pinch dried thyme

In 10-inch skillet, melt butter over medium-high heat. Add mushrooms, salt, and pepper and cook, stirring, until mushrooms are golden and liquid has evaporated, about 6 minutes. Add peas and thyme and cook until heated through, about 4 minutes longer. Makes 4 accompaniment servings.

Each serving: About 111 calories, 5g protein, 11g carbohydrate, 6g total fat (4g saturated), 16mg cholesterol, 292mg sodium.

Peas with Green Onions and Mint

Fresh mint is a very good match for peas; the green onions add an extra touch of flavor.

Prep: 10 minutes   Cook: 6 minutes

2	tablespoons butter or margarine
½	cup chopped green onions
1	bag (20 ounces) frozen peas, thawed
½	teaspoon salt
¼	teaspoon coarsely ground black pepper
¼	cup chopped fresh mint

1. In 10-inch skillet, melt butter over medium heat. Add green onions and cook until tender, about 2 minutes. Stir in peas, salt, and pepper and cook, stirring frequently, until heated through, about 3 minutes longer.

2. Remove skillet from heat; stir in mint. Makes 6 accompaniment servings.

Each serving: About 111 calories, 5g protein, 14g carbohydrate, 4g total fat (2g saturated), 10mg cholesterol, 340mg sodium.

SNOW PEAS AND SUGAR SNAP PEAS

Availability
Snow peas, year round; sugar snap peas, May through August

Buying Tips
Snow peas (also called Chinese pea pods) should have fresh-looking, flat, bright green pods; the pods are so tender that they are eaten. *Sugar snap peas,* a variety of snow peas, should look plump, bright green, and crisp. Avoid wilted, mottled, or brown-tipped pods. The peas resemble regular green peas, but the pod is always eaten along with the peas.

To Store
Place in a plastic bag. Refrigerate in the crisper drawer up to two days.

To Prepare
Rinse under cold running water. Remove the stem and the string from each pod; do not shell.

Mixed Pea Pod Stir-Fry

This sweet and tender-crisp medley celebrates the glorious flavor of fresh green vegetables.

Prep: 15 minutes   Cook: 16 minutes

1	teaspoon salt
8	ounces green beans, trimmed
2	teaspoons vegetable oil
4	ounces snow peas, trimmed and strings removed
4	ounces sugar snap peas, trimmed and strings removed
1	garlic clove, finely chopped
1	tablespoon soy sauce

1. In 12-inch skillet, combine *4 cups water* and salt; heat to boiling over high heat. Add green beans and cook 3 minutes. Drain; wipe skillet dry with paper towels.

2. In same skillet, heat oil over high heat. Add green beans and cook, stirring frequently (stir-frying), until they begin to brown, 2 to 3 minutes Add snow peas, sugar snap peas, and garlic; stir-fry until snow peas and sugar snap peas

Mixed Pea Pod Stir-Fry

are tender-crisp, about 1 minute longer. Stir in soy sauce and remove from heat. Makes 4 accompaniment servings.

♥ Each serving: About 63 calories, 3g protein, 8g carbohydrate, 2g total fat (0g saturated), 0mg cholesterol, 844mg sodium.

PEPPERS, HOT

Availability
Year round

Buying Tips
Purchase peppers that will provide the desired amount of heat to fit the recipe and to suit your taste. Depending on the variety of pepper, the degree of heat can range

from relatively mild to fiery hot. *Anaheim peppers* are long and tapering, usually green, and among the mildest. *Poblano peppers* are large tapered dark green peppers, that are moderately hot and are usually stuffed. The ever-popular *jalapeño pepper* is the workhorse of the well-spiced kitchen. It can be dark green or red and is often quite hot. Long curved *cayenne peppers* can be green or red and are a staple of Indian cooking. *Serrano peppers* are thin and small, with tapered tips, and are hotter still. The hottest of them all are the *habanero* and *Scotch bonnets*: Yellow, red, orange, or green, they resemble deflated little bells, 1 to 2 inches in diameter. They have a distinctive vegetablelike flavor that manages to hold its own even through the incendiary heat.

To Store

Refrigerate in the crisper drawer up to one week.

To Prepare

Hot peppers contain capsaicin, a colorless substance that can seriously irritate your skin and eyes. Wear rubber gloves while preparing hot peppers, and avoid touching your face, eyes, or other areas with delicate skin. Wash the gloves and your hands thoroughly with hot soapy water after handling hot peppers.

Remove the stems, seeds, and membranes (ribs) from the peppers. (Most of the heat is in the membranes and seeds; don't remove them if you prefer more heat.) Rinse the peppers under cold running water. Roast and peel Anaheim or poblano peppers (Roasted Peppers Master Recipe, page 448) before using in recipes.

PEPPERS, SWEET

Availability

Year round

Buying Tips

Buy peppers that are firm, shiny, and thick-fleshed. Avoid wilted or flabby peppers with cuts or soft spots. *Red peppers* are mature (ripe) *green peppers*, but *yellow* and *purple peppers* are different varieties. Long pale green *Italian frying peppers* are mild flavored and a good substitute for green peppers. *Pimientos* are mild thick-fleshed red peppers that are almost always canned.

To Store

Refrigerate in the crisper drawer up to one week.

To Prepare

Rinse peppers under cold running water. Trim the stem end and remove the seeds and white membranes (ribs). Use peppers whole, cut in half to stuff, or cut into strips, rings, or matchstick strips.

Roasted Peppers with Fresh Basil

Try these colorful peppers with any of our suggested toppings or mix a few together.

Prep: 35 minutes	
2	large red peppers, roasted (page 448)
2	large yellow peppers, roasted (page 448)
1	tablespoon extravirgin olive oil
¼	teaspoon salt or to taste
⅛	teaspoon ground black pepper
3	large fresh basil leaves, thinly sliced

1. Cut peppers lengthwise into ½-inch-wide strips. Pat dry with paper towels.

2. Place pepper strips on serving platter; drizzle with oil and sprinkle with salt and black pepper. To serve, top with basil leaves, or cover and refrigerate up to overnight. Makes 6 appetizer servings.

Each serving without additional toppings: About 38 calories, 1g protein, 4g carbohydrate, 2g total fat (0g saturated), 0mg cholesterol, 97mg sodium.

ADDITIONAL TOPPINGS

- Chopped fresh parsley, oregano, mint, chives, sage, marjoram, rosemary, or savory, or a combination
- Drained capers
- Finely chopped red onion
- Anchovy fillets, drained and chopped
- Minced garlic
- Crushed red pepper
- Chopped pitted olives, such as Kalamata or Gaeta
- Crumbled feta cheese

ROASTED PEPPERS MASTER RECIPE

1. Preheat broiler. Line broiling pan with foil. Cut each pepper lengthwise in half; remove and discard stems and seeds. Arrange peppers, cut side down, in prepared broiling pan. Place pan in broiler, 5 to 6 inches from heat source. Broil, without turning, until skin is charred and blistered, 8 to 10 minutes.

2. Wrap peppers in foil and allow to steam at room temperature 15 minutes or until cool enough to handle.

3. Remove peppers from foil. Peel skin and discard.

Sautéed Peppers and Onion

This brightly colored and flavored sauté goes well with grilled steaks, burgers, sweet or hot sausages, or roast chicken.

	Prep: 10 minutes Cook: 22 minutes
1	tablespoon vegetable oil
1	red pepper, cut into thin strips
1	yellow pepper, cut into thin strips
1	green pepper, cut into thin strips
1	large onion (12 ounces), thinly sliced
1/2	teaspoon salt
1/8	teaspoon ground black pepper

In 12-inch skillet, heat oil over medium heat. Add red, yellow, and green peppers, onion, salt, and black pepper and cook, stirring frequently, until vegetables are tender, about 20 minutes. Makes 4 accompaniment servings.

Each serving: About 67 calories, 1g protein, 8g carbohydrate, 4g total fat (0g saturated), 0mg cholesterol, 292mg sodium.

Sweet and Sour Peppers

Prepare peppers as directed but when peppers are tender, stir in **2 tablespoons sugar** and **2 tablespoons red wine vinegar**; cook 30 seconds longer.

Stuffed Italian Frying Peppers

Serve these peppers as part of an antipasto platter or Mediterranean-inspired buffet, hot or at room temperature. This recipe is easily doubled.

	Prep: 35 minutes Bake: 45 minutes
2	cups fresh 1/2-inch bread cubes (about 3 slices bread)
2	tablespoons olive oil
1	medium onion, chopped
2	garlic cloves, finely chopped
3/4	cup freshly grated Pecorino Romano cheese
1/3	cup chopped fresh parsley
4	Italian frying peppers (3 ounces each), tops removed and seeded

1. Preheat oven to 375°F. On cookie sheet, toast bread cubes until light golden, about 7 minutes.

2. Meanwhile, in 10-inch skillet, heat 1 tablespoon oil over medium heat. Add onion and garlic and cook, stirring, until tender, about 5 minutes. Transfer to large bowl.

3. Add cheese, parsley, and croutons to onion, tossing to combine. Spoon crouton mixture into peppers, pressing down gently to fill. Place peppers on their sides in 11" by 7" baking dish. Drizzle remaining 1 tablespoon oil over peppers and cover with foil. Bake 40 minutes. Remove foil and bake until peppers are tender, about 5 minutes longer. Makes 4 accompaniment servings.

Each serving: About 211 calories, 9g protein, 19g carbohydrate, 12g total fat (4g saturated), 15mg cholesterol, 282mg sodium.

Vegetarian Stuffed Peppers

If you like, add cooked sausage or shredded cheese to the rice filling to make this a more substantial dish.

Prep: 40 minutes Bake: 30 minutes	
1	tablespoon olive oil
1	medium onion, chopped
2	garlic cloves, finely chopped
8	ounces mushrooms, trimmed and thinly sliced (3 cups)
½	cup regular long-grain rice
1⅔	cups water
¼	cup chopped fresh basil
½	teaspoon salt
¼	teaspoon ground black pepper
4	red, yellow, and/or green peppers

1. Preheat oven to 400°F. In 3-quart saucepan, heat oil over medium-low heat. Add onion and garlic and cook, stirring frequently, until onion is tender, about 5 minutes. Add mushrooms and cook, stirring frequently, until mushrooms are tender and liquid has evaporated, about 5 minutes. Add rice, 1 cup water, basil, salt, and black pepper; heat to boiling. Reduce heat; cover and simmer until rice is tender and liquid has been absorbed, about 20 minutes.

2. Meanwhile, cut off top from each pepper; reserve tops. Remove seeds and cut thin slice from bottom of each pepper so it will sit flat. In 5-quart saucepot, heat *3 quarts water* to boiling. Add peppers and their tops and cook 5 minutes. Remove and place, stem side down, on paper towels to drain.

3. When drained, stand peppers in 8-inch square baking dish. Spoon rice mixture into peppers and replace tops. Pour remaining ⅔ cup water into baking dish. Cover with foil and bake until peppers are tender, about 30 minutes. Makes 4 accompaniment servings.

♥ Each serving: About 168 calories, 4g protein, 30g carbohydrate, 4g total fat (1g saturated), 0mg cholesterol, 296mg sodium.

PLANTAINS

Availability
Year round

Buying Tips
Plantains are related to the banana but they aren't as sweet. Unripe green plantains are very hard and starchy and are usually boiled. Ripe yellow plantains have a mild bananalike flavor. Very ripe plantains have dark brown to black skin and are slightly sweet.

To Store
Store plantains at room temperature, but refrigerate if they are very ripe.

To Prepare
Cut plantains crosswise into three or four pieces. Score the peel along the ridges, down to the flesh. Pull the peel away from the flesh and cut into pieces as directed.

Golden Sautéed Plantains

These are a great change of pace when you want an unusual side dish. Try them with roast pork or ham. If you can't find plantains at your market, substitute very green unripe bananas; the cooking time may be slightly shorter.

Prep: 10 minutes Cook: 20 minutes	
4	tablespoons butter or margarine
4	very ripe plantains (2¼ pounds), peeled and cut on diagonal into ½-inch-thick slices
½	teaspoon salt or 1 tablespoon brown sugar

1. In 12-inch skillet, melt 2 tablespoons butter over medium-high heat. Add half of plantains and cook until lightly browned, about 5 minutes per side. Transfer to warm plate; sprinkle lightly with half of salt or sugar. Keep warm.

2. Repeat with remaining plantains, butter, and salt or sugar. Makes 8 accompaniment servings.

Each serving: About 152 calories, 1g protein, 26g carbohydrate, 6g total fat (4g saturated), 16mg cholesterol, 207mg sodium.

POTATOES

Availability
Year round

Peak Season
October through December; new potatoes, April through June

Buying Tips
Buy potatoes that are well shaped and firm, without any blemishes or sprouts. Large cuts or bruises only mean you will have a lot of waste when peeling. Avoid potatoes with a greenish cast. Potatoes are categorized by the amount of starch in the flesh. *Baking potatoes,* such as russet, Idaho, and Burbank, are quite starchy: when baked, their flesh becomes fluffy and dry. *Waxy potatoes,* such as the red-skinned variety, hold their shape after cooking and are preferred for salads and boiling. When time is short, don't bother to peel them. *All-purpose potatoes,* such as Yukon Gold, have the qualities of both varieties and are, therefore, quite versatile. Not all small potatoes

are new potatoes. True *new potatoes* are baby potatoes that have been harvested before they are fully grown; they are a seasonal delicacy worth waiting for.

To Store
Store potatoes in a cool (45° to 50°F) dark place with good air circulation, up to several weeks (don't refrigerate). In warmer weather, potatoes will keep up to one week.

To Prepare
If recipe directs, peel the potatoes and remove any "eyes" with the end of the vegetable peeler or the tip of a small knife. Otherwise, scrub the potatoes with a vegetable brush under cold running water.

Basic Mashed Potatoes

Here is our recipe for fluffy potatoes, plus three easy variations. To achieve a perfectly smooth texture, use a ricer or food mill.

Prep: 25 minutes	Cook: 30 minutes
3	pounds all-purpose potatoes (9 medium), peeled and cut into 1-inch pieces
4	tablespoons butter or margarine, cut into pieces
1½	teaspoons salt
1	cup milk, warmed

1. In 4-quart saucepan, combine potatoes and enough *water* to cover; heat to boiling over high heat. Reduce heat; cover and simmer until tender, about 15 minutes. Drain.

2. Return potatoes to saucepan. Mash potatoes with butter and salt. Gradually add warm milk; continue to mash until smooth and well blended. Keep warm. Makes 8 accompaniment servings.

Each serving: About 204 calories, 4g protein, 32g carbohydrate, 7g total fat (4g saturated), 20mg cholesterol, 516mg sodium.

Mashed Potatoes with Garlic and Lemon

Prepare as directed in Step 1. Meanwhile, with garlic press, press **2 garlic cloves** into 1-quart saucepan with butter and salt. Cook over low heat until butter has melted and garlic is golden, 2 to 3 minutes. Add garlic mixture to potatoes with milk; mash. Stir in **2 tablespoons finely chopped parsley** and **1 teaspoon freshly grated lemon peel.**

Mashed Potatoes with Horseradish

Prepare as directed but add **2 tablespoons undrained prepared white horseradish** with milk.

Mashed Potatoes with Parsnips

Prepare as directed but substitute **1 pound parsnips,** peeled and cut into 1-inch pieces, for 1 pound potatoes and use only **¾ cup milk.**

Basil Mashed Potatoes

Fresh, fragrant basil and a hint of lemon make these potatoes a good match for Mediterranean-style main courses.

	Prep: 25 minutes Cook: 30 minutes
2	large bunches basil
3½	pounds baking potatoes (7 medium), peeled and cut into 1-inch pieces
6	strips (3" by ¾" each) lemon peel
6	garlic cloves, peeled
1½	teaspoons salt
4	tablespoons butter or margarine, cut into pieces
2	tablespoons extravirgin olive oil
½	teaspoon coarsely ground black pepper

1. Set aside 8 large basil sprigs. Thinly slice enough remaining basil leaves to equal ½ cup, loosely packed. (Reserve any remaining basil for another use.)

2. In 4-quart saucepan, combine reserved basil sprigs, potatoes, lemon peel, garlic, 1 teaspoon salt, and enough *water* to cover; heat to boiling over high heat. Reduce heat; cover and simmer until potatoes are tender, about 15 minutes. Drain, reserving ¾ cup potato water. Discard basil sprigs and lemon peel.

3. Return potatoes to saucepan. Mash potatoes with butter, oil, remaining ½ teaspoon salt, and pepper. Gradually add reserved potato water; mash until smooth and well blended. Stir in sliced basil leaves. Makes 8 accompaniment servings.

Each serving: About 207 calories, 4g protein, 28g carbohydrate, 9g total fat (4g saturated), 16mg cholesterol, 360mg sodium.

Mashed Potatoes with Caramelized Onions

Sweet caramelized onions folded into creamy mashed potatoes are especially inviting when served with roasted meats.

	Prep: 25 minutes Cook: 35 minutes
3	tablespoons olive oil
3	large red onions (2¼ pounds), thinly sliced
2	teaspoons salt
2½	pounds baking potatoes (5 medium), peeled and cut into 1-inch pieces
⅓	cup milk
⅛	teaspoon coarsely ground black pepper

1. In 12-inch skillet, heat oil over medium heat. Add onions and ¼ teaspoon salt; cook, stirring occasionally, until very tender and deep golden brown, about 30 minutes.

2. Meanwhile, in 4-quart saucepan, combine potatoes, enough *water* to cover, and 1 teaspoon salt; heat to boiling over high heat. Reduce heat; cover and simmer until tender, about 15 minutes. Drain.

3. Return potatoes to saucepan. Coarsely mash potatoes with milk, remaining ¾ teaspoon salt, and pepper. Stir in all but 2 tablespoons caramelized onions; heat through. Spoon potato mixture into serving bowl and top with remaining caramelized onions. Makes 6 accompaniment servings.

♡ Each serving: About 242 calories, 6g protein, 40g carbohydrate, 8g total fat (1g saturated), 2mg cholesterol, 808mg sodium.

Lowfat Mashed Potatoes

The natural buttery flavor of Yukon Gold potatoes makes them the perfect choice for this lowfat side dish.

Prep: 15 minutes   Cook: 25 minutes

2	pounds Yukon Gold potatoes, peeled and cut into 1-inch pieces
¾	cup lowfat milk (1%), warmed
2	tablespoons olive oil
¾	teaspoon salt
⅛	teaspoon ground black pepper

1. In 4-quart saucepan, combine potatoes and enough *water* to cover; heat to boiling over high heat. Reduce heat; cover and simmer until tender, about 15 minutes. Drain.

2. Return potatoes to saucepan. Mash potatoes with warm milk, oil, salt, and pepper until smooth and well blended. Makes 4 accompaniment servings.

♥ Each serving: About 244 calories, 5g protein, 39g carbohydrate, 8g total fat (1g saturated), 2mg cholesterol, 475mg sodium.

Baby Potatoes with Rosemary

For the best golden brown potatoes, roast them with olive oil and herbs in a hot oven. Instead of baby potatoes, you can also use larger potatoes cut into bite-size pieces.

Prep: 20 minutes   Roast: 30 to 40 minutes

5	pounds assorted small potatoes, such as red, white, purple, or golden, cut in half
¼	cup olive oil
2	tablespoons chopped fresh rosemary or thyme or 1 teaspoon dried rosemary or thyme
1½	teaspoons salt
½	teaspoon coarsely ground black pepper

Preheat oven to 425°F. In large roasting pan (17" by 11½"), toss potatoes, oil, rosemary, salt, and pepper to coat. Roast potatoes, turning occasionally, until golden and tender, 30 to 40 minutes. Makes 10 accompaniment servings.

♥ Each serving: About 232 calories, 4g protein, 41g carbohydrate, 6g total fat (1g saturated), 0mg cholesterol, 366mg sodium.

Pan-Roasted Potatoes

While roasting meat or poultry in the oven, pop in these potatoes. They'll turn out crispy on the outside and tender on the inside. If your oven temperature is lower than 350°F, just cook the potatoes a bit longer.

Prep: 10 minutes   Roast: 1 hour 30 minutes

6	medium all-purpose or baking potatoes (6 ounces each), each peeled and cut in half
2	tablespoons olive oil
½	teaspoon salt

Preheat oven to 350°F. In small roasting pan (13" by 9"), toss potatoes and oil to coat. Arrange cut sides down in pan. Roast until tender and golden, about 1 hour 30 minutes. Sprinkle with salt. Makes 6 accompaniment servings.

Each serving: About 129 calories, 2g protein, 20g carbohydrate, 5g total fat (1g saturated), 0mg cholesterol, 200mg sodium.

Oven Fries

A quick way to make crispy "fries" without frying. Just don't crowd them in the pan, or they won't crisp.

Prep: 10 minutes   Bake: 45 minutes

3	medium baking potatoes or sweet potatoes (8 ounces each), not peeled
1	tablespoon vegetable oil
½	teaspoon salt
⅛	teaspoon ground black pepper

1. Preheat oven to 425°F. Cut each potato lengthwise into quarters, then cut each quarter lengthwise into 3 wedges.

2. In jelly-roll pan, toss potatoes, oil, salt, and pepper to coat. Bake, turning occasionally, until tender, about 45 minutes. Makes 4 accompaniment servings.

♥ Each serving: About 156 calories, 4g protein, 28g carbohydrate, 4g total fat (0g saturated), 0mg cholesterol, 301mg sodium.

Baked Potatoes

Utterly simple and always satisfying.

Prep: 5 minutes	Bake: 45 minutes
6	medium baking potatoes (8 ounces each), not peeled
	choice of toppings: sour cream, butter or margarine, shredded Cheddar cheese, chopped fresh chives, crumbled cooked bacon

Preheat oven to 450°F. Wash potatoes and dry with paper towels; pierce with fork. Place directly on oven rack and bake until tender, about 45 minutes. If desired, slash top of potatoes; serve with choice of toppings. Makes 6 accompaniment servings.

Each serving without topping: About 166 calories, 3g protein, 38g carbohydrate, 0g total fat (0g saturated), 0mg cholesterol, 12mg sodium.

Home-Fried Potatoes

These are as good as (or better than) any roadside diner's. Cook the potatoes the night before, or use leftover cooked potatoes.

Prep: 30 minutes plus cooling	Cook: 40 minutes
4	medium all-purpose potatoes (6 ounces each), not peeled
4	tablespoons butter or margarine
1	small onion, chopped
¼	teaspoon salt

1. In 4-quart saucepan, combine potatoes and enough *water* to cover; heat to boiling over high heat. Reduce heat; cover and simmer until tender, 15 to 20 minutes. Drain.

2. Leave potato skins on, if you like. When cool enough to handle, cut potatoes into ¼-inch-thick slices.

3. In 12-inch skillet, melt butter over medium heat. Add potatoes and onion; cook until underside is golden, about 5 minutes. With wide spatula, turn potatoes; continue to cook over medium heat, turning several times, until evenly browned. Sprinkle with salt. Makes 4 accompaniment servings.

Each serving: About 291 calories, 4g protein, 44g carbohydrate, 12g total fat (7g saturated), 31mg cholesterol, 269mg sodium.

Scalloped Potatoes

These rich and creamy potatoes go directly from oven to table.

Prep: 30 minutes	Bake: 1 hour 30 minutes
3	tablespoons butter or margarine
1	small onion, chopped
3	tablespoons all-purpose flour
1	teaspoon salt
⅛	teaspoon ground black pepper
1½	cups milk, warmed
2	pounds all-purpose potatoes (6 medium), peeled and thinly sliced

1. Preheat oven to 375°F. In heavy 2-quart saucepan, melt butter over low heat. Add onion and cook until tender, about 5 minutes. Add flour and cook, stirring, 1 minute. With wire whisk, gradually whisk in milk. Cook over medium heat, stirring constantly with wooden spoon, until mixture has thickened and boils. Reduce heat and simmer, stirring frequently, 1 minute. Stir in salt and pepper; remove from heat.

2. Grease 9-inch square baking dish or shallow 2-quart casserole. Arrange half of potatoes in single layer in prepared dish; pour half of sauce on top. Repeat layers. Cover and bake 1 hour. Remove cover and bake until potatoes are tender and top is golden, about 30 minutes longer. Makes 6 accompaniment servings.

Each serving: About 199 calories, 5g protein, 28g carbohydrate, 8g total fat (5g saturated), 24mg cholesterol, 484mg sodium.

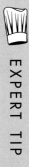

If you are cooking vegetables on the stove and want them to soften without browning, keep the flame low and stir frequently. If you want them to brown, turn the heat up at the end and stir occasionally.

DANIEL BOULUD

CHEF/OWNER, DANIEL AND CAFÉ BOULUD, NEW YORK CITY

EXPERT TIP

Twice-Baked Potatoes

One of America's favorite recipes. Other cheeses, including Parmesan, Roquefort, or Monterey Jack, can be substituted for the Cheddar cheese, if you like.

Prep: 15 minutes   Bake: 55 minutes

3	medium baking potatoes (8 ounces each), not peeled
2	tablespoons butter or margarine, cut into pieces
1	cup ricotta or cottage cheese
3	ounces sharp Cheddar cheese, shredded (¾ cup)
¼	teaspoon salt
⅛	teaspoon coarsely ground pepper
	chopped green onions or chives

1. Preheat oven to 450°F. Wash potatoes and dry with paper towels; pierce with fork. Place directly on oven rack and bake until tender, about 45 minutes.

2. Cut potatoes lengthwise in half. With spoon, scoop out flesh into bowl; reserve shells. Mash potatoes with butter. Stir in ricotta, ½ cup Cheddar, salt, and pepper. Spoon mixture into reserved potato shells, mounding slightly. Place in jelly-roll pan; sprinkle with remaining ¼ cup Cheddar.

3. Bake potatoes 10 minutes. Sprinkle with green onions. Makes 6 accompaniment servings.

Each serving: About 245 calories, 10g protein, 21g carbohydrate, 14g total fat (9g saturated), 46mg cholesterol, 263mg sodium.

Dilled Red Potatoes with Mint

Lots of fresh herbs make this potato salad one of the best, and it's equally appetizing hot or cold.

Prep: 15 minutes   Cook: 20 minutes

2	pounds small red potatoes, cut into quarters
1½	teaspoons salt
3	green onions, chopped
3	tablespoons chopped fresh dill
2	tablespoons chopped fresh mint
2	tablespoons olive oil
⅛	teaspoon coarsely ground black pepper

1. In 3-quart saucepan, combine potatoes, enough *water* to cover, and 1 teaspoon salt; heat to boiling over high heat. Reduce heat; cover and simmer until potatoes are tender, about 10 minutes.

2. Meanwhile, in large bowl, combine green onions, dill, mint, oil, remaining ½ teaspoon salt, and pepper.

3. Drain potatoes. Add hot potatoes to herb mixture in bowl and toss until mixed. Serve warm, or cover and refrigerate up to 6 hours. (If chilled, let stand at room temperature 30 minutes before serving.) Makes 8 accompaniment servings.

♥ Each serving: About 124 calories, 2g protein, 21g carbohydrate, 4g total fat (0g saturated), 0mg cholesterol, 301mg sodium.

Herbed Roasted Potatoes

Potato chunks tossed with parsley and butter cook into tender morsels when foil-wrapped.

Prep: 15 minutes   Bake: 30 minutes

2	tablespoons butter or margarine
1	tablespoon chopped fresh parsley
½	teaspoon freshly grated lemon peel
½	teaspoon salt
⅛	teaspoon coarsely ground black pepper
1½	pounds small red potatoes, cut in half

1. Preheat oven to 450°F. In 3-quart saucepan, melt butter with parsley, lemon peel, salt, and pepper over medium-low heat. Remove saucepan from heat; add potatoes and toss well to coat.

2. Place potato mixture in center of 24" by 18" sheet of heavy-duty foil. Fold edges over and pinch to seal tightly.

3. Place package in jelly-roll pan and bake until potatoes are tender when potatoes are pierced (through foil) with knife, about 30 minutes. Makes 6 accompaniment servings.

♥ Each serving: About 126 calories, 2g protein, 20g carbohydrate, 4g total fat (2g saturated), 10mg cholesterol, 241mg sodium.

Herbed Roasted Potatoes

Potato Latkes

These potato pancakes, a must for Hanukah, are best enjoyed right out of the frying pan, but if you must, they can be kept warm in a 250°F oven until ready to serve. If you are preparing a large batch several hours ahead, to reheat them, place on a rack set over a cookie sheet in a 375°F oven for about 10 minutes or until piping hot.

Prep: 35 minutes   Cook: 8 to 10 minutes per batch

2½	pounds baking potatoes (4 large)
1	medium onion, peeled
1	large egg
2	tablespoons all-purpose flour or matzoh meal
1	tablespoon chopped fresh parsley or dill
1	tablespoon fresh lemon juice
½	teaspoon baking powder
½	teaspoon salt
¼	teaspoon coarsely ground black pepper
¾	cup vegetable oil for frying
	applesauce or sour cream

1. Peel potatoes and onion and shred into colander. With hands, squeeze to press out as much liquid as possible. Place potato mixture in large bowl; stir in egg, flour, parsley, lemon juice, baking powder, salt, and pepper.

2. Preheat oven to 250°F. In 12-inch skillet, heat 3 tablespoons oil over medium heat until hot. Drop potato mixture by scant ¼ cups into hot oil to make 5 latkes. With back of spoon, flatten each latke into 3-inch round. Cook until underside is golden, 4 to 5 minutes. With slotted spatula, turn latkes and cook until second side is golden brown and crisp, 4 to 5 minutes longer. With slotted wide spatula, transfer latkes to paper towel–lined cookie sheet to drain; keep warm in oven.

3. Repeat with remaining potato mixture, stirring before frying each batch and using 3 tablespoons more oil for each new batch. Serve latkes hot with applesauce or sour cream. Makes about 20 latkes or 10 accompaniment servings.

Each latke without applesauce or sour cream: About 208 calories, 3g protein, 18g carbohydrate, 14g total fat (2g saturated), 21mg cholesterol, 152mg sodium.

Sweet Potato Pancakes
Prepare as directed but substitute **2 pounds sweet potatoes** for all-purpose potatoes.

Potatoes Anna

This potato cake gets its distinctive appearance from weighting the concentric circles of layered sliced potatoes during baking so they stick together. A nonstick skillet makes unmolding a snap.

Prep: 25 minutes   Cook/Bake: 40 minutes

4	medium baking potatoes (8 ounces each)
3	tablespoons butter or margarine
½	teaspoon salt
⅛	teaspoon ground black pepper

1. Preheat oven to 350°F. Peel potatoes and cut into paper-thin slices. In nonstick oven-safe 10-inch skillet (if skillet is not oven-safe, wrap handle with double layer of foil), melt butter over low heat. Remove skillet from heat. Beginning at outside edge of skillet, arrange one layer of potatoes in concentric circles, slightly overlapping slices. Sprinkle with some salt and pepper. Continue layering potatoes in concentric circles to make two or three more layers, sprinkling each layer with salt and pepper.

2. Lightly grease sheet of foil; place foil, greased side down, on top of potatoes. Place heavy 10-inch skillet on top to weight down potatoes. Cook over medium-high heat until underside is lightly browned, 10 to 15 minutes. Remove top skillet and foil. Carefully invert potatoes onto large flat plate. Slide potatoes back into skillet.

3. Place skillet in oven and bake until potatoes are tender, about 30 minutes. Slide onto serving plate. To serve, cut into wedges. Makes 8 accompaniment servings.

Each serving: About 110 calories, 2g protein, 15g carbohydrate, 5g total fat (3g saturated), 12mg cholesterol, 194mg sodium.

Parmesan Potatoes

Roasted red potatoes capped with melted Parmesan cheese are absolutely irresistible.

Prep: 10 minutes	Bake: 30 minutes
4	medium red potatoes (5 ounces each)
½	cup freshly grated Parmesan cheese
1	tablespoon butter or margarine, melted
¼	teaspoon coarsely ground black pepper

1. Preheat oven to to 450°F. Line jelly-roll pan with foil; lightly grease foil. Cut potatoes lengthwise in half and place, cut side down, on foil. Bake until tender, about 25 minutes.

2. Spread Parmesan on waxed paper. Brush cut side of each potato with melted butter, then dip in Parmesan. Return potatoes, Parmesan side up, to jelly-roll pan. Sprinkle with pepper. Bake until Parmesan melts, 5 to 7 minutes longer. Makes 4 accompaniment servings.

Each serving: About 196 calories, 8g protein, 26g carbohydrate, 7g total fat (4g saturated), 17mg cholesterol, 267mg sodium.

"Leftover" Mashed-Potato Pancakes

A great way to use leftover potatoes. In fact, make extra so you can enjoy this easy dish a second time.

Prep: 10 minutes	Cook: 6 minutes
1½	cups mashed potatoes
2	tablespoons plain dried bread crumbs
1	tablespoon freshly grated Parmesan cheese
1	tablespoon butter or margarine

1. With hands, shape potatoes into eight 2-inch patties. On waxed paper, combine bread crumbs and Parmesan. Coat patties with bread-crumb mixture, patting crumbs to cover.

2. Heat nonstick 10-inch skillet over medium heat; melt butter. Add patties and cook until golden and heated through, 2 to 3 minutes per side. Makes 4 accompaniment servings.

Each serving: About 129 calories, 3g protein, 16g carbohydrate, 7g total fat (3g saturated), 11mg cholesterol, 319mg sodium.

PUMPKIN

Availability
September through December

Peak Season
October

Buying Tips
Buy firm, bright-colored pumpkins, free from cuts or nicks. *Mini pumpkins* have a rich, sweet flavor. Other cooking pumpkins include *sugar, cheese,* and *pie pumpkins.* They are often cooked and used for pie filling, but canned solid-pack pumpkin is a very convenient, high-quality product. *Jack-o'-lantern pumpkins* have stringy, watery flesh and are best reserved for Halloween decorations.

To Store
Store pumpkins in a cool dry place up to one month.

To Prepare
Cut pumpkin in half or into quarters; remove the seeds and scrape out the stringy portions. Cut into large pieces. To prepare mini pumpkins, see Roasted Mini Pumpkins, page 458.

To Cook
To steam, in a saucepot, heat 1 inch of water to boiling over high heat; add pumpkin pieces and heat to boiling. Reduce heat to medium-high; cover and cook until tender, 25 to 30 minutes. Drain, cool, and peel. If desired, mash with butter, brown sugar, and cinnamon. Or, if using for pie filling, puree in a blender or food processor with knife blade attached. Do not add other ingredients. Place in a paper towel–lined sieve set over a bowl and let drain to remove excess liquid; puree should have the same thickness as solid-pack canned pumpkin. One pound of uncooked pumpkin yields about 1 cup puree.

Roasted Mini Pumpkins

Not only are these attractive, they also make great eating. Each mini pumpkin is a perfect single serving.

Prep: 10 minutes	Roast: 45 minutes
4	mini pumpkins
4	teaspoons butter or margarine
1/8	teaspoon salt
	pinch ground black pepper

1. Preheat oven to 400°F. Create a lid in each pumpkin by cutting top 1 inch from stem; remove seeds. Place one-fourth of butter, salt, and pepper in each cavity. Top with lids. Place in jelly-roll pan.

2. Roast until tender, about 45 minutes. Let stand 5 minutes before serving. Makes 4 accompaniment servings.

Each serving: About 75 calories, 2g protein, 10g carbohydrate, 4g total fat (2g saturated), 10mg cholesterol, 114mg sodium.

RADISHES

Availability
Year round

Peak Season
Round radishes, April and May; Asian varieties, October

Buying Tips
Radishes should be uniformly shaped, free from blemishes, firm, and bright red (or white, if icicle radishes).

To Store
If not serving within one day, remove the leaves and place the radishes in a plastic bag. Refrigerate up to one week.

To Prepare
Trim the radish roots and tops, if necessary. Rinse well under cold running water. If using as a garnish or in a relish tray, cut as desired and store in ice water in the refrigerator.

To Cook
Radishes can be sautéed in butter and served as a side dish; their flavor will be reminiscent of turnips.

RUTABAGAS

Availability
Year round

Peak Season
October through March

Buying Tips
Also called yellow turnip, wax turnip, and Swede. Rutabagas should be large, heavy, and without any decay or soft spots. Extremely large ones should be passed over, however. Rutabagas are usually coated with a thick protective wax, which isn't a problem, because they are always peeled.

To Store
Store at cool room temperature or in the refrigerator in the crisper drawer up to one month.

To Prepare
Cut the rutabaga into quarters, then peel using a small knife.

Mashed Rutabagas with Brown Butter

Mashed rutabagas have a silken texture and a slightly sweet flavor. If using older rutabagas, they will take longer to cook.

Prep: 10 minutes	Cook: 30 minutes
2	rutabagas (1 1/4 pounds each)
1 3/4	teaspoons salt
4	tablespoons butter or margarine
1/2	teaspoon sugar
1/4	cup milk, warmed

1. Cut each rutabaga into quarters; peel, then cut into 1-inch pieces. In 4-quart saucepan, combine rutabagas, enough *water* to cover, and 1 teaspoon salt; heat to boiling over high heat. Reduce heat to medium; cover and cook until tender, about 15 minutes. Drain.

2. In food processor with knife blade attached, combine rutabagas, 2 tablespoons butter, sugar, and remaining 3/4 teaspoon salt, and puree until smooth, occasionally scraping down side with rubber spatula. With processor running, gradually add milk until blended.

3. In small saucepan over medium heat, melt remaining 2 tablespoons butter; cook, stirring, until golden brown (do not let burn).

4. To serve, spoon rutabaga puree into bowl and pour brown butter over. Makes 12 accompaniment servings.

Each serving: About 67 calories, 1g protein, 7g carbohydrate, 4g total fat (3g saturated), 11mg cholesterol, 299mg sodium.

SALSIFY

Availability
Year round

Peak Season
October through March

Buying Tips
There are two types: a light brown, slender, parsnip-shaped root that is sometimes referred to as "true" salsify and a brownish-black skinned variety that is considerably larger and more regularly shaped. They are interchangeable in most recipes.

To Store
Place in a plastic bag. Refrigerate up to one week.

To Prepare
Scrub salsify under cold running water; cut off the tops. Peel and cut as directed. Salsify discolors easily; place peeled pieces into a bowl containing 8 cups of water and 1 tablespoon of lemon juice.

Buttered Salsify

One of the simplest and best ways to cook salsify.

Prep: 10 minutes   Cook: 20 minutes

2	tablespoons fresh lemon juice
1	pound salsify
1¼	teaspoons salt
1	tablespoon butter or margarine
	pinch ground black pepper
1	teaspoon chopped fresh parsley

1. In large bowl, combine 1 tablespoon lemon juice and *8 cups water.* With vegetable peeler, peel salsify; immediately place in lemon water to prevent browning.

2. Cut salsify into 1-inch pieces. In 3-quart saucepan, combine salsify, *8 cups water,* remaining 1 tablespoon lemon juice, and 1 teaspoon salt; heat to boiling over high heat. Boil until tender, about 10 minutes.

3. Drain salsify and return to saucepan. Add butter, remaining ¼ teaspoon salt, and pepper; cook, stirring frequently, until butter begins to brown, about 2 minutes. Transfer to serving dish and sprinkle with parsley. Makes 4 accompaniment servings.

Each serving: About 107 calories, 3g protein, 19g carbohydrate, 3g total fat (2g saturated), 8mg cholesterol, 485mg sodium.

SPINACH

Availability
Year round

Peak Season
September and October, March and April

Buying Tips
Buy spinach that is tender and fresh-looking with bright green leaves. Avoid spinach that is yellowish or wilted. Packaged *curly spinach* is more strongly flavored than *loose-leaf spinach.* Curly spinach is fleshier and, therefore, better for cooking than delicate flat-leaf spinach. *Baby spinach,* available in bags, has very tender, edible stems. Frozen spinach is a very handy and excellent-quality convenience product.

To Store
Place unwashed in a plastic bag. Refrigerate up to two days.

To Prepare
Trim tough stems. Wash spinach well in several changes of cool water, swishing to remove all the grit. Transfer to a colander to drain. To use spinach raw, dry in a salad spinner or pat dry with paper towels.

Spanakopita

Spinach pie in a flaky phyllo crust makes a great main course for supper or brunch. You can make the filling a day ahead—just store it in the refrigerator. The day of serving, prepare the phyllo crust, fill it, and pop it into the oven.

Prep: 40 minutes   Bake: 35 minutes

6	tablespoons butter or margarine
1	jumbo onion (1 pound), chopped
4	packages (10 ounces each) frozen chopped spinach, thawed and squeezed dry
1	package (8 ounces), feta cheese well drained and crumbled
1	cup part-skim ricotta cheese
3	large eggs
1/2	cup chopped fresh dill
1/4	teaspoon salt
1/4	teaspoon coarsely ground black pepper
10	sheets (16" by 12" each) fresh or frozen (thawed) phyllo

1. In 12-inch skillet, melt 2 tablespoons butter over medium-high heat. Add onion and cook, stirring occasionally, until tender and lightly browned, about 15 minutes.

2. Transfer to large bowl. Stir in spinach, feta, ricotta, eggs, dill, salt, and pepper until combined. Wipe skillet clean.

3. Preheat oven to 400°F. In same skillet, melt remaining 4 tablespoons butter. Remove phyllo from package; keep covered with damp towel to prevent from drying out. Lightly brush bottom and sides of 11" by 7" baking dish with some melted butter. On waxed paper, lightly brush 1 phyllo sheet with some melted butter. Place phyllo in baking dish, gently pressing phyllo against sides of dish and allowing to overhang sides. Lightly brush second sheet with melted butter; place over first sheet. Repeat layering with 3 more phyllo sheets.

4. Spread spinach filling evenly over phyllo in baking dish. Fold overhanging edges of phyllo over filling. Cut remaining 5 phyllo sheets crosswise in half. On waxed paper, lightly brush 1 phyllo sheet with melted butter. Place on top of filling. Repeat with remaining phyllo, brushing each sheet lightly with butter; tuck edges of phyllo under.

5. Bake until filling is hot in center and top of phyllo is golden, 35 to 40 minutes. Makes 8 main-dish servings.

Each serving: About 348 calories, 16g protein, 26g carbohydrate, 21g total fat (12g saturated), 138mg cholesterol, 759mg sodium.

Sautéed Spinach and Garlic

In five minutes, you'll have a satisfying side dish. To save time, use bags of prewashed baby spinach.

Prep: 15 minutes   Cook: 5 minutes

1	tablespoon vegetable oil
2	garlic cloves, crushed with side of chef's knife
2	bunches (10 to 12 ounces each) spinach, washed and dried very well, tough stems trimmed
1/4	teaspoon salt

In 5-quart saucepot, heat oil over medium-high heat. Add garlic and cook, stirring, until golden. Add spinach in batches; add salt. Cover and cook, stirring once, just until spinach wilts, about 4 minutes. Discard garlic, if you like. Makes 4 accompaniment servings.

Each serving: About 57 calories, 3g protein, 4g carbohydrate, 4g total fat (0g saturated), 0mg cholesterol, 232mg sodium.

Creamed Spinach

Parsley adds fresh flavor to frozen spinach, while the cream cheese and sour cream add richness and a delicate tang.

Prep: 20 minutes   Cook: 15 minutes

2	tablespoons butter or margarine
3	large shallots, finely chopped (about 3/4 cup)
2	tablespoons all-purpose flour
1/2	cup milk
3/4	teaspoon salt
1/4	teaspoon coarsely ground black pepper
1/8	teaspoon ground nutmeg
1	package (3 ounces) cream cheese, softened and cut into pieces
3	packages (10 ounces each) frozen chopped spinach, thawed and squeezed dry
1	cup loosely packed fresh parsley leaves
1/4	cup sour cream

1. In 4-quart saucepan, melt butter over medium-low heat. Add shallots and cook, stirring frequently, until tender, about 3 minutes. Add flour and cook, stirring, 1 minute. With wire whisk, gradually whisk in milk; heat to boiling, whisking

constantly. Reduce heat and simmer, stirring occasionally, until sauce has thickened and boils, about 2 minutes. Stir in salt, pepper, and nutmeg.

2. Remove from heat; stir in cream cheese until smooth. Stir in spinach, parsley, and sour cream; heat through (do not boil). Makes 6 accompaniment servings.

Each serving: About 180 calories, 7g protein, 14g carbohydrate, 12g total fat (7g saturated), 33mg cholesterol, 500mg sodium.

Indian-Style Creamed Spinach

To avoid diluting the flavor, make sure your spinach is very dry (use a salad spinner).

Prep: 20 minutes	Cook: 12 minutes
1	tablespoon butter or margarine
1	medium onion, chopped
2	teaspoons minced, peeled fresh ginger
2	garlic cloves, finely chopped
½	teaspoon ground coriander
½	teaspoon ground cumin
⅛	teaspoon ground red pepper (cayenne)
2	bunches (10 to 12 ounces each) spinach, washed and dried very well, tough stems trimmed
½	teaspoon salt
¼	cup heavy or whipping cream

1. In 5-quart Dutch oven, melt butter over medium heat. Add onion and cook, stirring frequently, until tender, about 5 minutes. Add ginger, garlic, coriander, cumin, and ground red pepper; cook, stirring, 1 minute.

2. Increase heat to high. Add spinach and salt; cook, stirring, just until spinach wilts, 2 to 3 minutes. Stir in cream and cook 2 minutes. Makes 4 accompaniment servings.

Each serving: About 122 calories, 4g protein, 9g carbohydrate, 9g total fat (5g saturated), 28mg cholesterol, 415mg sodium.

SQUASH, SUMMER

Availability
Year round

Peak Season
June through August

Buying Tips
Summer squash are picked while very young, before their skins have had time to mature and harden. *Zucchini* is the most common summer squash; some farmers' markets carry *yellow zucchini. Crookneck* squash is another popular summer squash. *Pattypan* squash is round and squat with firm flesh. If squash is allowed to mature, the skin will become hard and must be removed before cooking. Buy thin-skinned, shiny squash without blemishes or soft spots.

To Store
Refrigerate in the crisper drawer up to two or three days.

To Prepare
Scrub gently under cold running water. Trim both ends. Do not remove the seeds or skin unless the squash is mature.

Shredded Zucchini

This zucchini cooks up in minutes, retains a slight crunch, and has vibrant color.

Prep: 5 minutes	Cook: 3 minutes
2	small zucchini (5 ounces each), shredded (2 cups)
1	tablespoon butter or margarine, cut into pieces
¼	teaspoon salt

In 10-inch skillet, combine zucchini, butter, and salt; cook over medium-high heat, stirring frequently, until tender-crisp, about 3 minutes. Makes 4 accompaniment servings.

Each serving: About 35 calories, 1g protein, 2g carbohydrate, 3g total fat (2g saturated), 8mg cholesterol, 174mg sodium.

Zucchini Ribbons with Mint

Making long paper-thin strips of zucchini is an out-of-the-ordinary way to prepare it. If you don't have fresh mint, use parsley instead.

Prep: 10 minutes   Cook: 4 minutes

4	small zucchini (4 ounces each) or 2 medium zucchini (8 ounces each)
1	tablespoon olive oil
2	garlic cloves, crushed with side of chef's knife
½	teaspoon salt
2	tablespoons chopped fresh mint

1. Trim ends from zucchini. With vegetable peeler, peel long thin ribbons from each zucchini.

2. In 12-inch skillet, heat oil over medium heat. Add garlic and cook until golden; discard. Increase heat to high. Add zucchini and salt and cook, stirring, just until zucchini wilts, about 2 minutes. Remove from heat and stir in mint. Makes 4 accompaniment servings.

Each serving: About 49 calories, 1g protein, 4g carbohydrate, 4g total fat (0g saturated), 0mg cholesterol, 294mg sodium.

Parmesan-Broiled Squash

Sure to please kids and grownups alike, this quick dish can be made with zucchini, yellow squash, or both.

Prep: 10 minutes   Broil: 7 minutes

2	medium zucchini or yellow squash (8 ounces each), each cut crosswise in half, then lengthwise into ½-inch-thick slices
1	teaspoon olive oil
⅛	teaspoon salt
⅛	teaspoon ground black pepper
¼	cup freshly grated Parmesan cheese

1. Preheat broiler. In broiling pan without rack, toss zucchini and oil to coat; arrange in single layer and sprinkle with salt and pepper.

2. Place pan in broiler, 5 inches from heat source. Broil until zucchini is tender and begins to brown, 3 to 5 minutes per side. Sprinkle evenly with Parmesan and broil until bubbling, 30 to 60 seconds longer. Makes 4 accompaniment servings.

Each serving: About 54 calories, 4g protein, 4g carbohydrate, 3g total fat (1g saturated), 5mg cholesterol, 190mg sodium.

Squash Casserole

With its cracker topping and rich filling, this casserole doubles as a hearty side dish or light vegetarian main course.

Prep: 30 minutes   Bake: 20 minutes

2	tablespoons butter or margarine
1	large onion (12 ounces), thinly sliced
1	pound yellow squash (2 medium), cut into ½-inch-thick slices
1	pound zucchini (2 medium), cut into ½-inch-thick slices
½	teaspoon salt
1	garlic clove, finely chopped
⅛	teaspoon ground red pepper (cayenne)
2	tablespoons all-purpose flour
½	cup milk
½	cup reduced-fat sour cream
4	tablespoons freshly grated Parmesan cheese
½	cup saltine cracker crumbs

1. Preheat oven to 350°F. In 12-inch skillet, melt butter over medium heat. Add onion and cook, stirring frequently, until tender, about 5 minutes. Increase heat to medium-high. Add yellow squash, zucchini, and salt and cook, stirring occasionally, until tender, about 10 minutes. Stir in garlic and ground red pepper and cook 30 seconds. Reduce heat to low; sprinkle flour over vegetables and cook, stirring, 1 minute. Add milk and heat to boiling, stirring until browned bits are loosened from bottom of skillet. Remove from heat and stir in sour cream and 3 tablespoons Parmesan.

2. Spoon squash mixture into shallow 1½-quart baking dish. Sprinkle with cracker crumbs and remaining 1 tablespoon Parmesan. Bake until bubbling at edges, about 20 minutes. Makes 8 accompaniment servings.

Each serving: About 130 calories, 5g protein, 13g carbohydrate, 7g total fat (4g saturated), 17mg cholesterol, 307mg sodium.

SQUASH, WINTER

Availability
Year round, but less plentiful April through July

Peak Season
October through January

Buying Tips
Unlike summer squash, the skin of winter squash is thick and inedible, and the seeds are rarely eaten (except for pump-

kin). *Butternut* squash resembles an elongated pear and has orange-colored flesh. The skin can be removed with a vegetable peeler. *Buttercup* is similar, but turban-shaped with very hard skin. *Acorn* squash has ridges that makes peeling difficult, so it isn't. It has delicious flesh that is enhanced by sweet flavors, such as brown sugar and maple syrup. *Spaghetti squash* has unusual flesh: It separates into pastalike strands when scraped out of the cooked shell. *Delicata* squash has beautiful markings on its skin and its taste is reminiscent of sweet potatoes. *Sweet Dumpling* squash is closely related to Delicata but is round. *Hubbard* squash is very large and has hard, dry, sweet flesh. Buy winter squash with thick, hard skin; tender (softish) skin indicates immaturity and poor quality. Harmless bumpy "warts" appear on some varieties.

To Store
Refrigerate or store at cool room temperature up to two weeks.

To Prepare
Rinse under cold running water. Cut in half, or as directed. Scoop out and discard the seeds and stringy portion.

Maple Butternut Squash

Maple syrup provides a sweet note in this autumn-colored puree.

Prep: 20 minutes	Cook: 20 minutes
2	medium butternut squash (2 pounds each)
½	cup maple or maple-flavored syrup
4	tablespoons butter or margarine, cut into pieces
½	teaspoon salt
¼	teaspoon ground black pepper

1. Cut each squash lengthwise in half; discard seeds. With vegetable peeler, remove peel, then cut squash crosswise into 1-inch-thick slices.

2. In 5-quart saucepot, heat *1 inch water* to boiling over high heat; add squash. Reduce heat; cover and simmer until tender, about 15 minutes. Drain.

3. In large bowl, combine squash, maple syrup, butter, salt, and pepper. With mixer at low speed, beat until smooth. Spoon into serving bowl. Makes 10 accompaniment servings.

Each serving: About 151 calories, 2g protein, 28g carbohydrate, 5g total fat (3g saturated), 12mg cholesterol, 170mg sodium.

Rosemary-Roasted Butternut Squash

Hearty chunks of winter squash become aromatic and sweet when roasted with rosemary.

Prep: 10 minutes	Roast: 35 minutes
3	tablespoons butter or margarine
1	large butternut squash (3 pounds)
1	medium onion, chopped
1¼	teaspoons salt
¾	teaspoon dried rosemary, crumbled
¼	teaspoon coarsely ground black pepper

1. Preheat oven to 400°F. Place butter in small roasting pan (13" by 9"); place pan in oven until butter melts. Meanwhile, cut squash lengthwise in half; discard seeds. With vegetable peeler, remove peel, then cut squash into 2-inch pieces.

2. In large bowl, combine onion, salt, rosemary, and pepper. Add squash and toss to coat. Add squash mixture to melted butter in pan; toss to coat. Arrange squash in single layer and roast until tender, about 35 minutes. Makes 6 accompaniment servings

Each serving: About 148 calories, 2g protein, 25g carbohydrate, 6g total fat (4g saturated), 16mg cholesterol, 551mg sodium.

Thyme-Roasted Butternut Squash
Prepare as directed but substitute ½ **teaspoon dried thyme** and ⅛ **teaspoon nutmeg** for rosemary.

Spaghetti Squash with Tomatoes

We love the flavor of oven-roasted spaghetti squash, but use your microwave if you're in a hurry.

Prep: 10 minutes   Cook/Bake: 1 hour
1 medium spaghetti squash (2½ pounds), cut lengthwise in half and seeded
3 tablespoons butter or margarine
1 garlic clove, finely chopped
1 can (28 ounces) tomatoes, drained and chopped
½ teaspoon salt
¼ teaspoon ground black pepper
2 tablespoons chopped fresh parsley

1. Preheat oven to 400°F. Place squash, cut side down, in jelly-roll pan; pour ¼ *inch water* into pan. Bake 45 minutes. Turn squash, cut side up, and bake until very tender, about 15 minutes longer.

2. Meanwhile, in nonstick 12-inch skillet, melt 2 tablespoons butter over medium heat. Add garlic and cook, stirring, 1 minute. Stir in tomatoes, ¼ teaspoon salt, and ⅛ teaspoon pepper and cook, stirring, until flavors blend, about 5 minutes. Remove from heat and stir in parsley.

3. Using two forks, from squash, scrape out pulp in long strands and place on serving platter. Add remaining 1 tablespoon butter, remaining ¼ teaspoon salt, and remaining ⅛ teaspoon pepper and toss to mix. Spoon sauce over squash. Serve hot. Makes 6 accompaniment servings.

Each serving: About 127 calories, 2g protein, 16g carbohydrate, 7g total fat (4g saturated), 16mg cholesterol, 493mg sodium.

Spaghetti Squash with Tomatoes

Baked Acorn Squash

To ensure that the squash sits flat, trim about one-quarter inch off the bottom of each half.

Prep: 10 minutes   Bake: 35 minutes
2 small acorn squash (1 pound each), each cut lengthwise in half and seeded
2 tablespoons butter or margarine, cut into pieces
¼ cup packed brown sugar

1. Preheat oven to 350°F. Grease 13" by 9" baking dish.

2. Place squash, cut side down, in baking pan; bake 30 minutes. Turn cut side up. Place one-fourth of butter and brown sugar in each cavity. Bake until squash is tender and butter and brown sugar have melted, about 5 minutes longer. Makes 4 accompaniment servings.

Each serving: About 181 calories, 1g protein, 31g carbohydrate, 7g total fat (4g saturated), 16mg cholesterol, 69mg sodium.

Roasted Delicata Squash

Delicata is a lovely looking and good-tasting squash. Its beautiful green-and-cream-colored rind and pale orange flesh easily whet one's appetite.

Prep: 10 minutes   Roast: 1 hour

2	Delicata squash (1 pound each), each cut lengthwise in half and seeded
4	teaspoons butter or margarine
4	teaspoons brown sugar (optional)
¼	teaspoon salt
⅛	teaspoon ground black pepper

1. Preheat oven to 400°F. Place squash, cut side down, in jelly-roll pan; pour *¼ inch water* into pan. Roast 45 minutes.

2. Turn squash cut side up. Place one-fourth of butter, brown sugar if using, salt, and pepper in each cavity. Roast 15 minutes longer. Serve hot. Makes 4 accompaniment servings.

Each serving: About 94 calories, 2g protein, 14g carbohydrate, 4g total fat (2g saturated), 10mg cholesterol, 189mg sodium.

Roasted Buttercup Squash

High in beta-carotene and flavor, this buttercup squash is a great accompaniment for cold-weather meals.

Prep: 10 minutes   Roast: 1 hour

1	large buttercup squash (3 pounds), cut into quarters and seeded
4	teaspoons butter or margarine
⅛	teaspoon salt
	pinch ground black pepper

1. Preheat oven to 400°F. Place squash, cut side down, in jelly-roll pan; pour *¼ inch water* into pan. Roast 45 minutes.

2. Turn squash cut side up. Place one-fourth of butter, salt, and pepper into each cavity. Roast until very tender, about 15 minutes longer. Makes 4 accompaniment servings.

♥ Each serving: About 163 calories, 3g protein, 33g carbohydrate, 4g total fat (2g saturated), 10mg cholesterol, 124mg sodium.

SUNCHOKES

Availability
Year round

Peak Season
September through March

Buying Tips
Also called Jerusalem artichokes. Buy firm, irregularly shaped sunchokes that are free from mold.

To Store
Place in a plastic bag with a few holes poked in it. Refrigerate in the crisper drawer up to two weeks.

To Prepare
Scrub under cold running water. Peel and drop into cold water to prevent discoloration.

Roasted Sunchokes

Roasting brings out the subtle nutty flavor of this knobby tuber.

Prep: 15 minutes   Roast: 1 hour

2	pounds sunchokes (Jerusalem artichokes)
1	tablespoon olive oil
1	teaspoon salt
¼	teaspoon ground black pepper
	chopped fresh parsley

1. Preheat oven to 425°F. With vegetable brush, scrub sunchokes under cold running water. In medium roasting pan (14" by 10"), toss sunchokes, oil, salt, and pepper to coat.

2. Roast until tender, about 1 hour. To serve, sprinkle with parsley. Makes 8 accompaniment servings.

♥ Each serving: About 75 calories, 2g protein, 14g carbohydrate, 2g total fat (0g saturated), 0mg cholesterol, 294mg sodium.

SWEET POTATOES

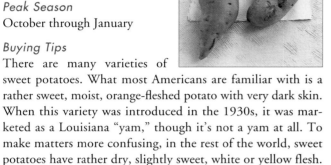

Availability
Year round

Peak Season
October through January

Buying Tips
There are many varieties of sweet potatoes. What most Americans are familiar with is a rather sweet, moist, orange-fleshed potato with very dark skin. When this variety was introduced in the 1930s, it was marketed as a Louisiana "yam," though it's not a yam at all. To make matters more confusing, in the rest of the world, sweet potatoes have rather dry, slightly sweet, white or yellow flesh. Look for sweet potatoes that feel heavy for their size and have no bruises, soft spots, or sign of sprouting. Handle them gently; they bruise easily.

To Store
Sweet potatoes are quite perishable. Store in a cool dark place up to one week. Do not refrigerate.

To Prepare
Scrub under cold running water.

To Cook
Sweet potatoes are often treated like their savory (white) cousins and mashed, sautéed, fried, or turned into pancakes. To bake sweet potatoes, preheat oven to 450°F and bake on a cookie sheet until tender, 45 minutes to 1 hour.

Pan-Roasted Sweet Potato Chunks

This is how to prepare sweet potatoes quickly: Cut them up and cook in a skillet on top of the stove.

Prep: 10 minutes	Cook: 22 minutes
1½	pounds sweet potatoes (2 large), peeled and cut into 1-inch pieces
2	tablespoons butter or margarine
¼	teaspoon salt
⅛	teaspoon ground black pepper

In 12-inch skillet, melt butter over medium-low heat. Add sweet potatoes; cover and cook, turning occasionally, until tender and browned, about 20 minutes. Sprinkle with salt and pepper. Makes 4 accompaniment servings.

♥ Each serving: About 180 calories, 2g protein, 30g carbohydrate, 6g total fat (4g saturated), 16mg cholesterol, 218mg sodium.

Praline Sweet Potatoes

These sweet potatoes are great for a crowd. Prepare the praline up to one week ahead and the sweet potatoes up to one day ahead. When ready to serve, spread the potatoes in a nine-inch square baking dish. Cover and reheat in a 350°F oven for forty-five minutes; remove the cover and bake fifteen minutes longer or until heated through. Sprinkle with the praline and serve.

Prep: 30 minutes	Cook: 45 minutes
5	pounds sweet potatoes (8 medium), peeled and cut crosswise into thirds
¼	cup sugar
¼	cup water
1	cup chopped pecans (4 ounces)
5	tablespoons butter or margarine
½	cup milk
1¼	teaspoons salt

1. In 8-quart saucepot, combine sweet potatoes and enough *water* to cover; heat to boiling over high heat. Reduce heat; cover and simmer until tender, about 25 minutes. Drain; return potatoes to saucepot.

2. Meanwhile, grease cookie sheet. In 1-quart saucepan, combine sugar and water; heat over low heat, stirring gently, until sugar has dissolved, about 1 minute. Increase heat to medium-high and boil rapidly, without stirring, until syrup has turned light golden brown, about 7 minutes. Working quickly, stir in pecans and 1 tablespoon butter until combined and butter melts. Spread pecan mixture in thin layer on cookie sheet; cool.

3. To sweet potatoes in saucepot, add milk, remaining 4 tablespoons butter, and salt. With mixer at low speed, beat sweet potatoes, frequently scraping down side with rubber spatula. Increase speed to medium; beat until smooth, about 2 minutes longer.

4. To serve, spoon potatoes into large bowl. Break pecan mixture into small pieces and sprinkle on top. Makes 12 accompaniment servings.

Each serving: About 329 calories, 4g protein, 47g carbohydrate, 15g total fat (5g saturated), 17mg cholesterol, 376mg sodium.

Candied Sweet Potatoes

If you wish, sprinkle with sliced almonds, chopped walnuts, or chopped pecans before serving. Or top with tiny marshmallows and broil about six inches away from the source of heat until lightly browned.

Prep: 25 minutes Cook/Bake: 1 hour 20 minutes	
4	large sweet potatoes (12 ounces each), each peeled, cut crosswise in half, and each half cut lengthwise into 3 wedges
2½	teaspoons salt
⅓	cup packed brown sugar
3	tablespoons butter or margarine, cut into pieces
⅛	teaspoon ground red pepper (cayenne)
2	tablespoons dry sherry (optional)

1. Preheat oven to 375°F. In 5-quart Dutch oven, combine sweet potatoes, enough *water* to cover, and 2 teaspoons salt; heat to boiling over high heat. Boil until tender, about 10 minutes. Drain.

2. Meanwhile, in nonstick 10-inch skillet, combine brown sugar, butter, remaining ½ teaspoon salt, and ground red pepper; heat over medium heat, stirring, until butter melts, about 1 minute. Stir in sherry, if using. Cook, stirring occasionally, 5 minutes longer.

3. Transfer potatoes to shallow 13" x 9" baking dish and top with brown-sugar mixture. Cover with foil and bake 30 minutes, stirring halfway through baking. Remove foil and bake until syrup is dark and very thick, 30 to 40 minutes, stirring halfway through. Makes 8 accompaniment servings.

Each serving: About 201 calories, 2g protein, 39g carbohydrate, 5g total fat (3g saturated), 12mg cholesterol, 499mg sodium.

TOMATOES

Availability
Year round

Peak Season
July through September

Buying Tips
Buy firm, plump, unblemished tomatoes. Size is not an indication of quality or flavor. Not so very long ago, only red tomatoes could be found in markets, but now there are orange, yellow, purple, green, and even striped varieties. Most tomatoes are picked unripe and allowed to ripen during shipping and storage. Vine-ripened tomatoes, usually locally grown and available mid-summer to early autumn, are picked as close to their flavorful peak as possible and have superior flavor.

Tomatoes are categorized by their shape. Round tomatoes range from the small *cherry tomatoes* to the large *beefsteak* variety. They are especially juicy and excellent in salads. *Plum tomatoes* are oval and have meatier flesh. *Roma tomatoes* are a popular West Coast plum tomato. They are best cooked into sauces. *Green tomatoes* have not been allowed to ripen; they have a nice lemonlike flavor.

To Store

Refrigeration dulls the flavor of tomatoes; only overripe tomatoes should be refrigerated. Store tomatoes, stem side up, at cool room temperature, out of direct sunlight, up to three or four days. As tomatoes ripen, their color deepens, but the amount of natural sugar remains the same.

To Prepare

Tomatoes do not usually have to be peeled before use. But if you wish to peel them, here's how: With a sharp knife, cut a small shallow X in the bottom of each tomato. Lower the tomatoes into a saucepot of boiling water for 1 minute. Remove with a slotted spoon, and plunge into very cold water; drain and gently remove the skin with a knife. To seed tomatoes, cut them crosswise in half and gently squeeze to remove the seeds.

Savory Tomato Tart

A dramatically beautiful main dish—for the most color, include the yellow tomato, but it's equally delicious with all red.

Prep: 45 minutes   Bake/Broil: 31 minutes

	Pastry for 11-inch Tart (page 687)
1	tablespoon olive oil
3	medium onions, thinly sliced
½	teaspoon salt
1	package (3½ ounces) goat cheese
1	ripe medium yellow tomato (8 ounces), cut into ¼-inch-thick slices
2	ripe medium red tomatoes (8 ounces each), cut into ¼-inch-thick slices
¼	cup Kalamata olives, pitted and chopped
½	teaspoon coarsely ground black pepper

1. Preheat oven to 425°F. Prepare dough for 11-inch tart and use to line tart pan as directed. Line tart shell with foil; fill with pie weights or dry beans. Bake 15 minutes: Remove foil with weights. Bake until golden, 5 to 10 minutes longer. If shell puffs up during baking, gently press it down with back of spoon.

2. Meanwhile, in nonstick 12-inch skillet, heat oil over medium heat. Add onions and ¼ teaspoon salt; cook, stirring frequently, until very tender, about 20 minutes.

Savory Tomato Tart

3. Turn oven control to broil. Spread onions over bottom of tart shell and crumble half of goat cheese on top. Arrange yellow and red tomatoes, alternating colors, in concentric circles over onion-cheese mixture. Sprinkle with remaining ¼ teaspoon salt and pepper. Crumble remaining goat cheese on top of tart.

4. Place tart on rack in broiling pan. Place pan in broiler about 7 inches from heat source. Broil until cheese has melted and tomatoes are heated through, 6 to 8 minutes. Sprinkle with olives. Makes 6 main-dish servings.

Each serving: About 420 calories, 8g protein, 33g carbohydrate, 29g total fat (15g saturated), 54mg cholesterol, 753mg sodium.

Cherry Tomato Gratin

The vibrant flavor of cherry tomatoes makes this gratin tasty.

Prep: 10 minutes   Bake: 20 minutes

¼	cup plain dried bread crumbs
¼	cup freshly grated Parmesan cheese
1	garlic clove, crushed with garlic press
¼	teaspoon coarsely ground black pepper
1	tablespoon olive oil
2	pints ripe cherry tomatoes
2	tablespoons chopped fresh parsley

1. Preheat oven to 425°F. In small bowl, combine bread crumbs, Parmesan, garlic, pepper, and oil until blended.

2. Place cherry tomatoes in shallow 1½-quart casserole or 9-inch deep-dish pie plate. Top with bread-crumb mixture and sprinkle with parsley. Bake until heated through and crumbs have browned, about 20 minutes. Makes 6 accompaniment servings.

Each serving: About 72 calories, 3g protein, 7g carbohydrate, 4g total fat (1g saturated), 3mg cholesterol, 121mg sodium.

Skillet Cherry Tomatoes

From start to finish, this cherry tomato side dish takes little more than five minutes.

Prep: 5 minutes   Cook: 3 minutes

1	tablespoon butter or margarine
1	pint ripe cherry tomatoes
1/8	teaspoon salt
	chopped parsley

In 10-inch skillet, melt butter over medium-high heat. Add cherry tomatoes and salt and cook, shaking skillet frequently, just until heated through and skins split, about 2 minutes. Sprinkle with parsley. Makes 4 accompaniment servings.

Each serving: About 36 calories, 0g protein, 2g carbohydrate, 3g total fat (2g saturated), 8mg cholesterol, 107mg sodium.

Skillet Cherry Tomatoes with Garlic
Prepare as directed but add **1 garlic clove,** finely chopped, to skillet with butter.

Broiled Parmesan Tomatoes

These warm and juicy tomatoes are guaranteed to be a hit.

Prep: 10 minutes   Broil: 3 minutes

1	tablespoon butter or margarine
1	garlic clove, finely chopped
1/4	cup freshly grated Parmesan cheese
4	small ripe plum tomatoes (3 ounces each), each cut lengthwise in half

1. Preheat broiler. In 1-quart saucepan, melt butter over low heat. Add garlic and cook until golden; remove from heat.
2. Spread Parmesan on waxed paper. Dip cut side of each tomato in melted-butter mixture, then in Parmesan; place, cheese side up, on rack in broiling pan. Sprinkle any remaining Parmesan on top; drizzle with any remaining butter mixture.
3. Place pan in broiler at closest position to heat source. Broil until Parmesan is golden, 3 to 4 minutes. Makes 4 accompaniment servings.

Each serving: About 72 calories, 3g protein, 4g carbohydrate, 5g total fat (3g saturated), 13mg cholesterol, 151mg sodium.

Fried Green Tomatoes

Here's a classic Southern way to fry up green tomatoes. Use them in BLT sandwiches for a refreshing change of pace.

Prep: 20 minutes   Cook: 3 minutes per batch

6	slices bacon
1	large egg white
1/4	teaspoon salt
1/2	cup cornmeal
1/4	teaspoon coarsely ground black pepper
3	medium green tomatoes (1 pound), cut into scant 1/2-inch-thick slices

1. In 12-inch skillet, cook bacon over medium heat until browned. With slotted spoon, transfer bacon to paper towels to drain; crumble. Set aside skillet with bacon drippings.
2. In pie plate, beat egg white and salt. On waxed paper, combine cornmeal and pepper. Dip tomatoes in egg mixture to coat both sides, then dip into cornmeal mixture, pressing so mixture adheres. Place on waxed paper.
3. Heat bacon drippings in skillet over medium-high heat. In batches, cook tomatoes until golden brown, about 1 1/2 minutes per side, transferring to paper towels to drain.
4. Transfer tomatoes to platter and top with bacon. Makes 6 accompaniment servings.

Each serving: About 189 calories, 4g protein, 13g carbohydrate, 13g total fat (5g saturated), 15mg cholesterol, 270mg sodium.

OVEN-DRIED TOMATOES

Preheat oven to 250°F. Peel 12 plum tomatoes (3 pounds; see page 469). Cut each lengthwise in half; scoop out seeds with small spoon. In a large bowl, toss tomatoes with 2 tablespoons extravirgin olive oil, 1/2 teaspoon dried basil, 1/2 teaspoon dried thyme, 1/2 teaspoon salt, and 1/4 teaspoon coarsely ground black pepper. Arrange tomatoes, cut side down, on wire rack set over cookie sheet. Bake until tomatoes are shriveled and partially dried, about 5 1/2 hours. Cool completely, then transfer to a ziptight plastic bag. Refrigerate up to 2 months, or freeze up to 6 months. Makes 24 tomato halves.

Broiled Tomato Halves

An easy way to add color to your dinner plate.

Prep: 15 minutes   Broil: 8 minutes

3	ripe medium tomatoes (6 ounces each), each cut crosswise in half
2	tablespoons butter or margarine
¾	cup fresh bread crumbs (about 1½ slices bread)
1	tablespoon chopped fresh parsley
¼	teaspoon salt
¼	teaspoon ground black pepper

1. Preheat broiler. Place tomatoes, cut side up, on rack in broiling pan.

2. In small skillet, melt butter over low heat. Brush each tomato half with some melted butter. Place pan in broiler 5 to 7 inches from heat source. Broil until heated through, 5 to 7 minutes. Remove from broiler.

3. Meanwhile, combine bread crumbs, parsley, salt, and pepper with butter remaining in skillet.

4. Evenly top each tomato half with bread-crumb mixture. Return tomatoes to broiler; broil until topping is golden brown, 3 to 5 minutes. Makes 6 accompaniment servings.

Each serving: About 66 calories, 1g protein, 6g carbohydrate, 4g total fat (2g saturated), 11mg cholesterol, 169mg sodium.

TURNIPS

Turnips
Availability
Year round

Peak Season
October through March

Buying Tips
Buy firm, unblemished turnips with fresh green tops, if attached. (Turnip greens can be cooked separately, just like beet greens. See Stir-Frying 101, page 436.)

To Store
Refrigerate the tops and turnips separately in plastic bags in the crisper drawer. Store turnips up to one week and the tops up to two days.

To Prepare
Rinse turnips under cold running water; peel. Leave whole, slice, or cut into pieces. Cook the turnips and the tops as directed in recipe.

Candied Turnips

A sugar glaze balances the mild bitterness of the turnips.

Prep: 10 minutes   Cook: 23 minutes

1½	pounds turnips, peeled and cut into 1-inch-thick wedges
1	teaspoon salt
2	tablespoons butter or margarine
⅓	cup sugar

1. In 12-inch skillet, combine turnips, enough *water* to cover, and salt; heat to boiling over high heat. Reduce heat; cover and simmer just until turnips are tender, 7 to 10 minutes. Drain; wipe skillet dry with paper towels.

2. In same skillet, melt butter over high heat. Add sugar and cook, stirring occasionally, until sugar has turned amber, about 2 minutes. Add turnips and cook, stirring frequently, until well coated and golden, about 5 minutes. Makes 6 accompaniment servings.

Each serving: About 101 calories, 1g protein, 17g carbohydrate, 4g total fat (2g saturated), 10mg cholesterol, 294mg sodium.

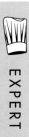

EXPERT TIP

Most people are familiar with grilling vegetables, such as eggplant, summer squash, and mushrooms. Grilled greens can also be delicious, especially sturdy ones like kale, collard, and chard, which can stand up to the heat. If you're a gardener or the recipient of vegetables from someone else's garden, this method is an especially appealing way to cook these greens. Simply remove any tough stems, brush them lightly with a little olive oil, and season with salt and pepper. Place on a medium-hot grill and cook on both sides until the edges char a little. Toss with some good vinegar, like a nutty sherry vinegar, and serve hot or at room temperature. You won't believe how good they are!

JOHN ASH

CULINARY DIRECTOR, FETZER VINEYARDS, CALIFORNIA

Curried Vegetable Stew

Serve over rice for a healthful vegetarian meal.

Prep: 15 minutes   Cook: 25 minutes

2	teaspoons olive oil
1	large sweet potato (12 ounces), peeled and cut into 1/2-inch pieces
1	medium onion, cut into 1/2-inch pieces
1	medium zucchini (8 ounces), cut into 1-inch pieces
1	small green pepper, cut into 3/4-inch pieces
1 1/2	teaspoons curry powder
1	teaspoon ground cumin
1	can (15 to 19 ounces) garbanzo beans, rinsed and drained
1	can (14 1/2 ounces) diced tomatoes
3/4	cup vegetable broth
1/2	teaspoon salt

1. In deep nonstick 12-inch skillet, heat oil over medium-high heat. Add sweet potato, onion, zucchini, and green pepper; cook, stirring, until vegetables are tender, 8 to 10 minutes. Add curry powder and cumin; cook 1 minute.

2. Add garbanzo beans, tomatoes with their juice, broth, and salt; heat to boiling over high heat. Reduce heat to medium-low; cover and simmer until vegetables are very tender but still hold their shape, about 10 minutes longer. Makes 4 main-dish servings.

Each serving: About 223 calories, 8g protein, 39g carbohydrate, 5g total fat (0g saturated), 0mg cholesterol, 790mg sodium.

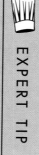

Make sure to amply salt the water when blanching or boiling vegetables; taste the water to make sure there is enough. When water is salted properly at the beginning, greens stay greener and vegetables emerge nicely seasoned, instead of tasting water logged.

DANIEL BOULUD

CHEF/OWNER, DANIEL AND CAFÉ BOULUD, NEW YORK CITY

EXPERT TIP

Moroccan Vegetable Stew

Spiced with cinnamon and crushed pepper, sweetened with prunes, and served over couscous, this Moroccan stew is richly flavored and satisfying.

Prep: 15 minutes   Cook: 40 minutes

1	tablespoon olive oil
1	medium butternut squash (about 2 pounds), peeled and cut into 1-inch pieces
2	carrots, peeled and cut into 1/4-inch-thick slices
1	medium onion, chopped
1	can (15 to 19 ounces) garbanzo beans, rinsed and drained
1	can (14 1/2 ounces) stewed tomatoes
1/2	cup pitted prunes, chopped
1/2	teaspoon ground cinnamon
1/2	teaspoon salt
1/8 to 1/4	teaspoon crushed red pepper
1 1/2	cups water
1	cup couscous (Moroccan pasta)
1 1/4	cups vegetable or chicken broth
2	tablespoons chopped fresh cilantro or parsley

1. In nonstick 12-inch skillet, heat oil over medium-high heat. Add squash, carrots, and onion and cook, stirring frequently, until onion is tender and golden, about 10 minutes.

2. Stir in garbanzo beans, tomatoes, prunes, cinnamon, salt, crushed red pepper, and water; heat to boiling. Reduce heat; cover and simmer until all vegetables are tender, about 30 minutes.

3. Meanwhile, prepare couscous as label directs, but use broth in place of water.

4. To serve, stir cilantro into stew and spoon over couscous. Makes 4 main-dish servings.

Each serving: About 474 calories, 14g protein, 95g carbohydrate, 6g total fat (1g saturated), 0mg cholesterol, 1,022mg sodium.

Succotash

Corn and lima beans, two staples of Native American cooking, are combined to make this simple dish. The name succotash comes from the Narraganset word for "ear of corn."

Prep: 10 minutes   Cook: 25 minutes

5	slices bacon
3	stalks celery, cut into ¼-inch-thick slices
1	medium onion, chopped
2	cans (15¼ to 16 ounces each) whole-kernel corn, drained
2	packages (10 ounces each) frozen baby lima beans
½	cup chicken broth
¾	teaspoon salt
¼	teaspoon coarsely ground black pepper
2	tablespoons chopped fresh parsley

1. In 12-inch skillet, cook bacon over medium-low heat until browned. With slotted spoon, transfer to paper towels to drain; crumble.

2. Discard all but 2 tablespoons bacon drippings from skillet. Add celery and onion and cook over medium heat, stirring, until vegetables are tender and golden, about 15 minutes. Stir in corn, frozen lima beans, broth, salt, and pepper; heat to boiling over high heat. Reduce heat; cover and simmer until heated through, 5 to 10 minutes longer. Stir in parsley and sprinkle with bacon. Makes 10 accompaniment servings.

Each serving: About 171 calories, 7g protein, 27g carbohydrate, 5g total fat (1g saturated), 5mg cholesterol, 458mg sodium.

Ciambotta

As with many vegetable stews, the ingredients for ciambotta *can be varied according to what you have on hand and the flavors you prefer. It can also be served at room temperature.*

Prep: 30 minutes   Cook: 30 minutes

3	tablespoons olive oil
1	medium onion, chopped
2	garlic cloves, finely chopped
2	red peppers, cut into 1-inch pieces
1½	pounds zucchini (3 medium), cut lengthwise in half, then into ½-inch pieces
1½	pounds ripe tomatoes, peeled, seeded, and chopped
¾	teaspoon salt
⅓	cup chopped fresh basil

1. In nonreactive 12-inch skillet, heat 2 tablespoons oil over medium heat. Add onion and garlic and cook, stirring frequently, until onion is tender, about 5 minutes. Add red peppers and cook, stirring frequently, until red peppers are tender-crisp, about 5 minutes longer.

2. Add remaining 1 tablespoon oil and zucchini; cook, stirring, until zucchini is tender-crisp, about 5 minutes. Add tomatoes and salt; heat to boiling. Reduce heat; cover and simmer until vegetables are very tender, about 10 minutes. Stir in basil. Makes 6 accompaniment servings.

Each serving: About 117 calories, 3g protein, 13g carbohydrate, 7g total fat (1g saturated), 0mg cholesterol, 305mg sodium.

The one rule I live by more than any other when it comes to cooking is that the better the ingredients, the less you have to do to make them taste good. This is particularly true of vegetables and fruits. Since you can't make them better than they are naturally, make every effort to use the best. What are the best? Foods that are in season, grown close to where you live, well tended in the garden, and harvested at the right moment. If you don't garden, a farmers' market where farmers sell their own produce is the best place for vegetables that are impeccably fresh and flavorful. Even if you can't use them right away, you'll find they will keep much longer, because they haven't been shipped for hundreds of miles.

DEBORAH MADISON
COOKBOOK AUTHOR

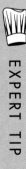

EXPERT TIP

Mashed Root Vegetables

This is comfort food of the highest order. Use just one vegetable or a combination for mashing with the potatoes.

Prep: 15 minutes   Cook: 25 minutes

2	pounds root vegetables, such as carrots, celery root (celeriac), parsnips, white turnips, or rutabaga, peeled and cut into 1-inch pieces (5 cups)
1	pound all-purpose potatoes (3 medium), peeled and cut into 1-inch pieces
2½	teaspoons salt
3	tablespoons butter or margarine, cut into pieces
¼	teaspoon ground black pepper
	pinch ground nutmeg

1. In 4-quart saucepan, combine root vegetables, potatoes, enough *water* to cover, and 2 teaspoons salt; heat to boiling over high heat. Boil until vegetables are tender, about 15 minutes. Drain.

2. Return vegetables to saucepan. Add butter, remaining ½ teaspoon salt, pepper, and nutmeg; mash until smooth and well blended. Makes 8 accompaniment servings.

Each serving: About 118 calories, 2g protein, 18g carbohydrate, 5g total fat (3g saturated), 12mg cholesterol, 534mg sodium.

Mediterranean Grilled Eggplant and Summer Squash

This summertime recipe can be served hot or cool and doubles easily. If you're feeding a crowd, grill the vegetables in batches.

 *Prep: 15 minutes   Grill: 10 minutes*

3	tablespoons olive oil
2	tablespoons red wine vinegar
2	teaspoons Dijon mustard
1	garlic clove, crushed with garlic press
¼	teaspoon salt
¼	teaspoon coarsely ground black pepper
1	medium zucchini (8 ounces), cut lengthwise into ¼-inch-thick slices
1	medium yellow squash (8 ounces), cut lengthwise into ¼-inch-thick slices
1	small eggplant (1¼ pounds), cut lengthwise into ¼-inch-thick slices
2	tablespoons chopped fresh mint
1	ounce ricotta salata or feta cheese, crumbled (¼ cup)

1. Prepare grill. Prepare vinaigrette: In small bowl, with wire whisk, mix oil, vinegar, mustard, garlic, salt, and pepper until blended; brush on one side of vegetable slices.

2. Place vegetables, vinaigrette side down, on grill over medium heat. Grill, turning once and brushing with remaining vinaigrette, until browned and tender, 10 to 15 minutes. Transfer vegetables to large platter as they are done.

3. To serve, sprinkle vegetables with mint and ricotta salata. Makes 6 accompaniment servings.

Each serving: About 114 calories, 3g protein, 9g carbohydrate, 8g total fat (2g saturated), 4mg cholesterol, 222mg sodium.

Mediterranean Grilled Eggplant and Summer Squash

Ratatouille

This Provençal classic is very flexible: Serve it hot or cold, or as a first course, salad, or a side dish to accompany meat, poultry, or fish.

Prep: 20 minutes   Cook: 1 hour

2	tablespoons olive oil
1	medium onion, chopped
1	small eggplant (1 pound), not peeled, cut into 1-inch pieces
¾	teaspoon salt
¼	teaspoon ground black pepper
1	yellow or red pepper, cut into 1-inch pieces
1	medium zucchini (8 ounces), cut into 1-inch pieces
2	large garlic cloves, finely chopped
1	can (28 ounces) tomatoes, chopped
⅛	teaspoon dried thyme
¼	cup chopped fresh basil or parsley

In nonreactive 5-quart saucepot, heat oil over medium heat. Add onion; cook until tender and golden, about 10 minutes. Add eggplant, salt, and black pepper; cook, stirring, until eggplant begins to brown, about 10 minutes. Stir in yellow pepper, zucchini, and garlic; cook 1 minute. Stir in tomatoes with their juice and thyme; heat to boiling. Reduce heat; cover and simmer until eggplant is tender, about 30 minutes. Remove from heat; stir in basil. Makes 8 accompaniment servings.

Each serving: About 81 calories, 2g protein, 12g carbohydrate, 4g total fat (0g saturated), 0mg cholesterol, 384mg sodium.

Soy sauce comes in many forms and varying degrees of saltiness. Try several to find one you like. Never buy nonbrewed soy sauce, made with caramel coloring and hydrolyzed soy protein: It's black and bitter. Look for naturally brewed and aged soy sauce made from soybeans, wheat, and water. It's reddish brown and deeply flavorful. If you are on a wheat-free diet, use authentic *tamari*, made from soybeans alone.

BARBARA TROPP
COOKBOOK AUTHOR

EXPERT TIP

Harvest Casserole

A great dish for a holiday turkey or ham.

Prep: 40 minutes   Bake: 1 hour

5	tablespoons butter or margarine
1	jumbo onion (1 pound), cut into ¼-inch-thick slices
2	garlic cloves, finely chopped
1	medium rutabaga (1 pound), peeled, cut into quarters, and thinly sliced
6	carrots (1 pound), peeled and thinly sliced
5	small parsnips (1 pound), peeled and thinly sliced
3	tablespoons all-purpose flour
2½	cups milk, warmed
1½	teaspoons salt
¼	teaspoon coarsely ground black pepper
¼	teaspoon ground nutmeg
¼	cup freshly grated Parmesan cheese
	chopped fresh parsley (optional)

1. Preheat oven to 375°F. In nonstick 10-inch skillet, melt 3 tablespoons butter over medium heat. Add onion and garlic; cook, stirring occasionally, until onion is golden brown and tender, about 15 minutes.

2. In shallow 2½-quart casserole, combine rutabaga, carrots, parsnips, and onion mixture and toss until combined. Cover and bake until vegetables are tender, about 45 minutes.

3. Meanwhile, prepare sauce: In heavy 2-quart saucepan, melt remaining 2 tablespoons butter over low heat. Add flour and cook, stirring, 1 minute. With wire whisk, gradually whisk in warm milk. Cook over medium heat, stirring constantly with wooden spoon, until mixture has thickened and boils. Reduce heat and simmer, stirring frequently, 5 minutes. Stir in salt, pepper, and nutmeg; remove from heat.

4. Add sauce to vegetables and toss to coat; sprinkle with Parmesan. Bake, uncovered, until sauce is bubbling and top is golden, about 15 minutes longer. To serve, sprinkle with parsley, if you like. Makes 8 accompaniment servings.

Each serving: About 235 calories, 6g protein, 29g carbohydrate, 11g total fat (7g saturated), 32mg cholesterol, 637mg sodium.

GUIDE TO GRILLED VEGETABLES

Preheat grill to medium-high

VEGETABLE (4 SERVINGS)	PREPARATION	SEASONING	GRILLING TIME
8 ears corn	Soak 15 minutes, then remove silk (leave husk on) or remove husks and silk.	Brush with 1 tablespoon oil.	45 minutes 20 minutes, turning occasionally
1½-pound eggplant	Cut crosswise into ½-inch-thick slices.	Brush with ¼ cup oil.	11 to 13 minutes per side
4 heads endive	Cut lengthwise in half.	Brush with 1 tablespoon oil.	10 to 12 minutes per side
2 medium fennel bulbs (1 pound each)	Cut lengthwise into ¼-inch-thick slices.	Brush with 4 teaspoons oil.	6 to 8 minutes per side
6 medium leeks	Remove dark green tops; blanch and cut lengthwise in half.	Toss with 1 tablespoon oil.	11 to 13 minutes per side
8 ounces large white mushrooms	Trim and thread onto skewers.	Brush with 2 teaspoons oil.	20 minutes, turning several times
4 large portobello mushrooms (about 1 pound)	Remove stems.	Brush with 4 teaspoons oil.	15 minutes per side
4 medium red or white onions	Cut crosswise into ½-inch-thick slices; secure with toothpicks.	Brush with 4 teaspoons oil.	12 to 14 minutes per side
2 bunches small green onions	Trim.	Toss with 4 teaspoons oil.	2 to 4 minutes, turning several times
4 red, green, or yellow peppers	Cut lengthwise into quarters.		10 to 12 minutes per side
2 heads radicchio (12 ounces each)	Cut lengthwise into quarters.	Brush with 2 tablespoons oil.	5 minutes per side
4 medium yellow squash or zucchini (8 ounces each)	Cut lengthwise into ¼-inch-thick slices.	Brush with 4 teaspoons oil.	5 minutes per side
4 medium tomatoes (8 ounces each)	Cut crosswise in half.	Brush cut sides with 2 tablespoons oil.	14 to 17 minutes per side
1 pint cherry tomatoes	Thread onto skewers.	Brush with 2 teaspoons oil.	5 to 7 minutes, turning several times

Vegetable Stir-Fry

Start with this basic recipe, then add other ingredients to suit your taste. Possibilities include Asian (toasted) sesame oil, thinly sliced radishes, hot chiles or crushed red pepper, or soy sauce.

Prep: 20 minutes   Cook: 18 minutes

1	tablespoon vegetable oil
2	garlic cloves, thinly sliced
1	teaspoon minced, peeled fresh ginger
1	small bunch broccoli (12 ounces), cut into flowerets (about 3 cups)
1	cup water
1	cup peeled and thinly sliced carrots
1	yellow pepper, cut into 1/2-inch pieces
6	mushrooms, trimmed and thinly sliced
3	green onions, cut on diagonal into 1-inch pieces
2	tablespoons hoisin sauce
1/4	teaspoon salt

In nonstick 12-inch skillet, heat oil over medium-high heat until hot. Add garlic and ginger and cook, stirring frequently (stir-frying), 1 minute. Add broccoli and stir-fry 1 minute. Increase heat to high; add water and cook 3 minutes. Add carrots and yellow pepper and stir-fry until liquid has evaporated, about 6 minutes. Add mushrooms, green onions, hoisin sauce, and salt; stir-fry until vegetables are tender and almost all liquid has evaporated, about 5 minutes longer. Makes 4 accompaniment servings.

Each serving: About 109 calories, 4g protein, 15g carbohydrate, 4g total fat (1g saturated), 0mg cholesterol, 355mg sodium.

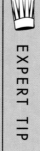

My favorite stir-fry tool is a broad wooden rice paddle. It fits the contours of a wok perfectly, it's lightweight, and it's very easy to hold. I've never found a better flipper. Look for a paddle that's 9 inches long and almost 8 inches across at the wide end.

BARBARA TROPP
COOKBOOK AUTHOR

EXPERT TIP

Sicilian Stewed Vegetables

In Southern Italy, this is the kind of tasty food you're likely to find served in almost every home.

Prep: 30 minutes   Cook: 1 hour

3	tablespoons olive oil
1	pound ripe plum tomatoes, chopped
2	small onions, sliced
2	stalks celery with leaves, thinly sliced
1/4	cup chopped fresh basil
2	garlic cloves, thinly sliced
1	small eggplant (1 pound), cut into 3/4-inch pieces
1	medium all-purpose potato (about 5 ounces), peeled and cut into 3/4-inch pieces
1/2	cup water
3/4	teaspoon salt
1/4	teaspoon ground black pepper
2	small zucchini (6 ounces each), each cut lengthwise in half, then crosswise into thin slices
1	yellow pepper, cut into thin strips

1. In nonreactive 12-inch skillet, heat 1 tablespoon oil over medium heat. Add tomatoes and cook, stirring occasionally, 10 minutes. Strain through food mill or coarse-mesh sieve into medium bowl. Wipe skillet clean.

2. In same skillet, heat remaining 2 tablespoons oil over medium heat. Add onions, celery, 2 tablespoons basil, and garlic and cook, stirring, until vegetables are tender, about 10 minutes. Add tomatoes and heat to boiling. Stir in eggplant, potato, 1/4 cup water, salt, and black pepper. Cover and simmer, stirring frequently, 20 minutes, adding more water if necessary to prevent sticking. Add zucchini, yellow pepper, remaining 2 tablespoons basil, and remaining 1/4 cup water; cover and simmer, stirring frequently and adding more water if necessary, until vegetables are tender, about 20 minutes.

3. Cover and let stand 10 minutes before serving. Makes 8 accompaniment servings.

Each serving: About 110 calories, 3g protein, 15g carbohydrate, 5g total fat (1g saturated), 0mg cholesterol, 237mg sodium.

Tzimmes

Though traditionally reserved for the Jewish New Year, this sweet and savory dish can be enjoyed anytime. Try it with roast chicken.

Prep: 25 minutes   Cook: 1 hour 25 minutes

1	tablespoon olive oil
1	medium onion, chopped
1	pound sweet potatoes (2 small), peeled and cut into 1-inch pieces
1	pound all-purpose potatoes (3 medium), peeled and cut into 1-inch pieces
3	carrots, peeled, cut lengthwise in half, and then into 1-inch pieces
¾	cup small pitted prunes
⅓	cup packed brown sugar
2½	cups water
¾	teaspoon salt
½	teaspoon freshly grated orange peel
¼	teaspoon coarsely ground black pepper
¼	teaspoon ground ginger
¼	teaspoon ground cinnamon
1½	teaspoons fresh lemon juice

In 3-quart saucepan, heat oil over medium-low heat. Add onion and cook until tender, about 5 minutes. Stir in sweet and all-purpose potatoes, carrots, prunes, brown sugar, water, salt, orange peel, pepper, ginger, and cinnamon; heat to boiling. Reduce heat; cover and simmer 1 hour. Remove cover and cook until slightly thickened, about 10 minutes longer. Stir in lemon juice. Makes 6 accompaniment servings.

♥ Each serving: About 243 calories, 3g protein, 54g carbohydrate, 3g total fat (0g saturated), 0mg cholesterol, 320mg sodium.

Potato and Turnip Gratin

Sliced turnips and potatoes smothered in cream and baked until golden are another candidate for the Thanksgiving table.

Prep: 50 minutes plus cooling   Bake: 25 minutes

6	medium all-purpose potatoes (about 5 ounces each), peeled and cut into ¼-inch-thick slices
3	medium turnips (about 5 ounces each), peeled and cut into ¼-inch-thick slices
2	teaspoons salt
2	tablespoons butter or margarine
1	medium onion, thinly sliced
1	cup heavy or whipping cream
4	tablespoons freshly grated Parmesan cheese
¼	teaspoon coarsely ground black pepper
⅛	teaspoon ground nutmeg
2	tablespoons plain dried bread crumbs

1. Preheat oven to 400°F. Generously grease shallow 2½-quart casserole.

2. In 4-quart saucepan, combine potatoes, turnips, enough *water* to cover, and 1 teaspoon salt; heat to boiling over high heat. Reduce heat; cover and simmer until tender, 8 to 10 minutes. Drain.

3. Meanwhile, in 2-quart saucepan, melt 1 tablespoon butter over medium heat. Add onion and cook until tender and golden, about 10 minutes. Stir in cream, 2 tablespoons Parmesan cheese, remaining 1 teaspoon salt, pepper, and nutmeg; cook 1 minute.

4. When cool enough to handle, in prepared casserole, arrange potato and turnip slices in concentric circles, overlapping slices. Evenly pour onion-cream mixture over potatoes and turnips.

5. Melt remaining 1 tablespoon butter. In cup, combine bread crumbs, remaining 2 tablespoons Parmesan, and melted butter. Evenly sprinkle over potato-turnip mixture. Bake gratin until bubbling and golden, about 25 minutes. Makes 8 accompaniment servings.

Each serving: About 241 calories, 5g protein, 22g carbohydrate, 16g total fat (9g saturated), 51mg cholesterol, 584mg sodium.

12

FRUITS

Vitamin-packed, fiber-rich fruits are important components of a well-balanced diet: The USDA recommends two to four servings per day. There are many delicious ways to meet this goal. Enjoy a refreshing fruit salad for lunch, or top a green salad with orange or grapefruit sections. Serve juicy grapes or figs with cheese as a snack or dessert, or slip sliced fruit into a meat sandwich (try sliced peaches with baked ham and Dijon mustard). Toss dried apricots or prunes into braised chicken dishes and beef or lamb stews, or eat ripe fruit out of hand and savor every sweet bite.

Over the years, more and more imported fruit (from Central America, South America, and New Zealand) has appeared in stores, making otherwise out-of-season fruit available. But practically every fruit has a season when it is at its flavorful peak and is most reasonably priced. Whenever possible, buy fruits in season from local farmers' markets; you will be rewarded with the most delicious produce possible.

Some fruits, such as apples, cherries, citrus fruits, pomegranates, and rhubarb, are purchased fully ripe and can be enjoyed immediately. Other fruits, especially those that have been shipped long distances, need further ripening. These include apricots, nectarines, peaches, pears, and plums. To ripen these fruits, place them in a closed paper (not plastic) bag or fruit-ripening bowl and leave at room temperature for a few days. Some fruits, such as bananas, kiwifruit, mangoes, melons, papayas, and persimmons, ripen best at room temperature, away from direct sunlight. Refrigerate all ripened fruits to keep them from becoming overripe.

All fruits with edible skins should be rinsed well before eating to remove any residual pesticides and surface bacteria. Some fruits, such as apples, may be covered with an edible wax coating to give them an attractive shine. If you wish, peel waxed fruit before eating.

Nothing beats the flavor of fresh seasonal fruit, but canned fruit is a good pantry staple for a quick lunch or dessert. Some canned fruits are better than others; we are especially fond of pears and apricots. Keep in mind that fruits canned in light syrup have a fresher flavor than those in heavy syrup.

In this chapter, we offer tempting recipes that are easy and delicious for just about every fruit you will find in your supermarket, local produce market, or farmers' market. Also included is how to choose each fruit, how to store it at home, how long it will keep, and the best way to prepare the fruit for eating out of hand or for cooking. We also felt it important to list not only when the fruit is available in the market, but also its peak season—when it will be at its flavorful best.

Berries and Cream Shortcake

APPLES

Availability
Year round

Peak Season
October through March

Buying Tips
Buy firm, crisp, well-shaped fruit. Apples range in color from bright green to deep red, depending on the variety. Avoid apples that are soft or have brown bruise spots.

If you are planning to cook apples, choose a variety that will work well in the particular recipe. Cooking apples are preferred for baking and pies. Some apples fall apart when cooked, so they make great applesauce. And some varieties are really at their best eaten out of hand.

Cortland A fine all-purpose apple, this large round apple remains firm when baked. Cortland is a good choice for fruit salads because the raw slices do not discolor.

Gala This New Zealand import is a cross between Kidd's Orange Red and Golden Delicious. It is sweet and crisp with red-streaked yellow skin and is good for cooking.

Golden Delicious Another good all-purpose apple with yellow-gold skin and a sweet flavor. Excellent for eating out of hand, pies, applesauce, and salads.

Granny Smith Very crisp and slightly acidic, this green-skinned apple is named for its original cultivator, an Aus-

tralian grandmother. Its slices hold their shape well during baking, so it's a good choice for pies.

Jonagold A crisp, yellow-fleshed apple that works well in pies, cobblers, and applesauce.

Macoun A cross between the McIntosh and Jersey Black, it has fragrant white flesh and is a good all-purpose apple.

McIntosh Round and juicy, this apple's flesh softens when cooked. Best for applesauce, eating out of hand, or in combination with firmer apples in pies.

Newtown Pippin A somewhat small apple with tart, firm flesh. Great in pies.

Red Delicious The most familiar red-skinned apple; best for eating out of hand.

Rome Beauty A large, aromatic apple that is excellent for baking whole.

Winesap A crisp pie apple with winelike juice.

To Store
The storage period for apples depends on the variety. In general, store apples in the crisper drawer in the refrigerator and use within two weeks.

To Prepare
Rinse apples and core. If the apples (except for Golden Delicious or Cortland) are to be peeled or sliced, sprinkle with lemon juice, vinegar, or a little vinaigrette (depending on their use) to prevent browning.

THE FASTEST BAKED APPLE

Our microwaved apples are ready in minutes instead of the usual hour in a standard oven. They make a nutritious breakfast or dessert with a generous dollop of plain or vanilla yogurt on top.

Prep: 10 minutes   Microwave: 7 to 9 minutes

Remove cores from large cooking apples (10 ounces each), such as Romes, but don't cut through to bottom. Peel one-third of way down. Stand apples in small individual bowls or 8-inch square baking dish. Place 1 teaspoon butter and 1 tablespoon brown sugar into cavity of each apple. Cover and cook on medium-high (70% power) until tender, about 9 minutes, turning halfway through cooking. Cover and let stand 5 minutes.

Each apple: About 234 calories, 0g protein, 52g carbohydrate, 5g total fat (3g saturated), 10mg cholesterol, 44mg sodium.

McIntosh Applesauce

Cooking the apples with the cores and peels adds flavor and body to applesauce, and pressing the mixture through a sieve makes it silky smooth. If the apples you use are red-skinned, the sauce will turn a lovely shade of pink.

Prep: 15 minutes	Cook: 15 minutes
1½ pounds cooking apples (6 small), preferably McIntosh	
¼ cup water	
⅓ cup sugar or more to taste	
1 teaspoon fresh lemon juice	

1. Cut apples into quarters but do not peel or remove cores. In 4-quart saucepan, combine apples and water; heat to boiling over high heat. Reduce heat; cover and simmer, stirring occasionally, until very tender, 10 to 15 minutes. Stir in sugar and lemon juice.

2. Press apple mixture through sieve or food mill set over large bowl; discard skin and seeds. Taste and add more sugar, if desired. Serve warm, or cover and refrigerate to serve chilled. Makes about 3½ cups.

♥ Each ½ cup: About 84 calories, 0g protein, 22g carbohydrate, 0g total fat (0g saturated), 0mg cholesterol, 0mg sodium.

Ginger Applesauce
Prepare as directed but add **1½ teaspoons grated, peeled fresh ginger** to apples.

Lemon Applesauce
Prepare as directed but add **2 strips (2" by 1" each) lemon peel** to apples.

Spiced Applesauce
Prepare as directed but add **1 cinnamon stick (3 inches)** and **3 whole cloves** to apples.

Horseradish Applesauce
Prepare as directed but after straining, stir **2 tablespoons bottled white horseradish** into applesauce. (Serve with pork.)

Cranberry Applesauce
Prepare as directed but add **1½ cups fresh or frozen cranberries** to apples.

Vermont Baked Apples

Choose a sweet apple that holds its shape when baked, such as Rome Beauty or Cortland. If you like, serve with whipped cream.

Prep: 10 minutes	Bake: 1 hour 45 minutes
6 large cooking apples (7 to 8 ounces each)	
3 tablespoons butter or margarine	
1 cup maple syrup or maple-flavored syrup	

1. Preheat oven to 350°F. Remove apple cores; beginning at stem, peel one-third of way down. Stand apples in shallow 13" by 9" baking dish. Place 1½ teaspoons butter into cavity of each apple. Pour maple syrup over and around apples.

2. Bake apples, basting occasionally with syrup in baking dish, until tender, about 1 hour 45 minutes. Serve hot, or cover and refrigerate to serve chilled. Makes 6 servings.

♥ Each serving: About 288 calories, 0g protein, 61g carbohydrate, 6g total fat (4g saturated), 16mg cholesterol, 63mg sodium.

Vermont Baked Apples

Apple-Oatmeal Crisp

The ultimate autumn dessert. Substitute Golden Delicious apples for the Granny Smiths if you prefer a sweeter dessert.

Prep: 20 minutes   Bake: 30 minutes

2¾	pounds Granny Smith apples (7 medium), peeled, cored, and cut into ¼-inch-thick slices
2	tablespoons fresh lemon juice
¾	cup packed brown sugar
2	tablespoons plus ⅓ cup all-purpose flour
½	cup old-fashioned oats, uncooked
¼	teaspoon ground cinnamon
6	tablespoons butter or margarine, cut into pieces

1. Preheat oven to 425°F. In 1½-quart baking dish, toss apples with lemon juice; add ½ cup brown sugar and 2 tablespoons flour and toss to coat.

2. In small bowl, combine oats, remaining ⅓ cup flour, and remaining ¼ cup brown sugar. With pastry blender or two knives used scissor-fashion, cut in butter until mixture resembles coarse crumbs. Sprinkle over apple mixture.

3. Bake until apples are tender and topping has lightly browned, 30 to 35 minutes. Cool slightly on wire rack to serve warm. Makes 6 servings.

Each serving: About 368 calories, 2g protein, 65g carbohydrate, 13g total fat (7g saturated), 31mg cholesterol, 128mg sodium.

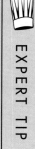

The easiest way to peel an apple is to first remove a circle of peel from the bottom and the top with a small knife or vegetable peeler. Then peel the entire apple going from top to bottom. This saves a lot of time.

JOANNE WEIR
TELEVISION HOST OF WEIR COOKING

EXPERT TIP

Apple Brown Betty

A betty is fruit baked under a bread crumb topping. Be indulgent: Pour a little heavy cream over each serving.

Prep: 35 minutes   Bake: 50 minutes

8	slices firm white bread, torn into ½-inch pieces
½	cup butter or margarine (1 stick), melted
1	teaspoon ground cinnamon
2½	pounds Granny Smith apples (6 medium), peeled, cored, and thinly sliced
⅔	cup packed brown sugar
2	tablespoons fresh lemon juice
1	teaspoon vanilla extract
¼	teaspoon ground nutmeg

1. Preheat oven to 400°F. Place bread pieces in jelly-roll pan; bake, stirring occasionally, until very lightly toasted, 12 to 15 minutes. Grease shallow 2-quart baking dish.

2. In medium bowl, combine melted butter and ½ teaspoon cinnamon. Add toasted bread pieces, tossing gently until evenly moistened.

3. In large bowl, combine apples, brown sugar, lemon juice, vanilla, nutmeg, and remaining ½ teaspoon cinnamon; toss to coat.

4. Place ½ cup toasted bread pieces in baking dish. Cover with half of apple mixture; top with 1 cup toasted bread pieces. Place remaining apple mixture on top and sprinkle evenly with remaining bread pieces, leaving 1-inch border around edges.

5. Cover with foil and bake 40 minutes. Remove foil and bake until apples are tender and bread pieces have browned, about 10 minutes longer. Let stand 10 minutes before serving. Makes 8 servings.

Each serving: About 319 calories, 3g protein, 51g carbohydrate, 13g total fat (7g saturated), 31mg cholesterol, 277mg sodium.

Outrageous Caramel Apples

Even better than the ones at the county fair! Roll them in nuts or your favorite candy.

	Prep: 35 minutes plus chilling Cook: 6 minutes
5	wooden ice-cream sticks
5	medium McIntosh or Macoun apples (5 to 6 ounces each)
¾	cup chopped peanuts, miniature candy-coated chocolate pieces, semisweet chocolate chips, flaked sweetened coconut, colored sprinkles, toffee bits, or other favorite topping
1	package (14 ounces) caramels, unwrapped
2	tablespoons water
3	squares (3 ounces) semisweet or white chocolate, melted

1. Insert ice-cream stick into stem end of each apple. Place peanuts on waxed paper.

2. Line jelly-roll pan with waxed paper; lightly oil.

3. In 2-quart saucepan, combine caramels and water; heat over low heat, stirring constantly, until melted and smooth. Remove from heat. Holding one apple by stick, dip into caramel mixture, spooning caramel over apple to coat completely. (If caramel mixture in saucepan begins to harden, warm over low heat to soften.) Dip caramel-coated apple into peanuts or candy to coat bottom, then place in prepared pan. Repeat with remaining apples, caramel, and peanuts.

4. Spoon melted chocolate into zip-tight plastic bag. With scissors, cut off one corner of bag to make small opening. Drizzle melted chocolate over apples. Refrigerate apples 15 minutes to allow chocolate to set. If not eating right away, loosely cover and refrigerate up to 2 days. Let apples stand at room temperature 15 minutes to soften caramel before eating. Makes 5 apples.

Each apple: About 599 calories, 10g protein, 99g carbohydrate, 23g total fat (10g saturated), 6mg cholesterol, 198mg sodium.

Apple Charlotte

This traditional French farmhouse dessert is simply intensely flavored applesauce baked in a buttery sliced-bread shell.

	Prep: 1 hour Bake: 20 minutes
1	lemon
5	pounds Golden Delicious apples, peeled, cored, and cut into ¾-inch pieces (15 cups)
6	tablespoons butter or margarine, softened
⅔	cup sugar
	pinch salt
15	slices firm white bread, crusts removed

1. From lemon, with vegetable peeler, remove 2 strips (3" by 1" each) peel; squeeze 1 tablespoon juice.

2. In 5-quart Dutch oven, combine apples, lemon peel, and 2 tablespoons butter. Cover and cook over medium-high heat, stirring occasionally, until apples are almost tender, about 15 minutes.

3. Discard lemon peel and stir in sugar. Increase heat to high. Cook, mashing apples with spoon and stirring frequently to prevent burning, until apples are tender and lightly caramelized and almost all liquid has evaporated, 15 to 25 minutes. Stir in lemon juice and salt.

4. Meanwhile, preheat oven to 425°F. Spread remaining 4 tablespoons butter over one side of bread slices. Line bottom and sides of 9" by 5" metal loaf pan with some of bread, placing buttered side against pan and trimming bread to fit.

5. Spoon apple mixture into bread-lined pan; top with remaining bread, placing buttered side up. Bake 20 minutes. Invert onto serving plate. To serve, cut into slices with serrated knife while warm. Makes 10 servings.

♥ Each serving: About 326 calories, 3g protein, 61g carbohydrate, 9g total fat (5g saturated), 19mg cholesterol, 290mg sodium.

APRICOTS

Availability
June and July

Buying Tips
Look for plump, juicy-looking, orange-yellow fruit; ripe apricots yield to gentle pressure.

To Store
Handle carefully; apricots bruise easily. Ripen at room temperature, then refrigerate for up to three days.

To Prepare
Wash apricots and cut in half to remove the pit; peel if desired. If the apricots are not to be eaten immediately, sprinkle with lemon juice to prevent browning.

Poached Apricots

Poaching is a great way to enhance the flavor of apricots that aren't as tasty as they could be. If you have some fresh blueberries or raspberries on hand, scatter them over the top.

Prep: 10 minutes   Cook: 20 minutes

1	large lemon
1	cup water
8	large apricots, each cut in half and pitted (pits reserved)
2/3	cup sugar
1/8	teaspoon vanilla extract

1. From lemon, grate ¾ teaspoon peel and squeeze 3 tablespoons juice.

2. In nonreactive 2-quart saucepan, combine water, apricot pits, sugar, and lemon juice and peel; heat to boiling over high heat. Reduce heat; cover and simmer 10 minutes.

3. Strain syrup through fine sieve into small bowl. Return syrup to same clean saucepan along with apricots and heat to boiling; reduce heat and simmer just until apricots begin to soften, about 2 minutes (they will continue to cook in hot syrup). Stir in vanilla. To serve, spoon warm apricots with some syrup into dessert dishes. Makes 4 servings.

Each serving: About 171 calories, 1g protein, 43g carbohydrate, 0g total fat (0g saturated), 0mg cholesterol, 1mg sodium.

BANANAS

Availability
Year round

Buying Tips
Yellow bananas are supermarket staples, but red and small yellow bananas are also available in some areas. Plantains (see Vegetables) are considered cooking bananas because they are not sweet.

If you want to eat bananas right away, buy solid yellow bananas with some brown flecks. Bananas that are somewhat green will ripen within a few days at room temperature. To hasten ripening, store in a closed paper bag.

To Store
After bananas ripen, they can be refrigerated for two or three days. (The skins will darken, but the fruit inside will remain ripe and fresh.) For longer storage, mash the fruit with a little lemon juice, pack into freezer containers (leaving ½-inch headspace), and freeze. Thaw in the refrigerator and use in cakes, cookies, and breads.

To Prepare
Peel and slice or cut up, depending on their use. If peeled or sliced bananas are not to be eaten immediately, sprinkle with a little lemon juice to prevent browning.

Banana Pops

An easy, fun treat for kids to enjoy. Use bananas that are firm and brown-speckled, but don't use overripe fruit.

Prep: 20 minutes plus freezing	
12	wooden ice-cream sticks
4	large ripe bananas, each peeled and cut crosswise into thirds
1	package (6 ounces) semisweet chocolate chips
2	tablespoons vegetable oil
½	cup flaked sweetened coconut, toasted
½	cup chopped salted peanuts or almond-brickle chips

1. Line cookie sheet with waxed paper. Insert ice-cream stick about 1 inch deep into one end of each banana piece.

2. In 1-quart saucepan, combine chocolate chips and oil; heat over low heat, stirring occasionally, until chocolate is melted and smooth. Pour into pie plate. Put coconut and peanuts on separate sheets of waxed paper.

3. Roll each banana piece in chocolate, then roll half of bananas in toasted coconut and half in peanuts. Place on prepared cookie sheet and freeze at least 30 minutes. Remove from freezer and let stand at room temperature 5 minutes before serving. Makes 12 servings.

Each serving: About 180 calories, 3g protein, 22g carbohydrate, 11g total fat (4g saturated), 0mg cholesterol, 52mg sodium.

Flambéed Bananas

In this classic dessert, be sure to use dark Jamaican rum: It gives the bananas an irresistible flavor.

Prep: 5 minutes Cook: 8 minutes	
3	tablespoons butter or margarine
¾	cup packed brown sugar
1	tablespoon fresh lemon juice
4	ripe medium bananas, each peeled, cut crosswise in half, and then lengthwise in half
⅓	cup dark Jamaican rum or brandy
	vanilla ice cream (optional)

1. In 12-inch skillet, melt butter over medium heat. Stir in brown sugar and lemon juice. Place bananas in single layer in skillet; cook until just slightly softened, about 2 minutes per side. Reduce heat to low.

2. In 1-quart saucepan, heat rum over low heat. With long match, carefully ignite rum; pour over bananas. Spoon rum over bananas until flames die out. Serve with ice cream, if you like. Makes 8 servings.

Each serving: About 179 calories, 1g protein, 34g carbohydrate, 5g total fat (3g saturated), 12mg cholesterol, 53mg sodium.

BERRIES

Availability
Year round, depending on variety

Peak Season
June through October

Buying Tips
Berries should be plump, fresh-looking, uniformly colored, and free of stems and leaves. Avoid crushed or bruised berries and cartons that are stained with berry juice. Beware of moldy fruit, because mold can spread from berry to berry. And don't be deceived by the dewy-looking water-sprayed berries at the market—the moisture will only accelerate the molding and decaying of the berries.

Blackberries
These purplish black, cone-shaped berries grow on climbing vines. For the best flavor, buy deeply colored berries. Choose large maroon *boysenberries* for their rich, tart taste; deep red *loganberries* which are long and tangy; medium to large dark purple *marionberries* which have small seeds and an intense flavor; and large black *olallieberries*, whose flavor ranges from sweet to tart.

Blueberries
The silvery "bloom" on this berry is a natural protective coating and a sign of freshness. Only buy berries that still have their bloom. Blueberry varieties range in color from purplish blue to almost black. Wild blueberries, also called *lowbush berries*, are pea-sized and quite tart; they hold their shape well in baked goods. Look for cultivated berries from June through August. Wild berries, most easily found along the coasts, are available in August and September. To store blueberries, refrigerate in their baskets for up to ten days.

Currants

Currants are red, white, and black . Red and white currants, found in farmers' markets in July and August, are sweet enough to eat out of hand and are often used in summer puddings. Black currants are made into liqueurs, syrups, and jams.

Dewberries

Dewberries resemble blackberries in appearance and flavor, but they grow on trailing ground-running vines. Look for them in the summer.

Gooseberries

Ranging in color from green (the most common) to amber to red, tart gooseberries are usually cooked into jams, sauces, or pies. Specialty food stores sometimes carry *Chinese (Cape) gooseberries,* an entirely different species that is covered with a balloonlike papery husk (peel the shell back for a dramatic-looking dessert garnish). Gooseberries are available in June and July. You'll most likely find them in farmers' markets.

Raspberries

Red raspberries are the most common, but also look for sweet apricot-colored berries and sweet-tart black raspberries in produce or farmers' markets. If red raspberries have darkened to a dusky shade, they are past their prime. There are two peak seasons: June and July and September and October.

Strawberries

Choose bright red berries with fresh green stems still attached: Pale or yellowish white strawberries are unripe and sour. Local strawberries are available from April to July, but strawberries are found year round.

To Store

Berries are very perishable and can deteriorate within twenty-four hours of purchase. You can store them in their baskets for a brief period, but to keep them for two or three days, place the (unwashed) berries in a paper towel–lined jelly-roll or baking pan, cover loosely with paper towels, and refrigerate.

To freeze berries, wash and drain, then spread in a single layer in a jelly-roll pan and place in the freezer. Once they're frozen, transfer to a heavy-duty zip-tight plastic bag and freeze for up to one year. Do not thaw or rinse frozen berries before using. Extend the cooking time ten to fifteen minutes for berry pies and five to ten minutes for muffins and quick breads.

To Prepare

Rinse fresh berries just before serving. Remove hulls from strawberries (with a huller or small knife) and any stems from the other berry varieties; drain well.

Three-Berry Charlotte

Ladyfingers enclose a delectable berry filling in this tempting do-ahead dessert. Make it when berries are at their peak of flavor.

	Prep: 45 minutes plus chilling
2	tablespoons fresh orange juice
1	tablespoon orange-flavored liqueur
1	package (3 ounces) sponge-type ladyfingers, split
1	pint strawberries, hulled and cut in half
1/3	cup sugar
3	tablespoons fresh lemon juice
1	envelope unflavored gelatin
1/4	cup cold water
1	cup heavy or whipping cream
1	cup raspberries
1	cup blackberries
1 1/2	cups mixed berries

1. Line 9" by 5" loaf pan with plastic wrap, allowing plastic wrap to extend over sides of pan. In cup, combine orange juice and liqueur. With pastry brush, lightly brush flat side of ladyfingers with juice mixture. Line long sides and bottom of loaf pan with ladyfingers, placing rounded side against pan.

2. In blender, puree strawberries with sugar and lemon juice until smooth. In 2-quart saucepan, evenly sprinkle gelatin over water; let stand 2 minutes to soften slightly. Cook over low heat, stirring frequently, until gelatin has completely dissolved, 2 to 3 minutes. Remove saucepan from heat; stir in strawberry puree.

3. Set saucepan in large bowl of ice water. With rubber spatula, stir just until mixture forms mound when dropped from spatula, 10 to 15 minutes. Remove saucepan from bowl of water.

4. In large bowl, with mixer at medium speed, beat cream until stiff peaks form. Fold one-third of whipped cream into strawberry mixture; fold strawberry mixture into remaining whipped cream. Gently fold in raspberries and blackberries. Spoon mixture into ladyfinger-lined pan. Cover and refrigerate at least 4 hours or up to overnight.

5. To serve, unmold charlotte onto serving plate; remove plastic wrap. Garnish with mixed berries. Makes 8 servings.

Each serving: About 225 calories, 3g protein, 26g carbohydrate, 12g total fat (7g saturated), 80mg cholesterol, 29mg sodium.

Raspberry Charlotte

Prepare as above but substitute **2 packages (10 ounces each) frozen raspberries in syrup,** thawed, for strawberries and use only ¼ **cup sugar.** In blender, puree raspberries with lemon juice and sugar until smooth; press through sieve and stir into dissolved gelatin.

Each serving: About 278 calories, 3g protein, 40g carbohydrate, 12g total fat (7g saturated), 80mg cholesterol, 30mg sodium.

Berries and Cream Shortcake

(pictured on page 480)

A tender cake, instead of a baking-powder biscuit, is the base for this showstopper. Assemble just before serving.

Prep: 40 minutes   Bake: 25 minutes
½ cup butter or margarine (1 stick), softened
1 cup plus 1 tablespoon sugar
1½ cups cake flour (not self-rising)
1½ teaspoons baking powder
¼ teaspoon salt
½ cup milk
2 large eggs
1 teaspoon vanilla extract
1 pint blueberries
½ pint strawberries, hulled and cut in half
½ pint raspberries
½ pint blackberries
½ cup seedless strawberry jam
1 cup heavy or whipping cream

1. Preheat oven to 350°F. Grease and flour two 8-inch round cake pans.

2. In large bowl, with mixer at low speed, beat butter and 1 cup sugar just until blended. Increase speed to high; beat until light and fluffy, about 5 minutes. Reduce speed to low; add flour, baking powder, salt, milk, eggs, and vanilla. Beat, frequently scraping bowl with rubber spatula, until well mixed. Increase speed to high; beat 2 minutes.

3. Spoon batter into prepared pans. Bake until toothpick inserted in center of cake comes out clean, 25 to 30 minutes. Cool in pans on wire racks 10 minutes. Remove cake from pans and cool completely on wire racks.

4. Meanwhile, in large bowl, gently combine blueberries, strawberries, raspberries, and blackberries with strawberry jam.

5. In small bowl, with mixer at medium speed, beat cream with remaining 1 tablespoon sugar until stiff peaks form.

6. Place one cake layer on cake plate; spread with half of whipped cream and top with half of fruit mixture. Place second cake layer on fruit mixture; top with remaining whipped cream and remaining fruit. Makes 10 servings.

Each serving: About 415 calories, 4g protein, 56g carbohydrate, 21g total fat (12g saturated), 102mg cholesterol, 261mg sodium.

Summer Pudding

A mix of summer berries, heated just until they release their juices, is layered with sliced bread to make this irresistible traditional English sweet. (In Britain, any dessert is called a pudding.)

Prep: 20 minutes plus cooling plus 24 hours to chill
Cook: 8 minutes

12	slices firm white bread, crusts removed
2	cups blueberries
2/3	cup sugar
2	cups sliced strawberries
2	cups raspberries
1	cup blackberries
	whipped cream (optional)

1. Arrange bread slices on wire racks to dry out while preparing filling.

2. In 3-quart saucepan, combine blueberries and sugar and heat to boiling over medium heat, stirring often; boil 1 minute. Stir in strawberries, raspberries, and blackberries and cook, stirring, 1 minute longer. Remove from heat; cool berry filling to room temperature.

3. Line deep 1½-quart bowl with plastic wrap, allowing plastic wrap to extend over side of bowl. Line bowl with some bread slices, trimming bread to fit; use bread scraps to fill any spaces. Spoon 2 cups berry filling into bread-lined bowl. Cover with layer of bread, trimming to fit as needed. Spoon remaining filling over bread and top with remaining bread.

4. Fold plastic wrap over filling. Place saucer just small enough to fit inside bowl on top of plastic wrap. Place several heavy cans on saucer to weight down pudding. Place pudding on plate to catch any overflow and refrigerate until pudding is firm and bread is saturated with berry juices, about 24 hours.

5. Remove cans and saucer and fold back plastic wrap. Invert pudding onto serving plate; remove bowl and discard plastic wrap. Spoon any excess juices over pudding. Serve with whipped cream, if you like. Makes 8 servings.

♡ Each serving without whipped cream: About 223 calories, 4g protein, 49g carbohydrate, 2g total fat (0g saturated), 0mg cholesterol, 209mg sodium.

Blueberry-Lemon Tiramisù

A summer alternative to traditional tiramisù, this rendition is light, fruity, and refreshing. If time is short, use one and one-half cups good-quality store-bought lemon curd.

Prep: 1 hour plus chilling

Lemon Curd

2	large lemons
3	large egg yolks
2	large eggs
1/3	cup sugar
6	tablespoons butter or margarine, cut into pieces

Tiramisù

	double recipe Best Blueberry Sauce (page 560)
1	lemon
1/4	cup sugar
1/4	cup water
1	package (7 ounces) Italian-style ladyfingers (savoiardi)
8	ounces mascarpone cheese
1/2	cup heavy or whipping cream

1. Prepare lemon curd: From 2 lemons, finely grate 1 tablespoon peel and squeeze 1/3 cup juice. In heavy nonreactive 2-quart saucepan, with wire whisk, beat grated lemon peel and juice, egg yolks, whole eggs, and sugar just until mixed. Add butter and cook over low heat, stirring constantly, until mixture coats back of spoon (do not boil, or mixture will curdle). Pour lemon curd through sieve into bowl; press plastic wrap onto surface and refrigerate until cool, about 45 minutes.

2. Meanwhile, prepare Best Blueberry Sauce; cool to room temperature. From lemon, with vegetable peeler, remove 3 strips (3" by 3/4" each) peel. In nonreactive, 1-quart saucepan, combine lemon peel, sugar, and water; heat over medium heat, stirring occasionally, until sugar has dissolved and mixture boils. Pour sugar syrup into small bowl; cool to room temperature.

3. Line bottom and short sides of 13" by 9" baking dish with ladyfingers. Discard lemon peel from syrup. Brush ladyfingers with syrup. Spread blueberry sauce over ladyfingers in bottom of dish.

4. In large bowl, with wire whisk, mix cooled lemon curd, mascarpone, and cream until smooth. Spoon mascarpone mixture evenly over blueberry sauce, spreading to cover completely. Cover and refrigerate until well chilled, at least 6 hours or up to overnight. Makes 12 servings.

Each serving: About 386 calories, 5g protein, 47g carbohydrate, 21g total fat (12g saturated), 133mg cholesterol, 129mg sodium.

Fresh Blueberry Fool

The perfect end to a summer night's dinner. This simplest of fruit desserts can also be made with raspberries, kiwifruit, strawberries, or peaches: just a few of the possibilities

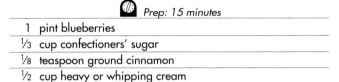 *Prep: 15 minutes*

1	pint blueberries
1/3	cup confectioners' sugar
1/8	teaspoon ground cinnamon
1/2	cup heavy or whipping cream

1. Set aside about ¾ cup blueberries. In large bowl, coarsely mash remaining blueberries. Stir in confectioners' sugar, cinnamon, and reserved whole blueberries.

2. In small bowl, with mixer at medium speed, beat cream until soft peaks form. Gently swirl blueberry mixture into whipped cream to create marbled effect. Makes 4 servings.

Each serving: About 182 calories, 1g protein, 21g carbohydrate, 11g total fat (7g saturated), 41mg cholesterol, 16mg sodium.

Make a warm berry compote to serve with cakes, sorbets, ice cream, or puddings. To do so, puree one cup of fruit and press through a sieve. Heat the fruit puree in a saucepan with one-quarter cup sugar, stirring until the sugar has dissolved. Stir in an additional two cups berries and heat just until warmed through.

JOANNE WEIR

TELEVISION HOST OF WEIR COOKING

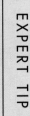

EXPERT TIP

Strawberry Shortcake

No seasonal dessert is more luscious than strawberry shortcake, and this biscuit-based version is the classic.

Prep: 30 minutes	*Bake: 20 minutes*
2	cups all-purpose flour
3/4	cup sugar
2	teaspoons baking powder
1/4	teaspoon salt
1/3	cup cold butter or margarine, cut into pieces
2/3	cup milk
2	pints strawberries
1	cup heavy or whipping cream

1. Preheat oven to 425°F. Grease 8-inch round cake pan.

2. In medium bowl, combine flour, 3 tablespoons sugar, baking powder, and salt. With pastry blender or two knives used scissor-fashion, cut in butter until mixture resembles coarse crumbs. Stir in milk just until mixture forms soft dough that leaves side of bowl.

3. On lightly floured surface, knead dough 10 times. With floured hands, pat evenly into cake pan and sprinkle with 1 tablespoon sugar. Bake until golden, 20 to 22 minutes.

4. Meanwhile, reserve 4 whole strawberries for garnish; hull remaining strawberries and cut in half or into quarters. In medium bowl, toss strawberries with remaining ½ cup sugar until sugar has dissolved.

5. Invert shortcake onto surface. With long serrated knife, cut shortcake horizontally in half. In bowl, with mixer at medium speed, beat cream just until soft peaks form.

6. Place bottom half of shortcake, cut side up, on cake plate; top with half of strawberry mixture and half of whipped cream. Place remaining shortcake, cut side down, on strawberry mixture. Spoon remaining strawberry mixture over, then top with remaining whipped cream. Garnish with reserved whole strawberries. Serves 10.

Each serving: About 321 calories, 4g protein, 41g carbohydrate, 16g total fat (10g saturated), 51mg cholesterol, 235mg sodium.

Strawberries in White Wine

Make this simple Italian treat with perfectly ripe, fragrant fruit.

Prep: 10 minutes

⅓	cup dry white wine, such as riesling or sauvignon blanc
2	tablespoons sugar
1	pint strawberries, hulled and cut in half

In small bowl, stir wine and sugar together until sugar has dissolved. Divide strawberries among four goblets. Pour wine mixture over fruit. Makes 4 servings.

♥ Each serving: About 61 calories, 0g protein, 12g carbohydrate, 0g total fat (0g saturated), 0mg cholesterol, 2mg sodium.

Peaches in Red Wine

Prepare as directed but substitute ⅓ **cup red wine** for white wine and **2 cups sliced, peeled peaches (3 to 4 peaches)** for strawberries. Makes 4 servings.

♥ Each serving: About 75 calories, 1g protein, 16g carbohydrate, 0g total fat (0g saturated), 0mg cholesterol, 1mg sodium.

Strawberries in White Wine

CACTUS PEARS

Availability
October through May

Peak Season
October and November

Buying Tips
Look for brightly colored cactus pears (also called *prickly pears*) minus their sharp spines (to be safe, pick up the fruit with a paper bag to protect your hands). When ripe, cactus pears yield to gentle pressure. Avoid shriveled or dried-out fruit.

To Store
Keep cactus pears at room temperature and use within two or three days.

To Prepare
Wearing rubber gloves or using a paper bag to protect your hands, peel a ripened cactus pear as you would an apple, being sure to cut away any spines. Slice for salads, or eat out of hand with a squeeze of lime or lemon juice.

CHERIMOYAS

Availability
November through May

Buying Tips
Pick large, uniformly green cherimoyas (custard apples) without bruises or blackened skin. Because ripe cherimoyas are very fragile, it is best to choose firm fruit and ripen at home. When ripe, cherimoyas yield to gentle pressure.

To Store
Ripen at room temperature, then refrigerate and use within one or two days.

To Prepare
Wash, then cut lengthwise in half or into quarters. Serve as you would melon wedges. Discard the seeds when eating.

CHERRIES

Availability
Sweet cherries, May through July; tart (sour) cherries, late June to mid-July

Buying Tips
Look for plump, brightly colored cherries with fresh-looking stems still attached: Stemless cherries are prone to mold. Avoid fruit that is soft, bruised, or moldy.

Sweet cherries, such as dark red *Bing* or golden *Rainier* (*Royal Anne*) varieties, make delicious summer eating. Fresh tart (sour) cherries can be found in farmers' markets or at roadside stands; they are excellent in pies.

To Prepare
Wash and remove stems just before using. To use in desserts and salads, remove the pits.

Cherry-Almond Clafouti

Sweet cherries baked in a custardlike pudding are a classic French country dessert. Serve right out of the oven.

Prep: 20 minutes	Bake: 40 minutes
1	pound dark sweet cherries, pitted
2	cups half-and-half or light cream
4	large eggs
⅓	cup sugar
2	tablespoons amaretto (almond-flavored liqueur)
⅔	cup all-purpose flour
	confectioners' sugar

1. Preheat oven to 350°F. Grease 10" by 1½" round baking dish. Place cherries in baking dish.

2. In medium bowl, with wire whisk, beat half-and-half, eggs, sugar, and amaretto until well mixed. Gradually whisk in flour until smooth. Or, in blender, process half-and-half, eggs, sugar, amaretto, and flour until smooth.

3. Pour egg mixture over cherries in baking dish. Bake until custard has set and knife inserted 1 inch from edge comes out clean (center will still jiggle), 40 to 45 minutes. Serve hot or warm, sprinkled with confectioners' sugar. Makes 12 servings.

Each serving: About 161 calories, 4g protein, 20g carbohydrate, 7g total fat (4g saturated), 86mg cholesterol, 38mg sodium.

COCONUTS

Availability
Year round

Peak Season
October through December

Buying Tips
Choose a coconut that is heavy for its size and sounds full of liquid when shaken. Avoid coconuts with moldy or wet eyes (the three indentations at one end).

To Store
Refrigerate and use within one week. Shredded fresh coconut will keep in the refrigerator for one or two days.

To Prepare

Pierce two of the eyes using a clean screwdriver or an ice pick and hammer; drain the liquid (or strain and reserve for another use). Bake the coconut in a preheated 350°F oven for fifteen minutes. Remove it from the oven and wrap in a kitchen towel. With the hammer, hit the coconut to break it into large pieces. With a knife, pry the coconut meat from the shell.

To shred With a vegetable peeler, remove the brown outer skin from the coconut meat. Shred the meat on the coarse side of a box grater or in a food processor fitted with the fine shredding blade. One 1½-pound coconut yields 4 to 5 cups of shredded coconut.

To toast Preheat the oven to 350°F. Evenly spread the shredded coconut in a jelly-roll pan. Bake until delicately browned, twenty to thirty minutes, stirring occasionally to toast evenly.

CRANBERRIES

Availability
September through mid-December

Buying Tips
Berries should be plump and firm, from light to dark red, with a glossy sheen. Avoid shriveled, discolored, or moist berries.

To Store
Refrigerate and use within two weeks. To freeze, place cranberries in the freezer in their original bag.

To Prepare
Rinse the cranberries and remove any stems; discard any shriveled fruit and drain well. To use, do not thaw frozen cranberries, just rinse with cold water and drain.

DATES

Availability
Year round

Buying Tips
The intensely sweet and moist Deglet Noor and Medjool dates are the most common varieties. Choose dates that are shiny, plump, and rich golden brown.

They are sold with and without pits and packaged or loose.

To Store
Refrigerate dates tightly wrapped for up to several weeks.

To Prepare
Remove pits, if necessary.

FIGS

Availability
June through November

Buying Tips
Varieties range in color from greenish yellow (*Kadota*) to dark purple (*Black Mission*) to green (*Calimyrna*). Buy slightly firm fruit that yields to gentle pressure. Avoid bruised or very soft fruit, or fruit with a sour odor.

To Store
Figs are very perishable; refrigerate and use within two days.

To Prepare
Wash figs and remove any stems.

To Serve
Eat figs out of hand, serve them as a first course topped with thinly sliced prosciutto, or for dessert with a soft, mild cheese.

Warm Figs with Walnuts

Figs seem so perfect just as they are, but prepared this way they're even better.

Prep: 10 minutes   Cook: 7 minutes

2	tablespoons butter or margarine
2	tablespoons brown sugar
6	ripe fresh figs, each trimmed and cut in half
⅛	teaspoon vanilla extract
	vanilla ice cream (optional)
¼	cup toasted chopped walnuts

1. In nonstick 12-inch skillet, melt butter over medium heat. Add brown sugar and cook, stirring, until sugar has melted slightly, about 2 minutes. Add figs and vanilla and cook, turning figs once, until softened, about 4 minutes.

2. Scoop ice cream, if using, into bowls and top with warm figs and syrup; sprinkle with walnuts. Makes 4 servings.

Each serving without ice cream: About 181 calories, 2g protein, 22g carbohydrate, 11g total fat (4g saturated), 16mg cholesterol, 63mg sodium.

GRAPEFRUIT

Availability
Year round

Peak Season
January through April

Buying Tips
Grapefruit can have seeds or be seedless; they can be pink-, red-, or white-fleshed. Select well-shaped fruit that is firm and heavy for its size. Brownish discolorations on the skin usually do not affect the eating quality. Avoid fruit that is soft or discolored at the stem end.

Pummelo (also called *pomelo* or *Chinese grapefruit*) looks like an overgrown grapefruit, but its flesh is sweeter and firmer. Because it is very seedy, it should be peeled, seeded, and sectioned like an orange (page 501) before eating.

To Store
Refrigerate grapefruit and use within one to two weeks.

To Prepare
Cut the fruit crosswise in half. With a knife, cut out the sections from between the membranes; leave the sections in place if serving the fruit in the shell. Remove any seeds.

Broiled Grapefruit

Serve this hot-and-juicy treat at breakfast time or as a healthful dessert. Instead of sugar, you can spoon on one tablespoon of honey, dark corn syrup, or orange marmalade. If you like sherry, sprinkle on a little after broiling.

Prep: 10 minutes   Broil: 10 minutes

1	medium grapefruit, cut in half
1	tablespoon brown sugar
1	tablespoon butter or margarine, cut into pieces

1. Preheat broiler. Section grapefruit and remove seeds.
2. Line broiling pan with foil. Place grapefruit halves in pan, sprinkle with brown sugar, then dot with butter. Place pan in broiler, about 5 inches from heat source. Broil until golden on top and heated through, about 10 minutes. Makes 2 servings.

Each serving: About 115 calories, 1g protein, 16g carbohydrate, 6g total fat (4g saturated), 16mg cholesterol, 61mg sodium.

GRAPES

Availability
Year round, depending on variety

Buying Tips
Bunches of grapes should be plump and fresh-looking, with individual grapes firmly attached to their stems. Avoid dry, brittle stems, shriveled grapes, or fruit leaking moisture.

Table grapes, used for eating rather than winemaking (although a few varieties do double duty), are categorized as seedless or with seeds. Seedless grapes, derived from European varieties, dominate the market and include *Thompson, Perlette, Flame,* and *Ruby Seedless.* Grapes with seeds usually are indigenous American varieties and have a distinct musky flavor. Lambruscas, such as the purple *Concord,* pale red *Delaware,* and red-purple *Catawba,* are prized for their pectin-rich juice and make fine jellies. Muscadine grapes, which include the sweet-juiced southern *Scuppernong,* are also great for jellies.

To Store
Refrigerate grapes in their perforated plastic bags and use within one week.

To Prepare
Rinse grapes well and dry with paper towels.

Grapes with Sour Cream

Even when you're pressed for time, you can make this easy treat.

 Prep: 10 minutes

2	cups seedless grapes
¼	cup sour cream
1	tablespoon brown sugar

In small bowl, gently stir grapes, sour cream, and brown sugar until well combined. Cover and refrigerate until ready to serve. Makes 4 servings.

♥ Each serving: About 100 calories, 1g protein, 18g carbohydrate, 3g total fat (2g saturated), 6mg cholesterol, 11mg sodium.

GUAVAS

Availability
September through November

Buying Tips
Depending on the variety, guavas have green to yellowish red skin. Ripe guavas yield to gentle pressure. As with other tropical fruits, it is best to buy firm, uncracked guavas and ripen them at home.

To Store
Ripen fruit at room temperature in a brown paper bag. Refrigerate guavas after ripening and use within two or three days.

To Prepare
Wash guavas and remove the skin. Cut large guavas into pieces for eating out of hand. The tiny seeds are edible but can be cut out before serving, if you wish.

KIWIFRUIT

Availability
Year round

Buying Tips
Kiwifruit should be slightly firm with very fuzzy skin. When fully ripe, they yield to gentle pressure.

To Store

Ripen kiwifruit at room temperature; refrigerate after ripening and use within one or two days. Firm unripened unwashed kiwifruit can be stored in a plastic bag in the refrigerator for up to several months.

To Prepare

With a sharp knife, peel off the skin, then cut into wedges or slices. Or cut unpeeled fruit crosswise in half and scoop out the pulp with a spoon.

KUMQUATS

Availability
November through April

Peak Season
November through December

Buying Tips
Buy firm, glossy, bright orange kumquats. They are often sold with some stems and leaves still attached. Avoid soft, blemished, or shriveled fruit.

To Store
Keep kumquats at room temperature for up to two days, or refrigerate and use within two weeks.

To Prepare
Wash the fruit and remove the stems, then cut in half to remove the seeds.

To Serve
Eat the entire fruit, peel and all. Add cut-up kumquats to fruit salads or leave them whole as a garnish.

LEMONS AND LIMES

Availability
Year round

Buying Tips
The fruits should be firm, brightly colored, and heavy for their size. Pale or greenish yellow lemons usually indicate fruit that is more acidic. Limes should be glossy-skinned; irregular purplish brown marks on the skin do not affect the quality. Avoid soft, shriveled, or hard-skinned fruits.

In addition to the familiar supermarket varieties, two fragrant, distinctively flavored varieties can sometimes be found in well-stocked produce markets. Thin-skinned *Meyer* lemons, more aromatic and sweeter than regular lemons, are favored by West Coast cooks. Small tart *key* limes (also known as *West Indian, bartender,* or *Mexican* limes) are so highly regarded that a pie was created for them. If you can't find fresh key limes, excellent bottled key lime juice is available.

To Store
Keep lemons and limes at room temperature for up to a few days, or refrigerate and use within two weeks.

To Prepare
When grating lemon or lime peel, be sure to grate only the zest: the thin colored part of the peel. The white pith underneath is very bitter. To get the most juice out of lemons or limes, press down on them while rolling them back and forth, or place in hot tap water for several minutes.

Fresh Lemon Gelatin

Tart and cooling, this old-fashioned gelatin dessert has a soft set. If you prefer a sweeter dessert, increase the sugar to two-thirds cup.

Prep: 10 minutes plus chilling	Cook: 2 minutes
1	envelope unflavored gelatin
1¼	cups cold water
⅔	cup fresh lemon juice
½	cup sugar

In nonreactive 1-quart saucepan, evenly sprinkle gelatin over ¼ cup water; let stand 2 minutes to soften slightly. Cook over low heat, stirring frequently, until gelatin has completely dissolved, 2 to 3 minutes. Remove from heat and add lemon juice and sugar, stirring until sugar has dissolved. Stir in remaining 1 cup water. Pour into small bowl; cover and refrigerate 4 hours or up to overnight. Makes 4 servings.

♥ Each serving: About 113 calories, 2g protein, 28g carbohydrate, 0g total fat (0g saturated), 0mg cholesterol, 4mg sodium.

LOQUATS

Availability
April through early May

Buying Tips
Look for fruit with deep-colored, orange-yellow skin that yields to gentle pressure.

To Store
Refrigerate loquats and use within two or three days.

To Prepare
Pull off the peel, cut in half, and remove the large central seeds for eating out of hand, or cut up to use in salads.

LYCHEES

Availability
late May through July

Buying Tips
Lychees are usually found in Asian markets. They have a bumpy, deep reddish brown shell that protects their slightly translucent soft white flesh. Choose blemish-free fruit.

To Store
Refrigerate lychees and use within one or two days.

To Prepare
With your thumb, beginning at the stem, pull off the skin as you would an orange; remove the seed (which clings tightly to the fruit) for eating lychees out of hand, or use in salads.

MANGOES

Availability
Year round

Peak Season
May through August

Buying Tips
Purchase plump fruit with a fresh, sweet aroma. Some varieties are speckled, but tiny black spots indicate very ripe fruit. Ripe mangoes yield to gentle pressure. Avoid oversoft, shriveled, or bruised fruit.

To Store
Let mangoes ripen at room temperature, then refrigerate and use within two or three days.

Mango Mousse

Sweet, thick cream of coconut is the secret behind this dessert—it tastes of the tropics.

Prep: 20 minutes plus chilling	Cook: 2 minutes
1	envelope unflavored gelatin
¼	cup cold water
2	large ripe mangoes, peeled and coarsely chopped (3 cups)
1	can (15 ounces) cream of coconut
½	cup fresh lime juice (4 large limes)
	fresh berries (optional)

1. In 1-quart saucepan, evenly sprinkle gelatin over water; let stand 2 minutes to soften gelatin slightly.

2. Meanwhile, in blender, combine mangoes, cream of coconut, and lime juice. Puree until smooth.

3. Heat gelatin over low heat, stirring frequently, until it has completely dissolved, 2 to 3 minutes. Add to mango mixture and process to combine. Pour into custard cups. Cover and refrigerate until well chilled, 4 hours or up to overnight. Serve with berries, if you like. Makes 8 servings.

Each serving: About 181 calories, 3g protein, 18g carbohydrate, 12g total fat (11g saturated), 0mg cholesterol, 38mg sodium.

MELONS

Availability
April through December, depending on variety

Buying Tips
Summer melons have a netted rind and thrive in hot climates. Winter melons, which are typically oblong in shape and can be grown in temperate climates, take longer to mature on the vine and appear later in markets.

Buy fully ripened melons for the most flavor and sweetness. (Only winter melons ripen after picking.) Melons should feel heavy for their size and exude a fruity aroma from the smooth (blossom) end. Avoid bruised or cracked melons or those with soft or damp spots. (See Watermelons, page 512.)

CUTTING A MANGO

With a sharp knife, cut a lengthwise slice from each side of the long flat seed, as close to the seed as possible. Peel seed section; cut off as much flesh as possible; discard seed.

Cut the mango pieces lengthwise into thick wedges. Use a knife to remove the peel from each wedge, cutting close to the peel.

For eating mango out of hand, score the flesh of each piece without cutting through the skin, and gently push it out to eat.

Canary

Oval in shape and with a bright yellow rind, this winter melon gives off a rich aroma when ripe. The sweet flesh tastes similar to honeydew. Look for canary melons from mid-June to mid-September.

Cantaloupe

Available June through September, this luscious melon has golden or greenish beige skin, covered with thick netting. The scar at the stem end should be smooth, without any stem remaining. When ripe, cantaloupe has a sweet aroma and salmon-colored flesh. It should feel tender but not mushy at the blossom end.

Casaba

Chartreuse yellow casaba is round with a point at one end. It has deep lengthwise furrows, and the flesh is cream-colored. When ripe, the rind is a rich yellow (but the stem end may remain light green), and the blossom end will yield to gentle pressure.

Cranshaw (Crenshaw)

Globe-shaped, with shallow furrows and a point at the stem end, this winter melon has a gold green rind that turns completely gold when the melon is ripe. The pink flesh has a rich aroma and the blossom end yields to gentle pressure. These melons are at their peak from July through October.

Honeydew, Honeyball

These melons are similar except that the honeyball is smaller. The rind is cream-colored and covered with patches of netting. When the melon is ripe, the skin should feel velvety and the rind should give slightly. Look for honeyballs from July through November, honeydews all year.

Although the flesh of the honeydew is usually green, there are several varieties that differ: They include the *Golden Honeydew,* the *Orange Honeydew,* and the *Temptation Honeydew.*

Persian

Resembling a large cantaloupe but with finer netting, the Persian melon has a dark green background that turns lighter green when ripe. The skin will yield to gentle pressure when ripe. The orange-pink flesh has a distinctive aroma. Persian melons are available from June through November.

Santa Claus

Available in December, this melon is large and oblong with yellow-green flesh and a lightly netted, green-gold rind that turns yellow when the melon is ripe. The blossom end will yield to gentle pressure.

To Store

Let melon ripen at room temperature, then refrigerate and use within two or three days. Keep well wrapped after cutting to prevent the melon from absorbing odors.

NECTARINES

Availability
May through September

Peak Season
June through August

Buying Tips
Buy plump, richly colored, smooth-skinned fruit. The color should be deep reddish to yellowish. Slightly firm nectarines ripen well at room temperature. Avoid hard, soft, or shriveled nectarines or any with a large proportion of green skin.

To Store
Let nectarines ripen at room temperature, then refrigerate and use within two or three days.

To Prepare
Wash the fruit, cut in half along the seam line, and remove the pit. Nectarine skin is quite thin, so it does not need to be peeled. To prevent browning, sprinkle with lemon juice.

Spiced Nectarines

You can substitute peeled peaches for the nectarines if they are the better choice at your market. Serve as an accompaniment to a pork roast or baked ham.

 Prep: 10 minutes   Cook: 15 minutes

1½	cups water
6	whole cloves
¼	teaspoon ground cinnamon
¼	teaspoon ground ginger
4	large nectarines, each peeled and cut into quarters
½	cup sugar
3	tablespoons fresh lemon juice

1. In 10-inch skillet, combine water, cloves, cinnamon, and ginger; heat to boiling over medium-high heat. Boil mixture 2 minutes.

2. Add nectarines to spice mixture; cook, stirring occasionally, until nectarines are tender, about 10 minutes. Just before nectarines are done, stir in sugar and lemon juice until sugar has dissolved. Refrigerate. Serve as condiment for meat or as dessert. Makes 8 accompaniment servings.

Each serving: About 92 calories, 1g protein, 23g carbohydrate, 0g total fat (0g saturated), 0mg cholesterol, 0mg sodium.

ORANGES

Availability
Year round

Peak Season
December through April

Buying Tips
Eating oranges, such as *Temple* and *navel*, are easily peeled and segmented. Other orange varieties, such as *Valencia, Pineapple,* and *Hamlin,* are valued for their abundant juice. Some specialty markets carry sweet, maroon-fleshed *Moro (blood)* oranges from late winter through early spring. Bitter oranges (also called Seville or sour oranges), which are used in Latino cooking and marmalades, have very thick skins and tart juice.

Oranges should be firm and heavy for their size. Strict state regulations guarantee tree-ripened fruit; a slight greenish color or russeting on the skin does not affect the quality.

To Store
Keep at room temperature for a few days, or refrigerate and use within two weeks.

To Prepare
Peel oranges and separate into segments; slice or cut into pieces. When grating orange peel, be sure to grate only the zest: the thin colored part of the peel. The white pith underneath is very bitter.

Orange Slices
Marinated in Marmalade

A super-simple dessert with triple orange flavor.

Prep: 15 minutes plus chilling	
5	medium navel oranges, peeled and sliced into rounds
½	cup sweet or bitter orange marmalade
1	tablespoon orange-flavored liqueur (optional)

Arrange orange slices on platter, overlapping them slightly; brush with marmalade. Sprinkle with liqueur, if you like. Cover and refrigerate at least 30 minutes or up to several hours. Makes 4 servings.

Each serving: About 179 calories, 2g protein, 47g carbohydrate, 0g total fat (0g saturated), 0mg cholesterol, 24mg sodium.

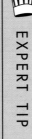

It's always a good idea to buy fruits from organic farmers who offer heirloom varieties that are grown for their superior flavor, are picked at their peak of ripeness, and have not been sprayed with pesticides.
- When you find yourself with some overripe fruit, turn it into a delicious batch of jam.
- Give fruit salads a flavor (and moisture) lift by sprinkling them with orange juice that's been blended with a little jam.

ALICE WATERS

CHEF/OWNER, CHEZ PANISSE, CALIFORNIA

EXPERT TIP

PREPARING CITRUS FRUITS

Using a vegetable peeler, remove the colored part of the citrus peel in strips. (Do not remove the bitter white pith.)

If directed, cut the citrus peel into thin slivers.

Cut a slice off the top and bottom of the fruit to steady it. Stand fruit upright on cutting board and cut off peel and white pith, turning the fruit as you cut.

Holding the fruit over a bowl to catch the juices, cut between the membranes to release the sections.

Oranges with Caramel

Serve as a light and elegant finale to a rich meal. When the caramel-drizzled orange rounds are refrigerated, the caramel melts into a luscious golden syrup.

Prep: 30 minutes plus chilling   Cook: 10 minutes

6	large navel oranges
2	tablespoons brandy (optional)
1	cup sugar

1. From oranges, with vegetable peeler, remove 6 strips (3" by ¾" each) peel. Cut strips lengthwise into slivers.

2. Cut remaining peel and white pith from oranges. Slice oranges into ¼-inch-thick rounds and place on deep platter, overlapping slices slightly. Sprinkle with brandy, if desired, and orange peel.

3. In 1½-quart saucepan, cook sugar over medium heat, stirring to dissolve any lumps, until sugar has melted and turned deep amber. Drizzle caramel over orange slices. Cover and refrigerate until caramel melts, about 2 hours. Makes 6 servings.

♥ Each serving: About 208 calories, 2g protein, 53g carbohydrate, 0g total fat (0g saturated), 0mg cholesterol, 2mg sodium.

Oranges with Caramel

ORANGES WITH CARAMEL

Cook the sugar over medium heat until melted, stirring constantly to dissolve any lumps.

Continue cooking until the syrup turns dark amber.

Carefully drizzle the caramel over the orange slices.

PAPAYAS

Availability
Year round

Buying Tips
Pick evenly colored gold-yellow fruit. Papayas are sometimes speckled with a few black spots; they do not affect the flavor or quality. The fruit should yield to gentle pressure. Fruit that is too hard will never fully ripen. Avoid oversoft, shriveled, or bruised fruit.

To Store
Ripen papayas at room temperature, then refrigerate and use within three or four days.

To Prepare
Cut papayas lengthwise in half and scoop out the black, peppery seeds. Peel and slice or simply cut up.

PASSION FRUIT

Availability
February through July

Buying Tips
Ripe passion fruit isn't very pretty (the skin is wrinkled and puckered), but the prize is the highly perfumed flesh inside. The skin is usually purple but may be yellow-gold.

To Store
Refrigerate ripe fruit and use within three days.

To Prepare
Cut the fruit crosswise in half and with a spoon, scoop out the pulp and seeds. If desired, strain the pulp through a fine sieve to remove the tiny edible seeds, pressing hard to extract all the juices. One passion fruit yields about two tablespoons pulp.

PEACHES

Availability
May through September

Buying Tips
Peaches are classified as *freestone,* which means the fruit easily separates from the pit, or *clingstone,* where the fruit clings tightly to the pit. The type does not affect the flavor.

Tree-ripened peaches have a sweet fruity aroma, yield to gentle pressure, and have the best flavor. Underripe peaches will soften at room temperature but will not get sweeter than when purchased. Avoid green, shriveled, or bruised fruit.

To Store
Refrigerate ripe peaches and use within five days.

To Prepare
Peel the fruit, cut in half along the seam line, and remove the pit. To peel, dip into rapidly boiling water for about fifteen seconds, then plunge into a bowl of cold water; slip off the skins. Some peaches are almost impossible to peel; simply use a vegetable peeler. To prevent browning, sprinkle peeled fruit with lemon juice.

5-MINUTE DESSERTS

GINGERED CREAM AND GRAPES
Serve halved red and green seedless grapes with a dollop of sour cream topped with coarsely chopped crystallized ginger or preserved ginger in syrup.

MINT MELON CUPS
Toss 1-inch chunks of honeydew and cantaloupe with fresh lime juice and honey. Garnish with a twist of lime peel.

BROILED AMARETTI PLUMS
Place fresh plum halves, cut side up, in ungreased broiler-safe pan. Sprinkle with crushed amaretti (almond-flavored) cookies and broil just until crumbs have lightly browned and plums are tender. Great with peeled peaches, too.

Peach Cobbler

A true summer treat, bursting with the flavor of ripe peaches and topped with lemon-scented biscuits. Serve with rich vanilla ice cream or softly whipped cream.

Prep: 45 minutes   Bake: 45 minutes

Peach Filling

6	pounds ripe medium peaches (16 to 18), peeled, pitted, and sliced (13 cups)
¼	cup fresh lemon juice
⅔	cup granulated sugar
½	cup packed brown sugar
¼	cup cornstarch

Lemon Biscuits

2	cups all-purpose flour
½	cup plus 1 teaspoon granulated sugar
2½	teaspoons baking powder
¼	teaspoon salt
1	teaspoon freshly grated lemon peel
4	tablespoons cold butter or margarine, cut into pieces
⅔	cup plus 1 tablespoon half-and-half or light cream

1. Prepare peach filling: Preheat oven to 425°F. In nonreactive 8-quart saucepot, toss peaches with lemon juice; add granulated and brown sugars, and cornstarch, tossing to coat. Heat over medium heat, stirring occasionally, until bubbling; boil 1 minute. Spoon hot peach mixture into 13" by 9" baking dish. Place baking dish on foil-lined cookie sheet to catch any overflow during baking. Bake 10 minutes.

2. Meanwhile, prepare biscuits: In medium bowl, combine flour, ½ cup granulated sugar, baking powder, salt, and lemon peel. With pastry blender or two knives used scissor-fashion, cut in butter until mixture resembles coarse crumbs. Stir in ⅔ cup half-and-half just until mixture forms soft dough that leaves side of bowl.

3. Turn dough onto lightly floured surface. With lightly floured hands, pat into 10" by 6" rectangle. With floured knife, cut rectangle lengthwise in half, then cut each half crosswise into 6 pieces.

4. Remove baking dish from oven. Arrange biscuits on top of fruit. Brush biscuits with remaining 1 tablespoon half-and-half and sprinkle with remaining 1 teaspoon granulated sugar. Return cobbler to oven and bake until filling is hot and bubbling and biscuits are golden, about 35 minutes longer. To serve warm, cool cobbler on wire rack about 1 hour. Makes 12 servings.

♥ Each serving: About 331 calories, 4g protein, 69g carbohydrate, 6g total fat (3g saturated), 16mg cholesterol, 199mg sodium.

PEARS

Availability
Year round

Buying Tips
Pears are picked unripe, then ripen during shipping and storage. Select well-shaped, fairly firm fruit; the color depends on the variety. Avoid shriveled, discolored, cut, or bruised fruit.

For cooking, *Bartlett, Anjou,* or *Bosc* pears are good choices. The elegant shape of the Bosc pear makes it especially appealing for poaching. Delicious eating pears include the *Comice, Seckel, Winter Nelis,* and *Kieffer* varieties. The *Asian* pear, a crisp and not very sweet relative of the common pear, is ubiquitous in West Coast farmers' markets and perfect for green salads or in combination with other fruits.

To Store
Knowing when a particular pear is ripe depends on the variety. Bartletts go from green to soft yellow, greenish brown Boscs turn the color of milk-chocolate, and Anjous yield to gentle

pressure. Let firm pears ripen at room temperature in a brown paper bag for a few days (it may even take up to a week), then refrigerate and use within three to five days. Never refrigerate pears in an airtight plastic bag: The centers will turn dark brown. Store pears away from strong-smelling foods, because they absorb odors easily. To prevent peeled or cut-up pears from browning, sprinkle with lemon juice.

To Prepare

Peel pears, if desired. Cut the fruit lengthwise in half and remove the core (use a small melon baller) and stem, if desired.

Zinfandel-Poached Pears

Easy and fat-free, the poaching liquid is reduced to a spicy ruby red syrup.

Prep: 20 minutes plus chilling	Cook: 45 to 60 minutes
1	bottle (750 ml) red zinfandel wine (about 3 cups)
2	cups cranberry-juice cocktail
1¼	cups sugar
1	cinnamon stick (3 inches)
2	whole cloves
½	teaspoon whole black peppercorns
8	medium Bosc pears with stems

1. In nonreactive 5-quart Dutch oven, combine wine, cranberry-juice cocktail, sugar, cinnamon, cloves, and peppercorns; heat just to boiling over high heat, stirring occasionally, until sugar has dissolved.

2. Meanwhile, peel pears, leaving stems on. With melon baller or small knife, remove cores by cutting through blossom end (bottom).

3. Place pears in wine mixture; heat to boiling. Reduce heat; cover and simmer, turning pears occasionally, until tender but not soft, 15 to 25 minutes.

4. With slotted spoon, carefully transfer pears to platter. Strain wine mixture through sieve into bowl; pour back into Dutch oven. Heat to boiling over high heat. Cook, uncovered, until liquid has reduced to 1½ cups, 15 to 30 minutes.

5. Cover pears and syrup separately and refrigerate until well chilled, at least 6 hours. To serve, spoon syrup over pears. Makes 8 servings.

♥ Each serving: About 352 calories, 1g protein, 76g carbohydrate, 1g total fat (0g saturated), 0mg cholesterol, 6mg sodium.

Lemon-Anise Poached Pears

Serve these tender pears and their bracing aromatic syrup in a large glass bowl, and garnish with glistening orange slices.

Prep: 20 minutes plus chilling	Cook: 1 hour
1	lemon
8	firm-ripe pears, such as Bosc or Anjou (8 to 9 ounces each), peeled and cored
6	cups water
1	cup sugar
3	whole star anise or 1 teaspoon anise seeds
1	small orange, thinly sliced

1. From lemon, with vegetable peeler, remove 3 strips (3" by ¾" each) peel; squeeze 2 tablespoons juice. In nonreactive 8-quart saucepot, combine pears, lemon peel, water, sugar, and star anise; heat to boiling over high heat. Reduce heat; cover and simmer until pears are tender, about 30 minutes. With slotted spoon, transfer pears to large bowl. Stir lemon juice into bowl with pears. Strain syrup through sieve into separate large bowl. Return syrup to saucepot.

2. Heat syrup to boiling over high heat; cook, uncovered, until reduced to 3 cups, about 15 minutes. Pour hot syrup over pears. Cover and refrigerate, turning occasionally, until pears are well chilled, at least 6 hours.

3. Serve pears with syrup, garnished with orange slices. Makes 8 servings.

♥ Each serving: About 236 calories, 1g protein, 61g carbohydrate, 1g total fat (0g saturated), 0mg cholesterol, 1mg sodium.

QUICK PEAR DESSERTS

CHOCOLATE PEARS
Microwave cored whole pears, covered, until tender; top with hot fudge sauce.

PEAR AND DRIED-CHERRY RICE PUDDING
Cook diced pears in nonstick skillet until tender. Stir into deli rice pudding along with some dried cherries.

PEAR SMOOTHIES
Peel very ripe pears; coarsely chop. Whirl in blender with milk, yogurt, honey, and ice until smooth.

Pear Dumplings

Pears wrapped in pastry and baked until golden will wow your guests. If you like, substitute Golden Delicious apples for the pears.

	Prep: 35 minutes plus chilling Bake: 40 minutes
1½	cups all-purpose flour
½	cup butter or margarine (1 stick), softened
1	package (3 ounces) cream cheese, softened
3	medium Bartlett pears (5 to 6 ounces each)
¼	cup packed brown sugar
¼	teaspoon ground cinnamon
1	large egg white, lightly beaten
2	teaspoons granulated sugar
	Custard Sauce (page 562)
6	whole cloves

1. In food processor with knife blade attached, process flour, butter, and cream cheese until mixture forms a ball. Remove from processor and divide in half. Flatten each half into small disk. Wrap each disk in plast wrap and refrigerate 30 minutes.

2. Meanwhile, peel pears. Cut each pear lengthwise in half; remove core. Set pear halves aside.

3. On floured surface, with floured rolling pin, roll 1 piece dough ⅛ inch thick. Using 7-inch round plate as guide, cut 3 rounds from dough. Reserve trimmings.

4. In cup, combine brown sugar and cinnamon. Sprinkle dough rounds with half of sugar mixture. Place 1 pear half, cut side up, on each dough round. Fold dough over pear, pinching edges to seal. Place dough-covered pear, seam side down, on ungreased large cookie sheet. Repeat with remaining dough, sugar mixture, and pears to make 6 dumplings in all.

5. Preheat oven to 375°F. Reroll dough trimmings and cut out some leaves. With pastry brush, brush dumplings with egg white and decorate with leaves. Brush with egg white and sprinkle with granulated sugar. Place two sheets foil under cookie sheet; crimp edges to form rim to catch any overflow during baking. Bake until pastry is golden, 40 to 45 minutes (there will be some leakage around pears). With wide spatula, immediately transfer dumplings to wire rack to cool slightly.

6. Meanwhile, prepare Custard Sauce.

7. To serve, place dumplings on dessert plates. Insert 1 whole clove in tip of each dumpling to resemble stem. Serve warm with custard sauce. Makes 6 servings.

Each serving without Custard Sauce: About 397 calories, 6g protein, 48g carbohydrate, 21g total fat (13g saturated), 57mg cholesterol, 212mg sodium.

Roasted Pears with Marsala

Roasting pears at high heat intensifies their flavor, and the Marsala adds a sweet nuttiness. Ruby port is a delicious alternative.

	Prep: 25 minutes Bake: 40 to 50 minutes
1	lemon
8	medium Bosc pears
2	teaspoons plus ⅓ cup sugar
½	cup sweet Marsala wine
⅓	cup water
2	tablespoons butter or margarine, melted

1. Preheat oven to 450°F. From lemon, with vegetable peeler, remove peel in strips (2½" by ½" each); squeeze juice.

2. With melon baller or small knife, remove cores from pears by cutting through blossom end (bottom) of unpeeled pears (do not remove stems). With pastry brush, brush cavity of each pear with lemon juice, then sprinkle each cavity with ¼ teaspoon sugar.

3. In shallow 1½- to 2-quart baking dish, combine lemon peel, wine, and water. Place remaining ⅓ cup sugar on waxed paper. With pastry brush, brush pears with melted butter, then roll in sugar to coat. Stand pears in baking dish. Sprinkle any remaining sugar into baking dish.

4. Bake pears, basting occasionally with syrup in dish, until tender, 40 to 45 minutes.

5. Cool slightly to serve warm, or cool completely and cover and refrigerate up to 1 day. Reheat to serve warm, if you like. Makes 8 servings.

♥ Each serving: About 201 calories, 1g protein, 45g carbohydrate, 4g total fat (2g saturated), 8mg cholesterol, 31mg sodium.

Roasted Pears with Marsala

PERSIMMONS

Availability

October through February

Buying Tips

The most common persimmon is the *Hachiya*. It is deep orange, heart-shaped, and eaten raw or cooked. This persimmon must be ripened until very soft and almost translucent before using, or it will be inedibly tannic. *Fuyu* persimmons are pale orange and squat with a light bloom covering the skin. They are preferred for salads and are firm even when ripe.

Buy slightly firm, plump fruit with smooth, unbroken skin and the stem cap still attached; ripen at home. If you buy soft-ripe fruit, transport it very carefully and use the same day. Avoid bruised or cracked fruit.

To Store

Ripen Hachiya persimmons at room temperature in a closed brown paper bag until very soft. Refrigerate and use within one or two days. Hachiya pulp freezes very well in an airtight freezer container for up to two months.

To Prepare

Remove the stem cap. To use Hachiya pulp, cut persimmon in half and, with a spoon, scoop out the soft flesh; discard the seeds. Puree in a blender or food processor, or press through a fine sieve. To enjoy Fuyu persimmons, simply peel and slice.

Persimmon-Date Pudding

The secret to this soothing pudding is Hachiya persimmons, fully ripened until translucent, soft, and jellylike.

Prep: 15 minutes	Bake: 50 to 60 minutes
1	cup all-purpose flour
1	cup sugar
2	teaspoons baking soda
1½	teaspoons baking powder
¼	teaspoon ground cinnamon
⅛	teaspoon ground ginger
	pinch ground cloves
1	cup walnuts, coarsely chopped
½	cup chopped pitted dates
½	cup dark seedless raisins
½	teaspoon freshly grated orange peel
1	cup persimmon pulp (1 to 2 large ripe Hachiya persimmons)
½	cup milk
2	tablespoons butter or margarine, melted
1	teaspoon vanilla extract
	Hard Sauce (page 562) or whipped cream

1. Preheat oven to 325°F. Grease 8-inch square baking dish. In large bowl, combine flour, sugar, baking soda, baking powder, cinnamon, ginger, and cloves. Stir in walnuts, dates, raisins, and orange peel.

2. Stir persimmon pulp, milk, melted butter, and vanilla into flour mixture until well combined. Spoon evenly into baking dish and bake until toothpick inserted in center comes out clean, 50 to 60 minutes.

3. Meanwhile, prepare Hard Sauce. Serve pudding warm with hard sauce or whipped cream. Makes 8 servings.

Each serving: About 386 calories, 5g protein, 66g carbohydrate, 14g total fat (3g saturated), 10mg cholesterol, 447mg sodium.

PINEAPPLES

Availability

Year round

Buying Tips

A pineapple's color depends on the variety: It can range from deep yellow to reddish brown to green. Pineapple is always picked ripe: It does not get sweeter with time, it only softens. Pick a pineapple that is slightly soft with a deep sweet fragrance. The leaves should be firm and green. Avoid fruit with soft spots or dark areas.

To Store

If you like, chill pineapples before serving.

To Prepare

For rings or chunks, cut off the crown and stem end. Stand the pineapple upright and slice off the rind and eyes. Place the fruit on its side and cut crosswise into ¼- to 1-inch-thick slices. Core the pineapple with a pineapple corer or knife and cut into chunks, if desired. For wedges, with a long serrated knife, cut fruit lengthwise in half, then into quarters, cutting from the crown to the stem. Slice off the core by cutting along the top of the wedges, then slide a knife between the rind and flesh, keeping the knife close to the rind. Leave the flesh in the shell and cut into ¼- to ½-inch-thick slices.

PLUMS

Availability
June through September

Buying Tips
A plum's sweetness does not increase as the fruit softens, so be sure to purchase ripe fruit. Its color is determined by the variety. Plums should be plump and evenly colored and yield to gentle pressure. If the powdery bloom is still on the skin, it's a sign they haven't been overhandled. Avoid hard, shriveled, or cracked plums.

Greengage A round, very sweet, perfumed fruit with greenish yellow skin. *Damson* and *Mirabelle* plums are members of the same family.

Italian prune plums These are purplish black, oval, freestone plums. Because the flesh is somewhat dry, this plum is best cooked or dried. Look for them from late summer through early autumn.

Santa Rosa One of the most popular plum varieties. Grown primarily in California, this excellent all-purpose plum has juicy, sweet-tart flesh. *Friar* and *Queen Anne* plums are related to the Santa Rosa and have similar qualities.

Wild plums Although the name varies depending on the locale (from the *Sierra* plum in the West to the *beach* plum along the Atlantic coast), these small plums grow in bunches and are primarily used to make jams and jellies.

To Store
Refrigerate ripe plums and use within five days.

To Prepare
Wash plums, then cut into each center to remove the pit, if desired. For serving, slice or cut up the fruit, with or without the skin. When cooked, the amount of sugar needed will depend on the variety.

Roasted Almond–Crusted Plums

This dessert is perfect with a scoop of vanilla ice cream.

Prep: 15 minutes Bake: 25 to 35 minutes
6 large plums (4 to 5 ounces each), each cut in half and pitted
3 tablespoons butter or margarine, softened
⅓ cup packed brown sugar
¼ cup all-purpose flour
⅓ cup sliced natural almonds

1. Preheat oven to 425°F. In shallow baking dish, arrange plums, cut side up, close together in one layer.

2. In medium bowl, beat butter and brown sugar until smooth. Stir in flour until blended. Stir in almonds. Sprinkle mixture evenly over plums. Bake until plums are tender, 25 to 35 minutes. Makes 6 servings.

Each serving: About 204 calories, 2g protein, 31g carbohydrate, 9g total fat (4g saturated), 16mg cholesterol, 64mg sodium.

Plum Kuchen

Kuchen, *German for "cake," originated in the Old World, but its many variations are enjoyed throughout America.*

Prep: 30 minutes   Bake: 30 to 35 minutes

5	large plums or 16 prune plums
1	cup all-purpose flour
½	cup sugar
1½	teaspoons baking powder
¼	teaspoon salt
¼	cup milk
¼	cup butter or margarine, softened, plus 3 tablespoons
1	large egg
¼	teaspoon ground cinnamon
	pinch ground nutmeg
⅓	cup apricot jam or currant jelly
1	tablespoon boiling water

1. Cut each plum in half and remove pit. If using large plums, cut each into 8 wedges. Preheat oven to 400°F. Grease 12" by 8" baking dish.

2. In large bowl, combine flour, ¼ cup sugar, baking powder, salt, milk, ¼ cup butter, and egg. With mixer at low speed, beat, frequently scraping bowl with rubber spatula, until mixture leaves side of bowl and clings to beaters.

3. Spread dough in prepared baking dish. Arrange plums, skin side up, in slightly overlapping rows.

4. In small saucepan, melt remaining 3 tablespoons butter over medium heat. Stir in remaining ¼ cup sugar, cinnamon, and nutmeg; spoon over plums. Bake until plums are tender, 30 to 35 minutes.

5. In small bowl, with fork, stir jelly with boiling water until smooth; with pastry brush, brush melted jelly over hot fruit. Serve warm. Makes 10 servings.

Each serving: About 222 calories, 3g protein, 34g carbohydrate, 9g total fat (5g saturated), 44mg cholesterol, 226mg sodium.

Peach or Nectarine Kuchen

Prepare as directed but substitute **5 medium peaches,** peeled and cut into 8 wedges, or **5 medium nectarines,** not peeled and cut into 8 wedges, for plums.

Each serving: About 276 calories, 3g protein, 43g carbohydrate, 11g total fat (7g saturated), 55mg cholesterol, 283mg sodium.

Plum Kuchen

POMEGRANATES

Availability
September through December, but most plentiful in October

Buying Tips
Select fresh-looking fruit that is heavy for its size. Avoid shriveled fruit, any with broken peel, or fruit with soft spots.

To Prepare
To eat out of hand, with a sharp knife held one inch from, and parallel to, the blossom end, make a shallow cut all around. With your fingers, pull off the top. Score the fruit (only cutting through the peel) into six wedges. Break the wedges apart.

To remove the seeds (which are very juicy and stain), immerse the wedges in a bowl of cold water; gently separate the seeds from the pith and peel, and let the seeds sink to the bottom of the bowl. Pomegranate seeds can be frozen in an airtight container for up to three months; rinse with cold water before serving.

To extract the juice, place the seeds in a blender and pulse until pureed, then strain through a paper towel–lined sieve. (A medium pomegranate yields about ½ cup juice.)

To Serve
Use the juice in fruit drinks. Eat the seeds out of hand, add to fruit salads, or sprinkle on as a garnish.

QUINCES

Availability
October and November

Buying Tips
Quinces are never eaten raw. Their hard flesh, tart flavor, and abundance of pectin, however, make them popular for jams and jellies. Buy quinces that are golden yellow (the skin changes from green to yellow as it ripens) with fuzzy skin. Depending on the variety, the fruit will be either round or pear-shaped. Avoid small, knotty, or bruised fruit.

To Store
Store for up to a few days at room temperature; quinces are very fragrant and will perfume the room. Or refrigerate in a perforated plastic bag for up to two weeks.

To Prepare
To poach, first peel the fruit. Using a heavy knife (the core is very hard), cut the fruit in half, remove all the seeds and every bit of core, and slice. In a saucepan, place the slices in one inch of boiling water over medium-high heat. Heat to boiling. Reduce heat; cover and simmer until tender and deep gold or rose-colored (the cooking time depends on the size of the slices). Add sugar to taste. (The cooked fruit will remain firm though tender.)

To Serve
The cooked fruit can be served as a sauce or dessert or used in puddings, pies, and tarts.

RHUBARB

Availability
April and May

Buying Tips
The stalks should be firm, crisp, and fairly thick. Rhubarb can range in color from pale pink to deep red; avoid flabby stalks.

To Store
Refrigerate rhubarb and use within three to five days.

To Prepare
Wash and trim the stalks, then cut off and discard any leaves (they are toxic and should not be eaten).

TANGERINES, TANGELOS, AND OTHER MANDARIN ORANGES

Availability
November through May

Buying Tips
Tangerines, tangelos, clementines, satsumas, and *ugli fruit* are all members of the mandarin orange family; they are sweet citrus fruit with loose-fitting, easy-to-peel skin and segments that come apart easily. No matter what type you purchase, buy fruit

that is heavy for its size. Some
popular varieties (with their seasons) include:

Tangerine Named for the
city of Tangiers. Look for fruits
with deep orange-red skin. They
are in season from November
through May.

Tangelo A cross between
the tangerine and grapefruit, this fruit has a mild flavor and
few seeds. The season runs from November to April.

Clementine Look for sweet, seedless, compact mandarins
from October to February.

Satsuma A super-juicy, virtually seedless favorite that's
easy to peel and separate into segments. Available from mid-
October to December.

Ugli fruit This looks like a large greenish grapefruit (and
has similar flesh) but is a bit sweeter. Dark spots on the skin
are harmless, but don't buy fruit with a dried-out stem end.
The season runs from December through May.

WATERMELONS

Availability
May through September

Buying Tips
Watermelons come in two sizes:
icebox (around 8 pounds) and
large (up to 20 pounds). The

flesh can be red, the classic color, or yellow, and some varieties
are seedless. Watermelons should be firm and symmetrically
shaped, either oblong or round, depending on the variety. The
side of the melon that touched the soil should be yellowish or
cream-colored, not pale green or white. The rind should have
a velvety bloom, giving it a dull, not shiny, appearance.

To test a whole melon for ripeness, slap the side of the
melon with the open palm of your hand; the sound should be
deep and resonant. A dull thud indicates an underripe melon,
and a hollow sounds means it is overripe and mushy.

Cut watermelon should have firm, deep red flesh with
dark brown or black seeds. Avoid melons with white streaks
running through the flesh.

To Store
Refrigerate whole watermelon and use within one week. After
cutting, cover the cut surface with waxed paper; use within
one or two days.

To Serve
For wedges, with a large knife, cut the whole melon in half
from stem to blossom end. Cut each piece lengthwise in half
and cut crosswise into slices of desired thickness. Or, cut the
melon flesh into bite-size chunks and discard the rind.

Watermelon Bowl

*For a great presentation, serve this colorful mixture of sweet sum-
mer fruits and minty syrup in the hollowed-out watermelon. It
makes a very large amount, so it's just right for casual summer
get-togethers.*

Prep: 1 hour plus chilling   Cook: 10 minutes

1½	cups water
1	cup sugar
1½	cups loosely packed fresh mint leaves and stems, chopped
3	tablespoons fresh lime juice
1	large watermelon (20 pounds), cut lengthwise in half
1	small cantaloupe
6	large plums, each cut in half and pitted
4	large nectarines, each cut in half and pitted
1	pound seedless green grapes

1. In 2-quart saucepan, combine water and sugar; heat to
boiling over medium heat, stirring occasionally until sugar has
dissolved. Cook 5 minutes. Stir in mint and lime juice and refrigerate until well chilled.

2. Meanwhile, cut watermelon flesh into bite-size pieces;
discard seeds. Cut cantaloupe flesh into bite-size pieces. Cut
plums and nectarines into wedges. Combine cut-up fruit with
grapes in very large bowl or in shell of watermelon. Hold sieve
over fruit and pour chilled syrup through. Gently toss to mix
well. Cover and refrigerate about 2 hours to blend flavors, stirring occasionally. Makes about 32 cups.

♥ Each cup: About 111 calories, 2g protein, 26g carbohydrate, 1g total
fat (0g saturated), 0mg cholesterol, 7mg sodium.

Anise Fruit Bowl
Prepare as directed opposite but substitute **2 tablespoons anise seeds** for mint.

MIXED FRUIT DESSERTS

Holiday Fruit Compote

Winter's most flavorful fruits are featured in this refreshing compote.

Prep: 30 minutes plus chilling Cook: 20 minutes	
3	navel oranges
2	cups water
2	tablespoons fresh lemon juice
1¼	cups sugar
1	cinnamon stick (3 inches)
1	red eating apple, not peeled, cored, and cut into thin wedges
1	pear, not peeled, cored and cut into thin wedges
3	pink or red grapefruit

1. From 1 orange, with vegetable peeler, remove 1-inch-wide continuous strip of peel.

2. In nonreactive 2-quart saucepan, combine water, lemon juice, sugar, cinnamon stick, and orange peel; heat to boiling over medium-high heat. Reduce heat; cover and simmer until syrup has thickened slightly, about 15 minutes. Remove from heat. Add apple and pear wedges; let stand 30 minutes at room temperature to soften fruit slightly.

3. Meanwhile, from 1 orange, with vegetable peeler, remove peel; cut into thin strips. Wrap in foil and set aside (for garnish) in refrigerator. Cut peel and white pith from grapefruits and remaining orange; discard. Holding oranges and grapefruits over bowl to catch juice, cut out sections from between membranes, allowing sections to drop into bowl. Squeeze juice from membranes into bowl.

4. Add apple mixture to orange and grapefruit sections; cover and refrigerate until well chilled, at least 4 hours or overnight. Garnish with orange-peel strips. Makes 12 servings.

♥ Each serving: About 131 calories, 1g protein, 34g carbohydrate, 0g total fat (0g saturated), 0mg cholesterol, 1mg sodium.

Blueberry-Mango Compote

A summery duo that can't be beat.

Prep: 15 minutes	
1	tablespoon dark Jamaican rum
1	tablespoon fresh lime juice
1	tablespoon sugar
2	large mangoes, peeled and cut into ¾-inch pieces
1	pint blueberries

In medium bowl, combine rum, lime juice, and sugar. Add mangoes and blueberries; toss to coat. Cover and refrigerate if not serving right away. Makes 6 servings.

♥ Each serving: About 97 calories, 1g protein, 24g carbohydrate, 0g total fat (0g saturated), 0mg cholesterol, 5mg sodium.

Dried Apricot, Prune, and Cherry Compote

This compote is made exclusively with dried fruits. It tastes great by itself but can also be served with crisp cookies or a generous dollop of vanilla yogurt.

Prep: 15 minutes plus cooling Cook: 15 minutes	
1	cup dried apricots (8 ounces), each cut into thirds
¼	cup packed brown sugar
3	strips (3" by 1" each) lemon peel
1	cinnamon stick (3 inches)
4	cups apple cider or apple juice
1	cup pitted prunes (8 ounces), each cut in half
½	cup dried tart cherries (4 ounces)
½	teaspoon vanilla extract

1. In 3-quart saucepan, combine apricots, brown sugar, lemon peel, cinnamon stick, and apple cider; heat to boiling over high heat. Reduce heat and simmer 5 minutes.

2. Spoon apricot mixture into large bowl; stir in prunes, cherries, and vanilla. Let cool to serve at room temperature, or cover and refrigerate. Store in refrigerator up to 1 week. Makes 8 servings.

♥ Each serving: About 257 calories, 2g protein, 67g carbohydrate, 0g total fat (0g saturated), 0mg cholesterol, 11mg sodium.

Ambrosia

Some ambrosias have gotten away from the pure simplicity of the original recipe—not ours.

Prep: 50 minutes   Bake: 15 minutes

1	fresh coconut
1	ripe pineapple
6	large navel oranges

1. Preheat oven to 350°F. Prepare coconut: Using hammer and screwdriver or large nail, puncture two of the three eyes (indentations) in coconut. Drain liquid. Bake coconut 15 minutes. Remove from oven and wrap in kitchen towel. With hammer, hit coconut to break it into large pieces. With knife, pry coconut meat from shell. With vegetable peeler, peel brown outer skin from coconut meat. With vegetable peeler or on large holes of grater, shred 1 cup coconut. (Wrap and refrigerate remaining coconut up to 2 days for another use.)

2. Prepare pineapple: Cut crown and stem end from pineapple. Stand pineapple on cutting board, cut off rind, and remove eyes. Cut pineapple lengthwise into quarters. Cut out core. Cut quarters lengthwise in half, then crosswise into pieces. Place in large bowl.

3. Prepare oranges: Cut ends off oranges; stand oranges on cutting board and cut off peel and white pith. Holding oranges over bowl with pineapple to catch juice, cut out sections from between membranes, allowing sections to drop in bowl. Squeeze juice from membranes into bowl.

4. Add shredded coconut to bowl and toss gently to combine. Makes 10 servings.

Each serving: About 240 calories, 3g protein, 31g carbohydrate, 14g total fat (12g saturated), 0mg cholesterol, 10mg sodium.

Mint Julep Cups

Bourbon and mint lend a gentle kick to fruit salad. It's just the thing to serve at a Kentucky Derby party.

Prep: 25 minutes plus chilling

1	pineapple
¼	cup bourbon
¼	cup chopped fresh mint leaves
2	tablespoons sugar
1	pint strawberries, hulled and thickly sliced

1. In separate large bowl, combine bourbon, mint, and sugar until blended.

2. Cut crown and stem end from pineapple. Stand pineapple on cutting board, cut off rind, and remove eyes. Cut pineapple lengthwise into quarters; remove core. Cut quarters lengthwise in half, then crosswise into thin slices. Place in bowl with bourbon mixture.

3. Add strawberries; stir to combine. Refrigerate about 2 hours to blend flavors. Makes 6 servings.

♥ Each serving: About 144 calories, 1g protein, 30g carbohydrate, 1g total fat (0g saturated), 0mg cholesterol, 4mg sodium.

CANDIED FRUITS

Candied fruits (fruits that have been preserved in sugar) are indispensable in many holiday recipes. They are sometimes crystallized (coated with granulated sugar) or glacéed (dipped into a glossy syrup). For the highest-quality candied fruits, shop at a store that specializes in European ingredients. Some candy stores also sell high-quality candied fruit. The supermarket variety is quite often tasteless and colorless.

Most candied fruit is simply sweetened and artificially colored. Examples include cherries, citrus peel, pineapple, oranges, and apricots. A few edibles are cultivated almost exclusively so they can be candied. Angelica is an herb related to parsley. Its stalk is candied and colored bright green; it is used to decorate fruit cakes and trifles. Citron is a large citrus fruit with thick skin; when candied it turns dull green. It is used in fruit cakes.

Three-Fruit Salad with Vanilla Bean Syrup

Perfect alone but also a delicious accompaniment to pound cake. If you don't have a vanilla bean, stir one-half teaspoon vanilla extract into the chilled syrup.

Prep: 30 minutes plus chilling   Cook: 10 minutes

2	large lemons
1	vanilla bean
¾	cup water
¾	cup sugar
3	ripe mangoes, peeled and cut into 1-inch pieces
2	pints strawberries, hulled and cut in half, or into quarters if large
1	medium honeydew melon, peeled and cut into 1-inch pieces

1. From 1 lemon, with vegetable peeler, remove 1-inch-wide continuous strip of peel; from lemons, squeeze ¼ cup juice. Cut vanilla bean lengthwise in half. With small knife, scrape seeds from vanilla bean; reserve seeds and pod.

2. In 1-quart saucepan, combine lemon peel, vanilla-bean seeds and pod, water, and sugar; heat to boiling over high heat. Reduce heat to medium and cook until syrup has thickened slightly, about 5 minutes. Pour syrup mixture through sieve into small bowl; stir in lemon juice. Cover and refrigerate syrup until chilled, about 2 hours.

3. Place mangoes, strawberries, and melon in large bowl; add syrup and toss. Makes 12 servings.

 Each serving: About 138 calories, 1g protein, 35g carbohydrate, 0g total fat (0g saturated), 0mg cholesterol, 13mg sodium.

Autumn Fruit Compote

Dried fruits and fresh apples are poached together for a sweet compote with just a touch of citrus and cinnamon. Serve after a rich entrée such as pork or roast goose.

Prep: 20 minutes plus chilling   Cook: 25 minutes

1	orange
1	lemon
4	medium Golden Delicious or Jonagold apples, each peeled, cored, and cut into 16 wedges
1	package (8 ounces) mixed dried fruit (with pitted prunes)
1	cup dried Calimyrna figs (6 ounces)
½	cup sugar
1	cinnamon stick (3 inches)
3	cups water

1. From orange and lemon, with vegetable peeler, remove peel in 1-inch-wide strips. From lemon, squeeze 2 tablespoons juice (reserve orange for another use).

2. In nonreactive 4-quart saucepan, combine apples, mixed dried fruit, figs, orange and lemon peels, lemon juice, sugar, cinnamon stick, and water; heat to boiling over high heat. Reduce heat; cover and simmer until apples are tender, 15 to 20 minutes.

3. Pour fruit mixture into bowl and refrigerate at least 4 hours to blend flavors. Serve chilled. Store in refrigerator up to 4 days. Makes 8 servings.

 Each serving: About 211 calories, 1g protein, 55g carbohydrate, 1g total fat (0g saturated), 0mg cholesterol, 8mg sodium.

This is a simple way to enjoy overripe fruit. Peel the fruit, if desired, and cut into bite-size pieces. Place in a nonreactive saucepan, and sprinkle with some fresh lemon juice (about 2 tablespoons per pound of fruit). Heat to boiling, then reduce the heat to a simmer and cook until the fruit forms a sauce. Remove from the heat and sweeten to taste with sugar, honey, or pure maple syrup. Serve as a dessert sauce or with roasted chicken or duck.

MOLLIE KATZEN

MOLLIE KATZEN'S COOKING SHOW

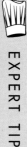

EXPERT TIP

Rhubarb-Strawberry Cobbler

We like this filling sweet-tart. If you prefer a sweeter version, just increase the sugar in the filling to three-quarters cup. Serve warm with vanilla ice cream.

Prep: 45 minutes	Bake: 20 minutes

1¼	pounds rhubarb, cut into 1-inch pieces (4 cups)
¾	cup plus 1 teaspoon sugar
¼	cup water
1	tablespoon cornstarch
1	pint strawberries, hulled and cut into quarters
1½	cups all-purpose flour
1½	teaspoons baking powder
½	teaspoon baking soda
¼	teaspoon salt
¼	teaspoon ground cinnamon
⅛	teaspoon ground nutmeg
4	tablespoons butter or margarine, cut into pieces
¾	cup plus 1 tablespoon heavy or whipping cream

1. Prepare filling: In nonreactive 3-quart saucepan, combine rhubarb and ½ cup sugar; heat to boiling over high heat, stirring constantly. Reduce heat to medium-low and cook until rhubarb is tender, about 8 minutes.

2. In cup, blend water and cornstarch until smooth. Stir strawberries and cornstarch mixture into rhubarb mixture; cook until mixture has thickened and boils, about 2 minutes. Remove from heat and keep warm.

3. Meanwhile, preheat oven to 400°F. In large bowl, combine flour, ¼ cup sugar, baking powder, baking soda, salt, cinnamon, and nutmeg. With pastry blender or two knives used scissor-fashion, cut in butter until mixture resembles coarse crumbs. Stir in ¾ cup cream just until mixture forms soft dough that leaves side of bowl.

4. On lightly floured surface, knead dough 6 to 8 times to mix thoroughly. With floured rolling pin, roll dough ½ inch thick. With 3-inch star-shaped cookie cutter or 2½-inch round cutter, cut out as many biscuits as possible. Press trimmings together; cut as above to make 8 biscuits in all.

5. Reheat rhubarb filling and pour into shallow 2-quart casserole or 11" by 7" baking dish. Place biscuits on top; with pastry brush, brush with remaining 1 tablespoon cream. Sprinkle with remaining 1 teaspoon sugar. Place baking dish on foil-lined cookie sheet to catch any overflow during baking. Bake until biscuits are golden brown and rhubarb is bubbling, about 20 minutes. Cool on wire rack about 15 minutes to serve warm. Makes 8 servings.

Each serving: About 336 calories, 4g protein, 47g carbohydrate, 15g total fat (9g saturated), 49mg cholesterol, 313mg sodium.

Rhubarb-Apple Crumble

A lowfat but irresistible homestyle dessert. The sweet oat topping is mixed with just a bit of butter for rich flavor.

Prep: 20 minutes	Bake: 45 minutes

⅓	cup granulated sugar
1	tablespoon cornstarch
1¼	pounds rhubarb, cut into ½-inch pieces (4 cups)
1¼	pounds Golden Delicious apples (3 medium), peeled, cored, and cut into 1-inch pieces
½	cup packed brown sugar
2	tablespoons butter or margarine, softened
¼	teaspoon ground cinnamon
⅓	cup old-fashioned or quick-cooking oats, uncooked
¼	cup all-purpose flour

1. Preheat oven to 375°F. In large bowl, combine granulated sugar and cornstarch. Add rhubarb and apples and toss to coat. Spoon mixture into 11" by 7" baking dish or shallow 2-quart casserole.

2. In medium bowl, with fingertips, mix brown sugar, butter, and cinnamon until blended. Stir in oats and flour until combined; sprinkle mixture over fruit in baking dish.

3. Bake until filling is hot and bubbling and topping has browned, about 45 minutes. Serve warm. Makes 6 servings.

♥ Each serving: About 252 calories, 2g protein, 53g carbohydrate, 5g total fat (2g saturated), 10mg cholesterol, 50mg sodium.

Rhubarb-Strawberry Cobbler

Nectarine and Cherry Crisp

Two favorite summertime fruits become the perfect foil for the crunchy topping.

Prep: 30 minutes   Bake: 1 hour to 1 hour 15 minutes

Nectarine and Cherry Filling

½	cup granulated sugar
3	tablespoons cornstarch
10	ripe medium nectarines (3 pounds), each cut in half, pitted, and cut into 6 wedges
1½	pounds dark sweet cherries, pitted
2	tablespoons fresh lemon juice
2	tablespoons cold butter or margarine, cut into small pieces

Oatmeal Topping

6	tablespoons butter or margarine, softened
⅔	cup packed brown sugar
1	large egg
2	teaspoons vanilla extract
1½	cups old-fashioned oats, uncooked
¾	cup all-purpose flour
¼	teaspoon baking soda
¼	teaspoon salt

1. Preheat oven to 375°F. In large bowl, combine granulated sugar and cornstarch. Add nectarines, cherries, lemon juice, and sugar mixture and toss together until evenly coated.

2. Spoon mixture into 13" by 9" baking dish; dot with butter. Place baking dish on foil-lined cookie sheet to catch any overflow during baking. Cover with foil and bake until mixture is gently bubbling, 40 to 50 minutes.

3. Meanwhile, prepare oatmeal topping: In large bowl, with mixer at medium-high speed, beat butter and brown sugar until smooth. Add egg and vanilla; beat until fluffy. With spoon, stir in old-fashioned oats, flour, baking soda, and salt until mixed. Cover and refrigerate until ready to use.

4. Drop topping by scant ¼ cups over fruit. Bake, uncovered, until topping has browned, 20 to 25 minutes. Cool slightly on wire rack to serve warm. Makes 12 servings.

♥ Each serving: About 317 calories, 5g protein, 56g carbohydrate, 10g total fat (5g saturated), 38mg cholesterol, 162mg sodium.

Blueberry-Peach Shortcakes

Another fabulous take on everyone's favorite midsummer dessert. If you prefer, use a mix of peaches and raspberries, or try a combination of your favorite berries. It will be just as delicious.

Prep: 30 minutes   Cook/Bake: 25 minutes

2	tablespoons fresh lemon juice
1	tablespoon cornstarch
1½	pints blueberries (3¾ cups)
1	cup plus 3 tablespoons sugar
6	medium peaches (2 pounds), each peeled and cut into 8 wedges
3	cups all-purpose flour
4½	teaspoons baking powder
¾	teaspoon salt
9	tablespoons cold butter or margarine, cut into pieces, plus 1 tablespoon butter or margarine, melted
1	cup plus 2 tablespoons milk
1	cup heavy or whipping cream

1. Preheat oven to 425°F. In cup, blend lemon juice and cornstarch until smooth.

2. In 3-quart saucepan, combine blueberries, ⅔ cup sugar, and cornstarch mixture; heat to boiling over medium-high heat, stirring. Reduce heat to medium; cook 1 minute. Stir in peaches; remove from heat.

3. Prepare biscuits: In large bowl, combine flour, ⅓ cup sugar, baking powder, and salt. With pastry blender or two knives used scissor-fashion, cut in cold butter until mixture resembles coarse crumbs. Stir in milk just until mixture forms soft dough that leaves side of bowl.

4. On lightly floured surface, knead dough 6 to 8 times to mix thoroughly. With lightly floured hands, pat dough until 1 inch thick.

5. With floured 3-inch round biscuit cutter, cut out as many biscuits as possible. Place biscuits 1 inch apart on ungreased large cookie sheet. Press trimmings together; cut as above to make 8 biscuits in all.

6. With pastry brush, brush biscuits with melted butter; sprinkle with 1 tablespoon sugar. Bake biscuits until golden, 15 to 20 minutes.

7. In medium bowl, beat cream with remaining 2 table-spoons sugar until soft peaks form. With fork, split warm biscuits horizontally in half. Spoon some blueberry-peach mixture onto bottom halves of biscuits; top with whipped cream, then with more blueberry-peach mixture. Cover with biscuit tops. Makes 8 servings.

Each serving without whipped cream: About 613 calories, 8g protein, 91g carbohydrate, 26g total fat (16g saturated), 80mg cholesterol, 658mg sodium.

Chocolate Fondue with Fruit

A fun ending to any meal.

Prep: 15 minutes   Cook: 5 minutes

6	squares (6 ounces) semisweet chocolate, coarsely chopped
½	cup half-and-half or light cream
½	teaspoon vanilla extract
4	small bananas, peeled and cut into ½-inch-thick slices
2 to 3	small pears, cored and cut into ½-inch-thick wedges
1	pint strawberries, hulled
½	cup finely chopped almonds, toasted

1. In heavy 1-quart saucepan, heat chocolate and half-and-half over low heat, stirring frequently, until chocolate has melted and mixture is smooth, about 5 minutes. Stir in vanilla; keep warm.

2. To serve, arrange bananas, pears, and strawberries on large platter. Spoon sauce into small bowl; place nuts in separate small bowl. With forks or toothpicks, have guests dip fruit into chocolate sauce, then into nuts. Makes 8 servings.

Each serving: About 249 calories, 4g protein, 36g carbohydrate, 13g total fat (5g saturated), 6mg cholesterol, 10mg sodium.

DRIED FRUITS

Dried fruits are great for snacking and stirring into cookies, muffins, and cakes. Sulfur dioxide is often used to preserve and enhance their color. Some sulfur-free dried fruits can be found at supermarkets and natural food stores, but they won't have the same bright color. Dried fruits can be stored in an airtight container in a dark dry place at room temperature for up to one year.

DRIED APPLES Dried apple rings are often added to fruit compotes. Health food–store varieties are usually firmer and more flavorful than the supermarket variety.

DRIED APRICOTS Don't be fooled by the color. Sometimes the darker, less attractive unsulfured apricots have the most flavor.

DRIED BANANAS Sold in strips, dried bananas can be cut up and used much like dried figs in cakes and muffins. Crisp banana chips are usually eaten as a snack, not for cooking.

DRIED BLUEBERRIES These lose a bit of their berry flavor in the drying process, but they are a nice addition to muffins and quick breads.

DRIED CHERRIES Available tart or sweet; dried sweet cherries are a delicious snack, while dried tart cherries are excellent in baked goods.

DRIED CRANBERRIES Sometimes called Craisins, they are sprayed with sugar syrup to tame their characteristic tartness.

DRIED DATES Use dried dates in small amounts, because they are very sweet. They are very sticky; cut them up with oiled kitchen scissors. Prechopped dates are very convenient but not as tasty.

DRIED FIGS The Calimyrna (actually the Turkish Symrna fig, grown in California) is favored for its moistness and rich flavor. Choose dried figs that look plump and appetizing, not dried out and dull.

DRIED PEACHES AND PEARS Best as a snack, because their delicate flavor doesn't always hold up to cooking.

PRUNES Sold pitted and unpitted. They are a quick source of energy and contain potassium, iron, and vitamins A and C.

RAISINS More than 30 percent of the table grapes grown in America are dried into raisins.

GOLDEN RAISINS Seedless Thompson grapes that have been treated with sulfur dioxide to retain their light color.

CURRANTS Also known as *Zante currants*, these are dried seedless grapes, totally unrelated to fresh currants. The name is derived from the grape variety's place of origin: Corinth, Greece.

13

SALADS AND SALAD DRESSINGS

Salad, in its most familiar guise, is a cool, crisp, refreshing collection of greens tossed with a piquant dressing. The possibilities, however, don't end with this expected combination. A salad can be created from a seemingly endless array of ingredients, each contributing different flavors and textures and sometimes even dictating different serving temperatures. Whether prepared with beans or bread, with grains or greens, or served chilled or warm, a salad is always welcome. It can also play a variety of roles. Of course, a salad can be an appetite-teasing first course or a tempting side dish, especially at summer barbecues and picnics. But bolstered with meat, chicken, or seafood, a salad can also serve as a satisfying but light main dish for warm-weather meals.

BUYING, PREPARING, AND STORING SALAD GREENS

Choose crisp-looking greens without bruised, yellowing, or brown-tipped leaves. Ever-popular iceberg lettuce should be heavy for its size and feel firm when squeezed.

As soon as you get home, wash, dry, and store the lettuce leaves. This will keep the greens fresh longer and provide a few day's worth of salad ready to put together when you are. Even prewashed greens should be washed and dried to refresh them

Mixed Greens with Pears and Pecans

and to rinse off any bacteria from the surface of the leaves.

No one wants a gritty salad, so wash the greens well. Separate the leaves, submerge them in a sink or large bowl of cold water, and gently agitate the greens to loosen the dirt. Lift the greens from the water, leaving the grit to sink to the bottom. Curly-leafed greens, as well as spinach and arugula, are especially sandy and dirt often gets trapped in the crevices of the leaves. Wash these greens in cool water: The slightly warmer temperature loosens dirt better than cold water. And if necessary, give the greens a second washing.

Dry salad greens thoroughly before using or storing. Not only do wet greens dilute the dressing and make for a less flavorful, soggy salad, but they won't keep well either. A salad spinner is an efficient way to dry greens, but they can also be patted dry with paper towels or clean kitchen towels. If you are washing spinach, arugula, or watercress, remove their tough stems after rinsing.

To store, wrap the rinsed and dried greens in a clean kitchen towel (or in a few paper towels), place in a plastic bag (pressing out all the excess air), and store in the vegetable crisper drawer of the refrigerator. Tender leaf lettuce will keep for two to three days; iceberg and other sturdy lettuces will hold for up to five days. Very delicate greens, such as arugula or watercress, will keep for only a day or so.

A GLOSSARY OF GREENS

Salad greens fall into either of two basic categories: delicate and tender or assertive and slightly bitter. Tender greens, such as lettuce, are served alone or combined with other vegetables. There are four types of lettuce: crisphead (iceberg) varieties are crisp and mild-flavored and stand up well to thicker dressings; butterhead (Bibb, Boston) is sweet-tasting and delicate and should be served with an appropriately light-bodied dressing; loose-leaf (oak leaf) is tender but has a slightly stronger flavor than butterhead; long-leaf (romaine) has long, firm, crisp leaves and is another candidate for rich, thick dressings.

Stronger-flavored greens (including members of the chicory family) are usually combined with sweeter lettuces to make a well-balanced salad. Flavorwise, their mild bitterness contrasts nicely with lettuce's natural sweetness, but greens such as red radicchio and pale Belgian endive are also invaluable as color elements in the salad palette.

Here are the basic characteristics of the different greens to help you make the right choice at the market.

Arugula Peppery arugula, also known as rugula or rocket, is a favorite ingredient in Italian-style salads. The older and larger the leaves, the more assertive the flavor. The leaves can be very gritty, so be sure to rinse them thoroughly before using.

Baby greens Available in bags or in bulk at many supermarkets, this combination of very young, tender salad greens is an Americanization of the French salad mixture, *mesclun*.

Belgian endive A member of the chicory family, Belgian endive is appreciated for its crisp texture and slightly bitter flavor. It can be expensive, but there is very little waste. The leaves should be very white, graduating to pale yellow tips. Do not buy endive that has turned green: It will be very bitter.

Bibb lettuce Also called limestone lettuce, it has cup-shaped leaves and is best with mild vinaigrettes.

Boston lettuce A loose-leaf lettuce with tender floppy leaves; sometimes called butterhead lettuce.

Chicory Although chicory is an entire family of mildly bitter greens, Americans use the term to identify a dark green variety with fringed leaves. It is also known as curly endive.

Chinese cabbage A tightly formed head of white leaves with wide stalks. Excellent with Asian-style vinaigrettes.

Dandelion Tart greens that make a pungent addition to a salad. Some cooks gather the wild variety in the spring.

Escarole Sharp-tasting escarole should have curly leaves with firm stems that snap easily.

Frisée A delicate pale green chicory with curly, almost spiky leaves. A favorite of French cooks, it is often combined with Roquefort cheese, bacon, or apples.

Iceberg lettuce A lettuce that is best appreciated for its refreshing crisp texture rather than for its mild flavor. Cut out the core before rinsing the leaves.

Mâche Also called lamb's lettuce, this nutty-tasting green has tiny tender leaves. Use within one day; it wilts easily.

Mesclun From the Provençal word for mixture, true mesclun is made up of wild baby greens from the hillsides in Southern France and often includes herbs and edible flowers. Here, it is commonly a mix of sweet lettuces and bitter greens such as arugula, dandelion, frisée, mizuna, oak leaf, mâche, sorrel, and radicchio.

Mizuma Small, feathery, delicately flavored green of Japanese origin; also called mizuna.

Napa cabbage Very similar to, and interchangeable with, Chinese cabbage, but shorter and rounder.

Oak leaf A variety of Boston lettuce with ruffled leaves. Green oak leaf is uniformly green, whereas red oak leaf has dark red tips and a slightly fuller flavor.

Radicchio The most common radicchio is round with white-veined ruby red leaves. It has an understated bitterness. *Radicchio di Treviso* has long, narrow red leaves that form a tapered head. Radicchio is available year round, but its peak season is midwinter to early spring.

Radish sprouts Innocent-looking sprouts with clover-shaped heads that really pack a peppery punch. Discard the roots and use sparingly in salads and sandwiches.

Romaine Its long, crisp, dark green leaves and slightly nutty flavor make romaine the preferred lettuce for classic Caesar salad.

Spinach Whether dark green and crinkled or flat, spinach leaves always need to be well washed to remove all the grit. Baby spinach, with its very tender edible stems, is increasingly available at supermarkets and specialty food stores.

Watercress Sold in bunches, watercress adds crisp texture and a mildly spicy flavor to salads. It is very perishable, so use within one or two days of purchase.

THE WELL-DRESSED SALAD

A delicious dressing pulls the salad ingredients together to create a mouthwatering ensemble. Choosing the right dressing is critical. Thick dressings, such as blue cheese or Russian, should be reserved for sturdy lettuce, such as iceberg or romaine. Delicate greens, such as Bibb, should be dressed with a thin-bodied vinaigrette to avoid crushing the leaves.

Vinaigrettes are the most versatile of all salad dressings. They are simple blends of vinegar (or another acidic ingredient), oil, and seasonings, such as shallots, Dijon mustard, fresh or dried herbs, salt, and pepper. These ingredients allow vinaigrettes to be infinitely adaptable and versatile. The flavor of a vinaigrette dressing is largely determined by the kind of oil and vinegar used.

Oil is the backbone of any vinaigrette. Olive oil is regarded as the perfect vinaigrette ingredient because its mildly fruity flavor goes well with greens. Full-flavored extravirgin olive oil is produced from the first pressing of tree-ripe olives and has a greenish tint. The olives are pressed a second time to make the familiar gold-colored olive oil (what we used to call pure olive oil). Light olive oil is made from the final pressing of the olives. The term "light" refers to its taste, not its calorie or fat content. Nut oils, especially walnut oil and hazelnut oil, make fine vinaigrettes with a hint of mild nutty flavor. Dark sesame oil can be used in small amounts in combination with lighter oils, but its flavor is too heavy to be the only oil in a dressing. Infused oils, such as basil oil or roasted garlic oil, also make unusual salad dressings. Sometimes, however, vegetable oil is preferred because its neutral taste allows the flavor of the other ingredients to shine through.

Vinegar is probably the most often used acidic ingredient in salad dressings. Red- and white-wine vinegars and cider vinegar are very popular and have a sharp taste. Rice and balsamic vinegars are much milder, and sherry vinegar has a somewhat bolder flavor. Just like infused oils, flavored vinegars are newly popular ways to add zest to salad dressings. Citrus juices, such as orange, lemon, or lime, make wonderful dressings, too.

The way in which a dressing is mixed will give different results, too. In a classic vinaigrette, the vinegar and seasonings are combined in a bowl. With a wire whisk or a fork, the oil is gradually added. At first, add the oil drop by drop, constantly whisking. As the dressing thickens, add the oil in a thin, steady stream until it is blended. This method temporarily emulsifies the ingredients (holds them together). You can also emulsify a dressing by vigorously shaking the ingredients together in a tightly closed jar—the jar is a handy way to store the vinaigrette, too. If a dressing is made in a blender, it will be especially thick. For a thin dressing, simply beat all of the ingredients together. If you like your vinaigrette slightly thickened, be sure it contains mustard, which stabilizes the dressing and keeps it emulsified longer. A vinaigrette can be stored at room temperature for up to twenty-four hours. For longer storage, keep it in the refrigerator. The oil in the dressing will firm up when chilled, so let it stand at room temperature until it thins. If the dressing separates, mix it until recombined.

Most salads are naturally lowfat—it's the dressing that hikes up the fat grams. In all of our recipes, we have used just enough oil to coat and flavor the ingredients. There are a number of tricks to slim down your salads. First, don't toss the salad with the dressing, but serve the dressing on the side so you can drizzle a small amount over your portion. You can substitute buttermilk or lowfat yogurt for mayonnaise or sour cream in many dressings, or use reduced-fat sour cream or mayonnaise. Or make an Asian-style vinaigrette with rice vinegar, soy sauce, and citrus juice, which will be delicious without a drop of fat.

To fill you up without extra fat, top your salad with plenty of crunchy veggies. Include celery, fennel, peppers, jicama, or blanched green beans. Fruits can accent the salad bowl as well. Try sliced apples or pears, melon balls, orange segments, or cubed papaya. Stay away from fatty ingredients such as avocados, nuts, bacon, and cheese. And for main-dish salads, smart choices include skinless chicken breast, water-packed tuna, shrimp, and beans.

PUTTING IT TOGETHER

If you are making a green salad, create your own blend of mixed greens or use the convenient bagged salad mixtures available at supermarkets. Cut or tear the salad greens into bite-size pieces. For the crispest salad, dress the well-dried greens just before serving. When making a salad of rice, beans, or potatoes, toss the cooked ingredients with the dressing while they're still warm so they can soak up all the flavor. When these starchy salads absorb the dressing, their flavor mellows, so taste and reseason the salad with salt and pepper and perhaps a splash of vinegar before serving.

Mixed Greens with Pears and Pecans

(pictured on page 520)

The sweetness of ripe pears and the crunchiness of buttery pecans make this an irresistible holiday salad.

Prep: 45 minutes

3	tablespoons red wine vinegar
2	teaspoons Dijon mustard
½	teaspoon salt
½	teaspoon coarsely ground black pepper
⅓	cup olive oil
3	ripe medium pears, each peeled, cored, and cut into 16 wedges
1	wedge Parmesan cheese (4 ounces)
2	small heads radicchio, cored and torn into large pieces
2	small heads Belgian endive, separated into leaves
2	small bunches arugula (4 ounces each), trimmed
½	cup pecans, toasted and coarsely chopped

1. Prepare dressing: In very large bowl, with wire whisk, mix vinegar, mustard, salt, and pepper. In thin, steady stream, whisk in oil until blended. Add pears, tossing to coat.

2. With vegetable peeler, remove enough shavings from wedge of Parmesan to measure 1 cup, loosely packed.

3. Add radicchio, endive, and arugula to pears; toss until mixed and coated with dressing. Top salad with Parmesan shavings and pecans. Makes 10 first-course servings.

Each serving: About 166 calories, 4g protein, 11g carbohydrate, 13g total fat (2g saturated), 4mg cholesterol, 244mg sodium.

Beet and Orange Salad

This elegant salad can be made in no time if you prepare its components the day before serving. Wash the watercress, wrap in damp towels, and refrigerate. Section the oranges and slice the cooked beets; refrigerate in separate containers.

Prep: 45 minutes   Cook: 35 minutes

10	medium beets (2½ pounds), tops removed
4	large navel oranges
¼	cup olive oil
¼	cup red wine vinegar
1	tablespoon Dijon mustard
1	teaspoon sugar
¾	teaspoon salt
¼	teaspoon coarsely ground black pepper
3	bunches watercress (4 ounces each), tough stems trimmed
1	medium red onion, thinly sliced

1. In 4-quart saucepan, combine beets and enough *water* to cover; heat to boiling over high heat. Reduce heat; cover and simmer until tender, about 30 minutes.

2. Meanwhile, from 1 orange, grate 1 teaspoon peel. Cut peel and white pith from oranges. Holding oranges over large bowl to catch juice, cut out sections from between membranes. Place sections in small bowl. Add oil, vinegar, mustard, orange peel, sugar, salt, and pepper to orange juice in bowl. With wire whisk, mix until blended.

3. Drain beets and rinse with cold running water. When cool enough to handle, peel and cut each beet in half, then crosswise into ¼-inch-thick slices.

4. Add beets, oranges, watercress, and onion to dressing in bowl; toss until mixed and coated with dressing. Makes 10 accompaniment servings.

Each serving: About 130 calories, 4g protein, 18g carbohydrate, 6g total fat (1g saturated), 0mg cholesterol, 304mg sodium.

Citrus Salad with Sherry Dressing

A splash of sherry gives this fruit salad Spanish flair.

Prep: 30 minutes

2	tablespoons dry sherry
1	tablespoon red wine vinegar
1	teaspoon Dijon mustard
1/4	teaspoon salt
1/8	teaspoon coarsely ground black pepper
2	tablespoons olive oil
1	large Granny Smith apple, cored and cut into paper-thin slices
2	large navel oranges
1	large pink grapefruit
1	bunch watercress (4 ounces), tough stems trimmed

1. Prepare dressing: In large bowl, with wire whisk, mix sherry, vinegar, mustard, salt, and pepper. In thin, steady stream, whisk in oil until blended.

2. Add apple slices to dressing in bowl and toss to coat. Cut peel and white pith from oranges and grapefruit. Holding oranges and grapefruit over small bowl to catch juice, cut out sections from between membranes. (If you like, squeeze juice from membranes and reserve for another use.) Add orange and grapefruit sections to dressing in bowl; toss to coat.

3. Arrange watercress on platter. Spoon fruit mixture and dressing over watercress. Makes 6 accompaniment servings.

Each serving: About 109 calories, 2g protein, 16g carbohydrate, 5g total fat (1g saturated), 0mg cholesterol, 127mg sodium.

Spinach and Bacon Salad

Slightly wilted spinach, crisp bacon, and a sweet-and-sour dressing work together to create one of the most popular salads of all. Have the ingredients ready and combine just before serving.

Prep: 15 minutes   Cook: 12 minutes

2	bunches (10 to 12 ounces each) spinach, washed and dried very well, tough stems trimmed
6	slices bacon, coarsely chopped
1	small onion, finely chopped
2	tablespoons sugar
1/3	cup cider vinegar
2	tablespoons olive oil
1/2	teaspoon salt

1. Tear spinach into bite-size pieces and place in bowl.

2. In 10-inch skillet, cook bacon over medium heat until browned, about 5 minutes. With slotted spoon, transfer bacon to paper towels to drain. Discard all but 2 tablespoons bacon drippings from skillet.

3. Add onion to skillet and cook over low heat until tender, about 5 minutes. Add sugar, stirring to coat. Stir in vinegar, oil, and salt; heat to boiling. Pour hot dressing over spinach. Add bacon and toss until well-mixed and coated with dressing. Serve immediately. Makes 6 first-course servings.

Each serving: About 152 calories, 4g protein, 10g carbohydrate, 11g total fat (3g saturated), 8mg cholesterol, 376mg sodium.

Citrus Salad with Sherry Dressing

Escarole and Bacon Salad

Bitter greens, bacon, croutons, and a warm dressing make a rewarding winter salad. If you wish, top each serving with a poached egg for a great lunch or light supper.

Prep: 20 minutes   Bake/Cook: 20 minutes

1	loaf French bread, cut into 1-inch cubes (3 cups)
4	tablespoons olive oil
4	large eggs (optional)
4	thick slices bacon, cut into 1-inch pieces
1	small garlic clove, finely chopped
3	tablespoons red wine vinegar
½	teaspoon salt
½	teaspoon coarsely ground pepper
1	head escarole or chicory or 2 heads frisée, torn into bite-size pieces

1. Preheat oven to 400°F. Place bread cubes in jelly-roll pan and drizzle with 1 tablespoon oil; toss until evenly coated. Bake until golden, 12 to 15 minutes.

2. Meanwhile, if serving with eggs, in nonstick 10-inch skillet, heat *1 inch water* to boiling; reduce heat to medium-low. Break eggs, one at a time, into cup; holding cup close to simmering water, slip in eggs. Cook until egg whites are set and egg yolks begin to thicken, 3 to 5 minutes. With slotted spoon, gently transfer poached eggs to medium bowl filled with warm water. Wipe skillet dry.

3. In same skillet, cook bacon over medium heat until browned. With slotted spoon, transfer to paper towels to drain. Discard all but 1 tablespoon bacon drippings from skillet.

4. Add remaining 3 tablespoons oil to skillet; remove from heat and stir in garlic (do not let brown). Immediately stir in vinegar, salt, and pepper.

5. In large bowl, place escarole, croutons, and bacon. Add hot dressing and toss until mixed and coated with dressing. Divide salad among plates. With slotted spoon, carefully place 1 poached egg on top of each salad, if desired. Makes 4 first-course servings.

Each serving without egg: About 381 calories, 10g protein, 34g carbohydrate, 23g total fat (5g saturated), 11mg cholesterol, 845mg sodium.

Each serving with egg: About 455 calories, 16g protein, 35g carbohydrate, 28g total fat (6g saturated), 223mg cholesterol, 985mg sodium.

Warm Arugula and Mushroom Salad

Peppery arugula leaves are coated with a warm mushroom dressing, then topped with Parmesan cheese shavings.

Prep: 25 minutes   Cook: 12 to 14 minutes

¼	cup chicken broth
3	tablespoons olive oil
2	tablespoons balsamic vinegar
2	tablespoons dry vermouth
½	teaspoon sugar
½	teaspoon salt
½	teaspoon coarsely ground black pepper
3	small bunches arugula (4 ounces each), trimmed
1	wedge Parmesan cheese (4 ounces)
3	garlic cloves, crushed with side of chef's knife
8	ounces shiitake mushrooms, stems removed and caps cut into quarters
8	ounces white mushrooms, trimmed and sliced
1	teaspoon chopped fresh rosemary or ¼ teaspoon dried rosemary, crumbled

1. In small bowl, mix broth, 2 tablespoons oil, vinegar, vermouth, sugar, salt, and pepper. Arrange arugula on large serving platter.

2. With vegetable peeler, remove enough shavings from wedge of Parmesan to measure 1 cup, loosely packed.

3. In nonstick 12-inch skillet, heat remaining 1 tablespoon oil over medium heat. Add garlic and cook just until golden. Increase heat to medium-high. Add shiitake and white mushrooms and rosemary; cook, stirring, until mushrooms are browned and liquid has evaporated, 8 to 10 minutes; discard garlic.

4. Add broth mixture to skillet; cook, stirring, 30 seconds. Immediately spoon mushrooms over arugula; top with Parmesan shavings. Makes 4 first-course servings.

Each serving: About 197 calories, 9g protein, 8g carbohydrate, 14g total fat (4g saturated), 10mg cholesterol, 596mg sodium.

Winter Vegetable Salad

Here, winter's bounty makes a terrific salad.

Prep: 30 minutes plus standing and chilling	Cook: 20 minutes
3	cups small cauliflower flowerets
3	cups small broccoli flowerets
2	carrots, peeled, cut lengthwise into quarters, then crosswise into 1-inch pieces (1¼ cups)
6	ounces green beans, trimmed and cut into 1-inch pieces (1½ cups)
½	cup Classic French Vinaigrette (page 545)

1. In 5-quart saucepot, heat *3 quarts water* to boiling over high heat. Add cauliflower and cook until tender-crisp, about 4 minutes. With slotted spoon, transfer to large bowl. Add broccoli, carrots, and green beans to saucepot and cook until tender-crisp, about 5 minutes. Drain; add to cauliflower.

2. Add dressing to vegetables and toss to coat. Cool to room temperature; cover and refrigerate at least 1 hour to blend flavors or up to 24 hours. Serve chilled or at room temperature. Makes 6 accompaniment servings.

Each serving: About 164 calories, 4g protein, 11g carbohydrate, 13g total fat (2g saturated), 0mg cholesterol, 283mg sodium.

Three-Bean Salad

If you can't find wax beans, double the amount of green beans.

Prep: 25 minutes plus chilling	Cook: 13 minutes
8	ounces green beans, trimmed and cut into 1-inch pieces (2 cups)
8	ounces wax beans, trimmed and cut into 1-inch pieces (2 cups)
1½	teaspoons salt
3	tablespoons olive or vegetable oil
3	tablespoons cider vinegar
2	tablespoons sugar
1	can (15 to 19 ounces) red kidney beans, rinsed and drained
¼	cup chopped onion

1. In 4-quart saucepan, heat *3 inches water* to boiling over high heat. Add green and wax beans and ½ teaspoon salt; heat to boiling. Cook until tender-crisp, 6 to 8 minutes. Drain. Rinse beans with cold running water to cool slightly; drain.

2. Meanwhile, prepare dressing: In large bowl, with wire whisk, mix oil, vinegar, sugar, and remaining 1 teaspoon salt until well blended. Add green and wax beans, kidney beans, and onion; toss until mixed and coated with dressing. Cover and refrigerate salad at least 2 hours to blend flavors or up to 24 hours. Makes 8 accompaniment servings.

Each serving: About 118 calories, 4g protein, 14g carbohydrate, 5g total fat (1g saturated), 0mg cholesterol, 441mg sodium.

New Caesar Salad

Our recipe uses mayonnaise instead of raw egg yolk to create the classic dressing, while baked bread cubes stand in for the more usual deep-fried croutons.

Prep: 15 minutes	Bake: 7 minutes
6	slices (½ inch thick) Italian bread
2	garlic cloves, each peeled and cut in half
3	tablespoons olive oil
¼	cup mayonnaise
¼	cup freshly grated Parmesan cheese
3	tablespoons fresh lemon juice
2	tablespoons water
2	teaspoons anchovy paste
1	head romaine lettuce, torn into bite-size pieces

1. Preheat oven to 400°F. Rub bread slices with cut side of garlic. Brush both sides of bread with 2 tablespoons oil. Cut bread into ½-inch cubes and place in jelly-roll pan. Bake until golden brown and crisp, about 7 minutes.

2. Meanwhile, prepare dressing: In large bowl, with wire whisk, mix mayonnaise, Parmesan, lemon juice, water, remaining 1 tablespoon oil, and anchovy paste until blended. Add lettuce and croutons; toss to coat. Makes 4 first-course servings.

Each serving: About 367 calories, 9g protein, 27g carbohydrate, 25g total fat (5g saturated), 14mg cholesterol, 604mg sodium.

Chopped Salad

Neat to eat, a chopped salad can be prepared from your favorite salad ingredients. Here's one of our favorite combinations.

Prep: 25 minutes

1	large head romaine lettuce (1¼ pounds), chopped into ½-inch pieces
1	bunch watercress (4 ounces), tough stems trimmed, coarsely chopped
1¼	pounds ripe tomatoes (2 large), cut into ½-inch pieces
1	medium cucumber (8 ounces), peeled, seeded, and cut into ½-inch pieces
1	cup radishes, cut into quarters
¼	cup Classic French Vinaigrette (page 545) or dressing of choice

In large bowl, combine romaine, watercress, tomatoes, cucumber, radishes, and dressing; toss to coat. Makes 8 accompaniment servings.

Each serving: About 67 calories, 2g protein, 5g carbohydrate, 5g total fat (1g saturated), 0mg cholesterol, 109mg sodium.

Chopped Greek Salad

Prepare as directed but add **4 ounces feta cheese,** crumbled (1 cup), **½ cup Kalamata olives,** pitted and coarsely chopped, and **¼ cup coarsely chopped fresh mint.**

Each serving: About 131 calories, 4g protein, 7g carbohydrate, 10g total fat (3g saturated), 13mg cholesterol, 420mg sodium.

Summer Corn Salad

A colorful salad created from farmstand-fresh summer vegetables.

Prep: 30 minutes   Cook: 10 minutes

12	ears corn, husks and silk removed
12	ounces green beans, trimmed and cut into ¼-inch pieces
½	cup cider vinegar
¼	cup olive oil
¼	cup chopped fresh parsley
1	teaspoon salt
½	teaspoon coarsely ground black pepper
1	red pepper, finely chopped
1	small sweet onion, such as Vidalia or Walla Walla, finely chopped

1. In 8-quart saucepot, heat *2 inches water* to boiling over high heat; add corn. Heat to boiling. Reduce heat; cover and simmer 5 minutes. Drain. When cool enough to handle, cut kernels from corncobs.

2. Meanwhile, in 2-quart saucepan, heat *1 inch water* to boiling over high heat; add green beans and heat to boiling. Reduce heat; simmer until tender-crisp, 3 to 5 minutes. Drain green beans. Rinse with cold running water; drain.

3. Prepare dressing: In large bowl, with wire whisk, mix vinegar, oil, parsley, salt, and black pepper until blended.

4. Add corn, green beans, red pepper, and onion to dressing in bowl; toss to coat. Serve, or cover and refrigerate up to 2 hours. Makes 12 accompaniment servings.

Each serving: About 179 calories, 5g protein, 31g carbohydrate, 6g total fat (1g saturated), 0mg cholesterol, 219mg sodium.

Warm Goat Cheese Salad

If you like, coat the goat cheese with the bread crumbs early in the day, then refrigerate for last-minute baking.

Prep: 15 minutes   Bake: 8 minutes

¼	cup plain dried bread crumbs
1	tablespoon chopped fresh parsley
1	tablespoon olive oil
¼	teaspoon coarsely ground pepper
1	log (5 to 6 ounces) mild goat cheese
8	ounces mixed baby salad greens (10 loosely packed cups)
3	tablespoons Classic French Vinaigrette (page 545)

1. Preheat oven to 425°F. In small bowl, stir bread crumbs, parsley, oil, and pepper until well blended. Slice goat cheese crosswise into 6 equal disks. Place on waxed paper; use bread-crumb mixture to coat cheese disks, patting crumbs to cover evenly.

2. Place crumb-coated cheese disks on cookie sheet and bake until crumbs are golden, 8 to 10 minutes.

3. In large bowl, toss salad greens with dressing to coat.

Divide greens among salad plates and top each serving with warm goat cheese disk. Makes 6 first-course servings.

Each serving: About 178 calories, 7g protein, 5g carbohydrate, 15g total fat (6g saturated), 20mg cholesterol, 264mg sodium.

Waldorf Salad

Serve this chunky salad alongside your favorite grilled chicken for a sweet and savory meal.

🕐 *Prep: 30 minutes*

⅓	cup mayonnaise
¼	cup sour cream
1	tablespoon fresh lemon juice
1	teaspoon honey
¼	teaspoon salt
2	red apples, such as Braeburn, Cortland, or Red Delicious, each cored, cut into 8 wedges, then crosswise into ¼-inch pieces
1	Granny Smith apple, cored, cut into 8 wedges, then crosswise into ¼-inch pieces
2	stalks celery, each cut lengthwise in half, then thinly sliced (½ cup)
½	cup walnuts, toasted and coarsely chopped
⅓	cup dark seedless raisins

Prepare dressing: In medium bowl, with wire whisk, mix mayonnaise, sour cream, lemon juice, honey, and salt until blended. Add red and Granny Smith apples, celery, walnuts, and raisins to dressing in bowl and toss until mixed and coated with dressing. Makes 8 accompaniment servings.

Each serving: About 181 calories, 2g protein, 16g carbohydrate, 14g total fat (2g saturated), 9mg cholesterol, 135mg sodium.

Layered Salad

Add extra layers of whatever strikes your fancy: shredded Cheddar or crumbled blue cheese; canned garbanzo beans, black beans, or kidney beans (rinsed and drained); very thinly sliced red cabbage, shredded carrots, or chopped red or green pepper. Substitute fennel for the celery, or top it all off with coarsely chopped pitted olives or crunchy toasted walnuts.

🕐 *Prep: 20 minutes*

½	head iceberg lettuce, chopped (6 cups)
1	pint cherry tomatoes, cut in half
6	stalks celery, cut on diagonal into thin slices
1	package (10 ounces) frozen baby peas, thawed
½	cup Classic French Vinaigrette (page 545) or dressing of choice

In 4-quart glass bowl, layer lettuce, cherry tomatoes, celery, and peas. Cover and refrigerate up to 4 hours. To serve, drizzle with dressing. Makes 8 accompaniment servings.

Each serving: About 122 calories, 3g protein, 8g carbohydrate, 9g total fat (1g saturated), 0mg cholesterol, 252mg sodium.

Mozzarella and Tomato Salad

For this simple combination to be at its absolute best, use only fresh mozzarella and vine-ripened summer tomatoes.

🕐 *Prep: 15 minutes*

2	ripe medium tomatoes (8 ounces each), thinly sliced
10	ounces fresh mozzarella, thinly sliced
2	tablespoons extravirgin olive oil
¼	teaspoon salt
¼	teaspoon ground black pepper
2	tablespoons thinly sliced fresh basil leaves

On large platter, arrange tomatoes and mozzarella in overlapping rows. Drizzle with oil and sprinkle with salt and pepper. Top with basil. Makes 4 accompaniment servings.

Each serving: About 285 calories, 14g protein, 8g carbohydrate, 22g total fat (1g saturated), 50mg cholesterol, 203mg sodium.

Kirby Cucumber Salad

The unwaxed skins of kirby cucumbers don't need to be peeled. If you can't find them, buy regular cucumbers and remove half of the peel in strips, creating a striped pattern. This salad can be made one day ahead, then covered and refrigerated.

Prep: 30 minutes plus standing and chilling
4 pounds kirby cucumbers, not peeled, thinly sliced
1 tablespoon salt
¾ cup distilled white vinegar
2 tablespoons sugar
2 tablespoons chopped fresh dill

1. In colander set over large bowl, toss cucumbers and salt; let stand 30 minutes at room temperature. Discard liquid in bowl. Pat cucumbers dry with paper towels.

2. In same clean bowl, combine vinegar, sugar, and dill. Add cucumbers and toss to coat. Cover and refrigerate, stirring occasionally, at least 1 hour to blend flavors or up to 4 hours. Makes 12 accompaniment servings.

♥ Each serving: About 30 calories, 1g protein, 7g carbohydrate, 0g total fat, (0g saturated), 0mg cholesterol, 149mg sodium.

Creamy Cucumber and Dill Salad

On hot summer days, serve these thinly sliced cucumbers as a cool side dish for grilled salmon.

Prep: 15 minutes plus standing and chilling
2 English (seedless) cucumbers, not peeled, thinly sliced
2 teaspoons salt
½ cup sour cream
2 tablespoons chopped fresh dill
2 teaspoons chopped fresh mint
1 teaspoon distilled white vinegar
⅛ teaspoon ground black pepper

1. In colander set over large bowl, toss cucumbers and salt; let stand 30 minutes at room temperature. Discard liquid in bowl. Pat cucumbers dry with paper towels.

2. In same clean bowl, combine sour cream, dill, mint, vinegar, and pepper. Add cucumbers, stirring to coat. Cover and refrigerate at least 1 hour to blend flavors or up to 4 hours. Makes 6 accompaniment servings.

Each serving: About 60 calories, 2g protein, 5g carbohydrate, 4g total fat (3g saturated), 8mg cholesterol, 203mg sodium.

Asian Cucumber Salad

An easy salad that goes well with spicy food.

Prep: 15 minutes plus standing and chilling	Cook: 3 minutes
2 English (seedless) cucumbers	
1 teaspoon salt	
¼ cup seasoned rice vinegar	
4 teaspoons sugar	

1. With vegetable peeler, remove 4 evenly spaced lengthwise strips of peel from each cucumber. Thinly slice cucumbers. In colander set over large bowl, toss cucumbers and ½ teaspoon salt; let stand 30 minutes at room temperature. Discard liquid in bowl. Pat cucumbers dry with paper towels.

2. In 6-inch skillet, combine vinegar and sugar; heat to boiling over high heat. Cook until sugar has dissolved. Transfer to same clean bowl and stir in remaining ½ teaspoon salt. Add cucumbers and toss to coat. Refrigerate 1 hour to blend flavors or up to 4 hours. Makes 8 accompaniment servings.

♥ Each serving: About 27 calories, 1g protein, 6g carbohydrate, 0g total fat, (0g saturated), 0mg cholesterol, 332mg sodium.

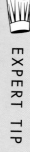

To add tasty crunch to your salads, quickly toast some seeds (pepita, sesame, sunflower) in a dry skillet; add a sprinkle of salt and a squirt of lemon or lime juice for some extra flavor. The aroma will bring your family to the dinner table in a flash.

MARY SUE MILLIKEN AND SUSAN FENIGER
TELEVISION HOSTS OF TOO HOT TAMALES

EXPERT TIP

Coleslaw with Vinaigrette

This flavorful coleslaw tastes best when thoroughly chilled.

Prep: 20 minutes plus chilling

2	tablespoons olive or vegetable oil
2	tablespoons red wine vinegar
1	tablespoon sugar
1	teaspoon salt
½	teaspoon caraway seeds or ¼ teaspoon celery seeds, crushed
1	small head green cabbage (1½ pounds), thinly sliced, tough ribs discarded (6 cups)
1	large red pepper, cut into 2" by ¼" matchstick strips

Prepare dressing: In large bowl, with wire whisk, mix oil, vinegar, sugar, salt, and caraway seeds until blended. Add cabbage and red pepper; toss to coat well. Cover and refrigerate at least 1 hour to blend flavors or up to 6 hours. Makes 6 accompaniment servings.

Each serving: About 75 calories, 1g protein, 8g carbohydrate, 5g total fat (1g saturated), 0mg cholesterol, 405mg sodium.

Asian Coleslaw

This refreshing Asian-style slaw is a tasty accompaniment for lime-grilled shrimp kabobs and ginger iced tea.

Prep: 35 minutes

⅓	cup seasoned rice vinegar
2	tablespoons vegetable oil
2	teaspoons Asian sesame oil
¾	teaspoon salt
1	medium head savoy cabbage (2½ pounds), thinly sliced, tough ribs discarded
1	bag (16 ounces) carrots, peeled and shredded
½	cup chopped fresh cilantro
4	green onions, thinly sliced

1. Prepare dressing: In large bowl, with wire whisk, mix vinegar, vegetable and sesame oils, and salt until blended.

2. Add cabbage, carrots, cilantro, and green onions to dressing in bowl; toss until mixed and coated with dressing. If not serving right away, cover and refrigerate up to 2 hours. Makes 12 accompaniment servings.

Each serving: About 69 calories, 2g protein, 10g carbohydrate, 3g total fat (0g saturated), 0mg cholesterol, 310mg sodium.

Light and Lemony Slaw

A crisp complement to any barbecue and lower in fat than the typical deli slaw. Its slight sweetness is also a nice change of pace.

Prep: 25 minutes

2	lemons
½	cup light mayonnaise
¼	cup reduced-fat sour cream
1	tablespoon sugar
1	teaspoon salt
½	teaspoon coarsely ground black pepper
¼	teaspoon celery seeds, crushed
1	large head green cabbage (3 pounds), thinly sliced, tough ribs discarded (12 cups)
4	carrots, peeled and shredded

1. From lemons, grate 1 teaspoon peel and squeeze ¼ cup juice. In large bowl, with wire whisk, mix lemon peel and juice, mayonnaise, sour cream, sugar, salt, pepper, and celery seeds until blended.

2. Add cabbage and carrots to dressing in bowl; toss to coat. Serve at room temperature, or cover and refrigerate up to 4 hours. Makes 12 accompaniment servings.

Each serving: About 80 calories, 2g protein, 10g carbohydrate, 4g total fat (1g saturated), 5mg cholesterol, 298mg sodium.

Cherry Tomato–Lemon Salad

Serve this tart salad at your next picnic or brunch. If your market does not have yellow cherry tomatoes, use red ones.

Prep: 20 minutes

2	lemons
2	pints red cherry tomatoes, cut in half
1	pint yellow cherry tomatoes, cut in half
2	tablespoons chopped fresh chives
2	tablespoons extravirgin olive oil
1	tablespoon sugar
¾	teaspoon salt
½	teaspoon coarsely ground black pepper

1. Cut peel and white pith from lemons. Cut each lemon crosswise into ¼-inch-thick rounds; cut into small pieces.

2. In medium bowl, toss lemons, red and yellow cherry tomatoes, chives, oil, sugar, salt, and pepper until coated. Makes 8 accompaniment servings.

Each serving: About 58 calories, 1g protein, 8g carbohydrate, 4g total fat (1g saturated), 0mg cholesterol, 226mg sodium.

Roasted Potato Salad

Roasted Potato Salad

Potatoes and shallots, roasted until tender and caramelized, become a spectacular salad when tossed with a lemon-Dijon dressing.

Prep: 25 minutes   Roast: 45 minutes

2	pounds red potatoes (12 medium), not peeled, cut into 1½-inch pieces
16	small shallots, peeled, or 2 medium red onions, each cut into 8 wedges
1	teaspoon salt
¼	teaspoon ground black pepper
2	tablespoons olive or vegetable oil
8	ounces French green beans *(haricots verts)* or regular green beans, trimmed
1	tablespoon fresh lemon juice
1	teaspoon Dijon mustard

1. Preheat oven to 425°F. In large roasting pan (17" by 11½"), sprinkle potatoes and shallots with salt and pepper. Drizzle with 1 tablespoon oil and toss. Roast 30 minutes.

2. After vegetables have roasted 30 minutes, stir in green beans. Roast, stirring occasionally, until all vegetables are tender, about 15 minutes longer.

3. Meanwhile, prepare dressing: In large bowl, with wire whisk, mix lemon juice, remaining 1 tablespoon oil, and mustard until blended and smooth. Add vegetables to dressing in bowl and toss to coat. Serve warm or at room temperature. Makes 6 accompaniment servings.

♥ *Each serving: About 212 calories, 5g protein, 39g carbohydrate, 5g total fat (1g saturated), 0mg cholesterol, 428mg sodium.*

Red Potato Salad

In France, potato salad is prepared with a shallot vinaigrette and the freshest, smallest red potatoes available. A bit of crumbled bacon over the top makes it even better.

Prep: 25 minutes plus cooling   Cook: 30 minutes

4	pounds small red potatoes, not peeled, cut into quarters or eighths if large
3½	teaspoons salt
4	slices bacon
3	large shallots, chopped (¾ cup)
⅓	cup cider vinegar
¼	cup olive oil
2	teaspoons sugar
2	teaspoons Dijon mustard
¼	teaspoon coarsely ground black pepper
2	green onions, chopped

1. In 5-quart saucepot, combine potatoes, enough *water* to cover, and 2 teaspoons salt; heat to boiling over high heat. Reduce heat; cover and simmer until tender, 10 to 12 minutes.

2. Meanwhile, in 10-inch skillet, cook bacon over medium-low heat until browned. With slotted spoon, transfer to paper towels to drain; crumble.

3. Discard all but 1 teaspoon bacon drippings from skillet. Reduce heat to low. Add shallots and cook, stirring, until tender, about 5 minutes. Remove from heat.

4. Prepare dressing: In large bowl, with wire whisk, mix shallots, vinegar, oil, sugar, mustard, remaining 1½ teaspoons salt, and pepper until blended.

5. Drain potatoes. Add hot potatoes to dressing in bowl. With rubber spatula, stir gently until potatoes absorb dressing. Let potatoes cool 30 minutes at room temperature, stirring occasionally. Stir in green onions.

6. If not serving right away, cover and refrigerate up to 4 hours. If chilled, let stand 30 minutes at room temperature before serving. To serve, sprinkle with crumbled bacon. Makes 12 accompaniment servings.

♥ Each serving: About 185 calories, 4g protein, 29g carbohydrate, 6g total fat (1g saturated), 2mg cholesterol, 456mg sodium.

Creamy Potato Salad

As familiar as this classic recipe may be, it is always welcome. For a variation, add one-quarter cup finely chopped smoked ham or two coarsely chopped hard-cooked eggs.

Prep: 20 minutes   Cook: 35 minutes

3	pounds all-purpose potatoes (9 medium), not peeled
½	cup mayonnaise
½	cup milk
2	tablespoons distilled white vinegar
2	tablespoons chopped green onion
1	teaspoon sugar
1	teaspoon salt
¼	teaspoon coarsely ground black pepper
2	large stalks celery, thinly sliced

1. In 4-quart saucepan, combine potatoes and enough *water* to cover; heat to boiling over high heat. Reduce heat; cover and simmer until tender, 25 to 30 minutes. Drain. When cool enough to handle, peel and cut potatoes into ¾-inch cubes.

2. Meanwhile, prepare dressing: In large bowl, with wire whisk, mix mayonnaise, milk, vinegar, green onion, sugar, salt, and pepper until blended. Add potatoes and celery to dressing; toss to coat. If not serving right away, cover and refrigerate up to 4 hours. Makes 10 accompaniment servings.

Each serving: About 198 calories, 3g protein, 27g carbohydrate, 9g total fat (2g saturated), 8mg cholesterol, 315mg sodium.

Lemony Potato Salad

Prepare as directed but substitute **3 tablespoons fresh lemon juice** and **1 teaspoon freshly grated lemon peel** for distilled white vinegar.

Tubetti Macaroni Salad

Carrots and celery add crunch to this lemon-scented salad. If the salad appears dry after chilling, stir in a touch of milk.

Prep: 25 minutes	Cook: 25 minutes
1	package (16 ounces) tubetti or ditalini pasta
2¾	teaspoons salt
4	carrots, peeled and cut into 2" by ¼" matchstick strips
1 to 2 lemons	
⅔	cup light mayonnaise
⅓	cup milk
2	stalks celery, cut into 2" by ¼" matchstick strips
2	green onions, thinly sliced

1. In large saucepot, cook pasta as label directs, using 2 teaspoons salt. After pasta has cooked 10 minutes, add carrots to pasta water and cook until carrots are just tender-crisp and pasta is done, 1 to 2 minutes longer.

2. Meanwhile, from lemon, grate 1 teaspoon peel and squeeze 3 tablespoons juice. Prepare dressing: In large bowl, with wire whisk, mix mayonnaise, milk, lemon peel and juice, and remaining ¾ teaspoon salt until blended.

3. Drain pasta and carrots; add to dressing in bowl along with celery and green onions; toss until mixed and coated with dressing. Serve at room temperature, or cover and refrigerate up to 4 hours. Makes 12 accompaniment servings.

♥ Each serving: About 202 calories, 5g protein, 33g carbohydrate, 5g total fat (1g saturated), 5mg cholesterol, 463mg sodium.

Japanese Rice Salad

Seasoned rice vinegar gives this salad its distinctive flavor.

Prep: 20 minutes plus cooling	Cook: 30 minutes
1½	cups regular long-grain rice
2	teaspoons salt
3	tablespoons seasoned rice vinegar
2	tablespoons vegetable oil
1	teaspoon grated, peeled fresh ginger
¼	teaspoon ground black pepper
4	ounces green beans, trimmed and cut into ¼-inch pieces
2	carrots, peeled and shredded
3	green onions, thinly sliced

1. Cook rice as label directs, using ½ teaspoon salt. Prepare dressing: In large bowl, with wire whisk, mix vinegar, oil, ginger, ½ teaspoon salt, and pepper. Add rice and toss to coat. Let cool, tossing occasionally with fork, 30 minutes.

2. Meanwhile, in 2-quart saucepan, heat *2 cups water* and remaining 1 teaspoon salt to boiling over high heat. Add green beans and cook until tender-crisp, 3 to 5 minutes. Drain and rinse with cold running water; drain.

3. Add green beans, carrots, and green onions to rice in bowl; toss until mixed and coated with dressing. Makes 8 accompaniment servings.

♥ Each serving: About 175 calories, 3g protein, 32g carbohydrate, 4g total fat (0g saturated), 0mg cholesterol, 484mg sodium.

White and Wild Rice Salad

Dress up a holiday buffet spread with this festive salad.

Prep: 25 minutes plus cooling	Cook: 50 to 60 minutes
½	cup wild rice
1½	teaspoons salt
¾	cup regular long-grain rice
⅓	cup dried cranberries or currants
2	tablespoons olive oil
2	tablespoons red wine vinegar
½	teaspoon freshly grated orange peel
¼	teaspoon ground black pepper
2	cups seedless red grapes, cut in half
2	stalks celery, thinly sliced (1 cup)
2	tablespoons chopped fresh parsley
½	cup pecans, toasted and coarsely chopped

1. Cook wild rice as label directs, using ½ teaspoon salt. Cook white rice as label directs, using ¼ teaspoon salt.

2. In small bowl, combine cranberries with just enough *boiling water* to cover; let stand 5 minutes. Drain.

3. Meanwhile, prepare dressing: In large bowl, with wire whisk, mix oil, vinegar, orange peel, remaining ¾ teaspoon salt, and pepper until blended. Add wild and white rice and cranberries; toss to coat. Let cool, tossing several times, 30 minutes.

4. Add grapes, celery, and parsley to rice; toss until mixed and coated with dressing. Transfer to serving bowl. Sprinkle with pecans. Makes 8 accompaniment servings.

Each serving: About 220 calories, 4g protein, 34g carbohydrate, 8g total fat (1g saturated), 0mg cholesterol, 452mg sodium.

Mediterranean Rice Salad

When tomatoes are ripe, juicy, and full of flavor, add some to this sprightly salad.

Prep: 25 minutes plus cooling	Cook: 30 minutes
2	cups water
1	cup regular long-grain rice
3	garlic cloves, finely chopped
1¼	teaspoons salt
3	tablespoons olive oil
1	small red onion, chopped
1	red pepper, chopped
1	medium zucchini (8 ounces), cut lengthwise into quarters, then crosswise into ½-inch-thick slices
2	tablespoons fresh lemon juice
⅓	cup Kalamata olives, pitted and coarsely chopped

1. In 2-quart saucepan, heat water to boiling over high heat. Add rice, garlic, and ½ teaspoon salt. Reduce heat; cover and simmer until rice is tender, about 17 minutes.

2. Meanwhile, in 10-inch skillet, heat 1 tablespoon oil over medium heat. Add onion and cook 2 minutes. Add red pepper, zucchini, and ¼ teaspoon salt and cook, stirring occasionally, until tender-crisp, about 4 minutes.

3. Prepare dressing: In large bowl, with wire whisk, mix lemon juice, remaining 2 tablespoons oil, and remaining ½ teaspoon salt until blended. Add rice, vegetable mixture, and olives; toss until mixed and coated with dressing. Cool to room temperature. Serve at room temperature, or cover and refrigerate up to 2 hours. Makes 6 accompaniment servings.

Each serving: About 214 calories, 3g protein, 30g carbohydrate, 9g total fat (1g saturated), 0mg cholesterol, 623mg sodium.

Couscous Salad

Couscous is quickly prepared and makes an excellent salad when paired with Moroccan-style spices and sweet dates.

Prep: 15 minutes plus chilling	Cook: 7 minutes
2	cups water
1⅓	cups couscous (Moroccan pasta)
¾	teaspoon salt
2	lemons
1	teaspoon ground cumin
1	teaspoon ground coriander
¼	teaspoon ground red pepper (cayenne)
⅛	teaspoon ground allspice
¼	cup olive oil
1	large carrot, peeled and shredded
1	red pepper, cut into ½-inch pieces
½	cup chopped pitted dates
⅓	cup Kalamata olives, pitted and coarsely chopped

1. In 2-quart saucepan, heat water to boiling. Add couscous and ½ teaspoon salt; remove from heat. Cover and let stand 5 minutes.

2. Meanwhile, from lemons, grate ½ teaspoon peel and squeeze ⅓ cup juice. In 6-inch skillet, heat cumin and coriander over low heat, stirring, until very fragrant, about 2 minutes. Transfer to large bowl and stir in ground red pepper and allspice. With wire whisk, whisk in oil, lemon peel and juice, and remaining ¼ teaspoon salt.

3. Add couscous to dressing in bowl; fluff with fork. Add carrot, red pepper, dates, and olives; fluff to combine. Cover and refrigerate 1 hour to blend flavors or up to 4 hours. Makes 8 accompaniment servings.

Each serving: About 234 calories, 4g protein, 35g carbohydrate, 9g total fat (1g saturated), 0mg cholesterol, 327mg sodium.

Wheat Berry Salad

This toothsome grain salad, which is lightly sweetened with dried cherries and tossed in a lemony vinaigrette, can be served as a hearty side dish or a light main course. Wheat berries, whole-wheat kernels with their outer bran still on, have a robust nutty flavor. They can be purchased at health food stores.

Prep: 25 minutes   Cook: 1 hour 45 minutes

2	cups wheat berries (1 pound)
3	tablespoons fresh lemon juice
1	tablespoon olive oil
1	large shallot, minced (¼ cup)
1	tablespoon Dijon mustard
2	teaspoons honey
1½	teaspoons salt
½	teaspoon coarsely ground black pepper
3	stalks celery, each cut lengthwise in half, then crosswise into ¼-inch-thick slices
¾	cup dried tart cherries, chopped
½	cup chopped fresh flat-leaf parsley leaves

1. In 4-quart saucepan, combine wheat berries and *8 cups water*; heat to boiling over high heat. Reduce heat; cover and simmer until wheat berries are just tender but still firm to the bite, about 1 hour 30 minutes.

2. Meanwhile, prepare dressing: In large bowl, with wire whisk, mix lemon juice, oil, shallot, mustard, honey, salt, and pepper until blended.

3. When wheat berries are cooked, drain. Add warm wheat berries, celery, cherries, and parsley to dressing in bowl; toss until mixed and coated with dressing. Serve at room temperature, or cover and refrigerate up to 4 hours. Makes 12 accompaniment servings.

♥ Each serving: About 149 calories, 4g protein, 31g carbohydrate, 2g total fat (0g saturated), 0mg cholesterol, 331mg sodium.

Barley Salad with Nectarines

Barley is another grain that makes a flavorful salad. You can use mangoes or peaches instead of the nectarines, if you prefer.

Prep: 30 minutes   Cook: 55 minutes

1	package (16 ounces) pearl barley
2¾	teaspoons salt
4	limes
⅓	cup olive oil
1	tablespoon sugar
¾	teaspoon coarsely ground black pepper
1½	pounds nectarines (4 medium), cut into ½-inch pieces
1	pound ripe tomatoes (2 large), seeded and cut into ½-inch pieces
4	green onions, thinly sliced
½	cup chopped fresh mint

1. In 4-quart saucepan, heat *6 cups water* to boiling over high heat. Add barley and 1½ teaspoons salt; heat to boiling. Reduce heat; cover and simmer until barley is tender and liquid has been absorbed, about 45 minutes. (Barley will have creamy consistency.)

2. Meanwhile, from limes, grate 1 tablespoon peel and squeeze ½ cup juice. Prepare dressing: In large bowl, with wire whisk, mix lime peel and juice, oil, sugar, pepper, and remaining 1¼ teaspoons salt until blended.

3. Rinse barley with cold running water; drain. Add barley, nectarines, tomatoes, green onions, and mint to dressing in bowl; stir gently until mixed and coated with dressing. If not serving right away, cover and refrigerate up to 1 hour. Makes 16 accompaniment servings.

♥ Each serving: About 172 calories, 4g protein, 30g carbohydrate, 5g total fat (1g saturated), 0mg cholesterol, 333mg sodium.

Tomato and Mint Tabbouleh

Tabbouleh, the popular bulgur wheat and vegetable salad, is one of the best ways to enjoy tomatoes, cucumbers, and herbs.

Prep: 20 minutes plus standing and chilling

1½	cups bulgur wheat
¼	cup fresh lemon juice
1½	cups boiling water
1	pound ripe tomatoes (3 medium), cut into ½-inch pieces
1	medium cucumber (8 ounces), peeled and cut into ½-inch pieces
3	green onions, chopped
¾	cup loosely packed fresh flat-leaf parsley leaves, chopped
½	cup loosely packed fresh mint leaves, chopped
1	tablespoon olive oil
¾	teaspoon salt
¼	teaspoon coarsely ground black pepper

1. In medium bowl, combine bulgur, lemon juice, and boiling water, stirring to mix. Let stand until liquid has been absorbed, about 30 minutes.

2. To bulgur mixture, add tomatoes, cucumber, green onions, parsley, mint, oil, salt, and pepper, stirring to mix. Cover and refrigerate at least 1 hour to blend flavors or up to 4 hours. Makes 12 accompaniment servings.

♥ Each serving: About 87 calories, 3g protein, 17g carbohydrate, 2g total fat (0g saturated), 0mg cholesterol, 157mg sodium.

The salad toss: The bigger the bowl, the better the tossing! Always use a bowl twice as big as the salad. The extra room will allow you to easily mix the ingredients together and to fully coat each item with the dressing without leaving a puddle in the bottom of the bowl. Remember: You can always add more dressing, so start with a small amount. Far and away, the best tool for tossing a salad is your hands. Your fingers can spread wider than a salad fork, which allows you to easily lift and separate the ingredients, as well as to thoroughly mix them, creating a well-balanced dish.

MARY SUE MILLIKEN AND SUSAN FENIGER
TELEVISION HOSTS OF TOO HOT TAMALES

EXPERT TIP

Tomato Aspic

The ultimate molded salad. We garnish ours with a dollop of dilled sour cream.

Prep: 15 minutes plus overnight to chill   Cook: 20 minutes

4	cups tomato juice
¼	cup celery leaves
6	whole allspice berries
2	whole cloves
2	envelopes unflavored gelatin
2	tablespoons fresh lemon juice
1	tablespoon sugar
½	teaspoon hot pepper sauce
1	container (8 ounces) sour cream
2	tablespoons mayonnaise
2	tablespoons chopped fresh dill

1. In 3-quart saucepan, heat 3½ cups tomato juice to boiling. Add celery leaves, allspice berries, and cloves. Reduce heat and simmer 15 minutes.

2. Meanwhile, pour remaining ½ cup tomato juice into large bowl. Evenly sprinkle gelatin over tomato juice. Let stand 2 minutes to soften gelatin slightly.

3. Strain hot tomato-juice mixture through sieve over softened gelatin. Stir until gelatin has completely dissolved. Stir in lemon juice, sugar, and hot pepper sauce. Pour into 8½" by 4½" glass loaf pan or 5-cup mold. Cover and refrigerate overnight.

4. To unmold, dip pan in large bowl of hot water for 10 seconds. Invert onto platter. In small bowl, combine sour cream, mayonnaise, and dill and stir until blended. Serve tomato aspic with dilled sour cream. Makes 8 accompaniment servings.

Each serving: About 120 calories, 3g protein, 9g carbohydrate, 9g total fat (4g saturated), 14mg cholesterol, 487mg sodium.

Cranberry-Orange Mold

To many families, a cranberry mold is an essential partner to the holiday turkey. This recipe, chock-full of cranberries and flavored with orange juice, is one of our favorites.

Prep: 15 minutes plus chilling and overnight to set

3	envelopes unflavored gelatin
3	cups cold water
1	package (8 servings) cranberry- or strawberry-flavored gelatin
2	cups orange juice
1	package (12 ounces) fresh cranberries
1¼	cups sugar
	lettuce leaves (optional)

1. In 4-quart saucepan, evenly sprinkle unflavored gelatin over 2 cups cold water; let stand 2 minutes to soften gelatin slightly. Cook over medium heat, stirring frequently until gelatin has completely dissolved. Remove saucepan from heat; add cranberry-flavored gelatin, stirring until it has completely dissolved. Stir in orange juice and remaining 1 cup cold water. Refrigerate until mixture mounds slightly when dropped from spoon, about 1 hour.

2. Meanwhile, in food processor with knife blade attached, combine cranberries and sugar; process until cranberries are finely chopped. Fold cranberry mixture into thickened gelatin. Pour into 10-inch Bundt pan or nonreactive 12-cup mold. Cover and refrigerate overnight.

3. To unmold, dip pan in large bowl of hot water for 10 seconds and invert onto platter lined with lettuce leaves, if desired. Makes 16 accompaniment servings.

♥ Each serving: About 130 calories, 2g protein, 31g carbohydrate, 0g total fat (0g saturated), 0mg cholesterol, 30mg sodium.

Thai Squid Salad

An abundance of fresh herbs and a sweet, pungent dressing contribute glorious flavor with a minimum of fat and calories.

Prep: 30 minutes   Cook: 12 minutes

2¼	teaspoons salt
3	tablespoons Asian fish sauce (nuoc nam, page 31)
3	tablespoons fresh lime juice
1	tablespoon sugar
¼	teaspoon crushed red pepper
½	small sweet onion, such as Vidalia or Walla Walla, very thinly sliced
1	carrot, peeled and shredded
1	pound cleaned squid
1	large head Boston lettuce, torn into bite-size pieces
½	cup loosely packed fresh mint leaves
½	cup loosely packed fresh cilantro leaves

1. In 4-quart saucepan, combine *3 quarts water* and 2 teaspoons salt; heat to boiling over high heat.

2. Meanwhile, in large bowl, combine fish sauce, lime juice, sugar, crushed red pepper, and remaining ¼ teaspoon salt and stir until sugar has dissolved. Stir in onion and carrot.

3. Rinse squid under cold running water. Slice squid bodies crosswise into very thin rings. Cut tentacles into several pieces if large. Add to boiling water and cook until tender and opaque, 30 seconds to 1 minute. Drain and add to dressing in bowl. Add lettuce, mint, and cilantro; toss until mixed and coated with dressing. Makes 4 first-course servings.

♥ Each serving: About 185 calories, 22g protein, 18g carbohydrate, 3g total fat (1g saturated), 264mg cholesterol, 954mg sodium.

Thai Chicken Salad

Prepare as directed but substitute **1 pound skinless, boneless chicken breasts,** grilled or broiled and thinly sliced, for cooked squid.

♥ Each serving: About 205 calories, 30g protein, 14g carbohydrate, 3g total fat (1g saturated), 66mg cholesterol, 978mg sodium.

Thai Grilled Beef Salad

Prepare as directed but substitute **1 pound flank or round steak,** grilled or broiled and cut into thin slices across the grain, for cooked squid.

Each serving: About 268 calories, 26g protein, 14g carbohydrate, 12g total fat (5g saturated), 56mg cholesterol, 971mg sodium.

Thai Vegetable Salad

Prepare as directed but substitute **1 cucumber,** peeled, seeded, and sliced, for cooked squid.

 Each serving: About 88 calories, 4g protein, 16g carbohydrate, 2g total fat (0g saturated), 0mg cholesterol, 907mg sodium.

Panzanella Salad with Tomato Vinaigrette

This classic Italian bread salad depends on a hearty loaf that won't get mushy when mixed with moist ingredients. We toss ours with a homemade tomato vinaigrette for the most flavor.

Prep: 35 minutes   Cook: 15 minutes
4   ounces pancetta or 4 slices bacon, cut into ¼-inch pieces
1   tablespoon olive oil
1   small loaf sourdough bread (6 ounces), cut into ½-inch cubes
2   tablespoons freshly grated Parmesan cheese
¼   teaspoon ground black pepper
4   small bunches arugula (4 ounces each), trimmed
1½ pints red and/or yellow cherry tomatoes, cut in half
Tomato Vinaigrette (page 545)

1. In nonstick 12-inch skillet, cook pancetta over medium heat until lightly browned. With slotted spoon, transfer to large serving bowl.

2. To pancetta drippings in skillet, add oil and bread cubes; cook, stirring occasionally, until bread cubes are lightly browned, about 10 minutes. Add croutons, Parmesan, and pepper to pancetta in bowl and toss to combine.

3. Add arugula and cherry tomatoes to croutons in bowl. Add Tomato Vinaigrette; toss until mixed and coated with dressing. Makes 6 main-dish servings.

Each serving: About 246 calories, 8g protein, 21g carbohydrate, 15g total fat (4g saturated), 13mg cholesterol, 562mg sodium.

Panzanella Salad with Tomato Vinaigrette

Italian Seafood Salad

Italians often serve this salad on Christmas Eve along with other fish dishes, but why not enjoy it throughout the year?

Prep: 50 minutes plus chilling	Cook: 15 minutes
1	pound sea scallops
2	pounds cleaned squid
1	small lemon, thinly sliced
2	pounds large shrimp, shelled and deveined (page 296)
²⁄₃	cup fresh lemon juice (4 lemons)
½	cup olive oil
1	small garlic clove, minced
½	teaspoon coarsely ground black pepper
4	large stalks celery, cut into ½-inch pieces
½	cup Gaeta or Niçoise olives (optional)
¼	cup loosely packed fresh parsley leaves

1. Pull off and discard tough crescent-shaped muscle from each scallop. Rinse squid; slice bodies crosswise into ¾-inch-thick rings. Cut tentacles into several pieces if large. In 5-quart saucepot, combine 2½ *inches water* and lemon; heat to boiling over high heat. Add shrimp. Reduce heat to medium; cook until shrimp are opaque throughout, 1 to 2 minutes. With slotted spoon, transfer shrimp to colander to drain; transfer to large bowl.

2. To boiling water in saucepot, add scallops; cook just until opaque throughout, 2 to 3 minutes. With slotted spoon, transfer to colander to drain; add to shrimp in bowl.

3. To boiling water in saucepot, add squid; cook until tender and opaque, 30 seconds to 1 minute. Drain in colander; add to shrimp and scallops in bowl.

4. Prepare dressing: In small bowl, with wire whisk, mix lemon juice, oil, garlic, and pepper until blended. Add celery, olives if using, and parsley to seafood in bowl; toss to mix. Add dressing and toss until mixed and coated with dressing. Cover and refrigerate salad at least 3 hours to blend flavors or up to 8 hours. Makes 12 first-course servings.

Each serving: About 255 calories, 31g protein, 6g carbohydrate, 11g total fat (2g saturated), 282mg cholesterol, 200mg sodium.

Niçoise Salad

As the story goes, the first Niçoise salad was created in eighteenth century France and it's been a hit ever since.

Prep: 35 minutes	Cook: 25 minutes
1	tablespoon white wine vinegar
1	tablespoon fresh lemon juice
1	tablespoon minced shallot
1	teaspoon Dijon mustard
1	teaspoon anchovy paste
¼	teaspoon sugar
¼	teaspoon coarsely ground black pepper
3	tablespoons extravirgin olive oil
1	pound medium red potatoes, not peeled, cut into ¼-inch-thick slices
8	ounces French green beans *(haricots verts)* or regular green beans, trimmed
1	head Boston lettuce, leaves separated
12	cherry tomatoes, each cut in half
1	can (12 ounces) solid white tuna in water, drained and flaked
2	large hard-cooked eggs, peeled and each cut into quarters
½	cup Niçoise olives

1. Prepare dressing: In small bowl, with wire whisk, mix vinegar, lemon juice, shallot, mustard, anchovy paste, sugar, and pepper until blended. In thin, steady stream, whisk in oil until blended.

2. In 3-quart saucepan, combine potatoes and enough *water* to cover; heat to boiling over high heat. Reduce heat; cover and simmer until tender, about 10 minutes. Drain.

3. Meanwhile, in 10-inch skillet, heat *1 inch water* to boiling over high heat. Add green beans; heat to boiling. Reduce heat to low and cook until tender-crisp, 6 to 8 minutes. Drain; rinse with cold running water. Drain.

4. To serve, pour half of dressing into medium bowl. Add lettuce leaves and toss to coat. Line large platter with dressed lettuce leaves. Arrange potatoes, green beans, cherry tomatoes, tuna, eggs, and olives in separate piles on lettuce. Drizzle remaining dressing over salad. Makes 4 main-dish servings.

Each serving: About 440 calories, 30g protein, 30g carbohydrate, 23g total fat (4g saturated), 140mg cholesterol, 716mg sodium.

Niçoise Salad

Best Chicken Salad

Plain or fancy, chicken salad is always a treat. Here's a basic recipe plus three of our favorite ways to make it extra special. If you don't want to poach a whole chicken, substitute three cups of deli-roasted chicken or leftover turkey.

Prep: 20 minutes plus cooling   Cook: 1 hour

1	chicken (3 pounds)
1½	teaspoons salt
3	stalks celery, finely chopped
¼	cup mayonnaise
2	teaspoons fresh lemon juice
¼	teaspoon ground black pepper

1. In 4-quart saucepan, combine chicken, 1 teaspoon salt, and enough *water* to cover; heat to boiling over high heat. Reduce heat; cover and simmer gently until chicken loses its pink color throughout, about 45 minutes. Let stand 30 minutes; drain (reserve broth for another use). When chicken is cool enough to handle, discard skin and bones; cut meat into bite-size pieces.

2. In bowl, combine celery, mayonnaise, lemon juice, remaining ½ teaspoon salt, and pepper; stir until blended. Add chicken and toss to coat. Makes 4 main-dish servings.

Each serving: About 337 calories, 36g protein, 2g carbohydrate, 20g total fat (4g saturated), 117mg cholesterol, 779mg sodium.

Basil and Dried Tomato Chicken Salad

Prepare as directed but add ¼ **cup chopped fresh basil** and **2 tablespoons finely chopped oil-packed dried tomatoes,** drained, to mayonnaise mixture.

Curry-Grape Chicken Salad

Prepare as directed but add **2 cups red or green seedless grapes,** cut in half, **1 teaspoon curry powder,** and **1 teaspoon honey** to mayonnaise mixture.

Lemon-Pepper Chicken Salad

Prepare as directed but use **1 tablespoon fresh lemon juice** and **½ teaspoon black pepper,** coarsely ground; add **½ teaspoon freshly grated lemon peel** to mayonnaise mixture.

Taco Salad

Better than a taco! Have all the ingredients chopped and ready to go for quick assembly. For a heartier dish, add drained canned beans or corn to the beef mixture.

Prep: 30 minutes   Cook: 20 minutes

2	teaspoons vegetable oil
1	medium onion, chopped
1	garlic clove, finely chopped
2	tablespoons chili powder
1	teaspoon ground cumin
1	pound ground beef chuck
1	can (8 ounces) tomato sauce
1	head iceberg lettuce, cut into quarters, cored, and very thinly sliced
1	large ripe tomato (10 ounces), finely chopped
1	ripe avocado, peeled, pitted, and chopped
4	ounces sharp Cheddar cheese, shredded (1 cup)
3	tablespoons sour cream
1	cup loosely packed small cilantro leaves
½	bag (5 ounces) tortilla chips

1. In 10-inch skillet, heat oil over medium heat. Add onion and cook, stirring occasionally, until tender, about 5 minutes. Stir in garlic, chili powder, and cumin and cook 30 seconds. Add ground beef, stirring to break up lumps with side of spoon; cook until no longer pink, about 5 minutes. Stir in tomato sauce and cook 5 minutes longer.

2. Divide lettuce among dinner plates. Spoon warm beef mixture on top of lettuce. Sprinkle with tomato, avocado, and Cheddar. Top each with some sour cream; sprinkle with cilantro. Tuck tortilla chips around edge of each plate. Makes 6 main-dish servings.

Each serving: About 506 calories, 22g protein, 21g carbohydrate, 38g total fat (15g saturated), 87mg cholesterol, 504mg sodium.

Szechuan Peanut-Noodle Salad

A tasty pasta salad packed with great Asian flavors. To serve cold, chill the pasta and toss with the vegetables just before serving.

Prep: 25 minutes   Cook: 25 minutes

1	package (16 ounces) linguine or spaghetti
2½	teaspoons salt
4	ounces snow peas, strings removed
½	cup creamy peanut butter
1	tablespoon grated, peeled fresh ginger
¼	cup soy sauce
2	tablespoons distilled white vinegar
2	teaspoons Asian sesame oil
¼	teaspoon hot pepper sauce
1	small cucumber (6 ounces), peeled, seeded, and cut into 2" by ¼" matchstick strips
¼	cup dry-roasted peanuts
1	green onion, chopped

1. In large saucepot, cook linguine as label directs, using 2 teaspoons salt.

2. Meanwhile, in 3-quart saucepan, combine *1 inch water* and snow peas; heat to boiling over high heat. Reduce heat and simmer 2 minutes; drain. Rinse with cold running water; drain. Cut snow peas lengthwise into ¼-inch-wide matchstick strips. Set aside.

3. Drain linguine, reserving 1 cup pasta water. Prepare dressing: In large bowl, with wire whisk, mix peanut butter, ginger, reserved pasta water, soy sauce, vinegar, sesame oil, remaining ½ teaspoon salt, and hot pepper sauce until smooth.

4. Add linguine to dressing in bowl and toss to coat. Add snow peas and cucumber; toss to combine. Sprinkle with peanuts and green onions. Makes 5 main-dish or 8 accompaniment servings.

Each main-dish serving: About 572 calories, 22g protein, 78g carbohydrate, 20g total fat (3g saturated), 0mg cholesterol, 1,794mg sodium.

Classic Tuna Salad

There are more ways to serve tuna salad than just between two slices of bread. Have fun personalizing your salad, then serve as an open-faced tuna melt or on a bed of greens.

Prep: 10 minutes

1	can (6 ounces) solid white tuna in water, drained and broken into pieces
2	stalks celery, finely chopped
3	tablespoons mayonnaise
2	teaspoons fresh lemon juice
¼	teaspoon ground black pepper

In small bowl, combine tuna, celery, mayonnaise, lemon juice, and pepper, flaking tuna with fork. If not serving right away, cover and refrigerate up to 4 hours. Makes 1⅓ cups or 2 main-dish servings.

Each serving: About 264 calories, 22g protein, 3g carbohydrate, 18g total fat (3g saturated), 45mg cholesterol, 462mg sodium.

Curried Tuna Salad

Prepare as directed but substitute ½ **Granny Smith apple,** finely chopped, for celery, and add **1 teaspoon curry powder** to tuna mixture.

Mexican-Style Tuna Salad

Prepare as directed but add **2 tablespoons chopped fresh cilantro** and **1 pickled jalapeño chile,** finely chopped, to tuna mixture.

Cobb Salad

A California classic, this salad appeals to both the eye and the palate. Make one large salad or, if you prefer, arrange on individual serving plates.

Prep: 25 minutes	Broil/Cook: 8 minutes

12	ounces skinless, boneless chicken breast halves
¼	teaspoon salt
⅛	teaspoon ground black pepper
6	slices bacon, coarsely chopped
1	head iceberg lettuce, thinly sliced (12 cups)
3	large hard-cooked eggs, peeled and coarsely chopped
1	large ripe tomato (10 ounces), cut into ½-inch pieces
1	ripe avocado, peeled, pitted, and cut into ½-inch pieces
3	ounces Roquefort cheese, crumbled (¾ cup)
	Classic French Vinaigrette (page 545)

1. Preheat broiler. Place chicken on rack in broiling pan and sprinkle with salt and pepper. Place pan in broiler 6 inches from heat source. Broil until chicken loses its pink color throughout, about 4 minutes per side. When cool enough to handle, cut into ½-inch pieces.

2. Meanwhile, in 10-inch skillet, cook bacon over medium heat until browned. Transfer bacon to paper towels to drain.

3. Line large platter with lettuce. Arrange eggs, tomato, avocado, Roquefort, chicken, and bacon in striped pattern over lettuce. Pass dressing separately. Makes 6 main-dish servings.

Each serving (without dressing): About 272 calories, 24g protein, 9g carbohydrate, 16g total fat (6g saturated), 157mg cholesterol, 537mg sodium.

Classic Egg Salad

The perfect egg salad, like other old-fashioned dishes, is a matter of individual taste. Our recipe leaves room for lots of creativity (see the variations below).

Prep: 10 minutes	Cook: 10 minutes plus standing

6	large eggs
¼	cup mayonnaise
1½	teaspoons Dijon or spicy brown mustard
¼	teaspoon salt

1. In 3-quart saucepan, place eggs and enough *cold water* to cover by at least 1 inch; heat to boiling over high heat. Immediately remove saucepan from heat and cover tightly; let stand 15 minutes. Pour off hot water and run cold water over eggs to cool. Peel eggs.

2. Coarsely chop eggs and transfer to medium bowl. Add mayonnaise, mustard, and salt and stir to combine. If not serving right away, cover and refrigerate up to 4 hours. Makes 2 cups or 4 main-dish servings.

Each serving: About 217 calories, 10g protein, 1g carbohydrate, 19g total fat (4g saturated), 327mg cholesterol, 359mg sodium.

Curried Egg Salad
Prepare as directed but add **4 teaspoons chopped mango chutney** and **½ teaspoon curry powder** to egg mixture.

Cobb Salad

Caesar-Style Egg Salad

Prepare as directed but use only ⅛ **teaspoon salt**. Add **2 tablespoons freshly grated Parmesan cheese** and **1 teaspoon anchovy paste** to egg mixture.

Mexican-Style Egg Salad

Prepare as directed but add ⅓ **cup chopped fresh cilantro** and ½ **teaspoon hot pepper sauce** to egg mixture.

Deli-Style Egg Salad

Prepare as directed but add ¼ **cup chopped celery** and ¼ **cup chopped red onion** to egg mixture.

SALAD DRESSINGS

Tomato Vinaigrette

This summer's-end salad dressing starts with a ripe tomato, which lends the dressing body and richness. It's perfect spooned over sliced tomatoes and feta cheese, spinach salad, or mixed greens.

 Prep: 15 minutes

1	small tomato (4 ounces), peeled and coarsely chopped
1	small shallot, cut in half
2	tablespoons olive oil
1	tablespoon red wine vinegar
1	tablespoon balsamic vinegar
2	teaspoons Dijon mustard with seeds
1	teaspoon chopped fresh oregano
1	teaspoon sugar
¼	teaspoon salt
¼	teaspoon ground black pepper

In blender, combine tomato, shallot, oil, red wine and balsamic vinegars, mustard, oregano, sugar, salt, and pepper; puree just until smooth. Transfer to bowl or jar. Cover and refrigerate up to 1 day. Makes about 1 cup.

Each tablespoon: About 19 calories, 0g protein, 1g carbohydrate, 2g total fat (0g saturated), 0mg cholesterol, 51mg sodium

Classic French Vinaigrette

Dijon mustard makes this vinaigrette smooth and delicious.

 Prep: 5 minutes

¼	cup red wine vinegar
1	tablespoon Dijon mustard
¾	teaspoon salt
½	teaspoon coarsely ground pepper
½	cup olive oil

In medium bowl, with wire whisk, mix vinegar, mustard, salt, and pepper until blended. In thin, steady stream, whisk in oil until blended. Cover and refrigerate dressing up to 1 week. Makes about ¾ cup.

Each tablespoon: About 82 calories, 0g protein, 0g carbohydrate, 9g total fat (1g saturated), 0mg cholesterol, 175mg sodium.

Blue Cheese Vinaigrette

Prepare as directed but add **2 ounces blue cheese,** crumbled (½ cup). Cover and refrigerate dressing up to 2 days. Makes about 1 cup.

Mustard-Shallot Vinaigrette

Prepare as directed but add **1 tablespoon minced shallot.** Cover and refrigerate up to 1 day. Makes about ¾ cup.

Here's the "wilted salad" restaurant trick: Place an oversized metal bowl directly on a burner over medium heat. Add a few tablespoons of dressing to the bowl and heat until warm; then add spinach or other greens and toss vigorously with tongs, coating every inch of the leaves and wilting the greens ever so slightly. Serve immediately.

MARY SUE MILLIKEN AND SUSAN FENIGER
TELEVISION HOSTS OF TOO HOT TAMALES

EXPERT TIP

Russian Dressing

Actually American in origin, this salad dressing includes mayonnaise and ketchup; early versions included Russian caviar. Serve over lettuce, hard-cooked eggs, or with cold poultry.

Prep: 10 minutes

¾	cup mayonnaise
¼	cup ketchup
1	tablespoon chopped fresh parsley
1	tablespoon grated onion (optional)
¼	teaspoon dry mustard
¼	teaspoon Worcestershire sauce
3	drops hot pepper sauce

In small bowl, stir mayonnaise, ketchup, parsley, onion if using, mustard, Worcestershire, and hot pepper sauce until well mixed. Cover and refrigerate up to 3 days. Makes about 1 cup.

Each tablespoon: About 78 calories, 0g protein, 1g carbohydrate, 8g total fat (1g saturated), 6mg cholesterol, 105mg sodium.

Creamy Blue Cheese Dressing

This versatile dressing can be served on mixed greens, lettuce and tomato wedges, chilled cooked vegetables, cold sliced roast beef, or even hard-cooked eggs.

Prep: 10 minutes

4	ounces blue cheese, crumbled (1 cup)
3	tablespoons half-and-half or light cream
½	cup mayonnaise
2	tablespoons white wine vinegar
1	teaspoon Dijon mustard
⅛	teaspoon salt
⅛	teaspoon ground black pepper

In small bowl, with fork, mash cheese with half-and-half until creamy; add mayonnaise, vinegar, mustard, salt, and pepper. With wire whisk, beat until well mixed. Cover and refrigerate up to 3 days. Makes about 1 cup.

Each tablespoon: About 79 calories, 2g protein, 1g carbohydrate, 8g total fat (2g saturated), 10mg cholesterol, 165mg sodium.

Poppy Seed Dressing

In the mood for a sweet-and-sour dressing? Spoon this gem over iceberg lettuce wedges or a colorful fresh fruit salad.

Prep: 10 minutes

1	cup vegetable oil
⅓	cup cider vinegar
½	cup sugar
1	tablespoon grated onion
1	tablespoon poppy seeds
1	teaspoon dry mustard
1	teaspoon salt

In blender, combine oil, vinegar, sugar, onion, poppy seeds, dry mustard, and salt; process until smooth and thick. Transfer to bowl or jar; cover and refrigerate up to 2 days. Stir well before using. Makes 1½ cups.

Each tablespoon: About 99 calories, 0g protein, 4g carbohydrate, 9g total fat (1g saturated), 0mg cholesterol, 97mg sodium.

Green Goddess Dressing

A touch of anchovy paste is the secret ingredient that gives Green Goddess its distinctive flavor.

Prep: 10 minutes

½	cup mayonnaise
¼	cup sour cream
½	cup loosely packed fresh parsley leaves
1	tablespoon red wine vinegar
1	teaspoon anchovy paste
¼	teaspoon ground black pepper

In blender, combine mayonnaise, sour cream, parsley, vinegar, anchovy paste, and pepper. Puree until smooth, scraping down sides of blender occasionally. Transfer to bowl or jar. Cover and refrigerate up to 3 days. Makes about ¾ cup.

Each tablespoon: About 78 calories, 0g protein, 1g carbohydrate, 8g total fat (2g saturated), 8mg cholesterol, 79mg sodium.

Honey-Lime Vinaigrette

Try this sweet and tangy fat-free dressing on sliced cucumbers or your favorite greens.

🕐 *Prep: 5 minutes*

⅓	cup fresh lime juice (2 to 3 limes)
4	teaspoons honey
1	tablespoon rice vinegar
⅛	teaspoon salt

In small bowl, with wire whisk, mix lime juice, honey, vinegar, and salt until blended. Cover and refrigerate up to 3 days. Makes about ½ cup.

♥ Each tablespoon: About 13 calories, 0g protein, 4g carbohydrate, 0g total fat (0g saturated), 0mg cholesterol, 37mg sodium.

Ranch Dressing

Buttermilk gives Ranch Dressing its characteristic tang and creaminess. Use the large holes on a box grater to grate the onion.

🕐 *Prep: 10 minutes*

½	cup buttermilk
⅓	cup mayonnaise
1	tablespoon chopped fresh parsley
½	teaspoon grated onion
¼	teaspoon salt
¼	teaspoon ground black pepper
1	garlic clove, cut in half

In small bowl, with wire whisk, mix buttermilk, mayonnaise, parsley, onion, salt, and pepper until blended; stir in garlic. Cover and refrigerate up to 3 days. Remove garlic before serving. Makes about ¾ cup.

Each tablespoon: About 48 calories, 0g protein, 1g carbohydrate, 5g total fat (1g saturated), 4mg cholesterol, 93mg sodium.

Tahini Dressing

Try this sesame-paste dressing on sautéed or broiled chicken or vegetables, as well as on salads.

🕐 *Prep: 10 minutes*

⅓	cup tahini (sesame seed paste)
2	tablespoons fresh lemon juice
4	teaspoons soy sauce
1	tablespoon honey (optional)
½	small garlic clove, minced
½	teaspoon ground black pepper

In small bowl, with wire whisk, mix tahini, lemon juice, soy sauce, honey if using, garlic, and pepper until smooth. Cover and refrigerate up to 2 days. Makes about ¾ cup.

Each tablespoon: About 41 calories, 1g protein, 2g carbohydrate, 4g total fat (0g saturated), 0mg cholesterol, 122mg sodium.

Japanese Miso Vinaigrette

Miso comes in different colors and flavor variances, but any one will make a tasty dressing.

🕐 *Prep: 10 minutes*

2	tablespoons miso (fermented soybean paste)
½	cup rice vinegar
¼	cup olive oil
1	tablespoon minced, peeled fresh ginger
1	tablespoon sugar

In small bowl, with wire whisk, stir miso into vinegar until smooth. In blender, combine miso mixture, oil, ginger, and sugar; puree until smooth. Transfer to bowl or jar. Cover and refrigerate up to 3 days. Makes about 1 cup.

Each tablespoon: About 38 calories, 0g protein, 1g carbohydrate, 4g total fat (0g saturated), 0mg cholesterol, 78mg sodium.

14

SAUCES, SALSAS, AND CONDIMENTS

In fashion, the right accessory can make or break an outfit; sauces are the accessories of the cooking world. Just as a beautiful necklace can bespangle a simple black dress, a fine sauce can elevate plain food from the ordinary to the sublime.

Sauces are typically described as liquid or semiliquid accompaniments to main courses or desserts. Most of the classic sauces are French. The basic ones are called "mother sauces": different ingredients are added to make an almost endless number of variations. For example, when béchamel sauce (which we know as white sauce) has Gruyère cheese added, it becomes Mornay sauce. Many of the traditional sauces are cooked, and most depend on butter and stock for body and flavor.

But the French dominance over the saucepot no longer exists. In fact, nowadays, many sauces aren't cooked at all and dont contain stock or butter. Today's sauces come from all around the world. Salsa, that sprightly chile-kissed sauce from south of the border, can be made with vegetables or fruits and goes with everything from grilled fish to tortilla chips. Some sauces, such as the Italian *salmoriglio* and the Argentinean *chimichurri,* are based on olive oil and a combination of fresh fragrant herbs.

Most sauces can be prepared ahead. In fact, many of them improve when their flavors have a chance to blend. Refrigerate tightly covered so their aromas don't affect other foods.

Peach Salsa, Tomato Salsa, and Tomatillo Salsa

Classic French butter sauces, such as hollandaise, béarnaise, and beurre blanc, are meant to be served warm. They cannot be reheated, or they will curdle. So keep them at serving temperature the way they do in restaraunts: To hold a butter sauce warm for up to twenty minutes (if held much longer, it could separate), place the bowl of sauce in a skillet of very hot, but not simmering, water. Whisk well before serving to dissolve any thin skin that may have formed. To hold for up to one hour, transfer the sauce, as soon as it is prepared, to a wide-mouthed vacuum bottle (rinse the bottle first with hot water to warm it), and seal. When ready to serve, transfer the sauce to a serving dish.

Sometimes, a thick sweet-and-tangy condiment is the preferred way to accent a main course. Intricately seasoned but easy to make Indian-inspired fruit chutneys are excellent with grilled meats. In this chapter, you'll also find an assortment of tasty cranberry sauces that are too good to be reserved for just the holiday turkey.

Dessert sauces are for the times when you want to gild the lily. A piece of chocolate cake can be wonderful, but when served in a pool of jewel-colored raspberry sauce, you are sure to collect compliments; it's also delicious with vanilla ice cream. And with only a little bit of effort, you can whip up an ethereal warm butterscotch sauce. If it takes you longer to eat the sauce-topped ice cream than it does to make the sauce, you are exercising great restraint.

White Sauce (Béchamel)

This classic sauce is the foundation for many popular dishes, including moussaka and macaroni and cheese.

Prep: 2 minutes   Cook: 15 minutes

2	tablespoons butter or margarine
2	tablespoons all-purpose flour
1	cup milk, warmed
½	teaspoon salt
	pinch ground nutmeg

In heavy 1-quart saucepan, melt butter over low heat. Add flour and cook, stirring, 1 minute. With wire whisk, gradually whisk in hot milk. Cook over medium heat, stirring constantly

with wooden spoon, until sauce has thickened and boils. Reduce heat and simmer, stirring frequently, 5 minutes. Remove from heat and stir in salt and nutmeg. Makes about 1 cup.

Each tablespoon: About 26 calories, 1g protein, 1g carbohydrate, 2g total fat (1g saturated), 6mg cholesterol, 94mg sodium.

Cheese Sauce

Prepare sauce as directed. Remove saucepan from heat. Add **4 ounces sharp Cheddar cheese,** shredded (1 cup); stir until cheese has melted and sauce is smooth. Makes about 1 cup.

Each tablespoon: About 54 calories, 2g protein, 2g carbohydrate, 4g total fat (3g saturated), 13mg cholesterol, 138mg sodium.

Mornay Sauce

Prepare sauce as directed. Remove saucepan from heat. Add **2 ounces Gruyère cheese,** shredded (½ cup); stir until cheese has melted and sauce is smooth. Makes about 1 cup.

Each tablespoon: About 40 calories, 2g protein, 1g carbohydrate, 3g total fat (2g saturated), 10mg cholesterol, 106mg sodium.

Hollandaise Sauce

A velvety, irresistible sauce to dress up vegetables or poached salmon. The traditional recipe uses undercooked eggs, but our updated version cooks them long enough to make them safe to eat.

Prep: 5 minutes   Cook: 10 minutes

3	large egg yolks
¼	cup water
2	tablespoons fresh lemon juice
½	cup butter (1 stick), cut into 8 pieces (do not use margarine)
¼	teaspoon salt

1. In heavy nonreactive 1-quart saucepan, with wire whisk, mix egg yolks, water, and lemon juice until well blended. Cook over medium-low heat, stirring constantly with wooden spoon or heat-safe rubber spatula, until egg-yolk mixture just begins to bubble at edge, 6 to 8 minutes.

2. Reduce heat to low. With wire whisk, whisk in butter one piece at a time until each addition is incorporated and

sauce has thickened. Remove from heat and stir in salt. Strain through sieve, if you like. Makes scant 1 cup.

Each tablespoon: About 62 calories, 1g protein, 0g carbohydrate, 7g total fat (4g saturated), 55mg cholesterol, 96mg sodium.

Despite any precautions you may take, egg yolk sauces and butter sauces sometimes separate. To repair a broken sauce, very slowly (at first drop by drop) whisk the sauce into a beaten egg yolk or into ¼ cup heavy cream that has been reduced by one-third and slightly cooled.

JAMES PETERSON
COOKBOOK AUTHOR

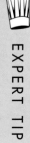

EXPERT TIP

Hollandaise Sauce

Béarnaise Sauce

Rich and delicious, this makes a wickedly delicious topping for steak, grilled chicken, vegetables, or poached eggs. If you don't have tarragon vinegar, use white wine vinegar and toss in an extra tablespoon of fresh tarragon.

Prep: 5 minutes   Cook: 30 minutes

½	cup tarragon vinegar
⅓	cup dry white wine
2	shallots, finely chopped
3	large egg yolks
¼	cup water
	pinch ground black pepper
½	cup cold butter (1 stick), cut into 8 pieces (do not use margarine)
1	tablespoon chopped fresh tarragon

1. In nonreactive 1-quart saucepan, combine vinegar, wine, and shallots; heat to boiling over high heat. Boil until liquid has reduced to ¼ cup, about 7 minutes. With back of spoon, press mixture through fine sieve into medium bowl.

2. With wire whisk, beat in egg yolks, water, and pepper. Set bowl over saucepan of *simmering water*. Cook, whisking constantly, until egg-yolk mixture bubbles around edge and has thickened, about 10 minutes.

3. Reduce heat to very low. With wire whisk, whisk in butter, one piece at a time, whisking to incorporate each piece of butter completely before adding more. Stir in tarragon. Makes 1 cup.

Each tablespoon: About 68 calories, 1g protein, 1g carbohydrate, 7g total fat (4g saturated), 55mg cholesterol, 60mg sodium.

Beurre Blanc

This suave and refined French sauce is often served with fish. The only challenge is controlling the heat so the butter doesn't melt completely when added. This is easily achieved, however, by moving the saucepan off the burner whenever you think it is getting too hot. Once you get used to the process, you'll love making this sauce. Vary it with herbs, your favorite citrus zest, or fresh ginger.

Prep: 5 minutes   Cook: 20 minutes

⅓	cup dry white wine
2	tablespoons white wine vinegar
⅓	cup finely chopped shallots
½	cup cold butter (1 stick), cut into 8 pieces (do not use margarine)
	pinch salt
	pinch ground pepper, preferably white

1. In heavy nonreactive 2-quart saucepan, combine wine, vinegar, and shallots; heat to boiling over high heat. Boil until liquid has reduced to almost 1 teaspoon, about 8 minutes.

2. Reduce heat to very low. With wire whisk, whisk in butter one piece at a time, whisking constantly to incorporate each addition of butter without letting it melt completely before adding more, until sauce is creamy and smooth.

3. Strain sauce through sieve, if desired; stir in salt and pepper. Serve, or set in pan of warm water (120°F) up to 20 minutes. Makes ½ cup strained or ⅔ cup unstrained sauce.

Each tablespoon (strained): About 112 calories, 0g protein, 1g carbohydrate, 11g total fat (7g saturated), 31mg cholesterol, 135mg sodium.

Beurre Rouge

Prepare as directed but substitute **6 tablespoons dry red wine** and **2 tablespoons red wine vinegar** for white wine and vinegar. Whisk in **2 tablespoons heavy cream or crème fraîche**, at room temperature, before adding butter.

Each tablespoon (strained): About 113 calories, 0g protein, 1g carbohydrate, 11g total fat (7g saturated), 31mg cholesterol, 135mg sodium.

Cumberland Sauce

A favorite British sauce that marries well with poultry, duck, ham, or venison.

Prep: 10 minutes   Cook: 10 minutes

1	large orange
1	large lemon
⅓	cup red currant jelly
¼	cup port wine
1	teaspoon cornstarch

1. From orange, grate ¼ teaspoon peel and squeeze ¼ cup juice. From lemon, grate ½ teaspoon peel and squeeze 2 tablespoons juice.

2. In nonreactive 1-quart saucepan, combine jelly, wine, and orange juice; heat to boiling over high heat. Reduce heat and simmer 5 minutes.

3. In cup, blend cornstarch and lemon juice until smooth. With wire whisk, stir cornstarch mixture and orange and lemon peels into sauce. Heat to boiling over high heat, stirring; boil 1 minute. Serve hot. Makes ¾ cup.

Each tablespoon: About 34 calories, 0g protein, 7g carbohydrate, 0g total fat (0g saturated), 0mg cholesterol, 4mg sodium.

Sauce Rémoulade

This richly flavored sauce, excellent with chilled shellfish or cooked vegetables, can also be spiced up Cajun-style. Omit the tarragon and Dijon, and heat it up with some Creole mustard and ground red pepper. Bam!

Prep: 20 minutes

⅓	cup mayonnaise
2	tablespoons sour cream
3	tablespoons finely chopped dill pickle
1	tablespoon chopped fresh parsley
¾	teaspoon chopped fresh tarragon or ¼ teaspoon dried tarragon
½	teaspoon chopped fresh chives
1	anchovy fillet, finely chopped
1	teaspoon capers, drained and chopped
1	teaspoon Dijon mustard

In small bowl, combine mayonnaise, sour cream, pickle, parsley, tarragon, chives, anchovy, capers, and mustard until well blended. Serve, or cover and refrigerate up to 1 day. Makes about ⅔ cup.

Each tablespoon: About 61 calories, 0g protein, 0g carbohydrate, 6g total fat (1g saturated), 6mg cholesterol, 143mg sodium.

Tartar Sauce

Serve this tasty sauce with Crab Cakes (page 289), shrimp, and baked, broiled, or fried fish.

Prep: 15 minutes

½	cup mayonnaise
¼	cup finely chopped dill pickle
1	tablespoon chopped fresh parsley
2	teaspoons milk
2	teaspoons distilled white vinegar
½	teaspoon finely chopped onion
½	teaspoon Dijon mustard

In small bowl, combine mayonnaise, pickle, parsley, milk, vinegar, onion, and mustard until well blended. Serve, or cover and refrigerate up to 2 days. Makes about ¾ cup.

Each tablespoon: About 68 calories, 0g protein, 0g carbohydrate, 7g total fat (1g saturated), 6mg cholesterol, 125mg sodium.

Salmoriglio Sauce

If you have oregano growing in your garden, chop enough to equal one tablespoon and use instead of dried oregano. It will make this favorite Sicilian sauce even better with grilled or roasted fish.

Prep: 10 minutes plus standing

¼	cup fresh lemon juice (about 2 lemons)
1	garlic clove, crushed with side of chef's knife
1	teaspoon dried oregano, crumbled
¼	teaspoon salt
¼	teaspoon coarsely ground black pepper
⅓	cup extravirgin olive oil

1. In medium bowl, combine lemon juice, garlic, oregano, salt, and pepper. Let stand 30 minutes.

2. With wire whisk, in thin, steady stream, whisk in oil until blended. Serve, or let stand up to 4 hours at room temperature. Whisk just before serving. Makes scant ⅔ cup.

Each tablespoon: About 66 calories, 0g protein, 1g carbohydrate, 7g total fat (1g saturated), 0mg cholesterol, 57mg sodium.

Sauce Gribiche

Another French classic: a piquant mayonnaise that goes especially well with cold poached fish.

Prep: 30 minutes

1	large hard-cooked egg
1	teaspoon Dijon mustard
1	teaspoon red wine vinegar
3	tablespoons mayonnaise
⅛	teaspoon salt
	pinch ground black pepper
1	tablespoon finely chopped cornichons or sour pickle
1	tablespoon chopped fresh parsley
1	teaspoon chopped fresh tarragon
1	teaspoon capers, drained and chopped

Remove white from hard-cooked egg and finely chop. In small bowl, mash yolk, mustard, and vinegar to a paste. Stir in mayonnaise, salt, and pepper until well combined. Stir in cornichons, parsley, tarragon, capers, and chopped egg white until well blended. Makes generous ⅔ cup.

Each tablespoon: About 81 calories, 1g protein, 2g carbohydrate, 8g total fat (1g saturated), 47mg cholesterol, 189mg sodium.

Roasted Red Pepper Sauce

Roast your own peppers for this zesty sauce and serve with grilled veal, poultry, or over toasted Italian bread.

Prep: 15 minutes plus cooling

2	large red peppers, roasted (page 448)
¼	cup pimiento-stuffed olives (salad olives)
⅓	cup fresh orange juice
2	tablespoons olive oil
2	tablespoons tomato paste

Cut roasted red peppers into large pieces. In food processor with knife blade attached, puree peppers, olives, orange juice, oil, and tomato paste until smooth. Serve, or cover and refrigerate up to 2 days. Makes 1½ cups.

Each tablespoon: About 17 calories, 0g protein, 1g carbohydrate, 1g total fat (0g saturated), 0mg cholesterol, 45mg sodium.

Roasted Garlic Sauce

The garlic may be roasted well in advance, squeezed out of its skin, and refrigerated until you are ready to use it.

Prep: 15 minutes plus cooling   Roast: 1 hour

2	heads garlic, not peeled
1	slice firm white bread, torn into pieces
3	tablespoons olive oil
2	tablespoons sour cream
2	teaspoons fresh lemon juice
½	teaspoon salt
⅓	cup water

1. Preheat oven to 350°F. Remove any loose papery skin from garlic, leaving head intact. Wrap each garlic head in foil and place in small baking dish. Roast until garlic has softened, about 1 hour. When cool enough to handle, separate garlic into cloves. Squeeze soft garlic from each clove into bowl.

2. In food processor with knife blade attached, puree garlic, bread, oil, sour cream, lemon juice, and salt until smooth. Add water and process until blended. Serve, or cover and refrigerate up to 1 day. Makes 1 cup.

Each tablespoon: About 39 calories, 1g protein, 3g carbohydrate, 3g total fat (1g saturated), 1mg cholesterol, 84mg sodium.

Chimichurri Sauce

This Argentinean herb vinaigrette is what stands in for steak sauce at Buenos Aires steakhouses. Drizzle it on sandwiches, or serve with grilled or roasted meats.

Prep: 20 minutes

1	large garlic clove, minced
½	teaspoon salt
1½	cups loosely packed fresh flat-leaf parsley leaves, chopped
1	cup loosely packed fresh cilantro leaves, chopped
¾	cup olive oil
2	tablespoons red wine vinegar
½	teaspoon crushed red pepper

1. With side of chef's knife, mash garlic and salt to a smooth paste.

2. In small bowl, combine garlic mixture, parsley, cilantro, oil, vinegar, and crushed red pepper until well blended. Serve, or cover and refrigerate up to 4 hours. Makes about 1 cup.

Each tablespoon: About 93 calories, 0g protein, 1g carbohydrate, 10g total fat (1g saturated), 0mg cholesterol, 76mg sodium.

Cilantro Sauce

As with many fresh herb-based sauces, this one is perfect on a buffet with beef tenderloin, cold roast turkey, or poached salmon.

Prep: 10 minutes

1	cup tightly packed fresh cilantro leaves
¾	cup light mayonnaise
¾	cup reduced-fat sour cream
2	teaspoons fresh lime juice
¼	teaspoon hot pepper sauce

In blender or in food processor with knife blade attached, puree cilantro, mayonnaise, sour cream, lime juice, and hot pepper sauce until smooth. Serve, or cover and refrigerate up to 1 day. Makes 1⅔ cups.

Each tablespoon: About 35 calories, 1g protein, 1g carbohydrate, 3g total fat (1g saturated), 5mg cholesterol, 59mg sodium.

Salsa Verde (Green Sauce)

Bright green and with an enticing flavor, this uncooked Italian sauce goes with almost any savory food, especially fish.

Prep: 20 minutes

1	large garlic clove, minced
¼	teaspoon salt
2	cups tightly packed fresh flat-leaf parsley leaves
8	anchovy fillets, drained and finely chopped (optional)
3	tablespoons capers, drained
1	teaspoon Dijon mustard
⅛	teaspoon ground black pepper
½	cup olive oil
3	tablespoons fresh lemon juice

1. With side of chef's knife, mash garlic and salt to a smooth paste.

2. In blender or in food processor with knife blade attached, puree parsley, anchovies if using, capers, garlic mixture, mustard, pepper, oil, and lemon juice until very smooth. Serve, or cover and refrigerate up to 4 hours. Makes about 1 cup.

Each tablespoon: About 69 calories, 1g protein, 2g carbohydrate, 7g total fat (1g saturated), 0mg cholesterol, 123mg sodium.

Asian Peanut Sauce

This time-honored sauce is still one of the best. Try it on thin spaghetti, sprinkled with chopped scallions and cilantro.

Prep: 5 minutes   Cook: 6 minutes

2	teaspoons vegetable oil
1	garlic clove, finely chopped
¼	teaspoon ground red pepper (cayenne)
⅓	cup creamy peanut butter
2	tablespoons brown sugar
2	tablespoons hoisin sauce
1	tablespoon tomato paste
1	cup water

1. In 1-quart saucepan, heat oil over medium heat. Add garlic and ground red pepper; cook, stirring constantly, 30 seconds. Add peanut butter, brown sugar, hoisin sauce, tomato

paste, and water; cook, stirring constantly, until sauce has thickened, about 5 minutes.

2. Serve warm or at room temperature, or cover and refrigerate up to 2 days. Reheat gently, adding a little water if too thick. Makes about 1½ cups.

Each tablespoon: About 33 calories, 1g protein, 3g carbohydrate, 2g total fat (0g saturated), 0mg cholesterol, 49mg sodium.

Sweet Corn Salsa

This deftly seasoned salsa tastes great made with fresh or frozen corn kernels. It keeps well in the refrigerator.

Prep: 20 minutes plus chilling   Cook: 10 minutes

8	ears corn, husks and silk removed, or 1 bag (20 ounces) frozen whole-kernel corn, thawed
3	tablespoons fresh lime juice (about 2 limes)
2	tablespoons olive oil
¾	teaspoon ground cumin
¾	teaspoon ground coriander
¾	teaspoon salt
½	teaspoon chili powder
1	large red pepper, finely chopped

1. If using fresh corn, with sharp knife, cut kernels from cobs. Heat 6-quart saucepot of *water* to boiling over high heat. Add corn kernels and heat to boiling; boil 30 seconds. Drain. Rinse with cold running water and drain.

2. In medium bowl, with wire whisk, mix lime juice, oil, cumin, coriander, salt, and chili powder until blended. Add corn and red pepper; toss until mixed and coated with dressing. Cover and refrigerate until well chilled, about 2 hours or up to 2 weeks. Makes about 5 cups.

Each ¼ cup: About 41 calories, 1g protein, 6g carbohydrate, 2g total fat (0g saturated), 0mg cholesterol, 93mg sodium.

Olive and Lemon Salsa

The sweet citrus flavor of oranges and lemons is the perfect foil for salty olives.

Prep: 15 minutes

2	small navel oranges
2	lemons
¼	cup coarsely chopped pimiento-stuffed olives (salad olives)
2	tablespoons chopped shallots
2	tablespoons chopped fresh parsley
½	teaspoon sugar
¼	teaspoon coarsely ground black pepper

1. Cut peel and white pith from oranges and lemons. Cut fruit into ¼-inch-thick slices; discard seeds. Cut slices into ½-inch pieces.

2. In small bowl, gently stir orange and lemon pieces, olives, shallots, parsley, sugar, and pepper until well mixed. Serve, or cover and refrigerate up to 1 day. Makes about 2 cups.

Each ¼ cup: About 28 calories, 1g protein, 7g carbohydrate, 1g total fat (0g saturated), 0mg cholesterol, 104mg sodium.

Orange-Fennel Salsa

Ideal with grilled fish or pork.

Prep: 20 minutes

3	small navel oranges
1	large fennel bulb (1½ pounds), trimmed and chopped
½	small red onion, thinly sliced
¼	cup chopped fresh cilantro leaves
1	jalapeño chile, seeded and minced
¼	teaspoon salt

1. Cut peel and white pith from oranges. Holding oranges over medium bowl to catch juice, cut out sections from between membranes, allowing sections to drop into bowl.

2. Add fennel, onion, cilantro, jalapeño, and salt; gently stir until well mixed. Serve, or cover and refrigerate up to 1 day. Makes about 3 cups.

Each ¼ cup: About 24 calories, 1g protein, 5g carbohydrate, 0g total fat (0g saturated), 0mg cholesterol, 94mg sodium.

Peach Salsa

(pictured on page 548)

Be patient. Wait until it is the height of peach season to make this. Spoon over grilled chicken breasts or pork chops.

Prep: 30 minutes plus chilling

1¾	pounds ripe peaches (5 medium), peeled, pitted, and chopped
2	tablespoons finely chopped red onion
1	tablespoon chopped fresh mint
1	teaspoon seeded, minced jalapeño chile
1	tablespoon fresh lime juice
⅛	teaspoon salt

In medium bowl, gently stir peaches, onion, mint, jalapeño, lime juice, and salt until well mixed. Cover and refrigerate 1 hour to blend flavors or up to 2 days. Makes about 3 cups.

♥ Each ¼ cup: About 23 calories, 0g protein, 6g carbohydrate, 0g total fat (0g saturated), 0mg cholesterol, 25mg sodium.

Plum Salsa

Serve with grilled pork or butterflied lamb.

Prep: 20 minutes plus chilling

1½	pounds ripe plums (6 to 8 medium), pitted and chopped
1	green onion, chopped
1	tablespoon chopped fresh basil
2	tablespoons balsamic vinegar
⅛	teaspoon salt

In medium bowl, gently stir plums, green onion, basil, vinegar, and salt until well mixed. Cover and refrigerate at least 1 hour to blend flavors or up to 2 days. Makes about 3 cups.

♥ Each ¼ cup: About 30 calories, 0g protein, 7g carbohydrate, 0g total fat (0g saturated), 0mg cholesterol, 25mg sodium.

Tomato Salsa

(pictured on page 548)

As a topping for burgers, this flavor-packed salsa is stiff competition for plain old ketchup.

Prep: 20 minutes plus chilling

1	large lime
1½	pounds ripe tomatoes (3 large), chopped
½	small red onion, finely chopped
1	small jalapeño chile, seeded and minced
2	tablespoons chopped fresh cilantro
¾	teaspoon salt
¼	teaspoon coarsely ground black pepper

From lime, grate ½ teaspoon peel and squeeze 2 tablespoons juice. In medium bowl, gently stir lime peel and juice, tomatoes, onion, jalapeño, cilantro, salt, and pepper until well mixed. Cover and refrigerate at least 1 hour to blend flavors or up to 2 days. Makes about 3 cups.

♥ Each ¼ cup: About 15 calories, 1g protein, 3g carbohydrate, 0g total fat (0g saturated), 0mg cholesterol, 151mg sodium.

Tomatillo Salsa

(pictured on page 548)

The tomatillo, sometimes called a Mexican green tomato, is actually related to the gooseberry. It has an acidic fruity flavor that is excellent with grilled meats and fish.

Prep: 25 minutes plus chilling

1	pound fresh tomatillos (about 10 medium), husked, washed well, and cut into quarters
¾	cup loosely packed fresh cilantro leaves, chopped
¼	cup finely chopped onion
1 or 2	serrano or jalapeño chiles, seeded and minced
1	garlic clove, minced
1	tablespoon olive oil
1	teaspoon sugar
½	teaspoon salt

1. In food processor with knife blade attached, coarsely chop tomatillos.

2. In medium bowl, gently stir tomatillos, cilantro, onion, serranos, garlic, oil, sugar, and salt until well mixed. Cover and refrigerate at least 1 hour to blend flavors or up to 3 days. Makes about 2 cups.

Each ¼ cup: About 34 calories, 1g protein, 3g carbohydrate, 2g total fat (0g saturated), 0mg cholesterol, 146mg sodium.

Watermelon Salsa

A great way to use up that last piece of watermelon. Both red and yellow watermelon work well here.

Prep: 30 minutes plus chilling	
1	piece (2½ pounds) watermelon, seeded and chopped
1	tablespoon finely chopped red onion
1	tablespoon chopped fresh cilantro
2	teaspoons seeded, minced jalapeño chile
2	tablespoons fresh lime juice
⅛	teaspoon salt

In medium bowl, gently stir watermelon, onion, cilantro, jalapeño, lime juice, and salt until well mixed. Cover and refrigerate at least 1 hour to blend flavors or up to 2 days. Makes about 3 cups.

Each ¼ cup: About 17 calories, 0g protein, 4g carbohydrate, 0g total fat (0g saturated), 0mg cholesterol, 26mg sodium.

Cranberry-Port Sauce

Serve this richly flavored cranberry sauce warm with baked ham, roast duck, pork, or venison.

Prep: 5 minutes Cook: 20 minutes	
½	12-ounce bag cranberries (1½ cups)
⅔	cup sugar
½	cup orange juice
⅓	cup port wine
⅛	teaspoon salt

In nonreactive 3-quart saucepan, combine cranberries, sugar, orange juice, port, and salt; heat to boiling over high heat, stirring occasionally. Reduce heat; cover and simmer, stirring occasionally, until thickened, about 15 minutes. Makes 1¾ cups.

Each ¼ cup: About 111 calories, 0g protein, 25g carbohydrate, 0g total fat (0g saturated), 0mg cholesterol, 43mg sodium.

Cranberry-Apple Sauce

Wonderful with ham as well as turkey.

Prep: 5 minutes plus chilling Cook: 15 minutes	
1	bag (12 ounces) cranberries
½	cup golden raisins
1	cup packed brown sugar
¾	cup water
2	tablespoons cider vinegar
1	cinnamon stick (3 inches)
	pinch ground cloves
	pinch salt
1	large Rome Beauty apple, peeled, cored, and chopped

1. In nonreactive 3-quart saucepan, combine cranberries, raisins, brown sugar, water, vinegar, cinnamon stick, cloves, and salt; heat to boiling over high heat.

2. Reduce heat; simmer, stirring occasionally, 6 minutes. Add apple and cook until most cranberries have popped and syrup has thickened slightly, about 4 minutes. Discard cinnamon stick.

3. Cover and refrigerate until well chilled, about 3 hours or up to 4 days. Makes about 4 cups.

Each ¼ cup: About 81 calories, 0g protein, 21g carbohydrate, 0g total fat, 0mg cholesterol, 15mg sodium.

Apricot-Cranberry Sauce with Fresh Ginger

The tart-sweet flavor of dried apricots is the perfect match for bright red cranberries.

Prep: 15 minutes plus standing and chilling	Cook: 15 minutes

- ½ cup dried apricot halves, cut into ¼-inch-wide strips
- ¾ cup cranberry-juice cocktail
- 1 bag (12 ounces) cranberries
- ⅔ cup sugar
- 1 tablespoon minced, peeled fresh ginger

1. In nonreactive 2-quart saucepan, soak apricots in cranberry-juice cocktail 10 minutes. Add cranberries, sugar, and ginger; heat to boiling over high heat.

2. Reduce heat to medium and cook, stirring occasionally, until most cranberries have popped and sauce has thickened slightly, about 10 minutes.

3. Cover and refrigerate until well chilled, about 3 hours or up to 4 days. Makes about 2½ cups.

♥ Each ¼ cup: About 95 calories, 0g protein, 25g carbohydrate, 0g total fat, 0mg cholesterol, 2mg sodium.

Southwestern-Style Cranberry Relish

This spicy sauce will liven things up at your Thanksgiving table.

Prep: 10 minutes plus chilling	Cook: 15 minutes

- 1 lemon
- 1 bag (12 ounces) cranberries
- 1 pickled jalapeño chile, finely chopped
- ½ cup honey
- ¼ cup cider vinegar
- 1 teaspoon mustard seeds
- ½ teaspoon salt
- ½ teaspoon ground black pepper

1. From lemon, with vegetable peeler, remove peel in 1-inch-wide strips. Cut strips crosswise into slivers. (Reserve lemon for another use.)

2. In nonreactive 2-quart saucepan, combine cranberries, lemon peel, pickled jalapeño, honey, vinegar, mustard seeds, salt, and pepper; heat to boiling over high heat. Reduce heat; simmer, stirring occasionally, until most cranberries have popped and mixture has thickened slightly, about 10 minutes.

3. Cover and refrigerate until well chilled, about 3 hours or up to 4 days. Makes about 2 cups.

♥ Each ¼ cup: About 90 calories, 0g protein, 24g carbohydrate, 0g total fat, 0mg cholesterol, 174mg sodium.

Cranberry-Fig Chutney

Don't serve this chutney just with turkey—try it with an Indian-style menu.

Prep: 15 minutes plus chilling	Cook: 35 minutes

- 1 bag (12 ounces) cranberries
- 1 package (8 ounces) dried Calimyrna figs, sliced
- 1 small onion, chopped
- ½ small lemon, chopped, seeds discarded
- 2 tablespoons minced, peeled fresh ginger
- 1 cup packed brown sugar
- 1 cup water
- ⅓ cup red wine vinegar
- ½ teaspoon salt
- ¼ teaspoon coarsely ground black pepper

1. In nonreactive 3-quart saucepan, combine cranberries, figs, onion, lemon, ginger, brown sugar, water, vinegar, salt, and pepper; heat to boiling over high heat. Reduce heat and simmer, stirring occasionally, 30 minutes.

2. Cover and refrigerate until well chilled, about 4 hours or up to 2 days. Makes about 4 cups.

♥ Each ¼ cup: About 103 calories, 1g protein, 27g carbohydrate, 0g total fat (0g saturated), 0mg cholesterol, 80mg sodium.

No-Cook Cranberry-Orange Relish

An easy no-fuss recipe.

Prep: 15 minutes plus chilling

- 1 bag (12 ounces) cranberries
- 1 medium orange, cut into pieces, seeds discarded
- ⅔ cup sugar

1. In food processor with knife blade attached, combine cranberries, orange, and sugar; pulse until coarsely chopped.

2. Cover and refrigerate until well chilled, about 2 hours or up to 2 days. Makes about 3 cups.

♥ Each ¼ cup: About 62 calories, 0g protein, 17g carbohydrate, 0g total fat (0g saturated), 0mg cholesterol, 1mg sodium.

Cranberry-Raisin Relish
Prepare as directed but use only ½ **cup sugar** and add ½ **cup dark seedless raisins.**

Dried Pear Chutney

Serve as an accompaniment to roast pork, ham, hamburgers, or poultry. Or serve with cream cheese and crackers as an appetizer.

Prep: 20 minutes plus chilling	Cook: 25 minutes
12	ounces dried pear halves, chopped (2 cups)
2	cups dark seedless and/or golden raisins
½	cup dried tart cherries
1	large red onion, finely chopped (1 cup)
1	tablespoon grated, peeled fresh ginger
⅓	cup sugar
1	tablespoon mustard seeds
1	cinnamon stick (3 inches)
¼	teaspoon salt
2½	cups pear nectar
1	cup water
¾	cup cider vinegar

1. In nonreactive 4-quart saucepan, combine dried pears, raisins, dried cherries, onion, ginger, sugar, mustard seeds, cinnamon stick, salt, pear nectar, water, and vinegar; heat to boiling over high heat, stirring occasionally. Reduce heat; simmer, stirring frequently, until pears are very tender, about 15 minutes.

2. Discard cinnamon stick. Cover and refrigerate until well chilled, about 4 hours or up to 1 month. Makes about 6 cups.

♥ Each ¼ cup: About 114 calories, 1g protein, 30g carbohydrate, 0g total fat (0g saturated), 0mg cholesterol, 28mg sodium.

Sweet Red Pepper Chutney

You can prepare and refrigerate this zesty-sweet relish up to two weeks before serving.

Prep: 25 minutes plus chilling	Cook: 50 minutes
1½	cups cider vinegar
1	cup sugar
6	large red peppers, chopped
3	firm medium pears, peeled, cored, and cut into ½-inch pieces
1	small red onion, chopped
⅓	cup dark seedless raisins
1½	teaspoons mustard seeds
1	teaspoon salt
⅛	teaspoon ground allspice

1. In nonreactive 5-quart Dutch oven, combine vinegar and sugar; heat to boiling over high heat. Boil 10 minutes.

2. Add red peppers, pears, onion, raisins, mustard seeds, salt, and allspice; heat to boiling. Reduce heat to medium-high and cook, stirring occasionally, until syrupy, about 30 minutes. Cover and refrigerate until well chilled, about 4 hours or up to 2 weeks. Makes about 6 cups.

♥ Each ¼ cup: About 62 calories, 0g protein, 16g carbohydrate, 0g total fat, 0mg cholesterol, 99mg sodium.

Sweet Red Pepper Chutney

Tomato Chutney

Deep red and richly flavored, this is a delicious accent for grilled meats and vegetables, or serve with cold meat sandwiches.

Prep: 25 minutes plus chilling   Cook: 55 minutes

3	pounds ripe tomatoes (9 medium), peeled and chopped
1	medium Granny Smith apple, peeled, cored, and coarsely grated
1	small onion, chopped
2	tablespoons minced, peeled fresh ginger
2	garlic cloves, finely chopped
1/3	cup golden raisins
1/3	cup packed brown sugar
1/2	teaspoon salt
1/4	teaspoon coarsely ground black pepper
1/2	cup cider vinegar

1. In heavy nonreactive 12-inch skillet, combine tomatoes, apple, onion, ginger, garlic, raisins, brown sugar, salt, pepper, and vinegar; heat to boiling over high heat. Reduce heat to medium; cook, stirring occasionally, until mixture has thickened, 45 to 50 minutes.

2. Cover and refrigerate until well chilled, about 4 hours or up to 2 weeks. Makes about 3½ cups.

♥ Each ¼ cup: About 59 calories, 1g protein, 15g carbohydrate, 0g total fat (0g saturated), 0mg cholesterol, 94mg sodium.

You can make chutney out of virtually any under-ripe fruit. Cut the fruit into small pieces and simmer it in almost enough light sugar syrup (page 774) to cover until the fruit has softened. With a slotted spoon, transfer the fruit to a bowl and boil down the cooking liquid until slightly syrupy. Add it to the fruit in the bowl along with vinegar to taste and spices, such as ginger and curry powder.

JAMES PETERSON
COOKBOOK AUTHOR

EXPERT TIP

Butterscotch Sauce

An old-fashioned favorite. Divine in an ice cream sundae but also wonderful with apple pie.

Prep: 5 minutes   Cook: 5 minutes

1	cup packed brown sugar
1/2	cup heavy or whipping cream
1/3	cup light corn syrup
2	tablespoons butter or margarine
1	teaspoon distilled white vinegar
1/8	teaspoon salt
1	teaspoon vanilla extract

In heavy 3-quart saucepan, combine brown sugar, cream, corn syrup, butter, vinegar, and salt; heat to boiling over high heat, stirring occasionally. Reduce heat and simmer 2 minutes. Remove saucepan from heat; stir in vanilla. Serve warm, or cover and refrigerate up to 1 week. Makes 1⅓ cups.

Each tablespoon: About 84 calories, 0g protein, 14g carbohydrate, 3g total fat (2g saturated), 11mg cholesterol, 38mg sodium.

Best Blueberry Sauce

Perfect with vanilla ice cream for a cooling, easy summer dessert.

Prep: 5 minutes   Cook: 5 to 8 minutes

3	cups blueberries
1/2 to 3/4	cup confectioners' sugar
3	tablespoons water
1 to 2	teaspoons fresh lemon or lime juice

1. In nonreactive 2-quart saucepan, combine blueberries, ½ cup confectioners' sugar, and water; cook over medium heat, stirring occasionally, until berries have softened and sauce has thickened slightly, 5 to 8 minutes.

2. Remove saucepan from heat; stir in 1 teaspoon lemon juice. Taste and stir in additional sugar and lemon juice, if desired. Serve warm, or cover and refrigerate up to 1 day. Reheat to serve, if you like. Makes about 2 cups.

♥ Each tablespoon: About 17 calories, 0g protein, 4g carbohydrate, 0g total fat (0g saturated), 0mg cholesterol, 1mg sodium.

Our Sublime Chocolate Sauce

You'll want to make a double batch of this! Keep it refrigerated for up to one week, gently reheating only the amount you want to use.

🕐 Prep: 5 minutes   Cook: 10 minutes

4	squares (4 ounces) unsweetened chocolate, chopped
1	cup heavy or whipping cream
¾	cup sugar
2	tablespoons light corn syrup
2	tablespoons butter or margarine
2	teaspoons vanilla extract

1. In heavy 2-quart saucepan, combine chopped chocolate, cream, sugar, and corn syrup; heat to boiling over high heat, stirring constantly. Reduce heat to medium. Cook at a gentle boil, stirring constantly, until sauce has thickened slightly, about 5 minutes.

2. Remove from heat; stir in butter and vanilla until smooth and glossy. Serve hot, or cool completely, then cover and refrigerate up to 1 week. Makes about 1¾ cups.

Each tablespoon: About 83 calories, 1g protein, 8g carbohydrate, 6g total fat (4g saturated), 14mg cholesterol, 14mg sodium.

Hot Fudge Sauce

Hot Fudge Sauce

Use this rich chocolaty sauce as a topping for ice cream or other desserts. Unsweetened cocoa powder makes it easy to prepare.

🕐 Prep: 5 minutes   Cook: 5 minutes

¾	cup sugar
½	cup unsweetened cocoa
½	cup heavy or whipping cream
4	tablespoons butter or margarine, cut into pieces
1	teaspoon vanilla extract

In heavy 1-quart saucepan, combine sugar, cocoa, cream, and butter; heat to boiling over high heat, stirring frequently. Remove saucepan from heat; stir in vanilla. Serve warm, or cool completely, then cover and refrigerate up to 2 weeks. Gently reheat before using. Makes about 1¼ cups.

Each tablespoon: About 75 calories, 1g protein, 9g carbohydrate, 5g total fat (3g saturated), 14mg cholesterol, 26mg sodium.

Lemon Sauce

Try this time-honored favorite the next time you bake gingerbread or applesauce cake.

🕐 Prep: 5 minutes   Cook: 5 minutes

1 to 2	large lemons
½	cup sugar
1	tablespoon cornstarch
⅔	cup water
1	tablespoon butter or margarine

1. From lemons, grate 1 teaspoon peel and squeeze ¼ cup lemon juice.

2. In nonreactive 2-quart saucepan, combine sugar and cornstarch until well blended. With wire whisk, whisk in water, lemon peel and juice, and butter. Heat to boiling over high heat, stirring constantly; boil 1 minute. Serve warm or at room temperature. Makes about 1¼ cups.

Each tablespoon: About 27 calories, 0g protein, 6g carbohydrate, 1g total fat (0g saturated), 2mg cholesterol, 6mg sodium.

Custard Sauce

This classic dessert sauce, also known as crème anglaise, goes beautifully with pies, tarts, plain cakes, and fruit. If you like, substitute one tablespoon of your favorite liqueur or brandy for the vanilla.

Prep: 5 minutes   Cook: 15 minutes

1¼	cups milk
4	large egg yolks
¼	cup sugar
1	teaspoon vanilla extract

1. In heavy 2-quart saucepan, heat milk to boiling over high heat.

2. Meanwhile, in medium bowl, with wire whisk, mix egg yolks and sugar until well blended. In thin, steady stream, whisk about ¼ cup hot milk into egg-yolk mixture. Gradually whisk remaining hot milk into egg-yolk mixture. Return mixture to saucepan; cook over medium heat, stirring constantly with wooden spoon, just until mixture has thickened slightly and coats back of spoon. Do not boil, or sauce will curdle.

3. Remove saucepan from heat; strain custard through sieve into clean bowl. Stir in vanilla. Serve warm, or cover and refrigerate up to 1 day. Makes about 1½ cups.

Each tablespoon: About 26 calories, 1g protein, 3g carbohydrate, 1g total fat (1g saturated), 37mg cholesterol, 7mg sodium.

Hard Sauce

The essential companion to any warm steamed pudding, but especially Christmas plum pudding.

Prep: 10 minutes

1	cup butter (2 sticks), softened (do not use margarine)
2	cups confectioners' sugar
¼	cup dark rum or brandy
1	teaspoon vanilla extract

1. In small bowl, with mixer at medium speed, beat butter until creamy. Reduce speed to low and gradually beat in confectioners' sugar until light and fluffy. Beat in rum and vanilla.

2. Serve, or transfer to airtight containers and refrigerate up to 1 month. Let stand at room temperature until soft enough to spread, about 30 minutes. Makes about 2 cups.

Each tablespoon: About 84 calories, 0g protein, 7g carbohydrate, 6g total fat (4g saturated), 16mg cholesterol, 59mg sodium.

Raspberry Sauce

Bright in color and tart in flavor, this red sauce dresses up cakes from Chocolate Truffle (page 663) to Angel Food (page 666), as well as tarts, puddings, ice cream, or fresh fruit.

Prep: 5 minutes   Cook: 5 minutes

1	package (10 ounces) frozen raspberries in syrup, thawed
2	tablespoons red currant jelly
2	teaspoons cornstarch

1. Into nonreactive 2-quart saucepan, with back of spoon, press raspberries through fine sieve; discard seeds. Stir in jelly and cornstarch. Heat to boiling over high heat, stirring constantly; boil 1 minute.

2. Serve at room temperature, or cover and refrigerate up to 2 days. Makes 1 cup.

Each tablespoon: About 26 calories, 0g protein, 7g carbohydrate, 0g total fat (0g saturated), 0mg cholesterol, 1mg sodium.

Sweetened Whipped Cream

Feel free to flavor the cream with vanilla or with one of the other tasty suggestions.

Prep: 10 minutes

1	cup heavy or whipping cream (preferably not ultrapasteurized), well chilled
1 to 2 tablespoons sugar	
1	teaspoon vanilla extract, ⅛ teaspoon almond extract, or 1 tablespoon brandy, rum, or orange-flavored liqueur

1. Chill medium bowl and beaters 20 minutes.

2. In chilled bowl, with mixer at medium speed, beat cream, sugar, and vanilla until soft peaks form. Do not overbeat, or cream will separate. Makes about 2 cups.

Each tablespoon: About 28 calories, 0g protein, 1g carbohydrate, 3g total fat (2g saturated), 10mg cholesterol, 3mg sodium.

FLAVORED BUTTERS

Flavored butters are an ideal way to gussy-up panfried or grilled steak or fish when unexpected company drops by. Prepare ahead and freeze to eliminate last-minute fussing.

Prep: 10 minutes

In medium bowl, beat ½ cup butter or margarine (1 stick), softened, with wooden spoon until creamy. Beat in flavor ingredients (below); blend well. Transfer flavored butter to waxed paper and shape into log about 6 inches long; wrap, twisting ends of waxed paper to seal. (Shape Roquefort Butter into two 6-inch-long logs.) Flavored butters can be refrigerated up to 2 days or frozen up to 1 month. To serve, cut into ½-inch-thick slices. Makes 12 servings each, except Roquefort Butter, which makes 24.

Ginger-Cilantro Butter

MAÎTRE D'HÔTEL BUTTER
Quite versatile; use on beef, chicken, veal, pork, and fish.
- 2 tablespoons chopped fresh parsley
- ¼ teaspoon freshly grated lemon peel
- 1 tablespoon fresh lemon juice

ANCHOVY BUTTER
For beef, swordfish, and veal.
- 2 tablespoons chopped fresh parsley
- 1 tablespoon anchovy paste
- ¼ teaspoon freshly grated lemon peel
- 1 teaspoon fresh lemon juice

HERB BUTTER
Good on beef, chicken, and fish.
- 2 tablespoons chopped fresh tarragon, dill, or chives
- ¼ teaspoon freshly grated lemon peel
- ⅛ teaspoon coarsely ground black pepper

ROQUEFORT BUTTER
Good on beef, chicken, and crackers.
- 4 ounces Roquefort cheese, softened
- ¼ teaspoon coarsely ground black pepper

SHALLOT AND RED WINE BUTTER
Good on beef and salmon.
- ½ cup dry red wine
- 2 tablespoons finely chopped shallots
- 1 tablespoon chopped fresh parsley

In heavy nonreactive 1-quart saucepan, heat wine to boiling over high heat. Add shallots and boil until liquid has reduced to 1 tablespoon; cool to room temperature. With wooden spoon, beat wine mixture and parsley into butter until well blended.

HORSERADISH BUTTER
Good on beef and tuna steaks.
- 2 tablespoons bottled white horseradish
- 2 tablespoons chopped fresh parsley

OLIVE BUTTER
Best on fish and chicken.
- ⅓ cup Kalamata olives, pitted and finely chopped
- 1 tablespoon chopped fresh parsley

PESTO BUTTER
Good on beef, veal, and chicken.
- 3 tablespoons freshly grated Parmesan cheese
- 2 tablespoons chopped fresh basil
- 1 teaspoon coarsely ground black pepper

GINGER-CILANTRO BUTTER
Good on chicken and fish.
- 2 tablespoons finely chopped fresh cilantro
- 2 teaspoons fresh lime juice
- ½ teaspoon grated, peeled fresh ginger

JALAPEÑO BUTTER
Good for pork, chicken, and fish.
- 4 green onions, white part only, finely chopped
- 2 tablespoons finely chopped fresh cilantro
- 1 jalapeño chile, seeded and minced
- 2 teaspoons fresh lime juice

CAPER BUTTER
Good on beef, veal, pork, fish, and chicken.
- 2 tablespoons capers, drained and finely chopped
- 1 tablespoon chopped fresh parsley
- ¼ teaspoon freshly grated lemon peel
- 2 teaspoons fresh lemon juice
- ¼ teaspoon coarsely ground black pepper

15

QUICK BREADS

Quick breads, as their name implies, are faster to prepare than their yeast-leavened cousins. Thanks to fast-acting leavening agents, these delicious breads don't require a rising period; just mix them up and pop them into the oven. Some of our favorite breads are from this wide-ranging category, and many of them—biscuits, muffins, coffee cakes, popovers, pancakes, and waffles—are especially appropriate for morning meals and a moist slice of banana, zucchini, or date-nut bread is sure to perk up even the dullest afternoon in a flash.

RISING TO THE OCCASION

Most quick breads rely on chemical leavenings, such as baking powder or baking soda, to make them rise. *Baking soda* is an alkali that forms carbon dioxide gas bubbles when combined with an acidic ingredient such as buttermilk, yogurt, chocolate, brown sugar, or molasses. Store baking soda in an airtight container in a cool dry place for up to one year.

Baking powder is a combination of baking soda and a dry acid, such as cream of tartar. Most commercial baking powders are double-acting: They start to produce gas bubbles as soon as they are moistened, then release more when heated in the oven. Baking powder can stay potent for up to six months if stored airtight in a cool dry place. Inactive baking powder

Basic Muffins with Variations

has been the cause of many a baking failure. To test it, stir ½ teaspoon baking powder into ¼ cup warm water; if it bubbles, it's ready for action.

Buttermilk was originally the liquid left over from churning butter, but it is now made from milk that has bacterial cultures added. It is a favorite baking ingredient: Its acidity balances sugar's sweetness, and it reacts with baking soda to give baked goods a fine crumb. It's a good ingredient to have on hand in your refrigerator; it lasts for a couple of weeks. Dehydrated buttermilk powder is also available. Reconstitute it according to the package directions.

In a pinch, a good substitute for buttermilk is sour cream (not reduced-fat) or plain lowfat yogurt blended with an equal amount of whole milk. You can also use "soured" milk: In a glass measuring cup, place 1 tablespoon fresh lemon juice or distilled white vinegar, then pour in enough whole milk to equal 1 cup. Stir and let stand for five minutes to thicken.

MIXING IT RIGHT

Unlike yeast breads, which are kneaded to activate the gluten in flour, quick breads are always mixed with a light hand. Simply combine the dry ingredients, add the liquids, and stir.

Before starting, be sure your baking powder or baking soda is active. All-purpose flour makes tender quick breads (bread flour contains too much gluten and is best saved for yeast breads). Except for recipes in which chilled butter or margarine is cut into the flour mixture, batters are easier to mix and bake better if all the ingredients are at room temperature.

After adding the liquids to the flour mixture, stir just until the batter is blended. If any lumps remain, they will disappear during baking. Do not overmix, or the bread will be tough, dense, and riddled with tunnels. Biscuit dough is usually kneaded a few times to blend the mixture together, but be gentle. Lastly, quick breads should be baked as soon as the batter is mixed, before the leavening loses its rising power.

BAKING SUCCESS

Bake quick breads in the center of the oven: If they're too high, the tops will brown too quickly; if too low, the bottoms could burn. If baking two loaves at once, be sure there is enough space between them so the air can circulate freely.

Always use the correct size pan. Loaf pans come in two standard sizes, 8½" by 4½" and 9" by 5". It may not seem as if there could be much difference, but the latter holds 2 cups more than the former! Loaf pans should be filled about two-thirds full. Smooth the top with a rubber spatula so the bread bakes uniformly. Don't be concerned if a lengthwise crack appears along the top during baking; it's very typical.

Muffin pans come in various sizes. Standard muffin-pan cups are about 2½" by 1¼", with 12 cups to the pan. There are also giant (4" by 2") and mini (1⅞" by ¾") muffin-pan cups. Regardless of the size, however, fill muffin-pan cups two-thirds to three-quarters full (to allow room for rising). If there are any empty cups, fill them with water to prevent the pan from warping during baking.

To test quick breads for doneness, use the toothpick test: Insert a wooden toothpick into the center of the bread. It should come out clean without any moist crumbs clinging. If not, bake the bread a few minutes longer, then test again. The bread could be done even if the crack in the top looks moist.

Two favorite quick breads—pancakes and waffles—have batters that tend to thicken as they stand, so thin them with additional milk or buttermilk as needed. To cook pancakes, preheat the griddle until very hot (a few drops of water sprinkled onto the surface should turn into tiny skittering balls) and lightly brush with oil. Pour the batter by scant ¼ cupfuls onto the hot griddle. Cook until the tops are bubbly, some of the bubbles burst, and the edges look dry. Turn the pancakes and cook until the underside is golden.

To cook waffles, preheat the waffle baker (iron) according to the manufacturer's directions. Pour enough batter into the center of the waffle baker so it spreads to within one inch of the edges. Close the baker and cook until the waffle stops steaming and the baker top lifts up easily; the waffles should be golden brown.

COOLING, STORING, AND REHEATING

Remove baked biscuits, scones, and muffins from their cookie sheets or pans immediately to prevent them from sticking; eat warm or at room temperature. Most fruit breads should be cooled in their pans for ten minutes to allow them to set before being unmolded. Invert them onto wire racks, then turn right side up to cool completely.

In general, the richer the batter (with eggs, butter, or fruit), the longer the baked bread will stay moist. Dense fruit breads are even better if made a day ahead so their flavors can blend; they'll also be firmer and easier to slice. Most muffins, biscuits, scones, and corn breads are best eaten the day they are made, or freeze to serve later.

To store fruit breads and muffins, cool completely. Wrap in plastic wrap and then in foil. Keep at room temperature for up to three days.

To freeze fruit breads, wrap tightly in plastic wrap and then in heavy-duty foil, pressing out the air. Freeze fruit breads for up to three months. Smaller items like muffins and biscuits can be frozen for up to one month. Thaw them, still wrapped, at room temperature.

Waffles can be frozen, too. Cook them until lightly browned, then cool completely on wire racks. Place on cookie sheets and freeze until firm, then seal in heavy-duty ziptight plastic bags and return to the freezer. To reheat, toast the frozen waffles in a toaster until golden brown.

Reheat fruit breads, wrapped in foil, at 400°F. Muffins, scones, and biscuits will take about ten minutes; loaves and coffee cakes about twenty minutes. Muffins also reheat well in the microwave oven. Loosely wrap each muffin in a paper towel and microwave on high for twenty seconds. Be careful, though: If the muffins have sugary add-ins such as chocolate chips or jam, they could get very hot, and if baked goods are reheated too long, they become tough.

Baking Powder Biscuits

If you like, prepare and refrigerate the flour-shortening mixture early in the day, then add the milk right before mixing. When cutting out the biscuits, press the cutter straight down: Do not twist it, or the biscuits may turn out lopsided.

Prep: 15 minutes   Bake: 12 minutes

2	cups all-purpose flour
1	tablespoon baking powder
½	teaspoon salt
¼	cup vegetable shortening
¾	cup milk

1. Preheat oven to 450°F. In large bowl, combine flour, baking powder, and salt. With pastry blender or two knives used scissor-fashion, cut in vegetable shortening until mixture resembles coarse crumbs. Stir in milk, stirring just until mixture forms soft dough that leaves side of bowl.

2. Turn dough onto lightly floured surface; knead 6 to 8 times, just until smooth. With floured rolling pin, roll dough ½ inch thick for high, fluffy biscuits or ¼ inch thick for thin, crusty biscuits.

3. With floured 2-inch biscuit cutter, cut out rounds, without twisting cutter. Arrange biscuits on ungreased cookie sheet, 1 inch apart for crusty biscuits or nearly touching for soft-sided biscuits.

4. Press trimmings together; reroll and cut out additional biscuits. Bake until golden, 12 to 15 minutes. Serve warm. Makes about 18 high biscuits or 36 thin biscuits.

Each high biscuit: About 86 calories, 2g protein, 12g carbohydrate, 3g total fat (1g saturated), 1mg cholesterol, 151mg sodium.

Buttermilk Biscuits

Prepare as directed but substitute ¾ **cup buttermilk** for milk and use only **2½ teaspoons baking powder;** add ½ **teaspoon baking soda** to flour mixture. Makes about 18 biscuits.

Drop Biscuits

Prepare as directed but use **1 cup milk.** Stir dough just until ingredients are blended. Drop heaping tablespoons of mixture, 1 inch apart, on ungreased cookie sheet. Makes about 20 biscuits.

Scones

Scones are a welcome treat for breakfast or as an afternoon snack with tea. For currant scones, stir one cup dried currants into the dry ingredients before adding the milk mixture.

Prep: 15 minutes   Bake: 22 minutes

2	cups all-purpose flour
2	tablespoons plus 2 teaspoons sugar
2½	teaspoons baking powder
¼	teaspoon salt
½	cup cold butter or margarine (1 stick), cut into pieces
¾	cup milk
1	large egg, separated

1. Preheat oven to 375°F. In large bowl, combine flour, 2 tablespoons sugar, baking powder, and salt. With pastry blender or two knives used scissor-fashion, cut in butter until mixture resembles coarse crumbs.

2. In 1-cup measuring cup, with fork, mix milk and egg yolk until blended. Make well in center of flour mixture and pour in milk mixture. Stir just until combined.

3. Turn dough onto lightly floured surface and knead 5 to 6 times, just until smooth. With lightly floured hands, pat into 7½-inch round. Transfer to ungreased cookie sheet.

4. With lightly floured knife, cut dough into 8 wedges (do not separate wedges). In small cup, lightly beat egg white. Brush scones with egg white and sprinkle with remaining 2 teaspoons sugar. Bake until golden brown, 22 to 25 minutes. Separate wedges. Serve warm, or cool on wire rack to serve later. Makes 8 scones.

Each scone: About 259 calories, 5g protein, 30g carbohydrate, 13g total fat (8g saturated), 61mg cholesterol, 361mg sodium.

Buttermilk Scones

Prepare as directed but use only **2 teaspoons baking powder.** Add ½ **teaspoon baking soda** to flour mixture. Substitute ¾ **cup buttermilk** for milk.

Rich Scones

This traditional Scottish quick bread is served warm, split in half, and slathered with butter, jam, or clotted cream.

⏱ Prep: 15 minutes   Bake: 15 minutes

3⅓	cups all-purpose flour
½	cup plus 1 tablespoon sugar
2	tablespoons baking powder
½	teaspoon salt
6	tablespoons cold butter or margarine, cut into pieces
1	cup plus 1 tablespoon half-and-half or light cream
2	large eggs, beaten

Rich Scones

1. Preheat oven to 400°F. Grease large cookie sheet.

2. In large bowl, mix flour, ½ cup sugar, baking powder, and salt. With pastry blender or two knives used scissor-fashion, cut in butter until mixture resembles coarse crumbs.

3. In small bowl, with fork, beat 1 cup half-and-half and eggs until blended. Make well in center of flour mixture and pour in half-and-half mixture. Stir just until combined.

4. Turn dough onto prepared cookie sheet (dough will be sticky). With lightly floured hands, pat dough into 9-inch round. Brush remaining 1 tablespoon half-and-half over dough and sprinkle with remaining 1 tablespoon sugar. With floured knife, cut dough into 8 wedges (do not separate).

5. Bake until golden, 15 to 20 minutes. Cool on cookie sheet 2 minutes; transfer to wire rack. Separate wedges and serve warm, or cool completely to serve later. Makes 8 scones.

Each scone: About 390 calories, 8g protein, 58g carbohydrate, 14g total fat (8g saturated), 88mg cholesterol, 628mg sodium

Lemon-Walnut Scones

Prepare as directed but add **1 teaspoon freshly grated lemon peel** to flour mixture; add **1 cup chopped walnuts (4 ounces)** with half-and-half mixture.

Currant Scones

Prepare as directed but add **¾ cup dried currants** with half-and-half mixture.

Basic Muffins

(pictured on page 564)

Easy, buttery muffins are a snap to prepare. To make chocolate chip muffins, stir three-quarter cup chocolate chips into the batter before baking. For orange muffins, add one teaspoon freshly grated orange peel to the dry ingredients.

⏱ Prep: 10 minutes   Bake: 20 minutes

2½	cups all-purpose flour
½	cup sugar
1	tablespoon baking powder
½	teaspoon salt
1	cup milk
½	cup butter or margarine (1 stick), melted
1	large egg
1	teaspoon vanilla extract

1. Preheat oven to 400°F. Grease twelve 2½" by 1¼" muffin-pan cups. In large bowl, combine flour, sugar, baking powder, and salt. In medium bowl, with fork, beat milk, melted butter, egg, and vanilla until blended. Add to flour mixture; stir just until flour is moistened (batter will be lumpy).

2. Spoon batter into prepared muffin-pan cups. Bake until toothpick inserted in center of muffin comes out clean, 20 to 25 minutes. Immediately remove muffins from pan. Serve muffins warm, or cool on wire rack to serve later. Makes 12 muffins.

Each muffin: About 225 calories, 4g protein, 30g carbohydrate, 10g total fat (6g saturated), 41mg cholesterol, 312mg sodium.

Jam-Filled Muffins

Prepare as directed but fill muffin-pan cups one-third full with batter. Drop **1 rounded teaspoon strawberry or raspberry preserves** in center of each cup batter; top with remaining batter. Bake as directed.

Blueberry or Raspberry Muffins

Prepare as directed, stirring **1 cup blueberries or raspberries** into batter.

Walnut or Pecan Muffins

Prepare as directed, stirring **½ cup chopped toasted walnuts or pecans** into batter. Sprinkle with **2 tablespoons sugar** before baking.

Bran Muffins

These healthful muffins will start your day off right. Add one-half cup raisins to the batter before baking, if you like.

Prep: 10 minutes plus standing	Bake: 20 minutes
1	cup milk
¼	cup vegetable oil
¼	cup light (mild) molasses
1	large egg, lightly beaten
1	cup whole-bran cereal (not bran flakes)
1	cup all-purpose flour
¼	cup sugar
1	tablespoon baking powder
½	teaspoon salt

1. Preheat oven to 400°F. Grease twelve 2½" by 1¼" muffin-pan cups. In medium bowl, with fork, beat milk, oil, molasses, egg, and cereal until blended; let stand 10 minutes.

2. Meanwhile, in large bowl, combine flour, sugar, baking powder, and salt. Add cereal mixture to flour mixture; stir just until flour is moistened (batter will be lumpy).

3. Spoon batter into prepared muffin-pan cups. Bake until golden and toothpick inserted in center of muffin comes out almost clean, 20 to 25 minutes. Immediately remove muffins from pan. Serve warm, or cool on wire rack to serve later. Makes 12 muffins.

Each muffin: About 154 calories, 3g protein, 22g carbohydrate, 7g total fat (1g saturated), 21mg cholesterol, 283mg sodium.

Carrot-Bran Muffins

Deliciously hearty and filled with fiber, these muffins will tide you over to your next meal.

Prep: 15 minutes plus standing	Bake: 30 minutes
1	cup milk
¼	cup vegetable oil
1	large egg, lightly beaten
1½	cups whole-bran cereal (not bran flakes)
1	cup shredded carrots
1¼	cups all-purpose flour
⅓	cup sugar
1	tablespoon baking powder
½	teaspoon salt
¼	teaspoon ground cinnamon
1	cup dark seedless raisins

1. Preheat oven to 400°F. Grease twelve 2½" by 1¼" muffin-pan cups. In medium bowl, with fork, beat milk, oil, egg, cereal, and carrots until blended; let stand 10 minutes.

2. Meanwhile, in large bowl, combine flour, sugar, baking powder, salt, and cinnamon. Add cereal mixture to flour mixture; stir just until flour is moistened (batter will be lumpy). Stir in raisins.

3. Spoon batter into prepared muffin-pan cups. Bake until muffins begin to brown and toothpick inserted in center of muffin comes out clean, about 30 minutes. Immediately remove muffins from pan. Serve warm, or cool on wire rack to serve later. Makes 12 muffins.

Each muffin: About 198 calories, 4g protein, 33g carbohydrate, 7g total fat (1g saturated), 21mg cholesterol, 309mg sodium.

Banana-Nut Muffins

Moist, flavorful muffins that are a sweet way to start the day.

Prep: 20 minutes   Bake: 25 minutes

2½	cups all-purpose flour
¾	cup sugar
1	tablespoon baking powder
¾	teaspoon salt
6	tablespoons cold butter or margarine, cut into pieces
1	cup walnuts (4 ounces), chopped
3	ripe small bananas, cut into pieces (2 cups)
⅓	cup milk
2	large eggs
½	teaspoon vanilla extract

1. Preheat oven to 400°F. Grease twelve 2½" by 1¼" muffin-pan cups. In large bowl, combine flour, sugar, baking powder, and salt. With pastry blender or two knives used scissor-fashion, cut in butter until mixture resembles coarse crumbs. Stir in walnuts.

2. In blender or in food processor with knife blade attached, process bananas, milk, eggs, and vanilla just until bananas are chopped. Add banana mixture to flour mixture; stir just until flour is moistened (batter will be lumpy).

3. Spoon batter into prepared muffin-pan cups. Bake until golden and toothpick inserted in center of muffin comes out clean, 25 to 30 minutes. Immediately remove muffins from pan. Serve warm, or cool on wire rack to serve later. Makes 12 muffins.

Each muffin: About 305 calories, 6g protein, 41g carbohydrate, 14g total fat (5g saturated), 52mg cholesterol, 341mg sodium.

REMOVING MUFFINS FROM PAN

Run a small metal spatula or knife around the inside of the muffin-pan cups. Invert the pan and rap on the counter to remove the muffins.

Blueberry-Corn Muffins

Enjoy summer's bounty of either blueberries or raspberries in these mouthwatering muffins.

Prep: 15 minutes   Bake: 20 minutes

1	cup all-purpose flour
1	cup cornmeal
½	cup sugar
2	teaspoons baking powder
1	teaspoon baking soda
½	teaspoon salt
1	cup buttermilk
¼	cup vegetable oil
1	large egg
2	teaspoons vanilla extract
1½	cups blueberries or raspberries

1. Preheat oven to 400°F. Grease twelve 2½" by 1¼" muffin-pan cups. In large bowl, combine flour, cornmeal, sugar, baking powder, baking soda, and salt. In small bowl, with fork, beat buttermilk, oil, egg, and vanilla until blended. Add buttermilk mixture to flour mixture; stir just until flour is moistened (batter will be lumpy). Fold in berries.

2. Spoon into prepared muffin-pan cups. Bake until toothpick inserted in center of muffin comes out clean, 20 to 25 minutes. Immediately remove muffins from pan. Serve warm, or cool on wire rack to serve later. Makes 12 muffins.

Each muffin: About 189 calories, 3g protein, 29g carbohydrate, 7g total fat (1g saturated), 19mg cholesterol, 311mg sodium.

Apple-Gingerbread Muffins

These muffins are packed with apple chunks and are full of the spicy flavor of ginger and the warmth of cinnamon.

Prep: 15 minutes   Bake: 25 minutes

2	cups all-purpose flour
¼	cup packed brown sugar
1	teaspoon baking soda
1	teaspoon ground cinnamon
½	teaspoon ground ginger
½	teaspoon salt
¼	teaspoon ground allspice
½	cup light (mild) molasses
¼	cup milk
4	tablespoons butter or margarine, melted
1	large egg
2	medium Golden Delicious or Rome Beauty apples, peeled and finely chopped (about 2 cups)
⅓	cup walnuts, chopped

1. Preheat oven to 400°F. Grease twelve 2½" by 1¼" muffin-pan cups. In large bowl, combine flour, brown sugar, baking soda, cinnamon, ginger, salt, and allspice. In small bowl, with fork, beat molasses, milk, melted butter, and egg until blended. Add molasses mixture to flour mixture; stir just until flour is moistened (batter will be lumpy). Gently stir in apples and walnuts.

2. Spoon into prepared muffin-pan cups. Bake until toothpick inserted in center of muffin comes out clean, about 25 minutes. Immediately remove muffins from pan. Serve warm, or cool on wire rack to serve later. Makes 12 muffins.

Each muffin: About 219 calories, 3g protein, 35g carbohydrate, 8g total fat (3g saturated), 29mg cholesterol, 256mg sodium.

When it comes to baking lofty popovers, the most critical element is the proper heat; popovers need a lot more than biscuits in order to rise. If you are using muffin-pan cups for your popovers, only fill the outer cups and leave the middle ones empty. This allows the heat to circulate more efficiently and evenly around the filled cups, giving popovers greater height.

MARION CUNNINGHAM
COOKBOOK AUTHOR

EXPERT TIP

Popovers

Popovers are crispy on the outside and hollow on the inside. Include these at your next brunch. Serve them fresh from the oven, or make ahead and reheat in a 400°F oven for fifteen minutes.

Prep: 10 minutes   Bake: 1 hour

3	large eggs
1	cup milk
3	tablespoons butter or margarine, melted
1	cup all-purpose flour
½	teaspoon salt

1. Preheat oven to 375°F. Generously grease eight 6-ounce custard cups or twelve 2½" by 1¼" muffin-pan cups with butter or vegetable oil. Place custard cups in jelly-roll pan for easier handling.

2. In blender, combine eggs, milk, melted butter, flour, and salt. Blend until smooth.

3. Pour about ⅓ cup batter into each prepared custard cup, or fill muffin-pan cups half-full. Bake 50 minutes, then, with tip of knife, quickly cut small slit in top of each popover to release steam; bake 10 minutes longer. Immediately remove popovers from cups, loosening with spatula if necessary. Serve hot. Makes 8 medium or 12 small popovers.

Each medium popover: About 159 calories, 5g protein, 14g carbohydrate, 9g total fat (5g saturated), 101mg cholesterol, 247mg sodium.

Giant Popovers

Generously grease six deep 8-ounce ceramic custard cups; place in jelly-roll pan. Prepare popovers as directed but use **6 eggs, 2 cups milk, 6 tablespoons butter or margarine,** melted, **2 cups flour,** and **1 teaspoon salt.** Bake 1 hour before cutting slit in top of popovers. Makes 6 giant popovers.

Each popover: About 394 calories, 13g protein, 36g carbohydrate, 22g total fat (12g saturated), 260mg cholesterol, 629mg sodium.

Golden Corn Bread

A slightly sweet batter that can be baked into a tender square, muffins, or corn sticks.

Prep: 10 minutes   Bake: 20 minutes

1	cup all-purpose flour
¾	cup cornmeal
3	tablespoons sugar
1	tablespoon baking powder
¾	teaspoon salt
⅔	cup milk
4	tablespoons butter or margarine, melted
1	large egg

1. Preheat oven to 425°F. Grease 8-inch square baking pan. In medium bowl, combine flour, cornmeal, sugar, baking powder, and salt. In small bowl, with fork, beat milk, melted butter, and egg until blended. Add egg mixture to flour mixture; stir just until flour is moistened (batter will be lumpy).

Golden Corn Bread

2. Spread batter evenly in prepared pan. Bake until golden and toothpick inserted in center comes out clean, 20 to 25 minutes. Cut corn bread into 9 squares; serve warm. Makes 9 servings.

Each serving: About 178 calories, 4g protein, 25g carbohydrate, 7g total fat (4g saturated), 40mg cholesterol, 425mg sodium.

Corn Muffins

Grease twelve 2½" by 1¼" muffin-pan cups. Prepare as directed but use **1 cup milk.** Spoon batter into prepared muffin-pan cups, filling each two-thirds full. Bake until golden and toothpick inserted in center of muffin comes out clean, about 20 minutes. Immediately remove muffins from pans. Serve warm, or cool on wire rack to serve later. Makes 12 muffins.

Each muffin: About 144 calories, 3g protein, 19g carbohydrate, 6g total fat (3g saturated), 31mg cholesterol, 322mg sodium.

Corn Sticks

Grease 14 corn-stick molds with vegetable oil. Heat molds in oven until hot, about 15 minutes. Meanwhile, prepare batter as directed. Remove molds from oven; spoon batter into molds. Bake until toothpick inserted in center of corn stick comes out clean, 15 to 20 minutes. Cool in molds on wire rack 10 minutes. Remove corn sticks from molds; serve warm. Makes 14 corn sticks.

Each corn stick: About 121 calories, 2g protein, 16g carbohydrate, 5g total fat (3g saturated), 26mg cholesterol, 273mg sodium.

Southern Corn Bread

For a golden brown crust, bake this unsweetened corn bread in a cast-iron skillet. Eat it warm!

Prep: 10 minutes   Bake: 25 minutes

4	tablespoons butter or margarine
1½	cups cornmeal
1	cup all-purpose flour
2	teaspoons baking powder
1	teaspoon salt
¼	teaspoon baking soda
1¾	cups buttermilk
2	large eggs

1. Preheat oven to 450°F. Place butter in 10-inch cast-iron skillet or 9-inch square baking pan; place in oven just until butter melts, 3 to 5 minutes. Tilt skillet to coat evenly.

2. Meanwhile, in large bowl, combine cornmeal, flour, baking powder, salt, and baking soda. In medium bowl, with fork, beat buttermilk and eggs until blended. Add melted butter to buttermilk mixture, then add to flour mixture. Stir just until flour is moistened (batter will be lumpy).

3. Pour batter into prepared skillet. Bake until golden at edges and toothpick inserted in center comes out clean, about 25 minutes. Serve warm. Makes 8 servings.

Each serving: About 243 calories, 7g protein, 35g carbohydrate, 8g total fat (4g saturated), 71mg cholesterol, 584mg sodium.

Cranberry-Orange Bread

Bake this tasty bread a day ahead to allow the flavors to develop.

Prep: 20 minutes	Bake: 55 minutes
1	large orange
2½	cups all-purpose flour
1	cup sugar
2	teaspoons baking powder
½	teaspoon baking soda
½	teaspoon salt
4	tablespoons butter or margarine, melted
2	large eggs
2	cups cranberries, coarsely chopped
¾	cup walnuts, chopped (optional)

1. Preheat oven to 375°F. Grease 9" by 5" metal loaf pan. From orange, grate 1 teaspoon peel and squeeze ½ cup juice.

2. In large bowl, combine flour, sugar, baking powder, baking soda, and salt. In small bowl, beat orange peel and juice, melted butter, and eggs until blended. With wooden spoon, stir egg mixture into flour mixture just until blended (batter will be stiff). Stir in cranberries and walnuts, if using.

3. Pour batter into prepared pan. Bake until toothpick inserted in center comes out clean, 55 to 60 minutes. Cool loaf in pan on wire rack 10 minutes; remove from pan and cool completely on wire rack. Makes 1 loaf, 12 slices.

Each slice without walnuts: About 223 calories, 4g protein, 40g carbohydrate, 5g total fat (3g saturated), 46mg cholesterol, 281mg sodium.

Blueberry-Lemon Tea Bread

A luscious bread packed with berries and dressed up with a tangy lemon glaze.

Prep: 25 minutes	Bake: 1 hour
2	cups all-purpose flour
1	teaspoon baking powder
½	teaspoon baking soda
½	teaspoon salt
½	cup butter or margarine (1 stick), softened
1⅓	cups sugar
2	large eggs
½	cup sour cream
1½	cups blueberries
¼	cup fresh lemon juice (2 lemons)

1. Preheat oven to 350°F. Grease and flour 8½" by 4½" metal loaf pan. In medium bowl, combine flour, baking powder, baking soda, and salt. In large bowl, with mixer at low speed, beat butter and 1 cup sugar just until blended. Increase speed to medium; beat until light and fluffy, about 5 minutes. Reduce speed to low; add eggs, one at a time, beating well after each addition, occasionally scraping bowl with rubber spatula.

2. Alternately add flour mixture and sour cream to egg mixture, beginning and ending with flour mixture, mixing just until blended. Gently stir in blueberries.

3. Pour batter into prepared pan. Bake until toothpick inserted in center comes out clean, about 1 hour. Cool loaf in pan on wire rack 10 minutes; remove from pan and place on rack. Place waxed paper under wire rack.

4. With cake tester or skewer, prick top and sides of warm loaf all over. Prepare lemon glaze: In small bowl, stir lemon juice and remaining ⅓ cup sugar. With pastry brush, brush top and sides of warm loaf with lemon glaze. Cool completely on rack. Makes 1 loaf, 12 slices.

Each slice: About 279 calories, 4g protein, 42g carbohydrate, 11g total fat (6g saturated), 60mg cholesterol, 285mg sodium.

Banana Bread

For the best flavor, wait until your bananas are completely ripe and covered with brown spots, but not blackened and soft.

Prep: 20 minutes   Bake: 1 hour 10 minutes

2½	cups all-purpose flour
2	teaspoons baking powder
¾	teaspoon salt
½	teaspoon baking soda
1½	cups mashed very ripe bananas (3 medium)
¼	cup milk
2	teaspoons vanilla extract
½	cup butter or margarine (1 stick), softened
1	cup sugar
2	large eggs

1. Preheat oven to 350°F. Evenly grease 9" by 5" metal loaf pan. In medium bowl, combine flour, baking powder, salt, and baking soda. In small bowl, combine bananas, milk, and vanilla.

2. In large bowl, with mixer at medium speed, beat butter and sugar until light and fluffy. Beat in eggs, one at a time. Reduce speed to low; alternately add flour mixture and banana mixture, beginning and ending with flour mixture, occasionally scraping bowl with rubber spatula. Beat just until blended.

3. Pour batter into prepared pan. Bake until toothpick inserted in center comes out clean, about 1 hour 10 minutes. Cool in pan on wire rack 10 minutes; remove from pan and cool completely on wire rack. Makes 1 loaf, 16 slices.

Each slice: About 206 calories, 3g protein, 33g carbohydrate, 7g total fat (4g saturated), 43mg cholesterol, 278mg sodium.

Banana-Nut Bread

Prepare bread as directed but fold **1 cup walnuts or pecans, (4 ounces)** coarsely chopped, into batter before baking.

Lowfat Banana Bread

For a whole-grain variation, substitute one-half cup whole-wheat flour for the same amount of all-purpose flour.

Prep: 20 minutes   Bake: 40 minutes

1¾	cups all-purpose flour
½	cup sugar
1	teaspoon baking powder
½	teaspoon baking soda
½	teaspoon salt
1	cup mashed very ripe bananas (2 medium)
⅓	cup fruit-based substitute for fat or unsweetened applesauce
2	large egg whites
1	large egg
¼	cup pecans, chopped

1. Preheat oven to 350°F. Grease 9" by 5" metal loaf pan. In large bowl, combine flour, sugar, baking powder, baking soda, and salt. In medium bowl, with fork, mix bananas, fat substitute, egg whites, and egg until well blended. Stir banana mixture into flour mixture just until flour mixture is moistened.

2. Pour batter into prepared pan; sprinkle with chopped pecans. Bake until toothpick inserted in center comes out almost clean, 40 to 45 minutes. Cool in pan on wire rack 10 minutes; remove from pan and cool completely on wire rack. Makes 1 loaf, 16 slices.

Each slice: About 119 calories, 3g protein, 23g carbohydrate, 2g total fat (0g saturated), 13mg cholesterol, 155mg sodium.

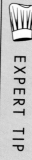

If you make muffins often, buy an ice-cream scoop. An ice-cream scoop makes filling muffin-pan cups a breeze by making it easy to scoop an equal amount of batter into each cup, which gives muffins a nice uniformity. Ice-cream scoops can be found in cookware shops, grocery stores, and restaurant supply stores. They are available in various sizes: small, medium, and large.

MARION CUNNINGHAM
COOKBOOK AUTHOR

EXPERT TIP

Date-Nut Bread

Serve slices of this dense, moist, old-fashioned favorite plain or slathered with cream cheese.

| Prep: 20 minutes plus cooling | Bake: 1 hour 15 minutes |

1½	cups chopped pitted dates
6	tablespoons butter or margarine, cut into pieces
1¼	cups boiling water
2	cups all-purpose flour
¾	cup sugar
1	teaspoon baking powder
½	teaspoon baking soda
½	teaspoon salt
1	large egg, lightly beaten
1	cup walnuts (4 ounces), coarsely chopped

1. In medium bowl, combine dates, butter, and boiling water; let stand until cool.

2. Preheat oven to 325°F. Grease 9" by 5" metal loaf pan.

In large bowl, combine flour, sugar, baking powder, baking soda, and salt. Stir egg into cooled date mixture; stir into flour mixture just until flour is moistened. Stir in walnuts.

3. Pour batter into prepared pan. Bake until toothpick inserted in center comes out clean, about 1 hour 15 minutes. Cool in pan on wire rack 10 minutes; remove from pan and cool completely on rack. Makes 1 loaf, 16 slices.

Each slice: About 232 calories, 3g protein, 35g carbohydrate, 10g total fat (3g saturated), 25mg cholesterol, 192mg sodium.

Zucchini Bread

Everyone loves zucchini bread—especially the baker. It delivers lots of flavor with very little effort.

| Prep: 20 minutes | Bake: 1 hour 10 minutes |

1½	cups all-purpose flour
¾	cup sugar
2¼	teaspoons baking powder
½	teaspoon ground cinnamon
½	teaspoon salt
⅓	cup vegetable oil
2	large eggs
1½	cups shredded zucchini (1 medium)
½	cup walnuts, chopped
½	teaspoon freshly grated orange peel

1. Preheat oven to 350°F. Grease 8½" by 4½" metal loaf pan. In large bowl, combine flour, sugar, baking powder, cinnamon and salt. In medium bowl, with fork, mix oil, eggs, zucchini, walnuts, and orange peel. Stir zucchini mixture into flour mixture just until flour is moistened.

2. Pour batter into prepared pan. Bake until toothpick inserted in center comes out clean, about 1 hour 10 minutes. Cool in pan on wire rack 10 minutes; remove from pan and cool completely on wire rack. Makes 1 loaf, 12 slices.

Each slice: About 209 calories, 4g protein, 26g carbohydrate, 10g total fat (1g saturated), 35mg cholesterol, 200mg sodium.

Date-Nut Bread

Traditional Irish Soda Bread

This bread is rich and tender, but it's even better when served warm with butter.

Prep: 15 minutes   Bake: 1 hour

4	cups all-purpose flour
¼	cup sugar
1	tablespoon baking powder
1½	teaspoons salt
1	teaspoon baking soda
6	tablespoons cold butter or margarine, cut into pieces
1½	cups buttermilk

1. Preheat oven to 350°F. Grease cookie sheet. In large bowl, combine flour, sugar, baking powder, salt, and baking soda. With pastry blender or two knives used scissor-fashion, cut in butter until mixture resembles coarse crumbs. Stir in buttermilk just until flour is moistened (dough will be sticky).

2. Turn dough onto well-floured surface; with lightly floured hands, knead 8 to 10 times to mix. (Do not overknead, or bread will be tough.) Shape into ball; place on prepared cookie sheet.

3. Dust dough lightly with all-purpose flour. With serrated knife or single-edge razor blade, in center, cut an X 4 inches long and about ¼ inch deep. Bake until toothpick inserted in center comes out clean, about 1 hour. Transfer loaf to wire rack to cool. Makes 1 loaf, 12 slices.

♥ Each slice: About 235 calories, 5g protein, 38g carbohydrate, 7g total fat (4g saturated), 17mg cholesterol, 609mg sodium.

Soda Bread with Currants and Caraway Seeds
Prepare as directed, stirring in **1½ cups dried currants** and **2 teaspoons caraway seeds** after adding buttermilk.

Classic Crumb Cake

The thick cinnamon-rich crumb topping on this coffee cake is irresistible—even better than from a bakery! Since our recipe yields two cakes, serve one fresh and freeze the other to enjoy later.

Prep: 40 minutes   Bake: 40 minutes

Crumb Topping

2	cups all-purpose flour
½	cup granulated sugar
½	cup packed brown sugar
1½	teaspoons ground cinnamon
1	cup butter or margarine (2 sticks), softened

Cake

2¼	cups all-purpose flour
2¼	teaspoons baking powder
½	teaspoon salt
½	cup butter or margarine (1 stick), softened
1¼	cups granulated sugar
3	large eggs
¾	cup milk
2	teaspoons vanilla extract

DUSTING PAN WITH FLOUR

Using a piece of folded paper towel or waxed paper, spread a thin layer of shortening inside the baking pan. Sprinkle about 1 tablespoon flour into the pan. Tilt to coat the bottom and side with the flour; invert the pan and tap out the excess flour.

1. Prepare crumb topping: In medium bowl, combine flour, granulated and brown sugars, and cinnamon until well blended. With fingertips, blend flour mixture and butter until mixture resembles coarse crumbs.

2. Prepare cakes: Preheat oven to 350°F. Grease and flour two 9-inch round cake pans. In medium bowl, combine flour, baking powder, and salt.

3. In large bowl, with mixer at low speed, beat butter and sugar until blended, frequently scraping bowl with rubber spatula. Increase speed to medium; beat until light and fluffy, about 2 minutes, occasionally scraping bowl. Reduce speed to low; add eggs, one at a time, beating well after each addition.

4. In cup, combine milk and vanilla. With mixer at low speed, alternately add flour mixture and milk mixture, beginning and ending with flour mixture, beating until smooth and occasionally scraping bowl.

5. Divide batter evenly between prepared pans. With hand, press crumb mixture to form ¾-inch chunks; sprinkle evenly over batter. Bake cakes until toothpick inserted in center comes out clean, 40 to 45 minutes. Cool in pans on wire  racks 15 minutes. With small metal spatula, loosen cakes from sides of pans. Invert cakes onto plates, then invert, crumb side up, onto wire racks to cool completely. Makes 2 crumb cakes, each 10 servings.

Each serving: About 330 calories, 4g protein, 44g carbohydrate, 16g total fat (9g saturated), 70mg cholesterol, 270mg sodium.

Fruit-Streusel Coffee Cake

This delectable coffee cake can be made with almost any seasonal fruit and it will be just as tempting.

Prep: 30 minutes   Bake: 50 minutes

Streusel Topping

¾	cup all-purpose flour
½	cup packed brown sugar
1	teaspoon ground cinnamon
4	tablespoons cold butter or margarine, cut into pieces

Cake

2¼	cups all-purpose flour
1½	teaspoons baking powder
½	teaspoon baking soda
½	teaspoon salt
¾	cup butter or margarine (1½ sticks), softened
1½	cups granulated sugar
3	large eggs
1	cup milk
1	teaspoon vanilla extract
1¼	pounds ripe pears, apples, or peaches, peeled and thinly sliced; or nectarines or plums, not peeled, thinly sliced (3 cups); or fresh or frozen rhubarb, cut into 1-inch pieces (4 cups); or 1 pint blueberries

1. Prepare topping: In medium bowl, combine flour, brown sugar, and cinnamon. With fingertips, blend flour mixture and butter until mixture resembles coarse crumbs.

2. Prepare cake: Preheat oven to 350°F. Grease and flour 13" by 9" baking pan. In medium bowl, combine flour, baking powder, baking soda, and salt.

3. In large bowl, with mixer at low speed, beat butter and sugar until blended, frequently scraping bowl with rubber spatula. Increase speed to high; beat until light and fluffy, about 2 minutes, occasionally scraping bowl. Reduce speed to low; add eggs, one at a time, beating well after each addition.

4. In cup, combine milk and vanilla. With mixer at low speed, alternately add flour mixture and milk mixture, beginning and ending with flour mixture, beating until smooth and occasionally scraping bowl.

5. Spread batter evenly in prepared pan. Arrange fruit slices on top, overlapping them slightly. Evenly sprinkle streusel topping over fruit.

6. Bake cake until toothpick inserted in center comes out clean, 50 to 55 minutes. Cool in pan on wire rack 10 minutes to serve warm, or cool completely in pan to serve later. Makes 15 servings.

Each serving: About 353 calories, 5g protein, 52g carbohydrate, 14g total fat (8g saturated), 78mg cholesterol, 317mg sodium.

Sour Cream Coffee Cake

Sour Cream Coffee Cake

A classic sour cream cake that has flavorful layers of streusel. It's even better the next day.

Prep: 30 minutes	*Bake: 1 hour 20 minutes*

²⁄₃	plus 1¾ cups sugar
²⁄₃	cup walnuts, finely chopped
1	teaspoon ground cinnamon
3¾	cups all-purpose flour
2	teaspoons baking powder
1	teaspoon baking soda
¾	teaspoon salt
½	cup butter or margarine (1 stick), softened
3	large eggs
2	teaspoons vanilla extract
1	container (16 ounces) sour cream

1. Preheat oven to 350°F. Grease and flour 9- to 10-inch tube pan with removable bottom. In small bowl, combine ²⁄₃ cup sugar, walnuts, and cinnamon. In medium bowl, combine flour, baking powder, baking soda, and salt.

2. In large bowl, with mixer at low speed, beat butter and remaining 1¾ cups sugar until blended, frequently scraping bowl with rubber spatula. Increase speed to high; beat until light and fluffy, about 2 minutes, occasionally scraping bowl. Reduce speed to low; add eggs, one at a time, beating well after each addition. Beat in vanilla.

3. With mixer at low speed, alternately add flour mixture and sour cream, beginning and ending with flour mixture, beating until smooth and occasionally scraping bowl.

4. Spoon one-third of batter into prepared pan. Sprinkle about ½ cup nut mixture evenly over batter, then top with one-third more batter. Sprinkle evenly with ½ cup more nut

mixture; top with remaining batter, then sprinkle with remaining nut mixture.

5. Bake coffee cake until toothpick inserted in center comes out clean, about 1 hour 20 minutes. Cool in pan on wire rack 10 minutes. Run thin

knife around cake to loosen from side and center tube of pan; lift tube to separate cake from pan side. Invert cake onto plate; slide knife under cake to separate from bottom of pan. Turn cake, nut-mixture side up, onto wire rack to cool completely. Makes 16 servings.

Each serving: About 388 calories, 6g protein, 55g carbohydrate, 17g total fat (8g saturated), 68mg cholesterol, 336mg sodium.

Easy Christmas Stollen

Ricotta cheese adds richness and moisture to this sweet bread.

Prep: 25 minutes   Bake: 1 hour

2¼	cups all-purpose flour
½	cup sugar
1½	teaspoons baking powder
¼	teaspoon salt
8	tablespoons butter or margarine (1 stick)
1	cup ricotta cheese
½	cup candied lemon peel
	or coarsely chopped red candied cherries
½	cup dark seedless raisins
⅓	cup slivered blanched almonds, toasted
1	teaspoon vanilla extract
½	teaspoon freshly grated lemon peel
1	large egg, lightly beaten
1	large egg yolk

1. Preheat oven to 325°F. Grease large cookie sheet. In large bowl, combine flour, sugar, baking powder, and salt. With pastry blender or two knives used scissor-fashion, cut in 6 tablespoons butter until mixture resembles fine crumbs. With spoon, stir in ricotta until mixture is moistened. Stir in candied lemon peel, raisins, almonds, vanilla, grated lemon peel, egg, and egg yolk until well mixed.

2. Turn dough onto lightly floured surface; gently knead dough 2 or 3 times to mix. With floured rolling pin, roll dough into 10" by 8" oval. Fold oval lengthwise almost in half, so that edges do not quite meet.

3. Place stollen on prepared cookie sheet. Bake until toothpick inserted in center comes out clean, about 1 hour. Transfer to wire rack. Melt remaining 2 tablespoons butter and brush over warm stollen. Cool completely. Makes 12 servings.

Each serving: About 298 calories, 7g protein, 38g carbohydrate, 14g total fat (7g saturated), 67mg cholesterol, 211mg sodium.

Pancakes

If your preference is for thinner pancakes, use a little more milk.

Prep: 15 minutes   Cook: 4 minutes per batch

1	cup all-purpose flour
2	tablespoons sugar
2½	teaspoons baking powder
½	teaspoon salt
1¼	cups milk
3	tablespoons butter or margarine, melted
1	large egg, lightly beaten
	vegetable oil for brushing pan

1. In bowl, combine flour, sugar, baking powder, and salt. Add milk, butter, and egg and stir until flour is moistened.

2. Heat griddle or 12-inch skillet over medium heat until drop of water sizzles; brush lightly with oil. Pour batter by scant ¼ cups onto hot griddle, making a few pancakes at a time. Cook until tops are bubbly, some bubbles burst, and

edges look dry. With wide spatula, turn and cook until underside is golden. Transfer to platter; keep warm.

3. Repeat with remaining batter, brushing griddle with more oil if necessary. Makes 3 servings.

Each serving: About 388 calories, 10g protein, 46g carbohydrate, 19g total fat (10g saturated), 116mg cholesterol, 981mg sodium.

Blueberry Pancakes

Prepare as directed but add **1 cup blueberries** to batter.

Buckwheat Pancakes

Prepare as directed but use ½ **cup all-purpose flour** and ½ **cup buckwheat flour.**

Banana Pancakes

Prepare as directed but add **1 very ripe medium banana,** mashed (about ½ cup), and ¼ **teaspoon baking soda;** use only ¾ **cup milk.**

Cornmeal Pancakes

Prepare as directed but add ¼ **cup cornmeal** to flour mixture.

Buttermilk Pancakes

A light and tender pancake with a mild tang. If you don't have buttermilk, use lowfat yogurt combined with milk; it will be just as good.

Prep: 15 minutes   Cook: 4 minutes per batch

1	cup all-purpose flour
2	tablespoons sugar
2	teaspoons baking powder
½	teaspoon baking soda
½	teaspoon salt
1¼	cups buttermilk, or 1 cup plain yogurt plus ¼ cup milk
3	tablespoons butter or margarine, melted
1	large egg, lightly beaten
	vegetable oil for brushing pan

1. In large bowl, combine flour, sugar, baking powder, baking soda, and salt. Add buttermilk, melted butter, and egg; stir just until flour is moistened.

2. Heat griddle or 12-inch skillet over medium heat until drop of water sizzles; brush lightly with oil. Pour batter by scant ¼ cups onto hot griddle, making a few pancakes at a time. Cook until tops are bubbly, some bubbles burst, and edges look dry. With wide spatula, turn and cook until underside is golden. Transfer to platter; keep warm.

Buttermilk Pancakes

3. Repeat with remaining batter, brushing griddle with more oil if necessary. Makes 3 servings.

Each serving: About 366 calories, 10g protein, 46g carbohydrate, 16g total fat (8g saturated), 106mg cholesterol, 1,167mg sodium.

Sour Cream Pancakes

Prepare as directed but substitute **1 container (8 ounces) sour cream** and ¼ **cup milk** for buttermilk.

Buttermilk Waffles

Crisp yet fluffy, these are worth getting out of bed for. Top with butter, syrup, or your favorite fresh fruit.

Prep: 15 minutes   Bake: 4 minutes per batch

1¾	cups all-purpose flour
1½	teaspoons baking powder
1	teaspoon baking soda
½	teaspoon salt
2	cups buttermilk
4	tablespoons butter or margarine, melted
2	large eggs, lightly beaten

1. Preheat waffle baker as manufacturer directs. In large bowl, combine flour, baking powder, baking soda, and salt. Add buttermilk, melted butter, and eggs; whisk until smooth.

2. When waffle baker is ready, pour batter into center until it spreads to within 1 inch of edges. Cover and bake as manufacturer directs; do not lift cover during baking.

3. When waffle is done, lift cover and loosen waffle with fork. Serve immediately with butter and maple syrup, or keep warm in oven (place waffle directly on oven rack to keep crisp). Reheat waffle baker before pouring in more batter. If batter becomes too thick upon standing, thin with a little more buttermilk. Makes eleven 4" by 4" waffles or 4 servings.

Each serving: About 388 calories, 13g protein, 48g carbohydrate, 16g total fat (9g saturated), 142mg cholesterol, 1,065mg sodium.

Pecan Waffles

Prepare as directed but add **1 tablespoon sugar** and **1 cup pecans (4 ounces),** chopped, to batter. Stir batter for each waffle before pouring.

Sweet Milk Waffles

Prepare as directed but omit baking soda; use **1 tablespoon baking powder.** Substitute **2 cups milk** for buttermilk.

Yeast Waffles

Waffles leavened with yeast are especially light and crisp. Start the batter the night before.

Prep: 15 minutes plus overnight to refrigerate
Bake: 4 minutes per batch

2	cups milk
4	tablespoons butter or margarine, cut into pieces
½	cup warm water (105° to 115°F)
1	package active dry yeast
1	teaspoon granulated sugar
2	cups all-purpose flour
2	tablespoons brown sugar
¾	teaspoon salt
2	large eggs, lightly beaten
¼	teaspoon baking soda

1. In 2-quart saucepan, combine milk and butter; heat over medium heat until butter melts. Remove from heat and cool to lukewarm.

2. Meanwhile, in large bowl, combine warm water, yeast, and granulated sugar; stir to dissolve. Let stand until foamy, about 5 minutes.

3. Add milk mixture, flour, brown sugar, and salt to yeast mixture; with wire whisk, beat until smooth. Cover with plastic wrap and refrigerate overnight.

4. Preheat waffle baker as manufacturer directs. Whisk eggs and baking soda into waffle batter.

5. When waffle baker is ready, pour batter into center until it spreads to within 1 inch of edges. Cover and bake as manufacturer directs; do not lift cover during baking.

6. When waffle is done, lift cover and loosen waffle with fork. Serve immediately with butter and maple syrup, or keep warm in oven (place waffle directly on oven rack to keep crisp). Reheat waffle baker before pouring in more batter. Makes eight 7-inch round waffles.

Each waffle: About 238 calories, 7g protein, 31g carbohydrate, 9g total fat (5g saturated), 77mg cholesterol, 363mg sodium.

16

YEAST BREADS

There's something magical about mixing flour and yeast with liquid and witnessing the transformation of the ingredients into a crusty, chewy loaf. Whether you enjoy the time-honored ritual of hands-on kneading or prefer using a bread machine, it's always satisfying to make bread at home. In this chapter, you'll find coffee cakes for breakfast or brunch, firm-slicing loaves for sandwiches or toast, flatbreads and rolls for serving alongside main courses, and pizzas that will make a meal. We have also included some easy batter breads: doughs that don't require kneading, just a vigorous bout of stirring.

TYPES OF YEAST

Yeast is the organism that makes bread rise. It reacts with the natural sugars in flour to create carbon dioxide gas, which is trapped in the dough and forces it to expand. If the yeast is too old (check the date on the package) or mixed with too hot (or too cold) water, the dough won't rise.

Dry yeast is the most convenient form of baker's yeast. It comes in ¼-ounce packages (three to a strip), jars, and in bulk. One ¼-ounce package of dry yeast equals 2¼ teaspoons of fresh yeast.

Overnight Sticky Buns

Fresh yeast, available in foil-wrapped 1-ounce cakes, is moist, crumbly, and tan-gray. It is very perishable; refrigerate and use within two weeks. To substitute fresh yeast for dry, use 1 teaspoon crumbled fresh yeast for each ½ teaspoon dry yeast. Yeast becomes activated when mixed with warm water (105° to 115°F). A small amount of sugar is often added to the water to encourage the formation of carbon dioxide. To check the water temperature, it is best to use an instant-read thermometer. Let the water-yeast mixture stand for about five minutes; it should look foamy or creamy, which indicates that the yeast is alive (active). If it doesn't, start over with fresh yeast.

Quick-rise yeast, a type of dry yeast, cuts the rising time of traditional yeast doughs by about 50 percent. This yeast requires very hot tap water (120° to 130°F) to be activated. When substituting quick-rise yeast for dry, follow the directions on the package.

Store yeast in the refrigerator. It is important to use it by the expiration date on the package, because the yeast quickly loses its potency after that date. You can also store yeast in the freezer, but freezing will not prolong its life.

KNOW YOUR FLOURS

A variety of flours can be used for bread making. Different flours contain varying amounts of gluten, which gives dough its strength and elasticity. Wheat flours milled from hard winter wheat are high in gluten and great for bread making. Soft-wheat flours, such as cake and pastry flours, are low in gluten and best for cakes and cookies.

Bread flour is made entirely from hard wheat, without chemicals and preservatives, and makes delicious, chewy, crusty loaves. *All-purpose flour* is a blend of hard and soft wheats and yields a more tender bread. All-purpose flour is available unbleached and bleached. Bleaching prolongs its shelf life and somewhat reduces the gluten content. You can use either bread or unbleached all-purpose flour, but since they absorb liquid at different rates, you will need more all-purpose flour when making a dough. *Whole-wheat flour* (which is milled from the whole grain and contains both the oil-rich bran and germ) and *rye flour* (which has very little gluten) are usually combined with bread or all-purpose flour. Cornmeal, oats, wheat germ, and stone-ground flours are also sometimes added to lend a nutty taste or coarse texture.

Store all-purpose and bread flours in airtight containers in a cool dry place for up to six months. Whole-grain flours spoil easily; they should be used within three months. For longer storage, keep flour in the freezer, but allow it to stand at room temperature for an hour before using for bread.

MIXING THE DOUGH

When mixing bread dough, use a large bowl and a sturdy wooden spoon. A thick pottery, glass, or ceramic bowl works best; these materials retain warmth better than metal. If you prefer, use a heavy-duty electric mixer to mix dough. Use the paddle to mix the ingredients into a soft dough, then switch to the dough hook to do the kneading.

Flour and yeast are the two basic ingredients in traditional bread making, but other ingredients are usually added as well. Salt slows the rising and enhances the flavor of bread. Fat (in the form of butter, margarine, oil, or eggs) adds richness, moistness, and softness to the crumb; breads that contain fat stay fresh longer. Fat also inhibits yeast growth, which is why rich doughs take longer to rise. Milk gives bread a tender, sweet crumb; buttermilk adds a slightly sour note. Sugar promotes tenderness and a golden crust.

Because yeast works best in a moderately warm environment, have all the ingredients at room temperature before you begin. The amount of flour needed to make the dough will vary according to the type of flour and the amount of humidity in the air (on a humid day, a dough will require more flour). Always use only enough flour to make a stiff dough that leaves the side of the bowl.

KNEADING THE DOUGH

Strong, steady kneading by hand or machine activates the gluten in flour, which strengthens the dough so it won't collapse when the yeast multiplies and gives off carbon dioxide gas. Knead in just enough flour to prevent the dough from sticking to the work surface (too much flour makes a dry, heavy loaf). Doughs that are sweet and rich or contain whole-grain flours should be somewhat sticky. If kneading in a heavy-duty mixer, take care not to overknead the dough; six to eight minutes is usually sufficient.

Place the dough on a lightly floured surface. To knead, fold about one-fourth of the dough onto the top of the dough mass, then push it down and away from you with the heel of

your hand. Give the dough a quarter turn.

Repeat until the dough is smooth and elastic and tiny blisters appear on the surface; this will usually take from eight to ten minutes.

RISING AND SHAPING THE DOUGH

Choose a bowl large enough to allow the dough to rise until double in volume without rising over the top of the bowl. Grease the bowl lightly but thoroughly with softened butter, margarine, or vegetable shortening. Gather the dough into a ball and place in the bowl; turn the dough to coat the top. Cover the bowl with plastic wrap to keep the surface of the dough moist and to prevent a crust from forming. Place the bowl in a warm, draft-free area, such as near a turned-on stove or water heater or in a warm closet.

If you wish, the dough can rise in the refrigerator for up to twelve hours. The cold temperature will slow the growth of the yeast, and the long rising period will improve the flavor of the bread. Before shaping the bread, remove the dough from the refrigerator and let it stand at room temperature for about two hours, or until it loses its chill.

The dough should rise until doubled. To test, press two fingers about ½ inch deep into the center of the dough. If the indentation stays, the dough has risen sufficiently.

To punch the dough down, gently push your fist into the center to deflate the dough (this distributes the carbon dioxide and makes a fine-textured bread). Batter breads are simply stirred down.

The bread is now ready to be shaped. If you have the time, place the dough on a lightly floured work surface, cover with plastic wrap, and let rest for fifteen minutes to relax the gluten, which makes the dough easier to work with. If indicated, cut the dough in half with a sharp knife.

For loaf breads, grease the pans. For round breads, lightly grease the cookie sheet or sprinkle with cornmeal as directed. Loosely cover the breads with plastic wrap and let stand in a warm place until doubled in volume. The finger test also works here, but if using loaf pans, don't let the loaves rise above the rims of the pans.

BAKING THE BREAD

Position a rack in the center of the oven and preheat for at least ten minutes. If baking two loaves at once, allow at least two inches between the pans. Some bakers use a baking stone, which promotes even browning and a crisp crust (although we get excellent results without a stone). If you have one, place it in the oven to preheat for at least twenty minutes.

Most loaves are slashed with a serrated knife or single-edge razor blade just before baking. This allows the carbon dioxide to escape, preventing the bread from bursting during baking. The tops of loaves are often brushed with beaten whole egg, yolk, or white, which is sometimes mixed with a little liquid. A whole-egg glaze makes the crust golden, yolk produces a dark brown crust, and egg white makes a shiny crust. For a crisp, chewy crust, the loaves are either sprayed with water from a mister, or steam is created by placing a metal pan containing ice cubes in the oven during baking.

Bread is done when it pulls away from the sides of the pan and is nicely browned. If tapped on the bottom with your knuckles (if necessary, remove the bread from the pans, protecting your hands with kitchen towels), the bread will sound hollow. The sides of the loaf should feel crisp and firm.

COOLING AND STORING

For the best texture and flavor, bread should be cooled completely before slicing. Remove the bread from the pan and place, right side up, on a wire cooling rack; cool completely, away from drafts, which can cause shrinkage. (If you *must* have warm bread, let it rest for at least twenty minutes before slicing; hot rolls, however, can be served immediately.)

Be sure bread is completely cool before wrapping or freezing. If it is still warm, condensation could form on the inside of the wrapper and hasten spoilage. Store breads tightly wrapped. Soft breads stay freshest in plastic bags, whereas crusty breads stay crispest in paper bags. Always store breads at room temperature. If stored in the refrigerator, they'll turn stale more quickly. Most breads will keep for three to five days.

To freshen a stale loaf, heat it in a 350°F oven for five to seven minutes. Use stale bread to make bread pudding, toast, croutons, or bread crumbs.

Most breads freeze well for up to three months. Cool completely, then place in a heavy-duty ziptight plastic bag and press out the air or tightly wrap in heavy-duty foil. To thaw, let stand at room temperature for about one hour, or wrap the frozen bread in foil (with an opening at the top so steam can escape) and heat in a 300°F oven for about twenty minutes.

White Bread

The all-American bread—beautiful tall loaves for sandwiches and toast or for serving with meals.

Prep: 25 minutes plus rising   Bake: 30 minutes
½   cup warm water (105° to 115°F)
2   packages active dry yeast
1   teaspoon plus ¼ cup sugar
2¼ cups milk, heated to warm (105° to 115°F)
4   tablespoons butter or margarine, softened
1   tablespoon salt
about 7½ cups all-purpose or bread flour

1. In large bowl, combine warm water, yeast, and 1 teaspoon sugar; stir to dissolve. Let stand until foamy, about 5 minutes. Add milk, butter, remaining ¼ cup sugar, salt, and 4 cups flour. Beat well with wooden spoon. Gradually stir in 3 cups flour to make soft dough.

2. Turn dough onto floured surface and knead until smooth and elastic, about 8 minutes, working in enough of remaining ½ cup flour just to keep dough from sticking.

3. Shape dough into ball; place in greased large bowl, turning dough to grease top. Cover bowl with greased plastic wrap and let rise in warm place (80° to 85°F) until doubled in volume, about 1 hour.

4. Grease two 9" by 5" metal loaf pans. Punch down dough. Turn dough onto lightly floured surface and cut in half. Shape each half into rectangle about 12" by 7". Roll up from a short side. Pinch seam and ends to seal. Place dough, seam side down, in prepared pans. Cover pans loosely with greased plastic wrap and let rise in warm place until almost doubled, about 1 hour.

5. Meanwhile, preheat oven to 400°F. Bake until browned and loaves sound hollow when lightly tapped on bottom, 30 to 35 minutes. Remove loaves from pans; cool on wire racks. Makes 2 loaves, 12 slices each.

♥ Each slice: About 187 calories, 5g protein, 34g carbohydrate, 3g total fat (2g saturated), 8mg cholesterol, 323mg sodium.

Cinnamon-Raisin Bread

Prepare as directed but stir **2 cups dark seedless raisins** into yeast mixture with milk. Spread each rectangle with **2 tablespoons butter or margarine,** softened, leaving ½-inch border. In small cup, combine ⅓ **cup firmly packed brown sugar** and **1 tablespoon ground cinnamon;** sprinkle over butter. Roll up each loaf from a short side. Pinch seam and ends to seal. Makes 2 loaves, 12 slices each.

♥ Each slice: About 244 calories, 5g protein, 47g carbohydrate, 4g total fat (2g saturated), 11mg cholesterol, 335mg sodium.

Buttermilk Bread

Buttermilk gives these loaves a delicious sour note.

Prep: 20 minutes plus rising   Bake: 25 minutes
¼   cup warm water (105° to 115°F)
1   package active dry yeast
1   teaspoon plus ¼ cup sugar
1½ cups buttermilk
8   tablespoons butter or margarine (1 stick)
2   teaspoons salt
about 4¾ cups all-purpose flour or bread flour

1. In large bowl, combine warm water, yeast, and 1 teaspoon sugar; stir to dissolve. Let mixture stand until foamy, about 5 minutes.

2. Meanwhile, in 1-quart saucepan, combine buttermilk, 6 tablespoons butter, and remaining ¼ cup sugar; heat over medium-low heat until warm (105° to 115°F). Add buttermilk mixture, salt, and 4½ cups flour to yeast mixture; beat with wooden spoon until blended.

3. Turn dough onto lightly floured surface and knead until smooth and elastic, about 10 minutes, working in enough of remaining ¼ cup flour just to keep dough from sticking. Shape dough into ball; place in greased large bowl, turning dough to grease top. Cover bowl with plastic wrap and let rise in warm place (80° to 85°F) until doubled in volume, about 1 hour.

4. Punch down dough. Turn dough onto lightly floured surface and cut in half; cover and let rest 15 minutes. Grease two 8½" by 4½" metal loaf pans.

Buttermilk Bread

Olive-Rosemary Loaves

Kalamata olives and fresh rosemary give this peasant loaf robust flavor. Using high-gluten bread flour guarantees your baking success.

Prep: 30 minutes plus rising   Bake: 30 minutes

1½	cups warm water (105° to 115°F)
4	tablespoons extravirgin olive oil
2	packages active dry yeast
1	tablespoon sugar
1	cup Kalamata or green olives, pitted and chopped
2	tablespoons finely chopped fresh rosemary
2	teaspoons salt
	about 5 cups bread flour or 5¼ cups all-purpose flour

1. In large bowl, combine ½ cup warm water, 3 tablespoons oil, yeast, and sugar; stir to dissolve. Let stand until foamy, about 5 minutes. Stir in remaining 1 cup warm water, olives, rosemary, salt, and 4 cups flour until combined.

2. Turn dough onto lightly floured surface and knead until dough is smooth and elastic, about 8 minutes, working in enough of remaining 1¼ cups flour just to keep dough from sticking.

3. Shape dough into ball; place in greased large bowl, turning dough to grease top. Cover bowl and let dough rise in warm place (80° to 85°F) until doubled in volume, about 1 hour.

4. Punch down dough. Turn dough onto lightly floured surface and cut in half; cover and let rest 15 minutes for easier shaping. Grease large cookie sheet.

5. Shape each dough half into 7½" by 4" oval; place 3 inches apart on prepared cookie sheet. Cover and let rise in warm place until doubled, about 1 hour.

6. Meanwhile, preheat oven to 400°F. Brush tops of loaves with remaining 1 tablespoon oil. With serrated knife or single-edge razor blade, cut three diagonal slashes across top of each loaf. Bake until golden and loaves sound hollow when tapped on bottom, about 30 minutes. Cool on wire rack. Makes 2 loaves, 12 slices each.

💙 Each slice: About 148 calories, 4g protein, 23g carbohydrate, 4g total fat (1g saturated), 0mg cholesterol, 296mg sodium.

5. Shape each dough half into rectangle about 9" by 6". Roll up from a short side. Pinch seam and ends to seal. Place, seam side down, in prepared pans. Cover and let rise in warm place until doubled in volume, about 1 hour.

6. Meanwhile, preheat oven to 375°F. Melt remaining 2 tablespoons butter. Just before baking, with serrated knife, cut a lengthwise ¼-inch-deep slash in top of each loaf. Brush loaves with melted butter. Bake until golden and loaves sound hollow when lightly tapped on bottom, 25 to 30 minutes. Remove loaves from pans; cool on wire racks. Makes 2 loaves, 12 slices each.

Each slice: About 145 calories, 3g protein, 22g carbohydrate, 5g total fat (3g saturated), 11mg cholesterol, 250mg sodium.

Baguettes

Long, crisp French baguettes taste best the day they are made. Eat one and freeze the other to have in reserve.

Prep: 20 minutes plus rising	Bake: 30 minutes
2	cups warm water (105° to 115°F)
1	package active dry yeast
1	tablespoon sugar
1	tablespoon plus ¼ teaspoon salt
	about 5 cups all-purpose flour or bread flour
1	large egg white

1. In large bowl, combine warm water, yeast, and sugar; stir to dissolve. Let stand until foamy, about 5 minutes. Add 1 tablespoon salt and 3 cups flour. Beat well with wooden spoon until smooth. Gradually stir in 1½ cups flour to make soft dough.

2. Turn dough onto lightly floured surface; knead until smooth and elastic, 6 to 8 minutes, working in enough of remaining ½ cup flour just to keep dough from sticking.

3. Shape dough into ball; place in greased large bowl, turning dough to grease top. Cover bowl with greased plastic wrap and let rise in warm place (80° to 85° F) until doubled in volume, about 1½ hours.

4. Grease two large cookie sheets. Punch down dough. Turn dough onto lightly floured surface and cut in half. With rolling pin, roll each dough half into 18" by 7" rectangle. From a long side, with hands, roll up tightly, rolling dough back and forth to taper ends. Place each loaf on diagonal on one prepared cookie sheet. Cover loosely with greased plastic wrap and let rise in warm place until almost doubled, about 1 hour.

5. Meanwhile, preheat oven to 400°F. With serrated knife or single-edge razor blade, cut five ¼-inch-deep diagonal slashes in top of each loaf. In small cup, beat egg white and remaining ¼ teaspoon salt; brush over loaves. Bake until well browned, 30 to 35 minutes, rotating cookie sheets between upper and lower oven racks halfway through baking. Transfer loaves to wire racks to cool. Makes 2 loaves, 8 slices each.

♥ Each slice: About 156 calories, 5g protein, 32g carbohydrate, 1g total fat (0g saturated), 0mg cholesterol, 477mg sodium.

Potato Bread

Mashed potatoes and eggs make these loaves moist and delectable. They make perfect toast or French toast the next day.

Prep: 1 hour 30 minutes plus rising	Bake: 25 minutes
3	medium all-purpose potatoes (about 1 pound), peeled and cut into 1-inch chunks
1	cup warm water (105° to 115°F)
2	packages active dry yeast
2	tablespoons sugar
4¼	teaspoons salt
4	tablespoons butter or margarine, softened
	about 9¾ cups all-purpose flour or 8¾ cups bread flour
2	large eggs

1. In 2-quart saucepan, combine potatoes and *4 cups water;* heat to boiling over high heat. Reduce heat; cover and simmer until potatoes are tender, about 15 minutes. Drain, reserving 1 cup potato water. Return potatoes to saucepan; mash until smooth.

2. In large bowl, combine warm water, yeast, and 1 tablespoon sugar; stir to dissolve. Let stand until foamy, about 5 minutes. Stir in 4 teaspoons salt, remaining 1 tablespoon sugar, butter, reserved potato water, and 3 cups flour.

3. With mixer at low speed, beat just until blended. Increase speed to medium; beat 2 minutes, occasionally scraping bowl with rubber spatula. Separate 1 egg. Cover egg white and reserve in refrigerator. Beat in remaining egg, egg yolk, and 1 cup flour to make a thick batter; continue beating 2 minutes, frequently scraping bowl. With wooden spoon, stir in mashed potatoes, then 5 cups all-purpose flour or 4 cups bread flour, 1 cup at a time, to make soft dough. (You may want to transfer mixture to larger bowl for easier mixing.)

4. Turn dough onto well-floured surface and knead until smooth and elastic, about 10 minutes, working in enough of remaining ¾ cup flour just to keep dough from sticking.

5. Shape dough into ball; place in greased large bowl, turning dough to grease top. Cover bowl with plastic wrap and let rise in warm place (80° to 85°F) until doubled in volume, about 1 hour.

6. Grease two 9" by 5" metal loaf pans. Punch down dough. Turn dough onto lightly floured surface and cut in half. Shape each dough half into rectangle about 12" by 7". Roll up from a short side. Pinch seam and ends to seal. Place, seam side down, in prepared pans. Cover pans and let rise in warm place until doubled, about 40 minutes, or refrigerate up to overnight.

7. Meanwhile, preheat oven to 400°F. (If dough has been refrigerated, remove plastic wrap and let stand 10 minutes before baking.) Beat reserved egg white with remaining ¼ teaspoon salt; brush over loaves. Bake until golden and loaves sound hollow when lightly tapped on bottom, 25 to 30 minutes. Remove loaves from pans; cool on wire racks. Makes 2 loaves, 12 slices each.

♥ Each slice: About 231 calories, 6g protein, 43g carbohydrate, 3g total fat (1g saturated), 23mg cholesterol, 439mg sodium.

TROUBLESHOOTING

- *Dough overrises in bowl:* To fix (otherwise, loaf could collapse in the oven or be heavy-textured), turn the dough onto a lightly floured work surface and knead for two to three minutes. Cover, let rest fifteen minutes, then shape as directed.
- *Bread is too pale:* Place the loaf directly on the oven rack and bake for five to ten minutes longer.
- *Bread is dry and crumbly:* The dough contained too much flour or the dough overrose.
- *Bread collapses in oven:* The shaped dough overrose in the pan. Don't let dough rise above the pan's rim.
- *Cracks in bread:* The dough contained too much flour or the pan was not large enough.
- *Holes in bread:* The dough wasn't kneaded enough (it's almost impossible to overknead by hand), rising time was too long, or the dough rose in too warm a place.

Round Rye Bread

A bit of sweetness from molasses and a generous dose of caraway seeds makes this a special sandwich bread.

Prep: 30 minutes plus rising	Bake: 35 minutes
½	cup warm water (105° to 115°F)
2	packages active dry yeast
1	teaspoon sugar
1½	cups buttermilk, at room temperature
⅓	cup light (mild) molasses
⅓	cup plus 2 tablespoons butter or margarine, softened
2	tablespoons caraway seeds
1½	teaspoons salt
2	cups rye flour
	about 4 cups all-purpose flour or 3½ cups bread flour

1. In large bowl, combine warm water, yeast, and sugar; stir to dissolve. Let stand until foamy, about 5 minutes. With wooden spoon, stir in buttermilk, molasses, ⅓ cup butter, caraway seeds, salt, and rye flour until smooth. Stir in 3½ cups all-purpose flour or 3 cups bread flour, 1 cup at a time, until mixture forms dough that leaves side of bowl.

2. Turn dough onto lightly floured surface and knead until smooth and elastic, about 8 minutes, working in enough of remaining ½ cup flour just to keep dough from sticking.

3. Shape dough into ball; place in greased large bowl, turning dough to grease top. Cover bowl with plastic wrap and let rise in warm place (80° to 85°F) until doubled in volume, about 1 hour.

4. Punch down dough. Turn dough onto lightly floured surface and cut in half; cover and let rest 15 minutes for easier shaping. Grease large cookie sheet.

5. Shape each dough half into 6-inch ball: Using the sides of your hands, tuck sides of dough under to meet in center. Rotate dough and repeat to form taut ball. Place on prepared cookie sheet and flatten slightly. Cover and let rise in warm place until doubled, about 1 hour.

6. Meanwhile, preheat oven to 350°F. Melt remaining 2 tablespoons butter; brush over loaves. Bake until loaves sound hollow when lightly tapped on bottom, 35 to 40 minutes. Transfer to wire racks to cool. Makes 2 loaves, 16 slices each.

♥ Each slice: About 122 calories, 3g protein, 21g carbohydrate, 3g total fat (2g saturated), 8mg cholesterol, 150mg sodium.

Whole Wheat–Oatmeal Bread

This recipe makes two slightly flat breads with a sweet flavor and dense texture.

Prep: 42 minutes plus rising   Bake: 35 minutes

2	cups warm water (105° to 115°F)
2	packages active dry yeast
½	teaspoon sugar
½	cup honey
4	tablespoons butter or margarine
1	cup quick-cooking or old-fashioned oats, uncooked
1	tablespoon salt
4	cups whole-wheat flour
1	large egg
	about 2½ cups all-purpose flour or 2 cups bread flour

1. In large bowl, combine ½ cup warm water, yeast, and sugar; stir to dissolve. Let stand until foamy, about 5 minutes. Stir in remaining 1½ cups warm water, honey, butter, oats, salt, and 2 cups whole-wheat flour until smooth. Stir in egg. Gradually stir in remaining 2 cups whole-wheat flour, then 2 cups all-purpose flour or 1½ cups bread flour.

2. Turn dough onto lightly floured surface and knead until smooth but slightly sticky, about 7 minutes, working in enough of remaining ½ cup flour just to keep dough from sticking.

3. Shape dough into ball; place in greased large bowl, turning dough to grease top. Cover bowl with plastic wrap and let rise in warm place (80° to 85°F) until doubled in volume, about 1 hour.

4. Punch down dough. Turn dough onto lightly floured surface and cut in half; cover and let rest 15 minutes. Grease large cookie sheet.

5. Shape each dough half into 7" by 4" oval; place on prepared cookie sheet. Cover and let rise in warm place until doubled, about 1 hour.

6. Meanwhile, preheat oven to 350°F. With serrated knife or single-edge razor blade, cut three to five ¼-inch-deep crisscross slashes across top of each loaf. Lightly dust tops of loaves with all-purpose flour. Bake until loaves sound hollow when lightly tapped on bottom, 35 to 40 minutes. Transfer to wire racks to cool. Makes 2 oval loaves, 12 slices each.

♥ Each slice: About 177 calories, 5g protein, 33g carbohydrate, 3g total fat (1g saturated), 14mg cholesterol, 315mg sodium.

Honey-Wheat Bread

Honey accentuates the sweetness of whole-wheat flour. These loaves emerge crusty from the oven but soften a bit when cool.

Prep: 25 minutes plus rising   Bake: 40 minutes

1½	cups warm water (105° to 115°F)
2	packages active dry yeast
1	teaspoon sugar
½	cup honey
⅓	cup butter or margarine, softened
1	large egg
1½	teaspoons salt
3	cups whole-wheat flour
	about 3 cups all-purpose flour

1. In large bowl, combine ½ cup warm water, yeast, and sugar; stir to dissolve. Let stand until foamy, about 5 minutes. Stir in remaining 1 cup warm water, honey, butter, egg, salt, and whole-wheat flour until smooth. Gradually stir in 2½ cups all-purpose flour.

2. Turn dough onto lightly floured surface and knead until smooth and elastic, 7 to 10 minutes, working in enough of remaining ½ cup flour to make slightly sticky dough.

3. Shape dough into ball; place in greased large bowl, turning dough to grease top. Cover bowl with plastic wrap and let rise in warm place (80° to 85°F) until doubled in volume, about 1½ hours.

4. Punch down dough. Turn dough onto lightly floured surface and cut in half; cover and let rest 10 minutes. On two ungreased cookie sheets, shape each dough half into 6" by 4½" oval. Cover loosely with plastic wrap; let rise in warm place until doubled, about 30 minutes. With serrated knife or single-edge razor blade, cut three 3-inch-long and ¼-inch-deep diagonal slashes across tops of loaves.

5. Meanwhile, preheat oven to 375°F. Lightly dust loaves with all-purpose flour. Bake until loaves sound hollow when lightly tapped on bottom, about 40 minutes. Transfer loaves to wire racks to cool. Makes 2 loaves, 12 slices each.

♥ Each slice: About 161 calories, 4g protein, 30g carbohydrate, 3g total fat (2g saturated), 16mg cholesterol, 175mg sodium.

Whole Wheat–Walnut Bread

Serve this bread with a selection of cheeses. It's great with blue or goat cheese.

Prep: 25 minutes plus rising	Bake: 30 minutes

½	cup milk, heated to warm (105° to 115°F)
1	package active dry yeast
1	cup warm water (105° to 115°F)
3	tablespoons butter or margarine, softened
2	tablespoons molasses
1½	teaspoons salt
2	cups whole-wheat flour
	about 1½ cups all-purpose or bread flour
2	cups walnuts (8 ounces), toasted and coarsely chopped

1. In large bowl, combine warm milk and yeast; stir to dissolve. Let stand until foamy, about 5 minutes. Stir in warm water, butter, molasses, salt, whole-wheat flour, and ½ cup all-purpose flour. Stir in ¾ cup all-purpose flour. Knead mixture in bowl until dough holds together.

2. Turn dough onto lightly floured surface and knead until dough is smooth and elastic, 7 to 10 minutes, working in enough of remaining ¼ cup all-purpose flour just to keep dough from sticking.

3. Shape dough into ball; place in greased large bowl, turning dough to grease top. Cover bowl with plastic wrap and let rise in warm place (80° to 85°F) until doubled in volume, about 1 hour.

4. Punch down dough. Turn dough onto lightly floured surface and knead in walnuts. Cut dough in half; cover and let rest 10 minutes. Grease two large cookie sheets.

5. Shape each dough half into 7" by 4" oval; place on prepared cookie sheets. Cover loosely with plastic wrap; let rise in warm place until doubled, about 45 minutes. With sharp knife or single-edge razor blade, cut three 3-inch-long and ¼-inch-deep diagonal slashes across tops of loaves.

6. Meanwhile, preheat oven to 375°F. Lightly dust loaves with all-purpose flour. Bake until loaves sound hollow when lightly tapped on bottom, about 30 minutes. Transfer loaves to wire rack to cool. Makes 2 loaves, 12 slices each.

Each slice: About 155 calories, 4g protein, 17g carbohydrate, 9g total fat (2g saturated), 5mg cholesterol, 165mg sodium.

Whole Wheat–Walnut Bread

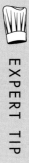

Try to resist adding extra flour if a bread dough seems soft. Although a soft dough is a little more difficult to handle, it usually makes a superior loaf.

NICK MALGIERI

DIRECTOR, BAKING PROGRAM, PETER KUMP'S NEW YORK COOKING SCHOOL

EXPERT TIP

Pumpernickel Bread

A medley of ingredients—molasses, chocolate, espresso powder, and prune juice—gives this loaf its distinctive dark color and complex flavor; dark rye flour makes it a hearty loaf.

Prep: 30 minutes plus rising   Bake: 40 minutes

¾	cup warm water (105° to 115°F)
2	packages active dry yeast
1	tablespoon brown sugar
2	teaspoons instant espresso-coffee powder
1	cup prune juice
⅓	cup light (mild) molasses
4	tablespoons butter or margarine, softened
1	square (1 ounce) unsweetened chocolate, melted
1	tablespoon caraway seeds
1	tablespoon salt
3	cups rye flour, preferably dark
½	cup whole-wheat flour
	about 2½ cups all-purpose flour
1	large egg white

1. In large bowl, combine ½ cup warm water, yeast, and brown sugar; stir to dissolve. Let mixture stand until foamy, about 5 minutes.

2. Meanwhile, in cup, dissolve espresso-coffee powder in remaining ¼ cup warm water. Stir into yeast mixture along with prune juice. Stir in molasses, butter, chocolate, caraway seeds, salt, and rye and whole-wheat flours until smooth. Gradually stir in 2 cups all-purpose flour. Knead mixture in bowl until dough holds together.

3. Turn dough onto lightly floured surface and knead until smooth and elastic, about 10 minutes, working in enough of remaining ½ cup all-purpose flour to make slightly sticky dough.

4. Shape dough into ball; place in greased large bowl, turning dough to grease top. Cover bowl with plastic wrap and let rise in warm place (80° to 85°F) until doubled in volume, about 1 hour.

5. Punch down dough. Turn dough onto floured surface; cut in half. Shape each dough half into ball: Using the sides of your hands, tuck sides of dough under to meet in center. Rotate dough and repeat to form taut balls. Grease two large cookie sheets. Place balls on prepared cookie sheets. Cover and let rise in warm place until doubled, about 1 hour.

6. Meanwhile, preheat oven to 350°F. With serrated knife or single-edge razor blade, cut three ¼-inch-deep slashes across top of each loaf. In small cup, beat egg white and *1 teaspoon water*; brush over loaves. Bake until loaves sound hollow when lightly tapped on bottom, about 40 minutes. Transfer to wire racks to cool. Makes 2 loaves, 12 slices each.

♥ Each slice: About 163 calories, 5g protein, 29g carbohydrate, 4g total fat (2g saturated), 5mg cholesterol, 316mg sodium.

Bread-Machine Multigrain Loaf

Bread machines have become the favorite appliance of many home bakers. To make this loaf, be sure to add the ingredients according to your machine's instructions. This recipe uses the setting for a one-and-one-half-pound whole-wheat loaf. Do not use the "delay" start mode; this dough contains buttermilk, which should not be left at room temperature for an extended period of time.

Prep: 10 minutes   Bake: per bread machine's instructions

2	cups whole-wheat flour
1	cup all-purpose flour
¼	cup bulgur wheat
¼	cup old-fashioned oats, uncooked
2	tablespoons toasted wheat germ
1½	teaspoons salt
1¼	cups buttermilk
¼	cup honey
3	tablespoons vegetable oil
1	package active dry yeast

Prepare recipe according to your bread machine's instructions. Makes 1 loaf, 16 slices.

♥ Each slice: About 143 calories, 4g protein, 25g carbohydrate, 3g total fat (0g saturated), 1mg cholesterol, 240mg sodium.

Quick-and-Easy Anadama Bread

We've streamlined this Early American cornmeal-molasses bread by turning it into a batter bread and using quick-rise yeast.

Prep: 25 minutes plus rising	*Bake: 30 minutes*
3	cups all-purpose flour
⅓	cup cornmeal
1	teaspoon salt
1	package quick-rise yeast
1	cup water
¼	cup light (mild) molasses
3	tablespoons butter or margarine, softened
1	large egg

1. In large bowl, combine 1 cup flour, cornmeal, salt, and yeast. In 1-quart saucepan, heat water and molasses over low heat until very warm (120° to 130°F). Meanwhile, grease 2-quart soufflé dish or deep casserole.

2. With mixer at low speed, gradually beat molasses mixture and butter into flour mixture just until blended. Increase speed to medium; beat 2 minutes, occasionally scraping bowl with rubber spatula. Beat in egg and 1 cup flour to make thick batter; continue beating 2 minutes, frequently scraping bowl. With wooden spoon, stir in remaining 1 cup flour to make soft dough.

3. Place dough in prepared soufflé dish; cover with plastic wrap and let rise in warm place (80° to 85°F) until doubled, about 1 hour.

4. Meanwhile, preheat oven to 375°F. Bake bread until browned and loaf sounds hollow when lightly tapped on bottom, 30 to 35 minutes. Remove loaf from soufflé dish; cool on wire rack. Makes 1 round loaf, 10 slices.

♥ Each slice: About 219 calories, 5g protein, 38g carbohydrate, 5g total fat (2g saturated), 31mg cholesterol, 279mg sodium.

Double-Cheese Batter Bread

Two kinds of sharp cheese contribute extra flavor to this batter bread. It makes terrific toast.

Prep: 25 minutes plus rising	*Bake: 35 minutes*
¾	cup warm water (105° to 115°F)
1	package active dry yeast
1	teaspoon plus 1 tablespoon sugar
6	ounces extrasharp Cheddar cheese, shredded (1½ cups)
¼	cup freshly grated Parmesan cheese
½	teaspoon salt
2½	cups all-purpose flour
2	large eggs

1. In large bowl, combine warm water, yeast, and 1 teaspoon sugar; stir to dissolve. Let stand until foamy, about 5 minutes. With wooden spoon or mixer at low speed, stir in Cheddar, Parmesan, remaining 1 tablespoon sugar, salt, and 1½ cups flour just until blended.

2. Separate 1 egg. Cover egg white and reserve in refrigerator. Beat remaining egg and remaining egg yolk into batter.

3. Stir batter vigorously or increase speed to medium and beat 3 minutes, frequently scraping bowl with rubber spatula. Stir in remaining 1 cup flour to make stiff batter that leaves side of bowl.

4. Cover bowl loosely with greased plastic wrap; let dough rise in warm place (80° to 85°F) until doubled in volume, about 1 hour.

5. Grease deep 1½-quart round casserole. Stir down batter; turn into prepared casserole. Cover loosely with greased plastic wrap; let rise in warm place until doubled in volume, about 45 minutes.

6. Meanwhile, preheat oven to 350°F. Beat reserved egg white; brush over top of loaf. Bake until loaf sounds hollow when tapped on bottom, about 35 minutes. Remove loaf from casserole and cool on wire rack. Makes 1 loaf, 12 slices.

Each slice: About 185 calories, 8g protein, 22g carbohydrate, 7g total fat (4g saturated), 52mg cholesterol, 234mg sodium.

Breadsticks

These breadsticks can be made well ahead. They keep perfectly for up to two weeks in an airtight container.

Prep: 40 minutes plus resting	Bake: 20 minutes per batch
2	packages quick-rise yeast
2½	teaspoons salt
	about 4¾ cups all-purpose flour
1⅓	cups very warm water (120° to 130°F)
½	cup olive oil
3	tablespoons caraway seeds, or sesame seeds, poppy seeds, or freshly grated Parmesan cheese

1. In large bowl, combine yeast, salt, and 2 cups flour. With wooden spoon, stir in very warm water; beat vigorously 1 minute. Stir in oil. Gradually stir in 2¼ cups flour. Stir in caraway seeds, if using.

2. Turn dough onto lightly floured surface and knead until smooth and elastic, about 8 minutes, working in enough of remaining ½ cup flour just to keep dough from sticking. Cover dough loosely with plastic wrap; let rest 10 minutes.

3. Preheat oven to 375°F. Grease two large cookie sheets. Cut dough in half. Cover one dough half; cut remaining dough half into 32 equal pieces. Shape each piece into 12-inch-long rope. Place ropes, 1 inch apart, on prepared cookie sheets. If not using caraway seeds, sprinkle with sesame seeds, poppy seeds, or Parmesan.

4. Bake breadsticks until golden and crisp, about 20 minutes, rotating cookie sheets between upper and lower oven racks halfway through baking. Transfer to wire racks to cool. Repeat with remaining dough. Makes 64 breadsticks.

Each breadstick: About 52 calories, 1g protein, 7g carbohydrate, 2g total fat (0g saturated), 0mg cholesterol, 91mg sodium.

Rosemary-Fennel Breadsticks

Prepare as directed but omit caraway, sesame, or poppy seeds or Parmesan. In Step 1, stir **2 teaspoons fennel seeds,** crushed, **1 teaspoon dried rosemary leaves,** crumbled, and **½ teaspoon coarsely ground black pepper** into dough. Proceed as directed.

Rosemary-Fennel Breadsticks

Quick Rolls

For an extra special touch, these easy rolls are sprinkled with sesame or poppy seeds before baking.

Prep: 30 minutes plus rising	Bake: 15 minutes
1	package quick-rise yeast
2	tablespoons sugar
1½	teaspoons salt
3¼	cups all-purpose flour or bread flour
1	cup very warm water (120° to 130°F)
3	tablespoons butter or margarine, softened
1	large egg
¼	cup sesame seeds or poppy seeds

1. In large bowl, combine yeast, sugar, salt, and 3 cups flour. With wooden spoon, gradually stir very warm water and butter into flour mixture to make soft dough.

2. Turn dough onto lightly floured surface; knead until smooth and elastic, about 5 minutes, working in enough of remaining ¼ cup flour just to keep dough from sticking. Shape into ball. Cover with plastic wrap and let rest 15 minutes. Grease large cookie sheet.

3. Cut dough into 12 equal pieces. On lightly floured surface, roll each piece of dough into ball. Place 2 inches apart on prepared cookie sheet. Cover and let rise in warm place (80° to 85°F) until doubled, about 30 minutes.

4. Meanwhile, preheat oven to 375°F. In small cup, beat egg and *1 teaspoon water;* brush over tops of rolls. Sprinkle with sesame seeds. Bake rolls until golden, 15 to 20 minutes. Serve rolls warm, or cool on wire racks to serve later. Makes 12 rolls.

♥ Each roll: About 184 calories, 5g protein, 29g carbohydrate, 5g total fat (2g saturated), 25mg cholesterol, 327mg sodium.

Refrigerator Rolls

Offer a basket of these soft, buttery rolls at your next holiday feast. (The dough can be made ahead and refrigerated overnight.)

Prep: 35 minutes plus rising   Bake: 15 minutes

1½	cups warm water (105° to 115°F)
2	packages active dry yeast
1	teaspoon plus ½ cup sugar
½	cup (1 stick) plus 2 tablespoons butter or margarine, softened
2	teaspoons salt
	about 6 cups all-purpose flour
1	large egg
	vegetable oil for brushing

1. In large bowl, combine ½ cup warm water, yeast, and 1 teaspoon sugar; stir to dissolve. Let stand until foamy, about 5 minutes. Stir in remaining 1 cup warm water, ½ cup butter, remaining ½ cup sugar, salt, and 2¼ cups flour. With wooden spoon or mixer at low speed, gradually beat in egg and ¾ cup flour; continue beating 2 minutes, scraping bowl frequently with rubber spatula. Stir in 2½ cups flour to make soft dough.

2. Turn dough onto lightly floured surface and knead until smooth and elastic, about 10 minutes, working in enough of remaining ½ cup flour just to keep dough from sticking to surface.

3. Shape dough into ball; place in greased large bowl, turning dough to grease top. Cover bowl with plastic wrap and let rise in warm place (80° to 85°F) until doubled in volume, about 1½ hours.

4. Punch down dough and turn; brush with oil. Cover bowl tightly with greased plastic wrap and refrigerate overnight or up to 24 hours. (Or, if you like, after punching down dough, shape into rolls as in Step 5. Cover and let rise until doubled, about 45 minutes, and bake as in Step 6.)

5. About 2½ hours before serving, remove dough from refrigerator. Grease 15½" by 10½" deep roasting pan. Cut dough into 30 equal pieces; shape into balls. Place balls in prepared pan; cover pan and let rise in warm place until doubled, about 1½ hours.

6. Meanwhile, preheat oven to 400°F. Bake until golden and rolls sound hollow when lightly tapped on bottom, 15 to 20 minutes. Melt remaining 2 tablespoons butter. With pastry brush, lightly brush melted butter over hot rolls. Serve warm. Makes 30 rolls.

Each roll: About 147 calories, 3g protein, 23g carbohydrate, 5g total fat (3g saturated), 17mg cholesterol, 197mg sodium.

Parker House Rolls

Prepare dough as directed in Steps 1 through 4. About 2½ hours before serving, melt **½ cup (1 stick) butter or margarine** in 17¼" by 11½" deep roasting pan. On lightly floured surface, with floured rolling pin, roll out dough ½ inch thick. With floured 2¾-inch round biscuit cutter, cut out as many rounds as possible. Knead trimmings together; reroll and cut out more rounds. Dip both sides of each dough round into melted butter; fold rounds in half and arrange in rows in prepared pan, letting rolls touch each other. Cover and let rise in warm place until doubled, about 1½ hours. Bake rolls 18 to 20 minutes. Serve warm, or cool on wire racks to serve later. Makes about 40 rolls.

Each roll: About 127 calories, 2g protein, 17g carbohydrate, 5g total fat (3g saturated), 18mg cholesterol, 165mg sodium.

Great Plains Oatmeal-Molasses Rolls

We've topped these light, tasty rolls with a butter-molasses glaze and oats for a beautiful presentation.

Prep: 1 hour plus rising   Bake: 45 minutes
1 cup boiling water
1 cup plus 2 tablespoons old-fashioned oats, uncooked
³⁄₄ cup warm water (105° to 115°F)
1 package active dry yeast
1 teaspoon sugar
5 tablespoons butter or margarine, softened
¹⁄₃ cup plus 2 teaspoons light (mild) molasses
1¹⁄₂ teaspoons salt
about 4¹⁄₄ cups all-purpose flour

1. In medium bowl, pour boiling water over 1 cup oats, stirring to combine. Let stand until oats have absorbed water and mixture has cooled to warm (105° to 115°F), 10 minutes.

2. Meanwhile, in small bowl, combine warm water, yeast, and sugar; stir to dissolve. Let mixture stand until foamy, about 5 minutes.

3. In large bowl, with mixer at low speed, beat 4 tablespoons butter until creamy. Add ¹⁄₃ cup molasses, beating until combined. Beat in oat mixture, yeast mixture, and salt just until blended. Gradually beat in 2 cups flour just until blended. With wooden spoon, stir in 2 more cups flour. Turn dough onto lightly floured surface and knead until smooth and elastic, about 5 minutes, working in enough of remaining ¹⁄₄ cup flour just to keep dough from sticking.

4. Shape dough into ball; place in greased large bowl, turning dough to grease top. Cover bowl with plastic wrap and let rise in warm place (80° to 85°F) until doubled in volume, about 1 hour. Grease 13" by 9" baking pan.

5. Punch down dough. On lightly floured surface, cut dough into 18 equal pieces. Shape each piece into ball and arrange in prepared pan in three rows of six balls each. Cover pan and let rise in warm place until doubled, about 1 hour.

6. Meanwhile, preheat oven to 350°F. Bake rolls until very lightly browned, about 30 minutes.

7. Melt remaining 1 tablespoon butter. Stir in remaining 2 teaspoons molasses.

8. After rolls have baked 30 minutes, remove from oven. Brush with molasses mixture and sprinkle with remaining 2 tablespoons oats. Bake rolls until golden, about 15 minutes longer. Serve warm, or cool on wire racks to serve later. Reheat if desired. Makes 18 rolls.

♥ Each roll: About 183 calories, 4g protein, 32g carbohydrate, 4g total fat (2g saturated), 9mg cholesterol, 230mg sodium.

Basic Pizza Dough

Try making this dough the night before to save some time; double the recipe and freeze half to have on hand for another meal. All-purpose flour makes a light crust, while bread flour gives it a chewy texture.

Prep: 40 minutes plus rising   Bake: 15 minutes
1¹⁄₄ cups warm water (105° to 115°F)
1 package active dry yeast
1 teaspoon sugar
2 tablespoons olive oil
2 teaspoons salt
about 4 cups all-purpose flour or 3¹⁄₂ cups bread flour
cornmeal for sprinkling

1. In large bowl, combine ¹⁄₄ cup warm water, yeast, and sugar; stir to dissolve. Let stand until foamy, about 5 minutes.

2. With wooden spoon, stir in remaining 1 cup warm water, oil, salt, and 1¹⁄₂ cups flour until smooth. Gradually add 2 cups all-purpose flour or 1¹⁄₂ cups bread flour, stirring until dough comes away from side of bowl.

3. Turn dough onto lightly floured surface and knead until smooth and elastic, about 10 minutes, working in enough of remaining ¹⁄₂ cup flour just to keep dough from sticking. Shape dough into ball; place in greased large bowl, turning dough to grease top. Cover bowl with plastic wrap and let rise in warm place (80° to 85°F) until doubled in volume, about 1 hour.

4. Punch down dough. Turn onto lightly floured surface and cut in half; cover and let rest 15 minutes. Or, if not using right away, place dough in greased large bowl, cover loosely with greased plastic wrap, and refrigerate up to 24 hours.

5. Sprinkle two large cookie sheets with cornmeal. Shape each dough half into ball. On one prepared cookie sheet, with floured rolling pin, roll one ball into 14" by 10" rectangle.

Fold edges in to form 1-inch rim. Repeat to make second pizza. Makes enough dough for 2 large pizzas, 4 main-dish servings each.

♥ Each ⅛ dough: About 262 calories, 7g protein, 49g carbohydrate, 4g total fat (1g saturated), 0mg cholesterol, 584mg sodium.

Quick Pizza Dough

In twenty-five minutes, this dough is ready to be turned into a fabulous pizza.

Prep: 25 minutes	Bake: 15 minutes
	about 2 cups all-purpose flour
1	package quick-rise yeast
¾	teaspoon salt
¾	cup very warm water (120° to 130°F)
	cornmeal for sprinkling

1. In large bowl, combine 2 cups flour, yeast, and salt. Stir in very warm water until blended and dough comes away from side of bowl. Turn onto lightly floured surface; knead until smooth and elastic, about 5 minutes.

2. Shape dough into one ball for one large rectangular pizza, two balls for two round 10-inch pizzas, or four balls for four 6-inch round pizzas. Place on cookie sheet (for four balls, use two cookie sheets). Cover loosely with greased plastic wrap; let rest 10 minutes.

3. Sprinkle large cookie sheet with cornmeal. Shape dough: To make one large pizza, on prepared cookie sheet, roll dough into 14" by 10" rectangle; fold edges in to form 1-inch rim. For two 10-inch pizzas, pat and stretch one ball into 10-inch round. Form 1-inch rim. Repeat to make second pizza. For four 6-inch pizzas, pat and stretch one ball into 6-inch round. Form ½-inch rim. Repeat to make three more pizzas. Makes enough dough for 1 large pizza, 2 medium pizzas, or 4 small pizzas; 4 main-dish servings.

♥ Each ¼: About 233 calories, 7g protein, 48g carbohydrate, 1g total fat (0g saturated), 0mg cholesterol, 438mg sodium.

Pizza Sauce

Here's a recipe for a zesty pizza sauce that's ready in just minutes.

Prep: 12 minutes	Cook: 20 minutes
1	tablespoon olive oil
1	large garlic clove, finely chopped
1	can (28 ounces) tomatoes in thick puree, chopped
¼	teaspoon salt

In nonreactive 2-quart saucepan, heat oil over medium heat. Stir in garlic and cook, stirring frequently, until golden, about 30 seconds. Add tomatoes with their puree and salt; heat to boiling over high heat. Reduce heat and simmer 10 minutes. Makes 3 cups.

Each ¼ cup: About 28 calories, 1g protein, 4g carbohydrate, 1g total fat (0g saturated), 0mg cholesterol, 153mg sodium.

Cheese Pizza

The champ of all pizzas. If you like, sprinkle the top with one teaspoon dried oregano or two to three tablespoons chopped fresh basil just before serving.

Prep: 40 minutes plus dough rising and resting		
	Bake: 15 minutes	
	Basic Pizza Dough (opposite) or Quick Pizza Dough (left)	
1	cup Pizza Sauce (above)	
2	tablespoons freshly grated Parmesan cheese	
4	ounces mozzarella cheese, shredded (1 cup)	

1. Prepare pizza dough (if using Basic Pizza Dough, reserve half of dough for separate pizza).

2. Meanwhile, prepare Pizza Sauce. Shape pizza dough as directed. Sprinkle with Parmesan. Spread sauce over Parmesan and top with mozzarella.

3. Preheat oven to 450°F. Let Basic Pizza Dough pizza rest 20 minutes or Quick Pizza Dough pizza rest 15 minutes. Bake until crust is golden, 15 to 20 minutes. Makes 4 main-dish servings.

♥ Each serving: About 391 calories, 14g protein, 55g carbohydrate, 12g total fat (5g saturated), 25mg cholesterol, 899mg sodium.

Grilled Pizza

Grilling gives pizza a crisp crust and great smoky flavor. Let the coals burn down until medium-hot, or the crust might scorch.

Prep: 35 minutes plus dough rising and resting
Grill: 10 minutes

	Basic Pizza Dough (page 596) or Quick Pizza Dough (page 597)
2	tablespoons olive oil
8	ounces fresh mozzarella cheese, thinly sliced
12	basil leaves
2	medium tomatoes (6 ounces each), thinly sliced
	salt
	ground black pepper

1. Prepare pizza dough (if using Basic Pizza Dough, reserve half of dough for separate pizza). Prepare grill.

2. Shape dough into two 10-inch rounds or four 6-inch rounds (do not form rims). Place dough rounds on grill rack over medium-hot coals; grill until underside of dough turns golden and grill marks appear, 2 to 5 minutes.

3. With tongs, turn crusts over. Brush lightly with some oil. Arrange mozzarella on crust, then top with basil and tomatoes. Grill until cheese begins to melt, 3 to 5 minutes longer. Drizzle with remaining oil and sprinkle with salt and pepper. Makes 4 main-dish servings.

Each serving: About 500 calories, 17g protein, 54g carbohydrate, 23g total fat (1g saturated), 40mg cholesterol, 629mg sodium.

MORE PIZZA TOPPINGS

Here are more delicious ideas for your pizzas. To keep the crust crispy, scatter cheese over the dough before topping with vegetables and other ingredients. Sprinkle fresh herbs over the pizza just before serving.
• Grilled radicchio, cooked crumbled pancetta or bacon, crumbled goat cheese, chopped fresh sage. • Sautéed cremini mushrooms, cooked sweet Italian sausage, thinly sliced fresh mozzarella cheese, dried oregano. • Coarsely chopped grilled eggplant, marinated artichoke hearts, chopped plum tomatoes, shredded mozzarella cheese, fresh basil leaves.

Focaccia

This bread's wonderfully chewy texture and fine crumb are due to three risings. Sprinkle either two tablespoons chopped fresh sage or one tablespoon chopped fresh rosemary over the focaccia just before baking, if you wish.

Prep: 25 minutes plus rising   Bake: 18 minutes

1½	cups warm water (105° to 115°F)
1	package active dry yeast
1	teaspoon sugar
5	tablespoons extravirgin olive oil
1½	teaspoons table salt
3¾	cups all-purpose flour or 3½ cups bread flour
1	teaspoon kosher salt or coarse sea salt

1. In large bowl, combine ½ cup warm water, yeast, and sugar; stir to dissolve. Let stand until foamy, about 5 minutes. Add remaining 1 cup warm water, 2 tablespoons oil, table salt, and flour; stir to combine.

2. Turn dough onto floured surface and knead until smooth and elastic, about 7 minutes. Dough will be soft; do not add more flour.

3. Shape dough into ball; place in greased large bowl, turning dough to grease top. Cover bowl with plastic wrap and let stand in warm place (80° to 85°F) until doubled in volume, about 1 hour.

4. Lightly oil 15½" by 10½" jelly-roll pan. Punch dough down and pat into prepared pan. Cover with plastic wrap and let rise in warm place until doubled, about 45 minutes.

5. With fingertips, make deep indentations, 1 inch apart, over entire surface of dough, almost to bottom of pan. Drizzle with remaining 3 tablespoons oil; sprinkle with kosher salt. Cover loosely with plastic wrap; let rise in warm place until doubled, about 45 minutes.

6. Meanwhile, preheat oven to 450°F. Bake focaccia on lowest oven rack until bottom is crusty and top is lightly browned, about 18 minutes. Transfer focaccia to wire rack to cool. Makes 12 servings.

Each serving: About 201 calories, 4g protein, 31g carbohydrate, 7g total fat (1g saturated), 0mg cholesterol, 537mg sodium.

Focaccia

Red Pepper Focaccia

Prepare as directed but do not sprinkle with kosher salt. In 12-inch skillet, heat **1 tablespoon olive oil** over medium heat. Add **4 red peppers,** sliced, and ¼ **teaspoon salt** and cook, stirring frequently, until tender, about 20 minutes. Cool to room temperature. Sprinkle over focaccia just before baking.

Dried Tomato and Olive Focaccia

Prepare as directed but do not sprinkle with kosher salt. Combine ½ **cup Gaeta olives,** pitted, ¼ **cup drained oil-packed dried tomatoes,** coarsely chopped, and 1½ **teaspoons kosher salt.** Sprinkle over focaccia just before baking.

Tomato Focaccia

Prepare as directed but drizzle with only **1 tablespoon olive oil.** Arrange **1 pound ripe plum tomatoes,** cut into ¼-inch-thick slices, over top; sprinkle with **1 tablespoon chopped fresh rosemary or 1 teaspoon dried rosemary,** crumbled, ½ **teaspoon coarsely ground black pepper,** and **1 teaspoon kosher salt.** Bake as directed.

Onion Focaccia

Prepare as directed but do not sprinkle with kosher salt. In 12-inch skillet, heat **2 teaspoons olive oil** over medium heat. Add **2 medium onions,** sliced, **1 teaspoon sugar,** and ½ **teaspoon salt,** and cook, stirring frequently, until golden brown, about 20 minutes. Cool to room temperature. Spread over focaccia just before baking.

Pissaladière

A specialty of Nice, France, this pizzalike tart is usually served as a snack or appetizer, but it makes a nice supper or brunch dish, too. You can prepare the dough in advance. Let it rise once, then freeze for up to three months. Defrost and follow the recipe.

Prep: 40 minutes plus rising	Cook/Bake: 55 minutes
1	cup warm water (105° to 115°F)
1	package active dry yeast
3	cups all-purpose flour
1¾	teaspoons salt
2	tablespoons olive oil
2	pounds onions, chopped
1	can (2 ounces) anchovy fillets, rinsed, drained, and coarsely chopped
⅓	cup pitted and halved Kalamata or Gaeta olives

1. In cup, combine ¼ cup warm water and yeast; stir to dissolve. Let stand until foamy, about 5 minutes.

2. In large bowl, combine flour and 1½ teaspoons salt. Stir in yeast mixture, remaining ¾ cup warm water, and 1 tablespoon oil. Turn dough onto lightly floured surface and knead until smooth and elastic, about 8 minutes. Shape dough into ball; place in greased large bowl, turning to grease top. Cover bowl with plastic wrap and let rise in warm place (80° to 85°F) until doubled in volume, about 45 minutes.

3. Meanwhile, in 12-inch skillet, heat remaining 1 tablespoon oil over low heat. Add onions and remaining ¼ teaspoon salt and cook, stirring frequently, until onions are very soft and golden, about 30 minutes. Cool.

4. Grease 15½" by 10½" jelly-roll pan. Punch down dough and pat into prepared pan. Cover loosely with plastic wrap and let rise 30 minutes.

5. Meanwhile, preheat oven to 425°F. With fingertips, make shallow indentations over surface of dough. Toss onions and anchovies and spread mixture over top. Place olives on onion mixture at 2-inch intervals. Bake on lowest oven rack until crust is golden, about 25 minutes. Cut into 32 squares. Makes 32 appetizers.

♥ Each square: About 73 calories, 2g protein, 12g carbohydrate, 2g total fat (0g saturated), 1mg cholesterol, 205mg sodium.

Cinnamon Bubble Ring

A giant bread ring made of pull-apart pieces that are laced with a delicious mixture of cinnamon and brown sugar.

Prep: 40 minutes plus rising	Bake: 45 minutes
¾	cup warm water (105° to 115°F)
2	packages active dry yeast
1	teaspoon plus ¾ cup granulated sugar
¾	cup (1½ sticks) butter or margarine, softened
1	teaspoon salt
	about 5½ cups all-purpose flour
3	large eggs
½	cup packed brown sugar
1	teaspoon ground cinnamon

1. In large bowl, combine ½ cup warm water, yeast, and 1 teaspoon granulated sugar; stir to dissolve. Let stand until foamy, about 5 minutes. Add remaining ¼ cup warm water and ½ cup butter; mix well. With wooden spoon, stir in remaining ¾ cup granulated sugar, salt, and 2 cups flour just until blended. Gradually beat in eggs and 1 cup flour. Stir in 2¼ cups more flour.

2. Turn dough onto lightly floured surface and knead until smooth and elastic, 8 to 10 minutes, working in enough of remaining ¼ cup flour just to keep dough from sticking. Cut dough in half and cut each half into 16 equal pieces. Cover and let dough rest 15 minutes.

3. Meanwhile, in small bowl, combine brown sugar and cinnamon. Melt remaining ¼ cup butter; set aside. Grease 9- to 10-inch tube pan.

4. Shape each piece of dough into tight ball. Place half of balls in prepared pan; brush with half of melted butter and sprinkle with half of sugar mixture. Repeat with remaining dough, melted butter, and sugar mixture. Cover pan with plastic wrap and let rise in warm place (80° to 85°F) until doubled in volume, about 1 hour.

5. Meanwhile, preheat oven to 350°F. Bake until browned and ring sounds hollow when lightly tapped, about 45 minutes. If top browns too quickly, cover with foil during last 15 minutes of baking. Cool ring in pan on wire rack 10 minutes; remove from pan. Serve warm, or cool on wire rack to serve later. Reheat if desired. Makes 16 servings.

Each serving: About 319 calories, 6g protein, 50g carbohydrate, 11g total fat (6g saturated), 63mg cholesterol, 249mg sodium.

Lemon-Almond Bubble Ring

Prepare as directed but combine ½ **cup granulated sugar, 1 tablespoon freshly grated lemon peel,** and ¾ **cup sliced almonds** and substitute for brown sugar–cinnamon mixture in Step 3. Sprinkle over dough. Makes 16 servings.

Each serving: About 343 calories, 7g protein, 50g carbohydrate, 13g total fat (6g saturated), 63mg cholesterol, 247mg sodium.

Bee-Sting Cake

Bee-sting (bienenstich in German), refers to the honey-nut glaze on this sweet yeast coffee cake. It is usually baked in a round pan, but we love the topping so much, we made our version in a jelly-roll pan to get a greater proportion of glaze to cake.

Prep: 40 minutes plus rising   Bake: 20 minutes

Cake

¼	cup warm water (105° to 115°F)
1	package active dry yeast
1	teaspoon plus ⅓ cup sugar
6	tablespoons butter or margarine, softened
1	large egg
1	large egg yolk
⅓	cup milk
1	teaspoon vanilla extract
¼	teaspoon salt
	about 3 cups all-purpose flour

Glaze

⅔	cup sugar
½	cup butter or margarine (1 stick)
½	cup honey
¼	cup heavy or whipping cream
2	teaspoons fresh lemon juice
1⅓	cups sliced natural almonds (5½ ounces)

1. Prepare cake: In cup, combine warm water, yeast, and 1 teaspoon sugar; stir to dissolve. Let mixture stand until foamy, about 5 minutes.

2. Meanwhile, in large bowl, with mixer at low speed, beat butter and remaining ⅓ cup sugar until blended, frequently scraping bowl with rubber spatula. Increase speed to high; beat until light and fluffy, about 3 minutes, occasionally scraping bowl. Reduce speed to low; beat in whole egg and egg yolk (mixture may look curdled). Beat in yeast mixture, milk, vanilla, salt, and 2½ cups flour until blended.

3. Turn dough onto lightly floured surface and knead until smooth and elastic, about 5 minutes, working in enough of remaining ½ cup flour to make slightly sticky dough.

4. Shape dough into ball; place in greased large bowl, turning dough to grease top. Cover bowl with plastic wrap and let rise in warm place (80° to 85°F) until doubled in volume, about 45 minutes.

5. Punch down dough; cover and let rest 15 minutes. Meanwhile, grease 15½" by 10½" jelly-roll pan. Line bottom and sides of pan with foil; grease foil.

6. Turn dough into prepared pan. With hand, press dough evenly into pan, making sure to press it into corners. Cover pan with plastic wrap and let rise in warm place until doubled, about 45 minutes.

7. Meanwhile, preheat oven to 375°F. Prepare glaze: In 2-quart saucepan, combine sugar, butter, honey, and cream; heat to boiling over medium heat, stirring frequently. Remove from heat; stir in lemon juice. Set aside to cool slightly, about 5 minutes.

8. Pour glaze over dough and scatter almonds over top. Place two sheets of foil underneath pan; crimp edges of foil to form rim to catch any overflow during baking. Bake cake until top is golden, 20 to 25 minutes. Cool in pan on wire rack 15 minutes. Run small knife between foil and edges of pan to loosen, then invert cake onto large cookie sheet. Gently peel off foil and discard. Immediately invert cake, almond side up, onto wire rack to cool completely. Makes 16 servings.

Each serving: About 339 calories, 5g protein, 43g carbohydrate, 17g total fat (8g saturated), 60mg cholesterol, 149mg sodium.

For a perfectly round loaf of bread, let the dough rise in a bowl or basket lined with a floured cloth or napkin. Unmold the dough onto a cookie sheet and remove the cloth before baking.

NICK MALGIERI

DIRECTOR, BAKING PROGRAM, PETER KUMP'S NEW YORK COOKING SCHOOL

EXPERT TIP

Coffee Cake Wreath

This versatile dough is shaped with your filling of choice to make a luscious coffee cake for brunch or snacks.

Prep: 40 minutes plus rising   Bake: 30 minutes

Cake

½	cup warm water (105° to 115°F)
2	packages active dry yeast
1	teaspoon plus ½ cup sugar
½	cup (1 stick) butter or margarine, softened
1	large egg
½	teaspoon salt
	about 3¼ cups all-purpose flour
	choice of filling (opposite)

Icing (optional)

1	cup confectioner's sugar
2	tablespoons milk

1. In cup, combine warm water, yeast, and 1 teaspoon sugar; stir to dissolve. Let stand until foamy, about 5 minutes.

2. Meanwhile, in large bowl, with mixer at low speed, beat butter and remaining ½ cup sugar until blended. Increase speed to high; beat until light and fluffy, about 2 minutes, occasionally scraping bowl with rubber spatula. Reduce speed to low; beat in egg until blended. Beat in yeast mixture, salt, and ½ cup flour (batter will look curdled) just until blended. With wooden spoon, stir in 2½ cups flour until blended.

3. Turn dough onto lightly floured surface and knead until smooth and elastic, about 8 minutes, working in enough of remaining ¼ cup flour just to keep dough from sticking.

4. Shape dough into ball; place in greased large bowl, turning dough to grease top. Cover bowl with plastic wrap and let rise in warm place (80° to 85°F) until doubled in volume, about 1 hour.

5. Meanwhile, prepare filling of choice; cover and refrigerate until ready to use.

6. Punch down dough. Turn dough onto lightly floured surface; cover and let rest 15 minutes. Meanwhile, grease large cookie sheet.

7. With floured rolling pin, roll dough into 18" by 12" rectangle. Spread filling of choice over dough to within ½ inch of edges.

8. Starting at a long side, roll up dough jelly-roll fashion. Carefully lift roll and place, seam side down, on prepared cookie sheet. Shape roll into ring; press ends together to seal. With knife or kitchen shears, cut ring at 1½-inch intervals, up to, but not completely through, inside dough edge. Gently pull and twist each cut piece to show filling. Dough will be soft, so use small metal spatula to help lift pieces. Cover and let rise in warm place until risen slightly, about 1 hour.

9. Meanwhile, preheat oven to 350°F. Bake coffee cake wreath until golden, 30 to 35 minutes. Transfer wreath to wire rack to cool.

10. Prepare icing, if using: In small bowl, mix confectioners' sugar with milk until smooth. When wreath is cool, drizzle with icing. Makes 1 coffee cake, about 16 slices.

Each slice without filling and icing: About 176 calories, 3g protein, 26g carbohydrate, 6g total fat (4g saturated), 29mg cholesterol, 136mg sodium.

Sweet Almond Filling

In food processor with knife blade attached, process ½ **cup whole blanched almonds** and ¼ **cup packed brown sugar** until almonds are finely ground. Add **4 ounces almond paste,** broken in chunks, and **2 large egg whites** and process until mixture is smooth. Makes about 1 cup.

Each tablespoon: About 71 calories, 2g protein, 7g carbohydrate, 4g total fat (0g saturated), 0mg cholesterol, 9mg sodium.

Lemon–Poppy Seed Filling

In small bowl, combine **1 can (12½ ounces) poppy seed filling** and **1 teaspoon freshly grated lemon peel.** Makes about 1 cup.

Each tablespoon: About 65 calories, 1g protein, 11g carbohydrate, 2g total fat (0g saturated), 0mg cholesterol, 11mg sodium.

Chocolate-Walnut Filling

In 1-quart saucepan, combine **3 squares (3 ounces) semi-sweet chocolate,** chopped, **1 square (1 ounce) unsweetened chocolate,** chopped, and **¾ cup lowfat sweetened condensed milk;** melt over low heat until smooth. Cool to room temperature. Stir in **½ cup walnuts,** toasted and chopped. Makes about 1 cup.

Each tablespoon: About 104 calories, 2g protein, 13g carbohydrate, 5g total fat (2g saturated), 2mg cholesterol, 16mg sodium.

Prune Filling

In 2-quart saucepan, combine **2 cups pitted, chopped prunes, 1¼ cups water,** and **2 strips (3" by ¾" each) lemon peel;** heat to boiling over high heat. Reduce heat to medium-low; cook, stirring occasionally, until liquid has been absorbed, 12 to 15 minutes. Remove lemon peel. In blender or in food processor with knife blade attached, blend prune mixture with **6 tablespoons sugar** to form a thick puree. Makes 1⅔ cups.

Each 1½ tablespoons: About 66 calories, 1g protein, 17g carbohydrate, 0g total fat (0g saturated), 0mg cholesterol, 1mg sodium.

Cinnamon-Sugar Filling

In small bowl, combine **½ cup packed brown sugar, ½ cup whole blanched almonds,** toasted and chopped, and **½ teaspoon ground cinnamon.** After rolling out dough, brush with **2 tablespoons butter or margarine,** melted, and sprinkle with sugar mixture. Makes about 1 cup.

Each tablespoon: About 65 calories, 1g protein, 8g carbohydrate, 4g total fat (1g saturated), 4mg cholesterol, 18mg sodium.

To divide dough easily into an equal number of pieces, press the dough into a small bowl or round cake pan; unmold and cut into wedges.

NICK MALGIERI

DIRECTOR, BAKING PROGRAM, PETER KUMP'S NEW YORK COOKING SCHOOL

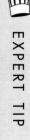

EXPERT TIP

Brioche

Rich and buttery brioche, a classic in French bread making, rests overnight in the refrigerator and is put into a preheated oven the next morning in time for breakfast. A heavy-duty mixer is a must for the stiff, sticky dough.

Prep: 25 minutes plus rising and overnight to refrigerate
Bake: 30 minutes

¾ cup milk, heated to warm (105° to 115°F)
1 package active dry yeast
1 teaspoon plus ¼ cup sugar
1 teaspoon salt
4 cups bread flour or all-purpose flour
6 large eggs
1 cup butter (2 sticks), softened and cut into pieces (do not use margarine)

1. In large bowl of heavy-duty mixer, combine warm milk, yeast, and 1 teaspoon sugar; stir to dissolve. Let stand until foamy, about 5 minutes. Stir in salt and 1 cup flour until blended. With mixer at low speed, beat in 1 egg. Continue beating, alternately adding remaining 3 cups flour and remaining 5 eggs until well incorporated. Gradually beat in butter until smooth.

2. Transfer dough to lightly buttered large bowl. Cover bowl with greased plastic wrap and let rise in warm place (80° to 85°F) until doubled in volume, about 2½ hours.

3. Meanwhile, lightly grease two 8½" by 4½" metal loaf pans. Punch down dough. Divide dough in half; place in prepared pans. Cover pans with lightly greased plastic wrap; refrigerate overnight.

4. Preheat oven to 350°F. Bake loaves until golden brown and toothpick inserted in center comes out clean, about 30 minutes. Removes loaves from pans; cool on wire racks. Makes 2 loaves, 12 slices each.

Each slice: About 188 calories, 5g protein, 19g carbohydrate, 10g total fat (6g saturated), 75mg cholesterol, 197mg sodium.

Overnight Sticky Buns

(pictured on page 582)

Make these rich, yummy rolls the night before serving. Let them rise overnight in the refrigerator, then bake and serve for breakfast. You can wrap any leftovers in foil and freeze; reheat, still wrapped, in a 350°F oven for fifteen to twenty minutes.

Prep: 1 hour plus rising and overnight to refrigerate
Bake: 30 minutes

Dough

¼	cup warm water (105° to 115°F)
1	package active dry yeast
1	teaspoon plus ¼ cup granulated sugar
¾	cup milk
4	tablespoons butter or margarine, softened
3	large egg yolks
1	teaspoon salt
	about 4 cups all-purpose flour

Filling

½	cup packed brown sugar
¼	cup dried currants
1	tablespoon ground cinnamon
4	tablespoons butter or margarine, melted

Topping

⅔	cup packed brown sugar
3	tablespoons butter or margarine
2	tablespoons light corn syrup
2	tablespoons honey
1¼	cups pecans (5 ounces), coarsely chopped

1. Prepare dough: In cup, combine warm water, yeast, and 1 teaspoon granulated sugar; stir to dissolve. Let stand until foamy, about 5 minutes.

2. In large bowl, with mixer at low speed, blend yeast mixture with milk, butter, remaining ¼ cup granulated sugar, egg yolks, salt, and 3 cups flour until blended. With wooden spoon, stir in ¾ cup flour.

3. Turn dough onto lightly floured surface and knead until smooth and elastic, about 5 minutes, working in enough of remaining ¼ cup flour just to keep dough from sticking.

4. Shape dough into ball; place in greased large bowl, turning dough to grease top. Cover bowl with plastic wrap and let rise in warm place (80° to 85°F) until doubled, about 1 hour.

5. Meanwhile, prepare filling: In small bowl, combine brown sugar, currants, and cinnamon; set aside. Reserve melted butter.

6. Prepare topping: In 1-quart saucepan, combine brown sugar, butter, corn syrup, and honey; heat over low heat, stirring occasionally, until brown sugar and butter have melted. Grease 13" by 9" baking pan; pour melted brown-sugar mixture into pan and sprinkle evenly with pecans.

7. Punch down dough. Turn dough onto lightly floured surface; cover and let rest 15 minutes. Roll dough into 18" by 12" rectangle. Brush dough with reserved melted butter and sprinkle with currant mixture. Starting at a long side, roll up dough jelly-roll fashion; place, seam side down, on surface. Cut dough crosswise into 20 slices.

8. Place slices, cut side down, on brown-sugar mixture in prepared pan in four rows of five slices each. Cover and refrigerate at least 12 hours or up to 15 hours.

9. Preheat oven to 375°F. Bake buns until golden, about 30 minutes. Remove from oven. Immediately place serving tray or jelly-roll pan over top of baking pan and invert; remove pan. Let buns cool slightly to serve warm, or cool on wire racks to serve later. Makes 20 buns.

Each bun: About 291 calories, 4g protein, 42g carbohydrate, 13g total fat (5g saturated), 50mg cholesterol, 195mg sodium.

Challah

This Jewish egg bread, made in the traditional double-braid shape, can be served anytime but is a must for holiday meals. If you wish, divide the dough in half and make two single-braided loaves instead.

Prep: 30 minutes plus rising	Bake: 30 minutes
¾ cup warm water (105° to 115°F)	
1 package active dry yeast	
1 teaspoon plus ¼ cup sugar	
3 large eggs, lightly beaten	
¼ cup vegetable oil	
1 teaspoon salt	
about 4¼ cups all-purpose flour or 3½ cups bread flour	

Challah

braid ropes, pinching ends to seal. Cut remaining third of dough into 3 pieces. With hands, roll each piece into 14-inch-long rope. Place ropes side by side and braid; pinch ends to seal. Place small braid on top of large braid. Tuck ends of top braid under bottom braid, stretching top braid if necessary; pinch ends to seal. Cover loosely with greased plastic wrap and let rise in warm place until doubled, about 45 minutes.

5. Meanwhile, preheat oven to 375°F. Brush reserved beaten egg over loaf. Bake until browned and loaf sounds hollow when lightly tapped on bottom, 30 to 35 minutes. Transfer loaf to wire rack to cool completely. Makes 1 loaf, 12 slices.

Each slice: About 250 calories, 7g protein, 40g carbohydrate, 7g total fat (1g saturated), 53mg cholesterol, 211mg sodium.

1. In large bowl, combine warm water, yeast, and 1 teaspoon sugar; stir to dissolve. Let stand until foamy, about 5 minutes. Measure 1 tablespoon beaten egg into small cup; cover and refrigerate. Add remaining eggs, oil, remaining ¼ cup sugar, salt, and 2 cups flour to yeast mixture; with wooden spoon, beat well. Stir in enough flour (about 1¾ cups all-purpose flour or 1¼ cups bread flour) to make soft dough.

2. Turn dough onto lightly floured surface and knead until smooth and elastic, about 8 minutes, working in enough of remaining ½ cup all-purpose flour or ¼ cup bread flour just to keep dough from sticking.

3. Shape dough into ball; place in greased large bowl, turning dough to grease top. Cover bowl with plastic wrap and let rise in warm place (80° to 85°F) until doubled in volume, about 1 hour.

4. Punch down dough. Grease large cookie sheet. Turn dough onto lightly floured surface and cut two-thirds of dough into 3 equal pieces; with hands, roll each piece into 13-inch-long rope. Place ropes side by side on prepared cookie sheet;

SPECIAL BUTTERS FOR YEAST BREADS

Try these delicious butters on your freshly baked bread.

MARMALADE OR STRAWBERRY BUTTER
In small bowl, with mixer at medium speed, beat 1 cup butter or margarine (2 sticks), softened, and ⅓ cup orange marmalade or strawberry preserves until blended. Cover and refrigerate up to 1 week. To use, let stand at room temperature 30 minutes for easier spreading. Makes about 1⅓ cups.

WHIPPED HONEY BUTTER
Prepare as directed for Marmalade Butter but omit marmalade and beat in 2 tablespoons honey and ⅛ teaspoon ground cinnamon. Makes about 1¼ cups.

FRESH STRAWBERRY BUTTER
Prepare as directed for Marmalade Butter but omit marmalade and beat in ½ pint strawberries, hulled and crushed, and 3 tablespoons confectioners' sugar. Cover and refrigerate up to 2 days. Makes about 2¼ cups.

Stollen

Stollen, studded with dried fruit and almonds, is Germany's Christmas bread. Give one as a fabulous holiday gift.

Prep: 45 minutes plus rising   Bake: 25 minutes per batch

½	cup warm water (105° to 115°F)
2	packages active dry yeast
1	teaspoon plus ½ cup granulated sugar
1	cup milk, heated to warm (105° to 115°F)
¾	cup butter or margarine (1½ sticks), softened
2	large eggs
1½	teaspoons salt
	about 6 cups all-purpose flour
1	cup slivered almonds (4 ounces), toasted
1	cup candied cherries, coarsely chopped
½	cup diced candied citron or candied lemon peel
½	cup golden raisins
	confectioners' sugar

1. In large bowl, combine warm water, yeast, and 1 teaspoon granulated sugar; stir to dissolve. Let stand until foamy, about 5 minutes. Add milk, butter, eggs, remaining ½ cup granulated sugar, salt, and 4 cups flour to yeast mixture; beat well with wooden spoon. Gradually stir in about 1½ cups flour to make soft dough.

2. Turn dough onto lightly floured surface and knead until smooth and elastic, about 8 minutes, working in enough of remaining ½ cup flour just to keep dough from sticking. Knead in almonds, cherries, citron, and raisins.

3. Shape dough into ball. Place in greased large bowl, turning dough to grease top. Cover bowl with plastic wrap and let rise in warm place (80° to 85°F) until doubled in volume, about 1½ hours.

4. Grease one large and one small cookie sheet. Punch down dough. Turn dough onto lightly floured surface and cut into thirds. Cover and refrigerate one piece of dough. With floured rolling pin, shape each remaining piece of dough into 12" by 7" oval. Fold each oval lengthwise almost in half so that edges do not quite meet. Place 3 inches apart on prepared large cookie sheet. Cover dough and let rise in warm place until doubled, 1 to 1½ hours.

5. After 30 minutes, remove remaining dough from refrigerator and repeat shaping; place on small cookie sheet. Cover and let rise in warm place until doubled, 1 to 1½ hours.

6. Meanwhile, preheat oven to 350°F. Bake stollen on large cookie sheet until browned, 25 to 30 minutes. Transfer to wire racks to cool. Bake remaining stollen; cool on wire rack. Dust stollen with confectioners' sugar before serving. Makes 3 loaves, 8 slices each.

Each slice: About 287 calories, 6g protein, 44g carbohydrate, 10g total fat (4g saturated), 35mg cholesterol, 232mg sodium.

Marzipan-Filled Stollen
Prepare stollen as directed through Step 3. Prepare marzipan filling: Crumble **1 tube or can (7 to 8 ounces) almond paste** into food processor with knife blade attached. Add **2 tablespoons butter or margarine,** softened, **2 tablespoons sugar,** and **1 large egg;** process until smooth. Shape dough into ovals. Spread one-third of filling lengthwise on half of each oval, leaving ½-inch border at edge; fold almost in half so that edges do not quite meet. Let rise and bake as directed.

Each slice: About 342 calories, 7g protein, 49g carbohydrate, 14g total fat (5g saturated), 46mg cholesterol, 245mg sodium.

Chocolate-Cherry Bread

A not-too-sweet bread studded with bits of bittersweet chocolate and dried tart cherries. We use Dutch-process cocoa instead of the more usual natural cocoa to give the bread a richer brown color.

Prep: 20 minutes plus rising   Bake: 20 minutes

¼	cup warm water (105° to 115°F)
1	package active dry yeast
3	teaspoons granulated sugar
⅓	cup unsweetened Dutch-process cocoa
⅓	cup packed brown sugar
1¾	teaspoons salt
	about 3½ cups all-purpose flour
1	cup freshly brewed coffee, cooled until warm (105° to 115°F)
4	tablespoons butter or margarine, softened
1	large egg, separated
¾	cup dried tart cherries
3	squares (3 ounces) bittersweet chocolate, coarsely chopped
1	teaspoon water

1. In cup, combine warm water, yeast, and 1 teaspoon granulated sugar; stir to dissolve. Let stand until foamy, about 5 minutes.

2. Meanwhile, in large bowl, combine cocoa, brown sugar, salt, and 3 cups flour.

3. With wooden spoon, stir warm coffee, butter, egg yolk (cover egg white and set aside in refrigerator), and yeast mixture into flour mixture. In bowl, with floured hands, knead several times to combine well.

4. Turn dough onto lightly floured surface and knead until smooth and elastic, about 10 minutes, working in enough of remaining $\frac{1}{2}$ cup flour just to keep dough from sticking. Knead in cherries and chocolate.

5. Shape dough into ball; place in greased large bowl, turning dough to grease top. Cover bowl with plastic wrap and let rise in warm place (80° to 85°F) until doubled in volume, about $1\frac{1}{2}$ hours.

6. Punch down dough. Turn dough onto lightly floured surface and cut in half; cover dough and let rest 15 minutes for easier shaping.

7. Shape each dough half into 5-inch ball: Using the sides of your hands, tuck sides of dough under to meet in center. Rotate and repeat to form taut ball. Place balls, 3 inches apart, in opposite corners, on ungreased large cookie sheet. Cover and let rise in warm place until doubled, 1 hour.

8. Preheat oven to 400°F. In cup, beat reserved egg white with water; use to brush tops of loaves. Sprinkle loaves with remaining 2 teaspoons granulated sugar. With serrated knife or single-edge razor blade, cut shallow X in top of each loaf. Bake until loaves are crusty, about 20 minutes. Transfer to wire racks to cool. Makes 2 loaves, 12 slices each.

Each slice: About 137 calories, 3g protein, 24g carbohydrate, 4g total fat (2g saturated), 14mg cholesterol, 202mg sodium.

Soft Pretzels

These soft pretzels, a specialty of Pennsylvania Dutch country that has swept the nation, are best served warm with mustard. Freeze them after shaping, if you like. Let them thaw, then dip in the baking-soda mixture and bake as directed. The pretzels can be sprinkled with sesame or poppy seeds in addition to the salt.

Prep: 30 minutes plus rising Bake: 16 minutes		
2	cups warm water (105° to 115°F)	
1	package active dry yeast	
1	teaspoon sugar	
1	teaspoon salt	
	about 4 cups all-purpose flour	
2	tablespoons baking soda	
1	tablespoon kosher or coarse sea salt	

1. In large bowl, combine $1\frac{1}{2}$ cups warm water, yeast, and sugar; stir to dissolve. Let stand until foamy, about 5 minutes. Add salt and 2 cups flour; beat well with wooden spoon. Gradually stir in $1\frac{1}{2}$ cups flour to make soft dough.

2. Turn dough onto floured surface and knead until smooth and elastic, about 6 minutes, kneading in enough of remaining $\frac{1}{2}$ cup flour just to keep dough from sticking.

3. Shape dough into ball; place in greased large bowl, turning dough to grease top. Cover bowl with plastic wrap and let rise in warm place (80° to 85°F) until doubled in volume, about 30 minutes.

4. Meanwhile, preheat oven to 400°F. Grease two cookie sheets. Punch down dough and cut into 12 equal pieces. Roll each piece into 24-inch-long rope. Shape ropes into loop-shaped pretzels.

5. In small bowl, whisk remaining $\frac{1}{2}$ cup warm water and baking soda until soda has dissolved.

6. Dip pretzels in baking-soda mixture and place $1\frac{1}{2}$ inches apart on prepared cookie sheets; sprinkle with kosher salt. Bake until browned, 16 to 18 minutes, rotating cookie sheets between upper and lower oven racks halfway through baking. Serve pretzels warm, or transfer to wire racks to cool. Makes 12 pretzels.

Each pretzel: About 167 calories, 5g protein, 33g carbohydrate, 1g total fat (0g saturated), 0mg cholesterol, 1,192mg sodium.

17

SANDWICHES

The first sandwich, created in 1762, was a matter of necessity; The Earl of Sandwich, an enthusiastic gambler, requested bread and meat dishes that he could consume while continuing to gamble. At that moment, the sandwich was born. Every culture has its sandwich: The Italians relish their paninis and calzones; the Mexicans enjoy tasty burritos; bagels and lox has long been a Jewish tradition; and the Croque Madame and Croque Monsieur are standard fare at Paris bistros. These days, you don't even need sliced bread to make a sandwich. It could just as easily be a filled and rolled-up flour tortilla—and the meat is optional, too. No one would think twice if a pita pocket was filled with a crisp Greek salad with olives and feta cheese or if a vegetable frittata was tucked between thin slabs of herbed focaccia.

You'll find lots of possibilities for sandwich fillings throughout this book (check the index). If you're in the mood for something that's not too rich and is on the traditional side, consider an old-fashioned tuna-, chicken-, or egg-salad filling, or try one of our new-wave recipes, such as Tuscan Tuna Salad on Focaccia or Turkey and Mango Roll-Ups. For a hot and hearty meal, try pulled pork barbecue on a soft bun, grilled sausages and peppers on a hero, Greek meatballs on a hard roll, or every kid's favorite, Sloppy Joes. Or substitute lamb for the ground beef in your burger, top with yogurt and mint, and serve with a warm pocketless pita. Grilled portobello mush-

Classic Italian Hero

rooms or garbanzo-bean falafel patties make terrific burgers, especially when layered with thickly sliced ripe tomatoes and some crisp green lettuce leaves.

Often you can make over a predictable sandwich by adding a tasty new condiment. Mayonnaise and mustard are always welcome and have their place. But why not try one of our flavored mayonnaises, such as Ginger-Sesame Mayonnaise or Chipotle Mayonnaise, to really wake up a sandwich.

SAFE SANDWICHES

The brown-bag lunch is an American tradition, but it should be carefully packed to ensure that the contents remain tasty and safe to eat.

If you are making a lot of sandwiches, use this simple assembly-line technique: Line up the bread slices in rows, apply the spreads, top with the fillings, and cover with the remaining bread. Wrap the sandwiches tightly in waxed paper or foil, or place in ziptight sandwich bags. Some ingredients (such as tomatoes, lettuce, and cucumbers) can make bread soggy, so it's best to wrap these items separately; add them to the sandwich just before eating.

Sandwiches containing meat, poultry, fish, or eggs should not stand at room temperature for longer than two hours: Warm temperatures encourage the growth of salmonella. Pack these sandwiches in insulated lunch boxes with portable ice packs to keep them at a safe cold temperature.

SLIM SANDWICHES

A sandwich doesn't have to be calorie- and fat-laden. Instead of high-fat mayonnaise, use one of the reduced-fat varieties (stir in some chopped fresh herbs for a flavor lift). Or hold the mayo and spread your bread with naturally lowfat mustard; specialty food stores carry a wide selection. Chutney, delicious by itself or when blended with mayonnaise or mustard, adds a delectable sweet-and-spicy dimension to a sandwich.

Many lunch meats are high in calories and sodium. Cured meat or sausage sandwiches should be occasional indulgences, not everyday fare. Look for alternatives such as grilled vegetables or skinless chicken breast, freshly roasted turkey breast, shrimp in a lowfat dressing, or water-packed tuna. Cheese is another high-fat sandwich ingredient that should be enjoyed in moderation. If you really must have it on your sandwich, try a reduced-fat version. Or make a spread of nonfat yogurt mixed with a bit of mustard.

Instead of ordering your sandwich at the deli counter, take a stroll by the salad bar. There are lots of candidates for a terrific sandwich just waiting to be piled onto bread (or into a pita) and drizzled with lowfat dressing: Artichoke hearts, roasted peppers, peperoncini, sprouts, shredded carrots, asparagus, sliced tomatoes, and tofu are all smart choices.

IT'S ALL IN THE BREAD

Sandwich fillings and breads are like color combinations: Some are a perfect match and some clash. Full-flavored fillings, such as corned beef, pastrami, and smoked salmon, are really at their best on hearty rye or pumpernickel. Delicate egg or fish salads are ideal on mildly flavored breads with soft textures; remove the crusts, if you like. Not-too-sweet pastries, such as brioche and croissants, make elegant sandwiches. When a sandwich has a foreign accent, the most obvious choice is a bread from the same region. For example, fresh mozzarella, arugula, and roasted red peppers, dressed with olive oil and balsamic vinegar, just seems to belong on crusty Italian bread. The sturdy bread can stand up to the oil and vinegar—softer breads would become soggy. Conversely, the humble Mexican tortilla is no longer reserved for south-of-the-border dishes such as burritos and tacos but is now turned into exotic wraps. These are, quite literally, sandwiches with a twist. And now, herb- or vegetable-flavored tortillas are taking the sandwich into the 21st century.

Perfectly Simple Tomato Sandwiches

These sandwiches are fabulous just the way they are, but we also like them with a few sprigs of watercress tucked in. Make them with absolutely ripe tomatoes.

🕐 Prep: 15 minutes

1	lemon
1/3	cup mayonnaise
1/4	teaspoon ground coriander
1/4	teaspoon salt
1/4	teaspoon coarsely ground black pepper
1	large round or oval loaf (1 pound) sourdough or other crusty bread
2	pounds ripe tomatoes (3 large), thickly sliced

1. From lemon, grate 1/2 teaspoon peel and squeeze 1 teaspoon juice. In small bowl, combine mayonnaise, lemon peel and juice, coriander, salt, and pepper until well blended.

2. Cut eight 1/2-inch-thick slices from center of bread. (Reserve ends for another use.) Toast bread, if desired. Spread mayonnaise mixture on each bread slice. Arrange tomato slices on 4 bread slices; top with remaining bread slices. To serve, cut each sandwich in half. Makes 4 main-dish servings.

Each serving: About 392 calories, 9g protein, 52g carbohydrate, 18g total fat (3g saturated), 11mg cholesterol, 742mg sodium.

Double Tomato–Brie Heroes

Dried and fresh tomatoes provide a double dose of flavor. For this recipe, we used dried tomatoes that were marinated in lightly salted oil with herbs. If you use the unseasoned variety, you may want to sprinkle them with some salt.

🕐 Prep: 20 minutes

1	jar (6 1/2 ounces) oil-packed dried tomatoes, drained and finely chopped
2	tablespoons extravirgin olive oil
2	tablespoons white wine vinegar
2	long loaves (8 ounces each) Italian bread, each cut horizontally in half
1	pound Brie cheese, rind left on, sliced
1	cup loosely packed fresh basil leaves
2	ripe medium tomatoes (12 ounces), sliced

In small bowl, combine dried tomatoes, oil, and vinegar. Spread dried-tomato mixture evenly on cut sides of bread. Arrange Brie on bottom halves of bread; top with basil and tomato slices. Replace tops of bread. To serve, cut each hero crosswise into 4 pieces. Makes 8 main-dish servings.

Each serving: About 374 calories, 20g protein, 39g carbohydrate, 16g total fat (0g saturated), 57mg cholesterol, 817mg sodium.

Frittata Sandwiches with Peppers and Onion

This tasty sandwich can be made in advance, wrapped in foil, and carried along to a picnic to serve warm. Focaccia, a pizzalike flatbread, can be found in the bread or deli section of some supermarkets and in specialty food stores.

Prep: 25 minutes   Cook/Bake: 32 minutes

2	tablespoons olive oil
2	medium onions, thinly sliced
8	ounces Italian frying peppers (about 4), thinly sliced
½	teaspoon salt
6	large eggs
¾	cup freshly grated Parmesan cheese
¼	cup chopped fresh parsley
¼	teaspoon ground black pepper
1	round or square focaccia (8 inches) or 1 loaf (12 ounces) Italian bread, cut horizontally in half

1. In 12-inch skillet, heat 1 tablespoon oil over medium heat. Add onions and cook, stirring frequently, until tender, about 5 minutes. Add frying peppers; sprinkle with ¼ teaspoon salt and cook until peppers are tender, about 12 minutes. Keep warm.

2. Meanwhile, preheat oven to 375°F. In large bowl, with wire whisk, beat eggs, Parmesan, parsley, remaining ¼ teaspoon salt, and pepper until well blended.

3. In nonstick oven-safe 10-inch skillet (if skillet is not oven-safe, wrap handle with double layer of foil), heat remaining 1 tablespoon oil over medium heat. Pour in egg mixture and cook until frittata begins to set around edge, 3 to 4 minutes.

4. Place skillet in oven. Bake until frittata is set, about 10 minutes.

5. Slide frittata onto bottom half of focaccia, trimming bread to fit if necessary; top with onion-pepper mixture. Replace top half of focaccia. To serve, cut into 4 wedges. Makes 4 main-dish servings.

Each serving: About 605 calories, 33g protein, 63g carbohydrate, 26g total fat (9g saturated), 339mg cholesterol, 1,311mg sodium.

FLAVORED MAYONNAISE

It's easy to transform mayonnaise into an extraordinary condiment that will add a boost of flavor to any simple sandwich.

ROASTED RED PEPPER MAYONNAISE
½ cup mayonnaise, ¼ cup finely chopped roasted red pepper, and 1 tablespoon chopped fresh parsley.

LEMON MAYONNAISE
½ cup mayonnaise, 1½ teaspoons fresh lemon juice, 1 teaspoon freshly grated lemon peel, and pinch ground black pepper.

GINGER-SESAME MAYONNAISE
½ cup mayonnaise, 2 small green onions, finely chopped, 1 tablespoon chopped fresh cilantro, 1 teaspoon minced, peeled fresh ginger, and ¼ teaspoon Asian sesame oil.

CHUTNEY MAYONNAISE
½ cup mayonnaise, ¼ cup mango chutney, finely chopped, and 1 tablespoon chopped fresh cilantro.

BASIL MAYONNAISE
½ cup mayonnaise, ¼ cup chopped fresh basil, and ⅛ teaspoon ground black pepper.

CHIPOTLE MAYONNAISE
½ cup mayonnaise, 1 finely chopped chipotle chile in adobo, 1 teaspoon adobo sauce, and ¼ teaspoon ground cumin.

PESTO MAYONNAISE
½ cup mayonnaise and 1 tablespoon plus 1 teaspoon pesto.

HORSERADISH MAYONNAISE
½ cup mayonnaise, 1 tablespoon bottled white horseradish, and 1 teaspoon fresh lemon juice.

PICKLED JALAPEÑO MAYONNAISE
½ cup mayonnaise, ¼ cup chopped fresh cilantro, and 1 to 2 pickled jalapeños, finely chopped.

Health Club Sandwiches

This carrot, sprout, and bean spread combo will satisfy your palate and ease your conscience.

Prep: 25 minutes   Cook: 2 minutes

2	tablespoons olive oil
2	teaspoons plus 1 tablespoon fresh lemon juice
1	teaspoon honey
⅛	teaspoon ground black pepper
3	carrots, peeled and shredded (1 cup)
2	cups alfalfa sprouts
1	garlic clove, finely chopped
½	teaspoon ground cumin
	pinch ground red pepper (cayenne)
1	can (15 to 19 ounces) garbanzo beans, rinsed and drained
1	tablespoon water
1	large ripe tomato (12 ounces), thinly sliced
1	bunch watercress, tough stems trimmed
12	slices multigrain bread, lightly toasted

1. In medium bowl, stir 1 tablespoon oil, 2 teaspoons lemon juice, honey, and ground black pepper until mixed. Add carrots and alfalfa sprouts; toss until mixed and evenly coated with dressing.

2. In 2-quart saucepan, heat remaining 1 tablespoon oil over medium heat. Add garlic, cumin, and ground red pepper and cook until very fragrant. Stir in garbanzo beans and remove from heat. Add remaining 1 tablespoon lemon juice and water; mash to a coarse puree.

3. Spread garbanzo-bean mixture on 8 toast slices. Place tomato slices and watercress over 4 garbanzo-topped toast slices. Top remaining 4 garbanzo-topped slices with alfalfa-sprout mixture and place on watercress-topped bread. Cover with 4 remaining toast slices. Cut sandwiches in half. Makes 4 main-dish servings.

Each serving: About 379 calories, 14g protein, 57g carbohydrate, 12g total fat (2g saturated), 0mg cholesterol, 545mg sodium.

Health Club Sandwiches

Smoked Salmon Sandwiches with Dill Cream Cheese

To turn this open-face sandwich into a heartier, more portable treat, top with an additional slice of pumpernickel that's been spread with cream cheese.

Prep: 15 minutes

1	package (3 ounces) cream cheese, softened
1	tablespoon minced shallot
1	tablespoon capers, drained and chopped
1	tablespoon chopped fresh dill plus additional sprigs
1	teaspoon fresh lemon juice
4	slices pumpernickel bread
6	ounces thinly sliced smoked salmon
	ground black pepper
4	teaspoons salmon caviar (optional)

In small bowl, stir cream cheese, shallot, capers, chopped dill, and lemon juice until well blended. Spread evenly on bread slices and arrange smoked salmon on top. Sprinkle lightly with pepper. Place 1 teaspoon caviar on each sandwich, if you like, and top with dill sprigs. Makes 4 main-dish servings.

Each serving: About 207 calories, 12g protein, 17g carbohydrate, 10g total fat (5g saturated), 33mg cholesterol, 1,224mg sodium.

Tuscan Tuna Salad on Focaccia

Tuna and cannellini beans is a popular combination in Italy. Tossed with a piquant dressing, it makes a great sandwich filling.

Prep: 15 minutes

1	can (15 to 19 ounces) white kidney beans (cannellini), rinsed and drained
½	cup chopped fresh basil
3	tablespoons capers, drained and chopped
2	tablespoons fresh lemon juice
2	tablespoons olive oil
½	teaspoon salt
¼	teaspoon coarsely ground black pepper
1	can (6 ounces) tuna packed in water, drained and flaked
1	bunch watercress (4 ounces), tough stems trimmed and sprigs cut in half
1	round or square focaccia (8 inches) or 4 pita breads, cut horizontally in half
2	ripe medium tomatoes (6 ounces each), thinly sliced

1. In large bowl, mash 1 cup beans. Stir in basil, capers, lemon juice, oil, salt, and pepper until well blended. Add tuna, watercress, and remaining beans; toss to mix.

2. Spoon tuna mixture onto bottom half of focaccia; top with tomato slices. Replace top half of focaccia. To serve, cut into 4 wedges. Makes 4 main-dish servings.

Each serving: About 522 calories, 33g protein, 69g carbohydrate, 14g total fat (3g saturated), 22mg cholesterol, 1,464mg sodium.

Oyster Po'Boys

A New Orleans classic: French rolls stuffed with crispy deep-fried oysters.

Prep: 20 minutes   Cook: 30 seconds per batch

	vegetable oil
¼	cup mayonnaise
1	tablespoon minced shallot
1	tablespoon chopped fresh parsley
1	tablespoon capers, drained and chopped
¼	teaspoon hot pepper sauce plus additional
1	cup fine cracker crumbs
¼	teaspoon ground red pepper (cayenne)
1	pint shucked oysters, drained
4	soft French bread rolls, each cut horizontally in half and lightly toasted
1	cup very thinly sliced iceberg lettuce

1. In heavy 3-quart saucepan, heat 2 inches oil over medium-high heat until temperature reaches 375°F on deep-fat thermometer.

2. Meanwhile, in small bowl, combine mayonnaise, shallot, parsley, capers, and ¼ teaspoon hot pepper sauce until well blended.

3. On waxed paper, combine cracker crumbs and ground red pepper. Coat 6 oysters with crumb mixture. With slotted spoon, carefully add oysters, all at once, to hot oil and cook until golden, about 30 seconds. With slotted spoon, transfer oysters to paper towels to drain. Repeat coating and frying with remaining oysters.

4. Spread mayonnaise mixture evenly on bottom halves of toasted rolls. Top with lettuce, then oysters. Replace top halves of rolls. Serve with hot pepper sauce. Makes 4 main-dish servings.

Each serving: About 504 calories, 16g protein, 49g carbohydrate, 27g total fat (4g saturated), 78mg cholesterol, 898mg sodium.

Pan Bagnat

Tuna salad sandwiches á la Française! It's best to make this large sandwich a day ahead to allow the juices to soak into the bread.

Prep: 30 minutes plus chilling

1	round loaf (8 inches) country-style bread (12 ounces)
1	garlic clove, cut in half
¼	cup extravirgin olive oil
2	tablespoons red wine vinegar
¼	teaspoon salt
⅛	teaspoon ground black pepper
3	ripe medium tomatoes (1 pound), sliced
½	cup loosely packed small fresh basil leaves
1	tablespoon fresh mint leaves
1	can (6 ounces) tuna packed in olive oil, drained and flaked
⅓	cup Mediterranean olives, such as Gaeta or Kalamata, pitted and chopped
2	green onions, chopped
1	tablespoon capers, drained
1	large hard-cooked egg, peeled and sliced

1. Cut bread horizontally in half. Remove enough soft center from each half to make 1-inch shell. (Reserve soft bread for another use.)

2. Rub inside of bread halves with cut side of garlic. In cup, stir oil, vinegar, salt, and pepper until blended. Drizzle about one-fourth of oil mixture over garlic-rubbed bread.

3. On bottom half of bread, arrange one-third of tomato slices; drizzle with about half of remaining oil mixture, then top with half of basil and all of mint.

4. In small bowl, combine tuna, olives, green onions, and capers. Spoon tuna mixture over herbs; top with sliced egg. Arrange remaining tomato slices and remaining basil on top. Drizzle with remaining oil mixture. Replace top half of bread.

5. Wrap sandwich tightly in foil and refrigerate at least 4 hours or up to 24 hours before serving to blend flavors and let juices moisten bread. To serve, cut into 4 wedges. Makes 4 main-dish servings.

Each serving: About 396 calories, 16g protein, 31g carbohydrate, 25g total fat (3g saturated), 68mg cholesterol, 1,111mg sodium.

Turkey and Mango Roll-Ups

A lime-spiked curried chutney adds zip to this rolled sandwich. If you can't find lavash, divide the filling ingredients among four 8- to 10-inch flour tortillas.

Prep: 25 minutes plus chilling

1	large lime
¼	cup light mayonnaise
3	tablespoons mango chutney, chopped
½	teaspoon curry powder
⅛	teaspoon paprika
1	lavash flatbread (7 ounces)
1	medium cucumber (8 ounces), peeled and thinly sliced
8	ounces thinly sliced smoked turkey breast
1	medium mango, peeled and finely chopped
6	large green-leaf lettuce leaves

1. From lime, grate ¼ teaspoon peel and squeeze 1 tablespoon juice. In bowl, combine mayonnaise, chutney, lime peel and juice, curry powder, and paprika until blended.

2. Unfold lavash; spread evenly with mayonnaise mixture. Arrange cucumber slices over mayonnaise, then top with turkey, mango, and lettuce. From a short side, roll lavash up, jelly-roll fashion.

3. Wrap lavash roll in foil and refrigerate at least 2 hours or up to 4 hours to blend flavors and let bread soften. To serve, trim ends, then cut lavash roll into 4 pieces. Makes 4 main-dish servings.

♥ Each serving: About 375 calories, 18g protein, 55g carbohydrate, 7g total fat (2g saturated), 29mg cholesterol, 939mg sodium.

Chicken Club Sandwiches

This is also a great way to use leftover turkey or chicken—you'll need about two cups shredded or sliced meat.

Prep: 20 minutes   Cook: 15 minutes

4	small skinless, boneless chicken breast halves (1 pound)
¼	cup Flavored Mayonnaise (page 611) or plain mayonnaise
8	slices bacon, each cut crosswise in half
12	slices firm white or whole-wheat bread
2	ripe medium tomatoes (12 ounces), thinly sliced
8	small romaine lettuce leaves

1. In 10-inch skillet, combine chicken and enough *cold water* to cover; heat to boiling over high heat. Reduce heat; cover and simmer until chicken loses its pink color throughout, 8 to 10 minutes. Drain and cool to room temperature.

2. Meanwhile, prepare Flavored Mayonnaise. In 12-inch skillet, cook bacon over medium heat until browned. Transfer bacon to paper towels to drain.

3. Spread about 1 teaspoon mayonnaise on each bread slice; top 4 bread slices with tomato slices and lettuce.

4. Cut chicken breasts on diagonal into thin slices. Place 4 more bread slices, mayonnaise side up, on top of lettuce. Arrange chicken and bacon on top and cover with remaining 4 bread slices.

5. To serve, cut each sandwich on diagonal into quarters. Use frilled toothpicks to hold slices together, if you like. Makes 4 main-dish servings.

Each serving: About 513 calories, 38g protein, 47g carbohydrate, 18g total fat (4g saturated), 83mg cholesterol, 800mg sodium.

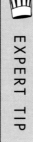

Whenever I use sliced or chopped fresh tomatoes, I first salt them lightly and then let them drain in a colander or on paper towels (5 minutes will do). I then pat them dry just before using. The salt pulls out the extra liquid and sharpens the flavor of the tomatoes. It make sandwiches tastier and also prevents them from getting soggy.

SARA MOULTON
TELEVISION HOST OF COOKING LIVE

EXPERT TIP

Open-Faced Steak and Mushroom Sandwiches

A hearty bistro-style meal.

Prep: 15 minutes   Cook: 30 minutes

2	tablespoons butter or margarine, softened
1	tablespoon plus 1 teaspoon chopped fresh tarragon
⅜	teaspoon ground black pepper
1	loaf (8 ounces) French bread, cut horizontally in half
3	teaspoons vegetable oil
1	beef flank steak (1¼ pounds)
¾	teaspoon salt
1	medium onion, thinly sliced
12	ounces mushrooms, trimmed and sliced
	pinch dried thyme
⅓	cup dry red wine

1. In small bowl, combine butter, 1 tablespoon tarragon, and ⅛ teaspoon pepper until well blended. Spread tarragon butter evenly on cut sides of bread. Cut each half into 4 pieces.

2. In heavy 12-inch skillet (preferably cast iron), heat 2 teaspoons oil over medium-high heat until very hot. Pat steak dry with paper towels and sprinkle with ¼ teaspoon salt and ⅛ teaspoon pepper. Add steak to skillet and cook 6 to 8 minutes per side for medium-rare or until desired doneness. Transfer steak to cutting board. Set aside.

3. Add remaining 1 teaspoon oil and onion to skillet; cook over medium heat, stirring frequently, until tender, about 5 minutes. Stir in mushrooms, thyme, remaining ½ teaspoon salt, and remaining ⅛ teaspoon pepper. Cook over medium-high heat until mushrooms are tender and liquid has evaporated, about 8 minutes. Stir in wine and boil 2 minutes. Remove from heat. Keep warm.

4. Holding knife almost parallel to cutting board, cut steak into thin slices across the grain; arrange on bread. Spoon mushroom mixture on top; sprinkle with remaining 1 teaspoon tarragon. Makes 4 main-dish servings.

Each serving: About 544 calories, 35g protein, 38g carbohydrate, 26g total fat (11g saturated), 89mg cholesterol, 946mg sodium.

Flank Steak Sandwiches with Chimichurri Sauce

Drizzled with the classic Argentinean herb vinaigrette and topped with onions, this is a great steak sandwich. If you can't find packaged grilled lavash, use Armenian flatbread instead.

Prep: 40 minutes   Cook: 30 minutes

	Chimichurri Sauce (page 554)
2	teaspoons olive oil
1	beef flank steak (1½ pounds)
¾	teaspoon salt
¼	teaspoon coarsely ground black pepper
2	large red onions, thinly sliced
1	package (14 ounces) lavash flatbreads, warmed

1. Prepare Chimichurri Sauce.

2. In heavy 12-inch skillet (preferably cast iron), heat oil over high heat until very hot. Pat steak dry with paper towels and sprinkle with ½ teaspoon salt and pepper.

3. Add steak to skillet; reduce heat to medium-high and cook 6 to 8 minutes per side for medium-rare or until desired doneness. Transfer steak to cutting board. Set aside.

4. Add onions and remaining ¼ teaspoon salt to skillet; cook over medium heat, stirring occasionally, until tender and browned, 12 to 15 minutes.

5. Holding knife almost parallel to cutting board, cut steak into thin slices across the grain. Drizzle 1 flatbread with 2 tablespoons chimichurri sauce; top with steak slices, onion, and additional 2 tablespoons sauce. Cover with remaining flatbread.

6. To serve, cut sandwich into 6 pieces. Pass remaining sauce separately. Makes 6 main-dish servings.

Each serving: About 625 calories, 33g protein, 56g carbohydrate, 27g total fat (7g saturated), 59mg cholesterol, 721mg sodium.

Flank Steak Sandwiches with Chimichurri Sauce

Roast Beef–Waldorf Club Sandwiches

Horseradish dressing and a crunchy celery-and-apple mixture make rare roast beef taste even better. A soak in ice water crisps the onion and tames its bite.

Prep: 20 minutes plus standing

4	very thin slices red onion
½	Golden Delicious apple, peeled and finely chopped (½ cup)
2	stalks celery, finely chopped
4	tablespoons reduced-fat mayonnaise
2	tablespoons sour cream
½	teaspoon fresh lemon juice
1	tablespoon bottled white horseradish
12	slices pumpernickel bread, lightly toasted, if desired
8	ounces thinly sliced rare roast beef
1	bunch (4 ounces) watercress, tough stems trimmed

1. In small bowl, combine onion with enough ice water to cover; let stand 15 minutes. Drain.

2. In separate small bowl, combine apple, celery, 2 tablespoons mayonnaise, 1 tablespoon sour cream, and lemon juice until well blended. In cup, combine horseradish, remaining 2 tablespoons mayonnaise, and remaining 1 tablespoon sour cream until blended.

3. Spread horseradish mixture evenly on 4 bread slices. Layer roast beef, onion, and watercress on top. Spread celery mixture evenly on 4 bread slices and place, celery mixture side up, over roast beef. Top with remaining bread slices. To serve, cut sandwiches in half. Makes 4 main-dish servings.

♥ Each serving: About 451 calories, 25g protein, 54g carbohydrate, 15g total fat (5g saturated), 50mg cholesterol, 842mg sodium.

Classic Italian Hero

(pictured on page 608)

If you feel the urge, build on the basic recipe by adding any of the ingredients listed below and/or whatever else you can think of.

 Prep: 15 minutes

¼	cup vinaigrette of choice
1	large loaf (12 ounces) Italian bread
4	ounces thinly sliced hot and/or sweet capocollo, prosciutto, soppressata, and/or salami
4	ounces mozzarella cheese, preferably fresh, thinly sliced shredded romaine lettuce or arugula, peperoncini, basil leaves, roasted red peppers, very thinly sliced red onions, pesto, olivada, and/or sliced ripe tomatoes

1. Prepare vinaigrette. Cut bread horizontally in half. Remove enough soft center from each half to make room for filling. (Reserve soft bread for another use.)

2. Brush vinaigrette evenly over cut sides of bread. Layer meats and cheese on bottom half of bread. Top with additional ingredients of your choice. Replace top half of bread. If not serving right away, wrap sandwich in foil and refrigerate up to 4 hours. Cut into 4 pieces. Makes 4 main-dish servings.

Each serving: About 430 calories, 20g protein, 36g carbohydrate, 23g total fat (7g saturated), 48mg cholesterol, 1,226mg sodium.

Muffuletta

A classic in New Orleans' French Quarter, where it's especially good at the Central Grocery. But you don't have to travel all that way; this recipe will "let the good times roll" at your house.

Prep: 25 minutes plus chilling

1¼	cups finely chopped celery with leaves
1	cup drained giardiniera (Italian mixed pickled vegetables), chopped
¾	cup green and black Mediterranean olives, such as Gaeta or Kalamata, pitted and chopped
⅓	cup chopped fresh parsley
1	garlic clove, minced
¼	cup olive oil
¼	teaspoon ground black pepper
1	round loaf (8 to 10 inches) soft French bread
4	ounces thinly sliced smoked ham
4	ounces thinly sliced Provolone cheese
4	ounces thinly sliced Genoa salami

1. In medium bowl, combine celery, giardiniera, olives, parsley, garlic, oil, and pepper until well mixed. Cover and refrigerate at least 4 hours or up to overnight to blend flavors.

2. Cut bread horizontally in half. Remove enough soft center from each half to make room for filling. (Reserve soft bread for another use). Onto bottom half of bread, spoon half of celery-olive mixture; layer ham, cheese, and salami on top. Spoon remaining celery-olive mixture over. Replace top half of bread.

3. Wrap sandwich in foil and refrigerate at least 4 hours or up to 24 hours to blend flavors and let juices soften bread. To serve, let stand at room temperature about 30 minutes, then cut into 6 wedges. Makes 6 main-dish servings.

Each serving: About 399 calories, 17g protein, 28g carbohydrate, 24g total fat (8g saturated), 41mg cholesterol, 1,615mg sodium.

Cucumber Tea Sandwiches

Utterly English and perfectly delicious, these classic sandwiches are a necessity at a tea party. A V-slicer or mandoline will make the thinnest cucumber slices.

Prep: 20 minutes plus chilling

1	English (seedless) cucumber
½	teaspoon salt
5	tablespoons butter or margarine, softened
16	very thin slices white or whole-wheat bread
32	fresh mint leaves (optional)

1. Cut cucumber lengthwise in half and remove seeds. Cut cucumber crosswise into paper-thin slices. In colander set over bowl, toss cucumber and salt. Cover and refrigerate 30 minutes, stirring occasionally. Discard liquid in bowl. Pat cucumber slices dry with paper towels.

2. Lightly spread butter on each bread slice. Arrange cucumber on 8 buttered slices; place 1 mint leaf, if using, in each corner of bread. Top with remaining bread slices. Trim crusts and cut each sandwich on diagonal into quarters.

3. If not serving right away, line jelly-roll pan with damp paper towels. Place sandwiches in pan; cover with additional damp paper towels to keep bread from drying out. Cover pan tightly with plastic wrap and refrigerate up to 4 hours. Makes 32 tea sandwiches.

Each sandwich: About 36 calories, 1g protein, 4g carbohydrate, 2g total fat (1g saturated), 5mg cholesterol, 74mg sodium.

Watercress and Radish Tea Sandwiches

These tea sandwiches look demure but have a peppery kick.

Prep: 20 minutes

8	very thin slices white or whole-wheat bread
3	tablespoons butter or margarine, softened
	pinch salt
	pinch ground black pepper
½	bunch watercress, tough stems trimmed
3	radishes, very thinly sliced

1. Lightly spread butter on each bread slice and sprinkle with salt and pepper. Arrange only very tender watercress sprigs on 4 buttered slices and top with radishes. Cover with remaining bread slices. Trim crusts and cut each sandwich on diagonal into quarters.

2. If not serving right away, line jelly-roll pan with damp paper towels. Place sandwiches in pan; cover with additional damp paper towels to keep bread from drying out. Cover pan tightly with plastic wrap and refrigerate up to 4 hours. Makes 16 tea sandwiches.

Each sandwich: About 39 calories, 1g protein, 4g carbohydrate, 2g total fat (1g saturated), 6mg cholesterol, 71mg sodium.

Dilled-Egg Tea Sandwiches

Use this recipe for large-size sandwiches as well as delicate tea sandwiches. They're tasty either way.

Prep: 40 minutes

3	large hard-cooked eggs, peeled and finely shredded
¼	cup mayonnaise
2	tablespoons chopped fresh dill
¼	teaspoon freshly grated lemon peel
¼	teaspoon ground black pepper
12	very thin slices white or whole-wheat bread

1. In medium bowl, combine eggs, mayonnaise, dill, lemon peel, and pepper. Spread evenly on 6 bread slices; top with remaining bread slices. Trim crusts and cut each sandwich into 3 equal rectangles.

2. If not serving right away, line jelly-roll pan with damp paper towels. Place sandwiches in pan; cover with additional damp paper towels to keep bread from drying out. Cover pan tightly with plastic wrap and refrigerate up to 4 hours. Makes 18 tea sandwiches.

Each sandwich: About 68 calories, 2g protein, 6g carbohydrate, 4g total fat (1g saturated), 37mg cholesterol, 95mg sodium.

Cheddar and Chutney Tea Sandwiches

This sweet-and-savory combination is a treat with a cup of tea, or even a cocktail.

 Prep: 15 minutes

3	tablespoons butter or margarine, softened
3	tablespoons mango chutney, finely chopped
8	very thin slices white or whole-wheat bread
4	ounces Cheddar cheese, shredded (1 cup)

1. In small bowl, combine butter and chutney until well blended. Spread evenly on bread slices. Sprinkle Cheddar on buttered side of 4 bread slices. Top with remaining bread. Trim crusts and cut each sandwich into 4 squares or triangles.

2. If not serving right away, line jelly-roll pan with damp paper towels. Place sandwiches in pan; cover with additional damp paper towels to keep bread from drying out. Cover pan tightly with plastic wrap and refrigerate up to 4 hours. Makes 16 tea sandwiches.

Each sandwich: About 78 calories, 2g protein, 6g carbohydrate, 5g total fat (3g saturated), 13mg cholesterol, 136mg sodium.

Smoked Salmon Tea Sandwiches

Using two different breads for these sandwiches is a nice touch but not absolutely necessary.

 Prep: 20 minutes

8	very thin slices white bread
8	very thin slices whole-wheat bread
6	tablespoons butter or margarine, softened, or whipped cream cheese
6	ounces very thinly sliced smoked salmon

1. Lightly spread butter on each bread slice. Arrange salmon on buttered side of white bread, trimming to fit. Top with whole-wheat bread. Trim crusts and cut each sandwich on diagonal into quarters.

2. If not serving immediately, line jelly-roll pan with damp paper towels. Place sandwiches in pan; cover with additional damp paper towels to keep bread from drying out.

Cover pan tightly with plastic wrap and refrigerate up to 4 hours. Makes 32 tea sandwiches.

Each sandwich: About 43 calories, 2g protein, 3g carbohydrate, 3g total fat (1g saturated), 7mg cholesterol, 166mg sodium.

Pinwheel Sandwiches

Use your favorite flavored cream cheese or garlic-and-herb cheese, if you prefer.

 Prep: 30 minutes

1	package (8 ounces) cream cheese, softened
4	small green onions, finely chopped
3	tablespoons chopped fresh parsley
4	radishes, minced
1/8	teaspoon salt
1/8	teaspoon ground black pepper
24	very thin slices white and/or whole-wheat bread, crusts trimmed

1. In small bowl, combine cream cheese, green onions, parsley, radishes, salt, and pepper until well blended. Place 2 bread slices together, overlapping them by 1 inch. With rolling pin, lightly flatten bread. Repeat with remaining bread. Gently spread cream cheese mixture on pairs of bread slices; from a short side, roll each pair up, jelly-roll fashion.

2. If not serving right away, line jelly-roll pan with damp paper towels. Place rolls in pan; cover with additional damp paper towels to keep bread from drying out. Cover pan tightly with plastic wrap and refrigerate up to 4 hours.

3. Cut each roll crosswise to make 4 pinwheels. Makes 48 pinwheel sandwiches.

Each sandwich: About 42 calories, 1g protein, 5g carbohydrate, 2g total fat (1g saturated), 5mg cholesterol, 71mg sodium.

18

DESSERTS

Here's a collection of scrumptious desserts that goes beyond cakes, pies, and frozen sweets: ethereal soufflés, melt-in-your-mouth meringues, creamy custards, phyllo pastries, choux and puff pastry desserts, an array of puddings, and other earthly delights. (And several that have been given reduced-fat makeovers, too.) Many desserts rely on eggs for their distinctive textures, which requires a certain amount of attention to detail, so here are some tips to help you with some of the basic techniques.

CUSTARDS

Custard, a cooked milk or cream mixture thickened with eggs and sweetened with sugar, can be baked for a dessert or cooked on top of the stove to make a silky dessert sauce (also called a stirred or pouring custard). The eggs for a custard should be stirred or whisked just until the yolks and whites are combined. Mix in the milk just until blended. If overbeaten, a custard mixture will become foamy, making it difficult to check the thickening progress of a stirred custard, and it will bake into tiny bubbles on the surface of a baked custard. To remove any chalazae (the white cords that anchor the yolk) and to ensure a smooth texture, strain the custard mixture. (With stirred custards, this is done after cooking.)

A moderate cooking temperature is necessary for perfect

Orange-Liqueur Soufflé

custard: Overbaked custards become tough and watery and overcooked stirred custards curdle. To prevent overcooking, baked custards are always cooked in a water bath (a large roasting pan filled with enough hot water to come halfway up the sides of the custards), which insulates the custards from the oven's heat so they cook evenly. For stirred custards, the yolks must be gradually heated to avoid curdling. A small amount of the hot milk is stirred into the yolks to warm them, then the yolk mixture is stirred back into the remaining hot milk.

Keep in mind that even though the center of a properly baked custard may jiggle when gently shaken, it will continue to cook and set up once removed from the oven. To test for doneness, insert a knife ½ inch into the custard, about 1 inch from the center; it should come out clean. Remove the custard promptly from its water bath or it will overcook. (Use a jar lifter.) Custard sauces must be stirred constantly with a wooden spoon over low heat to prevent scorching and overcooking. The sauce is cooked until thick enough to coat a spoon (if you draw your finger through the sauce on the back of the spoon, it will cut a distinct path). You can also check the doneness of the sauce with an instant-read thermometer: The temperature should range between 160° and 170°F. Never allow a custard sauce to come near the boiling point or it will curdle. Strain the custard into a bowl to remove any stray bits of cooked egg white. Cool the sauce with a piece of plastic wrap pressed directly onto the surface.

HIGH-RISING SOUFFLÉS

The secret to a beautifully risen soufflé? Perfectly beaten eggs whites. Room-temperature eggs beat to the highest volume, but eggs separate most easily when chilled. So, separate eggs when cold, but allow the whites to stand at room temperature for thirty minutes to warm them. Or place the whites in a heatproof bowl set in a larger bowl of hot (tap) water; stir briefly until they have warmed slightly.

Do not overbeat egg whites: Beat them just until stiff—not dry. Properly beaten whites fold easily into a soufflé mixture; overbeaten whites separate into cottony clumps. Fold about one-third of the whites into the batter to lighten the mixture, then fold the remaining whites into the batter just until blended.

Because soufflés need a blast of hot air to rise properly, be sure the oven is preheated thoroughly (allow at least twenty minutes) before baking. Position the rack in the lower third of the oven so the soufflé has plenty of room to rise. It is done when puffed and golden brown, with a somewhat soft, barely set center. Call your guests to the table before you remove the soufflé from the oven. When exposed to cool air, it will only keep its puff for three to five minutes.

THE MAGIC OF MERINGUES

Meringues are nothing more complicated than a beaten mixture of egg whites and sugar. There are two types of meringue, soft and hard, which simply depend on the proportion of sugar to egg whites. Soft meringue contains less sugar and is used mostly as a pie topping. Hard meringue contains more sugar and can be formed or piped into shapes such as disks (to become the delicious dessert called *dacquoise*) or shells (to hold fruit salads or other fillings) and then baked until crisp.

Don't make meringue on a humid or rainy day, because it will absorb the moisture from the air and end up soggy or "weep" (exude little beads of moisture). Beat room-temperature egg whites at high speed until soft peaks form. Then gradually beat in the sugar, two tablespoons at a time: If the sugar is added too quickly, it won't have enough time to completely dissolve, and the meringue won't set up. Continue beating just until stiff peaks form. Check to make sure that the sugar has dissolved: Rub a bit of the meringue between your fingers; it should feel smooth, not gritty.

To make crisp meringues that are lightly colored without any trace of stickiness, they are baked at a low temperature. To further ensure a dry interior, meringues are left in the turned-off oven while they cool—if removed too soon, the insides will be gummy. Meringue toppings are baked at a higher temperature until their peaks are browned.

GETTING TO KNOW GELATIN

Gelatin, which is odorless, tasteless, and colorless, is often used as a thickening agent in desserts. The most common form is powdered gelatin, which comes in individual envelopes. One envelope equals about 2½ teaspoons (¼ ounce) and will set about two cups of liquid.

Gelatin must always be dissolved: a simple two-step process. Sprinkle the gelatin over a small amount of cold liquid and allow to stand for about five minutes until it has softened and soaks up the liquid; this helps the gelatin to dissolve more efficiently. Add the softened gelatin to the bulk of the recipe's liquid. Stir it constantly over low heat until it has completely dissolved (if not, the dessert will be grainy and will not gel properly). To check that all the gelatin crystals have fully dissolved, lift a little of the gelatin into a spoon: There should be no visible crystals. Or, rub a little bit of the gelatin between your fingers.

If adding fruit to gelatin desserts, keep the fruit pieces small; gelatin pulls away from pieces that are too large. Raw papaya, kiwifruit, and pineapple contain enzymes that break down gelatin, preventing it from setting up.

To quick-chill gelatin, place the bowl of gelatin in a larger bowl of ice water and stir often with a rubber spatula until it has thickened and begins to mound but is not lumpy. Don't try to speed this process in the freezer.

Gelatin desserts are often molded. To remove a set dessert from a custard cup, a dip in water may not be needed, as long as the tight seal between the dessert and the mold can be broken. Sometimes a sharp rap on the counter is enough to break the seal; if necessary, run the tip of a knife around the inside of the mold. If the dessert is in a large mold, it will need to be loosened from the mold in warm water: Fill a large bowl with warm—not hot—water. Place the mold in the bowl and let stand for about ten seconds (no longer, or the gelatin could melt). Dry the outside of the mold with a kitchen towel. Place the serving plate on top of the mold, quickly invert it, and shake to release the dessert.

Fresh Apple Soufflés

A fresh fruit puree is the base for these little soufflés. So much sophistication and flavor for so few calories.

Prep: 45 minutes plus cooling	Bake: 12 minutes

4	cups peeled, cored and coarsely chopped apples, such as McIntosh or Cortland (4 to 5 medium)
1	tablespoon fresh lemon juice
1	tablespoon butter or margarine, melted
2	tablespoons plus ¼ cup sugar
6	large egg whites
½	teaspoon cream of tartar
1	teaspoon vanilla extract

1. In nonreactive 2-quart saucepan, combine apples and lemon juice. Cover and cook over medium-high heat until apples are soft, about 10 minutes. Remove cover and cook, stirring occasionally, until almost all liquid has evaporated and apples are reduced to 1 cup, about 10 minutes longer.

2. In blender with center of cover removed to allow steam to escape or in food processor with knife blade attached, puree apple mixture until smooth. Transfer to large bowl; cool to room temperature.

3. Meanwhile, preheat oven to 425°F. Brush six 6-ounce custard cups or ramekins with melted butter and sprinkle with 2 tablespoons sugar.

4. In large bowl, with mixer at high speed, beat egg whites and cream of tartar until soft peaks form when beaters are lifted. Sprinkle in remaining ¼ cup sugar, 1 tablespoon at a time, beating until sugar has dissolved. Add vanilla; continue beating until egg whites stand in stiff, glossy peaks when beaters are lifted. With rubber spatula, fold beaten egg whites, one-third at a time, into apple mixture just until blended.

5. Spoon into prepared custard cups. Place cups in jelly-roll pan for easier handling. Bake until soufflés have puffed and begin to brown, 12 to 15 minutes. Serve immediately. Makes 6 servings.

♥ Each serving: About 127 calories, 4g protein, 24g carbohydrate, 2g total fat (1g saturated), 5mg cholesterol, 75mg sodium.

Fresh Pear Soufflés

Prepare soufflés as directed but prepare pear puree instead of apple puree: In nonreactive 2-quart saucepan, combine **4 cups peeled, cored, and coarsely chopped fully ripe pears** (5 to 6 medium), **1 tablespoon fresh lemon juice,** and **2 teaspoons minced, peeled fresh ginger.** Cover and cook over medium-high heat until pears have softened, about 15 minutes. Remove cover and cook, stirring occasionally, until almost all liquid has evaporated and pears are reduced to 1 cup, 10 to 15 minutes longer. In blender with center of cover removed to allow steam to escape or in food processor with knife blade attached, puree pear mixture until smooth. Cool to room temperature. Fold beaten egg whites into pear puree and bake as directed.

Banana Soufflés

Prepare soufflés as directed but prepare banana puree instead of apple puree: In blender or in food processor with knife blade attached, puree **3 very ripe large bananas**, cut into large pieces, with **1 tablespoon fresh lemon juice** and **¼ teaspoon ground cinnamon** until smooth. Fold beaten egg whites into banana puree and bake as directed.

Peach or Apricot Soufflés

Prepare soufflés as directed but prepare peach or apricot puree instead of apple puree: Drain **1 can (1 pound, 13 ounces) peaches in heavy syrup or 2 cans (16 ounces each) apricots in heavy syrup.** In blender or food processor with knife blade attached, puree peaches or apricots until smooth. Transfer to 4-quart saucepan and heat to boiling over medium-high heat. Reduce heat to medium-low and cook, stirring occasionally, until puree has reduced to 1 cup, 15 to 20 minutes. Cool to room temperature. Stir in **1 tablespoon fresh lemon juice** and **⅛ teaspoon almond extract.** Fold beaten egg whites into fruit puree and bake as directed.

Chocolate Soufflés

These always make an impressive dessert. They are irresistible as individual soufflés, and spectacular baked as one large soufflé.

Prep: 20 minutes plus cooling   Bake: 25 minutes

1¼	cups plus 3 tablespoons granulated sugar
¼	cup all-purpose flour
1	teaspoon instant espresso-coffee powder
1	cup milk
5	squares (5 ounces) unsweetened chocolate, chopped
3	tablespoons butter or margarine, softened
4	large eggs, separated, plus 2 large egg whites
2	teaspoons vanilla extract
6	large egg whites
¼	teaspoon salt
	confectioners' sugar

1. In 3-quart saucepan, combine 1¼ cups granulated sugar, flour, and espresso powder. With wire whisk, gradually stir in milk until blended. Cook over medium heat, stirring constantly, until mixture has thickened and boils; boil, stirring, 1 minute. Remove from heat.

2. Stir in chocolate and butter until melted and smooth. With whisk, beat in egg yolks until well blended; stir in vanilla. Cool to lukewarm.

3. Meanwhile, preheat oven to 350°F. Grease eight 6-ounce custard cups or ramekins or 2-quart soufflé dish; sprinkle lightly with remaining granulated sugar.

4. In large bowl, with mixer at high speed, beat egg whites and salt just until stiff peaks form when beaters are lifted. With rubber spatula, gently fold one-third of beaten egg whites into chocolate mixture; fold back into remaining egg whites just until blended.

5. Spoon into prepared custard cups. (If using custard cups, place in jelly-roll pan for easier handling.) Bake until soufflés have puffed and centers are glossy, 25 to 30 minutes. Dust with confectioners' sugar. Serve immediately. Makes 8 servings.

Each serving: About 356 calories, 7g protein, 44g carbohydrate, 19g total fat (10g saturated), 122mg cholesterol, 178mg sodium.

Orange Liqueur Soufflé

(pictured on page 620)

Perhaps the most popular and elegant of all soufflés. Infuse it with your favorite orange liqueur: Grand Marnier, curaçao, or Triple Sec.

Prep: 20 minutes plus cooling   Bake: 30 minutes

4	tablespoons butter or margarine
⅓	cup all-purpose flour
⅛	teaspoon salt
1½	cups milk, warmed
½	cup plus 2 tablespoons granulated sugar
4	large egg yolks
⅓	cup orange-flavored liqueur
1	tablespoon freshly grated orange peel
6	large egg whites
	confectioners' sugar
	whipped cream (optional)

1. In heavy 2-quart saucepan, melt butter over low heat. Add flour and salt; cook, stirring, 1 minute. With wire whisk, gradually whisk in warm milk. Cook over medium heat, stirring with wooden spoon, until mixture has thickened and boils. Reduce heat and simmer 1 minute. Remove from heat.

2. With wire whisk, stir ½ cup granulated sugar into milk mixture. Gradually whisk in egg yolks, stirring rapidly to prevent curdling. Cool egg-yolk mixture to lukewarm, stirring occasionally. Stir in orange liqueur and orange peel.

3. Preheat oven to 375°F. Grease 2-quart soufflé dish with butter and evenly sprinkle with remaining 2 tablespoons granulated sugar.

4. In large bowl, with mixer at high speed, beat egg whites until stiff peaks form when beaters are lifted. Gently fold one-third of beaten egg whites into egg-yolk mixture; fold back into remaining egg whites just until blended.

5. Spoon mixture into prepared soufflé dish. If desired, to create top-hat effect (center will rise higher than edge), with back of spoon, make 1-inch-deep indentation all around top of soufflé about 1 inch from edge of dish. Bake until soufflé has puffed and is golden and knife inserted 1 inch from edge

comes out clean, 30 to 35 minutes. Dust with confectioners' sugar. Serve immediately. If desired, pass whipped cream to spoon onto each serving. Makes 8 servings.

Each serving: About 214 calories, 6g protein, 26g carbohydrate, 10g total fat (5g saturated), 128mg cholesterol, 162mg sodium.

Hazelnut Dacquoise

An exquisite combination of crunchy hazelnut meringue disks and layers of coffee and chocolate whipped creams. To make life easy, bake the meringues up to one week ahead, wrap in plastic wrap, and store in an airtight container.

Prep: 1 hour 30 minutes plus cooling and chilling
Bake: 45 minutes

1	cup hazelnuts (filberts), toasted and skinned (page 729)
1½	cups plus 4 tablespoons confectioners' sugar
2	tablespoons cornstarch
6	large egg whites
½	teaspoon cream of tartar
3	squares (3 ounces) semisweet chocolate, chopped
3	cups heavy or whipping cream
1	teaspoon vanilla extract
1	tablespoon instant espresso-coffee powder
	Chocolate Curls (page 681)

1. Preheat oven to 300°F. Line two large cookie sheets with foil. Using 8-inch round cake pan as guide, with toothpick, outline four circles on foil (two on each cookie sheet).

2. In food processor with knife blade attached, process hazelnuts, ¾ cup confectioners' sugar, and cornstarch until hazelnuts are finely ground.

3. In large bowl, with mixer at high speed, beat egg whites and cream of tartar until soft peaks form when beaters are lifted. Sprinkle in ¾ cup confectioners' sugar, 2 tablespoons at a time, beating until sugar has completely dissolved and egg whites stand in stiff, glossy peaks when beaters are lifted.

4. With rubber spatula, gently fold ground hazelnut mixture into beaten egg whites just until blended. Spoon one-fourth of meringue mixture (about 1¼ cups) inside each circle on prepared cookie sheets. With narrow metal spatula, spread meringue evenly to fill circles.

5. Bake meringues 45 minutes. Turn off oven; leave meringues in oven 1 hour to dry. Cool meringues on cookie sheets on wire racks 10 minutes. Carefully peel foil from meringues and cool completely. Store in airtight container at room temperature up to 1 week.

6. Assemble dacquoise: In heavy 1-quart saucepan, melt chocolate over low heat, stirring frequently, until smooth; cool. In small bowl, with mixer at medium speed, beat 1½ cups cream, 1 tablespoon confectioners' sugar, and ½ teaspoon vanilla until soft peaks form. With rubber spatula, fold half of cream mixture into cooled melted chocolate just until blended (do not overfold); fold in remaining whipped cream.

7. In cup, dissolve espresso powder in 2 tablespoons cream; set aside. In small bowl, with mixer at medium speed, beat remaining cream, remaining 3 tablespoons confectioners' sugar, and remaining ½ teaspoon vanilla until soft peaks form. Add espresso mixture and beat until stiff peaks form.

8. Reserve ¼ cup chocolate cream. Place one meringue layer on platter; with narrow metal spatula, spread with half of chocolate cream. Top with another meringue layer and spread with half of coffee cream. Repeat with remaining meringue layers and remaining cream fillings. Mound reserved chocolate cream on top. Refrigerate dacquoise 5 hours or up to overnight to soften layers slightly. To serve, arrange Chocolate Curls on top of dacquoise. Makes 12 servings.

Each serving without Chocolate Curls: About 383 calories, 5g protein, 27g carbohydrate, 30g total fat (15g saturated), 82mg cholesterol, 52mg sodium.

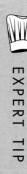

The color of caramel is best viewed against a white plate. Dip a skewer into the caramel from time to time and let drops of the caramel fall onto the plate. Caramel is most flavorful when it has just turned from amber to slightly reddish amber; immediately remove it from the heat to prevent it from burning.

ALICE MEDRICH
COOKBOOK AUTHOR

EXPERT TIP

Meringue Shells

Fill these versatile shells with whipped cream and berries or ice cream and chocolate sauce, or use to make Meringue Nests with Lemon Filling and Strawberries (right). Do not make meringues in humid weather: They will not stay crisp.

Prep: 15 minutes plus cooling	Bake: 2 hours
3	large egg whites
1/8	teaspoon cream of tartar
3/4	cup sugar
1/2	teaspoon vanilla extract

1. Preheat oven to 200°F. Line large cookie sheet with foil or parchment paper. In small bowl, with mixer at high speed, beat egg whites and cream of tartar until soft peaks form when beaters are lifted. Sprinkle in sugar, 2 tablespoons at a time, beating until sugar has dissolved. Add vanilla; continue beating until egg whites stand in stiff, glossy peaks when beaters are lifted.

2. Spoon meringue into 6 equal mounds on prepared cookie sheet, 4 inches apart. With back of tablespoon, spread each mound into 4-inch round. Make well in center of each round to form "nest."

3. Bake until meringues are firm and just begin to color, about 2 hours. Turn off oven; leave meringues in oven 1 hour or up to overnight to dry. If not leaving overnight, cool completely on cookie sheet on wire rack. Store meringue shells in airtight container. Makes 6 servings.

♥ Each serving: About 106 calories, 2g protein, 25g carbohydrate, 0g total fat (0g saturated), 0mg cholesterol, 28mg sodium.

PERFECT MERINGUE SHELLS

For symmetrically shaped meringue shells, mark circles on the foil with a toothpick. Use a saucer as a guide for large shells or a 1½-inch jar cap or cookie cutter for miniature shells.

Miniature Meringue Shells

Preheat oven to 200°F. Line two cookie sheets with foil or parchment paper. Prepare as directed in Step 1. Drop meringue by rounded teaspoons, 2 inches apart, on prepared cookie sheets. With back of teaspoon, make well in center of each mound to form "nest" about 1½ inches across. Bake until meringues are firm and just begin to color, about 1 hour. Turn off oven; leave meringues in oven 1 hour or up to overnight to dry. If not leaving overnight, cool completely on cookie sheet on wire rack. Store as directed. Makes 20 miniature shells.

♥ Each serving: About 32 calories, 0g protein, 8g carbohydrate, 0g total fat (0g saturated), 0mg cholesterol, 8mg sodium.

Meringue Nests with Lemon Filling and Strawberries

Make the meringue nests and the lemon filling up to two days ahead, and assemble the dessert just before serving.

Prep: 35 minutes plus chilling and cooling	Bake: 2 hours
	Lemon Filling (page 680)
	Meringue Shells (left)
1/2	cup heavy or whipping cream
1	pint strawberries, hulled and cut into quarters
2	tablespoons strawberry preserves
	mint leaves

1. Prepare Lemon Filling. While lemon filling is chilling, prepare Meringue Shells.

2. To serve, in small bowl, with mixer at medium speed, beat cream until stiff peaks form. With rubber spatula, gently fold whipped cream into lemon filling until blended.

3. In medium bowl, toss strawberries with preserves to coat evenly. Spoon lemon filling into meringue shells, dividing evenly. Top with strawberry mixture and garnish with mint leaves; place on dessert plates. Makes 6 servings.

Each serving: About 448 calories, 4g protein, 60g carbohydrate, 22g total fat (13g saturated), 200mg cholesterol, 159mg sodium.

Meringue Nests with Lemon Filling and Strawberries

Lime Pavlova

This dessert is very low in fat but rich in flavor; a creamy fresh lime filling is spooned into a crisp meringue nest. The meringue can be made several days ahead and stored in an airtight container. Fill up to four hours before serving.

Prep: 30 minutes plus cooling and chilling   Bake: 1 hour 15 minutes

3	large egg whites
¼	teaspoon cream of tartar
¼	teaspoon salt
½	cup sugar
1	teaspoon vanilla extract
4 to 6 limes	
1	can (14 ounces) lowfat sweetened condensed milk
1	container (8 ounces) plain lowfat yogurt
1	envelope unflavored gelatin
¼	cup cold water
5	strawberries, hulled and each cut in half

1. Preheat oven to 275°F. Line cookie sheet with foil. Using 9-inch round cake pan or plate as guide, with toothpick, outline circle on foil.

2. In medium bowl, with mixer at high speed, beat egg whites, cream of tartar, and salt until soft peaks form when beaters are lifted. Sprinkle in sugar, 2 tablespoons at a time, beating until sugar has dissolved. Add vanilla; continue beating until egg whites stand in stiff, glossy peaks when beaters are lifted.

3. Spoon meringue inside circle on cookie sheet. With back of tablespoon, make well in center to form "nest" about 1½ inches high at edge. Bake meringue 1 hour 15 minutes. Turn off oven; leave meringue in oven 1 hour to dry. Cool completely on cookie sheet on wire rack.

4. Meanwhile, prepare filling: From limes, grate 2 teaspoons peel and squeeze ½ cup juice. In medium bowl, with wire whisk, beat condensed milk, yogurt, and lime peel and juice until well blended.

5. In 1-quart saucepan, evenly sprinkle gelatin over cold water; let stand 2 minutes to soften gelatin. Cook over medium-low heat, stirring until gelatin has completely dissolved. Add gelatin to lime mixture and whisk until blended.

6. Set bowl with lime mixture in larger bowl filled with ice water. With rubber spatula, stir mixture occasionally until it begins to thicken, about 20 minutes. Remove bowl from water bath.

7. With metal spatula, carefully loosen and separate meringue shell from foil; place on serving plate. Spoon lime filling into meringue shell; refrigerate until set, about 1 hour. Garnish with strawberries and serve. Makes 10 servings.

♥ Each serving: About 234 calories, 7g protein, 45g carbohydrate, 2g total fat (2g saturated), 8mg cholesterol, 147mg sodium.

Raspberry-Pear Trifle

A trifle is a favorite holiday dessert that easily pleases a crowd. It can be made a day ahead.

Prep: 1 hour plus chilling   Cook: 10 minutes

2¼	cups milk
¾	cup plus 3 tablespoons sugar
¼	cup cornstarch
⅛	teaspoon salt
6	large egg yolks
¼	cup amaretto (almond-flavored liqueur)
3	cans (16 ounces each) pear halves in extra light syrup
1	package (10 ounces) frozen raspberries in light syrup, thawed
1	cup heavy or whipping cream
16	amaretti cookies, coarsely crushed (about 1¼ cups)
1	store-bought pound cake (10¾ to 12 ounces), cut into 1-inch cubes
	fresh raspberries (about ½ pint)

1. Prepare custard: In heavy 3-quart saucepan, combine 1¾ cups milk and ¾ cup sugar; heat over medium-high heat, stirring occasionally until sugar has dissolved and bubbles form around edge. Remove from heat.

2. Meanwhile, in medium bowl, with wire whisk, blend remaining ½ cup milk, cornstarch, and salt until smooth; beat in egg yolks until well combined.

3. Into egg-yolk mixture, stir about ⅓ cup hot milk mixture; gradually stir egg-yolk mixture back into milk mixture in saucepan. Cook over medium heat, stirring constantly, until mixture has thickened and boils. Stir in liqueur. Pour custard into clean bowl; press plastic wrap onto surface of custard. Refrigerate until well chilled, 3 hours or up to overnight.

4. Drain pear halves, reserving ⅓ cup syrup (discard remaining syrup). In blender, puree raspberries with their syrup and reserved syrup from pears until smooth.

5. In small bowl, with mixer at medium speed, beat cream and remaining 3 tablespoons sugar until stiff peaks form. Reserve 1 generous cup whipped cream for garnish. With rubber spatula, gently fold remaining whipped cream into chilled custard until blended.

6. Reserve ¼ cup amaretti cookie crumbs. In 4-quart glass trifle or serving bowl, place half of pound-cake cubes;

spoon half of raspberry mixture over pound cake. Arrange half of pear halves over raspberry mixture; sprinkle with half of cookie crumbs. Spread half of custard over crumb layer. Repeat layering.

7. Mound reserved whipped cream on top of trifle; sprinkle with reserved cookie crumbs and raspberries. Cover and refrigerate at least 2 hours to blend flavors or up to 24 hours. Makes 16 servings.

Each serving: About 318 calories, 4g protein, 46g carbohydrate, 13g total fat (7g saturated), 149mg cholesterol, 128mg sodium.

Tiramisù

This classic sweet is a favorite afternoon treat in Italy; literally, it means "pick me up."

Prep: 35 minutes plus chilling

1	cup hot espresso or very strong brewed coffee
3	tablespoons brandy
2	tablespoons plus ½ cup sugar
18	crisp Italian ladyfingers (savoiardi; 5 ounces)
½	cup milk
1	container (16 to 17½ ounces) mascarpone cheese
¾	cup heavy or whipping cream
	unsweetened cocoa
	Chocolate Curls (page 681)

1. In 9-inch pie plate, stir coffee, brandy, and 2 tablespoons sugar until sugar has dissolved; cool to room temperature. Dip both sides of 9 ladyfingers into coffee mixture, one at a time, to soak completely; arrange in single layer in 8-inch square baking dish.

2. In large bowl, stir milk and remaining ½ cup sugar until sugar has dissolved. Stir in mascarpone until blended.

3. In small bowl, with mixer at high speed, beat cream until soft peaks form. With rubber spatula, gently fold whipped cream into mascarpone mixture until blended. Spread half of mixture over ladyfingers in baking dish.

4. Dip remaining 9 ladyfingers into coffee mixture and arrange on top of mascarpone mixture. Spread with remaining mascarpone mixture. Refrigerate 3 hours or up to overnight.

5. Meanwhile, prepare Chocolate Curls.

6. Just before serving, dust with cocoa. Cut into squares and spoon into goblets or dessert dishes. Garnish with chocolate curls. Makes 12 servings.

Each serving: About 323 calories, 4g protein, 22g carbohydrate, 23g total fat (15g saturated), 55mg cholesterol, 59mg sodium.

Crème Caramel

A masterpiece of French dessert making: individual custards in their own caramel sauce.

Prep: 15 minutes plus cooling and chilling	Bake: 50 minutes
¼ plus ⅓ cup sugar	
4 large eggs	
2 cups milk	
1½ teaspoons vanilla extract	
¼ teaspoon salt	

1. Preheat oven to 325°F. In heavy 1-quart saucepan, heat ¼ cup sugar over medium heat, swirling pan occasionally, until sugar has melted and is amber in color. Immediately pour into six 6-ounce custard cups or ramekins.

2. In large bowl, with wire whisk, beat eggs and remaining ⅓ cup sugar until blended. Whisk in milk, vanilla, and salt until well combined; pour mixture through strainer into prepared custard cups.

3. Place custard cups in small baking pan; place on rack in oven. Carefully pour enough *very hot water* into pan to come halfway up sides of cups. Bake just until knife inserted 1 inch from center of custards comes out clean, 50 to 55 minutes. Transfer custard cups to wire rack to cool. Cover and refrigerate until well chilled, 3 hours or up to overnight.

4. To serve, run tip of small knife around edge of custards. Invert cups onto dessert plates, shaking cups gently until custards slip out, allowing caramel syrup to drip onto custards. Makes 6 servings.

Each serving: About 177 calories, 7g protein, 24g carbohydrate, 6g total fat (3g saturated), 153mg cholesterol, 177mg sodium.

Lowfat Crème Caramel

Lowfat milk and a moderate amount of eggs make this a guilt-free caramel custard.

Prep: 15 minutes plus cooling and chilling	Bake: 40 minutes
¾ cup sugar	
1 large egg	
2 large egg whites	
2 cups lowfat milk (1%)	
½ teaspoon vanilla extract	

1. Preheat oven to 350°F. In heavy 1-quart saucepan, heat ½ cup sugar over medium heat, swirling pan occasionally, until sugar has melted and is amber in color. Immediately pour into eight 4- to 5-ounce ramekins.

2. In large bowl, with wire whisk, beat egg, egg whites, and remaining ¼ cup sugar until well blended. Beat in milk and vanilla; pour into ramekins. Skim off foam.

3. Place ramekins in medium roasting pan; cover loosely with foil. Place pan on rack in oven. Carefully pour enough *very hot water* into pan to come halfway up sides of ramekins. Bake until knife inserted 1 inch from center comes out clean, 40 to 45 minutes. Transfer ramekins to wire rack to cool. Refrigerate until well chilled, 3 hours or up to overnight.

4. To serve, run tip of small knife around edge of custards. Invert ramekins onto dessert plates, shaking cups gently until custards slip out, allowing caramel syrup to drip onto custards. Makes 8 servings.

♥ Each serving: About 112 calories, 4g protein, 22g carbohydrate, 1g total fat (1g saturated), 29mg cholesterol, 52mg sodium.

CARAMEL

Always, immediately pour caramel into custard cups. Otherwise, it will overcook and harden.

Pumpkin Crème Caramel

When it comes to luscious holiday desserts, this one may even rival the ever-popular pumpkin pie.

Prep: 30 minutes plus cooling and chilling   Bake: 55 minutes

1¼	cups sugar
¼	cup water
6	strips (3" by 1" each) orange peel
1	can (12 ounces) evaporated milk
1	cup heavy or whipping cream
1	cup solid-pack pumpkin (not pumpkin-pie mix)
6	large eggs
¼	cup orange-flavored liqueur
1	teaspoon vanilla extract
1	teaspoon ground cinnamon
	pinch ground nutmeg
	pinch salt

1. In heavy 1-quart saucepan, combine ¾ cup sugar, water, and orange peel; heat to boiling over high heat. Cook 10 minutes. Discard orange peel; continue cooking sugar mixture until amber in color, about 3 minutes longer. Pour caramel into 9" by 5" loaf pan, tilting pan to coat bottom completely. (Use pot holders to protect your hands.)

2. In heavy 2-quart saucepan, combine evaporated milk, cream, and remaining ½ cup sugar; heat to boiling over medium-high heat, stirring occasionally until sugar has dissolved and bubbles form around edge.

3. Meanwhile, preheat oven to 350°F. In large bowl, with wire whisk, whisk pumpkin, eggs, liqueur, vanilla, cinnamon, nutmeg, and salt until blended.

4. Gradually whisk hot milk mixture into pumpkin mixture until smooth. Pour custard mixture into caramel-coated loaf pan. Place loaf pan in small roasting pan; place in oven. Carefully, pour enough *very hot water* into roasting pan to come halfway up sides of loaf pan. Bake until knife inserted 1 inch from edge of custard comes out clean (center will jiggle slightly), about 55 minutes.

5. Carefully remove loaf pan from water. Allow crème caramel to cool 1 hour in pan on wire rack; refrigerate overnight. To unmold, run tip of small knife around edges of custard. Invert onto serving plate, shaking pan gently until custard slips out, allowing caramel syrup to drip onto custard. Makes 12 servings.

Each serving: About 243 calories, 6g protein, 28g carbohydrate, 12g total fat (7g saturated), 143mg cholesterol, 85mg sodium.

BAIN MARIE

Place the custard cups or baking dish in a baking (or roasting) pan. Place the pan on the oven rack. Pour in enough very hot water (the water does not have to be boiling) to come halfway up the sides of the custard cups or dish.

Crème Brûlée

With its brittle caramelized top, this velvety custard has risen from obscurity to become a megastar of the dessert world.

Prep: 20 minutes plus cooling and chilling
Bake/Broil: 38 minutes

½	vanilla bean or 2 teaspoons vanilla extract
1½	cups heavy or whipping cream
1½	cups half-and-half or light cream
8	large egg yolks
⅔	cup granulated sugar
⅓ to ½	cup packed brown sugar

1. Preheat oven to 325°F. With knife, cut vanilla bean lengthwise in half; scrape out seeds and reserve. In heavy 3-quart saucepan, heat cream, half-and-half, and vanilla bean and seeds over medium heat until bubbles form around edge. Remove from heat. With slotted spoon, remove vanilla bean.

2. Meanwhile, in large bowl, with wire whisk, beat egg yolks and granulated sugar until well blended. Slowly stir in hot cream mixture until well combined. Pour cream mixture into ten 4- to 5-ounce broiler-proof ramekins or shallow 2½-quart casserole.

3. Place ramekins or casserole in large roasting pan; place pan in oven. Carefully pour enough *very hot water* into pan to come halfway up sides of ramekins. Bake just until set (mixture will still be slightly soft in center), 35 to 40 minutes. Transfer ramekins to wire rack to cool to room temperature. Cover and refrigerate until well chilled, at least 3 hours or up to overnight.

4. Up to 2 hours before serving, preheat broiler. Place brown sugar in small sieve; with spoon, press sugar through sieve to evenly cover tops of chilled custards.

5. Place ramekins in jelly-roll pan for easier handling. With broiler rack at closest position to heat source, broil crème brûlée just until sugar melts, 3 to 4 minutes. Serve, or refrigerate up to 2 hours. The melted brown sugar will form a delicious brittle crust. Makes 10 servings.

Each serving: About 307 calories, 4g protein, 25g carbohydrate, 21g total fat (12g saturated), 232mg cholesterol, 38mg sodium.

Panna Cotta with Raspberry Sauce

Panna Cotta with Raspberry Sauce

Panna cotta *means "cooked cream" in Italian, even though it is barely cooked at all.*

Prep: 20 minutes plus chilling	*Cook: 15 minutes*
1	envelope unflavored gelatin
1	cup milk
½	vanilla bean or 1½ teaspoons vanilla extract
1¾	cups heavy or whipping cream
¼	cup sugar
1	strip (3" by 1") lemon peel
1	cinnamon stick (3 inches)
	Raspberry Sauce (page 562)
	fresh raspberries

1. In 2-cup measuring cup, evenly sprinkle gelatin over milk; let stand 2 minutes to soften gelatin slightly. With knife, cut vanilla bean lengthwise in half; scrape out seeds and reserve.

2. In 1-quart saucepan, combine cream, sugar, lemon peel, cinnamon stick, and vanilla bean halves and seeds (do not add vanilla extract); heat to boiling over high heat, stirring occasionally. Reduce heat and simmer, stirring occasionally, 5 minutes. Stir in milk mixture; cook over low heat, stirring frequently, until gelatin has completely dissolved, 2 to 3 minutes.

3. Discard lemon peel, cinnamon stick, and vanilla bean from cream mixture. (Stir in vanilla extract, if using.) Pour cream mixture into medium bowl set in large bowl of ice water. With rubber spatula, stir mixture until it just begins to set, 10 to 12 minutes. Pour cream mixture into eight 4-ounce ramekins. Place ramekins in jelly-roll pan for easier handling. Cover and refrigerate panna cotta until well chilled and set, 4 hours or up to overnight.

4. Meanwhile, prepare Raspberry Sauce.

5. To unmold panna cotta, run tip of knife around edges. Tap side of each ramekin sharply to break seal. Invert onto plates. Spoon raspberry sauce around each panna cotta and sprinkle with raspberries. Makes 8 servings.

Each serving without Raspberry Sauce: About 228 calories, 3g protein, 9g carbohydrate, 20g total fat (13g saturated), 76mg cholesterol, 37mg sodium.

Cappuccino Mousse

For a fanciful presentation, serve this espresso-and-cream-flavored mousse in an assortment of coffee cups.

Prep: 30 minutes plus chilling   Cook: 2 minutes

1	envelope plus 1 teaspoon unflavored gelatin
⅓	plus ½ cup milk
1	cup espresso or very strong brewed coffee
½	cup plus 1 teaspoon sugar
2	tablespoons coffee-flavored liqueur
1⅓	cups heavy or whipping cream
	pinch ground cinnamon

1. In 1-quart saucepan, evenly sprinkle gelatin over ⅓ cup milk; let stand 5 minutes to soften gelatin slightly. Stir in espresso. Heat over low heat, stirring frequently, until gelatin has completely dissolved, 2 to 3 minutes. Remove from heat; add ½ cup sugar, stirring until dissolved. Stir in remaining ½ cup milk and liqueur. Transfer mixture to large bowl.

2. Place bowl in larger bowl of ice water. With rubber spatula, stir just until mixture mounds slightly when dropped from spoon, about 15 minutes. Remove from water bath.

3. Meanwhile, in medium bowl, with mixer at medium speed, beat 1 cup cream until soft peaks form. Fold one-third of cream into coffee mixture until well blended. Gently fold in remaining beaten cream. Spoon mixture into 8 coffee cups or 6-ounce custard cups. Cover and refrigerate until set, 4 hours or up to overnight.

4. Just before serving, in small bowl, beat remaining ⅓ cup cream, remaining 1 teaspoon sugar, and cinnamon until stiff peaks form. To serve, spoon dollop of whipped cream onto each mousse. Makes 8 servings.

Each serving: About 217 calories, 3g protein, 17g carbohydrate, 15g total fat (10g saturated), 58mg cholesterol, 30mg sodium.

Banana Icebox Cake

We've added bananas to this favorite mixture of chocolate wafer cookies and whipped cream to make it even more luscious.

 Prep: 30 minutes plus chilling

2	cups heavy or whipping cream
3	tablespoons confectioners' sugar
1	teaspoon vanilla extract
2	small ripe bananas, finely chopped
35	chocolate wafer cookies (part of 9-ounce package)
¼	cup semisweet chocolate chips

1. In large bowl, with mixer at medium speed, beat cream, confectioners' sugar, and vanilla until stiff peaks form. Spoon half of whipped cream into separate bowl; cover and refrigerate. With rubber spatula, gently fold bananas into remaining whipped cream.

2. On one side of each of 6 chocolate wafers, spread about 2 heaping teaspoons banana whipped cream. Stack wafers on top of one another. Top with plain wafer. Repeat with remaining wafers and remaining cream until all wafers are used, making 5 stacks of 7 wafers each.

3. Turn each stack on its side; place stacks, side by side, on serving platter. Cover with reserved whipped cream and sprinkle with chocolate chips. Cover and refrigerate 5 hours or up to overnight to soften wafers. To serve, slice cake on diagonal for striped effect. Makes 10 servings.

Each serving: About 302 calories, 3g protein, 26g carbohydrate, 22g total fat (12g saturated), 66mg cholesterol, 140mg sodium.

Plum Pudding with Hard Sauce

Our holiday steamed pudding is the perfect prepare-ahead recipe, because the flavor improves as the pudding ages. Hard Sauce, made with rum or brandy, is the ideal accompaniment. If you have one-quart decorative steamed pudding molds, by all means use them instead of bowls.

Prep: 1 hour   Cook: 2 hours

2¼	cups all-purpose flour
1	cup fresh bread crumbs (about 2 slices firm white bread)
1	teaspoon baking powder
1	teaspoon ground cinnamon
½	teaspoon salt
¼	teaspoon ground nutmeg
¼	teaspoon ground cloves
1	cup pitted prunes, chopped
1	cup pitted dates, chopped
¾	cup dark seedless raisins
½	cup walnuts, toasted and chopped
1	medium Granny Smith apple, peeled, cored, and shredded
1	teaspoon freshly grated lemon peel
1	cup butter or margarine (2 sticks), softened
1	cup packed light brown sugar
2	large eggs
⅔	cup buttermilk
½	cup dark molasses
⅓	cup dark rum or brandy
	Hard Sauce (page 562)

1. Generously grease two 1-quart heat-safe bowls. Cut two pieces of foil 2 inches larger than tops of bowls. Grease dull side of each piece of foil.

2. In large bowl, combine flour, bread crumbs, baking powder, cinnamon, salt, nutmeg, and cloves. Add prunes, dates, raisins, walnuts, apple, and lemon peel to flour mixture. With hands, thoroughly toss mixture until fruits are well coated and separate.

3. In separate large bowl, with mixer at low speed, beat butter and brown sugar until blended. Increase speed to high; beat until light and fluffy, about 1 minute. Reduce speed to medium; add eggs, one at a time, beating well after each addition. Beat in buttermilk, molasses, and rum (mixture will look curdled). With wooden spoon, stir butter mixture into flour mixture until well blended.

4. Divide batter evenly between prepared bowls; cover tightly with foil, greased side down, pressing foil against sides of bowls. Tightly tie string under rims of bowls to keep puddings from getting wet.

5. Place metal cookie cutter or small wire rack in each of two 5-quart saucepots. (Cookie cutters serve as steaming racks.) Pour in enough *water* to come 1½ inches up sides of pots. Set pudding bowls on top of cookie cutters. Cover and heat water to boiling over high heat. Reduce heat; simmer until toothpick inserted through foil in center of puddings comes out clean, about 2 hours.

6. Meanwhile, prepare Hard Sauce.

7. When puddings are done, cool in bowls on wire racks 5 minutes. Remove foil; run tip of small knife around edges of puddings. Invert onto serving plates. Serve hot with Hard Sauce. If making ahead, cool puddings completely in bowls, then wrap well in heavy-duty foil. Refrigerate up to 1 month, or freeze up to 3 months. To serve, cover and resteam pudding (thaw, if frozen) as directed in Step 5, 1 hour. Makes 2 puddings, 8 servings each.

Each serving without Hard Sauce: About 378 calories, 5g protein, 57g carbohydrate, 16g total fat (8g saturated), 58mg cholesterol, 266mg sodium.

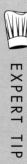

Silicon spatulas do not melt like those made of rubber, nor do they absorb flavors or odors like wooden spatulas; they have completely replaced the wooden spoons in my kitchen. They are especially good for stirring custards (they sweep the bottom and side of a pan completely and efficiently, which prevents scorching) and even for stirring ingredients into blazing hot caramel when making praline.

ALICE MEDRICH
COOKBOOK AUTHOR

EXPERT TIP

Bread-and-Butter Pudding

Cinnamon-raisin bread can be used in place of white bread for a just-as-tasty variation. Just reduce the ground cinnamon to one-half teaspoon.

Prep: 10 minutes plus standing   Bake: 50 to 60 minutes

½	cup sugar
¾	teaspoon ground cinnamon
4	tablespoons butter or margarine, softened
12	slices firm white bread
4	large eggs
3	cups milk
1½	teaspoons vanilla extract
	whipped cream (optional)

1. Preheat oven to 325°F. Grease 8-inch square baking dish. In cup, combine 1 tablespoon sugar and cinnamon. Spread butter on one side of bread slices. Arrange 4 bread slices in dish, overlapping slightly if necessary; lightly sprinkle with cinnamon mixture. Repeat to make two more layers.

2. In medium bowl, with wire whisk, beat eggs, milk, remaining sugar, and vanilla until well blended. Pour milk mixture over bread slices. Let stand 20 minutes, occasionally pressing bread down to absorb milk mixture.

3. Bake until knife inserted in center of pudding comes out clean, 50 to 60 minutes. Let stand 15 minutes to serve pudding warm, or cover and refrigerate to serve cold later. Top with whipped cream, if desired. Makes 8 servings.

Each serving: About 313 calories, 10g protein, 38g carbohydrate, 13g total fat (7g saturated), 135mg cholesterol, 364mg sodium.

Black-and-White Bread Pudding with White Chocolate Custard Sauce

For chocolate lovers: a sweet bread pudding with two kinds of chocolate. Serve it alone or with sinfully rich White Chocolate Custard Sauce. (We love the pudding served warm and the sauce cold.)

Prep: 40 minutes plus standing
Bake: 1 hour 15 minutes

1	loaf (16 ounces) sliced firm white bread
9	large eggs
4	cups milk
½	cup sugar
1	tablespoon vanilla extract
½	teaspoon salt
3	ounces white chocolate or white baking bar, grated
3	squares (3 ounces) semisweet chocolate, grated
	White Chocolate Custard Sauce (below)

1. Preheat oven to 325°F. Grease 13" by 9" baking dish. Place bread slices on large cookie sheet and bake in oven until lightly toasted, about 20 minutes, turning once. Place bread slices in prepared baking dish, overlapping slightly.

2. Meanwhile, in very large bowl, with wire whisk, beat eggs, milk, sugar, vanilla, and salt until well combined. Stir in grated white and semisweet chocolates. Pour milk mixture evenly over bread; let stand 20 minutes, occasionally pressing bread down to absorb milk mixture.

3. Cover baking dish with foil; bake 1 hour. Remove foil and bake until top is golden and knife inserted in center of pudding comes out clean, 15 to 20 minutes longer.

4. Meanwhile, prepare White Chocolate Custard Sauce. Serve bread pudding warm with custard sauce, or cover and refrigerate to serve cold later. Makes 16 servings.

Each serving without sauce: About 235 calories, 8g protein, 30g carbohydrate, 9g total fat (4g saturated), 128mg cholesterol, 296mg sodium.

White Chocolate Custard Sauce

Finely chop **3 ounces white chocolate or white baking bar;** place in large bowl. Set aside. In small bowl, with wire whisk, beat **4 large egg yolks** and ¼ **cup sugar** until well blended. In heavy 2-quart saucepan, heat **1 cup milk** and ¾ **cup heavy or whipping cream** over medium-high heat until bubbles form around edge. Into egg mixture, beat ⅓ cup hot milk mixture.

Slowly pour egg mixture back into milk mixture, stirring rapidly to prevent curdling. Reduce heat to low; cook, stirring constantly, until mixture has thickened slightly and coats back of spoon, about 5 minutes. (On thermometer, temperature should reach 160°F; do not boil, or sauce will curdle.) Pour milk mixture over white chocolate, stirring until chocolate melts and mixture is smooth. Serve custard sauce warm, or refrigerate to serve cold later. Makes about 2½ cups sauce.

Each tablespoon: About 41 calories, 1g protein, 3g carbohydrate, 3g total fat (2g saturated), 28mg cholesterol, 7mg sodium.

Indian Pudding

A baked cornmeal-and-molasses pudding that has been a New England favorite for many years. Top each serving with a scoop of vanilla ice cream.

Prep: 30 minutes   Bake: 2 hours

4	cups milk
⅔	cup cornmeal
½	cup light (mild) molasses
4	tablespoons butter or margarine, cut into pieces
¼	cup sugar
1	teaspoon ground ginger
1	teaspoon ground cinnamon
½	teaspoon salt
¼	teaspoon ground nutmeg
	whipped cream or vanilla ice cream (optional)

1. Preheat oven to 350°F. Grease shallow 1½-quart baking dish.

2. In small bowl, combine 1 cup milk and cornmeal. In 4-quart saucepan, heat remaining 3 cups milk to boiling over high heat. With wire whisk, whisk in cornmeal mixture; heat to boiling. Reduce heat and simmer, stirring frequently with wooden spoon to prevent lumps, until mixture is very thick, about 20 minutes. Remove from heat; stir in molasses, butter, sugar, ginger, cinnamon, salt, and nutmeg until well blended.

3. Pour batter evenly into prepared baking dish. Place baking dish in large roasting pan; place in oven. Carefully pour enough *very hot water* into roasting pan to come halfway up sides of baking dish. Cover with foil and bake pudding 1 hour. Remove foil and bake until lightly browned and just set, about 1 hour longer.

4. Remove baking dish from water. Cool pudding in pan on wire rack 30 minutes. Serve pudding warm with whipped cream or vanilla ice cream, if you like. Makes 8 servings.

Each serving: About 253 calories, 5g protein, 36g carbohydrate, 11g total fat (6g saturated), 33mg cholesterol, 271mg sodium.

Lemon Pudding Cake

A tried-and-true dessert that is just plain wonderful served from the baking dish while steaming hot. Try the orange version, too.

Prep: 20 minutes   Bake: 40 minutes

3	lemons
¾	cup sugar
¼	cup all-purpose flour
3	large eggs, separated
1	cup milk
4	tablespoons butter or margarine, melted
⅛	teaspoon salt

1. Preheat oven to 350°F. Grease 8-inch square baking dish. From lemons, grate 1 tablespoon peel and squeeze ⅓ cup juice. In large bowl, combine sugar and flour. With wire whisk, beat in egg yolks, milk, melted butter, and lemon peel and juice.

2. In small bowl, with mixer at high speed, beat egg whites and salt until soft peaks form when beaters are lifted. With rubber spatula, fold one-third of egg whites into lemon mixture; gently fold in remaining egg whites just until blended. Pour batter into prepared baking dish.

3. Set baking dish in medium roasting pan; place in oven. Carefully pour enough *very hot water* into roasting pan to come halfway up sides of baking dish. Bake until top is golden and set, about 40 minutes (batter will separate into cake and pudding layers). Cool in pan on wire rack 10 minutes. Serve hot. Makes 6 servings.

Each serving: About 256 calories, 5g protein, 32g carbohydrate, 12g total fat (7g saturated), 133mg cholesterol, 179mg sodium.

Orange Pudding Cake
Prepare as directed but in Step 1, use **¼ cup fresh lemon juice, ¼ cup fresh orange juice,** and **2 teaspoons freshly grated orange peel.**

Brownie Pudding Cake

Two desserts for the price of one! It separates during baking into a fudgy brownie on top of a silky chocolate pudding.

Prep: 20 minutes   Bake: 30 minutes

2	teaspoons instant-coffee powder (optional)
2	tablespoons plus 1¾ cups boiling water
1	cup all-purpose flour
¾	cup unsweetened cocoa
½	cup granulated sugar
2	teaspoons baking powder
¼	teaspoon salt
½	cup milk
4	tablespoons butter or margarine, melted
1	teaspoon vanilla extract
½	cup packed brown sugar
	whipped cream or vanilla ice cream (optional)

1. Preheat oven to 350°F. In cup, dissolve coffee powder in 2 tablespoons boiling water, if using.

2. In bowl, combine flour, ½ cup cocoa, granulated sugar, baking powder, and salt. In 2-cup measuring cup, combine milk, melted butter, vanilla, and coffee, if using. With wooden spoon, stir milk mixture into flour mixture until just blended. Pour into ungreased 8-inch square baking dish.

3. In small bowl, thoroughly combine brown sugar and remaining ¼ cup cocoa; sprinkle evenly over batter. Carefully pour remaining 1¾ cups boiling water evenly over mixture in baking dish; do not stir.

4. Bake 30 minutes (batter will separate into cake and pudding layers). Cool in pan on wire rack 10 minutes. Serve hot with whipped cream, if you like. Makes 8 servings.

♥ Each serving: About 238 calories, 4g protein, 43g carbohydrate, 7g total fat (5g saturated), 18mg cholesterol, 267mg sodium.

Brownie Pudding Cake

Rice Pudding

Cooking the rice very slowly in lots of milk makes this pudding especially creamy.

Prep: 10 minutes   Cook: 1 hour 15 minutes

4	cups milk
½	cup regular long-grain rice
½	cup sugar
¼	teaspoon salt
1	large egg
1	teaspoon vanilla extract

1. In heavy 4-quart saucepan, combine milk, rice, sugar, and salt; heat to boiling over medium-high heat. Reduce heat; cover and simmer, stirring occasionally, until rice is very tender, about 1 hour.

2. In small bowl, lightly beat egg; stir in ½ cup hot rice mixture. Slowly pour egg mixture back into rice mixture, stirring rapidly to prevent curdling. Cook, stirring constantly, until rice mixture has thickened, about 5 minutes (do not boil, or mixture will curdle). Remove from heat; stir in vanilla. Serve warm, or spoon into medium bowl and refrigerate until well chilled, about 3 hours. Makes 4 cups or 6 servings.

♥ Each serving: About 234 calories, 7g protein, 37g carbohydrate, 6g total fat (4g saturated), 58mg cholesterol, 187mg sodium.

Rich Rice Pudding

Prepare as directed and refrigerate. In small bowl, with mixer at medium speed, beat ½ **cup heavy or whipping cream** until soft peaks form. With rubber spatula, gently fold into rice pudding. Refrigerate until ready to serve, up to 4 hours. Makes 8 servings.

Vanilla Rice Pudding with Dried Cherries

The starchy nature of short-grain Arborio rice gives this pudding its unsurpassed creaminess.

Prep: 15 minutes plus cooling and chilling   Cook: 1 hour 40 minutes

½	vanilla bean or 1 tablespoon vanilla extract
6	cups milk
¾	cup sugar
¾	cup short-grain rice, preferably Arborio
½	cup dried cherries or raisins
2	tablespoons dark rum (optional)
¼	teaspoon salt
½	cup heavy or whipping cream

1. With knife, cut vanilla bean lengthwise in half; scrape out seeds and reserve.

2. In heavy 4-quart saucepan, combine milk, sugar, and vanilla bean halves and seeds; heat to boiling over medium-high heat, stirring occasionally. (If using vanilla extract, stir in with rum in Step 3.) Stir in rice and heat to boiling. Reduce heat; cover and simmer, stirring occasionally, until mixture is very creamy and has thickened slightly, about 1 hour 25 minutes (pudding will firm upon chilling). Discard vanilla bean.

3. Spoon rice pudding into large bowl; stir in dried cherries, rum, if using, and salt. Cool slightly, then cover and refrigerate until well chilled, 6 hours or up to overnight.

4. Up to 2 hours before serving, in small bowl, with mixer at medium speed, beat cream until stiff peaks form. Using rubber spatula, fold half of whipped cream into rice pudding, then fold in remaining cream. Makes 12 servings.

Each serving: About 212 calories, 5g protein, 31g carbohydrate, 8g total fat (5g saturated), 31mg cholesterol, 112mg sodium.

Sticky Toffee Pudding

This British pudding, with its sticky caramel topping, is outstanding when served warm with whipped cream.

Prep: 20 minutes plus standing and cooling
Bake/Broil: 31 minutes

1	cup chopped pitted dates
1	teaspoon baking soda
1½	cups boiling water
10	tablespoons butter or margarine (1¼ sticks), softened
1	cup granulated sugar
1	large egg
1	teaspoon vanilla extract
2	cups all-purpose flour
1	teaspoon baking powder
1	cup packed brown sugar
¼	cup heavy or whipping cream
	whipped cream (optional)

1. Preheat oven to 350°F. Grease 13" by 9" baking pan. In medium bowl, combine dates, baking soda, and boiling water; let stand 15 minutes.

2. In large bowl, with mixer at medium speed, beat 6 tablespoons butter until creamy. Beat in granulated sugar until light and fluffy. Add egg and vanilla; beat until blended. Reduce speed to low; add flour and baking powder, beating to combine. Add date mixture and beat until well combined (batter will be very thin). Pour batter into prepared pan. Bake until golden and toothpick inserted in center of pudding comes out clean, about 30 minutes.

3. Meanwhile, in 2-quart saucepan, combine brown sugar, cream, and remaining 4 tablespoons butter; heat to boiling over medium-high heat. Boil 1 minute; remove saucepan from heat.

4. Turn oven control to broil. Spread brown-sugar mixture evenly over top of hot pudding. Broil at position closest to heat source until bubbling, about 30 seconds. Cool in pan on wire rack 15 minutes. Serve warm with whipped cream, if you like. Makes 12 servings.

♥ Each serving: About 362 calories, 3g protein, 62g carbohydrate, 12g total fat (7g saturated), 50mg cholesterol, 259mg sodium.

Savarin

This light-textured yeast cake is soaked in a mild rum syrup.

Prep: 25 minutes plus rising and standing
Bake: 25 minutes

⅔	cup warm milk (105° to 115°F)
1	teaspoon plus 1 cup sugar
1	teaspoon active dry yeast
3	large eggs
2	cups all-purpose flour
1	teaspoon salt
6	tablespoons butter or margarine, melted and cooled
1½	cups water
6	strips (3" by ½" each) orange peel
⅓	cup dark rum
1	teaspoon vanilla extract

1. Grease and flour 9- to 10-inch tube pan. In large bowl, combine warm milk, 1 teaspoon sugar, and yeast; stir to dissolve. Let stand until foamy, about 5 minutes. Stir in eggs, flour, and salt until well combined. Cover and let rise in warm place (80° to 85°F) until doubled in volume, about 1 hour.

2. With wooden spoon, add melted butter, stirring until batter is thick, smooth, and elastic, about 5 minutes. Spoon batter into prepared pan; cover and let rise in warm place until doubled, about 45 minutes.

3. Meanwhile, preheat oven to 375°F. Bake until golden brown and toothpick inserted in center of cake comes out clean, about 25 minutes. Cool in pan on wire rack 5 minutes. Run thin knife around cake to loosen from side and center tube of pan; lift tube to separate cake from pan side. Slide knife under cake to separate from bottom of pan; invert cake onto wire rack. Turn cake, right side up, into deep-dish pie plate.

4. Meanwhile, in 3-quart saucepan, combine remaining 1 cup sugar, water, and orange peel. Heat to boiling over medium-high heat; boil 1 minute. Strain syrup through sieve set over bowl; discard orange peel. Stir in rum and vanilla.

5. With skewer or toothpick, poke holes, 1 inch apart, all over cake. Spoon 1½ cups warm syrup over cake. Continue spooning syrup over top and side of cake until most of syrup has been absorbed. Let stand 20 minutes before serving. Serve remaining syrup with cake. Makes 12 servings.

♥ Each serving: About 246 calories, 4g protein, 35g carbohydrate, 8g total fat (4g saturated), 71mg cholesterol, 276mg sodium.

Baklava

Crisp and nutty, this Near Eastern dessert is much easier to make than you might think. Cover the stack of phyllo sheets with a damp kitchen towel or plastic wrap so they don't dry out.

Prep: 30 minutes plus standing   Bake: 1 hour 25 minutes

4	cups walnuts (16 ounces), finely chopped
½	cup sugar
1	teaspoon ground cinnamon
1	package (16 ounces) fresh or frozen (thawed) phyllo
¾	cup butter or margarine (1½ sticks), melted
1	cup honey

1. Preheat oven to 300°F. Grease 13" by 9" baking dish. In large bowl, combine walnuts, sugar, and cinnamon.

2. Cut phyllo sheets into 13" by 9" rectangles; reserve leftover phyllo strips. In prepared baking dish, place 1 phyllo sheet; brush with some melted butter. Repeat to make five more phyllo layers; sprinkle with 1 cup walnut mixture.

3. Place 1 phyllo sheet over walnut mixture in baking dish; brush lightly with melted butter. Repeat to make five more phyllo layers, overlapping reserved phyllo strips to make additional rectangles, if necessary. Sprinkle 1 cup walnut mixture over phyllo. Repeat layering two more times, ending with walnut mixture.

4. Place remaining phyllo sheets on top of walnut mixture; brush lightly with melted butter. With sharp knife, cut lengthwise halfway through phyllo layers to make 3 equal strips; cut each strip crosswise halfway through layers into 4 pieces, then cut each rectangle on diagonal into 2 triangles. Bake until top is golden brown, about 1 hour 25 minutes.

5. Meanwhile, in 1-quart saucepan, heat honey over medium-low heat until hot but not boiling. Spoon hot honey evenly over hot baklava. Cool baklava in pan on wire rack at least 1 hour to absorb honey, then cover and let stand at room temperature up to 1 day. To serve, with knife, cut all the way through layers. Makes 24 servings.

Each serving: About 290 calories, 4g protein, 29g carbohydrate, 19g total fat (5g saturated), 16mg cholesterol, 152mg sodium.

Galatoboureko

Here is a Greek dessert composed of layers of phyllo surrounding a firm but creamy filling that is thickened with farina cereal.

Prep: 50 minutes plus standing	Bake: 35 minutes

6	cups milk
2	strips (3" by 1" each) orange peel
¾	cup quick-cooking enriched farina cereal
¾	cup sugar
4	large eggs
2	teaspoons vanilla extract
8	ounces fresh or frozen (thawed) phyllo
½	cup butter or margarine (1 stick), melted
	Lemon Syrup (page 640)

1. Preheat oven to 350°F. Grease 13" by 9" baking dish. In 3-quart saucepan, combine milk and orange peel; heat to boiling over medium-high heat. In small bowl, combine farina and sugar. Gradually sprinkle farina mixture into hot milk, stirring with wooden spoon; heat to boiling. Reduce heat and simmer, stirring, until mixture has thickened slightly, about 5 minutes. Remove from heat; discard orange peel.

2. In large bowl, with mixer at high speed, beat eggs and vanilla until well blended. Reduce speed to medium and gradually beat in hot farina mixture.

3. In prepared baking dish, place 1 phyllo sheet, allowing it to extend up sides of dish; brush with some melted butter. Repeat to make about five more layers; pour in farina mixture.

4. Cut remaining phyllo into 13" by 9" rectangles; reserve leftover phyllo strips. Place 1 phyllo sheet on top of farina mixture; brush with some melted butter. Repeat to make about six layers with remaining phyllo and melted butter, overlapping reserved phyllo strips to make additional rectangles, if necessary. With sharp knife, cut lengthwise through top phyllo layers to make 4 equal strips; cut each strip crosswise into 6 pieces. Bake until top is golden and puffy, about 35 minutes.

5. Meanwhile, prepare Lemon Syrup. Pour hot syrup over phyllo. Let galatoboureko stand at least 2 hours on wire rack to absorb syrup. To serve, with knife, cut all the way through layers. Serve warm, or cover and refrigerate up to 1 day to serve cold. Makes 24 servings.

Each serving: About 183 calories, 4g protein, 25g carbohydrate, 7g total fat (4g saturated), 54mg cholesterol, 139mg sodium.

Galatoboureko

Lemon Syrup

In 1-quart saucepan, combine ¾ **cup sugar,** ⅓ **cup water,** and **4 strips (3" by 1" each) lemon peel;** heat to boiling over medium heat, stirring occasionally. Reduce heat; simmer until syrup has thickened slightly, about 8 minutes. Discard lemon peel and stir in **1 tablespoon fresh lemon juice.**

Apple Strudel

Layer upon layer of delicate phyllo surround a tender apple filling. Try one of the variations, too.

Prep: 1 hour plus cooling   Bake: 35 minutes

8	tablespoons butter or margarine (1 stick)
4	pounds Granny Smith apples (8 large), peeled, cored, and cut into ½-inch pieces
½	cup dark seedless raisins
⅔	plus ¼ cup granulated sugar
¼	cup walnuts, toasted and ground
¼	cup plain dried bread crumbs
½	teaspoon ground cinnamon
¼	teaspoon ground nutmeg
8	sheets (16" by 12" each) fresh or frozen (thawed) phyllo confectioners' sugar

1. Prepare filling: In 12-inch skillet, melt 2 tablespoons butter over medium heat. Add apples, raisins, and ⅔ cup granulated sugar. Cook, stirring occasionally, 15 minutes. Increase heat to medium-high and cook until liquid has evaporated and apples are soft and golden, about 15 minutes longer. Remove from heat; let filling cool completely.

2. Meanwhile, in small bowl, stir ground walnuts, bread crumbs, remaining ¼ cup granulated sugar, cinnamon, and nutmeg until thoroughly combined.

3. Preheat oven to 400°F. In 1-quart saucepan, melt remaining 6 tablespoons butter. Cut two 24-inch lengths of waxed paper. Overlap two long sides by about 2 inches.

4. On waxed paper, place 1 phyllo sheet; lightly brush with some melted butter. Sprinkle with scant 2 tablespoons bread-crumb mixture. Repeat layering with remaining phyllo, melted butter, and crumb mixture; reserve about 1 tablespoon melted butter.

5. Spoon cooled apple filling along a long side of phyllo, leaving ¾-inch borders and covering about one-third of phyllo. Starting from filling side, roll phyllo up, jelly-roll fashion, using waxed paper to help lift roll. Place roll, seam side down, on diagonal, on ungreased large cookie sheet. Tuck ends of roll under; brush with reserved 1 tablespoon melted butter. Place two foil sheets under cookie sheet; crimp edges to form rim to catch any overflow during baking.

6. Bake strudel until phyllo is golden and filling is heated through, 35 to 40 minutes. If necessary, cover strudel loosely with foil during last 10 minutes of baking to prevent overbrowning. Cool on cookie sheet on wire rack about 20 minutes. To serve, dust with confectioners' sugar and cut into thick slices. Makes 10 servings.

Each serving: About 338 calories, 2g protein, 58g carbohydrate, 13g total fat (6g saturated), 25mg cholesterol, 192mg sodium.

PHYLLO

Fragile, paper-thin phyllo dough is traditionally used in Greek and Middle Eastern pastries, but it can also be used to make flaky phyllo tart and tartlet shells (page 688).

- Phyllo dough dries out quickly when exposed to air. Keep it covered with plastic wrap or a damp towel until ready to use. Leftover phyllo can be refrigerated, well wrapped in plastic wrap, for up to two weeks.
- Frozen phyllo dough should be thawed in the refrigerator overnight, not at room temperature. Never refreeze thawed phyllo dough, or it will become dry, brittle, and crumbly. (If you have a temperamental box of dough, poor shipping and handling was probably the culprit.) Frozen phyllo will keep for three to six months.
- Fresh phyllo dough is available at some Greek or Middle Eastern delicatessens and bakeries. It can be refrigerated for up to five days or frozen for up to three months.
- Bake phyllo until deep golden; this enhances the flavor and makes it crisp.
- Phyllo tart shells and cups can be baked a day ahead. Store in airtight containers and recrisp (if necessary) in a 350°F oven before filling and serving.

Apple Strudel

Dried Fruit Strudel

In 2-quart saucepan, combine **2 cups mixed dried fruit,** cut into 1-inch pieces, **1 cup dried figs,** cut into 1-inch pieces, **2 strips (3" by 1" each) lemon peel, 1 cinnamon stick (3 inches),** and **1¾ cups water;** heat to boiling over high heat, stirring occasionally. Reduce heat to medium; cook until all liquid has been absorbed and fruit is tender, about 20 minutes longer. Cool completely. Prepare and fill strudel as directed but substitute dried-fruit filling for apple filling. Bake strudel as directed.

Each serving: About 285 calories, 3g protein, 49g carbohydrate, 10g total fat (5g saturated), 19mg cholesterol, 175mg sodium.

Cherry Strudel

In 4-quart saucepan, combine **2 cans (16 ounces each) tart (sour) cherries packed in water,** drained (½ cup liquid reserved), **1 cup sugar, ¼ cup cornstarch, 1 tablespoon fresh lemon juice,** and **¼ teaspoon ground cinnamon;** heat to boiling over medium-high heat, stirring constantly. Reduce heat to medium-low; boil 1 minute. Remove from heat; stir in **½ teaspoon vanilla extract.** Cool completely. Prepare and fill strudel as directed but substitute cherry filling for apple filling. Bake as directed.

Each serving: About 280 calories, 3g protein, 47g carbohydrate, 10g total fat (5g saturated), 19mg cholesterol, 174mg sodium.

Cheese Strudel

In large bowl, with mixer at medium speed, beat **1 package (8 ounces) cream cheese,** softened, **¼ cup sugar,** and **1 tablespoon cornstarch** until thoroughly blended. With rubber spatula, fold in **1 cup ricotta cheese, 1 teaspoon freshly grated lemon peel,** and **½ teaspoon vanilla extract** until well combined. Cover and refrigerate filling while preparing phyllo. Prepare and fill strudel as directed but substitute cheese filling for apple filling. Bake as directed.

Each serving: About 301 calories, 6g protein, 23g carbohydrate, 21g total fat (12g saturated), 56mg cholesterol, 255mg sodium.

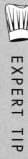

I like to try different apples in my desserts rather than sticking with the old familiar varieties. Simply sauté a few slices of the "new" apple to see if the flavor and texture is to your liking and will suit the dessert.

ALICE MEDRICH
COOKBOOK AUTHOR

EXPERT TIP

Strawberry Napoleons

Fresh strawberries and whipped cream are stacked between flaky phyllo triangles for a stylish dessert with professional pizzazz.

Prep: 45 minutes   Bake: 10 minutes

1	large egg white
1	teaspoon water
	pinch salt
4	sheets (16" by 12" each) fresh or frozen (thawed) phyllo
3	tablespoons butter or margarine, melted
1/3	cup plus 1 tablespoon sugar
1/2	cup sliced natural almonds
3/4	cup heavy or whipping cream
1/2	teaspoon vanilla extract
1	pint strawberries, hulled and sliced

1. Preheat oven to 375°F. In small bowl, lightly beat egg white, water, and salt; set aside. On surface, place 1 phyllo sheet; brush with some melted butter. Sprinkle with about 1 rounded tablespoon sugar. Repeat two more times with remaining phyllo sheets, melted butter, and sugar. Top with remaining phyllo sheet and brush with egg-white mixture.

2. With sharp knife, cut phyllo lengthwise into 3 equal strips, then cut each strip crosswise into 4 pieces. Cut each piece on diagonal to make 24 triangles. Place phyllo triangles on two ungreased large cookie sheets; sprinkle with almonds and 1 rounded tablespoon sugar. Bake until golden, about 10 minutes. With spatula, transfer phyllo to wire racks to cool.

3. Just before serving, in small bowl, with mixer at medium speed, beat cream, remaining 1 tablespoon sugar, and vanilla until stiff peaks form.

4. To assemble napoleons, place 1 phyllo triangle in center of each of eight dessert plates. Top each with about 1 tablespoon whipped cream and about 1 rounded tablespoon sliced strawberries. Cover each with second phyllo triangle, with points angled slightly away from points of bottom triangle. Top with remaining whipped cream and remaining strawberries; top each with third triangle. Serve immediately. Makes 8 servings.

Each serving: About 231 calories, 3g protein, 20g carbohydrate, 16g total fat (8g saturated), 42mg cholesterol, 124mg sodium.

Choux Pastry

This light, airy pastry is the basis for many glorious desserts, such as éclairs and cream puffs. Use the batter while it is still warm to get the highest puff possible.

Prep: 10 minutes   Cook: 5 minutes

1/2	cup butter or margarine (1 stick), cut into pieces
1	cup water
1/4	teaspoon salt
1	cup all-purpose flour
4	large eggs

In 3-quart saucepan, combine butter, water, and salt; heat over medium-high heat until butter melts and mixture boils. Remove from heat. Add flour all at once and, with wooden spoon, vigorously stir until mixture leaves side of pan and forms a ball. Add eggs to flour mixture, one at a time, beating well after each addition, until mixture is smooth and satiny. Shape and bake warm dough as directed in following recipes.

One recipe: About 1,566 calories, 39g protein, 98g carbohydrate, 113g total fat (64g saturated), 1,098mg cholesterol, 1,763mg sodium.

Vanilla Pastry Cream

This versatile cream is used to fill many classic desserts, such as Napoleons (page 646) and Éclairs (opposite). Be sure to cook the cream for the full two minutes, or it may not set up.

Prep: 5 minutes plus chilling   Cook: 10 minutes

2 1/4	cups milk
4	large egg yolks
2/3	cup sugar
1/4	cup all-purpose flour
1/4	cup cornstarch
1	tablespoon vanilla extract

1. In 3-quart saucepan, heat 2 cups milk over medium-high heat until bubbles form around edge. Meanwhile, in large bowl, with wire whisk, beat egg yolks, remaining 1/4 cup

milk, and sugar until combined; whisk in flour and cornstarch until blended. Gradually whisk hot milk into egg-yolk mixture.

2. Return milk mixture to saucepan; cook over medium-high heat, whisking constantly, until mixture has thickened and boils. Reduce heat to low and cook, stirring, 2 minutes.

3. Remove from heat and stir in vanilla. Pour pastry cream into shallow dish. Press plastic wrap onto surface of pastry cream. Refrigerate at least 2 hours or up to overnight. Makes 2¾ cups.

Each tablespoon: About 31 calories, 1g protein, 5g carbohydrate, 1g total fat (0g saturated), 21mg cholesterol, 7mg sodium.

Chocolate Pastry Cream

Prepare pastry cream as directed but add **3 squares (3 ounces) semisweet chocolate** and **1 square (1 ounce) unsweetened chocolate,** melted, with vanilla. Makes about 3 cups.

Each tablespoon: About 44 calories, 1g protein, 3g carbohydrate, 3g total fat (2g saturated), 23mg cholesterol, 37mg sodium.

Cream Puffs

The unfilled puffs can be frozen for up to one month, then re-crisped in the oven before filling. If you like, fill them with pastry cream instead of ice cream.

Prep: 30 minutes plus standing and cooling
Bake: 40 minutes

Choux Pastry (opposite)
Hot Fudge Sauce (page 561)
1 quart vanilla ice cream

1. Preheat oven to 400°F. Grease and flour large cookie sheet. Prepare Choux Pastry. Drop slightly rounded ¼ cups batter in 8 large mounds, 3 inches apart, on prepared cookie sheet. With moistened finger, gently smooth tops.

2. Bake until golden, 40 to 45 minutes. Remove puffs from oven; with tip of knife, make small slit in side of each puff to release steam. Turn off oven. Return puffs to oven and let stand 10 minutes. Transfer puffs to wire rack to cool completely. With serrated knife, cut each cooled puff horizontally in half; remove and discard any moist dough inside puffs.

3. Prepare Hot Fudge Sauce. To serve, place ½-cup scoop vanilla ice cream in bottom half of each cream puff; replace tops. Spoon Hot Fudge Sauce over puffs. Makes 8 servings.

Each serving: About 525 calories, 9g protein, 51g carbohydrate, 34g total fat (20g saturated), 202mg cholesterol, 339mg sodium.

Éclairs

Why buy éclairs? Nothing can compare to your first bite of a freshly prepared éclair made right at home.

Prep: 1 hour plus chilling, cooling, and standing   Bake: 40 minutes

Vanilla or Chocolate Pastry Cream (opposite)		
Choux Pastry (opposite)		
3	squares (3 ounces) semisweet chocolate, chopped	
3	tablespoons heavy or whipping cream	

1. Prepare Vanilla or Chocolate Pastry Cream; cover and refrigerate until ready to use.

2. Preheat oven to 400°F. Grease and flour large cookie sheet. Prepare Choux Pastry. Spoon dough into large pastry bag fitted with ½-inch plain tip. Pipe dough in lengths about 3½ inches long and ¾ inch wide, 1 inch apart, on prepared cookie sheet to make about 30 éclairs. With moistened finger, gently smooth tops.

3. Bake until golden, about 40 minutes. Remove éclairs from oven; with tip of knife, make small slit in end of each éclair to release steam. Return éclairs to oven and let stand 10 minutes. Transfer éclairs to wire rack to cool completely.

4. With small knife, make hole in one end of each éclair. Whisk pastry cream until smooth; spoon into clean large pastry bag fitted with ¼-inch plain tip. Pipe into éclairs.

5. In 6-inch skillet or 1-quart saucepan, combine chocolate and cream; heat over low heat, stirring frequently, until chocolate has melted and mixture is smooth. Remove from heat. Dip top of each éclair into chocolate mixture, smoothing with small spatula if necessary. Let stand on wire racks until chocolate sets. Makes about 30 éclairs.

Each éclair: About 116 calories, 3g protein, 12g carbohydrate, 6g total fat (4g saturated), 70mg cholesterol, 70mg sodium.

Praline Cream Puff Wreath

Also known as "Paris-Brest" (named in honor of the bicycle race between Paris and the city of Brest in Brittany), this is cream-puff dough baked in the shape of a bicycle wheel. We like to serve it at Christmas, so we call it a wreath).

Prep: 50 minutes plus chilling and cooling	Bake: 55 minutes
2	cups milk
3	large egg yolks
2/3	cup granulated sugar
3	tablespoons cornstarch
2	teaspoons vanilla extract
	Choux Pastry (page 642)
1/4	cup water
1/3	cup sliced natural almonds, toasted
1	cup heavy or whipping cream
1	tablespoon confectioners' sugar plus additional for dusting

1. Prepare pastry cream: In 3-quart saucepan, heat milk over medium-high heat until bubbles form around edge. Meanwhile, in medium bowl, with wire whisk, beat egg yolks, 1/3 cup granulated sugar, and cornstarch until well blended. Gradually whisk about half of hot milk into egg-yolk mixture. Return milk mixture to saucepan and cook, whisking constantly, until mixture has thickened and boils. Reduce heat to low and cook, stirring, 2 minutes.

2. Remove saucepan from heat; stir in vanilla. Pour pastry cream into medium bowl; press plastic wrap onto surface. Refrigerate until well chilled, 2 hours or up to overnight.

3. Meanwhile, prepare wreath: Preheat oven to 425°F. Grease and flour large cookie sheet. Using 8-inch cake pan or plate as guide, with tooth-pick, trace circle in flour on prepared cookie sheet. Prepare Choux Pastry.

4. Spoon dough into pastry bag fitted with 1/2-inch plain tip. Using tracing as guide, pipe dough in 1-inch-thick ring just inside circle. Pipe second ring outside of first, making sure dough rings touch. With remaining dough, pipe third ring on top of center seam of first two rings. With moistened finger, gently smooth dough rings where ends meet.

5. Bake wreath 20 minutes. Turn oven control to 375°F and bake until golden, about 25 minutes longer. Remove wreath from oven; with tip of knife, make several small slits to release steam. Bake 10 minutes longer. Transfer wreath to wire rack and cool completely.

6. While wreath is baking, prepare almond praline: Lightly grease cookie sheet. In 1-quart saucepan, combine remaining 1/3 cup granulated sugar and water; heat to boiling over medium-high heat, swirling pan occasionally, until sugar has dissolved. Boil mixture, without stirring, until amber in color, 5 to 7 minutes. Remove from heat and stir in almonds. Stir mixture over low heat just until it reliquifies. Immediately pour praline mixture onto prepared cookie sheet; spread with back of spoon to 1/2-inch thickness. Let praline cool on cookie sheet on wire rack until completely cool, about 10 minutes.

7. Break praline into small pieces. In food processor with knife blade attached, process praline to fine powder. With rubber spatula, gently fold praline into chilled pastry cream.

8. In small bowl, with mixer at medium speed, beat cream and 1 tablespoon confectioners' sugar just until stiff peaks form.

9. With long serrated knife, slice cooled wreath horizontally in half; remove and discard moist dough from inside. Spoon or pipe pastry cream into bottom of wreath; top with whipped cream. Replace top of wreath. Refrigerate up to 2 hours if not serving right away. To serve, dust with confectioners' sugar. Makes 12 servings.

Each serving: About 326 calories, 7g protein, 26g carbohydrate, 22g total fat (11g saturated), 178mg cholesterol, 177mg sodium.

Praline Cream Puff Wreath

Napoleons

This classic French pastry can be tailored to suit your taste. Use frozen or homemade puff pastry and fill with chocolate or vanilla pastry cream. Decorate with a vanilla glaze with lines of melted chocolate "feathered" through it, or simply dust generously with confectioners' sugar.

Prep: 25 minutes plus chilling and cooling   Bake: 25 minutes
Vanilla or Chocolate Pastry Cream (page 642)
1 sheet frozen puff pastry (half 17¼-ounce package), thawed
½ square (½ ounce) semisweet chocolate, chopped
1 cup confectioners' sugar
2 tablespoons water

1. Prepare Vanilla or Chocolate Pastry Cream; cover and refrigerate until ready to use.

2. Preheat oven to 400°F. On lightly floured surface, roll out puff pastry dough to 14" by 12" rectangle. Transfer rectangle to ungreased cookie sheet; with fork, prick all over. Cover dough with second ungreased cookie sheet.

3. Bake until edges of pastry are golden, 20 to 30 minutes. Remove top cookie sheet; bake until golden all over, about 5 minutes longer. Cool on cookie sheet on wire rack.

4. In heavy 1-quart saucepan, melt chocolate over low heat, stirring frequently, until smooth. With serrated knife, cut puff pastry lengthwise into 3 equal strips. With wire whisk, stir pastry cream until smooth. With narrow metal spatula, spread half of pastry cream over 1 puff pastry strip. Place second strip of pastry on top and spread with remaining pastry cream.

5. Place remaining pastry strip upside down on rack. Place melted chocolate in ziptight plastic bag with a corner cut. Mix confectioners' sugar with water until smooth; pour over pastry strip and smooth with metal spatula. Quickly pipe chocolate in lengthwise stripes, ¾ inch apart, over glaze. Drag tip of small knife crosswise through chocolate stripes at ½-inch intervals to make feathered design. Let glaze set. Place pastry strip, glaze side up, on top of pastry cream. Refrigerate up to 4 hours. To serve, with serrated knife, cut napoleon crosswise into 1-inch-thick slices. Makes 12 servings.

Each serving: About 273 calories, 4g protein, 38g carbohydrate, 11g total fat (3g saturated), 77mg cholesterol, 76mg sodium.

CHOUX PASTRY

Choux pastry dough is unique because it is cooked twice: first on the stove and then in the oven. (Its original name was *chaud*, or hot pastry, which eventually became *choux*.) The dough makes a light, airy, hollow pastry that is perfect for filling with ice cream, whipped cream, or pastry cream.

- When cooking the dough, be sure the butter is completely melted by the time the water comes to a full boil. If too much water evaporates, the dough will be dry.
- For the best results, use room-temperature eggs. Add them to the batter, one at a time, mixing well after each addition.
- For the highest puff, always shape and bake choux pastry dough while it is still warm.
- Bake the pastries until golden brown: Pale undercooked pastries collapse when removed from the oven.
- Choux dough creates a lot of steam when baked: This steam needs to be released or the pastries will become soggy. As soon as the pastries are removed from the oven, use the tip of a small knife to cut a slit into the side of each one.
- Unfilled choux dough pastries can be frozen in heavy-duty ziptight plastic bags for up to one month; simply recrisp in a 400°F oven for a few minutes before serving.

Crepes Suzette

For real table-side drama, flambé the crepes in a chafing dish, but they are just as enjoyable when prepared in the kitchen.

Prep: 30 minutes plus chilling   Cook: 10 minutes
12 Basic Crepes (page 318)
1 orange
4 tablespoons butter or margarine
2 tablespoons sugar
¼ cup orange-flavored liqueur

1. Prepare Basic Crepes. Prepare sauce: From orange, grate 1/2 teaspoon peel and squeeze 1/3 cup juice. In nonreactive 12-inch skillet, heat orange peel and juice, butter, and sugar over low heat, stirring until butter melts.

2. Fold crepes into quarters; arrange in sauce, overlapping if necessary, and heat through, turning crepes once.

3. In very small saucepan, heat liqueur over medium heat until hot; remove from heat. Carefully ignite liqueur with long match; pour flaming liqueur over crepes. When flame dies down, transfer crepes to dessert plates. Makes 6 servings.

Each serving: About 311 calories, 7g protein, 22g carbohydrate, 20g total fat (12g saturated), 156mg cholesterol, 411mg sodium.

Apple-Calvados Crepes

These crepes can be filled with almost any seasonal fruits. Calvados is French apple brandy; applejack is the American version. If you prefer, substitute apple juice.

Prep: 50 minutes plus chilling	Bake: 5 minutes

12	Basic Crepes (page 318)
5	tablespoons butter or margarine
3	pounds Golden Delicious apples (6 large), peeled, cored, and finely chopped
1/2	cup plus 1 tablespoon sugar
1/4	cup Calvados or applejack brandy

1. Prepare Basic Crepes. Preheat oven to 400°F. In 12-inch skillet, melt 4 tablespoons butter over medium-high heat. Stir in apples and 1/2 cup sugar; cover and cook until apples are soft, about 10 minutes. Remove cover and cook, stirring occasionally, until apples begin to caramelize, about 10 minutes. Stir in Calvados and remove from heat.

2. Spread scant 1/4 cup apple mixture down center of each crepe and roll up jelly-roll fashion. Arrange rolled crepes in single layer, seam side down, in shallow 3 1/2- to 4-quart baking dish. Dot with remaining 1 tablespoon butter and sprinkle with remaining 1 tablespoon sugar. Bake until heated through, about 5 minutes. Makes 6 servings.

Each serving: About 488 calories, 7g protein, 64g carbohydrate, 22g total fat (13g saturated), 161mg cholesterol, 430mg sodium.

Plum Filling

In 12-inch skillet, melt **3 tablespoons butter or margarine** over medium-high heat. Add **2 1/2 pounds ripe plums (10 large),** quartered and pitted, **2/3 cup granulated sugar,** and **pinch ground cloves.** Cook, stirring occasionally, until plums are tender, 15 to 20 minutes. Fill crepes and bake as directed.

Mixed Berry Filling

In medium bowl, toss **1 1/2 cups hulled and halved strawberries, 1 1/2 cups blueberries, 1 1/2 cups raspberries,** and **2/3 cup granulated sugar.** Fill crepes and bake as directed.

Banana Filling

In medium bowl, toss **2 large ripe bananas,** sliced, with **1/4 cup packed brown sugar.** Fill crepes and bake as directed.

PUFF PASTRY

Puff pastry dough gets its incredible flakiness from a special technique that creates hundreds of layers of buttery dough.

- When cutting puff pastry dough, use a very sharp knife or pizza wheel. Cut straight down: If cut on an angle, the pastry will be lopsided.

- To prevent the puff pastry dough from rising too much (the pastry will still be flaky and buttery), prick it well with a fork, or weight the pastry down with a cookie sheet.

- Puff pastry demands a quick initial blast of heat: This melts the butter in the dough while converting the water to steam, making it rise. To ensure your oven is hot enough, preheat it for at least twenty minutes.

- If buying frozen puff pastry, check the label. The best-tasting brands contain only flour, butter, salt, and water.

- Frozen puff pastry thaws very quickly, making it handy for last-minute desserts. Allow ten to twenty minutes thawing time. But be sure the pastry is still well chilled before baking, or it won't rise properly.

19

CAKES AND CAKE FROSTINGS

Say the word "cake" and a luscious layered dessert (perhaps topped with birthday candles) is what usually comes to mind. This all-American dessert, covered with a mantle of creamy frosting, may be one of the most enduring images in the ever-expanding world of desserts. But there are many other cakes to be enjoyed, some so moist and delicious they need only a sprinkling of confectioners' sugar to finish them off. And it cannot be denied that a thick slice of buttery pound cake surrounded by fresh fruit can be just as mouthwatering as an intricately composed nut torte that looks like it came from a European-style pastry shop. To satisfy everyone's sweet cravings, we offer cakes for every appetite and every occasion: fruitcakes for the holidays, cheesecakes for large parties, and a variety of enticing cakes that includes that perennial favorite—chocolate.

PERFECT CAKES EVERY TIME

The ingredients in cake recipes are carefully balanced and leave little room for inaccurate measuring or mixing. Always precisely measure out all the ingredients before mixing the batter.

Cake batters should be made with room-temperature ingredients. Remove butter, eggs, and dairy products from the

Easy Chocolate-Buttermilk Cake with White Chocolate Butter Frosting

refrigerator thirty minutes ahead of time. You can often use either butter or stick margarine, but butter has superior flavor. (Some recipes, however, use vegetable shortening, because it makes a tender cake with a delicate crumb.) Soften the butter just until malleable, not shiny and melting. To cut down on the softening time, you can cut the butter into small cubes. We use large eggs to make our cakes; do not use another size. Chilled eggs don't beat to their maximum volume, so either leave them out at room temperature, or place the whole eggs in a bowl of warm (tap) water for five minutes.

Flour is an important consideration in cake making. Although most of our recipes call for readily available all-purpose flour, some use cake flour. This low-protein flour has less gluten than other flours and produces tender cakes. If you don't have cake flour, you can use all-purpose bleached flour combined with cornstarch: For every cup of cake flour, spoon 2 tablespoons of cornstarch into a 1-cup measure. Spoon in enough all-purpose flour to fill the cup, then level the top. Do not substitute unbleached flour: It will make the cake heavy. When measuring flour, use the spoon-and-sweep method (see Basics, page 7).

Always use the recommended pan size. Don't guess: Measure the pan with a ruler if necessary. In some recipes, the bottom of the pan is lined with waxed paper for easy cake removal. To line a pan, place it on a piece of waxed paper. Use a pencil to trace around the bottom edge, and cut out the round.

If the recipe directs you, grease or grease and flour the pan(s). (Pans for chiffon and angel food cakes are not greased because these batters need to cling to the side of the pan as they rise). We like to use vegetable shortening to grease baking pans. Apply an even film of shortening using a folded piece of paper towel or waxed paper. When greasing a Bundt pan, be sure to get into all the crevices, or use nonstick cooking spray. To flour a greased pan, sprinkle a tablespoon or so of flour into the pan, tilting it to coat the bottom and side. Invert the pan and tap out the excess. In some chocolate cake recipes, cocoa is used instead of flour to dust the pan.

Preheat the oven thoroughly. It must be at the correct temperature when a cake is put in; it's a good idea to position the racks first. When baking two loaf or layer cakes, place a rack in the center of the oven. If baking more cakes, place the racks in the center and upper third of the oven. Stagger the pans so they are not directly above one another. Cake pans should never touch the sides of the oven or each other; allow at least 1 inch between them. For cakes baked in tube pans, position the oven rack in the lower third of the oven.

TYPES OF CAKES

Most cakes are variations on two themes, butter cakes and foam cakes, while cheesecakes form a separate category. Here are some tips for each.

Butter Cakes

Adored for their lush flavor and tender crumb, butter cakes rely on fat for their moistness and richness. The fat must be beaten well with the sugar to provide an aerated base upon which to build the batter. Beat the butter-and-sugar mixture with an electric mixer on medium speed until it is light and

fluffy, frequently scraping down the side of the bowl with a rubber spatula or as directed. Beat in the eggs, one a time, beating well after each addition. In some cases, the batter will look curdled, but it will come together when the dry ingredients are added. The dry ingredients don't have to be sifted together as long as they are combined thoroughly before being added.

Pour the batter into the prepared pan(s) and gently tap the pan(s) on a counter to break any large air bubbles that may have formed. Place the cake in the oven and bake for at least fifteen minutes before opening the oven door: A sudden temperature change could cause an underbaked cake to fall. The cake is done when a toothpick inserted in the center comes out clean. Some cakes also pull slightly away from the side of the pan. Or, lightly press the center of the cake with your finger: The top should spring back into place.

Cool the cake on a wire rack for just ten minutes (a hot cake is very tender and can break if removed from the pan too soon, while if allowed to stay in the pan too long, steam can collect, making the cake soggy and difficult to remove). Run a thin knife around the inside of the pan to release the cake from the side. Invert a second wire rack on top of the pan. Invert both racks along with the pan. Remove the top rack and the cake pan; peel off the waxed paper, if used. Replace the top rack and invert the cake again, so the top of the cake faces up; this way the cake will cool without retaining any marks from the rack. Cool completely before frosting.

Foam Cakes

Foam cakes depend on beaten whole eggs or egg whites for their light and airy texture. Angel food cake is extremely light because it doesn't contain any fat; it gets its great height from a large amount of beaten whites. Chiffon and sponge cakes, on the other hand, contain beaten whole eggs or egg yolks along with vegetable oil or melted butter for additional moisture. Patience is the key to success with foam cakes. It takes time to beat eggs (or egg whites) to their greatest volume. If a recipe calls for the eggs to be beaten until thick and lemon colored, expect it to take from three to ten minutes. (The time will depend on the number of eggs and the speed and power of the mixer.) When the beaters are lifted, the egg mixture should form a thick ribbon that holds it shape (for a few seconds) when it falls back into the bowl.

When combining the ingredients for these batters, fold them in with a rubber spatula, the larger the better. Folding prevents the beaten egg mixture from deflating. Cut down through the center of the batter, then draw the spatula across the bottom of the batter and up the side of the bowl. Flip the spatula over and draw it across the top of the batter. Give the bowl a quarter turn, and repeat the process until the batter is uniformly blended. Scrape the batter evenly into the cake pan with a rubber spatula, using a light hand (to deflate the batter as little as possible).

Bake the cake for the minimum recommended time, then check for doneness. The top should spring back when lightly pressed in the center. There may be a few cracks in the top of the cake, which is typical.

Cakes baked in tube pans are cooled upside down to hold their shape. Invert the pan and insert it over the neck of a tall bottle or funnel (some pans have small feet around the edge that keep the cake from touching the surface), and cool completely. To remove the cake from the pan, run a thin knife around the cake to loosen it from the side and center tube of the pan. Lift the cake and center tube together from the pan. Slide the knife under the cake to separate it from the pan bottom. Invert onto a wire rack and remove the center tube. Turn the cake, right side up, onto a wire rack to cool completely.

Sponge layer cakes are cooled just like butter cakes. Jelly-roll cakes are removed from the pan and rolled up with a towel. This helps them retain their shape when filled and rolled.

Cheesecakes

Cheesecakes are sinfully rich and delicious. There are two basic types: cream cheese and curd cheese (ricotta or cottage cheese, for example). Some cheesecakes have a crust, while others do not. The crust can be made of pastry dough, graham crackers, or cookies. The filling can be plain, flavored with citrus, or enriched with chocolate or pumpkin. The possibilities are almost limitless. In this chapter, we have included recipes that represent the very best cheesecakes.

To bake perfect cheesecakes, here are a few tips: Cream cheese must be well softened. Let it stand for at least one hour at room temperature. When baking cheesecakes, to prevent the butter in the crust from leaking out of the pan or to water-proof a pan that is placed in a water bath, the outside of the pan is often wrapped with heavy-duty foil. Cheesecakes should be baked until the centers barely jiggle; they will firm up during cooling and chilling. To help prevent cracking during cooling, run a thin knife around the edge of the cheesecake as soon as the cheesecake comes out of the oven.

FROSTING LAYER CAKES

Use a narrow metal spatula to spread frosting. It is easiest to frost a cake if it is elevated and can be turned. If you don't have a cake decorating stand, place the cake on a serving plate set on a large coffee can or inverted bowl.

We want to encourage you to partake in the pleasures of cake making, so we don't call for any special procedures for splitting cakes or leveling their tops. Simply brush off any crumbs and use a serrated knife to trim away any crisp edges. Place the first layer, rounded side down, on the serving plate. To keep the plate clean, tuck strips of waxed paper under the cake, covering the plate edge. Spread the cake layer with one-half to two-thirds cup frosting, spreading it almost to the edge. Top with the second cake layer, rounded side up. Thinly frost  the cake to set the crumbs and keep them in place; first coat the top of the cake, then the side. Finish the cake with a thicker layer of frosting. Where the top and side of the frosting meet, smooth it by sweeping and swirling the edge of the frosting toward the center of the cake. Then slip out the waxed paper strips and discard.

STORING CAKES

Always refrigerate cakes that contain fillings or frostings made with whipped cream, cream cheese, sour cream, yogurt, or eggs. If the cake layers were made with butter or margarine, they will harden in the refrigerator, so before serving, allow the cake to stand at room temperature for about thirty minutes.

Because of their high fat content, unfrosted butter cakes stay moist and fresh-tasting for two or three days. Store them at room temperature. Foam cakes contain little or no fat and dry out quickly; store at room temperature for up to two days.

To freeze butter cakes, place them, unwrapped, in the freezer until firm; wrap in plastic and then in heavy-duty foil. Frosted cakes can be frozen for up to two months, unfrosted cakes for up to six months. Do not freeze cakes with whipped-cream frostings or egg-based fillings. Foam cakes can be frozen in heavy-duty ziptight plastic bags for up to three months.

Yellow Cake

Make this versatile cake with shortening (for delicate flavor and crumb) or butter (for rich flavor). Either way, it will have the taste of old-fashioned goodness.

Prep: 45 minutes plus cooling	Bake: 30 minutes

2	cups all-purpose flour
2	teaspoons baking powder
1	teaspoon salt
½	cup vegetable shortening or ½ cup butter or margarine (1 stick), softened
1¼	cups sugar
3	large eggs
1	teaspoon vanilla extract
1	cup milk
	Chocolate Butter Frosting (page 677) or desired frosting

1. Preheat oven to 350°F. Grease and flour two 8-inch round cake pans or one 9-inch square baking pan, or line twenty-four 2½-inch muffin-pan cups with paper baking liners. (Preheat oven to 325°F if using 9-inch square pan.)

2. In medium bowl, combine flour, baking powder, and salt. In large bowl, with mixer at medium speed, beat shortening and sugar until light and fluffy, about 5 minutes. Add eggs, one at a time, beating well after each addition. Beat in vanilla. Reduce speed to low; add flour mixture alternately with milk, beginning and ending with flour mixture. Beat just until smooth, frequently scraping bowl with rubber spatula.

3. Divide batter between prepared pans; spread evenly. Bake until toothpick inserted in center comes out clean, about 30 minutes for 8-inch layers, 40 to 45 minutes for 9-inch square cake, or 20 to 25 minutes for cupcakes. Cool in pans on wire racks 10 minutes. Run thin knife around layers to loosen from sides of pans; invert onto racks to cool completely.

4. Meanwhile, prepare Chocolate Butter Frosting. Place one layer, rounded side down, on cake plate. With narrow metal spatula, spread ⅔ cup frosting over layer. Top with second layer, rounded side up. Spread remaining frosting over side and top of cake. Makes 12 servings.

Each serving with Chocolate Butter Frosting: About 526 calories, 5g protein, 66g carbohydrate, 28g total fat (13g saturated), 87mg cholesterol, 421mg sodium.

Orange Cake

Prepare cake as directed but add **1 teaspoon freshly grated orange peel** with vanilla. Frost with **Fluffy White Frosting** (page 679) or **Orange Butter Frosting** (page 677).

Each serving with Fluffy White Frosting: About 345 calories, 5g protein, 56g carbohydrate, 11g total fat (3g saturated), 56mg cholesterol, 312mg sodium.

Each serving with Orange Butter Frosting: About 494 calories, 5g protein, 77g carbohydrate, 19g total fat (8g saturated), 77mg cholesterol, 383mg sodium.

Silver White Cake

Made without egg yolks, this cake has a pristine ivory color that can be accented by a variety of frostings. Try Peppermint Whipped Cream Frosting (page 679), or fill with Lemon Filling (page 680), then frost with Fluffy White Frosting (page 679).

Prep: 50 minutes plus cooling	Bake: 30 minutes

2	cups cake flour (not self-rising)
2	teaspoons baking powder
1	teaspoon salt
4	large egg whites
1¼	cups sugar
½	cup vegetable shortening
1	teaspoon vanilla extract
¼	teaspoon almond extract
1	cup milk
	Chocolate Butter Frosting (page 677) or desired frosting

1. Preheat oven to 350°F. Grease and flour two 8-inch round cake pans.

2. In medium bowl, combine flour, baking powder, and salt. In medium bowl, with mixer at high speed, beat egg whites until soft peaks form when beaters are lifted. Sprinkle in ¼ cup sugar, 1 tablespoon at a time, beating until sugar has dissolved and egg whites stand in stiff, glossy peaks when beaters are lifted.

3. In large bowl, with mixer at low speed, beat shortening and remaining 1 cup sugar until blended. Increase speed to medium. Beat in vanilla and almond extracts. Reduce speed to low; add flour mixture alternately with milk, beginning and ending with flour mixture. Beat just until smooth, occasion-

ally scraping bowl with rubber spatula. Gently fold in beaten egg whites, one-third at a time, just until blended.

4. Divide batter between prepared pans; spread evenly. Bake until toothpick inserted in center comes out clean, about 30 minutes. Cool in pans on wire racks 10 minutes. Run thin knife around layers to loosen from sides of pans. Invert onto racks to cool completely.

5. Meanwhile, prepare Chocolate Butter Frosting. Place one layer, rounded side down, on cake plate. With narrow metal spatula, spread ⅔ cup frosting over layer. Top with second layer, rounded side up. Spread remaining frosting over side and top of cake. Makes 12 servings.

Each serving with Chocolate Butter Frosting: About 492 calories, 4g protein, 63 carbohydrate, 26g total fat (13g saturated), 34mg cholesterol, 423mg sodium.

Golden Butter Cake

This classic layer cake is a good candidate for frosting, but it is so moist that it can also be baked in a tube pan, dusted with confectioners' sugar, and enjoyed.

Prep: 45 minutes plus cooling	Bake: 23 minutes
3	cups cake flour (not self-rising)
1	tablespoon baking powder
½	teaspoon salt
1	cup butter or margarine (2 sticks), softened
2	cups sugar
4	large eggs
2	teaspoons vanilla extract
1	cup milk
	Silky Orange Butter Frosting (page 678) or desired frosting

1. Preheat oven to 350°F. Grease three 8-inch round cake pans. Line bottoms with waxed paper; grease and flour paper. Or grease and flour 9-inch fluted tube pan.

2. In medium bowl, combine flour, baking powder, and salt. In large bowl, with mixer at medium-high speed, beat butter and sugar until light and fluffy, about 5 minutes. Add eggs, one at a time, beating well after each addition. Beat in vanilla. Reduce speed to low; add flour mixture alternately with milk, beginning and ending with flour mixture. Beat just until smooth, scraping bowl with rubber spatula.

3. Divide batter among prepared cake pans; spread evenly. Place two pans on upper oven rack and one pan on lower oven rack so that pans are not directly above one another. Bake until toothpick inserted in center comes out clean, 23 to 28 minutes for 8-inch layers, or 50 to 55 minutes for tube pan. Cool in pans on wire racks 10 minutes. Run thin knife around layers to loosen from sides of pans. Or, if using fluted tube pan, run tip of knife around edge of cake to loosen. Invert onto racks. Remove waxed paper; cool completely.

4. Meanwhile, prepare Silky Orange Butter Frosting. Place one layer, rounded side down, on cake plate. With narrow metal spatula, spread ⅔ cup frosting over layer. Top with second layer, rounded side up, and spread with ⅔ cup frosting. Place remaining layer, rounded side up, on top. Spread remaining frosting over side and top of cake. Makes 16 servings.

Each serving with Silky Orange Butter Frosting: About 491 calories, 5g protein, 60g carbohydrate, 26g total fat (16g saturated), 120mg cholesterol, 432mg sodium.

Each serving without frosting: About 315 calories, 4g protein, 43g carbohydrate, 14g total fat (8g saturated), 86mg cholesterol, 305mg sodium.

Always preheat the oven for ten to fifteen minutes before putting in a cake. Be sure to put the cake right into the oven after mixing: If a batter sits at room temperature, it will lose some of its leavening power. Immediate baking is especially essential for batters leavened entirely by egg foam (angel food and sponge cakes), because the foam starts to deflate quickly.

SUSAN G. PURDY
COOKBOOK AUTHOR

EXPERT TIP

Banana Layer Cake

If you are a banana lover, this recipe is for you. Here, a generous amount of ripened bananas gives the cake lots of delicious flavor, while the buttermilk provides great texture. And, of course, the irresistible cream cheese frosting makes it all unforgettable. For the best results, use fully ripe (but not blackened) bananas.

Prep: 40 minutes plus cooling   Bake: 30 minutes

1	cup mashed fully ripe bananas (2 to 3 bananas)
¼	cup buttermilk
1	teaspoon vanilla extract
2	cups cake flour (not self-rising)
1	teaspoon baking powder
½	teaspoon baking soda
¼	teaspoon salt
⅛	teaspoon ground nutmeg
½	cup butter or margarine (1 stick), softened
1¼	cups sugar
2	large eggs
	Cream Cheese Frosting (page 679)

1. Preheat oven to 350°F. Grease three 8-inch round cake pans or one 13" by 9" baking pan. Line bottoms with waxed paper; grease paper. Dust pans with flour.

2. In small bowl, combine bananas, buttermilk, and vanilla. In medium bowl, combine flour, baking powder, baking soda, salt, and nutmeg.

3. In large bowl, with mixer at medium speed, beat butter and sugar until light and fluffy, about 5 minutes. Add eggs, one at a time, beating well after each addition. Reduce speed to low; add flour mixture alternately with banana mixture, beginning and ending with flour mixture. Beat just until smooth, frequently scraping bowl with rubber spatula.

4. Divide batter evenly among prepared pans; spread evenly. Place two pans on upper oven rack and one pan on lower oven rack so that pans are not directly above one another. Bake until toothpick inserted in center comes out clean, about 30 minutes for 8-inch layers or 35 to 40 minutes for 13" by 9" cake. Cool in pans on wire racks 10 minutes. Run thin knife around layers to loosen from sides of pans. Invert onto racks. Remove waxed paper; cool completely.

5. Meanwhile, prepare Cream Cheese Frosting. Place one layer, rounded side down, on cake plate. With narrow metal spatula, spread ½ cup frosting over layer. Top with second layer, rounded side up, and spread with ½ cup frosting. Place remaining layer, rounded side up, on top. Spread remaining frosting over side and top of cake. Makes 16 servings.

Each serving with Cream Cheese Frosting: About 362 calories, 3g protein, 54g carbohydrate, 15g total fat (9g saturated), 66mg cholesterol, 252mg sodium.

Spice Layer Cake

This recipe makes a triple layer cake that you'll want to serve again and again. The unusual brown butter frosting complements the aromatic spices beautifully.

Prep: 40 minutes plus cooling   Bake: 25 minutes

2⅔	cups all-purpose flour
2½	teaspoons baking powder
2	teaspoons ground cinnamon
1	teaspoon ground ginger
½	teaspoon salt
½	teaspoon ground nutmeg
¼	teaspoon ground cloves
1	cup butter or margarine (2 sticks), softened
1	cup granulated sugar
1	cup packed dark brown sugar
5	large eggs
1	cup milk
	Brown Butter Frosting (page 677) or desired frosting

1. Preheat oven to 350°F. Grease three 8-inch round cake pans. Line bottoms with waxed paper; grease paper. Dust pans with flour.

2. In medium bowl, combine flour, baking powder, cinnamon, ginger, salt, nutmeg, and cloves.

3. In large bowl, with mixer at low speed, beat butter and granulated and brown sugars until blended. Increase speed to medium; beat until light and fluffy, about 5 minutes, frequently scraping bowl with rubber spatula. Add eggs, one at a time, beating well after each addition. Reduce speed to low; add flour mixture alternately with milk, beginning and ending with flour mixture. Beat just until blended, scraping bowl.

4. Divide batter evenly among prepared pans; spread evenly. Place two pans on upper oven rack and one pan on lower oven rack so pans are not directly above one another. Bake until toothpick inserted in center comes out clean, 25 to 30 minutes. Cool in pans on wire racks 10 minutes. Run thin

Spice Layer Cake with Brown Butter Frosting

knife around layers to loosen from sides of pans. Invert onto racks. Remove waxed paper; cool completely.

5. Meanwhile, prepare Brown Butter Frosting. Place one layer, rounded side down, on cake plate. With narrow metal spatula, spread ½ cup frosting over layer. Top with second layer, rounded side up, and spread with ½ cup frosting. Place remaining layer, rounded side up, on top. Spread remaining frosting over side and top of cake. Makes 16 servings.

Each serving with Brown Butter Frosting: About 490 calories, 5g protein, 73g carbohydrate, 20g total fat (12g saturated), 116mg cholesterol, 360mg sodium.

Applesauce Spice Cake

For a quick snack, make this easy cake. You may already have all of the ingredients on hand.

	Prep: 20 minutes Bake: 40 minutes
2	cups all-purpose flour
1½	teaspoons ground cinnamon
1	teaspoon baking powder
½	teaspoon baking soda
½	teaspoon ground ginger
¼	teaspoon ground nutmeg
½	teaspoon salt
½	cup butter or margarine (1 stick), softened
¼	cup granulated sugar
1	cup packed dark brown sugar
2	large eggs
1¼	cups unsweetened applesauce
½	cup dark seedless raisins
	confectioners' sugar

1. Preheat oven to 350°F. Grease and flour 9-inch square baking pan.

2. In medium bowl, combine flour, cinnamon, baking powder, baking soda, ginger, nutmeg, and salt.

3. In large bowl, with mixer at low speed, beat butter and granulated and brown sugars until blended. Increase speed to medium-high; beat until light and fluffy, about 3 minutes. Add eggs, one at a time, beating well after each addition. Reduce speed to low; beat in applesauce. Mixture may appear curdled. Beat in flour mixture until smooth, occasionally scraping bowl with rubber spatula. Stir in raisins.

4. Scrape batter into prepared pan; spread evenly. Bake cake until toothpick inserted in center comes out clean, about 40 minutes. Cool completely in pan on wire rack. To serve, dust with confectioners' sugar. Makes 9 servings.

♥ Each serving: About 369 calories, 5g protein, 62g carbohydrate, 12g total fat (7g saturated), 75mg cholesterol, 383mg sodium.

Pineapple Upside-Down Cake

We cut the pineapple slices in half to fit more fruit into the pan. Plums or apples make delicious variations (you won't need the pineapple juice).

Prep: 30 minutes   Bake: 40 minutes

2	cans (8 ounces each) pineapple slices in juice
1/3	cup packed brown sugar
8	tablespoons butter or margarine (1 stick), softened
1	cup cake flour (not self-rising)
1	teaspoon baking powder
1/4	teaspoon salt
2/3	cup granulated sugar
1	large egg
1	teaspoon vanilla extract
1/3	cup milk

1. Preheat oven to 325°F. Drain pineapple slices in sieve set over bowl. Reserve 2 tablespoons juice. Cut 8 slices pineapple in half and drain on paper towels. Refrigerate remaining slices for another use.

2. In 10-inch oven-safe skillet (if skillet is not oven-safe, wrap handle with double layer of foil), heat brown sugar and 2 tablespoons butter over medium heat until melted. Stir in reserved pineapple juice and heat to boiling; boil 1 minute. Remove skillet from heat. Decoratively arrange pineapple in skillet, overlapping slices slightly to fit.

3. In small bowl, combine flour, baking powder, and salt. In large bowl, with mixer at high speed, beat remaining 6 tablespoons butter and granulated sugar until fluffy, frequently scraping bowl with rubber spatula. Reduce speed to low; beat in egg and vanilla until well blended. Add flour mixture alternately with milk, beginning and ending with flour mixture. Beat just until blended.

4. Spoon batter over pineapple; spread evenly with rubber spatula. Bake until toothpick inserted in center comes out clean, 40 to 45 minutes. Run thin knife around cake to loosen from side of skillet; invert onto serving plate. (If any pineapple slices stick to skillet, place on cake.) Serve warm or at room temperature. Makes 8 servings.

Each serving: About 302 calories, 3g protein, 46g carbohydrate, 13g total fat (8g saturated), 59mg cholesterol, 267mg sodium.

Plum Upside-Down Cake

Prepare as directed but substitute **1 pound plums** for pineapple. Cut plums into ½-inch-thick wedges. Heat brown sugar and 2 tablespoons butter in oven-safe skillet over medium heat until melted. Add plums and increase heat to high. Cook, stirring, until plums are glazed with brown-sugar mixture, about 1 minute.

Apple Upside-Down Cake

Prepare as directed but substitute **3 large Golden Delicious apples (1½ pounds)** for pineapple. Peel, core, and cut apples into ¼-inch-thick wedges. Heat brown sugar and 2 tablespoons butter in oven-safe skillet over medium heat until melted. Add apple wedges and cook over high heat until apples are fork-tender and begin to brown, 7 to 8 minutes.

Gingerbread

Because it's mixed by hand, this gingerbread has a dense, chewy texture. For a more cakelike consistency, beat the batter with an electric mixer for two full minutes. (One important tip: Measure the water after it comes to a boil.)

Prep: 15 minutes   Bake: 45 minutes

2	cups all-purpose flour
1/2	cup sugar
2	teaspoons ground ginger
1	teaspoon ground cinnamon
1/2	teaspoon baking soda
1/2	teaspoon salt
1	cup light (mild) molasses
1/2	cup butter or margarine (1 stick), cut into 4 pieces
3/4	cup boiling water
1	large egg, lightly beaten

1. Preheat oven to 350°F. Grease and flour 9-inch square baking pan.

2. In large bowl, combine flour, sugar, ginger, cinnamon, baking soda, and salt; stir until blended.

3. In small bowl, combine molasses and butter. Add boiling water and stir until butter melts. Add molasses mixture and beaten egg to flour mixture; whisk until smooth.

4. With rubber spatula, scrape batter into prepared pan. Bake gingerbread until toothpick inserted in center comes out

clean, 45 to 50 minutes. Cool in pan on wire rack. Serve gingerbread warm or at room temperature. Makes 9 servings.

Each serving: About 349 calories, 4g protein, 59g carbohydrate, 12g total fat (7g saturated), 51mg cholesterol, 324mg sodium.

Carrot Cake

Legend has it that George Washington enjoyed some carrot tea bread in 1783, and it remains one of America's favorite desserts.

Prep: 40 minutes plus cooling	*Bake: 55 minutes*

2½ cups all-purpose flour
2 teaspoons baking soda
2 teaspoons ground cinnamon
1 teaspoon baking powder
1 teaspoon salt
½ teaspoon ground nutmeg
4 large eggs
1 cup granulated sugar
¾ cup packed light brown sugar
1 cup vegetable oil
¼ cup milk
1 tablespoon vanilla extract
3 cups loosely packed shredded carrots (about 6 medium)
1 cup walnuts (4 ounces), chopped
¾ cup dark seedless raisins
Cream Cheese Frosting (page 679)

Carrot Cake with Cream Cheese Frosting

1. Preheat oven to 350°F. Grease 13" by 9" baking pan. Line bottom with waxed paper; grease paper. Dust pan with flour. Or grease and flour 10-inch Bundt pan.

2. In medium bowl, combine flour, baking soda, cinnamon, baking powder, salt, and nutmeg.

3. In large bowl, with mixer at medium-high speed, beat eggs and granulated and brown sugars until blended, about 2 minutes, frequently scraping bowl with rubber spatula. Beat in oil, milk, and vanilla. Reduce speed to low; add flour mixture and beat until smooth, about 1 minute, scraping bowl. Fold in carrots, walnuts, and raisins.

4. Spoon batter into prepared pan; spread evenly. Bake until toothpick inserted in center comes out almost clean, 55 to 60 minutes for 13" by 9" cake or about 1 hour for Bundt cake. Cool in pan on wire rack 10 minutes. Run thin knife

around cake to loosen from sides of pan. Or, if using Bundt pan, run tip of knife around edge of cake to loosen. Invert onto rack. Remove waxed paper; cool completely.

5. Meanwhile, prepare Cream Cheese Frosting. Transfer cooled cake to cake plate. With narrow metal spatula, spread frosting over sides and top of cake. Makes 16 servings.

Each serving with Cream Cheese Frosting: About 556 calories, 6g protein, 71g carbohydrate, 28g total fat (8g saturated), 77mg cholesterol, 443mg sodium.

Deluxe Carrot Cake

Prepare cake as directed but omit milk; fold in **1 can (8 to 8¼ ounces) crushed pineapple in unsweetened juice** with walnuts and raisins.

Blueberry Crumb Ring

In this simple coffee cake, part of the crumb mixture is set aside for the topping, and the remainder becomes the base for the batter.

Prep: 25 minutes   Bake: 1 hour

1	cup butter or margarine (2 sticks), softened
1½	cups sugar
1	teaspoon ground cinnamon
3½	cups all-purpose flour
2	teaspoons baking powder
½	teaspoon baking soda
½	teaspoon salt
1	container (8 ounces) sour cream
3	large eggs
2	teaspoons vanilla extract
2	cups fresh blueberries

1. Preheat oven to 350°F. Grease and flour 9- to 10-inch tube pan with removable bottom.

2. Prepare crumb mixture: In large bowl, with mixer at low speed, beat butter, 1 cup sugar, and cinnamon until blended. Increase speed to high and beat until light and fluffy. Reduce speed to low and add 2 cups flour. Beat until well blended and crumbly, occasionally scraping bowl with rubber spatula. Set aside 1 cup.

3. Prepare blueberry batter: In small bowl, combine remaining 1½ cups flour, baking powder, baking soda, and salt.

4. Add remaining ½ cup sugar, sour cream, eggs, and vanilla to crumb mixture in large bowl. With mixer at low speed, beat until blended, scraping bowl. Increase speed to high; beat 2 minutes, scraping bowl. Reduce speed to low; add flour mixture and beat just until blended. With rubber spatula, gently fold in 1½ cups blueberries.

5. Spoon batter into prepared pan; spread evenly. Sprinkle with remaining ½ cup blueberries, then reserved crumb topping. Bake until toothpick inserted in center comes out clean, about 1 hour. Cool in pan on wire rack 10 minutes. Run thin knife around cake to loosen from side and center tube of pan; lift tube to separate cake from pan side. Slide knife under cake to separate from bottom of pan. Invert onto wire rack and remove center tube. Turn cake, right side up, onto

rack to cool completely. Makes 16 servings.

Each serving: About 339 calories, 5g protein, 44g carbohydrate, 16g total fat (9g saturated), 77mg cholesterol, 311mg sodium.

Apple-Walnut Bundt Cake

An easy-to-make, dense cake filled with juicy apple chunks.

Prep: 25 minutes   Bake: 1 hour 15 minutes

3	cups all-purpose flour
1¾	cups granulated sugar
1	teaspoon baking soda
1	teaspoon ground cinnamon
¾	teaspoon salt
¼	teaspoon ground nutmeg
1	cup vegetable oil
½	cup apple juice
2	teaspoons vanilla extract
3	large eggs
1	pound Golden Delicious or Granny Smith apples (3 medium), peeled, cored, and coarsely chopped
1	cup walnuts (4 ounces), coarsely chopped
1	cup golden raisins
	confectioners' sugar

1. Preheat oven to 350°F. Grease and flour 10-inch Bundt pan.

2. In large bowl, combine flour, granulated sugar, baking soda, cinnamon, salt, nutmeg, oil, apple juice, vanilla, and eggs. With mixer at low speed, beat until well blended, frequently scraping bowl with rubber spatula. Increase speed to medium; beat 2 minutes, scraping bowl. With wooden spoon, stir in apples, walnuts, and raisins.

3. Spoon batter into prepared pan; spread evenly. Bake until cake pulls away from side of pan and toothpick inserted in center comes out clean, about 1 hour 15 minutes. Cool in pan on wire rack 10 minutes. Run tip of thin knife around edge of cake to loosen. Invert cake onto rack; cool completely. Dust with confectioners' sugar. Makes 16 servings.

Each serving: About 408 calories, 5g protein, 54g carbohydrate, 20g total fat (3g saturated), 40mg cholesterol, 202mg sodium.

Peanut Butter Cupcakes

These cupcakes are great for kids' parties. If you prefer, omit the chocolate topping and use your favorite frosting instead.

Prep: 10 minutes   Bake: 18 minutes

1¾	cups all-purpose flour
1	tablespoon baking powder
½	teaspoon salt
½	cup creamy or chunky peanut butter
¼	cup vegetable shortening
¾	cup sugar
2	large eggs
¾	teaspoon vanilla extract
1	cup milk
1	bar (4 ounces) semisweet or milk chocolate, cut into 18 pieces

1. Preheat oven to 350°F. Line eighteen 2½-inch muffin-pan cups with paper baking liners.

2. In bowl, combine flour, baking powder, and salt.

3. In large bowl, with mixer at medium speed, beat peanut butter and shortening until combined. Add sugar and beat until light and fluffy, about 3 minutes. Add eggs, one at a time, beating well after each addition. Beat in vanilla. Reduce speed to low; add flour mixture alternately with milk, beginning and ending with flour mixture, occasionally scraping bowl with rubber spatula.

4. Divide batter evenly among cups. Bake until toothpick inserted in center of cupcake comes out clean, about 18 minutes. Place 1 piece of chocolate on top of each cupcake; return to oven until chocolate melts, about 1 minute. With small metal spatula, spread chocolate over tops of cupcakes. Remove from pans and cool on wire rack. Makes 18 cupcakes.

Each cupcake: About 192 calories, 5g protein, 23g carbohydrate, 10g total fat (3g saturated), 26mg cholesterol, 193mg sodium.

Peanut Butter Cupcakes

COCOA CONFUSION?

There is a difference between natural and Dutch-process cocoas. Both, though, have rich chocolate flavor and contain only 8 to 24 percent fat—they are equally tasty.

In our kitchens, we usually use natural cocoa because it is readily available. Its acidity works in tandem with the baking soda in a batter to create carbon dioxide gas bubbles, which leaven cakes. Dutch-process cocoa (also called European-style) is treated with an alkali agent that neutralizes it and removes some of cocoa's acidity (the process was developed in the Netherlands in the mid-1800s, hence the name). This procedure changes the cocoa's chemical composition, so it doesn't need to be combined with baking soda. You'll find Dutch-process cocoa at specialty food stores and most supermarkets. Look closely at the label; some cocoas are alkalized even when the label doesn't clearly state it.

As a rule, don't swap cocoas; use what is recommended.

Easy Chocolate-Buttermilk Cake

This cake is so delectably moist and chocolaty, it can be served without any frosting at all.

(pictured on page 648)

Prep: 30 minutes plus cooling   Bake: 30 minutes

2¼	cups all-purpose flour
¾	cup unsweetened cocoa
1¾	cups sugar
2	teaspoons baking soda
1¼	teaspoons salt
1½	cups buttermilk
1	cup vegetable oil
3	large eggs
1½	teaspoons vanilla extract
	White Chocolate Butter Frosting (page 678) or desired frosting

1. Preheat oven to 350°F. Grease two 9-inch round cake pans or 10-inch Bundt pan. Dust pans with cocoa.

2. In large bowl, combine flour, cocoa, sugar, baking soda, and salt.

3. In medium bowl, with wire whisk, mix buttermilk, oil, eggs, and vanilla until blended. Add buttermilk mixture to flour mixture and whisk until smooth.

4. Divide batter between prepared layers or pour into Bundt pan; spread evenly. Bake until toothpick inserted in center comes out clean, about 30 minutes for 9-inch layers or about 40 minutes for Bundt cake. Cool in pans on wire racks 10 minutes. Run thin knife around layers to loosen from side of pan. Or, if using Bundt pan, run tip of knife around edge of cake to loosen. Invert onto racks to cool completely.

5. Meanwhile, prepare White Chocolate Butter Frosting. Place one layer, rounded side down, on cake plate. With narrow metal spatula, spread ⅔ cup frosting over layer. Top with second layer, rounded side up. Spread remaining frosting over side and top of cake. Makes 16 servings.

Each serving with White Chocolate Butter Frosting: About 527 calories, 5g protein, 61g carbohydrate, 31g total fat (12g saturated), 72mg cholesterol, 505 mg sodium.

Molten Chocolate Cakes

Molten Chocolate Cakes

When you cut into these warm cakes, their delectable molten centers flow out. You can assemble them up to twenty-four hours ahead and refrigerate, or freeze up to two weeks. If you refrigerate the cakes, bake them for ten minutes; if they are frozen, bake for sixteen minutes. Serve with whipped cream or vanilla ice cream.

Prep: 20 minutes   Bake: 8 minutes

4	squares (4 ounces) semisweet chocolate, chopped
½	cup butter or margarine (1 stick), cut into pieces
¼	cup heavy or whipping cream
½	teaspoon vanilla extract
¼	cup all-purpose flour
¼	cup sugar
2	large eggs
2	large egg yolks
	whipped cream or vanilla ice cream (optional)

1. Preheat oven to 400°F. Grease eight 6-ounce custard cups. Dust with sugar.

2. In heavy 3-quart saucepan, combine chocolate, butter, and cream; heat over low heat, stirring occasionally, until butter and chocolate melt and mixture is smooth. Remove from heat. Add vanilla; with wire whisk, stir in flour just until mixture is smooth.

3. In medium bowl, with mixer at high speed, beat sugar, eggs, and yolks until thick and lemon-colored, about 10 minutes. Fold egg mixture, one-third at a time, into chocolate mixture until blended.

4. Divide batter evenly among prepared custard cups. Place cups in jelly-roll pan. Bake until edge of cakes is set but center still jiggles, 8 to 9 minutes. Cool in pan on wire rack 3 minutes. Run thin knife around cakes to loosen from sides of cups; invert onto dessert plates. Serve immediately with whipped cream or ice cream, if desired. Makes 8 servings.

Each serving: About 281 calories, 4g protein, 20g carbohydrate, 22g total fat (12g saturated), 148mg cholesterol, 139mg sodium.

Rich Chocolate Cake

Here's a delicious chocolate cake that's guaranteed to please even your toughest critic.

Prep: 45 minutes plus cooling	Bake: 40 minutes
2	cups all-purpose flour
1	cup unsweetened cocoa
2	teaspoons baking powder
1	teaspoon baking soda
½	teaspoon salt
1	cup butter or margarine (2 sticks), softened
2	cups sugar
4	large eggs
2	teaspoons vanilla extract
1⅓	cups milk
	Fluffy White Frosting (page 679) or desired frosting

1. Preheat oven to 350°F. Grease 13" by 9" baking pan or three 8-inch round cake pans. Line bottom with waxed paper; grease and flour paper. Or line thirty-six 2½-inch muffin-pan cups with paper baking liners.

2. In medium bowl, combine flour, cocoa, baking powder, baking soda, and salt.

3. In large bowl, with mixer at low speed, beat butter and sugar until blended. Increase speed to high; beat until light and fluffy, about 5 minutes. Reduce speed to medium-low; add eggs, one at a time, beating well after each addition. Beat in vanilla. Mixture may appear grainy. Reduce speed to low; add flour mixture alternately with milk, beginning and ending with flour mixture. Beat until batter is smooth, occasionally scraping bowl with rubber spatula.

4. Pour batter into prepared pan. Bake until toothpick inserted in center comes out almost clean, 40 to 45 minutes for 13" by 9" cake or about 30 minutes for 8-inch layers. Cool in pan on wire rack 10 minutes. Run thin knife around cake to loosen from sides of pan. Invert cake or layers onto rack to cool completely. Or divide batter evenly among muffin-pan cups (bake as many cupcakes as fit on one rack in center of oven). Bake until toothpick inserted in center comes out almost clean, about 25 minutes. Repeat with remaining batter. Remove cupcakes from pans and cool completely.

5. Meanwhile, prepare Fluffy White Frosting. With narrow metal spatula, spread frosting on cake. Makes 13" by 9" cake, 20 servings; three 8-inch cake layers, 20 servings; or 36 cupcakes.

Each serving of 13" by 9" cake with Fluffy White Frosting: About 285 calories, 4g protein, 43g carbohydrate, 12g total fat (7g saturated), 70mg cholesterol, 291mg sodium.

Each cupcake with Fluffy White Frosting: About 156 calories, 2g protein, 24g carbohydrate, 6g total fat (4g saturated), 39mg cholesterol, 162mg sodium.

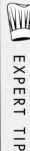

To ensure that cake layers rise evenly, give the pans a half-turn about halfway through the baking time. And don't leave the oven door open any longer than necessary, or the oven temperature will drop.

SUSAN G. PURDY
COOKBOOK AUTHOR

EXPERT TIP

Light Chocolate-Buttermilk Bundt Cake

Satisfy your chocolate cravings with this lowfat treat. If you skip the Mocha Glaze, you'll save forty-five calories per serving.

Prep: 30 minutes plus cooling   Bake: 45 minutes

2¼	cups all-purpose flour
1½	teaspoons baking soda
½	teaspoon baking powder
½	teaspoon salt
¾	cup unsweetened cocoa
1	teaspoon instant espresso-coffee powder
¾	cup hot water
2	cups sugar
⅓	cup vegetable oil
2	large egg whites
1	large egg
1	square (1 ounce) unsweetened chocolate, melted
2	teaspoons vanilla extract
½	cup buttermilk
	Mocha Glaze (right)

1. Preheat oven to 350°F. Grease 10-inch Bundt pan.

2. In medium bowl, combine flour, baking soda, baking powder, and salt.

3. In 2-cup measuring cup, stir cocoa, espresso-coffee powder, and hot water until blended.

4. In large bowl, with mixer at low speed, beat sugar, oil, egg whites, and egg until blended. Increase speed to high; beat until creamy, about 2 minutes. Reduce speed to low; beat in cocoa mixture, melted chocolate, and vanilla. Add flour mixture alternately with buttermilk, beginning and ending with flour mixture. Beat just until blended, occasionally scraping bowl with rubber spatula.

5. Scrape batter into prepared pan; spread evenly with rubber spatula. Bake until toothpick inserted in center comes out clean, about 45 minutes. Cool in pan on wire rack 10 minutes. Run tip of thin knife around edge of cake to loosen. Invert onto rack to cool completely.

6. Meanwhile, prepare Mocha Glaze. Place cake on cake plate; pour glaze over cooled cake. Makes 16 servings.

Mocha Glaze

In medium bowl, combine ¼ **teaspoon instant espresso-coffee powder** and **2 tablespoons hot water**; stir until dissolved. Stir in **3 tablespoons unsweetened cocoa, 3 tablespoons dark corn syrup,** and **1 tablespoon coffee-flavored liqueur** until blended. Add **1 cup confectioners' sugar;** stir until smooth.

♥ Each serving with Mocha Glaze: About 280 calories, 4g protein, 53g carbohydrate, 7g total fat (2g saturated), 14mg cholesterol, 232mg sodium.

♥ Each serving without Mocha Glaze: About 235 calories, 4g protein, 42g carbohydrate, 7g total fat (2g saturated), 14mg cholesterol, 226mg sodium.

Sacher Torte

This decadent Viennese chocolate dessert has two layers of apricot preserves and is covered with a chocolate glaze. Be traditional and serve the cake with schlag *(whipped cream). And, of course, for the best results, we use butter, not margarine.*

Prep: 45 minutes plus cooling   Bake: 40 minutes

Cake

¾	cup butter (1½ sticks), softened (do not use margarine)
¾	cup confectioners' sugar
6	large eggs, separated
1	teaspoon vanilla extract
3	squares (3 ounces) unsweetened chocolate, chopped
3	squares (3 ounces) semisweet chocolate, chopped
¼	teaspoon salt
¼	teaspoon cream of tartar
½	cup granulated sugar
¾	cup all-purpose flour
1	cup apricot preserves

Chocolate Glaze

3	squares (3 ounces) semisweet chocolate, chopped
2	tablespoons butter
1	teaspoon light corn syrup

1. Preheat oven to 350°F. Grease 9-inch springform pan. Line bottom of pan with waxed paper; grease paper. Dust pan with flour.

2. In large bowl, with mixer at medium speed, beat butter and confectioners' sugar until light and fluffy, about 3 minutes. Beat in egg yolks and vanilla until well blended.

3. In heavy 1-quart saucepan, melt unsweetened and semisweet chocolates over low heat, stirring frequently, until smooth. With mixer at medium speed, immediately beat melted chocolate into egg-yolk mixture until well blended; set aside. (Chocolate must be warm, about 130°F, when added to egg-yolk mixture, or batter will be too stiff.)

4. In medium bowl, with clean beaters and with mixer at high speed, beat egg whites, salt, and cream of tartar until soft peaks form when beaters are lifted. Sprinkle in granulated sugar, 2 tablespoons at a time, beating until sugar has dissolved and egg whites stand in glossy, stiff peaks when beaters are lifted (do not overbeat). With rubber spatula, gently fold beaten egg whites, one-third at a time, into chocolate mixture. Sprinkle flour, about ¼ cup at a time, over chocolate mixture; gently fold in just until blended.

5. Scrape batter into prepared pan; spread evenly. Bake until toothpick inserted in center comes out clean, 40 to 45 minutes. Cool in pan on wire rack 10 minutes. Run thin knife around cake to loosen from side of pan; remove pan side. Invert cake onto rack. Slip knife under cake to separate from bottom of pan; remove pan bottom. Remove waxed paper; cool cake completely on rack.

6. When cake is cool, cut horizontally into two layers. Place one layer, cut side up, on cake plate. In 1-quart saucepan, heat apricot preserves over medium-high heat until melted and bubbling. Strain through sieve set over small bowl. With pastry brush, brush half of preserves evenly over layer; replace top layer and spread evenly with remaining preserves. Let stand 10 minutes to set preserves slightly.

7. Prepare Chocolate Glaze: In heavy 1-quart saucepan, heat chocolate, butter, and corn syrup over low heat, stirring frequently, until chocolate and butter melt and mixture is smooth. Remove from heat and cool slightly, about 5 minutes.

8. Pour chocolate glaze over cake. With narrow metal spatula, spread glaze, allowing some to drip down side of cake; completely cover top and side of cake. Let stand 30 minutes to allow glaze to set. If not serving right away, refrigerate cake up to 4 hours. Let cake stand 20 minutes at room temperature before serving. Makes 10 servings.

Each serving: About 505 calories, 7g protein, 61g carbohydrate, 29g total fat (17g saturated), 171mg cholesterol, 276mg sodium.

Chocolate Truffle Cake

This exceptionally sinful chocolate dessert is easy to make, but it must be refrigerated for twenty-four hours before serving for the best flavor and texture. For the neatest slices, dip the knife into hot water before cutting each one.

Prep: 1 hour plus overnight to chill	Bake: 35 minutes
14	squares (14 ounces) semisweet chocolate, chopped
2	squares (2 ounces) unsweetened chocolate, chopped
1	cup butter (2 sticks; do not use margarine)
9	large eggs, separated
½	cup granulated sugar
¼	teaspoon cream of tartar
	confectioners' sugar

1. Preheat oven to 300°F. Remove bottom from 9" by 3" springform pan and cover with foil; wrap foil around back. Replace pan bottom. Grease and flour foil bottom and side of pan.

2. In heavy 2-quart saucepan, combine semisweet and unsweetened chocolates and butter; heat over low heat, stirring frequently, until melted and smooth. Pour chocolate mixture into large bowl.

3. In small bowl, with mixer at high speed, beat egg yolks and granulated sugar until very thick and lemon-colored, about 5 minutes. With rubber spatula, stir egg-yolk mixture into chocolate mixture until blended.

4. In separate large bowl, with clean beaters and with mixer at high speed, beat egg whites and cream of tartar until soft peaks form when beaters are lifted. With rubber spatula, gently fold beaten egg whites, one-third at a time, into chocolate mixture just until blended.

5. Scrape batter into prepared pan; spread evenly. Bake 35 minutes. (Do not overbake; cake will firm upon standing and chilling.) Cool completely in pan on wire rack; refrigerate overnight in pan.

6. Run thin knife, rinsed under very hot water and dried, around cake to loosen from side of pan; remove side of pan. Invert cake onto serving plate; unwrap foil from pan bottom and lift off pan. Carefully peel foil away from cake.

7. To serve, let cake stand 1 hour at room temperature. Dust with confectioners' sugar. Or dust heavily with confectioners' sugar over paper doily or stencil. Makes 20 servings.

Each serving: About 247 calories, 4g protein, 19g carbohydrate, 19g total fat (11g saturated), 120mg cholesterol, 125mg sodium.

Vanilla Pound Cake

This delicate, finely textured pound cake is not as sweet as some. It's perfect with an afternoon cup of tea.

Prep: 20 minutes   Bake: 1 hour to 1 hour 10 minutes

1½	cups butter or margarine (3 sticks), softened
2¼	cups granulated sugar
6	large eggs
1	tablespoon vanilla extract
¾	teaspoon salt
3	cups cake flour (not self-rising)
	confectioners' sugar

1. Preheat oven to 325°F. Grease and flour 10-inch Bundt pan.

2. In large bowl, with mixer at low speed, beat butter and granulated sugar just until blended. Increase speed to high; beat until light and fluffy, about 5 minutes, frequently scraping bowl with rubber spatula. Reduce speed to medium. Add eggs, one at a time, beating well after each addition. Add vanilla and salt. Increase speed to high; beat 3 minutes, scraping bowl. With wire whisk, stir in flour just until smooth.

3. Spoon batter into prepared pan; spread evenly. Bake until toothpick inserted near center comes out clean, 1 hour to 1 hour 10 minutes. Cool in pan on wire rack 10 minutes. Run tip of thin knife around edge of cake to loosen. Invert onto rack to cool completely. Dust with confectioners' sugar. Makes 20 servings.

Each serving: About 299 calories, 3g protein, 36g carbohydrate, 16g total fat (9g saturated), 101mg cholesterol, 247mg sodium.

My favorite pastry brush is made of goose feathers; the quills are braided together with white string. It is inexpensive and can be found in kitchenware stores and bakeware catalogues. The brush is pretty, delicate, useful, and durable. After using, simply rinse the feathers in warm soapy water and hang to dry.

SUSAN G. PURDY
COOKBOOK AUTHOR

EXPERT TIP

Marble Loaf Cake

Sour cream gives this marble cake an exceptionally moist crumb.

Prep: 20 minutes   Bake: 1 hour

1½	cups all-purpose flour
½	teaspoon baking powder
¼	teaspoon baking soda
¼	teaspoon salt
¾	cup butter or margarine (1½ sticks), softened
1¼	cups sugar
2	large eggs
1	teaspoon vanilla extract
½	cup sour cream
¼	cup unsweetened cocoa

1. Preheat oven to 350°F. Grease 9" by 5" metal loaf pan.

2. In small bowl, combine flour, baking powder, baking soda, and salt.

3. In large bowl, with mixer at low speed, beat butter and sugar until blended. Increase speed to high; beat until light and fluffy, about 5 minutes. Reduce speed to low; add eggs, one at a time, beating well after each addition, occasionally scraping bowl with rubber spatula. Beat in vanilla.

4. Add flour mixture alternately with sour cream, beginning and ending with flour mixture. Beat until smooth, occasionally scraping bowl.

5. Transfer half of batter to medium bowl. Add cocoa to batter remaining in large bowl and beat until blended. Alternately spoon vanilla and chocolate batters into pan. With knife, cut and twist through batters to create marbled effect.

6. Bake until toothpick inserted in center comes out clean, about 1 hour. Cool in pan on wire rack 10 minutes. Run thin knife around cake to loosen from sides of pan. Remove from pan; cool completely on rack. Makes 12 servings.

Each serving: About 280 calories, 3g protein, 34g carbohydrate, 15g total fat (9g saturated), 71mg cholesterol, 227mg sodium.

Almond Pound Cake

The addition of almond paste gives this cake delicious depth of flavor. To ensure that the almond paste is evenly blended, we use a heavy-duty standing mixer.

Prep: 20 minutes	Bake: 1 hour
3	cups cake flour (not self-rising)
1	tablespoon baking powder
½	teaspoon salt
1	tube or can (7 to 8 ounces) almond paste, crumbled
1¾	cups sugar
¾	cup butter or margarine (1½ sticks), softened
4	large eggs
2	teaspoons vanilla extract
1	cup milk
⅓	cup sliced natural almonds

1. Preheat oven to 350°F. Evenly grease and flour 10-inch tube pan.

2. In medium bowl, combine flour, baking powder, and salt. In large bowl, with heavy-duty mixer at low speed, beat almond paste and sugar until sandy consistency. (If not using heavy-duty mixer, combine almond paste and sugar in food processor with knife blade attached and pulse until mixture resembles fine crumbs. Transfer almond-paste mixture to mixer bowl and proceed as directed.) Beat in butter. Increase speed to high; beat until light and fluffy, about 5 minutes, frequently scraping bowl with rubber spatula. Reduce speed to low; add eggs, one at a time, beating well after each addition. Beat in vanilla just until blended.

3. With mixer at low speed, add flour mixture alternately with milk, beginning and ending with flour mixture. Beat until smooth, scraping bowl.

4. Spoon batter into prepared pan; spread evenly. Sprinkle almonds evenly on top. Bake until toothpick inserted in center comes out clean, about 1 hour. Cool in pan on wire rack 10 minutes. Run thin knife around cake to loosen from side and center tube of pan; lift tube to separate cake from pan side. Slide knife under cake to separate from bottom of pan. Invert onto wire rack and remove center tube. Turn cake, right side up, onto rack to cool completely. Makes 16 servings.

Each serving: About 344 calories, 6g protein, 46g carbohydrate, 16g total fat (7g saturated), 79mg cholesterol, 277mg sodium.

Lemon–Poppy Seed Pound Cake

This tangy-sweet cake keeps well. Store any leftover poppy seeds in the refrigerator. They turn rancid quickly at room temperature.

Prep: 25 minutes plus cooling	Bake: 1 hour 20 minutes
2	cups all-purpose flour
2	tablespoons poppy seeds
½	teaspoon baking powder
¼	teaspoon baking soda
¼	teaspoon salt
2	large lemons
¾	cup butter or margarine (1½ sticks), softened
1½	plus ⅓ cups sugar
4	large eggs
1	teaspoon vanilla extract
½	cup sour cream

1. Preheat oven to 325°F. Grease and flour 9" by 5" metal loaf pan.

2. In medium bowl, combine flour, poppy seeds, baking powder, baking soda, and salt. From lemons, grate 1 tablespoon peel and squeeze 3 tablespoons juice.

3. In large bowl, with mixer at low speed, beat butter and 1½ cups sugar until blended. Increase speed to high; beat until light and fluffy, about 5 minutes. Add eggs, one at a time, beating well after each addition, frequently scraping bowl with rubber spatula. Beat in lemon peel and vanilla. Reduce speed to low; add flour mixture alternately with sour cream, beginning and ending with flour mixture; beat just until smooth.

4. Spoon batter into prepared pan; spread evenly. Bake until toothpick inserted in center comes out clean, about 1 hour 20 minutes. Cool in pan on wire rack 10 minutes. Run thin knife around cake to loosen from sides of pan. Remove from pan; place on rack set over waxed paper.

5. In small bowl, combine lemon juice and remaining ⅓ cup sugar. With pastry brush, brush mixture over top and sides of warm cake. Cool completely. Makes 16 servings.

Each serving: About 267 calories, 4g protein, 36g carbohydrate, 12g total fat (7g saturated), 80mg cholesterol, 178mg sodium.

Angel Food Cake

Angel food cake, beloved for its clean flavor and light texture, has an added attraction—it's low fat.

Prep: 30 minutes   Bake: 35 minutes

1	cup cake flour (not self-rising)
½	cup confectioners' sugar
1⅔	cups egg whites (12 to 14 large egg whites)
1½	teaspoons cream of tartar
½	teaspoon salt
1¼	cups granulated sugar
2	teaspoons vanilla extract
½	teaspoon almond extract

1. Preheat oven to 375°F. Sift flour and confectioners' sugar through sieve set over small bowl.

2. In large bowl, with mixer at medium speed, beat egg whites, cream of tartar, and salt until foamy. Increase speed to medium-high; beat until soft peaks form when beaters are lifted. Sprinkle in granulated sugar, 2 tablespoons at a time, beating until sugar has dissolved and egg whites stand in stiff, glossy peaks when beaters are lifted. Beat in vanilla and almond extracts.

3. Transfer egg-white mixture to larger bowl. Sift flour mixture, one-third at a time, over beaten egg whites; fold in with rubber spatula just until flour mixture is no longer visible. Do not overmix.

4. Scrape batter into ungreased 9- to 10-inch tube pan; spread evenly. Bake until cake springs back when lightly pressed, 35 to 40 minutes. Invert cake in pan onto large metal funnel or bottle; cool completely in pan. Run thin knife around cake to loosen from side and center tube of pan. Remove from pan and place on cake plate. Makes 16 servings.

♥ Each serving: About 115 calories, 3g protein, 25g carbohydrate, 0g total fat (0g saturated), 0mg cholesterol, 114mg sodium.

Cappuccino Angel Food Cake

Prepare as directed but add **4 teaspoons instant espresso-coffee powder** and **½ teaspoon ground cinnamon** to egg whites before beating; use **1½ teaspoons vanilla extract** and omit almond extract. In cup, mix **1 tablespoon confectioners' sugar** with **⅛ teaspoon ground cinnamon;** sprinkle evenly over cooled cake.

Chocolate Angel Food Cake

Cocoa gives this angel food cake rich, satisfying chocolate flavor.

Prep: 30 minutes   Bake: 35 minutes

¾	cup cake flour (not self-rising)
½	cup unsweetened cocoa
1½	cups sugar
1⅔	cups egg whites (12 to 14 large egg whites)
1½	teaspoons cream of tartar
½	teaspoon salt
1½	teaspoons vanilla extract

1. Preheat oven to 375°F. Sift flour, cocoa, and ¾ cup sugar through sieve set over medium bowl.

2. In large bowl, with mixer at medium speed, beat egg whites, cream of tartar, and salt until foamy. Increase speed to medium-high; beat until soft peaks form when beaters are lifted. Sprinkle in remaining ¾ cup sugar, 2 tablespoons at a time, beating until sugar has dissolved and egg whites stand in stiff, glossy peaks when beaters are lifted. Beat in vanilla. Transfer egg-white mixture to larger bowl. Sift cocoa mixture, one-third at a time, over beaten egg whites; fold in with rubber spatula just until cocoa mixture is no longer visible. Do not overmix.

3. Scrape batter into ungreased 9- to 10-inch tube pan; spread evenly. Bake until cake springs back when lightly pressed, 35 to 40 minutes. Invert cake in pan onto large metal funnel or bottle; cool completely in pan. Run thin knife around cake to loosen from side and center tube of pan. Remove from pan and place cake on plate. Makes 16 servings.

♥ Each serving: About 118 calories, 4g protein, 25g carbohydrate, 0g total fat (0g saturated), 0mg cholesterol, 115mg sodium.

Hot Water Sponge Cake

This firm-textured, golden-colored sponge cake is leavened with both beaten eggs and baking powder for guaranteed height.

Prep: 20 minutes Bake: 35 minutes

6	large eggs
1¾	cups all-purpose flour
2	teaspoons baking powder
½	teaspoon salt
4	tablespoons butter or margarine, cut into 4 pieces
½	cup water
1	cup sugar
1½	teaspoons vanilla extract

1. Preheat oven to 350°F. Grease bottom of 9- to 10-inch tube pan (without removable bottom).

2. Place eggs in small bowl; set over medium bowl of warm water. Let stand until eggs are tepid, about 10 minutes. Sift flour, baking powder, and salt through sieve set over separate medium bowl.

3. In large bowl, with standing mixer at high speed, beat eggs until very foamy and doubled in volume, about 5 minutes. Meanwhile, combine butter and water in 1-quart saucepan and heat to boiling; remove from heat. Sprinkle sugar over eggs, 2 tablespoons at a time, and beat until eggs thicken slightly, about 2 minutes. Add vanilla. Reduce speed to low. Sift flour mixture over eggs and beat until blended and flour is no longer visible, frequently scraping bowl with rubber spatula. Add hot-water mixture and beat until blended, scraping bowl with rubber spatula.

4. Scrape batter into prepared pan; spread evenly. Bake until toothpick inserted in center comes out clean, 35 to 40 minutes. Invert tube cake in pan onto metal funnel or bottle; let cool completely. Run thin knife around cake to loosen from side and center tube of pan. Remove from pan and place on serving plate. Makes 16 servings.

❤ Each serving: About 157 calories, 4g protein, 24g carbohydrate, 5g total fat (2g saturated), 87mg cholesterol, 187mg sodium.

Lemon–Hot Water Sponge Cake

Prepare as directed but add **1 tablespoon freshly grated lemon peel** with flour mixture.

Walnut Torte

A torte (German for "cake") is a dense, moist cake in which finely ground nuts replace some or all of the flour.

Prep: 25 minutes plus cooling Bake: 25 minutes

3	cups walnuts (12 ounces)
1	cup sugar
3	tablespoons all-purpose flour
1	teaspoon baking powder
¼	teaspoon salt
6	large eggs, separated
1	cup heavy or whipping cream

1. Preheat oven to 350°F. Grease two 9-inch round cake pans. Line bottoms of pans with waxed paper; grease paper.

2. Chop 2 tablespoons walnuts and reserve for garnish. In blender or in food processor with knife blade attached, working in batches if necessary, finely grind remaining walnuts with ¼ cup sugar. In medium bowl, combine ground-walnut mixture, flour, baking powder, and salt; mix well.

3. In large bowl, with mixer at medium-high speed, beat egg whites until soft peaks begin to form when beaters are lifted. Sprinkle in ¼ cup sugar, 1 tablespoon at a time, beating until soft peaks form.

4. In small bowl, with same beaters and with mixer at high speed, beat egg yolks and remaining ½ cup sugar until thick and lemon-colored, about 3 minutes. With rubber spatula, gently fold half of nut mixture and half of egg yolks into beaten egg whites just until blended. Repeat with remaining nuts and yolks, folding just until blended. Do not overmix.

5. Scrape batter into prepared pans; spread evenly. Bake until cake springs back when lightly pressed, 25 to 30 minutes. Cool in pans on wire racks 5 minutes. Run thin knife around layers to loosen from sides of pans. Invert onto rack. Remove waxed paper; cool completely.

6. In small bowl, with mixer at medium-high speed, beat cream until soft peaks form. Place one layer, rounded side down, on cake plate. With narrow metal spatula, spread about half of whipped cream over layer. Top with second layer, rounded side up. Spread remaining whipped cream over top of cake; sprinkle with reserved chopped walnuts. Refrigerate until ready to serve, up to 4 hours. Makes 16 servings.

Each serving: About 282 calories, 6g protein, 18g carbohydrate, 22g total fat (5g saturated), 100mg cholesterol, 98mg sodium.

Vanilla Chiffon Cake

All this tall, handsome cake needs is a dusting of confectioners' sugar and some fresh berries served on the side. The citrus variation is tart, so if you prefer your desserts on the sweet side, use three-quarters cup orange juice and omit the lemon juice.

Prep: 20 minutes	Bake: 1 hour 15 minutes
2¼	cups cake flour (not self-rising)
1½	cups granulated sugar
1	tablespoon baking powder
1	teaspoon salt
¾	cup cold water
½	cup vegetable oil
5	large eggs, separated, plus 2 large egg whites
1	tablespoon vanilla extract
½	teaspoon cream of tartar
	confectioners' sugar

1. Preheat oven to 325°F. In large bowl, combine flour, 1 cup granulated sugar, baking powder, and salt. Make a well in center; add cold water, oil, egg yolks, and vanilla to well. With wire whisk, stir until smooth.

2. In separate large bowl, with mixer at high speed, beat egg whites and cream of tartar until soft peaks form when beaters are lifted. Sprinkle in remaining ½ cup granulated sugar, 2 tablespoons at a time, beating until sugar has dissolved and egg whites stand in stiff, glossy peaks when beaters are lifted. With rubber spatula, gently fold one-third of beaten egg whites into egg-yolk mixture, then fold in remaining egg whites until blended.

3. Scrape batter into ungreased 9- to 10-inch tube pan; spread evenly. Bake until cake springs back when lightly pressed, about 1 hour 15 minutes. Invert cake in pan onto large metal funnel or bottle; cool completely. Run thin knife around cake to loosen from side and center tube of pan. Remove from pan and place on serving plate. Dust with confectioners' sugar. Makes 16 servings.

Each serving: About 217 calories, 4g protein, 31g carbohydrate, 9g total fat (1g saturated), 66mg cholesterol, 264mg sodium.

Citrus Chiffon Cake

Prepare as directed but substitute **1 tablespoon freshly grated orange peel** and **1 teaspoon freshly grated lemon peel** for vanilla, and substitute **½ cup fresh orange juice** and **¼ cup fresh lemon juice** for cold water. In small bowl, combine **1 cup confectioners' sugar, 1 teaspoon freshly grated lemon peel, ¼ teaspoon vanilla extract,** and **about 5 teaspoons orange juice** to make smooth glaze; spoon over cooled cake.

Golden Sponge Cake

This cake is just made for soaking up fruit juices. Serve with fresh fruit or use as the base for a shortcake or trifle.

Prep: 20 minutes	Bake: 15 minutes
¾	cup all-purpose flour
2	tablespoons cornstarch
3	large eggs
½	cup sugar
1	tablespoon butter or margarine, melted

1. Preheat oven to 375°F. Grease and flour 9-inch square baking pan.

2. In small bowl, combine flour and cornstarch.

3. In large bowl, with mixer at high speed, beat eggs and sugar until thick and lemon colored and mixture forms ribbon when beaters are lifted, about 10 minutes, occasionally scraping bowl with rubber spatula. Fold in flour mixture until well blended, then fold in melted butter.

4. Scrape batter into prepared pan; spread evenly. Bake until cake is golden and springs back when lightly pressed, 15 to 20 minutes. Cool in pan on wire rack 10 minutes. Run thin knife around cake to loosen from sides of pan; invert onto rack to cool completely. Makes 8 servings.

♥ Each serving: About 148 calories, 4g protein, 24g carbohydrate, 4g total fat (2g saturated), 84mg cholesterol, 39mg sodium.

Vanilla Chiffon Cake

Jelly Roll

Jelly rolls are easy to make and look sensational on a decorative platter. Fill with your favorite jam or Lemon Filling (page 680).

Prep: 20 minutes plus cooling	Bake: 10 minutes
5	large eggs, separated
½	cup granulated sugar
1	teaspoon vanilla extract
½	cup all-purpose flour
	confectioners' sugar
⅔	cup strawberry jam

1. Preheat oven to 350°F. Grease 15½" by 10½" jelly-roll pan. Line with waxed paper; grease paper.

2. In large bowl, with mixer at high speed, beat egg whites until soft peaks form when beaters are lifted. Sprinkle in ¼ cup granulated sugar, 1 tablespoon at a time, beating until egg whites stand in stiff, glossy peaks when beaters are lifted. Do not overbeat.

3. In small bowl, with mixer at high speed, beat egg yolks, remaining ¼ cup granulated sugar, and vanilla until very thick and lemon colored, 8 to 10 minutes. Reduce speed to low; stir in flour until blended. With rubber spatula, gently fold egg-yolk mixture into beaten egg whites just until blended.

4. Evenly spread batter in prepared pan. Bake until cake springs back when lightly pressed, 10 to 15 minutes.

5. Meanwhile, sift confectioners' sugar onto clean kitchen towel. Run thin knife around edges of cake to loosen from sides of pan; invert onto towel. Carefully remove waxed paper. Trim ¼ inch from edges of cake. From a short side, roll cake up with towel jelly-roll fashion. Place rolled cake, seam side down, on wire rack; cool completely.

Jelly Roll

6. Unroll cooled cake. With narrow metal spatula, spread evenly with jam. Starting from same short side, roll cake up (without towel). Place rolled cake, seam side down, on platter and dust with confectioners' sugar. Makes 10 servings.

♥ Each serving: About 163 calories, 4g protein, 30g carbohydrate, 3g total fat (1g saturated), 106mg cholesterol, 40mg sodium.

Cannoli Cake Roll

This festive cake has a creamy ricotta and cream cheese filling.

Prep: 1 hour 30 minutes plus cooling and chilling
Bake: 10 minutes

Cake

	Jelly Roll (opposite), without jam
2	tablespoons orange-flavored liqueur
1	tablespoon water
1	tablespoon granulated sugar
	confectioners' sugar

Ricotta Filling

1¼	cups ricotta cheese
4	ounces Neufchâtel
½	cup confectioners' sugar
½	teaspoon vanilla extract
¼	teaspoon ground cinnamon
¼	cup semisweet chocolate mini-chips

Frosting

¾	cup heavy or whipping cream
3	tablespoons confectioners' sugar
2	tablespoons orange-flavored liqueur
½	teaspoon vanilla extract
¼	cup pistachio nuts, chopped
1	tablespoon semisweet chocolate mini-chips

1. Prepare and bake Jelly Roll as directed. Meanwhile, in cup, stir orange liqueur, water, and granulated sugar until sugar has dissolved.

2. Sift confectioners' sugar onto clean kitchen towel. When cake is done, run thin knife around edges of cake to loosen from sides of pan; invert onto towel. Carefully remove waxed paper. Brush cake with orange-liqueur mixture. From a long side, roll cake up with towel jelly-roll fashion. Place rolled cake, seam side down, on wire rack; cool completely.

3. Meanwhile, prepare ricotta filling: In food processor with knife blade attached, process ricotta, Neufchâtel, confectioners' sugar, vanilla, and cinnamon until smooth. Transfer filling to bowl; stir in chocolate chips. Cover and refrigerate filling while cake cools.

4. Gently unroll cooled cake. With narrow metal spatula, spread ricotta filling over cake, leaving ½-inch border. Starting from same long side, roll cake up (without towel). Place rolled cake, seam side down, on platter.

5. Prepare frosting: In small bowl, with mixer at medium speed, beat cream and confectioners' sugar until soft peaks form. With rubber spatula, fold in orange liqueur and vanilla. Spread whipped-cream frosting over cake. Refrigerate at least 2 hours or up to 6 hours before serving. Evenly sprinkle top of cake with pistachios and chocolate chips just before serving. Makes 14 servings.

Each serving: About 252 calories, 7g protein, 24g carbohydrate, 14g total fat (7g saturated), 110mg cholesterol, 81mg sodium.

If cracks form in your cheesecake despite your best efforts, simply hide them. Cover the top of the cake with fruit preserves, and add fresh berries, if you like. Dust lightly with confectioners' sugar just before serving.

SUSAN G. PURDY
COOKBOOK AUTHOR

EXPERT TIP

Old-Fashioned Fruitcakes

A generous amount of dried and candied fruits is soaked in brandy to add moistness and flavor to this cake, which has just enough batter to bind it all together. This recipe makes a dozen mini loaves—perfect for gift giving.

Prep: 1 hour 30 minutes plus 8 hours to stand and 1 month to ripen
Bake: 1 hour 30 minutes

3	cups dried figs, stemmed and chopped
2	cups pitted dates (14 ounces), chopped
2	cups golden raisins (12 ounces)
2	cups dark seedless raisins (12 ounces)
1	box (10 ounces) dried currants (2 cups)
1½	cups diced candied citron (about 11 ounces)
1	cup diced candied pineapple (7 ounces)
1	cup red candied cherries (8 ounces), coarsely chopped
1	cup diced candied orange peel (7 ounces)
1	cup brandy
3	cups all-purpose flour
½	teaspoon ground cinnamon
¼	teaspoon ground allspice
¼	teaspoon ground cloves
¼	teaspoon baking soda
2	cups butter or margarine (4 sticks), softened
1	box (16 ounces) dark brown sugar
6	large eggs
⅓	cup dark molasses
⅔	cup milk
5	cups pecans or walnuts (1¼ pounds)

1. In large bowl, combine figs, dates, golden and dark raisins, currants, citron, pineapple, cherries, orange peel, and brandy. Cover and let stand 8 hours or up to overnight, stirring several times.

2. Preheat oven to 275°F. Grease twelve 5¾" by 3¼" by 2" mini-loaf pans. Line bottoms with waxed paper; evenly grease paper.

3. In medium bowl, combine flour, cinnamon, allspice, cloves, and baking soda.

4. In large bowl, with mixer at low speed, beat butter and brown sugar until blended. Increase speed to medium-high; beat until light and fluffy, about 5 minutes, frequently scraping bowl with rubber spatula. Reduce speed to medium. Beat in eggs, one at a time, beating well after each addition. Beat in molasses. Reduce speed to low; beat in flour mixture alter-

nately with milk, beginning and ending with flour mixture, until blended, scraping bowl. Turn batter into larger bowl (for easier mixing). Stir in fruit mixture, including any brandy not absorbed by fruit, and pecans.

5. Spoon batter into prepared pans; spread evenly. Bake until toothpick inserted in center comes out clean, about 1 hour 30 minutes. Cool in pans on wire racks 15 minutes. Run thin knife around cakes to loosen from sides of pans and invert onto racks. Turn cakes, right side up, and cool completely. Remove waxed paper. Wrap cakes in plastic wrap, then in foil. Let stand in cool place, or refrigerate at least 1 month or up to 6 months before serving. Makes 12 cakes, 4 servings each.

Each serving: About 387 calories, 4g protein, 59g carbohydrate, 17g total fat (6g saturated), 48mg cholesterol, 126mg sodium.

Apricot-Pecan Fruitcake

A light fruitcake that has a mellow brandy flavor and is studded with chunks of tangy apricots and buttery pecans. You can make it up to one week ahead, but it's best to glaze it the day it's served.

Prep: 20 minutes plus cooling   Bake: 1 hour 10 to 20 minutes

2½	packages (6 ounces each) dried apricot halves (2½ cups), cut into ½-inch pieces
2	cups pecans (8 ounces), coarsely chopped, plus ⅔ cup pecan halves
1	tablespoon plus 2 cups all-purpose flour
2	teaspoons baking powder
1	teaspoon salt
1	cup butter or margarine (2 sticks), softened
1¼	cups sugar
5	large eggs
½	cup brandy
1	tablespoon vanilla extract
⅓	cup apricot preserves

1. Preheat oven to 325°F. Grease 9- to 10-inch tube pan.

2. In medium bowl, toss apricots and coarsely chopped pecans with 1 tablespoon flour. In medium bowl, combine remaining 2 cups flour, baking powder, and salt.

3. In large bowl, with mixer at low speed, beat butter and sugar until blended. Increase speed to high; beat until light and fluffy, about 5 minutes, occasionally scraping bowl with

rubber spatula. Reduce speed to low. Add eggs, brandy, vanilla, and flour mixture; beat until well blended, scraping bowl. Stir in apricot mixture.

4. Spoon batter into prepared pan; spread evenly. Arrange pecan halves on top of batter in two concentric circles. Bake until toothpick inserted in center comes out clean, 1 hour 10 to 20 minutes. Cool in pan on wire rack 10 minutes. Run thin knife around cake to loosen from side and center tube of pan; lift tube to separate cake from pan side. Slide knife under cake to separate from bottom of pan. Invert cake onto wire rack and remove center tube. Turn cake, right side up, onto rack to cool completely.

5. In 1-quart saucepan, heat apricot preserves over medium-high heat, stirring constantly, until melted and bubbling. Strain through sieve set over small bowl. With pastry brush, brush cooled cake with preserves. Or wrap cake and refrigerate up to 1 week, then brush with preserves before serving. Makes 24 servings.

Each serving: About 300 calories, 4g protein, 35g carbohydrate, 17g total fat (6g saturated), 65mg cholesterol, 233mg sodium.

Cranberry-Raisin Fruitcake
Prepare as directed but substitute **2 cups walnuts (8 ounces), toasted and coarsely chopped**, plus **⅔ cup walnut halves** for pecans and **1½ cups golden raisins** plus **1 cup dried cranberries** for apricots.

I like to use dental floss or strong button thread to cut cheesecake. Hold a length of the thread taut between your hands and slice down through the middle of the cake. Release one end of the thread and pull it through the cake. Repeat, making cuts like spokes in a wheel. You can also use a thin sharp knife dipped in hot water, then wiped off, but it's not as good a conversation starter.

SUSAN G. PURDY
COOKBOOK AUTHOR

EXPERT TIP

Deluxe Cheesecake

This is the classic New York–style cheesecake: very dense, rich, and baked in a pastry crust. Baking it at a low temperature and slowly cooling it in the oven are the keys to its perfect texture.

Prep: 45 minutes plus cooling and chilling
Bake: 50 minutes plus standing

½	cup butter or margarine (1 stick), softened
1½	cups sugar
3	large egg yolks
1¼	cups plus 3 tablespoons all-purpose flour
5	packages (8 ounces each) cream cheese, softened
5	large eggs
¼	cup milk
1	teaspoon freshly grated lemon peel

1. Preheat oven to 400°F. In small bowl, with mixer at low speed, beat butter and ¼ cup sugar until blended. Add 1 egg yolk and beat until well combined. Beat in 1¼ cups flour just until combined. Divide dough into almost equal parts; wrap slightly larger piece in plastic wrap and refrigerate.

2. With hand, press smaller piece of dough onto bottom of 10" by 2½" springform pan. Bake until golden, about 8 minutes; cool completely in pan on wire rack.

3. Turn oven control to 475°F. In large bowl, with mixer at medium speed, beat cream cheese just until smooth; gradually beat in remaining 1¼ cups sugar. Reduce speed to low. Beat in eggs, remaining 2 egg yolks, milk, remaining 3 tablespoons flour, and lemon peel just until blended, occasionally scraping bowl with rubber spatula.

4. Press remaining piece of dough around side of pan 1 inch from rim (do not bake). Scrape cream-cheese mixture into crust; bake 12 minutes. Turn oven control to 300°F; bake 30 minutes longer. Edge will be set, but center will still jiggle. Turn off oven; let cheesecake remain in oven 30 minutes. Remove cheesecake from oven; run thin knife around edge of cheesecake to prevent cracking during cooling. Cool completely in pan on wire rack. Cover and refrigerate until well chilled, at least 4 hours or up to overnight. Remove side of pan to serve. Makes 20 servings.

Each serving: About 359 calories, 7g protein, 24g carbohydrate, 27g total fat (16g saturated), 160mg cholesterol, 233mg sodium.

Strawberry Cheesecake
Top refrigerated cheesecake with **1 quart strawberries, hulled.**
Melt ½ **cup currant jelly;** brush over berries.

Chocolate Cheesecake

Calling all chocoholics! Here's a triple chocolate treat—chocolate wafers, semisweet chocolate, and cocoa.

Prep: 25 minutes plus cooling and chilling
Bake: 1 hour plus standing

1½	cups chocolate-wafer cookie crumbs (part of 9-ounce package)
3	tablespoons butter or margarine, melted
2	tablespoons plus 1 cup sugar
3	packages (8 ounces each) cream cheese, softened
¼	cup unsweetened cocoa
4	large eggs
¾	cup sour cream
1½	teaspoons vanilla extract
8	squares (8 ounces) semisweet chocolate, melted and cooled

1. Preheat oven to 325°F. In 9" by 3" springform pan, combine cookie crumbs, melted butter, and 2 tablespoons sugar; stir with fork until evenly moistened. With hand, press mixture firmly onto bottom of pan. Bake 10 minutes. Cool completely in pan on wire rack.

2. In large bowl, with mixer at low speed, beat cream cheese until smooth. Beat in remaining 1 cup sugar and cocoa until blended, occasionally scraping bowl with rubber spatula. Reduce speed to low. Add eggs, one at a time, beating just until blended, scraping bowl. Beat in sour cream and vanilla. Add melted chocolate and beat until well blended.

3. Pour chocolate mixture onto crust. Bake until cheesecake is set 2 inches from edge but center still jiggles, 50 to 55 minutes. Turn off oven; let cheesecake remain in oven with door ajar 1 hour. Remove from oven; run thin knife around edge of cheesecake to prevent cracking during cooling. Cool completely on wire rack. Cover loosely and refrigerate until well chilled, at least 6 hours or up to overnight. Remove side of pan to serve. Makes 16 servings.

Each serving: About 384 calories, 7g protein, 34g carbohydrate, 26g total fat (15g saturated), 111mg cholesterol, 237mg sodium.

Lemon-Ricotta Cheesecake

Ricotta cheese gives this cheesecake a lighter texture than most.

Prep: 20 minutes plus cooling and chilling
Bake: 1 hour 25 minutes plus standing

4	large lemons
1	cup vanilla-wafer crumbs (about 30 cookies)
4	tablespoons butter or margarine, melted
1¼	cups sugar
¼	cup cornstarch
2	packages (8 ounces each) cream cheese, softened
1	container (15 ounces) ricotta cheese
4	large eggs
2	cups half-and-half or light cream
2	teaspoons vanilla extract

1. Preheat oven to 375°F. From lemons, grate 4 teaspoons peel and squeeze ⅓ cup juice. In 9" by 3" springform pan, combine cookie crumbs, melted butter, and 1 teaspoon lemon peel; stir with fork until evenly moistened. Press mixture firmly onto bottom of pan. Tightly wrap outside of pan with heavy-duty foil. Bake until crust is deep golden, about 10 minutes. Cool completely in pan on wire rack.

2. Turn oven control to 325°F. In small bowl, stir sugar and cornstarch until blended. In large bowl, with mixer at medium speed, beat cream cheese and ricotta until very smooth, about 5 minutes; slowly beat in sugar mixture. Reduce speed to low; beat in eggs, half-and-half, lemon juice, vanilla, and remaining 3 teaspoons lemon peel just until blended, frequently scraping bowl with rubber spatula.

3. Scrape cream-cheese mixture onto crust. Bake 1 hour 15 minutes. Turn off oven; let cheesecake remain in oven 1 hour longer. Remove from oven and transfer to wire rack; remove foil. Run thin knife around edge of cheesecake to prevent cracking during cooling. Cool completely in pan on wire rack. Cover and refrigerate cheesecake until well chilled, at least 6 hours or up to overnight. Remove side of pan to serve. Makes 16 servings.

Each serving: About 324 calories, 8g protein, 25g carbohydrate, 22g total fat (13g saturated), 117mg cholesterol, 182mg sodium.

Lemon-Ricotta Cheesecake

Pumpkin Cheesecake

Pumpkin pie, move over. Here's a deliciously creamy dessert that is bound to be a hit at your next Thanksgiving dinner.

Prep: 30 minutes plus cooling and chilling
Bake: 1 hour 25 minutes

Crumb Crust

1	cup graham-cracker crumbs (8 rectangular graham crackers)
3	tablespoons butter or margarine, melted
2	tablespoons sugar

Pumpkin Filling

2	packages (8 ounces each) cream cheese, softened
1¼	cups sugar
1	can (15 ounces) solid-pack pumpkin (not pumpkin-pie mix)
¾	cup sour cream
2	tablespoons bourbon or 2 teaspoons vanilla extract
1	teaspoon ground cinnamon
½	teaspoon ground allspice
¼	teaspoon salt
4	large eggs

Sour Cream Topping

1	cup sour cream
3	tablespoons sugar
1	teaspoon vanilla extract

1. Preheat oven to 350°F. In 9" by 3" springform pan, combine graham-cracker crumbs, melted butter, and sugar; stir with fork until evenly moistened. With hand, press mixture firmly onto bottom of pan. Tightly wrap outside of pan with heavy-duty foil. Bake 10 minutes. Cool completely in pan on wire rack.

2. Prepare pumpkin filling: In large bowl, with mixer at medium speed, beat cream cheese until smooth. Slowly beat in sugar until blended, about 1 minute, frequently scraping bowl with rubber spatula. Reduce speed to low. Beat in pumpkin, sour cream, bourbon, cinnamon, allspice, and salt. Add eggs, one at time, beating after each addition, just until blended.

3. Scrape pumpkin mixture onto crust and place in large roasting pan. Place pan on oven rack. Carefully pour enough *very hot water* into roasting pan to come 1 inch up side of springform pan. Bake until center of cake barely jiggles, about 1 hour 10 minutes.

4. Meanwhile, prepare sour-cream topping: In small bowl, with wire whisk, beat sour cream, sugar, and vanilla until smooth. Remove cheesecake from water bath (leave water bath in oven); spread sour-cream mixture evenly over top. Return cake to water bath and bake 5 minutes longer.

5. Remove cheesecake from water bath and transfer to wire rack; remove foil. Run thin knife around edge of cheesecake to prevent cracking during cooling. Cool completely in pan on wire rack. Cover and refrigerate until well chilled, at least 6 hours or up to overnight. Remove side of pan to serve. Makes 16 servings.

Each serving: About 307 calories, 5g protein, 29g carbohydrate, 19g total fat (11g saturated), 101mg cholesterol, 217mg sodium.

Monster Snake Cake

Kids will love it! This easier-to-make-than-you-think cake is prepared from a mix.

Prep: 1 hour plus 2 hours cooling   Bake: 30 minutes

1	recipe Yellow Cake (page 652) or 1 package yellow cake mix for 2-layer cake
1	cup butter or margarine (2 sticks), softened
1	package (16 ounces) confectioners' sugar
⅓	cup half-and-half or light cream
2	teaspoons vanilla extract
	green food-color paste
1	package (11 ounces) jelly rings
1	blue nonmelting candy-coated chocolate piece
¼	cup yellow nonmelting candy-coated chocolate pieces
7 to 10	white candy-coated licorice candies
3	pieces candy corn

1. Grease two 8-inch round cake pans. Line bottoms with waxed paper; grease. Dust pans with flour. Prepare Yellow Cake as recipe directs or yellow cake mix as label directs.

2. Divide batter between prepared pans; spread evenly. Bake and cool as directed for 8-inch layers.

3. Prepare frosting: In large bowl, with mixer at low speed, beat butter, confectioners' sugar, half-and-half, and vanilla just until blended. Increase speed to medium and beat, occasionally scraping bowl with rubber spatula, until frosting

is smooth and is an easy spreading consistency. Stir in enough green food-color paste to tint frosting bright green.

4. Using 2½-inch biscuit cutter, cut out round in center of each cake layer. Without removing round, cut each layer in half to make 4 C-shaped pieces and 4 small semicircles.

5. On large piece of heavy cardboard, Styrofoam board, or cutting board covered with foil (finished cake measures approximately 28" by 9"), place C-shaped pieces of cake end to end, alternating the direction to create a curvy snake.

6. Place one semicircle of cake at one end, cut sides together, to complete tail. Repeat at other end to complete neck. Place remaining two semicircles at neck end to form open mouth. With narrow metal spatula, spread frosting over cake.

7. Garnish cake: Reserve 1 jelly ring; cut remaining jelly rings in half. Place jelly-ring halves along top edge of cake for scales. Place reserved jelly ring on head for eye and place blue candy in center for pupil. Use yellow candies to decorate body, white licorice candies for teeth, and candy corn for eyelashes. Makes 24 servings.

Each serving without decorations: About 412 calories, 3g protein, 52g carbohydrate, 23g total fat (12g saturated), 65mg cholesterol, 290mg sodium.

FROSTINGS AND FILLINGS

Classic Butter Frosting

This is the simplest of frostings.

 Prep: 10 minutes

½	cup butter or margarine (1 stick), softened
1	package (16 ounces) confectioners' sugar
4 to 6	tablespoons milk, half-and-half, or light cream
1½	teaspoons vanilla extract

In large bowl, with mixer at medium-low speed, beat butter, confectioners' sugar, 3 tablespoons milk, and vanilla until smooth and blended. Beat in additional milk as needed for easy spreading consistency. Increase speed to medium-high;

beat frosting until light and fluffy, about 1 minute. Makes about 2⅓ cups.

Each tablespoon: About 71 calories, 0g protein, 12g carbohydrate, 3g total fat (2g saturated), 7mg cholesterol, 26mg sodium.

Lemon Butter Frosting

Prepare as directed but omit vanilla and use **2 tablespoons fresh lemon juice, 2 tablespoons milk,** and **1 teaspoon freshly grated lemon peel.** Use only **1 to 2 tablespoons milk** as needed for easy spreading consistency.

Orange Butter Frosting

Prepare as directed for Lemon Butter Frosting but substitute **orange juice** for lemon juice and **orange peel** for lemon peel.

Brown Butter Frosting

In small skillet, over medium heat, cook butter until melted and lightly browned; let cool. Prepare as directed.

Chocolate Butter Frosting

The combination of semisweet and unsweetened chocolates gives this frosting its perfect flavor balance.

Prep: 15 minutes

¾	cup butter or margarine (1½ sticks), softened
2	cups confectioners' sugar
1	teaspoon vanilla extract
4	squares (4 ounces) semisweet chocolate, melted and cooled
2	squares (2 ounces) unsweetened chocolate, melted and cooled

In large bowl, with mixer at low speed, beat butter, confectioners' sugar, and vanilla until almost combined. Add semisweet and unsweetened chocolates. Increase speed to high; beat frosting until light and fluffy, about 1 minute. Makes about 2½ cups.

Each tablespoon: About 75 calories, 0g protein, 8g carbohydrate, 5g total fat (3g saturated), 9mg cholesterol, 36mg sodium.

White Chocolate Butter Frosting

Use this sweet frosting on your favorite chocolate cake.

Prep: 15 minutes

1	cup butter (2 sticks), softened (do not use margarine)
2	cups confectioners' sugar
6	ounces white chocolate, Swiss confectionery bars, or white baking bars, melted and cooled
3	tablespoons milk

In large bowl, with mixer at low speed, beat butter, confectioners' sugar, white chocolate, and milk just until combined. Increase speed to high; beat until light and fluffy, about 2 minutes, frequently scraping bowl with rubber spatula. Makes about 3½ cups.

Each tablespoon: About 62 calories, 0g protein, 6g carbohydrate, 4g total fat (3g saturated), 9mg cholesterol, 37mg sodium.

Silky Vanilla Butter Frosting

Butter is beaten into a flour-thickened base to make an exquisitely light and creamy frosting. Make sure the frosting base is completely cooled before beating in the butter.

Prep: 10 minutes plus cooling   Cook: 8 minutes

1	cup sugar
½	cup all-purpose flour
1⅓	cups milk
1	cup butter or margarine (2 sticks), softened
1	tablespoon vanilla extract

1. In 2-quart saucepan, thoroughly combine sugar and flour. With wire whisk, gradually stir in milk until smooth. Cook over medium-high heat, stirring frequently, until mixture has thickened and boils. Reduce heat to low; cook 2 minutes, stirring constantly. Remove from heat; cool completely.

2. In medium bowl, with mixer at medium speed, beat butter until light and fluffy. Gradually beat in milk mixture; beat in vanilla. Makes about 3¼ cups.

Each tablespoon: About 55 calories, 0g protein, 5g carbohydrate, 4g total fat (2g saturated), 10mg cholesterol, 39mg sodium.

Silky Lemon Butter Frosting

Prepare as directed but substitute **1 tablespoon freshly grated lemon peel** for vanilla extract.

Silky Orange Butter Frosting

Prepare as directed but substitute **1 teaspoon freshly grated orange peel** for vanilla extract.

Silky Chocolate Butter Frosting

Chocolate lovers will put this at the top of their list.

Prep: 10 minutes plus cooling   Cook: 8 minutes

¾	cup sugar
¼	cup all-purpose flour
3	tablespoons unsweetened cocoa
1	cup milk
1	cup butter or margarine (2 sticks), softened
4	squares (4 ounces) semisweet chocolate, melted and cooled
1	tablespoon vanilla extract

1. In 2-quart saucepan, combine sugar, flour, and cocoa. With wire whisk, gradually stir in milk until smooth. Cook over medium heat, stirring frequently, until mixture has thickened and boils. Reduce heat to low; cook 2 minutes, stirring constantly. Remove from heat; cool completely.

2. In medium bowl, with mixer at medium speed, beat butter until creamy. Gradually beat in milk mixture, melted chocolate, and vanilla. Makes 3 cups.

Each tablespoon: About 64 calories, 0g protein, 6g carbohydrate, 5g total fat (3g saturated), 11mg cholesterol, 42mg sodium.

After using a vanilla bean to make custard, dry off the bean and bury it in your sugar canister. Vanilla-scented sugar can be used in most baked goods with great success. (The vanilla bean will keep the sugar flavorful for up to one year.)

SUSAN G. PURDY
COOKBOOK AUTHOR

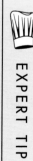

EXPERT TIP

Whipped Cream Frosting

For the times when a cake needs no more embellishment than some freshly whipped cream.

🕐 *Prep: 5 minutes*

2	cups heavy or whipping cream
¼	cup confectioners' sugar
1	teaspoon vanilla extract

In small bowl, with mixer at medium speed, beat cream, confectioners' sugar, and vanilla until stiff peaks form. Makes about 4 cups.

Each tablespoon: About 28 calories, 0g protein, 1g carbohydrate, 3g total fat (2g saturated), 10mg cholesterol, 3mg sodium.

Coffee Whipped Cream Frosting

Prepare as directed but dissolve **2 teaspoons instant-coffee powder** in **2 teaspoons hot water;** add to cream.

Orange Whipped Cream Frosting

Prepare as directed but substitute **2 tablespoons orange-flavored liqueur** for vanilla extract.

Peppermint Whipped Cream Frosting

Beat cream as directed but omit sugar and vanilla extract. Fold in ¼ **cup crushed peppermint candy.**

Cocoa Whipped Cream Frosting

Prepare as directed but use ½ **cup confectioners' sugar** and add ½ **cup unsweetened cocoa.**

Fluffy White Frosting

This irresistible marshmallowlike frosting is best enjoyed the day it is made. If you're planning on frosting a chocolate cake, omit the lemon juice.

🕐 *Prep: 15 minutes   Cook: 7 minutes*

2	large egg whites
1	cup sugar
¼	cup water
2	teaspoons fresh lemon juice (optional)
1	teaspoon light corn syrup
¼	teaspoon cream of tartar

1. In medium bowl set over 3- to 4-quart saucepan filled with *1 inch simmering water* (bowl should sit about 2 inches above water), with hand-held mixer at high speed, beat egg whites, sugar, water, lemon juice if using, corn syrup, and cream of tartar until soft peaks form and mixture reaches 160°F on candy thermometer, about 7 minutes.

2. Remove bowl from pan; beat egg-white mixture until stiff, glossy peaks form, 5 to 10 minutes longer. Makes about 3 cups.

 Each tablespoon: About 17 calories, 0g protein, 4g carbohydrate, 0g total fat (0g saturated), 0mg cholesterol, 2mg sodium.

Fluffy Harvest Moon Frosting

Prepare as directed but substitute **1 cup packed dark brown sugar** for white sugar and omit lemon juice.

Cream Cheese Frosting

The classic frosting for carrot cake, but do try it with banana or spice layer cakes, too.

🕐 *Prep: 10 minutes*

2	packages (3 ounces each) cream cheese, slightly softened
6	tablespoons butter or margarine, softened
3	cups confectioners' sugar
1½	teaspoons vanilla extract

In large bowl, with mixer at low speed, beat cream cheese, butter, confectioners' sugar, and vanilla just until blended. Increase speed to medium. Beat until smooth and fluffy, about 1 minute, frequently scraping bowl with rubber spatula. Makes about 2½ cups.

Each tablespoon: About 66 calories, 0g protein, 9g carbohydrate, 3g total fat (2g saturated), 9mg cholesterol, 30mg sodium.

Custard Buttercream

This is an updated version of a classic buttercream, which uses raw egg yolks; instead, we cook the yolks into a smooth custard. To incorporate the ingredients properly, the custard and the butter should be at the same temperature (the butter should be soft and spreadable, but not melting, or the frosting will become oily). Be sure to use only unsalted butter.

Prep: *15 minutes plus cooling*   **Cook:** *8 minutes*

⅔	cup milk
4	large egg yolks
¾	cup sugar
1	cup unsalted butter (2 sticks), softened (do not use margarine or salted butter)
2	teaspoons vanilla extract or 2 tablespoons flavored liqueur or brandy of choice

1. In 1-quart saucepan, heat milk to boiling over medium heat. Meanwhile, in small bowl, with wire whisk, beat egg yolks and sugar until blended. Gradually whisk hot milk into egg-yolk mixture. Return mixture to saucepan; cook over medium heat, stirring constantly, just until mixture thickens slightly and coats back of wooden spoon. (Do not boil, or custard will curdle.) Remove from heat; strain through sieve set over large bowl. Cool to room temperature.

2. With mixer at medium speed, beat butter into custard, 1 tablespoon at a time, beating until completely blended after each addition. (If mixture begins to look oily, refrigerate 20 minutes or set bowl in larger bowl of ice water 10 minutes. If butter does not incorporate perfectly and small butter flecks remain, let stand 15 minutes longer, then beat at high speed until buttercream is smooth before proceeding.) Beat in vanilla. Makes about 2⅓ cups.

Each tablespoon: About 69 calories, 0g protein, 4g carbohydrate, 6g total fat (3g saturated), 37mg cholesterol, 4mg sodium.

Amaretto Buttercream

Prepare as directed but use **1 cup milk, 6 large egg yolks, 1 cup sugar,** and **1½ cups unsalted butter (3 sticks);** gradually beat in ⅓ **cup amaretto liqueur.** Makes about 3½ cups.

Lemon Filling

This vibrant pucker-producing filling is always popular. It makes enough to fill two or three cake layers.

Prep: *15 minutes plus chilling*   **Cook:** *8 minutes*

3	large lemons
1	tablespoon cornstarch
6	tablespoons butter, cut into pieces (do not use margarine)
¾	cup sugar
4	large egg yolks

1. From lemons, grate 1 tablespoon peel and squeeze ½ cup juice. In 2-quart saucepan, with wire whisk, mix cornstarch and lemon peel and juice until blended. Add butter and sugar. Heat to boiling over medium-high heat, stirring constantly; boil 1 minute.

2. In small bowl, lightly beat egg yolks. Into egg yolks, beat ¼ cup hot lemon mixture; pour egg mixture back into lemon mixture in saucepan, beating rapidly to prevent curdling. Reduce heat to low; cook, stirring constantly, until mixture has thickened (do not boil), about 5 minutes. Pour into medium bowl. Press plastic wrap onto surface. Refrigerate until chilled, about 3 hours or up to 3 days. Makes about 1 cup.

Each tablespoon: About 93 calories, 1g protein, 11g carbohydrate, 6g total fat (3g saturated), 65mg cholesterol, 46mg sodium.

Ganache

Ganache is a thick, creamy chocolate filling meant to be slathered between layers of your favorite cake.

Prep: *15 minutes plus chilling*

1	cup heavy or whipping cream
2	tablespoons sugar
2	teaspoons butter or margarine
10	squares (10 ounces) semisweet chocolate, chopped
1	teaspoon vanilla extract
1 to 2	tablespoons brandy or orange- or almond-flavored liqueur (optional)

1. In 2-quart saucepan, combine cream, sugar, and butter; heat to boiling over medium-high heat. Remove saucepan from heat.

2. Add chocolate to cream mixture and with wire whisk, whisk until chocolate melts and mixture is smooth. Stir in vanilla and brandy, if using. Pour into jelly-roll pan and refrigerate until spreadable, at least 30 minutes. Makes 2 cups.

Each tablespoon: About 74 calories, 1g protein, 6g carbohydrate, 6g total fat (3g saturated), 11mg cholesterol, 6mg sodium.

CHOCOLATE GARNISHES

Chocolate Curls

Use these curls to garnish ice cream, cakes, and pies.

Prep: 15 minutes plus chilling	
1	package (6 ounces) semisweet chocolate chips
2	tablespoons vegetable shortening

1. In heavy 1-quart saucepan, combine chocolate chips and shortening; heat over low heat, stirring frequently, until melted and smooth.

2. Pour chocolate mixture into foil-lined or disposable 5¾" by 3¼" loaf pan. Refrigerate until chocolate is set, about 2 hours.

3. Remove chocolate from pan. Using vegetable peeler and working over waxed paper, draw blade across surface of chocolate to make large curls. If chocolate is too cold and curls break, let chocolate stand about 30 minutes at room temperature until slightly softened. To avoid breaking curls, use toothpick or wooden skewer to transfer.

Chocolate Wedges

A spectacular way to dress up cakes, ice cream, and pies.

Prep: 15 minutes plus chilling	
1	package (6 ounces) semisweet chocolate chips
2	tablespoons vegetable shortening

1. In heavy 1-quart saucepan, combine chocolate chips and shortening; heat over low heat, stirring frequently, until melted and smooth.

2. On waxed paper, with toothpick, trace circle using bottom of 9-inch round cake pan as guide; cut out circle. Invert cake pan; moisten bottom with water. Place waxed-paper circle on bottom of pan (water will prevent paper from moving).

3. With narrow metal spatula, spread melted chocolate mixture evenly over waxed paper. Refrigerate until chocolate is firm, about 30 minutes.

4. Heat blade of long thin knife with hot water; wipe dry. Quickly but gently, cut chocolate into wedges.

Chocolate Leaves

Only use nontoxic leaves, available at florist shops, such as lemon, gardenia, grape, magnolia, nasturtium, rose, and violet.

Prep: 30 minutes plus chilling	
12	lemon leaves
1	package (6 ounces) semisweet chocolate chips
¼	cup vegetable shortening

1. Wash leaves in warm soapy water; pat thoroughly dry with paper towels.

2. In heavy 1-quart saucepan, combine chocolate chips and shortening; heat over low heat, stirring frequently, until melted and smooth.

3. With pastry brush or small metal spatula, spread layer of melted chocolate mixture on underside (back) of each leaf (underside will give more distinct leaf design). Place chocolate-coated leaves, chocolate side up, on waxed paper–lined cookie sheet. Refrigerate until chocolate is firm, about 30 minutes.

4. With cool hands, carefully and gently peel each leaf away from chocolate.

TOXIC LEAVES

Do not allow these leaves to come in contact with chocolate or any other foods: amaryllis, azalea, caladium, daffodil, delphinium, dieffenbachia, English ivy, hydrangea, jonquil, larkspur, laurel, lily of the valley, mistletoe, narcissus, oleander, rhododendron.

20

PIES AND TARTS

It's hard to pick a favorite pie or tart; there are so many to choose from. Whether they're bursting with seasonal fruit, filled with a creamy custard, or topped with meringue or streusel, they're all delicious. And let's not forget the crust! There's no mystery to making a fine crust, one that is flavorful, flaky, and tender. Just follow our perfected mixing and rolling techniques, and you'll find that it's as . . . easy as pie.

INGREDIENTS

The flavor and texture of a baked piecrust depend on two main ingredients: flour and fat. For the tenderest crust, use all-purpose flour. Bread flour has too much gluten, and cake flour is too delicate.

The single most important factor in the quest for tender pastry is the fat. Butter gives a dough rich flavor, crispness, and color; vegetable shortening makes it flaky. Margarine yields a crumbly crust, so it isn't always a good substitute for butter. (Some cooks use lard, which admittedly makes a very tender and flaky crust, but one with a slightly savory flavor that doesn't always suit a pie, so we don't recommend it.) Instead of choosing one fat over another, we use both butter and shortening to give piecrust the best qualities of each. Tart

Strawberry Cheese Pie

dough has a higher proportion of butter, so it bakes into a crisp crust that holds its shape when removed from the tart pan, while Italian crostata dough is 100 percent butter to give it rich flavor and a cookielike crunch.

To keep the fat in the dough chilled and firm, use ice water (remove the ice cubes first) to bring the ingredients together. If you wish, substitute 1 tablespoon of distilled white vinegar for an equal amount of the water. The acid in the vinegar helps relax the flour's gluten and makes the pastry tender. And be sure both the butter and shortening are well chilled. The pieces of fat should hold their shape—not soften and melt into the flour. The kitchen should be cool, too. If you *must* make pie on a hot day, chill the flour.

MIXING THE DOUGH

- A pastry blender is the best utensil for blending fat and flour together. But you can also use two dinner knives, scissor-fashion, to cut in the fat until the mixture resembles coarse crumbs. Work quickly so the fat remains firm and cold. Use a fork to toss and combine the mixture (don't stir it), then sprinkle in the water, 1 tablespoon at a time, mixing lightly after each addition, just until the dough is moist enough to hold together. (The mixture will no longer look "dusty.") Too much water will toughen the crust, and not enough will make the dough too crumbly to roll out. The amount of water needed will vary, depending on the humidity in the air and the dryness of the flour.

- Handle the dough as little as possible, or you'll end up with a tough crust. Be especially aware of this if you make the dough in a food processor: Process the dough just until it barely comes together. If the dough needs more water, mix it in with a fork.

- Shape the dough into one or more disks, depending on the recipe. Wrap each disk tightly in waxed paper or plastic wrap and chill for at least thirty minutes or up to overnight before rolling it out. This allows the water to distribute itself throughout the dough and gives the gluten a chance to relax, making the dough easier to roll out and less likely to shrink. If it's been chilled overnight, allow the dough to stand at room temperature for about thirty minutes to soften it slightly or it will crack when rolled out.

ROLLING OUT THE DOUGH

To prevent sticking, dust the work surface lightly but thoroughly with flour. Rub the rolling pin with flour, too. If you wish, sprinkle a little flour on top of the dough.

It's easy to roll dough into a circle. Start in the center and roll out the dough, rolling up to—but not over—the edge. Give the dough a quarter turn. Repeat rolling and rotating until you have rolled out an even circle. This roll-and-rotate technique helps prevent dough from sticking to the work surface. If needed, slip a narrow metal spatula under the dough and toss some flour underneath to reflour the surface. If the dough tears, just moisten the edges and press them together.

THE PERFECT FIT

The right pan makes all the difference between a crisp, well-browned crust and a pale, soggy one. A glass pie plate is our first choice, followed by a metal pan with a dull surface (shiny pans reflect the heat away from the crust; they're fine for crumb crusts). A standard 9-inch pie plate is 1 inch deep; we use it for most of our pies. But some fruit pies call for a deep-dish pie plate (9 inches wide by 1½ to 2 inches deep) so the filling won't overflow. For tarts, use a fluted pan with a removable bottom, which makes for easy removal of the tart.

There are two ways to transfer rolled-out dough to a pie plate or tart pan; both work well. Use the method you are most comfortable with: Loosely roll the dough onto the rolling pin, position the pin at one side of the pie plate, and unroll the dough. Alternatively, fold the rolled-out dough into quarters, set it into the pie plate, and unfold.

Fit the dough into the pie plate by gently easing it onto the bottom and against the side with your fingertips (or use a small ball of excess dough), taking care to press out all the air pockets. Never stretch the dough to fit, or the crust may shrink during baking. To help reduce shrinkage in single-crust pies, chill the piecrust for ten to fifteen minutes.

DECORATIVE PIE EDGES

From classic to creative, these borders are the perfect way to add a professional finish to homemade pies. Forked, scalloped, fluted, and rope edges are pretty on almost any 1- or 2-crust pie. The appliqué leaf edge is best for 1-crust pies, but to have enough dough to work with, you will need to prepare dough for a 2-crust pie. For the best results, chill the pastry so it is firm (but not hard) enough to work with.

Forked Edge
With kitchen shears, trim the dough edge even with the rim of the pie plate. With floured fork tines, press the dough edge at even intervals all around the rim.

Scalloped Edge
With kitchen shears, trim the dough edge, leaving a 1-inch overhang. Fold the overhang under; form a stand-up edge. Place the thumb and forefinger of one hand, 1 inch apart, on the inner side of the pastry edge. With the forefinger of your other hand, gently pull the dough down toward the outer edge to form a scallop. Repeat all around.

Crimped Edge
With kitchen shears, trim the dough edge, leaving a 1-inch overhang. Fold the overhang under; form a stand-up edge. Push one index finger against the inside edge of the rim; with the index finger and thumb of other hand, pinch dough to flute. Repeat all around the edge, leaving ¼ inch between each flute.

Fluted Edge
With kitchen shears, trim the dough edge, leaving a 1-inch overhang. Fold the overhang under, then form a stand-up

edge. Place the thumb and forefinger of one hand, $\frac{1}{2}$ inch apart, on the outside of the pastry edge; pinch the dough into a V shape. Simultaneously, with the forefinger of your other hand on the inner side of the pastry edge, push the dough to define the shape. Repeat all around.

Rope Edge

With kitchen shears, trim the dough edge, leaving a 1-inch overhang. Fold the overhang under; form a stand-up edge. Pinch the dough edge at a 45° angle between your thumb and forefinger. At the same time, slightly twist the dough outward. Repeat all around the edge at 1-inch intervals.

Turret Edge

With kitchen shears, trim the dough edge, leaving a 1-inch overhang. Fold the overhang under; form a stand-up edge. With a knife, cut the dough at $\frac{1}{2}$-inch intervals. Fold the dough pieces down, alternating toward and away from the rim.

Leaf or Heart Edge

Prepare Pastry Dough for 2-Crust Pie (page 686). Roll out the dough for the bottom crust and place it in the pie plate as directed; trim the edge even with the rim of the plate. Roll out the remaining disk of dough $\frac{1}{8}$ inch thick. With a floured small knife or small cookie cutter, cut out leaves or hearts. Lightly brush the dough edge with water. Gently press the shapes, slightly overlapping them, onto the dough edge.

PIE TOPS AND GLAZES

Finish off your double-crust pies with one of these decorative possibilities. Top crusts always have slits or some other opening to release the steam.

If you wish, glaze the top crust before baking. To brown the crust, brush with milk, half-and-half, or heavy cream. For a shiny top, brush with lightly beaten egg white. For a golden crust, brush with beaten whole egg or egg yolk. To add a bit of sparkle, sprinkle lightly with granulated sugar.

Window Top

Prepare Pastry Dough for 2-Crust Pie (page 686). Roll out the dough for the bottom crust and place in the pie plate as directed; fill. Roll out the remaining disk into a 12-inch round; center it over the filling. Trim the edge, leaving a 1-inch overhang. Form a stand-up edge and make a decorative edge. With a small knife, cut a 4-inch X in the center of the top crust; gently fold back the points to make a square opening.

Lattice Top

Prepare Pastry Dough for 2-Crust Pie (page 686). Roll out the dough for the bottom crust and place in the pie plate as directed; fill. Roll out the remaining disk into a 12-inch round; with a pastry wheel or small knife, cut the dough into $\frac{1}{2}$-inch-wide strips. Moisten the edge of the bottom crust with water. Place half of the pastry strips about $\frac{3}{4}$ inch apart across the top of the pie; press the strips at both ends to seal. To complete the lattice, place an equal number of strips across (at right angles to) the first strips. Trim the edge, leaving a 1-inch overhang, then moisten and press the strips at both ends to seal. Turn the overhang up and over the ends of the strips; pinch to seal. Make a high stand-up edge to hold in the juices; form decorative edge.

Appliqué Top

Prepare Pastry Dough for 2-Crust Pie (page 686). Roll out the dough for the bottom crust and place in the pie plate as directed; fill. Roll out the remaining dough disk into a 12-inch round; center it over the filling. Trim the edge, leaving a 1-inch overhang. Form a stand-up edge and make a decorative edge. Roll out the trimmings. Use a small knife dipped in flour to cut free-form shapes, such as apples, hearts, or leaves (use the back of the knife to mark veins in the leaves). Brush the undersides of the dough shapes with water; place, moistened side down, on top of the pie in a decorative arrangement.

BAKING IT RIGHT

To catch any overflow, bake the pie on a sheet of foil with the edges crimped, or place on a foil-lined cookie sheet. Bake the pie in the lower third of the oven so the bottom crust crisps and the top doesn't overbrown (if the top is browning too fast, cover it loosely with foil, see page 686).

Before serving, always cool fruit pies on a wire rack so the filling can set.

STORAGE

Fruit pies can be covered and stored at room temperature overnight. For longer storage, refrigerate. Before serving, you can freshen pies by warming them in the oven. Meringue pies are best the day they are made. Pies with cream or custard fillings should be refrigerated as soon as they are cool, especially in warm weather. After serving, refrigerate leftovers.

Pastry Dough for 2-Crust Pie

Every cook should know how to make a from-scratch piecrust. Our perfect recipe gets its flavor from butter and its flakiness from vegetable shortening.

Prep: 15 minutes plus chilling	
2¼	cups all-purpose flour
½	teaspoon salt
½	cup cold butter or margarine (1 stick), cut into pieces
¼	cup vegetable shortening
4 to 6 tablespoons ice water	

1. In large bowl, combine flour and salt. With pastry blender or two knives used scissor-fashion, cut in butter and shortening until mixture resembles coarse crumbs.

2. Sprinkle in ice water, 1 tablespoon at a time, mixing lightly with fork after each addition, until dough is just moist enough to hold together.

3. Shape dough into two disks, one slightly larger than the other. Wrap each disk in plastic wrap and refrigerate 30 minutes or up to overnight. (If chilled overnight, let stand 30 minutes at room temperature before rolling.)

4. On lightly floured surface, with floured rolling pin, roll larger disk of dough into 12-inch round. Gently roll dough round onto rolling pin and ease into pie plate, pressing dough against side of plate. Trim edge, leaving 1-inch overhang. Reserve trimmings for decorating pie, if you like. Spoon filling into crust.

5. Roll remaining disk of dough into 12-inch round. Cut

¾-inch circle out of center and cut 1-inch slits to allow steam to escape during baking; center dough over filling. Or make desired pie top (page 685). Fold overhang under; make decorative edge (page 684). Bake as directed in recipe. Makes enough dough for one 9-inch 2-crust pie.

Each ¹⁄₁₀th pastry: About 235 calories, 3g protein, 23g carbohydrate, 15g total fat (7g saturated), 25mg cholesterol, 210mg sodium.

Food Processor Pastry Dough

In food processor with knife blade attached, pulse flour and salt to mix. Evenly distribute butter and shortening on top of flour mixture; pulse just until mixture resembles coarse crumbs. With processor running, pour ¼ **cup ice water** through feed tube. Immediately stop motor and pinch dough; it should be just moist enough to hold together. If not, with fork, stir in up to **2 tablespoons additional ice water.** Refrigerate and roll as directed.

Shortening Pastry Dough

Prepare as directed but use ¾ **cup vegetable shortening** and omit butter; use **1 teaspoon salt.**

Vinegar Pastry Dough

Prepare as directed but substitute **1 tablespoon distilled white vinegar** for 1 tablespoon ice water.

PROTECTING EDGES OF PIECRUST

Fold a 12-inch square of foil into quarters. With scissors, cut out an 8-inch round from middle. Unfold foil and place over pie, folding foil edges around piecrust to cover it.

Place a 12-inch square of foil over pie. Fold foil edges around piecrust to cover it.

Pastry Dough for 1-Crust Pie

Chilling a piecrust before baking helps it retain its shape.

Prep: 15 minutes plus chilling

1¼	cups all-purpose flour
¼	teaspoon salt
4	tablespoons cold butter or margarine, cut into pieces
2	tablespoons vegetable shortening
3 to 5 tablespoons ice water	

1. In large bowl, combine flour and salt. With pastry blender or two knives used scissor-fashion, cut in butter and shortening until mixture resembles coarse crumbs.

2. Sprinkle in ice water, 1 tablespoon at a time, mixing lightly with fork after each addition, until dough is just moist enough to hold together.

3. Shape dough into disk; wrap in plastic wrap. Refrigerate 30 minutes or up to overnight. (If chilled overnight, let stand 30 minutes at room temperature before rolling.)

4. On lightly floured surface, with floured rolling pin, roll dough into 12-inch round. Ease into pie plate, gently pressing dough against side of plate.

5. Make decorative edge (page 684) as desired. Refrigerate or freeze until firm, 10 to 15 minutes. Fill and bake as directed in recipe. Makes enough dough for one 9-inch crust.

Each ⅒th pastry: About 123 calories, 2g protein, 13g carbohydrate, 7g total fat (4g saturated), 12mg cholesterol, 104mg sodium.

Pastry for 9-Inch Tart

This recipe makes enough dough to nicely fit a nine-inch tart pan.

Prep: 15 minutes plus chilling

1	cup all-purpose flour
¼	teaspoon salt
6	tablespoons cold butter or margarine, cut into pieces
1	tablespoon vegetable shortening
2 to 3 tablespoons ice water	

1. In large bowl, combine flour and salt. With pastry blender or two knives used scissor-fashion, cut in butter and shortening until mixture resembles coarse crumbs.

2. Sprinkle in ice water, 1 tablespoon at a time, mixing lightly with fork after each addition, until dough is just moist enough to hold together.

3. Shape dough into disk; wrap in plastic wrap. Refrigerate 30 minutes or up to overnight. (If chilled overnight, let stand 30 minutes at room temperature before rolling.)

4. On lightly floured surface, with floured rolling pin, roll dough into 11-inch round. Ease dough into 9-inch tart pan with removable bottom. Fold overhang in and press dough against side of pan so it extends ⅛ inch above rim. Refrigerate or freeze until firm, 10 to 15 minutes. Fill and bake as directed in recipe. Makes enough pastry for one 9-inch tart shell.

Each ⅛th pastry: About 151 calories, 2g protein, 13g carbohydrate, 10g total fat (6g saturated), 23mg cholesterol, 160mg sodium.

Pastry for 11-Inch Tart

Tart pastry is a bit richer than pie pastry and bakes up crisper.

Prep: 15 minutes plus chilling

1½	cups all-purpose flour
½	teaspoon salt
½	cup cold butter or margarine (1 stick), cut into pieces
2	tablespoons vegetable shortening
3 to 4 tablespoons ice water	

1. In large bowl, combine flour and salt. With pastry blender or two knives used scissor-fashion, cut in butter and shortening until mixture resembles coarse crumbs.

2. Sprinkle in ice water, 1 tablespoon at a time, mixing lightly with fork after each addition, until dough is just moist enough to hold together.

3. Shape dough into disk; wrap in plastic wrap. Refrigerate 30 minutes or up to overnight. (If chilled overnight, let stand 30 minutes at room temperature before rolling.)

4. On lightly floured surface, with floured rolling pin, roll dough into 14-inch round. Ease dough into 11-inch tart pan with removable bottom. Fold overhang in and press dough against side of pan so it extends ⅛ inch above rim. Refrigerate or freeze until firm, 10 to 15 minutes. Fill and bake as directed in recipe. Makes enough pastry for one 11-inch tart shell.

Each ⅟12th pastry: About 148 calories, 2g protein, 13g carbohydrate, 10g total fat (5g saturated), 21mg cholesterol, 175mg sodium.

Prebaked Piecrust or Tart Shell

For the best flavor and texture, be sure to bake piecrust until golden all over.

Prep: 15 minutes plus chilling   Bake: 20 minutes

Pastry Dough for 1-Crust Pie, Pastry for 9-Inch Tart, or Pastry for 11-Inch Tart (page 687)

1. Prepare pastry dough as directed through chilling.
2. Preheat oven to 425°F. Use dough to line 9-inch pie plate, 9-inch tart pan with removable bottom, or 11-inch tart pan with removable bottom. If using pie plate, make decorative edge. Refrigerate or freeze until firm, 10 to 15 minutes.

3. Line pie or tart shell with foil; fill with pie weights or dry beans. Bake 15 minutes. Remove foil with weights; bake until golden, 5 to 10 minutes longer. If shell puffs up during baking, gently press it down with back of spoon. Cool on wire rack. Fill (and bake) as directed in recipe. Makes 1 piecrust or tart shell.

Phyllo Tart Shell

Phyllo crusts are elegant and versatile, and although they have rich flavor, they contain much less butter than other crusts. Use them for any recipe that calls for a baked piecrust or tart shell, or fill with Vanilla Pastry Cream (page 642) and fresh fruit.

Prep: 15 minutes   Bake: 15 minutes

3 tablespoons butter or margarine, melted
5 sheets (16" by 12" each) fresh or frozen (thawed) phyllo dough

1. Preheat oven to 375°F. Lightly brush 9-inch pie plate, including rim, with melted butter.
2. Place 1 sheet of phyllo on surface; brush with melted butter. (Keep remaining phyllo covered to prevent it from drying out.) Place phyllo sheet over pie plate; gently pat sheet onto bottom and against side of pie plate. Brush second sheet of phyllo with melted butter. Place second sheet on top of first sheet at slight angle. Gently pat phyllo onto bottom and against side of pie plate. Repeat layering with remaining

phyllo and melted butter. Roll phyllo overhang toward center to form rim.
3. Bake until golden, about 15 minutes. Cool on wire rack. Fill with desired filling. Makes 1 tart shell.

Each 1/10th pastry: About 59 calories, 1g protein, 5g carbohydrate, 4g total fat (2g saturated), 9mg cholesterol, 81mg sodium.

Phyllo Tartlet Shells

Use these just like the large phyllo shell for desserts, or fill them with your favorite spread and serve as appetizers.

Prep: 10 minutes   Bake: 15 minutes

3 tablespoons butter or margarine, melted
6 sheets (16" by 12" each) fresh or frozen (thawed) phyllo dough

1. Preheat oven to 375°F. Lightly brush eight 2½-inch muffin-pan cups with melted butter.
2. Place 1 sheet of phyllo on surface; brush with melted butter. Place second sheet of phyllo on top; brush with melted butter. Repeat with third sheet. Cut layered phyllo into eight 4-inch squares. Place a phyllo square in each prepared muffin-pan cup, gently patting phyllo onto bottom and against side of cup. Repeat buttering and layering with remaining 3 sheets of phyllo; cut into 8 squares and place crosswise over phyllo in muffin-pan cups, patting into place.
3. Bake until golden, about 15 minutes. Cool in pan on wire rack 15 minutes; remove phyllo shells from muffin-pan cups. Fill as desired. Makes 8 tartlet shells.

Each shell: About 81 calories, 1g protein, 7g carbohydrate, 5g total fat (3g saturated), 12mg cholesterol, 113mg sodium.

No-Roll Nut Crust

This flavorful crust will make a banana-, chocolate-, or coconut cream pie even more special.

Prep: 10 minutes   Bake: 20 minutes

1 cup all-purpose flour
½ cup walnuts, toasted
¼ cup sugar
⅓ cup cold butter or margarine, cut into pieces

1. Preheat oven to 375°F. In food processor with knife blade attached, process flour and walnuts until nuts are finely ground. Add sugar; pulse to mix. Add butter and pulse until mixture looks sandy.

2. Press nut mixture evenly onto bottom and up side of 9-inch pie plate.

3. Bake until lightly browned, about 20 minutes. Cool on wire rack. Fill as recipe directs. Makes one 9-inch crust.

Each 1/10th pastry: About 157 calories, 2g protein, 16g carbohydrate, 10g total fat (4g saturated), 16mg cholesterol, 63mg sodium.

Graham Cracker–Crumb Crust

For the freshest flavor, make your own cookie crumbs. Personalize your crusts by using your favorite cookies to make the crumbs.

Prep: 10 minutes   Bake: 10 minutes

1¼	cups graham-cracker crumbs (11 rectangular graham crackers)
4	tablespoons butter or margarine, melted
1	tablespoon sugar

1. Preheat oven to 375°F.

2. In 9-inch pie plate, with fork, mix crumbs, melted butter, and sugar until crumbs are evenly moistened. Press mixture firmly onto bottom and up side of pie plate, making small rim.

3. Bake 10 minutes; cool on wire rack. Fill as recipe directs. Makes one 9-inch crust.

Each 1/10th crust: About 105 calories, 1g protein, 12g carbohydrate, 6g total fat (3g saturated), 12mg cholesterol, 137mg sodium.

Chocolate Wafer–Crumb Crust
Prepare as directed but substitute **1¼ cups chocolate-wafer crumbs (24 cookies)** for graham-cracker crumbs.

Each 1/10th crust: About 108 calories, 1g protein, 12g carbohydrate, 7g total fat (3g saturated), 13mg cholesterol, 130mg sodium.

Vanilla Wafer–Crumb Crust
Prepare as directed but substitute **1¼ cups vanilla-wafer crumbs (35 cookies)** for graham-cracker crumbs.

Each 1/10th crust: About 92 calories, 1g protein, 9g carbohydrate, 6g total fat (3g saturated), 12mg cholesterol, 80mg sodium.

MAKING COOKIE CRUMBS

To make cookie crumbs, place the cookies in a heavy-duty zip-tight plastic bag and crush them with a rolling pin or meat mallet. Cookies can also be crushed in a food processor or blender. For about 1 cup crushed cookie crumbs, use approximately twenty 2¼-inch chocolate wafers, 14 gingersnaps, 22 vanilla wafers, or 7 rectangular plain or chocolate graham crackers.

Apple Pie

Make with a combination of apples, such as Braeburn, Granny Smith, and Golden Delicious. You can also use half brown sugar and half granulated sugar.

Prep: 45 minutes plus chilling   Bake: 1 hour 20 minutes

	Pastry Dough for 2-Crust Pie (page 686)
⅔	cup sugar
2	tablespoons all-purpose flour
½	teaspoon ground cinnamon
⅛	teaspoon salt
3	pounds cooking apples (9 medium), peeled, cored, and thinly sliced
1	tablespoon fresh lemon juice
1	tablespoon butter or margarine, cut into pieces

1. Prepare pastry dough as directed through chilling.

2. Preheat oven to 425°F. In large bowl, combine sugar, flour, cinnamon, and salt. Add apples and lemon juice; gently toss to combine.

3. Use larger disk of dough to line 9-inch pie plate. Spoon apple filling into crust; dot with butter. Roll out remaining disk of dough; cut center circle and 1-inch slits to allow steam to escape during baking. Place over filling and make decorative edge.

4. Place pie on foil-lined cookie sheet to catch any overflow during baking. Bake 20 minutes. Turn oven control to 375°F; bake until filling bubbles in center, about 1 hour longer. If necessary, cover pie loosely with foil during last 20 minutes of baking to prevent overbrowning. Cool on wire rack 1 hour to serve warm, or cool completely to serve later. Makes 10 servings.

Each serving: About 369 calories, 3g protein, 55g carbohydrate, 16g total fat (8g saturated), 28mg cholesterol, 251mg sodium.

Apple Crumb Pie

This old-fashioned recipe has sour cream in the filling to give it a subtle tang and creaminess.

Prep: 40 minutes plus chilling	*Bake: 1 hour 35 minutes*

Pastry Dough for 1-Crust Pie (page 687)

⅔	cup granulated sugar
3	tablespoons cornstarch
¾	teaspoon ground cinnamon
3	pounds Granny Smith apples (7 large), peeled, cored, and cut into ¾-inch pieces
⅓	cup dark seedless raisins
⅔	cup all-purpose flour
⅓	cup packed brown sugar
3	tablespoons cold butter or margarine, cut into pieces
1	container (8 ounces) sour cream
1	teaspoon vanilla extract

1. Prepare pastry dough as directed through chilling.

2. In large bowl, combine granulated sugar, cornstarch, and ½ teaspoon cinnamon. Add apples and raisins; toss to combine.

3. Preheat oven to 400°F. Use dough to line 9½-inch deep-dish pie plate; make decorative edge. Refrigerate or freeze until firm, 10 to 15 minutes.

4. Meanwhile, prepare topping: In medium bowl, combine flour, brown sugar, and remaining ¼ teaspoon cinnamon. With pastry blender or two knives used scissor-fashion, cut in butter until mixture resembles coarse crumbs; set aside.

5. Add sour cream and vanilla to apple mixture and toss well to coat evenly. Spoon into chilled pie shell. Sprinkle crumb topping evenly over apples.

6. Place pie on foil-lined cookie sheet to catch any overflow. Bake 1 hour. Turn oven control to 350°F; bake until filling bubbles in center, 35 to 45 minutes longer. If necessary, cover pie loosely with foil during last 20 minutes of baking to prevent overbrowning. Cool slightly on wire rack to serve warm, or cool completely to serve later. Makes 10 servings.

Each serving: About 403 calories, 4g protein, 64g carbohydrate, 16g fat (9g saturated), 32mg cholesterol, 155mg sodium.

Apple Tarte Tatin

This classic French dessert is simply a caramelized apple tart. Serve it warm with ice cream.

Prep: 1 hour 10 minutes plus chilling	*Bake: 25 minutes*

Pastry for 9-Inch Tart (page 687)

6	tablespoons butter or margarine
1	cup sugar
1	tablespoon fresh lemon juice
3¾	pounds Golden Delicious apples (9 medium), peeled, cored, and each cut in half

1. Prepare pastry dough as directed but roll into 12-inch round and transfer to cookie sheet. Refrigerate.

2. Preheat oven to 425°F. In heavy 10-inch skillet with oven-safe handle (if skillet is not oven-safe, wrap handle in double layer of foil), combine butter, sugar, and lemon juice; cook over medium-high heat until butter melts and mixture bubbles. Place apples in skillet, overlapping them. Cook 10 minutes, turning apples to cook evenly. Carefully turn apples rounded side down; cook until syrup has thickened and is amber in color, 8 to 12 minutes longer. Remove from heat.

3. Place dough on top of apples in skillet; fold edge of dough under to form rim around apples. With knife, cut six ¼-inch slits in dough so steam can escape during baking. Bake until crust is golden, about 25 minutes.

4. When tart is done, place large platter on top. Wearing oven mitts to protect your hands, quickly turn skillet upside down to unmold tart. Cool 30 minutes to serve warm, or cool completely to serve later. Makes 10 servings.

Each serving: About 342 calories, 2g protein, 52g carbohydrate, 16g total fat (9g saturated), 37mg cholesterol, 198mg sodium.

Peach Tarte Tatin

Prepare as directed but substitute **3¾ pounds firm-ripe peaches (11 medium),** peeled, halved, and pitted, for apples. Bake and cool as directed.

Pear Tarte Tatin

Prepare as directed but substitute **3¾ pounds firm-ripe Bosc pears (about 7),** peeled, cored, and cut lengthwise in half, for apples. Bake and cool as directed.

Apple Tarte Tatin

Apple Galette

This no-fuss free-form tart is baked on a cookie sheet instead of in a tart pan for a more casual look.

Prep: 40 minutes plus chilling	*Bake: 45 minutes*

Pastry Dough for 1-Crust Pie (page 687)
2 pounds Golden Delicious apples (6 medium)
¼ cup sugar
2 tablespoons butter or margarine, cut into pieces
2 tablespoons apricot preserves

1. Prepare pastry dough as directed through chilling.

2. Preheat oven to 425°F. On lightly floured surface, with floured rolling pin, roll dough into 15-inch round. Transfer to ungreased large cookie sheet; refrigerate.

3. Peel apples; cut in half. With melon baller, remove cores. Cut apples crosswise into ¼-inch-thick slices. Arrange apple slices on dough round in concentric circles, overlapping slices and leaving 1½-inch border. Sprinkle apples evenly with sugar and dot with butter. Fold border of dough over apples.

4. Place two sheets of foil under cookie sheet; crimp foil edges to form rim to catch any overflow during baking. Bake galette until apples are tender, about 45 minutes. Place cookie sheet on wire rack.

5. In small saucepan, melt apricot preserves over low heat until bubbling. Brush preserves over apples. Cool galette slightly to serve warm. Makes 8 servings.

Each serving: About 270 calories, 2g protein, 39g carbohydrate, 12g total fat (6g saturated), 23mg cholesterol, 162mg sodium.

Apricot Streusel Pie

The season for apricots is short. You may only see them once, so buy them to make this intensely flavored summer treat. If you like your pies on the sweet side, use the larger amount of sugar for the fruit filling.

Prep: 1 hour plus chilling	*Bake: 1 hour 15 minutes*

Pastry Dough for 1-Crust Pie (page 687)
1 cup all-purpose flour
6 tablespoons butter or margarine, softened
⅓ cup packed brown sugar
½ cup sliced natural almonds
1 to 1¼ cups sugar
3 tablespoons cornstarch
2 pounds ripe apricots,
   not peeled, pitted and cut into quarters (6 cups)
2 teaspoons fresh lemon juice

1. Prepare pastry dough as directed through chilling.

2. Preheat oven to 425°F. Use dough to line 9-inch pie plate; make decorative edge. Refrigerate or freeze until firm, 10 to 15 minutes.

3. Line pie shell with foil; fill with pie weights or dry beans. Bake 15 minutes. Remove foil with weights; bake until golden, 5 to 10 minutes longer. If shell puffs up during baking, gently press it down with back of spoon. Transfer to wire rack to cool.

4. Meanwhile, prepare streusel topping: In medium bowl, with fingertips, combine flour, butter, and brown sugar until mixture almost holds together. Add almonds and squeeze mixture into ball; set aside.

5. In large bowl, combine sugar and cornstarch. Add apricots and lemon juice; toss to combine. Spoon apricot filling into cooled pie shell. Crumble topping over filling.

6. Place pie on foil-lined cookie sheet to catch any overflow during baking. Bake until filling bubbles in center, about 55 minutes. If necessary, cover pie loosely with foil during last 20 minutes of baking to prevent overbrowning. Cool on wire rack 1 hour to serve warm, or cool completely to serve later. Makes 10 servings.

Each serving: About 422 calories, 5g protein, 64g carbohydrate, 17g total fat (8g saturated), 31mg cholesterol, 179mg sodium.

Warm Banana-Pecan Tart

To keep last-minute preparation to a minimum, bake the crust up to two days ahead. Prepare the toasted pecan cream up to one day in advance and refrigerate. Then simply assemble the tart just before serving.

Prep: 1 hour plus chilling	Bake/Broil: 32 minutes
Pastry for 11-Inch Tart (page 687)	
½	cup pecans, toasted
½	cup plus 1 tablespoon sugar
3	large egg yolks
1	tablespoon cornstarch
¾	cup half-and-half or light cream
2	tablespoons butter or margarine, cut into pieces
1	teaspoon vanilla extract
5	ripe medium bananas (about 2 pounds)

1. Prepare pastry dough as directed through chilling.

2. Prepare pecan cream: In blender or in food processor with knife blade attached, combine pecans and ¼ cup sugar; process until pecans are very finely ground.

3. In small bowl, with wire whisk, stir egg yolks, ¼ cup sugar, and cornstarch until blended. In 2-quart saucepan, heat half-and-half to simmering over medium-high heat. While whisking constantly, gradually pour about half of simmering cream into egg-yolk mixture in bowl. Return egg-yolk mixture to saucepan and cook over low heat, stirring constantly, until mixture has thickened (do not boil), 4 to 5 minutes. Stir in pecan mixture, butter, and vanilla until butter melts. Transfer pecan-cream mixture to medium bowl. Press plastic wrap onto surface and refrigerate at least 30 minutes or up to overnight.

4. Meanwhile, preheat oven to 425°F. Use dough to line 11-inch tart pan with removable bottom. Refrigerate or freeze until firm, 10 to 15 minutes.

5. Line tart shell with foil; fill with pie weights or dry beans. Bake 15 minutes. Remove foil with weights; bake until golden, 5 to 10 minutes longer. If shell puffs up during baking, gently press it down with back of spoon. Turn oven control to broil.

6. Cut bananas on diagonal into thin slices. Arrange banana slices, overlapping slightly, in tart shell. Spoon chilled pecan-cream filling over bananas and sprinkle with remaining 1 tablespoon sugar. Cover edge of shell with foil to prevent overbrowning. Place at position closest to heat source and broil until top is lightly caramelized, 1 to 2 minutes. Carefully remove side of pan. Serve warm. Makes 12 servings.

Each serving: About 315 calories, 4g protein, 36g carbohydrate, 18g total fat (8g saturated), 85mg cholesterol, 203mg sodium.

Double Blueberry Pie

In this old New England recipe, the blueberry flavor is maximized by stirring raw berries into the cooked filling. We like it with a simple gingersnap crust to make it especially easy for casual summer entertaining.

Prep: 30 minutes plus chilling	Bake: 8 minutes
1⅔	cups gingersnap cookie crumbs (about 25 cookies)
5	tablespoons butter or margarine, melted
2	tablespoons plus ½ cup sugar
2	tablespoons cornstarch
2	tablespoons cold water
3	pints blueberries
	whipped cream (optional)

1. Preheat oven to 375°F. In 9-inch pie plate, with fork, mix cookie crumbs, melted butter, and 2 tablespoons sugar until moistened. With hand, press mixture firmly onto bottom and up side of pie plate. Bake 8 minutes. Cool on wire rack.

2. Meanwhile, in 2-quart saucepan, blend cornstarch and water until smooth. Add half of blueberries and remaining ½ cup sugar to cornstarch mixture; heat to boiling over medium-high heat, pressing blueberries against side of saucepan with back of spoon. Boil, stirring constantly, 1 minute. Remove from heat; stir in remaining blueberries.

3. Pour blueberry filling into cooled crust. Press plastic wrap onto surface and refrigerate until thoroughly chilled, about 5 hours. Serve with whipped cream, if desired. Makes 10 servings.

Each serving: About 241 calories, 2g protein, 42g carbohydrate, 8g total fat (4g saturated), 16mg cholesterol, 201mg sodium.

Very Blueberry Pie

We like to serve this pie with cinnamon-scented whipped cream. Or, if you prefer, add a pinch of cinnamon or grated lemon peel to the filling. If using wild blueberries, increase the cornstarch to one-third cup; they tend to be juicier than cultivated berries.

Prep: 25 minutes plus chilling   Bake: 1 hour 20 minutes

	Pastry Dough for 2-Crust Pie (page 686)
¾	cup sugar
¼	cup cornstarch
	pinch salt
6	cups blueberries (about 3 pints)
1	tablespoon fresh lemon juice
2	tablespoons butter or margarine, cut into pieces

1. Prepare pastry dough as directed through chilling.
2. Preheat oven to 425°F.

3. In large bowl, combine sugar, cornstarch, and salt. Add blueberries and lemon juice; toss to combine.

4. Use larger disk of dough to line 9-inch pie plate. Spoon blueberry filling into crust; dot with butter. Roll out remaining disk of dough; cut out center circle and 1-inch slits to allow steam to escape during baking. Place over filling and make decorative edge.

5. Place pie on foil-lined cookie sheet to catch any overflow during baking. Bake 20 minutes. Turn oven control to 375°F; bake until filling bubbles in center and crust is golden, about 1 hour longer. If necessary, cover pie loosely with foil during last 20 minutes of baking to prevent overbrowning. Cool on wire rack 1 hour to serve warm, or cool completely to serve later. Makes 10 servings.

Each serving: About 374 calories, 4g protein, 53g carbohydrate, 17g total fat (8g saturated), 31mg cholesterol, 253mg sodium.

Very Blueberry Pie

Tart Cherry Pie

If you see tart (sour) cherries in your farmers' market, buy enough to make several desserts, and also freeze some. Invest in a cherry pitter; it makes quick work of removing the pits.

Prep: 1 hour plus chilling   Bake: 1 hour 20 to 30 minutes
Pastry Dough for 2-Crust Pie (page 686)
1 cup sugar
¼ cup cornstarch
pinch salt
2¼ pounds tart (sour) cherries, pitted (4½ cups)
1 tablespoon butter or margarine, cut into pieces

1. Prepare pastry dough as directed through chilling.

2. Preheat oven to 425°F. In large bowl, combine sugar, cornstarch, and salt. Add cherries and toss to combine.

3. Use larger disk of dough to line 9-inch pie plate. Spoon cherry filling into crust; dot with butter. Roll out remaining disk of dough; cut out center circle and 1-inch slits to allow steam to escape during baking. Place dough over filling; make decorative edge.

4. Place pie on foil-lined cookie sheet to catch any overflow during baking. Bake 20 minutes. Turn oven control to 375°F; bake until filling bubbles in center, 1 hour to 1 hour 10 minutes longer. If necessary, cover pie loosely with foil during last 20 minutes of baking to prevent overbrowning. Cool on wire rack 1 hour to serve warm, or cool completely to serve later. Makes 10 servings.

Each serving: About 381 calories, 4g protein, 57g carbohydrate, 16g total fat (8g saturated), 28mg cholesterol, 239mg sodium.

Frozen Tart Cherry Pie

Prepare as directed but use **1¼ cups sugar, 1 bag (20 ounces) frozen tart cherries,** thawed (with their juice), and **⅓ cup cornstarch.**

Canned Cherry Pie

Prepare as directed but use **2 cans (16 ounces each) pitted tart (sour) cherries packed in water.** Drain; reserve ½ cup cherry juice. In medium bowl, combine **¾ cup sugar, ¼ cup cornstarch, ⅛ teaspoon ground cinnamon,** and **pinch salt.** Add reserved cherry juice, cherries, and **½ teaspoon vanilla;** toss to combine.

Peach-Blueberry Galette

Blueberries and peaches are perfect for summer pastries such as this rustic-looking treat.

Prep: 30 minutes plus chilling   Bake: 40 minutes
Pastry Dough for 1-Crust Pie (page 687)
⅓ cup plus 2 tablespoons sugar
2 tablespoons cornstarch
2 pounds ripe peaches (6 large), peeled, pitted, and each cut into 6 wedges
1 cup blueberries
2 teaspoons fresh lemon juice
1 tablespoon butter or margarine, cut into pieces

1. Prepare pastry dough as directed through chilling.

2. Preheat oven to 425°F. In large bowl, combine ⅓ cup sugar and cornstarch. Add peaches, blueberries, and lemon juice; toss to combine.

3. On floured surface, roll dough into 14-inch round. Trim edges even. Transfer dough to ungreased large cookie sheet. Spoon fruit filling onto dough, leaving 2-inch border; dot with butter. Fold border of dough over fruit.

4. Sprinkle dough and filling with remaining 2 tablespoons sugar. Place two sheets of foil under cookie sheet; crimp foil edges to form rim to catch any overflow. Bake until filling bubbles in center, about 40 minutes. Cool on wire rack 30 minutes to serve warm, or cool completely to serve later. Makes 8 servings.

Each serving: About 266 calories, 3g protein, 41g carbohydrate, 11g total fat (5g saturated), 19mg cholesterol, 146mg sodium.

Peach Pie

Don't let the summer go by without making at least one fresh peach pie!

Prep: 35 minutes plus chilling	Bake: 1 hour 5 to 20 minutes

Pastry Dough for 2-Crust Pie (page 686)

¾	cup sugar
¼	cup cornstarch
	pinch salt
3	pounds ripe peaches, (9 large) peeled, pitted, and sliced (7 cups)
1	tablespoon fresh lemon juice
1	tablespoon butter or margarine, cut into pieces

1. Prepare pastry dough as directed through chilling.

2. Preheat oven to 425°F. In large bowl, combine sugar, cornstarch, and salt. Add peaches and lemon juice; gently toss to combine.

3. Use larger disk of dough to line 9-inch pie plate. Spoon peach filling into crust; dot with butter. Roll out remaining disk of dough; cut out center circle and 1-inch slits to allow steam to escape during baking. Place dough over filling and make decorative edge.

4. Place pie on foil-lined cookie sheet to catch any overflow during baking. Bake 20 minutes. Turn oven control to 375°F; bake until filling bubbles in center, 45 to 60 minutes longer. If necessary, cover pie loosely with foil during last 20 minutes of baking to prevent overbrowning. Cool on wire rack 1 hour to serve warm, or cool completely to serve later. Makes 10 servings.

Each serving: About 360 calories, 4g protein, 52g carbohydrate, 16g total fat (8g saturated), 28mg cholesterol, 236mg sodium.

Plum Pie

Prepare pie as directed but substitute **3 pounds tart plums (9 large),** pitted and sliced, for peaches; use **1 cup sugar.**

Pear Pie

Prepare as directed but substitute **3 pounds ripe pears,** peeled, cored, and sliced, for peaches; add **⅛ teaspoon ground nutmeg** to sugar mixture. Bake 20 minutes at 425°F. Turn oven control to 375°F; bake until filling bubbles in center, about 45 minutes longer.

Peach Pie

Plum Frangipane Tart

Make this tart with red or black plums—it will be equally good.

Prep: 30 minutes plus chilling	Bake: 1 hour 20 minutes

Pastry for 11-Inch Tart (page 687)

1	tube or can (7 to 8 ounces) almond paste, crumbled
4	tablespoons butter or margarine, softened
½	cup sugar
¼	teaspoon salt
2	large eggs
2	teaspoons vanilla extract
¼	cup all-purpose flour
1¼	pounds ripe plums (5 large), pitted and each cut into 6 wedges

1. Prepare pastry dough as directed through chilling.

2. Preheat oven to 425°F. Use dough to line 11-inch tart pan with removable bottom. Refrigerate or freeze until firm, 10 to 15 minutes.

3. Line tart shell with foil; fill with pie weights or dry beans. Bake 15 minutes. Remove foil with weights; bake until golden, 5 to 10 minutes longer. If shell puffs up during baking, gently press it down with back of spoon. Remove from oven; turn oven control to 375°F.

4. Meanwhile, in large bowl, with mixer at low speed, beat almond paste, butter, sugar, and salt until almond paste is crumbly. Increase speed to medium-high and beat until well blended, about 3 minutes, frequently scraping bowl with rubber spatula. (There may be some tiny lumps.) Add eggs and vanilla; beat until smooth. With wooden spoon, stir in flour.

5. Pour almond-paste mixture into warm tart shell. Arrange plums in concentric circles over filling. Bake until golden, 50 to 60 minutes. Cool in pan on wire rack. When cool, carefully remove side of pan. Makes 12 servings.

Each serving: About 342 calories, 6g protein, 37g carbohydrate, 20g total fat (8g saturated), 66mg cholesterol, 274mg sodium.

Cranberry-Almond Tart

Prepare as directed but omit plums. Bake almond filling until golden, about 20 minutes. Cool in pan on wire rack. In 2-quart saucepan, combine **1 cup cranberries, ¾ cup sugar, ⅓ cup water,** and **½ teaspoon freshly grated orange peel;** heat to boiling over high heat. Reduce heat; simmer until cranberries pop and mixture has thickened slightly, about 5 minutes. Stir in additional **2 cups cranberries.** Set aside until cool. When cool, carefully remove side of pan; spoon cranberry topping over almond filling.

Raspberry Tart

The unsurpassed flavor of fresh raspberries is glorified in this tangy tart. It's made in a springform pan to give it a handmade look, but use a tart pan if you prefer.

Prep: 20 minutes plus chilling	Bake: 1 hour 5 minutes
Pastry for 9-Inch Tart (page 687)	
⅔ cup sugar	
¼ cup all-purpose flour	
4 cups raspberries (about four ½ pints)	
1 cup heavy or whipping cream (optional)	

1. Prepare pastry dough as directed through chilling.

2. Preheat oven to 425°F. Roll dough into 11-inch round; fold into quarters. Ease dough onto bottom and 1 inch up side of 9-inch springform pan. Refrigerate or freeze until firm, 10 to 15 minutes.

3. Line tart shell with foil; fill with pie weights or dry beans. Bake 15 minutes. Remove foil with weights; bake until golden, 5 to 10 minutes longer. If shell puffs up during baking, gently press it down with back of spoon. Remove from oven; turn oven control to 375°F.

4. In bowl, combine sugar and flour. Add raspberries and gently toss to combine. Spoon raspberry filling into tart shell. Bake until filling bubbles in center, about 45 minutes.

5. Cool completely in pan on wire rack. When cool, carefully remove side of pan. Serve with whipped cream, if desired. Makes 8 servings.

Each serving without cream: About 260 calories, 3g protein, 39g carbohydrate, 11g total fat (6g saturated), 23mg cholesterol, 160mg sodium.

Waterproofing a prebaked crust is the perfect way to protect a crust that's going to hold a moist filling. Here's how: Right before the crust finishes baking, beat an egg white just enough to break it up. As soon as the crust comes out of the oven, brush the inside with a thin coating of egg white and then slide the crust back into the oven for 1 minute to set the white.

When a pie filling is particularly juicy, as fresh fruit and berry fillings often are, I like to scatter stale cake, cookie, or bread crumbs (good juice catchers) over the bottom of the crust before spooning in the filling.

DORIE GREENSPAN
COOKBOOK AUTHOR

EXPERT TIP

Rhubarb Pie

Turning rhubarb into a sweet-tart pie is a celebration of spring.

Prep: 30 minutes plus chilling	Bake: 1 hour 20 to 40 minutes

Pastry Dough for 2-Crust Pie (page 686)

1½ cups sugar
¼ cup cornstarch
pinch salt
2 pounds rhubarb, trimmed and cut into ½-inch pieces (7 cups)
1 tablespoon butter or margarine, cut into pieces

1. Prepare pastry dough as directed through chilling.

2. Preheat oven to 425°F. In large bowl, combine sugar, cornstarch, and salt. Add rhubarb and toss to combine.

3. Use larger disk of dough to line 9-inch pie plate. Spoon rhubarb filling into crust; dot with butter. Roll out remaining diskof dough; cut out center circle and 1-inch slits to allow steam to escape during baking. Place dough over filling and make decorative edge.

4. Place pie on foil-lined cookie sheet to catch any overflow during baking. Bake 20 minutes. Turn oven control to 375°F; bake until filling bubbles in center and crust is golden, 1 hour to 1 hour 20 minutes longer. If necessary, cover pie loosely with foil during last 20 minutes of baking to prevent overbrowning. Cool on wire rack 1 hour to serve warm, or cool completely to serve later. Makes 10 servings.

Each serving: About 387 calories, 4g protein, 59g carbohydrate, 16g total fat (8g saturated), 28mg cholesterol, 239mg sodium.

Mince Pie

Our gussied-up mincemeat almost tastes homemade.

Prep: 25 minutes plus chilling	Bake: 30 to 40 minutes

Pastry Dough for 2-Crust Pie (page 686)
1 jar (28 ounces) ready-to-use mincemeat
1 large cooking apple, peeled and finely chopped
1 cup walnuts (4 ounces), coarsely broken
½ cup packed brown sugar
2 tablespoons brandy or rum (optional)
1 tablespoon fresh lemon juice
Hard Sauce (page 562) or sliced sharp Cheddar cheese

1. Prepare pastry dough as directed through chilling.

2. Preheat oven to 425°F. In medium bowl, stir together mincemeat, apple, walnuts, brown sugar, brandy, and lemon juice until well combined.

3. Use larger disk of dough to line 9-inch pie plate. Spoon mincemeat filling into crust. Roll out remaining disk of dough; cut out center circle and 1-inch slits to allow steam to escape during baking. Place dough over filling and make decorative edge.

4. Bake until golden, 30 to 40 minutes. Cool on wire rack 1 hour to serve warm, topped with Hard Sauce, or cool completely to serve later. Makes 10 servings.

Each serving without Hard Sauce: About 538 calories, 6g protein, 76g carbohydrate, 24g total fat (8g saturated), 25mg cholesterol, 428mg sodium.

Maple-Walnut Pie

The subtle flavor of maple is a perfect match for walnuts. For even more maple flavor, serve the pie with maple syrup–sweetened whipped cream.

Prep: 25 minutes plus chilling	Bake: 1 hour 10 to 20 minutes

Pastry Dough for 1-Crust Pie (page 687)
1 cup maple or maple-flavored syrup
4 tablespoons butter or margarine, melted
3 tablespoons sugar
¼ teaspoon salt
3 large eggs
2 cups walnuts (8 ounces)

1. Prepare pastry dough as directed through chilling.

2. Preheat oven to 425°F. Use dough to line 9-inch pie plate; make high stand-up edge. Refrigerate or freeze until firm, 10 to 15 minutes.

3. Line pie shell with foil; fill with pie weights or dry beans. Bake 15 minutes. Remove foil with weights; bake until golden, 5 to 10 minutes longer. If shell puffs up during baking, gently press it down with back of spoon. Turn oven control to 350°F.

4. In medium bowl, with wire whisk, mix maple syrup, butter, sugar, salt, and eggs until blended. Spread walnuts over bottom of pie shell; carefully pour egg mixture over walnuts.

Bake until knife inserted 1 inch from edge comes out clean, 50 to 60 minutes. Cool on wire rack at least 1 hour for easier slicing. Makes 10 servings.

Each serving: About 437 calories, 7g protein, 42g carbohydrate, 28g total fat (8g saturated), 89mg cholesterol, 233mg sodium.

Double Berry Linzer Tart

To give this fine Austrian tart holiday flair, we've added fresh cranberries to the traditional raspberry jam.

	Prep: 30 minutes plus chilling Bake: 40 minutes
1	cup cranberries
¼	plus ⅓ cup packed brown sugar
¼	cranberry-juice cocktail
	pinch plus ¼ teaspoon salt
¾	cup seedless raspberry jam
⅔	cup hazelnuts (filberts), toasted and skinned (page 729)
1¼	cups all-purpose flour
6	tablespoons butter or margarine, softened
1	large egg
½	teaspoon vanilla extract
¼	teaspoon baking powder
¼	teaspoon ground cinnamon
	confectioners' sugar (optional)

1. In nonreactive 1-quart saucepan, combine cranberries, ¼ cup brown sugar, cranberry-juice cocktail, and pinch salt; heat to boiling over medium-high heat. Reduce heat to medium; cook, stirring occasionally, until cranberries pop and mixture has thickened slightly, about 6 minutes. Stir in raspberry jam; refrigerate until cool, about 30 minutes.

2. Meanwhile in blender or in food processor with knife blade attached, process hazelnuts and ¼ cup flour until nuts are very finely ground.

3. In large bowl, with mixer at low speed, beat butter and remaining ⅓ cup brown sugar until blended. Increase speed to medium-high; beat until light and fluffy, about 3 minutes. With mixer at medium speed, beat in egg and vanilla until smooth, about 1 minute. Reduce speed to low. Add hazelnut mixture, remaining 1 cup flour, baking powder, cinnamon, and remaining ¼ teaspoon salt; beat just until combined.

4. With floured hands, press two-thirds of dough onto bottom and up side of 9-inch tart pan with removable bottom.

Double Berry Linzer Tart

Trim edge even with rim of pan. Wrap tart shell and remaining dough in plastic wrap and refrigerate until disk of dough is firm enough to shape, about 30 minutes.

5. Spoon cooled filling into tart shell. On lightly floured surface, divide remaining dough into 10 equal pieces. With floured hands, roll each piece into 8½-inch-long rope. Place 5 ropes, 1½ inches apart, across top of tart. Place remaining 5 ropes at right angle to first ropes to make lattice pattern. Or, if desired, weave dough ropes to create "fancy" lattice pattern. Trim ends of ropes even with edge of tart and press ends to seal. With hands, roll any dough trimmings into ¼-inch-thick ropes. Press ropes around edge of tart to make finished edge. If ropes break, press pieces together.

6. Preheat oven to 400°F. Bake until filling bubbles and crust is lightly browned, about 40 minutes. Cool in pan on wire rack at least 1 hour. When cool, carefully remove side of pan. Dust with confectioners' sugar, if desired. Makes 10 servings.

Each serving: About 290 calories, 4g protein, 43g carbohydrate, 12g total fat (5g saturated), 40mg cholesterol, 175mg sodium.

Pecan Pie

This Southern classic couldn't be richer or more delicious.

Prep: 25 minutes plus cooling and chilling   Bake: 1 hour 5 minutes

	Pastry Dough for 1-Crust Pie (page 687)
1¾	cups pecan halves (7 ounces)
¾	cup dark corn syrup
½	cup packed brown sugar
4	tablespoons butter or margarine, melted
1	teaspoon vanilla extract
3	large eggs

1. Prepare pastry dough as directed through chilling.

2. Preheat oven to 425°F. Use dough to line 9-inch pie plate; make decorative edge. Refrigerate or freeze until firm, 10 to 15 minutes.

3. Line pie shell with foil; fill with pie weights or dry beans. Bake 15 minutes. Remove foil with weights; bake until golden, 5 to 10 minutes longer. If shell puffs up during baking, gently press it down with back of spoon. Cool on wire rack. Turn oven control to 350°F.

4. Coarsely chop 1 cup pecans.

5. In large bowl, with wire whisk, mix corn syrup, brown sugar, melted butter, vanilla, and eggs until blended. Stir in chopped pecans and remaining pecan halves.

6. Pour pecan filling into cooled pie shell. Bake until filling is set around edges but center jiggles slightly, 45 to 50 minutes. Cool on wire rack at least 1 hour for easier slicing. Makes 12 servings.

Each serving: About 353 calories, 4g protein, 38g carbohydrate, 22g total fat (7g saturated), 74mg cholesterol, 177mg sodium.

Chocolate Pecan Pie

Prepare as directed but use ¾ **cup packed dark brown sugar** and add **2 squares (2 ounces) unsweetened chocolate,** melted, to filling with butter.

Deluxe Cheese Pie

This is like having a scrumptious classic cheesecake, but it's made in a fraction of the time.

Prep: 20 minutes plus cooling and chilling   Bake: 45 minutes

	Graham Cracker–Crumb Crust (page 689)
1½	packages (8 ounces each) cream cheese, softened
½	cup plus 2 tablespoons sugar
2	large eggs
½	teaspoon vanilla extract
1	container (8 ounces) sour cream

1. Preheat oven to 350°F. Prepare crust as directed. Cool.

2. In medium bowl, with mixer at low speed, beat cream cheese and ½ cup sugar until smooth, occasionally scraping side of bowl with rubber spatula. Add eggs and vanilla; beat just until combined.

3. Pour cheese filling into cooled crust. Bake until set, about 30 minutes.

4. Blend sour cream and remaining 2 tablespoons sugar. Spread evenly over top of hot pie. Bake until set, about 5 minutes. Cool pie on wire rack. Refrigerate at least 2 hours for easier slicing or up to overnight. Makes 10 servings.

Each serving: About 337 calories, 6g protein, 27g carbohydrate, 23g total fat (14g saturated), 102mg cholesterol, 262mg sodium.

Strawberry Cheese Pie

(pictured on page 682)

Prepare as directed but omit sour-cream mixture; cool pie completely. Arrange **1½ pints strawberries,** hulled and cut in half, on top of pie. In small saucepan, heat ⅓ **cup red currant jelly** over medium-low heat until melted and bubbling; brush over strawberries.

Slipped Custard Pie

To prevent the crust from becoming soggy, the custard and crust are baked separately, then the custard is "slipped" into the crust.

Prep: 20 minutes plus chilling and cooling   Bake: 45 minutes

	Pastry Dough for 1-Crust Pie (page 687)
2	cups milk
4	large eggs
½	cup sugar
¼	teaspoon salt
1	teaspoon vanilla extract
½	teaspoon butter or margarine, softened
	pinch ground nutmeg

1. Prepare dough as directed through chilling.

2. Preheat oven to 425°F. Use dough to line 9-inch pie plate. Refrigerate or freeze until firm, 10 to 15 minutes.

3. Line pie shell with foil; fill with pie weights or dry beans. Bake 15 minutes. Remove foil with weights; bake until golden, 5 to 10 minutes longer. If shell puffs up during baking, press it down with back of spoon. Cool on wire rack. Turn oven control to 350°F.

4. Meanwhile, in 2-quart saucepan, heat milk over medium-high heat until bubbles form around edge. In medium bowl, with wire whisk, beat eggs, sugar, salt, and vanilla until blended. Slowly pour hot milk into egg mixture, whisking rapidly to prevent curdling.

5. Use butter to grease separate 9-inch pie plate; set pie plate in shallow baking pan on oven rack. Pour egg mixture into prepared pie plate; sprinkle with nutmeg. Pour enough *boiling water* into baking pan to come halfway up side of pie plate. Bake until knife inserted about 1 inch from edge comes out clean, about 25 minutes. Cool on wire rack.

6. When custard is cool, run tip of small knife around custard; gently shake to loosen bottom of custard. Hold far edge of pie plate over far edge of cooled pie shell. Tilt custard gently, and as it slips into shell, quickly pull plate away until  custard rests in shell. Let filling settle a few minutes; serve warm. Makes 8 servings.

Each serving: About 280 calories, 7g protein, 31g carbohydrate, 14g total fat (7g saturated), 131mg cholesterol, 266mg sodium.

Slipped Coconut-Custard Pie
Prepare as directed but add ½ **cup flaked sweetened coconut** to egg mixture.

Pilgrim Pumpkin Pie

Our forefathers would have appreciated this pie's subtle seasoning. For a spicier pie, add one-eighth teaspoon ground white pepper, or serve with whipped cream flavored with ground ginger.

Prep: 25 minutes plus chilling   Bake: 1 hour 10 minutes

	Pastry Dough for 1-Crust Pie (page 687)
1	can (15 ounces) solid-pack pumpkin (not pumpkin-pie mix) or 2 cups mashed cooked pumpkin
1	can (12 ounces) evaporated milk
¾	cup packed brown sugar
2	large eggs
1	teaspoon ground cinnamon
½	teaspoon ground ginger
½	teaspoon salt
¼	teaspoon ground nutmeg
¼	cup heavy or whipping cream (optional)

1. Prepare pastry dough as directed through chilling.

2. Preheat oven to 425°F. Use dough to line 9-inch pie plate; make high stand-up edge. Refrigerate or freeze until firm, 10 to 15 minutes.

3. Line pie shell with foil; fill with pie weights or dry beans. Bake 15 minutes. Remove foil with weights; bake until golden, 5 to 10 minutes longer. If shell puffs up during baking, gently press it down with back of spoon. Turn oven control to 375°F.

4. In large bowl, with wire whisk, mix pumpkin, evaporated milk, brown sugar, eggs, cinnamon, ginger, salt, and nutmeg until well combined. Place piecrust-lined pie plate on oven rack; carefully pour in pumpkin filling. Bake until knife inserted 1 inch from edge comes out clean, about 50 minutes. Cool on wire rack at least 1 hour or up to 6 hours.

5. Garnish pie with whipped cream, if you like. Makes 10 servings.

Each serving: About 267 calories, 6g protein, 36g carbohydrate, 11g total fat (6g saturated), 66mg cholesterol, 282mg sodium.

Grandma's Sweet Potato Pie

In many families, sweet potato pie is served along with (or in place of) pumpkin pie at holiday meals.

	Prep: 1 hour plus chilling Bake: 1 hour
	Pastry Dough for 1-Crust Pie (page 687)
2	small sweet potatoes (1 pound), not peeled,
	or 2 cans (16 to 17 ounces each) sweet potatoes, drained
1½	cups half-and-half or light cream
¾	cup packed brown sugar
3	large eggs
1	teaspoon ground cinnamon
¾	teaspoon ground ginger
½	teaspoon salt
¼	teaspoon ground nutmeg

1. Prepare pastry dough as directed through chilling.

2. Meanwhile, if using fresh sweet potatoes, in 3-quart saucepan, combine sweet potatoes and enough *water* to cover; heat to boiling over high heat. Reduce heat; cover and simmer until tender, about 30 minutes. Drain.

3. Preheat oven to 425°F. Use dough to line 9-inch pie plate; make decorative edge. Refrigerate or freeze 10 to 15 minutes to firm dough.

4. When cool enough to handle, peel sweet potatoes and cut into large pieces. In large bowl, with mixer at low speed, beat sweet potatoes until smooth. Add half-and-half, brown sugar, eggs, cinnamon, ginger, salt, and nutmeg; beat until well blended.

5. Line pie shell with foil; fill with pie weights or dry beans. Bake 15 minutes. Remove foil with weights; bake until golden, 5 to 10 minutes longer. If shell puffs up during baking, gently press it down with back of spoon. Cool on wire rack at least 10 minutes. Turn oven control to 350°F.

6. Spoon sweet-potato filling into cooled pie shell. Bake until knife inserted 1 inch from edge comes out clean, about 40 minutes. Cool on wire rack 1 hour to serve warm, or cool slightly, then refrigerate to serve later. Makes 10 servings.

Each serving: About 290 calories, 5g protein, 39g carbohydrate, 13g total fat (7g saturated), 89mg cholesterol, 265mg sodium.

Chocolate Truffle Tart

So unbelievably decadent, all you'll need is one thin slice!

	Prep: 20 minutes plus chilling and cooling Bake: 40 minutes
	Pastry for 9-Inch Tart (page 687)
6	squares (6 ounces) semisweet chocolate, coarsely chopped
½	cup butter or margarine (1 stick)
¼	cup sugar
1	teaspoon vanilla extract
3	large eggs
½	cup heavy or whipping cream
	softly whipped cream (optional)

1. Prepare pastry dough as directed through chilling.

2. Preheat oven to 425°F. Use dough to line 9-inch tart pan with removable bottom. Trim edge even with rim of pan. Refrigerate or freeze until firm, 10 to 15 minutes.

3. Line tart shell with foil; fill with pie weights or dry beans. Bake 15 minutes. Remove foil with weights; bake until golden, 5 to 10 minutes longer. If shell puffs up during baking, gently press it down with back of spoon. Cool in pan on wire rack. Turn oven control to 350°F.

4. Meanwhile, in heavy 2-quart saucepan, melt chocolate and butter over very low heat, stirring frequently, until smooth. Add sugar and vanilla, stirring until sugar has dissolved. In small bowl, with wire whisk, lightly beat eggs and cream. Whisk ⅓ cup warm chocolate mixture into egg mixture; stir egg mixture back into chocolate mixture in saucepan until blended.

5. Pour warm chocolate filling into cooled tart shell. Bake until custard is set but center still jiggles slightly, about 20 minutes.

6. Cool in pan on wire rack. When cool, carefully remove side of pan. Refrigerate until chilled, about 4 hours. Serve with whipped cream, if desired. Makes 12 servings.

Each serving: About 306 calories, 4g protein, 22g carbohydrate, 24g total fat (14g saturated), 103mg cholesterol, 206mg sodium.

Lemon Tart

A piquant tart that can be served on its own or accented with fresh berries. Be sure to make a high pastry rim to contain all the delicious filling.

Prep: 25 minutes plus chilling and cooling   Bake: 50 minutes

	Pastry for 9-Inch Tart (page 687)
4 to 6	lemons
4	large eggs
1	cup granulated sugar
1/3	cup heavy or whipping cream
	confectioners' sugar

1. Prepare pastry dough as directed through chilling.

2. Preheat oven to 425°F. Use dough to line 9-inch tart pan with removable bottom; press dough up side so it extends 1/4 inch above rim of pan. Refrigerate or freeze until firm, 10 to 15 minutes.

3. Line tart shell with foil; fill with pie weights or dry beans. Bake 15 minutes. Remove foil with weights; bake until golden, 5 to 10 minutes longer. If shell puffs up during baking, gently press it down with back of spoon. Cool in pan on wire rack. Turn oven control to 350°F.

4. From lemons, grate 1½ teaspoons peel and squeeze 2/3 cup juice. In medium bowl, with wire whisk, beat eggs, granulated sugar, and lemon peel and juice until well combined. Whisk in cream.

5. Carefully pour lemon filling into cooled tart shell. Place tart on foil-lined cookie sheet to catch any overflow during baking. Bake until filling is set but center still jiggles slightly, about 30 minutes. Cool completely on wire rack. Just before serving, dust with confectioners' sugar. Makes 8 servings.

Each serving: About 324 calories, 5g protein, 40g carbohydrate, 17g total fat (9g saturated), 143mg cholesterol, 195mg sodium.

Black Bottom Pie

Deserving of its classic status, this pie is both rich and light; it is layered with rum and chocolate custards and topped with cream.

Prep: 40 minutes plus cooling and chilling   Bake: 10 minutes

	Chocolate Wafer–Crumb Crust (page 689)
1	teaspoon unflavored gelatin
2	tablespoons cold water
1½	cups milk
3/4	cup sugar
4	large egg yolks
2	squares (2 ounces) unsweetened chocolate, melted
1/2	teaspoon vanilla extract
2	teaspoons dark rum or 1 teaspoon vanilla extract
2	cups heavy or whipping cream

1. Prepare crust as directed. Cool completely.

2. In cup, evenly sprinkle gelatin over cold water; let stand 2 minutes to soften gelatin slightly.

3. Meanwhile, in 2-quart saucepan, combine milk and 1/2 cup sugar; cook over medium heat, stirring, until bubbles form around edge.

4. In small bowl, with wire whisk, lightly beat egg yolks. Beat about 1/3 cup hot milk mixture into egg yolks. Slowly pour egg-yolk mixture back into milk mixture, whisking rapidly to prevent curdling. Cook over low heat, stirring constantly, until mixture has thickened slightly and coats back of spoon, about 10 minutes. (Temperature on thermometer should reach about 160°F; do not boil, or mixture will curdle.)

5. Transfer 1 cup milk mixture to small bowl. Stir in melted chocolate and vanilla until blended. Pour into cooled crust; refrigerate.

6. Over low heat, add softened gelatin to remaining milk mixture in saucepan; stir until gelatin has completely dissolved. Remove from heat. Stir in rum. Cool to room temperature, stirring occasionally.

7. In bowl, with mixer, beat cream with remaining 1/4 cup sugar until stiff peaks form. Whisk half of whipped cream into cooled gelatin mixture. Refrigerate remaining whipped cream. Spoon gelatin-cream mixture over chocolate layer. Cover; refrigerate until firm, about 3 hours. To serve, mound remaining whipped cream over filling. Makes 10 servings.

Each serving: About 409 calories, 5g protein, 31g carbohydrate, 31g total fat (18g saturated), 168mg cholesterol, 171mg sodium.

Frozen Key Lime Pie

Quick, refreshing, and light. What could be better during the heat of summer?

Prep: 20 minutes plus cooling and freezing	Bake: 10 minutes

Graham Cracker–Crumb Crust (page 689)

4	limes
1	can (14 ounces) sweetened condensed milk
1	cup heavy or whipping cream

1. Prepare crust as directed. Cool completely.

2. From limes, grate 1 tablespoon peel and squeeze ½ cup juice. In large bowl, with wire whisk, stir condensed milk and lime peel and juice until well blended.

3. In large bowl, with mixer at medium speed, beat cream until stiff peaks form. Fold whipped cream, one-third at a time, into lime mixture just until blended.

4. Pour mixture into cooled crust. Cover and freeze at least 3 hours or up to 1 month. Let pie stand 10 minutes at room temperature for easier slicing. Makes 10 servings.

Each serving: About 319 calories, 5g protein, 36g carbohydrate, 18g total fat (11g saturated), 59mg cholesterol, 196mg sodium.

Lemon Meringue Pie

Here is our favorite recipe for this classic lemon masterpiece, crowned with billowing meringue.

Prep: 45 minutes plus chilling and cooling	Bake: 30 minutes

Pastry Dough for 1-Crust Pie (page 687)

4 to 6	lemons
1½	cups sugar
⅓	cup cornstarch
¼	teaspoon plus pinch salt
1½	cups water
3	large eggs, separated, plus 1 large egg white
2	tablespoons butter or margarine, cut into pieces
¼	teaspoon cream of tartar

1. Prepare pastry dough as directed through chilling.

2. Preheat oven to 425°F. Use dough to line 9-inch pie plate; make decorative edge. Refrigerate or freeze until firm, 10 to 15 minutes.

Frozen Key Lime Pie

3. Line pie shell with foil; fill with pie weights or dry beans. Bake 15 minutes. Remove foil with weights; bake until golden, 5 to 10 minutes longer. If pastry puffs up during baking, press it down with back of spoon. Cool on wire rack.

4. Meanwhile, from lemons, grate 1 tablespoon peel and squeeze ¾ cup juice; set aside. In 2-quart saucepan, combine 1 cup sugar, cornstarch, and ¼ teaspoon salt; stir in water. Cook over medium heat, stirring constantly, until mixture has thickened and boils; boil 1 minute. Remove from heat.

5. In small bowl, with wire whisk, beat egg yolks. Stir in ⅓ cup hot cornstarch mixture until blended; slowly pour egg-yolk mixture back into cornstarch mixture in saucepan, stirring rapidly to prevent curdling. Place saucepan over low heat and cook, stirring constantly, until filling is very thick, about 4 minutes. Remove from heat; stir in butter until melted, then gradually stir in lemon peel and juice until blended. Pour into cooled pie shell.

6. Turn oven control to 400°F. In small bowl, with mixer at high speed, beat egg whites, cream of tartar, and remaining pinch salt until soft peaks form when beaters are lifted. Sprinkle in remaining ½ cup sugar, 2 tablespoons at a time, beating until sugar has completely dissolved and egg whites stand in stiff, glossy peaks when beaters are lifted.

7. Spread meringue over filling to edge of pie shell. Decoratively swirl meringue with back of spoon. Bake until meringue is golden, about 10 minutes. Cool on wire rack away from drafts. Refrigerate at least 3 hours for easier slicing or up to 2 days. Makes 10 servings.

Each serving: About 321 calories, 4g protein, 52g carbohydrate, 11g total fat (5g saturated), 82mg cholesterol, 224mg sodium.

Desperate conditions require desperate measures. When I have to roll out dough and my kitchen is hot and steamy, as it can be in summer, I cool down the counter by filling a roasting pan with ice cubes and running the bottom of the pan across the counter. Of course, if you've a marble board that you use for rolling—a nice convenience—you can just pop it into the refrigerator for a preroll chill.

DORIE GREENSPAN
COOKBOOK AUTHOR

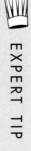

EXPERT TIP

Banana Cream Pie

This is also delicious in piecrust (page 688) or No-Roll Nut Crust (page 688).

Prep: 30 minutes plus cooling and chilling   Bake: 10 minutes

	Vanilla Wafer–Crumb Crust (page 689)
¾	cup sugar
⅓	cup cornstarch
¼	teaspoon salt
3¾	cups milk
5	large egg yolks
2	tablespoons butter or margarine, cut into pieces
1¾	teaspoons vanilla extract
3	ripe medium bananas
¾	cup heavy or whipping cream

1. Prepare crust as directed. Cool completely.

2. Meanwhile, prepare filling: In 3-quart saucepan, combine sugar, cornstarch, and salt; stir in milk. Cook over medium heat, stirring constantly, until mixture has thickened and boils; boil 1 minute. In small bowl, with wire whisk, lightly beat egg yolks; beat in ½ cup hot milk mixture. Slowly pour egg-yolk mixture back into milk, stirring rapidly to prevent curdling. Cook over low heat, stirring constantly, until mixture has thickened, about 2 minutes. Remove from heat. Add butter and 1½ teaspoons vanilla; stir until butter melts. Transfer to medium bowl. Press plastic wrap onto surface. Refrigerate, stirring occasionally, until cool, about 1 hour.

3. Slice 2 bananas. Spoon half of filling into crust. Arrange sliced bananas on top; spoon remaining filling evenly over bananas. Press plastic wrap onto surface; refrigerate at least 4 hours or up to overnight.

4. To serve, prepare topping: In small bowl, with mixer at medium speed, beat cream and remaining ¼ teaspoon vanilla until stiff peaks form; spread over filling. Slice remaining banana; arrange around edge of pie. Makes 10 servings.

Each serving: About 367 calories, 6g protein, 41g carbohydrate, 21g total fat (12g saturated), 162mg cholesterol, 216mg sodium.

Coconut Cream Pie

Prepare as directed but omit bananas; fold ¾ **cup sweetened flaked coconut** into filling before spooning into crust. Refrigerate and top with whipped cream as directed. To serve, sprinkle with ¼ **cup sweetened flaked coconut,** toasted.

Chocolate Cream Pie

Win friends and influence people with this indulgent dessert.

Prep: 35 minutes plus cooling and chilling	*Bake: 10 minutes*

Chocolate Wafer–Crumb Crust (page 689)
¾ cup sugar
⅓ cup cornstarch
½ teaspoon salt
3¾ cups milk
5 large egg yolks
3 squares (3 ounces) unsweetened chocolate, melted
2 tablespoons butter or margarine, cut into pieces
2 teaspoons vanilla extract
1 cup heavy or whipping cream
Chocolate Curls (page 681; optional)

1. Prepare crust as directed. Cool.

2. Meanwhile, in heavy 3-quart saucepan, combine sugar, cornstarch, and salt; with wire whisk, stir in milk until smooth. Cook over medium heat, stirring constantly, until mixture has thickened and boils; boil 1 minute. In small bowl, with wire whisk, lightly beat egg yolks. Beat ½ cup hot milk mixture into beaten egg yolks. Slowly pour egg-yolk mixture back into milk mixture, stirring rapidly to prevent curdling. Cook over low heat, stirring constantly, until mixture is very thick or until temperature on thermometer reaches 160°F.

3. Remove saucepan from heat and stir in melted chocolate, butter, and vanilla until butter melts and mixture is smooth. Pour hot chocolate filling into cooled crust; press plastic wrap onto surface. Refrigerate until filling is set, about 4 hours.

4. Meanwhile, make Chocolate Curls, if using.

5. To serve, in small bowl, with mixer at medium speed, beat cream until stiff peaks form; spoon over chocolate filling. Top with chocolate curls, if desired. Makes 10 servings.

Each serving: About 417 calories, 7g protein, 38g carbohydrate, 28g total fat (16g saturated), 171mg cholesterol, 329mg sodium.

Chocolate Cream Pie

Italian Triple Berry Tart

You can make the filling and crust a day ahead. Just fold in the whipped cream and top with berries when ready to serve.

Prep: 30 minutes plus chilling	*Bake: 20 minutes*

Pastry for 11-Inch Tart (page 687)
⅓ cup sugar
2 tablespoons cornstarch
3 large egg yolks
1 cup milk
2 tablespoons butter or margarine, cut into pieces
1 teaspoon vanilla extract
½ cup heavy or whipping cream
2 cups blueberries (about 1 pint)
2 cups raspberries (about 1 pint)
2 cups blackberries (about 1 pint)
confectioners' sugar

1. In small bowl, with wire whisk, combine sugar and cornstarch until blended. Add egg yolks and stir. In 2-quart saucepan, heat milk to simmering over medium-high heat. While beating constantly with wire whisk, gradually pour about half of simmering milk into egg-yolk mixture. Return egg-yolk mixture to saucepan and cook, whisking constantly, until pastry cream has thickened and boils; reduce heat and simmer, stirring, 1 minute. Remove from heat; stir in butter and vanilla until butter melts. Transfer pastry cream to medium bowl; press plastic wrap onto surface. Refrigerate until well chilled, at least 2 hours or up to 6 hours.

2. Prepare pastry dough as directed through chilling.

3. Preheat oven to 425°F. Use dough to line 11-inch tart pan with removable bottom. Refrigerate or freeze 10 to 15 minutes to firm dough.

4. Line tart shell with foil; fill with pie weights or dry beans. Bake 15 minutes. Remove foil with weights; bake until golden, 5 to 10 minutes longer. If shell puffs up during baking, gently press it down with back of spoon. Cool completely in pan on wire rack.

5. Up to 2 hours before serving, in small bowl, with mixer at medium speed, beat cream until stiff peaks form. Whisk pastry cream until smooth; gently fold in whipped cream until blended. Spoon pastry-cream filling into tart shell. In large bowl, gently toss blueberries, raspberries, and blackberries. Spoon over filling and dust with confectioners' sugar. Makes 12 servings.

Each serving: About 290 calories, 4g protein, 30g carbohydrate, 18g total fat (10g saturated), 95mg cholesterol, 212mg sodium.

Puff Pastry Variation

Prepare as directed but instead of making tart shell, bake Puff Pastry Strip: Preheat oven to 400°F. Unfold **1 sheet (half 17¼-ounce package) frozen puff pastry,** thawed, and place on ungreased large cookie sheet. With rolling pin, roll pastry into 12" by 9" rectangle. Cut a ¼-inch-wide strip from each long side. Lightly brush both long edges of pastry sheet with water; place pastry strips on top to build up long edges. Press pastry lightly to adhere. With fork, prick center portion of pastry all over. Bake until deep golden, 20 to 25 minutes; prick again with fork halfway through baking. Transfer to wire rack to cool completely. Fill with pastry cream and top with berries as directed. Makes 10 servings.

White Russian Pie

An exquisite double coffee–flavored pie made with espresso and coffee liqueur.

Prep: 45 minutes plus cooling and chilling   Bake: 10 minutes
Chocolate Wafer–Crumb Crust (page 689)
1   envelope plus 1 teaspoon unflavored gelatin
¾   cup milk
1   cup espresso or very strong brewed coffee
1   cup sugar
3   tablespoons coffee-flavored liqueur
1½   cups heavy or whipping cream

1. Prepare crust as directed. Cool completely.

2. In 1-quart saucepan, evenly sprinkle gelatin over ¼ cup milk; let stand 2 minutes to soften gelatin slightly.

3. Stir espresso into gelatin mixture. Cook over medium-low heat, stirring, until gelatin has dissolved. Stir in sugar and cook, stirring, just until sugar has dissolved. Stir in remaining ½ cup milk and coffee liqueur.

4. Pour coffee mixture into medium bowl. Place bowl in larger bowl of ice water and stir frequently until mixture mounds when dropped from spoon, about 15 minutes. Remove from ice bath.

5. In small bowl, with mixer at medium speed, beat ¾ cup cream until stiff peaks form. With rubber spatula, fold whipped cream into coffee mixture until blended. Spoon coffee filling into cooled crust. Refrigerate until pie is well chilled and set, at least 3 hours or up to 24 hours.

6. Up to 2 hours before serving, beat remaining ¾ cup cream until stiff peaks form. Spoon whipped cream over pie. Makes 10 servings.

Each serving: About 336 calories, 3g protein, 35g carbohydrate, 20g total fat (12g saturated), 64mg cholesterol, 155mg sodium.

Strawberry Mousse Pie

We prefer a graham-cracker crust with this filling. Make this recipe when you have sweet tasty berries.

Prep: 1 hour plus cooling and chilling   Bake: 10 minutes

	Graham Cracker–Crumb Crust (page 689)
1	envelope plus 1 teaspoon unflavored gelatin
⅓	cup water
2	pints strawberries (about 6 cups), hulled, plus additional for garnish
¾	cup sugar
1	tablespoon fresh lemon juice
½	cup heavy or whipping cream

1. Prepare crust as directed. Cool completely.

2. In 1-quart saucepan, evenly sprinkle gelatin over water; let stand 2 minutes to soften gelatin slightly.

3. Meanwhile, in medium bowl, mash 2 pints strawberries, leaving some lumps. Stir in sugar and lemon juice.

4. Cook gelatin mixture over medium-low heat, stirring frequently until gelatin has completely dissolved. Stir gelatin mixture into strawberry mixture.

5. Place bowl with strawberry mixture in larger bowl of ice water and stir frequently until mixture mounds when dropped from spoon, 10 to 15 minutes. Remove bowl from ice bath.

6. In small bowl, with mixer at medium speed, beat cream until stiff peaks form. With rubber spatula, fold whipped cream into strawberry mixture until blended. Return bowl with strawberry mixture to ice bath; stir occasionally until mixture mounds when dropped from spoon, about 3 minutes longer.

7. Spoon strawberry filling into cooled crust. Refrigerate until pie is chilled and set, at least 3 hours or up to 24 hours. To serve, top with whole strawberries. Makes 10 servings.

Each serving: About 230 calories, 2g protein, 32g carbohydrate, 11g total fat (6g saturated), 29mg cholesterol, 138mg sodium.

Chocolate Cream Angel Pie

This time-tested favorite is made with whipped chocolate cream nestled in a meringue crust. Heavenly!

Prep: 30 minutes plus cooling   Bake: 1 hour

3	large egg whites
¼	teaspoon cream of tartar
¼	teaspoon salt
2¼	cups confectioners' sugar
2½	teaspoons vanilla extract
½	cup unsweetened cocoa
1	teaspoon instant espresso-coffee powder
1	teaspoon hot water
2	tablespoons milk
2	cups heavy or whipping cream
	Chocolate Curls (page 681)

1. Preheat oven to 300°F. Line 9-inch pie plate with foil, extending foil over rim of plate. Press foil against pie plate; grease and flour.

2. In small bowl, with mixer at high speed, beat egg whites, cream of tartar, and salt until soft peaks form when beaters are lifted. Sprinkle in 1 cup confectioners' sugar, 2 tablespoons at a time, beating until sugar has dissolved. Add 1 teaspoon vanilla; continue beating until egg whites stand in stiff, glossy peaks when beaters are lifted.

3. With large spoon, spread meringue evenly over bottom and up side of pie plate, extending meringue ½ inch above rim of pie plate. Bake 1 hour. Turn off oven and let meringue remain in oven 1 hour to dry. Cool shell completely in pie plate on wire rack. Lift shell from pie plate and peel off foil. Place shell on serving plate.

4. Meanwhile, prepare filling: Sift cocoa with remaining 1¼ cups confectioners' sugar. In cup, dissolve espresso powder in hot water; stir in milk. In large bowl, with mixer at medium speed, beat cream, espresso, and remaining 1½ teaspoons vanilla until soft peaks form. Reduce speed to low; gradually beat in cocoa mixture until thoroughly blended and stiff peaks form.

5. With rubber spatula, spread chocolate cream into cooled meringue shell. If not serving right away, cover pie and refrigerate until ready to serve, up to 4 hours. Garnish with chocolate curls. Makes 10 servings.

Each serving: About 289 calories, 3g protein, 31g carbohydrate, 18g total fat (11g saturated), 66mg cholesterol, 95mg sodium.

Frozen Peanut Butter Pie

Serve this treat with a spoonful of Hot Fudge Sauce.

Prep: 30 minutes plus cooling and freezing	*Bake: 10 minutes*

Chocolate Wafer–Crumb Crust (page 689)
1 package (8 ounces) Neufchâtel, softened
1 cup creamy peanut butter
1 cup plus 2 tablespoons confectioners' sugar
2 tablespoons milk
2 teaspoons vanilla extract
1 cup heavy or whipping cream
¼ cup salted peanuts, chopped
Hot Fudge Sauce (page 561)

1. Prepare crust as directed. Cool completely.

2. In large bowl, with mixer at medium speed, beat Neufchâtel, peanut butter, and 1 cup confectioners' sugar until blended. Add milk and vanilla; beat until smooth.

3. In small bowl, with clean beaters and mixer at medium speed, beat cream and remaining 2 tablespoons confectioners' sugar until stiff peaks form.

4. With rubber spatula, gently fold whipped cream, half at a time, into peanut-butter mixture until blended. Spoon filling into cooled crust; sprinkle with peanuts. Cover pie with plastic wrap and freeze at least 6 hours or up to 24 hours.

5. Prepare Hot Fudge Sauce. Let pie stand 10 minutes at room temperature for easier slicing. Serve with hot fudge sauce. Makes 16 servings.

Each serving without Hot Fudge Sauce: About 298 calories, 8g protein, 19g carbohydrate, 22g total fat (9g saturated), 39mg cholesterol, 233mg sodium.

Cream Cheese and Fruit Tartlets

You'll need mini muffin pans to make these dainty tarts. Use a different combination of fresh fruits for each tartlet.

Prep: 45 minutes plus chilling and cooling	*Bake: 15 minutes*

Pastry for 9-Inch Tart (page 687)
1 container (8 ounces) soft cream cheese
3 tablespoons sugar
1 tablespoon milk
¾ teaspoon vanilla extract
  sliced, peeled kiwifruit; halved strawberries;
  drained canned mandarin-orange sections;
  and halved small seedless red and green grapes
mint leaves

1. Prepare pastry dough as directed through chilling.

2. Preheat oven to 425°F. Divide dough in half. Roll each half into 12-inch rope; cut each rope into twelve 1-inch pieces. Press piece of dough evenly onto bottom and up side of each of 24 mini muffin-pan cups (1¾" by 1"). With toothpick, prick each shell all over. Bake until golden, about 15 minutes. Cool in pans on wire rack 5 minutes. Remove tart shells from pans; cool completely on rack.

3. Meanwhile, in small bowl, with whisk, beat cream cheese, sugar, milk, and vanilla until blended. Spoon filling into shells. Top each tartlet with some kiwifruit, strawberries, orange sections, or grapes. Refrigerate up to 1 hour. Garnish with mint leaves. Makes 24 tartlets.

Each tartlet without fruit: About 90 calories, 1g protein, 6g carbohydrate, 7g total fat (4g saturated), 18mg cholesterol, 89mg sodium.

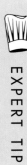

When I'm making dough for a pie or tart, I often double the recipe so I can also prepare a crust for the freezer. I roll out the extra dough, fit it into a pie plate or tart pan, and slide it into the freezer. When it's hard, I wrap it airtight in foil, pressing the foil against the contours of the crust, then wrap the whole set-up in a heavy-duty ziptight plastic bag, pressing out all the air. The crust can be frozen for up to a month and baked straight from the freezer—no defrosting necessary.

DORIE GREENSPAN
COOKBOOK AUTHOR

EXPERT TIP

21

COOKIES AND CONFECTIONS

Cookies are simply one of the most delicious and popular treats that you can make—and one of the simplest. Here is our collection of favorite recipes chosen from the thousands of cookies we've baked over the years, and some tips to help guarantee your baking success. And to satisfy your sweet tooth, you'll also find chocolate candies and other treats.

TYPES OF COOKIES

Bar cookies couldn't be easier. Mix up some dough, spread in a pan, then bake, cool, and cut.

Drop cookies are made by dropping spoonfuls of soft dough onto cookie sheets.

Molded cookies are made from a stiff dough that is formed by hand into balls, logs, pretzels or similar shapes, or baked in individual molds.

Pressed cookies are made from a moderately stiff dough that is squeezed through a cookie press or pastry bag to create a specific shape.

Refrigerator cookies (also called icebox cookies) begin with a chilled stiff dough that is sliced and baked.

Classic Sugar Cookies

Rolled cookies are made from a stiff dough that is rolled out and then cut into shapes, usually with cookie cutters.

COOKIE SHEET SAVVY

Good-quality cookie sheets are one of the secrets to perfect cookies. Heavy-gauge metal cookie sheets that have a dull finish turn out the most evenly browned cookies; aluminum is ideal. Double-thick insulated cookie sheets discourage overbaking and are a good investment. Dark cookie sheets can overbrown the bottoms of cookies. If your cookie sheets are old and discolored, line them with foil. Better still, purchase new ones.

The air in your oven should circulate freely around the cookie sheet(s). The sheet should be at least 2 inches smaller in length and width than your oven. Cookie sheets should be rimless (or have only one or two turned-up edges) to allow for the best air circulation.

Grease cookie sheets only when a recipe directs you to. Some cookies have a high fat content, so greasing isn't necessary. Vegetable shortening is best for greasing cookie sheets because butter sometimes browns as it melts in the oven. Nonstick cookie sheets and silcone nonstick baking liners are good alternatives to greasing and flouring.

For even spreading when greasing is required, use a crumpled piece of paper towel. To flour a cookie sheet, sprinkle the greased sheet evenly with a little flour, then tap off the excess. For easy cleanup, line cookie sheets with foil (dull side up).

Never place cookie dough on a hot cookie sheet; always let cookie sheets cool between batches. A hot cookie sheet will melt the dough before it has a chance to set. If the recipe calls for greased sheets, regrease for each batch.

BAKING SUCCESS

- While butter and margarine are interchangeable in some cookie recipes, for the best flavor and texture, use butter.
- If you prefer margarine, make sure it contains 80 percent fat. Spreads (diet, whipped, liquid, or soft) have a high water content, which results in tough cookies that lack flavor.
- For the tenderest cookies, once the flour has been added, mix the dough just until blended.
- Use a measuring spoon to scoop up equal portions of dough to make consistently shaped cookies that will bake in the same amount of time.
- For drop cookies, place spoonfuls of dough 2 inches apart unless the recipe directs otherwise.
- Dust the work surface lightly and evenly with flour before rolling out dough. Rub the rolling pin well with flour to keep it from sticking to the dough, or lightly dust the top of the dough with flour.
- When rolling out chilled dough, roll out one portion at a time; keep the remaining dough covered in the refrigerator.
- If a chilled dough cracks when rolled, let it stand at room temperature to soften slightly, then try again.
- For evenly baked cookies, bake one sheet of cookies at a time in the center of the oven. If you want to bake two sheets at a time, position the racks in the upper and lower thirds of the oven. Halfway through baking, rotate the cookie sheets between the upper and lower oven racks (unless directed otherwise) and rotate them front to back.
- Bake cookies for the minimum suggested baking time, then check for doneness. If not done, watch them carefully for the remainder of the time to avoid overbaking.
- Unless a recipe directs otherwise, cool cookies briefly on the cookie sheet to firm slightly, then transfer to wire racks to cool completely: Hot cookies are too soft to be moved immediately to racks. Cool bar cookies completely in the pan before cutting.

STORING AND SHIPPING COOKIES

Store soft and crisp cookies in separate containers with tight-fitting covers. If stored together, the crisp cookies could soften and the soft cookies could firm up. Crisp cookies that soften can be recrisped in a 300°F oven for three to five minutes. Soft cookies can be kept soft by adding a piece of apple or bread to the container; change it every other day or so. (This technique also works for soft cookies that have hardened.) Store bar cookies in the pan they were baked in, tightly covered with foil or plastic wrap.

To freeze baked cookies, thoroughly cool them first. Place in sturdy airtight containers, cushioned with crumpled waxed paper, if necessary. If the cookies have been decorated, freeze them until hard in a single layer on a cookie sheet, then pack for storage, separating the layers with waxed paper. To thaw, unwrap the cookies and let them stand for about ten minutes at room temperature.

To freeze unbaked cookie dough, wrap tightly in heavy-duty foil and store in a container. For refrigerator cookies, wrap the logs of dough in heavy-duty foil. Freeze for up to six months; thaw in the refrigerator. Remember to label each package with the contents and date.

Avoid mailing brittle cookies; chewy, soft drop, or bar cookies are the best choices. Line a sturdy cardboard box or tin with waxed paper or bubble wrap. Wrap the cookies individually or in pairs, back to back, with plastic wrap. Cushion each layer with crumpled newspaper. Fill any empty spaces with crumpled paper or bubble wrap, and be sure to mark the wrapped package "fragile."

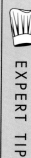

I wrap most of the cookies I make in clear cellophane. You could also use waxed paper but not plastic wrap (it's too hard to handle). If they are bar cookies, wrap them individually. But if they are round, wrap them together, bottoms touching.

MAIDA HEATTER

COOKBOOK AUTHOR

EXPERT TIP

Good Housekeeping's Fudgy Brownies

Ultrarich with lots of deep dark chocolate flavor, these brownies are fabulous with or without the pecan topping. For a moist, fudgy texture, do not overbake.

Prep: 10 minutes   Bake: 30 minutes

1¼	cups all-purpose flour
½	teaspoon salt
¾	cup butter or margarine (1½ sticks)
4	squares (4 ounces) unsweetened chocolate, chopped
4	squares (4 ounces) semisweet chocolate, chopped
2	cups sugar
1	tablespoon vanilla extract
5	large eggs, beaten

Praline-Iced Brownies

1. Preheat oven to 350°F. Grease 13" by 9" baking pan. In small bowl, combine flour and salt.

2. In heavy 4-quart saucepan, melt butter and unsweetened and semisweet chocolates over low heat, stirring frequently, until smooth. Remove from heat. With wooden spoon, stir in sugar and vanilla. Add eggs; stir until well mixed. Stir flour mixture into chocolate mixture just until blended. Spread batter evenly in prepared pan.

3. Bake until toothpick inserted 1 inch from edge comes out clean, about 30 minutes. Cool completely in pan on wire rack. When cool, cut lengthwise into 4 strips, then cut each strip crosswise into 6 pieces. Makes 24 brownies.

Each brownie: About 206 calories, 3g protein, 26g carbohydrate, 11g total fat (6g saturated), 60mg cholesterol, 121mg sodium.

Praline-Iced Brownies

Prepare brownies as directed; cool. In 2-quart saucepan, heat **5 tablespoons butter or margarine** and **⅓ cup packed brown sugar** over medium-low heat until mixture has melted and bubbles, about 5 minutes. Remove from heat. With wire whisk, beat in **3 tablespoons bourbon or 1 tablespoon vanilla extract plus 2 tablespoons water;** stir in **2 cups confectioners' sugar** until smooth. With small metal spatula, spread topping over room-temperature brownies; sprinkle **½ cup pecans,** toasted and coarsely chopped, over topping. Cut brownies lengthwise into 8 strips, then cut each strip crosswise into 8 pieces. Makes 64 brownies.

Each brownie: About 297 calories, 3g protein, 39g carbohydrate, 15g total fat (8g saturated), 66mg cholesterol, 147mg sodium.

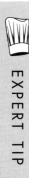

When it comes to baking cookies, the indicated time can only be used as a rough guide: Ovens vary. You must check before the time is up. You must be prepared for the cookies to bake either in more or less time than a recipe says. Watch the cookies. Check on them. Test them. Don't let them burn. And don't take them out before they are ready.

MAIDA HEATTER

COOKBOOK AUTHOR

EXPERT TIP

Almond Shortbread Brownies

These two-tone brownies feature a trufflelike layer nestled on a delicious almond shortbread crust.

Prep: 1 hour plus cooling   Bake: 40 to 50 minutes

1	cup whole natural almonds (4 ounces), toasted
¾	cup confectioners' sugar
1¾	cups butter or margarine (3½ sticks), softened
2¾	cups all-purpose flour
¼	teaspoon almond extract
5	squares (5 ounces) unsweetened chocolate, chopped
3	large eggs
2	cups granulated sugar
¼	teaspoon salt
2	teaspoons vanilla extract
6	squares (6 ounces) semisweet chocolate, chopped
⅓	cup heavy or whipping cream
½	cup sliced almonds, toasted

1. Preheat oven to 350°F. Line 15½" by 10½" jelly-roll pan with foil, extending foil over rim.

2. In blender or in food processor with knife blade attached, process whole almonds with ¼ cup confectioners' sugar until nuts are finely ground.

3. In large bowl, with mixer at low speed, beat ¾ cup butter and remaining ½ cup confectioners' sugar until blended. Increase speed to high and beat mixture until light and fluffy. Reduce speed to low; beat in ground-almond mixture, 1¾ cups flour, and almond extract just until blended (dough will be stiff).

4. With hands, pat dough onto bottom of prepared pan. Bake until golden, 20 to 25 minutes. Cool in pan on wire rack.

5. Meanwhile, in heavy 2-quart saucepan, melt unsweetened chocolate and remaining 1 cup butter over low heat, stirring frequently, until smooth. Remove from heat. Cool slightly, about 10 minutes.

6. In large bowl, with mixer at high speed, beat eggs, granulated sugar, salt, and 1 teaspoon vanilla until ribbon forms when beaters are lifted, 5 to 10 minutes. Beat in cooled chocolate mixture until blended. With wooden spoon, stir in remaining 1 cup flour. Pour chocolate-flour mixture over

shortbread crust. Bake until toothpick inserted 1 inch from edge comes out almost clean, 20 to 25 minutes. Cool in pan on wire rack.

7. In heavy 2-quart saucepan, melt semisweet chocolate with cream over low heat, stirring frequently until smooth. Remove from heat; stir in remaining 1 teaspoon vanilla. Lift foil with brownie out of pan; peel foil away from sides. With small metal spatula, spread chocolate glaze over brownie. Sprinkle almond slices over top. Let stand at room temperature until set, about 2 hours, or refrigerate 30 minutes.

8. When set, cut lengthwise into 6 strips, then cut each strip crosswise into 12 pieces. Makes 72 brownies.

Each brownie: About 127 calories, 2g protein, 13g carbohydrate, 8g total fat (4g saturated), 22mg cholesterol, 57mg sodium.

Almond Cheesecake Brownies

Sinfully rich brownies are marbled with a ribbon of cheesecake.

Prep: 30 minutes   Bake: 35 minutes

1¼	cups all-purpose flour
¾	teaspoon baking powder
½	teaspoon salt
½	cup butter or margarine (1 stick)
4	squares (4 ounces) unsweetened chocolate, chopped
4	squares (4 ounces) semisweet chocolate, chopped
2	cups sugar
5	large eggs
2½	teaspoons vanilla extract
1½	packages (8 ounces each) cold cream cheese
¾	teaspoon almond extract

1. Preheat oven to 350°F. Grease 13" by 9" baking pan. In small bowl, combine flour, baking powder, and salt.

2. In heavy 4-quart saucepan, melt butter and unsweetened and semisweet chocolates over low heat, stirring, until smooth. Remove from heat. With wooden spoon, beat in 1½ cups sugar. Add 4 eggs and 2 teaspoons vanilla; beat until well blended. Stir in flour mixture just until blended.

3. In small bowl, with mixer at medium speed, beat cream cheese until smooth; gradually beat in remaining ½ cup sugar. Beat in remaining 1 egg, almond extract, and remaining ½ teaspoon vanilla just until blended.

4. Spread 1½ cups chocolate batter in prepared pan. Spoon cream-cheese mixture in 6 large dollops on top of chocolate mixture (cream-cheese mixture will cover most of chocolate batter). Spoon remaining chocolate batter over and between cream cheese in 6 large dollops. With tip of knife, cut and twist through mixtures to create marbled effect.

5. Bake until toothpick inserted in center comes out almost clean, 35 to 40 minutes. Cool completely in pan on wire rack.

6. When cool, cut lengthwise into 4 strips, then cut each strip crosswise into 6 pieces. Makes 24 brownies.

Each brownie: About 238 calories, 4g protein, 26g carbohydrate, 14g total fat (8g saturated), 70mg cholesterol, 159mg sodium.

Cocoa Brownies

Whip up these easy saucepan brownies on the spur of the moment with pantry staples.

Prep: 10 minutes	Bake: 25 minutes
½	cup all-purpose flour
½	cup unsweetened cocoa
¼	teaspoon baking powder
¼	teaspoon salt
½	cup butter or margarine (1 stick)
1	cup sugar
2	large eggs
1	teaspoon vanilla extract
1	cup walnuts (4 ounces), coarsely chopped (optional)

1. Preheat oven to 350°F. Grease 9-inch square baking pan. In bowl, combine flour, cocoa, baking powder, and salt.

2. In 3-quart saucepan, melt butter over low heat. Remove from heat and stir in sugar. Stir in eggs, one at a time, until well blended; add vanilla. Stir flour mixture into sugar mixture until blended. Stir in nuts, if using. Spread batter evenly in prepared pan.

3. Bake until toothpick inserted 2 inches from center comes out almost clean, about 25 minutes. Cool completely in pan on wire rack.

4. When cool, cut into 4 strips, then cut each strip crosswise into 4 pieces. Makes 16 brownies.

Each brownie: About 132 calories, 2g protein, 17g carbohydrate, 7g total fat (4g saturated), 42mg cholesterol, 110mg sodium.

Fudgy Lowfat Brownies

Moist, chocolaty, and lowfat. Need we say more? Serve with cold skim milk for a healthful and delicious treat.

Prep: 15 minutes	Bake: 18 minutes
1	teaspoon instant espresso-coffee powder
1	teaspoon hot water
¾	cup all-purpose flour
½	cup unsweetened cocoa
½	teaspoon baking powder
¼	teaspoon salt
3	tablespoons butter or margarine
¾	cup sugar
2	large egg whites
¼	cup dark corn syrup
1	teaspoon vanilla extract

1. Preheat oven to 350°F. Grease 8-inch square baking pan. In cup, dissolve espresso powder in hot water; set aside. In large bowl, combine flour, cocoa, baking powder, and salt.

2. In 2-quart saucepan, melt butter over low heat. Remove from heat. With wooden spoon, stir in sugar, egg whites, corn syrup, espresso, and vanilla until blended. Stir sugar mixture into flour mixture just until blended (do not overmix). Pour batter into prepared pan.

3. Bake until toothpick inserted in center comes out almost clean, 18 to 22 minutes. Cool brownies completely in pan on wire rack.

4. When cool, cut brownies into 4 strips, then cut each strip crosswise into 4 pieces. If brownies are difficult to cut, use knife dipped in hot water and dried; repeat as necessary. Makes 16 brownies.

♡ Each brownie: About 103 calories, 2g protein, 19g carbohydrate, 3g total fat (2g saturated), 6mg cholesterol, 88mg sodium.

Blondies

For pecan lovers—these scrumptious bars are sometimes known as butterscotch brownies.

Prep: 10 minutes   Bake: 30 minutes

1	cup all-purpose flour
2	teaspoons baking powder
1	teaspoon salt
6	tablespoons butter or margarine
1¾	cups packed light brown sugar
2	teaspoons vanilla extract
2	large eggs
1½	cups pecans (6 ounces), coarsely chopped

1. Preheat oven to 350°F. Grease 13" by 9" baking pan. In small bowl, combine flour, baking powder, and salt.

2. In 3-quart saucepan, melt butter over low heat. Remove from heat. With wooden spoon, stir in brown sugar and vanilla; add eggs, stirring until well blended. Stir flour mixture into sugar mixture just until blended. Stir in pecans. Spread batter evenly in prepared pan.

3. Bake until toothpick inserted 2 inches from edge of pan comes out clean, about 30 minutes. Do not overbake; blondies will firm as they cool. Cool completely in pan on wire rack.

4. When cool, cut lengthwise into 4 strips, then cut each strip crosswise into 6 pieces. Makes 24 blondies.

Each blondie: About 159 calories, 2g protein, 21g carbohydrate, 8g total fat (2g saturated), 25mg cholesterol, 179mg sodium.

Coconut Blondies

Prepare as directed, stirring in ¾ **cup flaked sweetened coconut** with pecans.

Chocolate Chip Blondies

Prepare as directed through Step 2. Let batter stand 15 minutes; stir in **1 package (6 ounces) semisweet chocolate chips.** Proceed as directed.

Chocolate Swirl Peanut Butter Blondies

Irresistible to kids and grown-ups alike.

Prep: 20 minutes   Bake: 25 minutes

2½	cups all-purpose flour
1½	teaspoons baking powder
½	teaspoon salt
3	squares (3 ounces) semisweet chocolate, chopped
1	square (1 ounce) unsweetened chocolate, chopped
1	cup creamy peanut butter
½	cup butter or margarine (1 stick), softened
1¾	cups packed light brown sugar
3	large eggs
2	teaspoons vanilla extract
1	package (6 ounces) semisweet chocolate chips (1 cup)

1. Preheat oven to 350°F. In medium bowl, combine flour, baking powder, and salt. In heavy 1-quart saucepan, melt semisweet and unsweetened chocolates, stirring frequently, until smooth.

2. In large bowl, with mixer at medium speed, beat peanut butter, butter, and brown sugar until light and fluffy, about 2 minutes. Add eggs and vanilla; beat until blended. Reduce speed to low; beat in flour mixture just until blended (dough will be stiff).

3. Place one-third of dough (about 1¾ cups) in separate large bowl. Stir in melted chocolate until blended; stir in ¾ cup chocolate chips.

4. With hand, pat half of remaining plain peanut butter dough onto bottom of ungreased 13" by 9" baking pan to form thin layer. In random pattern, drop chocolate dough and remaining plain peanut butter dough on top of peanut butter layer; lightly pat. Sprinkle remaining chocolate chips on top.

5. Bake until toothpick inserted in center comes out clean, 25 to 30 minutes. Cool completely in pan on wire rack.

6. When cool, cut lengthwise into 4 strips, then cut each strip crosswise into 6 pieces. Makes 24 blondies.

Each blondie: About 273 calories, 6g protein, 34g carbohydrate, 14g total fat (6g saturated), 37mg cholesterol, 184mg sodium.

Lowfat Butterscotch Blondies

These chewy treats are one of our test kitchen's favorites.

Prep: 15 minutes   Bake: 35 minutes

1	cup all-purpose flour
½	teaspoon baking powder
¼	teaspoon salt
3	tablespoons butter or margarine
¾	cup packed dark brown sugar
2	large egg whites
⅓	cup dark corn syrup
2	teaspoons vanilla extract
2	tablespoons finely chopped pecans

1. Preheat oven to 350°F. Grease 8-inch square baking pan. In bowl, combine flour, baking powder, and salt.

2. In large bowl, with mixer at medium speed, beat butter and brown sugar until well blended, about 2 minutes. Reduce speed to low; beat in egg whites, corn syrup, and vanilla until smooth. Beat in flour mixture just until combined. Spread batter evenly in prepared pan. Sprinkle with pecans.

3. Bake until toothpick inserted in center comes out clean and edges are lightly browned, 35 to 40 minutes. Cool completely in pan on wire rack.

4. When cool, cut into 4 strips, then cut each strip crosswise into 4 pieces. Makes 16 blondies.

Each blondie: About 117 calories, 1g protein, 21g carbohydrate, 3g total fat (1g saturated), 6mg cholesterol, 94mg sodium.

Walnut Shortbread

Here's a shortbread with a delicate nutty flavor.

Prep: 20 minutes   Bake: 25 minutes

½	cup walnuts, toasted
1½	cups all-purpose flour
½	cup sugar
½	cup butter or margarine (1 stick), softened

1. Preheat oven to 325°F. In food processor with knife blade attached, process walnuts with ½ cup flour until nuts are finely ground.

2. In medium bowl, combine remaining 1 cup flour, sugar, and walnut mixture until blended.

3. With fingertips, blend butter into walnut mixture until well combined and crumbly. With hand, press dough onto bottom of ungreased 9-inch square baking pan.

4. Bake until light golden, 25 to 30 minutes. While still warm, cut into 4 strips, then cut each strip crosswise into 6 pieces. Cool completely in pan on wire rack.

5. When cool, with small metal spatula, carefully remove cookies from pan. Makes 24 cookies.

Each cookie: About 94 calories, 1g protein, 11g carbohydrate, 5g total fat (3g saturated), 10mg cholesterol, 39mg sodium.

Scottish Shortbread

The combination of cake flour and all-purpose flour makes a tender melt-in-your-mouth shortbread.

Prep: 20 minutes   Bake: 40 minutes

1½	cups cake flour (not self-rising)
1½	cups all-purpose flour
½	cup sugar
¼	teaspoon salt
1½	cups butter (3 sticks), cut into pieces and softened

1. Preheat oven to 325°F. In large bowl, combine cake and all-purpose flours, sugar, and salt. Knead butter into flour mixture until well blended and mixture holds together. (Or, in food processor with knife blade attached, pulse cake and all-purpose flours and salt to blend. Add butter and pulse until mixture resembles coarse crumbs.)

2. Divide dough in half; with hand, pat onto bottom of two 8-inch round cake pans. With fork, prick dough all over to make attractive pattern.

3. Bake until golden, about 40 minutes. Remove from oven; immediately run knife around edges of pans to loosen shortbread, then cut each shortbread round into 16 wedges. Cool completely in pans on wire racks.

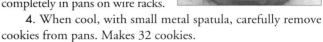

4. When cool, with small metal spatula, carefully remove cookies from pans. Makes 32 cookies.

Each cookie: About 128 calories, 1g protein, 12g carbohydrate, 9g total fat (5g saturated), 23mg cholesterol, 106mg sodium.

Mississippi Mud Bars

Dense as mud, rich as a millionaire, and they freeze well. Don't tell anyone, but they taste great frozen.

Prep: 20 minutes plus cooling   Bake: 35 minutes

Mud Cake

¾	cup butter or margarine (1½ sticks)
1¾	cups granulated sugar
¾	cup unsweetened cocoa
4	large eggs
2	teaspoons vanilla extract
½	teaspoon salt
1½	cups all-purpose flour
½	cup pecans, chopped
½	cup flaked sweetened coconut
3	cups mini marshmallows

Fudge Topping

5	tablespoons butter or margarine
1	square (1 ounce) unsweetened chocolate, chopped
⅓	cup unsweetened cocoa
⅛	teaspoon salt
¼	cup evaporated milk (not sweetened condensed milk) or heavy or whipping cream
1	teaspoon vanilla extract
1	cup confectioners' sugar
½	cup pecans, coarsely broken
¼	cup flaked sweetened coconut

1. Preheat oven to 350°F. Grease and flour 13" by 9" baking pan.

2. Prepare mud cake: In 3-quart saucepan, melt butter over low heat. With wire whisk, stir in granulated sugar and cocoa. Remove from heat. Beat in eggs, one at a time. Beat in

Mississippi Mud Bars

vanilla and salt until well blended. With wooden spoon, stir in flour just until blended; stir in pecans and coconut. Spread batter in prepared pan (batter will be thick).

3. Bake 25 minutes. Remove from oven. Sprinkle marshmallows in even layer on top of cake. Return to oven and bake until marshmallows are puffed and golden, about 10 minutes longer. Cool completely in pan on wire rack.

4. When cake is cool, prepare fudge topping: In heavy 2-quart saucepan, melt butter and chocolate over low heat, stirring frequently, until smooth. With wire whisk, stir in cocoa and salt until smooth. Stir in evaporated milk and vanilla (mixture will be thick); beat in confectioners' sugar until smooth and blended. Pour hot topping over cake.

5. Cool fudge-topped cake 20 minutes; sprinkle pecans and coconut over top. Serve at room temperature or chilled. To store, leave cake in pan and wrap. To serve, cut lengthwise into 4 strips, then cut each strip crosswise into 8 pieces. Makes 32 bars.

Each bar: About 204 calories, 3g protein, 26g carbohydrate, 11g total fat (5g saturated), 44mg cholesterol, 125mg sodium.

LINING PAN WITH FOIL

Invert the baking pan so it is bottom side up. Mold a length of foil, shiny side facing out, over the pan, pressing the foil firmly to set the shape. Lift up the foil.

Turn the pan right side up. Lower the foil "pan" into the baking pan; smooth it to create a tight fit.

Lemon Bars

A tangy-sweet treat that has been an American favorite for years.

Prep: 15 minutes   Bake: 30 minutes

1½	cups plus 3 tablespoons all-purpose flour
½	cup plus 1 tablespoon confectioners' sugar
¾	cup butter or margarine (1½ sticks), cut into pieces
2	large lemons
3	large eggs
1	cup granulated sugar
½	teaspoon baking powder
½	teaspoon salt

1. Preheat oven to 350°F. Line 13" by 9" baking pan with foil, extending foil over rim; lightly grease foil.

2. In medium bowl, combine 1½ cups flour and ½ cup confectioners' sugar. With pastry blender or two knives used scissor-fashion, cut in butter until mixture resembles coarse crumbs. Transfer crumb mixture to prepared pan. With floured hand, pat firmly onto bottom of pan.

3. Bake until lightly browned, 15 to 17 minutes.

4. Meanwhile, from lemons, grate 1 teaspoon peel and squeeze ⅓ cup juice. In large bowl, with mixer at high speed, beat eggs until thick and lemon-colored, about 3 minutes. Reduce speed to low. Add granulated sugar, remaining 3 tablespoons flour, baking powder, salt, and lemon peel and juice; beat, occasionally scraping bowl with rubber spatula, until blended. Pour lemon filling over warm crust.

5. Bake until filling is just set and golden around edges, about 15 minutes. Transfer pan to wire rack. Dust remaining 1 tablespoon confectioners' sugar over warm filling. Cool completely in pan on wire rack.

6. When cool, cut lengthwise into 3 strips, then cut each strip crosswise into 12 pieces. Makes 36 bars.

Each bar: About 93 calories, 1g protein, 12g carbohydrate, 4g total fat (3g saturated), 28mg cholesterol, 83mg sodium.

Raisin Spice Bars

You don't need a mixer to make these toothsome cookies, which are reminiscent of the New England favorite, hermits.

Prep: 10 minutes   Bake: 18 minutes

2	cups all-purpose flour
2/3	cup packed brown sugar
2	teaspoons ground cinnamon
1½	teaspoons ground ginger
½	teaspoon baking soda
½	teaspoon salt
2	large eggs
2/3	cup light (mild) molasses
6	tablespoons butter or margarine, melted
2	teaspoons vanilla extract
¾	cup dark seedless raisins

1. Preheat oven to 375°F. Grease 13" by 9" baking pan.

2. In large bowl, with wooden spoon, stir flour, brown sugar, cinnamon, ginger, baking soda, and salt until combined. Stir in eggs, molasses, butter, and vanilla just until blended. Stir in raisins. Spread batter evenly in prepared pan.

3. Bake until golden around edges, 18 to 22 minutes. Cool completely in pan on wire rack.

4. When cool, cut lengthwise into 6 strips, then cut each strip crosswise into 4 pieces. Makes 24 bars.

♥ Each bar: About 135 calories, 2g protein, 24g carbohydrate, 4g total fat (2g saturated), 25mg cholesterol, 115mg sodium.

Date and Nut Squares

A chewy, wholesome bar that is extremely easy to make and requires very little cleanup.

Prep: 15 minutes   Bake: 30 to 35 minutes

½	cup butter or margarine (1 stick)
1	cup packed light brown sugar
1¼	cups all-purpose flour
1	teaspoon baking soda
1	cup pecans (4 ounces), chopped
1	cup pitted dates, chopped
1	large egg

1. Preheat oven to 350°F. Evenly grease 9-inch square baking pan.

2. In 3-quart saucepan, melt butter and brown sugar over medium-low heat, stirring occasionally until smooth. Remove from heat. With wooden spoon, beat in flour, baking soda, pecans, dates, and egg until well blended. Spread batter evenly in prepared pan.

3. Bake until toothpick inserted in center comes out clean, 30 to 35 minutes. Cool completely in pan on wire rack.

4. When cool, cut into 4 strips, then cut each strip crosswise into 4 pieces. Makes 16 squares.

Each square: About 221 calories, 2g protein, 30g carbohydrate, 11g total fat (4g saturated), 29mg cholesterol, 147mg sodium.

Honey Granola Breakfast Bars

Instead of eating overly sweet and high-fat store-bought bars, make your own. These are easy enough to mix in one bowl.

Prep: 15 minutes   Bake: 30 to 35 minutes

2	cups old-fashioned oats, uncooked
1	cup all-purpose flour
¾	cup packed light brown sugar
¾	cup dark seedless raisins
½	cup toasted wheat germ
¾	teaspoon ground cinnamon
¾	teaspoon salt
½	cup vegetable oil
½	cup honey
1	large egg
2	teaspoons vanilla extract

1. Preheat oven to 350°F. Grease 13" by 9" baking pan.

2. In large bowl, with wooden spoon, combine oats, flour, brown sugar, raisins, wheat germ, cinnamon, and salt until blended. Stir in oil, honey, egg, and vanilla until well combined. With wet hand, pat oat mixture into prepared pan.

3. Bake until light golden around edges, 30 to 35 minutes. Cool completely in pan on wire rack.

4. When cool, cut lengthwise into 4 strips, then cut each strip crosswise into 4 pieces. Makes 16 bars.

Each bar: About 242 calories, 4g protein, 39g carbohydrate, 9g total fat (1g saturated), 13mg cholesterol, 119mg sodium.

Raspberry-Walnut Streusel Bars

An easy and delicious treat: Raspberry jam is sandwiched between a buttery cookie bottom and a crumbly streusel top.

Prep: 30 minutes	Bake: 45 minutes
¾	cup butter or margarine (1½ sticks), softened
1	cup sugar
½	teaspoon freshly grated lemon peel
½	teaspoon ground cinnamon
2	large egg yolks
1	teaspoon vanilla extract
2	cups all-purpose flour
¼	teaspoon salt
1	cup walnuts (4 ounces), toasted and chopped
½	cup seedless raspberry jam

1. Preheat oven to 350°F. Evenly grease 9-inch square baking pan.

2. In large bowl, with mixer at medium speed, beat butter, sugar, lemon peel, and cinnamon until light and fluffy, occasionally scraping bowl with rubber spatula. Reduce speed to low; beat in egg yolks and vanilla until well combined, frequently scraping bowl. Add flour and salt and beat just until blended, occasionally scraping bowl. With wooden spoon, stir in walnuts (mixture will be crumbly).

3. With lightly floured hand, pat half of dough evenly onto bottom of prepared pan. Spread raspberry jam over dough, leaving ¼-inch border all around. With lightly floured hands, pinch off 1-inch pieces of remaining dough and drop randomly on top of jam (it's okay if dough pieces touch); do not pat.

4. Bake until golden, 45 to 50 minutes. Cool completely in pan on wire rack.

5. When cool, cut into 4 strips, then cut each strip crosswise into 6 pieces. Makes 24 bars.

Each bar: About 176 calories, 2g protein, 22g carbohydrate, 10g total fat (4g saturated), 33mg cholesterol, 86mg sodium.

Peanut Butter Cookies

Great as an afternoon snack or special treat to sneak into a paper bag lunch. If you like, instead of crosshatching the cookies with a fork, lightly press mini nonmelting chocolate-covered candies into the top of each cookie before baking.

Prep: 15 minutes	Bake: 15 minutes per batch
1¼	cups all-purpose flour
1	teaspoon baking soda
¼	teaspoon salt
1	cup creamy peanut butter
½	cup butter or margarine (1 stick), softened
½	cup packed brown sugar
¼	cup granulated sugar
1	large egg
½	teaspoon vanilla extract

1. Preheat oven to 350°F. In small bowl, combine flour, baking soda, and salt.

2. In large bowl, with mixer at medium speed, beat peanut butter, butter, brown and granulated sugars, egg, and vanilla until combined, occasionally scraping bowl with rubber spatula. Reduce speed to low. Add flour mixture and beat just until blended.

3. Drop dough by heaping tablespoons, 2 inches apart, on two ungreased large cookie sheets. With fork, press crisscross pattern into top of each cookie. Bake until lightly browned, 15 to 20 minutes, rotating cookie sheets between upper and lower oven racks halfway through baking. With wide spatula, transfer cookies to wire racks to cool completely.

4. Repeat forming and baking with remaining dough. Makes about 36 cookies.

Each cookie: About 100 calories, 3g protein, 9g carbohydrate, 6g total fat (2g saturated), 13mg cholesterol, 114mg sodium.

Lowfat Oatmeal-Raisin Cookies

If you thought the words "delicious" and "lowfat" could never be used to describe the same cookie, think again. This one's chewy and sweet, yet it has only two grams of fat per cookie.

Prep: 15 minutes   Bake: 10 minutes per batch

2	cups all-purpose flour
1	teaspoon baking soda
½	teaspoon salt
½	cup light corn-oil spread (1 stick), 56% to 60% fat
¾	cup packed dark brown sugar
½	cup granulated sugar
2	large egg whites
1	large egg
2	teaspoons vanilla extract
1	cup quick-cooking oats, uncooked
½	cup dark seedless raisins

1. Preheat oven to 375°F. Grease two large cookie sheets. In medium bowl, combine flour, baking soda, and salt.

2. In large bowl, with mixer at low speed, beat corn-oil spread and brown and granulated sugars until well combined. Increase speed to high; beat until mixture is light and fluffy. Add egg whites, whole egg, and vanilla; beat until blended. With wooden spoon, stir in flour mixture, oats, and raisins until combined.

3. Drop dough by level tablespoons, 2 inches apart, on prepared cookie sheets. Bake until golden, 10 to 12 minutes, rotating cookie sheets between upper and lower oven racks halfway through baking. With wide spatula, transfer cookies to wire racks to cool completely.

4. Repeat with remaining dough. Makes about 48 cookies.

♥ Each cookie: About 67 calories, 1g protein, 12g carbohydrate, 2g total fat (0g saturated), 4mg cholesterol, 72mg sodium.

Grandmother's Oatmeal-Raisin Cookies

A classic cookie-jar favorite. For crisp cookies, bake until the tops are golden; for softer, chewier cookies, bake just until the edges are golden, about twelve minutes.

Prep: 15 minutes   Bake: 15 minutes per batch

¾	cup all-purpose flour
½	teaspoon baking soda
¼	teaspoon salt
½	cup butter or margarine (1 stick), softened
½	cup granulated sugar
⅓	cup packed brown sugar
1	large egg
2	teaspoons vanilla extract
1½	cups old-fashioned or quick-cooking oats, uncooked
¾	cup dark seedless raisins or chopped pitted prunes

1. Preheat oven to 350°F. In small bowl, combine flour, baking soda, and salt.

2. In large bowl, with mixer at medium speed, beat butter and granulated and brown sugars until light and fluffy. Beat in egg and vanilla until blended. Reduce speed to low; beat in flour mixture just until blended. With wooden spoon, stir in oats and raisins.

3. Drop dough by heaping tablespoons, 2 inches apart, on two ungreased large cookie sheets. Bake until golden, about 15 minutes, rotating cookie sheets between upper and lower oven racks halfway through baking. With wide spatula, transfer cookies to wire racks to cool completely.

4. Repeat with remaining dough. Makes about 24 cookies.

Each cookie: About 113 calories, 2g protein, 17g carbohydrate, 4g total fat (2g saturated), 19mg cholesterol, 94mg sodium.

Grandmother's Oatmeal-Raisin Cookies

Chocolate Wows

After one bite of these decadent cookies, you will understand why we call them "Wows."

Prep: 20 minutes   Bake: 15 minutes per batch

⅓	cup all-purpose flour
¼	cup unsweetened cocoa
1	teaspoon baking powder
¼	teaspoon salt
6	squares (6 ounces) semisweet chocolate, chopped
½	cup butter or margarine (1 stick)
2	large eggs
¾	cup sugar
1½	teaspoons vanilla extract
2	cups pecans (8 ounces), chopped
1	package (6 ounces) semisweet chocolate chips (1 cup)

1. Preheat oven to 325°F. Grease two large cookie sheets. In small bowl, combine flour, cocoa, baking powder, and salt.

2. In heavy 2-quart saucepan, melt chocolate and butter over low heat, stirring frequently, until smooth. Remove from heat and cool.

3. In large bowl, with mixer at medium speed, beat eggs and sugar until light and lemon colored, about 2 minutes, frequently scraping bowl with rubber spatula. Reduce speed to low. Add cooled chocolate mixture, flour mixture, and vanilla; beat just until blended. Increase speed to medium; beat 2 minutes. With wooden spoon, stir in pecans and chocolate chips.

4. Drop batter by rounded teaspoons, 2 inches apart, on prepared cookie sheets. With small metal spatula, spread batter into 2-inch rounds. Bake until tops are shiny and cracked, about 15 minutes, rotating cookie sheets between upper and lower oven racks halfway through baking. Cool 10 minutes on cookie sheet. With wide spatula, transfer cookies to wire racks to cool completely.

5. Repeat with remaining batter. Makes about 48 cookies.

Each cookie: About 102 calories, 1g protein, 9g carbohydrate, 7g total fat (3g saturated), 14mg cholesterol, 45mg sodium.

Chocolate Wows

Chocolate Chip Cookies

Who can say no to a chocolate chip cookie?

Prep: 15 minutes   Bake: 10 minutes per batch

1¼	cups all-purpose flour
½	teaspoon baking soda
½	teaspoon salt
½	cup butter or margarine (1 stick), softened
½	cup packed brown sugar
¼	cup granulated sugar
1	large egg
1	teaspoon vanilla extract
1	package (6 ounces) semisweet chocolate chips (1 cup)
½	cup walnuts, chopped (optional)

1. Preheat oven to 375°F. In small bowl, combine flour, baking soda, and salt.

2. In large bowl, with mixer at medium speed, beat butter and brown and granulated sugars until light and fluffy. Beat in egg and vanilla until well combined. Reduce speed to low; beat in flour mixture just until blended. With wooden spoon, stir in chocolate chips and walnuts, if using.

3. Drop dough by rounded tablespoons, 2 inches apart, on two ungreased cookie sheets. Bake until golden around edges, 10 to 12 minutes, rotating cookie sheets between upper and lower oven racks halfway through baking. With wide spatula, transfer cookies to wire racks to cool completely.

4. Repeat with remaining dough. Makes about 36 cookies.

Each cookie: About 80 calories, 1g protein, 11g carbohydrate, 4g total fat (2g saturated), 13mg cholesterol, 79mg sodium.

White Chocolate–Macadamia Cookies

Prepare as directed but substitute ¾ **cup white baking chips** for semisweet chocolate chips and **1 cup chopped macadamia nuts (4 ounces)** for walnuts.

Each cookie: About 110 calories, 1g protein, 11g carbohydrate, 7g total fat (3g saturated), 13mg cholesterol, 84mg sodium.

Pecan Lace Cookies

These perfect special-occasion cookies, are very delicate and elegant. If you like, they can be given a graceful shape by quickly molding them, while still warm, over a rolling pin. Store, layered between waxed paper, in a large shallow container. They're heavenly with ice cream or sorbet.

Prep: 20 minutes	Bake: 5 minutes per batch
¼	cup packed brown sugar
¼	cup light corn syrup
3	tablespoons butter, cut into pieces (do not use margarine)
½	cup pecans, finely chopped
6	tablespoons all-purpose flour
¼	teaspoon vanilla extract

1. Preheat oven to 375°F. Grease large cookie sheet.

2. In 2-quart saucepan, combine brown sugar, corn syrup, and butter; heat to simmering over medium heat, stirring, until butter has melted and mixture is smooth. Remove saucepan from heat. With wooden spoon, stir in pecans, flour, and vanilla.

3. Drop batter by level teaspoons, 3 inches apart, on prepared cookie sheet to make 6 to 8 cookies (depending on size of cookie sheet). Bake until lightly browned, 5 to 7 minutes. Cool on cookie sheet on wire rack about 1 minute to set slightly; with wide spatula, quickly transfer cookies to wire racks to cool completely.

4. Repeat with remaining batter. Makes about 36 cookies.

Each cookie: About 39 calories, 0g protein, 4g carbohydrate, 2g total fat (1g saturated), 3mg cholesterol, 13mg sodium.

Drop Sugar Cookies

Here's our recipe for a simple, old-fashioned cookie that will quickly disappear from your cookie jar.

Prep: 10 minutes	Bake: 10 minutes per batch
1⅓	cups all-purpose flour
¾	teaspoon baking powder
¼	teaspoon salt
½	cup butter or margarine (1 stick), softened
1	cup sugar
1	large egg
1	teaspoon vanilla extract

1. Preheat oven to 350°F. In small bowl, combine flour, baking powder, and salt.

2. In large bowl, with mixer at medium speed, beat butter and sugar until light and fluffy. Beat in egg and vanilla until blended. Reduce speed to low; beat in flour mixture just until combined, scraping bowl with rubber spatula.

3. Drop dough by heaping teaspoons, 2 inches apart, on two ungreased cookie sheets. Bake until browned around edges, 10 to 12 minutes, rotating cookie sheets between upper and lower oven racks halfway through baking. With wide spatula, transfer cookies to wire racks to cool completely.

4. Repeat with remaining dough. Makes about 42 cookies.

Each cookie: About 54 calories, 1g protein, 8g carbohydrate, 2g total fat (1g saturated), 11mg cholesterol, 46mg sodium.

Old-Fashioned Whoopie Pies

You may remember these from your childhood: soft, cakelike cookies sandwiched with fluffy marshmallow creme.

Prep: 30 minutes plus cooling   Bake: 12 minutes

2	cups all-purpose flour
1	cup sugar
½	cup unsweetened cocoa
1	teaspoon baking soda
¼	teaspoon salt
¾	cup milk
6	tablespoons butter or margarine, melted
1	large egg
1	teaspoon vanilla extract
	Marshmallow Creme Filling (below)

1. Preheat oven to 350°F. Grease two large cookie sheets.

2. In large bowl, with wooden spoon, mix flour, sugar, cocoa, baking soda, salt, milk, butter, egg, and vanilla until well blended.

3. Drop 12 heaping tablespoons batter, 2 inches apart, on each prepared cookie sheet. Bake until puffy and toothpick inserted in center comes out clean, 12 to 14 minutes, rotating cookie sheets between upper and lower oven racks halfway through baking. With wide spatula, transfer cookies to wire racks to cool completely.

4. When cool, prepare Marshmallow Creme Filling. Spread 1 rounded tablespoon filling on flat side of 12 cookies. Top with remaining cookies. Makes 12 whoopie pies.

Marshmallow Creme Filling

In large bowl, with mixer at medium speed, beat **6 tablespoons butter or margarine,** softened, until creamy. Reduce speed to low; gradually beat in **1 cup confectioners' sugar** until blended. Beat in **1 jar (7 to 7½ ounces) marshmallow creme (about 1½ cups)** and **1 teaspoon vanilla extract** until well combined.

Each whoopie pie: About 360 calories, 4g protein, 59g carbohydrate, 13g total fat (8g saturated), 51mg cholesterol, 292mg sodium.

Sour Cream Cookies

A hint of fresh lemon makes these special.

Prep: 15 minutes   Bake: 10 minutes per batch

1	cup all-purpose flour
¼	teaspoon baking soda
¼	teaspoon salt
6	tablespoons butter or margarine, softened
½	cup sugar
½	cup sour cream
1	teaspoon freshly grated lemon peel
½	teaspoon vanilla extract

1. Preheat oven to 350°F. Grease two cookie sheets. In small bowl, combine flour, baking soda, and salt.

2. In large bowl, with mixer at medium speed, beat butter until creamy. Gradually add sugar and beat until light and fluffy. Beat in sour cream, lemon peel, and vanilla. Reduce speed to low; beat in flour mixture just until blended.

3. Drop dough by rounded teaspoons, 1 inch apart, on prepared cookie sheets. Bake until set and golden around edges, 10 to 12 minutes, rotating cookie sheets between upper and lower oven racks halfway through baking. Cool 1 minute on cookie sheets; with wide spatula, transfer cookies to wire racks to cool completely.

4. Repeat with remaining dough. Makes about 36 cookies.

Each cookie: About 49 calories, 0g protein, 6g carbohydrate, 3g total fat (2g saturated), 7mg cholesterol, 46mg sodium.

Coconut Cookies

Every bite of these homey treats delivers great coconut flavor.

Prep: 20 minutes   Bake: 15 minutes per batch

2¾	cups all-purpose flour
1	teaspoon baking powder
½	teaspoon salt
1	cup butter or margarine (2 sticks), softened
1	cup sugar
1	large egg
2	tablespoons milk
1	teaspoon vanilla extract
1½	cups flaked sweetened coconut

1. Preheat oven to 325°F. In medium bowl, combine flour, baking powder, and salt.

2. In large bowl, with mixer at medium speed, beat butter and sugar until light and fluffy. Beat in egg, milk, and vanilla. Reduce speed to low; beat in flour mixture just until blended. With wooden spoon, stir in coconut (dough will be crumbly). With hands, press dough together.

3. Drop dough by rounded teaspoons, 2 inches apart, on two ungreased cookie sheets. With fork, make crosshatch pattern in each cookie, flattening to ¼-inch thickness. Bake until lightly browned around edges, 15 to 17 minutes, rotating cookie sheets between upper and lower oven racks halfway through baking. With wide spatula, transfer cookies to wire racks to cool completely.

4. Repeat shaping and baking with remaining dough. Makes about 72 cookies.

Each cookie: About 45 calories, 0g protein, 5g carbohydrate, 2g total fat (2g saturated), 7mg cholesterol, 41mg sodium.

Coconut Macaroons

Though a traditional Passover dessert, these chewy flourless cookies are good any time of the year.

Prep: 10 minutes   Bake: 25 minutes

3	cups flaked sweetened coconut
¾	cup sugar
4	large egg whites
¼	teaspoon salt
1	teaspoon vanilla extract
⅛	teaspoon almond extract

1. Preheat oven to 325°F. Line two cookie sheets with parchment paper or foil.

2. In large bowl, stir coconut, sugar, egg whites, salt, vanilla, and almond extract until well combined.

3. Drop batter by rounded teaspoons, 1 inch apart, on prepared cookie sheets. Bake until set and lightly golden, about 25 minutes, rotating cookie sheets between upper and lower oven racks halfway through baking. Cool 1 minute on cookie sheets; with wide spatula, transfer cookies to wire racks to cool completely. Makes about 42 cookies.

Each cookie: About 41 calories, 1g protein, 6g carbohydrate, 2g total fat (2g saturated), 0mg cholesterol, 32mg sodium.

Chocolate Coconut Macaroons
Prepare as directed, stirring **2 tablespoons unsweetened cocoa** and **1 square (1 ounce) semisweet chocolate,** grated, into coconut mixture.

Almond Macaroons

We've rolled classic macaroons in sliced almonds to give them an elegant finish.

Prep: 20 minutes   Bake: 18 minutes

1	tube or can (7 to 8 ounces) almond paste, cut into 1-inch pieces
⅓	cup confectioners' sugar
1	large egg white
½	cup sliced natural almonds

1. Preheat oven to 325°F. Evenly grease and flour large cookie sheet.

2. In small bowl, with mixer at low speed, beat almond paste until crumbly. Add confectioners' sugar and egg white; beat until well blended (dough will be wet and sticky).

3. Place almonds on waxed paper. With lightly floured hands, roll dough into 1-inch balls. Roll balls in almonds, gently pressing to coat. Place balls, 1 inch apart, on prepared cookie sheet.

4. Bake until golden, 18 to 20 minutes. With wide spatula, transfer cookies to wire racks to cool completely. Makes about 30 cookies.

Each cookie: About 50 calories, 1g protein, 5g carbohydrate, 3g total fat (0g saturated), 0mg cholesterol, 3mg sodium.

Jumbo Gingersnaps

The ginger-molasses flavor in these soft, chewy crackle-top cookies is just perfect. Their generous size makes them especially festive, but you can also make smaller cookies.

Prep: 20 minutes	Bake: 15 minutes
2	cups all-purpose flour
2	teaspoons ground ginger
1	teaspoon baking soda
1/2	teaspoon ground cinnamon
1/2	teaspoon salt
1/4	teaspoon ground black pepper (optional)
3/4	cup vegetable shortening
1/2	cup plus 2 tablespoons sugar
1	large egg
1/2	cup dark molasses

1. Preheat oven to 350°F. In medium bowl, combine flour, ginger, baking soda, cinnamon, salt, and pepper if using.

2. In large bowl, with mixer at medium speed, beat shortening and 1/2 cup sugar until light and fluffy. Beat in egg until blended; beat in molasses. Reduce speed to low; beat in flour mixture just until blended.

3. Place remaining 2 tablespoons sugar on waxed paper. Roll 1/4 cup dough into ball; roll in sugar to coat evenly. Repeat with remaining dough to make 10 balls in all. Place balls, 3 inches apart, on ungreased large cookie sheet. Or, for small cookies, roll dough into balls by slightly rounded tablespoons and place 2 inches apart on two ungreased cookie sheets.

4. Bake until set, about 15 minutes for large cookies, or 9 to 11 minutes for smaller cookies, rotating cookie sheets between upper and lower oven racks halfway through baking. Cookies will be very soft and may appear moist in cracks. Cool 1 minute on cookie sheets on wire racks; with wide spatula, transfer cookies to wire racks to cool completely. Makes 10 giant cookies or about 30 small cookies.

Each giant cookie: About 323 calories, 3g protein, 42g carbohydrate, 16g total fat (4g saturated), 21mg cholesterol, 258mg sodium.

Almond Crescents

A classic holiday favorite, these crescents also make a welcome gift. Butter is essential to the exquisite texture and flavor.

Prep: 45 minutes plus chilling	Bake: 20 minutes per batch
1	cup blanched whole almonds (4 ounces), lightly toasted
1/2	cup granulated sugar
1/4	teaspoon salt
1	cup butter (2 sticks), softened (do not use margarine)
2	cups all-purpose flour
1	teaspoon almond extract
1/2	teaspoon vanilla extract
3/4	cup confectioners' sugar

1. In food processor with knife blade attached, process almonds, 1/4 cup granulated sugar, and salt until almonds are very finely ground.

2. In large bowl, with mixer at low speed, beat butter and remaining 1/4 cup granulated sugar until blended, occasionally

Almond Crescents

scraping bowl with rubber spatula. Increase speed to high; beat until light and fluffy, about 3 minutes. Reduce speed to low. Gradually add flour, ground-almond mixture, almond extract, and vanilla and beat until blended. Divide dough in half; wrap each piece and refrigerate until dough is firm enough to handle, about 1 hour, or freeze about 30 minutes.

3. Preheat oven to 325°F. Working with one piece of dough at a time, with lightly floured hands, shape rounded teaspoons of dough into 2" by ½" crescents. Place crescents, 1 inch apart, on two ungreased cookie sheets.

4. Bake until lightly browned around edges, about 20 minutes, rotating cookie sheets between upper and lower oven racks halfway through baking. With spatula, transfer cookies to wire racks set over waxed paper. Immediately dust confectioners' sugar over cookies until well coated; cool completely.

5. Repeat with remaining dough. Makes about 72 cookies.

Each cookie: About 58 calories, 1g protein, 6g carbohydrate, 4g total fat (2g saturated), 7mg cholesterol, 34mg sodium.

Walnut or Pecan Crescents

Prepare crescents as directed but substitute **1 cup walnuts or pecans** (not toasted) for almonds and omit almond extract.

Hazelnut Crescents

Prepare crescents as directed but substitute **1 cup toasted, skinned hazelnuts (filberts)** (below) for almonds and omit almond extract.

TOASTING NUTS

Toasting nuts brings out their flavor, and in the case of nuts such as hazelnuts, allows the skins to be removed.

To toast almonds, pecans, walnuts, or hazelnuts, preheat the oven to 350°F. Spread the shelled nuts in a single layer on a cookie sheet. Bake, stirring occasionally, until lightly browned and fragrant, about 10 minutes. Toast hazelnuts until the skins begin to peel away. Let the nuts cool completely before chopping.

To skin hazelnuts, wrap the still-warm toasted nuts in a clean kitchen towel and let stand for about 10 minutes. Using the towel, rub off as much of the skins as possible (all of the skin may not come off).

Pecan Tassies

The miniature pastry cups for these tiny pecan pies are made from an especially tender cream cheese dough.

Prep: 40 minutes plus chilling	Bake: 30 minutes
1	package (3 ounces) cream cheese, softened
½	cup butter or margarine, softened, plus 1 tablespoon, melted
1	cup all-purpose flour
2	tablespoons granulated sugar
1	cup pecans (4 ounces), toasted and finely chopped
⅔	cup packed brown sugar
1	large egg
1	teaspoon vanilla extract

1. Preheat oven to 350°F. In large bowl, with mixer at high speed, beat cream cheese and ½ cup butter until creamy. Reduce speed to low; add flour and granulated sugar and beat until well combined. Cover and refrigerate 30 minutes.

2. In medium bowl, with wooden spoon, mix pecans, brown sugar, egg, 1 tablespoon melted butter, and vanilla.

3. With floured hands, divide chilled dough into 24 equal pieces (dough will be very soft). With floured fingertips, gently press each piece of dough evenly onto bottom and up sides of ungreased 1¾" by 1" miniature muffin-pan cups. Spoon heaping teaspoon pecan filling into each pastry cup.

4. Bake until filling has set and crust is golden, about 30 minutes. With small knife, loosen cookie cups from muffin-pan cups; transfer to wire racks to cool. Makes 24 cookies.

Each cookie: About 131 calories, 1g protein, 12g carbohydrate, 9g total fat (4g saturated), 24mg cholesterol, 60mg sodium.

Pine Nut Tassies

Substitute ¾ **cup pine nuts (pignoli),** toasted, for pecans. In food processor with knife blade attached, process pine nuts and brown sugar until nuts are finely ground; add to filling mixture. Spoon into prepared pastry-lined muffin-pan cups; sprinkle with additional ¼ **cup pine nuts** (not toasted). Bake tassies as directed.

Raspberry Linzer Thumbprints

These cookies have all the delicious flavor of a classic Austrian linzertorte: a nutty crust and a raspberry jam filling.

Prep: 45 minutes plus cooling	*Bake: 20 minutes per batch*

1	cup hazelnuts (filberts), toasted and skinned (page 729) plus ⅓ cup (not toasted)
½	cup sugar
¾	cup butter or margarine (1½ sticks), cut into pieces
1	teaspoon vanilla extract
¼	teaspoon salt
1¾	cups all-purpose flour
¼	cup seedless raspberry jam

1. Preheat oven to 350°F.

2. In food processor with knife blade attached, process 1 cup toasted hazelnuts and sugar until nuts are finely ground. Add butter, vanilla, and salt and process until blended. Add flour and process just until evenly combined. Remove knife blade and press dough together with hands.

3. Finely chop remaining ⅓ cup hazelnuts; spread on waxed paper. Roll dough into 1-inch balls (dough may be slightly crumbly). Roll balls in nuts, gently pressing to coat.

4. Place balls, 1½ inches apart, on two ungreased large cookie sheets. With thumb, make small indentation in center of each ball. Fill each indentation with ¼ teaspoon jam.

5. Bake until lightly golden around edges, about 20 minutes, rotating cookie sheets between upper and lower oven racks halfway through baking. With wide spatula, transfer cookies to wire racks to cool completely.

6. Repeat with remaining balls and raspberry jam. Makes about 48 cookies.

Each cookie: About 74 calories, 1g protein, 7g carbohydrate, 5g total fat (2g saturated), 8mg cholesterol, 42mg sodium.

Snickerdoodles

These fragrant cookies are perfect for the cookie jar.

Prep: 25 minutes	*Bake: 12 minutes per batch*

3	cups all-purpose flour
2	teaspoons cream of tartar
1	teaspoon baking soda
1	cup butter or margarine (2 sticks), softened
1⅓	cups plus ¼ cup sugar
2	large eggs
1	teaspoon vanilla extract
1½	teaspoons ground cinnamon

1. Preheat oven to 375°F. In large bowl, combine flour, cream of tartar, and baking soda.

2. In large bowl, with mixer at medium speed, beat butter and 1⅓ cups sugar until light and fluffy. Beat in eggs, one at a time, beating well after each addition; beat in vanilla. Reduce speed to low; beat in flour mixture until well blended.

3. In small bowl, combine remaining ¼ cup sugar and cinnamon. Roll dough into 1-inch balls. Roll in cinnamon-sugar to coat evenly. Place balls, 1 inch apart, on two ungreased cookie sheets.

4. Bake cookies until set and slightly crinkled on top, about 12 minutes, rotating cookie sheets between upper and lower oven racks halfway through baking. Cool cookies 1 minute on cookie sheet; with wide spatula, transfer cookies to wire racks to cool completely.

5. Repeat with remaining dough. Makes about 54 cookies.

Each cookie: About 81 calories, 1g protein, 11g carbohydrate, 4g total fat (2g saturated), 17mg cholesterol, 61mg sodium.

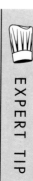

Baking pan liner (a.k.a. baking parchment) is a great help. Cookies hold their shape better when baked on parchment paper. And you can shape cookies on separate pieces of the paper, then just slide a cookie sheet under one of the filled papers to bake the cookies. What's more, you will not have any cookie sheets to wash.

MAIDA HEATTER
COOKBOOK AUTHOR

EXPERT TIP

Lemon Icebox Cookies

This dough is wonderful to have on hand in the freezer so you can bake fresh cookies whenever you wish. It's also the base for three delicious variations.

Prep: 20 minutes plus chilling	Bake: 10 minutes per batch

1²/₃	cups all-purpose flour
1	teaspoon baking powder
¼	teaspoon baking soda
⅛	teaspoon salt
3	lemons
½	cup butter or margarine (1 stick), softened
¾	cup sugar
1	large egg yolk

1. In medium bowl, combine flour, baking powder, baking soda, and salt. From lemons, grate 1 tablespoon peel and squeeze 2 tablespoons juice.

2. In large bowl, with mixer at medium speed, beat butter and sugar until light and fluffy. Beat in egg yolk and lemon peel and juice until combined. Reduce speed to low; beat in flour mixture just until blended.

3. Divide dough in half. On waxed paper, form one piece of dough into 12-inch log. Repeat with remaining dough. Wrap each log and refrigerate overnight, or freeze until very firm, at least 2 hours.

4. Preheat oven to 375°F. Grease and flour two large cookie sheets, or line with parchment paper or foil. Cut one log crosswise into ¼-inch-thick slices. Place slices, 1 inch apart, on prepared cookie sheets.

5. Bake until set and golden brown around edges, 10 to 12 minutes, rotating cookie sheets between upper and lower oven racks halfway through baking. With wide spatula, transfer cookies to wire racks to cool completely.

6. Repeat with remaining dough. Makes about 96 cookies.

Each cookie: About 25 calories, 0g protein, 3g carbohydrate, 1g total fat (1g saturated), 5mg cholesterol, 21mg sodium.

Lemon-Anise Icebox Cookies

Prepare as directed, beating **2 teaspoons anise seeds** into dough with lemon peel.

Lemon Icebox Cookies

Orange Icebox Cookies

Prepare as directed but substitute **1 tablespoon freshly grated orange peel** and **2 tablespoons fresh orange juice** for lemon peel and lemon juice.

Lemon-Walnut Icebox Cookies

Prepare as directed, stirring **1 cup walnuts (4 ounces),** finely chopped, into dough after adding flour.

Each cookie: About 33 calories, 0g protein, 4g carbohydrate, 2g total fat (1g saturated), 5mg cholesterol, 21mg sodium.

Spicy Almond Slices

These easy almond-flecked cookies are flavor packed.

Prep: 25 minutes plus chilling   Bake: 10 minutes per batch

3½	cups all-purpose flour
1	tablespoon ground cinnamon
1	teaspoon baking soda
½	teaspoon ground cloves
½	teaspoon ground nutmeg
½	teaspoon salt
1	cup butter or margarine (2 sticks), softened
1	cup granulated sugar
¾	cup packed dark brown sugar
2	large eggs
1	teaspoon vanilla extract
2	cups sliced blanched almonds (8 ounces)

1. In medium bowl, combine flour, cinnamon, baking soda, cloves, nutmeg, and salt. In large bowl, with mixer at medium speed, beat butter and granulated and brown sugars until light and fluffy. Beat in eggs, one at a time; add vanilla. Reduce speed to low; beat in flour mixture just until blended. With wooden spoon, mix in almonds (dough will be stiff).

2. Divide dough in half. Shape each half into 10" by 3" by 1" rectangle; wrap each piece and refrigerate overnight, or freeze until very firm, at least 2 hours.

3. Preheat oven to 375°F. Cut one rectangle crosswise into ¼-inch-thick slices; keep remaining dough refrigerated. Place slices, 1 inch apart, on two ungreased cookie sheets.

4. Bake until browned around edges, 10 to 12 minutes, rotating cookie sheets between upper and lower oven racks halfway through baking. With wide spatula, transfer cookies to wire racks to cool completely.

5. Repeat with remaining dough. Makes about 78 cookies.

Each cookie: About 79 calories, 1g protein, 9g carbohydrate, 4g total fat (2g saturated), 12mg cholesterol, 58mg sodium.

Classic Sugar Cookies

(pictured on page 710)

Our tender, delicate butter cookie is sure to become a favorite in your house. Decorate with colored sugar or Ornamental Frosting (page 739), if you like.

Prep: 1 hour 30 minutes plus chilling   Bake: 12 minutes per batch

3	cups all-purpose flour
½	teaspoon baking powder
½	teaspoon salt
1	cup butter (2 sticks), softened (do not use margarine)
1½	cups sugar
2	large eggs
1	teaspoon vanilla extract

1. In large bowl, combine flour, baking powder, and salt. In large bowl, with mixer at low speed, beat butter and sugar until blended. Increase speed to high; beat until light and fluffy, about 5 minutes. Reduce speed to low; beat in eggs and vanilla until mixed, then beat in flour mixture just until blended, occasionally scraping bowl with rubber spatula. Shape dough into four equal disks; wrap each disk and refrigerate overnight, or freeze until firm enough to roll, at least 2 hours.

2. Preheat oven to 350°F. On lightly floured surface, with floured rolling pin, roll one piece of dough until slightly less than ¼ inch thick; keep remaining dough refrigerated. With floured 3- to 4-inch cookie cutters, cut dough into as many cookies as possible; reserve trimmings for rerolling. Place cookies, 1 inch apart, on two ungreased large cookie sheets.

3. Bake until golden around edges, 12 to 15 minutes, rotating cookie sheets between upper and lower oven racks halfway through baking. With wide spatula, transfer cookies to wire racks to cool completely.

4. Repeat with remaining dough and trimmings. Makes about 72 cookies.

Each cookie: About 61 calories, 1g protein, 8g carbohydrate, 3g total fat (2g saturated), 13mg cholesterol, 47mg sodium.

Jam-Filled Sugar Cookies

Prepare, chill, and roll dough as directed. With 2½-inch fluted round or other decorative cutter, cut dough into rounds; with smaller cutter (1 to 1¼ inches), cut out and remove centers from half of rounds. Reserve centers for rerolling. Bake as directed; cool completely. Using **1 cup seed-less raspberry jam,** warmed, spread whole rounds with thin layer of jam. Top with cutout rounds. Makes 36 cookies.

Each cookie: About 144 calories, 2g protein, 23g carbohydrate, 5g total fat (3g saturated), 26mg cholesterol, 98mg sodium.

Holiday Sugar Cookies

This easy-to-handle dough is perfect for Christmas cutouts.

Prep: 30 minutes plus chilling   Bake: 10 minutes per batch
2¼ cups all-purpose flour
1½ teaspoons baking powder
¼ teaspoon salt
¾ cup butter or margarine (1½ sticks), softened
1 cup sugar
1 large egg
1 tablespoon milk
2 teaspoons freshly grated lemon peel or vanilla extract

1. In medium bowl, combine flour, baking powder, and salt. In large bowl, with mixer at medium speed, beat butter and ¾ cup sugar until light and fluffy. Beat in egg, milk, and lemon peel until well combined. Reduce speed to low; beat in flour mixture just until blended. Shape dough into disk; wrap and refrigerate at least 2 hours or up to overnight.

2. Preheat oven to 350°F. Grease and flour two large cookie sheets. On lightly floured surface, with floured rolling pin, roll half of dough ⅛ inch thick; keep remaining dough refrigerated. With floured 3-inch assorted cookie cutters, cut dough into as many cookies as possible; reserve trimmings for rerolling. Place cookies, 1 inch apart, on prepared cookie sheets. If desired, with drinking straw or skewer, make ¼-inch hole in top of each cookie for hanging. Sprinkle some of remaining ¼ cup sugar over cookies.

3. Bake until golden, about 10 minutes, rotating cookie sheets between upper and lower oven racks halfway through baking. With wide spatula, transfer cookies to wire racks to cool completely. Repeat with remaining dough and trimmings. Makes about 42 cookies.

Each cookie: About 76 calories, 1g protein, 10g carbohydrate, 4g total fat (2g saturated), 14mg cholesterol, 66mg sodium.

Finnish Almond Cookies

Thin, crisp, and buttery, these Scandinavian treats are traditionally served with cups of freshly brewed coffee.

Prep: 25 minutes   Bake: 12 minutes per batch
¾ cup butter or margarine (1½ sticks), softened
¼ cup plus 2 tablespoons sugar
1 large egg, separated
1 teaspoon almond extract
2 cups all-purpose flour
1 cup sliced blanched almonds (4 ounces)

1. Preheat oven to 375°F. In large bowl, with mixer at medium speed, beat butter and ¼ cup sugar until light and fluffy. Beat in egg yolk and almond extract until blended. Reduce speed to low; gradually beat in flour. If dough is dry and crumbly, sprinkle with *1 tablespoon water;* beat just until blended. Divide dough in half.

2. Sprinkle large ungreased cookie sheet with flour (if your cookie sheet has rim on four sides, use it upside down). With floured rolling pin, on cookie sheet, roll one piece of dough into 10½" by 9" rectangle. Lightly beat egg white. With pastry brush, brush dough with some egg white; sprinkle with half of almonds and 1 tablespoon sugar. Cut dough crosswise into seven 1½-inch-wide strips; cut each strip crosswise into 3 pieces.

3. Bake until edges are lightly browned, 12 to 15 minutes. If any cookies have not browned around edges, return to oven and bake several minutes longer. With wide spatula, transfer cookies to wire rack to cool completely.

4. Repeat with remaining dough, almonds, and sugar. Makes 42 cookies.

Each cookie: About 73 calories, 1g protein, 7g carbohydrate, 5g total fat (2g saturated), 14mg cholesterol, 35mg sodium.

Gingerbread Cutouts

Most gingerbread cookie doughs need to be chilled; ours can be rolled out right away. For wreath or tree decorations, tie a loop of nylon fishing line through a hole in each cookie for hanging.

Prep: 45 minutes plus cooling and decorating
Bake: 12 minutes per batch

½	cup sugar
½	cup light (mild) molasses
1½	teaspoons ground ginger
1	teaspoon ground allspice
1	teaspoon ground cinnamon
1	teaspoon ground cloves
2	teaspoons baking soda
½	cup butter or margarine (1 stick), cut into pieces
1	large egg, beaten
3½	cups all-purpose flour
	Ornamental Frosting (page 739)

1. In 3-quart saucepan, combine sugar, molasses, ginger, allspice, cinnamon, and cloves; heat to boiling over medium heat, stirring occasionally with wooden spoon. Remove from heat; stir in baking soda (mixture will foam up). Stir in butter until melted. Stir egg, then flour.

2. On floured surface, knead dough until thoroughly blended. Divide dough in half; wrap one piece in plastic wrap and set aside.

3. Preheat oven to 325°F. With floured rolling pin, roll remaining piece of dough slightly less than ¼ inch thick. With floured 3- to 4-inch assorted cookie cutters, cut dough into as many cookies as possible; reserve trimmings for rerolling. Place cookies, 1 inch apart, on two ungreased large cookie sheets. If desired, with drinking straw or skewer, make ¼-inch hole in top of each cookie for hanging.

4. Bake until brown around edges, about 12 minutes, rotating cookie sheets between upper and lower oven racks halfway through baking. With wide spatula, transfer cookies to wire racks to cool completely. Repeat with remaining dough and trimmings.

5. When cookies are cool, prepare Ornamental Frosting; use to decorate cookies as desired. Allow frosting to dry completely, about 1 hour. Makes about 36 cookies.

Each cookie without frosting: About 93 calories, 1g protein, 15g carbohydrate, 3g total fat (2g saturated), 13mg cholesterol, 100mg sodium.

Apricot-Raspberry Rugelach

A cream cheese dough crust gives these rugelach traditional taste.

Prep: 1 hour plus chilling   **Bake:** 35 to 40 minutes

1	cup butter or margarine (2 sticks), softened
1	package (8 ounces) cream cheese, softened
¾	cup granulated sugar
1	teaspoon vanilla extract
¼	teaspoon salt
2	cups all-purpose flour
1	cup walnuts (4 ounces), chopped
¾	cup dried apricots, chopped
¼	cup packed brown sugar
1½	teaspoons ground cinnamon
½	cup seedless raspberry preserves
1	tablespoon milk

1. In large bowl, with mixer at low speed, beat butter and cream cheese until blended and creamy. Beat in ¼ cup granulated sugar, vanilla, and salt. Beat in 1 cup flour. With wooden spoon, stir in remaining 1 cup flour just until blended. Divide dough into four equal disks. Wrap each disk and refrigerate until firm, at least 2 hours or up to overnight.

2. Prepare filling: In medium bowl, combine walnuts, apricots, brown sugar, ¼ cup plus 2 tablespoons granulated sugar, and ½ teaspoon cinnamon until well mixed. Line two large cookie sheets with foil; grease foil.

3. On lightly floured surface, with floured rolling pin, roll one disk of dough into 9-inch round; keep remaining dough refrigerated. Spread 2 tablespoons raspberry preserves over dough. Sprinkle with ½ cup walnut mixture, gently pressing filling to adhere. With pastry wheel or sharp knife, cut dough into 12 equal wedges. Starting at curved edge, roll up each wedge, jelly-roll fashion. Place cookies, point side down, ½ inch apart, on prepared cookie sheet. Repeat with remaining dough, one disk at a time.

4. Preheat oven to 325°F. In cup, combine remaining 2 tablespoons granulated sugar and remaining 1 teaspoon cinnamon. With pastry brush, brush rugelach with milk. Evenly sprinkle cinnamon-sugar on top.

5. Bake until golden, 35 to 40 minutes, rotating cookie sheets between upper and lower oven racks halfway through baking. With wide spatula, immediately transfer rugelach to wire racks to cool completely. Makes 48 rugelach.

Each rugelach: About 116 calories, 1g protein, 12g carbohydrate, 7g total fat (4g saturated), 16mg cholesterol, 67mg sodium.

Meringue Fingers

These ethereal meringue cookies are dipped into chocolate, which gives them fabulous flavor.

Prep: 25 minutes plus cooling Bake: 1 hour	
3	large egg whites
1/4	teaspoon cream of tartar
1/8	teaspoon salt
1/2	cup sugar
1	teaspoon vanilla extract
2	squares (2 ounces) semisweet chocolate, chopped
1	teaspoon vegetable shortening

1. Preheat oven to 200°F. Line two large cookie sheets with foil or parchment paper.

2. In small bowl, with mixer at high speed, beat egg whites, cream of tartar, and salt until soft peaks form when beaters are lifted. Beating at high speed, gradually sprinkle in sugar, 2 tablespoons at a time, beating until sugar has dissolved. Add vanilla; continue beating until meringue stands in stiff, glossy peaks when beaters are lifted.

3. Spoon meringue into pastry bag fitted with 1/2-inch star tip. Pipe meringue into 3 inch lengths, 1 inch apart, on prepared cookie sheets.

4. Bake cookies until set, about 1 hour, rotating cookie sheets between upper and lower oven racks halfway through baking. Cool 10 minutes on cookie sheets on wire racks; then, with spatula, transfer cookies to wire racks to cool completely.

5. When cookies have cooled, in heavy 1-quart saucepan, melt chocolate and shortening over low heat, stirring frequently, until smooth; remove from heat. Dip one end of each cookie into melted chocolate; let dry on wire racks set over waxed paper. Makes about 48 cookies.

Each cookie: About 16 calories, 0g protein, 3g carbohydrate, 0g total fat (0g saturated), 0mg cholesterol, 10mg sodium.

Ladyfingers

Tender and versatile ladyfingers can be served plain or layered with custard and turned into a dessert.

Prep: 25 minutes Bake: 10 minutes	
4	large eggs, separated
1/8	teaspoon salt
3/4	cup granulated sugar
1	teaspoon vanilla extract
3/4	cup all-purpose flour
	confectioners' sugar

1. Preheat oven to 350°F. Grease and flour two large cookie sheets.

2. In small bowl, with mixer at high speed, beat egg whites and salt until soft peaks form when beaters are lifted. Beating at high speed, gradually sprinkle in 1/4 cup granulated sugar, 1 tablespoon at a time, beating until sugar has dissolved and whites stand in stiff, glossy peaks when beaters are lifted.

3. In large bowl, with same beaters and with mixer at medium speed, beat egg yolks, remaining 1/2 cup granulated sugar, and vanilla until very thick and lemon-colored. With rubber spatula, fold in one-third of flour, then gently fold in remaining flour just until blended. Gently fold one-third of beaten egg whites into egg-yolk mixture. Fold in remaining egg whites just until blended.

4. Spoon half of batter into large pastry bag fitted with 1/2-inch plain tip. Pipe batter into 3-inch lengths, 1 inch apart, on prepared cookie sheets. If you like, with moistened finger, smooth edges. Lightly dust ladyfingers with confectioners' sugar. Repeat with remaining batter.

5. Bake until golden brown, 10 to 13 minutes, rotating cookie sheets between upper and lower oven racks halfway through baking. With wide spatula, transfer ladyfingers to wire racks to cool completely. Makes about 48 ladyfingers.

Each cookie: About 30 calories, 1g protein, 5g carbohydrate, 1g total fat (0g saturated), 18mg cholesterol, 11mg sodium.

Spritz Cookies

Don't reserve these buttery cookies just for the holidays; they're good at any time of the year.

Prep: 15 minutes	Bake: 10 minutes per batch
1	cup butter or margarine (2 sticks), softened
¾	cup confectioners' sugar
1	teaspoon vanilla extract
⅛	teaspoon almond extract
2	cups all-purpose flour
⅛	teaspoon salt

1. Preheat oven to 350°F. In large bowl, with mixer at medium speed, beat butter and confectioners' sugar until light and fluffy. Beat in vanilla and almond extract. Reduce speed to low; add flour and salt and beat until well combined.

2. Spoon one-third of batter into cookie press fitted with pattern of choice. Press cookies, 1 inch apart, on two ungreased cookie sheets.

3. Bake until golden brown around edges, 10 to 12 minutes, rotating cookie sheets between upper and lower oven racks halfway through baking. With wide spatula, transfer cookies to wire racks to cool completely.

4. Repeat with remaining dough. Makes about 60 cookies.

Each cookie: About 48 calories, 0g protein, 5g carbohydrate, 3g total fat (2g saturated), 8mg cholesterol, 36mg sodium.

Chocolate Spritz Cookies

Prepare as directed but use **1 cup confectioners' sugar.** Add **2 squares (2 ounces) unsweetened chocolate,** chopped, melted, and cooled after beating butter and sugar.

Almond Spritz Cookies

In food processor with knife blade attached, process **¾ cup whole natural almonds, toasted,** and **¼ cup confectioners' sugar** until nuts are finely ground. Prepare as directed, using **¼ teaspoon almond extract** and **2¼ cups flour.** Add ground almonds. Dough will be quite stiff. Makes about 72 cookies.

Brandy Snaps

These lacy cookies are a welcome addition to any homemade cookie assortment. Make them in dry weather or they will be sticky.

Prep: 25 minutes	Bake: 5 minutes per batch
½	cup butter (1 stick) (do not use margarine)
3	tablespoons light (mild) molasses
½	cup all-purpose flour
½	cup sugar
1	teaspoon ground ginger
¼	teaspoon salt
2	tablespoons brandy

1. Preheat oven to 350°F. Grease large cookie sheet.

2. In 2-quart saucepan, melt butter with molasses over medium-low heat, stirring occasionally, until smooth. Remove from heat. With wooden spoon, stir in flour, sugar, ginger, and salt until blended and smooth; stir in brandy. Set saucepan in bowl of hot water to keep warm.

Brandy Snaps

3. Drop 1 teaspoon batter on prepared cookie sheet; with small metal spatula, spread in circular motion to make 4-inch round (during baking, batter will spread and fill in any thin areas). Repeat to make 4 rounds in all, placing them 2 inches apart. (Do not place more than 4 cookies on sheet.)

4. Bake until golden brown, about 5 minutes. Cool 30 to 60 seconds on cookie sheet on wire rack, just until edges have set; then, with wide spatula, quickly flip cookies over.

5. Working as quickly as possible, roll up each cookie around handle (½-inch diameter) of wooden spoon or dowel. If cookies become too hard to roll, briefly return to oven to soften. As each cookie is shaped, slip off spoon handle and cool completely on wire racks.

6. Repeat with remaining batter. Makes about 24 cookies.

Each cookie: About 72 calories, 0g protein, 8g carbohydrate, 4g total fat (2g saturated), 10mg cholesterol, 64mg sodium.

Almond Tuiles

Our delicate almond cookies are curved to resemble terra-cotta roof tiles (tuiles), but you can make them flat, too.

Prep: 30 minutes	Bake: 5 minutes per batch
3	large egg whites
¾	cup confectioners' sugar
½	cup all-purpose flour
6	tablespoons butter, melted (do not use margarine)
¼	teaspoon salt
¼	teaspoon almond extract
⅔	cup sliced almonds

1. Preheat oven to 350°F. Grease large cookie sheet.

2. In large bowl, with wire whisk, beat egg whites, confectioners' sugar, and flour until blended and smooth. Beat in melted butter, salt, and almond extract until blended.

3. Drop 1 heaping teaspoon batter on prepared cookie sheet; with small metal spatula, spread in circular motion to make 3-inch round. Repeat to make 4 cookies in all, placing them 3 inches apart. (Do not place more than 4 cookies on sheet.) Sprinkle with some almonds (do not overlap).

4. Bake until golden around edges, 5 to 7 minutes. With wide spatula, quickly lift cookies, one at a time, and drape over rolling pin to curve cookies. When firm, transfer to wire racks to cool completely. (If you like, omit shaping and cool cookies flat.) If cookies become too firm to shape, briefly return to oven to soften.

5. Repeat with remaining batter and almonds. (Batter will become slightly thicker upon standing.) Makes about 30 cookies.

Each cookie: About 56 calories, 1g protein, 5g carbohydrate, 4g total fat (2g saturated), 6mg cholesterol, 48mg sodium.

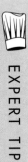

EXPERT TIP

Very buttery doughs can be difficult to roll out and transfer to a baking pan, even for bakers with lots of experience. So I like to roll the dough between lightly floured sheets of plastic wrap. Lift the plastic wrap from time to time so that it doesn't roll into the dough and create creases. When the dough is rolled out, peel the plastic wrap off the top of the dough and invert the dough into the pan. If the dough is very soft at this point, you can chill it (with the remaining sheet of plastic still in place) for 3 to 5 minutes. With the plastic still covering the dough, fit the dough onto the bottom of the pan, then peel away the plastic wrap.

DORIE GREENSPAN
COOKBOOK AUTHOR

Almond-Anise Biscotti

Soaking the anise seeds in liqueur softens them and releases their delicious flavor.

	Prep: 25 minutes plus cooling Bake: 55 minutes
1	tablespoon anise seeds, crushed
1	tablespoon anise-flavored aperitif or liqueur
2	cups all-purpose flour
1	cup sugar
1	cup whole almonds (4 ounces), toasted and coarsely chopped
1	teaspoon baking powder
1/8	teaspoon salt
3	large eggs

1. Preheat oven to 325°F. In medium bowl, combine anise seeds and anise-flavored aperitif; let stand 10 minutes.

2. Grease large cookie sheet. In large bowl, combine flour, sugar, chopped almonds, baking powder, and salt. With wire whisk, beat eggs into anise mixture. With wooden spoon, stir egg mixture into flour mixture until blended. Divide dough in half. On prepared cookie sheet, with floured hands, shape each half into 15-inch log, placing them 3 inches apart (dough will be sticky).

3. Bake until golden and toothpick inserted in center comes out clean, about 40 minutes. Cool 10 minutes on cookie sheet on wire rack; then transfer logs to cutting board. With serrated knife, cut each log crosswise on diagonal into 1/4-inch-thick slices. Place slices, cut side down, on two ungreased cookie sheets. Bake 15 minutes, turning slices over once and rotating cookie sheets between upper and lower oven racks halfway through baking. With spatula, transfer biscotti to wire racks to cool completely. Makes about 84 biscotti.

♥ Each biscotti: About 33 calories, 1g protein, 5g carbohydrate, 1g total fat (0g saturated), 8mg cholesterol, 12mg sodium.

Chocolate–Dried Cherry Biscotti

Flavor-rich cocoa is paired with tart dried cherries to give these classic twice-baked treats a new point of view.

	Prep: 30 minutes plus cooling Bake: 45 minutes
1	teaspoon instant espresso-coffee powder
1	teaspoon hot water
2 1/2	cups all-purpose flour
3/4	cup unsweetened cocoa
1	tablespoon baking powder
1/2	teaspoon salt
2	squares (2 ounces) semisweet chocolate, chopped
1/2	cup butter or margarine (1 stick), softened
1 1/3	cups sugar
3	large eggs
3/4	cup dried tart cherries, coarsely chopped

1. Preheat oven to 350°F. Grease and flour large cookie sheet. In cup, dissolve espresso powder in hot water; set aside. In medium bowl, combine flour, cocoa, baking powder, and salt. In heavy 1-quart saucepan, melt chocolate over low heat, stirring frequently, until smooth. Cool.

2. In large bowl, with mixer at medium speed, beat butter and sugar until light and fluffy. At low speed, add eggs, one at a time, until blended, then add chocolate and espresso and beat until blended. Add flour mixture and beat just until blended. With hand, knead in cherries until combined.

3. With floured hands, divide dough in half. On ungreased large cookie sheet, shape each half into 12" by 3" loaf, placing them 3 inches apart. With pastry brush, brush off any excess flour.

4. Bake 30 minutes. Cool on cookie sheet on wire rack until easy to handle, about 10 minutes, then transfer loaves to cutting board. With serrated knife, cut each loaf crosswise on diagonal into 1/2-inch-thick slices. Place slices, cut side down, on same cookie sheet. Return to oven and bake 15 to 20 minutes to dry biscotti. With wide spatula, transfer biscotti to wire racks to cool completely. Biscotti will harden as they cool. Makes about 48 biscotti.

Each biscotti: About 83 calories, 1g protein, 14g carbohydrate, 3g total fat (2g saturated), 17mg cholesterol, 79mg sodium.

Palmiers

Though palmiers are traditionally made with classic puff pastry, our version uses quick puff pastry, which turns out beautifully flaky and buttery cookies in half the time. The dough rolls can be refrigerated for up to one week or frozen for up to three weeks. Then simply slice and bake them.

Prep: 35 minutes plus overnight to chill
Bake: 15 minutes per batch

1½	cups butter (3 sticks), cut into pieces (do not use margarine)
3	cups all-purpose flour
¾	cup sour cream
1	cup sugar

1. In large bowl, with pastry blender or two knives used scissor-fashion, cut butter into flour until mixture resembles coarse crumbs. Stir in sour cream. On lightly floured surface, knead dough just until it holds together; flatten into 8" by 6" rectangle. Wrap in plastic wrap and refrigerate overnight.

2. Preheat oven to 400°F. Sprinkle ½ cup sugar on surface. Cut dough in half. With lightly floured rolling pin, roll one half of dough to 14-inch square; keep remaining dough refrigerated. Using side of your hand, make indentation down along center of dough. Starting from one side, tightly roll dough up to indentation. Roll up other side of dough until it meets first roll, incorporating as much sugar as possible into dough; refrigerate. Repeat with remaining piece of dough and the remaining ½ cup sugar.

3. With serrated knife, cut dough scroll crosswise into ¼-inch-thick slices. (Refrigerate if too soft to slice.) Place slices, 2 inches apart, on ungreased cookie sheet. Bake 10 minutes. With wide spatula, carefully turn cookies over and bake until sugar has caramelized and cookies are deep golden, about 5 minutes longer. Cool 1 minute on cookie sheet; then, with wide spatula, transfer cookies to wire racks to cool completely.

4. Repeat slicing, baking, and cooling with remaining dough scroll. Makes about 72 cookies.

Each cookie: About 69 calories, 1g protein, 7g carbohydrate, 4g total fat (3g saturated), 11mg cholesterol, 40mg sodium.

Ornamental Frosting

This glossy, hard-drying frosting is often made with raw egg whites, but we prefer meringue powder, which is available at many supermarkets and at cake supply stores.

 Prep: 5 minutes

1	package (16 ounces) confectioners' sugar
3	tablespoons meringue powder
⅓	cup warm water
	assorted food colorings (optional)

1. In large bowl, with mixer at medium speed, beat confectioners' sugar, meringue powder, and water until stiff and knife drawn through leaves path, about 5 minutes.

2. If desired, tint frosting with food colorings. Keep tightly covered to prevent drying out. With small metal spatula, artists' paintbrushes, or decorating bags with small plain tips, decorate cookies with frosting. (You may need to thin frosting with a little warm water to obtain right spreading or piping consistency.) Makes about 3 cups.

Each tablespoon: About 39 calories, 0g protein, 10g carbohydrate, 0g total fat (0g saturated), 0mg cholesterol, 2mg sodium.

CONFECTIONS

Candy is always a luscious indulgence, so when you make your own, use only the best ingredients to make every calorie worthwhile. Homemade candies are perfect for holiday gift-giving, wonderful to serve with after-dinner coffee, and great to have on hand for an afternoon pick-me-up.

SUGAR SYRUP TEMPERATURES

Many candies are made with sugar syrup. As the syrup cooks, its temperature rises and the liquid begins to evaporate. In general, a syrup that is cooked to a high temperature makes candy with a harder texture because it contains less liquid than one cooked to a lower temperature.

Accurate temperature readings are crucial in candy making. For the best results, always use a candy thermometer.

SUGAR SYRUP STAGES

Note that each stage includes a range of temperatures; this allows (the cook) some leeway. To use this method (which we suggest only as an alternative to using a candy thermometer), remove the pan of syrup from the heat. Drop a half spoonful of the hot syrup into a bowl of very cold (not iced) water. Let the syrup stand for 30 seconds; gather the syrup up into a mass and remove from the water to check its consistency.

THREAD (230° to 234°F) Syrup forms a fine thin thread in the air as it falls from the spoon.

SOFT BALL (234° to 240°F) Syrup can be formed into a soft ball that can be flattened easily.

FIRM BALL (244° to 248°F) Syrup can be formed into a firm ball that cannot be flattened.

HARD BALL (250° to 266°F) Syrup can be formed into a hard ball that holds it shape.

SOFT CRACK (270° to 290°F) Syrup can be pulled into soft, pliable threads.

HARD CRACK (300° to 310°F) Syrup forms hard, brittle threads that can be broken when removed from water.

CARAMEL (320° to 350°F) Syrup turns nut brown and caramelizes. (We like to judge caramel by its color: the deeper the color, the fuller the flavor.)

When attaching the thermometer to the pan, be sure the tip of the thermometer doesn't touch the bottom of the pan, or you may get an inaccurate reading.

We don't recommend the old-fashioned "cold water" test, although you may want to refer to the chart (left), which details the various stages of cooked sugar syrups and their temperature ranges.

When cooking a sugar syrup, as the liquid evaporates and the amount of syrup decreases, sugar crystals form on the side of the saucepan. These crystals must be dissolved, or they can make candy grainy. Dip a pastry brush into cold water; rub the brush firmly against the sugar crystals to wash the crystals into the cooking syrup. Repeat this procedure all around the inside of the saucepan until no sugar crystals remain.

Do not make sugar syrup-based candies in rainy or humid weather. Sugar syrup attracts the moisture in the air, so the candy will either not set properly or be sticky.

CHOCOLATE AND COCOA

Because of its unique flavor and smooth texture, chocolate is an essential component in all kinds of sweets, including candies. There are many different kinds of chocolates available, and they are rarely interchangeable. See Chocolate and Cocoa Powder, page 744.

Chocolate has two enemies: water and high heat. If a single drop of water gets into chocolate while it's melting, the chocolate can thicken and "seize" (form a dull, thick paste). Chocolate can, however, be melted in a measured amount of liquid, about 1 tablespoon for every ounce of chocolate. Keep in mind that chocolate melted over too high a heat clumps up and becomes grainy, so melt it carefully over low heat.

To chop chocolate, use a sharp heavy knife and a clean, odor-free cutting board; be sure both are absolutely dry. Chop the chocolate into ¼-inch (or smaller) pieces. In recipes in which a hot liquid is added to chocolate, it can be chopped in a food processor. In general, however, don't use the processor for chopping chocolate, because the friction and heat generated by the spinning blade could melt the chocolate.

To melt chocolate, place the chopped chocolate in a heavy-bottomed saucepan; stir almost constantly over low heat until melted, watching carefully to avoid scorching. Or, place the chocolate in the top of a double boiler over very hot, not simmering, water and stir until melted. Alternatively, place it in a microwave-safe bowl and microwave, uncovered, at 50 percent (medium) power, stirring occasionally (the chocolate may look shiny and solid but will melt when stirred).

Store chocolate and cocoa in a cool dry place. During hot weather, store chocolate, double-wrapped, in the refrigerator (the crisper drawer is ideal). Ignore any pale streaks that form on the surface of the chilled chocolate—it's simply the cocoa butter separating out.

Melt Away Chocolate Mints

Serve these melt-in-your-mouth mints as an elegant finale to a special dinner.

Prep: 25 minutes plus chilling and standing Cook: 8 minutes
16 squares (16 ounces) semisweet chocolate, chopped
2 tablespoons vegetable shortening
½ cup heavy or whipping cream
1 tablespoon peppermint extract
2 tablespoons unsweetened cocoa

1. Line bottom of 8-inch square baking pan with waxed paper. In heavy 3-quart saucepan, melt chocolate and shortening over low heat, stirring frequently, until smooth. Remove from heat.

2. Meanwhile, in small saucepan, heat cream to simmering over medium heat. Immediately add hot cream and peppermint extract to chocolate mixture; with wire whisk, mix until blended and smooth.

3. Pour mixture into prepared pan, tilting pan to spread mixture evenly. Refrigerate until firm, about 1½ hours.

4. With small metal spatula, loosen chocolate mixture from sides of pan. Lightly dust cutting board with cocoa; invert pan onto board. Remove pan and discard waxed paper. Let candy stand 10 minutes at room temperature to soften slightly. With sharp knife, cut chocolate mixture into 8 strips, then cut each strip crosswise into 8 pieces. Layer between waxed paper in airtight container. Refrigerate up to 1 week. Makes 64 mints.

Each mint: About 45 calories, 0g protein, 5g carbohydrate, 3g total fat (2g saturated), 3mg cholesterol, 2mg sodium.

Chocolate and Hazelnut Truffles

Use the best chocolate to give these truffles European flair. If you wish, add two tablespoons of coffee-, orange-, or almond-flavored liqueur to the melted-chocolate mixture.

Prep: 25 minutes plus chilling
8 ounces bittersweet chocolate or 6 squares (6 ounces) semisweet chocolate plus 2 squares (2 ounces) unsweetened chocolate, coarsely chopped
½ cup heavy or whipping cream
3 tablespoons butter, cut into pieces and softened (do not use margarine)
⅓ cup hazelnuts (filberts), toasted and skinned (page 729), finely chopped
3 tablespoons unsweetened cocoa

1. Line 8½" by 4½" loaf pan with plastic wrap; smooth out wrinkles. In food processor with knife blade attached, process chocolate until finely ground.

2. In 1-quart saucepan, heat cream to simmering over medium-high heat. Add to chocolate in food processor and puree until smooth. Add butter and process until smooth.

3. Pour chocolate mixture into prepared pan; spread evenly. Refrigerate until cool and firm enough to handle, about 3 hours.

4. Remove chocolate mixture from pan by lifting edges of plastic wrap. Invert chocolate block onto cutting board; discard plastic wrap. Cut chocolate lengthwise into 4 strips, then cut each strip crosswise into 8 pieces. (To cut chocolate easily, dip knife in hot water and wipe dry; repeat as needed.) With cool hands, quickly roll each square into ball. Roll 16 truffles in chopped hazelnuts and remaining 16 truffles in cocoa. Place in single layer in waxed paper–lined airtight container. Refrigerate up to 1 week, or freeze up to 1 month. Remove from freezer 5 minutes before serving. Makes 32 truffles.

Each truffle: About 66 calories, 1g protein, 5g carbohydrate, 6g total fat (3g saturated), 8mg cholesterol, 13mg sodium.

Chocolate-Walnut Fudge

A rich and creamy fudge that couldn't be easier, thanks to the addition of sweetened condensed milk.

Prep: 25 minutes plus chilling

1	pound bittersweet chocolate or 16 squares (16 ounces) semisweet chocolate, chopped
1	can (14 ounces) sweetened condensed milk
1	cup walnuts (4 ounces), coarsely chopped
1	teaspoon vanilla extract
⅛	teaspoon salt

1. Line 8-inch square baking pan with plastic wrap; smooth out wrinkles. In heavy 2-quart saucepan, melt chocolate with condensed milk over medium-low heat, stirring constantly, until smooth. Remove from heat.

2. Stir in walnuts, vanilla, and salt. Scrape chocolate mixture into prepared pan; spread evenly. Refrigerate until firm, about 3 hours.

3. Remove fudge from pan by lifting edges of plastic wrap. Invert fudge onto cutting board; discard plastic wrap. Cut fudge into 8 strips, then cut each strip crosswise into 8 pieces. Layer between waxed paper in airtight container. Store at room temperature up to 1 week, or refrigerate up to 1 month. Makes 64 pieces.

Each piece: About 67 calories, 1g protein, 8g carbohydrate, 4g total fat (2g saturated), 2mg cholesterol, 13mg sodium.

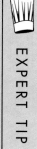

To prevent honey, molasses, or corn syrup from sticking to a measuring cup or spoon, oil the measuring cup or lightly spray with nonstick cooking spray.

SUSAN G. PURDY
COOKBOOK AUTHOR

EXPERT TIP

Creamy Penuche

This sweet can best be described as brown sugar fudge. The name penuche (pah-NOO-chee) comes from the Mexican word for brown sugar.

Prep: 15 minutes plus cooling   Cook: 25 minutes

4	tablespoons butter (do not use margarine)
2	cups heavy or whipping cream
2	tablespoons light corn syrup
1½	cups granulated sugar
1½	cups packed dark brown sugar
2	ounces white chocolate or white baking bar, chopped
1½	cups walnuts (6 ounces), toasted and coarsely chopped

1. Grease 8-inch square baking pan. Line pan with foil, extending foil over rim on two opposite sides; grease foil.

2. In heavy 4-quart saucepan, melt butter over medium heat. Add cream, corn syrup, and granulated and brown sugars; cook over high heat, stirring frequently, until sugars have completely dissolved and mixture is bubbling. With pastry brush dipped in cold water, wash down sugar crystals on side of saucepan.

3. Set candy thermometer in place and continue cooking, without stirring, until temperature reaches 234° to 240°F (soft-ball stage), 15 to 20 minutes.

4. Remove saucepan from heat. Without stirring, cool mixture to 210°F, about 8 minutes. Sprinkle chopped white chocolate over mixture; let stand 1 minute.

5. With wooden spoon, stir in walnuts just until mixed (do not overmix). Immediately pour mixture into prepared pan (do not scrape mixture from saucepan).

6. Cool in pan on wire rack until firm but still warm, about 30 minutes. Remove candy from pan by lifting edges of foil and place on cutting board. Cut candy into 8 strips, then cut each strip crosswise into 8 pieces. Cool completely on foil on wire rack. With spatula, lift candy away from foil. Layer between waxed paper in airtight container. Store at room termperature up to 3 weeks. Makes about 64 pieces.

Each piece: About 95 calories, 1g protein, 11g carbohydrate, 6g total fat (2g saturated), 12mg cholesterol, 14mg sodium.

Peanut Brittle

Nibble this old-time treat on its own, or crush it and serve over ice cream. For variety, try other nuts, such as almonds or cashews.

Prep: 5 minutes plus cooling   Cook: 30 minutes

1	cup sugar
½	cup light corn syrup
¼	cup water
2	tablespoons butter or margarine
1	cup salted peanuts
½	teaspoon baking soda

1. Lightly grease large cookie sheet.

2. In heavy 2-quart saucepan, combine sugar, corn syrup, water, and butter; cook over medium heat, stirring constantly, until sugar has dissolved and syrup is bubbling.

3. Set candy thermometer in place and continue cooking, stirring frequently, until temperature reaches 300° to 310°F (hard-crack stage), 20 to 25 minutes. (Once temperature reaches 220°F, it will rise quickly, so watch carefully.) Stir in peanuts.

4. Remove from heat and stir in baking soda (mixture will bubble vigorously); immediately pour onto prepared sheet. With two forks, quickly lift and stretch peanut mixture into 14" by 12" rectangle.

5. Cool brittle completely on cookie sheet on wire rack. With hands, break brittle into small pieces. Layer between waxed paper in airtight container. Store at room temperature up to 1 month. Makes about 1 pound.

Each ounce: About 146 calories, 2g protein, 22g carbohydrate, 6g total fat (2g saturated), 4mg cholesterol, 103mg sodium.

Gold Rush Nut Brittle

Prepare as directed but use only ¾ cup **salted peanuts;** stir in ¾ **cup sliced blanched almonds** and ¾ **cup pecans,** coarsely broken, with peanuts. Makes about 1¼ pounds.

Pralines

This is the classic pecan candy from the South. Use dark brown sugar if you prefer a richer flavor.

Prep: 15 minutes   Cook: 25 minutes

½	cup (1 stick) butter, cut into pieces (do not use margarine)
2	cups granulated sugar
1	cup packed light brown sugar
1	cup heavy or whipping cream
2	tablespoons light corn syrup
2	cups pecans (8 ounces), toasted and coarsely chopped
1	teaspoon vanilla extract

1. Grease two or three cookie sheets.

2. In heavy 3-quart saucepan, combine butter, granulated and brown sugars, cream, and corn syrup; cook over medium heat, stirring occasionally, until sugars have dissolved and syrup is bubbling.

3. Set candy thermometer in place and continue cooking, without stirring, until temperature reaches 230° to 234°F (thread stage), about 8 minutes.

4. Add pecans and vanilla; stir until bubbling subsides. Heat to boiling. Continue cooking until candy temperature reaches 244° to 248°F (firm-ball stage).

5. Remove saucepan from heat and stir vigorously until syrup has thickened and turns opaque, about 3 minutes.

6. Working quickly, drop mixture by tablespoons, at least 1 inch apart, on prepared cookie sheets (stir briefly over low heat if mixture gets too thick). Cool pralines completely. Layer between waxed paper in airtight container. Store at room temperature up to 1 week, or freeze up to 3 months. Makes about 40 pralines.

Each praline: About 144 calories, 1g protein, 17g carbohydrate, 9g total fat (3g saturated), 14mg cholesterol, 29mg sodium.

CHOCOLATE AND COCOA POWDER

We always use pure chocolate products and avoid artificially flavored compound (summer) coatings or premelted chocolate, which include large amounts of vegetable fats.

Unsweetened chocolate is simply ground cocoa beans. Professionals call it chocolate liquor. It's not very tasty on its own, so it is combined with sugar and other ingredients in recipes.

Bittersweet chocolate has been sweetened, but the amount of sugar varies greatly from brand to brand. Some bittersweet chocolates list the percentage of chocolate liquor on the label; a brand with 70 percent will be more bitter than one with 64 percent. Most European chocolate bars are bittersweet, and some is now produced in the U.S.

Semisweet chocolate is similar to bittersweet chocolate, although it is usually a bit sweeter. It is available in individually wrapped one-ounce squares and in bulk. It can be used instead of bittersweet chocolate.

Sweet chocolate is usually sold under a brand name (and used to make German chocolate cake) and should not be confused with bitter- or semisweet chocolate.

Milk chocolate contains dried milk powder and a high proportion of sugar. It is essentially an eating chocolate—it's not usually used for baking.

White chocolate is not really a chocolate but rather vanilla-flavored, sweetened cocoa butter (a by-product of chocolate processing), although some mid-priced brands substitute vegetable fat for the cocoa butter.

Unsweetened cocoa powder provides the rich chocolate flavor in many desserts. There are two kinds of cocoa powder: natural and Dutch-processed; check the label. In baking, the two are not interchangeable. They react differently when combined with baking soda or baking powder. However, for a cup of hot cocoa, use your favorite.

Natural cocoa powder, with its full, rich flavor, is the most common cocoa in American kitchens. Unless stated otherwise, we used it for the recipes in this book.

Dutch-processed cocoa powder (so named because the technique was developed in the Netherlands) has been treated with an alkali to mellow cocoa's natural bitterness and to give baked goods a darker color.

Candied Citrus Peel

This makes a lovely gift when packed into pretty tins or glass jars.

Prep: 20 minutes plus overnight to dry
Cook: 1 hour 30 minutes

3	large grapefruit or 5 large navel oranges
3½	cups sugar
1½	cups water

1. With knife, score peel of each grapefruit into quarters, cutting through peel and white pith. Remove peel from grapefruit. (Refrigerate pulp for another use.) Cut grapefruit peel crosswise into ¼-inch-wide strips. Or, if using oranges, cut peel lengthwise into ¼-inch-wide strips.

2. In 4-quart saucepan, combine peel and enough *water* to cover; heat to boiling over high heat. Boil 5 minutes; drain. Repeat 2 more times, draining peel well and using fresh water each time.

3. In deep heavy 12-inch skillet, combine 2½ cups sugar with water; heat to boiling over high heat, stirring until sugar has dissolved. With pastry brush dipped in cold water, wash down sugar crystals on side of saucepan.

4. Set candy thermometer in place and continue cooking, stirring occasionally, until temperature reaches 230° to 234°F (thread stage), about 15 minutes.

5. Add drained peel to sugar syrup and stir to coat evenly. Reduce heat and partially cover; simmer, stirring occasionally, until peel has absorbed most of syrup, about 1 hour. Remove cover and continue cooking, stirring gently, until all syrup has been absorbed.

6. On waxed paper, place remaining 1 cup sugar. With tongs, lift a few pieces of peel from skillet and lightly roll in sugar. Arrange sugared peel in single layer on wire racks set over waxed paper. Let peel dry at least 12 hours or up to overnight. If necessary, dry longer; peel should be dry on the outside but still moist on the inside. Store candied peel at room temperature in airtight container up to 1 month. Makes about 2 pounds.

♥ Each ounce: About 90 calories, 0g protein, 23g carbohydrate, 0g total fat (0g saturated), 0mg cholesterol, 0mg sodium.

Toffee Almond Crunch

This crunch is also delicious without the chocolate topping.

Prep: 25 minutes plus cooling and standing   Cook: 30 minutes

1¾	cups sugar
⅓	cup light corn syrup
¼	cup water
1	cup butter or margarine (2 sticks), cut into pieces
2	cups blanched slivered almonds (8 ounces), lightly toasted and finely chopped
2	squares (2 ounces) unsweetened chocolate, chopped
2	squares (2 ounces) semisweet chocolate, chopped
1	teaspoon vegetable shortening

1. Lightly grease 15½" by 10½" jelly-roll pan.

2. In heavy 2-quart saucepan, combine sugar, corn syrup, and water; cook over medium heat, stirring occasionally, until sugar has dissolved and syrup is bubbling. Stir in butter.

3. Set candy thermometer in place and continue cooking, stirring frequently, until temperature reaches 300° to 310°F (hard-crack stage), about 20 minutes. (Once temperature reaches 220°F, it will rise quickly, so watch carefully.) Remove from heat.

4. Reserve ⅓ cup almonds. Stir remaining 1⅔ cups almonds into hot syrup. Immediately pour hot mixture into prepared jelly-roll pan; working quickly, with two forks, spread mixture evenly. Cool candy completely in pan on wire rack.

5. Meanwhile, in heavy 1-quart saucepan, melt unsweetened and semisweet chocolates and shortening over low heat, stirring, until smooth. Remove from heat; cool slightly.

6. Lift out candy, in one piece, and place on cutting board. With narrow metal spatula, spread warm chocolate evenly over candy; sprinkle with reserved ⅓ cup almonds, gently pressing them into chocolate. Let stand until chocolate has set, about 1 hour.

7. Use sharp knife to help break hardened candy into pieces. Layer between waxed paper in airtight container. Store in refrigerator up to 1 month. Makes about 1¾ pounds.

Each ounce: About 189 calories, 2g protein, 19g carbohydrate, 13g total fat (6g saturated), 18mg cholesterol, 73mg sodium.

Toffee Almond Crunch

Wrap your homemade candies in creative packaging for gifts as pretty as they are delicious.

- Collect unusual (and unbreakable) containers, such as Shaker-style wooden boxes that can be trimmed with a length of sheer or velvet ribbon.
- Antique tin boxes and baking pans (flea market finds) of various shapes and sizes can be lined with colored cellophane and tied up with raffia.
- Collect old vanilla bottles. They can look charming tied to the top of a box of candy.
- Old Mason jars are perfect for packing candied citrus peel. Hot-glue tiny pine cones to the jar, along with a bit of greenery.

CHRISTINE MCCABE

PHOTO STYLIST

EXPERT TIP

22

FROZEN DESSERTS

A frozen dessert (including ice cream and its cousins sherbet, granita, sorbet, ice, and frozen yogurt) stands alone in the world of sweets. In a single taste, its richness and flavor satisfies, its smooth, melting texture comforts, and its coolness refreshes. Old-fashioned ice cream brings out the child in us, probably because it evokes memories of carefree summer days with ice-cream trucks and dripping cones—a time when calories didn't count. Yet there is nothing childish about an elegant, intensely flavored fruit sorbet or granita, fat-free treats that have the same endearing qualities as ice cream.

With today's ice-cream makers, preparing homemade frozen desserts is a breeze. Many of our desserts, however, do not even require a machine, just the freezer compartment of your refrigerator. Nothing beats the flavor of freshly made frozen desserts prepared from juicy seasonal fruits, the very best chocolate, or fragrant vanilla beans. In this chapter, we have also included spectacular ice-cream cakes and other showstoppers that are made with high-quality, store-bought ice cream and surprisingly little effort.

ICE CREAM AND FAMILY

Ice cream Dairy-rich ice cream is one of life's culinary luxuries. Most are prepared with an egg-custard base, giving the

Banana-Split Cake

ice cream an unsurpassable silkiness. These ice creams may also be called frozen custard, French ice cream, or gelato. Philadelphia-style ice cream doesn't contain egg yolks, resulting in a slightly icy texture that emphasizes the flavor of the cream. Frozen yogurt is a reduced-fat cousin of ice cream.

Sherbet A frozen combination of fruit juice (usually citrus), sugar, and milk, cream, or egg whites.

Sorbet Smooth-textured sorbet is usually made from a sweetened fruit puree without dairy products.

Ices Made from sweetened fruit purees or juices, ices are beaten with a mixer after an initial freezing to incorporate air and produce a lighter texture; it is frozen again until firm.

Granita Italian in origin, granita has the same ingredients as sorbet, but it is chilled in a (baking) pan and stirred frequently during freezing to achieve a granular, icy texture (*granita* comes from the Latin word for grain).

MAKING ICE CREAM AT HOME

Using an ice-cream machine used to be quite a job because most of them required crushed ice and rock salt to chill the canister in its housing. Now there are a variety of ice-cream makers, and they are all easy and fun to use. Regardless of their design, they all have dashers that beat the ice-cream mixture during freezing to incorporate air; otherwise, the mixture would freeze solid (like an ice cube).

Popular, inexpensive models use regular ice cubes and regular salt. The salt lowers the temperature of the ice-water mixture to the subzero level needed to freeze the ice-cream base. If you use one of these machines, be sure to have plenty of ice and at least two pounds of salt on hand. The kind of salt does not matter; either table or kosher is fine. And because you might be using quite a lot of ice, you may want to buy it rather than make enough ice cubes at home.

Some machines have removable canisters that are frozen ahead of time. The most expensive ice-cream machines contain their own freezer units. Some cooks, however, still prefer the old-fashioned crushed ice and rock salt models because they have the ability to make large quantities of ice cream. If you have a smaller machine but need to make more ice cream than the canister allows, just prepare it in batches. You will need fresh ice and salt for each batch, however, so make sure you have enough on hand.

Regardless of the machine you use, the technique for making ice cream (or one of its cousins) is the same. First and most importantly: Only use the ripest, juiciest, most flavorful fruit at the peak of its season. Flavorless fruit makes bland, characterless ice cream. Shop at farmers' markets, U-pick farms, roadside stands, or the most reliable produce store in town. Frozen fruit is preferable to mediocre fresh fruit.

The base mixture, whether prepared from a custard, fruit puree, or other combination, must be well chilled before freezing. Press plastic wrap or waxed paper directly onto the custard base to prevent a skin from forming on the surface. If you want to speed the chilling process, place the mixture in a metal bowl set into a larger bowl of ice water; stir often until well chilled.

Since frozen mixtures dull one's taste buds, ice creams must be well sweetened to intensify their flavors. For the smoothest frozen desserts, sugar syrups are often used. Be sure the syrup is well chilled before using.

It is certainly tempting to serve freshly frozen ice cream as soon as it is ready, but it will improve if allowed to rest in the freezer for a few hours first. The flavors will deepen and the texture will be firmer and, therefore, easier to scoop. Transfer the ice cream from the machine canister to an airtight container and cover tightly. Most homemade frozen desserts are best eaten within a few days.

Some of these recipes call for slightly softened ice cream, which is easier to spread. The best place to soften ice cream is in the refrigerator. It will usually take twenty to thirty minutes. Check it often.

Rich Vanilla-Bean Ice Cream

Using a vanilla bean instead of vanilla extract makes this classic extra special. The yolks in the custard base make it sinfully rich.

Prep: 5 minutes plus chilling and freezing	Cook: 15 minutes
1	vanilla bean or 1 tablespoon vanilla extract
¾	cup sugar
3	cups half-and-half or light cream
4	large egg yolks
⅛	teaspoon salt
1	cup heavy or whipping cream

1. Chop vanilla bean, if using, into ¼-inch pieces. In blender, process vanilla bean and sugar until vanilla bean is very finely ground.

2. In heavy 3-quart saucepan, heat half-and-half to boiling over medium-high heat.

3. Meanwhile, in medium bowl, with wire whisk, whisk egg yolks, vanilla-sugar mixture, and salt until smooth. Gradually whisk half-and-half into egg-yolk mixture. Return mixture to saucepan and cook over medium heat, stirring constantly, just until mixture coats back of spoon (do not boil, or it will curdle). Remove saucepan from heat.

4. Strain custard through sieve into large bowl; add heavy cream and vanilla extract, if using. Press plastic wrap onto surface of custard. Refrigerate until well chilled, at least 2 hours or up to overnight.

5. Freeze in ice-cream maker as manufacturer directs. Makes about 5 cups or 10 servings.

Each serving: About 261 calories, 4g protein, 19g carbohydrate, 19g total fat (11g saturated), 144mg cholesterol, 71mg sodium.

No-Cook Vanilla Ice Cream

This is an example of Philadelphia-style ice cream: egg-free but creamy and delicious.

Prep: 5 minutes plus freezing	
2	cups half-and-half or light cream
2	cups heavy or whipping cream
¾	cup sugar
1	tablespoon vanilla extract
⅛	teaspoon salt

In large bowl, stir half-and-half, heavy cream, sugar, vanilla, and salt until sugar has completely dissolved. Freeze in ice-cream maker as manufacturer directs. Makes about 6½ cups or 13 servings.

Each serving: About 177 calories, 2g protein, 3g carbohydrate, 18g total fat (11g saturated), 64mg cholesterol, 52mg sodium.

Old-Fashioned Vanilla Ice Cream

The flour-based custard makes a velvety ice cream.

Prep: 5 minutes plus chilling and freezing	Cook: 15 minutes
1	cup sugar
3	tablespoons all-purpose flour
½	teaspoon salt
3	cups milk
3	large eggs
1½	cups heavy or whipping cream
4	teaspoons vanilla extract

1. In heavy 3-quart saucepan, combine sugar, flour, and salt; stir in milk until well blended. Cook over medium heat, stirring frequently, until mixture has thickened and boils. Remove saucepan from heat.

2. In medium bowl, with wire whisk, lightly beat eggs; stir in about ½ cup of hot milk mixture. Over medium heat, slowly pour egg mixture back into milk mixture in saucepan, stirring rapidly to prevent curdling. Remove saucepan from heat. Strain custard through sieve into large bowl. Press plastic wrap onto surface of custard. Refrigerate until well chilled, about 3 hours or up to overnight.

3. Add heavy cream and vanilla to custard. Freeze in ice-cream maker as manufacturer directs. Makes about 6½ cups or 13 servings.

Each serving: About 216 calories, 4g protein, 20g carbohydrate, 13g total fat (8g saturated), 95mg cholesterol, 142mg sodium.

Chocolate-Chip Ice Cream

Prepare Old-Fashioned Vanilla Ice Cream as directed. Immediately after churning, stir **1 package (4 ounces) sweet cooking chocolate,** chopped, into ice cream until well mixed.

Each serving: About 260 calories, 4g protein, 26g carbohydrate, 16g total fat (10g saturated), 95mg cholesterol, 143mg sodium.

Strawberry Ice Cream

Prepare custard for Old-Fashioned Vanilla Ice Cream as directed in Steps 1 and 2. While custard is chilling, in medium bowl, crush **1 quart strawberries,** hulled with ½ **cup sugar** and **2 tablespoons fresh lemon juice;** refrigerate until well chilled, at least 1 hour or up to 4 hours. Stir strawberry mixture into chilled custard. Freeze in ice-cream maker as manufacturer directs. Makes about 11 cups or 22 servings.

Each serving: About 154 calories, 3g protein, 19g carbohydrate, 8g total fat (5g saturated), 56mg cholesterol, 84mg sodium.

Peach Ice Cream

Prepare custard for Old-Fashioned Vanilla Ice Cream as directed in Steps 1 and 2. When custard is almost chilled, in blender or in food processor with knife blade attached, puree **10 to 12 ripe medium peaches,** peeled, pitted, and cut into pieces, with ½ **cup sugar** until smooth. (There should be 3 cups.) Add peach puree and ¼ **teaspoon almond extract,** instead of vanilla, to chilled custard. Freeze in ice-cream maker as manufacturer directs. Makes about 11 cups or 22 servings.

Each serving: About 171 calories, 3g protein, 24g carbohydrate, 8g total fat (5g saturated), 56mg cholesterol, 84mg sodium.

Chocolate Ice Cream

A delightfully intense chocolate experience.

Prep: 25 minutes plus chilling and freezing

	Rich Vanilla-Bean Ice Cream (page 748) or No-Cook Vanilla Ice Cream (page 749)
3	squares (3 ounces) unsweetened chocolate, chopped
2	squares (2 ounces) semisweet chocolate, chopped

1. Prepare Rich Vanilla-Bean Ice Cream as directed in Steps 1 through 4, reserving ¼ cup heavy cream, or prepare No-Cook Vanilla Ice Cream, reserving ¼ cup heavy cream and using only 1 teaspoon vanilla.

2. In heavy 2-quart saucepan, melt unsweetened and semisweet chocolates with reserved cream over low heat, stirring, until smooth; remove from heat.

3. Stir 1 cup ice-cream mixture into chocolate mixture; stir back into ice-cream mixture. Freeze in ice-cream maker as manufacturer directs. Makes about 6 cups or 12 servings.

Each serving: About 277 calories, 4g protein, 21g carbohydrate, 21g total fat (13g saturated), 120mg cholesterol, 61mg sodium.

Rum-Raisin Ice Cream

Be sure to use dark Jamaican rum for the best flavor.

Prep: 25 minutes plus chilling and freezing

½	cup dark seedless raisins
⅓	cup dark Jamaican rum
	Rich Vanilla-Bean Ice Cream (page 748) or No-Cook Vanilla Ice Cream (page 749)

1. In nonreactive 1-quart saucepan, combine raisins and rum; heat to boiling over medium heat. Remove saucepan from heat; cover and let stand 20 minutes. Drain, reserving raisins and liquid separately.

2. Meanwhile, prepare Rich Vanilla-Bean Ice Cream as directed in Steps 1 through 4, or prepare No-Cook Vanilla Ice Cream as directed. Add raisin liquid to cream mixture. Freeze in ice-cream maker as manufacturer directs. Stir in raisins immediately after churning. Makes 5½ cups or 11 servings.

Each serving: About 273 calories, 4g protein, 22g carbohydrate, 17g total fat (10g saturated), 131mg cholesterol, 65mg sodium.

Raspberry Ice Cream

A luxurious dessert. Top with Best Blueberry Sauce (page 560) or Raspberry Sauce (page 562).

Prep: 10 minutes plus chilling and freezing

4	cups fresh (about 3 half-pints) or frozen raspberries, thawed
¾	cup sugar
⅛	teaspoon salt
1	cup heavy or whipping cream
1	cup milk

1. In blender or in food processor with knife blade attached, puree raspberries until smooth. With spoon, press raspberries through sieve into large bowl; discard seeds.

2. With wire whisk, stir sugar and salt into raspberry puree until sugar has completely dissolved. Whisk in cream and milk. Cover and refrigerate until well chilled, about 1 hour or up to 4 hours.

3. Freeze in ice-cream maker as manufacturer directs. Makes about 4 cups or 8 servings.

Each serving: About 224 calories, 2g protein, 28g carbohydrate, 12g total fat (7g saturated), 45mg cholesterol, 63mg sodium.

Raspberry Ice Cream and Cantaloupe Sorbet

Orange Sherbet

No need to pull out your ice-cream machine for this rich and creamy sorbet.

Prep: 10 minutes plus chilling and freezing
Cook: 10 minutes

1½	cups milk
½	cup sugar
5	large oranges
⅛	teaspoon salt

1. In heavy 2-quart saucepan, combine milk and sugar; cook over medium-high heat, stirring occasionally, until bubbles form around edge and sugar has completely dissolved, about 2 minutes. Pour into medium bowl; press plastic wrap onto surface. Refrigerate until well chilled, about 1 hour or up to 4 hours.

2. From oranges, grate 1 teaspoon peel and squeeze 2 cups juice. Stir orange peel and juice and salt into chilled milk mixture. Pour into 9-inch square metal baking pan; cover and freeze until firm, at least 4 hours.

3. With spoon, scoop sherbet into food processor with knife blade attached. Process sherbet until smooth but still frozen. Return mixture to pan; cover and freeze until firm, 1 to 2 hours longer.

4. To serve, let sherbet stand at room temperature until just soft enough to scoop, about 10 minutes. Makes about 4 cups or 8 servings.

♥ Each serving: About 104 calories, 2g protein, 21g carbohydrate, 2g total fat (1g saturated), 6mg cholesterol, 60mg sodium.

5-Minute Frozen Peach Yogurt

A food processor makes quick work of this dessert. Try it with strawberries, blueberries, or your favorite combination of flavorful frozen fruits.

Prep: 15 minutes plus standing

1	bag (20 ounces) frozen unsweetened peach slices
1	container (8 ounces) plain lowfat yogurt
1	cup confectioners' sugar
1	tablespoon fresh lemon juice
⅛	teaspoon almond extract

1. Let frozen peaches stand at room temperature 10 minutes. In food processor with knife blade attached, process peaches until fruit resembles finely shaved ice, occasionally scraping down side with rubber spatula.

2. With processor running, add yogurt, confectioners' sugar, lemon juice, and almond extract; process until mixture is smooth and creamy, occasionally scraping down side. Serve immediately. Makes about 4 cups or 8 servings.

♥ Each serving: About 107 calories, 2g protein, 25g carbohydrate, 1g total fat (0g saturated), 2mg cholesterol, 20mg sodium.

Strawberry-Orange Ice

A sweet, refreshing treat to make with fresh strawberries from your local farmers' market. If you like, substitute one-quarter cup orange-flavored liqueur for one-quarter cup orange juice.

Prep: 15 minutes plus freezing

3	pints strawberries, hulled
1¾	cups orange juice
½	cup fresh lemon juice (about 3 large lemons)
1½	cups sugar
⅛	teaspoon salt

1. In blender or in food processor with knife blade attached, in batches, puree strawberries with orange and lemon juices, sugar, and salt until smooth. Transfer strawberry mixture to 13" by 9" metal baking pan.

2. Cover and freeze, stirring occasionally, until partially frozen, about 4 hours. Place large bowl in refrigerator to chill.

3. Spoon strawberry mixture into chilled bowl. With mixer at medium speed, beat until smooth but still frozen. Return mixture to pan; cover and freeze until firm, at least 3 hours or up to 6 hours.

4. To serve, let strawberry ice stand at room temperature until just soft enough to scoop, about 10 minutes. Makes about 9 cups or 18 servings.

♥ Each serving: About 93 calories, 1g protein, 24g carbohydrate, 0g total fat (0g saturated), 0mg cholesterol, 17mg sodium.

Lemon Ice in Lemon Cups

Serve these at your next dinner party with a sprightly sprig of mint on each.

Prep: 30 minutes plus freezing	Cook: 5 minutes

6	large lemons
1	cup sugar
1	envelope unflavored gelatin
2¼	cups water

1. Cut off top one-third of each lemon. Grate peel from lemon tops. Wrap 1 teaspoon grated peel in plastic wrap for garnish and refrigerate; reserve remaining grated peel. Squeeze ¾ cup juice from lemons. With melon baller, remove all pulp and membrane; discard. Cut thin slice off bottom of each lemon cup so it sits flat. Place lemon cups in plastic bag and freeze until ready to fill.

2. In 2-quart saucepan, combine sugar and gelatin; stir in water. Let stand 2 minutes to soften gelatin slightly. Cook over medium-low heat, stirring constantly, until gelatin has completely dissolved. Remove saucepan from heat. Stir in lemon juice and reserved grated peel.

3. Pour lemon mixture into 9-inch square metal baking pan. Cover and freeze, stirring occasionally, until partially frozen, about 2 hours. Place large bowl in refrigerator to chill.

4. Spoon lemon mixture into chilled bowl. With mixer at medium speed, beat until smooth but still frozen. Return mixture to pan; cover and freeze until partially frozen, about 2 hours. Return bowl to refrigerator. Spoon lemon mixture into chilled bowl and beat until smooth but still frozen. Cover and freeze until firm, about 3 hours.

5. Spoon lemon ice into frozen lemon cups. Sprinkle with remaining 1 teaspoon grated lemon peel. Serve immediately, or freeze up to 2 hours. Makes 6 servings.

♥ Each serving: About 141 calories, 1g protein, 36g carbohydrate, 0g total fat (0g saturated), 0mg cholesterol, 3mg sodium.

GRANITAS

Cover and freeze the granita mixture until partially frozen, about 2 hours. Stir with a fork to break up the chunks. Cover and freeze until the mixture is completely frozen, at least 3 hours or up to overnight. To serve, let the granita stand at room temperature until slightly softened, about 15 minutes. Use a metal spoon to scrape across the surface of the granita, transferring the ice shards to chilled dessert dishes or wine goblets without packing them.

Raspberry or Blackberry Granita

Berries make a richly colored granita that tastes like summer.

Prep: 15 minutes plus cooling and freezing	Cook: 5 minutes

1	cup sugar
1¼	cups water
3	pints raspberries or blackberries
2	tablespoons fresh lime juice

1. In 2-quart saucepan, combine sugar and water; heat to boiling over high heat, stirring until sugar has dissolved. Reduce heat to medium and cook 1 minute. Set saucepan in bowl of ice water until syrup is cool.

2. Meanwhile, in blender or in food processor with knife blade attached, puree raspberries until smooth. With spoon, press puree through sieve into medium bowl; discard seeds.

3. Stir sugar syrup and lime juice into puree; pour into 9-inch square metal baking pan. Cover, freeze, and scrape as directed for granitas (left). Makes about 8 cups or 16 servings.

♥ Each serving: About 71 calories, 0g protein, 18g carbohydrate, 0g total fat (0g saturated), 0mg cholesterol, 0mg sodium.

Strawberry Granita

Make this granita with flavorful ripe strawberries for the quintessential early-summer dessert.

Prep: 10 minutes plus cooling and freezing   Cook: 8 minutes

½	cup sugar
1	cup water
2	pints strawberries, hulled
1	tablespoon fresh lemon juice

1. In 2-quart saucepan, combine sugar and water; heat to boiling over high heat, stirring until sugar has dissolved. Reduce heat to medium and cook 5 minutes. Set saucepan in bowl of ice water until syrup is cool.

2. Meanwhile, in blender or in food processor with knife blade attached, puree strawberries until smooth. Stir strawberry puree and lemon juice into sugar syrup; pour into 9-inch square metal baking pan. Cover, freeze, and scrape as directed for granitas (opposite). Makes about 6 cups or 12 servings.

♥ Each serving: About 49 calories, 0g protein, 12g carbohydrate, 0g total fat (0g saturated), 0mg cholesterol, 1mg sodium.

Coffee Granita

A Neapolitan tradition. If you like, use decaffeinated espresso.

Prep: 10 minutes plus cooling and freezing

⅔	cup sugar
2	cups hot espresso coffee
	unsweetened whipped cream (optional)

In medium bowl, stir sugar and espresso until sugar has completely dissolved. Pour into 9-inch square metal baking pan; cool. Cover, freeze, and scrape as directed for granitas (opposite). Serve granita with whipped cream, if you like. Makes about 5 cups or 10 servings.

If you do not have an espresso coffeemaker, use 3 cups water and 1⅓ cups ground espresso coffee in an automatic drip coffee maker.

♥ Each serving without whipped cream: About 53 calories, 0g protein, 14g carbohydrate, 0g total fat (0g saturated), 0mg cholesterol, 1mg sodium.

Clementine Granita

Frozen desserts aren't just summer fare. Clementines and tangerines are winter fruits that make a terrific granita.

Prep: 15 minutes plus cooling and freezing   Cook: 8 minutes

16	clementines or 8 tangerines
⅔	cup sugar
1	cup water

1. From clementines, with vegetable peeler, remove 3 strips (3" by ½" each) peel; squeeze 2½ cups juice.

2. In 2-quart saucepan, combine clementine peel, sugar, and water; heat to boiling over high heat, stirring until sugar has dissolved. Reduce heat to medium; cook 5 minutes. Set saucepan in bowl of ice water until syrup is cool; discard peel.

3. Stir clementine juice into sugar syrup; pour into 9-inch square metal baking pan. Cover, freeze, and scrape as directed for granitas (opposite). Makes about 6 cups or 12 servings.

♥ Each serving: About 66 calories, 0g protein, 16g carbohydrate, 0g total fat (0g saturated), 0mg cholesterol, 1mg sodium.

Lemon Granita

This simple, zesty granita has an invigorating tang.

Prep: 10 minutes plus cooling and freezing   Cook: 10 minutes

1	cup sugar
2	cups water
4	large lemons

1. In 2-quart saucepan, combine sugar and water; heat to boiling over high heat, stirring until sugar has dissolved. Reduce heat to medium and cook 5 minutes. Set saucepan in bowl of ice water until syrup is cool.

2. Meanwhile, from lemons, grate 2 teaspoons peel and squeeze ¾ cup juice.

3. Stir lemon peel and juice into sugar syrup; pour into 9-inch square metal baking pan. Cover, freeze, and scrape as directed for granitas (opposite). Makes about 4 cups or 8 servings.

♥ Each serving: About 103 calories, 0g protein, 27g carbohydrate, 0g total fat (0g saturated), 0mg cholesterol, 1mg sodium.

Watermelon Granita

The ultimate summer refreshment.

Prep: 15 minutes plus cooling and freezing	Cook: 5 minutes
1	cup sugar
¾	cup water
1	piece watermelon (5½ pounds), rind and seeds removed and flesh cut into bite-size pieces (9 cups)
2	tablespoons fresh lime juice

1. In 2-quart saucepan, combine sugar and water; heat to boiling over high heat, stirring until sugar has dissolved. Reduce heat to medium and cook 1 minute. Set saucepan in bowl of ice water until syrup is cool.

2. Meanwhile, in blender or in food processor with knife blade attached, in batches, puree watermelon until smooth. With spoon, press watermelon puree through sieve into large bowl; discard watermelon fibers.

3. Stir sugar syrup and lime juice into watermelon puree; pour into 9-inch square metal baking pan. Cover, freeze, and scrape as directed for granitas (page 752). Makes about 9 cups or 18 servings.

♥ Each serving: About 69 calories, 0g protein, 17g carbohydrate, 0g total fat (0g saturated), 0mg cholesterol, 2mg sodium.

Pink Grapefruit Sorbet

A welcome change from the usual flavors; serve it with a splash of vodka or dark rum.

Prep: 20 minutes plus cooling and freezing	Cook: 15 minutes
3	large pink or red grapefruit
1	cup sugar
¼	cup light corn syrup
4	cups water
	drop red food coloring (optional)

1. From grapefruit, with vegetable peeler, remove 3 strips (4" by ¾" each) peel; squeeze 2 cups juice.

2. In 2-quart saucepan, combine sugar, corn syrup, grapefruit peel, and water; heat to boiling over high heat, stirring until sugar has dissolved. Reduce heat to medium and cook

2 minutes. Set saucepan in bowl of ice water until syrup is cool; discard peel.

3. Strain grapefruit juice through sieve into large bowl. With spoon, press pulp to extract juice; discard pulp. Stir in sugar syrup and food coloring, if using. Pour into 9-inch square metal baking pan; cover and freeze, stirring occasionally, until partially frozen, about 4 hours.

4. In food processor with knife blade attached, process sorbet until smooth but still frozen. Return to pan; cover and freeze until almost firm, 3 to 4 hours.

5. To serve, process sorbet in food processor until smooth. Makes about 5 cups or 10 servings

♥ Each serving: About 120 calories, 0g protein, 31g carbohydrate, 0g total fat (0g saturated), 0mg cholesterol, 11mg sodium.

Chocolate Sorbet

An alternative to rich ice cream, with lots of chocolate flavor.

Prep: 10 minutes plus chilling and freezing	Cook: 12 minutes
¾	cup sugar
2½	cups water
2	squares (2 ounces) unsweetened chocolate, chopped
¼	cup light corn syrup
1½	teaspoons vanilla extract

1. In 2-quart saucepan, combine sugar and water; heat to boiling over high heat, stirring until sugar has dissolved. Reduce heat to medium and cook 3 minutes. Remove from heat.

2. In heavy 1-quart saucepan, combine chocolate and corn syrup; heat over low heat, stirring frequently, until chocolate is melted and smooth.

3. With wire whisk, stir 1 cup sugar syrup into chocolate mixture until well blended. Stir chocolate mixture into remaining sugar syrup in saucepan; stir in vanilla. Pour into medium bowl; cover and refrigerate until well chilled, about 1½ hours.

4. Freeze in ice-cream maker as manufacturer directs. Makes about 4 cups or 8 servings.

♥ Each serving: About 141 calories, 1g protein, 29g carbohydrate, 4g total fat (2g saturated), 0mg cholesterol, 14mg sodium.

Peach Sorbet

Fragrant ripe peaches are a must for this sorbet.

Prep: 15 minutes plus chilling and freezing	Cook: 6 minutes
1¼	cups sugar
½	cup water
3	tablespoons fresh lemon juice
3	pounds fully ripe peaches, peeled, pitted, and sliced (7 to 8 cups)

1. In 2-quart saucepan, combine sugar and water; heat to boiling over high heat, stirring until sugar has dissolved. Reduce heat to medium and cook 3 minutes. Set saucepan in bowl of ice water until syrup is cool; stir in lemon juice.

2. In blender or in food processor with knife blade attached, in batches, puree peaches with sugar syrup until smooth; pour into large bowl. Cover and refrigerate until well chilled, about 2 hours.

3. Freeze in ice-cream maker as manufacturer directs. Makes about 7½ cups or 15 servings.

♥ Each serving: About 95 calories, 0g protein, 25g carbohydrate, 0g total fat (0g saturated), 0mg cholesterol, 0mg sodium.

Cantaloupe Sorbet

If your ice-cream maker is large enough, the recipe can easily be doubled. This sorbet is best eaten the day it's made.

Prep: 15 minutes plus chilling and freezing	Cook: 8 minutes
1	lemon
½	cup sugar
½	cup water
1	ripe cantaloupe (3 to 3½ pounds), rind and seeds removed and flesh chopped (4 cups)

1. From lemon, with vegetable peeler, remove 2 strips (3" by 1" each) peel; squeeze 1 tablespoon juice. In 2-quart saucepan, combine lemon peel, sugar, and water; heat to boiling over high heat, stirring until sugar has dissolved. Reduce heat to medium and cook 5 minutes. Set saucepan in bowl of ice water until syrup is cool; stir in lemon juice. Strain syrup through sieve into large bowl.

2. In blender or in food processor with knife blade attached, in batches, puree cantaloupe until smooth. Stir puree into sugar syrup. Cover and refrigerate until well chilled, 2 to 4 hours.

3. Freeze in ice-cream maker as manufacturer directs. Makes about 3½ cups or 7 servings.

♥ Each serving: About 88 calories, 1g protein, 22g carbohydrate, 0g total fat (0g saturated), 0mg cholesterol, 8mg sodium.

Cantaloupe Cream Sherbet
Prepare as directed, adding ½ **cup heavy or whipping cream** to cantaloupe mixture.

Rocky-Road Freeze

You don't need an ice-cream maker to whip up this sweet treat. If you like, spoon into a Graham Cracker Crust (page 689).

Prep: 15 minutes plus overnight to freeze	
1	can (14 ounces) sweetened condensed milk
½	cup chocolate-flavored syrup
2	cups heavy or whipping cream
1	cup miniature marshmallows
½	cup semisweet chocolate chips
½	cup salted peanuts, chopped

1. In small bowl, combine condensed milk and chocolate syrup until blended.

2. In large bowl, with mixer at medium speed, beat cream just until stiff peaks form. Fold chocolate mixture, marshmallows, chocolate chips, and peanuts into whipped cream just until combined. Cover bowl and freeze overnight.

3. To serve, let mixture stand about 15 minutes at room temperature for easier scooping, then scoop into dessert dishes. Makes about 4½ cups or 12 servings.

Each serving: About 351 calories, 5g protein, 35g carbohydrate, 23g total fat (13g saturated), 66mg cholesterol, 95mg sodium.

Banana-Split Cake

(pictured on page 746)

A fabulous freeze-ahead finale for your next party.

Prep: 35 minutes plus chilling and freezing
Bake: 12 minutes

	Hot Fudge Sauce (page 561)
14	creme-filled chocolate sandwich cookies
3	tablespoons butter or margarine, melted
1	pint vanilla ice cream
4	ripe medium bananas
1	pint chocolate ice cream
1	pint strawberry ice cream
½	cup heavy or whipping cream
¼	cup walnuts, broken into small pieces
	maraschino cherries

1. Preheat oven to 350°F. Prepare Hot Fudge Sauce; let stand to cool completely. In plastic bag, with rolling pin, finely crush cookies.

2. In 9" by 3" springform pan, with fork, stir cookie crumbs and melted butter until evenly moistened. With hand, press cookie mixture firmly onto bottom of pan. Bake until crust is slightly darker at edge, 12 to 14 minutes. Place crust in freezer until well chilled, about 30 minutes.

3. Meanwhile, place vanilla ice cream in refrigerator to soften slightly, about 30 minutes. With narrow metal spatula, evenly spread vanilla ice cream over crust; cover and freeze until firm, about 45 minutes.

4. Cut 3 bananas lengthwise in half. Pour cooled fudge sauce over vanilla ice cream; arrange bananas on top. Cover and freeze cake until fudge sauce is firm, about 1 hour. Meanwhile, place chocolate ice cream in refrigerator to soften slightly, about 30 minutes.

5. Evenly spread chocolate ice cream over fudge sauce and bananas. Cover and freeze until firm, about 20 minutes.

6. Meanwhile, place strawberry ice cream in refrigerator to soften slightly. Spread strawberry ice cream evenly over chocolate ice cream. Cover and freeze until firm, about 3 hours or up to 2 days.

7. To serve, in small bowl, with mixer at medium speed, beat cream until soft peaks form. Cut remaining banana on diagonal into ½-inch-thick slices. Dip small knife in hot water, shaking off excess; run knife around edge of pan to loosen cake. Remove side of pan; place cake on platter. With narrow metal spatula, spread whipped cream on top of cake. Arrange banana slices over whipped cream; sprinkle with walnuts and top with cherries. Let stand about 10 minutes at room temperature for easier slicing. Makes 16 servings.

Each serving: About 324 calories, 4g protein, 38g carbohydrate, 19g total fat (10g saturated), 52mg cholesterol, 158mg sodium.

Raspberry Baked-Alaska Pie

A showstopping dessert that is sure to win you applause.

Prep: 40 minutes plus freezing   Bake: 2 minutes

3	pints vanilla ice cream
2	packages (3 ounces each) soft ladyfingers, split in half
⅓	cup orange-flavored liqueur
1	package (10 ounces) frozen raspberries in syrup, slightly thawed
4	large egg whites
¾	cup sugar
4	teaspoons water
¼	teaspoon cream of tartar
¼	teaspoon salt

1. Transfer ice cream to large bowl and place in refrigerator to soften slightly, about 30 minutes. Line bottom and side of 9-inch deep-dish pie plate with about two-thirds of ladyfingers, rounded side down, allowing ends to extend beyond pie plate rim. Drizzle with half of liqueur.

2. In medium bowl, crush raspberries. Drop dollops of raspberries over ice cream in large bowl; with knife, cut through raspberries and ice cream once or twice to create marbled effect. With large serving spoon, carefully transfer half of ice cream into pie plate, keeping marbled effect; place bowl of remaining ice cream in freezer. Arrange remaining ladyfingers on top of ice cream in pie plate; drizzle with remaining liqueur. Spoon remaining ice cream evenly over ladyfingers. Cover and freeze until firm, at least 4 hours.

3. In medium bowl set over saucepan of simmering water, with mixer at medium speed, beat egg whites, sugar, water, cream of tartar, and salt until soft peaks form when beaters are lifted or until temperature on thermometer

reaches 160°F, 10 to 14 minutes. Place bowl on surface; continue to beat egg whites until stiff peaks form when beaters are lifted, 8 to 10 minutes longer. With spoon, quickly spread meringue over top of pie, sealing meringue to edge and making decorative swirls with back of spoon. Freeze, uncovered, up to 6 hours.

4. To serve, preheat oven to 500°F. Bake pie until meringue is lightly browned, 2 to 3 minutes. Makes 12 servings.

♥ Each serving: About 281 calories, 5g protein, 45g carbohydrate, 9g total fat (5g saturated), 81mg cholesterol, 140mg sodium.

CUTTING FROZEN DESSERTS

To cut ice cream cakes or pies, dip a thin knife into hot water. Plunge the point into the center of the dessert, cutting all the way through. Using an up-and-down sawing motion, cut through to the outside edge.

Sorbet-and-Cream Cake

Here's a colorful dessert for a festive meal. Substitute raspberry and passion fruit sorbets, or your favorite flavors, for the strawberry and mango if you prefer.

Prep: 30 minutes plus freezing and chilling
Bake: 10 minutes

1	cup vanilla wafer crumbs (30 cookies)
4	tablespoons butter or margarine, melted
½	teaspoon freshly grated lime peel
2	pints vanilla ice cream
1	pint strawberry sorbet
1	pint mango sorbet
1	pint lemon sorbet
1	ripe mango, peeled and sliced
	fresh raspberries

1. Preheat oven to 375°F. In 9" by 3" springform pan, with fork, stir wafer crumbs, melted butter, and lime peel until crumbs are evenly moistened. With hand, press mixture firmly onto bottom of pan. Bake crust 10 minutes. Place in freezer until well chilled, about 30 minutes.

2. Meanwhile, place 1 pint vanilla ice cream and strawberry, mango, and lemon sorbets in refrigerator to soften slightly, about 30 minutes.

3. Arrange alternating scoops of vanilla ice cream and strawberry, mango, and lemon sorbets over crust in two layers; with rubber spatula, press down to eliminate air pockets. Place in freezer until ice cream is firm, about 30 minutes.

4. Meanwhile, place remaining 1 pint vanilla ice cream in refrigerator to soften slightly. With narrow metal spatula, evenly spread vanilla ice cream over ice-cream layers. Cover and freeze until firm, at least 4 hours or up to 1 day.

5. To serve, dip small knife in hot water, shaking off excess; run knife around edge of pan to loosen cake. Remove side of pan; place cake on platter. Let stand about 15 minutes at room temperature for easier slicing. Decorate top of cake with mango slices and raspberries. Makes 20 servings.

Each serving: About 161 calories, 1g protein, 27g carbohydrate, 6g total fat (3g saturated), 18mg cholesterol, 63mg sodium.

Biscuit Tortoni

This rich frozen Italian dessert gets its light texture from a mixture of whipped cream and meringue.

Prep: 15 minutes plus freezing	Cook: 10 minutes
3	large egg whites
¼	cup plus 2 tablespoons sugar
3	tablespoons water
¼	teaspoon cream of tartar
1	cup heavy or whipping cream
2	tablespoons sweet sherry or Marsala wine
½	cup amaretti cookie crumbs (10 cookies)

1. Line twelve 2½-inch muffin-pan cups with paper baking liners. In medium bowl set over saucepan of simmering water, with mixer at medium speed, beat egg whites, sugar, water, and cream of tartar until soft peaks form when beaters are lifted or until temperature on thermometer reaches 160°F, 10 to 14 minutes. Transfer to large bowl; beat until stiff peaks form when beaters are lifted, 8 to 10 minutes longer.

2. In medium bowl, with same beaters and mixer at high speed, beat cream and sherry just until stiff peaks form. Gently fold whipped cream into egg whites until blended; fold in cookie crumbs. Spoon evenly into paper-lined cups. Freeze until firm, about 2 hours. Makes 12 servings.

Each serving: About 120 calories, 2g protein, 11g carbohydrate, 8g total fat (5g saturated), 27mg cholesterol, 24mg sodium.

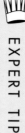

Taking a minute to wrap desserts properly for freezing is time well spent. For ice cream, rigid plastic containers with tight-fitting lids work well. For other frozen desserts, place the dessert in the freezer until hard, then wrap tightly, first with plastic wrap and then with heavy-duty foil. The plastic wrap forms a tight seal, while the heavy foil protects the dessert from moisture and punctures.

ELINOR KLIVANS
COOKBOOK AUTHOR

EXPERT TIP

Tartufo

*These chocolate-coated ice-cream balls are intended to resemble truffles (*tartufo *means "truffle" in Italian).*

Prep: 30 minutes plus freezing	
1	pint chocolate or vanilla ice cream
2	tablespoons brandy
6	maraschino cherries, stems removed
1	cup fine amaretti cookie crumbs (20 cookies)
1½	cups semisweet chocolate chips
4	tablespoons butter or margarine, cut into pieces
2	tablespoons light corn syrup

1. Place ice cream in refrigerator to soften slightly, about 30 minutes. Line small cookie sheet with waxed paper and place in freezer. Meanwhile, in cup, pour brandy over cherries. Place amaretti crumbs on waxed paper.

2. Working quickly, with large ice-cream scoop (⅓ cup), scoop ball of ice cream. With ice cream still in scoop, gently

ICE CREAM TREATS

MINI ICE CREAM SANDWICHES
Spread flat side of 2 chocolate- or vanilla-wafer cookies with thin layer of creamy peanut butter. Sandwich small scoop of your favorite ice cream between two peanut butter–coated sides.

WAFFLES AND ICE CREAM
Lightly toast 1 frozen Belgian waffle; top with vanilla ice cream or frozen yogurt and frozen (thawed) strawberries or raspberries in syrup.

ICE CREAM PARFAITS
Pour some almond-flavored liqueur over 1 scoop coffee ice cream; top with whipped cream and crushed amaretti cookies.

ICE CREAM DRINK
In blender, combine 2 tablespoons orange-flavored liqueur with 2 scoops peach or vanilla ice cream; blend until smooth. Pour into tall glass; top with whipped cream.

S'MORE SUNDAE
Spoon 1 tablespoon fudge sauce over graham cracker; top with 1 scoop chocolate ice cream and marshmallow topping.

press 1 cherry deep into center of ball; reshape ice cream around cherry. Release ice-cream ball on top of amaretti crumbs and roll to coat well. Place on prepared cookie sheet in freezer. Repeat to make 6 ice-cream balls. Freeze until firm, at least 1½ hours.

3. In medium bowl set over saucepan of simmering water, heat chocolate chips with butter and corn syrup, stirring occasionally, until chocolate and butter have melted and mixture is smooth. Remove pan from heat, but leave bowl in place to keep chocolate warm for easier coating.

4. Remove 1 ice-cream ball from freezer; place in slotted spoon and slip ice-cream ball into melted chocolate, turning quickly to coat thoroughly. Return to cookie sheet. Repeat with remaining ice-cream balls. Freeze until chocolate is firm, about 1 hour. If not serving right away, wrap in foil and freeze up to 1 day.

5. To serve, let tartufo stand at room temperature until slightly softened, about 10 minutes. Makes 6 servings.

Each serving: About 476 calories, 5g protein, 59g carbohydrate, 27g total fat (15g saturated), 36mg cholesterol, 133mg sodium.

Tulipes

For an elegant presentation at a dinner party or other special occasion serve your favorite ice cream in these delicate cookie shells.

Prep: 30 minutes   Bake: 5 minutes per batch

3	large egg whites
¾	cup confectioners' sugar
½	cup all-purpose flour
6	tablespoons butter, melted (do not use margarine)
½	teaspoon vanilla extract
¼	teaspoon salt
1	quart ice cream or sorbet

1. Preheat oven to 350°F. Grease large cookie sheet. In large bowl, with wire whisk, beat egg whites, confectioners' sugar, and flour until well blended. Beat in melted butter, vanilla, and salt.

2. Make 2 cookies by dropping batter by heaping tablespoons, 4 inches apart, on prepared cookie sheet. With narrow metal spatula, spread batter to form 4-inch rounds. Bake cookies until golden around edges, 5 to 7 minutes.

Tulipes

3. Place two 2-inch-diameter glasses upside down on surface. With spatula, quickly lift 1 hot cookie and gently shape over bottom of glass. Shape second cookie. When cookies are cool, transfer to wire rack. (If cookies become too firm to shape, return them to cookie sheet and place in oven to soften slightly.)

4. Repeat Steps 2 and 3 with remaining batter. (Batter will become slightly thicker upon standing.) Store tulipes in single layer in airtight container at room temperature. To serve, place on dessert plates and fill with ice cream. Makes about 12 tulipes.

Each serving with ice cream: About 192 calories, 3g protein, 22g carbohydrate, 11g total fat (7g saturated), 35mg cholesterol, 155mg sodium.

23

BEVERAGES

Beginning the day with a cup of coffee or tea is a time-honored ritual that should never become mundane. Here are the basics for making perfect coffee and tea every day, as well as beverages for more festive occasions, including party-size punches, eggnogs, and hot winter treats. When the weather is warm, serve one of our fruit juice–based thirst quenchers. And when you need a quick meal on the run, whip up a thick and creamy fruit smoothie.

COFFEE

Coffee starts out as a bean, actually the seed of the fruit of the coffee plant. Most coffees are named for their places of origin: Colombia, Sumatra, Java, and Kona are just a few of the most common. Coffee stores often combine different coffee beans to make proprietary blends.

Coffee beans are roasted to bring out their flavor and aroma. The four basic roasting categories are light, medium, medium dark, and high. But there are also many roasting variances within these categories, which give each coffee its personality. Most American coffee is medium roast and usually brewed in a drip or percolator coffeepot. French-roast coffee is darker and oilier, and Italian-roast coffee is roasted almost to

Limeade

the point of carbonization (blackening). These darker roasts are usually prepared in an espresso machine to make the strong, intense European-style coffees that have established themselves as the new favorites. How finely or coarsely coffee is ground depends on the method of brewing: For espresso, a fine grind is needed, whereas coffee headed for a drip pot is more coarsely ground.

Coffee rapidly loses its flavor and aroma when exposed to air, moisture, heat, and light (in that order). So the freshness of the coffee you purchase is very important. Because grinding exposes the beans to air, many coffee aficionados prefer to grind their coffee beans at home right before brewing.

Store ground coffee or coffee beans in an airtight container; the brown bags most coffee stores use do not keep coffee very fresh. Store the coffee you use on a daily basis in a cool dark location; the coffee will retain its flavor for two to three weeks. If you must store coffee longer, store airtight in the freezer for up to one month. After that, the flavor will suffer. Once coffee is removed from the freezer for any length of time, store in a cool dry place. Do not return it to the freezer.

If you are using chilled ground coffee or beans, return them to the refrigerator or freezer as soon as possible; cold coffee attracts humidity, so when brewed, the coffee will taste weak. Unopened cans of vacuum-packed coffee and jars of instant coffee will keep for up to one year in a cool dry place. Once they're opened, follow the storage suggestions above.

BREWING HOT COFFEE

For the best results, use only the grind of coffee recommended for your coffeemaker. Follow the manufacturer's directions, or use ¾ cup (6 ounces) fresh cold water and 1 to 2 tablespoons ground coffee per cup. Proceed as directed.

PERCOLATOR COFFEE

For stovetop percolators, just before serving, place a measured amount of cold water into the bottom of the percolator. Return the stem and basket to the pot. Measure the coffee into the basket; replace the basket lid and cover the pot. Over high heat, heat the water to boiling. Reduce the heat to low and perk for 5 to 8 minutes. Remove from the heat and remove the basket and stem. Let stand for 1 to 2 minutes before serving to allow any sediment to settle to the bottom.

DRIP COFFEE

For nonelectric drip coffeemakers (including paper and gold-washed filters), just before serving, bring the water to a boil; remove from the heat and let stand about 15 seconds. Line the cone with a paper filter if the manufacturer directs. Pour enough water over the coffee to moisten, wait about 30 seconds, then pour the remaining water through the filter, in batches, if necessary. When the dripping is completed, remove the basket and discard the grounds.

For electric drip coffeemakers, just before serving, measure the coffee into the basket and line with a paper filter, if directed. Measure the water and pour into the water compartment of the machine. Replace the pot and turn on the machine; let the coffee drip through the coffee basket.

TEA

Tea, which was first sipped over two thousand years ago in China, was originally appreciated for its medicinal qualities. And although China is still one of the world's largest tea producers, it is also grown in Sri Lanka, Japan, India, and Africa. There are thousands of varieties of teas, but they all fall into four general categories: black, green, oolong, and herbal. We often use tea bags for convenience, but tea lovers agree that for the best flavor, you should use loose tea.

Full-flavored *black tea* is the most popular tea in the world. The leaves are fermented to develop their tannins—the longer the leaves ferment, the less astringent and the darker the brewed tea. Some examples include Assam, Keemun, Darjeeling, and Ceylon. Earl Grey is a blend of black teas and oil of bergamot, a small acidic orange. Black teas are graded according to the size of the leaves. Orange Pekoe is neither orange in color nor in flavor; rather, its name indicates long, well-formed leaves.

Green tea leaves are dried but unfermented, so the resulting mild brew reflects the flavor of the tea in its natural state. Green tea is beloved by the Japanese, and some of the best green teas are Japanese in origin. The highest grade is Gunpowder, so called because the leaves are rolled into small balls that resemble gunshot.

The leaves for *oolong tea* are only partially fermented, so the tea has the qualities of both black and green teas. The most prized is Formosa Oolong, which has a peachlike flavor and deep amber color.

Herbal teas are not classified as true teas. They are made from the dried leaves or flower buds of herbs and plants, which are often blended with other aromatic ingredients, such as citrus peels and spices. They are usually caffeine-free, unless they are blended with black tea or maté, a Latin American plant whose leaves are brewed as a caffeinated beverage.

Loose tea and tea bags should be stored at cool room temperature. After opening tea, transfer it to an airtight container and use within six months.

BREWING HOT TEA

Use ¾ cup (6 ounces) freshly boiled water and 1 rounded teaspoon loose tea (or 1 tea bag) for each cup of tea. Preheat the teapot by rinsing it out with boiling water. Measure the loose tea into the hot teapot (or into a tea ball before placing into the teapot). Pour freshly boiled water over the tea. Cover the teapot and let steep for 3 to 5 minutes. Do not judge the strength of the tea by its color: Some fully brewed teas are light, while others are dark. Stir the tea to make sure the flavor is distributed evenly. Pour it through a small strainer into a teacup (or remove the tea ball or tea bag before pouring).

Irish Coffee

This heady drink was popularized in San Francisco, where it has become the perfect beverage for a foggy night.

🕐 *Prep: 5 minutes*

5	ounces strong freshly brewed coffee
1	jigger (3 tablespoons) Irish whiskey
2 to 3	teaspoons sugar
¼	cup whipped cream

In heatproof stemmed glass or mug, stir coffee, whiskey, and sugar until sugar has dissolved. Top with whipped cream. Serve hot. Makes 1 serving.

One serving: About 254 calories, 1g protein, 12g carbohydrate, 11g total fat (7g saturated), 42mg cholesterol, 15mg sodium.

Spiced Hot Tea

You can personalize this brew by adding the spices in different proportions. It makes great iced tea, too.

🕐 *Prep: 5 minutes plus steeping   Cook: 10 minutes*

5	cups cold water
6	whole cloves
6	whole allspice berries
1	cinnamon stick (3 inches)
5	tea bags of choice
	honey
	lemon or orange wedges (optional)

1. In nonreactive 2-quart saucepan, combine water, cloves, allspice, and cinnamon stick; heat to boiling over high heat. Cover and boil 5 minutes. Remove from heat.

2. Add tea bags to hot spice mixture in saucepan; cover and steep 3 to 5 minutes.

3. To serve, pour tea through small sieve into mugs. Into each mug, stir about 1½ teaspoons honey, or to taste. Serve with lemon or orange wedges, if you like. Makes about 5 cups or 4 servings.

♥ Each serving: About 4 calories, 0g protein, 1g carbohydrate, 0g total fat (0g saturated), 0mg cholesterol, 9mg sodium.

Best Iced Tea

Here's how to brew the clearest and most sparkling iced tea ever.

🕐 *Prep: 5 minutes plus steeping*

8	cups cold water
8	tea bags of choice
	ice cubes
	granulated or superfine sugar
	thin lemon slices

1. In nonreactive 3-quart saucepan, heat 4 cups cold water to boiling over high heat. Remove from heat and stir in tea bags. Cover and steep 5 minutes.

2. Stir again and remove tea bags. Pour tea into heatproof 2½-quart pitcher. Add remaining 4 cups cold water. Cover and let stand until ready to serve.

3. Fill tall glasses with ice cubes and pour tea over. Serve with sugar and lemon slices. Makes 8 cups or 8 servings.

♥ Each serving: About 5 calories, 0g protein, 2g carbohydrate, 0g total fat (0g saturated), 0mg cholesterol, 8mg sodium.

Iced Tea with Lemon and Mint

Prepare as directed but add **1 lemon,** thinly sliced, and **1 cup loosely packed fresh mint leaves** with tea bags.

Iced Tea with Fruit Juice

Prepare as directed but substitute **4 cups peach, apricot, or raspberry juice or nectar or lemonade** for 4 cups cold water.

ICED COFFEE AND TEA

Iced coffee is at its best when brewed with twice the usual amount of ground coffee, because the coffee is diluted by the (melting) ice cubes. Or use regular-strength brewed iced coffee and serve over coffee ice cubes. They're easy to prepare: Pour cool brewed coffee into ice-cube trays and freeze.

The perfect glass of iced tea is sparkling clear, but when refrigerated, iced tea turns cloudy. To make clear iced tea, brew the tea with half the usual amount of boiling water, then add enough cold water to cool the tea. If you must refrigerate iced tea, stir a little boiling water into the chilled tea until it clears.

Hearty Hot Cocoa

Classic, soothing, and delicious.

Prep: 5 minutes   Cook: 8 minutes

²/₃	cup unsweetened cocoa
½	cup sugar
¾	cup water
5¼	cups milk
½	teaspoon vanilla extract
6	marshmallows or whipped cream

1. In heavy 3-quart saucepan, stir cocoa, sugar, and water until smooth. Heat to boiling over medium-high heat.

2. Stir in milk; heat until tiny bubbles form around edge (do not boil). Remove from heat and stir in vanilla.

3. Pour into cups or mugs and top each serving with marshmallow or dollop of whipped cream. Makes 6 cups or 6 servings.

Each serving: About 241 calories, 9g protein, 38g carbohydrate, 8g total fat (5g saturated), 30mg cholesterol, 110mg sodium.

Ice Cream Soda

Vary this traditional soda-fountain treat with different flavors of syrup and ice cream. For a professional look, "hook" the ice cream onto the lip of the glass.

Prep: 5 minutes

¼	cup milk
2 to 3	tablespoons chocolate-flavored or fruit-flavored syrup
1	scoop vanilla ice cream
	plain seltzer or club soda, chilled
	whipped cream (optional)

Pour milk into tall glass; stir in syrup. Add ice cream and enough seltzer to almost fill glass; stir. Top with whipped cream, if desired. Serve with iced-tea spoon and straw. Makes 1 serving.

One serving: About 272 calories, 5g protein, 46g carbohydrate, 10g total fat (6g saturated), 38mg cholesterol, 128mg sodium.

Mango-Strawberry Smoothie

Mango-Strawberry Smoothie

All you need to whip up a fruit-filled smoothie for breakfast or a snack is a blender. Blend different fruits and juices with the yogurt and ice cubes to vary the drinks. If you use frozen fruit, skip the ice cubes.

Prep: 5 minutes

1	cup fresh or frozen unsweetened strawberries
1	cup mango or apricot nectar
½	cup plain or vanilla yogurt
4	ice cubes

In blender, process strawberries, mango nectar, yogurt, and ice cubes until smooth and frothy. Pour into two tall glasses. Serve with straws, if you like. Makes 2 servings.

Each serving: About 129 calories, 4g protein, 27g carbohydrate, 1g total fat (1g saturated), 3mg cholesterol, 44mg sodium.

Peach Smoothie

Prepare as directed but substitute **1 cup peeled, sliced fresh or frozen unsweetened peaches** for strawberries and **1 cup peach juice or nectar or apple juice** for mango nectar.

Banana Smoothie

Prepare as directed but substitute **1 ripe medium banana** for strawberries and **1 cup pineapple or orange juice** for mango nectar. Add ½ **teaspoon vanilla extract,** if desired.

Limeade

(pictured on page 760)

Some people find limeade even more refreshing than lemonade. This one is especially good with fresh berries added—try sliced strawberries, raspberries, or blueberries.

Prep: 25 minutes plus standing and chilling
Cook: 10 minutes

2	cups sugar
3½	cups cold water
1¼	cups fresh lime juice (about 10 limes)
	ice cubes

1. In 2-quart saucepan, combine sugar and water; heat to boiling over high heat, stirring until sugar has dissolved. Reduce heat to medium and cook 2 minutes. Remove from heat; cover and let stand 10 minutes.

2. Add lime juice to sugar syrup in saucepan; pour limeade into heatproof 1½-quart pitcher. Cover and refrigerate until well chilled, about 3 hours. To serve, fill tall glasses with ice cubes and pour limeade over. Makes about 6 cups or 6 servings.

♥ Each serving: About 272 calories, 0g protein, 71g carbohydrate, 0g total fat (0g saturated), 0mg cholesterol, 1mg sodium.

Ginger Limeade

Prepare as directed but combine **6 quarter-size slices fresh ginger** with sugar and water.

Lemonade

There's nothing like good old-fashioned lemonade. It's like drinking summer from a glass.

Prep: 25 minutes plus standing and chilling
Cook: 10 minutes

2	cups sugar
2	cups cold water
1	lemon, thinly sliced (optional)
2	cups fresh lemon juice (about 10 large lemons)
	ice cubes

1. In 2-quart saucepan, combine sugar and water; heat to boiling over high heat, stirring until sugar has dissolved. Reduce heat to medium and cook 2 minutes. Remove from heat; add sliced lemon, if using. Cover and let stand 10 minutes.

2. Add lemon juice to sugar syrup in saucepan; pour lemonade through sieve into heatproof 1½-quart pitcher. Discard lemon slices. Cover and refrigerate until well chilled, about 3 hours. To serve, fill tall glasses with ice cubes and pour lemonade over. Makes about 5 cups or 5 servings.

♥ Each serving: About 334 calories, 0g protein, 88g carbohydrate, 0g total fat (0g saturated), 0mg cholesterol, 2mg sodium.

Mint Lemonade

Prepare as directed but add **1 cup loosely packed fresh mint leaves** with the sliced lemon.

Black Cow

This dish is also known as a root beer float. Serve in frosty glasses (pop them in the freezer until well chilled).

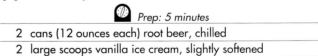 Prep: 5 minutes

2	cans (12 ounces each) root beer, chilled
2	large scoops vanilla ice cream, slightly softened

Pour root beer into two chilled tall glasses. Top each with scoop of ice cream. Serve with iced-tea spoons and straws, if you like. Makes 2 servings.

♥ Each serving: About 257 calories, 2g protein, 47g carbohydrate, 7g total fat (4g saturated), 29mg cholesterol, 78mg sodium.

Holiday Champagne Punch

This pretty punch is refreshing and only slightly sweet.

Prep: 20 minutes   Freeze: 3 hours

1	pint strawberries
1	pound seedless green grapes, stemmed
2	cups orange juice
¼	cup orange-flavored liqueur
1	bottle (1 liter) ginger ale, chilled
1	bottle (750 milliliters) champagne or sparkling white wine, chilled
1	bunch fresh mint

1. Prepare ice ring: Fill 5-cup ring mold with *¼ inch cold water*; freeze until hard, about 45 minutes. Reserve 8 strawberries; hull and slice remaining strawberries. On top of ice in ring mold, decoratively arrange half of sliced strawberries and ½ cup grapes. Add just enough *water* to cover to prevent fruit from floating. Freeze until hard, about 45 minutes. Repeat with remaining strawberry slices, another ½ cup grapes, and enough *water* to cover fruit; freeze until hard, about 45 minutes.

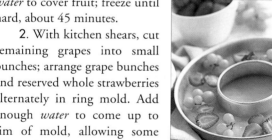

2. With kitchen shears, cut remaining grapes into small bunches; arrange grape bunches and reserved whole strawberries alternately in ring mold. Add enough *water* to come up to rim of mold, allowing some fruit to be exposed above water; freeze until hard, about 45 minutes or up to 6 hours.

3. About 15 minutes before serving, in 5-quart punch bowl or bowl large enough to hold ice ring, combine orange juice and orange liqueur. Stir in ginger ale and champagne.

4. Unmold ice ring and turn, fruit side up. Tuck small mint sprigs between grapes and strawberries. Add ice ring to punch bowl. Makes about 10 cups or 20 servings.

♥ Each serving: About 85 calories, 0g protein, 14g carbohydrate, 0g total fat (0g saturated), 0mg cholesterol, 7mg sodium.

Sangria

This sparkling summer refresher looks lovely in a glass pitcher.

Prep: 15 minutes

2	oranges
2	lemons
1	bottle (750 milliliters) dry red wine, chilled
¼	cup brandy
¼	cup orange-flavored liqueur
⅓	cup sugar
3	cups plain seltzer or club soda, chilled
	ice cubes (optional)

1. With vegetable peeler, remove peel from 1 orange and 2 lemons. (Refrigerate lemons for another use.) Squeeze juice from both oranges.

2. In 2½-quart pitcher, combine wine, orange juice, brandy, orange liqueur, and sugar; stir until sugar has completely dissolved.

3. Stir in orange and lemon peels and seltzer. To serve, half-fill wine glasses with ice, if desired, and pour sangria over. Makes about 7 cups or 14 servings.

♥ Each serving: About 82 calories, 0g protein, 7g carbohydrate, 0g total fat (0g saturated), 0mg cholesterol, 14mg sodium.

White Sangria

Prepare as directed but substitute **1 bottle (750 milliliters) dry white wine** for red wine and add **1 ripe peach,** peeled, pitted, and cut into thin wedges, **or 1 cup sliced unsweetened frozen peaches** with citrus peel in Step 3.

Hot Mulled Wine

If you wish, add other whole spices, such as cardamom pods, all-spice berries, or even black peppercorns. The toasted sliced almonds are a traditional Scandinavian garnish.

Prep: 10 minutes   Cook: 20 minutes

2	cups sugar
1	cup water
1	small orange, thinly sliced
1	small lemon, thinly sliced
3	cinnamon sticks (3 inches each)
8	whole cloves
1	bottle (750 milliliters) dry red wine

1. In nonreactive 4-quart saucepan, combine sugar, water, orange, lemon, cinnamon sticks, and cloves; heat to boiling over high heat, stirring until sugar has dissolved. Reduce heat to medium and cook 3 minutes.

2. Add wine to saucepan and heat, stirring, until hot (do not boil). Serve hot. Makes 8 generous cups or 16 servings.

♥ Each serving: About 170 calories, 0g protein, 28g carbohydrate, 0g total fat (0g saturated), 0mg cholesterol, 5mg sodium.

Hot Mulled Wine

Wassail

This classic Christmas beverage is traditionally made with wine, ale, or hard cider, but we like this less potent combination of sweet cider and apple brandy.

Prep: 10 minutes   Cook: 25 minutes

½	gallon apple cider or juice
1	lemon, thinly sliced
2	tablespoons brown sugar
2	cinnamon sticks (3 inches each)
12	whole allspice berries
12	whole cloves
6	lady apples or 1 Golden Delicious apple
1	cup applejack or apple brandy

1. In nonreactive 5-quart Dutch oven, combine cider, lemon slices, brown sugar, cinnamon sticks, and allspice berries; heat to boiling over medium-high heat. Reduce heat and simmer 10 minutes.

2. Insert 2 cloves into each lady apple or all cloves into Golden Delicious apple. Add apples and applejack to cider and cook until heated through, about 2 minutes. Makes about 8 cups or 16 servings.

♥ Each serving: About 108 calories, 0g protein, 18g carbohydrate, 0g total fat (0g saturated), 0mg cholesterol, 5mg sodium.

Holiday Eggnog

Here's an updated version of eggnog that uses cooked eggs to guarantee that it's salmonella-free. To keep the eggnog chilled, float a pint of vanilla ice cream in the punch bowl.

Prep: 10 minutes plus chilling   **Cook:** 25 minutes

12	large eggs
1¼	cups sugar
½	teaspoon salt
2	quarts milk
1	cup dark rum (optional)
2	tablespoons vanilla extract
1	teaspoon ground nutmeg plus additional for sprinkling
1	cup heavy or whipping cream

1. In heavy 4-quart saucepan, with wire whisk, beat eggs, sugar, and salt until blended. Gradually stir in 1 quart milk and cook over low heat, stirring constantly, until custard thickens and coats the back of a spoon (temperature on thermometer should reach 160°F), about 25 minutes. (Do not boil, or mixture will curdle.)

2. Pour custard into large bowl; stir in remaining 1 quart milk, rum if using, vanilla, and 1 teaspoon nutmeg. Cover and refrigerate until chilled, at least 3 hours or up to 1 day.

3. To serve, in small bowl, with mixer at medium speed, beat cream until soft peaks form. With wire whisk, gently fold whipped cream into custard mixture.

4. Pour eggnog into chilled 5-quart punch bowl; sprinkle with nutmeg. Makes about 16 cups or 32 servings.

Each serving: About 124 calories, 4g protein, 11g carbohydrate, 7g total fat (4g saturated), 98mg cholesterol, 93mg sodium.

Light Eggnog

With less fat than classic eggnog, this holiday treat is easy to enjoy.

Prep: 15 minutes plus chilling   **Cook:** 15 minutes

6	large eggs
6	large egg whites
2	quarts milk
1¼	cups sugar
¼	cup cornstarch
½	teaspoon salt
1	cup dark rum (optional)
2	tablespoons vanilla extract
1	teaspoon ground nutmeg plus additional for sprinkling

1. In large bowl, with wire whisk, beat eggs and egg whites until blended. In heavy 3-quart saucepan, with clean wire whisk, mix 1 quart milk, sugar, cornstarch, and salt until blended. Heat to boiling over medium-high heat, stirring constantly, until mixture has thickened slightly; boil 1 minute. Gradually whisk about 1 cup simmering milk into egg mixture; pour egg mixture back into milk, whisking constantly.

2. With wooden spoon, stir mixture constantly until thermometer reaches 160°F, about 3 minutes. (Do not boil, or it will curdle.) Pour custard into large bowl; stir in remaining 1 quart milk, rum if using, vanilla, and 1 teaspoon nutmeg. Cover and refrigerate until well chilled, at least 3 hours or up to 1 day.

3. Pour eggnog into chilled 5-quart punch bowl; sprinkle with nutmeg. Makes about 13 cups or 26 servings.

Each serving: About 112 calories, 5g protein, 15g carbohydrate, 4g total fat (2g saturated), 60mg cholesterol, 109mg sodium.

If you serve white wine with appetizers or the first course and then red wine with the main course, there's no need to wash the glasses in between. Simply pour out any remaining white wine and pour in the red.

Wine glasses do not need to be elaborate, expensive, or cut crystal. In fact, the best wine glasses are simple ones that are clear, not colored, and have no facets or design. Simple glasses allow you to see the wine. And for super-casual occasions, you don't even need stemmed glasses. Tumblers are perfect! After all, any glass you put wine into becomes a wine glass.

KAREN MACNEIL

CHAIRMAN OF WINE PROGRAMS, CULINARY INSTITUTE OF AMERICA AT GREYSTONE

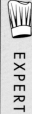

EXPERT TIP

Warm Spiced Cider

This holiday favorite makes a large batch for a crowd of holiday carolers or revelers.

Prep: 10 minutes   Cook: 30 minutes

1	large orange
12	whole cloves
1	lemon
6	cinnamon sticks (3 inches each)
1	gallon apple cider

1. Cut two ½-inch-thick slices from middle of orange. Insert 6 cloves into skin of each orange slice, spacing cloves evenly. Cut remaining orange into thin slices for garnish. With vegetable peeler, from lemon, remove 1-inch-wide continuous strip of peel. (Refrigerate lemon for another use.)

2. In nonreactive 5-quart saucepot, combine clove-studded orange slices with cloves, lemon peel, cinnamon sticks, and apple cider; heat to boiling over high heat. Reduce heat; cover and simmer 15 minutes.

3. Pour hot cider into 5-quart heatproof punch bowl. Float remaining orange slices in cider. Makes about 16 cups or 20 servings.

Each serving: About 95 calories, 0g protein, 24g carbohydrate, 0g total fat (0g saturated), 0mg cholesterol, 6mg sodium.

Fizzy Cranberry-Lemonade Punch

One of the easiest and most refreshing punches. If you wish, offer guests vodka or dark rum on the side to "spike" their drinks.

Prep: 5 minutes

4	cups cranberry-juice cocktail, chilled
1	container (6 ounces) frozen lemonade concentrate, thawed
1	bottle (1 liter) plain seltzer or club soda, chilled
	ice cubes (optional)
1	small orange, cut into ¼-inch-thick slices and each slice cut in half

In large pitcher, stir cranberry-juice cocktail and lemonade concentrate until blended. Stir in seltzer and ice cubes, if you like. Add orange slices and serve. Makes about 9 cups or 12 servings.

Each serving: About 81 calories, 0g protein, 21g carbohydrate, 0g total fat (0g saturated), 0mg cholesterol, 23mg sodium.

Italian Lemon Cordial

Known as limoncello, *this after-dinner drink is best served in tiny glasses right from the freezer so it's very cold and syrupy.*

Prep: 10 minutes plus 1 week standing, cooling, and chilling
Cook: 5 minutes

6	lemons
1	bottle (750 milliliters) 100-proof vodka
1¾	cups sugar
3¼	cups water

1. From lemons, with vegetable peeler, remove peel in strips. (Refrigerate lemons for another use.) Pour vodka into 8-cup glass measuring cup or large pitcher and add lemon peel. Cover measuring cup with plastic wrap and let stand 1 week at room temperature.

2. After 1 week, pour vodka through paper towel–lined sieve set over large bowl. Discard lemon peel.

3. In 2-quart saucepan, combine sugar and water; heat to boiling over high heat, stirring until sugar has dissolved. Reduce heat to medium and cook 2 minutes. Remove from heat and cool completely.

4. Add cooled syrup to vodka in bowl. Pour cordial into small decorative bottles with tight-fitting stoppers or lids. Store in refrigerator up to 3 months or in freezer up to 6 months. Serve very cold. Makes about 6½ cups or 34 servings.

Each serving: About 89 calories, 0g protein, 10g carbohydrate, 0g total fat (0g saturated), 0mg cholesterol, 0mg sodium.

24

CANNING AND FREEZING

Before refrigeration, cooks fought a constant battle against spoilage, working hard to put up enough food to feed their families until the next harvest. Now, putting up food is as easy as wrapping it and freezing. In this chapter, we concentrate on the most popular and modern methods of food preservation: canning and freezing. And we offer a number of small-batch recipes that use less produce to take into account the needs of urban cooks and smaller families who want to enjoy healthful homemade canned goods. Also included are recipes for freezer jams, which are not processed in boiling-water baths, but instead, simply stored in the freezer.

Always use the freshest, ripest, and most flavorful produce available. Some varieties of fruits and vegetables are better than others for freezing or canning because they retain truer color, flavor, and texture. Check with your county or state cooperative extension service or state college of agriculture for information on these varieties.

In food preservation, the enemies are the microorganisms that cause food to spoil: yeast, mold, and bacteria. The naturally occuring changes (caused by enzymes) in fruit are also responsible for its deterioration (when strawberries go soft, it's enzymes at work). By killing these microorganisms or by arresting their growth, spoilage can be averted or delayed. The various methods of preservation accomplish this by either re-

Three-Berry Skillet Jam

moving the oxygen that micoorganisms and enzymes need to survive (vacuum-sealed canning jars), using extreme temperatures (high temperature boiling-water baths kill them, while freezing retards their growth), increasing the acidity (microbes can't exist in high-acid conditions, thus the use of vinegar in pickling), or reducing the amount of life-sustaining water (as for dehydrated foods, a method we don't address here).

CANNING

Today, most people process fruits and vegetables because they enjoy it, not because they have to. (Processing means heating food in canning jars at high temperatures for periods long enough to kill the spoilage-causing microorganisms and enzymes that would alter the food's flavor, texture, and color.) The fruits and vegetables for homemade pickles, jams, preserves, and jellies can come from an urban farmers' market or the field out back. Making homemade canned goods is a satisfying pleasure, and nothing produced commercially can equal the quality or flavor.

It is important to know the acidity level of the food being preserved. Every food contains natural acid; when measured on a pH scale (the abbreviation for "potential of hydrogen"), the lower the pH, the higher the acidity (not vice versa). Our canning recipes take the acidity level of the ingredients into account, so you don't need to look it up.

High-acid foods have a pH of 4.6 or below; low-acid foods have a pH rating above 4.6. Fruits (except figs), fruit juices, fruit jams and jellies, and vinegar-pickled foods are high-acid. Low-acid foods include vegetables, meats, seafood, and poultry, as well as soups and other combination foods that are mostly high-acid but contain some low-acid vegetables. (Stewed tomatoes with onion, celery, and green pepper are a good example.)

The harmful microbes in high-acid foods are killed by the high temperature of a boiling-water (212°F at sea level) bath. But the pathogens in low-acid foods can only be destroyed by the extremely high temperature (240°F) obtained in a steam-pressure canner. Since most cooks prefer to pickle or freeze low-acid foods, we haven't included pressure-canning instructions. For information on pressure-canning or canning foods at high altitudes, contact your local cooperative extension service or state college of agriculture.

Equipment for Canning Fruits and Vegetables

- Boiling water–bath canning pot: If you plan on doing a lot of canning, you may want to purchase a very large canning pot. It comes with a canning basket to hold the jars and a tight-fitting lid. However, any large stockpot will do, as long as it is deep enough so the pot's rim will be 3 to 4 inches above the tops of the jars and large enough so the jars don't touch each other. Instead of a wire canning basket, you can use any sturdy heatproof rack that will fit in the pot; round wire cooling racks work well. If your improvised rack needs a little extra support to hold heavy jars, place several metal jar bands underneath the center of the rack.

- Jars: Tempered glass canning jars, sometimes called Mason jars, are the only recommended jars for home canning. Their special two-piece lids ensure a vacuum-tight seal that discourages spoilage. We do not recommend European-style glass jars with rubber seals and wire clamps; they make nice canisters for dry goods but aren't trustworthy for preserving. If you want versatile jars that can be used in either the freezer or a canning pot, buy jars with straight or tapered sides; jars with "shoulders" don't work in the freezer.

  Jars range in size from four ounces to half gallon. Use the size recommended in the recipe, especially for hot-water-bath–processed foods; if you use larger jars than recommended, the heat that kills harmful microorganisms may not penetrate all the way through the food or preserves may not

set up properly. Wide-mouthed jars are easier to fill than narrow ones. The jars are reusable, but check carefully before reusing for any signs of wear, like cracks or chips.

  Do not reuse jars from commercial food, such as mayonnaise, because the glass could break when exposed to high heat, and the canning lids won't fit properly.

- Caps: The most common cap is made of two pieces: a flat lid with a rubberlike sealing compound on the underside and a metal screw band that holds the lid in place during processing. You must use new lids each time you can food. Undamaged screw bands, however, can be reused.

- Utensils for canning: A wide-mouthed funnel for transferring the food to the jars and a jar-lifter to grip the jars so they can be easily lifted in and out of the boiling water, while not essential, facilitate the canning process. To remove air bubbles, use a narrow rubber spatula (a metal spatula or knife could chip the glass).

Canning Steps

- Prepare jars and caps for processing. Check the jars to be sure there are no chips, nicks, or cracks. Wash the jars, lids, and screw bands in hot soapy water; rinse. (If desired, wash and dry in the dishwasher and keep hot until ready to use.) The jars must be heated before canning to prevent breakage. Submerge the jars in enough water to cover; heat to boiling. Remove from the heat; cover. Leave the jars in the hot water for at least 10 minutes. Place the lids and bands in a saucepan with enough water to cover; bring to a simmer (180° F). Remove from the heat, cover, and keep hot until ready to use. Remove the jars, one at a time, as needed.

- Pack jars. Raw fruit can be packed into hot jars (cold pack), or it can be slightly cooked (hot pack). In the chart Canning Fruits and Tomatoes in a Boiling Water Bath on page 776, we offer the recommended pack method (although some fruits can be prepared either way). **Important:** Do not prepare more food than your canner can hold at one time. The jars (and food, if directed) for each batch must be hot and the syrup, water, or juice must be boiling.

  Raw or cold pack is generally preferred for delicate fruits that would become too soft if cooked. Firmly pack the unheated raw food into hot jars, then cover with boiling liquid to within 1/2 inch from the tops of the jars. You will need about 1/2 to 1 1/2 cups of liquid for every 4 cups of food.

Hot pack is the method used for firm fruit that will hold up well to a brief cooking period. Cooking makes food more pliable and easier to pack, therefore requiring fewer jars. Hot foods, either precooked or heated in liquid, should be packed loosely into hot jars and covered with boiling liquid to ½ inch from the rim. The amount of headspace is

important: If a jar has too little headspace, the food may swell and force itself under the lid, breaking the seal. With too much headspace, the food at the top of the jar could discolor.

After filling each jar, run a narrow rubber spatula between the food and the side of the jar to remove any air bubbles. The bubbles may not be visible; they could be trapped between the pieces of food.

Using a clean damp cloth, thoroughly wipe the jar rims and threads to remove any drips of food or liquid. Cover the jars with the hot lids. Screw on the bands just until tightened; do not force.

- Process jars. The food must be processed in a boiling-water bath immediately after packing to maintain the proper temperature for processing. The processing time will vary according to the type of fruit, the method of packing, and the size of the jars.

  To process food in a boiling-water bath: Place the canning basket in the canning pot. Fill the pot halfway with hot water; heat to simmering over high heat. In another pot or kettle, heat additional water to boiling. Using a jar-lifter, carefully place the filled jars in the basket (if using a rack, place the jars far enough apart so the water can circulate freely). The water should come 1 to 2 inches above the jars; add boiling water if needed.

  Cover the canner and heat the water to boiling. Start timing as soon as the water comes to a full boil; check often. Reduce the heat to maintain a gentle boil for the time indicated in the recipe. If necessary, add boiling water to keep the jars properly covered.

- Cool jars. In a draft-free place, prepare an area for cooling. Line the surface with folded kitchen towels (contact with a cold hard surface could break the jars). With a jar-lifter, remove the jars from the pot and place on the towels, allowing 1 to 2 inches between the jars so the air can circulate freely. (If any liquid has boiled out of the jars, do not open to add more.) Cool to room temperature, at least 12 hours or up to 24 hours.

- Test jars for airtight seal. When the jars are cool, check the seals. Press the center of each lid; if it is flat, the jar is sealed. To double-check, unscrew the band and pick up the jar by the lid; if the lid stays attached, all is well. If

the lid has a slight dome in the center that can be pressed down or if the lid comes off easily, the jar is not sealed properly. It must be refrigerated, and used within twenty-four hours, or reprocessed (reheat the food and pack into a clean hot jar with a new lid).

- Store jars properly. Wipe the top edges of the jars with a clean damp cloth to remove any food residue. Do not return the screw bands to the jars: They can corrode and become difficult to remove. Label the jars: Include the name of the contents and the date processed. Store the jars in a cool dark place, preferably between 50° and 70°F. When stored under ideal conditions, home-processed foods will keep for about a year; after that, changes in the flavor, color, and texture will affect the quality.

  Before eating processed food, check the jar carefully for signs of spoilage. Do not taste or use any canned food if the lids are loose; there are any gas bubbles; there is spurting liquid; the contents are soft, mushy, moldy, or slimy; there is sediment at the bottom of the jar; or any unpleasant odor is present. Destroy the food immediately in such a manner that it cannot be accidentally eaten by children or pets. Thoroughly wash any surface that may have come in contact with the spoiled food and discard any kitchen sponges used during cleanup.

Canning Fruit

Whether fruit is canned in syrup, fruit juice, or water, the processing time is the same. Sugar adds flavor and helps retain fruit's color, but it is not needed to prevent spoilage. Fruit canned in water or juice, however, will be lower in calories.

If you want to make your own fruit juice for canning, prepare it just before packing the fruit or making the sugar syrup. Place ripe, juicy fruit in a large nonreactive saucepan. With a potato masher or large spoon, crush the fruit well. Over low heat, stirring frequently, heat to simmering. Strain through a double layer of cheesecloth; discard the fruit pulp.

To make a sugar syrup for canning, in a medium nonreactive saucepan, heat water or fruit juice and sugar over high heat, stirring until the sugar has dissolved. If directed, stir in ascorbic acid. Reduce the heat to low; keep hot (do not boil).

> *Light Sugar Syrup*
> 4 cups water or juice and 1⅓ cups sugar. Yields 4½ cups.
> *Medium Sugar Syrup*
> 4 cups water or juice and 2 cups sugar. Yields 5 cups.
> *Heavy Sugar Syrup*
> 4 cups water or juice and 4 cups sugar. Yields 6 cups.

Use only fresh fruits that are in perfect condition and full of flavor. Rinse the fruit well, either under cold running water or in several changes of water, lifting the fruit out of the water after rinsing so the dirt stays off. Prepare the fruit as directed in the Canning Fruits and Tomatoes in a Boiling Water Bath chart (page 776). To prevent the fruit from darkening, dip in an ascorbic-acid solution according to the instructions on page 780.

To Can Jams, Jellies, and Other Fruit Spreads

Fruit that isn't quite at the right stage of ripeness or is not the right size or shape for canning can be transformed into a delicious fruit spread. If you have a large quantity of fruit and the inclination to do so, make a big batch of jam. And remember, you don't always have to pull out the canning pot for water-bath processing. Excellent jams can be prepared for storage right in your freezer.

Equipment for Fruit Spreads

- Cooking utensils: To encourage fast heating and the quick evaporation of any excess liquid, use a broad flat-bottomed 8-quart Dutch oven for large-batch recipes and a 12-inch skillet for small-batch skillet jams. Don't use unlined aluminum pots or skillets, as they can react with the acid in fruit and affect the flavor and color.

- Utensils for canning: A wide-mouthed funnel for transferring the food to the jars and a jar-lifter to grip the jars so they can be easily lifted in and out of boiling water will facilitate the canning process.

- Jars: For processed spreads, use tempered glass canning jars with two-piece lids. For freezer jams, the glass jars must have straight sides without "shoulders," or use plastic freezer-safe food containers with tight-fitting lids. Do not use jelly jars that are topped with melted paraffin. Paraffin does not create an airtight seal that will protect against bacterial growth.

Steps in Making Jams and Other Fruit Spreads

- Assemble all your equipment and prepare the jars or containers before you start.

- Prepare and measure all the ingredients. Do not double the recipes: Make one batch at a time.

- Prepare jars for jams or fruit spreads. Check all the jars to be sure there are no chips, nicks, or cracks. Wash the jars, lids, and screw bands or freezer containers in hot soapy water; rinse. The jars must be heated before canning to prevent breakage. Submerge the jars in enough water to cover; heat to boiling. Remove from the heat; cover. Leave the jars in the hot water for at least 10 minutes. Place the lids and bands in a saucepan with enough water to cover; bring to a simmer (180° F). Remove from the heat, cover, and keep hot until ready to use. Remove the jars, one at a time, as needed.

  For freezer jams: Slowly pour boiling water into and over the outside of clean freezer-safe containers or jars. Invert onto a clean kitchen towel and drain dry. Or place the clean containers or jars in the dishwasher. Run the rinse cycle using very hot water (at least 150°F or higher). Leave them in the dishwasher until ready to use.

  For other fruit spreads: Place the clean jars in a large bowl or pot and cover with boiling water. Let stand for 10 minutes.

Use a jar-lifter or tongs to remove the jars from the hot water; invert onto a clean kitchen towel and let drain dry.

- Prepare fruit. Gently rinse the fruit, either with cold running water or in several changes of water, lifting the fruit out for each change of water. Drain. If necessary, finely chop the fruit, using a knife or a food processor with the knife blade attached. Do not puree: the spread will not set. Cook as directed.

    Pectin is a naturally occurring substance found in varying amounts in fruits. It causes jellies and jams to jell; underripe fruit contains more pectin than fully ripe fruit. Some recipes use commerical pectin to set mixtures properly. Commercial pectin comes in powdered and liquid forms: They are not interchangeable.

    If the recipe calls for the fruit to come to a "rolling boil," heat it until the mixture forms bubbles all across its surface that cannot be stirred down.

- Skim off foam. Remove the pan from the heat. Use a large metal spoon to skim the foam from the surface.

- Pack jars. For freezer jams, pack the jam into containers to ½ inch from the tops; cover tightly. Freeze. For processed spreads, preferably using a wide-mouthed funnel, fill and close the jars one at a time. For jellies, fill the jars to ⅛ inch from the tops; for jams, fill to ¼ inch from tops. Wipe the rims of the jars with a clean damp cloth. Cover the jars with the lids, then screw on the bands.

- Process fruits spreads in a boiling-water bath according to the instructions on page 773.

- Cool jars. Remove the jars from the boiling-water bath and cool as directed on page 773.

- Test the jars for an airtight seal according to the instructions on page 773.

- Store jars properly. Keep freezer jams frozen for up to 1 year. Refrigerate after opening; use within 3 weeks. Keep processed fruit spreads in a cool dark dry place for up to 1 year. After opening, store in the refrigerator for up to 3 weeks.

FREEZING

Freezing is a great way to preserve fruits and vegetables. It retards the growth of microorganisms that cause spoilage and slows the enzyme activity that makes fruit tough and unpalatable. (For meats, poultry, and seafood, see the Storing sections of their respective chapters.) Freezing also maintains the natural color and flavor of food better than other methods of preservation. Frozen produce doesn't last forever, however. For the best flavor and texture, all home-frozen fruits and vegetables should be used within nine months.

The Right Wrap

Frozen food must be wrapped properly to prevent "freezer burn" (a tough, dry surface that forms when food is exposed to the air in the freezer) and other conditions that reduce the quality of food. Protect your frozen food by using materials designed specifically for the freezer. For long-term freezer storage (more than a month), use glass jars suitable for canning and freezing (with straight sides and two-piece lids), plastic freezer-safe containers, waxed cardboard cartons, foil containers, or heavy-duty ziptight plastic bags. The wrapping materials for food must be moisture-proof; use heavy-duty foil, freezer paper, or freezer plastic wrap. For short-term storage, regular (not heavy-duty) wraps can be used.

Secure wrapped packages with freezer tape. Use waterproof felt-tip pens or markers for writing on labels, freezer tape, or freezer paper.

PICKLES AND RELISHES

To most people, pickles are vinegar-preserved cucumbers, but many other fruits and vegetables can also be pickled in vinegar or brine. (Brine-pickling requires controlled temperatures and a good amount of attention, so we have concentrated on vinegar-pickling.) Vegetables are low-acid foods but when pickled, the vinegar raises their acidity so they can be processed safely in a boiling-water bath.

To process pickles and relishes, follow the steps for canning fruits and tomatoes. But, pickle recipes include one important additional ingredient: salt (canning, pickling, or kosher; also called pure salt). Iodized and table salts are not used because they make brine cloudy and turn some pickles dark.

CANNING FRUITS AND TOMATOES IN A BOILING WATER BATH

HOW TO PREPARE	HOW TO PACK	MINUTES TO PROCESS	
		PINTS	QUARTS
Apples Cut apples in half or into quarters; core and peel. Slice, if desired. Treat to prevent darkening.	*Hot pack:* In light or medium sugar syrup, heat apples to boiling; simmer 5 minutes. Pack into hot jars to ½ inch from tops. Cover with boiling sugar syrup; leave ½-inch headspace. Adjust caps.	20 minutes	20 minutes
Applesauce Make sweetened or unsweetened applesauce, using your favorite recipe.	*Hot pack:* Heat applesauce to boiling. Pour bubbling applesauce into hot jars; leave ½-inch headspace. Adjust caps.	20 minutes	20 minutes
Apricots For cold pack, use unpeeled apricots. For hot pack, peel apricots. To peel, plunge fruit into boiling water for 30 seconds; transfer to cold water to help loosen skins. Cut in half; remove pits. Treat to prevent darkening.	*Cold pack:* Pack unpeeled apricots into hot jars to ½ inch from tops. Cover with boiling light or medium sugar syrup; leave ½-inch headspace. Adjust caps. *Hot pack:* Cook peeled apricots, a few at a time, in light or medium syrup just until heated through. Pack into hot jars to ½ inch from tops. Cover with boiling sugar syrup; leave ½-inch headspace. Adjust caps.	25 minutes 20 minutes	30 minutes 25 minutes
Berries Wash berries; drain. Remove stems. Use cold pack for soft berries (blackberries, boysenberries, dewberries, loganberries, raspberries, youngberries). Use hot pack for firm berries (blueberries, currants, elderberries, gooseberries, huckleberries).	*Cold pack:* Pack berries into hot jars to ½ inch from tops; gently shake jars to pack tightly. Cover with boiling light or medium sugar syrup; leave ½-inch headspace. Adjust caps. *Hot pack:* Measure berries into saucepot. Add ¼ to ½ cup sugar for each 4 cups; let stand 2 hours. Over medium-low heat, cook until sugar has dissolved and mixture boils. Pack mixture into hot jars; leave ½-inch headspace (add boiling water or sugar syrup to cover fruit if needed). Adjust caps.	15 minutes 15 minutes	20 minutes 15 minutes
Cherries Remove stems and pits from cherries.	*Cold pack:* Pour ½ cup boiling light or medium sugar syrup for sweet cherries or medium or heavy sugar syrup for sour cherries into each hot jar. Fill jar with cherries and shake to pack cherries down to ½ inch from tops. Cover cherries with boiling sugar syrup; leave ½-inch headspace. Adjust caps.	25 minutes	25 minutes

HOW TO PREPARE	HOW TO PACK	MINUTES TO PROCESS	
		PINTS	QUARTS
Cherries (continued from previous page)	*Hot pack:* In saucepot, add ½ cup sugar for each 4 cups cherries. Cover; heat until sugar has dissolved and mixture is hot. Pack into hot jars; leave ½-inch headspace (add boiling light or medium sugar syrup if needed). If using cherries for baking, heat cherries, one layer at a time, in extra-light syrup just until hot. Adjust caps.	15 minutes	20 minutes
Peaches Peel peaches (see Apricots); cut in half. Remove pits. Scrape (red) fibers from cavities (they could turn brown). Slice, if desired. Treat to prevent darkening.	*Cold pack:* Pack peaches into hot jars to ½ inch from tops (pack halves, cavity side down, in overlapping layers.) Cover with boiling light or medium sugar syrup; leave ½-inch headspace. Adjust caps. *Hot pack:* Cook peaches, a few at a time, in medium or heavy sugar syrup until heated through. Pack as for Apricots.	25 minutes 20 minutes	30 minutes 25 minutes
Pears Cut pears in half or into quarters; core and peel. Treat to prevent darkening.	*Hot pack*: In saucepot, in light sugar syrup, heat one layer of pears to boiling; simmer 5 minutes. Pack pears into hot jars to ½ inch from tops. Cover with boiling sugar syrup; leave ½-inch headspace. Adjust caps.	20 minutes	25minutes
Plums Use firm, meaty varieties of plums, not very juicy ones. Wash; prick skins if left whole to prevent bursting. For Italian prune plums and other freestone varieties, cut in half and remove pits, if desired.	*Hot pack:* In saucepot, heat medium or heavy sugar syrup to boiling; add one layer of plums. Simmer 2 minutes. If plums are whole, remove saucepot from heat. Cover; let stand 20 to 30 minutes (to plump plums). Pack plums into hot jars to ½ inch from tops. Cover whole or halved plums with boiling sugar syrup; leave ½-inch headspace. Adjust caps.	20 minutes	25 minutes
Rhubarb Cut unpeeled rhubarb stalks into 1-inch pieces; measure into large glass or ceramic bowl. Add ½ cup sugar for each 4 cups; mix well. Let stand 3 to 4 hours to draw out juices.	*Hot pack:* In saucepot, heat mixture to boiling; boil 30 seconds. Pack rhubarb mixture into hot jars; leave ½-inch headspace (add boiling water to cover fruit if needed). Adjust caps.	15 minutes	15 minutes
Tomatoes Use only firm-ripe—not overripe—tomatoes (tomatoes lose their acidity as they mature). Plunge tomatoes into boiling water 30 seconds to loosen skins. Transfer to cold water; drain. Peel and cut out stem ends. Leave whole or cut in half or into quarters.	*Hot pack:* In saucepot, place tomatoes; add water to cover. Heat to boiling; simmer 5 minutes. Add salt, if desired. To each hot quart jar, add 2 tablespoons bottled lemon juice; add 1 tablespoon bottled lemon juice to each pint jar. Pack hot tomatoes and cooking liquid into hot jars; leave ½-inch headspace. Adjust caps.	40 minutes	45 minutes

Some casserole dishes can go directly from freezer to oven. Be sure to preheat the oven if the casserole is glass or ceramic: Placing a casserole in a cold oven and then turning it on can cause breakage. Most nonplastic containers designed for use in microwave ovens are suitable for freezing.

Freezing Success

- Chill foods and liquids before packing.

- Wipe edges of containers or jar rims clean.

- When wrapping food in freezer wrap or when using plastic bags, press out as much air as possible before sealing.

- Leave enough headspace in containers to allow room for expansion. For containers with wide-top openings, leave ¾ inch for pints and 1 inch for quarts. For containers with narrow openings, leave ¾ inch for pints and 1½ inches for quarts. Vegetables that are packed loosely don't need headspace.

- Drugstore-wrap flat foods (opposite), such as steaks.

- To securely seal soft foods in bags with metal ties, press out the air; twist the bag top, leaving headspace if the recipe directs. Fold the twisted top down and fasten the metal tie around the doubled-over top.

- Label each package with the name of the food and the date packed. Add other information if you like, such as the number of servings, the use-by date, and thawing directions.

- Put only as much unfrozen food into your freezer as will freeze within twenty-four hours. (The rule of thumb is: 2 to 3 pounds of food for each cubic foot of freezer space.) Overloading a freezer slows the freezing process, and foods that freeze too slowly could lose quality. Overloading also raises the temperature of the freezer and affects the quality of the food already in the freezer. Check the manufacturer's instructions to see how much unfrozen food you can place in the freezer at one time.

- Place packages against the freezing plates or coils and leave enough space between them so the air can circulate. Freeze foods at 0°F or lower. After the packages are frozen, move them close together.

- Store frozen food at 0°F or lower. The quality of food deteriorates rapidly at higher temperatures: Use a freezer thermometer for the most accurate reading.

What Not to Freeze
Knowing how to freeze is only one factor; knowing what to freeze is equally important.

- Salad greens and unblanched raw vegetables turn limp and soggy when thawed.

- Whole eggs in the shell expand and the shells crack. Hard-cooked egg whites turn tough and rubbery. Shelled whole eggs, egg whites, and yolks can be frozen. See Storing Eggs on page 308.

- Creamed cottage cheese changes texture and becomes grainy, so only freeze dry-curd or uncreamed cottage cheese.

- Sour cream separates when frozen and thawed.

- Heavy cream does not whip well after freezing. Instead, whip the cream and then freeze. To use, thaw in the refrigerator.

- Potatoes aren't always good candidates for freezing. If frozen raw, they turn mushy; frozen boiled potatoes become tough when thawed; and potatoes cooked in stews or soups turn out spongy. But mashed, stuffed, and scalloped potatoes freeze well.

- Poultry should never be stuffed before freezing. Freeze whole poultry unstuffed, then thaw; stuff just before roasting.

- Fluffy white frosting that is made with egg whites does not hold up to freezing and thawing.

- Frozen custard becomes tough and watery when thawed.

- Cream fillings in cakes and pies become watery when thawed.

- Frozen meringue pie toppings toughen when thawed.

- Mayonnaise salads become greasy after thawing.

- Fried foods become soggy when thawed.

Thawing and Using Frozen Food

- Thawed frozen food spoils much more quickly than fresh food. Thaw only as much food as you can use.

- The best way to thaw food is unopened in the refrigerator. If you must, food can be thawed at room temperature for up to two hours; then complete the thawing in the refrigerator.

- To thaw in the microwave, use the defrost cycle as the manufacturer directs. Protect the corners of wrapped foods, since they will cook before the center is thawed. If you can use foil in your microwave (check the owner's manual), for square-shaped foods, cut two 6-inch squares of foil and cut each into two triangles. Place a triangle on each corner and mold it over the dish. For rectangular-shaped foods, shield the ends with 3-inch-wide foil strips. Halfway through cooking, check the food under the foil to be sure it is thawing at about the same rate as the center.

- Thaw food in water only as a last resort. Place waterproof packages in cold water, changing the water when it loses its chill. Never thaw food in hot water.

- Frozen cooked foods should be reheated at their regular cooking temperature. The exact cooking time may vary with the dish, but there is an easy way to tell when the food is done. Insert a thin knife into the center of the food for a few seconds. Withdraw the knife and touch the blade; if it is very warm, the food is heated through.

Refreezing Thawed Food

Food that is frozen raw, then cooked, can be successfully refrozen. For example, if you use thawed beef to make a stew, the stew can be frozen. However, most thawed or partially thawed food should be carefully evaluated before refreezing. If you want to refreeze partially frozen food, feel the unopened package. If the food still feels semifrozen and it hasn't warmed above 40°F, it can be refrozen. But the flavor and texture are likely to deteriorate after the second freezing. Baked goods, such as breads, cookies, and plain unfrosted cakes, can be frozen, thawed, and refrozen (although they won't be at their best). Use refrozen food as soon as possible to minimize any further loss of quality.

Freezing Fruit

There are three ways to freeze fruit: in syrup, in sugar, and unsweetened. The method you choose depends on how you plan to use the fruit. While some fruits can be frozen without sweetening, most have better flavor and texture if packed with sugar or in syrup.

Berries with moisture-proof cell structures, like raspberries, cranberries, and blueberries, can be frozen unsweetened on trays, then packed in plastic bags. These frozen berries are excellent in baked goods; they can be stirred (frozen) into batters.

DRUGSTORE-WRAPPING FOOD

Tear off enough freezer wrap to go around food 1½ times.

Bring ends of wrap together.

Fold paper over about 1 inch and crease along fold.

Continue to make folds until wrap is tight against food. Press out air at ends.

Fold each end to a point.

Fold ends under, tightly against food. Seal with freezer tape.

Some fruits, such as apples, turn brown when exposed to air: They need to be treated with ascorbic acid. During canning season, most supermarkets carry commercial ascorbic acid-based products; follow the package directions. Ascorbic acid is sometimes added to canning syrup as well. Pure ascorbic acid is available at drugstores in powdered, crystallized, or tablet form (crush the tablets).

The chart Freezing Fruit lists the fruits that freeze well and the best method for preparing them. It's as easy as one, two, three.

Preparing Fruit for Freezing

Rinse the fruit well; take care not to bruise tender fruit, especially berries. Prepare as the recipe directs. For the best results, prepare only a few containers at a time, especially if the fruit is prone to darkening.

To prevent fruit from darkening, treat it with an ascorbic acid solution, prepared from a commercial mix. Or, in a large bowl, combine 4 quarts water, 2 tablespoons salt, and 2 tablespoons cider or white vinegar. Drop the peeled or cut fruit into the solution as soon as the fruit is prepared; let stand a few minutes, then remove the fruit and rinse well. Drain on paper towels.

Packing Fruit for Freezing

- Use freezer containers or glass canning jars; wash and dry.
- To pack fruit in syrup, prepare the sugar syrup: In a large bowl, mix the hot water and sugar until the sugar has dissolved; cool the syrup completely. Each pint container usually takes ½ to ⅔ cup syrup.

Light Sugar Syrup
  4 cups hot water and 1⅓ cups sugar. Yields 4½ cups.
Medium Sugar Syrup
  4 cups hot water and 2 cups sugar. Yields 5 cups.
Heavy Sugar Syrup
  4 cups hot water and 4 cups sugar. Yields 6 cups.

For fruit that darkens when cut, add ascorbic acid to the syrup. Dissolve the ascorbic acid in 1 to 2 tablespoons cold water. Just before using the syrup, gently stir in the dissolved ascorbic acid, taking care not to beat in any air bubbles. Pour about ½ cup of the syrup into the container; fill the container with fruit and add enough syrup to cover the fruit, leaving ½-inch headspace. Press the fruit down under the syrup and hold it in place with a small piece of crumpled foil; remove foil. Close and seal the container.

- To pack fruit in sugar, cut the fruit into a bowl and sprinkle with the amount of sugar specified. If directed, dissolve ascorbic-acid in a small amount of water and sprinkle over the fruit. With a rubber spatula, gently mix the fruit and sugar until the fruit releases its juices and the sugar has dissolved. Transfer to containers or jars, then close and seal.

- To pack unsweetened fruit, place the prepared fruit in a container or jar. If specified, sprinkle dissolved ascorbic acid over the fruit and mix well just before packing. If packing fruit in water, dissolve ascorbic acid in the water before covering the fruit; leave ½-inch headspace. Or cover crushed or sliced fruit with its own unsweetened juice and ascorbic acid, then press the fruit down under the syrup and hold it in place with a small piece of crumpled foil. Close and seal.

- To tray-freeze fruit before packing to prevent it from sticking together, spread the fruit in a single layer, without touching, in a jelly-roll pan. Freeze until hard, 1 to 2 hours. Pack into heavy-duty ziptight plastic bags, pressing out all the air.

To Thaw and Use Frozen Fruit

- Thaw fruit in its sealed container in the refrigerator or in a pan of cold water.

- To serve the fruit uncooked, serve it as soon as it has thawed (while a few ice crystals remain).

- To serve the fruit cooked, thaw it just until the pieces can be separated, then cook it as you would fresh fruit. Add sugar to taste, keeping in mind whether or not the fruit was sweetened before freezing; if needed, add 1 to 2 tablespoons water.

Freezing Vegetables

For the best results when freezing vegetables, use impeccably fresh and flavorful produce. All vegetables (except green onions, sweet and hot peppers, and chopped onions) must be blanched in boiling water before being frozen to reduce the enzyme activity that can change their color, flavor, texture, and nutritive value. Cooling the vegetables properly after blanching is equally important.

Preparing Vegetables for Freezing

Vegetables should be tender, fresh, and at their peak-of-eating quality. Wash vegetables thoroughly and drain. Sort them according to their size, unless being cut up. Prepare each vegetable as directed in the Freezing Vegetables chart (page 786).

FREEZING FRUIT

See Packing Fruit for Freezing, opposite.

HOW TO PREPARE	IN SYRUP	IN SUGAR	UNSWEETENED
Apples Wash; peel and core crisp apples. Slice apples into 2 quarts ascorbic acid solution, prepared according to manufacturer's directions. Remove and drain well on paper towels.	Use heavy syrup. Add $\frac{1}{2}$ teaspoon ascorbic acid to each 4 cups syrup. Pack, covered with syrup.		For pie apples: In boiling water to cover, cook apple slices 2 minutes. Plunge into ice water to cool; drain. Tray-freeze (page 780).
Applesauce Wash apples; peel, if desired. Core and slice. To each 4 cups apples, add $\frac{1}{3}$ cup water and $\frac{1}{4}$ teaspoon ascorbic acid. Cook until tender. Press apples through food mill; discard peels. Stir $\frac{1}{4}$ cup sugar (optional) into each 4 cups hot puree. Cool; pack into containers or jars, leaving $\frac{1}{2}$-inch headspace.			
Apricots Wash carefully to avoid bruising; peel, if desired. Leave apricots whole or cut in half and remove pits. If not peeled, heat in boiling water 30 seconds to prevent skin from toughening during freezing.	Use light, medium, or heavy syrup. Add $\frac{1}{2}$ teaspoon ascorbic acid to each 4 cups syrup. Pack, covered with syrup.	Mix $\frac{1}{2}$ cup sugar and $\frac{1}{4}$ teaspoon ascorbic acid for each 4 cups fruit; let stand until sugar has dissolved. Pack fruit and juice into containers	
Bananas Mash bananas with a little lemon juice. Thawed mixture may discolor but is excellent for baked goods.			
Blackberries Remove any stems or leaves. Rinse carefully, removing less than perfect berries.	Use medium or heavy syrup. Pack berries into containers; shake gently to fill empty spaces. Cover with syrup.	Mix each 4 cups berries with $\frac{3}{4}$ cup sugar.	Tray-freeze (page 780).

FREEZING FRUIT

See Packing Fruit for Freezing, page 780.

HOW TO PREPARE	IN SYRUP	IN SUGAR	UNSWEETENED
Blueberries Remove stems. Gently rinse and drain. For syrup pack, steam over boiling water 1 minute; cool.	Pack as for blackberries.	Mix each 4 cups berries with $2/3$ cup sugar.	Tray-freeze (page 780).
Boysenberries See Blackberries.			
Cherries, Sweet Rinse; remove stems and pits.	Use medium or heavy syrup. Add $1/2$ teaspoon ascorbic acid to each 4 cups syrup. Pack as for blackberries.		If desired, do not remove pits. Tray-freeze (page 780). Rinse cherries before using.
Cherries, Tart (Sour) Rinse; remove stems and pits.	Pack as for blackberries.	Mix each 4 cups cherries with 1 cup sugar.	Tray-freeze (page 780).
Cranberries			Leave in original bags; freeze. Rinse before using.
Dewberries See Blackberries.			Tray-freeze (page 780).
Gooseberries Remove blossom ends. Rinse and drain.	Pack as for blackberries.		Tray-freeze (page 780).
Grapefruit Peel and cut into sections. Remove all membranes and seeds; reserve any juice.	Use light, medium, or heavy syrup; use juice as part of the syrup. Add $1/2$ teaspoon ascorbic acid to each 4 cups syrup. Pack, covered with syrup.		
Grapes Remove stems; rinse. Leave seedless grapes whole; cut table grapes with seeds in half and seed. Leave grapes for jelly or juice whole.	Use light or medium syrup. Pack, covered with syrup.		Tray-freeze (page 780).

FREEZING FRUIT

See Packing Fruit for Freezing, page 780.

HOW TO PREPARE	IN SYRUP	IN SUGAR	UNSWEETENED
Huckleberries See Blackberries.			
Kiwifruit Peel firm but ripe fruit; cut into ¼-inch-thick slices.			Tray-freeze (page 780).
Loganberries See Blackberries.			
Mangoes Peel ripe mangoes; cut flesh away from seed and cut into chunks.	Pack as for apricots.		
Nectarines Wash nectarines; peel, if desired. Cut in half; remove pits. Slice, if desired.	Pack as for apricots.		
Oranges Peel and cut into sections, or slice. Remove all membranes and seeds; reserve any juice.	Pack as for grapefruit.		
Peaches Peel firm but ripe peaches. (For better quality, peel without first dipping into boiling water.) Cut fruit in half; remove pits. Slice, if desired.	Pack as for apricots.	Pack as for apricots.	
Pears Peel firm-ripe pears. Cut in half; remove cores. If desired, cut into quarters, or slice. Drop into 8 cups ascorbic acid solution, prepared according to manufacturer's directions. Remove and drain well on paper towels.	Use light, medium, or heavy syrup. Heat syrup to boiling; add pears and boil 1 to 2 minutes, depending on size. Drain; cool pears and syrup. (For better quality, add ¾ teaspoon ascorbic acid to each 4 cups syrup.) Pack, covered with syrup.		

FREEZING FRUIT

See Packing Fruit for Freezing, page 780.

HOW TO PREPARE	IN SYRUP	IN SUGAR	UNSWEETENED
Persimmons Choose orange-colored, soft-ripe fruit. Peel; press through food mill. Puree made from native variety needs no sugar. Pack puree from cultivated varieties (Hachiya, Fuyu) with or without sugar. For each 4 cups puree, add ⅛ teaspoon ascorbic acid.		Mix each 4 cups puree with 1 cup sugar.	Pack puree into containers, leaving ½-inch headspace.
Pineapple Peel. Cut into slices or lengthwise wedges; remove core. Or cut into sticks or chunks. Do not use frozen fresh pineapple in gelatin mixtures; they will not set.	Use light or medium syrup. Pack, covered with syrup.	Mix each 8 cups fruit with 1 cup sugar; let stand until sugar has dissolved.	Pack into containers. If sliced, stack with 2 pieces freezer paper between slices. Or, tray-freeze chunks (page 780).
Plums Wash; leave whole or cut in half. Remove pits. If desired, cut into quarters.	For cut-up fruit, use medium or heavy syrup. Add ½ teaspoon ascorbic acid to each 4 cups syrup.	Mix each 5 cups fruit with 1 cup sugar; let stand until sugar has dissolved.	Pack whole fruit into containers or ziptight plastic bags.
Raspberries See Blackberries.			
Rhubarb Trim crisp, well-colored rhubarb stalks. Cut into 1- to 2-inch pieces. Blanch in boiling water 1 minute; drain and cool.	Use medium or heavy syrup. Pack, covered with syrup.	Mix each 4 cups rhubarb with 1 cup sugar; let stand until sugar has dissolved.	Tray-freeze (page 780).
Strawberries Rinse; hull. Slice large berries.	Use light, medium, or heavy syrup. Pack, covered with syrup.	Mix each 4 cups berries with ½ cup sugar; let stand until sugar has dissolved.	Pack into containers or jars. For better color, dissolve 1 teaspoon ascorbic acid in 4 cups water; cover berries with mixture. Or tray-freeze (page 780).
Youngberries See Blackberries.			

Blanching vegetables is an essential step before freezing for some produce. Carefully follow the blanching time for each vegetable, because underblanching stimulates enzyme activity and is worse than no blanching at all. To blanch: Fill an 8-quart saucepot halfway with water and bring to a full boil over high heat. Do not add salt. Place a small amount of vegetables (about 4 cups) in a wire basket or strainer so they can be lowered into and removed from the water at the same time. Completely immerse the basket in the boiling water; cover and start timing immediately (do not wait for the water to boil).

Meanwhile, fill a large bowl halfway with cold water; add one tray of ice cubes. Set aside. As soon as the blanching time is up, lift out the vegetables and plunge them into the iced water to stop the cooking and to cool them quickly. Stir the vegetables several times while cooling; the cooling time should not exceed the blanching time. Drain thoroughly. The blanching water may be reused (return it to a full boil), but the cooling water must be replenished with ice cubes for each batch of vegetables.

Packing Vegetables for Freezing

- Put vegetables without liquid into freezer-safe containers without headspace, or pack into heavy-duty ziptight plastic bags, pressing out all the air. Seal, label, and freeze. Pack pureed vegetables, such as potatoes, in heavy-duty ziptight plastic bags, pressing out all the air, or in freezer containers, leaving ½ inch headspace.

- Smaller vegetables and cut-up vegetables can be tray-frozen before packing, if desired, to keep the pieces from sticking together when packed. To tray-freeze vegetables: Spread the blanched, cooled, and drained vegetables in a single layer, without touching, in a jelly-roll pan. Freeze until hard, 1 to 2 hours. Pack the vegetables into freezer-safe containers or heavy-duty ziptight plastic bags; do not leave headspace. Seal, label, and freeze.

Cooking Frozen Vegetables

Frozen vegetables should be cooked just until tender. Since blanching partially cooks them, the cooking time will be shorter than for fresh vegetables. Most can be cooked without thawing. Leafy vegetables, such as spinach, cook more evenly if thawed just enough to separate the leaves. Corn on the cob should be completely thawed before being cooked so the cobs can heat through in the same time it takes to cook the kernels.

For a one-pint package of frozen lima beans, use 1 cup water. For corn on the cob, use 2 to 3 inches of water. For other frozen vegetables, use ½ cup of water. Salt the water lightly, if desired.

In a 2-quart saucepan over high heat, heat the water to boiling. Add the frozen vegetables and heat again to boiling, separating the pieces with a fork. Reduce the heat to medium and cover. Simmer just until the vegetables are tender. Drain, season as desired, and serve.

Whenever you have time, prepare a favorite casserole for the freezer. First line the casserole dish with heavy-duty foil. Ladle in the casserole mixture and freeze. Transfer the frozen casserole block to a heavy-duty ziptight plastic bag, label, and date. When you're ready to cook, unwrap the frozen block and slip it back into its original casserole dish. This way, you won't tie up the casserole dish for weeks or months.

JEAN ANDERSON
COOKBOOK AUTHOR

EXPERT TIP

FREEZING VEGETABLES

See Packing Vegetables for Freezing, page 785.

HOW TO PREPARE	FOR 4 QUARTS WATER	BLANCHING	SPECIAL INSTRUCTIONS
Asparagus Break off tough ends of spears and remove "scales"; rinse. Cut spears in lengths to fit package or into 2-inch pieces.	Large spears Medium spears Small spears	3 minutes 2 minutes 1½ minutes	Tray-freeze, if desired. For spears, pack alternating tip and stem ends.
Avocado Select avocados that are soft-ripe, not mushy. Peel. Cut in half, remove seed, and mash. Whole or sliced avocados do not freeze well.			To each cup of mashed avocado, add rounded ½ teaspoon ascorbic acid. Leave ½-inch headspace.
Basil Puree ¼ cup packed leaves with 1 tablespoon oil; freeze in ice cube trays. Do not freeze whole basil leaves.			Remove cubes from trays; transfer to ziptight plastic bags. Add cubes to soups or stews.
Beans, green or wax Trim ends. Leave whole, slice lengthwise for French-cut, or cut into 2-inch pieces.	Whole French-cut 2-inch pieces	3 minutes 3 minutes 3 minutes	Tray-freeze, if desired.
Beans, lima	Fordhook Baby	3 minutes 1 minutes	Tray-freeze, if desired.
Beet greens See Greens.			
Beets Select beets not larger than 3 inches. Trim tops and roots. Cook in boiling water until tender. Drain and peel. Leave whole, slice, or cube.	Fully cook; do not blanch.		Tray-freeze cut-up beets, if desired.
Broccoli Rinse; trim stem ends. Cut broccoli lengthwise into stalks with flowerets no larger than 1½ inches across.	Stalks	3 minutes	
Brussels sprouts Trim outer leaves and root ends. Sort by size.	Large Medium Small	5 minutes 4 minutes 3 minutes	

HOW TO PREPARE	FOR 4 QUARTS WATER	BLANCHING	SPECIAL INSTRUCTIONS
Carrots			
Peel. Leave small carrots whole; cut larger carrots lengthwise into strips, slice, or cube.	Whole Strips, slices, or cubes	5 minutes 3 minutes	Tray-freeze cut-up carrots, if desired.
Cauliflower			
Separate into 1-inch flowerets. Rinse.	Add 4 teaspoons salt to water.	3 minutes	
Collards			
See Greens.			
Corn, whole-kernel or cream-style			
Remove husks and silk. Cook corn on the cob in boiling water 4 minutes. Drain; cool. For whole-kernel corn, cut kernels from cob at about $\frac{2}{3}$ depth of kernels. For cream-style, cut off kernels where they meet cob; scrape off pulp.	Do not blanch.		Tray-freeze whole corn kernels, if desired. Pack cream-style corn, leaving $\frac{1}{2}$-inch headspace.
Corn, on the cob			
Remove husks and silk. Sort ears by size.	Large Medium Small	10 minutes 8 minutes 6 minutes	Wrap ears individually in foil, then pack in ziptight plastic bags.
Greens			
(beet or turnip tops, collards, kale, mustard greens, spinach, Swiss chard) Trim tough ribs and stems. Rinse well to remove all grit. Cut into pieces as desired.	Collards Other greens	3 minutes 2 minutes	Leave $\frac{1}{2}$-inch headspace.
Herbs			
Rinse; drain and pat dry. *For mint, oregano, parsley, and sage,* remove leaves from stems. *For chervil, dill, marjoram, rosemary, savory, tarragon, and thyme,* keep leaves on their stems.	Do not blanch.		Wrap sprigs or leaves in foil, then place in ziptight plastic bags. Use frozen herbs in cooked dishes.
Kale			
See Greens.			
Kohlrabi			
Select kohlrabi not larger than 2 inches. Trim tops and roots; peel. Leave whole or cut into $\frac{1}{2}$-inch cubes.	Whole Cubes	3 minutes 1 minute	

FREEZING VEGETABLES

See Packing Vegetables for Freezing, page 785.

HOW TO PREPARE	FOR 4 QUARTS WATER	BLANCHING	SPECIAL INSTRUCTIONS
Mushrooms Trim stem ends. If mushrooms are larger than 1 inch across, slice or cut into quarters. Cook 2 cups mushrooms in about 2 tablespoons oil. Cool.	Fully cook; do not blanch.		Leave ½-inch headspace.
Mustard greens See Greens.			
Okra Remove stems without cutting into pods. Blanch; drain and cool. Leave whole or slice.	Large Small	5 minutes 3 minutes	
Onions Peel; chop. No cooking needed.	Do not blanch.		Tray-freeze, if desired. Pack in convenient amounts.
Parsnips Select smooth, young roots. Trim tops. Peel, then slice or cube.	Slices	3 minutes	
Pea pods, Chinese (snow peas), snap peas Remove stems and strings from pea pods; do not shell.	Medium	2 minutes	
Peas, green Shell.		1½ minutes	Tray-freeze, if desired.
Peppers, sweet or hot Remove stems, membranes, and seeds from sweet peppers. If desired, roast sweet red, yellow, or orange peppers and peel. Leave whole, cut in half, slice, or chop. Remove stems from hot peppers; leave whole.	Do not blanch.		Tray-freeze, if desired.
Pumpkin, mashed Cut into large chunks; peel. Remove seeds and stringy portion. Steam until tender; mash.	Fully cook; do not blanch.		Leave ½-inch headspace.

How to Prepare	For 4 quarts Water	Blanching	Special Instructions
Rutabagas Peel; cut into ½-inch chunks. Cook in boiling water until tender; drain.	Cubes; mashed Fully cook; do not blanch.	2 minutes	If mashed, leave ½-inch headspace.
Spinach See Greens.			
Squash, summer *(zucchini, yellow crookneck)* Do not peel; cut into ½-inch-thick slices.	Slices	3 minutes	
Squash, winter *(acorn, banana, butternut, Delicious, Hubbard)* See Pumpkin.			
Sweet Potatoes Bake until tender; cool and peel. Leave whole, cut in half, slice, or mash. To keep from darkening after cooking, dip whole or cut-up potatoes in 4 cups water mixed with ½ cup lemon juice. Stir 2 tablespoons orange juice into 4 cups mashed sweet potatoes.	Fully cook; do not blanch.		If mashed, leave ½-inch headspace.
Swiss chard See Greens.			
Tomatoes Plunge into boiling water 30 seconds to loosen skin. Peel and cut out stem ends. Cut into quarters. Cook until heated through (do not add water); cool.	Fully cook; do not blanch.		Leave ½-inch headspace.
Turnip greens See Greens.			
Turnips Trim and peel; slice or cut into ½-inch cubes.	Slices, cubes	3 minutes	

Freezer Strawberry Jam

Jewel-like freezer jam is especially fresh-tasting. Peak-of-the-season farmstand strawberries work best.

Prep: 35 minutes plus overnight to stand	Cook: 8 minutes

- 5 half-pint freezer-safe containers with tight-fitting lids
- 1 quart fully ripe strawberries, hulled
- 4 cups sugar
- 2 tablespoons fresh lemon juice
- ¾ cup water
- 1 package (1¾ ounces) powdered fruit pectin

1. Prepare containers and lids for freezer jams (page 774).

2. In large bowl, thoroughly crush enough strawberries to equal 2 cups. Stir in sugar and lemon juice until thoroughly mixed; let stand 10 minutes.

3. In 1-quart saucepan, combine water and pectin and heat to boiling over high heat. Boil, stirring constantly, 1 minute. Stir pectin mixture into fruit until sugar has dissolved and mixture is no longer grainy, 3 to 4 minutes. A few sugar crystals will remain.

4. Quickly ladle jam into containers to within ½ inch of tops. Wipe container rims clean; cover with lids.

5. Let stand at room temperature until set, about 24 hours. Refrigerate up to 3 weeks, or freeze up to 1 year. To use, place frozen jam in refrigerator until thawed, about 4 hours. Makes five 8-ounce containers.

♥ Each tablespoon: About 43 calories, 0g protein, 11g carbohydrate, 0g total fat (0g saturated), 0mg cholesterol, 1mg sodium.

Freezer Raspberry Jam

Here's a quick way to prepare ruby red raspberry jam.

Prep: 30 minutes plus overnight to stand	Cook: 10 minutes

- 4 half-pint freezer-safe containers with tight-fitting lids
- 2 pints fully ripe raspberries
- 4 cups sugar
- 1 pouch (3 ounces) liquid fruit pectin
- 2 tablespoons fresh lemon juice

1. Prepare containers and lids for freezer jams (page 774).

2. In large bowl, thoroughly crush raspberries. If you like, with spoon, press half of crushed berries through sieve into medium bowl to remove seeds; discard seeds. In large bowl, combine berries. Stir in sugar until thoroughly mixed; let stand 10 minutes.

3. In bowl, combine pectin and lemon juice. Stir pectin mixture into fruit until sugar has dissolved and mixture is no longer grainy, 3 to 4 minutes. A few sugar crystals will remain.

4. Quickly ladle jam into containers to within ½ inch of tops. Wipe container rims clean; cover with lids.

5. Let stand at room temperature until set, about 24 hours. Refrigerate up to 3 weeks, or freeze up to 1 year. To use, place frozen jam in refrigerator until thawed, about 4 hours. Makes four 8-ounce containers.

♥ Each tablespoon: About 52 calories, 0g protein, 13g carbohydrate, 0g total fat (0g saturated), 0mg cholesterol, 0mg sodium.

Apricot Skillet Jam

Fresh apricots make the best jam. Use perfectly ripe fruit for the most flavor.

Prep: 30 minutes plus chilling	Cook: 10 minutes

- 2 half-pint jars with tight-fitting lids
- 1 pound fresh apricots, pitted and finely chopped (3 cups)
- 1 cup sugar
- 2 tablespoons fresh lemon juice
- 2 tablespoons powdered fruit pectin

1. Prepare jars and lids for jam (page 774).

2. In heavy nonstick 12-inch skillet, combine apricots, sugar, lemon juice, and pectin; heat to boiling over high heat, stirring constantly. Boil, stirring constantly, until apricots have softened, 2 to 3 minutes. Remove from heat.

3. Quickly ladle hot jam into hot jars. Wipe jar rims and threads clean; cover with lids and place in refrigerator until jam has set, about 6 hours. Refrigerate up to 3 weeks. Makes two 8-ounce jars.

♥ Each tablespoon: About 30 calories, 0g protein, 8g carbohydrate, 0g total fat (0g saturated), 0mg cholesterol, 1mg sodium.

SKILLET JAMS

Prepare jars and lids for jams (page 774). Press ½ cup crushed blackberries and/or raspberries, if using, through sieve to remove seeds, if you like. In heavy nonstick 12-inch skillet, combine fruit, pectin, and butter. Heat to boiling over high heat, stirring constantly. Stir in sugar and heat to boiling, stirring constantly; boil 1 minute. Remove skillet from heat. Quickly ladle hot jam into hot jars. Wipe jar rims and threads clean; cover with lids. Refrigerate until set, about 6 hours. Refrigerate up to 3 weeks. Each recipe makes two 8-ounce jars.

JAM	FRUIT MIXTURE	POWDERED FRUIT PECTIN	BUTTER OR MARGARINE	SUGAR
Blackberry-Blueberry Skillet Jam	2 cups each blackberries and blueberries, crushed	2 tablespoons	½ teaspoon	¾ cup
Three-Berry Skillet Jam (pictured on page 770)	1 cup each blackberries, raspberries, and sliced strawberries, crushed	4 teaspoons	½ teaspoon	1 cup
Strawberry Skillet Jam	2 cups sliced strawberries, crushed	4 teaspoons	½ teaspoon	1 cup
Raspberry Skillet Jam	3 cups raspberries, crushed	4 teaspoons	½ teaspoon	1½ cups
Blueberry Skillet Jam	2 cups blueberries, crushed	2 tablespoons	½ teaspoon	1 cup
Peach Skillet Jam	1 pound peaches, peeled, pitted, and mashed with 2 teaspoons fresh lemon juice	2 tablespoons	½ teaspoon	1 cup

Mint Jelly

The classic American accompaniment to roast leg of lamb.

Prep: 5 minutes plus preparing jars and lids for jam and standing
Cook: 15 minutes plus processing

4	half-pint canning jars and lids
1½	cups apple juice
½	cup cider vinegar
¼	cup dried mint
3½	cups sugar
1	pouch (3 ounces) liquid fruit pectin

1. Prepare jars and lids for jam (page 774). Fill canner halfway with *water*; cover and heat to simmering over high heat.

2. Meanwhile, in nonreactive 4-quart saucepan, combine apple juice and vinegar; heat to boiling over high heat. Re-move from heat. Stir in mint; cover and let stand 10 minutes.

3. Strain mixture through small sieve into 2-cup measuring cup; discard mint. If necessary, add enough *water* to apple-juice mixture to equal 1¾ cups. Wipe saucepan clear.

4. In same saucepan, combine juice mixture and sugar; heat to boiling over high heat, stirring constantly. Stir in pectin. Cook, stirring constantly, until mixture comes to rolling boil; boil 1 minute. Remove from heat. With spoon, skim off any foam.

5. Quickly ladle hot jelly into hot jars to within ¼ inch of tops. Wipe jar rims and threads clean; cover quickly with lids and screw bands on securely but not too tightly. Process in boiling water bath (page 773) 10 minutes; cool jars and test for airtight seal (page 773). Makes four 8-ounce jars.

♥ Each tablespoon: About 46 calories, 0g protein, 12g carbohydrate, 0g total fat (0g saturated), 0mg cholesterol, 1mg sodium.

All-Season Apple Jelly

Try one of the variations to brighten up your morning toast.

Prep: 5 minutes plus preparing jars and lids for jam
Cook: 15 minutes plus processing

4	half-pint canning jars and lids
4	cups apple juice
1	package (1¾ ounces) powdered fruit pectin
5	cups sugar

1. Prepare jars and lids for jam (page 774). Fill canner halfway with *water;* cover and heat to simmering over high heat.

2. Meanwhile, in nonreactive 5-quart Dutch oven, combine apple juice and pectin. Heat to boiling over high heat, stirring constantly; immediately stir in sugar. Cook, stirring constantly, until mixture comes to rolling boil; boil 1 minute. Remove from heat. With spoon, skim off any foam.

3. Quickly ladle hot jelly into hot jars to within ¼ inch of tops. Wipe jar rims and threads clean; cover quickly with lids and screw bands on securely but not too tightly. Process in boiling water bath (page 773) 10 minutes; cool jars and test for airtight seal (page 773). Makes four 8-ounce jars.

♥ Each tablespoon: About 70 calories, 0g protein, 18g carbohydrate, 0g total fat (0g saturated), 0mg cholesterol, 2mg sodium.

Apple-Cider Jelly

Prepare as directed but substitute **4 cups apple cider** for apple juice.

Spiced Apple Jelly

With vegetable peeler, remove peel from **1 large navel orange.** With string, tie **12 cloves, 2 cinnamon sticks** (3 inches each), and **orange peel** in double thickness of cheesecloth. Prepare jelly as directed. Add spice bag to pot with apple juice and pectin. Before ladling jelly, discard spice bag.

Grape Jelly

Prepare as directed but substitute **2 cups unsweetened grape juice** and **1 cup water** for apple juice; use only **3½ cups sugar.** Makes three 8-ounce jars.

Jalapeño Pepper Jelly

This sweet and spicy jelly makes a great accompaniment to meat and chicken dishes, or dollop onto crackers that are spread with cream cheese for a flavor-packed appetizer.

Prep: 20 minutes plus preparing jars and lids for jam
Cook: 25 minutes plus processing

6	half-pint canning jars and lids
8	large green peppers, each cut into quarters
6	jalapeño chiles or hot red chiles, seeded
6	cups sugar
½	cup distilled white vinegar
1	package (6 ounces) liquid fruit pectin
4	drops green food coloring (optional)

1. Prepare jars and lids for jam (page 774). Fill canner halfway with *water.* Cover; heat to simmering over high heat.

2. Meanwhile, in blender or in food processor with knife blade attached, process green peppers and jalapeños until very finely chopped. Transfer pepper mixture to sieve set over large bowl. With spoon, press pepper mixture until all liquid is removed. (There should be about 2 cups liquid.) Discard peppers.

3. In nonreactive 8-quart saucepot, combine sugar, pepper liquid, and vinegar; heat to boiling over high heat. Boil 10 minutes. Stir in pectin and food coloring, if using. Cook, stirring constantly, until mixture comes to rolling boil; boil 1 minute. Remove from heat. With spoon, skim off any foam.

4. Quickly ladle hot jelly into hot jars to within ¼ inch of tops. Wipe jar rims and threads clean; cover quickly with lids and screw bands on securely but not too tightly. Process jars in boiling water bath (page 773) 10 minutes; cool jars and test for airtight seal (page 773). Makes six 8-ounce jars.

♥ Each tablespoon: About 50 calories, 0g protein, 13g carbohydrate, 0g total fat (0g saturated), 0mg cholesterol, 0mg sodium.

Spiced Sherry Jelly

Cream sherry has a rich, sweet flavor that makes it the perfect match for the spices in this jelly.

Prep: 5 minutes plus preparing jars and lids for jam
Cook: 15 minutes plus processing

4	half-pint canning jars and lids
1	cinnamon stick (3 inches)
½	teaspoon whole cloves
½	teaspoon whole allspice berries
2½	cups cream sherry
½	cup water
¼	cup fresh lemon juice
1	package (1¾ ounces) powdered fruit pectin
3	cups sugar

1. Prepare jars and lids for jam (page 774). Fill canner halfway with *water;* cover and heat to simmering over high heat.

2. With string, tie cinnamon stick, cloves, and allspice in double thickness of cheesecloth.

3. In nonreactive 3-quart saucepan, combine sherry, water, lemon juice, pectin, and spice bag; heat to boiling over high heat, stirring frequently. Immediately stir in sugar. Cook, stirring constantly, until mixture comes to rolling boil; boil

1 minute. Discard spice bag. Remove saucepan from heat. With spoon, skim off any foam.

4. Quickly ladle hot jelly into hot jars to within ¼ inch of tops. Wipe jar rims and threads clean; cover quickly with lids and screw bands on securely but not too tightly. Process in boiling water bath (page 773) 10 minutes; cool jars and test for airtight seal (page 773). Makes four 8-ounce jars.

♥ Each tablespoon: About 53 calories, 0g protein, 11g carbohydrate, 0g total fat (0g saturated), 0mg cholesterol, 2mg sodium.

White Grape–Wine Jelly

Serve this delicately spiced, clear jelly as an accompaniment to pork or chicken, or spread on bread or crackers.

Prep: 5 minutes plus preparing jars and lids for jam
Cook: 15 minutes plus processing

6	half-pint canning jars and lids
1	lemon
8	whole cloves
1	cinnamon stick (3 inches)
2½	cups white grape juice
1½	cups Riesling wine
1	package (1¾ ounces) powdered fruit pectin
4½	cups sugar

1. Prepare jars and lids for jam (page 774). Fill canner halfway with *water;* cover and heat to simmering over high heat.

2. From lemon, with vegetable peeler, remove 3-inch strip peel; squeeze 1 tablespoon juice. With string, tie cloves and cinnamon stick in double thickness of cheesecloth.

3. In heavy nonreactive 8-quart saucepot, combine grape juice, wine, pectin, lemon peel and juice, and spice bag; heat to boiling over high heat, stirring frequently. Immediately stir in sugar. Cook, stirring constantly, until mixture comes to rolling boil; boil 1 minute. Discard spice bag. Remove saucepot from heat. With spoon, skim off any foam.

4. Quickly ladle hot jelly into hot jars to within ¼ inch of tops. Wipe jar rims and threads clean; cover quickly with lids and screw bands on securely but not too tightly. Process in boiling water bath (page 773) 10 minutes; cool jars and test for airtight seal (page 773). Makes six 8-ounce jars.

♥ Each tablespoon: About 67 calories, 0g protein, 16g carbohydrate, 0g total fat (0g saturated), 0mg cholesterol, 3mg sodium.

Spiced Sherry Jelly

Strawberry Jam

Strawberry Jam

Here's an old-fashioned way to make a large batch of thick and delicious jam.

Prep: 25 minutes plus preparing jars and lids for jam
Cook: 20 minutes plus processing

8	half-pint canning jars and lids
2	quarts fully ripe strawberries, hulled
6	cups sugar
¼	cup fresh lemon juice
1	pouch (3 ounces) liquid fruit pectin

1. Prepare jars and lids for jam (page 774). Fill canner halfway with *water;* cover and heat to simmering over high heat.

2. Meanwhile, in large bowl, crush enough strawberries to equal 4 cups, leaving berries slightly chunky.

3. In heavy nonreactive 8-quart saucepot, combine strawberries, sugar, and lemon juice; heat to boiling over high heat, stirring constantly. Boil rapidly 1 minute, stirring constantly; stir in pectin. Cook until mixture comes to rolling boil; boil 1 minute. Remove from heat. With spoon, skim off any foam.

4. Quickly ladle hot jam into hot jars to within ¼ inch of tops. Wipe jar rims and threads clean; cover quickly with lids and screw bands on securely but not too tightly. Process in boiling water bath (page 773) 10 minutes; cool jars and test for airtight seal (page 773). Makes eight 8-ounce jars.

💗 Each tablespoon: About 39 calories, 0g protein, 10g carbohydrate, 0g total fat (0g saturated), 0mg cholesterol, 0mg sodium.

Tomato-Pear Preserves

Enjoy this unusual preserve on thickly cut toast or with cold sliced meat or roasted chicken.

Prep: 25 minutes plus preparing jars and lids for jam
Cook: 2 hours 20 minutes plus processing

4	large lemons
3	pounds firm-ripe tomatoes (9 medium), peeled and cut into bite-size pieces
2	pounds firm-ripe Bartlett or Bosc pears (4 medium), peeled, cored, and cut into bite-size pieces
3	tablespoons minced, peeled fresh ginger
4½	cups sugar
¼	teaspoon salt
4	one-pint canning jars and lids

1. From lemons, with vegetable peeler, remove peel along with some white pith. Cut peel into 2" by ⅛" strips; squeeze ¾ cup juice from lemons.

2. In 2-quart saucepan, combine lemon peel and enough *water* to cover; heat to boiling over high heat. Reduce heat; cover and simmer until lemon peel is tender, about 10 minutes. Drain.

3. In heavy nonreactive 8-quart saucepot, combine tomatoes, pears, ginger, and lemon peel and juice; heat to boiling over high heat. Reduce heat; simmer, stirring frequently, 1 hour. Add sugar and salt; simmer, stirring occasionally, until fruit becomes translucent and mixture has thickened slightly, about 1 hour longer. With spoon, skim off any foam.

4. Meanwhile, prepare jars and lids for jam (page 774). Fill canner halfway with *water;* cover and heat to simmering over high heat.

5. Quickly ladle simmering preserves into hot jars to within ¼ inch of tops. (Keep preserves simmering while filling jars.) Wipe jar rims and threads clean; cover quickly with lids and screw bands on securely but not too tightly. Process in boiling water bath (page 773) 20 minutes; cool jars and test for airtight seal (page 773). Makes four 16-ounce jars.

♥ Each tablespoon: About 34 calories, 0g protein, 9g carbohydrate, 0g total fat (0g saturated), 0mg cholesterol, 5mg sodium.

Sweet Cherry Jam

Who can resist homemade cherry jam? Take the time to find perfectly ripe fruit for the best results.

Prep: 45 minutes plus preparing jars and lids for jam
Cook: 20 minutes plus processing

5	half-pint canning jars and lids
2	pounds dark sweet cherries
5	cups sugar
¼	cup fresh lemon juice
1	pouch (3 ounces) liquid fruit pectin

1. Prepare jars and lids for jam (page 774). Fill canner halfway with *water.* Cover; heat to simmering over high heat.

2. Meanwhile, remove pits from cherries; finely chop enough cherries to equal 3 cups.

3. In heavy nonreactive 8-quart saucepot, combine cherries, sugar, and lemon juice; heat to boiling over high heat, stirring constantly; stir in pectin. Cook until mixture comes to rolling boil; boil 1 minute. Remove from heat. With spoon, skim off any foam.

4. Quickly ladle hot jam into hot jars to within ¼ inch of tops. Wipe jar rims and threads clean; cover quickly with lids and screw bands on securely but not too tightly. Process in boiling water bath (page 773) 10 minutes; cool jars and test for airtight seal (page 773). Makes five 8-ounce jars.

♥ Each tablespoon: About 56 calories, 0g protein, 14g carbohydrate, 0g total fat (0g saturated), 0mg cholesterol, 0mg sodium.

Tart Cherry Jam

Prepare as directed but substitute **2 pounds tart cherries** for sweet cherries, use only **4½ cups sugar,** and omit lemon juice. Remove pits from cherries and finely chop enough cherries to equal about 2½ cups. Makes three 8-ounce jars.

♥ Each tablespoon: About 98 calories, 0g protein, 25g carbohydrate, 0g total fat (0g saturated), 0mg cholesterol, 1mg sodium.

Pear Marmalade

Here, pears are combined with thinly sliced orange peel, fresh ginger, and a touch of allspice to make an unusually delectable marmalade. Use any variety of pear you like.

Prep: 30 minutes plus preparing jars and lids for jam
Cook: 1 hour plus processing

3	large oranges
6	pounds pears (12 large), peeled, cored, and coarsely chopped (12 cups)
2	tablespoons minced, peeled fresh ginger
4	cups sugar
⅓	cup fresh lemon juice
½	teaspoon ground allspice
7	half-pint canning jars and lids

1. From oranges, with vegetable peeler, remove peel along with some white pith. Cut enough peel into 2" by ⅛" strips to equal ¾ cup. Coarsely chop enough oranges to equal 1½ cups; discard seeds.

Pear Marmalade

2. In heavy nonreactive 8-quart saucepot, combine pears, oranges and peel, ginger, sugar, lemon juice, and allspice; heat to boiling over high heat, stirring frequently. Reduce heat to medium-high; cook, stirring frequently, until mixture is very thick, about 45 minutes. With spoon, skim off any foam.

3. Meanwhile, prepare jars and lids for jam (page 774). Fill canner halfway with *water;* cover and heat to simmering over high heat.

4. Quickly ladle simmering marmalade into hot jars to within ¼ inch of tops. (Keep marmalade simmering while filling jars.) Wipe jar rims and threads clean; cover quickly with lids and screw bands on securely but not too tightly. Process in boiling water bath (page 773) 15 minutes; cool jars and test for airtight seal (page 773). Makes seven 8-ounce jars.

♥ Each tablespoon: About 43 calories, 0g protein, 11g carbohydrate, 0g total fat (0g saturated), 0mg cholesterol, 0mg sodium.

Peach Butter

An exquisitely delicious spread that has the rich flavor of ripe peaches and just a touch of cinnamon.

Prep: 30 minutes plus preparing jars and lids for jam
Cook: 1 hour 30 minutes plus processing

6	pounds ripe peaches (18 to 20 medium), peeled, pitted, and cut into quarters
2½	cups sugar
½	teaspoon ground cinnamon
4	half-pint canning jars and lids

1. In heavy nonreactive 8-quart saucepot, cook peaches over medium heat, stirring, until very soft, about 20 minutes. Remove from heat. In batches, in blender with center part of cover removed to let steam escape, or in food processor with knife blade attached, puree peaches until smooth.

2. Return peach puree to clean saucepot; stir in sugar and cinnamon. Heat peach mixture to boiling over high heat. Reduce heat to medium-low; cook, stirring frequently, until puree has thickened and mixture mounds when dropped from spoon, about 1 hour.

3. Meanwhile, prepare jars and lids for jam (page 774). Fill canner halfway with *water;* cover and heat to simmering over high heat.

4. Quickly ladle simmering peach butter into hot jars to within ¼ inch of tops. (Keep mixture simmering while filling jars.) Wipe jar rims and threads clean; cover quickly with lids and screw bands on securely but not too tightly. Process in boiling water bath (page 773) 10 minutes; cool jars and test for airtight seal (page 773). Makes four 8-ounce jars.

♥ Each tablespoon: About 44 calories, 0g protein, 11g carbohydrate, 0g total fat (0g saturated), 0mg cholesterol, 0mg sodium.

Blushing Apple Butter

Cranberries tint this apple butter pink. Plan ahead: Make a batch to give as gifts during the holidays.

Prep: 30 minutes plus preparing jars and lids for jam
Cook: 1 hour 30 minutes

2	lemons
3¾	pounds Granny Smith apples (8 large), peeled, cored, and thinly sliced
1	cup cranberries
1½	cups apple cider or apple juice
1½	cups sugar
5	half-pint jars with tight-fitting lids

1. From lemons, with vegetable peeler, remove 3 strips (3" by 1" each) peel; squeeze 3 tablespoons juice. In heavy nonreactive 5-quart Dutch oven, combine apples, cranberries, lemon peel and juice, and apple cider; heat to boiling over high heat. Reduce heat; simmer, stirring occasionally, until apples are very soft, about 10 minutes.

2. Stir in sugar; heat to boiling over high heat. Reduce heat to medium; partially cover and cook, stirring occasion-ally, until apple butter is very thick, about 1 hour. (Mixture may sputter and splash, so be careful when stirring.)

3. Meanwhile, prepare jars and lids for jam (page 774). In batches, in blender with center part of cover removed to let  steam escape, or in food processor with knife blade attached, puree apple butter until smooth.

Blushing Apple Butter

4. Ladle hot apple butter into clean jars; wipe jar rims and threads clean. Cover tightly. Refrigerate up to 3 weeks. Makes five 8-ounce jars.

♥ Each tablespoon: About 31 calories, 0g protein, 8g carbohydrate, 0g total fat (0g saturated), 0mg cholesterol, 0mg sodium.

Watermelon-Rind Pickles

These pickles look especially nice, because a little of the red flesh is left on the rind.

Prep: 30 minutes plus overnight to refrigerate and
preparing jars and lids for canning
Cook: 1 hour 40 minutes plus processing

	rind from 1 medium watermelon (10 pounds)
½	cup kosher, canning, or pickling salt
6	cinnamon sticks (3 inches each)
2	teaspoons whole cloves
4	cups sugar
2	cups distilled white vinegar
2	cups water
5	one-pint canning jars and lids

Watermelon-Rind Pickles

1. Trim and discard outer dark green skin from watermelon rind. Cut enough rind into 1-inch pieces to equal 14 cups, leaving about ⅛-inch red flesh. In very large bowl, combine salt and *6 cups water,* stirring until salt has dissolved; add watermelon rind. If necessary, add enough *water* to cover. Cover and refrigerate overnight.

2. Next day, pour rind mixture into colander to drain. Rinse with cold running water; drain. In heavy nonreactive 8-quart saucepot, combine rind and enough *water* to cover; heat to boiling over high heat. Reduce heat and simmer 20 minutes; drain and return to pot.

3. With string, tie cinnamon sticks and cloves in double thickness of cheesecloth. Add sugar, vinegar, water, and spice bag to saucepot. Heat to boiling over high heat. Reduce heat; cover and simmer, stirring frequently, 45 minutes.

4. Meanwhile, prepare the jars and lids for canning (page 772). Fill canner halfway with *water;* cover and heat to simmering over high heat.

5. Discard spice bag. Spoon hot pickle mixture into hot jars to within ½ inch of tops. Immediately ladle simmering syrup into hot jars to within ¼ inch of top, making sure rind is completely covered with syrup. (Keep syrup simmering while filling jars.) Wipe jar rims and threads clean; cover quickly with lids and screw bands on securely but not too

tightly. Process in boiling water bath (page 773) 10 minutes; cool the jars and test for airtight seal (page 773). Makes five 16-ounce jars.

♥ Each ¼ cup: About 84 calories, 0g protein, 22g carbohydrate, 0g total fat (0g saturated), 0mg cholesterol, 177mg sodium.

To turn apple jelly into herbal jelly, lightly bruise a sprig or two of fresh rosemary and push down into a jar of hot jelly just before sealing. Or lightly bruise a small pesticide-free leaf of rose or lemon geranium and place in the bottom of a jelly jar. Fill the jar with hot jelly, then lay another geranium leaf on top. Seal and process as recipe directs.

JEAN ANDERSON
COOKBOOK AUTHOR

EXPERT TIP

Home-Style Chutney

This chutney gets its full flavor from a tempting mix of fruits and vegetables; it is a fine accompaniment to grilled lamb.

Prep: 40 minutes plus preparing jars and lids for canning
Cook: 2 hours 15 minutes plus processing

2 to 3	medium oranges
3	pounds ripe nectarines (6 large), pitted and cut into wedges
1½	pounds Granny Smith apples (3 large), peeled, cored, and cut into ½-inch pieces
1	pound firm-ripe tomatoes (3 medium), cut into ½-inch pieces
3	medium onions, cut into ½-inch pieces
3	tablespoons minced, peeled fresh ginger
1	package (16 ounces) light brown sugar
2¼	cups distilled white vinegar
2	teaspoons dry mustard
1	teaspoon salt
¼	teaspoon ground red pepper (cayenne)
1	cup dark seedless raisins
6	half-pint canning jars and lids

1. From oranges, grate 2 tablespoons peel and squeeze ⅔ cup juice. In nonreactive 5-quart Dutch oven, combine nectarines, apples, tomatoes, onions, ginger, orange peel and juice, brown sugar, vinegar, mustard, salt, and ground red pepper. Heat to boiling over high heat, stirring frequently. Reduce heat and simmer 1 hour. Add raisins; cook, stirring frequently, until mixture is very thick, about 45 minutes.

2. Meanwhile, prepare the jars and lids for canning (page 772). Fill canner halfway with *water;* cover and heat to simmering over high heat.

3. Ladle simmering chutney into hot jars to within ¼ inch of tops. (Keep chutney simmering while filling jars.) Wipe jar rims and threads clean; cover quickly with lids and screw bands on securely but not too tightly. Process in boiling water bath (page 773) 10 minutes; cool jars and test for airtight seal (page 773). Makes six 8-ounces jars.

♥ Each tablespoon: About 34 calories, 0g protein, 9g carbohydrate, 0g total fat (0g saturated), 0mg cholesterol, 27mg sodium.

Bread-and-Butter Pickles

Take a jar of these sweet pickles to your next family barbecue. Use absolutely fresh kirby cucumbers from a farmers' market or farm stand for the best results.

Prep: 20 minutes plus standing and preparing jars and lids for canning
Cook: 45 minutes plus processing

4	pounds very firm unwaxed cucumbers (4 to 6 inches long), cut into ¼-inch-thick slices
3	large onions, thinly sliced
½	cup kosher, canning, or pickling salt
8	cups ice cubes (3 trays)
5	cups sugar
5	cups cider vinegar
1	teaspoon ground turmeric
1½	teaspoons celery seeds
1½	teaspoons mustard seeds
6	one-pint canning jars and lids

1. In 8-quart enamel, stainless steel, or glass container, combine cucumbers, onions, salt, and enough *cold water* to cover. Stir until salt has dissolved; stir in ice. Cover and let stand in cool place 3 hours. Drain vegetables and rinse with cold running water; drain.

2. In nonreactive 8-quart saucepot, combine sugar, vinegar, turmeric, celery seeds, and mustard seeds; heat to boiling over high heat. Reduce heat; simmer, stirring, 30 minutes.

3. Meanwhile, prepare the jars and lids for canning (page 772). Fill canner halfway with *water;* cover and heat to simmering over high heat.

4. Add cucumbers and onions to pot; heat to boiling. Spoon hot vegetables into hot jars to within ½ inch of tops. Immediately ladle simmering syrup over vegetables to within ¼ inch from tops, making sure vegetables are completely covered with syrup. (Keep syrup simmering while filling jars.) Wipe jar rims and threads clean; cover quickly with lids and screw bands on securely but not too tightly. Process in boiling water bath (page 773) 10 minutes; cool jars and test for airtight seal (page 773). Makes six 16-ounce jars.

♥ Each ¼ cup: About 95 calories, 0g protein, 25g carbohydrate, 0g total fat (0g saturated), 0mg cholesterol, 292mg sodium.

Peppery Dilled Beans

These tangy green beans have great dill flavor. They look their best when tightly packed into the jars.

Prep: 45 minutes plus preparing jars and lids for canning
Cook: 10 minutes plus processing

2½	pounds green beans
6	half-pint canning jars and lids
2½	cups distilled white vinegar
2	cups water
¼	cup kosher, canning, or pickling salt
1	garlic clove, peeled
6	dill sprigs
¾	teaspoon crushed red pepper

1. Trim green beans to ¼ inch shorter than height of glass canning jars.

2. Prepare jars and lids for canning (page 772). Fill canner halfway with *water*. Cover canner and heat to simmering over high heat.

3. In nonreactive 2-quart saucepan, combine vinegar, water, salt, and garlic; heat to boiling over high heat. In each hot jar, place 1 dill sprig and ⅛ teaspoon crushed red pepper. Pack green beans tightly into jars. Discard garlic and immediately ladle in simmering liquid to within ¼ inch of tops. (Keep liquid simmering while filling jars.) Wipe jar rims and threads clean; cover quickly with lids and screw bands on securely but not too tightly. Process jars in boiling water bath (page 773) 10 minutes; cool and test for airtight seal (page 773). Makes six 8-ounce jars, 6 servings each.

❤ Each serving: About 9 calories, 0g protein, 2g carbohydrate, 0g total fat (0g saturated), 0mg cholesterol, 583mg sodium.

Corn Relish

Jars of colorful corn relish are pretty enough to share with friends.

Prep: 40 minutes plus preparing jars and lids for canning
Cook: 35 minutes plus processing.

5	one-pint canning jars and lids
12	ears corn, husks and silk removed
2	green peppers, finely chopped (1½ cups)
2	red peppers, finely chopped (1½ cups)
1	pound firm-ripe medium tomatoes, chopped (1½ cups)
2	medium onions, chopped (1 cup)
1½	cups sugar
3	cups cider vinegar
4	teaspoons kosher, canning, or pickling salt
1	teaspoon celery seeds
1	teaspoon dry mustard
1	teaspoon ground turmeric

1. Prepare jars and lids for canning (page 772). Fill canner halfway with *water*. Cover canner and heat to simmering over high heat.

2. With sharp knife, cut 8 cups kernels from corncobs.

3. In nonreactive 5-quart Dutch oven, combine corn, green and red peppers, tomatoes, onions, sugar, vinegar, salt, celery seeds, dry mustard, and turmeric; heat to boiling over high heat. Reduce heat; simmer, stirring, 20 minutes.

4. Ladle simmering relish into hot jars to within ¼ inch of tops. (Keep relish simmering while filling jars.) Wipe jar rims and threads clean; cover quickly with lids and screw bands on securely but not too tightly. Process in boiling water bath (page 773) 15 minutes; cool jars and test for airtight seal (page 773). Makes five 16-ounce jars.

❤ Each tablespoon: About 16 calories, 0g protein, 4g carbohydrate, 0g total fat (0g saturated), 0mg cholesterol, 60mg sodium.

Giardiniera

Usually served as part of an Italian antipasto. If you like, combine it with some peperoncini and oil-cured black olives.

Prep: 1 hour plus preparing jars and lids for canning
Cook: 20 minutes plus processing

5	one-pint canning jars and lids
1	small head cauliflower (1½ pounds), cut into small flowerets (3 cups)
2	large red peppers, cut into 1-inch pieces
5	large carrots, peeled and thickly sliced (2 cups)
4	large stalks celery, thickly sliced (2 cups)
1	jar (5 ounces) green olives, drained
1	cup sugar
4½	cups distilled white vinegar
1½	cups water
2	tablespoons kosher, canning, or pickling salt
½	teaspoon mustard seeds
¼	teaspoon crushed red pepper

1. Prepare jars and lids for canning (page 772). Fill canner halfway with *water;* cover canner and heat to simmering over high heat.

2. In large bowl, combine cauliflower, red peppers, carrots, celery, and olives. In nonreactive 4-quart saucepan, combine sugar, vinegar, water, and salt; heat to boiling over high heat, stirring occasionally. Reduce heat to low.

Giardiniera

3. In each hot jar, place some mustard seeds and crushed red pepper; pack vegetables tightly into hot jars to within ½ inch of tops. Immediately ladle simmering syrup over vegetables to within ¼ inch of tops, making sure vegetables are completely covered with syrup. (Keep syrup simmering while filling jars.) Wipe jar rims and threads clean; cover quickly with lids and screw bands on securely but not too tightly. Process in boiling water bath (page 773) 20 minutes; cool jars and test for airtight seal (page 773). Makes five 16-ounce jars.

💙 Each ¼ cup: About 34 calories, 0g protein, 8g carbohydrate, 0g total fat (0g saturated), 0mg cholesterol, 443mg sodium.

Pickled Okra

Tender okra pods preserved with dill, garlic, and crushed red pepper are an old-time Southern favorite.

Prep: 20 minutes plus preparing jars and lids for canning
Cook: 20 minutes plus processing

8	half-pint canning jars and lids
3½	cups distilled white vinegar
2	cups water
¼	cup kosher, canning, or pickling salt
8	garlic cloves, peeled
8	dill sprigs
2	teaspoons crushed red pepper
1¼	pounds small firm okra, stems trimmed

1. Prepare jars and lids for canning (page 772). Fill canner halfway with *water;* cover and heat to simmering over high heat.

2. In nonreactive 2-quart saucepan, combine vinegar, water, and salt; heat to boiling over high heat.

3. In each hot jar, place 1 garlic clove, 1 dill sprig, and ¼ teaspoon crushed red pepper. Tightly pack okra, stem end up, into hot jars. Immediately ladle simmering liquid over okra to within ¼ inch of tops, making sure okra is completely covered with liquid. (Keep liquid simmering while filling jars.) Wipe jar rims and threads clean; cover with lids and screw bands on securely but not too tightly. Process in boiling water bath (page 773) 10 minutes; cool jars and test for airtight seal (page 773). Makes eight 8-ounce jars, 4 servings each.

💙 Each serving: About 11 calories, 0g protein, 3g carbohydrate, 0g total fat (0g saturated), 0mg cholesterol, 874mg sodium.

INDEX

* indicates heart healthy recipes;
+ indicates quick recipes

A

Acini di pepe, 340
Acorn squash, baked, 464
Adjustable-blade slicer, 11
Adobo-style chili, 151
Adzuki, 372
Aïoli, easy, 40
Al dente, 28
Ale, 27
All-purpose flour, 584
Almond(s)
    *-anise biscotti, 738
    cheesecake brownies, 714–15
    cherry- clafouti, 493
    cranberry- tart, 697
    crescents, 728–29, **728**
    Finnish, cookies, 733
    green beans amandine, 409
    lemon- bubble ring, 601
    macaroons, 727
    paste, 31
    pound cake, 665
    roasted –crusted plums, 509
    shortbread brownies, 714
    spicy, slices, 732
    spritz, 736
    sweet, filling, 602
    toasting, 729
    trout amandine, 263
    tuiles, 737

Alphabet pasta, 340
Amaranth, 381
Amaretti, broiled, plums, 503
Amaretti cookies, 31
Amaretto, buttercream, 680
Ambrosia, 514
Anasazi, 372
Anchovy(ies), 254, 258
    butter, 563
    *linguine with broccoli rabe and, 349
*Angel food cake, 666
Angel hair, 340
Anise
    *almond-, biscotti, 738
    beef kabobs, 115
    cornish hens with -orange glaze, 228
    fruit bowl, 513
    lemon-, icebox cookies, 731
    *lemon-, poached pears, 505
Appaloosa beans. *See* Heirloom beans
Appenzeller, 329
Appetizer(s), 35–55
    adding twist to, 47
    baba ganoush, 38
    bite-size bacon quiches, 49
    +black bean dip, 40
    brandade, 285
    buffalo-style chicken wings, 51
    caraway-cheese crisps, 45
    caviar in potato nests, 50
    cheddar crisps, 336
    chicken and beef saté, 52
    chicken liver pâté, 44

chili nuts, 42
*Chinese dumplings, 52–53
chorizo and black bean nachos, 47
clams casino, 55
+classic Swiss fondue, **326,** 333
curried cheddar puffs, 50
curried nuts, 42
do-ahead strategies for, 36
dried tomato filling, 43
easy aïoli, 40
easy spicy cheese straws, 46
empanaditas, 48
fried calamari fra diavolo, 301
gravlax, 54
Greek cheese pastries, 49
herbed yogurt-cheese dip, 40
+hot-pepper nuts, 42
+hummus, 39
+lacy parmesan crisps, 336, **336**
marinated mixed olives, 43
meze, 39
mini crab cakes, 51, **51**
mini spanakopita, 50
mozzarella in carrozza, 335, **335**
mozzarella with dried tomatoes, 337
oysters rockefeller, 55
parmesan-pepper sticks, 45
*pickled shrimp, 43
*pissaladière, 600
potted cheddar and beer spread, 37
potted shrimp, 41
*+prosciutto with melon, 53
prosciutto with other fruit, 53

prosciutto-wrapped asparagus, 47
*+quick quesadillas, 45
roasted eggplant dip with herbs, 38
+roasted red pepper dip, 37, **37**
salmon pâté, 44
samosas, 48–49
savory ricotta cheesecake, 337
serving, 36
*shrimp cocktail, 54
smoked salmon filling, 43
+smoked trout pâté, 44
soft-shell crabs with lemon-caper
    sauce, 288
*+steamed soft-shell clams, 287
sweet and spicy nuts, 42
Swiss cheese crisps, 45
+tapenade, 41
+tomato and ricotta salata bruschetta, **34,** 46
tomato-basil cream cheese logs, 41
tortilla spirals, 42–43
tzatziki, 38
warm layered bean dip, 39
Apple(s), 482–85
autumn fruit compote, 515
blushing, butter, 797, **797**
brown betty, 484
butternut-, soup, 60, **60**
-calvados crepes, 647
canning, 776
*charlotte, 485
*chestnut and, stuffing, 245
*cranberry- sauce, 557
crepes filled with, and gruyère, 319
crumb pie, 690
*-curry sauce, 214
*fastest baked, 482
freezing, 781
*fresh, soufflés, 623
fresh ham with spiced, glaze, 144
fruit-stuffed veal roast, 130
galette, 692
-gingerbread muffins, 571
ham steak with, chutney, 156
jelly
    *all-season, 792
    -cider, 792
    spiced, 792
    turning into herbal jelly, 798
*Northwest fruit stuffing, 246
-oatmeal crisp, 484
outrageous caramel, 485
peeling, 484
pie, 689
pork crown roast with, stuffing, 142–43, **143**
*+puffy, pancake, 321
red snapper with bacon and, 284

*rhubarb-, crumble, 517
strudel, 640–41, **641**
stuffed pork chops, 155
tarte tatin, 690, **691**
and thyme roast chicken, **184,** 190
upside-down cake, 656
varieties, 482
*Vermont baked, 483, **483**
+waldorf salad, 529
-walnut bundt cake, 658
Apple corer, 11
Applesauce
canning, 776
cranberry, 483
freezing, 781
ginger, 483
horseradish, 483
lemon, 483
*McIntosh, 483
*spice cake, 655
spiced, 483
Appliqué pie top, 685
Apricot(s), 486
-balsamic sauce, 201
bulgur pilaf with, 397
canning, 776
*-cranberry sauce with fresh ginger, 558
*dried, prune, and cherry compote, 513
freezing, 781
-ginger chicken, 224
*-glazed chicken, 200–201
-pecan fruitcake, 672–73
*+poached, 486
-raspberry rugelach, 734–35
*rosemary-, chicken, 196
*+skillet jam, 790
soufflés, 623
streusel pie, 692
Arborio, 383, **383**
Arctic char, 254
Aromatic rice, 382–83, 384
Arrabbiata sauce, 343
*Arroz con pollo, 205
Artichoke(s), 403–5
baked, with parmesan stuffing, **400,** 404–5
braised baby, with olives, 404
with roasted-red-pepper-and-basil sauce, 405
Arugula, 522
*radiatori with, cherry tomatoes,
    and pancetta, 346
veal with tomato and, salad, 136, **136**
warm, and mushroom salad, 526
Asiago, 329
Asparagus, 406–7
cream of, soup, 62
freezing, 786

lamb navarin, 175
*penne with salmon and, 354
prosciutto-wrapped, 47
quiche, 317
quick cream of, soup, 63
roasted, 407
scallop and, stir-fry, 294, **294**
+sesame stir-fried, 407
+with lemon-caper vinaigrette, 406
*ziti with roasted, 350, **350**
Avocado(s), 407–8
freezing, 786
+guacamole, 408

B
Baby greens, 522
Bacon, 140
bite-size, quiches, 49
brussels sprouts with, 416
brussels sprouts with, and chestnuts, 416
choucroute garni, 153, **153**
cod, cabbage, and, in parchment, 273
cottage cheese and, puffs, 334
escarole and, salad, 526
-horseradish stuffed eggs, 325
oven-baked pepper, 149
panfried calf's liver and, 182
*parsnips, swiss chard, and, stuffing, 248
*+pasta with, and peas, 353
red snapper with, and apples, 284
+sautéed lima beans with, 410
+scallops with, and cream, 295
spinach, cheddar, and, filling, 311
spinach and, salad, 525
trout with cornmeal and, 263
Bain marie, **630**
*Baked ziti, 365
Baking dish, 8
Baking pan, 8
liner for, 730
lining, with foil, **719**
Baking powder, 15, 565
+ biscuits, 567, **567**
Baklava, 638
Balsamic (vinegar)
apricot-, sauce, 201
*chicken and pears, 214
+-glazed pork chops, 155
-glazed swordfish with greens, 266
-rosemary sauce, 161
+-swordfish with, glaze, 266
Banana(s), 486–87
cream pie, 705
filling (for crepes), 647
*+flambéed, 487
freezing, 781

Banana(s) (continued)
+icebox cake, 632
layer cake, 654
*lowfat, bread, 574
-nut bread, 574
-nut muffins, 570
pancakes, 580
pops, 487
smoothie, 765
soufflés, 623
-split cake, **746,** 756
warm, -pecan tart, 693
Baguettes, 588
Barbecue(d), 159. *See also* Grilled
all-American, chicken, 219
beef ribs, 116
+catfish, 271
North Carolina–style chicken, 222
oven-spareribs, 146
pork spareribs, **160,** 161
pulled pork, 152
Bar cookies, 711, 712
Barley, 381, **381**
*hearty mushroom- soup, 70
*mushroom-, pilaf, 396
+salad with nectarines, 536
Basil
artichokes with roasted-red-pepper-and-,
sauce, 405
chicken breasts stuffed with dried tomatoes
and, 200
and dried tomato chicken salad, 542
freezing, 786
lemon-, stuffed eggs, 325, **325**
mashed potatoes, 451
mayonnaise, 611
*red snapper in parchment with tomatoes
and, 281
roasted peppers with fresh, 447
*rolled turkey breast with, mayonnaise,
233, 233–34
*spaghetti with pesto, 347
Thai beef with, 111, **111**
*Thai chicken with, 216, **216**
tomato-, cream cheese logs, 41
+veal stuffed with fontina, prosciutto, and, 137
Basmati rice, 382, **383**
Bass, California cioppino, 303
Baste, 28
Beans, 371–80
black, 372, **373**
+cakes, 378
*Caribbean-flavored, soup, 72
chorizo and, nachos, 47
*classic, soup, 72
*cumin rice with, 387

+dip, 40
*quick "baked," 378
* salsa, 214
and salsa filling, 310
*spicy, soup, 64
*three-bean vegetarian chili, 375, **375**
buying and storing, 371
cooking, 372
flavoring, 389
hoppin' John, 374
*Italian white, and spinach soup, 63
leftover cooked, 378
*old-fashioned baked, 376
pasta e fagioli with canned, 82
pasta e fagioli with sausage, 82, **82**
*+quick "baked," 378
*+red, and rice, 379
refried, 378–79
shell, 410–11
*peas and fava beans, 410–11, **411**
+sautéed lima beans with bacon, 410
soaking, 372
split pea soup with ham, 67
three-, salad, 527
*Tuscan cabbage and, 418–19
types of, 372–73
white kidney, 373, **373**
braised lamb shanks with, and vegetables,
172, 173
*French-style, 376–77
*Italian, and spinach soup, 63
*+quick "baked," 378
*three-bean vegetarian chili, 375, **375**
*Tuscan, bruschetta, 46
*Tuscan, with sage, 376
Béarnaise sauce, 551
Beat, 28
Beaujolais Nouveau, 26
Beaujolais, 26
Beef, 91–126
anise, kabobs, 115
boeuf bourguignon, 99
braciole, 103
braised oxtails, 102
*brisket with chunky BBQ sauce, 117
brisket with mushrooms, 104–5
buying, 91–92
carbonnades à la flamande, 100
chicken and, saté, 52
cooking, 92
corned beef hash, 118
cured, 92
eye round au jus, 95
fajitas, 113
+filet mignon with mustard-caper
sauce, 107

grading, 87
grillades, 103
ground, 118
buying, 118
Cajun meat loaf, **122,** 122
chili, 99
classic bolognese sauce, 358
+classic hamburgers, 119
cooking, 118
Danish meatballs, 120
Greek burgers, 119
Greek meatballs, 121
grilled hamburgers, 119
Italian stuffed cabbage, 123
leaner meatballs, 226
Mexican meatballs, 120
picadillo, 125
*+rigatoni with "sausage" sauce, 358
Roquefort burgers, 119
sausage and pepper meat loaf, 123
and sausage lasagna, 362–63, **363**
sloppy joes, 126
spaghetti and meatballs, 357
storing, 118
"Susan's" meat loaf, 121
tamale pie, 125
teriyaki burgers, 119
Tex-Mex burgers, 119, **119**
two-alarm chili, 124
London broil, 105
New England boiled dinner, **106,** 107
oven-barbecued, brisket with mop sauce,
105, **105**
popular cuts, **93**
pot roast
country, 102
with root vegetables, 100–101, **101**
provençal, stew (daube), 98
rib roast
carving, **94**
with creamy horseradish sauce, 95
herb-crusted, **86,** 94
ribs
barbecued, 116
deviled short, 97
Korean-style sesame short, **116,** 116–17
*roast beef-waldorf club sandwiches, 616–17
roasting times, 91
ropa vieja, 104
with snow peas and carrots, 115
spicy tangerine, **112,** 113
steak
+au poivre, 108
+Cajun, 110
+chicken-fried, 108
doneness, 108

+flank, sandwiches with chimichurri sauce, 616, **616**
flank, with chimichurri sauce, 114
flank, with red onion marmalade, 109
open-faced, and mushroom sandwiches, 615
*orange-glazed, 115
+pizzaiola, 109, **109**
*sesame, 111
+Tuscan pan seared strip, 110
+ with red wine sauce, 110
stir-fried, and broccoli, 114
storing, 91–92
stroganoff, 98
tenderloin
Asian-flavored, 97
roasted, 97
sauces for, 97
Southwestern-flavored, 97
spice-rubbed, 115
stuffed, with mushroom gravy, 96
Thai, with basil, 111, **111**
*Thai grilled, salad, 538–39
*-vegetable soup, 81
Beefalo, 90
Beer, 27
+-batter fried shrimp, 297
-braised bratwurst dinner, 162
cooking with, 28
potted cheddar and, spread, 37
serving and storing, 27
Beet(s), 411–13
freezing, 786
*Harvard, 412
hearty borscht, 80–81
and orange salad, 524
*pickled, 412–13
red flannel hash, 118
roasted, and onions, 412
Beet greens, freezing, 786
Belgian endive, 432, 522
+butter-braised, 432
Benedict eggs, 148, 320–21
Berry(ies), 487–92.
See also specific varieties
canning, 776
compote, 491
and cream shortcake, **480,** 489
mixed, filling (for crepes), 647
three-berry charlotte, 488–89
+Beurre blanc, 551
Beurre rouge, 552
Beverage(s), 761–69. *See also* Beer; Wine
*+black cow, 765
coffee, 761
brewing hot, 762
drip, 762

iced, 763
+Irish, 763
percolator, 762
tea, 762
eggnog
holiday, 768
+light, 768
*fizzy cranberry-lemonade punch, 769
*+hearty hot cocoa, 764
*holiday champagne punch, 766
*+hot mulled wine, 767, **767**
*+ice cream soda, 764
*Italian lemon cordial, 769
*lemonade, 765
mint, 765
limeade, **760,** 765
ginger, 765
*+sangria, 766
white, 766
smoothie
banana, 765
*+mango-strawberry, 764
peach, 764
tea
black, 762
brewing hot, 762
green, 762
herbal, 762
iced, 763
*+best, 763
with fruit juice, 763
with lemon and mint, 763
oolong, 762
*+spiced hot, 763
warm spiced cider, 769
*wassail, 767
Bibb lettuce, 522
Biscotti
*almond-anise, 738
chocolate-dried cherry, 738
Biscuit(s)
+baking powder, 567
buttermilk, 567
drop, 567
ham, 148
Biscuit tortoni, 758
Bison, 90
Bisque, 58
shrimp, 75
Bittersweet chocolate, 744
Black beans, 372, **373**
See also under Beans
Black beluga lentils, 374, **374**
Blackberry(ies), 487
berries and cream shortcake,
480, 489

-blueberry skillet jam, 791
freezing, 781
*granita, 752
*summer pudding, 490
three-berry charlotte, 488–89
Black bottom pie, 703
*+Black cow, 765
Black-eyed peas, 372, **372**
hoppin' John, 374
Black rice, 383
Blanch, 28
Blend, 28
Blind bake, 28
Blintzes, cheese, 320
Blondies, 716
chocolate chip, 716
chocolate swirl peanut butter, 716
coconut, 716
*lowfat butterscotch, 717
Blueberry(ies), 487
*+best, sauce, 560
blackberry-, skillet jam, 791
-corn muffins, 570
crumb ring, 658
*double, pie, 693
freezing, 782
+fresh, fool, 490
-lemon tea bread, 573
-lemon tiramisù, 490–91
*+-mango compote, 513
muffins, 569
pancakes, 580
peach-, galette, 695
-peach shortcakes, 518
skillet jam, 791
very pie, 694, **694**
Blue cheese, 329, **329**
+creamy, dressing, 546
sauce, 201
vinaigrette, 545
Bluefish, 254
+fennel-crusted, 269
Bock beer, 27
Boil, 28
Bok choy, 413
+stir-fried, 413
stir-fried shrimp with, 299
Bordeaux, 26
Borscht, hearty, 80–81
Boston bluefish, 254
Boston lettuce, 522
Boeuf bourguignon, 99
Bouillabaisse, 305
chicken, 208
Boysenberries, freezing, 782
Braciole, 103

Brains, 179
Braise, 28
Braising
    beef, 92
    lamb, 167
    meat, 89
    pork, 142
    veal, 128
Brandade, 285
Bratwurst, beer-braised, dinner, 162
Bread(s)
    moist stuffing, 246
    quick, 565–81
        baking, 566
        +baking powder biscuits, 567
        banana, 574
            *lowfat, 574
            -nut, 574
        blueberry-lemon tea, 573
        buttermilk scones, 567
        classic crumb cake, 576–77
        cooking, storing, and reheating, 566
        corn
            golden, 572, **572**
            muffins, 572
            *southern, 572–73
            sticks, 572
        *cranberry-orange, 573
        date-nut, 575
        drop biscuits, 567
        dusting pan with flour, **576**
        easy Christmas stollen, 579
        fruit-streusel coffee cake, 577
        mixing, 565–66
        muffins
            apple-gingerbread, 571
            banana-nut, 570
            basic, **564,** 568–69
            blueberry, 569
            blueberry-corn, 570
            bran, 569
            carrot-bran, 569
            jam-filled, 569
            pecan, 569
            raspberry, 569
            walnut, 569
        popovers, 571
            giant, 571
        scones, 567
            buttermilk, 567
            currant, 568
            lemon-walnut, 568
            rich, 568, **568**
        soda bread
            with currants and caraway seeds, 576
            *traditional Irish, 576

        sour cream coffee cake,
            578, 578–79
        waffles
            +buttermilk, 581
            pecan, 581
            sweet milk, 581
            yeast, 581
    yeast, 583–607
        *baguettes, 588
        baking, 585
        *basic pizza dough, 596–97
        bee-sting cake, 601
        *bread-machine multigrain loaf, 592
        breadsticks, 594
            rosemary-fennel, 594, **594**
        brioche, 603
        buttermilk, 586–87, **587**
        butters for, 605
        *challah, 604–5, **605**
        chocolate-cherry, 606
        cinnamon bubble ring, 600
        *cinnamon-raisin, 586
        coffee cake wreath, 602–3
        cooling, 585
        double-cheese batter, 593
        flours in, 584
        focaccia, 598–99, **599**
        forming round, 601
        *great plains oatmeal-molasses
            rolls, 596
        *honey-wheat, 590
        kneading dough, 584
        lemon-almond bubble ring, 601
        marzipan-filled stollen, 606
        mixing dough, 584
        olive-rosemary loaves, 587
        overnight sticky buns, 604
        parker house rolls, 595
        *pissaladière, 600
        *potato, 588–89
        *pumpernickel, 592
        *quick-and-easy anadama, 593
        *quick pizza dough, 597
        *quick rolls, 594–95
        refrigerator, 595
        rising and shaping dough, 584–85
        *round rye, 589
        *soft pretzels, 607
        stollen, 606
        storing, 585
        troubleshooting, 589
        *white, 586
        whole wheat–oatmeal, 590
        whole wheat–walnut, 591, **591**
        yeasts in, 583
*Bread-and-butter pickles, 799

Bread-and-butter pudding, 634
Bread crumbs, 15
    grating fresh, **405**
    *scrod with lemon-garlic, 273
Breaded pork tenderloin, +152–53
Bread flour, 584
*Bread-machine multigrain loaf, 592
Breadsticks, 594
    rosemary-fennel, 594, **594**
Bresaola, 92
Brie, **329,** 329
    +double tomato- heroes, 610–11
Brining, 142, 236
Brioche, 603
Brisket
    with mushrooms, 104–5
    *with chunky BBQ sauce, 117
Bristle brushes, 10
Broad beans, 372–73. *See also* Fava
Broccoflower, 413
Broccoli, 414–15
    cream of, soup, 62
    freezing, 786
    Italian sausage and, rabe, 165
    *light fettuccine alfredo, 352
    *linguine with, 350
    +quick cream of, soup, 62
    rabe, 414
        with garbanzo beans, 415
        *linguine with, and anchovies, 349
    +stir-fried, 414
    stir-fried beef and, 114
    vegetable stir-fry, 478
Broiling
    beef, 92
    lamb, 167
    meat, 89–90
    pork, 142
    veal, 128
Broth, 28, 57, 58. *See also* Stock
    chicken, 84
    mussels in saffron-tomato, 74
    pressure cooker chicken, 84
    *vegetable, 83
Brown, 28
*Brown beef stock, 83
Brown butter frosting, 677
Brownie(s)
    almond cheesecake, 714–15
    almond shortbread, 714
    cocoa, 715
    *fudgy lowfat, 715
    Good Housekeeping's fudgy, 713
    praline-iced, **713,** 713
Brownie pudding cake, 636, **636**
Brown lentils, 374

*Brown rice, **383,** 384
   *and vegetable pilaf, 387
Bruschetta
   +tomato and ricotta salata, **34,** 46
   *Tuscan white bean, 46
Brussels sprouts, 415–16
   with bacon, 416
   freezing, 786
   sautéed, 415
Bucatini, 340
Bûcheron, **330**
Buckwheat, 381
   pancakes, 580
Buffalo, 90
Buffalo-style chicken wings, 51
Buffets, 23
Bulgur, 381, **381**
   *+basic, 397
   *pilaf with apricots, 397
Bundt pan, 9
Burgundy, 26
Butter(s). *See also* Jams; Jellies;
   Marmalade(s); Preserves
   anchovy, 563
   caper, 563
   fresh strawberry, 605
   ginger-cilantro, 563, **563**
   herb, 563
   horseradish, 563
   jalapeño, 563
   maître d'hôtel, 563
   marmalade, 605
   olive, 563
   pesto, 563
   roquefort, 563
   shallot and red wine, 563
   strawberry, 605
   whipped honey, 605
Butter beans, 373. *See also* Lima beans
Butter cakes, 650
*Buttercup squash, roasted, 465
Butterfly, 28
Butterflying shrimp, **297**
Buttermilk, 565
   biscuits, 567
   easy chocolate, cake, **648,** 660
   light chocolate-, bundt cake, 662
   bread, 586–87, **587**
   +pancakes, 580, **580**
   scones, 567
   *spicy, -grilled chicken, 221
   *waffles, 581
Butternut squash
   -apple soup, 60, **60**
   maple, 463
   rosemary-roasted, 463

   thyme-roasted, 463
   *Winter vegetable chili, 379
Butterscotch
   *lowfat, blondies, 717
   +sauce, 560
Buttons, 330, **330**

C

Cabbage. *See also* Coleslaw; Green cabbage;
   Napa cabbage; Red cabbage
   cod, and bacon in parchment, 273
   Italian stuffed, 123
   stuffed, with dill, 162
Cabernet sauvignon, 26
Cactus pears, 492
+Caesar salad, new, 527
Cajun meat loaf, **122,** 122
+Cajun steaks, 110
Cake(s), 649–77
   *angel food, 666
      cappuccino, 666
      *chocolate, 666
   *applesauce spice, 655
   apple-walnut bundt, 658
   banana
      +icebox, 632
      layer, 654
      -split, **746,** 756
   blueberry crumb ring, 658
   *brownie pudding, 636, **636**
   cannoli cake roll, 671
   carrot, 657, **657**
      deluxe, 657
   cheese
      cracks in, 671
      deluxe, 673
      pumpkin, 676
   chiffon
      citrus, 669
      vanilla, **668,** 669
   chocolate, 674
      *angel food, 666
      cheese, 674
      easy, -buttermilk, with white chocolate
         butter frosting, **648,** 660
      *light, -buttermilk bundt, 662
      marble loaf, 664
      +molten, **660,** 660–61
      rich, 661
      sacher torte, 662–63
      truffle, 663
   dental floss in cutting, 673
   fruit
      apricot-pecan, 672–73
      cranberry-raisin, 673
      old-fashioned, 672

   gingerbread, 656–57
   golden butter, 653
   *golden sponge, 669
   *jelly roll, **670,** 670–71
   layer
      banana, 654
      frosting, 651
      spice, 654–55, **655**
   lemon
      pudding, 635
      -ricotta, 674, **675**
   making perfect, 649–50, 651
   monster snake, 676–77
   orange, 652
   +peanut butter cup, 659, **659**
   pound
      almond, 665
      lemon–poppy seed, 665
      vanilla, 664
   preheating oven for baking, 653
   silver white, 652–53
   sorbet-and-cream, 757
   spice layer, 654–55, **655**
   sponge
      *hot water, 667
      lemon–hot water, 667
   storing, 651
   strawberry, 674
   types of, 650–51
   upside-down
      apple, 656
      pineapple, 656
      plum, 656
   walnut torte, 667
   yellow, 652
Cake frostings and fillings,
   651, 677–80
   amaretto buttercream, 680
   brown butter, 677
   +chocolate butter, 677
   +classic butter, 677
   +cream cheese, 679
   +custard buttercream, 680
   fluffy harvest moon, 679
   *+fluffy white, 679
   ganache, 680–81
   lemon butter, 677
   +lemon filling, 680
   mocha glaze, 662
   orange butter, 677
   +silky chocolate butter, 678
   silky lemon butter, 678
   silky orange butter, 678
   *silky vanilla butter, 678
   +whipped cream, 679
      cocoa, 679

Cake frostings and fillings (continued)
  coffee, 679
  orange, 679
  peppermint, 679
  +white chocolate butter, 678
Cake pan, 9
Calamari, 256. *See also* Squid
  fried, fra diavolo, 301
*Caldo verde, 61
Calf's liver
  panfried, and bacon, 182
  Venetian-style, 182
Calvados, 31
Camembert, **329**, 329
Canary melon, 499
Canning, 771–75
  equipment for, 772
  equipment for fruit spreads, 774–75
  fruits, 774
  pickles and relishes, 775
  steps in, 772–73
Cannoli cake roll, 671
Cantaloupe, 499
  *peachy melon soup, 84
  *sorbet, **750,** 755
Capelli d' angelo, 340
Capellini, 340
Caper(s), 31
  asparagus with lemon- vinaigrette, 406
  butter, 563
  chicken breasts with lemon-sauce, 213
  dried tomato- stuffed eggs, 325
  mustard-, sauce, 107
  sauce, 260
  skate with brown butter, lemon,
    and, 281
Capon(s), 193
  roasting times, 188
Caponata, 430–31
Cappuccino
  angle food cake, 666
  mousse, 632
Caramel, **629**
  color of, 625
  oranges with, 502, **502**
  pumpkin crème, 630
Caramelize, 28
Caramelized onions, 442, **442**
  with raisins, 442
Caramelized shallots, 442
Carbonnades à la flamande, 100
Cardoon, 419
  sautéed, with parsley, 419
Carrot(s), 419–21
  beef with snow peas and, 115
  -bran muffins, 569

cake, 657, **657**
  deluxe, 657
candied, 420
freezing, 787
*giardiniera, 801, **801**
ginger candied, 420
harvest casserole, 476
hot-and-sour, 421
+shredded, 420
spicy curried, soup, 60–61
vegetable stir-fry, 478
Carving
  ham, **147**
  leg of lamb, **170**
  meat, 90
  rib roast, **94**
  roast chicken, **189**
  roast turkey, **231**
Casaba, 499
Casserole(s), 8
  *country captain, 204, **204**
  eggplant and lamb, 178
  freezing, 785
  harvest, 476
  polenta and sausage, **164,** 165
  squash, 462
Catfish, 254
  +barbecued, 271
  fried, 270
  +jerk, with grilled pineapple, 270
Cauliflower, 421–23
  cream of, soup, 62
  curried, with potatoes and peas,
    423, **423**
  curry-roasted, 422
  freezing, 787
  *giardiniera, 801, **801**
  with golden raisins and pine nuts, 422
  polonaise, 421
  roasted, 422
Cavatelli, 340, **341**
Caviar, 258
  in potato nests, 50
Celeriac. *See* Celery root
Celery, 423–24
  braised, 424
  butter-braised, 424
Celery root, 424–25
  with mashed potatoes, 425
  rémoulade, 425
Cellophane noodles, 340
*Challah, 604–5, **605**
Champagne, 26
Chardonnay, 25
Chayote, 425–26
  +sautéed, 426

Cheddar cheese, 329, **331**
  +and chutney tea sandwiches, 619
  caraway-, crisps, 45
  cheddar crisps, 336
  curly mac 'n' cheese, 364–65
  curried, puffs, 50
  double-, batter bread, 593
  easy spicy, straws, 46
  potted, and beer spread, 37
  puffy, grits, 394
  *reduced-fat macaroni and cheese, 365
  spinach, and bacon filling, 311
  +Welsh rabbit, 336
Cheese, 327–37. *See also* specific types
  blintzes, 320
  buying, 327–28
  classic, soufflé, 315
  cooking with, 328
  glossary for, 329–32
  serving, 328, 337
  storing, 328
  strudel, 641
Cheesecake(s), 651
  chocolate, 674
  deluxe, 673
  lemon -ricotta, 674, **675**
Cherimoyas, 492
Cherry(ies), 493
  -almond chafouti, 493
  canned, pie, 695
  canning, 776–77
  chocolate-, bread, 606
  chocolate-dried, biscotti, 738
  *+dried, couscous, 393
  *dried apricot, prune, and, compote, 513
  freezing sweet, 782
  freezing sour, 782
  frozen tart, pie, 695
  *nectarine and, crisp, 518
  pear and dried-, rice pudding, 505
  strudel, 641
  *sweet jam, 795
  tart, pie, 695
  *tart, soup, 85
  *tart jam, 795
  vanilla rice pudding with dried, 637
Cherry tomatoes. *See under* Tomato(es)
Chestnut(s), 426
  *and apple stuffing, 245
  brussels sprouts with bacon and, 416
  *roasted, 426
Chianti, 26
Chicken
  All-American barbecue(d), 219
  apricot-ginger, 224
  *arroz con pollo, 205

*baked "fried," 198–99
baked lime, 198
*balsamic, and pears, 214
and beef saté, 52
bouillabaisse, 208
breasts
    *apricot-glazed, 200–201
    *+grilled, saltimbocca, 223, **223**
    +grilled, with cumin, coriander, and
        lime, 221
    with lemon-caper sauce, 213
    *+lemon-rosemary, 221
    with pecan crust, 212
    *roasted tandoori-style, 199
    roulades, 202, **202**
    skinning and boning, **212**
    stuffed with dried tomatoes and basil, 200
    tonnato, 211
    *+with green peppercorns, 213
    *with mushrooms and tarragon, 212
    *+with six quick sauces, 214–15
broiled teriyaki, 217
*broth, 84
buffalo-style, wings, 51
buying, 185
cacciatore, 205
citrus-sage, 218–19
club sandwiches, 615
and coconut milk soup, 77
coq au vin, 202–3
*country captain casserole, 204, **204**
couscous, 208
creole, gumbo, 209, **209**
crepes with, spinach, and mushroom filling, 319
curry, 206
cutting up
    butterflying, **202**
    raw, **195**
enchiladas, 239
ginger-grilled, for a crowd, 220
*Greek-style lemon soup, 76
ground, 224
    shepherd's pie, 224–25, **225**
    +Texas burgers, 225
herb, 198
*Jamaican jerk, kabobs, 218, **218**
liver, 179
    +marsala, 181
    +with mushrooms and onions, 181
meatballs, 207
mole, 203
+new, cordon bleu, 215
North Carolina–style barbecued, 222
+paella, **370,** 389
parmigiana, 135
picnic, with three sauces, 201

Portuguese mixed grill, 222
*poule au pot with tarragon, 210
pressure cooker, broth, 84
removing skin from raw, **200**
roast(ed)
    apple and thyme, **184,** 190
    carving, **189**
    fennel-rubbed, 192–93
    with forty cloves of garlic, 190–91
    with green olives and sherry, 193
    with herb butter, 191
    lemon, 194–95
    mahogany, 194
    Peking, 192
    *tandoori-style, breasts, 199
    tarragon, 191
    *thyme-, and vegetables,
        196, **197**
    times, 188
*rosemary-apricot, 196
salad
    basil and dried tomato, 542
    best, 542
    curry-grape, 542
    lemon-pepper, 542
soup with rice, *78
southern fried, 217
south-of-the-border, soup, 78, **79**
southwest, 199
*spicy buttermilk-grilled, 221
spicy peanut, 207
+Szechwan, 215
*tandoori-style grilled, 220
tarragon broiled, 219
*Thai, salad, 538
*Thai, with basil, 216, **216**
thighs provençal, 210
Turkish, in walnut sauce, 211
*Vietnamese noodle soup, 77
*with rosemary dumplings, 206–7
+with tomato-olive relish, 223
+Chicken-fried steak, 108
Chicken liver pâté, 44
Chicken stock, 85, 217
Chickpeas, 373.
    See also Garbanzo beans
Chicory, 426–27, 522
Chilean sea bass, 254
Chili
    beef, 99
        Cincinnati, 124
        two-alarm, 124
    pork
        adobo-style, 151
        New Mexican green, 151
    three-bean vegetarian, 375, **375**

turkey
    grilled, with -cumin rub, 237
    *white, 237
    *winter vegetable, 379
Chili beans, 373. *See also* Red beans
Chili nuts, 42
Chili powder, 31
+Chimichurri sauce, 554
    flank steak sandwiches with, 616, **616**
    flank steak with, 114
Chinese cabbage, 416, 522
Chinese dumplings, 52–53, **53**
Chinese peas, freezing, 788
Chipotles en adobo, 31, **31**
Chocolate, 740–41, 744. *See also* Brownies;
    Cocoa; Fudge
    black-and-white bread pudding with white
        chocolate custard sauce, 634–35
    cakes
        *angel food, 666
        brownie pudding, 636, **636**
        cheese, 674
        easy, -buttermilk, **648,** 660
        light, -buttermilk bundt, 662
        marble loaf, 664
        +molten, **660,** 660–61
        rich, 661
        sacher torte, 662–63
        truffle, 663
    -cherry bread, 606–607
    coconut macaroons, 727
    creamy penuche, 742
    -dried cherry biscotti, 738
    +fondue with fruit, 518
    frostings and fillings
        +butter, 677
        ganache, 680–81
        +silky, butter, 678
        +white, butter, 678
    garnishes, 681
    and hazelnut truffles, 741
    ice cream, 750
    melt-away, mints, 741
    +our sublime, sauce, 561
    pastry cream, 643
    pears, 505
    pie
        black bottom, 703
        cream, 706, **706**
        cream angel, 708
        pecan, 700
    *sorbet, 754
    soufflés, 624
    spritz, 736
    swirl peanut butter blondies, 716
    truffle tart, 702

Chocolate (continued)
-walnut filling, 603
-walnut fudge, 742
white
  +butter frosting, 678
  custard sauce, 634–35
  –macadamia cookies, 725
wows, 724, **724**
Chocolate chip
blondies, 716
cookies, 724–25
ice cream, 749
Chop, 14
Chorizo sausage, 31, 140
and black bean nachos, 47
+paella, **370,** 389
Choucroute garni, 153, **153**
Choux pastry, 642, 646
Chowder, 58. *See also* Soups
garden vegetable, 64
Manhattan clam, 73
New England clam, 73
oyster-corn, 75
summertime corn, **65,** 65
yankee cod, 74
Chutney, 560
cheddar and, tea sandwiches, 619
*cranberry-fig, 558
*dried pear, 559
ham steak with apple, 156
*home-style, 799
mayonnaise, 611
*sweet red pepper, 559, **559**
*tomato, 560
Ciambotta, 473
Cider
warm spiced, 769
*wassail, 767
Cilantro, 31
gazpacho with, cream, 66
ginger-. butter, 563
+sauce, 554
Cincinnati chili, 124
Cinnamon bubble ring, 600
*Cinnamon-raisin bread, 586
Cinnamon stick, 31
Cinnamon-sugar filling, 603
Citrus chiffon cake, 669
Citrus-sage chicken, 218–19
Citrus salad with sherry dressing, 525, **525**
Clam(s), 251, 253, 255
casino, 55
*+Chinese steamed, 287
*linguine with white, sauce, 355
Manhattan, chowder, 73
New England, chowder, 73

sauce
  *linguine with red, 344
  *quick white, 355
scrubbing and shucking, **286**
*+steamed soft-shell, 287
*Clementine, granita, 753
Coarse chop, 14
Cobbler
*peach, 504
rhubarb-strawberry, **516,** 517
Cobb salad, 544, **544**
Cocoa, 740–41, 744
brownies, 715
natural and Dutch-process, 659
*+hearty hot, 764
whipped cream frosting, 679
Coconut(s), 493–94
ambrosia, 514
blondies, 716
chocolate, macaroons, 727
cookies, 726–27
cream pie, 705
macaroons, 727
rice, 384
slipped -custard pie, 701
Coconut milk, 31
chicken, and soup, 77
Cod, 254
*bouillabaisse, 305
brandade, 285
+broiled, steaks Montauk, 269
cabbage, and bacon in
  parchment, 273
-fish cakes, 271
+lemon-thyme, 274
salt, Portuguese-style, 286
salt, salad, 285
veracruz, 268
yankee, chowder, 74
Coffee, 761
brewing hot, 762
drip, 762
*granita, 753
iced, 763
+Irish, 763
percolator, 762
tea, 762
whipped cream frosting, 679
Coffee cake
classic crumb, 576–77
fruit-streusel, 577
sour cream, **578,** 578–79
wreath, 602
  chocolate-walnut filling, 603
  cinnamon-sugar filling, 603
  *lemon-poppy seed filling, 602

*prune, 603
sweet almond filling, 602
Colander, 10
Colby, 330, **330**
Coleslaw. *See also* Cabbage
Asian, 531
+hot, with poppy seed dressing, 418
with vinaigrette, 531
Collards, 435
freezing, 787
Compote(s), 491
autumn fruit, 515
*+blueberry-mango, 513
*dried apricot, prune, and cherry, 513
Conchiglie, 340, **341**
Confections, 740–45
*candied citrus peel, 744
chocolate and hazelnut truffles, 741
chocolate-walnut fudge, 742
creamy penuche, 742
gold rush nut brittle, 743
melt-away chocolate mints, 741
peanut brittle, 743
pralines, 743
storing, 745
sugar syrup, 740
toffee almond crunch, 745, **745**
Consommé, 57, 58
Converted rice, 382, **383**
Cookie crumbs, making, 689
Cookies, 711–39
almond
  *-anise biscotti, 738
  cheesecake brownies, 714–15
  crescents, 728–29
  macaroons, 727
  shortbread brownies, 714
  spritz, 736
  tuiles, 737
apricot-raspberry rugelach, 734–35
baking, 712, 713
blondies, 716
brandy snaps, **736,** 736–37
chocolate chip, 724–25
chocolate chip blondies, 716
chocolate coconut macaroons, 727
chocolate-dried cherry biscotti, 738
chocolate spritz, 736
chocolate swirl peanut butter blondies, 716
chocolate wows, 724, **724**
classic sugar, **710,** 732
cocoa brownies, 715
coconut, 726–27
coconut blondies, 716
coconut macaroons, 727
date and nut squares, 720

drop sugar, 725
Finnish almond, 733
*fudgy lowfat brownies, 715
*gingerbread cutouts, 734
Good Housekeeping's fudgy brownies, 713
grandmother's oatmeal-raisin, 722, **723**
hazelnut crescents, 729
holiday sugar, 733
honey granola breakfast bars, 720
jam-filled sugar, 732–33
jumbo gingersnaps, 728
*ladyfingers, 735
lemon-anise icebox, 731
lemon bars, 719
lemon icebox, 731, **731**
lemon-walnut icebox, 731
*lowfat butterscotch blondies, 717
*lowfat oatmeal-raisin, 722
*meringue fingers, 735
Mississippi mud bars, **718,** 718–19
old-fashioned whoopie pies, 726
orange icebox, 731
ornamental frosting, 739
palmiers, 739
peanut butter, 721
pecan crescents, 729
pecan lace, 725
pecan tassies, 729
pine nut tassies, 729
praline-iced brownies, 713
*raisin spice bars, 720
raspberry linzer, 730
raspberry-walnut streusel bars, 721
Scottish shortbread, 717
snickerdoodles, 730
sour cream, 726
spicy almond slices, 732
spritz, 736
storing and shipping, 712
types of, 711
walnut shortbread, 717
walnut crescents, 729
white chocolate–macadamia, 725
Cookie sheets, 9, 711–12
Cooking terms, 28–30
Cooling racks, 10
Coq au vin, 202–3
+Cordon bleu, new chicken, 215
Core, 28
Corkscrew, 10
Corn, 427–29
blueberry-, muffins, 570
cream of
quick, soup, 63
creamy, pudding, 427
freezing, 787

grilled sweet, 428–29
*Louisiana maquechoux, 428
oyster-, chowder, 75
*relish, 800
+sautéed fresh, 429
*succotash, 473
*summer, salad, 528
summertime, chowder, 65, **65**
sweet, salsa, 555
West Texas creamed, 428
Corn bread
golden, 572, **572**
*southern, 572–73
stuffing
country sausage, 245
southwestern, 244
Corned beef, 92
hash, 118
Cornichons, 31
Cornish hens, 226
with anise-orange glaze, 228
buying, 186
milanese, 228, **228**
molasses-glazed, 227
roasting times, 188
with wild rice and mushroom stuffing, 227
Cornmeal, 381, **381**
broiled polenta wedges, 394
creamy polenta, 394
creamy polenta with sausage and mushrooms, **395,** 395
crust, 238
pancakes, 580
rosemary polenta wedges, 394
spoonbread, 396, **396**
trout with, and bacon, 263
Corn muffins, 572
Corn sticks, 572
Cottage cheese, **330**
and bacon puffs, 334
old-fashioned cheese mold with fresh fruit, 334
Country ham, 140
*whole Smithfield, 148
Couscous, 381, **381,** 393
chicken, 208
*+dried cherry, 393
*+lime, 393
*+Moroccan, 393
Moroccan-style lamb with, 171, **171**
salad, 535
*+sun-dried tomato and green-onion, 393
Cowpeas, 372
See also Black-eyed peas
Crab(s), 256–57
*boil, 289

buying, 287
+cakes, 289
mini, 51, **51**
remoulade, 290
rolled sole stuffed with, 276–77, **276**
sherried, quiche, 317
soft-shell
cleaning, 289
with lemon-caper sauce, 288
panfried, 288, **288**
Crab boil, 31
Cranberry(ies), 494
-almond tart, 697
applesauce, 483
*-apple sauce, 557
*apricot- sauce with fresh ginger, 558
beans, 372
double berry linzer tart, 699, **699**
*-fig chutney, 558
*+fizzy, -lemonade punch, 769
freezing, 782
no-cook, -orange relish, 558–59
*-orange bread, 573
*-orange mold, 538
*+-port sauce, 557
-raisin fruitcake, 673
-raisin relish, 559
southwestern-style, relish, 558
*wild rice pilaf with dried, 393
Cranshaw, 499
Crawfish
Étouffée, 298
Cream, 29
+scallops with bacon and, 295
scallops with leeks and, 294–95
+tubetti with lemon and, 360–61
Cream cheese, 44, 329, **330**
+ frosting, 679
and fruit tartlets, 709
old-fashioned cheese mold with fresh fruit, 334
+pinwheel sandwiches, 619
+scrambled eggs with, 320
scrambled eggs with, and salmon, 320
+smoked salmon sandwiches with dill, 612–13
tomato-basil, logs, 41
Creamed onions and peas, 442
Creamed pearl onions, 442
Creamed spinach, 460–61
Cream puffs, 643
Crème brûlée, 630–31
Crème caramel, 629
*lowfat, 629
Crenshaw, 499
Creole chicken gumbo, 209, **209**

Crepes
  apple-calvados, 647
  basic, 318
  with chicken, spinach, and
    mushroom filling, 319
  filled with apples and gruyère, 319
  with pipérade filling, 318
  suzette, 646–47
Creste di gallo, 340, **341**
Crimp, 29
Crimped pie edge, 684, **684**
Croutons, 539
Crumb-topped onions, 443
Crustaceans, 256–57
  buying live, 252
Cubes, 14
Cucumber(s), 429–30
  *Asian, salad, 530
  *+cool, soup, 67
  creamy, and dill salad, 530
  gazpacho with cilantro cream, 66
  *kirby, salad, 530
  *salad, 52
  +sautéed, with dill, 429
  stir-fried, and radishes, 430
  tea sandwiches, 618
Culls, 257
*+Cumberland sauce, 552
Curdle, 29
Cured beef, 92
Currants, 488
  soda bread with, and caraway
    seeds, 576
Currant scones, 568
Curry(ied)
  *apple sauce, 214
  *-apricot sauce, 234
  cauliflower with potatoes and
    peas, 423
  cheddar puffs, 50
  chicken, 206
  egg salad, 544
  -grape chicken salad, 542
  lentil soup, 68
  nuts, 42
  -roasted cauliflower, 422
  rub, 177
  +shrimp, 296
  +vegetable stew, 472
Curry powder, 31
+Custard buttercream, 680
+Custard sauce, 562
Custard cups, 9
Cut in, 29
Cutting boards, 10

D
Dabs, 254
Dandelion, 522
Dandelion greens, 435
Danish Blue, **329**
Danish meatballs, 120
Date(s), 494
  *dried fruit kugel, 366
  -nut bread, 575, **575**
  and nut squares, 720
  persimmon- pudding, 508
Dayboat shrimp, 257
Deglaze, 29
Delicata, roasted, squash, 465
Dessert(s), 621–47. *See also* Cakes;
  Frozen desserts; Pies; Tarts
  apple-calvados crepes, 647
    banana filling, 647
    mixed berry filling, 647
    plum filling, 647
  bain marie, **630**
  baklava, 638
  banana, 623
    +icebox cake, 632
  cappuccino mousse, 632
  choux pastry, 642, 646
  cream puffs, 643
  créme brûlée, 630–31
  crème caramel, 629
    *lowfat, 629
    pumpkin, 630
  crepes suzette, 646–47
  custards, 621
  éclairs, 643
  5-minute, 503
  galatoboureko, 639, **639**
  gelatins, 622
  meringues, 622
    hazelnut dacquoise, 625
    *lime pavlova, 627
    *minature, shells, 626
    nests with lemon filling and
      strawberries, 626, **627**
    *shells, 626
  napoleons, 646
  panna cotta with raspberry sauce,
    631, **631**
  pastry cream
    chocolate, 643
    +vanilla, 642–43
  plum pudding with hard sauce, 633
  praline cream puff wreath, 644, **645**
  pudding cake
    brownie, 636, **636**
    lemon, 635
    orange, 635

  puddings
    black-and-white bread, with white chocolate
      custard sauce, 634–34
    bread-and-butter, 634
    Indian, 635
    *rice, 636
    rich rice, 637
    *sticky toffee, 637
    vanilla rice, with dried cherries, 637
  puff pastry, 647
  raspberry-pear trifle, 628
  *savarin, 638
  soufflés, 622
    banana, 623
    chocolate, 624
    +fresh apple, 623
    fresh pear, 623
    orange liqueur, **624**, 624–25
    peach or apricot, 623
  strawberry napoleons, 642
  strudel
    apple, 640–41, **641**
    cheese, 641
    cherry, 641
    dried fruit, 641
  tiramisù, 628–29
Devein, 29
Dewberry(ies), 488
  freezing, 782
Dietary Guidelines for Americans, 16
Dijon (mustard), 32
  orange-, sauce, 161
  *sauce, 215
Dill(ed)
  creamy cucumber and, salad, 530
  -egg tea sandwiches, 618
  -pepper topping, 269
  +red potatoes with mint, 454
  roasted green beans with, vinaigrette, 409
  +sautéed cucumbers with, 429
  +smoked salmon sandwiches with, cream
    cheese, 612–13
  stuffed cabbage with, 162
  veal nuggets with sour cream–, sauce, 138
Dinner parties, 23–24
Ditalini, 340
Dollop, 29
Dot, 29
Double boiler, 8
Dough
  *basic pizza, 596–97
  dividing into equal pieces, 603
  for 11-inch tart, 687
  fitting, into pan, 684
  flaky turnover, 48
  food processor, 686

homemade pasta, 366–67
mixing, 683–84
for 9-inch tart, 687
for 1-crust pie, 687
*quick pizza, 597
rolling out, 684
shortening, 686
for 2-crust pie, 686
vinegar, 686
Dredge, 29
Drippings, 29
Drizzle, 29
Drop biscuits, 567
Drop cookies, 711, 712
Drugstore-wrapped food, **779**
Dry beer, 27
Dry Jack cheese, 331, **331**
Dry yeast, 583
Duck, 240
*breast of, with mango chutney
    sauce, 242
chipotle-glazed, 241
ginger-glazed, 241
red-cooked, 241
roasting, 243
spiced, 240
Duckling(s)
buying, 186
roasting times, 188
Dumpling(s)
*chicken with rosemary, 206–7
*Chinese, 52–53, **53**
pear, 506
Durum, 31
Dust, 29
Dutch oven, 8
Dutch processed cocoa powder, 744

E
Éclairs, 643
Edam, 329
Egg(s), 307–25. *See also* Crepes; Pancakes
bearnaise sauce, 551
beating whites, 309, **309**
benedict, 148, 320–21
cheese blintzes, 320
choosing, 307–8
cooking, 308–9, 319
dilled-, tea sandwiches, 618
and food safety, 307
+French toast, 322
    overnight baked, 322
frittata
    +chive and goat cheese, 313
    Italian sausage and mozzarella, 314
    +potato-salsa, 312

potato and ham, 313
spaghetti, 314
hollandaise sauce, 550, **551**
+huevos rancheros, 317
+lemon-and-parsley-baked, 324
measuring, 311
omelets
    +basic, 310–11
    +basic fluffy, 312
    black bean and salsa filling, 310
    creamy mushroom filling, 310
    +egg white, 311
    garden vegetable, 311
    quick no-cook fillings for, 312
    red pepper and goat cheese filling, 311
    spinach, cheddar, and bacon filling, 311
    western filling, 311
pickled, 325
quiche
    asparagus, 317
    bite-size bacon, 49
    lorraine, 316
    mushroom, 317
    sherried crab, 317
salad
    Caesar-style, 544–45
    classic, 544
    curried, 544
    deli-style, 545
    Mexican-style, 545
schnitzel á la Holstein, 134
scrambled
    with cream cheese and salmon, 320
    +with cream cheese, 320
separating, 309, 319
spinach roulade with mushrooms,
    322–23, **323**
spinach strata, 324
storing, 308
stuffed, 324–25
    bacon-horseradish, 325
    dried tomato-caper, 325
    lemon-basil, 325, **325**
    pimiento-studded, 325
sweet onion tart with herbs, 316
using leftover whites and yolks, 313
Egg beater, 11
Eggnog
holiday, 768
+light, 768
Egg noodles, 340
*buttered, with herbs, 360
*dried fruit kugel, 366
Eggplant, 430–31
caponata, 430–31
glazed Japanese, 431

and lamb casserole, 178
+Mediterranean grilled, and summer squash,
    474, **475**
ratatouille, 476
roasted, dip with herbs, 38
roasted, parmesan, 431
Sicilian stewed vegetables, 478
Elbow macaroni, 340
Emmental, **330,** 332
Empanaditas, 48
Emulsify, 29
Enchiladas, chicken, 239
Entertaining, 22–25
slow roasting meat while, 96
Equipment, 7
knives, 12
for the microwave, 9–10
for mixing, 12
in the oven, 8–9
on the stove, 7–8
utensils, 10–11
Escarole, 432, 522
and bacon salad, 526
*rice and, stuffing, 247
+with raisins and pignoli, 432
Espresso coffee powder, instant, 31
Explorateur, **329,** 332

F
Fajitas, 113
+Falafel, 380
Farfalle, 340, **341**
with Gorgonzola sauce, 352
Farmer cheese, 330, **330**
Farro, 381
Fats, trimming, 18
Fava beans, 372–73
*peas and, 410–11, **411**
Feathered game, 240
Fennel, 433–34
*baked scrod with, and potatoes, 272–73
braised, with parmesan, 434
+crusted bluefish, 269
*orange-, pasta, 360
*+orange-, salsa, 555
+-orange pork chops, 159
pork roast with, and garlic, 144
and potato gratin, 433
roasted, 433
rosemary-, breadsticks, 594
-rubbed roast chicken, 192–93
Ferment, 29
Feta cheese, 330, **330**
Greek cheese pastries, 49
shrimp and tomatoes in feta-tomato
    sauce, 297

Fettuccini, 340
  alfredo, 352
  homemade, 367
  *light, alfredo, 352
  pasta primavera, **338,** 351
Fig(s), 494–95
  *cranberry-, chutney, 558
  +warm, with walnuts, 495
+Filet mignon with mustard-caper sauce, 107
Fine chop, 14
Finnish almond cookies, 733
Fish, 250–305. *See also* Shellfish; *specific varieties*
  buying, 251–52
  buying and storing frozen, 252–53
  cooking, 253
  cubed, 267
  fat content of, 252–53
  fillets, 252
    turning, in frying pan, **271**
  flat, 253
  knowledge of, 253–56
  *+oven-fried, 274–75
  processed, 259
  round, 253
  *salt-baked, 261
  sauces for, 277
  smoked, 259
  storing, 252, 258
  types of, 254–55
Fish cakes, 270
  cod, 271
  Mexican, 272
  +old-fashioned, 272
Fish sauce, 31
Five-spice powder, 31
*Fizzy cranberry-lemonade punch, 769
Flageolets, 373, **373**
Flaked crabmeat, 256–57
Flaky turnover pastry, 48
*+Flambéed bananas, 487
Flank steak
  with red onion marmalade, 109
  sandwiches with chimichurri sauce, 616, **616**
  + with chimichurri sauce, 114
Flounder, 254
  *+Asian-style, baked in parchment, 276
  +baked, with savory crumb topping, 275
  +crispy, 275
  *+grilled whole, 258
  parmesan cheese fillets, 275
  sesame seed fillets, 275
Flour, 29
Fluted pie edge, 684
Foam cakes, 650–51
Focaccia, 598–99, **599**
  dried tomato and olive, 599

onion, 599
  red pepper, 599
  tomato, 599
Foie gras, fresh, 180–81
Foil, lining baking pan with, **719**
Fold, 29
Fondue
  +chocolate, with fruit, 518
  +classic Swiss, **326,** 333
Fontina cheese, 330, **330**
  +veal stuffed with, prosciutto, and
    basil, 137
Food labels, 19
Food processor pastry dough, 686
Food pyramid, 17–18, **17**
Food safety, 14–15
  with eggs, 307–308
  with fish, 251–53
  with meat, 90–91
  with poultry, 187
  with sandwiches, 609
Forked pie edge, 684
Fork-tender, 29
Freezing, 775, 778–89
  casseroles, 785
  fruit, 779–80, 781–84
  poultry, 187
  refreezing thawed food, 779
  success in, 778–79
  thawing and using frozen food, 778–79
  vegetables, 780, 785–89
French-fried onion rings, 443
+French toast, 322
  overnight baked, 322
Fresh foie gras, 180–81
Fresh ham with spiced apple glaze, 144
Fresh yeast, 583
Frisée, 522
Frittata
  chive and goat cheese, 313
  Italian sausage and mozzarella, **306,** 314
  potato and ham, 313
  +potato-salsa, 312
  sandwiches with peppers and onion, 611
  spaghetti, 314
Frozen desserts, 747–59. *See also* Ice: Granita;
    Ice cream; Sherbet; Sorbet
  banana-split cake, **746,** 756
  biscuit tortoni, 758
  cutting, 757
  raspberry baked-Alaska pie, 756–57
  rocky-road freeze, 755
  sorbet-and-cream cake, 757
  tartufo, 758–59
  tulipes, 759, **759**
  wrapping, 758

Fruit(s), 481–519. *See also* specific
  candied, 514
  canning, 774
    equipment for, 772
  canning, in boiling water bath, 776–77
  dried, 519
  eating overripe, 515
  freezing, 779–80, 781–84
  *holiday, compote, 513
  old-fashioned cheese mold with fresh, 334
  organic, 519
  preparing citrus, **501**
Fruit spreads
  equipment for, 774
  steps in making, 774–75
Fudge
  chocolate-walnut, 742
  +hot, sauce, 561, **561**
*Fudgy lowfat brownies, 715
Fusilli, 340

G
Galette, peach-blueberry, 695
Game, 90
Ganache, 680–81
Garbanzo beans, **372,** 373
  broccoli rabe with, 415
  +falafel, 380
Garlic, 434
  mashed potatoes with, and lemon, 450–51
  pork roast with fennel and, 144
  roast chicken with forty cloves of, 190–91
  roasted, 434
  +roasted, sauce, 553
  +sautéed, and garlic, 460
  *scrod with lemon-, bread crumbs, 273
  skillet cherry tomatoes with, 470
  *+spaghetti with oil, and, 347
Garnishes
  chocolate, 681
  for soups, 58
Gazpacho with cilantro cream, 66
Gemelli, 340, **341**
Gewürztraminer, 25
*Giardiniera, 801, **801**
Giblet gravy, 231
Giblets, 231
Ginger(ed)
  applesauce, 483
  apricot-, chicken, 224
  *apricot-cranberry sauce with fresh, 558
  +cabbage with, and cumin, 418
  candied carrots, 420
  *Chinese sauce, 214
  -cilantro butter, 563
  cream and grapes, 503

*fried rice, 388
-glazed duck, 241
-grilled chicken for a crowd, 220
pickled, 278
saving peel, 78
-sesame mayonnaise, 611
Gingerbread, 656–57
apple-, muffins, 571
+cutouts, 734
Ginger limeade, 765
Gingersnaps, jumbo, 728
Glaze(s), 29
melba, 147
tomato and onion, 147
Glutinous rice, 383
*Gnocchi, 368–69
ricotta, with browned butter and sage, 369, **369**
Goat, 90
Goat cheese, **330,** 330–31
+chive and, frittata, 313
red pepper, and, filling, 311
+warm, salad, 528–29
Goose, 243
buying, 186
crispy roasted, with orange sauce, 243
roasting times, 188
Gooseberry(ies), 488
freezing, 782
Gorgonzola, 329, **329**
farfalle with, sauce, 352
Gouda, 331
Goulash, Hungarian pork, 150
+Graham cracker-crumb crust, 689
Grains
buying and storing, 380
cooking, 380–81
types of, 381
Grandules, 373. *See also* Pigeon peas
Granita, 747, 752
*clementine, 753
*coffee, 753
*lemon, 753
*raspberry or blackberry, 752
*strawberry, 753
scraping, **752**
*watermelon, 754
Granola
hazelnut-honey, 398
honey-, breakfast bars, 720
Grape(s), 496
curry-, chicken salad, 542
freezing, 782–83
gingered cream and, 503
jelly, 792
*white, –wine jelly, 793
*+with sour cream, 496

Grapefruit, 495
+broiled, 495
freezing, 782
*pink, sorbet, 754
Grater, 10
Gravlax, 54
Gravy
ham and grits with red-eye, 156
stuffed beef tenderloin with mushroom, 96
*traditional roast turkey with giblet, 229–31, **230**
Great Northern beans, 373, **373**
pasta e fagioli with sausage, 82, **82**
*+quick "baked," 378
Green beans, 408
amandine, 409
freezing, 786
with hazelnuts, 409
*peppery dilled, 800
roasted, with dill vinaigrette, 409
*sesame, 409
three-bean salad, 527
+wax and, with lemon and mint, 408
Green cabbage, 417
+hot slaw with poppy seed dressing, 418
southern-style, 418
*Tuscan cabbage and beans, 418–19
+with ginger and cumin, 418
+Green goddess dressing, 546
Green lentils, 374, **374**
Green onions, 443–44. *See also* Onions
peas with, and mint, 445
+sautéed, 444
Greens, 435
balsamic-glazed swordfish with, 266
freezing, 787
grilled, 471
southern-style, 435
stir-frying, 436
+Green sauce, 554
Griddle, 8
Grill, 29
Grillades, 103
Grilled. *See also* Barbecue(d)
+*chicken breasts saltimbocca, 223, **223**
+chicken breasts with cumin, coriander, and lime, 221
hamburgers, 119
+lamb chops with spice rub, 177
leg of lamb with mint and oregano, 176
+spiced salmon steaks, 264
+squid, 302
sweet corn, 428–29
*Thai snapper packets, 282
turkey with chili-cumin rub, 237
veal chops, 137

*+whole flounder, 258
+whole sea bass with lemon and herbs, 260
Grilling, 20–22, 403
beef, 92
lamb, 167
meat, 89–90
pork, 142
safety in, 22
veal, 128
Grill pan, 8
Grits
Hominy, 381, **381**
puffy cheddar, 394
Grouper, 254
Gruyère, 331
crepes filled with apples and, 319
mornay sauce, 550
-spinach soufflé, 315
+Guacamole, 408
Guavas, 496
Gumbo, 58. *See also* Soups
creole chicken, 209, **209**
sausage and shrimp, **300,** 301

H
Haddock, 254
kedgeree, 284–85
Halal meat, 88
Halibut, 254
braised in red wine, 267
Greek-style grilled, 268, **268**
Ham, 138, 140. *See also* Prosciutto
biscuits, 148
carving whole, **147**
country, 140
fresh, with spiced apple glaze, 144
and grits with red-eye gravy, 156
melba glaze for, 147
and melon, 148
more ways to enjoy, 148
new chicken cordon bleu, 215
*pineapple glazed, 147
potato and, frittata, 313
+southwestern steak, 161
split pea soup with, 67
*steak with apple chutney, 156
tomato and onion glaze for, 147
*whole Smithfield, 148
Hamburger(s), 119. *See also* Sandwiches
+classic, 119
Greek, 119
grilled, 119
Roquefort, 119
salmon, 278
teriyaki, 119

Hamburger(s) (continued)
+Texas chicken, 225
Tex-Mex, 119, **119**
+Hard sauce, 562
*Harvard beets, 412
Hash
corned beef, 118
red flannel, 118
Havarti, 331
Hazelnut(s)
chocolate and, truffles, 741
crescents, 729
dacquoise, 625
green beans with, 409
-honey granola, 398
skinning, 729
toasting, 729
Heart pie edge, 685
Heirloom beans, 373
Herb(s)(ed)
butter, 563
*buttered noodles with, 360
chicken, 198
-crusted rib roast, **86,** 94
dried, 16
freezing, 787
fresh, 15–16
+grilled whole sea bass with lemon and, 260
lamb rib roast, 170
pasta squares, 367, **367**
roast chicken with, butter, 191
roasted eggplant dip with, 38
roasted potatoes, 454, **455**
storage of fresh, 15–16
sweet onion tart with, 316
*+turkey cutlets, 236
yogurt-cheese dip, 40
Herbes de Provence rub, 177
High-altitude cooking, 13
Hoisin sauce, 31
Hollandaise sauce, 550, **551**
Home-fried potatoes, 453
Homemade pasta dough, 366–67
Hominy, 381
Hominy grits, 381, **381**
Honey, 15
creamy -mustard sauce, 201
granola breakfast bars, 720
*-lime vinaigrette, 547
preventing sticking, 742
+-wheat bread, 590
Honeyball, 499
Honeydew, 499
*three-fruit salad with vanilla bean syrup, 515
Hoppin' John, 374

Horseradish
applesauce, 483
bacon-, stuffed eggs, 325
butter, 563
creamy, sauce, 95
mashed potatoes with, 451
mayonnaise, 611
todding, 269
Hot-and-sour carrots, 421
+Hot fudge sauce, 561, **561**
Hot pepper sauce, 15
Huckleberries, freezing, 783
+Huevos rancheros, 317
+Hummus, 39

I
Ice(s), 747
lemon, in lemon cups, 752
*strawberry-orange, 751
Iceberg lettuce, 522
Ice cream, 747
chocolate, 750
chocolate-chip, 749
home-made, 747–48
no-cook vanilla, 749
old-fashioned vanilla, 749
peach, 749
raspberry, 750, **750**
rich vanilla-bean, 748
rum-raisin, 750
*+soda, 764
strawberry, 749
treats, 758
Ice-cream maker, 11
Ingredients, glossary of, 31–33
Instant rice, 382
Irish stew, 174
Italian sausage
beef and, lasagna, 362–63, **363**
and broccoli rabe, 165
creamy polenta with, and mushrooms, 395, **395**
Italian stuffed cabbage, 123
jambalaya, 388
and mozzarella frittata, **306,** 314
Neapolitan pasta sauce, 359
pasta e fagioli with sausage, 82, **82**
*penne with, 358–59
and pepper meat loaf, 123
and peppers, 166
and shrimp gumbo, **300,** 301

J
Jalapeño
butter, 563
lime-, topping, 269
*pepper jelly, 792

Jam(s). See also Butters; Jellies; Marmalade; Preserves
*apricot skillet, 790
blackberry-blueberry, 791
blueberry skillet, 791
-filled muffins, 569
-filled sugar cookies, 732–33
*freezer raspberry, 790
*freezer strawberry, 790
peach skillet, 791
raspberry skillet, 791
skillet, 791
*strawberry, 794
strawberry skillet, 791
*sweet cherry, 795
*tart cherry, 795
three-berry skillet, 791
Jambalaya, 388
Jarlsberg, **330,** 332
Jell(ies). See also Butters; Jams; Marmalade; Preserves
*all-season apple, 792
apple-cider, 792
grape, 792
*japapeño pepper, 792
*mint, 791
spiced apple, 792
*spiced sherry, 793, **793**
*white grape–wine, 793
Jelly roll, **670,** 670–71
Jelly-roll pan, 9
Jerky, 92
Jicama, 437
Juicer, 11
Julienne, 29
Juniper berries, 31

K
Kabob(s), 171
anise beef, 115
*Jamaican jerk chicken, 218, **218**
oregano–red wine vinegar, 116
rosemary lamb, 177
sesame-ginger, 116
*+shrimp and scallop, 303
swordfish, 265, **265**
Kale, 435
*caldo verde, 61
freezing, 787
Kamut, 381
+Kasha with mushrooms, 397
Kedgeree, 284–85
Key lime, frozen, pie, 704, **704**
Kidney(s), 179
sautéed veal, with mustard, 183
Kielbasa and red cabbage, 163, **163**

*Kirby cucumber salad, 530
Kirsch, 31
Kitchen scissors, 11
Kiwifruit, 496–97
  freezing, 783
Knead, 29
Knives, 12, 13–14
Kohlrabi, 437
  freezing, 787
  sautéed, 437
Kosher meat, 88
Kuchen
  nectarine, 510
  peach, 510
  plum, 510
Kumquats, 497

L

*Ladyfingers, 735
Lager, 27
Lamb, 166–79
  braised shanks, with white beans and
    vegetables, **172, 173**
  buying, 166
  cooking, 167
  eggplant and, casserole, 178
  *+glazed rosemary chops, 175
  grading, 87
  *Greek-style shanks, 174
  +grilled chops, with spice rub, 177
  ground, 166
    Greek meatballs, 121
    shepherd's pie, 178–79
  herbed rib roast, 170
  Irish stew, 174
  leg of
    aromatic, 176
    carving, **170**
    grilled, with mint and oregano, 176
    roasted, with pistachio-mint crust, 169
    rosemary, 169
  *Moroccan-style, with couscous,
    171, **171**
  navarin, 175
  popular cuts, **168**
  roasting times, **167**
  rosemary, kabobs, 177
  steak
    *with red pepper relish, 173
  storing, 166
Lasagna, 340
  beef and sausage, 362–63, **363**
  northern-style, 361
  pasta for, 364
  rolls, 364
  vegetable, 362

Latkes, potato, 456
Lattice pie top, 685
+Layered salad, 529
Leaf pie edge, 685
Leavening, 29
Leek(s), 437–39
  +braised, 438
  scallops with, and cream, 294–95
  vichyssoise, 66
  vinaigrette, 438, **438**
+"Leftover" mashed-potato pancakes, 457
Lemon(s), 497
  -almond bubble ring, 601
  +-and-parsley-baked eggs, 324
  -anise icebox cookies, 731
  *–anise poached pears, 505
  applesauce, 483
  +asparagus with -caper vinaigrette, 406
  bars, 719
  -basil stuffed eggs, 325, **325**
  blueberry-, tea bread, 573
  blueberry- tiramisù, 490–91
  *bow ties with tomatoes and, 346
  butter frosting, 677
  chicken breasts with, -caper sauce, 213
  +filling, 680
  *fresh, gelatin, 497
  *granita, 753
  Greek-style, soup, 76
  -grilled pork chops, 159
  +grilled whole sea bass with, and herbs, 260
  -hot water sponge cake, 667
  icebox cookies, 731
  ice in lemon cups, 752
  -marinated mushrooms, 440
  mashed potatoes with garlic and, 450–51
  mayonnaise, 611
  meringue nests with, filling and strawberries,
    626, **627**
  meringue pie, 704–5
  +olive and, salsa, 555
  -Parmesan rice, 384
  -parsley rice, 384
  -pepper chicken salad, 542
  +-poppy seed filling, 602
  –poppy seed pound cake, 665
  pudding cake, 635
  -ricotta cheesecake, 674, **675**
  roast, chicken, 194–95
  -roasted chicken for a crowd, 195
  *+-rosemary chicken breasts, 221
  sauce, 51
  *sauce, 561
  *scrod with -garlic bread crumbs, 273
  silky, butter frosting, 678
  syrup, 640

tart, 703
+-thyme cod, 274
topping, 269
+tubetti with, and cream, 360–61
-walnut icebox cookies, 731
-walnut scones, 568
+wax and green beans with, and
  mint, 408
Lemonade, 765
  *+fizzy cranberry-, punch, 769
  mint, 765
Lemony potato salad, 533
Lentil(s), 374, **374**
  *curried, soup, 68
  *French, with shallots and brandy, 377
  *German, soup, 68
  *Indian-style, 377
  salmon and, 278, **279**
Lettuce. *See also* specific varieties
  spicy shredded pork in, cups, 156–57
Lima bean(s), 373, **373**
  freezing, 786
  +sautéed, with bacon, 410
  *succotash, 473
Limburger, 331
Lime(s), 497. *See also* Key lime
  baked, chicken, 198
  *+couscous, 393
  +grilled chicken breasts with cumin,
    coriander, and, 221
  honey-, vinaigrette, 547
  -jalapeño topping, 269
  *pavlova, 627
Limeade, **760,** 765
  ginger, 765
Linguine, 340, **341**
  *with broccoli, 350
  *with broccoli rabe and anchovies, 349
  *with mushroom sauce, 351
  *with red clam sauce, 344
  *with white clam sauce, 355
Liver
  beef, 179
  chicken, 179
  pork, 179
Loaf pan, 9
Lobster, 257
  bisque, 290–91
  buying, 257
  +steamed, 290
Loganberry(ies)
  freezing, 783
London broil, 105
Long-grain rice, 382–83
Loquats, 498
Lychees, 498

M

Macadamia, white chocolate–, cookies, 725
Macaroni
  curly mac 'n' cheese, 364–365
  *reduced-fat, and cheese, 365
  *tubetti salad, 534
Macaroon(s)
  almond, 727
  chocolate coconut, 727
  coconut, 727
Mâche, 522
Mackerel, 254
Madeira, 26
  sweetbreads braised with, 183
Mafalde, 340
Main-dish pie(s)
  chicken shepherd's, 224–25, **225**
  savory tomato tart, **468,** 469
  tamale, 125
  *turkey, with cornmeal crust, 238
Maître d'hôtel butter, 563
Malt liquor, 27
Manchego, 331
Mandarin oranges, 511–12
Mango(es), 498
  *+blueberry- compote, 513
  *breast of duck with, chutney sauce, 242
  cutting, **499**
  freezing, 783
  mousse, 498
  *+-strawberry smoothie, 764, **764**
  *three-fruit salad with vanilla bean
    syrup, 515
  *turkey and, roll-ups, 614
Mango chutney, 31
Manicotti, 340, **341**
Maple butternut squash, 463
Maple-glazed pork tenderloins, 158
Maple syrup, 32
Maple-walnut pie, 698
Marble loaf cake, 664
Marinate, 29
Marzipan-filled stollen, 606
Marmalade(s). *See also* Butter(s); Jams;
    Jellies; Preserves
  flank steak with red onion, 109
  *pear, 796
Marsala, 32
  +chicken livers, 181
  *roasted pears with, 506, **507**
  +turkey, with mushrooms, 234–35
  +veal scallopini, 135
Marshmallow creme filling, 726
Mascarpone, **330,** 331
Mashed root vegetables, 474
Matchstick strips, 14

Mayonnaise
  basil, 234, 611
  chipotle, 611
  chutney, 611
  ginger-sesame, 611
  horseradish, 611
  lemon, 611
  pesto, 611
  pickled jalapeño, 611
  roasted red pepper, 611
Maytag Blue, **329**
Measuring, 12–13
Measuring cups, 10
Measuring spoons, 10
Meat, 87–183. *See also* Beef; Lamb; Pork;
    Variety; Veal
  buying, 87–88
  carving, 90
  cooking techniques, 89–90
  and food safety, 90–91
  grading, 87–88
  Halal, 88
  kosher, 88
  natural, 88
  organic, 88
  salting, 101
  slow roasting, when entertaining, 96
  storing, 88
  variety, 179–83
Meatball(s)
  chicken/turkey, 207
  Danish, 120
  Greek, 121
  leaner, 226
  Mexican, 120
Meat loaf
  Cajun, **122,** 122
  sausage and pepper, 123
  "Susan's", 121
  turkey, 226
Meat thermometer with poultry, 188–89, **189**
Mediterranean diet, 19
Medium-grain rice, 383
Melba glaze, 147
Melon(s), 498–500
  ham and, 148
  mint, cups, 503
  *+prosciutto with, 53
Melon baller, 11
Meringue(s)
  +fingers, 735
  nests with lemon filling and
    strawberries, 626, **627**
  shells, 626
    *miniature, 626
    perfect, 626

Merlot, 26
Merluzzo, 255
Mesclun, 522
Microwave, equipment for, 9–10
Milanese
  Cornish hens, 228, **228**
  *risotto, 391
Milk chocolate, 744
Millet, 381
Mince, 14
  pies, 698
Minestrone with pesto, **56,** 69
Mint
  dilled red potatoes with, 454
  grilled leg of lamb with, and oregano, 176
  +jelly, 791
  *julep cups, 514
  lemonade, 765
  melon cups, 503
  pasta with squash and, 348
  peas with green onions and
  roasted leg of lamb with pistachio- crust, 169
  tomato and, tabbouleh, 537
  +wax and green beans with lemon and, 408
  +zucchini ribbons with, 462
Miso, 32, 373
  soup, 69
Mixing bowls, 10
Mixing equipment, 12
Mizuma, 522
Mocha glaze, 662
Molasses, 32
  -glazed Cornish hens, 227
  *great plains oatmeal, rolls, 596
Molded cookies, 711
Mole, 203
  chicken, 203
Mollusks, 252, 255
  buying, 252
Monkfish, 254
  *bouillabaisse, 305
  *Peruvian seafood soup, 304
  Portuguese-style, 277
Monterey Jack, 331, **331**
  *+quick quesadillas, 45
  warm layered bean dip, 39
Mornay sauce, 550
Moroccan pasta, 381
Mortar and pestle, 11
Mostaccioli, 340
Mousse
  cappuccino, 632
  mango, 498
  strawberry, pie, 708
Mozzarella, 331, **331**
  +and tomato salad, 529

in carrozza, 335, **335**
with dried tomatoes, 337
Italian sasuage and, frittata, **306,** 314
veal parmigiana, 135
Muenster, 331, **331**
Muffins
apple-gingerbread, 571
banana-nut, 570
basic, **564,** 568–69
blueberry, 569
blueberry-corn, 570
bran, 569
carrot-bran, 569
jam-filled, 569
pecan, 569
raspberry, 569
removing from pan, **570**
walnut, 569
Muffin tins, 9
Mung beans, 373
Mushroom(s), 439–40
*-barley pilaf, 396
brisket with, 104–5
*chicken breasts with, and tarragon, 212
+chicken livers with, and onions, 181
Cornish hens with wild rice and stuffing, 227
cream of, soup, 59
creamy, filling, 310
*creamy, sauce, 215
creamy polenta with sausage and, 395, **395**
crepes with chicken spinach, and, filling, 319
freezing, 788
+grilled portobello, salad, 439
*hearty, -barley soup, 70
+kasha with, 397
lemon-marinated, 440
open-faced steak and, sandwiches, 615
pasta primavera, **338,** 351
+peas with, 445
quiche, 317
risotto, 392
sauce, 234
*linguine with, 351
+sautéed mixed, 440
spinach-, stuffing, 96
spinach roulade with, 322–23, **323**
stuffed beef tenderloin with, gravy, 96
+turkey marsala with, 234–35
veal and, stew, 131
warm arugula and, salad, 526
and wild rice soup, 71, **71**
wild rice with, 392
Mussels, 251, 253, 255
Billi-Bi, 76
*bouillabaisse, 305
moules à la mariniére, 292

in saffron-tomato broth, 74
scrubbing and debearding, 291
*seafood fra diavolo, **356,** 357
*with tomatoes and white wine, 291, **291**
Mustard. *See also* Dijon (mustard)
-caper sauce, 107
creamy honey- sauce, 201
dipping sauce, 55
sauce, 54
sautéed veal kidneys with, 183
shallot vinaigrette, 545
Mustard greens, 435. *See also* Greens
freezing, 788

N
Nachos, chorizo and black bean, 47
Napa cabbage, 416–17, 522
pickled, 416
stir-fry, 417
Napoleons, 646
strawberry, 642
Natural cocoa powder, 744
Navy beans, 373, **373**
*old-fashioned baked, 376
Neapolitan pasta sauce, 359
Nectarine(s), 500
*and cherry crisp, 518
*barley salad with, 536
freezing, 783
kuchen, 510
*+spiced, 500
New England boiled dinner, **106,** 107
Niçoise salad, 540, **541**
Noodles
*buttered, with herbs, 360
cellophane, 340
Chinese-style egg, 340
*pad Thai, **354,** 354–55
Szechuan peanut-, salad, 543
udon, 340
*Vietnamese, soup, 77
Nuts. *See also* specific
chili, 42
curried, 42
+hot-pepper, 42
sweet and spicy, 42
toasting, 729

O
Oak leaf, 522
Oatmeal
apple- crisp, 484
grandmother's, -raisin cookies, 722, **723**
*great plains, -molasses rolls, 596
*lowfat, raisin cookies, 722
*whole wheat–-, bread, 590

Ocean perch, 254
Okra, 440–41
freezing, 788
+fried, 440
*pickled, 801
with tomatoes, 441
Old Bay seasoning, 32
Olive(s), 32, **32**
+and lemon salsa, 555
braised baby artichokes with, 404
butter, 563
+chicken with tomato-, relish, 223
dried tomato and, focaccia, 599
marinated mixed, 43
roast chicken with green, and sherry, 193
-rosemary loaves, 587
+tapenade, 41
tomato-, sauce, 234
Olive oil, 15, 32
Omega-3 fatty acids, 251
Omelet(s)
+basic, 310–11
+basic fluffy, 312
black bean and salsa filling, 310
creamy mushroom filling, 310
+egg white, 311
garden vegetable, **310,** 311
quick no-cook fillings for, 312
red pepper and goat cheese filling, 311
spinach, cheddar, and bacon filling, 311
western filling, 311
Onion(s), 441–43. *See also* Green onions
caramelized, 442, **442**
caramelized, with raisins, 442
+chicken livers with mushrooms, and, 181
chopping, 14
creamed, and peas, 442
creamed pearl, 442
crumb-topped, 443
flank steak with red, marmalade, 109
focaccia, 599
freezing, 788
French, soup, 59
French-fried, rings, 443
frittata sandwiches with peppers and, 611
*mashed potatoes with caramelized, 451
oven-roasted, 443
*pasta with peas and, 360
roasted beets and, 412
sautéed peppers with, 448
*+sun-dried tomato and green-, couscous, 393
sweet, tart with herbs, 316
Open-faced steak and mushroom sandwiches, 615
Orange(s), 500–501
beet and, salad, 524
butter frosting, 677

Orange(s) (continued)
  cake, 652
  *candied citrus peel, 744
  cornish hens with anise-, glaze, 228
  *cranberry-, bread, 573
  *cranberry-, mold, 538
  crispy roasted goose with, sauce, 243
  Dijon sauce, 161
  +fennel-, pork chops, 159
  *-fennel pasta, 360
  +-fennel salsa, 555
  freezing, 783
  +-ginger pork medallions, 154
  -glazed pork rolls, 152
  *-glazed steak, 115
  icebox cookies, 731
  liqueur soufflé, 624–25
  *sherbet, 751
  silky, butter frosting, 678
  *slices marinated in marmalade, 501
  *strawberry-, ice, 751
  whipped cream frosting, 679
  *with caramel, 502, **502**
Orange roughy, 254
Orecchiette, 340, **341**
Ornamental frosting, 739
Orzo, 340, **341**
Osso buco
  *style turkey, 237
  *with gremolata, **132**, 133
Oven, equipment for, 8–9
Oven-dried tomatoes, 470
*+Oven-fried fish, 274–75
*Oven fries, 452
Oxtails, braised, 102
Oyster(s), 251, 255–56
  +panfried, 292
  +pan roast, 293
  +po'boys, 613
  Rockefeller, 55
  scalloped, 292
Oyster-corn chowder, 75

P
*Pad Thai, **354**, 354–55
+Paella, **370**, 389
Palmiers, 739
Pan bagnat, 614
Pancake(s), 579
  banana, 580
  blueberry, 580
  buckwheat, 580
  +buttermilk, 580, **580**
  cornmeal, 580
  +"leftover" mashed potato, 457
  +puffy, 321

  *+puffy apple, 321
  sour cream, 580
  sweet potato, 456
Pancake syrup, 15
Pancetta, 32, **32**
  *radiatori with arugula, cherry tomatoes
    and, 346
  *spaghetti all'Amatriciana, 359
Panfrying, 29
  beef, 92
  lamb, 167
  meat, 89
  pork, 142
  veal, 128
Panna cotta with raspberry sauce, 631, **631**
Pantry, storage in, 15
Panzanella salad with tomato vinaigrette,
  539, **539**
Papayas, 503
Pappardelle, 340, 367
Parboil, 29
Parboiled rice, 382
Parchment
  *+Asian-style flounder baked in, 276
  cod, cabbage, and bacon in, 273
  *red snapper in, with tomatoes and
    basil, 281
Pare, 29
Parker house rolls, 595
Parmesan cheese, 331–32, **332**
  baked artichokes with, stuffing, **400**, 404–5
  braised fennel with, 434
  +broiled, tomatoes, 470
  +-broiled squash, 462
  fillets, 275
  +lacy, crisps, 336, **336**
  lemon-, rice, 384
  -pepper sticks, 45
  potatoes, 457
  roasted eggplant, 431
  topping, 269
  veal parmigiana, 135
Parmigiana
  chicken, 135
  veal, 135
Parsley
  lemon-, rice, 384
  sautéed cardoons with, 419
Parsnips, 444
  candied, 420
  harvest casserole, 476
  mashed potatoes with, 451
  pureed, 444
  roasted, 444–45
  *swiss chard, and bacon stuffing, 248
Passion fruit, 503

Pasta, 339–42
  baked ziti, 365
  bow ties
    *with a trio of peas, 348
    *with tomatoes and lemon, 346
  *buttered noodles with herbs, 360
  buying and storing, 339
  *confetti, 360
  curly mac 'n' cheese, 364–65
  *dried fruit kugel, 366
  farfalle, with gorgonzola sauce, 352
  fettuccine
    alfredo, 352
    *light alfredo, 352
  *gnocchi, 368–69
    ricotta, with browned butter and
      sage, 369, **369**
  homemade, dough, 367
  jumbo cheese ravioli, 368
  lasagna
    beef and sausage, 362–63, **363**
    northern-style, 361
    pasta for, 364
    rolls, 364
    vegetable, 362
  linguine
    *white white clam sauce, 355
    *with broccoli, 350
    +with fresh tomato sauce, 345
    *with mushroom sauce, 351
    *with red clam sauce, 344
  *linguine with broccoli rabe and anchovies, 349
  *orange-fennel, 360
  *pad Thai, **354**, 354–55
  pasta e fagioli with canned beans, 82
  pasta e fagioli with sausage, 82, **82**
  *pasta e piselli, 67
  penne
    with tomato cream, 344, **344**
    + with no-cook tomato sauce, 346
    +with salmon and asparagus, 354
    *with sausage, 358–59
    + with spinach and raisins, 349
  preparation, 342
  primavera, **338**, 351
  *radiatori with arugula, cherry tomatoes,
    and pancetta, 346
  *reduced-fat macaroni and cheese, 365
  rigatoni
    baked, and peas, 366
    *+with "sausage" sauce, 358
  *seafood fra diavolo, **356**, 357
  spaghetti
    +all'Amatriciana, 359
    and meatballs, 357
    with walnuts, 348

*+with oil and garlic, 347
*with pesto, 347
*with roasted tomatoes, 345
with squash and mint, 348
tips, 342, 345
+tubetti with lemon and cream, 360–61
types of, 340, **341**
*+with bacon and peas, 353
*+with browned butter and sage, 361
*with fresh tomato sauce, 345
*with peas and onion, 360
*with tuna puttanesca, 353
*ziti with roasted asparagus, 350, **350**
Pasta sauces
Arrabbiata, 343
big batch tomato, 343
classic bolognese, 358
marinara, 343
Neapolitan, 359
*quick white clam, 355
Pasteurize, 29
Pastina, 340
Pastrami, 92
Pastry. *See* Dough
Pastry bag, 11
Pastry blender, 11
Pastry brush, 11, 664
Pea(s), 445
+and fava beans, 410–11, **411**
baked rigatoni and, 366
*bow ties with a trio of, 348
*braised veal chops with tomatoes and, 131
creamed onions and, 442
curried cauliflower with potatoes and, 423, **423**
with green onions and mint, 445
+layered salad, 529
*pasta e piselli, 67
*pasta with, and onion, 360
*+pasta with bacon and, 353
quick cream of, soup, 63
*shrimp risotto with baby, **390,** 391
+with mushrooms, 445
Pea beans, 373. *See also* Navy beans
Peach(es), 503–4
blueberry-, shortcakes, 518
-blueberry galette, 695
*butter, 796–97
canning, 777
*cobbler, 504
5-minute frozen, yogurt, 751
freezing, 783
ice cream, 749
*in red wine, 492
kuchen, 510
pie, 696, **696**
*salsa, 556

skillet jam, 791
smoothie, 764
*sorbet, 755
soufflés, 623
tarte tatin, 690
Peanut(s)
+Asian, sauce, 554–55
brittle, 743
spicy, chicken, 207
spicy, sauce, 52
Szechuan, -noodle salad, 543
Peanut butter, 15
chocolate swirl, blondies, 716
cookies, 721
+cupcakes, 659, **659**
frozen, pie, 709
Pea pods, freezing, 788
Pear(s), 504–7
*and red wine soup, 85
*balsamic chicken and, 214
canning, 777
chocolate, 505
dried, chutney, 559
and dried-cherry rice pudding, 505
dumplings, 506
freezing, 783
*fresh, soufflés, 623
*lemon-anise poached, 505
*marmalade, 796, **796**
mixed greens with, and pecans, **520,** 524
*northwest fruit stuffing, 246
raspberry-, trifle, 628
*roasted, with marsala, 506, **507**
smoothies, 505
tarte tatin, 690
*tomato-, preserves, 795
*zinfandel-poached, 505
Pecan(s)
apricot-, fruitcake, 672–73
chicken breast with, crust, 212
crescents, 729
lace cookies, 725
mixed greens with pears and, **520,** 524
muffins, 569
pie, 700
chocolate, 700
pralines, 743
tassies, 729
toasting, 729
warm banana-, tart, 693
wheat berries with brown butter and, 398
Penne, 340
*with no-cook tomato sauce, 346
*with salmon and asparagus, 354
*with sausage, 358–59
+with tomato cream, 344, **344**

Pepper(s), 32–33
artichokes with roasted-, -and- basil
sauce, 405
dill-, topping, 269
focaccio, 599
freezing, 788
frittata sandwiches with, and onion, 611
*giardiniera, 801, **801**
and goat cheese filling, 311
hot, 446–47
Italian sausage and, 166
*lamb steak with, relish, 173
lemon-, chicken salad, 542
+roasted, dip, 37, **37**
+roasted, sauce, 553
sweet, 447–49
+chutney, 559
roasted, 448, **448**
roasted, with fresh basil, 447
sautéed, with onion, 448
stuffed Italian frying, 448
sweet and sour, 448
*vegetarian stuffed, 449
Pepper Jack rice, 384
Peppermint, whipped cream frosting, 679
*Peppery dilled beans, 800, **800**
Persian melons, 500
*Persian rice pilaf, 386
Persimmons, 508
-date pudding, 508
freezing, 784
Pesto
butter, 563
mayonnaise, 611
minestrone with, **56,** 69
Pheasant, 240
Phyllo, 640
+tart shell, 688
+tartlet shells, 688
Picadillo, 125
+Piccata, veal, 136–37
*Pickled beets, 412–13
Pickled Chinese cabbage, 416
Pickled eggs, 325
Pickled ginger, 278
Pickled jalapeño mayonnaise, 611
*Pickled okra, 801
Pickles, 775
*bread-and-butter, 799
watermelon-rind, 798, **798**
Picnics, 16
Pie(s), 683–709. *See also* Main-dish pies; Tarts
apple, 689
crumb, 690
galette, 692
tarte tatin, 690, **691**

Pie(s) (continued)

apricot streusel, 692
baking, 685
banana cream, 705
black bottom, 703
blueberry
*double, 693
very, 694, **694**
cherries
canned, 695
frozen tart, 695
tart, 695
chocolate
cream, 706, **706**
cream angel, 708
pecan, 700
coconut cream, 705
decorative edges, 684–85
deluxe cheese, 700
fit into pan, 684
frozen key lime, 704, **704**
frozen peanut butter, 709
grandma's sweet potato, 702
ingredients in, 683
lemon meringue, 704–5
malnut-walnut, 698
mince, 698
peach, 696, **696**
-blueberry galette, 695
tarte tatin, 690
pear, 696
tarte tatin, 690
pecan, 700
pilgrim pumpkin, 701
plum, 696
raspberry baked-Alaska, 756–57
rhubarb, 698
slipped coconut-custard, 701
slipped custard, 701
storage, 685
strawberry cheese, **682,** 700
strawberry mousse, 708
tops and glazes, 685
warm banana-pecan tart, 692
White Russian, 707
Piecrust(s). *See also* Dough
chocolate wafer–crumb, 689
cornmeal, 238
freezing, 709
+graham cracker–crumb, 689
no-roll nut, 688–89
+phyllo tartlet shells, 688
+phyllo tart shell, 688
prebaked, 688
protecting edges, **686**
tart shell, 688

vanilla wafer–crumb, 689
waterproofing a prebaked, 697
Pie plate, 9
Pigeon peas, 373
+Pignoli, escarole with raisins and, 432
Pike, 254
Pinch, 29
Pineapple(s), 508–9
ambrosia, 514
freezing, 784
*-glazed ham, 147
+jerk catfish with grilled, 270
*mint julep cups, 514
*teriyaki pork chops with grilled, slices, 158–59
upside-down cake, 656
Pine nut(s), 33
cauliflower with golden raisins, 422
tassies, 729
Pink beans, 373, **373**
*+quick "baked," 378
Pinot noir, 26
Pinto beans, 373, **373**
warm layered, dip, 39
Pipe, 30
Pistachio, roasted leg of lamb with -mint crust, 169
*Pissaladière, 600
Pizza
*cheese, 597
grilled, 598
toppings, 598
*Pizza dough, 596–97
Pizza sauce, 597
Plantains, 449
+golden sautéed, 449
Plum(s), 509–10
broiled amaretti, 503
canning, 777
filling (for crepes), 647
frangipane tart, 696–97
freezing, 784
kuchen, 510
*+pork tenderloin cutlets with, glaze, 157, **157**
pudding with hard sauce, 633
roasted almond–crusted, 509
*salsa, 556
upside-down cake, 656
Poach, 30
Polenta
broiled polenta wedges, 394
creamy, 394
creamy, with sausage and mushrooms, 395, **395**
rosemary polenta wedges, 394
and sausage casserole, **164,** 165
Polish sausage, 140
Pollock, 254

Pomegranates, 510–11
Popovers, 571
giant, 571
Poppy seed
+dressing, 546
hot slaw with, 418
*lemon-, filling, 602
lemon-, pound cake, 665
Porcini mushrooms, 33
Pork, 138–66. *See also* Bacon; Ham; Sausage
adobo-style chili, 151
+balsamic-glazed, chops, 155
beer-braised bratwurst dinner, 162
breakfast patties, 163
brining, 142
buying, 138, 140–41, 149
chops
+fennel-orange, 159
lemon-grilled, 159
Sicilian stuffed, 149
stuffed, 155
*teriyaki, with grilled pineapple slices, 158–59
choucroute garni, 153, **153**
cooking, 142
grading, 87
ground, 141
stuffed cabbage with dill, 162
Hungarian goulash, 150
Neapolitan pasta sauce, 359
+orange-ginger, medallions, 154
orange-glazed, rolls, 152
popular cuts, **139**
pulled, barbecue, 152
ribs
barbecued, spareribs, **160,** 161
Mexican-style spare, 150
oven-barbecued spare, 146
roast
with caraway seeds, 145
Caribbean, 146, **146**
crown, with apple stuffing, 142–43, **143**
with fennel and garlic, 144
French, 145
with fresh sage, 144–45
roasting times, 141
smoked cuts, **140**
spicy shredded, in lettuce cups, 156–57
storing, 138, 140–41
+sweet and savory, 154
tenderloin
*breaded, 152–53
maple-glazed, 158
+spice-rubbed, 158
*+with plum glaze, 157, **157**
Port, 26

Port-Salut, 332
+Portobello mushroom, grilled, salad, 439
Port sauce with prunes, 181
Potato(es), 450–57
    anna, 456
    *baby, with rosemary, 452
    *baked, 453
    *baked scrod with fennel and, 272–73
    bread, 588–89
    *caldo verde, 61
    caviar in, nests, 50
    curried cauliflower with, and peas, 423, **423**
    *dilled red, with mint, 454
    fennel and, gratin, 433
    *gnocchi, 368–69
    and ham frittata, 313
    herbed roasted, 454, **455**
    home-fried, 453
    latkes, 456
    mashed
        basic, 450
        basil, 451
        celery root with, 425
        with garlic and lemon, 450–51
        with horseradish, 451
        +"leftover", pancakes, 457
        *lowfat, 452
        with parsnips, 451
        *with caramelized onions, 451
    *oven fries, 452
    pan-roasted, 452
    parmesan, 457
    salads
        creamy, 533
        lemony, 533
        *red, 533
        *roasted, 532
    +-salsa frittata, 312
    samosas, 48–49
    scalloped, 453
    shepherd's pie, 178–79
    shrimp and, in feta-tomato sauce, 297
    and turnip gratin, 479
    twice-baked, 454
    *tzimmes, 479
    vichyssoise, 66
Potato masher, 11
Potpies. *See* Main-dish pies
Pot roast with root vegetables, 100–101, **101**
Poultry, 185–249. *See also* Capons; Chicken;
    Cornish hens; Duck; Goose; Turkey
    all-natural, 186
    buying, 185–87
    carving tips for, **189**
    and food safety, 187
    free-range, 185–86

freezing, 187
frozen, 186
Halal, 186
handling and storage, 187
Kosher, 186
meat thermometer with, 188–89, **189**
organic, 185
roasting, 188–89, 191
    times for, 188
stuffing, 244
    *chestnut and apple, 245
    country sausage and corn bread, 245
    moist bread, 246
    *northwest fruit, 246
    *parsnips, swiss chard, and bacon, 248
    *rice and escarole, 247
    southwestern corn bread, 244
    *wild rice and vegetable, 247
thawing, 187
white and dark meat, 187
Pound, 30
Praline(s), 743
    cream puff wreath, 644, **645**
    -iced brownies, **713,** 713
    sweet potatoes, 466–67
Prawns, 257
Preheat, 30
Preserves. *See also* Butters; Jams;
    Jellies; Marmalade
    *tomato-pear, 795
Pressed cookies, 711
Pretzels, soft, 607
Prick, 30
Processed fish, 258
Proof, 30
Prosciutto, 33, 140. *See also* Ham
    *+grilled chicken breasts saltimbocca,
        223, **223**
    with other fruit, 53
    +veal stuffed with fontina, and basil, 137
    *+with melon, 53
    -wrapped asparagus, 47
*Provençal sauce, 214
Provolone, **331,** 332
Prune(s)
    *dried apricot, and cherry compote, 513
    *dried fruit kugel, 366
    *filling, 603
    port sauce with, 181
Pudding(s), *see also* Desserts
    creamy corn, 427
    pear and dried-cherry rice, 505
    persimmon-date, 508
    *summer, 490
    Yorkshire, 94
Puff pastry, 647

Pulled pork barbecue, 152
*Pumpernickel bread, 592
Pumpkin(s), 457–58
    cheescake, 676
    crème caramel, 630
    freezing, 788
    Pilgrim, pie, 701
    roasted mini, 458
Punch down, 30
Puree, 30
Pureed soups, 58
Puy, 374, **374**
Pyramid, 330, **330**

Q

Quail, 240
    pan-roasted, 242
*+Quesadillas, quick, 45
Queso blanco, 332
Quiche(s)
    asparagus, 317
    bite-size bacon, 49
    lorraine, 316
    mushroom, 317
    sherried crab, 317
Quick-rise yeast, 583
Quinces, 510–11
Quinoa, 381, **381,** 398

R

Rabbit, 248
    braised in red wine, 248–49
    niçoise, 249, **249**
Raclette, 332, 333
Radiatori, 340, **341**
    *with arugula, cherry tomatoes, and
        pancetta, 346
Radicchio, 522
Radish(es), 458
    stir-fried cucumbers and, 430
    +watercress and, tea sandwiches, 618
Radish sprouts, 522
Raisin(s)
    cauliflower with golden, and
        pine nuts, 422
    *cinnamon-, bread, 586
    cranberry-, relish, 559
    cranberry- fruitcake, 673
    +escarole with, and pignoli, 432
    grandmother's oatmeal-, cookies, 722, **723**
    *lowfat oatmeal-, cookies, 722
    *penne with spinach and, 349
    rum-, ice cream, 750
    *spice bars, 720
Ramps, 443–44
+Ranch dressing, 547

Raspberry(ies), 488
    apricot-, rugelach, **734,** 734–35
    baked-Alaska pie, 756–57
    berries and cream shortcake, **480,** 489
    charlotte, 489
    *freezer, jam, 790
    freezing, 784
    *granita, 752
    ice cream, 750, **750**
    linzer thumbprints, 730
    muffins, 569
    panna cotta with, sauce, 631, **631**
    -pear trifle, 628
    *+sauce, 562
    skillet jam, 791
    *summer pudding, 490
    tart, 697
    three-berry charlotte, 488–89
    -walnut streusel bars, 721
Ratatouille, 476
Rattlesnake beans. *See* Heirloom beans
Ravioli
    easy wonton, 368
    jumbo cheese, 368
Red beans, 373. *See* Red kidney beans
Red cabbage, 417–19
    braised sweet-and-sour, 417
    kielbasa and, 163, **163**
Red kidney beans, 373, **374**
    *+and rice, 379
    *+quick "baked," 378
    three-bean salad, 527
    *three-bean vegetarian chili, 375, **375**
Red lentils, 374, **374**
Red snapper, 254
    with bacon and apples, 284
    California cioppino, 303
    +Chinese-style steamed, **250,** 260
    *Grilled Thai, packets, 282
    *in parchment with tomatoes and basil, 281
    *livornese, 282–83, **283**
    *+Tunisian, fillets, 282
Reduce, 30
Reduced-fat cheese, 332
Red wine(s), 26
    beurre rouge, 552
    halibut braised in, 267
    oregano–, vinegar kabobs, 116
    *peaches in, 492
    *pear and, soup, 85
    rabbit braised in, 248–49
    serving, 768
    shallot and, butter, 563
Red winter wheat, 381
Refried beans, 378–79
Refrigerator cookies, 711

Refrigerator rolls, 595
Refrigerators, 15
Relish(es), 775
    +chicken with tomato-olive, 223
    *corn, 800
    cranberry-raisin, 559
    *lamb steak with red pepper, 173
    *no-cook cranberry-orange, 558–59
    *roasted scrod with tomato, 274
    *southwestern-style cranberry, 558
Render, 30
Rhubarb, 510–11
    *-apple crumble, 517
    canning, 777
    freezing, 784
    pie, 698
    -strawberry cobbler, **516,** 517
Ribs
    barbecued, spareribs, **160,** 161
    barbecued beef, 116
    deviled short, 97
    Korean-style sesame short, **116,** 116–17
    Mexican-style spare, 150
    oven-barbecued spare, 146
Rice
    Asian, 384
    *baked, 385
    *brown, 384
    *brown, and vegetable pilaf, 387
    buying and storing, 382
    *chicken soup with, 78
    coconut, 384
    cooking, 382
    *cumin, with black beans, 387
    *and escarole stuffing, 247
    *ginger fried, 388
    green, 385
    hoppin' John, 374
    *+hot fluffy, 384
    *+Indian-spiced, 386–87
    jambalaya, 388
    lemon-parmesan, 384
    lemon-parsley, 384
    *Mexican red, 385
    mushroom and wild, soup, 71, **71**
    pepper Jack, 384
    pilaf
        *Persian, 386
        with vermicelli, 386
    *+red beans and, 379
    risotto
        *milanese, 391
        mushroom, 392
        *shrimp, with baby peas, **390,** 391
    salad
        *Japanese, 534

    Mediterranean, 535
    white and wild, 534–35
    types of, 382–83
    wild, 383
        *and vegetable stuffing, 247
        Cornish hens with, and mushroom stuffing, 227
        mushroom and, soup, 71, **71**
        with mushrooms, 392
        pilaf, with dried cranberries, 393
*Rice pudding, 636
    rich, 637
    vanilla, with dried cherries, 637
Rice stick noodles
    *pad Thai, **354,** 354–55
Rice sticks, 340
Ricotta, **330,** 332
    gnocchi with browned butter and sage, 369, **369**
    lemon-, cheesecake, 674, **675**
    *+pasta with bacon and peas, 353
    savory ricotta cheesecake, 337
Ricotta salata, **330,** 332
    +tomato and, bruschetta, **34,** 46
Riesling, 25
Rigatoni, 340
    baked, and peas, 366
    *+with "sausage" sauce, 358
Risotto, 383
    *Milanese, 391
    *mushroom, 392
    *shrimp, with baby peas, **390,** 391
Roast(ing), 30
    beef, 92
    duck, 243
    lamb, 167
    meat, 89, 96
    pork, 142
    poultry, 188–89, 191
    veal, 128
Roasting pan, 8
Rock cod, 254
Rockfish, 254
Rock lobster, 257
Rolled cookies, 711, 737
Rolling boil, 30
Rolling pins, 10
Romaine, 522
Romano, **332,** 332
Roquefort, 329, **329**
    burgers, 119
    butter, 563
Rosé, 26
Rosemary
    *-apricot chicken, 196
    *baby potatoes with, 452

balsamic- sauce, 161
*chicken with, dumplings, 206–7
-fennel breadsticks, 594
*+glazed, lamb chops, 175
lamb kabobs, 177
leg of lamb, 169
*+lemon-, chicken breasts, 221
olive-, loaves, 587
polenta wedges, 394
-roasted butternut squash, 463
*roast turkey breast, 232
Rotini, 340, **341**
    curly mac 'n' cheese, 364–65
    *pasta with tuna puttanesca, 353
Roulades, chicken, 202, **202**
Ruler, 11
Rum-raisin ice cream, 750
Ruote, 340, **341**
+Russian dressing, 546
Rutabaga(s), 458–59
    freezing, 789
    harvest casserole, 476
    mashed, with brown butter, 458–59
Rye, 381
Rye bread
    *round, 589

S

Sacher torte, 662–63
Safety. *See also* Food safety
    with grill, 22
Sage
    citrus-, chicken, 218–19
    *+pasta with browned butter and, 361
    pork roast with fresh, 144–45
    ricotta gnocchi with browned butter and, 369,
        369
    trout with brown butter and, 263
    *Tuscan white beans with, 376
Salad(s), 521–45
    adding crunch to, 530
    Asian coleslaw, 531
    *Asian cucumber, 530
    *barley, with nectarines, 536
    basil and dried tomato chicken, 542
    beet and orange, 524
    best chicken, 542
    buying, preparing and storing salad greens, 521
    Caesar-style egg, 544–45
    +cherry tomato–lemon, 532
    +chopped, 528
    chopped Greek, 528
    +citrus, with sherry dressing, 525, **525**
    classic egg, 544
    +classic tuna, 543
    cobb, 544, **544**

coleslaw with vinaigrette, 531
couscous, 535
*cranberry-orange mold, 538
creamy cucumber and dill, 530
croutons for, 539
*cucumber, 52
curried egg, 544
curried tuna, 543
curry-grape chicken, 542
deli-style egg, 545
escarole and bacon, 526
+grilled portobello mushroom, 439
Italian seafood, 540
*Japanese rice, 534
*kirby cucumber, 530
+layered, 529
lemon-pepper chicken, 542
+light and lemony slaw, 531
Mediterranean rice, 535
Mexican-style egg, 545
Mexican-style tuna, 543
mixed greens with pears and
    pecans, **520**, 524
+mozzarella and tomato, 529
+new Caesar, 527
Niçoise, 540, **541**
panzanella, with tomato vinaigrette, 539, **539**
potato
    creamy, 533
    lemony, 533
    *red, 533
    *roasted, 532, **532**
salt cod, 285
+spinach and bacon, 525
*summer corn, 528
Szechuan peanut-noodle, 543
taco, 542
*Thai chicken, 538
Thai grilled beef, 538–39
*Thai squid, 538
*Thai vegetable, 539
three-bean, 527
*three-fruit, with vanilla bean syrup, 515
*tomato and mint tabbouleh, 537
tomato aspic, 537
tossing, 537
*tubetti macaroni, 534
+turkey cutlets with chopped, 235, **235**
types of greens in, 522
veal with tomato and argula, 136, **136**
+waldorf, 529
warm arugula and mushroom, 526
+warm goat cheese, 528–29
*wheat berry, 536
white and wild rice, 534–35
wilted, 545

winter vegetable, 527
Salad dressings, 523
    blue cheese vinaigrette, 545
    +classic French vinaigrette, 545
    +creamy blue cheese, 546
    +green goddess, 546
    *+honey-lime vinaigrette, 547
    +Japanese miso vinaigrette, 547
    mustard-shallot vinaigrette, 545
    +poppy seed, 546
    +ranch, 547
    +Russian, 546
    +tahini, 547
    +tomato vinaigrette, 545
Salad spinner, 11
Salmon, 254
    +baked, fillets, 280
    +broiled, steaks, 264
    burgers, 278
    +cakes, 280
    cold poached, steaks with watercress
        sauce, 263
    +five-spice, fillets, 280
    gravlax, 54
    +grilled spiced, steaks, 264
    and lentils, 278, **279**
    pâté, 44
    *penne with, and asparagus, 354
    poached whole, 259
    scrambled eggs with cream cheese and, 320
    smoked, 258
        filling, 43
        +tea sandwiches, 619
        +with dill cream cheese, 612–13
    +steaks teriyaki, 264
    tarragon-roasted, 259
Salmonella, 307
Salmon trout, 254
Salmoriglio sauce, 553
Salsa(s), 555–57. *See also* Sauces
    *black bean, 214
    black bean and, filling, 310
    +olive and lemon, 555
    *+orange-fennel, 555
    *peach, 556
    *plum, 556
    +potato-, frittata, 312
    sweet corn, 555
    tomatillo, 556–57
    *tomato, 556
    *watermelon, 557, **557**
+Salsa verde, 554
Salsify, 459
    +buttered, 459
Salt, 33
*Salt-baked fish, 261

Salt cod, 254, 258
    Portuguese-style, 286
    salad, 285
*+Saltimbocca, grilled chicken breasts, 223, **223**
Salting
    meat, 101
    turkey, 236
Samosas, 48–49
Sandwich(es), 609–19. *See also* Hamburgers
    bread for, 610
    +cheddar and chutney tea, 619
    chicken club, 615
    +classic Italian hero, **608,** 617
    cucumber tea, 618
    dilled-egg tea, 618
    +double tomato–brie heroes, 610–11
    flank steak, with chimichurri sauce, 616, **616**
    frittata, with peppers and onion, 610–11
    +health club, 612, **612**
    muffuletta, 617
    open-faced grilled, 148
    open-faced steak and mushroom, 615
    +oyster po'boys, 613
    pan bagnat, 614
    +perfectly simple tomato, 610
    +pinwheel, 619
    *roast beef-waldorf club, 616–17
    safe, 609
    slim, 610
    sloppy joes, 126
    +smoked salmon, with dill cream cheese, 612–13
    +smoked salmon tea, 619
    *turkey and mango roll-ups, 614
    *+Tuscan tuna salad on focaccia, 612–13
    +watercress and radish tea, 618
    zesty spread, 148
*+Sangria, 766
    white, 766
Santa Claus melon, 500
Sauce(s), 549–63. *See also* Toppings
    *apple curry, 214
    apricot-balsamic, 201
    *apricot-cranberry, with fresh ginger, 558
    Asian barbecue, 161
    +Asian peanut, 554–55
    balsamic-rosemary, 161
    béarnaise, 551
    béchamel, 550
    for beef tenderloin, 97
    *+best blueberry, 560
    +beurre blanc, 551
    beurre rouge, 552
    *black bean, 214
    blue-cheese, 201
    *breast of duck, with mango chutney, 242

brisket with chunky BBQ, 117
    +butterscotch, 560
    caper, 260
    cheese, 550
    +chimichurri, 554
    *Chinese ginger, 214
    +cilantro, 554
    *+cranberry-port, 557
    creamy honey-mustard, 201
    creamy horseradish, 95
    *creamy mushroom, 215
    crispy roasted goose with orange, 243
    *+cumberland, 552
    *curry-apricot, 234
    +custard, 562
    *Dijon, 215
    for fish, 277
    +flank steak with chimichurri, 114
    +gribiche, 553
    +hard, 562
    +hollandaise, 550, **551**
    +hot fudge, 561, **561**
    lemon, 51, 561
    mop, 105
    mornay, 550
    *mushroom, 234
    mustard, 54
    mustard-caper, 107
    mustard dipping, 55
    orange-dijon, 161
    +our sublime chocolate, 561
    *pear-balmamic, 181
    pizza, 597
    port, with prunes, 181
    *provençal, 214
    *+raspberry, 562
    repairing a broken, 550
    roasted garlic, 553
    +roasted red pepper, 553
    salmoriglio, 553
    salsa verde, 554
    sauce rémoulade, 552
    shrimp and potatoes in feta-tomato, 297
    soft-shell crabs with lemon-caper, 288
    sour cream–dill
        veal nuggets with, 138
    *southwestern-style cocktail, 55
    *soy dipping, 53
    spicy peanut, 52
    +tartar, 552
    *tomato-olive, 234
    Turkish chicken in walnut, 211
    for vegetables, 406
    watercress, 264
    +white, 550
    white chocolate custard, 634–35

Saucepan, 7
Saucepot, 8
Sauerkraut
    choucroute garni, 153, **153**
    Hungarian pork goulash, 150
Sausage(s), 140. *See also* Chorizo sausage;
        Italian sausage
    country, and corn bread stuffing, 245
    polenta and, casserole, **164,** 165
    Portuguese mixed grill, 222
Sauté, 30
Sautéing meat, 89
Sauternes, 25
Sauvignon blanc, 25
*Savarin, 638
Savoiardi, 33
Scald, 30
Scallions, 443–44
Scalloped pie edge, 684
Scallops, 256
    and asparagus stir-fry, 294, **294**
    with leeks and cream, 294–95
    +panfried, 295
    pan roast, 293
    provençal, 293
    *seafood paella, 304
    *+shrimp and, kabobs, 303
    +with bacon and cream, 295
Scarlet runner beans. *See* Heirloom beans
Scones, 567
    buttermilk, 567
    currant, 568
    lemon-walnut, 568
    rich, 568, **568**
Score, 30
Scottish shortbread, 717
Scrambled eggs
    with cream cheese, 320
    with cream cheese and salmon, 320
Scrod, 254
    *baked, with fennel and potatoes, 272–73
    *roasted, with tomato relish, 274
    *with lemon-garlic bread crumbs, 273
Sea bass
    +Chinese-style steamed, **250,** 260
    +grilled whole, with lemon and herbs, 260
Seafood. *See also* Fish; *specific varieties*
    Italian, salad, 540
    *paella, 304
Sear, 30
Semolina, 33
Sesame oil, Asian, 33
Shad, 254
    +broiled, 280–81
    broiled with roe, 281
    +sauéed roe, 284

Shallot(s), 443–44
    +beurre blanc, 551
    caramelized, 442
    *French lentils with, and brandy, 377
    mustard-, vinaigrette, 545
    and red wine butter, 563
    roast turkey breast with caramelized, 232–33
Shave, 30
Shell beans, 372. *See also* Cranberry beans
Shellfish. *See also* Fish; *specific varieties*
    buying, 251–52
    buying and storing frozen, 252–53
    storing, 252
    types of, 255–56
Shepherd's pie, 178–79
Sherbet, 747
    *orange, 751
Sherry, 26
    roast chicken with green olives and, 193
Shortcake(s)
    berries and cream, **480,** 489
    blueberry-peach, 518
    strawberry, 491
Shortening pastry dough, 686
Short-grain rice, 383, 385
Shred, 30
Shrimp, 257
    *+and scallop kabobs, 303
    +beer-batter fried, 297
    bisque, 75
    *bouillabaisse, 305
    butterflying, **297**
    buying and storing, 253
    California cioppino, 303
    *cocktail, 54
    +curry, 296
    deveining, **296**
    Étouffée, 298
    Italian seafood salad, 540
    jambalaya, 388
    *pad Thai, **354,** 354–55
    *Peruvian seafood soup, 304
    *pickled, 43
    and potatoes in feta-tomato sauce, 297
    potted, 41
    *risotto with baby peas, **390,** 391
    sausage and, gumbo, **300,** 301
    *seafood fra diavolo, **356,** 357
    *seafood paella, 304
    shelling and deveining, **296**
    stir-fried, with bok choy, 299
    tempura, 299
    Thai, 298
Shuck, 30
Sieve, 10
Sift, 30

Simmer, 30
Skate, 255
    +with brown butter, lemon, and capers, 281
Skewers, 11
Skillets, 8
Skim, 30
Sloppy joes, 126
Smelt, 255
    +fried, 261
Smoked fish, 258
Smoked salmon, 258
Smoked salmon filling, 43
+Smoked salmon sandwiches with dill cream
        cheese, 612–13
+Smoked salmon tea sandwiches, 619
Smoked tongue, 182
+Smoked trout pâté, 44
Smoothie
    banana, 765
    *+mango-strawberry, 764, **764**
    peach, 764
Snap peas, freezing, 788
Snickerdoodles, 730
Snow peas, 446
    beef with, and carrots, 115
    freezing, 788
    *+mixed pea pod stir-fry, 446, **446**
Soba, 340
Soda bread
    with currants and caraway seeds, 576
    *traditional Irish, 576
Soft peaks, 30
*Soft pretzels, 607
Soft-shell crabs, 257
    panfried, 288, **288**
    with lemon-caper sauce, 288
Sole, 255
    rolled, stuffed with crab, 276–77, **276**
Sorbet, 747
    -and-cream cake, 757
    *cantaloupe, **750,** 755
    *chocolate, 754
    *peach, 755
    *pink grapefruit, 754
Sorrel soup, 61
Soufflé(s), *see also* Desserts
    classic cheese, 315
    cottage cheese and bacon puffs, 334
    gruyère-spinach, 315
    southwestern, 315, **315**
Soup(s), 57–85. *See also* Bisque; Broths;
        Chowder(s); Stock
    *beef-vegetable, 81
    Billi-Bi, 76
    butternut-apple, 60, **60**
    *caldo verde, 61

*Caribbean-flavored black bean, 72
*chicken, with rice, 78
chicken and coconut milk, 77
*classic black bean, 72
*+cool cucumber, 67
cream of
    asparagus, 62
    broccoli, 62
    cauliflower, 62
    mushroom, 59
    quick, asparagus, 63
    +quick, broccoli, 62
    quick, corn, 63
    quick, pea, 63
    quick, squash, 63
    spinach, 62
*curried lentil, 68
French onion, 59
garnishing, 58
gazpacho with cilantro cream, 66
*German lentil, 68
*Greek-style lemon, 76
hearty borscht, 80–81
*hearty mushroom-barley, 70
*Italian white bean and spinach, 63
lobster bisque, 290–91
minestrone with pesto, **56,** 69
miso, 69
mushroom and wild rice, 71, **71**
mussels in saffron-tomato broth, 74
pasta e fagioli with canned beans, 82
pasta e fagioli with sausage, 82
*pasta e piselli, 67
*peachy melon, 84
*pear and red wine, 85
*Peruvian seafood, 304
pureed, 58
sausage and shrimp gumbo, **300,** 301
seasonal, 61
sorrel, 61
south-of-the-border chicken, 78, **79**
*spicy black bean, 64
spicy curried carrot, 60–61
storing, 58
*tart cherry, 85
*turkey, 80
Tuscan vegetable, 70
types of, 58
vichyssoise, 66
*Vietnamese noodle, 77
Sour cream
    coffee cake, **578,** 578–79
    cookies, 726
    *+grapes with, 496
    veal nuggets with, –dill sauce, 138
Southern fried chicken, 217

Soybeans, 373
*Soy dipping sauce, 53
Soy sauce, 15, 33, 476
Spaghetti, 340
    *all'Amatriciana, 359
    frittata, 314
    with meatballs, 357
    *+pasta with bacon and peas, 353
    with walnuts, 348
    *with pesto, 347
    *with roasted tomatoes, 345
Spaghetti squash
    with tomatoes, 464, **464**
Spanakopita, 460
Spanish mackerel, 254
Sparkling wine, 26
Spatulas, 10
    silicon, 633
Spelt, 381
Spice layer cake, 654–55, **655**
Spices, 15
Spinach, 459–61, 522
    +and bacon salad, 525
    cheddar, and bacon filling, 311
    creamed, 460–61
    cream of, soup, 62
    crepes with chicken, and mushroom filling, 319
    freezing, 789
    Indian-style creamed, 461
    *Italian white bean and, soup, 63
    lasagna rolls, 364
    mini spanakopita, 50
    -mushroom stuffing, 96
    new chicken cordon bleu, 215
    pasta e fagioli with sausage, 82, **82**
    *penne with, and raisins, 349
    roulade with mushrooms, 322–23, **323**
    +sautéed, and garlic, 460
    spanakopita, 460
    strata, 324
    stuffed breast of veal, 130–31
    vegetable lasagna, 362
Split peas, 373
    soup, with ham, 67
Spoonbread, 396, **396**
Springform pan, 9
Spritz cookies, 736
Squab, 240
Squash
    pasta primavera, **338,** 351
    quick cream of, soup, 63
    summer, 461–62
        casserole, 462
        freezing, 789
        +Mediterranean grilled eggplant and,
            474, **475**

    +parmesan-broiled, 462
    pasta with, and mint, 348
    +shredded zucchini, 461
    +zucchini ribbons with mint, 462
    winter, 463–65
        baked acorn squash, 464
        freezing, 789
        maple butternut squash, 463
        *roasted buttercup squash, 465
        roasted Delicata squash, 465
        rosemary-roasted butternut squash, 463
        spaghetti squash with tomatoes, 464, **464**
        thyme-roasted butternut squash, 463
Squid, 256. *See also* Calamari
    cleaning, 302
    +grilled, 302
    *seafood paella, 304
    stuffed, 302
    *Thai, salad, 538
Star anise, 33
`+Steak au poivre, 108
+Steak pizzaiola, 109
+Steak with red wine sauce, 110
Steam, 30
Steamer, 11
Steamers, 255
Stelline, **341**
Stew(s)
    beef, 117, 171
    *bouillabaisse, 305
    California cioppino, 303
    chicken bouillabaisse, 208
    ciambotta, 473
    creamy veal, 133
    *curried vegetable, 472
    Irish, 174
    Moroccan vegetable, 472
    Provençal, (Daube) 98
    veal and mushroom, 131
    veal with gremolata, 133
Stewing
    beef, 92, 117
    lamb, 167
    meat, 89
    pork, 142
    veal, 128
Sticky rice, 383
Stiff peaks, 30
Stilton, 329, **329**
Stir-fry(ied), 30, 403
    beef and broccoli, 114
    beef with snow peas and carrots, 115
    +bok choy, 413
    +broccoli, 414
    cucumbers and radishes, 430
    greens, 435

    *+mixed pea pod, 446, **446**
    +napa cabbage, 417
    pork, 142
    scallop and asparagus, 294, **294**
    +sesame, asparagus, 407
    shrimp with bok choy, 299
    spicy tangerine beef, **112,** 113
    +Szechwan chicken, 215
    Thai beef with basil, 111, **111**
    tofu with vegetables, 399, **399**
    vegetable, 478
Stock(s), 57–58. *See also* Broths
    *brown beef, 83
Stockpot, 8
Stollen, 606
    easy Christmas, 579
    marzipan-filled, 606
Stout, 27
Stove, equipment for, 7–8
Stovetop smoking, 155
Strainer, 10
Strata, spinach, 324
Strawberry(ies), 488
    berries and cream shortcake, **480,** 489
    butter, 605
    cheesecake, 674
    cheese pie, **682,** 700
    *freezer, jam, 790
    freezing, 784
    fresh, butter, 605
    *granita, 753
    ice cream, 749
    *+in white wine, 492
    jam, 794, **794**
    *+mango-, smoothie, 764, **764**
    meringue nests with lemon filling and,
        626, **627**
    *mint julep cups, 514
    mousse pie, 708
    napoleons, 642
    *-orange ice, 751
    rhubarb-, cobbler, **516,** 517
    shortcake, 491
    skillet jam, 791
    *summer pudding, 490
    *three-fruit salad with vanilla bean syrup, 515
String cheese, 332
Striped bass, 255
    *roasted, 261
Stroganoff, beef, 98
Stuffed beef tenderloin with mushroom gravy, 96
Stuffed breast of veal, 130–31
Stuffed cabbage with dill, 162
Stuffed eggs, 324
    bacon-horseradish, 325
    dried tomato–caper, 325

lemon-basil, 325, **325**

pimiento-studded, 325

Stuffed Italian frying peppers, 448

Stuffed pork chops, 155

+Stuffed squid, 302

Stuffed veal roast, 128–129

Stuffing, 244

*chestnut and apple, 245

cornish hens with wild rice and mushroom, 227

country sausage and corn bread, 245

moist bread, 246

*northwest fruit, 246

*parsnips, swiss chard, and bacon, 248

*rice and escarole, 247

southwestern corn bread, 244

spinach-mushroom, 96

*wild rice and vegetable, 247

*Succotash, 473

Sugar cookies

classic, **710**, 732

drop, 725

holiday, 733

jam-filled, 732–33

Sugar snap peas

*+mixed pea pod stir-fry, 446, **446**

pasta primavera, **338**, 351

Sugar syrup, 740, 774, 780

Sunchokes, 465

*roasted, 465

Sweetbreads, 179

braised with madeira, 183

Sweet chocolate, 744

+Sweetened whipped cream, 562

Sweet potato(es), 466–67

candied, 467

freezing, 789

grandma's, pie, 702

pancakes, 456

*pan-roased, chunks, 466

praline, 466–67

*tzimmes, 479

Sweet rice, 383

Swiss chard, 435

freezing, 789

*parsnips, and bacon stuffing, 248

Swiss cheese, 332

+classic, fondue, **326**, 333

crisps, 45

Swordfish, 255

balsamic-glazed, with greens, 266

kabobs, 265, **265**

+steaks broiled with maître d'hôtel butter, 265

+with balsamic glaze, 266

Syrup, lemon, 640

T

*Tabbouleh, tomato and mint, 536

Table setting, 24

Taco salad, 542

Tagliatelle, 340

Tahini, 33

+dressing, 547

Taleggio, 332

Tamale pie, 125

Tangelos, 511–12

Tangerines, 511–12

Tapenade, 33

+Tapenade, 41

Tarragon

broiled chicken, 219

*chicken breasts with mushrooms and, 212

*poule au pot with, 210

roast chicken, 191

-roasted salmon, 259

Tart(s). *See also* Pies

chocolate truffle, 702

cranberry-almond, 697

cream cheese and fruit, 709

double berry linzer, 699, **699**

Italian triple berry, 706–7

lemon, 703

pastry for 9-inch, 687

pastry for 11-inch, 687

+phyllo, shell, 688

+phyllo, tartlet shells, 688

plum frangipane, 696–97

prebaked piecrust or, shell, 688

raspberry, 697

+Tartar sauce, 553

Tart pan, 9

Tartufo, 758–59

Tea

black, 762

brewing hot, 762

green, 762

herbal, 762

iced, 763

*+best, 763

with fruit juice, 763

with lemon and mint, 763

oolong, 762

*+spiced hot, 763

Tempeh, 373

Temper, 30

Tender-crisp, 30

Thermometers, 10–11

Three-bean salad, 527

Thyme

apple and, roast chicken, **184**, 190

+lemon-, cod, 274

-roasted butternut squash, 463

*-roasted chicken and vegetables, 196, **197**

Tilapia, 255

Tilefish, 255

Tiramisù, 628–29

blueberry-lemon, 490–91

Toast, 30

Toffee almond crunch, 745, **745**

Tofu, 373

"egg salad", 399

miso soup, 69

stir-fried, with vegetables, 399, **399**

Tomatillo salsa, 556–57

Tomato(es), 467–71

*and mint tabbouleh, 537

+and ricotta salata bruschetta, **34**, 46

aspic, 537

basil and dried, chicken salad, 542

-basil cream cheese logs, 41

bow ties with, and lemon, 346

*braised veal chops with, and peas, 131

+broiled halves, 471

+broiled parmesan, 470

canning, 777

canning, in boiling water bath, 776–77

cherry

+gratin, 469

+—lemon salad, 532

*radiatori with arugula, and pancetta, 346

+skillet, 470

+skillet with garlic, 470

chicken breasts stuffed with dried, and basil, 200

+chicken with -olive relish, 223

chopped, 615

*chutney, 560

ciambotta, 473

classic bolognese sauce, 358

+double —brie heroes, 610–11

dried, 33

dried, and green onion couscous, 393

dried, and olive focaccia, 599

dried, -caper stuffed eggs, 325

dried, filling, 43

dried, topping, 269

focaccia, 599

freezing, 789

fried green, 470

gazpacho with cilantro cream, 66

Manhattan clam chowder, 73

+mozzarella and, salad, 529

mozzarella with dried, 337

mussels in saffron- broth, 74

*mussels with, and white wine, 291, **291**

Neapolitan pasta sauce, 359

okra with, 441

Tomato(es) (continued)
  *-olive sauce, 234
  and onion glaze, 147
  oven-dried, 470
  panzanella salad with, vinaigrette, 539, **539**
  *penne with sausage, 358
  +perfectly simple, sandwiches, 610
  *red snapper in parchment with, and basil, 281
  *+rigatoni with "sausage" sauce, 358
  *roasted scrod with, relish, 274
  *salsa, 556
  sauces
    big batch, 343
    *linguine with fresh, 345
    marinara, 343
    *penne with, cream, 344, **344**
    *penne with no-cook, 346
  savory, tart, **468,** 469
  shrimp and potatoes in feta-, sauce, 297
  sliced, 615
  *spaghetti all'Amatriciana, 359
  spaghetti squash with, 464, **464**
  *spaghetti with roasted, 345
  +veal with, and arugula salad, 136, **136**
  vinaigrette, 545
Tongs, 11, 176
Tongue, 179
  smoked, 182
Tonnato
  chicken breasts, 211
  vitello, 134
Topping(s). See also Sauces
  baked flounder with savory crumb, 275
  dill-pepper, 269
  dried tomato, 269
  horseradish, 269
  lemon, 269
  lime-jalapeño, 269
  parmesan, 269
Tortilla spirals, 42–43, **42**
Toss, 30
Toxic leaves, 681
Tripe-crème cheese, 332
Triticale, 381
Trout, 255
  amandine, 263
  with brown butter and sage, 263
  with cornmeal and bacon, 263
  grenobloise, 263
  meuniére, 262, **262**
  +smoked, pâté, 44
Truffles, chocolate and hazelnut, 741
Tube pan, 9
Tubetti, 340
  *macaroni salad, 534
  +with lemon and cream, 360–61

Tulipes, 759, **759**
Tuna, 252, 255
  pan bagnat, 614
  pan-seared, 267
  *pasta with, puttanesca, 353
  salad
    +classic, 543
    curried, 543
    Mexican-style, 543
  Sicilian, 266
  *+Tuscan, salad on focaccia, 613
Turbot, 255
Turkey, 229. See also Chicken; Poultry
  *and mango roll-ups, 614
  breast
    with caramelized shallots, 232–33
    *rolled, with basil mayonnaise, 233, **233**
    *rosemary roast, 232
    *white, chili, 237
  brining, 236
  buying, 186
  charcoal-grilled whole, 236
  cutlets
    *+herbed, 236
    *sautéed, 234
    +with chopped salad, 235, **235**
  ground, 224
    meat loaf, 226
  +marsala with mushrooms, 234–35
  meatballs, 207
  +old-fashioned creamed, 240
  *potpie with cornmeal crust, 238
  roast
    carving, **231**
    *traditional, with giblet gravy,
      229–31, **230**
  roasting times, 188
  *soup, 80
  tetrazzini, 239
  *thighs osso buco–style, 237
Turnip(s), 471
  candied, 471
  freezing, 789
  lamb navarin, 175
  potato and, gratin, 479
Turnip greens, freezing, 789
Turret pie edge, 685
Turtle beans, 372. See also Black beans
Tzatziki, 38
*Tzimmes, 479

U
Udon noodles, 340
Unsweetened chocolate, 744
Unsweetened cocoa powder, 744
Utensils, 10–11

V
Valencia, 383
Vanilla
  chiffon cake, **668,** 669
  no-cook, ice cream, 749
  old-fashioned, ice cream, 749
  pastry cream, 642–43
  pound cake, 664
  rice pudding with dried cherries, 637
  rich, -bean ice cream, 748
  in scenting sugar, 678
  +silky, butter frosting, 678
  three-fruit salad with, bean syrup, 515
Variety meats, 178–83, **180.**
  See also specific varieties
Veal, 126–38
  *braised, chops with tomatoes and peas, 131
  buying, 126, 128
  cooking, 128
  creamy, stew, 133
  cutlets, 126, 128
  cuts, **127**
  grading, 87
  grilled, chops, 137
  and mushroom stew, 131
  no-frills, chops, 137
  nuggets with sour cream–dill sauce, 138
  *osso buco with gremolata, **132,** 133
  parmigiana, 135
  +piccata, 136–37
  roast
    fruit-stuffed, 130
    rib, 129
    stuffed, 128–29
  roasting times, **128**
  sautéed, kidneys with mustard, 183
  +scallopini marsala, 135
  schnitzel á la Holstein, 134
  stew with gremolata, 133
  storing, 126, 128
  stuffed breast of, 130–31
  +stuffed with fontina, prosciutto, and basil, 137
  vitello tonnato, 134
  Wiener schnitzel, 134
  +with tomato and arugula salad, 136, **136**
Vegetable(s), 401–79. See also specific varieties
  *beef-, soup, 81
  braised lamb shanks with white beans and,
    172, 173
  *broth, 83
  *brown rice and, pilaf, 387
  buying and storing, 401–2
  ciambotta, 473
  cooking, 402–3, 453, 472, 473
  *curried, stew, 472
  eating raw, 474

eating wild, 422
equipment for canning, 772
freezing, 780, 785–89
garden, chowder, 64
garden, filling, 311
grilled, 471, 477
grilling, 428
harvest casserole, 476
mashed root, 474
Moroccan, stew, 472
picking out, 411
pot roast with root, 100–101, **101**
preparing, 402, 413
ratatouille, 476
samosas, 48–49
sauce from, 420
sauces for, 406
Sicilian stewed, 478
stir-fried tofu with, 399, **399**
stir-fry, 478
*Thai, salad, 539
*three-bean vegetarian chili, 375, **375**
*thyme-roasted chicken and, 196, **197**
Tuscan, soup, 70
*tzimmes, 479
*wild rice and, stuffing, 247
winter, salad, 527
*winter vegetable chili, 379
Vegetable oil, 15
Vegetable peeler, 11
Venison, 90
Vermicelli, 340
   *+pasta with bacon and peas, 353
   rice pilaf with, 386
Vichyssoise, 66
*Vietnamese noodle soup, 77
Vinaigrette(s), 523, 531
   +asparagus with lemon-caper, 406
   leeks, 438, **438**
   roasted green beans with dill, 409
Vinegar, 15, 33, 523. *See also* Balsamic (vinegar)
   pastry dough, 686
Vitello tonnato, 134

W

Waffle(s)
   +buttermilk, 581
   pecan, 581
   sweet milk, 581
   yeast, 581
+Waldorf salad, 529

Walnut(s)
   apple-, bundt cake, 658
   chocolate-, filling, 603
   chocolate-, fudge, 742
   creamy penuche, 742
   crescents, 729
   +hot pepper nuts, 42
   lemon-, icebox cookies, 731
   lemon-, scones, 568
   maple-, pie, 698
   muffins, 569
   raspberry-, streusel bars, 721
   shortbread, 717
   spaghetti with, 348
   toasting, 729
   torte, 667
   Turkish chicken in, sauce, 211
   +warm figs with, 495
   whole wheat–, bread, 591, **591**
*Wassail, 767
Watercress, 522
   + and radish tea sandwiches, 618
   cold poached salmon steaks with,
      sauce, 263
   sauce, 264
Watermelon(s), 512–13
   *bowl, 512
   *granita, 754
   *salsa, 557
*Watermelon-rind pickles, 798, **798**
Wax beans
   +and green beans with lemon and
      mint, 408
   freezing, 786
   three-bean salad, 527
   +with lemon and mint, 408
+Welsh rabbit, 336
Wheat, 381
Wheat beer, 27
Wheat berr(ies), 381
   with brown butter and pecans, 398
   +salad, 536
Wheat bread
   *honey-, 590
   *whole, –oatmeal, 590
   whole, –walnut, 591, **591**
Whip, 30
+Whipped cream frosting, 679
Whisk, 11, 30
Whitebait, 255
White beans. *See under* Beans

*White bread, 586
White chocolate, 744. *See also under* Chocolate
*White grape–wine jelly, 793
White sangria, 766
White sauce (béchamel), 550
White wine(s), 25
   *-mussels with tomatoes and, 291, **291**
   serving, 768
   *+strawberries in, 492
Whiting, 255
*Whole wheat–oatmeal bread, 590
*Whole wheat–walnut bread, 591, **591**
Wiener schnitzel, 134
Wine, 25–27. *See also* Red wine; White wine
   body of, 28
   cooking with, 28
   *+hot mulled, 767, **767**
   serving, 26–27
   storing, 27
   vintage of, 28
Wonton wrappers, 33

Y

Yams. *See* Sweet potatoes
Yankee beans, 373. *See also* Navy beans
Yeast waffles, 581
Yellow cake, 652
Yellowtail, 254
Yogurt
   *+5-minute frozen peach, 751
   herbed, -cheese dip, 40
   tzatziki, 38
Yorkshire pudding, 94
Youngberries, freezing, 784

Z

Zest, 30
Zester, 11
Zinfandel, 26
   *-poached pears, 505
Ziti, 340
   *baked, 365
   *with roasted asparagus, 350, **350**
Zucchini
   bread, 575
   ciambotta, 473
   ratatouille, 476
   +ribbons with mint, 462
   +shredded, 461
   Sicilian stewed vegetables, 478
   vegetable lasagna, 362

ACKNOWLEDGMENTS

Credits

COPY EDITORS: Brenda Goldberg, Barbara Machtiger, Sydne Matus, Deri Reed, Miriam Rubin, and Judith Sutton ■ PROOFREADERS: Nancy Frank, Lisa Geller, Judith B. Johnson, Roseanne Klass, Cyndi Marsico, Linnea Leedham Ochs, and Michael Ricca ■ INPUTTERS: Diane Boccadoro, Ginjer L. Clarke, Laura Furst, Kate W. Harris, Janet Kopito, Maryellen LoBosco, and Ann McNamara.

Photography Credits

BRIAN HAGIWARA for Basics, Poultry, Fish and Shellfish, Salad and Salad Dressings, Sauces, Salsas and Condiments, and Frozen Desserts with John Waldie, photographer's assistant; Dora Jonassen, food stylist; Christine McCabe, prop stylist; Jee Levine and Marie Baker-Lee, food stylist assistants; Amy Lord, hand model. ■ RITA MAAS for Appetizers, Eggs, Beans, Rice and Other Grains, Vegetables, Beverages, and Canning and Freezing with Matt Kesterson, photographer's assistant; Brett Kurzweil, Michael Pederson, and William Smith, food stylists; Cathy Cook, Barbara Fritz, and Marina Malchin, prop stylists; Tracy Harlor, Peter Occolowitz, and Lisa Wasserman, food stylist assistants. ■ ANN STRATTON for Soups, Cheese, Fruits, Yeast Breads, Desserts, and Pies and Tarts with Andy Aronson, Matthew Begun, Natasha Drazich, Matthew Huber, Christopher McLellan, Daemian Smith, and Leslie Van Stelten, photographer's assistants; Rori Spinelli, food stylist; Betty Alfenito, Philippa Brathwaite, Robyn Glaser, and Cristina Wressell, prop stylists; Laurie Cearley and Suzanne Gruber, food stylist assistants; Sarita Goosey and Robin Herrick, prop stylist assistants. ■ MARK THOMAS for Meat, Pasta and Pasta Sauces, Quick Breads, Sandwiches, Cakes and Cake Frostings, and Cookies and Confections with Peter Baiamonte, Janie Cloin, Yoshi Takagai, Angel Tucker, and Amy Sessler, photographer's assistants; A.J. Battifarano, Anne Disrude, and Dora Jonassen, food stylists; Nancy Micklin, prop stylist; Margarette Adams, Marie Baker-Lee, Lisa Homa, and Jee Levine, food stylist assistants.

Acknowledgments

Many thanks to everyone who gave so generously of their time and talent to make this book a reality. ■ TO OUR FRIENDS IN THE FOOD INDUSTRY: Marlys Bielunski, National Cattleman's Beef Association; Robin Kline, National Pork Producer's Council; Nancy Tringali National Chicken Council; Howard Helmer, American Egg Board; Carolyn Hughes at the California Fig Advisory Board; Marilyn Wilkinson at California Tree Fruit Agreement; Duplin Winery; Teresa Cearley; and Carol Santos. ■ FOR ADVICE AND BEAUTIFUL PRODUCTS FOR PHOTOGRAPHY: The folks at All-Clad Metalcrafters; Le Creuset; Alex Lee at Oxo; Gretchen Holt, Mark Misilli, Joy Noto and Diane Schwartz at the Meyer Corporation. ■ FOR ADVICE ON TABLE ETIQUETTE: Cardel Ltd. and Tiffany & Company ■ TO COLLEAGUES AT GOOD HOUSEKEEPING: Ellen Levine, Sarah Scrymser, Richard Eisenberg, Scott Yardley, Gina Davis, Suzie Bolotin, Debbie Goldsmith, Sharon Franke, Delia Hammock, Cathy Lo, Lori Conforti, MaryAnn Svec, Lisa Troland, and Herta Guhl. ■ TO OUR BOOK TEAM who approached every word, recipe, taste, photo, and query with enthusiasm and a fresh eye, you have our eternal admiration and appreciation. Deborah Mintcheff, editor and tweaker par excellence; Lisa Brainerd Burge, shaper of chapters; Rick Rodgers, wordmeister; Sandy Gluck, Lori Longbotham, Gina Miraglia, Sara Reynolds, Fraya Berg, Wendy Kalin, Maryanne Marinelli, food lovers who all produce delicious recipes that work; Maryanne Bannon, managing editor, guardian angel, traffic cop, counselor. ■ TO BTD (A.K.A. SANTA'S WORKSHOP): Sabrina Bowers, Kimberly Johnston, Daniel Rodney, Beth Tondreau, and Mary Wirth who all merrily made text, recipes, and images into a beautiful, easy-to-use book. ■ AT HEARST BOOKS: Elizabeth Rice, Jacqueline Deval, and Monica Taitt. IT WAS A JOY TO WORK WITH SO MANY GIFTED PEOPLE.

Special thanks to friends and colleagues who contributed so generously of their expertise and knowledge for our expert tips.

JODY ADAMS, chef/owner Rialto and Red Clay, Massachusetts ■ BRUCE AIDELLS, chef/owner Aidells Sausage Company; coauthor with Denis Kelly *The Complete Meat Cookbook* and *Real Beer & Good Eats* ■ JEAN ANDERSON, award-winning author *Jean Anderson Cooks, The Nutrition Bible,* and *The American Century Cookbook* ■ JOHN ASH, Culinary Director, Fetzer Vineyards, Hopland, California; award-winning author *From the Earth to the Table: John Ash's Wine Country Cuisine* ■ LIDIA MATTICCHIO BASTIANICH, television host of *Lidia's Italian Table;* author *Lidia's Italian Table* and *La Cucina di Lidia;* owner Felidia, Becco, and Frico Bar, New York City and Lidia's Kansas City, Missouri ■ DANIEL BOULUD, chef/owner Daniel and Café Boulud, New York City; author with D. Greenspan *The Café Boulud Cookbook;* author *Cooking with Daniel Boulud* ■ SHIRLEY O. CORRIHER, award-winning author *CookWise* ■ MARION CUNNINGHAM, award-winning author *Fannie Farmer Cookbook* ■ NATHALIE DUPREE, award-winning author *Nathalie Dupree's Comfortable Entertaining* and *Nathalie Dupree's Quick Meals for Busy Days;* television host ■ BETTY FUSSELL, author *The Story Of Corn, I Hear America Cooking,* and *Home Bistro* ■ DORIE GREENSPAN, award-winning author *Baking with Julia* and *Desserts by Pierre Hermé* ■ MAIDA HEATTER, award-winning author *Maida Heatter's Book of Great Desserts* and *Maida Heatter's Book of Great Chocolate Desserts* ■ BARBARA KAFKA, award-winning author *Soup, A Way of Life* and *Roasting, A Simple Art* ■ MOLLIE KATZEN, author *Moosewood Cookbook* and *Vegetable Heaven;* televison host of *Mollie Katzen's Cooking Show* ■ ELINOR KLIVANS, award-winning author *125 Cookies to Bake, Nibble, and Savor* and *Bake and Freeze Chocolate Desserts* ■ KAREN MACNEIL, chairman of wine programs at the Culinary Institute of America at Greystone, California; author *The Wine Primer* ■ CHRISTINE MCCABE, photo stylist *Good Housekeeping* and *Redbook* magazines; *Family Circle Easy Gardening* ■ MAX MCCALMAN, Maître Fromager, Picholine, New York City ■ DEBORAH MADISON, award-winning author *Vegetarian Cooking for Everyone* and *The Savory Way* ■ NICK MALGIERI, director of the baking program Peter Kump's New York Cooking School; award-winning author *Chocolate* and *How to Bake* ■ ALICE MEDRICH, author *Chocolate and the Art of Low Fat Desserts,* and *Alice Medrich's Cookies and Brownies* ■ MARY SUE MILLIKEN AND SUSAN FENIGER, television hosts of Food Network's *Too Hot Tamales;* chef/owners Border Grill restaurants in Santa Monica and Las Vegas and Ciudad in Los Angeles. ■ SARA MOULTON, televison host of Food Network's *Cooking Live* and *Cooking Live Primetime;* Executive Chef *Gourmet Magazine;* Food Editor *Good Morning America* ■ JAMES PETERSON, award-winning author *Sauces, The Essentials of Cooking,* and *A New Look at the French Classics* ■ SUSAN G. PURDY, award-winning author *The Family Baker, Let Them Eat Cake,* and *Have Your Cake and Eat It, Too* ■ STEVE RAICHLEN, award-winning author *Steve Raichlen's Healthy Latin Cooking* and *Barbecue Bible* ■ ERIC RIPERT, executive chef/co-owner, Le Bernadin; coauthor *Le Bernadin Cookbook, Four Star Simplicity* ■ ANNE ROSENZWEIG, chef/owner The Lobster Club; author *The Arcadia Seasonal Mural and Cookbook* ■ CHRIS SCHLESINGER, chef/owner East Coast Grill, Cambridge, Massachusetts and Back Eddy, Westport, Massachusetts; coauthor *Thrill of the Grill* and *License to Grill* ■ MICHELE SCICOLONE, author *Savoring Italy* and *A Fresh Taste of Italy* ■ MARIE SIMMONS, author *The Good Egg, Fresh & Fast,* and *A to Z Puddings* ■ BARBARA TROPP, author *The Modern Art of Chinese Cooking* and *China Moon Cookbook* ■ ALICE WATERS, chef/owner Chez Panisse Restaurant and Café, Berkeley, California; author *Chez Panisse Café Cookbook* and *Chez Panisse Vegetables Cookbook* ■ JASPER WHITE, author *Cooking from New England* and *Lobster at Home* ■ JOANNE WEIR, television host of *Weir Cooking;* author *You Say Tomato.*

Bacon, 16-ounce package, diced, cooked	$1\frac{1}{2}$ cups pieces
Beans, dry 1 pound 1 cup	2 cups 2 to $2\frac{1}{2}$ cups cooked
Berries	See individual varieties.
Blackberries, 1 pint	about 2 cups
Blueberries, 1 pint	about 3 cups
Bread crumbs, dried 8-ounce package	$2\frac{1}{4}$ cups
Bread crumbs, fresh 1 slice bread	$\frac{1}{2}$ cup bread crumbs
Butter or margarine $\frac{1}{4}$-pound stick 1 pound	$\frac{1}{2}$ cup or 8 tablespoons 4 sticks or 2 cups
Cabbage, 1 pound coarsely sliced	about 4 to 5 cups
Celery, 1 medium bunch sliced/diced	about 4 cups
Cheddar cheese, 4 ounces	1 cup shredded
Cherries, 1 pound	about 2 cups pitted
Chicken, cooked $2\frac{1}{2}$-pound to 3-pound chicken, diced meat	about $2\frac{1}{2}$ cups
Cocoa, unsweetened, 8-ounce can	2 cups
Coconut, flaked, $3\frac{1}{2}$ ounces	$1\frac{1}{3}$ cups
Cookies, crushed chocolate wafers, 20 $2\frac{1}{4}$-inch gingersnaps, 15 vanilla wafers, 22	about 1 cup fine crumbs about 1 cup fine crumbs about 1 cup fine crumbs

Cottage cheese, 8 ounces	1 cup
Couscous, 1 cup	about $2\frac{1}{2}$ cups cooked
Crackers, crushed graham, 7 5" by $2\frac{1}{2}$" crackers saltine, 28	about 1 cup fine crumbs about 1 cup fine crumbs
Cranberries, 12-ounce bag	3 cups
Cream, heavy or whipping, 1 cup	about 2 cups whipped cream
Cream cheese 3-ounce package 8-ounce package	6 tablespoons 1 cup
Currants, dried, 5 ounces	about 1 cup
Dates, dry, pitted, 10-ounce container	about 2 cups
Egg whites, large 1 1 cup	about 2 tablespoons 8 to 10 egg whites
Egg yolks, large, 1 cup	12 to 14 egg yolks
Flour, 1 pound all-purpose cake whole-wheat	about $3\frac{1}{2}$ cups about 4 cups about $3\frac{3}{4}$ cups
Gelatin, unflavored, to gel 2 cups liquid	1 envelope
Green or red bell pepper, 1 large	about 1 cup chopped
Hominy grits, 1 cup	about $4\frac{1}{2}$ cups cooked
Honey, liquid, 16 ounces	$1\frac{1}{3}$ cups